THE EARTH AND ITS PEOPLES

A Global History

SIXTH EDITION

Richard W. Bulliet
Columbia University

Pamela Kyle Crossley
Dartmouth College

Daniel R. Headrick
Roosevelt University

Steven W. Hirsch
Tufts University

Lyman L. Johnson
University of North Carolina—Charlotte

David Northrup
Boston College

CENGAGE
Learning·

Australia • Brazil • Mexico • Singapore • United Kingdom • Unit

CI

CENGAGE
Learning·

The Earth and Its Peoples: A Global History, **Sixth Edition, Advantage Edition**

Richard W. Bulliet, Pamela Kyle Crossley, Daniel R. Headrick, Steven W. Hirsch, Lyman L. Johnson, and David Northrup

Product Director: Suzanne Jeans

Product Manager: Brooke Barbier

Content Developer: Lauren Floyd

Associate Content Developer: Cara Swan

Product Assistant: Katie Coaster

Media Developer: Kate MacLean

Marketing Brand Manager: Melissa Larmon

Manufacturing Planner: Sandee Milewski

Art and Design Direction, Production Management, and Composition: PreMediaGlobal

Cover Image: Vase decorated with scenes from the "Gengzhi tu": Winnowing of rice and feeding of the silkworms. 18th century, Qing Dynasty. Green porcelain, 43 cm. Musee des Arts Asiatiques-Guimet, Paris, France/© RMN-Grand Palais/Art Resource, NY. Photo: Thierry Ollivier

For product information and technology assistance, contact us at **Cengage Learning Customer & Sales Support, 1-800-354-9706.**

For permission to use material from this text or product, submit all requests online at **www.cengage.com/permissions.** Further permissions questions can be e-mailed to **permissionrequest@cengage.com.**

Library of Congress Control Number: 2014932005

Student Edition:

ISBN-13: 978-1-285-44563-2

ISBN-10: 1-285-44563-5

Cengage Learning
200 First Stamford Place, 4th Floor
Stamford, CT 06902
USA

Cengage Learning is a leading provider of customized learning solutions with office locations around the globe, including Singapore, the United Kingdom, Australia, Mexico, Brazil, and Japan. Locate your local office at **www.cengage.com/global**.

Cengage Learning products are represented in Canada by Nelson Education, Ltd.

To learn more about Cengage Learning Solutions, visit **www.cengage.com.**

Purchase any of our products at your local college store or at our preferred online store **www.cengagebrain.com.**

Printed in the United States of America
1 2 3 4 5 6 7 18 17 16 15 14

Brief Contents

PART ONE   **The Emergence of Human Communities, to 500 B.C.E.   1**
1   Nature, Humanity, and History, to 3500 B.C.E.   2
2   The First River-Valley Civilizations, 3500–1500 B.C.E.   23
3   The Mediterranean and Middle East, 2000–500 B.C.E.   49
4   New Civilizations Outside the West Asian Core Area, 2300 B.C.E.–350 C.E.   78

PART TWO   **The Formation of New Cultural Communities, 1000 B.C.E.–400 C.E.   109**
5   Greece and Iran, 1000–30 B.C.E.   111
6   An Age of Empires: Rome and Han China, 753 B.C.E.–330 C.E.   143
7   India and Southeast Asia, 1500 B.C.E.–1025 C.E.   174
8   Peoples and Civilizations of the Americas, 1200 B.C.E.–1400 C.E.   198

PART THREE **Growth and Interaction of Cultural Communities, 300 B.C.E.–1200 C.E.   227**
9   Networks of Communication and Exchange, 300 B.C.E.–1100 C.E.   228
10   The Sasanid Empire and the Rise of Islam, 200–1200   247
11   Christian Societies Emerge in Europe, 600–1200   272
12   Inner and East Asia, 400–1200   297

PART FOUR   **Interregional Patterns of Culture and Contact, 1200–1550   321**
13   Mongol Eurasia and Its Aftermath, 1200–1500   322
14   Latin Europe, 1200–1500   350
15   Southern Empires, Southern Seas, 1200–1500   374
16   The Maritime Revolution, to 1550   401

PART FIVE   **The Globe Encompassed, 1500– 1750   433**
17   Transformations in Europe, 1500–1750   435
18   The Diversity of American Colonial Societies, 1530–1770   462
19   The Atlantic System and Africa, 1550–1800   488
20   Between Europe and China, 1500–1750   515
21   East Asia in Global Perspective   540

PART SIX   **Revolutions Reshape the World, 1750–1870   561**
22   The Early Industrial Revolution, 1760–1851   562
23   Revolutionary Changes in the Atlantic World, 1750–1850   589
24   Land Empires in the Age of Imperialism, 1800–1870   615
25   Nation Building and Economic Transformation in the Americas, 1800–1890   640

PART SEVEN **Global Diversity and Dominance, 1750–1945   673**
26   Varieties of Imperialism in Africa, India, Southeast Asia, and Latin America, 1750–1914   675
27   The New Power Balance, 1850–1900   704
28   The Crisis of the Imperial Order, 1900–1929   732
29   Revolutions in Living, 1900–1950   757
30   The Collapse of the Old Order, 1929–1949   784

PART EIGHT **Perils and Promises of a Global Community, 1945 to the Present   815**
31   The Cold War and Decolonization, 1945–1975   816
32   The End of the Cold War and the Challenge of Economic Development and Immigration, 1975–2000   843
33   New Challenges in a New Millennium   874

Contents

Preface   ix

PART 1
THE EMERGENCE OF HUMAN COMMUNITIES,
TO 500 B.C.E.   1

1
NATURE, HUMANITY, AND HISTORY, TO
3500 B.C.E.   2
African Genesis   2
Technology and Culture in the Ice Age   8
ENVIRONMENT + TECHNOLOGY: The Iceman   13
The Agricultural Revolutions   14
Life in Neolithic Communities   18
Conclusion   21
IMPORTANT EVENTS TO 3500 B.C.E.   22

2
THE FIRST RIVER-VALLEY CIVILIZATIONS,
3500–1500 B.C.E.   23
Mesopotamia   25
DIVERSITY + DOMINANCE: Violence and Order in the
Babylonian New Year's Festival   32
Egypt   36
The Indus Valley Civilization   44
Conclusion   47
IMPORTANT EVENTS 3500 B.C.E. TO 1500 B.C.E.   48

3
THE MEDITERRANEAN AND MIDDLE EAST,
2000–500 B.C.E.   49
The Cosmopolitan Middle East,
    1700–1100 B.C.E.   50
The Aegean World, 2000–1100 B.C.E.   56
The Assyrian Empire, 911–612 B.C.E.   59
Israel, 2000–500 B.C.E.   63
Phoenicia and the Mediterranean,
    1200–500 B.C.E.   67
ENVIRONMENT + TECHNOLOGY: Ancient Textiles
and Dyes   70
Failure and Transformation, 750–550 B.C.E.   75

Conclusion   76
IMPORTANT EVENTS 2000 B.C.E. TO 500 B.C.E.   77

4
NEW CIVILIZATIONS OUTSIDE THE
WEST ASIAN CORE AREA,
2300 B.C.E.–350 C.E.   78
Early China, 2000–221 B.C.E.   79
DIVERSITY + DOMINANCE: Human Nature and Good
Government in the Analects of Confucius and
the Legalist Writings of Han Fei   88
Nubia, 2300 B.C.E.–350 C.E.   92
Pastoral Nomads of the Eurasian Steppes,
    1000–100 B.C.E.   95
Celtic Europe, 1000–50 B.C.E.   100
Conclusion   103
IMPORTANT EVENTS 2300 B.C.E. TO 350 C.E.   105
ISSUES IN WORLD HISTORY: Animal
Domestication   106

PART 2
THE FORMATION OF NEW CULTURAL
COMMUNITIES, 1000 B.C.E.–400 C.E.   109

5
GREECE AND IRAN, 1000–30 B.C.E.   111
Ancient Iran, 1000–500 B.C.E.   112
The Rise of the Greeks, 1000–500 B.C.E.   119
The Struggle of Persia and Greece,
    546–323 B.C.E.   129
The Hellenistic Synthesis, 323–30 B.C.E.   135
ENVIRONMENT + TECHNOLOGY: Ancient
Astronomy   138
Conclusion   140
IMPORTANT EVENTS 1000 B.C.E. TO 30 B.C.E.   142

6
AN AGE OF EMPIRES: ROME AND HAN
CHINA, 753 B.C.E.–330 C.E.   143
Rome's Creation of a Mediterranean Empire,
    753 B.C.E.–330 C.E.   144
DIVERSITY + DOMINANCE: Socioeconomic Mobility,
Winners and Losers in Imperial Rome and Han
China   150

The Origins of Imperial China,
221 B.C.E.–220 C.E.   *160*
Conclusion   *171*
IMPORTANT EVENTS 1000 B.C.E. TO 220 C.E.   *173*

7

INDIA AND SOUTHEAST ASIA, 1500 B.C.E.–1025 C.E.   174

Foundations of Indian Civilization,
1500 B.C.E.–300 C.E.   *175*
Imperial Expansion and Collapse,
324 B.C.E.–650 C.E.   *184*
ENVIRONMENT + TECHNOLOGY: Indian
Mathematics   *190*
Southeast Asia, 50–1025 C.E.   *192*
Conclusion   *196*
IMPORTANT EVENTS 1500 B.C.E. TO
1025 C.E.   *197*

8

PEOPLES AND CIVILIZATIONS OF THE AMERICAS, 1200 B.C.E.–1400 C.E.   198

Formative Civilizations of the Olmec and Chavín,
1200–200 B.C.E.   *199*
Classic-Era Culture and Society in Mesoamerica,
200–900   *203*
The Postclassic Period in Mesoamerica to
1400   *208*
Northern Peoples   *211*
Andean Civilizations, 200–1400   *214*
DIVERSITY + DOMINANCE: Burials as Historical
Texts   *218*
Conclusion   *221*
IMPORTANT EVENTS 1200 B.C.E. TO 1400 C.E.   *223*
ISSUES IN WORLD HISTORY: Oral Societies and the
Consequences of Literacy   *224*

PART 3
GROWTH AND INTERACTION OF CULTURAL COMMUNITIES, 300 B.C.E.–1200 C.E.   227

9

NETWORKS OF COMMUNICATION AND EXCHANGE, 300 B.C.E.–1100 C.E.   228

The Silk Road   *229*
The Indian Ocean Maritime System   *233*
Routes Across the Sahara   *235*
ENVIRONMENT + TECHNOLOGY: Camel
Saddles   *237*
Sub-Saharan Africa   *238*

The Spread of Ideas   *242*
Conclusion   *245*
IMPORTANT EVENTS 300 B.C.E. TO 1100 C.E.   *245*

10

THE SASANID EMPIRE AND THE RISE OF ISLAM, 200–1200   247

The Sasanid Empire, 224–651   *248*
The Origins of Islam   *250*
The Rise and Fall of the Caliphate, 632–1258   *254*
Islamic Civilization   *262*
DIVERSITY + DOMINANCE: Secretaries, Turks, and
Beggars   *266*
Conclusion   *270*
IMPORTANT EVENTS 200–1200   *271*

11

CHRISTIAN SOCIETIES EMERGE IN EUROPE, 600–1200   272

The Byzantine Empire, 600–1200   *273*
Early Medieval Europe, 600–1000   *276*
The Western Church   *282*
ENVIRONMENT + TECHNOLOGY: Iron
Production   *283*
Kievan Russia, 900–1200   *287*
Western Europe Revives, 1000–1200   *289*
The Crusades, 1095–1204   *292*
Conclusion   *295*
IMPORTANT EVENTS 300–1200   *296*

12

INNER AND EAST ASIA, 400–1200   297

The Sui and Tang Empires, 581–755   *297*
DIVERSITY + DOMINANCE: Law and Society in China
and Japan   *304*
China and Its Rivals   *306*
New Kingdoms in East Asia   *314*
Conclusion   *318*
IMPORTANT EVENTS 200–1200   *319*

PART 4
INTERREGIONAL PATTERNS OF CULTURE AND CONTACT, 1200–1550   321

13

MONGOL EURASIA AND ITS AFTERMATH, 1200–1500   322

The Rise of the Mongols, 1200–1260   *323*
The Mongols and Islam, 1260–1500   *328*
Regional Responses in Western Eurasia   *332*

Mongol Domination in China, 1271–1368   335
The Early Ming Empire, 1368–1500   339
ENVIRONMENT + TECHNOLOGY: From Gunpowder to Guns   342
Centralization and Militarism in East Asia, 1200–1500   343
Conclusion   348
IMPORTANT EVENTS 1200–1500   349

14

LATIN EUROPE, 1200–1500   350

Rural Growth and Crisis   350
Urban Revival   356
DIVERSITY + DOMINANCE: Persecution and Protection of Jews, 1272–1349   360
Learning, Literature, and the Renaissance   363
Political and Military Transformations   368
Conclusion   372
IMPORTANT EVENTS 1200–1500   373

15

SOUTHERN EMPIRES, SOUTHERN SEAS, 1200–1500   374

Tropical Africa and Asia   375
New Islamic Empires   379
Indian Ocean Trade   384
ENVIRONMENT + TECHNOLOGY: The Indian Ocean Dhow   385
Social and Cultural Change   390
The Western Hemisphere   394
Conclusion   399
IMPORTANT EVENTS 1200–1500   400

16

THE MARITIME REVOLUTION, TO 1550   401

Global Maritime Expansion Before 1450   402
European Expansion, 1400–1550   408
Encounters with Europe, 1450–1550   415
DIVERSITY + DOMINANCE: Kongo's Christian King   418
Conclusion   427
IMPORTANT EVENTS TO 1500   428
ISSUES IN WORLD HISTORY: Climate and Population to 1500   430

PART 5

THE GLOBE ENCOMPASSED, 1500–1750   433

17

TRANSFORMATIONS IN EUROPE, 1500–1750   435

Culture and Ideas   436
Social and Economic Life   445
ENVIRONMENT + TECHNOLOGY: Mapping the World   450
Political Innovations   452
Conclusion   460
IMPORTANT EVENTS 1500–1750   461

18

THE DIVERSITY OF AMERICAN COLONIAL SOCIETIES, 1530–1770   462

The Columbian Exchange   463
Spanish America and Brazil   465
DIVERSITY + DOMINANCE: Race and Ethnicity in the Spanish Colonies: Negotiating Hierarchy   472
English and French Colonies in North America   475
Colonial Expansion and Conflict   484
Conclusion   486
IMPORTANT EVENTS 1500–1770   487

19

THE ATLANTIC SYSTEM AND AFRICA, 1550–1800   488

Plantations in the West Indies   489
Plantation Life in the Eighteenth Century   491
ENVIRONMENT + TECHNOLOGY: Hurricanes and the Caribbean Plantation Economy   494
Creating the Atlantic Economy   500
Africa, the Atlantic, and Islam   506
Conclusion   512
IMPORTANT EVENTS 1500–1800   514

20

BETWEEN EUROPE AND CHINA, 1500–1750   515

The Ottoman Empire, to 1750   516
DIVERSITY + DOMINANCE: Islamic Law and Ottoman Rule   520
The Safavid Empire, 1502–1722   526
The Mughal Empire, 1526–1739   529
The Russian Empire, 1500–1725   531
The Maritime Worlds of Islam, 1500–1750   535
Conclusion   538
IMPORTANT EVENTS 1500–1750   538

21

EAST ASIA IN GLOBAL PERSPECTIVE   540

East Asia and Europe   541

The Imjin War and Japanese Unification   545

Tokugawa Japan and Choson Korea to 1800   546

ENVIRONMENT + TECHNOLOGY: East Asian
Porcelain   548

From Ming to Qing   551

Conclusion   557

IMPORTANT EVENTS 1500–1800   558

ISSUES IN WORLD HISTORY: The Little Ice Age   559

PART 6

REVOLUTIONS RESHAPE THE WORLD,
1750–1870   561

22

THE EARLY INDUSTRIAL REVOLUTION,
1760–1851   562

Causes of the Industrial Revolution   563

The Technological Revolution   567

DIVERSITY + DOMINANCE: Adam Smith and the
Division of Labor   568

The Impact of the Early Industrial Revolution   576

New Economic and Political Ideas   582

The Limits of Industrialization Outside the
West   585

Conclusion   587

IMPORTANT EVENTS 1750–1854   588

23

REVOLUTIONARY CHANGES IN THE
ATLANTIC WORLD, 1750–1850   589

Prelude to Revolution: The Eighteenth-Century
Crisis   590

The American Revolution, 1775–1800   595

The French Revolution, 1789–1815   599

ENVIRONMENT + TECHNOLOGY: The
Guillotine   605

Revolution Spreads, Conservatives Respond,
1789–1850   608

Conclusion   613

IMPORTANT EVENTS 1750–1850   614

24

LAND EMPIRES IN THE AGE OF IMPERIALISM,
1800–1870   615

The Ottoman Empire   616

The Russian Empire   624

The Qing Empire   628

DIVERSITY + DOMINANCE: Chinese Responses to
Imperialism   636

Conclusion   638

IMPORTANT EVENTS 1800–1908   639

25

NATION BUILDING AND ECONOMIC
TRANSFORMATION IN THE AMERICAS,
1800–1890   640

Independence in Latin America,
1800–1830   641

The Problem of Order, 1825–1890   646

The Challenge of Social and Economic
Change   656

ENVIRONMENT + TECHNOLOGY: Industrializing
Sugar Agriculture in Cuba   664

Conclusion   667

IMPORTANT EVENTS 1800–1890   669

ISSUES IN WORLD HISTORY: State Power, the Census,
and the Question of Identity   670

PART 7

GLOBAL DIVERSITY AND DOMINANCE,
1750–1945   673

26

VARIETIES OF IMPERIALISM IN AFRICA, INDIA,
SOUTHEAST ASIA, AND LATIN AMERICA,
1750–1914   675

Changes and Exchanges in Africa   676

DIVERSITY + DOMINANCE: Two Africans Recall the
Arrival of the Europeans   680

India under British Rule   686

Southeast Asia and the Pacific   692

Imperialism in Latin America   695

The World Economy and the Global
Environment   699

Conclusion   702

IMPORTANT EVENTS 1750–1914   703

27

THE NEW POWER BALANCE,
1850–1900   704

New Technologies and the World Economy   705

Social Changes   710

ENVIRONMENT + TECHNOLOGY: Railroads and
Immigration   711

Socialism and Labor Movements   716

Nationalism and the Rise of Italy, Germany, and
    Japan   718
The Great Powers of Europe, 1871–1900   725
China, Japan, and the Western Powers   728
Conclusion   730
IMPORTANT EVENTS 1850–1910   730

28
THE CRISIS OF THE IMPERIAL ORDER, 1900–1929   732

Origins of the Crisis in Europe and the Middle
    East   732
The "Great War" and the Russian Revolutions,
    1914–1918   734
Peace and Dislocation in Europe,
    1919–1929   741
China and Japan: Contrasting Destinies   745
The New Middle East   749
DIVERSITY + DOMINANCE: The Middle East After
World War I   750
Conclusion   755
IMPORTANT EVENTS 1900–1929   756

29
REVOLUTIONS IN LIVING, 1900–1950   757

New Technology Outside the Industrialized
    World   758
New Ways of Living in the Industrialized
    World   761
ENVIRONMENT + TECHNOLOGY: New
Materials   766
A New India, 1905–1947   768
Mexico, Argentina, and Brazil, 1917–1949   774
Sub-Saharan Africa, 1900–1945   778
Conclusion   782
IMPORTANT EVENTS 1900–1950   782

30
THE COLLAPSE OF THE OLD ORDER, 1929–1949   784

The Stalin Revolution   785
The Depression   787
DIVERSITY + DOMINANCE: Women, Family Values,
and the Russian Revolution   790
The Rise of Fascism   792
East Asia, 1931–1945   795
The Second World War   798
The Character of Warfare   805

Conclusion   809
IMPORTANT EVENTS 1920s–1949   810
ISSUES IN WORLD HISTORY: Famines and
Politics   812

PART 8
PERILS AND PROMISES OF A GLOBAL COMMUNITY, 1945 TO THE PRESENT   815

31
THE COLD WAR AND DECOLONIZATION, 1945–1975   816

The Cold War   817
ENVIRONMENT + TECHNOLOGY: The Green
Revolution   820
Decolonization and Nation Building   827
Beyond a Bipolar World   834
Conclusion   840
IMPORTANT EVENTS 1945–1975   841

32
THE END OF THE COLD WAR AND THE CHALLENGE OF ECONOMIC DEVELOPMENT AND IMMIGRATION, 1975–2000   843

Postcolonial Crises and Asian Economic
    Expansion   844
DIVERSITY + DOMINANCE: The Struggle for Women's
Rights in an Era of Global Political and Economic
Change   850
The End of the Bipolar World   854
The Challenge of Population Growth   859
Unequal Development and the Movement of
    Peoples   864
Technological and Environmental Change   868
Conclusion   871
IMPORTANT EVENTS 1970–2000   872

33
NEW CHALLENGES IN A NEW MILLENNIUM   874

Globalization and Economic Crisis   875
The Question of Values   884
ENVIRONMENT + TECHNOLOGY: Global
Warming   888
Global Culture   889
IMPORTANT EVENTS 2000–2012   895

Index   I-1

Preface

In preparing the sixth edition of this book, we examined the flow of topics from chapter to chapter and decided that certain rearrangements within chapters and in the order of chapters would accommodate the needs of instructors and students better than the template they had followed since the first edition. The first change was reversing the order of the third and fourth chapters to have early Mediterranean and Middle Eastern history directly follow the discussion of the origins of civilization in the Nile Valley and Mesopotamia.

The second change addressed the problem of when and how to discuss the history of pre-Columbian America. The time span to be covered, ranging from roughly 1500 B.C.E. to 1500 C.E., was too long to fit easily into the book's division into eight parts. The new structure we have adopted relocates the long pre-Aztec and pre-Inka narrative from Part III, Growth and Interaction of Cultural Communities, to the end of Part II, The Formation of New Cultural Communities. This change puts the status of the earliest civilizations in the Western Hemisphere on the same footing as the civilizations of early Greece, China, and South and Southeast Asia. It has the added benefit of making the history of East Asia in the Tang and Song periods directly precede the history of the Mongol empire, which allows instructors to have an uninterrupted focus on East Asia. The histories of the Aztecs and Inkas have been shifted to the chapter on tropical history located in Part IV, Interregional Patterns of Culture and Contact. This allows for a discussion of the overall influence of tropical environments and places them in close proximity to our treatment of the coming of Europeans to the New World.

A third structural change has shortened the length of the book from 34 to 33 chapters. To lessen the impression that Europe's domination of the world should always be the primary focus of student attention between the eighteenth and mid-twentieth centuries we have combined the two separate chapters on European imperialism, Chapters 26 and 28 in previous editions, into one. We feel that this change provides a better balance between the saga of European imperialism, accounts of resistance to imperialism, and the rise of independence movements in different parts of the world.

In a related change, we have relocated the chapter dealing with the histories of India, Latin America, and Africa in the first half of the twentieth century from after World War II, the old Chapter 31, to a position between the world wars. The aim of this chapter, titled "Revolutions in Living," is to portray that period not only as a time of political change in parts of the world subjected to European imperialism, but also as one of transformation of daily lives of people in both the industrialized and nonindustrialized worlds. The added focus of the chapter fills a gap between discussion of the Industrial Revolution in the eighteenth and nineteenth centuries and the advent of major technological changes in the post-World War II era.

Finally in this new edition, contributor and East Asian specialist Michael Wert of Marquette University brought a fresh perspective to many of our chapters dealing with East Asia, helping ensure that our coverage is at the forefront of emerging scholarship.

The authors believe that these changes, along with myriad smaller changes detailed below, significantly enhance the overall goal of *The Earth and Its Peoples*, namely, to be a textbook that speaks not only for the past but also to today's student and teacher. Students and instructors alike should take away from this text a broad, and due to the changes, more flowing impression of human societies beginning as sparse and disconnected communities reacting creatively to local circumstances; experiencing ever more intensive stages of contact, interpenetration, and cultural expansion and amalgamation; and arriving at a twenty-first-century world in which people increasingly visualize a single global community.

Process, not progress, is the keynote of this book: a steady process of change over time, at first experienced differently in various regions, but eventually connecting peoples and traditions from all parts of the globe. Students should come away from this book with a sense that the problems and promises of their world are rooted in a past in which people of every sort, in every part of the world, confronted problems of a similar character and coped with them as best they could. We believe that our efforts will help students see where their world has come from and learn thereby something useful for their own lives.

Central Themes and Goals
We subtitled *The Earth and Its Peoples* "A Global History" because the book explores the common challenges and experiences that unite the human past. Although the dispersal of early humans to every livable environment resulted in a myriad of different economic, social, political, and cultural systems, all societies displayed

analogous patterns in meeting their needs and exploiting their environments. Our challenge was to select the particular data and episodes that would best illuminate these global patterns of human experience.

To meet this challenge, we adopted two themes for our history: "technology and the environment" and "diversity and dominance." The first theme represents the commonplace material bases of all human societies at all times. It grants no special favor to any cultural group even as it embraces subjects of the broadest topical, chronological, and geographical range. The second theme expresses the reality that every human society has constructed or inherited structures of domination. We examine practices and institutions of many sorts: military, economic, social, political, religious, and cultural, as well as those based on kinship, gender, and literacy. Simultaneously we recognize that alternative ways of life and visions of societal organization continually manifest themselves both within and in dialogue with every structure of domination.

With respect to the first theme, it is vital for students to understand that technology, in the broad sense of experience-based knowledge of the physical world, underlies all human activity. Writing is a technology, but so is oral transmission from generation to generation of lore about medicinal or poisonous plants. The magnetic compass is a navigational technology, but so is Polynesian mariners' hard-won knowledge of winds, currents, and tides that made possible the settlement of the Pacific islands.

All technological development has come about in interaction with environments, both physical and human, and has, in turn, affected those environments. The story of how humanity has changed the face of the globe is an integral part of our first theme. Yet technology and the environment do not explain or underlie all important episodes of human experience. The theme of "diversity and dominance" informs all our discussions of politics, culture, and society. Thus when narrating the histories of empires, we describe a range of human experiences within and beyond the imperial frontiers without assuming that imperial institutions are a more fit topic for discussion than the economic and social organization of pastoral nomads or the lives of peasant women. When religion and culture occupy our narrative, we focus not only on the dominant tradition but also on the diversity of alternative beliefs and practices.

Organization

The *Earth and Its Peoples* uses eight broad chronological divisions to define its conceptual scheme of global historical development.

In **Part One: The Emergence of Human Communities, to 500 B.C.E.**, we examine important patterns of human communal organization primarily in the Eastern Hemisphere. Small, dispersed human communities living by foraging spread to most parts of the world over tens of thousands of years. They responded to enormously diverse environmental conditions, at different times in different ways, discovering how to cultivate plants and utilize the products of domestic animals. On the basis of these new modes of sustenance, population grew, permanent towns appeared, and political and religious authority, based on collection and control of agricultural surpluses, spread over extensive areas.

Part Two: The Formation of New Cultural Communities, 1000 B.C.E.–400 C.E., introduces the concept of a "cultural community," in the sense of a coherent pattern of activities and symbols pertaining to a specific human community. While all human communities develop distinctive cultures, including those discussed in Part One, historical development in this stage of global history prolonged and magnified the impact of some cultures more than others. In the geographically contiguous African-Eurasian landmass, as well as in the Western Hemisphere, the cultures that proved to have the most enduring influence traced their roots to the second and first millennia B.C.E.

Part Three: Growth and Interaction of Cultural Communities, 300 B.C.E.–1200 C.E., deals with early episodes of technological, social, and cultural exchange and interaction on a continental scale both within and beyond the framework of imperial expansion. These are so different from earlier interactions arising from more limited conquests or extensions of political boundaries that they constitute a distinct era in world history, an era that set the world on the path of increasing global interaction and interdependence that it has been following ever since.

In **Part Four: Interregional Patterns of Culture and Contact, 1200–1550**, we look at the world during the three and a half centuries that saw both intensified cultural and commercial contact and increasingly confident self-definition of cultural communities in Europe, Asia, Africa, and the Americas. The Mongol conquest of a vast empire extending from the Pacific Ocean to eastern Europe greatly stimulated trade and interaction. In the West, strengthened European kingdoms began maritime expansion in the Atlantic, forging direct ties with sub-Saharan Africa and entering into conflict with the civilizations of the Western Hemisphere.

Part Five: The Globe Encompassed, 1500–1750, treats a period dominated by the global effects of European expansion and continued economic growth. European ships took over, expanded, and extended the maritime trade of the Indian Ocean, coastal Africa, and the Asian rim of the Pacific Ocean. This maritime commercial enterprise had its counterpart in European colonial empires in the Americas and a new Atlantic trading system. The contrasting capacities and fortunes of traditional land empires and new maritime empires, along with the exchange of domestic plants and animals between the hemispheres, underline the technological and environmental dimensions of this first era of complete global interaction.

In **Part Six: Revolutions Reshape the World, 1750–1870**, the word *revolution* is used in several senses: in the political sense of governmental overthrow, as in France and the Americas; in the metaphorical sense of radical transformative change, as in the Industrial Revolution; and in the broadest sense of a perception of a profound change in circumstances and worldview. Technology and environment lie at the core of these developments. With the rapid ascendancy of the Western belief that science and technology could overcome all challenges—environmental or otherwise—technology became an instrument not only of transformation but also of domination, to the point of threatening the integrity and autonomy of cultural traditions in nonindustrial lands and provoking strong movements of resistance.

Part Seven: Global Diversity and Dominance, 1750–1945, examines the development of a world arena in which people conceived of events on a global scale. Imperialism, international economic connections, and world-encompassing ideological tendencies, such as nationalism and socialism, present the picture of a globe becoming increasingly involved with European political and ideological concerns. Two world wars arising from European rivalries provide a climax to these developments, and European exhaustion affords other parts of the world new opportunities for independence and self-expression.

For **Part Eight: Perils and Promises of a Global Community, 1945 to the Present,** we divide the period since World War II into three time periods: 1945–1975, 1975–2000, and 2000 to the present. The challenges of the Cold War and postcolonial nation building dominate much of the period and unleash global economic, technological, and political forces that become increasingly important in all aspects of human life. With the end of the Cold War, however, new forces come to the fore. Technology is a key topic in Part Eight because of its integral role in both the growth and the problems of a global community. However, its many benefits in improving the quality of life become clouded by negative impacts on the environment.

Features and New Pedagogical AIDS   As with previous editions, the sixth edition offers a number of valuable features and pedagogical aids designed to pique student interest in specific world history topics and help them process and retain key information. Historical essays for each of the eight parts called Issues in World History are specifically designed to alert students to broad and recurring conceptual issues that are of great interest to contemporary historians; this feature has proved to be an instructor and student favorite. The Environment and Technology feature, which has been a valuable resource in all prior editions of *The Earth and Its Peoples*, serves to illuminate the major theme of the text by demonstrating the shared material bases of all human societies across time. Finally, Diversity and Dominance, also core to the theme of the text, is the primary source feature that brings a myriad of real historical voices to life in a common struggle for power and autonomy.

Changes in this Edition   Here are a few highlights:

- Chapter 4 descriptions of early civilizations in the Western Hemisphere have been shifted to Chapter 8 in order to facilitate a more unified discussion of Pre-Columbian America.

- Chapter 4 also contains a substantial new section on pastoral nomadism in the Eurasian steppe. Chapter 6 has a new Diversity and Dominance feature, "Socioeconomic Mobility: Winners and Losers in Imperial Rome and Han China."

- Chapter 8 has been extensively revised. Discussion of the Olmec and Chavín have been moved from Chapter 3 and the discussion of the Toltec, Tiwanaku, Wari, and Chimú civilizations expanded. Discussion of the Aztec and Inka civilizations appears in Chapter 15.

- Chapter 9 includes discussion of early Egyptian archaeological site of Nabta Playa.

- Chapter 12 contains expanded coverage of Korea.

- Chapter 13 contains expanded coverage of Vietnam and Yunnan province in southwest China.

- Chapter 14 has expanded coverage of eastern Europe and the Ottoman empire.

- Chapter 15 bears a new title, "Southern Empires, Southern Seas," and includes treatment of the Aztec and Inka empires that were previously covered much earlier in the book.

- Chapter 16 reflects new research on South Asian and Polynesian maritime cultures.

- Chapter 17 includes expanded coverage of early capitalism, including a discussion of stock markets and speculative bubbles like the Tulip, South Sea, and Mississippi Company frenzies.

- Chapter 19 includes a new feature, "Hurricanes and the Caribbean Plantation Economy."

- Chapter 20 has expanded to include the history of Russia, hence a new opening that features a Russian popular hero and the change of title to "Territorial Empires Between Europe and China."

- Chapter 21 has a new discussion of Korean history and the Imjin War.

- Chapters 22–23 have been reversed in sequence to provide better continuity to discussions of revolutions in Europe and parallel changes in the Americas.

- Chapter 22 includes a new discussion of proto-industrialization as well as augmented discussions of the spread of industrialization to continental Europe and North America and the early career of Karl Marx. The section "Protest and Reform" has been broadly revised to include machine breaking in the textile sector and rural resistance to mechanization in the Captain Swing riots.

- Chapter 25 has a new feature: "Industrializing Sugar Agriculture in Cuba."

- Chapter 26 combines accounts of European imperialism that were previously contained in this chapter and in Chapter 28.

- Chapter 27 features a revised discussion of early Japanese industrialization as well as an expanded treatment of Marx and Marxism and a new discussion of Mikhail Bakunin and anarchism.

- Chapter 29 combines in a new chapter a discussion of technology and lifestyle changes that occurred between 1900 and 1945 with accounts of political movements in India, Latin America, and Africa that were previously located in Chapter 31. Highlights include an Environment and Technology feature, "New Materials."

- Chapter 31 includes an updated discussion about the Cold War confrontation between West and East plus a revised discussion of apartheid and South Africa's struggle for independence.

- Chapter 33 updates world affairs through the first half of 2013 and incorporates new statistical information on maps.

Formats   To accommodate different academic calendars and approaches to the course, *The Earth and Its Peoples* is available in three formats. There is a one-volume version containing all 33 chapters, along with a two-volume edition: Volume I: To 1550 (Chapters 1–16) and Volume II: Since 1500 (Chapters 16–33). Volume II includes an Introduction that surveys the main developments set out in Volume I and provides a groundwork for students studying only the period since 1500.

ANCILLARIES

A wide array of supplements accompany this text to assist students with different learning needs and to help instructors master today's various classroom challenges.

Instructor Resources   Aplia™ [ISBN: 9781285767949] is an online interactive learning solution that improves comprehension and outcomes by increasing student effort and engagement. Founded by a professor to enhance his own courses, Aplia provides automatically graded assignments with detailed, immediate explanations on every question. The interactive assignments have been developed to address the major concepts covered in *The Earth and Its Peoples* and are designed to promote critical thinking and engage students more fully in learning. Question types include questions built around animated maps, primary sources such as newspaper extracts, or imagined scenarios, like engaging in a conversation with a historical figure or finding a diary and being asked to fill in some blanks; more in-depth primary source question sets address a major topic with a number of related primary sources and questions that promote deeper analysis of historical evidence. Many of the questions incorporate images, video clips, or audio clips. Students get immediate feedback on their work (not only what they got right or wrong, but why), and they can choose to see another set of related questions if they want more practice. A searchable eBook is available inside the course as well so that students can easily reference it as they work. Map-reading and writing tutorials are also available to get students off to a good start.

Aplia's simple-to-use course management interface allows instructors to post announcements, upload course materials, host student discussions, e-mail students, and manage the gradebook; a knowledgeable and friendly support team offers assistance and personalized support in customizing assignments to the instructor's course schedule. To learn more and view a demo for this book, visit www.aplia.com.

MindTap Reader for *The Earth and Its Peoples* is an eBook specifically designed to address the ways students assimilate content and media assets. MindTap Reader combines thoughtful navigation ergonomics, advanced student annotation, note-taking, and search tools, and embedded media assets such as video and MP3 chapter summaries, primary source documents with critical thinking questions, and interactive (zoomable) maps. Students can use the eBook as their primary text or as a multimedia companion to their printed book. The MindTap Reader eBook is available within the MindTap and Aplia online offerings found at www.cengagebrain.com.

Online PowerLecture with Cognero® This PowerLecture is an all-in-one online multimedia resource for class preparation, presentation, and testing. Accessible through Cengage.com/login with your faculty account, you will find the following available for download.

The **Test Bank**, offered in Cognero® format, contains multiple-choice and essay questions for each chapter. Cognero® is a flexible, online system that allows you to author, edit, and manage test bank content for *The Earth and Its People*, sixth edition. Create multiple test versions instantly and deliver through your LMS from your classroom, or wherever you may be, with no special installs or downloads required.

The **Instructor's Manual** contains for each chapter: an outline and summary; critical thinking questions; in-class activities; lecture launching suggestions; a list of key terms with definitions; and suggested readings and Web resources.

The *Microsoft® PowerPoint® presentations* are ready-to-use, visual outlines of each chapter. These presentations are easily customized for your lectures. These PowerPoint Lecture Tools include presentations of only lecture or only images, as well as combined lecture and image presentations.

History CourseMate Cengage Learning's History CourseMate brings course concepts to life with interactive learning, study tools, and exam preparation tools that support the printed textbook. Use Engagement Tracker to monitor student engagement in the course and watch student comprehension soar as your class works with the printed textbook and the textbook-specific website. An interactive eBook allows students to take notes, highlight, search, and interact with embedded media (such as quizzes, flashcards, primary sources, and videos). Learn more at **www.cengage.com/coursemate**.

CourseReader CourseReader is an online collection of primary and secondary sources that lets you create a customized electronic reader in minutes. With an easy-to-use interface and assessment tool, you can choose exactly what your students will be assigned—simply search or browse Cengage Learning's extensive document database to preview and select your customized collection of readings. In addition to print sources of all types (letters, diary entries, speeches, newspaper accounts, etc.), their collection includes a growing number of images and video and audio clips.

Each primary source document includes a descriptive headnote that puts the reading into context and is further supported by both critical thinking and multiple-choice questions designed to reinforce key points. For more information visit **www.cengage.com/coursereader**.

Cengagebrain.com Save your students time and money. Direct them to **www.cengagebrain.com** for choice in formats and savings and a better chance to succeed in your class. Cengagebrain.com, Cengage Learning's online store, is a single destination for more than 10,000 new textbooks, eTextbooks, eChapters, study tools, and audio supplements. Students have the freedom to purchase a-la-carte exactly what they need when they need it. Students can save 50% on the electronic textbook, and can pay as little as $1.99 for an individual eChapter.

Reader Program Cengage Learning publishes a number of readers, some containing exclusively primary sources, others a combination of primary and secondary sources, and some designed to guide students through the process of historical inquiry. Visit Cengage.com/history for a complete list of readers.

Custom Options Nobody knows your students like you, so why not give them a text that is tailor-fit to their needs? Cengage Learning offers custom solutions for your course—whether it's making a small modification to The Earth and Its Peoples to match your syllabus or combining multiple sources to create something truly unique. You can pick and choose chapters, include your own material, and add additional map exercises along with the Rand McNally Atlas to create a text that fits the way you teach. Ensure that your students get the most out of their textbook dollar by giving them exactly what they need. Contact your Cengage Learning representative to explore custom solutions for your course.

Student Resources   *Writing for College History,* first edition [ISBN: 9780618306039]   Prepared by Robert M. Frakes, Clarion University. This brief handbook for survey courses in American history, Western Civilization/European history, and world civilization guides students through the various types of writing assignments they encounter in a history class. Providing examples of student writing and candid assessments of student work, this text focuses on the rules and conventions of writing for the college history course.

The History Handbook, second edition [ISBN: 9780495906766]   Prepared by Carol Berkin of Baruch College, City University of New York and Betty Anderson of Boston University. This book teaches students both basic and history-specific study skills such as how to read primary sources, research historical topics, and correctly cite sources. Substantially less expensive than comparable skill-building texts, *The History Handbook* also offers tips for Internet research and evaluating online sources.

Doing History: Research and Writing in the Digital Age, second edition [ISBN: 9781133587880]   Prepared by Michael J. Galgano, J. Chris Arndt, and Raymond M. Hyser of James Madison University. Whether you're starting down the path as a history major, or simply looking for a straightforward and systematic guide to writing a successful paper, you'll find this text to be an indispensible handbook to historical research. This text's "soup to nuts" approach to researching and writing about history addresses every step of the process, from locating your sources and gathering information, to writing clearly and making proper use of various citation styles to avoid plagiarism. You'll also learn how to make the most of every tool available to you—especially the technology that helps you conduct the process efficiently and effectively.

The Modern Researcher, sixth edition [ISBN: 9780495318705]   Prepared by Jacques Barzun and Henry F. Graff of Columbia University. This classic introduction to the techniques of research and the art of expression is used widely in history courses, but is also appropriate for writing and research methods courses in other departments. Barzun and Graff thoroughly cover every aspect of research, from the selection of a topic through the gathering, analysis, writing, revision, and publication of findings, presenting the process not as a set of rules but through actual cases that put the subtleties of research in a useful context. Part One covers the principles and methods of research; Part Two covers writing, speaking, and getting one's work published.

Rand McNally Historical Atlas of the World, second edition [ISBN: 9780618841912]   This valuable resource features over 70 maps that portray the rich panoply of the world's history from preliterate times to the present. They show how cultures and civilization were linked and how they interacted. The maps make it clear that history is not static. Rather, it is about change and movement across time. The maps show change by presenting the dynamics of expansion, cooperation, and conflict. This atlas includes maps that display the world from the beginning of civilization; the political development of all major areas of the world; expanded coverage of Africa, Latin America, and the Middle East; the current Islamic World; and the world population change in 1900 and 2000.

ACKNOWLEDGMENTS

In preparing the sixth edition, we benefited from the critical readings of many colleagues. Our sincere thanks go in particular to contributor Michael Wert of Marquette University who lent his fresh perspective to our coverage of East Asia. We thank Beatrice Manz of the History Department at Tufts University who provided guidance on the new Pastoral Nomads section in Part I. We are also indebted to the following instructors who lent their insight over various editions: Hedrick Alixopuilos, Santa Rosa Junior College; Hayden Bellenoit, U.S. Naval Academy; Dusty Bender, Central Baptist College; Cory Crawford, Ohio University; Adrian De Gifis, Loyola University New Orleans; Peter de Rosa, Bridgewater State University; Aaron Gulyas, Mott Community College; Darlene Hall, Lake Erie College; Vic Jagos, Scottsdale Community College; Adrien Ivan, Vernon College; Andrew Muldoon, Metropolitan State College of Denver; Percy Murray, Shaw University; Dave Price, Santa Fe College; Anthony Steinhoff, University of Tennessee-Chattanooga; Anara Tabyshalieva, Marshal University; Susan Autry, Central Piedmont Community College; Christopher Cameron, University of North Carolina at Charlotte; Anna Collins, Arkansas Tech University; William Connell, Christopher Newport University; Gregory Crider, Winthrop University; Shawn Dry, Oakland Community College; Nancy Fitch, California State University, Fullerton; Christine Haynes, University of North Carolina at Charlotte; Mark Herman, Edison College; Ellen J. Jenkins, Arkansas Tech University; Frank Karpiel, The Citadel; Ken Koons, Virginia Military Institute; David Longfellow, Baylor University; Heather Lucas, Georgia Perimeter College; Jeff Pardue, Gainesville State College; Craig Patton, Alabama A & M University; Amanda Pipkin, University of North Carolina at Charlotte; Linda Scherr, Mercer County Community College; Robert Sherwood,

Georgia Military College; Brett Shufelt, Copiah-Lincoln Community College; Peter Thorsheim, University of North Carolina at Charlotte; Kristen Walton, Salisbury University; Christopher Ward, Clayton State University; William Wood, Point Loma Nazarene University.

When textbook authors set out on a project, they are inclined to believe that 90 percent of the effort will be theirs and 10 percent that of various editors and production specialists employed by their publisher. How very naïve. This book would never have seen the light of day had it not been for the unstinting labors of the great team of professionals who turned the authors' words into beautifully presented print. Our debt to the staff of Cengage Learning remains undiminished in the sixth edition. Brooke Barbier, product manager, has offered us firm but sympathetic guidance throughout the revision process. Tonya Lobato, senior content developer, offered astute and sympathetic assistance as the authors worked to incorporate many new ideas and subjects into the text. Carol Newman, senior content project manager, moved the work through the production stages to meet a challenging schedule. Abbey Stebing did an outstanding job of photo research.

We thank also the many students whose questions and concerns, expressed directly or through their instructors, shaped much of this revision. We continue to welcome all readers' suggestions, queries, and criticisms. Please contact us at our respective institutions.

ABOUT THE AUTHORS

RICHARD W. BULLIET   Professor of Middle Eastern History at Columbia University, Richard W. Bulliet received his Ph.D. from Harvard University. He has written scholarly works on a number of topics: the social and economic history of medieval Iran (The Patricians of Nishapur and Cotton, Climate, and Camels in Early Islamic Iran), the history of human-animal relations (The Camel and the Wheel and Hunters, Herders, and Hamburgers), the process of conversion to Islam (Conversion to Islam in the Medieval Period), and the overall course of Islamic social history (Islam: The View from the Edge and The Case for Islamo-Christian Civilization). He is the editor of the Columbia History of the Twentieth Century. He has published four novels, coedited The Encyclopedia of the Modern Middle East, and hosted an educational television series on the Middle East. He was awarded a fellowship by the John Simon Guggenheim Memorial Foundation and was named a Carnegie Corporation Scholar.

PAMELA KYLE CROSSLEY   Pamela Kyle Crossley received her Ph.D. in Modern Chinese History from Yale University. She is currently the Robert and Barbara Black Professor of History at Dartmouth College. Her books include The Wobbling Pivot: An Interpretive History of China Since 1800; What Is Global History?; A Translucent Mirror: History and Identity in Qing Imperial Ideology; The Manchus; Orphan Warriors: Three Manchu Generations and the End of the Qing World; and (with Lynn Hollen Lees and John W. Servos) Global Society: The World Since 1900.

DANIEL R. HEADRICK   Daniel R. Headrick received his Ph.D. in History from Princeton University. Professor of History and Social Science, Emeritus, at Roosevelt University in Chicago, he is the author of several books on the history of technology, imperialism, and international relations, including The Tools of Empire: Technology and European Imperialism in the Nineteenth Century; The Tentacles of Progress: Technology Transfer in the Age of Imperialism; The Invisible Weapon: Telecommunications and International Politics; Technology: A World History; Power Over Peoples: Technology, Environments and Western Imperialism, 1400 to the Present; and When Information Came of Age: Technologies of Knowledge in the Age of Reason and Revolution, 1700–1850. His articles have appeared in the Journal of World History and the Journal of Modern History, and he has been awarded fellowships by the National Endowment for the Humanities, the John Simon Guggenheim Memorial Foundation, and the Alfred P. Sloan Foundation.

STEVEN W. HIRSCH   Steven W. Hirsch holds a Ph.D. in Classics from Stanford University and is currently Associate Professor of Classics and History at Tufts University. He has received grants from the National Endowment for the Humanities and the Massachusetts Foundation for Humanities and Public Policy. His research and publications include The Friendship of the Barbarians: Xenophon and the Persian Empire, as well as articles and reviews in the Classical Journal, the American Journal of Philology, and the Journal of Interdisciplinary History. He is currently completing a comparative study of ancient Greco-Roman and Chinese civilizations.

LYMAN L. JOHNSON   Professor Emeritus of History at the University of North Carolina at Charlotte, Lyman L. Johnson earned his Ph.D. in Latin American History from the University of Connecticut. A two-time Senior Fulbright-Hays Lecturer, he also has received fellowships from the Tinker Foundation, the Social Science Research Council, the National Endowment for the Humanities, and the American

Philosophical Society. His recent books include Workshop of Revolution: Plebeian Buenos Aires and the Atlantic World, 1776-1810; Death, Dismemberment, and Memory; The Faces of Honor (with Sonya Lipsett-Rivera); Aftershocks: Earthquakes and Popular Politics in Latin America (with Jürgen Buchenau); Essays on the Price History of Eighteenth-Century Latin America (with Enrique Tandeter); and Colonial Latin America (with Mark A. Burkholder). He also has published in journals, including the Hispanic American Historical Review, the Journal of Latin American Studies, the International Review of Social History, Social History, and Desarrollo Económico. He has served as president of the Conference on Latin American History.

DAVID NORTHRUP David Northrup earned his Ph.D. in African and European History from the University of California, Los Angeles. He has published scholarly works on African, Atlantic, and world history. His most recent books are How English Became the Global Language, the third edition of Africa's Discovery of Europe, 1450–1850, and the Diary of Antera Duke, an Eighteenth-Century African Slave Trader. He taught at a rural secondary school on Nigeria, Tuskegee Institute in Alabama, Boston College, and Venice International University and is a past president of the World History Association.

NOTE ON SPELLING AND USAGE

Where necessary for clarity, dates are followed by the letters C.E. or B.C.E. The abbreviation C.E. stands for "Common Era" and is equivalent to A.D. (anno Domini, Latin for "in the year of the Lord"). The abbreviation B.C.E. stands for "before the Common Era" and means the same as B.C. ("before Christ"). In keeping with our goal of approaching world history without special concentration on one culture or another, we chose these neutral abbreviations as appropriate to our enterprise. Because many readers will be more familiar with English than with metric measurements, however, units of measure are generally given in the English system, with metric equivalents following in parentheses.

In general, Chinese has been Romanized according to the pinyin method. Exceptions include proper names well established in English (e.g., Canton, Chiang Kaishek) and a few English words borrowed from Chinese (e.g., kowtow). Spellings of Arabic, Ottoman Turkish, Persian, Mongolian, Manchu, Japanese, and Korean names and terms avoid special diacritical marks for letters that are pronounced only slightly differently in English. An apostrophe is used to indicate when two Chinese syllables are pronounced separately (e.g., Chang'an).

For words transliterated from languages that use the Arabic script—Arabic, Ottoman Turkish, Persian, Urdu—the apostrophe indicating separately pronounced syllables may represent either of two special consonants, the hamza or the ain. Because most English-speakers do not hear the distinction between these two, they have not been distinguished in transliteration and are not indicated when they occur at the beginning or end of a word. As with Chinese, some words and commonly used place-names from these languages are given familiar English spellings (e.g., Quran instead of Qur'an, Cairo instead of al-Qahira). Arabic romanization has normally been used for terms relating to Islam, even where the context justifies slightly different Turkish or Persian forms, again for ease of comprehension.

Before 1492 the inhabitants of the Western Hemisphere had no single name for themselves. They had neither a racial consciousness nor a racial identity. Identity was derived from kin groups, language, cultural practices, and political structures. There was no sense that physical similarities created a shared identity. America's original inhabitants had racial consciousness and racial identity imposed on them by conquest and the occupation of their lands by Europeans after 1492. All of the collective terms for these first American peoples are tainted by this history. Indians, Native Americans, Amerindians, First Peoples, and Indigenous Peoples are among the terms in common usage. In this book the names of individual cultures and states are used wherever possible. Amerindian and other terms that suggest transcultural identity and experience are used most commonly for the period after 1492.

There is an ongoing debate about how best to render Amerindian words in English. It has been common for authors writing in English to follow Mexican usage for Nahuatl and Yucatec Maya words and place-names. In this style, for example, the capital of the Aztec state is spelled Tenochtitlán, and the important late Maya city-state is spelled Chichén Itzá. Although these forms are still common even in the specialist literature, we have chosen to follow the scholarship that sees these accents as unnecessary. The exceptions are modern place-names, such as Mérida and Yucatán, which are accented. A similar problem exists for the spelling of Quechua and Aymara words from the Andean region of South America. Although there is significant disagreement among scholars, we follow the emerging consensus and use the spellings khipu (not quipu), Tiwanaku (not Tiahuanaco), and Wari (not Huari). In this edition we have introduced the now common spelling Inka (not Inca) but keep Cuzco for the capital city (not Cusco), since this spelling facilitates locating this still-important city on maps.

PART ONE

◆

THE EMERGENCE OF HUMAN COMMUNITIES, TO 500 B.C.E.

CHAPTER 1
Nature, Humanity, and History, to 3500 B.C.E.

CHAPTER 2
The First River-Valley Civilizations, 3500–1500 B.C.E.

CHAPTER 3
The Mediterranean and Middle East, 2000–500 B.C.E.

CHAPTER 4
New Civilizations Outside the West Asian Core Area, 2300 B.C.E.–350 C.E.

Human beings evolved over several million years from primates in Africa. Able to walk upright and possessing large brains, hands with opposable thumbs, and the capacity for speech, early humans used teamwork and created tools to survive in diverse environments. They spread relatively quickly to almost every habitable area of the world, hunting and gathering wild plant products. Around 10,000 years ago some groups began to cultivate plants, domesticate animals, and make pottery vessels for storage. These developments led to permanent settlements—at first small villages but eventually larger towns.

The earliest complex societies arose in the great river valleys of Mesopotamia, Egypt, Pakistan, and northern China. In these arid regions agriculture depended on river water, and centers of political power arose to organize the labor required to dig and maintain irrigation channels. Kings and priests dominated these early societies from the urban centers, helped by administrators, scribes, soldiers, merchants, craftsmen, and others with specialized skills. Surplus food grown in the countryside by a dependent peasantry sustained the activities of these groups.

As they sought access to raw materials, especially metals, certain centers came to dominate broader expanses of territory. This development also stimulated long-distance trade and diplomatic relations between major powers. Artisans made weapons, tools, and ritual objects from bronze, and culture and technology spread to neighboring regions, such as southern China, Nubia, Syria-Palestine, Anatolia, and the Aegean.

In the Western Hemisphere, different geographical circumstances led to distinctive patterns of technological and cultural response. These early civilizations in southern Mexico and the Andean region of South America are discussed in Part 2.

1

NATURE, HUMANITY, AND HISTORY, TO 3500 B.C.E.

P aintings and engravings on stone created tens of thousands of years ago by early humans have been found on every continent. Someone in Central Africa carved this image of cattle around 5000 B.C.E., when the Sahara was not a desert but a verdant savanna supporting numerous species of wildlife. Why the image was carved and what significance it originally held will likely remain a mystery, but for us it is a beautiful work of art that reveals much about our human ancestry.

Long before the invention of writing, societies told themselves stories about how human beings and the natural world were created. Some, like the Yoruba (yoh-roo-bah) people of West Africa, related that the first humans came down from the sky; others, like the Hopi of southwest North America, claimed that they emerged out of a hole in the earth. Although such creation myths typically explain how a people's way of life, social divisions, and cultural system arose, historical accuracy in the modern sense was not their primary purpose. As with the story of Adam and Eve in the Hebrew Bible, their goal was to define the moral principles that people thought should govern their dealings with the supernatural world, with each other, and with the rest of nature.

In the nineteenth century evidence began to accumulate about the actual origins of humanity. Natural scientists were finding remains of early humans who resembled apes. Other discoveries suggested that the familiar ways of life based on farming and herding did not arise within a generation or two of creation, as many myths suggested, but tens of thousands of years after humans first appeared. This evidence provides insights into human identity that are as meaningful as those propounded by the creation myths.

AFRICAN GENESIS

The discovery in the mid-nineteenth century of the remains of ancient creatures that had both humanlike and apelike features generated excitement and controversy. The finds upset many people because they challenged religious beliefs about human origins. Others welcomed the new evidence for what some had long suspected: that the physical characteristics of modern humans had evolved over incredibly long periods of time.

Interpreting the Evidence   In 1856 in the Neander Valley of Germany, laborers discovered fossilized bones of a creature with a body much like that of modern humans but with a face that had heavy brow ridges and a low forehead, like the faces of apes. Although we now know these were Neanderthals, a type of human common in Europe and the Middle East from 135,000 to 25,000 years ago, in the mid-nineteenth century the idea of humans that different from modern people was so novel that some scholars thought they must be deformed individuals from recent times.

Three years after the Neanderthal finds, Charles Darwin, a young English naturalist (student of natural history), published *On the Origin of Species*, in which he argued that the time frame for all biological life was far longer than most people supposed. Darwin based his conclusion on the pioneering research of others and on his own investigations of fossils and living plant and animal species in Latin America. He proposed that the great diversity of living species and the profound changes in them over time could be explained by natural selection, the process by which biological variations that enhance a population's ability to survive become dominant in that species. He theorized that, over long periods of time, the changes brought about by this process could lead to the **evolution** of distinct new species.

Turning to the sensitive subject of human evolution in *The Descent of Man* (1871), Darwin summarized the growing consensus among naturalists that human beings had come into existence through the same process of natural selection. Because humans shared so many physical similarities with African apes, he proposed Africa as the home of the first humans, even though there was no fossil evidence at the time to support his hypothesis.

The next major discoveries pointed to Asia, rather than Africa, as the original human home. On the Indonesian island of Java in 1891, Eugene Dubois uncovered an ancient skullcap of what was soon called Java man. In 1929 near Peking (an old form of Beijing [bay-jeeng]), China, W. C. Pei discovered a similar skullcap of what became known as Peking man.

By then, even older fossils had been found in southern Africa. In 1924 Raymond Dart found the skull of a creature that he named *Australopithecus africanus* (aw-strah-loh-PITH-uh-kuhs ah-frih-KAH-nuhs) (African southern ape), which he argued was transitional between apes and early humans. For many years most specialists disputed Dart's idea because, although *Australopithecus africanus* walked upright like a human, its brain was the size of an ape's.

Since 1950, Louis and Mary Leakey and their son Richard, along with many others, have discovered a wealth of early human fossils in the exposed sediments of the Great Rift Valley of eastern Africa. These finds are strong evidence for Dart's hypothesis and for Darwin's guess that the tropical habitat of the African apes was the cradle of humanity.

The development of modern archaeological techniques has added to our knowledge. Rather than collect isolated bones, researchers sift the neighboring soils to extract the fossilized remains of other creatures, seeds, and even pollen existing at the time, documenting the environment in which early humans lived. They can also measure the age of most finds by the rate of molecular change in potassium, contained in minerals in lava flows, or in carbon from wood and bone.

A major new approach was made possible by the full decipherment of the human genetic code in 2003. Researchers have been able to extrapolate backward from genetic differences among contemporary human populations to answer such questions as: when language first emerged; the approximate size and location in Northeast Africa of the ancestral human population and the date when some of its members moved out of the continent; the paths taken by migrating groups as humans ultimately spread to all habitable parts of the planet; and when the skin color of the various human populations developed.

By combining these forms of evidence with the growing understanding of how other species adapt to their natural environments, researchers can trace the evolutionary changes that produced modern humans over the course of millions of years.

Human Evolution

Biologists classify **australopithecines** (aw-strah-loh-PITH-uh-seen) and humans as members of a family of primates known as **hominids** (HOM-uh-nid). Primates are members of a class of warm-blooded, four-limbed, social animals known as mammals that came to prominence about 65 million years ago. The first hominids are now dated to about 7 million years ago.

Among living primates, modern humans are most closely related to the African apes—chimpanzees and gorillas. Since Darwin's time it has been popular (and controversial) to say that we are descended from apes. In fact, apes and humans share a common ancestor. Over 99 percent of human DNA, the basic genetic blueprint, is identical to that of the great apes. But three traits distinguish humans from apes and other primates. The earliest of these traits to appear was **bipedalism** (walking upright on two legs). Being upright frees the forelimbs from any role in locomotion and enhances an older primate trait: a hand with a long, opposable thumb that can work with the fingers to manipulate objects skillfully. Modern humans' second distinctive trait is a very large brain. Besides enabling humans to think abstractly, experience profound emotions, and construct complex social relationships, this larger brain controls the fine motor movements of the hand and of the tongue, increasing humans' tool-using capacity and facilitating the development of speech. The physical possibility of language, however, depends on a third distinctive human trait: the location of the larynx (voice box). In humans it lies much lower in the neck than in any other primate.

These critical biological traits are due to natural selection, the preservation of genetic changes that enhanced the ability of the ancestors of modern humans to survive and reproduce. Major shifts in the world's climate led to evolutionary changes in human ancestors and other species. Falling temperatures culminated in the **Great Ice Age,** or Pleistocene (PLY-stuh-seen) epoch, extending from about 2 million to about 9000 B.C.E. (see Chronology). These temperature changes and altered rainfall and vegetation imposed great strains on plant and animal species, causing large numbers of new species to evolve.

Beginning approximately 4.5 million years ago, several species of australopithecines evolved in southern and eastern Africa. In northern Ethiopia in 1974, Donald Johanson unearthed a well-preserved skeleton of a twenty-five-year-old female, whom he nicknamed Lucy. Mary Leakey's discovery of fossilized footprints in Tanzania in 1977 provided spectacular visual evidence that australopithecines walked on two legs.

Bipedalism evolved because it provided australopithecines with some advantage for survival. Some studies suggest that walking and running on two legs is very energy efficient. Another theory is that bipeds survived better because they could carry armfuls of food back to their mates and children.

Climate changes between 2 and 3 million years ago led to the evolution of a new species, the first to be classified in the same genus (*Homo*) with modern humans. At Olduvai (ol-DOO-vy) Gorge in northern Tanzania in the early 1960s, Louis Leakey discovered the fossilized remains of a creature that he named **Homo habilis** (HOH-moh HAB-uh-luhs) (handy human). What most distinguished *Homo habilis* from the australopithecines was a brain that was nearly 50 percent larger. Greater intelligence may have enabled *Homo habilis* to locate things to eat throughout the seasons of the year. Seeds and other fossilized remains found in ancient *Homo habilis* camps indicate that the new species ate a greater variety of more nutritious foods than did australopithecines.

By 1 million years ago *Homo habilis* and all the australopithecines had become extinct. In their habitat lived a new hominid, **Homo erectus** (HOH-moh ee-REK-tuhs) (upright human), which first appeared in eastern Africa about 1.8 million years ago. (It is uncertain whether *Homo erectus* evolved from *Homo habilis* or both species descended from *Australopithecus*.) These creatures possessed brains a third larger than those of *Homo habilis*, which presumably accounted for their better survivability. A nearly complete skeleton of a twelve-year-old male of the species discovered by Richard Leakey in 1984 on the shores of Lake Turkana in Kenya shows that *Homo erectus* closely resembled modern people from the neck down. *Homo erectus* was very successful in dealing with different environments and underwent hardly any biological changes for over a million years.

Sometime between 400,000 and 100,000 years ago, a new human species emerged: **Homo sapiens** (HOH-moh SAY-pee-enz) (wise human). The brains of *Homo sapiens* were a third larger than those of *Homo erectus*, whom they gradually superseded. Although this species was anatomically similar to people today, archaeological and genetic evidence suggest that a further development around 50,000 years ago produced the first behaviorally modern humans, with the intellectual and social capabilities that we have.

There is no scholarly consensus on when, why, or how humans developed the capacity to speak. In the absence of tangible evidence, this question has even been labeled "the hardest problem in science." Assuming that the shape of the throat and low position of the larynx are essential to vocalizing a wide range of sounds, it ought to be relevant that these features were still evolving in *Homo habilis* and *Homo erectus*. Some scholars link the development of language in the fullest sense to the period around 50,000 years ago when *Homo sapiens* began to migrate out of Africa and employed a larger, more sophisticated set of tools that can be sorted into functional categories.

This slow but remarkable process of physical evolution, which distinguished humans from other primates, was one part of what was happening. Equally remarkable was the way in which humans were extending their habitat.

Evolution of the Human Brain *These drawings of skulls show the extensive cranial changes associated with the increase in brain size during 5 million years of evolutionary change. Seen here are the skulls of a chimpanzee,* Australopithecus, Homo Habilis, Homo Erectus, Neanderthal, *and* Homo Sapiens.

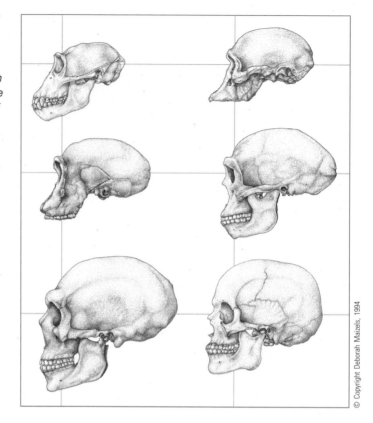

© Copyright Deborah Maizels, 1994

Migrations from Africa   Early humans first expanded their range in eastern and southern Africa. Then they ventured out of Africa, perhaps following migrating herds of animals or searching for more abundant food supplies in a time of drought. The reasons are uncertain, but the end results are vividly clear: humans successfully colonized diverse environments, including deserts and arctic lands. This dispersal demonstrates early humans' talent for adaptation.

Homo erectus was the first human species to inhabit all parts of Africa and to be found outside Africa. Java man and Peking man were members of this species. At that time, Java was not an island but was part of the Southeast Asian mainland. During the Pleistocene, massive glaciers of frozen water spread out from the poles and mountains. At their peak such glaciers covered a third of the earth's surface and contained so much frozen water that ocean levels were lowered by over 450 feet (140 meters), exposing land bridges between many places now isolated by water.

DNA and fossil evidence suggest that *Homo sapiens* also first evolved in Africa. The ancestral group from which all modern humans are descended may have comprised as few as 5,000 individuals. From this population, a band of several hundred people initially moved out of Northeast Africa around 50,000 years ago, and their descendants rapidly spread across the planet (although some scientists dispute this "African Genesis" and hold that distinct groups of *Homo sapiens* evolved from *Homo erectus* populations in Africa, Europe, China, and Southeast Asia).

© Cengage Learning

MAP 1.1 Human Dispersal to 10,000 Years Ago

Early migrations from Africa into southern Eurasia were followed by treks across land bridges during ice ages, when giant ice sheets lowered ocean levels. Boats may also have been employed.

Recent excavations and DNA analysis have shown that early modern humans coexisted and interbred with other species of *Homo* that are now extinct: Neanderthals and Denisovans (whose bone fragments were recently discovered in Siberia). The small and small-brained *Homo floresiensis*, whose remains were recently excavated in Indonesia, only died out about 12,000 years ago.

Ultimately modern humans displaced older human populations, probably because they were better able to survive environmental conditions in the Ice Age, though some scholars believe the Neanderthals were absorbed into the *Homo sapiens* population through interbreeding.

The Great Ice Age enabled modern humans to penetrate into the Americas and even the Arctic. During glacial periods, people would have been able to cross a land bridge from Siberia to Alaska, perhaps beginning around 18,000 B.C.E., though some scholars believe that the first migrations occurred as early as 35,000 to 25,000 B.C.E. Over thousands of years the population of the Americas grew and spread throughout the hemisphere, penetrating southern South America by 10,500 B.C.E. As they spread, these humans adapted to environments that included polar extremes, tropical rain forests, and high mountain ranges as well as deserts, woodlands, and prairies.

About 46,000 years ago, modern humans, traveling by boat from Java, colonized New Guinea and Australia when both were part of a single landmass, and others crossed the land bridge then existing between the Asian mainland and Japan. When global temperatures rose and the glaciers melted, submerging the land bridges and increasing the extent of ocean between Southeast Asia and Australia, the peoples of the Western Hemisphere and Australia were virtually isolated from the rest of the world for at least 15,000 years.

As populations migrated, they underwent minor evolutionary changes that helped them adapt to extreme environments. One such change was in skin color. The deeply pigmented skin of today's indigenous inhabitants of the tropics (and presumably of all early humans) reduces harmful effects of the harsh tropical sun such as sunburn and skin cancer. At some point between 20,000 and 5,000 years ago, pale skin became characteristic of Europeans living in northern latitudes with far less sunshine, especially during winter months. The loss of pigment enabled their skin to produce more vitamin D from sunshine.

As distinctive as skin color seems, it represents a very minor biological change. What is far more remarkable is that widely dispersed human populations vary so little in their genetic makeup. Whereas other species need to evolve physically to adapt to new environments, modern humans have been able to adapt technologically, changing their eating habits and devising new forms of tools, clothing, and shelter. As a result, human communities have become culturally diverse while remaining physically homogeneous.

TECHNOLOGY AND CULTURE IN THE ICE AGE

Evidence of early humans' splendid creative abilities came to light in 1940 near Lascaux in southern France. Youths who stumbled onto the entrance to a vast underground cavern found its walls covered with paintings of animals, including many that had been extinct for thousands of years. Other ancient cave paintings have been found in Spain, Africa, Australia, and elsewhere. The artistic quality of ancient cave art is vivid evidence that the biologically modern people who made such art were intellectually modern as well.

The production of similar art and specialized tools over wide areas and long periods of time demonstrates that skills and ideas were deliberately passed along within societies. These learned patterns of action and expression constitute **culture**. Culture includes both material objects, such as dwellings, clothing, tools, and crafts, and nonmaterial values, beliefs, and languages. While some animals also learn new ways, their activities are determined primarily by inherited instincts. Among humans, instincts are less important than the cultural traditions that each generation learns from its elders.

Food Gathering and Stone Tools   When archaeologists examine the remains of ancient human sites, the first thing that jumps out at them is the abundant evidence of human toolmaking. Because the tools that survive are mostly made of stone, the extensive period of history from the appearance of the first fabricated stone tools around 2.6 million years ago until the appearance of metal tools around four thousand years ago has been called the **Stone Age**.

The name can be misleading because not all tools were made of stone. Early humans also made useful objects out of bone, skin, wood, plant fibers, and other materials less likely than stone to survive the ravages of time. Early scholars recognized two phases of the Stone Age: the **Paleolithic** (pay-lee-oh-LITH-ik) (Old Stone Age), down to 8000 B.C.E., and the **Neolithic** (NEE-OH-LITH-IK) (New Stone Age), which is associated with the rise of agriculture. Modern scientists have developed more complex schemes with many subdivisions.

Most early human activity centered on gathering food. Like the australopithecines, early humans depended heavily on vegetable foods such as leaves, seeds, and grasses, but during the Ice Age the consumption of highly nutritious animal flesh increased. Moreover, unlike australopithecines, humans regularly made tools. These two changes—increased meat eating and toolmaking—appear to be closely linked.

Specimens of crude early tools found in the Great Rift Valley of eastern Africa reveal that *Homo habilis* made tools by chipping flakes off the edges of volcanic stones. The razor-sharp edges of such flakes are highly effective for skinning and butchering wild animals.

Lacking the skill to hunt and kill large animals, small-brained *Homo habilis* probably obtained animal protein by scavenging meat from kills made by animal predators or resulting from accidents. This species probably used large stone "choppers" for cracking open bones to get at the nutritious marrow. The fact that such tools are found far from the volcanic outcrops where they were quarried suggests that people carried them long distances for use at kill sites and camps.

Members of *Homo erectus* were also scavengers, but their larger brains made them more clever. They made more effective tools for butchering large animals, including a hand ax formed by removing chips from both sides of a stone to produce a sharp outer edge. The hand ax was an efficient multipurpose tool, suitable for skinning and butchering animals, for scraping skins clean for use as clothing and mats, for sharpening wooden tools, and for digging up edible roots. Since a hand ax can also be hurled accurately for nearly 100 feet (30 meters), it might also have been used as a projectile to fell animals. *Homo erectus* even hunted elephants by driving them into swamps, where they became trapped and died.

Members of *Homo sapiens* were far more skillful hunters. Using their superior intelligence and an array of finely made tools, they tracked and killed large animals. Sharp stone flakes chipped from carefully prepared rock cores were used in combination with other materials. Attaching a stone point to a wooden shaft made a spear. Embedding several sharp stone flakes in a bone handle produced a sawing tool.

Indeed, members of *Homo sapiens* were so successful as hunters that they may have caused a series of ecological crises. Between 40,000 and 13,000 years ago the giant mastodons and mammoths gradually disappeared from Africa, Southeast Asia, and northern Europe. In North America around 11,000 years ago, three-fourths of the large mammals became extinct, including giant bison, camels, ground sloths, stag-moose, giant cats, mastodons, and mammoths. In Australia there was a similar event. However, since these extinctions occurred during severe cold spells at the end of the Ice Age, it is difficult to distinguish the effects of climate change and human predation.

Despite the evidence for hunting, anthropologists do not believe that early humans depended primarily on meat for their food. The few surviving present-day **foragers** (hunting and food-gathering peoples) in Africa derive the bulk of their day-to-day nourishment from wild vegetable foods, with meat reserved for feasts. The same was probably true for Stone Age peoples, even though tools for gathering and processing vegetable foods have left few traces because they were made of perishable materials. Ancient humans would have used skins and mats woven from leaves for collecting fruits, berries, and wild seeds. They would have dug edible roots out of the ground with wooden sticks.

Both meat and vegetables become tastier and easier to digest when they are cooked. The first cooked foods were probably found by accident after wildfires. Humans may have been setting fires deliberately as early as 1.4 million years ago, and maintaining hearths around 500,000 years ago. However, only with the appearance of clay cooking pots some 18,000 years ago in East Asia is there hard evidence of cooking.

Gender Roles and Social Life   Researchers have studied the behavior and organization of nonhuman primates for clues about very early human society. Gorillas and chimpanzees live in groups consisting of several adult males and females and their offspring. Status varies with age and sex, and a dominant male usually heads the group. Sexual unions between males and females generally do not result in long-term pairing. Instead, the strongest ties are those between a female and her children and among siblings. Adult males are often recruited from neighboring bands.

Very early human groups likely shared some of these primate traits, but long before the advent of modern *Homo sapiens* the two-parent family would have been common. We can only guess how this change developed, but it is likely that

Making Stone Tools

About 35,000 years ago the manufacture of stone tools became highly specialized. Small blades chipped from a rock core were mounted in a bone or wooden handle. Not only were such composite tools more varied than earlier all-purpose hand axes, but the small blades also required fewer rock cores—an important consideration where suitable rocks were scarce.

From Jacques Bordaz, Tools of the Old and New Stone Age. Copyright 1970 by Jacques Bordaz. Redrawn by the permission of Addison-Wesley Educational Publishers, Inc.

physical and social evolution were linked. Big-headed humans with large brains have to be born in a less mature state than other mammals so that they can pass through the narrow birth canal. Other large mammals are mature at two or three years of age; humans are not able to care for themselves until the age of twelve to fifteen. The need of human infants and children for much longer nurturing makes care by mothers, fathers, and other family members a biological imperative.

The human reproductive cycle also became unique. In many other species sexual contact is biologically restricted to a special mating season of the year or to the fertile part of the female's menstrual cycle. Moreover, among other primates the choice of mate is usually not a matter for long deliberation. To a female baboon in heat any male will do, and to a male baboon any receptive female is a suitable sexual partner. In contrast, adult humans can mate at any time and are much choosier about their partners. Once they mate, frequent sexual contact promotes deep emotional ties and long-term bonding.

An enduring bond between human parents made it much easier for vulnerable offspring to receive the care they needed during the long period of their childhood. Working together, mothers and fathers could nurture dependent children of different ages at the same time, unlike other large mammals, whose females must raise their offspring nearly to maturity before beginning another reproductive cycle. Spacing births close together also would have enabled humans to multiply more rapidly than other large mammals.

Researchers studying present-day foragers infer that Ice Age women would have done most of the gathering and cooking (which they could do while caring for small children). Older women past childbearing age would have been the most knowledgeable and productive food gatherers. Men, with stronger arms, would have been more suited than women to hunting, particularly for large animals. Since the male hunters will only occasionally have succeeded in bringing down their prey, while the women gatherers provided the bulk of the band's daily diet, it is likely that women held a respected position in early human societies.

All recent foragers have lived in small bands. The community has to have enough members to defend itself from predators and divide responsibility for collection and preparation of foods. However, too many members would exhaust the food available in its immediate vicinity. The band has to move at regular intervals to follow migrating animals and take advantage of seasonally ripening plants in different places. Archaeological evidence from Ice Age campsites suggests that early humans, too, lived in highly mobile bands.

Hearths and Cultural Expressions   Because frequent moves were necessary, early hunter-gatherers did not lavish much time on housing. Natural shelters under overhanging rocks or in caves were favorite camping places to which bands returned at regular intervals. Where the climate was severe or where natural shelters did not exist, people erected huts of branches, stones, bones, skins, and leaves. Large, solid structures were common in fishing villages that grew up along riverbanks and lakeshores, where the abundance of fish permitted people to occupy the same site year-round.

Animal skin cloaks were probably an early form of clothing. Although the oldest evidence of fibers woven into cloth dates from about 26,000 years ago, the appearance of the body louse around 70,000 years ago has been linked to people beginning to wear close-fitting garments. An "Iceman" from 5,300 years ago, whose frozen remains were found in the European Alps in 1991, was wearing many different garments made of animal skins sewn together with cord fashioned from vegetable fibers and rawhide (see Environment and Technology: The Iceman).

Although accidents, erratic weather, and disease might take a heavy toll on a foraging band, day-to-day existence was probably not particularly hard or unpleasant. Studies suggest that, in plant- and game-rich areas, obtaining necessary food, clothing, and shelter would have occupied only from three to five hours a day. This would have left a great deal of time for artistic endeavors, toolmaking, and social life.

The foundations of science, art, and religion were built during the Stone Age. Basic to human survival was extensive knowledge about the natural environment. Gatherers learned which local plants were best for food and when they were available, and hunters gained intimate knowledge of the habits of game animals. People learned how to use plant and animal parts for clothing, twine, building materials, and dyes; minerals for paints and stones for tools; as well as natural substances effective for medicine and consciousness altering. It is very likely that the transmission of such knowledge involved verbal communication, even though direct evidence for language appears only in later periods.

Early music and dance have left no traces, but there is abundant evidence of painting and drawing. Because many cave paintings feature wild animals that were

ENVIRONMENT + TECHNOLOGY

The Iceman

The discovery of the well-preserved remains of a man at the edge of a melting glacier in the European Alps in 1991 provided detailed information about everyday technologies of the fourth millennium B.C.E. Not just the body of this "Iceman" was well preserved. His clothing, his tools, and even the food in his stomach survived in remarkably good condition.

Dressed from head to toe for the cold weather of the mountains, the fifty-year-old man was wearing a fur hat fastened under the chin with a strap, a vest of different colored deerskins, leather leggings and loincloth, and a padded cloak made of grasses. His calfskin shoes also were padded with grass for warmth and comfort. The articles of clothing had been sewn together with fiber and leather cords. He carried a birch-bark drinking cup.

In a leather fanny pack he carried small flint tools for cutting, scraping, and punching holes, as well as some tinder for making a fire. He also carried a leather quiver with flint-tipped arrows, but his 6-foot (1.8-meter) bow was unfinished, lacking a bowstring. In addition, he had a flint knife and a tool for sharpening flints. His most sophisticated tool, indicating the dawning of the age of metals, was a copper-bladed ax with a wooden handle.

His death was violent, caused either by a small arrowhead lodged in his shoulder or a blow to the head. In his stomach, researchers found the remains of the meat-rich meal he had eaten not long before he died.

© Smetek/STERN/Picture Press

The Iceman *This is an artist's rendition of what the Iceman might have looked like. Notice his tools, remarkable evidence of the technology of his day.*

hunted for food, some believe they were meant to record hunting scenes or formed part of magical and religious rites to ensure successful hunting. However, a newly discovered cave in southern France features rhinoceroses, panthers, bears, and other animals that probably were not hunted. Other drawings include people dressed in animal skins and smeared with paint. In many caves there are stencils of human hands. Are these the signatures of the artists or the world's oldest graffiti? Some scholars suspect that other marks in cave paintings and on bones from this period may represent efforts at counting or writing. Other theories suggest that cave and rock art represent concerns with fertility, efforts to educate the young, or elaborate mechanisms for time reckoning.

Without written texts it is difficult to know about the religious beliefs of early humans. Sites of deliberate human burials from about 100,000 years ago give some hints. The fact that an adult was often buried with stone implements, food, clothing, and red-ochre powder suggests that early people revered their leaders, relatives, and companions enough to honor them after death and may imply a belief in an afterlife where such items would be useful.

Today we recognize that the Old Stone Age, whose existence was scarcely dreamed of two centuries ago, was a formative period. Important in its own right, it also laid the foundation for major changes ahead as human communities passed from being food gatherers to food producers.

The Agricultural Revolutions

For most of human existence people ate only wild plants and animals. But around 10,000 years ago global climate changes seem to have induced some societies to enhance their food supplies with domesticated plants and animals. More and more people became food producers over the following millennia. Although hunting and gathering did not disappear, this transition from foraging to food production was one of the great turning points in history because it fostered a rapid increase in population and greatly altered humans' relationship to nature.

Because agriculture arose in combination with new kinds of stone tools, archaeologists called this period the Neolithic, or New Stone Age, and the rise of agriculture the Neolithic Revolution. But that name can be misleading: first, stone tools were not its essential component, and second, it was not a single event but a series of separate transformations in different parts of the world. A better term is **Agricultural Revolutions**, which emphasizes that the central change was in food production and that agriculture arose independently in many places. In most cases agriculture included the domestication of animals as well as the cultivation of new food crops.

The Transition to Plant Cultivation   Food gathering gave way to food production in stages spread over hundreds of generations. The process may have begun when forager bands, returning year after year to the same seasonal camps, deliberately scattered the seeds of desirable plants in locations where they would thrive and discouraged the growth of competing plants by clearing them away. Such semicultivation could have supplemented food gathering for many generations. Eventually, families choosing to concentrate on food production would have settled permanently near their fields.

The presence of new, specialized tools for agriculture first alerted archaeologists to the beginning of a food production revolution. These included polished stone

A Neolithic House

This reconstruction of an early permanent human habitation has single door and no windows. Simple dwellings were constructed of mud-brick over a timber frame or of wattle and daub, a lattice of branches covered with a sticky composite of mud, straw, etc. The roof is thatched, a layering of dried vegetation that sheds water.

Herv Champollion/akg-images/Newscom

heads to work the soil, sharp stone chips embedded in bone or wooden handles to cut grain, and stone mortars to pulverize grain. Since stone axes were not very efficient for clearing away shrubs and trees, farmers used fire to get rid of unwanted undergrowth (the ashes were a natural fertilizer).

The transition to agriculture occurred first in the Middle East. By 8000 B.C.E. humans, by selecting the highest-yielding strains, had transformed certain wild grasses into the domesticated grains now known as emmer wheat and barley. They also discovered that alternating the cultivation of grains and pulses (plants yielding edible seeds such as lentils and peas) helped maintain soil fertility. Women, the principal gatherers of wild plant foods, had the expertise to play a major role in this transition to plant cultivation, but the heavy work of clearing the fields would have fallen to men.

Plants domesticated in the Middle East spread to Greece as early as 6000 B.C.E., to the light-soiled plains of central Europe and along the Danube River shortly after 4000 B.C.E., and then to other parts of Europe over the next millennium. Early farmers in Europe and elsewhere practiced shifting cultivation, also known as swidden agriculture. After a few growing seasons, the fields were left fallow (abandoned to natural vegetation) for a time to restore their fertility, and new fields were cleared nearby. From around 2600 B.C.E. people in central Europe began using ox-drawn wooden plows to till heavier and richer soils.

Wheat and barley could not spread farther south because the rainfall patterns in most of Africa were unsuited to their growth. Instead, separate Agricultural Revolutions took place in Saharan and sub-Saharan Africa, beginning almost as early as in the Middle East. During a particularly wet period after 8000 B.C.E., people in what is now the eastern Sahara began to cultivate sorghum, a grain derived from wild grasses they had previously gathered. Over the next three thousand years the Saharan farmers domesticated pearl millet, black-eyed peas, a kind of peanut, sesame, and gourds. In the Ethiopian highlands, farmers domesticated finger millet and a grain called tef. The return of drier conditions about 5000 B.C.E. led many Saharan farmers to move to the Nile Valley, where the annual flooding of the river provided moisture for farming. People in the rain forests of equatorial West Africa domesticated rice and yams.

Rice, which thrives in warm and wet conditions, was probably first domesticated in the Yangzi River Valley in central China, possibly as early as 10,000 B.C.E., and by 3000 B.C.E. it had made its way to Southeast Asia and India. In India several pulses domesticated about 2000 B.C.E. (including hyacinth beans, green grams, and black grams) were cultivated along with rice.

The inhabitants of the American continents were domesticating other crops by about 5000 B.C.E.: maize (mayz), or corn, in Mexico, manioc in Brazil and Panama, and beans and squash in Mesoamerica. By 4000 B.C.E., the inhabitants of Peru were developing potatoes and quinoa (kee-NOH-uh), a protein-rich seed grain. Insofar as their climates and soils permitted, other farming communities throughout the Americas adopted these crops, along with tomatoes and peppers.

Domesticated Animals and Pastoralism

The first domesticated animals were probably dogs descended from wolves that were used initially to help hunters track game and later to herd other domesticated animals as well as provide protection and companionship. There is much debate about the place, date, and process of domestication. Experts have argued for Siberia, the Middle East, and Europe as the site of the first domestication. The time of domestication may go back 30,000 years or more, though the first known burial of a dog with a human—a sure sign of the relationship—is from around 14,000 B.C.E.

The domestication of animals expanded rapidly during the Neolithic period, as other animals were domesticated to provide meat, milk, and energy. Refuse heaps outside some Middle East villages during the centuries after 7000 B.C.E. show that sheep and goat bones gradually replaced gazelle bones. As wild sheep and goats scavenged for food scraps around villages, the tamer animals probably accepted human control and protection in exchange for a ready supply of food. Selective breeding for desirable characteristics such as high milk production and long wooly coats eventually led to distinct breeds of sheep and goats.

Elsewhere, other animal species were domesticated during the centuries before 3000 B.C.E.: wild cattle in northern Africa or the Middle East; donkeys in northern

Ancient Dog Burial
This husky-like dog, buried 7000 years ago in Siberia, was interred along with, and in the same manner as humans. This, and the fact that he ate the same food as humans, suggests that he was seen as a companion and helper. Skeletal damage has also been interpreted as showing that he carried heavy loads and may have been repeatedly injured on hunts.

Vladimir Bazaliiskii/Robert Losey/Sandra Garvie-Lok/Mietje Germonpre/ Jennifer Leonard/Andrew Allen/Anne Katzenberg/Mikhail Sablin

Africa; water buffalo in China; and humped-back Zebu (ZEE-boo) cattle in India. Varieties of domesticated animals spread from one region to another.

Once cattle became tame enough to be yoked to plows, they became essential to grain production. In addition, animal droppings provided valuable fertilizer. In the Americas, however, comparatively few species of wild animals were suitable for domestication, and domesticated animals could not spread from elsewhere because the land bridge to Asia had been submerged by raised sea levels. In the Western Hemisphere, therefore, domesticated llamas provided transport and wool, while guinea pigs and turkeys furnished meat. Hunting remained the most important source of meat for Amerindians.

In the more arid parts of Africa and in some regions of western and Central Asia, pastoralism, a way of life dependent on large herds of small and large stock, predominated. As the Sahara approached its maximum dryness around 2500 B.C.E., pastoralists replaced farmers, who migrated southward (see Chapter 9). Moving their herds to new pastures and watering places throughout the year made pastoralists almost as mobile as foragers and discouraged accumulation of bulky possessions and construction of substantial dwellings. Early herders probably relied more heavily on milk than on meat, since killing animals reduced their herds. During wet seasons, they may also have done some hasty crop cultivation or bartered meat and skins for plant foods with nearby farming communities.

Agriculture and Ecological Crisis   Why did the Agricultural Revolutions occur? Some theories assume that people were drawn to food production by its obvious advantages, such as the promise of a secure food supply. It has recently been suggested that people in the Middle East might have settled down so they could grow enough grains to ensure themselves a ready supply of beer.

However, most experts believe that climate change drove people to abandon hunting and gathering in favor of agriculture or pastoralism. With the end of the Great Ice Age, the temperate lands became exceptionally warm between 6000 and 2000 B.C.E., the era when people in many parts of the world adopted agriculture. The precise nature of the crisis probably varied. Shortages of wild food in the Middle East caused by a dry spell or population growth may have prodded people to take up food production. Elsewhere, a warmer, wetter climate could turn grasslands into forest, reducing supplies of game and wild grains.

In many drier parts of the world, where wild food remained abundant, people did not take up agriculture. The inhabitants of Australia continued to rely exclusively on foraging until recent centuries. Many Amerindians in the arid grasslands from Alaska to the Gulf of Mexico hunted bison, others in the Pacific Northwest took up salmon-fishing, and east of the Mississippi River food gatherers thrived on abundant supplies of fish, shellfish, and aquatic animals. In Africa, in the equatorial rain forest and in the southern part of the continent, conditions favored retention of the older ways. The reindeer-based societies of northern Eurasia were also unaffected by the spread of farming.

Whatever the causes, the gradual adoption of food production transformed most parts of the world. A hundred thousand years ago there were fewer than 2 million people, and their range was largely confined to the temperate and tropical regions of

Africa and Eurasia. The population may have fallen even lower during the last glacial epoch, between 32,000 and 13,000 years ago. Then, as the glaciers retreated and people took up agriculture, their numbers rose. World population may have reached 10 million by 5000 B.C.E. and then mushroomed to between 50 million and 100 million by 1000 B.C.E.[1] This increase led to important changes in social and cultural life.

LIFE IN NEOLITHIC COMMUNITIES

Evidence that an ecological crisis may have driven people to food production has prompted a reexamination of the assumption that farmers enjoyed better lives than foragers. Modern studies demonstrate that food producers have to work much harder and for much longer periods than do food gatherers, clearing and cultivating land, guiding herds to pastures, and guarding them from predators.

Although early farmers were less likely to starve because they could store food between harvests, their diet was less varied and nutritious than that of foragers. Skeletal remains show that Neolithic farmers were shorter on average than earlier food-gathering peoples. Farmers were also more likely to die at an earlier age because people in permanent settlements were more exposed to diseases. Their water was contaminated by human waste; disease-bearing vermin and insects infested their bodies and homes; and they could catch new diseases from their domesticated animals.

The Triumph of Food Producers   So how did farmers displace foragers? Some researchers have envisioned a violent struggle between practitioners of the two ways of life; others have argued for a more peaceful transition. In most cases, farmers seem to have displaced foragers by gradual infiltration rather than by conquest.

The key to the food producers' expansion may have been the fact that their small surpluses gave them a long-term advantage in population growth by ensuring higher survival rates during times of drought or other crisis. Archaeologist Colin Renfrew argues that over a few centuries farming population densities in Europe could have increased by a factor of 50 to 100. As population rose, individuals who had to farm far from their native village would have formed a new settlement close to their fields. A steady, nonviolent expansion of only 12 to 19 miles (20 to 30 kilometers) a generation could have repopulated the whole of Europe between 6500 and 3500 B.C.E.[2] So gradual a process need not have provoked sharp conflicts with existing foragers, who simply could have stayed clear of the agricultural frontier or gradually adopted agriculture themselves. New studies that map genetic changes also attest to a gradual spread of agricultural people across Europe from southeast to northwest.[3]

The expanding farming communities were organized around kinship and marriage. Nuclear families (parents and their children) probably lived in separate households but felt solidarity with all those related to them by descent from common

---

[1]Colin McEvedy and Richard Jones, *Atlas of World Population History* (New York: Penguin Books, 1978), 13–15.

[2]Colin Renfrew, *Archaeology and Language: The Puzzle of Indo-European Origins* (New York: Cambridge University Press, 1988), 125, 150.

[3]Cavalli-Sforza, L. Luca, Paolo Menozzi, and Alberto Piazza, *The History and Geography of Human Genes* (Princeton, NJ: Princeton University Press, 1994).

ancestors. These kinship units, known as lineages (LIN-ee-ij) or clans, acted together to defend their common interests and land. Some societies trace descent equally through both parents, but most give greater importance to descent through either the mother (matrilineal [mat-ruh-LIN-ee-uhl] societies) or the father (patrilineal [pat-ruh-LIN-ee-uhl] societies). It is important not to confuse tracing descent through women (matrilineality) with the rule of women (matriarchy [MAY-tree-ahr-key]).

Cultural Expressions   Kinship systems influenced early agricultural people's outlook on the world. Burials of elders might be occasions for elaborate ceremonies expressing their descendants' group solidarity. Plastered skulls found in the ancient city of Jericho (JER-ih-koh) may be evidence of such early ancestor reverence or worship.

A society's religious beliefs tend to reflect its relations to nature. The religion of food gatherers centered on sacred groves, springs, and wild animals, while pastoralists worshiped the sky-god who controlled the rains and guided their migrations. In contrast, the religion of many farming communities centered on the Earth Mother; since women bear children, a female deity was logically believed to be the source of all new life.

The worship of ancestors, gods of the heavens, and earthly nature and fertility deities varied from place to place, and many societies combined the different elements. A recently discovered complex of stone structures in the Egyptian desert that was in use by 5000 B.C.E. includes burial chambers presumably for ancestors, a calendar circle, and pairs of upright stones that frame the rising sun at the summer solstice. The builders must have been deeply concerned with the cycle of the seasons and how they were linked to the movement of heavenly bodies. Other **megaliths** (meaning "big stones") were erected elsewhere. Observation and worship of the sun are evident at the famous Stonehenge site in England, constructed about 2000 B.C.E. Megalithic burial chambers dating from 4000 B.C.E. are evidence of ancestor rituals in western and southern Europe. The early ones appear to have been communal burial chambers, erected by descent groups to mark their claims to farmland. In the Middle East, the Americas, and other parts of the world, giant earth burial mounds may have served similar functions.

Another fundamental contribution of the Neolithic period was the dissemination of the large language families that form the basis of most languages spoken today. The root language of the giant Indo-European language family arose around 5000 B.C.E., probably in the region north of the Black and Caspian Seas. Its spread to the south and west across Europe and south and east into Anatolia (modern Turkey), Iran, and the Indian subcontinent may have been the work of pioneering agriculturalists. In the course of this very gradual expansion, Celtic, Germanic, Romance, Slavic, Iranian, and Indian languages developed. Similarly, the Afro-Asiatic language family of the Middle East and northern Africa may have been the result of food producers' expansion, as might the spread of the Sino-Tibetan family in East and Southeast Asia.

Early Towns and Specialists   Most early farmers lived in small villages, but in some parts of the world a few villages grew into more densely populated towns that were centers of trade and specialized crafts. These towns had grander dwellings and ceremonial buildings, as well as large structures for storing surplus food until the next harvest. Farmers could make most of the buildings, tools, and containers they needed in their spare time, but in large communities some craft specialists devoted their full time to making products of unusual complexity or beauty.

Two early towns in the Middle East that have been extensively excavated are Jericho on the west bank of the Jordan River and Çatal Hüyük (cha-TAHL hoo-YOOK) in central Turkey (Map 2.1 shows their locations). Jericho, located near a natural spring, was an unusually large and elaborate agricultural settlement around 8000 B.C.E. whose round, mud-brick dwellings may have been modeled on hunters' tents. A millennium later, rectangular buildings with finely plastered walls and floors and wide doorways opened onto central courtyards. A massive stone wall surrounding the 10-acre (4-hectare) settlement defended it against attacks.

The ruins of Çatal Hüyük, an even larger town, date to between 7000 and 5000 B.C.E. and cover 32 acres (13 hectares). Its residents also occupied plastered mud-brick rooms with elaborate decorations, but Çatal Hüyük had no defensive wall. Instead, the walls of the town's outermost houses formed a continuous barrier without doors or large windows. Residents entered their house by means of ladders through holes in the roof.

Çatal Hüyük prospered from long-distance trade in obsidian, a hard volcanic rock that craftspeople made into tools, weapons, mirrors, and ornaments. Other residents made fine pottery, wove baskets and woolen cloth, made stone and shell

Neolithic Goddess

Many versions of a well-nourished and pregnant female figure were found at Çatal Hüyük. Here she is supported by twin leopards whose tails curve over her shoulders. To those who inhabited the city some 8,000 years ago, the figure likely represented fertility and power over nature.

beads, and worked leather and wood. House sizes varied, but there is no evidence of a dominant class or centralized political structure. Fields around the town produced crops of barley and emmer wheat, as well as vegetables. Pigs were kept along with goats and sheep. Yet wild foods—acorns, wild grains, and game animals—still featured prominently in the residents' diet.

Wall paintings, remarkably similar to earlier cave paintings, reveal the continuing importance of hunting. Scenes depict people adorned with the skins of wild leopards, and men were buried with weapons of war and hunting, not the tools of farming.

There is a religious shrine for every two houses. Many rooms contain depictions of horned wild bulls, female breasts, goddesses, leopards, and handprints. Rituals involved burning grains, legumes, and meat as offerings, but there is no evidence of live animal sacrifice. Statues of plump female deities far outnumber statues of male deities, suggesting that the inhabitants primarily venerated a goddess of fertility. According to the site's principal excavator, "it seems extremely likely that the cult of the goddess was administered mainly by women."[4]

Metalworking became an important specialized occupation in the late Neolithic period. At Çatal Hüyük objects of copper and lead—metals that occur naturally in a fairly pure form—date to about 6400 B.C.E. In many parts of the world silver and gold were also worked at an early date. Because of their rarity and softness, those metals did not replace stone tools and weapons but were used primarily to make decorative or ceremonial objects. The discovery of many such objects in graves suggests they were symbols of status and power.

The emergence of towns and individuals engaged in crafts and other specialized occupations added to the workload of agriculturalists. Extra food had to be produced for nonfarmers such as priests and artisans. Added labor was needed to build permanent houses, town walls, and towers, not to mention religious structures and megalithic monuments. It is not known whether these tasks were performed freely or coerced.

CONCLUSION

The theory of evolution, supported by an enormous body of evidence, leads to far-reaching conclusions. Every living species evolved from a common ancestor. Humans are descended from earlier hominid species that evolved in Africa beginning about 7 million years ago, and every modern human being is descended from communities that evolved in Africa 50,000 years ago, with some groups then migrating to the other habitable continents. However diverse their cultures became, all human communities are directly related—to each other, to all other living species, and to the earth.

More than 2 million years ago there was a dramatic increase in the variety of tools early humans made—above all from stone, but also from bone, skin, wood, and plant fiber. Paleolithic families enjoyed a primarily vegetarian diet, though their skill at making weapons also made them effective hunters. Work was divided along gender lines, with women responsible for food gathering, cooking, and child

---

[4]James Mellaart, *Çatal Hüyük: A Neolithic Town in Anatolia* (New York: McGraw-Hill, 1967), 202.

rearing, and men for activities such as hunting because of their greater upper-body strength. Humans acquired a profound knowledge of the natural world that helped them create clothing, medicine, and other useful products. Cave and rock art opens a tantalizing window onto their imaginative and spiritual lives.

Research suggests that climate change drove the first human communities to abandon hunting and gathering and adopt the practices of agriculture and pastoralism. In the warmer era following the Great Ice Age around 9000 B.C.E., populations on every major continent except Australia underwent this great transformation, selecting high-yield strains of plants for cultivation and breeding livestock for the consumption of meat and dairy products. By 5000 B.C.E. wheat and barley had been domesticated in the Middle East; sorghum in Africa; rice in India and Southeast Asia; and corn, beans, and squash in Mesoamerica. After the dog, the first animals to be domesticated were sheep, goats, and cattle. Many people living in far northern and southern latitudes never adopted agriculture, but for those who did the consequences were enormous. In less than 10,000 years the global human population increased from 2 to 10 million.

Farming and settled life in the Neolithic period brought plagues of animal-borne diseases and a more labor-intensive way of life, but also the prosperity that gave rise to the first towns, trade, and specialized occupations. Human beings' intimate relationship to their ancestors, the earth, and seasonal cycles of death and rebirth is revealed by archaeological sites with a clearly religious significance—from the megalithic monuments of northern Europe to the household shrines at Çatal Hüyük. However foreign the world of our ancestors may seem, the scientific study of prehistory has brought us much closer to understanding it.

IMPORTANT EVENTS TO 3500 B.C.E.	
2,500,000–2,000,000 B.C.E.	Earliest stone tools; hunting and gathering (foraging) societies
2,000,000–8,000 B.C.E.	Paleolithic (Old Stone Age)
1,900,000–350,000 B.C.E.	*Homo erectus*
500,000 B.C.E.	Use of fire for cooking
400,000–130,000 B.C.E.	Archaic *Homo sapiens*
150,000 B.C.E.	Modern *Homo sapiens* in Africa
100,000 B.C.E.	Modern humans in Eurasia
70,000 B.C.E.	First known cave art
50,000 B.C.E.	Modern humans in Australia
30,000 B.C.E.	First cave paintings
13,000 B.C.E.	Modern humans in Americas
9000 B.C.E.–present	Holocene
8000–2000 B.C.E.	Neolithic (New Stone Age); earliest agriculture

2

THE FIRST RIVER-VALLEY CIVILIZATIONS, 3500–1500 B.C.E.

T he *Epic of Gilgamesh*, whose roots date to before 2000 B.C.E., defines *civilization* as the people of ancient Mesopotamia (present-day Iraq) understood it. Gilgamesh, an early king (who may be depicted on the sculpture shown here), sends a temple prostitute to tame Enkidu (EN-kee-doo), a wild man who lives like an animal in the grasslands. Using her sexual charms to win Enkidu's trust, the temple prostitute tells him:

> Come with me to the city, to Uruk (OO-rook), to the temple of Anu and the goddess Ishtar ... to Uruk, where the processions are and music, let us go together through the dancing to the palace hall where Gilgamesh presides.[1]

She clothes Enkidu and teaches him to eat cooked food, drink beer, and bathe and oil his body. Her words and actions signal the principal traits of civilized life in ancient Mesopotamia.

The Mesopotamians, like other peoples throughout history, equated civilization with their own way of life, but *civilization* is an ambiguous concept, and the charge that a particular group is "uncivilized" has been used throughout human history to justify many distressing acts. Thus it is important to explain the common claim that the first advanced civilizations emerged in Mesopotamia and Egypt sometime before 3000 B.C.E.

Scholars agree that certain political, social, economic, and technological traits are indicators of **civilization**: (1) cities as administrative centers, (2) a political system based on control of a defined territory rather than kinship connections, (3) many people engaged in specialized, non-food-producing activities, (4) status distinctions based largely on accumulation of substantial wealth by some groups, (5) monumental building, (6) a system for keeping permanent records, (7) long-distance trade, and (8) major advances in science and the arts. The earliest societies exhibiting these traits developed in the floodplains of great rivers: the Tigris (TIE-gris) and Euphrates (you-FRAY-teez) in Iraq, the Indus in Pakistan, the Yellow (Huang He [hwang huh]) in China, and the Nile in Egypt. The periodic flooding of the rivers deposited fertile silt and provided water for agriculture, but it also

---

[1]David Ferry, *Gilgamesh: A New Rendering in English Verse* (New York: Noonday Press, 1992).

© Cengage Learning

MAP 2.1   River-Valley Civilizations, 3500–1500 B.C.E.

The earliest complex societies arose in the floodplains of large rivers: in the valley of the Tigris and Euphrates Rivers in Mesopotamia and the Nile River in Egypt, in the third millennium B.C.E. in the valley of the Indus River in Pakistan, and in the second millennium B.C.E. in the valley of the Yellow River in China.

threatened lives and property. To protect themselves and channel the forces of nature, people living near the rivers created new technologies and forms of political and social organization.

In this chapter we trace the rise of complex societies in Mesopotamia, Egypt, and the Indus River Valley from approximately 3500 to 1500 B.C.E. (China, developing slightly later, is discussed in Chapter 4.) Our starting point roughly coincides with the origins of writing, allowing us to observe aspects of human experience not revealed by archaeological evidence alone.

MESOPOTAMIA

Mesopotamia means "land between the rivers" in Greek. The name reflects the centrality of the Euphrates and Tigris Rivers to the way of life in this region. Mesopotamian civilization developed in the plain alongside and between the rivers, which originate in the mountains of eastern Anatolia (modern Turkey) and empty into the Persian Gulf. This is an alluvial plain—a flat, fertile expanse built up over many millennia by silt that the rivers deposited.

Mesopotamia lies mostly within modern Iraq. To the north and east, an arc of mountains extends from northern Syria and southeastern Anatolia to the Zagros (ZAG-ruhs) Mountains, which separate the plain from the Iranian Plateau. The Syrian and Arabian deserts lie to the west and southwest, the Persian Gulf to the southeast.

Settled Agriculture in an Unstable Landscape

Although the first domestication of plants and animals took place in the "Fertile Crescent" region of northern Syria and southeastern Anatolia around 8000 B.C.E., agriculture did not come to southern Mesopotamia until approximately 5000 B.C.E. Lacking adequate rainfall (at least 8 inches [20 centimeters] is needed annually), farming in hot, dry southern Mesopotamia depended on irrigation—the artificial provision of water to crops. At first, people probably took advantage of the occasional flooding of the rivers into nearby fields, but the floods could be sudden and violent and tended to come at the wrong time for grain agriculture—in the spring when the crop was ripening in the field. Moreover, the floods sometimes caused the rivers to suddenly change course, cutting off fields and population centers from water and river communication. Shortly after 3000 B.C.E. the Mesopotamians learned to construct canals to carry water to more distant fields.

By 4000 B.C.E. farmers were using ox-drawn plows to turn over the earth. An attached funnel dropped a carefully measured amount of seed into the furrow. Barley was the main cereal crop because of its ability to tolerate hot, dry conditions and withstand the salt drawn to the surface by evaporation. Fields were left fallow (unplanted) every other year to replenish the nutrients in the soil. Date palms provided food, fiber, and wood, while garden plots produced vegetables. Reed plants, which grew on the riverbanks and in the marshy southern delta, could be woven into mats, baskets, huts, and boats. Fish was a dietary staple. Herds of sheep and goats, which grazed on fallow land or beyond the zone of cultivation, provided wool, milk, and meat. Donkeys, originally domesticated in Northeast Africa, and cattle carried or pulled burdens; in the second millennium B.C.E. they were joined by newly introduced camels from Arabia and horses from the mountains.

Sumerians and Semites   The people living in Mesopotamia at the start of the "historical period"—the period for which we have written evidence—were the **Sumerians**. Archaeological evidence places them in southern Mesopotamia by 5000 B.C.E. and perhaps even earlier. The Sumerians created the framework of civilization in Mesopotamia during a long period of dominance in the fourth and third millennia B.C.E. Other peoples lived in Mesopotamia as well. Personal names recorded in inscriptions from northern cities from as early as 2900 B.C.E. reveal the presence of people who spoke a **Semitic** (suh-MIT-ik) language. (*Semitic* refers to a family of languages spoken in parts of western Asia and northern Africa, including ancient Hebrew, Aramaic [ar-uh-MAY-ik], Phoenician [fi-NEE-shuhn], and modern Arabic.) Possibly the descendants of nomads who had migrated into the Mesopotamian plain from the western desert, these Semites seem to have lived in peace with the Sumerians, adopting their culture and sometimes achieving positions of wealth and power.

By 2000 B.C.E. the Semitic peoples had become politically dominant, and from this time forward the Semitic language Akkadian (uh-KAY-dee-uhn) supplanted Sumerian, although the Sumerian cultural legacy was preserved. Sumerian-Akkadian dictionaries were compiled and Sumerian literature was translated. This cultural synthesis parallels a biological merging of Sumerians and Semites through intermarriage. Other ethnic groups, including mountain peoples such as the Kassites (KAS-ite) as well as Elamites (EE-luh-mite) and Persians from Iran, played a part in Mesopotamian history. But not until the arrival of Greeks in the late fourth century B.C.E. was the Sumerian-Semitic cultural heritage of Mesopotamia fundamentally altered.

Cities, Kings, and Trade   Mesopotamia was a land of villages and cities. Groups of farming families banded together in villages to protect one another; work together at key times in the agricultural cycle; and share tools, barns, and threshing floors. Village society also provided companionship and a pool of potential marriage partners.

Most cities evolved from villages. When a successful village grew, small satellite villages developed nearby and eventually merged with the main village to form an urban center. Historians use the term **city-state** to designate these self-governing urban centers and the agricultural territories they controlled.

Scholars have long believed that the earliest cities and complex societies arose in southern Mesopotamia in the fourth millennium B.C.E., as a result of the need to organize labor to create and maintain irrigation channels. However, recent archaeological discoveries in northern Mesopotamia, where agriculture first developed in this part of the world and was sustained by rainfall, are suggesting a more complicated picture, as a number of sites in northeast Syria appear to have developed urban centers, bureaucracy, and other elements of social complexity at roughly the same time.

Cities needed food, and many Mesopotamian city dwellers went out each day to labor in nearby fields. However, some urban residents did not engage in food production but instead specialized in crafts, manufacturing pottery, artwork, and clothing, as well as weapons, tools, and other objects forged out of metal. Others served the gods or carried out administrative duties. These urban specialists depended on the surplus food production from the villages in their vicinity. In return, the city provided rural districts with military protection against bandits and raiders and a market where villagers could acquire manufactured goods produced by urban specialists.

Stretches of uncultivated land, either desert or swamp, served as buffers between the many small city-states of early Mesopotamia. Nevertheless, disputes over land, water rights, and movable property often sparked hostilities between neighboring cities and prompted most to build protective walls of sun-dried mud bricks.

Southern Mesopotamians opened new land to agriculture by building and maintaining irrigation networks. Canals brought water to fields far from the rivers, and dams raised the level of the river so that water could flow by gravity into the canals. Drainage ditches carried water away from flooded fields before evaporation could draw salt and minerals harmful to crops to the surface. Dikes protected fields near the riverbanks from floods. Because the rivers carried so much silt, clogged channels needed constant dredging.

Successful construction and maintenance of these irrigation systems required leaders who were able to organize large numbers of people to work together. Other projects called for similar coordination: the harvest, sheep shearing, the construction of fortification walls and large public buildings, and warfare. Little is known about the political institutions of early Mesopotamian city-states, although there are traces of a citizens' assembly that may have evolved from the traditional village council. The two centers of power attested in written records are the temple and the palace of the king.

Each city had one or more centrally located temples that housed the cult (a set of religious practices) of the deity or deities who watched over the community. The temples owned extensive agricultural lands and stored the gifts that worshipers donated. The leading priests, who controlled the shrines and managed their wealth, played prominent political and economic roles in early communities.

In the third millennium B.C.E. the *lugal* (LOO-gahl), or "big man"—we would call him a king—emerged in Sumerian cities. A plausible theory maintains that certain men chosen by the community to lead the armies in time of war extended their authority in peacetime and assumed key judicial and ritual functions. The location of the temple in the city's heart and the less prominent location of the king's palace attest to the later emergence of royalty.

The priests and temples retained influence because of their wealth and religious mystique, but they gradually became dependent on the palace. Normally, the king portrayed himself as the deity's earthly representative and saw to the upkeep and building of temples and the proper performance of ritual. Other royal responsibilities included maintaining city walls and defenses, extending and repairing irrigation channels, guarding property rights, warding off outside attackers, and establishing justice.

Some city-states became powerful enough to dominate others. Sargon (SAHR-gone), ruler of the city of Akkad (AH-kahd) around 2350 B.C.E., was the first to unite many cities under one king and capital. Sargon and the four family members who succeeded him over a period of 120 years secured their power in several ways. They razed the walls of conquered cities and installed governors backed by garrisons of Akkadian troops, and they gave land to soldiers to ensure their loyalty. Being of Semitic stock, they adapted the cuneiform (kyoo-NEE-uh-form) system of writing used for Sumerian (discussed later in the chapter) to express their own language.

For reasons that remain obscure, the Akkadian state fell around 2230 B.C.E. The Sumerian language and culture became dominant again in the cities of the southern plain under the Third Dynasty of Ur (2112–2004 B.C.E.). Through campaigns of conquest and marriage alliances, this dynasty of five kings flourished for a century. Although not controlling territories as extensive as those of the Akkadians, they maintained tight control by means of a rapidly expanding bureaucracy of administrators and obsessive record keeping. Messengers and well-maintained road stations enabled rapid communication, and an official calendar, standardized weights and measures, and uniform writing practices increased the efficiency of the central administration.

In the northwest the kings erected a great wall 125 miles (201 kilometers) in length to keep out the nomadic Amorites (AM-uh-rite), but in the end nomad incursions combined with an Elamite attack from the southeast toppled the Third Dynasty of Ur. The Semitic Amorites founded a new city at **Babylon**, not far from Akkad. Toward the end of a long reign, **Hammurabi** (HAM-uh-rah-bee) (r. 1792–1750 B.C.E.) launched a series of aggressive military campaigns, and Babylon became the capital of what historians call the "Old Babylonian" state, which stretched beyond Sumer and Akkad into the north and northwest from 1900 to 1600 B.C.E. Hammurabi's famous Law Code, inscribed on a polished black stone pillar, provided judges with a lengthy set of examples illustrating principles to use in deciding cases (and thereby left us a fascinating window on the activities of everyday life). Many offenses were met with severe physical punishments and, not infrequently, the death penalty.

The far-reaching conquests of some states were motivated, at least in part, by the need to obtain vital resources. The alternative was to trade for raw materials, and long-distance commerce flourished in most periods. Evidence of boats used in river and sea trade appears as early as the fifth millennium B.C.E. Recent archaeological discoveries outside the core zone in southern Mesopotamia—in Anatolia, northern Mesopotamia, and Iran—are demonstrating that cities and complex societies were evolving across western Asia, probably as a consequence of the long-distance trade networks. Wool, barley, and vegetable oil were exported in exchange for wood from cedar forests in Lebanon and Syria, silver from Anatolia, gold from Egypt, copper from the eastern Mediterranean and Oman (on the Arabian peninsula), and tin from Afghanistan. Precious stones used for jewelry and carved figurines came from Iran, Afghanistan, and Pakistan.

In the third millennium B.C.E. merchants were primarily employed by the palace or temple, the only two institutions with the financial resources and long-distance connections to organize the collection, transport, and protection of goods. Merchants exchanged surplus food from the estates of kings or temples for raw materials and luxury goods. In the second millennium B.C.E. more commerce came into the hands of independent merchants, and guilds (cooperative associations formed by merchants) became powerful forces in Mesopotamian society. Items could be bartered—traded for one another—or valued in relation to fixed weights of precious metal, primarily silver, or measures of grain.

**Mesopotamian
Society**

Urbanized civilizations generate social divisions—variations in the status and legal and political privileges of certain groups of people. The rise of cities, specialization of labor, centralization of power, and the use of written records enabled some groups to amass unprecedented wealth. Temple leaders and kings controlled large agricultural estates, and the palace administration collected taxes from subjects. An elite class acquired large landholdings, and soldiers and religious officials received plots of land in return for their services.

The Law Code of Hammurabi in eighteenth-century B.C.E. Babylonia reflects social divisions that may also have been valid at other times. Society was divided into three classes: (1) the free, landowning class, largely living in the cities, which included royalty, high-ranking officials, warriors, priests, merchants, and some artisans and shopkeepers; (2) the class of dependent farmers and artisans, whose legal attachment to royal, temple, or private estates made them the primary rural workforce; and (3) the class of slaves, primarily employed in domestic service. Penalties for crimes prescribed in the Law Code depended on the class of the offender, with the most severe punishments reserved for the lower orders.

Slavery was not as prevalent and fundamental to the economy as it would be in the later societies of Greece and Rome (see Chapters 5 and 6). Many slaves came from mountain tribes, either captured in war or sold by slave traders. Others were people unable to pay their debts. Normally slaves were not chained, but they were identified by a distinctive hairstyle; if given their freedom, a barber shaved off the

Mesopotamian Cylinder Seal *Seals indicated the identity of an individual and were impressed into wet clay or wax to "sign" legal documents or to mark ownership of an object. This seal, produced in the period of the Akkadian Empire, depicts Ea (second from right), the god of underground waters, symbolized by the stream with fish emanating from his shoulders; Ishtar, whose attributes of fertility and war are indicated by the date cluster in her hand and the pointed weapons showing above her wings; and the sun-god Shamash, cutting his way out of the mountains with a jagged knife, an evocation of sunrise.*

telltale mark. In the Old Babylonian period, as the class of people who were not dependent on the temple or palace grew in numbers and importance, the amount of land and other property in private hands increased, and the hiring of free laborers became more common. Slaves, dependent workers, and hired laborers were all compensated with commodities such as food and oil in quantities proportional to their age, gender, and tasks.

The daily lives of ordinary Mesopotamians, especially those in villages or on large estates in the countryside, left few archaeological or written remains. Peasants built houses of mud brick and reed, which quickly disintegrate, and they had few metal possessions. Being illiterate, they left no written record of their lives.

It is likewise difficult to discover much about the experiences of women. The written sources were produced by male **scribes**—trained professionals who applied their reading and writing skills to tasks of administration—and for the most part reflect elite male activities. Anthropologists theorize that women lost social standing and freedoms in societies where agriculture superseded hunting and gathering (see Chapter 1). In hunting-and-gathering societies women provided most of the community's food from their gathering activities, and this work was highly valued. But in Mesopotamia food production depended on the heavy physical labor of plowing, harvesting, and digging irrigation channels, jobs usually performed by men. Since food surpluses permitted families to have more children, bearing and rearing children became the primary occupation of many women, preventing them from acquiring the specialized skills of the scribe or artisan. However, women could own property, maintain control of their dowry (a sum of money given by the woman's father to support her in her husband's household), and even engage in trade. Some worked outside the household in textile factories and breweries or as prostitutes, tavern keepers, bakers, or fortunetellers. Non-elite women who stayed at home helped with farming, planted vegetable gardens, cooked, cleaned, fetched water, tended the household fire, and wove baskets and textiles.

The standing of women seems to have declined further in the second millennium B.C.E., perhaps because of the rise of an urbanized middle class and an increase in private wealth. The laws favored the rights of husbands. Although Mesopotamian society was generally monogamous, a man could take a second wife if the first gave him no children, and in later Mesopotamian history kings and wealthy men had several wives. Marriage alliances arranged between families made women into instruments for preserving and increasing family wealth. Alternatively, a family might decide to avoid a daughter's marriage—and the resulting loss of a dowry—by dedicating her to the service of a deity as a "god's bride." Constraints on women's lives that eventually became part of Islamic tradition, such as largely confining themselves to the home and wearing veils in public (see Chapter 9), may have originated in the second millennium B.C.E.

Gods, Priests, and Temples   The Sumerian gods embodied the forces of nature. When the Semitic peoples became dominant, they equated their deities with those of the Sumerians. Myths of the Sumerian gods were transferred to their Semitic counterparts, and many of the same rituals continued to be practiced. People imagined the gods as anthropomorphic (an-thruh-puh-MORE-fik)—like humans in form and conduct. They thought the gods had bodies and senses, sought nourishment from sacrifice, enjoyed the worship and obedience of humanity, and were driven by lust, love, hate, anger, and envy. The Mesopotamians feared their gods, believing them responsible for the natural disasters that occurred without warning in their environment, and sought to appease them.

The public, state-organized religion is most visible in the archaeological record. Cities built temples and showed devotion to the divinities who protected the community. The temple precinct, encircled by a high wall, contained the shrine of the chief deity; open-air plazas; chapels for lesser gods; housing, dining facilities, and offices for priests and other temple staff; and craft shops, storerooms, and service buildings. The most visible part of the temple compound was the **ziggurat** (ZIG-uh-rat), a multistory, mud-brick, pyramid-shaped tower approached by ramps and stairs. Scholars are not certain of the ziggurat's function and symbolic meaning.

A temple was considered the god's residence, and the statue in its interior shrine was believed to be occupied by the deity's life force. Priests anticipated and met every need of the divine image in a daily cycle of waking, bathing, dressing, feeding, moving around, entertaining, soothing, and revering. These efforts reflected the claim of the Babylonian Creation Myth that humankind had been created from the blood of a vanquished rebel deity in order to serve the gods. Several thousand priests may have staffed a large temple like that of the chief god Marduk at Babylon.

Priests passed their hereditary office and sacred lore to their sons, and their families lived on rations of food from the deity's estates. The amount a priest received depended on his rank within a complicated hierarchy of status and specialized function. The high priest performed the central acts in the great rituals. Certain priests made music to please the gods. Others exorcised evil spirits. Still others interpreted dreams and divined the future by examining the organs of sacrificed animals, reading patterns in the rising incense smoke, or casting dice.

Harder to determine are the everyday beliefs and religious practices of the common people. Scholars do not know how much access the general public had to the temple buildings, although individuals did place votive statues in the sanctuaries, believing that these miniature replicas of themselves could continually seek the deity's favor. The survival of many **amulets** (small charms meant to protect the bearer from evil) and representations of a host of demons suggests widespread belief in magic—the use of special words and rituals to manipulate and control the forces of nature. For example, people believed that a headache was caused by a demon that could be driven out of the ailing body. In return for a gift or sacrifice, a god or goddess might reveal information about the future. We do know that elite and common folk came together in great festivals such as the twelve-day New Year's Festival held each spring in Babylon to mark the beginning of a new agricultural cycle (see Diversity and Dominance: Violence and Order in the Babylonian New Year's Festival).

Technology and Science   The term *technology*, from the Greek word *techne*, meaning "skill" or "specialized knowledge," normally refers to the tools and machines that humans use to manipulate the physical world. Many scholars now use the term more broadly for any specialized knowledge used to transform the natural environment and human society.

DIVERSITY + DOMINANCE

Violence and Order in the Babylonian New Year's Festival

The twelve-day Babylonian New Year's Festival was one of the most important religious celebrations in ancient Mesopotamia. Fragmentary documents of the third century B.C.E. (fifteen hundred years after Hammurabi) provide most of our information, but because of the continuity of culture over several millennia, the later Babylonian New Year's Festival preserves many of the beliefs and practices of earlier epochs.

In the first days of the festival, most activities took place in inner chambers of the temple of Marduk, patron deity of Babylon, attended only by high-ranking priests. A key ceremony was a ritualized humiliation of the king, followed by a renewal of the institution of divinely sanctioned kingship:

On the fifth day of the month Nisannu ... they shall bring water for washing the king's hands and then shall accompany him to the temple Esagil. The *urigallu*-priest shall leave the sanctuary and take away the scepter, the circle, and the sword from the king. He shall bring them before the god Bel [Marduk] and place them on a chair. He shall leave the sanctuary and strike the king's cheek. He shall accompany the king into the presence of the god Bel. He shall drag him by the ears and make him bow to the ground. The king shall speak the following only once: "I did not sin, lord of the countries. I was not neglectful of the requirements of your godship. I did not destroy Babylon. The temple Esagil, I did not forget its rites. I did not rain blows on the cheek of a subordinate." ... [The *urigallu*-priest responds:] "The god Bel will listen to your prayer. He will exalt your kingship. The god Bel will bless you forever. He will destroy your enemy, fell your adversary." After the *urigallu*-priest

says this, the king shall regain his composure. The scepter, circle, and sword shall be restored to the king.

Also in the early days of the festival, a priest recited the entire Babylonian Creation Epic to the image of Marduk. After relating the origins of the gods from the mating of two primordial creatures, Tiamat, the female embodiment of the salt sea, and Apsu, the male embodiment of fresh water, the myth tells how Tiamat gathered an army of older gods and monsters to destroy the younger generation of gods.

All the Anunnaki [the younger gods], the host of gods gathered into that place tongue-tied; they sat with mouths shut for they thought, "What other god can make war on Tiamat? No one else can face her and come back." ... Lord Marduk exulted, ... with racing spirits he said to the father of gods, "Creator of the gods who decides their destiny, if I must be your avenger, defeating Tiamat, saving your lives, call the Assembly, give me precedence over all the rest; ... now and for ever let my word be law; I, not you, will decide the world's nature, the things to come. My decrees shall never be altered, never be annulled, but my creation endures to the ends of the world." ... He took his route towards the rising sound of Tiamat's rage, and all the gods besides, the fathers of the gods pressed in around him, and the lord approached Tiamat.... When Tiamat heard him her wits scattered, she was possessed and shrieked aloud, her legs shook from the crotch down, she gabbled spells, muttered maledictions, while the gods of war sharpened their weapons.... The lord shot his net to entangle Tiamat, and the pursuing tumid wind, Imhullu, came from behind and beat in her face. When the mouth gaped open to suck him down he drove Imhullu in, so that the mouth would not shut but wind raged through her belly; her carcass blown up, tumescent. She gaped. And now he shot the arrow that split the belly, that pierced the gut and cut the womb....

He split it apart like a cockle-shell; with the upper half he constructed the arc of sky, he pulled down the bar and set a watch on the waters, so they should never escape.... He projected positions for the Great Gods conspicuous in the sky, he gave them a starry aspect as constellations; he measured the year, gave it a beginning and an end, and to each month of the twelve three rising stars.... Through her ribs he opened gates in the east and west, and gave them strong bolts on the right and left; and high in the belly of Tiamat he set the zenith. He gave the moon the luster of a jewel, he gave him all the night, to mark off days, to watch by night each month the circle of a waxing waning light.... When Marduk had sent out the moon, he took the sun and set him to complete the cycle from this one to the next New Year....

Then Marduk considered Tiamat. He skimmed spume from the bitter sea, heaped up the clouds, spindrift of wet and wind and cooling rain, the spittle of Tiamat. With his own hands from the steaming mist he spread the clouds. He pressed hard down the head of water, heaping mountains over it, opening springs to flow: Euphrates and Tigris rose from her eyes, but he closed the nostrils and held back their springhead. He piled huge mountains on her paps and through them drove water-holes to channel the deep sources; and high overhead he arched her tail, locked-in to the wheel of heaven; the pit was under his feet, between was the crotch, the sky's fulcrum. Now the earth had foundations and the sky its mantle....

Marduk considered and began to speak to the gods assembled in his presence. This is what he said, "In the former time you inhabited the void above the abyss, but I have made Earth as the mirror of Heaven, I have consolidated the soil for the foundations, and there I will build my city, my beloved home. A holy precinct shall be established with sacred halls for the presence of the king. When you come up from the deep to join the Synod you will find lodging and sleep by night. When others from heaven descend to the Assembly, you too will find lodging and sleep by night. It shall be BABYLON the home of the gods. The masters of all crafts shall build it according to my plan." ... Now that Marduk has heard what it is the gods are saying, he is moved with desire to create a work of consummate art. He told Ea the deep thought in his heart.

> "Blood to blood
> I join,
> blood to bone
> I form
> an original thing,
> its name is MAN,
> aboriginal man
> is mine in making.
> "All his occupations
> are faithful service...."

Ea answered with carefully chosen words, completing the plan for the gods' comfort. He said to Marduk, "Let one of the kindred be taken; only one need die for the new creation. Bring the gods together in the Great Assembly; there let the guilty die, so the rest may live."

Marduk called the Great Gods to the Synod.... The king speaks to the rebel gods, "Declare on your oath if ever before you spoke the truth, who instigated rebellion? Who stirred up Tiamat? Who led the battle? Let the instigator of war be handed over; guilt and retribution are on him, and peace will be yours for ever."

The Great Gods answered the Lord of the Universe, the king and counselor of gods, "It was Kingu who instigated rebellion, he stirred up that sea of bitterness and led the battle for her." They declared him guilty, they bound and held him down in front of Ea, they cut his arteries and from his blood they created man; and Ea imposed his servitude.

Much of the subsequent activity of the festival, which took place in the temple courtyard and streets, was a reenactment of the events of the Creation Myth. The festival occurred at the beginning of spring, when the grain shoots were beginning to emerge, and its essential symbolism concerns the return of natural life to the world. The Babylonians believed that the natural world had an annual life cycle consisting of birth, growth, maturity, and death. In winter the cycle drew to a close, and there was no guarantee that life would return to the world. Babylonians hoped proper performance of the New Year's Festival would encourage the gods to grant a renewal of time and life, in essence to re-create the world.

Questions for Analysis

1. According to the Creation Epic, how did the present order of the universe come into being? What does the violent nature of this creation tell us about the Mesopotamian view of the physical world and the gods?

2. How did the symbolism of the events of the New Year's Festival, with its ritual reading and reenactment of the story of the Creation Myth, validate such concepts as kingship, the primacy of Babylon, and mankind's relationship to the gods?

3. What is the significance of the distinction between the "private" ceremonies celebrated in the temple precincts and the "public" ceremonies that took place in the streets of the city? What does the festival tell us about the relationship of different social groups to the gods?

Source: PRITCHARD, JAMES, ANCIENT NEAR EASTERN TEXTS RELATING TO THE OLD TESTAMENT. © 1969 by Princeton University Press. Reprinted by permission of Princeton University Press.

An important example of the broader type of technology is writing, which first appeared in Mesopotamia before 3300 B.C.E. The earliest inscribed tablets, found in the chief temple at Uruk, date from a time when the temple was the most important economic institution in the community. According to a plausible recent theory, writing originated from a system of tokens used to keep track of property—such as sheep, cattle, or wagon wheels—when increases in the amount of accumulated wealth and the complexity of commercial transactions strained people's memories. The tokens, made in the shape of the commodity, were sealed in clay envelopes, and pictures of the tokens were incised on the outside of the envelopes as a reminder of what was inside. Eventually, people realized that the incised pictures were an adequate record, making the tokens inside the envelope redundant. These pictures were the first written symbols. Each symbol represented an object, and it could also stand for the sound of the word for that object if the sound was part of a longer word.

The usual method of writing involved pressing the point of a sharpened reed into a moist clay tablet. Because the reed made wedge-shaped impressions, the early realistic pictures were increasingly stylized into a combination of strokes and wedges, a system known as **cuneiform** (Latin for "wedge-shaped") writing. Mastering this system required years of training and practice. Several hundred signs were in use at any one time, as compared to the twenty-five or so signs in an alphabetic system. The prestige and regular employment that went with their position may have made scribes reluctant to simplify the cuneiform system. In the Old Babylonian period, the growth of private commerce brought an increase in the number of people who could read and write, but only a small percentage of the population was literate.

The earliest Mesopotamian documents are economic, but cuneiform came to have wide-ranging uses. Written documents marked with the seal of the participants became the primary proof of legal actions. Texts were written about political, literary, religious, and scientific topics. Cuneiform is not a language but rather a system of writing. Developed originally for the Sumerian language, it was later adapted to the Akkadian language of the Mesopotamian Semites as well as to other languages of western Asia, such as Hittite, Elamite, and Persian.

Other technologies enabled the Mesopotamians to meet the challenges of their physical environment. Wheeled carts and sledlike platforms dragged by cattle were used to transport goods in some locations. In the south, where numerous water channels cut up the landscape, boats and barges predominated. In northern Mesopotamia, donkeys were the chief pack animals for overland caravans before the advent of the camel around 1200 B.C.E. (see Chapter 9).

The Mesopotamians had to import metals, but they became skilled in metallurgy, refining ores containing copper and alloying them with arsenic or tin to make **bronze**. Craftsmen poured molten bronze into molds to produce tools and weapons. The cooled and hardened bronze took a sharper edge than stone, was less likely to break, and was more easily repaired. Stone implements remained in use among poor people, who could not afford bronze.

Widely available clay was used to make dishware and storage vessels. By 4000 B.C.E. the potter's wheel, a revolving platform spun by hands or feet, made possible the rapid production of vessels with precise and complex shapes. Mud bricks, dried in the sun or baked in an oven for greater durability, were the primary building material. Construction of city walls, temples, and palaces required practical knowledge of architecture and engineering. For example, the reed mats that Mesopotamian builders laid between the mud-brick layers of ziggurats served the same stabilizing purpose as girders in modern high-rise construction.

Early military forces were nonprofessional militias of able-bodied men called up for short periods when needed. The powerful states of the later third and second millennia B.C.E. built up armies of well-trained and well-paid full-time soldiers. In the early second millennium B.C.E. horses appeared in western Asia, and the horse-drawn chariot came into vogue. Infantry found themselves at the mercy of swift chariots carrying a driver and an archer who could easily run them down. Mesopotamian soldiers also used increasingly effective siege machinery that enabled them to climb over, undermine, or knock down the walls protecting the cities of their enemies.

Mesopotamians used a base-60 number system in which numbers were expressed as fractions or multiples of 60 (in contrast to our base-10 system; this is the origin of the seconds and minutes we use in calculating time today). Advances in mathematics and careful observation of the skies made the Mesopotamians sophisticated practitioners of astronomy. Priests compiled lists of omens or unusual sightings on earth and in the heavens, together with a record of the events that coincided with them. They consulted these texts at critical times, for they believed that the recurrence of such phenomena could provide clues to future developments. The underlying premise was that the elements of the material universe, from the microscopic to the macrocosmic, were interconnected in mysterious but undeniable ways.

EGYPT

No place exhibits the impact of the natural environment on the history and culture of a society better than ancient Egypt. Located at the intersection of Asia and Africa, Egypt was protected by surrounding barriers of desert and a harborless, marshy seacoast. Whereas Mesopotamia was open to migration or invasion and was dependent on imported resources, Egypt's natural isolation and material self-sufficiency fostered a unique culture that for long periods had relatively little to do with other civilizations.

The Land of Egypt: "Gift of the Nile"   The fifth-century B.C.E. Greek traveler Herodotus (he-ROD-uh-tuhs) justifiably called Egypt the "gift of the Nile." The world's longest river, the Nile flows northward from Lake Victoria and several large tributaries in the highlands of tropical Africa, carving a narrow valley between a chain of hills on either side, until it reaches the Mediterranean Sea. Though bordered mostly by desert, the banks of the river support lush vegetation. About 100 miles (160 kilometers) from the Mediterranean, the Nile divides into channels to form a triangular delta. Most of the population, then as now, lived on the twisting, green ribbon of land alongside the river or in the Nile Delta. The rest of the country, 90 percent or more, is a bleak and inhospitable desert of mountains, rocks, and dunes. The ancient Egyptians distinguished between the low-lying, life-sustaining dark soil of the "Black Land" along the river and the elevated, deadly "Red Land" of the desert.

The river was the main means of travel and communication, with the most important cities located upstream away from the Mediterranean. Because the river flows from south to north, the Egyptians called the southern part of the country "Upper Egypt" and the northern delta "Lower Egypt." In most periods the southern boundary of Egypt was the First Cataract of the Nile, the northernmost of a series of impassable rocks and rapids below Aswan (AS-wahn) (about 500 miles [800 kilometers] south of the Mediterranean). At times Egyptians' control extended farther south into what they called "Kush" (later Nubia, today part of southern Egypt and northern Sudan). The Egyptians also settled a chain of large oases west of the river, green and habitable "islands" in the midst of the desert.

While the hot, sunny climate favored agriculture, rain rarely falls south of the delta, and agriculture was entirely dependent on river water. Each September the

MAP 2.2 Ancient Egypt

The Nile River, flowing south to north, carved out of the surrounding desert a narrow green valley that became heavily settled in antiquity.

river overflowed its banks, spreading water into the bordering basins, and irrigation channels carried water farther out into the valley to increase the area suitable for planting. Unlike the Tigris and Euphrates, the Nile flooded at exactly the right time for grain agriculture. When the waters receded, they left behind a moist, fertile layer of mineral-rich silt in which farmers could easily plant their crops. An Egyptian creation myth featured the emergence of a life-supporting mound of earth from a primeval swamp.

The level of the flood's crest determined the abundance of the next harvest. "Nilometers," stone staircases with incised units of measure placed along the river's edge, gauged the flood surge. When the flood was too high, dikes protecting inhabited areas were washed out, and much damage resulted. When the floods were too low for several years, less land could be cultivated, and the country experienced famine and decline. The ebb and flow of successful and failed regimes seems to have been linked to the cycle of floods. Nevertheless, remarkable stability

characterized most eras, and Egyptians viewed the universe as an orderly and beneficent place.

Egypt was well endowed with natural resources and far more self-sufficient
than Mesopotamia. Egyptians used papyrus reeds growing in marshy areas to
make sails, ropes, and a kind of paper. Hunters pursued the abundant wild animals
and birds in the marshes and on the edge of the desert, and fishermen netted fish
from the river. Building stone was quarried and floated downstream from southern
Egypt. Clay for mud bricks and pottery could be found almost everywhere. The
state organized armed expeditions and forced labor to exploit copper and turquoise
deposits in the Sinai Desert to the east and gold from Nubia to the south.

The farming villages that appeared in Egypt as early as 5500 B.C.E. relied on
domesticated plant and animal species that had originated several millennia earlier
in western Asia. Egypt's emergence as a focal point of civilization stemmed, at least
in part, from a gradual change in climate from the fifth to the third millennium
B.C.E. Until then, the Sahara, the vast region that is now the world's largest desert,
had a relatively mild and wet climate, and its lakes and grasslands supported a variety of plant and animal species as well as populations of hunter-gatherers (see
Chapter 9). As the Sahara became a desert, displaced groups migrated into the
Nile Valley, where they developed a sedentary way of life.

Divine Kingship   The increase in population led to more complex political
organization, including a form of local kingship. Later gen-
erations of Egyptians saw the conquest of these smaller units and the unification of
all Egypt by Menes (MEH-neez), a ruler from the south, as a pivotal event. Kings of
Egypt bore the title "Ruler of the Two Lands"—Upper and Lower Egypt—and wore
two crowns symbolizing the unification of the country. In contrast to Mesopotamia,
Egypt was unified early in its history.

Historians organize Egyptian history using the system of thirty dynasties
(sequences of kings from the same family) identified by Manetho, an Egyptian
from the third century B.C.E. The rise and fall of dynasties often reflect the dominance of different parts of the country. More generally, scholars refer to the
"Old," "Middle," and "New Kingdoms," each a period of centralized political
power and brilliant cultural achievement, punctuated by "Intermediate Periods" of
political fragmentation and cultural decline. Although experts debate the specific
dates for these periods, the chronology on page 48 reflects current opinion.

The Egyptian state centered on the king, often known by the New Kingdom
term **pharaoh**, from an Egyptian phrase meaning "palace." From the time of the
Old Kingdom, if not earlier, Egyptians considered the king to be a god sent to
earth to maintain **ma'at** (muh-AHT), the divinely authorized order of the universe.
He was the indispensable link between his people and the gods, and his benevolent
rule ensured the welfare and prosperity of the country.

So much depended on the kings that their deaths called forth elaborate efforts to
ensure the well-being of their spirits on their perilous journey to rejoin the gods. Massive resources were poured into the construction of royal tombs, the celebration of
elaborate funerary rites, and the sustenance of the kings' spirits in the afterlife by perpetual offerings in funerary chapels attached to the royal tombs. Early rulers were
buried in flat-topped, rectangular tombs made of mud brick. Around 2630 B.C.E.

Solar Ship of King Khufu *This full-size ship (143 feet [43.6 meters] long and 19.5 feet [5.9 meters] wide) was buried in a pit at the base of the Great Pyramid ca. 2500 B.C.E. While it was probably intended to carry the resurrected king along with the sun-god Ra across the sky, it may also have been used to transport Khufu's embalmed body to Giza. Ships equipped with sails and oars were well suited for travel on the peaceful Nile and sometimes were used for voyages on the more turbulent Mediterranean and Red Seas.*

Andrea Thompson Photography/Getty Images

Djoser (JO-sur), a Third Dynasty king, constructed a stepped **pyramid** consisting of a series of stone platforms laid one on top of the other at Saqqara (suh-KAHR-uh), near Memphis. Rulers in the Fourth Dynasty filled in the steps to create the smooth-sided, limestone pyramids that have become the most memorable symbol of ancient Egypt. Between 2550 and 2490 B.C.E. the pharaohs Khufu (KOO-foo) and Khafre (KAF-ray) erected huge pyramids at Giza, several miles north of Saqqara.

Egyptians accomplished this construction with stone tools (bronze was still expensive and rare) and no machinery other than simple levers, pulleys, and rollers. What made it possible was almost unlimited human muscle power. Calculations of the human resources needed to build a pyramid within the lifetime of the ruler suggest that large numbers of people must have been pressed into service for part of each year, probably during the flood season when no agricultural work could be done. Although this labor was compulsory, the Egyptian masses probably regarded it as a kind of religious service that helped ensure prosperity. The age of the great pyramids lasted only about a century, although pyramids continued to be built on a smaller scale for two millennia.

Administration and Communication   Ruling dynasties usually placed their capitals in the area of their original power base. **Memphis**, near the apex of the delta (close to Cairo, the modern capital), held this central position during the Old Kingdom. **Thebes**, far to the south, supplanted it during the Middle and New Kingdom periods.

The extensive administrative system began at the village level and progressed to the districts into which the country was divided and, finally, to the central government in the capital city. Bureaucrats kept track of land, products, and people, extracting as taxes a substantial portion of the country's annual revenues—at times

Michelle Burgess/SuperStock

Pyramids of Menkaure, Khafre, and Khufu at Giza, ca. 2500 B.C.E. *With a width of 755 feet (230 meters) and a height of 480 feet (146 meters), the Great Pyramid of Khufu is the largest stone structure ever built. The construction of these massive edifices depended on relatively simple techniques of stonecutting, transport (the stones were floated downriver on boats and rolled to the site on sledges), and lifting (the stones were dragged up the face of the pyramid on mud-brick ramps). However, the surveying and engineering skills required to level the platform, lay out the measurements, and securely position the blocks were very sophisticated and have withstood the test of time.*

as much as 50 percent. This income supported the palace, bureaucracy, and army, as well as the construction and maintenance of temples and great monuments celebrating the ruler's reign. The government maintained a monopoly over key sectors of the economy and controlled long-distance trade, unlike in Mesopotamia, where commerce increasingly fell into the hands of an acquisitive urban middle class.

The hallmark of the administrative class was literacy. A writing system had been developed by the beginning of the Early Dynastic period. **Hieroglyphics** (high-ruh-GLIF-iks), the earliest form of this system, were picture symbols standing for words, syllables, or individual sounds. Hieroglyphic writing long continued to be used on monuments and ornamental inscriptions. By 2500 B.C.E., however, a cursive script, in which the original pictorial nature of the symbol was less apparent, had been developed for the everyday needs of administrators and copyists. The Egyptians used writing for many purposes other than administrative record keeping. Their written literature included tales of adventure and magic, love poetry, religious hymns, and instruction manuals on technical subjects. Scribes in workshops attached to the temples made copies of traditional texts. They worked with ink on a writing material made from the **papyrus** (puh-PIE-ruhs) reed. The plant grew only in Egypt but was in demand throughout the ancient world and was exported in large quantities.

When the monarchy was strong, officials were appointed and promoted on the basis of ability and accomplishment. The king gave them grants of land cultivated by dependent peasants. Low-level officials were assigned to villages and district capitals, while high-ranking officials served in the royal capital. When Old Kingdom officials died, they were buried in tombs around the monumental tomb of the king so that they could serve him in death as they had in life.

Throughout Egyptian history there was an underlying tension between the centralizing power of the monarchy and the decentralizing tendencies of the bureaucracy. One sign of the breakdown of royal power in the late Old Kingdom and First Intermediate Period was the placement of officials' tombs in their home districts, where they spent much of their time and exercised power more or less independently, rather than near the royal tomb. Another sign was the tendency of administrative posts to become hereditary. The early monarchs of the Middle Kingdom restored centralized control by reducing the power and prerogatives of the old elite and creating a new class of loyal administrators.

It has often been said that Egypt lacked real cities because the political capitals were primarily extensions of the palace and central administration. Compared to Mesopotamia, a far larger percentage of Egyptians lived in rural villages and engaged in agriculture, and Egypt's wealth derived to a higher degree from the land and its products. But there were towns and cities in ancient Egypt, although they were less crucial to the economic and cultural dynamism of the country than were Mesopotamian urban centers. Unfortunately, archaeologists have been unable to excavate many ancient urban sites in Egypt because they lie beneath modern communities.

During the Old and Middle Kingdoms, Egypt's foreign policy was essentially isolationist. Technically, all foreigners were considered enemies. When necessary, local militia units backed up a small standing army of professional soldiers. Nomadic groups in the eastern and western deserts and Libyans to the northwest were a nuisance rather than a real danger and were readily handled by the Egyptian military. Egypt's interests abroad focused on maintaining access to valuable resources rather than on acquiring territory. Trade with the coastal towns of the Levant (luh-VANT) (modern Israel, the Palestinian territories, Lebanon, and Syria) brought in cedar wood. In return, Egypt exported grain, papyrus, and gold.

In all periods the Egyptians had a particularly strong interest in goods from the south. Nubia had rich sources of gold (Chapter 4 examines the rise of a civilization in Nubia that, though considerably influenced by Egypt, created a vital and original culture that lasted for more than two thousand years), and the southern course of the Nile offered the easiest passage to sub-Saharan Africa. In the Old Kingdom, Egyptian noblemen led donkey caravans south to trade for gold, incense, and products of tropical Africa such as ivory, dark ebony wood, and exotic jungle animals. A line of forts along the southern border protected Egypt from attack. In the early second millennium B.C.E. Egyptian forces struck south into Nubia, extending the border to the Third Cataract of the Nile and taking possession of the gold fields. Still farther to the south, perhaps in the coastal region of present-day Sudan or Eritrea, lay the fabled land of Punt (poont), source of the fragrant myrrh resin burned on the altars of the Egyptian gods.

**The People
of Egypt**
The million to million and a half inhabitants of Egypt included various physical types, ranging from dark-skinned people related to the populations of sub-Saharan Africa to lighter-skinned people akin to the populations of North Africa and western Asia. Although Egypt did not experience the large-scale migrations and invasions common in Mesopotamia, settlers periodically trickled into the Nile Valley and assimilated with the people already living there.

Although some Egyptians had higher status and more wealth and power than others, in contrast to Mesopotamia no formal class structure emerged. At the top of the social hierarchy were the king and high-ranking officials. In the middle were lower-level officials, local leaders, priests and other professionals, artisans, and well-to-do farmers. At the bottom were peasants, who made up the vast majority of the population.

Any account of the lives of ordinary Egyptians is largely conjectural; the villages of ancient Egypt, like those of Mesopotamia, left few traces in the archaeological or literary record. In tomb paintings of the elite, artists indicated status by pictorial conventions, such as obesity for their wealthy and comfortable patrons, baldness and deformity for the working classes. Egyptian poets frequently used metaphors of farming and hunting, and papyrus documents preserved in the hot, dry sands tell of property transactions and legal disputes among ordinary people.

Peasants living in rural villages engaged in the seasonally changing tasks of agriculture: plowing, sowing, tending emerging shoots, reaping, threshing, and storing grain or other products of the soil. They maintained and extended the irrigation network of channels, basins, and dikes. Meat from domesticated animals—cattle, sheep, goats, and poultry—and fish supplemented a diet based on wheat or barley, beer, and vegetables. Villagers shared implements, work animals, and storage facilities and helped one another at peak times in the agricultural cycle and in the construction of houses and other buildings. They prayed and feasted together at festivals to the local gods. Periodically they had to contribute labor to state projects. If taxation or compulsory service was too great a burden, flight into the desert was the only escape.

Some information is available about the lives of women of the upper classes, but it is filtered through the brushes and pens of male artists and scribes. Tomb paintings show women of the royal family and elite classes accompanying their husbands and engaging in typical domestic activities. They are depicted with dignity and affection, though they are clearly subordinate to the men. The artistic convention of depicting men with a dark red and women with a yellow flesh tone implies that the elite woman's proper sphere was indoors, away from the searing sun. In the beautiful love poetry of the New Kingdom, lovers address each other in terms of apparent equality and express emotions of romantic love.

Legal documents show that Egyptian women could own property, inherit property from their parents, and will their property to whomever they wished. Marriage, usually monogamous, was not confirmed by any legal or religious ceremony and essentially constituted a decision by a man and woman to establish a household together. Either party could dissolve the relationship, and the divorced woman retained rights over her dowry. At certain times queens and queen-mothers played significant behind-the-scenes roles in the politics of the court, and priestesses sometimes supervised the cults of female deities. In general, the limited evidence suggests that women in ancient Egypt were treated more respectfully and had more legal rights and social freedom than women in Mesopotamia and other ancient societies.

Belief and Knowledge

Egyptian religion was rooted in the landscape of the Nile Valley and the vision of cosmic order that it evoked. The consistency of their environment—the sun rose every day in a clear and cloudless sky, and the river flooded on schedule every year, ensuring a bounteous harvest—persuaded the Egyptians that the natural world was a place of recurrent cycles and periodic renewal. The sky was imagined to be a great ocean surrounding the inhabited world. The sun-god Re (ray) traversed this blue waterway in a boat by day, then returned through the Underworld at night, fighting off the attacks of demonic serpents so that he could be born anew in the morning. In one especially popular story Osiris (oh-SIGH-ris), a god who once ruled Egypt, was slain by his jealous brother Seth, who then scattered the dismembered pieces. Isis, Osiris's devoted sister and wife, found and reconstructed the remnants, and Horus, his son, took revenge on Seth. Osiris was restored to life and installed as king of the Underworld, and his example gave people hope of a new life in a world beyond this one.

The king, who was seen as Horus and as the son of Re, was thus associated with both the return of the dead to life and the life-giving and self-renewing sun-god. He was the chief priest of Egypt, intervening with the gods on behalf of his land and people. Egyptian rulers zealously built new temples, refurbished old ones, and made lavish gifts to the gods. Much of the country's wealth was directed to religious activities in a ceaseless effort to win the gods' favor, maintain the continuity of divine kingship, and ensure the renewal of the life-giving forces that sustained the world.

The many gods of ancient Egypt were diverse in origin and nature. Some were normally depicted with animal heads; others were always given human form. Few myths about the origins and adventures of the gods have survived, but there must have been a rich oral tradition. Many towns had temples for locally prominent deities. When a town became the capital of a ruling dynasty, the chief god of that town became prominent across the land. Thus did Ptah (puh-TAH) of Memphis, Re of Heliopolis (he-lee-OP-uh-lis), and Amon (AH-muhn) of Thebes become gods of all Egypt, serving to unify the country and strengthen the monarchy. As in Mesopotamia, some temples possessed extensive landholdings worked by dependent peasants, and the priests who administered the deity's wealth were influential locally and sometimes even throughout the land.

Cult activities were carried out in the inner reaches of the temples, off limits to all but the priests who served the needs of the deity by attending to his or her statue. During great festivals, the priests paraded a boat-shaped litter carrying the shrouded statue and cult items of the deity around the town, an event that brought large numbers of people into contact with the deity in an outpouring of devotion and celebration. However, little is known about the day-to-day beliefs and practices of the common people. In the household family members made small offerings to Bes, the grotesque god of marriage and domestic happiness, to local deities, and to the family's ancestors. They relied on amulets and depictions of demonic figures to protect the bearer and ward off evil forces. In later times Greeks and Romans commented that the devotion to magic was especially strong in Egypt.

Egyptians believed in the afterlife and made extensive preparations for safe passage to the next world and a comfortable existence once they arrived there. A common belief was that death was a journey beset with hazards. The Egyptian Book of the Dead, present in many excavated tombs, contained rituals and spells to protect the journeying spirit. The final challenge was the weighing of the deceased's heart in the presence of the judges of the Underworld to determine whether the person had led a good life and deserved to reach the ultimate blessed destination.

Obsession with the afterlife led to great concern about the physical condition of the cadaver, and Egyptians perfected techniques of mummification to preserve the dead body. The idea probably grew out of the early practice of burying the dead in the hot, dry sand on the edge of the desert, where bodies decomposed slowly. The elite classes utilized the most expensive kind of mummification. Vital organs were removed, preserved, and stored in stone jars laid out around the corpse. Body cavities were filled with various packing materials. The cadaver, immersed for long periods in dehydrating and preserving chemicals, eventually was wrapped in linen. The **mummy** was then placed in one or more decorated wooden caskets and deposited in a tomb.

The form of the tomb reflected the wealth and status of the deceased. Common people made do with simple pit graves or small mud-brick chambers. The privileged classes built larger tombs. Kings erected pyramids and other grand edifices, employing subterfuge to hide the sealed chamber containing the body and treasures, as well as curses and other magical precautions to foil tomb robbers. Rarely did they succeed, however, and archaeologists have seldom discovered an undisturbed royal tomb. The tombs, usually built at the edge of the desert so as not to tie up valuable farmland, were filled with pictures, food, and the objects of everyday life to provide whatever the deceased might need in the next life. Small figurines called shawabtis (shuh-WAB-tees) were included to play the part of servants and take the place of the deceased in case the afterlife required periodic compulsory labor. The elite classes attached chapels to their tombs and left endowments to subsidize the daily attendance of a priest and offerings of foodstuffs to sustain their spirits for all eternity.

The ancient Egyptians made remarkable advances in many areas of knowledge. The process of mummification taught them about human anatomy, and Egyptian doctors were in demand in the courts of western Asia. They developed mathematics to measure the dimensions of fields and to calculate the quantity of agricultural produce owed to the state. Through careful observation of the stars they constructed the most accurate calendar in the world, and they knew that the appearance of the star Sirius on the horizon shortly before sunrise meant that the Nile flood surge was imminent. Pyramids, temple complexes, and other monumental building projects called for great skill in engineering. Long underground passageways were excavated to connect mortuary temples by the river with tombs near the desert's edge. On several occasions Egyptian kings dredged out a canal more than 50 miles (80 kilometers) long in order to join the Nile Valley to the Red Sea and expedite the transport of goods.

THE INDUS VALLEY CIVILIZATION

Civilization arose almost as early in South Asia as in Mesopotamia and Egypt. In the fertile floodplain of the Indus River, farming created the food surplus essential to urbanized society.

Natural Environment A plain of more than 1 million acres (400,000 hectares) stretches from the mountains of western Pakistan east to the Thar (tahr) Desert in the Sind (sinned) region of modern Pakistan. Over many centuries silt carried downstream and deposited by the Indus River has elevated the riverbed and its banks above the level of the plain. Twice a year the river overflows and inundates surrounding land as far as 10 miles (16 kilometers). In March and April melting snow from the Pamir (pah-MEER) and Himalaya (him-uh-LAY-uh) mountain ranges feeds the floods. In August, the great monsoon (seasonal wind) blowing off the ocean to the southwest brings rains that cause a second flood. Farmers in this region of little rainfall are thus able to plant and harvest two crops a year. In ancient times the Hakra (HAK-ruh) River (sometimes referred to as the Saraswati), which has since dried up, ran parallel to the Indus about 25 miles (40 kilometers) to the east and supplied water to a second cultivable area.

Adjacent regions shared many cultural traits with this core area. To the northeast is the Punjab, where five rivers converge to form the main course of the Indus. Lying beneath the towering Himalaya range, the Punjab receives considerably more rainfall than the central plain but is less prone to flooding. Settlements spread as far east as Delhi (DEL-ee) in northwest India. Settlement also extended south into the great delta where the Indus empties into the Arabian Sea, and southeast into India's hook-shaped Kathiawar (kah-tee-uh-WAHR) Peninsula, an area of alluvial plains and coastal marshes. The Indus Valley civilization covered an area much larger than the zone of Mesopotamian civilization.

Material Culture   The Indus Valley civilization flourished from approximately 2600 to 1900 B.C.E. Although archaeologists have located several hundred sites, the culture is best known from the remains of two great cities first discovered eighty years ago. Since the ancient names of these cities are unknown, they are referred to by modern names: **Harappa** and **Mohenjo-Daro** (moe-hen-joe–DAHR-oh). Unfortunately, the high water table at these sites makes excavation of the earliest levels of settlement nearly impossible.

Settled agriculture in this region dates back to at least 5000 B.C.E. The precise relationship between the Indus Valley civilization and earlier cultural complexes in the Indus Valley and in the hilly lands to the west is unclear. Also unclear are the forces that gave rise to urbanization, population increase, and technological advances in the mid-third millennium B.C.E. Nevertheless, the case for continuity with the earlier cultures seems stronger than the case for a sudden transformation due to the arrival of new peoples.

Man from Mohenjo-Daro, ca. 2600–1900 B.C.E. *This statue of a seated man wearing a cloak and headband was carved from a soft stone called steatite. It is often called the "Priest-King" because some scholars believe it may represent someone with religious and secular authority, but the true identity and status of this person are unknown.*

Scala/Art Resource, NY

This society produced major urban centers. Harappa, 3.5 miles (5.6 kilometers) in circumference, may have housed a population of 35,000. Mohenjo-Daro was several times larger. High, thick brick walls surrounded each city, and the streets were laid out in a rectangular grid. Covered drainpipes carried away waste. The consistent width of streets and length of city blocks and the uniformity of the mud bricks used in construction suggest a strong central authority. The seat of this authority may have been the citadel—an elevated, enclosed compound containing large buildings. Scholars think the well-ventilated structures nearby were store-houses of grain for feeding the urban population and for export. The presence of barracks may point to some regimentation of skilled artisans.

Different centers may have had different functions. Mohenjo-Daro dominates the great floodplain of the Indus. Harappa, which is nearly 500 miles (805 kilo-meters) to the north, is on a frontier between farmland and herding land, and it may have served as a "gateway" for procuring the copper, tin, and precious stones of the northwest. Coastal towns in the south gathered fish and highly prized sea-shells and engaged in seaborne trade with the Persian Gulf.

Mohenjo-Daro and Harappa have been extensively excavated, and published accounts of the Indus Valley civilization tend to treat them as the norm. Most peo-ple, however, lived in smaller settlements, which exhibit the same artifacts and the same standardization of styles and shapes as the large cities. Some scholars attribute this standardization to extensive exchange of goods within the zone of Indus Valley civilization, rather than to the urban centers' control of the smaller settlements.

There is a greater quantity of metal in the Indus Valley than in Mesopotamia and Egypt, and most metal objects are utilitarian tools and other everyday objects. In contrast, more jewelry and other decorative metal objects have been unearthed in Mesopotamia and Egypt. Apparently metals were available to a broad cross-section of the population in the Indus Valley, while primarily reserved for the elite in the Middle East.

Technologically, the Indus Valley people showed skill in irrigation, used the potter's wheel, and laid the foundations of large public buildings with mud bricks fired to rocky hardness in kilns (sun-dried bricks would have dissolved quickly in floodwaters). They had a system of writing with more than four hundred signs. Archaeologists have recovered thousands of inscribed seal stones and copper tablets, but no one has been able to decipher these documents.

The people of the Indus Valley had widespread trading contacts. They had ready access to the metals and precious stones of eastern Iran and Afghanistan, as well as to ore deposits in western India, building stone, and timber. Goods were moved on rivers within the zone of Indus Valley culture. Indus Valley seal stones have been found in the Tigris-Euphrates Valley, indicating that Indus Valley mer-chants served as middlemen in long-distance trade, obtaining raw materials from the northwest and shipping them to the Persian Gulf. The undeciphered writing on seal stones may represent the names of merchants who stamped their wares.

We know little about the political, social, economic, and religious institutions of Indus Valley society. Attempts to link artifacts and images to cultural features charac-teristic of later periods of Indian history (see Chapter 7)—including a system of heredi-tary occupational groups with priests predominating, bathing tanks like those later found in Hindu temples, depictions of gods and sacred animals on seal stones, a cult of the mother-goddess—are highly speculative. Further knowledge about this society awaits additional archaeological finds and the deciphering of the Indus Valley script.

Transformation of the Indus Valley Civilization
The Indus Valley cities were abandoned sometime after 1900 B.C.E. Archaeologists once thought that invaders destroyed them, but they now believe this civilization suffered "systems failure"—a breakdown of the fragile interrelationship of political, social, and economic systems that sustained order and prosperity. The cause may have been one or more natural disasters, such as an earthquake or massive flooding. Gradual ecological changes may also have played a role as the Hakra river system dried up and salinization (an increase in the amount of salt in the soil, inhibiting plant growth) and erosion increased.

Towns no longer on the river, ports separated from the sea by silt deposits in the deltas, and the loss of fertile soil and water would have necessitated the relocation of populations and a change in the livelihood of those who remained. The causes and pace of change probably varied in different areas. The urban centers eventually succumbed, however, and village-based farming and herding took their place. As the interaction between regions lessened, regional variation replaced the standardization of technology and style of the previous era. It is important to keep in mind that in most cases like this the majority of the population adjusts to the new circumstances. But members of the elite, who depend on the urban centers and complex political and economic structures, lose the source of their authority and are merged with the population as a whole.

CONCLUSION

It is no accident that the first civilizations to develop high levels of political centralization, urbanization, and technology were situated in river valleys where rainfall was insufficient for reliable agriculture. Dependent on river water to irrigate the cultivated land that fed their populations, Mesopotamia, Egypt, and the Indus Valley civilization channeled considerable human resources into the construction and maintenance of canals, dams, and dikes. This effort required the formation of political centers that could organize the necessary labor force.

In both Egypt and Mesopotamia, kingship emerged as the dominant political form. The Egyptian king's divine origins and symbolic association with the forces of renewal made him central to the welfare of the entire country and gave him religious authority superseding the temples and priests. Egyptian monarchs lavished much of the country's wealth on their tombs, believing that a proper burial would ensure the continuity of kingship and the attendant blessings that it brought to the land and people. Mesopotamian rulers, who were not normally regarded as divine but still dominated the religious institutions, built new cities, towering walls, splendid palaces, and religious edifices as lasting testaments to their power.

The unpredictable and violent floods in the Tigris-Euphrates Basin were a constant source of alarm for the people of Mesopotamia. In contrast, the predictable, opportune, and gradual Nile floods were eagerly anticipated events in Egypt. The relationship with nature stamped the religious outlooks of both peoples, since their gods embodied the forces of the environment. Mesopotamians nervously tried to appease their harsh deities so as to survive in a dangerous world, whereas Egyptians largely trusted in and nurtured the supernatural powers that, they believed, guaranteed orderliness and prosperity. The Egyptians also believed that, although the journey to the next world was beset with hazards, the righteous spirit that overcame them could look forward to a blessed existence. In contrast, Gilgamesh, the hero of the Mesopotamian epic, is tormented by terrifying visions of the afterlife: disembodied spirits of the dead stumbling around in the darkness of the Underworld for all eternity, eating dust and clay and slaving for the heartless gods of that realm.

Although the populations of Egypt and Mesopotamia were ethnically heterogeneous, both regions experienced a remarkable degree of cultural continuity. New immigrants readily assimilated to the dominant language, belief system, and lifestyles of the civilization. Mesopotamia developed sharp social divisions that were reflected in the class-based penalties set down in the Law Code of Hammurabi, whereas Egyptian society was less urban and less stratified. Mesopotamian women's apparent loss of freedom and legal privilege in the second millennium B.C.E. also may have been related to the higher degree of urbanization and class stratification in this society. In contrast, Egyptian pictorial documents, love poems, and legal records indicate respect and greater equality for women in the valley of the Nile.

Because of the lack of readable texts, we can say very little about the political institutions, social organization, and religious beliefs of the Indus Valley people. However, they clearly possessed technologies on a par with those found in Mesopotamia and Egypt—a writing system, irrigation, bronze-casting, and techniques for producing monumental architecture. The striking uniformity in the planning and construction of cities and towns and in the shapes and styles of artifacts argues for easy communication and some kind of interdependence among the far-flung Indus Valley settlements, as does the relatively rapid collapse of this civilization as a result of ecological changes.

IMPORTANT EVENTS 3500 B.C.E. TO 1500 B.C.E.

3100–2575 B.C.E.	Early Dynastic
3000–2350 B.C.E.	Early Dynastic (Sumerian)
2600 B.C.E.	Beginning of Indus Valley civilization
2575–2134 B.C.E.	Old Kingdom
2350–2230 B.C.E.	Akkadian (Semitic)
2134–2040 B.C.E.	First Intermediate Period
2112–2004 B.C.E.	Third Dynasty of Ur (Sumerian)
2040–1640 B.C.E.	Middle Kingdom
1900 B.C.E.	End of Indus Valley civilization
1900–1600 B.C.E.	Old Babylonian (Semitic)
1640–1532 B.C.E.	Second Intermediate Period
1532–1070 B.C.E.	New Kingdom
1500–1150 B.C.E.	Kassite

3

THE MEDITERRANEAN AND MIDDLE EAST, 2000–500 B.C.E.

Ancient peoples' stories—even when not historically accurate—provide valuable insights into how they thought about their origins and identity. One famous story concerned the founding of the city of Carthage (KAHR-thuhj) in present-day Tunisia, which for centuries dominated the waters and water-borne commerce of the western Mediterranean. Tradition held that Dido and her supporters fled the Phoenician city-state of Tyre (tire) in southern Lebanon after her husband was murdered by her brother, the king. Landing on the North African coast, they made contact with local people, who offered them as much land as a cow's hide could cover. Cleverly cutting the hide into narrow strips, they marked out a substantial territory for Kart Khadasht, the "New City" (called *Carthago* by their Roman enemies).

This story highlights the spread of cultural patterns from older centers to new regions, as well as the migration of Late Bronze Age and Early Iron Age peoples in the Mediterranean lands and western Asia. Trade, diplomatic contacts, military conquests, and the relocation of large numbers of people spread knowledge, beliefs, practices, and technologies.

By the early first millennium B.C.E. many societies of the Eastern Hemisphere were entering the **Iron Age**, using iron in addition to bronze for tools and weapons. Iron offered several advantages. It was a single metal rather than an alloy, and there were many sources of iron ore. Once the technology had been mastered—iron has to be heated to a higher temperature than bronze, and its hardness depends on the amount of carbon added during the forging process—iron tools were found to have harder, sharper edges than bronze tools.

The first part of this chapter resumes the story of Mesopotamia and Egypt in the second millennium B.C.E.: their relations with neighboring peoples, the development of a prosperous, "cosmopolitan" network of states in the Middle East, and the period of destruction and decline that set in around 1200 B.C.E. We also look at how the Minoan and Mycenaean civilizations of the Aegean Sea were inspired by the technologies and cultural patterns of the older Middle Eastern centers and prospered from participation in long-distance trade networks. The remainder of the chapter examines the resurgence of this region in the Early Iron Age, from

1000 to 500 B.C.E. The focus is on three societies: the Assyrians of northern Mesopotamia; the Israelites of Israel; and the Phoenicians of Lebanon and their colonies in the western Mediterranean, mainly Carthage. After the decline of the ancient centers dominant throughout the third and second millennia B.C.E., these societies evolved into new political, cultural, and commercial centers.

THE COSMOPOLITAN MIDDLE EAST, 1700–1100 B.C.E.

Both Mesopotamia and Egypt succumbed to outside invaders in the seventeenth century B.C.E. Eventually the outsiders were either ejected or assimilated, and conditions of stability and prosperity were restored. Between 1500 and 1200 B.C.E. a number of large states dominated the Middle East, controlling the smaller states and kinship groups (peoples with simple political structures living in relatively small groups based on perceived descent from common ancestors) as they interacted, competed with, and sometimes fought against one another for control of valuable commodities and trade routes.

The Late Bronze Age in the Middle East was a "cosmopolitan" era of widely shared cultures and lifestyles. Diplomatic relations and commercial contacts between states fostered the flow of goods and ideas, and elite groups shared similar values and enjoyed a relatively high standard of living. The peasants in the countryside, who constituted the majority of the population, saw some improvement in their standard of living but reaped fewer benefits from the increasing contacts and trade.

Western Asia   By 1500 B.C.E. Mesopotamia was divided into two distinct political zones: Babylonia in the south and Assyria in the north. The city of Babylon had gained political and cultural ascendancy over the southern plain under the dynasty of Hammurabi in the eighteenth and seventeenth centuries B.C.E. (see Chapter 2). Subsequently Kassites (KAS-ite) from the Zagros (ZAH-groes) Mountains to the east migrated into southern Mesopotamia, and by 1460 B.C.E. a Kassite dynasty ruled in Babylon. The Kassites retained names in their native language but otherwise embraced Babylonian language and culture and intermarried with the native population. During their 250 years in power, the Kassite rulers of Babylonia defended their core area and traded for raw materials, but they did not pursue territorial conquest.

The Assyrian kingdom in northern Mesopotamia was more ambitious. As early as the twentieth century B.C.E. (the "Old Assyrian" period), the city of Ashur (AH-shoor) on the northern Tigris anchored a busy trade route stretching across the northern plain to the Anatolian Plateau. Assyrian merchant families settled outside the walls of Anatolian cities and exchanged textiles and tin (a component of bronze) for Anatolian silver. After 1400 B.C.E. a resurgent "Middle Assyrian" kingdom engaged in campaigns of conquest and expansion of its economic interests.

Other dynamic states emerged on the periphery of the Mesopotamian heartland, including Elam in southwest Iran and Mitanni (mih-TAH-nee) in the broad plain between the upper Euphrates and Tigris Rivers. Most formidable of all were the **Hittites** (HIT-ite), who became the foremost power in Anatolia from around 1700 to 1200 B.C.E. From their capital at Hattusha (haht-tush-SHAH), near present-day Ankara (ANG-kuh-ruh) in central Turkey, they deployed the fearsome new technology of horse-drawn war chariots. The Hittites exploited Anatolia's rich metal deposits to play a key role in international commerce.

© Cengage Learning

MAP 3.1 The Middle East in the Second Millennium B.C.E.

Although warfare was not uncommon, treaties, diplomatic missions, and correspondence in Akkadian cuneiform fostered cooperative relationships between states. All were tied together by extensive networks of exchange centering on the trade in metals, and peripheral regions, such as Nubia and the Aegean Sea, were drawn into the web of commerce.

The Hittites also first developed a technique for making tools and weapons of iron. Heating the ore until it was soft enough to shape, they pounded it to remove impurities and then plunged it into cold water to harden. They kept knowledge of this process secret because it provided military and economic advantages. In the disrupted period after 1200 B.C.E., blacksmiths from the Hittite core area may have migrated and spread iron technology.

During the second millennium B.C.E. Mesopotamian political and cultural concepts spread across western Asia. Akkadian (uh-KAY-dee-uhn) became the language of diplomacy and correspondence between governments. The Elamites (EE-luh-mite) and Hittites, among others, adapted the cuneiform system to write their own languages. In the Syrian coastal city-state of Ugarit (OO-guh-reet), thirty cuneiform symbols were used to write consonant sounds, an early use of the alphabetic principle and a considerable advance over the hundreds of signs required in conventional cuneiform and hieroglyphic writing. Mesopotamian myths, legends, and styles of art and architecture were widely imitated. Newcomers who had learned and improved on the lessons of Mesopotamian civilization often put pressure on the old core area. The small, fractious city-states of the third millennium B.C.E. had been concerned only with their immediate neighbors in southern Mesopotamia. In contrast, the larger states of the second millennium B.C.E. interacted politically, militarily, and economically in a geopolitical sphere encompassing all of western Asia.

New Kingdom Egypt   After flourishing for nearly four hundred years (see Chapter 2), the Egyptian Middle Kingdom declined in the seventeenth century B.C.E. As officials in the countryside became increasingly independent and new groups migrated into the Nile Delta, central authority broke down and Egypt entered a period of political fragmentation and economic decline. Around 1640 B.C.E. northern Egypt came under foreign rule for the first time, at the hands of the Hyksos (HICK-soes), or "Princes of Foreign Lands."

Historians are uncertain who the Hyksos were and how they came to power. Semitic peoples had been migrating from the Syria-Palestine region (present-day Syria, Jordan, Lebanon, Israel, and the Palestinian territories) into the eastern Nile Delta for centuries. In the chaotic conditions of this time, various groups may have cooperated to establish control, first in the delta and then in the middle of the country. The Hyksos possessed advantageous military technologies, such as the horse-drawn war chariot and a composite bow, made of wood and horn that had greater range and velocity than the simple wooden bow. They intermarried with Egyptians, used the Egyptian language, and maintained Egyptian institutions and culture. Nevertheless, in contrast to the easy assimilation of outsiders such as the Kassites in Mesopotamia, the Egyptians, with their strong ethnic identity, continued to regard the Hyksos as "foreigners."

As with the formation of the Middle Kingdom five hundred years earlier, the reunification of Egypt under a native dynasty was accomplished by princes from Thebes. After three decades of warfare, Kamose (KAH-mose) and Ahmose (AH-mose) expelled the Hyksos from Egypt and inaugurated the New Kingdom, which lasted from about 1532 to 1070 B.C.E.

A century of foreign domination had injured Egyptian pride and shattered the isolationist mindset of earlier eras. New Kingdom Egypt was an aggressive and expansionist state. By extending its territorial control north into Syria-Palestine and south into Nubia, Egypt won access to timber, gold, and copper (bronze metallurgy took hold in Egypt around 1500 B.C.E.), as well as taxes and tribute payments from the conquered peoples. The occupied territories provided a buffer zone, protecting Egypt from attack. In Nubia, Egypt imposed direct control and pressed the native population to adopt Egyptian language and culture. In the Syria-Palestine region, in contrast, the Egyptians stationed garrisons at strategically placed forts and supported cooperative local rulers.

In this period of innovation, Egypt fully participated in the diplomatic and commercial networks linking the states of western Asia. Egyptian soldiers, administrators, diplomats, and merchants traveled widely, bringing back new fruits and vegetables, new musical instruments, and new technologies, such as an improved potter's wheel and weaver's loom.

One woman held the throne of New Kingdom Egypt. When her husband died, Queen **Hatshepsut** (hat-SHEP-soot) claimed the royal title for herself (r. 1473–1458 B.C.E.). In inscriptions she often used the male pronoun for herself, and drawings and sculptures show her wearing the long, conical beard of the Egyptian ruler.

Around 1470 B.C.E. Hatshepsut sent a naval expedition down the Red Sea to the fabled land of Punt (poont), probably near the coast of eastern Sudan or Eritrea. Hatshepsut was seeking the source of myrrh (murr), a reddish-brown resin from the hardened sap of a local tree, which the Egyptians burned on the altars of their gods and used in medicines and cosmetics. When the expedition returned with myrrh and sub-Saharan luxury goods—ebony, ivory, cosmetics, live monkeys, panther skins—Hatshepsut celebrated the achievement in a great public display and in words and pictures on the walls of her mortuary temple at Deir el-Bahri (DARE uhl–BAH-ree). She may have used the success of this expedition to bolster her claim to the throne. After her death, her image was defaced and her name blotted out wherever it appeared, presumably by officials opposed to a woman ruler.

A century later another untraditional ruler ascended the throne as Amenhotep (ah-muhn-HOE-tep) IV, but he soon began to refer to himself as **Akhenaten** (ah-ken-AHT-n) (r. 1353–1335 B.C.E.), meaning "beneficial to the Aten" (AHT-n) (the disk of the sun). Changing his name was one way to spread his belief in Aten as the supreme deity. He closed the temples of other gods, challenging the age-old supremacy of the chief god Amon (AH-muhn) and the power and influence of his priests. Some scholars have credited Akhenaten with the invention of monotheism— the belief in one exclusive god. It is likely, however, that Akhenaten was attempting to reassert the superiority of the king over the priests and to renew belief in the king's divinity. Worship of Aten was confined to the royal family: the people of Egypt were pressed to revere the divine ruler.

Akhenaten built a new capital at modern-day Amarna (uh-MAHR-nuh), halfway between Memphis and Thebes. He transplanted thousands of Egyptians to construct the site and serve the ruling elite. Akhenaten and his artists created a new style that broke with the conventions of earlier art: the king, his wife Nefertiti (nef-uhr-TEE-tee), and their daughters were depicted in fluid, natural poses with strangely elongated heads and limbs and swelling abdomens.

Akhenaten's reforms were strongly resented by government officials and priests whose privileges and wealth were linked to the traditional system. After his death the temples were reopened; Amon was reinstated as chief god; the capital was returned to Thebes; and the institution of kingship was weakened to the advantage of the priests. The boy-king Tutankhamun (tuht-uhnk-AH-muhn) (r. 1333–1323 B.C.E.),

The Mortuary Temple of Queen Hatshepsut at Deir el-Bahri, Egypt, ca. 1460 B.C.E. *This beautiful complex of terraces, ramps, and colonnades featured relief sculptures and texts commemorating the famous expedition to Punt. Hatshepsut, facing resistance from traditionalists opposed to a woman ruling Egypt, sought to prove her worth by publicizing the opening of direct contact with the source of highly prized myrrh.*

famous solely because his was the only royal tomb found by archaeologists that had not been pillaged by robbers, reveals both in his name (meaning "beautiful in life is Amon") and in his insignificant reign the ultimate failure of Akhenaten's revolution.

The rulers of a new dynasty, the Ramessides (RAM-ih-side), returned to the policy of conquest and expansion that Akhenaten had neglected. The greatest of these monarchs, **Ramesses II** (RAM-ih-seez), ruled for sixty-six years (r. 1290–1224 B.C.E.) and dominated his age. Ramesses undertook monumental building projects all over Egypt. Living into his nineties, he had many wives and may have fathered more than a hundred children. Since 1990 archaeologists have been excavating a network of corridors and chambers carved deep into a hillside near Thebes, where many sons of Ramesses were buried.

Commerce and Communication   Early in his reign Ramesses II fought the Hittites to a draw in a major battle at Kadesh in northern Syria (1285 B.C.E.). Subsequently, diplomats negotiated a treaty, which was strengthened by Ramesses's marriage to a Hittite princess. At issue was control of Syria-Palestine, strategically located between the great powers of the Middle East and at the end of the east-west trade route across Asia. Inland cities—such as Mari (MAH-ree) on the upper Euphrates and Alalakh (UH-luh-luhk) in western Syria—received overland caravans. Coastal towns—particularly Ugarit and the Phoenician towns of the Lebanese seaboard—extended commerce to the lands ringing the Mediterranean Sea.

Ramesses II in a War Chariot Attacks Nubian Enemies *This is a restoration of a 13th-century B.C.E. painting on the wall of a temple at Beit el Wali. Other paintings depict the pharaoh attacking Asiatic enemies and making offerings to the high god Amon.*

Any state seeking to project its power needed metals for tools, weapons, and ornamentation, and commerce in metals energized the long-distance trade of the time. Assyrians were interested in silver from Anatolia (discussed previously), and the Egyptians had a passion for Nubian gold (see Chapter 4). Copper came from Anatolia and Cyprus, tin from Afghanistan and possibly the British Isles. Both ores had to be carried long distances and pass through a number of hands before reaching their final destinations.

New modes of transportation expedited communications and commerce across great distances and inhospitable landscapes. Horses, domesticated by nomadic peoples in Central Asia, were brought into Mesopotamia through the Zagros Mountains around 2000 B.C.E. and reached Egypt before 1600 B.C.E. The speed of travel and communication made possible by horses contributed to the creation of large states and empires, enabling soldiers and government agents to cover great distances quickly. Swift, maneuverable horse-drawn chariots became the premier instrument of war. The team of driver and archer could run up and unleash a volley of arrows or trample terrified foot-soldiers.

Sometime after 1500 B.C.E. in western Asia, but not for another thousand years in Egypt, people began to make common use of camels, though the animal may have been domesticated a millennium earlier in southern Arabia. Thanks to their strength and ability to go long distances without water, camels were able to travel across barren terrain. Their physical qualities eventually led to the emergence of a new kind of desert nomad and the creation of cross-desert trade routes (see Chapter 9).

THE AEGEAN WORLD, 2000–1100 B.C.E.

The influence of Mesopotamia, Syria-Palestine, and Egypt was felt as far away as the Aegean Sea, a gulf of the eastern Mediterranean. The emergence of the Minoan (mih-NO-uhn) civilization on the island of Crete and the Mycenaean (my-suh-NEE-uhn) civilization of Greece is another manifestation of the fertilizing influence of older centers on outlying lands and peoples, who then struck out on their own unique paths of cultural evolution. With few deposits of metals and little timber, Aegean peoples had to import these commodities, as well as additional food supplies, from abroad. As a result, the rise, success, and eventual fall of the Minoan and Mycenaean societies were closely tied to their commercial and political relations with other peoples in the region.

Minoan Crete   By 2000 B.C.E. the island of Crete was home to the first European civilization to have complex political and social structures and advanced technologies like those found in western Asia and northeastern Africa. Archaeologists named this civilization **Minoan** after King Minos, who, in Greek legend, ruled a naval empire in the Aegean and kept the monstrous Minotaur (MIN-uh-tor) (half-man, half-bull) in a mazelike labyrinth built by the ingenious inventor Daedalus (DED-ih-luhs). Thus later Greeks recollected a time when Crete had been home to many ships and skilled craftsmen.

The ethnicity of the Minoans is uncertain, and their writing has not been deciphered. But the distribution of Cretan pottery and other artifacts around the Mediterranean and Middle East testifies to widespread trading connections. Egyptian, Syrian, and Mesopotamian influences can be seen in the design of the Minoan palaces, centralized government, and system of writing. The absence of identifiable representations of Cretan rulers, however, contrasts sharply with the grandiose depictions of kings in the Middle East and suggests a different conception of authority. Also noteworthy is the absence of fortifications at the palace sites and the presence of high-quality indoor plumbing.

Statuettes of women with elaborate headdresses and serpents coiling around their limbs may represent fertility goddesses. Colorful frescoes (paintings done on the moist plaster surfaces of walls) in the palaces portray groups of women in frilly skirts conversing or watching performances. We do not know whether pictures of young acrobats vaulting over the horns and back of an onrushing bull show a religious activity or mere sport. The stylized depictions of scenes from nature on vases—plants with swaying leaves and playful octopuses winding their tentacles around the surface of the vase—communicate a delight in the beauty and order of the natural world.

All the Cretan palaces except at Cnossus (NOSS-suhs), along with the houses of the elite and peasants in the countryside, were deliberately destroyed around 1450 B.C.E. Because Mycenaean Greeks took over at Cnossus, most historians regard them as the culprits.

Mycenaean Greece   Speakers of an Indo-European language ancestral to Greek migrated into the Greek peninsula around 2000 B.C.E. Through intermarriage, blending of languages, and melding of cultural practices, the indigenous population and the newcomers created the first Greek culture. For centuries this society remained simple and static. Farmers and shepherds lived in Stone Age conditions, wringing a bare living from the land. Then, sometime around 1600 B.C.E., life changed relatively suddenly.

In 1876 a German businessman, Heinrich Schliemann (SHLEE-muhn), discovered a circle of graves at **Mycenae** (my-SEE-nee), in southern Greece. These deep, rectangular **shaft graves** contained the bodies of men, women, and children and were filled with gold jewelry and ornaments, weapons, and utensils. Clearly, some people in this society had acquired wealth, authority, and the capacity to mobilize human labor. Subsequent excavation uncovered a large palace complex, massive walls, more shaft graves, and other evidence of a rich and technologically advanced civilization that lasted from around 1600 to 1150 B.C.E.

How can the sudden rise of Mycenae and other centers in mainland Greece be explained? These early Greeks were clearly influenced by the Minoan palaces, centralized economy, and administrative bureaucracy, as well as the writing system. They adopted Minoan styles of architecture, pottery, and fresco and vase painting. The sudden accumulation of power and wealth may have resulted from the profits from trade and piracy and perhaps also from pay and booty brought back by mercenaries (soldiers who served for pay in foreign lands).

This first advanced civilization in Greece is called "Mycenaean" because Mycenae was the first site excavated. Other excavated centers reveal similar features: a hilltop location and high, thick fortification walls made of stones so large that later Greeks believed the giant, one-eyed Cyclopes (SIGH-kloe-pees) of legend had lifted them into place. The fortified citadel provided refuge for the entire community in time of danger and contained the palace and administrative complex. A large central hall with an open hearth and columned porch was surrounded by courtyards, living quarters for the royal family and their retainers, offices, storerooms, and workshops. Palace walls were covered with brightly painted frescoes depicting scenes of war, the hunt, and daily life, as well as decorative motifs from nature.

Nearby lay the tombs of the rulers and leading families: shaft graves at first; later, grand beehive-shaped structures made of stone and covered with a mound of earth. Large houses belonging to the aristocracy lay just outside the walls. The peasants lived on the lower slopes and in the plain below, close to the land they worked.

Additional information is provided by over four thousand baked clay tablets written in a script called **Linear B**, which uses pictorial signs to represent syllables and is an early form of Greek. Palace administrators kept track of people, animals, and objects in exhaustive detail, listing the number of chariot wheels in storerooms, the rations paid to workers, and the gifts dedicated to various gods. The government exercised a high degree of control over the economy, organizing grain production and the wool industry from raw material to finished product. The tablets reveal little, however, about the political and legal system, social structure, gender relations, and religious beliefs. They tell nothing about historical figures (not even the name of a single Mycenaean king), particular historical events, or relations with other Mycenaean centers or foreign peoples.

Long-distance contact and trade were made possible by the seafaring skill of Minoans and Mycenaeans. Commercial vessels depended primarily on wind and sail. In general, ancient sailors preferred to sail in daylight hours and keep the land in sight. Their light, wooden vessels with low keels could run up onto the beach, allowing the crew to go ashore to eat and sleep at night.

Cretan and Greek pottery and crafted goods are found not only in the Aegean but also in other parts of the Mediterranean and Middle East. The oldest artifacts are Minoan; then Minoan and Mycenaean objects are found side by side; and eventually Greek wares replace Cretan goods altogether. Such evidence indicates that Cretan merchants pioneered trade routes and established trading posts and were later joined by Mycenaean traders, who supplanted them in the fifteenth century B.C.E.

The numerous Aegean pots found throughout the Mediterranean and Middle East once contained such products as wine and olive oil. Other possible exports include textiles, weapons, and other crafted goods, as well as slaves and mercenary soldiers. Aegean sailors also may have transported the trade goods of other peoples.

As for imports, amber (a translucent, yellowish-brown fossilized tree resin used for jewelry) from northern Europe and ivory carved in Syria have been discovered at Aegean sites, and the large population of southern Greece may have relied on imports of grain. Above all, the Aegean lands needed metals, both gold and the copper and tin needed to make bronze. Several sunken ships carrying copper ingots have been found on the floor of the Mediterranean. Only the elite classes owned metal goods, which may have been symbols of their superior status.

Mycenaeans were tough, warlike, and acquisitive, trading with those who were strong and taking from those who were weak. In the fourteenth and thirteenth centuries B.C.E. these qualities led them into conflict with the Hittite kings of Anatolia. Documents in the archives at the Hittite capital refer to the king and land of Ahhijawa (uh-key-YAW-wuh), most likely a Hittite rendering of *Achaeans* (uh-KEY-uhns), a term used by Homer for the Greeks. They indicate that relations were sometimes friendly, sometimes strained, and that the people of Ahhijawa took advantage of Hittite preoccupation or weakness. The *Iliad*, Homer's tale of the Achaeans' ten-year siege and eventual destruction of Troy, a city on the fringes of Hittite territory controlling the sea route between the Mediterranean and Black Seas, should be seen against this backdrop of Mycenaean belligerence and opportunism. Archaeology has confirmed a destruction at Troy around 1200 B.C.E.

The Fall of Late Bronze Age Civilizations Hittite difficulties with Ahhijawa and the attack on Troy foreshadowed the troubles that culminated in the destruction of many of the old centers of the Middle East and Mediterranean around 1200 B.C.E. In this period, for reasons not well understood, large numbers of people were on the move. As migrants swarmed into one region, they displaced other peoples, who then joined the tide of refugees.

Around 1200 B.C.E. unidentified invaders destroyed the Hittite capital, Hattusha, and the Hittite kingdom in Anatolia came crashing down. The tide of destruction moved south into Syria, and the great coastal city of Ugarit was swept away. Egypt managed to beat back two attacks: an assault on the Nile Delta around 1220 B.C.E. by "Libyans and Northerners coming from all lands," and a major invasion by the "Sea Peoples" about thirty years later. Although the Egyptian ruler claimed a great victory, the Philistines (FIH-luh-steen) occupied the coast of Palestine (this is the origin of the name subsequently used for this region). Egypt soon surrendered all its territory in Syria-Palestine and lost contact with the rest of western Asia. The Egyptians also lost their foothold in Nubia, opening the way for the emergence of the native kingdom centered on Napata (see Chapter 4).

Among the invaders listed in the Egyptian inscriptions are the Ekwesh (ECK-wesh), who could be Achaeans—that is, Greeks. In these troubled times it is easy to imagine the participation of opportunistic Mycenaeans. The Mycenaean centers also saw trouble coming; at some sites they began to build more extensive fortifications and took steps to guarantee the water supply of the citadels. But their efforts were in vain, and nearly all the palaces were destroyed in the first half of the twelfth century B.C.E.

How these events came about is unclear. The archaeological record contains no trace of foreign invaders. An attractive explanation combines external and internal factors, since it is likely to be more than coincidence that the demise of Mycenaean civilization occurred at roughly the same time as the fall of other great civilizations in the region. Since the Mycenaean ruling class depended on the import of vital commodities and the profits from trade, the destruction of major trading partners and disruption of trade routes would have weakened their position. Competition for limited resources may have led to internal unrest and, ultimately, political collapse.

The end of Mycenaean civilization illustrates the interdependence of the major centers of the Late Bronze Age. It also highlights the consequences of political and economic collapse. The destruction of the palaces ended the domination of the ruling class. The massive administrative apparatus revealed in the Linear B tablets disappeared. The technique of writing was forgotten, since it had been known only to a few palace officials and was no longer useful. Archaeological studies indicate the depopulation of some regions of Greece and an inflow of people to other regions that had escaped destruction. The Greek language persisted, and a thousand years later people were still worshiping gods mentioned in the Linear B tablets. People also continued to make the vessels and implements that they were familiar with, although with a marked decline in artistic and technical skill in a much poorer society. The cultural uniformity of the Mycenaean Age gave way to regional variations in shapes, styles, and techniques, reflecting increased isolation of different parts of Greece.

Thus perished the cosmopolitan world of the Late Bronze Age in the Mediterranean and Middle East. Societies that had long prospered through complex links of trade, diplomacy, and shared technologies now collapsed in the face of external violence and internal weakness, and the peoples of the region entered a centuries-long "Dark Age" of poverty, isolation, and loss of knowledge.

THE ASSYRIAN EMPIRE, 911–612 B.C.E.

A number of new centers emerged in western Asia and the eastern Mediterranean in the centuries after 1000 B.C.E. The most powerful and successful was the **Neo-Assyrian Empire** (911–612 B.C.E.). Compared to the flat expanse of Babylonia to the south, the Assyrian homeland in northern Mesopotamia is hillier and has a more temperate climate and greater rainfall.

Peasant farmers, accustomed to defending themselves against raiders from the mountains to the east and north and the arid plain to the west, provided the foot-soldiers for the revival of Assyrian power. The rulers of the Neo-Assyrian Empire led a ceaseless series of campaigns: westward across the plain and desert as far as the Mediterranean, north into mountainous Urartu (ur-RAHR-too) (modern Armenia), east across the Zagros range onto the Iranian Plateau, and south along the Tigris River to Babylonia. These campaigns provided immediate booty and the long-term prospect of tribute and taxes. They also secured access to vital resources such as iron and silver and gave the Assyrians control of international commerce. Driven by pride, greed, and religious conviction, the Assyrians defeated the other great kingdoms of the day. At its peak their empire stretched from Anatolia, Syria-Palestine, and Egypt in the west, across Armenia and Mesopotamia, and as far as western Iran. The Assyrians created a new kind of empire, larger in extent than anything seen before and dedicated to the enrichment of the imperial center at the expense of the subjugated periphery.

God and King   The king was literally and symbolically the center of the Assyrian universe. All the land belonged to him, and all the people, even the highest-ranking officials, were his servants. Assyrians believed that the gods chose the king as their earthly representative. Normally the king selected one of his sons to succeed him, then had the choice confirmed by divine oracles and the Assyrian elite. In the revered ancient city of Ashur the high priest anointed the new king's head with oil and gave him the insignia of kingship: a crown and scepter. The kings also were buried in Ashur.

Messengers and spies brought the king information from every corner of the empire. The king appointed officials, heard complaints, dictated correspondence to an army of scribes, and received foreign envoys. He was the military leader, responsible for planning campaigns, and was often away from the capital commanding operations in the field.

The king also devoted much of his time to supervising the state religion, attending elaborate public and private rituals, and overseeing the upkeep of the temples. He made no decisions of state without consulting the gods through rituals of divination, and all actions were carried out in the name of Ashur, the chief god. Military victories were cited as proof of Ashur's superiority over the gods of the conquered peoples.

Relentless government propaganda secured popular support for military campaigns that mostly benefited the king and the nobility. Royal inscriptions posted throughout the empire catalogued recent victories, extolled the unshakeable determination of the king, and promised ruthless punishments to anyone who resisted. Relief sculptures depicting hunts, battles, sieges, executions, and deportations covered the walls of the royal palaces. Looming over most scenes was the king, larger than anyone else, muscular and fierce. Few visitors to the Assyrian court could fail to be awed and intimidated.

Conquest and Control   Superior military organization and technology lay behind Assyria's unprecedented conquests. Early armies consisted of men who served in return for grants of land and peasants and slaves contributed by large landowners. Later, King Tiglathpileser (TIG-lath-pih-LEE-zuhr) (r. 744–727 B.C.E.) created a core army of professional soldiers made up of Assyrians and the most formidable subject peoples. At its peak the Assyrian state could mobilize a half-million troops, including light-armed bowmen and slingers who launched stone projectiles, armored spearmen, cavalry equipped with bows or spears, and four-man chariots.

MAP 3.2 The Assyrian Empire

From the tenth to the seventh century B.C.E., the Assyrians of northern Mesopotamia created the largest empire the world had yet seen, extending from the Iranian Plateau to the eastern shore of the Mediterranean and containing a diverse array of peoples.

Iron weapons gave Assyrian soldiers an advantage over many opponents, and cavalry provided speed and mobility. Assyrian engineers developed machinery and tactics for besieging fortified towns. They dug tunnels under the walls, built mobile towers for archers, and applied battering rams to weak points. Couriers and signal fires provided long-distance communication, while a network of spies gathered intelligence.

The Assyrians used terror tactics to discourage resistance and rebellion, inflicting harsh punishments and publicizing their brutality: civilians were thrown into fires, prisoners were skinned alive, and the severed heads of defeated rulers hung on city walls. **Mass deportation**—the forced uprooting of entire communities and resettlement elsewhere—broke the spirit of rebellious peoples. Although this tactic had a long history in the ancient Middle East, the Neo-Assyrian monarchs used it on an unprecedented scale, and up to 4 million people may have been relocated. Deportation also shifted human resources from the periphery to the center, where the deportees worked on royal and noble estates, opened new lands for agriculture, and built palaces and cities.

The Assyrians never discovered an effective method of governing an empire of such vast distances, varied landscapes, and diverse peoples. Control tended to be tight at the center and in lands closest to the core area, and less so farther away.

The Assyrian kings waged many campaigns to reinstate control over territories subdued in previous wars. Provincial officials oversaw the collection of tribute and taxes, maintained law and order, raised troops, undertook public works, and provisioned armies and administrators passing through their territory. Provincial governors were subject to frequent inspections by royal overseers.

The Assyrians ruthlessly exploited the wealth and resources of their subjects. Military campaigns and administration were funded by plunder and tribute. Wealth from the periphery was funneled to the center, where the king and nobility grew rich. Triumphant kings expanded the ancestral capital and religious center at Ashur and built magnificent new royal cities encircled by high walls and containing ornate palaces and temples. Dur Sharrukin (DOOR SHAH-roo-keen), the "Fortress of Sargon," was completed in a mere ten years by a massive labor force composed of prisoners of war and Assyrian citizens who owed periodic service to the state.

Nevertheless, the Assyrian Empire was not simply parasitic. There is some evidence of royal investment in provincial infrastructure. The cities and merchant classes thrived on expanded long-distance commerce, and some subject populations were surprisingly loyal to their Assyrian rulers.

Assyrian Society and Culture

The Assyrian elite class was bound to the monarch by oaths of obedience, fear of punishment, and the expectation of rewards, such as land grants or shares of booty and taxes. Skilled professionals—priests, diviners, scribes, doctors, and artisans—were similarly bound.

Surviving sources primarily shed light on the deeds of kings and elites, and only a little is known about the lives and activities of the millions of Assyrian subjects. The government did not distinguish between native Assyrians and the increasingly large number of immigrants and deportees in the Assyrian homeland. All were referred to as "human beings," entitled to the same legal protections and liable for the same labor and military service. Over time the inflow of outsiders changed the ethnic makeup of the core area.

The vast majority of subjects worked on the land. The agricultural surpluses they produced allowed substantial numbers of people—the standing army, government officials, religious experts, merchants, artisans, and other professionals in the towns and cities—to engage in specialized activities.

Individual artisans and small workshops in the towns manufactured pottery, tools, and clothing, and most trade took place at the local level. The state fostered long-distance trade, since imported luxury goods—metals, fine textiles, dyes, gems, and ivory—brought in substantial customs revenues and found their way to the royal family and elite classes. Silver was the basic medium of exchange, weighed out for each transaction in a time before the invention of coins.

Assyrian scholars preserved and built on the achievements of their Mesopotamian predecessors. When archaeologists excavated the palace of Ashurbanipal (ah-shur-BAH-nee-pahl) (r. 668–627 B.C.E.), one of the last Assyrian kings, at Nineveh (NIN-uh-vuh), they discovered more than twenty-five thousand tablets or fragments. The **Library of Ashurbanipal** contained official documents as well as literary and scientific texts. Some were originals that had been brought to the capital; others were copies made at the king's request. The "House of Knowledge" referred to in some documents may have been an academy that attracted learned men to the imperial center. Much of what we know about Mesopotamian art, literature, science, and earlier history comes from discoveries at Assyrian sites.

ISRAEL, 2000–500 B.C.E.

The small land of Israel probably appeared insignificant to the Assyrian masters of western Asia, but it would play an important role in world history. Two interconnected dramas played out here between 2000 and 500 B.C.E. First, a loose collection of nomadic groups engaged in herding and caravan traffic became a sedentary, agricultural people, developed complex political and social institutions, and became integrated into the commercial and diplomatic networks of the Middle East. Second, these people transformed the austere cult of a desert god into the concept of a single, all-powerful, and all-knowing deity, in the process creating ethical and intellectual traditions that underlie the beliefs and values of Judaism, Christianity, and Islam.

The land and people at the heart of this story have gone by various names: Canaan, Israel, Palestine; Hebrews, Israelites, Jews. For the sake of consistency, the people are referred to here as *Israelites*, the land they occupied in antiquity as **Israel**.

Israel is a crossroads, linking Anatolia, Egypt, Arabia, and Mesopotamia. Its natural resources are few. The Negev Desert and the vast wasteland of the Sinai (SIE-nie) lie to the south. The Mediterranean coastal plain was usually in the hands of others, particularly the Philistines, throughout much of this period. Galilee to the north, with its sea of the same name, was a relatively fertile land of grassy hills and small plains. The narrow ribbon of the Jordan River runs down the eastern side of the region into the Dead Sea, so named because its high salt content is toxic to life.

Origins, Exodus, and Settlement   Information about ancient Israel comes partly from archaeological excavations and documents such as the royal annals of Egypt and Assyria. Fundamental, but also problematic, are the texts preserved in the **Hebrew Bible** (called the Old Testament by Christians), a compilation of several collections of materials that originated with different groups and advocated particular interpretations of past events. Traditions about the Israelites' early history were long transmitted orally. Not until the tenth century B.C.E. were they written down in a script borrowed from the Phoenicians. The text that we have today dates from the fifth century B.C.E., with a few later additions, and reflects the point of view of the priests who controlled the Temple in Jerusalem. The Hebrew language of the Bible reflects the speech of the Israelites until about 500 B.C.E., when it was supplanted by Aramaic. Although historians disagree about how accurately this document represents Israelite history, it provides a foundation to be used critically and tested against archaeological discoveries.

The history of ancient Israel follows a familiar pattern in the ancient Middle East: nomadic pastoralists, occupying marginal land between the inhospitable desert and settled agricultural areas, sometimes engaged in trade and sometimes raided the farms and villages of settled peoples, but eventually they settled down to an agricultural way of life and later developed a unified state.

The Hebrew Bible tells the story of Abraham and his descendants. Born in the city of Ur in southern Mesopotamia, Abraham rejected the idol worship of his homeland and migrated with his family and livestock across the Syrian Desert. Eventually he arrived in the land of Israel, which had been promised to him and his descendants by the Israelite god, Yahweh.

These "recollections" of the journey of Abraham (who, if he was a real person, probably lived around 1800 B.C.E.) may compress the experiences of generations of pastoralists who migrated from the grazing lands between the upper reaches of the Tigris and Euphrates Rivers to the Mediterranean coastal plain. They camped by a permanent water source in the dry season, then drove herds of sheep, cattle, and donkeys to a well-established sequence of grazing areas during the rest of the year. The animals provided them with milk, cheese, meat, and cloth.

The nomadic Israelites and the settled peoples were suspicious of one another. This friction between herders and farmers permeates the biblical story of the innocent shepherd Abel, who was killed by his farmer brother Cain, and the story of Sodom (SOE-duhm) and Gomorrah (guh-MORE-uh), two cities that Yahweh destroyed because of their wickedness.

In the Hebrew Bible, Abraham's son Isaac and then his grandson Jacob became the leaders of this migratory group of herders. In the next generation the squabbling sons of Jacob's several wives sold their brother Joseph as a slave to passing merchants heading for Egypt. Through luck and ability Joseph became a high official at the pharaoh's court. Thus he was in a position to help his people when drought struck and forced the Israelites to migrate to Egypt. The sophisticated Egyptians looked down on these rough herders and eventually enslaved them and put them to work on royal building projects.

Several points need to be made about this biblical account. First, the Israelite migration to Egypt and later enslavement may have been connected to the rise and fall of the Hyksos. Second, although surviving Egyptian sources do not refer to Israelite slaves, they do complain about Apiru (uh-PEE-roo), a derogatory term applied to caravan drivers, outcasts, bandits, and other marginal groups. Some scholars believe there may be a connection between the similar-sounding terms *Apiru* and *Hebrew*. Third, the period of alleged Israelite slavery coincided with the ambitious building programs launched by several New Kingdom pharaohs. However, there is little archaeological evidence of an Israelite presence in Egypt.

According to the Hebrew Bible, the Israelites were led out of captivity by Moses, an Israelite with connections to the Egyptian royal family. The narrative of their departure, the Exodus, is overlaid with folktale motifs, including the ten plagues that Yahweh inflicted on Egypt to persuade the pharaoh to release the Israelites, and the miraculous parting of the waters of the Red Sea that enabled the refugees to escape. Oral tradition may have embellished memories of a real emigration from Egypt followed by years of wandering in the wilderness of Sinai.

During their forty years in the desert, as reported in the Hebrew Bible, the Israelites entered into a "covenant" or pact with their god, Yahweh: they would be his "Chosen People" if they promised to worship him exclusively. This covenant was confirmed by tablets that Moses brought down from the top of Mount Sinai, inscribed with the Ten Commandments that set out the basic tenets of Jewish belief and practice. The Commandments prohibited murder, adultery, theft, lying, and envy and demanded respect for parents and rest from work on the Sabbath, the seventh day of the week.

The biblical account proceeds to tell how Joshua, Moses's successor, led the Israelites from the east side of the Jordan River into the land of Canaan (KAY-nuhn) (modern Israel and the Palestinian territories), where they attacked and destroyed Canaanite (KAY-nuh-nite) cities. Archaeological evidence confirms the destruction of some Canaanite towns between 1250 and 1200 B.C.E., though not precisely the towns mentioned in the biblical account. Shortly thereafter, lowland sites were resettled and new sites were established in the hills. The material culture of the new settlers was cruder but continued Canaanite patterns. Most scholars doubt that Canaan was conquered by a unified Israelite army. In a time of widespread disruption, movements of peoples, and decline and destruction of cities throughout this region, it is more likely that Israelite migrants took advantage of the disorder and were joined by other groups and even refugees from the Canaanite cities.

The new coalition of peoples invented a common ancestry. The "Children of Israel," as they called themselves, were divided into twelve tribes supposedly descended from the sons of Jacob and Joseph. Each tribe was installed in a different part of the country and led by one or more chiefs. Such leaders usually had limited power and were primarily responsible for mediating disputes and seeing to the welfare and protection of the group. Certain charismatic figures, famed for their daring in war or genius in arbitration, were called "Judges" and enjoyed a special standing that transcended tribal boundaries. The tribes also shared access to a shrine in the hill country at Shiloh (SHIE-loe), which housed the Ark of the Covenant, a sacred chest containing the tablets that Yahweh had given Moses.

Rise of the Monarchy   The troubles afflicting the eastern Mediterranean around 1200 B.C.E. also brought the Philistines to the coastal plain of Israel, where they came into frequent conflict with the Israelites. Their wars were memorialized in Bible stories about the long-haired strongman Samson, who toppled a Philistine temple, and the shepherd boy David, whose slingshot felled the towering warrior Goliath. A religious leader named Samuel recognized the need for a strong central authority and anointed Saul as the first king of Israel around 1020 B.C.E. When Saul perished in battle, the throne passed to David (r. ca. 1000–960 B.C.E.). Many scholars regard the biblical account for the period of the monarchy as more historically reliable than the earlier parts, although some maintain that the archaeological record still does not match up very well with that narrative and that the wealth and power of the early kings have been greatly exaggerated.

A gifted musician, warrior, and politician, David oversaw Israel's transition from tribal confederacy to unified monarchy. He strengthened royal authority by making the captured hill city of Jerusalem his capital. Soon after, David brought the Ark to Jerusalem, making the city the religious as well as political center of the kingdom. A census was taken to facilitate the collection of taxes, and a standing army, with soldiers paid by and loyal to the king, was established. These innovations enabled David to win military victories and expand Israel's borders.

The reign of David's son Solomon (r. ca. 960–920 B.C.E.) marked the high point of the Israelite monarchy. Alliances and trade linked Israel with near and distant lands. Solomon and Hiram, the king of Phoenician Tyre, dispatched a fleet into the Red Sea to bring back gold, ivory, jewels, sandalwood, and exotic animals. The story of the visit to Solomon by the queen of Sheba may be mythical, but it reflects the reality of trade with Saba (SUH-buh) in south Arabia (present-day Yemen) or the Horn of Africa (present-day Somalia). The wealth gained from military and commercial ventures supported a lavish court life, a sizable bureaucracy, and an intimidating chariot army that made Israel a regional power. Solomon undertook an ambitious building program employing slaves and the compulsory labor of citizens. To strengthen the link between religious and secular authority, he built the **First Temple** in Jerusalem. The Israelites now had a central shrine and an impressive set of rituals that could compete with other religions in the area.

The Temple priests became a powerful and wealthy class, receiving a share of the annual harvest in return for making animal sacrifices to Yahweh on behalf of the community. The expansion of Jerusalem, new commercial opportunities, and the increasing prestige of the Temple hierarchy changed the social composition of Israelite society. A gap between urban and rural, rich and poor, polarized a people that previously had been relatively homogeneous. Fiery prophets, claiming revelation from Yahweh, accused the monarchs and aristocracy of corruption, impiety, and neglect of the poor.

The Israelites lived in extended families, several generations residing together under the authority of the eldest male. Male heirs were of paramount importance, and first-born sons received a double share of the inheritance. If a couple had no son, they could adopt one, or the husband could have a child by the wife's slave attendant. If a man died childless, his brother was expected to marry his widow and sire an heir.

In early Israel, because women provided vital goods and services that sustained the family, they were respected and had some influence with their husbands. Unlike men, however, they could not inherit property or initiate divorce, and a woman caught in extramarital relations could be put to death. Peasant women labored with other family members in agriculture or herding in addition to caring for the house and children. As the society became urbanized, some women worked outside the home as cooks, perfumers, wet nurses, prostitutes, and singers of laments at funerals. A few women reached positions of power, such as Deborah the Judge, who led troops in battle against the Canaanites. "Wise women" composed sacred texts in poetry and prose. This reality has been obscured, in part by the male bias of the Hebrew Bible, in part because the status of women declined as Israelite society became more urbanized.

Fragmentation and Dispersal   After Solomon's death around 920 B.C.E., resentment over royal demands for money and labor and the neglect of tribal prerogatives split the monarchy into two kingdoms: Israel in the north, with its capital at Samaria (suh-MAH-ree-yuh); and Judah (JOO-duh) in the southern territory around Jerusalem. The two were sometimes at war, sometimes allied.

This period saw the final formulation of **monotheism**, the belief in Yahweh as the one and only god. Nevertheless, many Israelites were attracted to the ecstatic rituals of the Canaanite storm-god Baal (BAHL) and the fertility goddess Asherah (uh-SHARE-uh). Prophets condemned the adoption of foreign ritual and threatened that Yahweh would punish Israel severely.

The two Israelite kingdoms and other small states in the region laid aside their rivalries to mount a joint resistance to the Neo-Assyrian Empire, but to no avail. In

721 B.C.E. the Assyrians destroyed the northern kingdom of Israel and deported much of its population to the east. New settlers were brought in from Syria, Babylon, and Iran, changing the area's ethnic, cultural, and religious character. The kingdom of Judah survived more than a century longer, sometimes rebelling, sometimes paying tribute to the Assyrians or the Neo-Babylonian kingdom (626–539 B.C.E.) that succeeded them. When the Neo-Babylonian monarch Nebuchadnezzar (NAB-oo-kuhd-nez-uhr) captured Jerusalem in 587 B.C.E., he destroyed the Temple and deported to Babylon the royal family, the aristocracy, and many skilled workers such as blacksmiths and scribes.

The deportees prospered so well in their new home "by the waters of Babylon" that half a century later most of their descendants refused the offer of the Persian monarch Cyrus (see Chapter 5) to return to their homeland. This was the origin of the **Diaspora** (die-ASS-peh-rah)—a Greek word meaning "dispersion" or "scattering." This dispersion outside the homeland of many Jews—as we may now call these people, since an independent Israel no longer existed—continues to this day. To maintain their religion and culture, the Diaspora communities developed institutions like the synagogue (Greek for "bringing together"), a communal meeting place that served religious, educational, and social functions.

Several groups of Babylonian Jews did make the long trek back to Judah in the later sixth and fifth centuries B.C.E. They rebuilt the Temple in modest form and edited the Hebrew Bible into roughly its present form.

The loss of political autonomy and the experience of exile had sharpened Jewish identity. With an unyielding monotheism as their core belief, Jews lived by a rigid set of rules. Dietary restrictions forbade the eating of pork and shellfish and mandated that meat and dairy products not be consumed together. Ritual baths were used to achieve spiritual purity. The Jews venerated the Sabbath (Saturday, the seventh day of the week) by refraining from work and from fighting, following the example of Yahweh, who, according to the Bible, rested on the seventh day after creating the world (this is the origin of the concept of the week and the weekend). These strictures and others, including a ban on marrying non-Jews, tended to isolate the Jews from other peoples, but they also fostered a powerful sense of community and the belief that the Jews were protected by a watchful and beneficent deity.

PHOENICIA AND THE MEDITERRANEAN, 1200–500 B.C.E.

While the Israelite tribes were forging a united kingdom, the people who occupied the Mediterranean coast to the north were developing their own distinctive civilization. Historians follow the Greeks in calling them **Phoenicians** (fi-NEE-shun), though they referred to themselves as "Can'ani"—Canaanites. Despite few written records and archaeological remains disturbed by frequent migrations and invasions, some of their history can be reconstructed.

The Phoenician City-States   When the eastern Mediterranean was disturbed by violent upheavals and mass migrations around 1200 B.C.E., many Canaanite settlements in the Syria-Palestine region were destroyed. Aramaeans (ah-ruh-MAY-uhn)—nomadic pastoralists similar to the early Israelites—migrated into the interior portions of Syria. Farther south, Israelite herders and farmers settled in the interior of present-day Israel. The Philistines

Phoenician Ivory Panel, Ninth to Eighth Century B.C.E. *This panel, originally covered with gold leaf and inlaid with red carnelian and blue lapis lazuli, depicts a lioness devouring a boy. Produced in Phoenicia, perhaps as tribute for the Assyrian king, it was probably part of a wooden throne. It was found in a well in the palace area of the Assyrian capital Nimrud, where it was discarded when the city was destroyed in the late seventh century* B.C.E.

occupied the southern coast and introduced iron-based metallurgy to this part of the world.

By 1100 B.C.E. Canaanite territory had shrunk to a narrow strip of present-day Lebanon between the mountains and the sea. Rivers and rocky spurs of Mount Lebanon sliced the coastal plain into a series of small city-states, chief among them Byblos (BIB-loss), Berytus (buh-RIE-tuhs), Sidon (SIE-duhn), and Tyre. The inhabitants of this densely populated area adopted new political forms and turned to seaborne commerce and new kinds of manufacture for their survival. A thriving trade in raw materials (cedar and pine, metals, incense, papyrus), foodstuffs (wine, spices, salted fish), and crafted luxury goods (carved ivory, glass, and textiles colored with a highly prized purple dye extracted from the murex snail) brought considerable wealth to the Phoenician city-states and gave them an important role in international politics (see Environment and Technology: Ancient Textiles and Dyes).

The Phoenicians developed earlier Canaanite models into an "alphabetic" system of writing with about two dozen symbols, in which each symbol represented a sound. (The Phoenicians represented only consonants, leaving the vowel sounds to be inferred by the reader. The Greeks later added symbols for vowel sounds, creating the first truly alphabetic system of writing—see Chapter 5.) Little Phoenician writing survives, however, probably because scribes used perishable papyrus.

Before 1000 B.C.E. Byblos was the most important Phoenician city-state. It was a distribution center for cedar timber from the slopes of Mount Lebanon and for papyrus from Egypt. King Hiram, who came to power in 969 B.C.E., was responsible for Tyre's rise to prominence. According to the Hebrew Bible, he formed a close alliance with the Israelite king Solomon and provided skilled Phoenician craftsmen and cedar wood for building the Temple in Jerusalem. In return, Tyre gained access to silver, food, and trade routes to the east and south. In the 800s B.C.E. Tyre took control of nearby Sidon and dominated the Mediterranean coastal trade.

Located on an offshore island, Tyre was practically impregnable. It had two harbors connected by a canal, a large marketplace, a magnificent palace complex with treasury and archives, and temples to the gods Melqart (MEL-kahrt) and Astarte (uh-STAHR-tee). Some of its thirty thousand inhabitants lived in suburbs on the mainland. Its one weakness was its dependence on the mainland for food and fresh water.

Little is known about the internal affairs of Tyre and other Phoenician cities. The names of a series of kings are preserved, and the scant evidence suggests that the political arena was dominated by leading merchant families. Between the ninth and seventh centuries B.C.E. the Phoenician city-states contended with Assyrian aggression, followed in the sixth century B.C.E. by the expansion of the Neo-Babylonian kingdom and later the Persian Empire (see Chapter 5). The Phoenician city-states preserved their autonomy by playing the great powers off against one another when possible and by accepting a subordinate relationship to a distant master when necessary.

Expansion into the Mediterranean   After 900 B.C.E. Tyre turned its attention westward, establishing colonies on Cyprus, a copper-rich island 100 miles (161 kilometers) from the Syrian coast. By 700 B.C.E. a string of settlements in the western Mediterranean formed a "Phoenician triangle" composed of the North African coast from western Libya to Morocco; the south and southeast coast of Spain, including Gades (GAH-days) (modern Cadiz [kuh-DEEZ]) on the Strait of Gibraltar, controlling passage between the Mediterranean and the Atlantic Ocean; and the islands of Sardinia, Sicily, and Malta off the coast of Italy. Many settlements were situated on promontories or offshore islands in imitation of Tyre. The Phoenician trading network spanned the entire Mediterranean.

Frequent and destructive Assyrian invasions of Syria-Palestine and the lack of arable land to feed a swelling population probably motivated Tyrian expansion. Overseas settlement provided an outlet for excess population, new sources of trade goods, and new trading partners. Tyre maintained its autonomy until 701 B.C.E. by paying tribute to the Assyrian kings. In that year it finally fell to an Assyrian army that stripped it of much of its territory and population, allowing Sidon to become the leading city in Phoenicia.

Carthage's Commercial Empire   Historians know far more about **Carthage** and the other Phoenician colonies in the western Mediterranean than they do about the Phoenician homeland. Much of this comes from Greek and Roman reports of their wars with the western Phoenician communities. For example, the account of the origins of Carthage that begins this chapter comes from Roman sources but probably is based on a Carthaginian original. Archaeological excavation has roughly confirmed the city's traditional foundation date of 814 B.C.E. The new settlement grew rapidly and soon dominated other Phoenician colonies in the west.

ENVIRONMENT + TECHNOLOGY

Ancient Textiles and Dyes

Throughout human history the production of textiles—cloth for clothing, blankets, carpets, and coverings of various sorts—required an expenditure of human labor second only to the work necessary to provide food. Nevertheless, textile production in antiquity has left few archaeological traces. The plant fibers and animal hair used for cloth quickly decompose except in rare circumstances. Some textile remains have been found in the hot, dry conditions of Egypt, the cool, arid Andes of South America, and the peat bogs of northern Europe. But most of our knowledge of ancient textiles depends on the discovery of equipment used in textile production—such as spindles, loom weights, and dyeing vats—and on pictorial representations and descriptions in texts.

Cloth production usually has been the work of women for a simple but important reason. Responsibility for child rearing limits women's ability to participate in other activities but does not consume all their time and energy. In many societies textile production has been complementary to child-rearing activities, for it can be done in the home, is relatively safe, does not require great concentration, and

Felt decoration depicting a fenix/Hermitage, St. Petersburg, Russia/De Agostini Picture Library/A. Dagli Orti/ The Bridgeman Art Library

Scythian Felt Cloth from Pazyryk, ca. 500 B.C.E. *Found in a subterranean tomb in Siberia, the textile was preserved by the permafrost. It depicts a winged figure with a human upper body and antlers.*

Located just outside the present-day city of Tunis in Tunisia, on a promontory jutting into the Mediterranean, Carthage stretched between the original hilltop citadel and a double harbor. The inner harbor could accommodate 220 warships. A watchtower allowed surveillance of the surrounding area, and high walls made it impossible to see in from the outside. The outer commercial harbor was filled with docks for merchant ships and shipyards. In case of attack, the harbor could be closed off by a huge iron chain.

Government offices ringed a large central square where magistrates heard legal cases outdoors. The inner city was a maze of narrow, winding streets, multistory apartment buildings, and sacred enclosures. Farther out was a sprawling suburban district where the wealthy built spacious villas amid fields and vegetable gardens. This entire urban complex was enclosed by a wall 22 miles (35 kilometers) in can be interrupted without consequence. The growing and harvesting of plants such as cotton or flax (from which linen is made) and the shearing of wool from sheep and, in the Andes, llamas are outdoor activities, but the subsequent stages of production can be carried out inside the home. The basic methods of textile production did not change much from early antiquity until the late eighteenth century C.E., when the fabrication of textiles was transferred to mills and mass production began.

When textile production has been considered "women's work," most of the output has been for household consumption. However, women weavers in Peru developed new raw materials, new techniques, and new decorative motifs around three thousand years ago. They began to use the wool of llamas and alpacas in addition to cotton. Three women worked side by side and passed the weft from hand to hand in order to produce a fabric of greater width. Women weavers also introduced embroidery and decorated garments with new religious motifs, such as the jaguar-god. Their high-quality textiles were given as tribute to the elite and were used to trade for luxury goods.

More typically, men dominated commercial production. In ancient Phoenicia, fine textiles with bright, permanent colors became a major export product. Most prized was the red-purple known as Tyrian purple because Tyre was the major source. Persian and Hellenistic kings wore robes dyed this color, and a white toga with a purple border was the sign of a Roman senator.

The production of Tyrian purple was an exceedingly laborious process. The spiny dye-murex snail lives on the sandy Mediterranean bottom at depths ranging from 30 to 500 feet (10 to 150 meters). Nine thousand snails were needed to produce 1 gram (0.035 ounce) of dye. The dye was made from a colorless liquid in the snail's hypobranchial gland. The gland sacs were removed, crushed, soaked with salt, and exposed to sunlight and air for some days; then they were subject to controlled boiling and heating.

Huge mounds of broken shells on the Phoenician coast are testimony to the ancient industry. The snail may have been rendered nearly extinct at many locations, and some scholars speculate that Phoenician colonization in the Mediterranean was motivated in part by the search for new sources of snails.

length. At the most critical point—the 2–½-mile-wide (4-kilometer) isthmus connecting the promontory to the mainland—the wall was over 40 feet (13 meters) high and 30 feet (10 meters) thick and had high watchtowers.

With a population of roughly 400,000, Carthage was one of the largest cities in the world by 500 B.C.E. The population was ethnically diverse, including people of Phoenician stock, indigenous peoples ancestral to modern-day Berbers, and immigrants from other Mediterranean lands as well as sub-Saharan Africa. The Phoenicians readily intermarried with other peoples.

Each year two "judges" were elected from upper-class families to serve as heads of state and carry out administrative and judicial functions. The real seat of power was the Senate, where members of the leading merchant families, who sat for life, directed the affairs of the state. An inner circle of thirty or so senators made the

© Cengage Learning

MAP 3.3 Colonization of the Mediterranean

In the ninth century B.C.E., the Phoenicians of Lebanon began to explore and colonize parts of the western Mediterranean, including the coast of North Africa, southern and eastern Spain, and the islands of Sicily and Sardinia. The Phoenicians were primarily interested in access to valuable raw materials and trading opportunities.

crucial decisions. The leadership occasionally convened an Assembly of the citizens to elect public officials or vote on important issues, particularly when they were divided or wanted to stir up popular enthusiasm for some venture.

There is little evidence at Carthage of the kind of social and political unrest that plagued Greece and Rome. A merchant aristocracy (unlike an aristocracy of birth) was not a closed group, and a climate of economic and social mobility allowed newly successful families and individuals to push their way into the circle of influential citizens. Insofar as everyone benefited from the riches of empire, the masses were usually ready to defer to those who made prosperity possible.

Carthaginian power rested on its navy, which dominated the western Mediterranean for centuries. Phoenician towns provided a network of friendly ports. The Carthaginian fleet consisted of fast, maneuverable galleys (warships propelled by oars). Each bore a sturdy, pointed ram in front that could pierce the hull of an enemy vessel below the water line, while marines (soldiers aboard a ship) fired weapons. Innovations in the placement of benches and oars eventually made room for as many as 170 rowers. The Phoenicians and their Greek rivals set the standard for naval technology in this era.

Carthaginian foreign policy, reflecting the economic interests of the dominant merchant class, focused on protecting the sea lanes, gaining access to raw materials, and fostering trade. Indeed, Carthage claimed the waters of the western Mediterranean as its own. Foreign merchants were free to sail to Carthage to market their goods, but if they tried to operate elsewhere on their own, they risked having their ships sunk by the Carthaginian navy. Treaties between Carthage and other states included formal recognition of this maritime commercial monopoly.

The archaeological record provides few clues about the commodities traded by the Carthaginians. These may have included perishable goods—foodstuffs, textiles, animal skins, slaves—and raw metals whose Carthaginian origin would not be evident. Carthaginian ships carried goods manufactured elsewhere, and products brought to Carthage by foreign traders were re-exported.

There is also evidence for trade with sub-Saharan Africa. Hanno (HA-noe), a Carthaginian captain of the fifth century B.C.E., claimed to have sailed through the Strait of Gibraltar into the Atlantic Ocean and to have explored the West African coast. Other Carthaginians explored the Atlantic coast of Spain and France and secured control of an important source of tin in the "Tin Islands," probably Cornwall in southwestern England.

War and Religion   The Carthaginian state did not directly rule a large territory. A belt of fertile land in northeastern Tunisia, owned by Carthaginians but worked by native peasants and imported slaves, provided a secure food supply. Beyond this core area the Carthaginians ruled most of their "empire" indirectly and allowed other Phoenician communities in the western Mediterranean to remain independent. These Phoenician communities looked to Carthage for military protection and followed its lead in foreign policy. Only Sardinia and southern Spain were put under the direct control of a Carthaginian governor and garrison, presumably to safeguard their agricultural, metal, and manpower resources.

Carthage's focus on trade may explain the unusual fact that citizens were not required to serve in the army: they were of more value in other capacities, such as

The Tophet of Carthage *Here, from the seventh to second centuries B.C.E., the cremated bodies of sacrificed children were buried. Archaeological excavation has confirmed the claim in ancient sources that the Carthaginians sacrificed children to their gods at times of crisis. Stone markers, decorated with magical signs and symbols of divinities as well as family names, were placed over ceramic urns containing the ashes and charred bones of one or more infants or, occasionally, older children.*

Werner Forman Archive/Glow Images

trading activities and the navy. Since the indigenous North African population was not politically or militarily well organized, Carthage had little to fear close to home. When Carthage was drawn into a series of wars with the Greeks and Romans from the fifth through third centuries B.C.E., it relied on mercenaries from the most warlike peoples in its dominions or from neighboring areas. These well-paid mercenaries were under the command of Carthaginian officers; generals were chosen by the Senate and kept in office for as long as they were needed. In contrast to most ancient states, the Carthaginians separated military command from civilian government.

Like the deities of Mesopotamia (see Chapter 2), the gods of the Carthaginians—chief among them Baal Hammon (BAHL ha-MOHN), a male storm-god, and Tanit (TAH-nit), a female fertility figure—were powerful and capricious entities who had to be appeased by anxious worshipers. Roman sources report that members of the Carthaginian elite would sacrifice their own male children in times of crisis. Excavations at Carthage and other western Phoenician towns have turned up *tophets* (TOE-fet)—walled enclosures where thousands of small, sealed urns containing the burned bones of children lay buried. Originally practiced by the upper classes, child sacrifice became more common and involved broader elements of the population after 400 B.C.E.

Plutarch (PLOO-tawrk), a Greek who lived around 100 C.E., long after the demise of Carthage, wrote the following on the basis of earlier sources:

> *The Carthaginians are a hard and gloomy people, submissive to their rulers and harsh to their subjects, running to extremes of cowardice in times of fear and of cruelty in*

times of anger; they keep obstinately to their decisions, are austere, and care little for amusement or the graces of life.[1]

We should not take the hostile opinions of Greek and Roman sources at face value. Still, it is clear that the Carthaginians were perceived as different and that cultural barriers, leading to misunderstanding and prejudice, played a significant role in the conflicts among these peoples of the ancient Mediterranean. In Chapter 6 we follow the protracted and bloody struggle between Rome and Carthage for control of the western Mediterranean.

FAILURE AND TRANSFORMATION, 750–550 B.C.E.

The extension of Assyrian power over the entire Middle East had enormous consequences for all the peoples of the region. In 721 B.C.E. the Assyrians destroyed the northern kingdom of Israel and deported a substantial portion of the population, and for over a century the southern kingdom of Judah faced relentless pressure. Assyrian threats and demands for tribute spurred the Phoenicians to explore and colonize the western Mediterranean. Tyre's fall to the Assyrians in 701 B.C.E. accelerated the decline of the Phoenician homeland, but the western colonies, especially Carthage, flourished. Even Egypt, for so long impregnable behind its desert barriers, fell to Assyrian invaders in the mid-seventh century B.C.E. Southern Mesopotamia was reduced to a protectorate, with Babylon alternately razed and rebuilt by Assyrian kings of differing dispositions. Urartu and Elam, Assyria's nearby rivals, were destroyed.

By 650 B.C.E. Assyria stood supreme in western Asia. But the arms race with Urartu, the frequent expensive campaigns, and the protection of lengthy borders had sapped Assyrian resources. Assyrian brutality and exploitation aroused the hatred of conquered peoples. At the same time, changes in the ethnic composition of the army and the population of the homeland had reduced popular support for the Assyrian state.

Two new political entities spearheaded resistance to Assyria. First, Babylonia had been revived by the Neo-Babylonian, or Chaldaean (chal-DEE-uhn), dynasty (the Chaldaeans had infiltrated southern Mesopotamia around 1000 B.C.E.). Second, the Medes (MEED), an Iranian people, were extending their kingdom on the Iranian Plateau in the seventh century B.C.E. The two powers launched a series of attacks on the Assyrian homeland that destroyed the chief cities by 612 B.C.E. The destruction systematically carried out by the victorious attackers led to the depopulation of northern Mesopotamia.

The Medes took over the Assyrian homeland and the northern plain as far as eastern Anatolia, but most of the territory of the old empire fell to the **Neo-Babylonian kingdom** (626–539 B.C.E.), thanks to the energetic campaigns of kings Nabopolassar (NAB-oh-poe-lass-uhr) (r. 625–605 B.C.E.) and Nebuchadnezzar (r. 604–562 B.C.E.). Babylonia underwent a cultural renaissance. The city of Babylon was enlarged and adorned, becoming the greatest metropolis of the world

---

[1]Plutarch, *Moralia*, 799 D, trans. B. H. Warmington, *Carthage* (Harmondsworth, England: Penguin, 1960), 163.

in the sixth century B.C.E. Old cults were revived, temples rebuilt, festivals resurrected. The related pursuits of mathematics, astronomy, and astrology reached new heights.

CONCLUSION

The Late Bronze Age in the Middle East was a "cosmopolitan" era of shared lifestyles and technologies. Patterns of culture that had originated long before in Egypt and Mesopotamia persisted into this era. Peoples such as the Amorites, Kassites, and Chaldaeans, who migrated into the Tigris-Euphrates plain, were largely assimilated into the Sumerian-Semitic cultural tradition, adopting its language, religious beliefs, political and social institutions, and forms of artistic expression. Similarly, the Hyksos, who migrated into the Nile Delta and controlled much of Egypt for a time, adopted the ancient ways of Egypt. When the founders of the New Kingdom finally ended Hyksos domination, they reinstituted the united monarchy and the religious and cultural traditions of earlier eras.

The Late Bronze Age expansion of commerce and communication stimulated the emergence of new civilizations, including those of the Minoans and Mycenaean Greeks in the Aegean Sea. These new civilizations borrowed heavily from the technologies and cultural practices of Mesopotamia and Egypt, creating dynamic syntheses of imported and indigenous elements.

Ultimately, the very interdependence of the societies of the Middle East and eastern Mediterranean made them vulnerable to the destructions and disorder of the decades around 1200 B.C.E. The entire region slipped into a "Dark Age" of isolation, stagnation, and decline that lasted several centuries. The early centuries after 1000 B.C.E. saw a resurgence of political organization and international commerce, as well as the spread of technologies and ideas. The Assyrians created an empire of unprecedented size and diversity through superior organization and military technology, and they maintained it through terror and deportations of subject peoples.

The Israelites began as nomadic pastoralists and then settled permanently in Canaan. Conflict with the Philistines forced them to adopt a more complex political structure, and under the monarchy Israelite society grew more urban and economically stratified. While the long, slow evolution of the Israelites from wandering groups of herders to an agriculturally based monarchy followed a common pattern in ancient western Asia, the religious and ethical concepts that they formulated were unique and have had a powerful impact on world history.

After the upheavals of the Late Bronze Age, the Phoenician city-states along the coast of Lebanon flourished. Under pressure from the Neo-Assyrian Empire, the Phoenicians, with Tyre in the lead, began spreading westward into the Mediterranean. Carthage became the most important city outside the Phoenician homeland. Ruled by leading merchant families, it extended its commercial empire throughout the western Mediterranean, maintaining power through naval superiority.

The far-reaching expansion of the Assyrian Empire was the most important factor in the transformation of the ancient Middle East. The Assyrians destroyed many older states and, directly or indirectly, displaced large numbers of people. Their brutality, as well as the population shifts that resulted from their deportations, undercut support for their state. The Chaldaeans and Medes led resistance to Assyrian rule. After the swift collapse of Assyria, the Chaldaeans expanded the Neo-Babylonian kingdom, enlarged the city of Babylon, and presided over a cultural renaissance.

IMPORTANT EVENTS 2000 B.C.E. TO 500 B.C.E.	
2000 B.C.E.	Rise of Minoan civilization on Crete; early Greeks arrive in Greece
1800 B.C.E.	Abraham migrates to Canaan
1700–1200 B.C.E.	Hittites dominant in Anatolia
1640–1532 B.C.E.	Hyksos dominate northern Egypt
1600 B.C.E.	Rise of Mycenaean civilization in Greece
1532 B.C.E.	Beginning of New Kingdom
1470 B.C.E.	Queen Hatshepsut dispatches expedition to Punt
1460 B.C.E.	Kassites assume control of southern Mesopotamia
1450 B.C.E.	Destruction of Minoan palaces in Crete
1353 B.C.E.	Akhenaten launches reforms
1290–1224 B.C.E.	Reign of Ramesses the Great
1250–1200 B.C.E.	Israelite occupation of Canaan
1200 B.C.E.	Destruction of Hittite kingdom
1200–1150 B.C.E.	Destruction of Mycenaean centers in Greece
1200–1150 B.C.E.	Sea Peoples attack Egypt
1150 B.C.E.	Philistines settle southern coast of Israel
1070 B.C.E.	End of New Kingdom
1000 B.C.E.	Jerusalem made Israelite capital
920 B.C.E.	Division into two kingdoms of Israel and Judah
911 B.C.E.	Rise of Neo-Assyrian Empire
814 B.C.E.	Foundation of Carthage
750 B.C.E.	Kings of Kush control Egypt
744–727 B.C.E.	Reforms of Tiglathpileser
721 B.C.E.	Assyrian conquest of northern kingdom
671 B.C.E.	Assyrian conquest of Egypt
626–539 B.C.E.	Neo-Babylonian kingdom
612 B.C.E.	Fall of Assyria
587 B.C.E.	Capture of Jerusalem

4

NEW CIVILIZATIONS OUTSIDE THE WEST ASIAN CORE AREA, 2300 B.C.E.–350 C.E.

Around 2200 B.C.E. an Egyptian official named Harkhuf (HAHR-koof) set out from Aswan (AS-wahn), on the southern boundary of Egypt, for a place called Yam, far to the south in the land that later came to be called Nubia. He brought gifts from the Egyptian pharaoh for the ruler of Yam, and he returned home with three hundred donkeys loaded with incense, ebony, ivory, and other exotic products from tropical Africa. Despite the diplomatic fiction of exchanging gifts, we should probably regard Harkhuf as a brave and enterprising merchant. He returned with something so special that the eight-year-old boy pharaoh, Pepi II, could not contain his excitement. He wrote:

> Come north to the residence at once! Hurry and bring with you this pygmy whom you brought from the land of the horizon-dwellers live, hale, and healthy, for the dances of the god, to gladden the heart, to delight the heart of king Neferkare [Pepi] who lives forever! When he goes down with you into the ship, get worthy men to be around him on deck, lest he fall into the water! When he lies down at night, get worthy men to lie around him in his tent. Inspect ten times at night! My majesty desires to see this pygmy more than the gifts of the mine-land and of Punt![1]

Scholars identify Yam with Kerma, later the capital of the kingdom of Nubia, on the upper Nile in modern Sudan. For Egyptians, Nubia was a wild and dangerous place. Yet it was developing a more complex political organization, and this illustration demonstrates how vibrant the commerce and cultural interaction between Nubia and Egypt would later become.

In this chapter we discuss other parts of the world outside the core area in western Asia that has been central to this point: East Asia, sub-Saharan Africa, the Eurasian steppes, and continental Europe. These societies emerged later than those in Mesopotamia, Egypt, and the Indus Valley and in more varied ecological conditions—sometimes independently, sometimes under the influence of older centers. Whereas the older river-valley civilizations were largely self-sufficient, many of

---

[1]Quoted in Miriam Lichtheim, ed., *Ancient Egyptian Literature: A Book of Readings* (Berkeley: University of California Press, 1978).

the new civilizations discussed in the previous chapter and in this chapter were shaped by networks of long-distance trade. In the second millennium B.C.E. a civilization based on irrigation agriculture arose in the valley of the Yellow River and its tributaries in northern China. In the same epoch, in Nubia (southern Egypt and northern Sudan), the first complex society in tropical Africa continued to develop from the roots observed earlier by Harkhuf. The first millennium B.C.E. also witnessed the rise of a new kind of nomadism on the Eurasian steppes and the spread of Celtic peoples across much of continental Europe. These societies represent a variety of responses to different environmental and historical circumstances. However, they have certain features in common and collectively point to a distinct stage in the development of human societies.

EARLY CHINA, 2000–221 B.C.E.

On the eastern edge of the vast Eurasian landmass, Neolithic cultures developed as early as 8000 B.C.E. A more complex civilization evolved in the second and first millennia B.C.E. Under the Shang and Zhou dynasties, many of the elements of classical Chinese civilization emerged and spread across East Asia. As in Mesopotamia, Egypt, and the Indus Valley, the rise of cities, specialization of labor, bureaucratic government, writing, and other advanced technologies depended on the exploitation of a great river system—the Yellow River (Huang He [hwahng-HUH]) and its tributaries—to support intensive agriculture.

Geography and Resources   China is isolated by formidable natural barriers: the Himalaya (him-uh-LAY-uh) mountain range on the southwest; the Pamir (pah-MEER) and Tian Mountains and the Takla Makan (TAH-kluh muh-KAHN) Desert on the west; and the Gobi (GO-bee) Desert and the treeless, grassy hills and plains of the Mongolian steppe to the northwest and north. To the east lies the vast Pacific Ocean. Although China's separation was not total—trade goods, people, and ideas moved back and forth between China, India, and Central Asia—in many respects its development was distinctive.

Most of East Asia is covered with mountains, making overland travel and transport difficult. The great river systems of eastern China, however—the Yellow and the Yangzi (yang-zuh) Rivers and their tributaries—facilitate east-west movement. In the eastern river valleys dense populations practiced intensive agriculture; on the steppe lands of Mongolia, the deserts and oases of Xinjiang (shin-jyahng), and the high plateau of Tibet sparser populations lived largely by herding. The climate zones of East Asia range from the dry, subarctic reaches of Manchuria in the north to the lush, subtropical forests of the south, and a rich variety of plant and animal life are adapted to these zones.

Within the eastern agricultural zone, the north and the south have quite different environments. Each region developed distinctive patterns for land use, the kinds of crops grown, and the organization of agricultural labor. The monsoons that affect India and Southeast Asia (see Chapter 2) drench southern China with heavy rainfall in the summer, the most beneficial time for agriculture. In northern China rainfall is much more erratic. As in Mesopotamia and the Indus Valley, Chinese civilization developed in relatively adverse conditions on the northern plains, a demanding environment that stimulated important technologies and political traditions as well as the philosophical and religious views that became hallmarks of Chinese civilization. By the third century C.E., however, the gradual flow of population toward the warmer southern lands caused the political and intellectual center to move south.

The eastern river valleys and North China Plain contained timber, stone, scattered deposits of metals, and, above all, potentially productive land. Winds blowing from Central Asia deposit a yellowish-brown dust called **loess** (less) (these particles suspended in the water give the Yellow River its distinctive hue and name). Over the ages a thick mantle of soil has accumulated that is extremely fertile and soft enough to be worked with wooden digging sticks.

In this landscape, agriculture required the coordinated efforts of large numbers of people. Forests had to be cleared. Earthen dikes were constructed to protect nearby fields from recurrent floods on the Yellow River. To cope with the periodic droughts, reservoirs were dug to store river water and rainfall. Retaining walls partitioned the hillsides into flat arable terraces.

The staple crops in the northern region were millet, a grain indigenous to China, and wheat, which had spread to East Asia from the Middle East. Rice, which requires a warmer climate, prospered in the Yangzi River Valley. The cultivation of rice required a great outlay of labor. Rice paddies—the fields where rice is grown—must be flat and surrounded by water channels to bring and lead away water according to a precise schedule. Seedlings sprout in a nursery and are transplanted to the paddy, which is then flooded. Flooding eliminates weeds and rival plants and supports microscopic organisms that keep the soil fertile. When the crop is ripe, the paddy is drained; the rice stalks are harvested with a sickle; and the edible kernels are separated out. The reward for this effort is a harvest that can feed more people per cultivated acre than any other grain, which explains why the south eventually became more populous than the north.

The Late Neolithic: Artifacts and Legends

Archaeological evidence shows that the Neolithic population of China grew millet, raised pigs and chickens, and used stone tools. Workers made pottery on a wheel and fired it in high-temperature kilns. Some also pioneered the production of silk cloth, first raising silkworms on the leaves of mulberry trees, then carefully unraveling their cocoons to produce silk thread. They built walls of pounded earth by hammering the soil inside temporary wooden frames until it became hard as cement. By 2000 B.C.E. the Chinese had begun to make bronze (a thousand years after the beginnings of bronze-working in the Middle East).

In later times legends depicted the early rulers of China, starting with the Yellow Emperor, as ideal and benevolent masters in a tranquil Golden Age. They were followed by a dynasty called Xia (shah), who were in turn succeeded by the **Shang** (shahng) dynasty. Since scholars are uncertain about the historical reality of the Xia, Chinese history really begins with the rise of the Shang.

The Shang Period, 1766–1045 B.C.E.

Little is known about how the Shang rose to dominance around 1766 B.C.E., since written documents only appear toward the end of Shang rule. These documents are the so-called oracle bones, the shoulder bones of cattle and the bottom shells of turtles employed by Shang rulers to obtain information from ancestral spirits and gods.

The writing on the oracle bones concerns the king, his court, weather and its impact on agriculture, warfare against enemies, and religious practices, with little about other aspects of Shang society. The same limitations apply to the archaeological record, primarily treasure-filled tombs of the Shang ruling class.

The earliest known oracle bone inscriptions date to the thirteenth century B.C.E., but the system was already so sophisticated that some scholars believe writing in China could be considerably older. In the Shang writing system the several hundred characters (written symbols) were originally pictures of objects that become simplified over time, with each character representing a one-syllable word for an object or idea. It is likely that only a small number of people at court used this system. Nevertheless, the Shang writing system is the ancestor of the systems still used in China and elsewhere in East Asia today. Later Chinese writing developed thousands of more complex characters that provide information about both the meaning of the word and its sound.

Scholars have reconstructed the major features of Shang religion from the oracle bones. The supreme god, Di (dee), who resides in the sky and unleashes the power of storms, is felt to be distant and unconcerned with the fate of humans, and cannot be approached directly. When people die, their spirits survive in the same supernatural sphere as Di and other gods of nature. These ancestral spirits, organized in a heavenly hierarchy that mirrors the social hierarchy on earth, can intervene in human affairs. The Shang ruler has direct access to his more recent ancestors, who have access to earlier generations, who can, in turn, intercede with Di. Thus the ruler is the crucial link between Heaven and earth, using his unrivaled access to higher powers to promote agricultural productivity and protect his people from natural and man-made disasters. This belief, which persisted throughout Chinese history, has been an extremely effective rationale for authoritarian rule.

The king was often on the road, traveling to the courts of his subordinates to reinforce their loyalty, but it is uncertain how much territory in the North China Plain was effectively controlled by the Shang. Excavations at sites elsewhere in China show artistic and technological traditions so different that they are probably the products of independent groups. Both the lack of writing elsewhere in early China and the Han-era conception that China had always been unified obscure from us the probable ethnic, linguistic, and cultural diversity of early China.

The Shang elite were a warrior class reveling in warfare, hunting, exchanging gifts, feasting, and drinking. They fought with bronze weapons and rode into battle on horse-drawn chariots, a technology that originated in western Asia. Frequent military campaigns provided these warriors with a theater for brave achievements and yielded considerable plunder. Many prisoners of war were taken in these campaigns and made into slaves and sacrificial victims.

Excavated tombs of Shang royal and elite families, primarily from the vicinity of Anyang (ahn-yahng), contain large quantities of valuable objects made of metal, jade, bone, ivory, shell, and stone, including musical instruments, jewelry, mirrors, weapons, and bronze vessels. These vessels, intricately decorated with stylized depictions of real and imaginary animals, were used to make offerings to ancestral spirits. Possession of bronze objects was a sign of status and authority. The tombs also contain the bodies of family members, servants, and prisoners of war who were killed at the time of the burial. It appears that the objects and people were intended to serve the main occupant of the tomb in the afterlife.

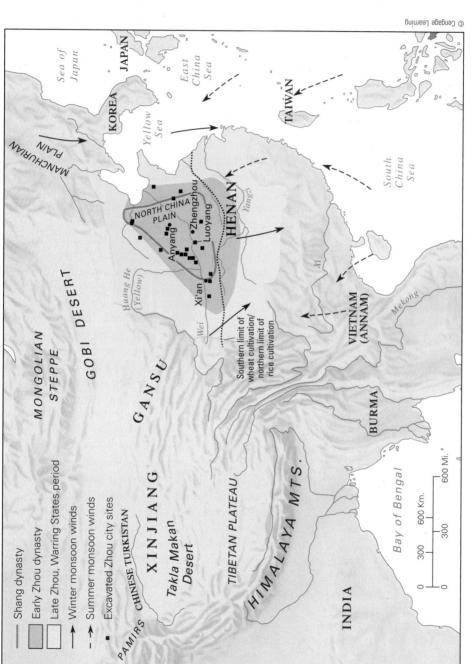

© Cengage Learning

MAP 4.1   China in the Shang and Zhou Periods, 1750–221 B.C.E.

The Shang dynasty arose in the second millennium B.C.E. in the floodplain of the Yellow River. While southern China benefits from the monsoon rains, northern China depends on irrigation. As population increased, the Han Chinese migrated from their eastern homeland to other parts of China, carrying with them their technologies and cultural practices. Other ethnic groups predominated in more outlying regions, and the nomadic peoples of the northwest constantly challenged Chinese authority.

Shang cities are not well preserved in the archaeological record, partly because of the climate of northern China and partly because of the building materials used. With stone in short supply, cities were protected by massive walls of pounded earth, and buildings were constructed with wooden posts and dried mud. A number of sites appear to have served at different times as centers of political control and religion, with palaces, administrative buildings and storehouses, royal tombs, shrines of gods and ancestors, and houses of the nobility. The common people lived in agricultural villages outside these centers.

The Zhou Period, 1045– 221 B.C.E.   In the mid-eleventh century B.C.E. the Shang were overthrown by the **Zhou** (joe), whose homeland lay several hundred miles to the west, in the valley of the Wei (way) River. While the ethnic origin of the Zhou is unclear (their traditions acknowledged that their ancestors had lived for generations among the western "barbarians"), they took over many elements of Shang culture. The Zhou line of kings was the longest lasting and most revered of all dynasties in Chinese history. The two founders were Wen, a vassal ruler who, after being held prisoner for a time by his Shang overlord, initiated a rebellion of disaffected Shang subjects; and his son, Wu, who mounted a successful attack on the Shang capital and was enthroned as the first ruler of the new dynasty.

Wu justified his achievement in a manner that became the norm throughout subsequent Chinese history. Claiming that the last Shang ruler was depraved and tyrannical, neglecting to honor gods and ancestors and killing and abusing his subjects, he invoked the highest Zhou deity, Tian (tyehn) ("Heaven"), who was more compassionate than the aloof Di of the Shang. Wu declared that Heaven granted authority and legitimacy to a ruler as long as he looked out for the welfare of his subjects; the monarch, accordingly, was called the "Son of Heaven." The proof of divine favor was the prosperity and stability of the kingdom. But if the ruler persistently failed in these duties and neglected the warning signs of flood, famine, invasion, or other disasters, Heaven could withdraw this "Mandate" and transfer it to another, more worthy ruler and family. This theory of the **Mandate of Heaven**, which validated the institution of monarchy by connecting the religious and political spheres, served as the foundation of Chinese political thought for three thousand years.

Much more is known about the early centuries of Zhou rule (the Western Zhou Period, 1045–771 B.C.E.) than the preceding Shang era because of the survival of written texts, above all the *Book of Documents*, a collection of decrees, letters, and other historical and pseudo-historical (some allegedly written by the early emperors of legend) records, and the *Book of Songs*, an anthology of 305 poems, ballads, and folksongs that illuminate the lives of rulers, nobles, and peasants. Additionally, members of the Zhou elite recorded their careers and cited honors received from the rulers in bronze inscriptions.

To consolidate his power, King Wu distributed territories to his relatives and allies, which they were to administer and profit from so long as they remained loyal to him. These regional rulers then apportioned pieces of their holdings to their supporters, creating a pyramidal structure of political, social, and economic relations often referred to as "feudal," borrowing terminology from the European Middle Ages.

When Wu died, his son and heir, Cheng (chung), was too young to assume full powers, and for a time the kingdom was run by his uncles, especially the Duke of

Zhou. The Duke of Zhou is one of the most famous figures in early Chinese history, in large part because the philosopher Confucius later celebrated him as the ideal administrator who selflessly served as regent for his young nephew at a delicate time for the new dynasty, then dutifully returned power as soon as the lawful ruler came of age.

The early Zhou rulers constructed a new capital city in their homeland (near modern Xi'an), and other urban centers developed in succeeding centuries. Cities were laid out on a grid plan aligned with the north polar star, with gates in the fortification walls opening to the cardinal directions and major buildings facing south. This was in keeping with an already ancient concern, known as *feng shui* (fung shway) ("wind and water"), to orient structures so that they would be in a harmonious relationship with the terrain, the forces of wind, water, and sunlight, and the invisible energy perceived to be flowing through the natural world.

Alongside the new primacy of the Zhou deity Tian and continuation of religious practices inherited from the Shang era, new forms of divination developed. One increasingly popular method involved throwing down a handful of long and short stalks of the milfoil or yarrow plant and interpreting the patterns they formed. Over time a multilayered text was compiled, called the *Book of Changes*, that explained in detail the meanings of each of the sixty-four standard patterns formed by the stalks. In later ages this practice and the accompanying text also came to be used as a vehicle for self-examination and contemplation of the workings of the world.

The *Book of Songs* provides extraordinary glimpses into the lives, activities, and feelings of a diverse cross-section of early Chinese people—elite and common, male and female, urban and rural. We can glean much from these poems about the situation of women in early China. Some describe men and women choosing each other and engaging in sex outside of marriage. Other poems tell of arranged marriages in which the young woman anxiously leaves home and birth family behind and journeys to the household of an unknown husband and new family. One poem describes the different ways that infant boys and girls were welcomed into an aristocratic family. The male was received like a little prince: placed on a bed, swaddled in expensive robes, and given a jade scepter to play with as a symbol of his future authority; the female was placed on the floor and given the weight from a weaving loom to indicate her future obligations of subservience and household labor.

Over the period from the eleventh to eighth centuries B.C.E. the power of the Zhou monarch gradually eroded, largely because of the feudal division of territory and power. In 771 B.C.E. the Zhou capital was attacked by a coalition of enemies, and the dynasty withdrew to a base farther east, at Luoyang (LWOE-yahng). This change ushers in the Eastern Zhou Period (770–221 B.C.E.), a long era in which the Zhou monarchs remained as figureheads, given only nominal allegiance by the rulers of many virtually independent states scattered across northern and central China.

The first part of the Eastern Zhou era is called the Spring and Autumn Period (770–481 B.C.E.) because of the survival of a text, the *Spring and Autumn Annals*, that provides a spare historical record of events in the small eastern state of Lu. Later writers added commentaries that fleshed out this skeletal record. The states of this era were frequently at odds with one another and employed various tactics to protect themselves and advance their interests, including diplomatic initiatives, shifting alliances, and coups and assassinations as well as conventional warfare. The overall trend was gradual consolidation into a smaller number of larger and more powerful kingdoms.

Warfare was a persistent feature of the period, and there were important transformations in the character and technology of war. In the Shang and early Zhou periods, warfare largely had been conducted by members of the elite, who rode in chariots, treated battle as an opportunity for displays of skill and courage, and adhered to a code of heroic conduct. But in the high-stakes conflicts of the Eastern Zhou era, there was a shift to much larger armies made up of conscripted farmers who fought bloody battles, unconstrained by noble etiquette, in which large numbers were slaughtered. Some men undertook the study of war and composed handbooks, such as Sunzi's *Art of War*. Sunzi (soon-zuh) approaches war as a chess game in which the successful general employs deception, intuits the energy potential inherent in the landscape, and psychologically manipulates both friend and foe. The best victories are achieved without fighting so that one can incorporate the unimpaired resources of the other side.

Technological advances also impacted warfare. In the last centuries of the Zhou, the Chinese learned from the nomadic peoples of the northern steppes to put fighters on horseback. By 600 B.C.E. iron began to replace bronze as the primary metal for tools and weapons. There is mounting evidence that ironworking also came to China from the nomadic peoples of the northwest. Metalworkers in China were the first in the world to forge steel by removing carbon during the iron-smelting process.

Another significant development was the increasing size and complexity of the governments that administered Chinese states. Rulers ordered the careful recording of the population, the land, and its agricultural products so that the government could compel peasants to donate labor for public works projects (digging and maintaining irrigation channels and building roads, defensive walls, and palaces), conscript them into the army, and collect taxes. Skilled officials supervised the expanding bureaucracies of scribes, accountants, and surveyors and advised the rulers on various matters. Thus there arose a class of educated and ambitious men who traveled from state to state offering their services to the rulers—and their theories of ideal government.

Confucianism, Daoism, and Chinese Society

The Eastern Zhou era, despite being plagued by political fragmentation, frequent warfare, and anxious uncertainty, was also a time of great cultural development. The two most influential "philosophical" systems of Chinese civilization—Confucianism and Daoism—had their roots in this period, though they would be further developed and adapted to changing circumstances in later times.

Kongzi (kohng-zuh) (551–479 B.C.E.), known in the West by the Latin form of his name, **Confucius**, withdrew from public life after unsuccessful efforts to find employment as an official and adviser to several rulers of the day. He attracted a circle of students to whom he presented his wide-ranging ideas on morality, conduct, and government. His sayings were handed down orally by several generations of disciples before being compiled in written form as the *Analects* (see Diversity and Dominance: Human Nature and Good Government in the *Analects* of Confucius and the Legalist Writings of Han Fei). This work, along with a set of earlier texts that were believed (probably wrongly) to have been edited by Confucius—the *Book of Documents*, the *Book of Songs*, the *Book of Changes*, and the *Spring and Autumn Annals*—became the core texts of Confucianism.

Confucius drew upon traditional institutions and values but gave them new shape and meaning. He looked back to the early Zhou period as a Golden Age of wise rulers and benevolent government, models to which the people of his own "broken" society should return. He also placed great importance on the "rituals," or forms of behavior, that guide people in their daily interactions with one another, since these promote harmony in human relations.

For Confucius the family was the fundamental component of society, and the ways in which family members regulated their conduct in the home prepared them to serve as subjects of the state. Each person had his or her place and duties in a hierarchical order that was determined by age and gender. The "filiality" of children to parents, which included obedience, reverence, and love, had its analogue in the devotion of subjects to the ruler. Another fundamental virtue for Confucius was *ren* (ruhn), sometimes translated as "humaneness," which traditionally meant the feelings between family members and was now expanded into a universal ideal of benevolence and compassion that would, ideally, pervade every activity. Confucianism placed immense value on the practical task of making society function smoothly at every level. It provided a philosophical and ethical framework for conducting one's life and understanding one's place in the world. But it was not a religion. While Confucius urged respect for gods, ancestors, and religious traditions, he felt that such supernatural matters were unknowable.

Confucius's ideas were little known in his own time, but his teachings were preserved and gradually spread to a wider audience. Some disciples took Confucianism in new directions. Mengzi (muhng-zuh) (known in the West as Mencius, 371–289 B.C.E.), who did much to popularize Confucian ideas in his age, believed in the essential goodness of all human beings and argued that, if people were shown the right way by virtuous leaders, they would voluntarily do the right thing. Xunzi (shoon-zuh) (ca. 310–210 B.C.E.), on the other hand, concluded that people had to be compelled to make appropriate choices. (This approach led to the development of a school of thought called Legalism, discussed later in this chapter.) As we shall see in Chapter 6, in the era of the emperors a revised Confucianism became the dominant political philosophy and the core of the educational system for government officials.

If Confucianism emphasized social engagement, its great rival, **Daoism** (DOW-ism), urged withdrawal from the empty formalities, rigid hierarchy, and distractions of Chinese society. Laozi (low-zuh) is regarded as the originator of Daoism, although virtually nothing is known about him, and some scholars doubt his existence. Laozi is credited with the foundational text of Daoism, the *Classic of the Way of Virtue,* a difficult book full of ambiguity and paradox, beautiful poetic images, and tantalizing hints of "truths" that cannot be adequately explained with words. It raises questions about whether the material world in which we operate is real or a kind of dream that blocks us from perceiving a higher reality. It argues that education, knowledge, and rational analysis are obstacles to understanding and that we would be better off cultivating our senses and trusting our intuitions. The primal world of the distant past was happy and blessed before civilization and "knowledge" corrupted it. The Daoist sage strives to lead a tranquil existence by retreating from the stresses and obligations of a chaotic society. He avoids useless struggles, making himself soft and malleable so that the forces that buffet people can flow harmlessly around him. He chooses not to "act" because such action almost always leads to a different outcome from the one desired, whereas inaction may bring the desired outcome. And he has no fear of death because, for all we know, death may be merely a transformation to another plane of existence. In the end, in a world that is always changing and lacks any absolute morality or meaning, all that matters is the individual's fundamental understanding of, and accommodation to, the *Dao,* the "path" of nature.

Daoism, like Confucianism, would continue to evolve for many centuries, adapting to changes in Chinese society and incorporating many elements of traditional religion, mysticism, and magic. Although Daoism and Confucianism may appear to be thoroughly at odds regarding the relationship of the individual and the larger society, many Chinese through the ages have drawn on both traditions, and it has been said that the typical Chinese scholar-official was a Confucian in his work and public life but a Daoist in the privacy of his study.

The classical Chinese patterns of family and property took shape in the later Zhou period. The kinship structures of the Shang and early Zhou periods, based on the clan (a relatively large group of related families), gave way to the three-generation family of grandparents, parents, and children as the fundamental social unit. Fathers had absolute authority over women and children, arranged marriages for their offspring, and could sell the labor of family members. Only men could conduct rituals and make offerings to the ancestors, though women helped maintain the household's ancestral shrines. A man was limited to one wife but was permitted additional sexual partners, who had the lower status of concubines. A man whose wife died had a duty to remarry in order to produce male heirs to keep alive the cult of the ancestors, whereas women were discouraged from remarrying.

Asian Art & Archaeology, Inc./Corbis

Chinese Bronze Bells *This set of 65 bells was discovered in the tomb of Marquis Yi, the ruler of one of the warring states in the fifth century* B.C.E. *Bells in different sizes were central components of ancient Chinese "orchestras." In the Eastern Zhou era, each state had its own distinctive set of instruments, an assertion of independence and local pride.*

DIVERSITY + DOMINANCE

Human Nature and Good Government in the Analects of Confucius and the Legalist Writings of Han Fei

While monarchy (the rule of one man) was the standard form of government in ancient China and was rarely challenged, political theorists and philosophers thought a great deal about the qualities of the ideal ruler, his relationship to his subjects, and the means by which he controlled them. These considerations about how to govern people were inevitably molded by fundamental assumptions about the nature of human beings. In the Warring States Period, as the major states struggled desperately with one another for survival and expansion, such discussions took on a special urgency, and the Confucians and Legalists came to represent two powerful, and largely contradictory, points of view.

The Analects are a collection of sayings of Confucius, probably compiled and written down several generations after he lived, though some elements may have been added even later. They cover a wide range of matters, including ethics, government, education, music, and rituals. Taken as a whole, they are a guide to living an honorable, virtuous, useful, and satisfying life. While subject to reinterpretation according to the circumstances of the times, Confucian principles have had a great influence on Chinese values and behavior ever since.

Han Fei (280–233 B.C.E.), who was, ironically, at one time the student of a Confucian teacher, became a Legalist writer and political adviser to the ruler of the ambitious state of Qin. Eventually he lost out in a power struggle at court and was forced to kill himself.

The following selections illuminate the profound disagreements between Confucians and Legalists over the essential nature of human beings and how the ruler should conduct himself in order to most effectively govern his subjects and protect his kingdom.

Confucius

4:5 Confucius said: "Riches and honors are what all men desire. But if they cannot be attained in accordance with the *dao* [*the way*] they should not be kept. Poverty and low status are what all men hate. But if they cannot be avoided while staying in accordance with the *dao*, you should not avoid them. If a Superior Man departs from *ren* [humaneness], how can he be worthy of that name? A Superior Man never leaves *ren* for even the time of a single meal. In moments of haste he acts according to it. In times of difficulty or confusion he acts according to it."

16:8 Confucius said: "The Superior Man stands in awe of three things: (1) He is in awe of the decree of Heaven. (2) He is in awe of great men. (3) He is in awe of the words of the sages. The inferior man does not know the decree of Heaven; takes great men lightly and laughs at the words of the sages."

4:14 Confucius said: "I don't worry about not having a good position; I worry about the means I use to gain position. I don't worry about being unknown; I seek to be known in the right way."

7:15 Confucius said: "I can live with coarse rice to eat, water for drink and my arm as a pillow and still be happy. Wealth and honors that one possesses in the midst of injustice are like floating clouds."

13:6 Confucius said: "When you have gotten your own life straightened out, things will go well without your giving orders. But if your own life isn't straightened out, even if you give orders, no one will follow them."

12:2 Zhonggong asked about the meaning of *ren*. The Master said: "Go out of your home as if you were receiving an important guest. Employ the people as if you were assisting at a great ceremony. What you don't want done to yourself, don't do to others. Live in your town without stirring up resentments, and live in your household without stirring up resentments."

1:5 Confucius said: "If you would govern a state of a thousand chariots (a small-to-middle-size state), you must pay strict attention to business, be true to your word, be economical in expenditure and love the people. You should use them according to the seasons."

2:3 Confucius said: "If you govern the people legalistically and control them by punishment, they will avoid crime, but have no personal sense of shame. If you govern them by means of virtue and control them with propriety, they will gain their own sense of shame, and thus correct themselves."

12:7 Zigong asked about government. The Master said, "Enough food, enough weapons and the confidence of the people." Zigong said, "Suppose you had no alternative but to give up one of these three, which one would be let go of first?" The Master said, "Weapons." Zigong said, "What if you had to give up one of the remaining two, which one would it be?" The Master said, "Food. From ancient times, death has come to all men, but a people without confidence in its rulers will not stand."

12:19 Ji Kang Zi asked Confucius about government saying: "Suppose I were to kill the unjust, in order to advance the just. Would that be all right?"

Confucius replied: "In doing government, what is the need of killing? If you desire good, the people will be good. The nature of the Superior Man is like the wind, the nature of the inferior man is like the grass. When the wind blows over the grass, it always bends."

2:19 The Duke of Ai asked: "How can I make the people follow me?" Confucius replied: "Advance the upright and set aside the crooked, and the people will follow you. Advance the crooked and set aside the upright, and the people will not follow you."

2:20 Ji Kang Zi asked: "How can I make the people reverent and loyal, so they will work positively for me?" Confucius said, "Approach them with dignity, and they will be reverent. Be filial and compassionate and they will be loyal. Promote the able and teach the incompetent, and they will work positively for you."

Han Fei

Past and present have different customs; new and old adopt different measures. To try to use the ways of a generous and lenient government to rule the people of a critical age is like trying to drive a runaway horse without using reins or whips. This is the misfortune that ignorance invites....

Humaneness [*ren*] may make one shed tears and be reluctant to apply penalties, but law makes it clear that such penalties must be applied. The ancient kings allowed law to be supreme and did not give in to their tearful longings. Hence it is obvious that humaneness cannot be used to achieve order in the state....

The best rewards are those that are generous and predictable, so that the people may profit by them. The best penalties are those that are severe and inescapable, so that the people will fear them. The best laws are those that are uniform and inflexible, so that the people can understand them....

Hardly ten men of true integrity and good faith can be found today, and yet the offices of the state number in the hundreds.... Therefore the way of the enlightened ruler is to unify the laws instead of seeking for wise men, to lay down firm policies instead of longing for men of good faith....

When a sage rules the state, he does not depend on people's doing good of themselves; he sees to it that they are not allowed to do what is bad. If he depends on people's doing good of themselves, then within his borders he can count fewer than ten instances of success. But if he sees to it that they are not allowed to do what is bad, then the whole state can be brought to a uniform level of order. Those who rule must employ measures that will be effective with the majority and discard those that will be effective with only a few. Therefore they devote themselves not to virtue but to law....

When the Confucians of the present time counsel rulers, they do not praise those measures that will bring order today, but talk only of the achievements of the men who brought order in the past.... No ruler with proper standards will tolerate them. Therefore the enlightened ruler works with facts and discards useless theories. He does not talk about deeds of humaneness and rightness, and he does not listen to the words of scholars....

Nowadays, those who do not understand how to govern invariably say, "You must win the hearts of the people!"... The reason you cannot rely on the wisdom of the people is that they have the minds of little children. If the child's head is not shaved, its sores will spread; and if its boil is not lanced, it will become sicker than ever ... for it does not understand that the little pain it suffers now will bring great benefit later....

Now, the ruler presses the people to till the land and open up new pastures so as to increase their means of livelihood, and yet they consider him harsh; he draws up a penal code and makes the punishments more severe in order to put a stop to evil, and yet the people consider him stern.... He makes certain that everyone within his borders understands warfare and sees to it that there are no private exemptions from military service; he unites the strength of the state and fights fiercely in order to take its enemies captive, and yet the people consider him violent.... [These] types of undertaking all ensure order and safety to the state, and yet the people do not have sense enough to rejoice in them.

Questions for Analysis

1. What do Confucius and Han Fei believe about the nature of human beings? Are they intrinsically good and well-behaved, or bad and prone to misbehave?

2. What are the qualities of an ideal ruler for Confucius and Han Fei?

3. By what means can the ruler influence his subjects in Confucian thought? How should the ruler compel obedience in the people in Legalist thought?

4. What do Confucians and Legalists think about the value of the past as a model for the present?

5. Why might Confucius's passionate concern for ethical behavior on the part of officials and rulers arise at a time when the size and power of governments were growing?

Sources: Confucius selections from "The Analects of Confucius," translated by A. Charles Muller, from http://www.acmuller.net/con-dao/analects.html. Reprinted by permission of Charles Muller. Han Fei selections from *Sources of Chinese Tradition,* Vol. 1 (paper) by De Bary, William Theodore and Lufrano, Richard. Copyright © 2000 by Columbia University Press. Reprinted with permission of the publisher.

In Chinese tradition the concept of **yin/yang** represented the complementary nature of male and female roles in the natural order. The male principle (yang) was equated with the sun: active, bright, and shining; the female principle (yin) corresponded to the moon: passive, shaded, and reflective. Male toughness was balanced by female gentleness, male action and initiative by female endurance and need for completion, and male leadership by female supportiveness. In its earliest form, the theory considered yin and yang as equal and alternately dominant, like night and day, creating balance in the world. However, as a result of the changing role of women in the Zhou period and the pervasive influence of Confucian ideology, the male principle came to be seen as superior to the female.

The Warring States Period, 481–221 B.C.E.   The second half of the Eastern Zhou era is conventionally called the Warring States Period (480–221 B.C.E.) because the scale and intensity of rivalry and warfare between the states accelerated. More successful states conquered and absorbed less capable rivals, and by the beginning of the third century B.C.E. only seven major states remained. Each state sought security by any and all means: building walls to protect its borders; putting into the field the largest possible armies; experimenting with military organization, tactics, and technology; and devising new techniques of administration to produce the greatest revenues. Some wars were fought against non-Chinese peoples living on the margins of the states' territories or even in enclaves within the states. In addition to self-defense, the aim of these campaigns was often to increase the territory available for agriculture, since cultivated land was, ultimately, the source of wealth and manpower. The conquered peoples assimilated over time, becoming Chinese in language and culture.

The most innovative of all the states of this era was Qin (chin), on the western edge of the "Central States" (the term used for the Chinese lands of north and central China). Coming from the same Wei River Valley frontier region as the Zhou long before, and exposed to barbarian influences and attacks, the Qin rulers commanded a nation of hardy farmers and employed them in large, well-trained armies. The very vulnerability of their circumstances may have inspired the Qin rulers of the fourth and third centuries B.C.E. to take great risks, for they were the first to put into practice the philosophy and methods of the Legalist school of political theorists.

In the mid-fourth century B.C.E. Lord Shang was put in charge of the Qin government. He maintained that the Confucians were mistaken in looking to an idealized past for solutions and naïve in thinking that the ruler should worry about his subjects' opinions. In Lord Shang's view, the ruler should trust his own judgment and employ whatever means are necessary to compel obedience and good behavior in his subjects. In the end, Legalists were willing to sacrifice individual freedom to guarantee the security and prosperity of the state. To strengthen the ruler, Lord Shang moved to weaken the Qin nobility, sending out centrally appointed district governors, abolishing many of the privileges of the nobility, and breaking up large estates by requiring property to be divided equally among the surviving sons. Although he eventually became entangled in bitter intrigue at court and was killed in 338 B.C.E., the Qin rulers of the third century B.C.E. continued to employ Legalist advisers and pursue Legalist policies, and, as we shall see in Chapter 6, they converted the advantages gained from this approach into a position of unprecedented power.

NUBIA, 2300 B.C.E.–350 C.E.

Since the first century B.C.E. the name *Nubia* has been applied to a 1,000-mile (1,600-kilometer) stretch of the Nile Valley lying between Aswan and Khartoum (kahr-TOOM) and straddling the southern part of the modern nation of Egypt and the northern part of Sudan. Nubia is the only continuously inhabited territory connecting sub-Saharan Africa (the lands south of the Sahara Desert) with North Africa. For thousands of years it has served as a corridor for trade between tropical Africa and the Mediterranean. Nubia was richly endowed with natural resources such as gold, copper, and semiprecious stones.

Nubia's location and natural wealth, along with Egypt's hunger for Nubian gold, explain the early rise of a civilization with a complex political organization, social stratification, metallurgy, monumental building, and writing. Scholars have moved away from the traditional view that Nubian civilization simply imitated Egypt, and they now emphasize the mutually beneficial interactions between Egypt and Nubia and the growing evidence that Nubian culture also drew on influences from sub-Saharan Africa.

Early Cultures and Egyptian Domination 2300–1100 B.C.E.

The central geographical feature of Nubia, as of Egypt, is the Nile River. This part of the Nile flows through a landscape of rocky desert, grassland, and fertile plain. River irrigation was essential for agriculture in a climate that was severely hot and, in the north, nearly without rainfall. Six cataracts, barriers formed by large boulders and rapids, obstructed boat traffic. Boats operating between the cataracts and caravans skirting the river made travel and trade possible.

In the fifth millennium B.C.E. bands of people in northern Nubia made the transition from seminomadic hunting and gathering to a settled life based on grain agriculture and cattle herding. From this time on, the majority of the population lived in agricultural villages alongside the river. Even before 3000 B.C.E. Egyptian craftsmen worked in ivory and in ebony wood—products of tropical Africa that came through Nubia.

Nubia enters the historical record around 2300 B.C.E. in Old Kingdom Egyptian accounts of trade missions to southern lands. At that time Aswan, just north of the First Cataract, was the southern limit of Egyptian control. As we saw with the journey of Harkhuf at the beginning of this chapter, Egyptian officials stationed there led donkey caravans south in search of gold, incense, ebony, ivory, slaves, and exotic animals from tropical Africa. This was dangerous work, requiring delicate negotiations with local Nubian chiefs to secure protection, but it brought substantial rewards to those who succeeded.

During the Middle Kingdom (ca. 2040–1640 B.C.E.), Egypt adopted a more aggressive stance toward Nubia. Seeking to control the gold mines in the desert east of the Nile and to cut out the Nubian middlemen who drove up the cost of luxury goods from the tropics, the Egyptians erected a string of mud-brick forts on islands and riverbanks south of the Second Cataract. The forts regulated the flow of trade goods and protected the southern frontier of Egypt against Nubians and nomadic raiders from the desert. There seem to have been peaceable relations but little interaction

MAP 4.2 Ancient Nubia

The land route alongside the Nile River as it flows through Nubia has long served as a corridor connecting sub-Saharan Africa with North Africa. Centuries of Egyptian occupation, as well as time spent in Egypt by Nubian hostages, mercenaries, and merchants, led to a marked Egyptian cultural influence in Nubia.

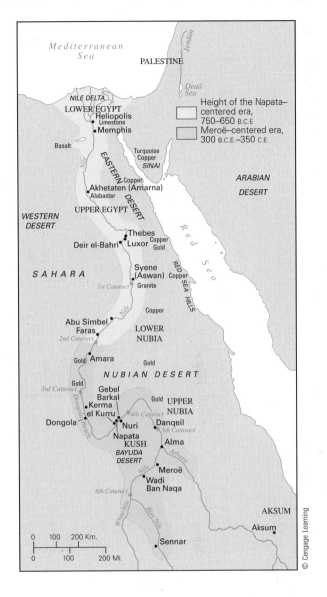

between the Egyptian garrisons and the indigenous population of northern Nubia, which continued to practice its age-old farming and herding ways.

Farther south, where the Nile makes a great U-shaped turn in the fertile plain of the Dongola Reach, a more complex political entity was evolving from the chiefdoms of the third millennium B.C.E. The Egyptians gave the name **Kush** to the kingdom whose capital was located at Kerma, one of the earliest urbanized centers in tropical Africa. Beginning around 1750 B.C.E. the kings of Kush built fortification walls and monumental structures of mud brick. The dozens or even hundreds of servants and wives sacrificed for burial with the kings, as well as the rich objects found in their tombs, testify to the wealth and power of the rulers of Kush and imply a belief in an afterlife in which attendants and possessions would be useful. Kushite craftsmen were skilled in metalworking, whether for weapons or jewelry, and produced high-quality pottery.

During the expansionist New Kingdom (ca. 1532–1070 B.C.E.), the Egyptians penetrated more deeply into Nubia (see Chapter 3). They destroyed Kush and its capital (recent archaeological excavations have shown that the Egyptians constructed a new town and palace complex a half-mile north of the abandoned native city) and extended their frontier to the Fourth Cataract. A high-ranking Egyptian official called "Overseer of Southern Lands" or "King's Son of Kush" ruled Nubia from a new administrative center at Napata (nah-PAH-tuh), near Gebel Barkal (JEB-uhl BAHR-kahl), the "Holy Mountain," believed to be the home of a local god. Exploiting the mines of Nubia, Egypt supplied gold to the states of the Middle East. Fatalities were high among native workers in the brutal desert climate, and the army had to ward off attacks from desert nomads.

Five hundred years of Egyptian domination in Nubia left many marks. The Egyptian government imposed Egyptian culture on the native population. Children from elite families were brought to the Egyptian royal court to guarantee the good behavior of their relatives in Nubia; they absorbed Egyptian language, culture, and religion, which they later carried home with them. Other Nubians served as archers in the Egyptian armed forces. The manufactured goods that they brought back to Nubia have been found in their graves. The Nubians built towns on the Egyptian model and erected stone temples to Egyptian gods, particularly Amon. The frequent depiction of Amon with the head of a ram may reflect a blending of the chief Egyptian god with a Nubian ram deity.

The Kingdom of Meroë, 800 B.C.E.–350 C.E.   Egypt's weakness after 1200 B.C.E. led to the collapse of its authority in Nubia. In the eighth century B.C.E. a powerful new native kingdom emerged in southern Nubia. Its history can be divided into two parts. During the early period, between the eighth and fourth centuries B.C.E., Napata, the former Egyptian headquarters, was the primary center. During the later period, from the fourth century B.C.E. to the fourth century C.E., the center was farther south, at **Meroë** (MER-oh-ee), near the Sixth Cataract.

For half a century, from around 712 to 660 B.C.E., the kings of Nubia ruled all of Egypt as the Twenty-fifth Dynasty, conducting themselves in the age-old manner of Egyptian rulers. They were addressed by royal titles, depicted in traditional costume, and buried according to Egyptian custom. However, they kept their Nubian names and were depicted with the physical features of sub-Saharan Africans. They also inaugurated an artistic and cultural renaissance, building on a monumental scale for the first time in centuries and reinvigorating Egyptian art, architecture, and religion. The Nubian kings resided at Memphis, the Old Kingdom capital, while Thebes, the New Kingdom capital, was the residence of a celibate female member of the king's family who was titled "God's Wife of Amon."

The Nubian dynasty made a disastrous mistake in 701 B.C.E. when it offered help to local rulers in Palestine who were struggling against the Assyrian Empire. The Assyrians retaliated by invading Egypt and driving the Nubian monarchs back to their southern domain by 660 B.C.E. Napata again became the chief royal residence and religious center of the kingdom. However, Egyptian cultural influences remained strong. Court documents continued to be written in Egyptian hieroglyphs, and the mummified remains of the rulers were buried in modestly sized sandstone pyramids along with hundreds of shawabti (shuh-WAB-tee) figurines.

By the fourth century B.C.E. the center of gravity had shifted south to Meroë, perhaps because Meroë was better situated for agriculture and trade, the economic mainstays of the Nubian kingdom. As a result, sub-Saharan cultural patterns gradually replaced Egyptian ones. Egyptian hieroglyphs gave way to a new set of symbols, still essentially undeciphered, for writing the Meroitic language. People continued to worship Amon as well as Isis, an Egyptian goddess connected to fertility and sexuality, but those deities had to share the stage with Nubian deities like the lion-god Apedemak. Meroitic art combined Egyptian, Greco-Roman, and indigenous traditions.

Women of the royal family played an important role in Meroitic politics, another reflection of the influence of sub-Saharan Africa. In their matrilineal system the king was succeeded by the son of his sister. Nubian queens sometimes ruled by themselves and sometimes in partnership with their husbands, playing a part in warfare, diplomacy, and the building of temples and pyramid tombs. They are depicted in scenes reserved for male rulers in Egyptian imagery, smiting enemies in battle and being suckled by the mother-goddess Isis.

Meroë was a huge city for its time, more than a square mile in area, dominating fertile grasslands and converging trade routes. Great reservoirs were dug to catch precious rainfall, and the city was a major center for iron smelting. Although much of the city is still buried under the sand, in 2002 archaeologists using a magnetometer to detect buried structures discovered a large palace. The Temple of Amon was approached by an avenue lined with stone rams, and the walled precinct of the "Royal City" was filled with palaces, temples, and administrative buildings. The ruler, who may have been regarded as divine, was assisted by a professional class of officials, priests, and army officers.

Meroë collapsed in the early fourth century C.E., overrun by nomads from the western desert who had become more mobile because of the arrival of the camel in North Africa. It had already been weakened when profitable commerce with the Roman Empire was diverted to the Red Sea and to the rising kingdom of Aksum (AHK-soom) (in present-day Ethiopia). Thus the end of the Meroitic kingdom was as closely linked to Nubia's role in long-distance commerce as its beginning.

PASTORAL NOMADS OF THE EURASIAN STEPPES, 1000–100 B.C.E.

Early Nomadism   **Nomads** (from a Greek word meaning "wanderers") are people who do not have a single, settled place of residence, but rather move from one temporary encampment to another, usually as a strategy for feeding themselves. For most of human history people were nomadic hunter-gatherers, moving about in search of wild plants they could harvest and animals they could kill. It was only with the Agricultural Revolutions—the domestication of plants and animals—beginning around 10,000 years ago that human groups were able to settle in one place, build permanent homes, acquire more possessions, and create more complex societies (see Chapter 1).

The domestication of herd animals, such as sheep, goats, and cattle, made possible a new kind of nomadism in which people lived off the products of their animals, consuming the meat, milk and other dairy products, clothing themselves with hair and hides, and utilizing animal manure to fuel fires. We have already seen several examples of nomadic peoples, initially living on the fringes of the settled, agricultural areas in early western Asia and, in some cases, eventually settling down and assimilating to the cultures of the more advanced agricultural peoples—the Amorites who migrated into southern Mesopotamia and founded Babylon in the early second millennium B.C.E. (see Chapter 2); the Aramaeans who settled in Syria-Palestine and whose language, Aramaic, became widespread in that region; and the early Israelites, whose migratory lifestyle was remembered in the traditions about the patriarchs Abraham, Isaac and Jacob (see Chapter 3). Many scholars believe that the proto-Indo-Europeans, speakers of the language or languages ancestral to the large family of Indo-European languages found across much of Europe and Asia, were nomadic herders who migrated from an original homeland north of the Black and Caspian Seas beginning in the third millennium B.C.E. They are believed to have first domesticated horses, which enhanced their ability to herd other animals (see Chapter 1).

Steppe Nomads   Our concern here is with a new kind of pastoral nomadism that arose across the vast Eurasian Steppes in the first millennium B.C.E. **Steppe**—a word of Russian origin—is used to describe an ecological zone characterized by treeless, grass- and shrub-covered plains and marked by a relatively arid climate with too little precipitation for agriculture and radical extremes of temperature from summer to winter and day to night. The Eurasian Steppes extend from Hungary in eastern Europe across Ukraine and southern Russia, Central Asia, Mongolia, and southern Siberia. The peoples who occupied these lands became horse-riding warriors, driving their herds to seasonal camping grounds and being careful not to overexploit pastures and water sources to the point that they could not recover and be used again. They didn't wander randomly, but rather operated within certain territorial bounds worked out with other groups. Normally they relocated to familiar encampments appropriate to their needs in different seasons. The success of this way of life also depended on a symbiotic interaction of the nomads with settled agricultural peoples, often by trading animal products (live animals, meat, hides, wool, cheese) for agricultural products and manufactured goods (metalwork and textiles), sometimes by raiding and stealing.

Because they lacked the technology of writing, we know relatively little about these peoples and must depend on the information provided by archaeology and the accounts of nomads in the records of literate ancient peoples. Greek and Roman texts tell us something about the peoples on the western range of the steppes, while Chinese sources inform us about the peoples of the eastern side. While there were, no doubt, significant ethnic and linguistic differences among these peoples, they shared many features of technology, culture, and political and social organization, due, in large part, to their mobility and the speed with which objects and ideas could move across this open landscape. Indeed, the steppe was the conduit by which products, such as wheat, and technologies, including bronze

Scythian Gold Pectoral *This gold pectoral (decorative item worn over the breast), found in Ukraine and dating to the fourth century B.C.E., displays the beauty and quality of craftsmanship of Scythian art. The lower register shows griffins attacking a horse, while two men with quivers examine a fleece shirt in the upper register.*

Ria Novosti/Alamy

and iron metalworking, chariots, and cavalry warfare, traveled from western and Central Asia to East Asia.

While the origins of pastoral nomadism on the steppe are shrouded in the mists of prehistory, a picture begins to emerge in the centuries just after 1000 B.C.E. The first Greek historian, **Herodotus** (fifth century B.C.E.), claims that the nomadic Cimmerians, driven out of their northern homelands by another nomadic people, the **Scythians**, invaded Anatolia (modern Turkey) in the seventh century B.C.E., and the Cimmerians are also mentioned in Assyrian records from the late eighth and seventh centuries B.C.E.

The Scythians   Herodotus devoted many pages to an account of the Scythian lands and peoples. The Greeks used the term *Scythian* in a very broad and general way to describe peoples living to the north and east of their Aegean homeland: the lands north of the Black and Caspian Seas, or present-day Ukraine and southern Russia. While the Greeks lumped together various peoples who probably would not have regarded themselves as belonging to the same ethnic group, the Scythians were, according to most experts, speakers of languages belonging to the Iranian subgroup of the Indo-European language family. Because Greeks had established colonies around the coasts of the Black Sea, Herodotus was able to travel in this region, and his report, based primarily on information derived from Greek traders who traveled far inland and Scythian natives who interacted with the Greeks, is generally reliable. Some scholars have suggested that Herodotus is also employing the Scythians as a "mirror," emphasizing how different they were in lifestyle, culture, and values from the Greeks as an indirect way of highlighting aspects of Greek civilization.

For Herodotus, the fundamental quality of the Scythians was that they were nomads, people without cities or permanent homes who migrated with their herds of sheep, goats, and cattle and their prized horses, transporting their few possessions and living in carts. They belonged to tribal kinship groups ruled by kings. They are depicted as exceedingly warlike and savage; their chief god is equated with the Greek god of war, Ares, and they are said to drink the blood of their enemies, to cut off their enemies' heads as trophies, and to make goblets out of the skulls and napkins and coats from the skins. They had no images of the gods, no shrines and no altars, and employed a sacrificial ritual quite different from that of the Greeks that sometimes included human sacrifice. When their kings died, they were accompanied in the grave by murdered servants, guards, and horses. In an amusing passage, Herodotus betrays his puzzlement at how they threw brush (presumably cannabis, the plant source for marijuana) on a fire and appeared to be drunk, and how they cleaned their bodies by cavorting in cannabis steam baths. Herodotus also makes clear that not all Scythians were strictly nomadic; some engaged in a mixed pastoral and agricultural economy, and some (perhaps influenced by the nearby Greek settlers) were settled agriculturalists. These observations reinforce the idea that nomadic pastoralists required some form of access to agricultural peoples and the food and goods that they produced.

Herodotus then describes what he sees as the disastrous attempt of the Persian king Darius to invade the lands of the Scythians at the end of the sixth century B.C.E. Because the Scythians lacked permanent settlements and cultivated fields, there were no obvious targets for the Persians to attack and hold hostage. And because the nomads were exceedingly mobile, they were able to move away from the invaders, drawing them ever further into unknown territory and practicing a "scorched earth" policy of burning the grass and destroying the wells. They clearly felt that there was no shame in retreating, and when, at one point, the Persians were finally drawn up for battle with a contingent of Scythian troops, a hare darted across an open space and all the Scythians took off in pursuit of it. At this point, the Persian king realized that the Scythians were toying with him, and it was all he could do to make a successful escape home with part of his army. Herodotus is obviously taking pleasure at the discomfiture of the powerful Persians, and he may misunderstand Darius's purpose in the invasion—to drive the Scythians far from Persian-controlled lands. Nevertheless, he has brilliantly illustrated the unique difficulties that nomads presented to even powerful ancient states and empires, many of whom found it cheaper to just buy off the nomads by giving them "gifts" in return for not attacking.

China and the Nomads   Chinese sources provide glimpses of the nomadic peoples living at the other end of the Eurasian Steppes, and these accounts usually match up very closely with those of Herodotus and other Greek and Roman sources, proving the relative cultural and technological uniformity of the Eurasian steppe nomads. Again, it appears that an economy based on pastoral nomadism was taking shape on the steppes in central and eastern Asia in the early first millennium B.C.E. As the Chinese states of the Spring and Autumn and Warring States periods came under increasing pressure from raiding by swift-moving, horse-borne warriors, they began to build walls along their northern frontiers to keep the raiders out, and in the late fourth century

B.C.E. the forward-thinking ruler of the state of Zhao took the unprecedented step of outfitting some of his troops with trousers and mounting them on horseback.

Our fullest Chinese account of the northern nomads comes from **Sima Qian** (Sih-muh Chyen) (ca. 100 B.C.E.), who in many ways corresponds to Herodotus as "the father of history" in East Asia. Like Herodotus, he may have been using his description of the Xiongnu (Shawng-noo) nomads to highlight characteristic aspects of Chinese civilization. Sima Qian served at the court of the Han emperor Wu and therefore had access to records in the imperial archives and earlier historical texts, as well as some experience traveling on official business among the barbarians.

Sima Qian reports that the Xiongnu had no cities, no fixed dwellings, no agriculture, and no writing. They migrated with their herds to pastures and sources of water. They were trained as warriors from an early age, and for this reason the young and fit were given preference over the old and useless. Though tough and warlike by nature, they felt no shame in retreating when necessary. Their armies lacked discipline and order, and they largely fought for their own personal gain. They swooped in like birds and vanished just as quickly, and they cut off the heads of their vanquished enemies. As with the Scythians, human sacrifice was a component of royal funerals. In Sima Qian's account, a former Chinese official who has defected to the nomads points out that, unlike the Chinese, their lives are simple and unencumbered by excessive rules, rituals, or bureaucracy. Again, the Xiongnu either controlled or were allied to groups that practiced agriculture, which gave them access to items they could not produce themselves. Many scholars believe that the Xiongnu and several other nomadic peoples on the East Asian steppe spoke Turkic languages, while the Yuezhi (Yweh-juhr), located further west, spoke an Indo-European language.

In addition to information from ancient texts like those of Herodotus and Sima Qian, archaeological excavation has illuminated our understanding of the culture of pastoral nomads. Because of the lack of permanent settlements, the primary targets of archaeology have been the large burial mounds of the elite. In a number of cases the permafrost of Siberia has preserved materials, such as textiles, that normally do not survive in the archaeological record. The art of the nomads—mainly golden jewelry, horse fittings, and colorful carpets and other textiles—is beautiful to the modern eye, with its emphasis on animals, real and fantastic, often shown in combat and in twisting, interlocked poses that conform gracefully to the surface on which they are displayed.

As we will see in subsequent chapters, the nomadic pastoralists of the steppe were, at the least, a constant nuisance to the sedentary agricultural peoples living on their borders. Under normal circumstances the relatively small, fractious tribal groups were as prone to fight each other as to raid the lands and possessions of the farmers in neighboring areas. However, from time to time they united in great confederacies under charismatic leaders, and then they presented a serious military threat even to great states and empires. The Han Chinese emperors would be at war for centuries with the Xiongnu; the Parthians would take over Iran and much of Mesopotamia and become Rome's only great-power rival (see Chapter 6); the late Roman Empire would be hard-pressed by Avars and Huns; and in the medieval period the Mongols and several Turkic peoples would overrun most of Asia (see Chapter 13). While nomadism has become increasingly rare in the industrialized and urbanized modern world, it has been estimated that 30 to 40 million people still practice this ancient way of life, primarily in Central Asia and the West African Sahel region.

CELTIC EUROPE, 1000–50 B.C.E.

The southern peninsulas of Europe—present-day Spain, Italy, and Greece—share in the mild climate of all the Mediterranean lands and are separated from "continental" Europe to the north by high mountains (the Pyrenees and Alps). Consequently, the history of southern Europe in antiquity is primarily connected to that of the Mediterranean and Middle East, at least until the Roman conquests north of the Alps (see Chapters 3, 5, and 6).

Continental Europe (including the modern nations of France, Germany, Switzerland, Austria, the Czech Republic, Slovakia, Hungary, Poland, and Romania)— was well suited to agriculture and herding. It contained broad plains with good soil and had a temperate climate with cold winters, warm summers, and ample rainfall. It was well endowed with natural resources such as timber and metals, and large, navigable rivers facilitated travel and trade.

Humans had lived in this part of Europe for many thousands of years (see Chapter 1), but their lack of any system of writing severely limits our knowledge of the earliest inhabitants. Around 500 B.C.E., as Celtic peoples spread from their original homeland across a substantial portion of Europe, they came into contact with the literate societies of the Mediterranean and thereby entered the historical record. Information about the early **Celts** (kelts) comes from the archaeological record, the accounts of Greek and Roman travelers and conquerors, and the oral traditions of Celtic Wales and Ireland that were written down during the European Middle Ages.

The Spread of the Celts

The term *Celtic* refers to a branch of the large Indo-European family of languages found throughout Europe and in western and southern Asia. Scholars link the Celtic language group to archaeological remains first appearing in parts of present-day Germany, Austria, and the Czech Republic after 1000 B.C.E. Many early Celts lived in or near hill-forts—lofty natural locations made more defensible by earthwork fortifications. By 500 B.C.E. Celtic elites were trading with Mediterranean societies for crafted goods and wine. This contact may have stimulated the new styles of Celtic manufacture and art that appeared at this time.

These new cultural features coincided with a period in which Celtic groups migrated to many parts of Europe. The motives behind these population movements, the precise timing, and the manner in which they were carried out are not well understood. Celts occupied nearly all of France and much of Britain and Ireland, and they merged with indigenous peoples to create the Celtiberian culture of northern Spain. Other Celtic groups overran northern Italy (they sacked Rome in 490 B.C.E.), raided into central Greece, and settled in central Anatolia (modern Turkey). By 300 B.C.E. Celtic peoples were spread across Europe north of the Alps, from present-day Hungary to Spain and Ireland. Their traces remain in many place names in Europe today.

These widely diffused Celtic groups shared elements of language and culture, but there was no Celtic "nation," for they were divided into hundreds of small, loosely organized kinship groups. In the past scholars built up a generic picture of Celtic society derived largely from the observations of Greek and Roman writers. Current scholarship is focusing attention on the differences as much as the similarities among Celtic peoples. It is unlikely that the ancient Celts identified themselves as belonging to anything akin to our modern conception of "Celtic civilization."

Greek and Roman writers were struck by the appearance of male Celts—their burly size, long red hair, shaggy mustaches, and loud, deep voices—and by their strange apparel, trousers (usually an indication of horse-riding peoples) and twisted gold neck collars. Particularly terrifying were the warriors who fought naked and made trophies of the heads of defeated enemies. Surviving accounts describe the Celts as wildly fond of war, courageous, childishly impulsive and emotional, and fond of boasting and exaggeration, yet quick-witted and eager to learn.

Celtic Society   One of the best sources of information about Celtic society is the account of the Roman general Gaius Julius Caesar, who conquered Gaul (present-day France) between 58 and 51 B.C.E. Many Celtic groups in Gaul had once been ruled by kings, but by the time of the Roman invasion they periodically chose public officials, perhaps under Greek and Roman influence.

Celtic society was divided into an elite class of warriors, professional groups of priests and bards (singers of poems about glorious deeds of the past), and commoners. The warriors owned land and flocks of cattle and sheep and monopolized both wealth and power. The common people labored on their land. The Celts built houses (usually round in Britain, rectangular in France) out of wattle and daub—a wooden framework filled in with clay and straw—with thatched straw roofs. Several such houses belonging to related families might be surrounded by a wooden fence for protection.

The warriors of Welsh and Irish legend reflect a stage of political and social development less complex than that of the Celts in Gaul. They raided one another's flocks, reveled in drunken feasts, and engaged in contests of strength and wit. At banquets warriors would fight to the death just to claim the choicest cut of the meat, the "hero's portion."

Druids, the Celtic priests in Gaul and Britain, formed a well-organized fraternity that performed religious, judicial, and educational functions. Trainees spent years memorizing prayers, secret rituals, legal precedents, and other traditions. The priesthood was the one Celtic institution that crossed tribal lines. The Druids sometimes headed off warfare between feuding groups and served as judges in cases involving Celts from different groups. In the first century C.E. the Roman government attempted to stamp out the Druids, probably because of concern that they might serve as a rallying point for Celtic opposition to Roman rule and also because of their involvement in human sacrifices.

The Celts supported large populations by tilling the heavy but fertile soils of continental Europe. Their metallurgical skills probably surpassed those of the Mediterranean peoples. Celts on the Atlantic shore of France built sturdy ships that braved ocean conditions, and they developed extensive trade networks along Europe's large, navigable rivers. One lucrative commodity was tin, which Celtic traders from southwest England brought to Greek buyers in southern France. By the first century B.C.E. some hill-forts were evolving into urban centers.

Women's lives were focused on child rearing, food production, and some crafts. Their situation was superior to that of women in the Middle East and in the Greek and Roman Mediterranean. Greek and Roman sources depict Celtic women as strong and proud. Welsh and Irish tales portray clever, self-assured women who sit at banquets with their husbands and engage in witty conversation. Marriage was a partnership to which both parties contributed property. Each had the right to inherit the estate if the other died. Celtic women also had greater freedom in their sexual relations than did their southern counterparts.

Tombs of elite women have yielded rich collections of clothing, jewelry, and furniture for use in the next world. Daughters of the elite were married to leading

Universal History Archive/Getty Images

The Gundestrup Cauldron *This silver vessel was found in a peat bog in Denmark, but it must have come from elsewhere. It is usually dated to the second or first century B.C.E. On the inside right are Celtic warriors on horse and on foot, with lozenge-shaped shields and long battle-horns. On the inside left is a horned deity, possibly Cernunnos.* .

members of other tribes to create alliances. When the Romans invaded Celtic Britain in the first century C.E., they sometimes were opposed by Celtic tribes headed by queens, although some experts see this as an abnormal circumstance created by the Roman invasion itself.

Belief and Knowledge

Historians know the names of more than four hundred Celtic gods and goddesses, mostly associated with particular localities or kinship groups. More widely revered deities included Lug (loog), the god of light, crafts, and inventions; the horse-goddess Epona (eh-POH-nuh); and the horned god Cernunnos (KURN-you-nuhs). "The Mothers," three goddesses depicted together holding symbols of abundance, probably played a part in a fertility cult. Halloween and May Day preserve the ancient Celtic holidays of Samhain (SAH-win) and Beltaine (BEHL-tayn), respectively, which took place at key moments in the agricultural cycle.

The early Celts did not build temples but instead worshiped wherever they felt the presence of divinity—at springs, groves, and hilltops. At the sources of the Seine and Marne Rivers in France, archaeologists have found huge caches of wooden statues thrown into the water by worshipers.

The burial of elite members of early Celtic society in wagons filled with extensive grave goods suggests belief in some sort of afterlife. In Irish and Welsh legends, heroes and gods pass back and forth between the natural and supernatural worlds much more readily than in the mythology of many other cultures, and magical occurrences are commonplace. Celtic priests set forth a doctrine of reincarnation—the rebirth of the soul in a new body.

The Roman conquest from the second century B.C.E. to the first century C.E. of Spain, southern Britain, France, and parts of central Europe curtailed the evolution of Celtic society, as the peoples in these lands were largely assimilated to Roman ways (see Chapter 6). As a result, the inhabitants of modern Spain and France speak languages that are descended from Latin. From the third century C.E. on, Germanic invaders weakened the Celts still further, and the English language has a Germanic base. Only on the western fringes of the European continent—in Brittany (northwest France), Wales, Scotland, and Ireland—did Celtic peoples maintain their language, art, and culture into modern times.

Conclusion

Environment and Organization

The civilizations of early China, Nubia, the Eurasian Steppes, and the Celts emerged in very different ecological contexts in widely separated parts of the Eastern Hemisphere, and the patterns of organization, technology, behavior, and belief that they developed were, in large part, responses to the challenges and opportunities of those environments.

In the North China Plain, as in the river-valley civilizations of Mesopotamia and Egypt, the presence of great, flood-prone rivers and the lack of dependable rainfall led to the formation of powerful institutions capable of organizing large numbers of people to dig and maintain irrigation channels and build dikes. An authoritarian central government has been a recurring feature of Chinese history from at least as early as the Shang monarchy.

In Nubia, the initial impetus for the formation of a strong state was the need for protection from desert nomads and from the Egyptian rulers who coveted Nubian gold and other resources. Control of these resources and of the trade route between sub-Saharan Africa and the north, as well as the agricultural surplus to feed administrators and specialists in the urban centers, made the rulers and elites of Kerma, Napata, and Meroë wealthy and powerful.

Pastoral nomads found ways to exploit the challenging environment of the Eurasian Steppes. The very nature of their lifestyle, based on migrating with their herds of domesticated animals to seasonal camping grounds, meant that they had no permanent settlements and maintained small, kinship-based groups. Thus, under normal circumstances, their political organization was relatively simple. However, in moments of crisis or when a charismatic military leader came to the fore, they could unite in formidable confederacies.

The Celtic peoples of continental Europe never developed a strong state. They occupied fertile lands with adequate rainfall for agriculture, grazing territory for flocks, and timber for fuel and construction. Kinship groups dominated by warrior elites and controlling compact territories were the usual form of organization. The Celtic elites of central Europe initially traded for luxury goods with the Mediterranean; when they began to expand into lands to the west and south after 500 B.C.E., they came into even closer contact with Mediterranean peoples. Eventually many Celtic groups were incorporated into the Roman Empire.

Religion and Power

In these, as in most human societies, the elites used religion to bolster their position. The Shang rulers of China were indispensable intermediaries between their kingdom and powerful and protective ancestors and gods. Bronze vessels were used to make offerings to ancestral spirits, and divination by means of oracle bones delivered information of value to the ruler and kingdom. Their Zhou successors developed the concept of the ruler as divine Son of Heaven who ruled in accord with the Mandate of Heaven.

In its religious practices, as in other spheres, the civilization that developed in Nubia was powerfully influenced by its interactions with the more complex and technologically advanced neighboring society in Egypt. Nubian rulers built temples and pyramid tombs on the Egyptian model, but they also synthesized Egyptian and indigenous gods, beliefs, and rituals.

While not much is known about the religious beliefs and practices of the steppe nomads, their mobility and lack of permanent settlements may account for the fact that they didn't build monumental religious shrines. Greco-Roman and Chinese accounts report, and archaeology confirms, that they sacrificed animals, and sometimes human victims, to their gods. The elaborate goods found in elite burials imply belief in an afterlife, and shamans were able to make contact with the gods and the dead.

Among the Celtic peoples of Gaul and Britain, the Druids constituted an elite class of priests who performed vital religious, legal, and educational functions.

However, the Celts did not construct temples and ceremonial centers, and instead worshiped hundreds of gods and goddesses in natural surroundings, where they felt the presence of divinity.

A Tale of Two Hemispheres   This chapter has moved beyond the core area of the two oldest complex human societies (Mesopotamia and Egypt), and the neighboring peoples who came under their cultural influence, to focus on East Asia, sub-Saharan Africa, continental Europe, and the vast steppe region linking Europe, Central, and East Asia. It thus continues the discussion of the rise of complex societies in the Eastern Hemisphere.

The societies in the other half of the world, the Western Hemisphere, are discussed in Chapter 8. These civilizations—the Olmec in Mesoamerica and Chavín in South America—while contemporary with the societies featured in this chapter, emerged several millennia later than the earliest complex societies in the Eastern Hemisphere. Scholars have debated why powerful civilizations appeared many centuries later in the Western Hemisphere than in the Eastern Hemisphere, and recent theories have focused on environmental differences. The Eastern Hemisphere was home to a far larger number of wild plant and animal species that were particularly well suited to domestication. In addition, the natural east-west axis of the huge landmass of Europe and Asia allowed for the relatively rapid spread of domesticated plants and animals to climatically similar zones along the same latitudes. Settled agriculture led to population growth, more complex political and social organization, and increased technological sophistication. In the Americas, by contrast, there were fewer wild plant and animal species that could be domesticated, and the north-south axis of the continents made it more difficult for domesticated species to spread because of variations in climate at different latitudes. As a result, the processes that foster the development of complex societies evolved somewhat more slowly.

IMPORTANT EVENTS 2300 B.C.E. TO 350 C.E.

1750 B.C.E.	Rise of kingdom of Kush based on Kerma
1750–1045 B.C.E.	Shang dynasty
1500 B.C.E.	Egyptian conquest of Nubia
1200–900 B.C.E.	Rise of Olmec civilization, centered on San Lorenzo
1045–221 B.C.E.	Zhou dynasty
1000 B.C.E.	Decline of Egyptian control in Nubia
1000 B.C.E.	Origin of Celtic culture in Central Europe
900–250 B.C.E.	Chavín civilization in the Andes
750 B.C.E.	Rise of kingdom based on Napata
600–400 B.C.E.	Ascendancy of Tres Zapotes and Olmec decline
390 B.C.E.	Celts sack Rome
356–338 B.C.E.	Lord Shang brings Legalist reforms to Qin state

Animal Domestication

Because the earliest domestication of plants and animals took place long before the existence of written records, we cannot be sure how and when humans first learned to plant crops and make use of tamed animals. Historians usually link the two processes as part of an Agricultural Revolution, but they were not necessarily connected.

The domestication of plants is much better understood than the domestication of animals. Foraging bands of humans primarily lived on wild seeds, fruits, and tubers. Eventually some humans tried planting seeds and tubers, favoring varieties that they particularly liked, and a variety that may have been rare in the wild became more common. When such a variety suited human needs, usually by having more food value or being easier to grow or process, people stopped collecting the wild types and relied on farming and further developing their new domestic type.

In the case of animals, the basis of selection to suit human needs is less apparent. Experts looking at ancient bones and images interpret changes in hair color, horn shape, and other visible features as indicators of domestication. But these visible changes did not generally serve human purposes. It is usually assumed that animals were domesticated for their meat, but even this is questionable. Dogs, which may have become

Nomadic Pastoralists on the Eurasian Steppe *The domestication of animals engendered a new form of nomadism, enabling certain populations to live in the treeless grasslands of the steppe and move with their animals and portable dwellings to a sequence of water sources and grazing grounds.*

Paul Harris/Getty Images

domestic tens of thousands of years before any other species, were not eaten in most cultures, and cats, which became domestic much later, were eaten even less often. As for the uses most commonly associated with domestic animals, some of the most important, such as milking cows, shearing sheep, and harnessing oxen and horses to pull plows and vehicles, first appeared hundreds and even thousands of years after domestication.

Cattle, sheep, and goats became domestic around ten thousand years ago in the Middle East and North Africa. Coincidentally, wheat and barley were being domesticated at roughly the same time in the same general area. This is the main reason historians generally conclude that plant and animal domestication are closely related. Yet other major meat animals, such as chickens, which originated as jungle fowl in Southeast Asia, and pigs, which probably became domestic separately in several parts of North Africa, Europe, and Asia, have no agreed-upon association with early plant domestication. Nor is plant domestication connected with the horses and camels that became domestic in western Asia and the donkeys that became domestic in the Sahara region around six thousand years ago. Moreover, though the wild forebears of these species were probably eaten, the domestic forms were usually not used for meat.

In the Middle East humans may have originally kept wild sheep, goats, and cattle for food, though wild cattle were large and dangerous and must have been hard to control. It is questionable whether, in the earliest stages, keeping these animals captive for food would have been more productive than hunting. It is even more questionable whether the humans who kept animals for this purpose had any reason to anticipate that life in captivity would cause them to become domestic.

Human motivations for domesticating animals can be better assessed after a consideration of the physical changes involved in going from wild to domestic. Genetically transmitted tameness, defined as the ability to live with and accept handling by humans, lies at the core of the domestication process. In separate experiments with wild rats and foxes in the twentieth century, scientists found that wild individuals with strong fight-or-flight tendencies reproduce poorly in captivity, whereas individuals with the lowest adrenaline levels have the most offspring in captivity. In the wild, the same low level of excitability would have made these individuals vulnerable to predators and kept their reproduction rate down. However, early humans probably preferred the animals that seemed the tamest and destroyed those that were most wild. In the rat and fox experiments, after twenty generations or so, the surviving animals were born with much smaller adrenal glands and greatly reduced fight-or-flight reactions. Since adrenaline production normally increases in the transition to adulthood, many of the low-adrenaline animals also retained juvenile characteristics, such as floppy ears and pushed-in snouts, both indicators of domestication.

Historians disagree about whether animal domestication was a deliberate process or the unanticipated outcome of keeping animals for other purposes. Some assume that domestication was an understood and reproducible process. Others argue that, since a twenty-generation time span for wild cattle and other large quadrupeds would have amounted to several human lifetimes, it is unlikely that the people who ended up with domestic cows had any recollection of how the process started. This would also rule out the possibility that people who had unwittingly domesticated one species would have attempted to repeat the process with other species, since they did not know what they and their ancestors had done to produce genetically transmitted tameness.

Historians who assume that domestication was an understood and reproducible process tend to conclude that humans domesticated every species that could be domesticated. This is unlikely. Twentieth-century efforts to domesticate bison, eland, and elk have not fully succeeded, but they have generally not been maintained for as long as twenty generations. Rats and foxes have more rapid reproduction rates, and the experiments with them succeeded.

Animal domestication is probably best studied on a case-by-case basis as an unintended result of other processes. In some instances, sacrifice probably played a key role. Religious traditions of animal sacrifice rarely utilize, and sometimes prohibit, the ritual killing of wild animals. It is reasonable to suppose that the practice of capturing wild animals and holding them for sacrifice eventually led to the appearance of genetically transmitted tameness as an unplanned result.

Horses and camels were domesticated relatively late, and most likely not for meat consumption. The societies within which these animals first appeared as domestic species already had domestic sheep, goats, and cattle for meat, and they used oxen to carry loads and pull plows and carts. Horses, camels, and later reindeer may represent successful experiments with substituting one draft animal for another, with genetically transmitted tameness an unexpected consequence of separating animals trained for riding or pulling carts from their wilder kin.

Once human societies had developed the full range of uses of domestic animals—meat, eggs, milk, fiber, labor, transport—the likelihood of domesticating more species diminished. In the absence of concrete knowledge of how domestication had occurred, it was usually easier for people to move domestic livestock to new locations than to attempt to develop new domestic species. Domestic animals accompanied human groups wherever they ventured, and this practice triggered enormous environmental changes as domestic animals, and their human keepers, competed with wild species for food and living space.

PART TWO

THE FORMATION OF NEW CULTURAL COMMUNITIES, 1000 B.C.E.–400 C.E.

CHAPTER 5
Greece and Iran, 1000–30 B.C.E.

CHAPTER 6
An Age of Empires: Rome and Han China, 753 B.C.E.–330 C.E.

CHAPTER 7
India and Southeast Asia, 1500 B.C.E.–1025 C.E.

CHAPTER 8
Peoples and Civilizations of the Americas, 1200 B.C.E.–1400 C.E.

From 1000 B.C.E. to 400 C.E. important changes occurred in the ways of life established in the river-valley civilizations in the two previous millennia, and the scale of human institutions and activities increased. On the shores of the Mediterranean and in Iran, India, and Southeast Asia, new centers arose in lands watered by rainfall and worked by a free peasantry. Similarly, in the Americas new political and religious centers developed in southern Mesoamerica and in the Andes. These societies developed new patterns of political and social organization and economic activity, at the same time moving in new intellectual, artistic, and spiritual directions.

The rulers of the empires of this era constructed extensive networks of roads and promoted urbanization, measures that brought more rapid communication, trade over greater distances, and the broad diffusion of religious ideas, artistic styles, and technologies. Large cultural zones unified by common traditions emerged—Iranian, Hellenistic, Roman, Hindu, Mesoamerican, Andean, and Chinese—and exercised substantial influence on subsequent ages.

The expansion of agriculture and trade and improvements in technology led to population increases, the spread of cities, and the growth of new social classes. In many places iron replaced bronze as the preferred metal for weapons, tools, and utensils, and metals were available to more people than in the preceding age. People using iron tools cleared extensive forests around the Mediterranean, in India, and in eastern China, while iron weapons gave an advantage to the armies of Greece, Rome, and imperial China. Progress in metallurgy developed much more slowly in the Americas. Copper and copper-alloy production developed first in the Andes and only reached Mesoamerica after 500 C.E. Iron was only introduced with the arrival of Europeans.

New systems of writing, more easily and rapidly learned, moved the preservation and transmission of knowledge out of the control of specialists and gave birth to new ways of thinking, new genres of literature, and new types of scientific endeavor.

5

GREECE AND IRAN, 1000–30 B.C.E.

The Greek historian Herodotus (heh-ROD-uh-tuhs) (ca. 485–425 B.C.E.) describes a famine on the island of Thera in the Aegean Sea in the seventh century B.C.E. that caused the desperate inhabitants to send out a portion of young men to found a new settlement called Cyrene on the coast of North Africa (modern Libya). This is one of our best descriptions of the process by which Greeks spread from their homeland to many parts of the Mediterranean and Black Seas between the eighth and sixth centuries B.C.E., carrying their language, technology, and culture with them. Cyrene became a populous and prosperous city-state, largely thanks to its exports of silphium—a plant valued for its medicinal properties—as seen on this painted cup with an image of Arcesilas, the ruler of Cyrene, supervising the weighing and transport of the product.

Greek Cyrene quietly submitted to the Persian king Cambyses (kam-BIE-sees) in the 520s B.C.E., in one of the more peaceful encounters of the city-states of Greece with the Persian Empire. This event reminds us that the Persian Empire (and the Hellenistic Greek kingdoms that succeeded it) brought together, in eastern Europe, western Asia, and northwest Africa, peoples and cultural systems that had little direct contact previously, thereby stimulating new cultural syntheses. The claim has often been made that the rivalry and wars of Greeks and Persians from the sixth to fourth centuries B.C.E. were the first act of a drama that has continued intermittently ever since: the clash of the civilizations of East and West, of two peoples and two ways of life that were fundamentally different and almost certain to come into conflict. Some see current tensions between the United States and Middle Eastern states such as Iran, Iraq, and Afghanistan as the latest manifestation of this age-old conflict.

Ironically, Greeks and Persians had more in common than they realized. Both spoke languages belonging to the same Indo-European language family found throughout Europe and western and southern Asia. Many scholars believe that all the ancient peoples who spoke languages belonging to this family inherited fundamental cultural traits, forms of social organization, and religious outlooks from their shared past.

ANCIENT IRAN, 1000–500 B.C.E.

Iran, the "land of the Aryans," links western Asia with southern and Central Asia, and its history has been marked by this mediating position. In the sixth century B.C.E. the vigorous Persians of southwest Iran created the largest empire the world had yet seen. Heirs to the long legacy of Mesopotamian culture, they introduced distinctly Iranian elements and developed new forms of political and economic organization in western Asia.

Relatively little written material from within the Persian Empire has survived, so we are forced to view it mostly through the eyes of the ancient Greeks—outsiders who were ignorant at best, often hostile, and interested primarily in events that affected themselves. (Iranian groups and individuals are known in the Western world by Greek approximations of their names; thus these familiar forms are used here, with the original Iranian names given in parentheses.) This Greek perspective leaves us less informed about developments in the central and eastern portions of

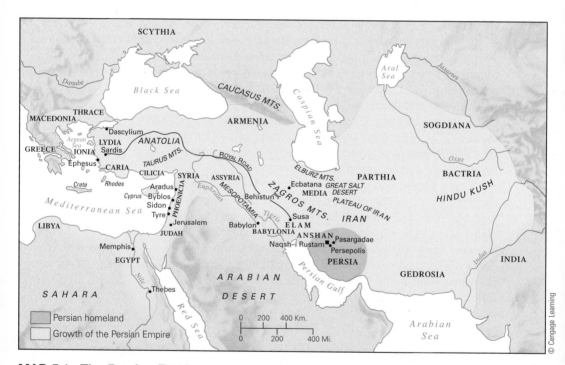

MAP 5.1 The Persian Empire

Between 550 and 522 B.C.E., the Persians of southwest Iran, under their first two kings, Cyrus and Cambyses, conquered each of the major states of western Asia—Media, Babylonia, Lydia, and Egypt. The third king, Darius I, extended the boundaries as far as the Indus Valley to the east and the European shore of the Black Sea to the west. The first major setback came when the fourth king, Xerxes, failed in his invasion of Greece in 480 B.C.E. The Persian Empire was considerably larger than its predecessor, the Assyrian Empire. For their empire, the Persian rulers developed a system of provinces, governors, regular tribute, and communication by means of royal roads and couriers that allowed for efficient operations for two centuries.

the Persian Empire. Nevertheless, recent archaeological discoveries and close analysis of the limited written material from within the empire can supplement and correct the perspective of the Greek sources.

Geography and Resources

Iran is bounded by the Zagros (ZUHG-roes) Mountains to the west, the Caucasus (KAW-kuh-suhs) Mountains and Caspian Sea to the northwest and north, the mountains of Afghanistan and the desert of Baluchistan (buh-loo-chi-STAN) to the east and southeast, and the Persian Gulf to the southwest. The northeast is less protected by natural boundaries, and from that direction Iran was open to attacks by the nomads of Central Asia.

The fundamental topographical features of Iran are high mountains at the edges, salt deserts in the interior depressions, and mountain streams draining into interior salt lakes and marshes. Ancient Iran never had a dense population. The best-watered and most populous parts of the country lie to the north and west; aridity increases and population decreases as one moves south and east. On the interior plateau, oasis settlements sprang up beside streams or springs. The Great Salt Desert, which covers most of eastern Iran, and Baluchistan in the southeast corner were extremely inhospitable. Scattered settlements in the narrow plains beside the Persian Gulf were cut off from the interior plateau by mountain barriers.

In the first millennium B.C.E. irrigation enabled people to move down from the mountain valleys and open the plains to agriculture. To prevent evaporation of precious water in the hot, dry climate, they devised underground irrigation channels. Constructing and maintaining these channels and the vertical shafts that provided access to them was labor-intensive. Normally, local leaders oversaw the expansion of the network in each district. Activity accelerated when a strong central authority organized large numbers of laborers. Even so, human survival depended on a delicate ecological balance, and a buildup of salt in the soil or a falling water table sometimes forced the abandonment of settlements.

Iran's mineral resources—copper, tin, iron, gold, and silver—were exploited on a limited scale in antiquity. Mountain slopes, more heavily wooded than they are now, provided fuel and materials for building and crafts. Because this austere land could not generate much of an agricultural surplus, objects of trade tended to be minerals and crafted goods such as textiles and carpets.

The Rise of the Persian Empire

In antiquity many groups of people, whom historians refer to collectively as "Iranians" because they spoke related languages and shared certain cultural features, spread across western and Central Asia—an area comprising not only the modern state of Iran but also Turkmenistan, Afghanistan, and Pakistan. Several of these groups arrived in western Iran near the end of the second millennium B.C.E. The first to achieve a complex level of political organization were the Medes (*Mada* in Iranian). They settled in the northwest and came under the influence of the ancient centers in Mesopotamia and Urartu (modern Armenia and northeast Turkey). The Medes played a major role in the destruction of the Assyrian Empire in the late seventh century B.C.E. According to Greek sources, Median kings extended their control westward across Assyria into Anatolia (modern Turkey) and also southeast toward the Persian Gulf, a region occupied by another Iranian people, the Persians (*Parsa*). However, some scholars doubt the Greek testimony about a well-organized Median kingdom controlling such extensive territories.

The Persian rulers—called Achaemenids (a-KEY-muh-nid) because they traced their lineage back to an ancestor named Achaemenes—cemented their relationship with the Median court through marriage. **Cyrus** (*Kurush*), the son of a Persian chieftain and a Median princess, united the various Persian tribes and overthrew the Median monarch around 550 B.C.E. His victory should perhaps be seen less as a conquest than as an alteration of the relations between groups, for Cyrus placed both Medes and Persians in positions of responsibility and retained the framework of Median rule. The differences between these two Iranian peoples were not great, and the Greeks could not readily tell them apart.

The early inhabitants of western Iran had a patriarchal family organization: the male head of the household had nearly absolute authority over family members. Society was divided into three social and occupational classes—warriors, priests, and peasants—with warriors being the dominant element. A landowning aristocracy, they took pleasure in hunting, fighting, and gardening. The king was the most illustrious member of this group. The priests, or Magi (*magush*), were ritual specialists who supervised the proper performance of sacrifices. The common people—peasants—were primarily village-based farmers and shepherds.

Over the course of two decades the energetic Cyrus (r. 550–530 B.C.E.) redrew the map of western Asia. In 546 B.C.E. he defeated the kingdom of Lydia, and all Anatolia, including the Greek city-states on the western coast, came under Persian control. In 539 B.C.E. he swept into Mesopotamia and overthrew the Neo-Babylonian dynasty that had ruled since the decline of Assyrian power (see Chapter 3). A skillful propagandist, Cyrus showed respect to the Babylonian priesthood and native traditions.

After Cyrus lost his life in 530 B.C.E. while campaigning against nomadic Iranians in the northeast, his son Cambyses (*Kambujiya*, r. 530–522 B.C.E.) set his sights on Egypt, the last of the great ancient kingdoms of the Middle East. After the Persians prevailed in a series of bloody battles, they sent exploratory expeditions south to Nubia and west to Libya. Greek sources depict Cambyses as a cruel and impious madman, but contemporary documents from Egypt show him operating in the same practical vein as his father, cultivating local priests and notables and respecting native traditions.

When Cambyses died in 522 B.C.E., a Persian nobleman distantly related to the royal family, **Darius I** (duh-RIE-uhs) (*Darayavaush*), seized the throne. His success in crushing many early challenges to his rule testifies to his skill, energy, and ruthlessness. From this reign forward, Medes played a lesser role, and the most important posts went to members of leading Persian families. Darius (r. 522–486 B.C.E.) extended Persian control eastward as far as the Indus Valley and westward into Europe, where he bridged the Danube River and chased the nomadic Scythian (SITH-ee-uhn) peoples north of the Black Sea. The Persians erected a string of forts in Thrace (modern-day northeast Greece and Bulgaria) and by 500 B.C.E. were on the doorstep of Greece. Darius also promoted the development of maritime routes. He dispatched a fleet to explore the waters from the Indus Delta to the Red Sea, and he completed a canal linking the Red Sea with the Nile.

Imperial Organization   The empire of Darius I was the largest the world had yet seen. Stretching from eastern Europe and Libya to Pakistan, from southern Russia to Sudan, it encompassed multiple ethnic groups and many forms of social and political organization. Darius can rightly be considered a second founder of the Persian Empire, after Cyrus, because he created a new organizational structure that was maintained throughout the remaining two centuries of the empire's existence.

Darius divided the empire into about twenty provinces, each under the supervision of a Persian **satrap** (SAY-trap), or governor, who was often related or connected by marriage to the royal family. The satrap's court was a miniature version of the royal court. The tendency for the position of satrap to become hereditary meant that satraps' families lived in the province governed by their head, acquired knowledge about local conditions, and formed connections with the local elite. The farther a province was from the center of the empire, the more autonomy the satrap had, because slow communications made it impractical to refer most matters to the central administration.

One of the satrap's most important duties was to collect and send tribute to the king. Darius prescribed how much precious metal each province was to contribute annually. Some of it was disbursed for necessary expenditures, but most was hoarded. As precious metal was taken out of circulation, the price of gold and silver rose, and provinces found it increasingly difficult to meet their quotas. Evidence from Babylonia indicates a gradual economic decline setting in by the fourth century B.C.E. The increasing burden of taxation and official corruption may have inadvertently caused the economic downturn.

Well-maintained and patrolled royal roads connected the outlying provinces to the heart of the empire. Way stations were built at intervals to receive important travelers and couriers carrying official correspondence. Military garrisons controlled strategic points, such as mountain passes, river crossings, and important urban centers.

The king had numerous wives and children. Women of the royal family could become pawns in the struggle for power, as when Darius strengthened his claim to the throne by marrying two daughters and a granddaughter of Cyrus. Greek sources portray Persian queens as vicious intriguers, poisoning rival wives and plotting to win the throne for their sons. However, a recent study suggests that the Greek stereotype misrepresents the important role played by Persian women in protecting family members and mediating conflicts.[1] Both Greek sources and documents within the empire reveal that Persian elite women were politically influential, possessed substantial property, traveled, and were prominent on public occasions.

The king and his court moved with the seasons, living in luxurious tents on the road and in palaces in the ancient capitals of Mesopotamia and Iran. Besides the royal family, the king's large entourage included several other groups: (1) the sons of Persian aristocrats, who were educated at court and also served as hostages for their parents' good behavior; (2) many noblemen, who were expected to attend the king when they were not otherwise engaged; (3) the central administration,

---

[1]Maria Brosius, *Women in Ancient Persia, 559–331 B.C.* (Oxford and New York: Oxford University Press, 1996).

including officials and employees of the treasury, secretariat, and archives; (4) the royal bodyguard; and (5) countless courtiers and slaves. Long gone were the simple days when the king hunted and caroused with his warrior companions. Inspired by Mesopotamian conceptions of monarchy, the king of Persia had become an aloof figure of majesty and splendor: "The Great King, King of Kings, King in Persia, King of countries." He referred to everyone, even the Persian nobility, as "my slaves," and anyone who approached him had to bow down before him.

The king owned vast tracts of land throughout the empire. Some of it he gave to his supporters. Donations called "bow land," "horse land," and "chariot land" in Babylonian documents obliged the recipient to provide the corresponding form of military service. Scattered around the empire were gardens, orchards, and hunting preserves belonging to the king and high nobility. The *paradayadam* (meaning "walled enclosure"—the term has come into English as *paradise*), a green oasis in an arid landscape, advertised the prosperity that the king could bring to those who loyally served him.

Surviving administrative records from the Persian homeland reveal how the complex tasks of administration were managed. Government officials distributed food and other essential commodities to large numbers of workers of many different nationalities. Some of these workers may have been prisoners of war brought to the center of the empire to work on construction projects, maintain and expand the irrigation network, and farm the royal estates. Workers were divided into groups of men, women, and children. Women received less than men of equivalent status, but pregnant women and women with babies received additional support. Men and women performing skilled jobs received more than their unskilled counterparts. Administrators were provided with authorizations to requisition food and other necessities while traveling on official business.

The central administration was not based in the Persian homeland but closer to the geographical center of the empire, in Elam and Mesopotamia, where it could employ the trained administrators and scribes of those ancient civilizations. The administrative center of the empire was Susa, the ancient capital of Elam, in southwest Iran near the present-day border with Iraq. It was to Susa that Greeks and others went with requests and messages for the king. A party of Greek ambassadors would need at least three months to make the journey. Additional time spent waiting for an audience with the Persian king, delays due to weather, and the duration of the return trip probably kept the ambassadors away from home a year or more.

However, on certain occasions the kings returned to one special place back in the homeland. Darius began construction of a ceremonial capital at **Persepolis** (per-SEH-poe-lis) (*Parsa*). An artificial platform was erected, and on it were built a series of palaces, audience halls, treasury buildings, and barracks. Here, too, Darius and his son Xerxes (ZERK-sees), who completed the project, were inspired by Mesopotamian traditions, for the great Assyrian kings had created new fortress-cities as advertisements of their wealth and power.

Ideology and Religion   Darius's approach to governing can be seen in the luxuriant relief sculpture that covers the foundations, walls, and stairwells of the buildings at Persepolis. Representatives of all the peoples of the empire—recognizable by their distinctive hair, beards, dress, hats, and footwear—are depicted bringing gifts to the king. In this exercise in what today we would call public relations or propaganda, Darius crafted a vision of an empire of vast extent and abundant resources in which all the subject peoples willingly cooperate. On his tomb Darius subtly contrasted the character of his rule with that of the Assyrian Empire, the Persians' predecessors in these lands (see Chapter 3). Where Assyrian kings had gloried in their power and depicted subjects staggering under the weight of a giant platform that supported the throne, Darius's artists showed erect subjects shouldering the burden willingly and without strain.

What actually took place at Persepolis? This opulent retreat in the homeland was the scene of events of special significance for the king and his people: the New Year's Festival, coronation, marriage, death, and burial. The kings from Darius on were buried in elaborate tombs cut into the cliffs at nearby Naqsh-i Rustam (NUHK-shee ROOS-tuhm).

Another perspective on what the Persian monarchy claimed to stand for is provided by several dozen royal inscriptions that have survived. At Naqsh-i Rustam, Darius makes the following claim:

> Ahuramazda (ah-HOOR-uh-MAZZ-duh) [the chief deity], when he saw this earth in commotion, thereafter bestowed it upon me, made me king.... By the favor of Ahuramazda I put it down in its place.... I am of such a sort that I am a friend to right, I am not a friend to wrong. It is not my desire that the weak man should have wrong done to him by the mighty; nor is that my desire, that the mighty man should have wrong done to him by the weak.[2]

As this inscription makes clear, behind Darius and the empire stands the will of god. Ahuramazda made Darius king, giving him a mandate to bring order to a world in turmoil and ensure that all people be treated justly. Ahuramazda is the great god of a religion called **Zoroastrianism** (zo-roe-ASS-tree-uh-niz-uhm), and it is probable that Darius and his successors were Zoroastrians.

The origins of this religion are shrouded in uncertainty. The *Gathas*, hymns in an archaic Iranian dialect, are said to be the work of Zoroaster (zo-roe-ASS-ter) (*Zarathushtra*), who probably lived in eastern Iran sometime between 1700 and 500 B.C.E. He revealed that the world had been created by Ahuramazda, "the wise lord," but its original state of perfection and unity had been badly damaged by the attacks of Angra Mainyu (ANG-ruh MINE-yoo), "the hostile spirit," backed by a host of demons. The struggle between good and evil plays out over thousands of years, with good ultimately destined to prevail. Humanity is a participant in this cosmic struggle, and individuals are rewarded or punished in the afterlife for their actions in life.

Darius has brilliantly joined the moral theology of Zoroastrianism to political ideology. In essence, he is claiming that the divinely ordained mission of the empire is to bring all the scattered peoples of the world back together again under a regime of justice and thereby to restore the perfection of creation.

---

[2]Quoted in Roland G. Kent, *Old Persian: Grammar, Texts, Lexicon,* 2d ed. (New Haven, CT: American Oriental Society, 1953), 138, 140.

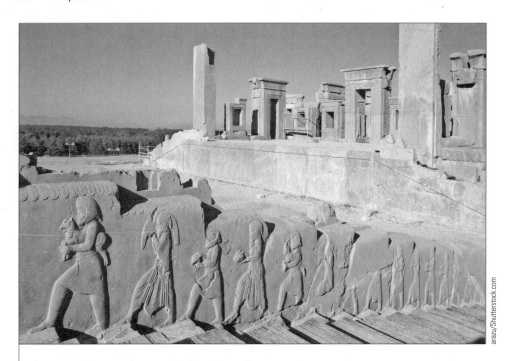

Sculpted Images on a Stairwell at Persepolis, ca. 500 B.C.E. *Persepolis, in the Persian homeland, was built by Darius I and his son Xerxes, and it was used for ceremonies of special importance to the Persian king and people–coronations, royal weddings, funerals, and the New Year's Festival. Relief images like these on the stone foundations, walls, and stairways, representing members of the court and embassies bringing gifts, broadcast a vision of the grandeur and harmony of the Persian Empire.*

In keeping with this Zoroastrian worldview, the Persians were sensitive to the beauties of nature and venerated beneficent elements, such as water, which was not to be polluted by human excretion, and fire, which was worshiped at fire altars. Corpses were exposed to wild beasts and the elements to prevent them from putrefying in the earth or tainting the sanctity of fire. Persians were also expected to keep promises and tell the truth. In his inscriptions Darius castigated evildoers as followers of "the Lie."

Zoroastrianism was one of the great religions of the ancient world. It preached belief in one supreme deity, held humans to a high ethical standard, and promised salvation. It traveled across western Asia with the advance of the Persian Empire, and it may have exerted a major influence on Judaism and thus, indirectly, on Christianity. God and the Devil, Heaven and Hell, reward and punishment, and the Messiah and the End of Time all appear to be legacies of this profound belief system. Because of the accidents of history—the fall of the Achaemenid Persian Empire in the later fourth century B.C.E. and the Islamic conquest of Iran in the seventh century C.E. (see Chapter 9)—Zoroastrianism has all but disappeared, except among a relatively small number of Parsees, as Zoroastrians are now called, in Iran and India.

THE RISE OF THE GREEKS, 1000–500 B.C.E.

Because Greece was a relatively resource-poor region, the cultural developments of the first millennium B.C.E. were only possible because the Greeks had access to raw materials and markets abroad. Greek merchants, mercenaries, and travelers were in contact with other peoples and brought home foreign goods and ideas. Under the pressure of population, poverty, war, or political crisis, Greeks settled in other parts of the Mediterranean and Black Sea, bringing their language and culture and influencing other societies. Encounters with the different practices and beliefs of other peoples stimulated the formation of a Greek identity and sparked interest in geography, ethnography, and history. A two-century-long rivalry with the Persian Empire helped shape the destinies of the Greek city-states.

Geography and Resources   Greece is part of an ecological zone encompassing the Mediterranean Sea and the lands surrounding it. This zone is bounded by the Atlantic Ocean to the west, the several ranges of the Alps to the north, the Syrian Desert to the east, and the Sahara to the south. The lands lying within this zone have a similar climate, a similar sequence of seasons, and similar plants and animals. In summer a weather front near the entrance of the Mediterranean impedes the passage of storms from the Atlantic, allowing hot, dry air from the Sahara to creep up over the region. In winter the front dissolves and ocean storms roll in, bringing waves, wind, and cold. It was relatively easy for people to migrate to new homes within this ecological zone without altering familiar cultural practices and means of livelihood.

Greek civilization arose in the lands bordering the Aegean Sea: the Greek mainland, the Aegean islands, and the western coast of Anatolia. Southern Greece is a dry and rocky land with small plains separated by low mountain ranges. No navigable rivers ease travel or the transport of commodities. The small islands dotting the Aegean were inhabited from early times. People could sail from Greece to Anatolia almost without losing sight of land. The sea was always a connector, not a barrier. From about 1000 B.C.E. Greeks began settling on the western edge of Anatolia. Broad and fertile river valleys near the coast made Ionia, as the ancient Greeks called this region, a comfortable place.

Greek farmers depended on rainfall to water their crops. The limited arable land, thin topsoil, and sparse rainfall in the south could not sustain large populations. Farmers planted grain (mostly barley, which was hardier than wheat) in the flat plain, olive trees at the edge of the plain, and grapevines on the terraced lower slopes of the foothills. Sheep and goats grazed in the hills during the growing season. In northern Greece, where the rainfall is greater and the land opens out into broad plains, cattle and horses were more abundant. These lands had few metal deposits and little timber, but both building stone, including fine marble, and clay for the potter were abundant.

The Greek mainland has a deeply pitted coastline with many natural harbors. A combination of circumstances—the difficulty of overland transport, the availability of good anchorages, and the need to import metals, timber, and grain—drew the Greeks to the sea. They obtained timber from the northern Aegean, gold and iron from Anatolia, copper from Cyprus, tin from the western Mediterranean, and grain

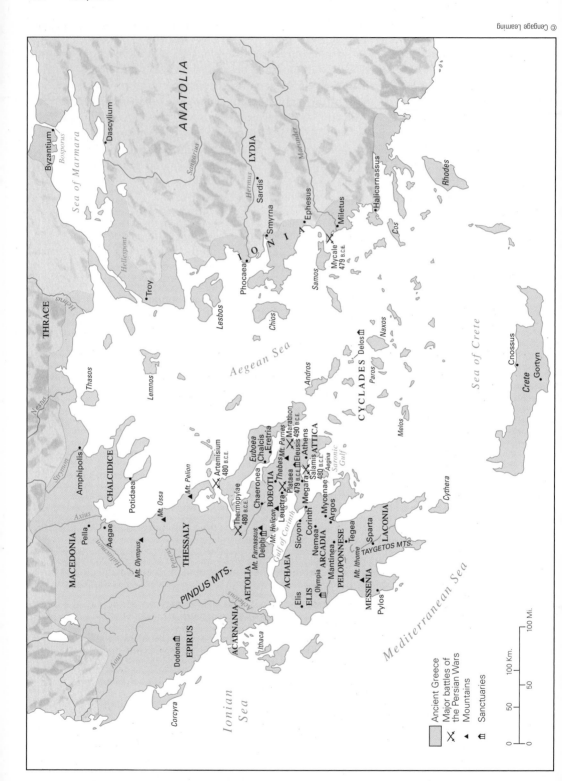

ANATOLIA

Byzantium

Bosporus

Dascylium

Sea of Marmara

LYDIA

Sardis

Hermus

Maeander

Halicarnassus

Rhodes

Smyrna

Ephesus

Phocaea

Miletus

Cos

I O N I A

Mycale
479 B.C.E.

Hellespont

Samos

Troy

Lesbos

Chios

Aegean Sea

THRACE

Hebrus

Nestus

Thasos

Lemnos

Andros

CYCLADES Delos

Naxos

Paros

Sea of Crete

Cnossus

Gortyn

Crete

Melos

Strymon

Amphipolis

CHALCIDICE

Potidaea

Mt. Pelion

Artemisium
480 B.C.E.

Euboea
Chalcis
Eretria

Cythera

Axius

MACEDONIA

Pella

Aegae

Mt. Ossa

THESSALY

Thermopylae
480 B.C.E.

Mt. Parnes
Marathon
490 B.C.E.

Chaeronea

BOEOTIA

Thebes

Eleusis

Mt. Helicon

Plataea
479 B.C.E.

Salamis ATTICA
480 B.C.E.

Athens

Aegina

*Saronic
Gulf*

Mt. Olympus

Mt. Parnassus

Delphi

Mt. Haliacmon

Peneus

PINDUS MTS.

AETOLIA

Mt. Parnassus

Gulf of Corinth

Leuctra

Megara

Sicyon

Corinth

Mycenae

Nemea

Argos

ACARNANIA

Achelous

ACHAEA

Elis

ELIS

Olympia

Mantinea

ARCADIA

Tegea

Sparta

LACONIA

TAYGETOS MTS.

PELOPONNESE

Mt. Ithone

MESSENIA

Pylos

Ithaca

Dodona

EPIRUS

Axus

Corcyra

*Ionian
Sea*

Mediterranean Sea

Ancient Greece

Major battles of
the Persian Wars

Mountains

Sanctuaries

0   50   100 Km.

0   50   100 Mi.

from the Black Sea, Egypt, and Sicily. Sea transport was much cheaper and faster than overland transport. Thus, some Greeks reluctantly embarked upon the sea in their small, frail ships, hugging the coastline or island-hopping where possible.

The Emergence of the Polis   The first flowering of Greek culture in the Mycenaean civilization of the second millennium B.C.E., described in Chapter 3, was largely an adaptation to the Greek terrain of the imported institutions of Middle Eastern palace-dominated states. For several centuries after the destruction of the Mycenaean palace-states, Greece lapsed into a "Dark Age" (ca. 1150–800 B.C.E.), a time of depopulation, poverty, and backwardness that left few traces in the archaeological record.

During the Dark Age, the Greeks were largely isolated from the rest of the world. The importation of raw materials, especially metals, had been the chief source of Mycenaean prosperity. Lack of access to resources lay behind the poverty of the Dark Age. With fewer people to feed, the land was largely given over to grazing animals. Although there was continuity of language, religion, and other aspects of culture, there was a sharp break with the authoritarian Mycenaean political structure and centralized control of the economy. This opened the way for the development of new political, social, and economic forms rooted in the Greek environment.

The isolation of Greece ended by 800 B.C.E. when Phoenician ships began to visit the Aegean (see Chapter 3), inaugurating what scholars term the "Archaic" period of Greek history (ca. 800–480 B.C.E.). Soon Greek ships were also plying the waters of the Mediterranean in search of raw materials, trade opportunities, and fertile farmland.

New ideas arrived from the east, such as the depiction of naturalistic human and animal figures and imaginative mythical beasts on painted pottery. The most auspicious gift of the Phoenicians was a writing system. The Phoenicians used twenty-two symbols to represent the consonants in their language, leaving the vowel sounds to be inferred by the reader. To represent Greek vowel sounds, the Greeks utilized some of the Phoenician symbols for which there were no equivalent sounds in the Greek language. This was the first true alphabet, a system of writing that fully represents the sounds of spoken language. An alphabet offers tremendous advantages over systems of writing such as cuneiform and hieroglyphics, whose signs represent entire words or syllables. Because cuneiform and hieroglyphics

MAP 5.2 Ancient Greece

By the early first millennium B.C.E. Greek-speaking peoples were dispersed throughout the Aegean region, occupying the Greek mainland, most of the islands, and the western coast of Anatolia. The rough landscape of central and southern Greece, with small plains separated by ranges of mountains, and the many islands in the Aegean favored the rise of hundreds of small, independent communities. The presence of adequate rainfall meant that agriculture was organized on the basis of self-sufficient family farms. As a result of the limited natural resources of this region, the Greeks had to resort to sea travel and trade with other lands in the Mediterranean to acquire metals and other vital raw materials.

required years of training and the memorization of hundreds of signs, they were known only by a scribal class whose elevated social position stemmed from their mastery of the technology. With an alphabet only a few dozen signs are required, and people can learn to read and write in a relatively short period of time.

Some scholars maintain that the Greeks first used alphabetic writing for economic purposes, such as to keep inventories of a merchant's wares. Others propose that it was created to preserve the oral epics so important to the Greeks. Whatever its first use, the Greeks soon applied the new technology to new forms of literature, law codes, religious dedications, and epitaphs on gravestones. This does not mean, however, that Greek society immediately became literate in the modern sense. For many centuries, Greece remained a primarily oral culture: people used storytelling, rituals, and performances to preserve and transmit information. Many of the distinctive intellectual and artistic creations of Greek civilization, such as theatrical drama, philosophical dialogues, and political and courtroom oratory, resulted from the dynamic interaction of speaking and writing.

The early Archaic period saw a veritable explosion of population. Studies of cemeteries in the vicinity of Athens show a dramatic population increase (perhaps fivefold or more) during the eighth century B.C.E. This was probably due, in part, to more intensive use of the land, as farming replaced herding and families began to work previously unused land on the margins of the plains. The accompanying shift to a diet based on bread and vegetables rather than meat may have increased fertility and life span. Another factor was increasing prosperity based on the importation of food and raw materials. Rising population density caused villages to merge and become urban centers. Freed from agricultural tasks, some members of the society were able to develop specialized skills in other areas, such as crafts and commerce.

Greece at this time consisted of hundreds of independent political entities, reflecting the facts of Greek geography—small plains separated by mountain barriers. The Greek **polis** (POE-lis) (usually translated "city-state") consisted of an urban center and the rural territory it controlled. City-states came in various sizes, with populations as small as several thousand or as large as several hundred thousand in the case of Athens.

Most urban centers had certain characteristic features. A hilltop *acropolis* (uh-KRAW-poe-lis) ("top of the city") offered refuge in an emergency. The town spread out around the base of this fortified high point. An *agora* (ah-go-RAH) ("gathering place") was an open area where citizens came together to ratify decisions of their leaders or to assemble with their weapons before military ventures. Government buildings were located there, but the agora developed into a marketplace as well, since vendors everywhere set out their wares wherever crowds gather. Fortified walls surrounded the urban center; but as the population expanded, new buildings went up beyond the perimeter.

City and country were not as sharply distinguished as they are today. The urban center depended on its agricultural hinterland to provide food, and many people living within the walls of the city worked on nearby farms during the day. Unlike the dependent workers on the estates of Mesopotamia, the rural populations of the Greek city-states were free members of the community.

Each polis was fiercely jealous of its independence and suspicious of its neighbors, leading to frequent conflict. By the early seventh century B.C.E. the Greeks had developed a new kind of warfare, waged by **hoplites** (HAWP-lite)—heavily armored infantrymen who fought in close formation. Protected by a helmet, a breastplate, and leg guards, each hoplite held a round shield over his own left side and the right side of the man next to him and brandished a thrusting spear, keeping a sword in reserve. The key to victory was maintaining the cohesion of one's own formation while breaking open the enemy's line. Most of the casualties were suffered by the defeated army in flight.

There was a close relationship between hoplite warfare and agriculture. Greek states were defended by armies of private citizens—mostly farmers—called up for brief periods of crisis, rather than by a professional class of soldiers. Although this kind of fighting called for strength to bear the weapons and armor, as well as courage to stand one's ground in battle, no special training was needed. Campaigns took place when farmers were available, in the windows of time between major tasks in the agricultural cycle. When a hoplite army marched into the fields of another community, the enraged farmers of that community, who had toiled to develop their land and buildings, rarely refused the challenge. Though brutal and terrifying, the clash of two hoplite lines provided a quick decision. Battles rarely lasted more than a few hours, and the survivors could promptly return home to tend their farms.

The expanding population soon surpassed the capacity of the small plains, and many communities sent excess population abroad to establish independent "colonies" in distant lands (see the story at the beginning of this chapter). Not every colonist left willingly. Sources tell of people being chosen by lot and forbidden to return on pain of death. Others, seeing an opportunity to escape from poverty, avoid the constraints of family, or find adventure, voluntarily sought their fortunes on the frontier. After obtaining the approval of the god Apollo from his sanctuary at Delphi, the colonists departed, carrying fire from the communal hearth of the "mother-city," a symbol of the kinship and religious ties that would connect the two communities. They settled by the sea in the vicinity of a hill or other natural refuge. The "founder," a prominent member of the mother-city, allotted parcels of land and drafted laws for the new community. In some cases the indigenous population was driven away or reduced to semiservile status; in other cases there was intermarriage between colonists and natives.

A wave of colonization from the mid-eighth through mid-sixth centuries B.C.E. spread Greek culture far beyond the land of its origins. New settlements sprang up in the northern Aegean area, around the Black Sea, and on the Libyan coast of North Africa. In southern Italy and on the island of Sicily another Greek core area was established. Greek colonists were able to transplant their entire way of life because of the general similarity in climate and ecology in the Mediterranean lands.

Greeks began to use the term *Hellenes* (HELL-leans) (*Graeci* is what the Romans later called them) to distinguish themselves from *barbaroi* (the root of the English word *barbarian*). Interaction with new peoples and exposure to their different practices made the Greeks aware of the factors that bound them together: their language, religion, and lifestyle. It also introduced them to new ideas and technologies. Developments first appearing in the colonial world traveled back to the Greek homeland—urban planning, new forms of political organization, and new intellectual currents.

Coinage was invented in the early sixth century B.C.E., probably in Lydia (western Anatolia), and soon spread throughout the Greek world and beyond. A coin was a piece of metal whose weight and purity, and thus value, were guaranteed by the state. Silver, gold, bronze, and other metals were attractive choices for a medium of exchange: sufficiently rare to be valuable, relatively lightweight and portable, virtually indestructible, and therefore permanent. Prior to the invention of coinage, people weighed out quantities of metal in exchange for items they wanted to buy. Coinage allowed for more rapid exchanges of goods as well as for more efficient record keeping and storage of wealth. It stimulated trade and increased the total wealth of the society. Even so, international commerce could still be confusing because different states used different weight standards that had to be reconciled, just as people have to exchange currencies when traveling today.

By reducing surplus population, colonization helped relieve pressures within Archaic Greek communities. Nevertheless, this was an era of political instability. Kings ruled the Dark Age societies depicted in Homer's *Iliad* and *Odyssey*, but at some point councils composed of the heads of noble families superseded the kings. This aristocracy derived its wealth and power from ownership of large tracts of land. Peasant families worked this land, occupying small plots and handing over a portion of the crop to the owner. Debt-slaves, who had borrowed money or seed from the lord and lost their freedom when unable to repay the loan, also worked the land. Also living in a typical community were free peasants, who owned small farms, and urban-based craftsmen and merchants, who began to constitute a "middle class."

In the mid-seventh and sixth centuries B.C.E. in one city-state after another, a **tyrant**—a person who seized and held power in violation of the normal political traditions of the community—gained control. Greek tyrants were often disgruntled or ambitious members of the aristocracy who were backed by the emerging middle class. New opportunities for economic advancement and the declining cost of metals meant that more and more men could acquire arms and serve as hoplite soldiers in the local militias. These individuals must have demanded increased political rights as the price of their support for the tyrant.

Ultimately, the tyrants were unwitting catalysts in an evolving political process. Some were able to pass their positions on to their sons, but eventually the tyrant-family was ejected. Authority in the community developed along one of two lines: toward oligarchy (OLL-ih-gahr-key), the exercise of political privilege by the wealthier members of society, or toward **democracy**, the exercise of political power by all free adult males.

Greek religion encompassed a wide range of cults and beliefs. The ancestors of the Greeks brought a collection of sky-gods with them when they entered the Greek peninsula at the end of the third millennium B.C.E. Male gods predominated, but several female deities had important roles. Some gods represented forces in nature: for example, Zeus sent storms and lightning, and Poseidon was master of the sea and earthquakes. The two great epic poems of Homer, the *Iliad* and *Odyssey*, which Greek schoolboys memorized and professional performers recited, put a distinctive stamp on the personalities of these deities. The Homeric gods were anthropomorphic (an-thruh-puh-MORE-fik)—that is, conceived as humanlike in appearance (though taller, more beautiful, and far more powerful than mere mortals) and humanlike in their displays of emotion. Indeed, the chief difference between them and human beings was humans' mortality.

Worship of the gods at state-sponsored festivals was as much an expression of civic identity as of personal piety. **Sacrifice**, the central ritual of Greek religion, was performed at altars in front of the temples that the Greeks built to be the gods' places of residence. Greeks gave their gods gifts, often as humble as a small cake or a cup of wine poured on the ground, in the hope that the gods would favor and protect them. In more spectacular forms of sacrifice, a group of people would kill one or more animals, spray the altar with the victim's blood, burn parts of its body so that the aroma would ascend to the gods on high, and enjoy a rare feast of meat.

Greek individuals and communities sought advice or predictions about the future from oracles—sacred sites where they believed the gods communicated with humans. Especially prestigious was the oracle of Apollo at Delphi in central Greece. Petitioners left gifts in the treasuries, and the god responded to their questions through his priestess, who gave forth obscure utterances. Because most Greeks were farmers, a popular form of worship was the fertility cult, in which members worshiped and sought to enhance the productive forces in nature (usually conceived as female). This kind of popular religion is often hidden from modern view because of our dependence on literary texts privileging the values of an educated, urban elite.

New Intellectual Currents
The changes taking place in Greece in the Archaic period—new technologies, increasing prosperity, and social and political development—led to innovations in intellectual outlook and artistic expression. One distinctive feature of the period was a growing emphasis on the uniqueness and rights of the individual.

We see clear signs of individualism in the new lyric poetry—short verses in which the subject matter is intensely personal, drawn from the experience of the poet and expressing his or her feelings. Archilochus (ahr-KIL-uh-kuhs), a soldier and poet living in the first half of the seventh century B.C.E., made a surprising admission:

> *Some barbarian is waving my shield, since I was obliged to leave that perfectly good piece of equipment behind under a bush. But I got away, so what does it matter? Let the shield go; I can buy another one equally good.*[3]

Here Archilochus is poking fun at the heroic ideal that regarded dishonor as worse than death. In challenging traditional values and expressing personal views, lyric poets paved the way for the modern Western conception of poetry.

Some daring thinkers rejected traditional religious conceptions and sought rational explanations for events in nature. For example, in the sixth century B.C.E. Xenophanes (zeh-NOFF-uh-nees) called into question the kind of gods that Homer had popularized.

> *But if cattle and horses or lions had hands, or were able to draw with their hands and do the works that men can do, horses would draw the forms of the gods like horses, and cattle like cattle, and they would make their bodies such as they each had themselves.*[4]

---

[3]Richmond Lattimore, *Greek Lyrics*, 2nd ed. (Chicago: University of Chicago Press, 1960), 2.

[4]G. S. Kirk and J. E. Raven, *The Presocratic Philosophers: A Critical History with a Selection of Texts* (Cambridge, England: Cambridge University Press, 1957), 169.

Bildarchiv Preussischer Kulturbesitz/Art Resource, NY

Vase Painting Depicting a Sacrifice to the God Apollo, ca. 440 B.C.E. *For the Greeks, who believed in a multitude of gods who looked and behaved like humans, the central act of worship was the sacrifice, the ritualized offering of a gift. Sacrifice created a relationship between the human worshiper and the deity and raised expectations that the god would bestow favors in return. Here we see a number of male devotees, wearing their finest clothing and garlands in their hair, near a sacred outdoor altar and statue of Apollo. The god is shown at the far right, standing on a pedestal and holding his characteristic bow and laurel branch. The first worshiper offers the god bones wrapped in fat. All of the worshipers will feast on the meat carried by the boy.*

These early philosophers were primarily concerned with how the world was created, what it is made of, and why changes occur. Some postulated various combinations of earth, air, fire, and water as the primal elements that combine or dissolve to form the numerous substances found in nature. One advanced the theory that the world is composed of microscopic atoms (from a Greek word meaning "indivisible") moving through the void of space, colliding randomly and combining in various ways to form many substances. This model, in some respects startlingly similar to modern atomic theory, was essentially a lucky intuition, but it attests to the sophistication of these thinkers. Most of these thinkers came from Ionia and southern Italy, where Greeks were in close contact with non-Greek peoples. The shock of encountering different ideas may have stimulated new lines of inquiry.

In Ionia in the sixth century B.C.E., a group of men referred to as logographers (loe-GOG-ruff-er) ("writers of prose accounts"), taking advantage of the nearly infinite capacity of writing to store information, gathered data on a wide range of topics, including ethnography (description of foreign people's physical characteristics and cultural practices), the geography of unfamiliar lands, foundation stories of important cities, and the origins of famous Greek families. They were the first to write in prose—the language of everyday speech—rather than poetry, which had long facilitated the memorization essential in an oral society. *Historia*, "investigation/research," was the Greek term for the method they used to collect, sort, and select information. An important successor to these early researchers was **Herodotus** (ca. 485–425 B.C.E.), who published his *Histories* in the later fifth century B.C.E. Early parts of the work are filled with the geographic and ethnographic reports, legends, and marvels dear to the logographers, but in later sections Herodotus focuses on the great event of the previous generation: the wars between the Greeks and the Persian Empire.

Herodotus declared his new conception of his mission in the first lines of the book:

> I, *Herodotus of Halicarnassus, am here setting forth my history, that time may not draw the color from what man has brought into being, nor those great and wonderful deeds, manifested by both Greeks and barbarians, fail of their report, and, together with all this, the reason why they fought one another.*[5]

In seeking to discover *why* Greeks and Persians came to blows, Herodotus became a historian, directing the all-purpose techniques of *historia* to the narrower service of *history* in the modern sense. For this achievement he is known as the "father of history."

Athens and Sparta

The two preeminent Greek city-states of the late Archaic and Classical periods were Athens and Sparta. The different character of these communities underscores the potential for diversity in human societies, even those arising in similar environmental and cultural contexts.

The ancestors of the Spartans migrated into the Peloponnese (PELL-uh-puh-neze), the southernmost part of the Greek mainland, around 1000 B.C.E. For a time Sparta followed a typical path of development, participating in trade and fostering the arts. Then in the seventh century B.C.E. something altered the character of the Spartan state. Like many other parts of Greece, the Spartan community was feeling the effects of increasing population and a shortage of arable land. However, instead of sending out colonists, the Spartans invaded the fertile plain of neighboring Messenia. They took over Messenia and reduced the native population to the status of helots (HELL-ut), or state-owned serfs, who became the most abused and exploited population on the Greek mainland.

Fear of a helot uprising led to the evolution of the unique Spartan way of life. The Spartan state became a military camp in a permanent state of preparedness. Territory in Messenia and Laconia (the Spartan homeland) was divided into several thousand lots and assigned to Spartan citizens. Helots worked the land and turned over a portion of what they grew to their Spartan masters, who were freed from food production and able to spend their lives in military training and service.

The Spartan soldier was the best in Greece, and the professional Spartan army was superior to the citizen militias of other Greek states. The Spartans, however, paid a huge personal price for their military readiness. At age seven, boys were taken from their families and put into barracks, where they were toughened by severe discipline, beatings, and deprivation. A Spartan male's whole life was

---

[5]Herodotus, *The History*, trans. David Grene (Chicago: University of Chicago Press, 1988), 33. (Herodotus 1.1)

subordinated to the needs of the state. Sparta essentially stopped the clock, declining to participate in the economic, political, and cultural renaissance taking place in the Archaic Greek world. There were no longer any poets or artists at Sparta. To maintain equality among citizens, precious metals and coinage were banned, and Spartans were forbidden to engage in commerce. The fifth-century B.C.E. Athenian historian Thucydides (thoo-SID-ih-dees) remarked that in his day Sparta appeared to be little more than a large village and that no future observer of the ruins of the site would be able to guess its power.

The Spartans, practicing a foreign policy that was cautious and isolationist, cultivated a mystique by rarely putting their reputation to the test. Reluctant to march far from home for fear of a helot uprising, the Spartans maintained regional peace through the Peloponnesian League, a system of alliances between Sparta and its neighbors.

In comparison with other Greek city-states, Athens possessed an unusually large and populous territory: the entire region of Attica, containing a number of moderately fertile plains and well suited for cultivation of olive trees. In addition to the urban center of Athens, located 5 miles (8 kilometers) from the sea where the sheer-sided Acropolis towered above the plain, the peninsula was dotted with villages and a few larger towns.

In 594 B.C.E., however, Athens was on the verge of civil war, and a respected member of the elite class, Solon, was appointed lawgiver and granted extraordinary powers. Solon divided Athenian citizens into four classes based on the annual yield of their farms. Those in the top three classes could hold state offices. Members of the lowest class, with little or no property, could participate in meetings of the Assembly. This arrangement, which made political rights a function of wealth, was far from democratic, but it broke the monopoly on power of a small circle of aristocratic families. Solon also abolished the practice of enslaving individuals for failure to repay their debts, thereby guaranteeing the freedom of Athenian citizens.

Nevertheless, political turmoil continued until 546 B.C.E., when an aristocrat named Pisistratus (pie-SIS-truh-tuhs) seized power. To strengthen his position and weaken the aristocracy, the tyrant enticed the largely rural population to identify with the urban center of Athens, where he was the dominant figure. He undertook a number of monumental building projects, including a Temple of Athena on the Acropolis. He also instituted or expanded several major festivals that drew people to Athens for religious processions, performances of plays, and athletic and poetic competitions.

Pisistratus passed the tyranny on to his sons, but with Spartan assistance the Athenians turned the tyrant-family out in the last decade of the sixth century B.C.E. In the 460s and 450s B.C.E. **Pericles** (PER-eh-kleez) and his political allies took the last steps in the evolution of Athenian democracy, transferring all power to popular organs of government: the Assembly, Council of 500, and People's Courts. Men of moderate or little means now could participate fully in the political process, being selected by lot to fill even the highest offices and being paid for public service so they could take time off from their work. The focal point of Athenian political life became the Assembly of all citizens. Several times a month proposals were debated; decisions were made openly, and any citizen could speak to the issues of the day.

During this century and a half of internal political evolution, Athens's economic clout and international reputation rose steadily. From the time of Pisistratus, Athenian exports, especially olive oil, became increasingly prominent all around the Mediterranean, crowding out the products of other Greek commercial powerhouses such as Corinth. Extensive trade increased the numbers and wealth of the middle class and helps explain why Athens took the path of increasing democratization.

THE STRUGGLE OF PERSIA AND GREECE, 546–323 B.C.E.

For many Greeks of the fifth and fourth centuries B.C.E., Persia was the great enemy and the wars with Persia were crucial events. The Persians probably were more concerned about threats farther east. Nevertheless, the encounters of Greeks and Persians over a period of two centuries were of profound importance for the history of the eastern Mediterranean and western Asia.

Early Encounters   Cyrus's conquest of Lydia in 546 B.C.E. led to the subjugation of the Greek cities on the Anatolian seacoast. In the years that followed, local groups or individuals who collaborated with the Persian government ruled their home cities with minimal Persian interference. All this changed when the Ionian Revolt, a great uprising of Greeks and other subject peoples on the western frontier, broke out in 499 B.C.E. The Persians needed five years and a massive infusion of troops and resources to stamp out the insurrection.

The failed revolt led to the **Persian Wars**—two Persian attacks on Greece in the early fifth century B.C.E. In 490 B.C.E. Darius dispatched a force to punish Eretria (er-EH-tree-uh) and Athens, two mainland states that had aided the Ionian rebels. Eretria was betrayed to the Persians, and the survivors were marched off to permanent exile in southwest Iran. The Athenians probably would have suffered a similar fate if their hoplites had not defeated the more numerous but lighter-armed Persian troops in a sharp engagement at Marathon, 26 miles (42 kilometers) from Athens.

In 480 B.C.E. Darius's son and successor, Xerxes (*Khshayarsha*, r. 486–465 B.C.E.), set out with a huge invasionary force consisting of the Persian army, contingents from all the peoples of the empire, and a large fleet of ships drawn from maritime subjects. Crossing the narrow Hellespont strait, Persian forces descended into central and southern Greece. Xerxes sent messengers ahead to most Greek states, demanding "earth and water"—tokens of submission.

Many Greek communities acknowledged Persian overlordship. But an alliance of southern Greek states bent on resistance was formed under the leadership of the Spartans. This Hellenic League initially failed to halt the Persian advance. At the pass of Thermopylae (thuhr-MOP-uh-lee) in central Greece, three hundred Spartans and their king gave their lives to buy time for their allies to escape. However, after the city of Athens had been sacked, the Persian navy was lured into the narrow straits of nearby Salamis (SAH-lah-miss), sacrificing their advantage in numbers and maneuverability, and suffered a devastating defeat. The following spring (479 B.C.E.), the Persian land army was routed at Plataea (pluh-TEE-uh), and the immediate threat to Greece receded. A number of factors account for the outcome: the Persians' difficulty in supplying their very large army in a distant land; their tactical error at Salamis; the superiority of heavily armed Greek hoplite soldiers over lighter-armed Asiatic infantry; and the tenacity of people defending their homeland and liberty.

The Greeks then went on the offensive. Athens's stubborn refusal to submit and the vital role played by the Athenian navy, which made up half the allied fleet, had earned the city a large measure of respect. The next phase of the war—driving the Persians away from the Aegean and liberating Greek states still under Persian control—was naval. Thus Athens replaced land-based, isolationist Sparta as leader of the campaign against Persia. In 477 B.C.E. the Delian (DEE-lih-yuhn) League was formed. Initially a voluntary alliance of Greek states to prosecute the war against Persia, in less than twenty years Athenian-led League forces swept the Persians from the waters of the eastern Mediterranean and freed all Greek communities except those in distant Cyprus.

The Height of Athenian Power The Classical period of Greek history (480–323 B.C.E.) begins with the successful defense of the Greek homeland. Ironically, the Athenians, who had played such a crucial role, exploited these events to become an imperial power. A string of successful campaigns and the passage of time led many of their complacent Greek allies to contribute money instead of military forces. The Athenians used the money to build up and staff their navy. Eventually they saw the other members of the Delian League as their subjects and demanded annual contributions and other signs of submission. States that deserted the League were brought back by force, stripped of their defenses, and subordinated to Athens.

Athens's mastery of naval technology transformed Greek warfare and politics and brought great power and wealth to Athens itself. Unlike commercial ships, whose stable, round-bodied hulls were propelled by a single square sail, military vessels could not risk depending on the wind. By the late sixth century B.C.E. the **trireme** (TRY-reem), a sleek, fast vessel powered by 170 rowers, had become the premier warship. Athenian crews, by constant practice, became the best in the eastern Mediterranean, able to reach speeds of 7 knots and perform complex maneuvers.

The effectiveness of the Athenian navy had significant consequences at home and abroad. The emergence at Athens of a democratic system in which each male citizen had an equal share is connected to the new primacy of the fleet. Hoplites, who had to provide their own armor and weapons, were members of the middle and upper classes. Rowers, in contrast, came from the lower classes, but because they were the source of Athens's power, they could insist on full rights.

The navy allowed Athens to project its power farther than would be possible with a hoplite militia, which could be kept in arms for only short periods of time. In previous Greek wars, the victorious state could not occupy a defeated neighbor permanently and was satisfied with booty and, perhaps, minor adjustments to boundary lines. Athens was able to continually dominate and exploit other, weaker communities in an unprecedented way.

Athens used its power to promote its economic interests. Its port, Piraeus (pih-RAY-uhs), became the most important commercial center in the eastern Mediterranean. The money collected from the subject states helped subsidize the increasingly expensive Athenian democracy as well as construction of beautiful buildings on the Acropolis, including the majestic new temple of Athena, the Parthenon. The Athenian leader Pericles redistributed the profits of empire to the many Athenians working on the construction and decoration of these monuments and gained extraordinary popularity.

Other cultural achievements were supported indirectly by the profits of empire. Wealthy Athenians paid the production costs of the tragedies and comedies performed at state festivals, and the most creative artists and thinkers in the Greek world were drawn to Athens. Traveling teachers called Sophists ("wise men") provided instruction in logic and public speaking to pupils who could afford their fees. The new discipline of rhetoric—the construction of attractive and persuasive arguments—gave those with training and quick wits a great advantage in politics and the courts.

These new intellectual currents came together in 399 B.C.E. when the philosopher **Socrates** (ca. 470–399 B.C.E.) was brought to trial. A sculptor by trade, Socrates spent most of his time in the company of young men who enjoyed conversing with him and observing him deflate the pretensions of those who thought themselves wise. He wryly commented that he knew one more thing than everyone else: that he knew nothing. At his trial, Socrates easily disposed of the charges of corrupting the youth and not believing in the gods of the city. He argued that the real basis of the hostility he faced was twofold: (1) He was being held responsible for the actions of several of his aristocratic students who had tried to overthrow the Athenian democracy. (2) He was being blamed for the controversial teachings of the Sophists, which were widely believed to contradict traditional religious beliefs and undermine morality.

In Athenian trials, juries of hundreds of citizens decided guilt and punishment, often motivated more by emotion than by legal principles. The vote that found Socrates guilty was close. But his lack of contrition in the penalty phase—he proposed that he be rewarded for his services to the state—led the jury to condemn him to death by drinking hemlock. Socrates's disciples regarded his execution as a martyrdom, and smart young men such as Plato withdrew from public life and dedicated themselves to the philosophical pursuit of knowledge and truth.

This period witnesses an important stage in the transition from orality to literacy. Socrates himself wrote nothing, preferring to converse with people. His student Plato (ca. 428–347 B.C.E.) may represent the first truly literate generation that gained much knowledge from books and habitually wrote down their thoughts. On the outskirts of Athens Plato founded the Academy, where young men could pursue a course of higher education. Yet even Plato retained traces of the orality of the world in which he had grown up. He wrote dialogues—an oral form—in which his protagonist, Socrates, uses the "Socratic method" of question and answer to reach a deeper understanding of values such as justice, excellence, and wisdom. Plato refused to write down the most advanced stages of the philosophical and spiritual training that took place at his Academy. He believed that full apprehension of a higher reality, of which our own sensible world is but a pale reflection, could be entrusted only to "initiates" who had completed the earlier stages.

Replica of the trireme 'Olympia' at sea (photo)/Private Collection/Ancient Art and Architecture Collection Ltd./Mike Andrews/The Bridgeman Art Library

Replica of Ancient Greek Trireme *Greek warships had a metal-tipped ram in front to pierce the hulls of enemy vessels and a pair of steering rudders in the rear. Though equipped with masts and sails, in battle these warships were propelled by 170 rowers. This modern, full-size replica, manned by international volunteer crews, is helping scholars to determine attainable speeds and maneuvering techniques.*

The third of the great classical philosophers, Aristotle (384–322 B.C.E.), came from Stagira in the northern Aegean. After several decades of study at Plato's Academy, he was chosen by the king of Macedonia, Philip II, who had a high regard for Greek culture, to tutor his son Alexander. Later, Aristotle returned to Athens to found his own school, the Lyceum. Of a very different temperament than the mystical Plato, Aristotle collected and categorized a vast array of knowledge. He lectured and wrote about politics, philosophy, ethics, logic, poetry, rhetoric, physics, astronomy, meteorology, zoology, and psychology, laying the foundations for many modern disciplines.

Inequality in Classical Greece   Athens, the inspiration for the concept of democracy in the Western tradition, was a democracy only for the relatively small percentage of inhabitants who were citizens—free adult males of pure Athenian ancestry. Excluding women, children, slaves, and foreigners, this group amounted to 30,000 or 40,000 people out of a total population of approximately 300,000—only 10 or 15 percent.

Slaves, mostly of foreign origin, constituted perhaps one-third of the population of Attica in the fifth and fourth centuries B.C.E., and the average Athenian family owned one or more. Slaves were needed to run the shop or work on the farm while the master attended meetings of the Assembly or served on one of the boards that oversaw the day-to-day activities of the state. The slave was a "living piece of property," required to do any work, submit to any sexual acts, and receive any punishments the owner ordained. Most Greek slaves were domestic servants, often working on the same tasks as the master or mistress. Close daily contact between owners and slaves meant that a relationship often developed, making it hard for slave owners to deny the essential humanity of their slaves. Still, Aristotle rationalized the institution of slavery by arguing that *barbaroi* (non-Greeks) lacked the capacity to reason and thus were better off under the direction of rational Greek owners.

The position of women varied across Greek communities. The women of Sparta, who were expected to bear and raise strong children, were encouraged to exercise, and they enjoyed a level of public visibility and outspokenness that shocked other Greeks. Athens may have been at the opposite extreme as regards the confinement and suppression of women. Ironically, the exploitation of women in Athens, as of slaves, made possible the high degree of freedom enjoyed by men in the democratic state. Greek men justified the confinement of women by claiming that they were naturally promiscuous and likely to introduce other men's children into the household.

Athenian marriages were unequal affairs. A new husband might be thirty, reasonably well educated, a veteran of war, and experienced in business and politics. Under law he had nearly absolute authority over the members of his household. He arranged his marriage with the parents of his prospective wife, who was likely to be a teenager brought up with no formal education and only minimal training in weaving, cooking, and household management. Coming into the home of a husband she hardly knew, she had no political rights and limited legal protection. The primary function of marriage was to produce children, preferably male. It is likely that many more girls than boys were victims of infanticide—the killing through exposure of unwanted children.

Husbands and wives had limited contact. The man spent the day outdoors attending to work or political responsibilities; he dined with male friends at night; and usually he slept alone in the men's quarters. The woman stayed home to cook, clean, raise the children, and supervise the servants, going out only to attend funerals and religious rituals and to make discreet visits to female relatives. During the three-day Thesmophoria (thes-moe-FOE-ree-uh) festival, the women of Athens lived together and managed their own affairs in a great encampment, carrying out mysterious rituals to enhance the fertility of the land. The appearance of assertive women on the Athenian stage is also suggestive. Although the plays were written by men and probably reflect a male fear of strong women, the playwrights must have had models in their mothers, sisters, and wives.

The inequality of men and women posed obstacles to creating a "meaningful relationship" between the sexes. To find his intellectual and emotional equal, a man often looked to other men. Bisexuality was common in ancient Greece, as much a product of the social structure as of biological inclinations. A common pattern was that of an older man wooing a youth, in the process mentoring him and initiating him into the community of adult males.

Failure of the City-State and Triumph of the Macedonians

The emergence of Athens as an imperial power in the half century after the Persian invasion aroused the suspicions of other Greek states and led to open hostilities between former allies. In 431 B.C.E. the **Peloponnesian War** broke out, a nightmarish struggle between the Athenian and Spartan alliance systems that involved most of the Greek world.

In this war unlike any previous Greek war, the Athenians used their naval power to insulate themselves from the dangers of a siege by land. In mid-century they had built three long walls connecting the city with the port of Piraeus and the adjacent shoreline. When the war began, Pericles, devising an unprecedented strategy, refused to engage the Spartan-led armies that invaded Attica each year, knowing that, as long as Athens controlled the sea lanes and was able to provision itself, the enemy hoplites must soon return to their farms and the city could not be starved into submission.

The Peloponnesian War dragged on for nearly three decades with great loss of life and squandering of resources. It sapped the morale of all Greece and ended only with the surrender of Athens after defeat in a naval battle in 404 B.C.E. Because the Persian Empire had bankrolled the construction of ships by the Spartan alliance, Sparta finally was able to take the conflict into Athens's own element, the sea.

The victorious Spartans, who had entered the war championing "the freedom of the Greeks," took over Athens's overseas empire until their own increasingly highhanded behavior aroused the opposition of other city-states. Indeed, the fourth century B.C.E. was a time of nearly continuous skirmishing among Greek states. The independent polis, from one point of view the glory of Greek culture, was also fundamentally flawed because it fostered rivalry, fear, and warfare among neighboring communities.

Internal conflict in the Greek world allowed the Persians to recoup old losses. By the terms of the King's Peace of 387 B.C.E., to which most of the states of war-weary Greece subscribed, all of western Asia, including the Greek communities of the Anatolian seacoast, were conceded to Persia. The Persian king became the guarantor of a status quo that kept the Greeks divided and weak. Luckily for the Greeks, rebellions in Egypt, Cyprus, and Phoenicia as well as intrigues among some of the satraps in the western provinces diverted Persian attention from thoughts of another Greek invasion.

Meanwhile, in northern Greece developments were taking place that would irrevocably alter the balance of power. Philip II (r. 359–336 B.C.E.) transformed his previously backward kingdom of Macedonia into the premier military power in the Greek world. (Although southern Greeks had long doubted the "Greekness" of the rough and rowdy Macedonians, many modern scholars regard their language and culture as Greek at base, though much influenced by contact with non-Greek neighbors.) Philip made a number of improvements to the traditional hoplite formation. He increased the striking power and mobility of his force by equipping soldiers with longer thrusting spears and less armor. Because horses thrived in the broad plains of the north, he experimented with the coordinated use of infantry and cavalry. His engineers also developed new kinds of siege equipment, including the first catapults—machines using the power of twisted cords to hurl arrows or stones great distances. For the first time it became possible to storm a fortified city rather than wait for starvation to take effect.

In 338 B.C.E. Philip defeated a coalition of southern states and established the Confederacy of Corinth as an instrument for controlling the Greek city-states. Philip had himself appointed military commander for a planned all-Greek campaign against Persia, and his generals established a bridgehead on the Asiatic side of the Hellespont. Philip apparently was following the advice of Greek thinkers who had pondered the lessons of the Persian Wars of the fifth century B.C.E. and urged a crusade against the national enemy as a means of unifying their quarrelsome countrymen.

We will never know how far Philip's ambitions extended, for an assassin killed him in 336 B.C.E. When **Alexander** (356–323 B.C.E.), his son and heir, crossed into Asia in 334 B.C.E., his avowed purpose was to exact revenge for Xerxes' invasion a century and half before. He defeated the Persian forces of King Darius III (r. 336–330 B.C.E.) in three pitched battles in Anatolia and Mesopotamia, and he ultimately campaigned as far as the Punjab region of modern Pakistan. After more than two centuries of domination in the Middle East, the Achaemenid Persian Empire had fallen.

Alexander the Great, as he came to be called, maintained the framework of Persian administration in the lands he conquered, recognizing that it was well adapted to local circumstances and familiar to the subject peoples. At first, he replaced Persian officials with his own Macedonian and Greek comrades. To control strategic points in his expanding empire, he established a series of Greek-style cities, beginning with Alexandria in Egypt, and settled wounded and aged former soldiers in them. After his decisive victory in northern Mesopotamia (331 B.C.E.), he began to experiment with leaving cooperative Persian officials in place. He also admitted some Persians and other Iranians into his army and the circle of his courtiers, and he adopted elements of Persian dress and court ceremonial. Finally, he married several Iranian women who had useful royal or aristocratic connections, and he pressed his leading subordinates to do the same.

Scholars have reached widely varying conclusions about why Alexander adopted these policies, which were fiercely resented by the Macedonian nobility. Alexander may have operated from a combination of pragmatic and idealistic motives. He set off on his Asian campaign with visions of glory, booty, and revenge. But the farther east he traveled, the more he began to see himself as the legitimate successor of the Persian king (a claim facilitated by the death of Darius III at the hands of subordinates). Besides recognizing that he had responsibilities to all the diverse peoples who fell under his control, he also may have realized the difficulty of holding down so vast an empire by brute force and without the cooperation of important elements among the conquered peoples. In this, he was following the example of the Achaemenids.

THE HELLENISTIC SYNTHESIS, 323–30 B.C.E.

Alexander died suddenly in 323 B.C.E. at the age of thirty-two, with no clear plan for the succession. This event ushered in a half century of chaos as the most ambitious and ruthless of his officers struggled for control of the vast empire. When the dust cleared, the empire had been broken up into three major kingdoms, each ruled by a Macedonian dynasty—the Seleucid (sih-LOO-sid), Ptolemaic (tawl-uh-MAY-ik), and Antigonid (an-TIG-uh-nid) kingdoms. Each kingdom faced a unique set of circumstances, and although they frequently were at odds with one another, a rough balance of power prevented any one from gaining the upper hand and enabled smaller states to survive by playing off the great powers.

Historians call the epoch ushered in by Alexander the "**Hellenistic Age**" (323–30 B.C.E.) because the lands in northeastern Africa and western Asia that came under Greek rule became "Hellenized"—that is, powerfully influenced by Greek culture. This was a period of large kingdoms with heterogeneous populations, great cities, powerful rulers, pervasive bureaucracies, and vast disparities in wealth—a far cry from the small, homogeneous, independent city-states of Archaic and Classical Greece. It was a cosmopolitan age of long-distance trade and communications, which saw the rise of new institutions like libraries and universities, new kinds of scholarship and science, and the cultivation of sophisticated tastes in art and literature.

The Seleucids, who took over the bulk of Alexander's conquests, faced the greatest challenges. The Indus Valley and Afghanistan soon split off, and over the course of the third and second centuries B.C.E. Iran was lost to the Parthians. From their capital at Syrian Antioch (AN-tee-awk), the Seleucid monarchs controlled Mesopotamia, Syria, and parts of Anatolia. Their sprawling territories were open to attack from many directions, and, like the Persians before them, they had to deal with many ethnic groups organized under various political and social forms. In the countryside, where most of the native peoples resided, the Seleucids largely maintained the Persian administrative system. They also continued Alexander's policy of founding Greek-style cities throughout their domains. These cities served as administrative centers and were also used to attract colonists from Greece, since the Seleucids needed Greek soldiers, engineers, and administrators.

The dynasty of the **Ptolemies** (TAWL-uh-meze) ruled Egypt and sometimes laid claim to adjacent Syria-Palestine. The people of Egypt belonged to only one ethnic group and were easily controlled because the vast majority were farmers in villages alongside the Nile. The Ptolemies essentially perfected an administrative structure devised by the pharaohs to extract the surplus wealth of this populous and productive land. The Egyptian economy was centrally planned and highly controlled. Vast revenues poured into the royal treasury from rents (the king owned most of the land), taxes of all sorts, and royal monopolies on olive oil, salt, papyrus, and other key commodities.

The Ptolemies ruled from **Alexandria**, the first of the new cities laid out by Alexander himself. Whereas Memphis and Thebes, the capitals of ancient Egypt, had been located upriver, Alexandria was situated where the westernmost branch of the Nile runs into the Mediterranean Sea, linking Egypt and the Mediterranean world. In the language of the bureaucracy, Alexandria was technically "beside Egypt" rather than in it, as if to emphasize the gulf between rulers and subjects.

The Ptolemies also encouraged the immigration of Greeks from the homeland and, in return for their skills and collaboration in the military or civil administration, gave them land and a privileged position in the new society. But the Ptolemies did not plant Greek-style cities throughout the Egyptian countryside. Only the last Ptolemy, Queen Cleopatra (r. 51–30 B.C.E.), even bothered to learn the language of her Egyptian subjects. Periodic insurrections in the countryside were signs of the Egyptians' growing resentment of the Greeks' exploitation and arrogance.

The Antigonid dynasty ruled a compact and ethnically homogeneous kingdom in the Macedonian homeland and northern Greece. Garrisons at strong-points gave the Antigonids a toehold in central and southern Greece, and the shadow of Macedonian intervention always hung over the south. The southern states met the threat by banding together into confederations, such as the Achaean (uh-KEY-uhn) League in the Peloponnese, in which member-states maintained local autonomy but pooled resources and military power.

Athens and Sparta, the two leading cities of the Classical period, stood out from these confederations. The Spartans clung to the myth of their own invincibility and made a number of heroic but futile stands against Macedonian armies. Athens, which held a special place in the hearts of all Greeks because of the artistic and literary accomplishments of the fifth century B.C.E., pursued a policy of neutrality. The city became a large museum, filled with the relics and memories of a glorious past, as well as a university town that attracted the children of the well-to-do from all over the Mediterranean and western Asia.

In an age of cities, the greatest city of all was Alexandria, with a population of nearly half a million. At its heart was the royal compound, containing the palace and administrative buildings, as well as the magnificent Mausoleum of Alexander. (The first Ptolemy had stolen the body of Alexander on its way back to Macedonia for burial, seeking legitimacy for his dynasty by claiming the blessing of the great conqueror, who was declared to be a god.) Two harbors linked the commerce of the Mediterranean with the Red Sea and Indian Ocean. A great lighthouse—the first of its kind, a multistory tower with a fiery beacon visible at a distance of 30 miles (48 kilometers)—was one of the wonders of the ancient world.

Alexandria gained further luster from its famous Library, with several hundred thousand volumes, and from its Museum, or "House of the Muses" (divinities who presided over the arts and sciences), a research institution supporting the work of the greatest poets, philosophers, doctors, and scientists of the day. These well-funded institutions made possible significant advances in sciences such as mathematics, medicine, and astronomy (see Environment and Technology: Ancient Astronomy).

Greek residents of Alexandria enjoyed citizenship in a Greek-style polis with an Assembly, a Council, and officials who dealt with local affairs. Public baths and shaded arcades offered places to relax and socialize with friends. Ancient plays were revived in the theaters, and musical performances and demonstrations of oratory took place in the concert halls. Gymnasia, besides providing facilities for exercise, were where young men of the privileged classes were schooled in athletics, music, and literature. Jews had their own civic government, officials, and law courts and predominated in two of the five main residential districts. Other quarters were filled with the sights, sounds, and smells of ethnic groups from Syria, Anatolia, and the Egyptian countryside.

In all the Hellenistic states, ambitious members of the indigenous populations learned the Greek language and adopted elements of Greek lifestyle, since this put them in a position to become part of the privileged and wealthy ruling class. For the ancient Greeks, to be Greek was primarily a matter of language and lifestyle rather than physical traits. In the Hellenistic Age there was a spontaneous synthesis of Greek and indigenous ways. Egyptians migrated to Alexandria, and Greeks

Ancient Astronomy

Long before the advent of writing, people studied the appearance and movement of objects in the sky and used this information for a variety of purposes. Ancient hunters, herders, and farmers all coordinated their activities with the cycle of seasons during the year so that they could follow the migrations of prey, find appropriate pastures for domestic animals, and perform vital agricultural tasks.

Ancient farmers drew on an intimate knowledge of the night sky. Hesiod (**HEE-see-uhd**), who lived around 700 B.C.E., composed a poem called *Works and Days* describing the annual cycle of tasks on a Greek farm. How did the ancient Greeks, with no clocks, calendars, or newspapers, know where they were in the cycle of the year? They oriented themselves by close observation of natural phenomena such as the movements of planets, stars, and constellations in the night sky. Hesiod gives the following advice for determining the proper times for planting and harvesting grain:

> Pleiades rising in the dawning sky,
> Harvest is nigh.
> Pleiades setting in the waning night,
> Plowing is right.

The Pleiades (**PLEE-uh-dees**) are a cluster of seven stars visible to the naked eye. The ancient Greeks observed that individual stars, clusters, and constellations moved from east to west during the night and appeared in different parts of the sky at different times of the year. (In fact, the apparent movement of the stars is due to the earth's rotation on its axis and orbit around the sun against a background of unmoving stars.) Hesiod is telling his audience that, when the Pleiades appear above the eastern horizon just before the light of the rising sun makes all the other stars invisible (in May on the modern calendar), a sensible farmer will cut down his grain crop. Some months later (in our September), when the Pleiades dip below the western horizon just before sunrise, it is time to plow the fields and plant seeds for the next year's harvest.

Farmers such as Hesiod were primarily concerned with the seasons of the year. However, there was also a need to divide the year up into smaller units. The moon, so easily visible in the night sky and with clear phases, offered the unit of the month. Unfortunately, the lunar and solar cycles do not fit comfortably together, since twelve lunar months falls eleven days short of the solar cycle of a 365-day year. Ancient peoples wrestled with ways of reconciling the two cycles, and the months of varying lengths and leap years in our present-day calendar are the legacy of this dilemma.

The complex societies that arose from the fourth millennium B.C.E. onward had additional needs for information derived from astronomical observation, and these needs reflected the distinctive characteristics of those societies. In ancient Egypt an administrative calendar was essential for record keeping and the regular collection of taxes by the government. The Egyptians discovered that a calendar based on lunar months could be kept in harmony with the solar year by inserting an extra month five times over a nineteen-year cycle. They also learned from experience that the flooding of the Nile River—so vital for Egyptian agriculture—happened at the time when Sirius, the brightest star in the sky, rose above the eastern horizon just before the sun came up.

In the second millennium B.C.E., the Babylonians began to make and record very precise naked-eye observations of the movements of the sun, the moon, and the visible planets, of occasional eclipses, and of other unusual celestial occurrences. Believing that the phenomena they saw in the sky sometimes contained messages and warnings of disaster, the rulers supported specialists who observed, recorded, and interpreted these "signs" from the gods. Using a sophisticated system of mathematical notation, they figured out the regularities of certain cycles and were able to predict future occurrences of eclipses and the movements of the planets.

Whereas Babylonian science observed and recorded data, Greek philosophers tried to figure out why the heavenly bodies moved as they did and what the actual structure of the *kosmos* (Greek for an "orderly arrangement") was. Aristotle pointed out that because the earth's shadow, as seen on the face of the moon during a lunar eclipse, was curved, the earth must be a sphere. Eratosthenes (**eh-ruh-TOSS-thih-nees**) made a surprisingly accurate calculation of the circumference of the earth. Aristarchus (**ah-ris-TAWR-kiss**) calculated the distances and relative sizes of the moon and sun. He also argued against the prevailing notion that the earth was the center of the universe, asserting that the earth and other planets revolved around the sun. Other Greek theorists pictured the earth as a sphere at the center of a set of concentric spheres that rotated, carrying along the seven visible "planets"— the moon, Mercury, Venus, the sun, Mars,

De Agostini/Getty Images

Tower of the Winds, Athens, Second Century B.C.E. *Designed in the Hellenistic period by the astronomer Andronicus of Cyrrhus, the eight sides are decorated with images of the eight directional winds. Sundials on the exterior showed the time of day, and a water-driven mechanism inside the tower revealed the hours, days, and phases of the moon.*

Jupiter, Saturn—with the outermost ring containing the stars that maintain a fixed position relative to one another.

As a result of the conquests of Alexander the Great, Mesopotamia came under Greek control and Greek astronomers gained access to the many centuries of accumulated records of Babylonian observers. This more precise information allowed Greek thinkers to further refine their models for the structure and movement of celestial objects.

The Greek conception of the universe, in the form set down by the second-century C.E. astronomer Claudius Ptolemy, became the basis of scientific thinking about these matters for the next 1,400 years in the Islamic Middle East and Christian Europe.

Source: From *Hesiod: Works and Days and Theogony*, translated by Stanley Lombardo. Copyright © 1993. Reprinted by permission of Hackett Publishing Company.

and Egyptians intermarried in the villages of the countryside. Greeks living amid the monuments and descendants of the ancient civilizations of Egypt and western Asia were exposed to the mathematical and astronomical wisdom of Mesopotamia, the elaborate mortuary rituals of Egypt, and the many attractions of foreign religious cults. With little official planning or blessing, stemming for the most part from the day-to-day experiences and actions of ordinary people, a great multicultural experiment unfolded as Greek and Middle Eastern cultural traits clashed and merged.

CONCLUSION

Profound changes took place in the lands of the eastern Mediterranean and western Asia in the first millennium B.C.E., with Persians and Greeks playing pivotal roles. Let us compare the impacts of these two peoples and assess the broad significance of these centuries.

The empire of the Achaemenid Persians was the largest empire yet to appear in the world, encompassing a wide variety of landscapes, peoples, and social, political, and economic systems. How did the Persians manage this diverse collection of lands for more than two centuries? The answer did not lie entirely in brute force. The Persian government demonstrated flexibility and tolerance in its handling of the laws, customs, and beliefs of subject peoples. Persian administration, superimposed on top of local structures, left a considerable role for native institutions.

The Persians also displayed a flair for public relations. Their brand of Zoroastrian religion underlined the authority of the king as the appointee of god, champion of justice, and defender of world order against evil and destructive forces. In their art and inscriptions, the Persian kings broadcast an image of a benevolent empire in which the dependent peoples gladly contributed to the welfare of the realm.

Western Asia underwent significant changes in the period of Persian supremacy. By imposing a uniform system of law and administration and by providing security and stability, the Persian government fostered prosperity, at least for some. It also organized labor on a large scale to construct an expanded water distribution network and work the extensive estates of the Persian royal family and nobility.

Most difficult to assess is the cultural impact of Persian rule. A new synthesis of the long-dominant culture of Mesopotamia with Iranian elements is most visible in the art, architecture, and inscriptions of the Persian monarchs. The Zoroastrian religion may have spread across the empire and influenced other religious traditions, such as Judaism, but Zoroastrianism does not appear to have had broad, popular appeal. The Persian administration relied heavily on the scribes and written languages of its Mesopotamian, Syrian, and Egyptian subjects, and literacy remained the preserve of a small, professional class. Thus the Persian language does not seem to have been widely adopted by inhabitants of the empire.

Nearly two centuries of trouble with the Greeks on their western frontier vexed the Persians, but they were primarily concerned with the security of their eastern and northeastern frontiers, where they were vulnerable to attack by the nomads of Central Asia. The technological differences between Greece and Persia were not great. The only significant difference was the hoplite arms and military formation used by the Greeks, which often allowed them to prevail over the Persians. The Persian king's response in the later fifth and fourth centuries B.C.E. was to hire Greek mercenaries to employ hoplite tactics for his benefit.

Alexander's conquests brought changes to the Greek world almost as radical as those experienced by the Persians. Greeks spilled out into the sprawling new frontiers in northeastern Africa and western Asia, and the independent city-state became inconsequential in a world of large kingdoms. The centuries of Greek domination had a far more pervasive cultural impact on the Middle East than did the Persian period. Whereas Alexander had been inclined to preserve the Persian administrative apparatus, leaving native institutions and personnel in place, his successors relied almost exclusively on a privileged class of Greek soldiers, officers, and administrators.

Equally significant were the foundation of Greek-style cities, which exerted a powerful cultural influence on important elements of the native populations, and a system of easily learned alphabetic Greek writing, which led to more widespread literacy and more effective dissemination of information. The result was that the Greeks had a profound impact on the peoples and lands of the Middle East, and Hellenism persisted as a cultural force for a thousand years. And even after Islam spread over this region in the seventh century C.E., it absorbed and maintained elements of the Hellenistic legacy (see Chapter 10).

A final point should be made about the Greeks, one that is particularly apt for students of world history who are learning about the diversity of ways in which humans have addressed the challenges of living in the natural world and among other humans. Readers of this book are encouraged to compare Greek civilization to another great contemporary civilization where the sheer distance and lack of communication precluded any possibility of borrowing—ancient China in the Zhou era (see Chapter 4). Beyond discovering that the similarities are great, one is struck by the fact that the most innovative developments in both civilizations took place during periods of political fragmentation and persistent rivalry and warfare—the Archaic and Classical periods of Greek history and the Spring and Autumn and Warring States periods in China—rather than in the more stable centuries of imperial rule under the Roman and Han emperors (in Chapter 6 we will be making comparisons between Rome and early imperial China). The differences between Greek and early Chinese civilization are equally revealing and underlie the ways in which Western and East Asian civilizations have diverged, with implications for our own times.

IMPORTANT EVENTS 1000 B.C.E. TO 30 B.C.E.

ca. 1000 B.C.E.	Persians settle in southwest Iran
ca. 800 B.C.E.	Resumption of Greek contact with eastern Mediterranean
ca. 700 B.C.E.	Beginning of hoplite warfare
594 B.C.E.	Solon reforms laws at Athens
550 B.C.E.	Cyrus overthrows Medes
546 B.C.E.	Cyrus conquers Lydia
546–510 B.C.E.	Pisistratus and sons hold tyranny at Athens
539 B.C.E.	Cyrus takes control of Babylonia
530–522 B.C.E.	Conquest of Egypt
499–494 B.C.E.	Ionian Greeks rebel against Persia
490 B.C.E.	Athenians check Persian punitive expedition at Marathon
480–479 B.C.E.	Xerxes' invasion of Greece
477 B.C.E.	Athens becomes leader of Delian League
461–429 B.C.E.	Pericles dominant at Athens; Athens completes evolution to democracy
431–404 B.C.E.	Peloponnesian War
399 B.C.E.	Trial and execution of Socrates
387 B.C.E.	King's Peace makes Persia arbiter of Greek affairs
359 B.C.E.	Philip II becomes king of Macedonia
338 B.C.E.	Philip takes control of Greece
334–323 B.C.E.	Alexander the Great defeats Persia and creates huge empire
200 B.C.E.	First Roman intervention in the Hellenistic East
30 B.C.E.	Roman annexation of Egypt, the last Hellenistic kingdom

6

An Age of Empires: Rome and Han China, 753 b.c.e.–330 c.e.

According to Chinese sources, in the year 166 c.e. a group of travelers identifying themselves as envoys from Andun, the king of distant Da Qin, arrived at the court of the Chinese emperor Huan, one of the Han dynasty rulers. Andun was Marcus Aurelius Antoninus, the emperor of Rome. As far as we know, these travelers were the first "Romans" to reach China, although they probably were residents of one of the eastern provinces of the Roman Empire, and they probably stretched the truth in claiming to be official representatives of the Roman emperor. More likely they were merchants hoping to set up a profitable trading arrangement at the source of the silk so highly prized in the West. Chinese officials, however, were in no position to disprove their claim, since there was no direct contact between the Roman and Chinese Empires.

We do not know what became of these travelers, and their mission apparently did not lead to more regular contact between the empires. Even so, the episode raises some interesting points. First, the last centuries b.c.e. and the first centuries c.e. saw the emergence of two manifestations of a new kind of empire. Second, Rome and China were linked by far-flung international trading networks encompassing the entire Eastern Hemisphere, and they were dimly aware of each other's existence.

The Roman Empire encompassed all the lands surrounding the Mediterranean Sea as well as sizable portions of continental Europe and the Middle East. The Han Empire stretched from the Pacific Ocean to the oases of Central Asia. The largest empires the world had yet seen, they succeeded in centralizing control to a greater degree than earlier empires; their cultural impact on the lands and peoples they dominated was more pervasive; and they were remarkably stable and lasted for many centuries.

Thousands of miles separated Rome and Han China; neither influenced the other. Why did two such unprecedented political entities flourish at the same time? And why did they develop roughly similar solutions to certain problems? Historians have put forth theories stressing supposedly common factors—such as climate change and the pressure of nomadic peoples from Central Asia on the Roman and Chinese frontiers—but no theory has won general support.

ROME'S CREATION OF A MEDITERRANEAN EMPIRE, 753 B.C.E.–330 C.E.

Rome's central location contributed to its success in unifying Italy and then all the lands ringing the Mediterranean Sea. The middle of three peninsulas that jut from the European landmass into the Mediterranean, the boot-shaped Italian peninsula and the large island of Sicily constitute a natural bridge almost linking Europe and North Africa. Italy was a crossroads in the Mediterranean, and Rome was a cross-roads within Italy. Rome lay at the midpoint of the peninsula, about 15 miles (24 kilometers) from the western coast, where a north-south road intersected an east-west river route. The Tiber River on one side and a double ring of seven hills on the other afforded natural protection to the site.

Italy is a land of hills and mountains. The Apennine range runs along its length like a spine, separating the eastern and western coastal plains, while the arc of the Alps shields it on the north. Many of Italy's rivers are navigable, and passes through the Apennines and through the snowcapped Alps allowed merchants and armies to travel overland. The mild Mediterranean climate affords a long growing season and conditions suitable for a wide variety of crops. The hillsides, largely denuded of cover today, were well forested in ancient times, providing timber for construction and fuel. The region of Etruria in the northwest was rich in iron and other metals.

Even though as much as 75 percent of the total area of the Italian peninsula is hilly, there is still ample arable land in the coastal plains and river valleys. Much of this land has extremely fertile volcanic soil and sustained a much larger population than was possible in Greece. While expanding within Italy, the Roman state created effective mechanisms for tapping the human resources of the countryside.

A Republic of Farmers, 753–31 B.C.E. Popular legend maintained that Romulus was cast adrift on the Tiber River as a baby, was nursed by a she-wolf, and founded the city of Rome in 753 B.C.E. Archaeological research, however, shows that the Palatine Hill was occupied as early as 1000 B.C.E. The merging of several hilltop communities to form an urban nucleus, made possible by the draining of a swamp on the site of the future Roman Forum (civic center), took place shortly before 600 B.C.E. The Latin speech and cultural patterns of the inhabitants of the site were typical of the indigenous population of most of the peninsula. However, tradition remembered Etruscan immigrants arriving in the seventh century B.C.E. (the Etruscans, from the region north of Rome, were linguistically and culturally different and more technologically advanced than other peoples in Italy), and Rome came to pride itself on offering refuge to exiles and outcasts.

Agriculture was the essential economic activity in the early Roman state, and land was the basis of wealth. As a consequence, social status, political privilege, and fundamental values were related to land ownership. Most early Romans were self-sufficient farmers who owned small plots of land. A small number of families managed to acquire large tracts of land. The heads of these wealthy families were members of the Senate—a "Council of Elders" that played a dominant role in the politics of the Roman state. According to tradition, there were seven kings of Rome between 753 and 507 B.C.E. The first was Romulus; the last was the tyrannical Tarquinius Superbus. In 507 B.C.E. members of the senatorial class, led by Brutus "the Liberator," deposed Tarquinius Superbus and instituted a *res publica*, a "public possession," or republic.

The **Republic,** which lasted from 507 to 31 B.C.E., was not a democracy in the modern sense. Sovereign power resided in an Assembly of the male citizens where the votes of the wealthy classes counted for more than the votes of poor citizens. Each year a slate of officials was chosen, with members of the elite competing vigorously to hold offices in a prescribed order. The culmination of a political career was to be selected as one of the two consuls who presided over meetings of the Senate and Assembly and commanded the army on military campaigns.

The real center of power was the **Senate.** Technically an advisory council, first to the kings and later to the annually changing Republican officials, the Senate increasingly made policy and governed. Senators nominated their sons for public offices and filled Senate vacancies from the ranks of former officials. This self-perpetuating body, whose members served for life, brought together the state's wealth, influence, and political and military experience.

The inequalities in Roman society led to periodic conflict between the elite (called "patricians" [puh-TRISH-uhn]) and the majority of the population (called "plebeians" [pluh-BEE-uhn]), a struggle known as the Conflict of the Orders. On several occasions the plebeians refused to work or fight, and even physically withdrew from the city, in order to pressure the elite to make political concessions. One result was publication of the laws on twelve stone tablets ca. 450 B.C.E., which served as a check on arbitrary decisions by judicial officials. Another important reform was the creation of new officials, the tribunes (TRIH-byoon), who were drawn from the nonelite classes and who could veto, or block, actions of the Assembly or officials that threatened the interests of the lower orders. The elite, though forced to give in on key points, found ways to blunt the reforms, in large part by bringing the plebeian leadership into an expanded elite.

The basic unit of Roman society was the family, made up of the several living generations of family members plus domestic slaves. The oldest living male, the *paterfamilias*, exercised absolute authority over other family members. More generally, important male members of the society possessed *auctoritas*, a quality that elicited obedience from their inferiors.

Complex ties of obligation, such as the **patron/client relationship,** bound together individuals of different classes. Clients sought the help and protection of patrons, men of wealth and influence. A patron provided legal advice and representation, physical protection, and loans of money in tough times. In turn, the client was expected to follow his patron into battle, work on his land, and support him in the political arena. Throngs of clients awaited their patrons in the morning and accompanied them to the Forum for the day's business. Especially large retinues brought great prestige. Middle-class clients of aristocrats might be patrons of poorer men. In Rome inequality was accepted, institutionalized, and turned into a system of mutual benefits and obligations.

Historical sources rarely report the activities of Roman women, largely because they played no public role, and nearly all our information pertains to the upper classes. In early Rome, a woman was like a child in the eyes of the law. She started out under the absolute authority of her paterfamilias, and when she married, she came under the jurisdiction of the paterfamilias of her husband's family. Unable to own property or represent herself in legal proceedings, she depended on a male guardian to protect her interests.

Map legend:
- Roman Empire by death of Augustus, 14 C.E.
- Roman territory added by death of Hadrian, 138 C.E.
- Parthian Empire
- ✕ Major battles

© Cengage Learning

MAP 6.1 The Roman Empire

The Roman Empire came to encompass all the lands surrounding the Mediterranean Sea, as well as parts of continental Europe. When Augustus died in 14 C.E., he left instructions to his successors not to expand beyond the limits he had set, but Claudius invaded southern Britain in the mid-first century and the soldier-emperor Trajan added Romania early in the second century. Deserts and seas provided solid natural boundaries, but the long and vulnerable river border in central and eastern Europe would eventually prove expensive to defend and vulnerable to invasion by Germanic and Central Asian peoples.

Despite these limitations, Roman women were less constrained than their Greek counterparts (see Chapter 5). Over time they gained greater personal protection and economic freedom: for instance, some employed a form of marriage that left a woman under the jurisdiction of her father and independent after his death. There are many stories of strong women with great influence on their husbands or sons who helped shape Roman history. From the first century B.C.E. on, Roman poets confess their love for educated and outspoken women.

Early Romans believed in invisible forces known as *numina*. Vesta, the living, pulsating energy of fire, dwelled in the hearth. Janus guarded the door. The Penates watched over food stored in the cupboard. Other deities resided in nearby hills, caves, grottoes, and springs. Romans made small offerings of cakes and liquids to win the favor of these spirits. Certain gods had larger spheres of operation—for example, Jupiter was the god of the sky, and Mars initially was a god of agriculture as well as war.

Statue of a Roman Carrying Busts of His Ancestors, First Century B.C.E. *Roman society was extremely conscious of status, and the status of an elite Roman family was determined in large part by the public achievements of ancestors and living members. A visitor to a Roman home found portraits of distinguished ancestors in the entry hall, along with labels listing the offices they held. Portrait heads were carried in funeral processions.*

Alinari/Art Resource, NY

The Romans labored to maintain the *pax deorum* ("peace of the gods"), a covenant between the gods and the Roman state. Boards of priests drawn from the aristocracy performed sacrifices and other rituals to win the gods' favor. In return, the gods were expected to support the undertakings of the Roman state.

When the Romans came into contact with the Greeks of southern Italy (see Chapter 5), they equated their major deities with Greek gods—for example, Jupiter with Greek Zeus, Mars with Greek Ares—and they took over the myths attached to those gods.

Expansion in Italy and the Mediterranean   Around 500 B.C.E. Rome was a relatively unimportant city-state in central Italy. Three and a half centuries later, Rome was the center of a huge empire encompassing virtually all the lands surrounding the Mediterranean Sea. Expansion began slowly and then picked up momentum, reaching a peak in the third and second centuries B.C.E. Some scholars attribute this expansion to the greed and aggressiveness of a people fond of war. Others observe that the structure of the Roman state encouraged war, because the two consuls had only one year in office in which to gain military glory. The Romans invariably claimed that they were only defending themselves. The pattern was that the Romans, feeling insecure, expanded the territory under their control in order to provide a buffer against attack. However, each new conquest became vulnerable and led to further expansion.

The chief instrument of Roman expansion was the army. All male citizens owning a specified amount of land were subject to service. The Roman soldiers' equipment—body armor, shield, spear, and sword—was not far different from that of Greek hoplites, but the Roman battle line was more flexible than the phalanx, being subdivided into units that could maneuver independently. Roman armies were famous for their training and discipline. One observer noted that a Greek army would lazily seek a naturally defended hilltop to camp for the night, but a Roman army would always laboriously fortify an identical camp in the plain.

Rome's conquest of Italy was sparked by friction between the hill tribes of the Apennines, who drove their herds to seasonal grazing grounds, and the farmers of the coastal plains. In the fifth century B.C.E. Rome led a league of central Italian cities organized for defense against the hill tribes. On several occasions in the fourth century B.C.E. the Romans protected the wealthy and sophisticated cities of Campania, the region on the Bay of Naples possessing the richest farmland in Italy. By 290 B.C.E., in the course of three wars with the Samnite tribes of central Italy, the Romans had extended their "protection" over nearly the entire peninsula.

Unlike the Greeks, who were reluctant to share the privileges of citizenship with outsiders, the Romans often granted some or all of the political, legal, and economic privileges of Roman citizenship to conquered populations. They co-opted the most influential people in the conquered communities and made Rome's interests their interests. Rome demanded soldiers from its Italian subjects, and a seemingly inexhaustible reservoir of manpower was a key element of its military success. In a number of crucial wars, Rome was able to endure higher casualties than the enemy and to prevail by sheer numbers.

Between 264 and 202 B.C.E. Rome fought two protracted and bloody wars against the Carthaginians, those energetic descendants of Phoenicians from

Lebanon who had settled in present-day Tunisia and dominated the commerce of the western Mediterranean (see Chapter 3). The Roman state emerged as the unchallenged master of the western Mediterranean and acquired its first overseas provinces in Sicily, Sardinia, and Spain. Between 200 and 146 B.C.E. a series of wars pitted the Roman state against the major Hellenistic kingdoms in the eastern Mediterranean. The Romans were at first reluctant to occupy such distant territories and withdrew their troops at the conclusion of several wars. But when the settlements that they imposed failed to take root—often because Rome's "friends" in the Greek world did not understand that they were expected to be deferential and obedient clients to their Roman patron—the frustrated Roman government took over direct administration of these lands. The conquest of the Celtic peoples of Gaul (modern France; see Chapter 4) by Rome's most brilliant general, Gaius Julius Caesar, between 59 and 51 B.C.E. led to Rome's first territorial acquisitions in Europe's heartland.

At first the Romans resisted extending their system of governance and citizenship rights to the distant provinces. Indigenous elite groups willing to collaborate with the Romans were given considerable autonomy, including responsibility for local administration and tax collection. Every year a senator who recently had held a high office was dispatched to each province to serve as governor. Accompanied by a small retinue of friends and relations who served as advisers and deputies, he was responsible for defending the province against outside attack and internal disruption, overseeing the collection of taxes and other revenues due Rome, and deciding legal cases.

Over time, this system of provincial administration proved inadequate. Officials were chosen because of their political connections and often lacked competence. Yearly changes of governor meant that incumbents had little time to gain experience or make local contacts. Although many governors were honest, some unscrupulously extorted huge sums of money from the provincial populace. While governing an ever-larger Mediterranean empire, the Romans were still relying on the institutions and attitudes that developed when Rome was merely a city-state.

The Failure of the Republic   Rome's success in creating a vast empire unleashed forces that eventually destroyed the Republican system of government.

The frequent wars and territorial expansion of the third and second centuries B.C.E. produced profound changes in the Italian landscape. Most of the wealth generated by the conquest and control of new provinces ended up in the hands of the upper classes. Italian farmers were away from home on military service for long periods of time, and while they were away, investors took over their farms by purchase, deception, or intimidation. The small, self-sufficient farms of the Italian countryside, whose peasant owners had been the backbone of the Roman legions, were replaced by *latifundia*, literally "broad estates," or ranches.

The owners of these large estates grazed herds of cattle or grew crops—such as grapes for wine—that brought in big profits, rather than growing wheat, the staple food of ancient Italy. As a result, the population in the burgeoning cities of Italy became dependent on expensive imported grain. Meanwhile, the cheap slave labor provided by prisoners of war made it hard for peasants who had lost their farms to find work in the countryside (see Diversity and Dominance: Socioeconomic Mobility, Winners and Losers in Imperial Rome and Han China). When they moved to Rome

Socioeconomic Mobility, Winners and Losers in Imperial Rome and Han China

Throughout human history, most people have been born into societies in which there was little opportunity or likelihood that they could significantly improve their social or economic circumstances. However, in complex and urbanized civilizations like imperial Rome or Han China, economic advancement (which is, then, generally linked to a higher social status) is more achievable for various reasons, including conditions of peace and stability favorable to commerce brought by the imperial power, the construction of roads over which goods can be conveyed, increased wealth and higher standards of living for many, the presence of large numbers of potential customers in urban centers, and innovative technologies for producing high-quality products. However, two further points need to be made. First, in situations of open economic competition, there are losers as well as winners. And, second, the existence of new forms of wealth and its acquisition by new groups of people tends to destabilize and threaten traditional institutions and values. We are fortunate in having texts from early imperial Rome and Han China that illustrate these processes from the vantage point of "the losers."

Juvenal wrote poetic satires at Rome in the late first and early second centuries C.E. Of course satire, by its very nature, exaggerates, but to be effective and funny it has to be based on something real. The main speaker in Juvenal's Third Satire is a friend of the poet named Umbricius, who has decided to abandon the ever more dangerous and frustrating city of Rome for a quieter town on the Bay of Naples.

...'There is no room in the city
for respectable skills,' he said, 'and no
    reward for one's efforts.
Today my means are less than yesterday;
    come tomorrow,
the little left will be further reduced...

What can I do in Rome? I can't tell lies;
    if a book
is bad I cannot praise it and beg for a
    copy; the stars
in their courses mean nothing to me;
    I'm neither willing nor able
to promise a father's death; I've never
    studied the innards
of frogs; I leave it to others to carry
    instructions and presents
to a young bride from her lover; none will
    get help from me
in a theft; that's why I never appear on a
    governor's staff;...
Who, these days, inspires affection except
    an accomplice – one
whose conscience boils and seethes with
    unspeakable secrets?...
I shan't mince words. My fellow Romans,
    I cannot put up with a city of Greeks...
They make for the Esquiline, or the wil-
    low's Hill, intent on becoming
the vital organs and eventual masters of
    our leading houses.
Nimble wits, a reckless nerve, and a ready
    tongue...
What of the fact that the nation excels in
    flattery, praising
the talk of an ignorant patron, the looks
    of one who is ugly...
the whole country's a play. You chuckle,
    he shakes with a louder
guffaw; he weeps if he spots a tear in the
    eye of his patron,
yet he feels no grief; on a winter's day if
    you ask for a brazier,
he dons a wrap; if you say 'I'm warm,' he
    starts to perspire.
So we aren't on equal terms; he always has
    the advantage
who night and day alike is able to take his
    expression
from another's face, to throw up his hands
    and cheer if his patron

*produces an echoing belch or pees in a
    good straight line...
There's no room here for any Roman...
That same man, moreover, provides a
    cause and occasion
for universal amusement if his cloak is
    ripped and muddy,
if his toga is a little stained, and one of his
    shoes gapes open...
Of all that luckless poverty involves,
    nothing is harsher
than the fact that it makes people funny.'*

Umbricius complains about the difficulty that educated, middle-class Romans like Juvenal and himself have in finding gainful employment and making a decent living. They cannot compete with the swarms of "Greeks" (by which he means people from the Greek-speaking Eastern Mediterranean, which would include Greeks proper, Syrians, and Egyptians), who are such accomplished actors, flatterers, and liars that they ingratiate themselves with the rich and powerful and get all the good jobs and contracts. The real Romans, who have too much dignity to stoop to this level, are left on the outside looking in. As they descend into poverty in a city in which the cost of lodging, food, and everything else is exorbitantly high, they are scorned and humiliated.

We see in this poem a resurgence of long-standing Roman prejudice toward the Greeks. Ironically, the presence of so many Easterners in Rome is a product of the empire, both because large numbers of prisoners of war initially serving as slaves in Italy gained their freedom and Roman citizenship, and because the capital city was a magnet attracting the most able and ambitious people in the empire to come to Rome to make their fortune.

A striking Han Chinese parallel to Juvenal's *Third Satire* can be found in an essay on friendship written by Wang Fu. He lived in the first half of the second century CE and never obtained an official post, leading him to complain that the system was not operating with fairness.

People compete to flatter and to get close to those who are wealthy and prominent... People are also quick to snub those who are poor and humble... If a person makes friends with the rich and prominent, he will gain the benefits of influential recommendations for advancement in office and the advantages of generous presents and other emoluments. But if he makes friends with the poor and humble, he will lose money either from giving them handouts or from unrepaid loans... This is the reason that crafty, calculating individuals can worm their way up the official ladder while ordinary scholars slip ever more into obscurity. Unless the realm has a brilliant ruler, there may be no one to discern this... Alas! The gentlemen of today speak nobly but act basely. Their words are upright, but their hearts are false. Their actions do not reflect their words, and their words are out of harmony with their thoughts... In their lofty speeches they refer to virtuous and righteous persons as being worthy. But when they actually recommend people for office, they consider only such requirements as influence and prominence. If a man is just an obscure scholar, even if he possesses the virtue of Yan Hui and Min Ziqian, even if he is modest and diligent, even if he has the ability of Yi Yin and Lu Shang, even if he is filled with the most devoted compassion for the people, he is clearly not going to be employed in this world.

As Wang Fu sees it, men of ambition focused all their attention on cultivating the rich and powerful in order to get the recommendations that led to official appointments, and in the process they ignored their real friends, whereas men of talent who could not or would not play this game were overlooked and scorned for their poverty. While appointment to public office was supposed to be meritocratic, based, first, on knowledge of the classic Confucian texts as determined by an exam and then by performance in office, Wang Fu's essay makes clear that what mattered most was connections to powerful people and the recommendations those people made to their peers in the government.

Questions for Analysis

1. What kinds of abilities lead to success in imperial Rome and China?
2. Are the authors of these two texts just whining because they have had little success, or are they justified in claiming that the situation is unfair?
3. How are the new circumstances of increased socioeconomic mobility damaging traditional institutions and values?

Sources: First selection [translated by Niall Rudd, *Juvenal, The Satires* (Oxford 1992)]. Second selection [translated by Lily Hwa, in Patricia Buckley Ebrey (ed.), *Chinese Civilization*, A Sourcebook, 2nd ed. (The Free Press, 1993)].

and other cities, they found no work there either, and they lived in dire poverty. The growing urban masses, idle and prone to riot, would play a major role in the political struggles of the late Republic.

One consequence of the decline of peasant farmers in Italy was a shortage of men who owned the property required for military service. At the end of the second century B.C.E. Gaius Marius—a "new man," as the Romans called politically active individuals who did not belong to the traditional ruling class—accepted into his legions poor, propertyless men and promised them farms upon retirement from military service. These troops became devoted to Marius and helped him get elected to an unprecedented (and illegal) six consulships.

Between 88 and 31 B.C.E., a series of ambitious individuals—Sulla, Pompey, Julius Caesar, Mark Antony, and Octavian—commanded armies more loyal to them than to the state. Their use of Roman troops to increase their personal power led to bloody civil wars. The city of Rome was taken by force on several occasions, and victorious commanders executed opponents and controlled the state.

The Roman Principate, 31 B.C.E.–330 C.E.   Julius Caesar's grandnephew and heir, Octavian (63 B.C.E.–14 C.E.), eliminated all rivals by 31 B.C.E. and carefully set about refashioning the Roman system of government. He maintained the forms of the Republic—the offices, honors, and privileges of the senatorial class—but fundamentally altered the realities of power. A military dictator in fact, he never called himself king or emperor, claiming merely to be *princeps*, "first among equals," in a restored Republic. Thus, the period following the Republic is called the **Principate.**

Augustus, one of the many honorific titles that the Senate gave Octavian, connotes prosperity and piety, and it became the name by which he is best known to posterity. Augustus's patience and intuitive grasp of human nature enabled him to manipulate all the groups in Roman society. When he died in 14 C.E., after forty-five years of carefully veiled rule, few could remember the Republic. During his reign

Egypt and parts of the Middle East and central Europe were added to the empire, leaving only the southern half of Britain and modern Romania to be added later.

Augustus allied himself with the *equites* (EH-kwee-tays), the class of well-to-do Italian merchants and landowners second in wealth and social status to the senatorial class. This body of competent and self-assured individuals became the core of a new, paid civil service that helped run the Roman Empire. At last Rome had a governmental bureaucracy up to the task of managing a large empire with considerable honesty, consistency, and efficiency.

So popular was Augustus when he died that four members of his family succeeded to the position of "emperor" (as we call it) despite serious personal and political shortcomings. However, because of Augustus's calculated ambiguity about his role, the position of emperor was never automatically regarded as hereditary, and after the mid-first century C.E. other families obtained the post. In theory the early emperors were affirmed by the Senate; in reality they were chosen by the armies. By the second century C.E. a series of very capable emperors instituted a new mechanism of succession: each adopted a mature man of proven ability as his son and trained him as his successor.

While Augustus had felt it important to appeal to Republican traditions and conceal the source and extent of his power, this became less necessary over time, and later emperors exercised their authority more overtly. In imitation of Alexander the Great and the Hellenistic kings, many Roman emperors were officially deified (regarded as gods) after death. A cult of the living emperor developed as a way to increase the loyalty of subjects.

During the Republic a body of laws had developed, including decrees of the Senate, bills passed in the Assembly, and the practices of public officials who heard cases. In the later Republic legal experts began to analyze laws and legal procedures to determine the underlying principles; then they applied these principles to the creation of new laws required by a changing society. These experts were less lawyers in the modern sense than teachers, though they were sometimes consulted by officials or the parties to legal actions.

During the Principate the emperor became a major source of new laws. Roman law was studied and codified with a new intensity by the class of legal experts, and their interpretations often had the force of law. The basic divisions of Roman law— persons, things, and actions—reveal the importance of property and the rights of individuals in Roman eyes. The culmination of this long process of development and interpretation of the law was the sixth century C.E. Digest of Justinian. Roman law has remained the foundation of European law to this day.

An Urban Empire
The Roman Empire of the first three centuries C.E. was an "urban" empire. This does not mean that most people lived in cities. Perhaps 80 percent of the 50 to 60 million people in the empire engaged in agriculture and lived in villages or isolated farms. The empire, however, was administered through a network of towns and cities, and the urban populace benefited most.

Numerous towns had several thousand inhabitants, while a few major cities had several hundred thousand. Rome itself had approximately a million residents.

The largest cities strained the technological capabilities of the ancients; providing adequate food and water and removing sewage were always problems.

In Rome the upper classes lived in elegant townhouses on one of the hills. The house was centered around an *atrium*, a rectangular courtyard with an open sky-light that let in light and rainwater for drinking and washing. Surrounding the atrium were a large dining room for dinner and drinking parties, an interior garden, a kitchen, and possibly a private bath. Bedrooms were on the upper level. The floors were decorated with pebble mosaics, and the walls and ceilings were covered with frescoes (paintings done directly on wet plaster) of mythological scenes or out-door vistas, giving a sense of openness in the absence of windows. The typical aris-tocrat also owned a number of villas in the Italian countryside to which the family could retreat to escape the pressures of city life.

The poor lived in crowded slums in the low-lying parts of the city. Damp, dark, and smelly, with few furnishings, these wooden tenements were susceptible to fre-quent fires. Fortunately, Romans could spend much of the day outdoors, working, shopping, eating, and socializing.

The cities, towns, and even the ramshackle settlements that sprang up on the edge of frontier forts were miniature replicas of the capital city in political organi-zation and physical layout. A town council and two annually elected officials drawn from the local elite ran regional affairs with considerable autonomy. This "munici-pal aristocracy" imitated the manners and conduct of Roman senators, enhancing their status by endowing their communities with attractive elements of Roman urban life—civic buildings, temples, gardens, baths, theaters, amphitheaters—and putting on games and public entertainments.

In the countryside hard work and drudgery were relieved by occasional holi-days and village festivals and by the everyday pleasures of sex, family, and conver-sation. Rural people had to fend for themselves in dealing with bandits, wild animals, and other hazards of country life. They had little direct contact with the Roman government other than occasional run-ins with bullying soldiers and the dreaded arrival of the tax collector.

The concentration of land ownership in ever fewer hands was temporarily reversed by the distribution of farms to veteran soldiers during the civil wars of the late Republic, but it resumed in the era of the emperors. However, after the era of conquest ended in the early second century C.E., slaves were no longer plenti-ful or inexpensive, and landowners needed a new source of labor. "Tenant farm-ers" cultivated plots of land in return for a portion of their crops. The landowners lived in the cities and hired foremen to manage their estates. Thus wealth was con-centrated in the cities but was based on the productivity of rural laborers.

Some urban dwellers got rich from manufacture and trade. Commerce was greatly enhanced by the thousands of miles of well-built roads and by the **pax romana** ("Roman peace"), the safety and stability guaranteed by Roman might. Grain, meat, vegetables, and other bulk foodstuffs usually were exchanged locally because transportation was expensive and many products spoiled quickly. How-ever, the city of Rome imported massive quantities of grain from Sicily and Egypt to feed its huge population, and special naval squadrons performed this vital task.

Glass, metalwork, delicate pottery, and other fine manufactured products were exported throughout the empire. The centers of production, originally located in

Italy, moved into the provinces as knowledge of the necessary skills spread. Other merchants traded in luxury items from far beyond the boundaries of the empire, especially silk from China and spices from India and Arabia.

Roman armies stationed on the frontiers were a large market that promoted the prosperity of border provinces. The revenues collected by the central government transferred wealth from the rich interior provinces like Gaul (France) and Egypt, first to Rome to support the emperor and the central government, then to the frontier provinces to subsidize the armies.

Romanization—the spread of the Latin language and Roman way of life—was strongest in the western provinces, whereas Greek language and culture, a legacy of the Hellenistic kingdoms, predominated in the eastern Mediterranean (see Chapter 5). Modern Portuguese, Spanish, French, Italian, and Romanian evolved from the Latin language. The Roman government did not force Romanization; many provincials chose to adopt Latin and the cultural habits that went with it. There were advantages to speaking Latin and wearing a *toga* (the traditional cloak worn by Roman male citizens), just as people in today's developing nations see advantages in moving to the city, learning English, and wearing Western clothing. Latin facilitated dealings with the Roman administration and helped merchants get contracts to supply the military. Many also were drawn to the aura of success surrounding the language and culture of the dominant people.

The empire gradually granted Roman citizenship, with its privileges, legal protections, and exemptions from some types of taxation, to people living outside Italy. Men who completed a twenty-six-year term of service in the native military units that backed up the Roman legions were granted citizenship and could pass this coveted status on to their descendants. Emperors made grants of citizenship to individuals or entire communities as rewards for good service. Finally, in 212 C.E. the emperor Caracalla granted citizenship to all free, adult, male inhabitants of the empire.

The gradual extension of citizenship mirrored the empire's transformation from an Italian dominion into a commonwealth of peoples. As early as the first century C.E. some of the leading literary and intellectual figures came from the provinces. By the second century even the emperors hailed from Spain, Gaul, and North Africa.

The Rise of Christianity

During this period of general peace and prosperity, events were taking place in the East that, though little noted at the moment, would be of great historical significance. The Jewish homeland of Judaea (see Chapter 3), roughly equivalent to present-day Israel, came under direct Roman rule in 6 C.E. Over the next half century Roman governors insensitive to the Jewish belief in one god provoked opposition to Roman rule. Many waited for the arrival of the Messiah, the "Anointed One," a military leader who would drive out the Romans and liberate the Jewish people.

This is the context for the career of **Jesus**, a young Jewish carpenter from the Galilee region in northern Israel. Since the portrait of Jesus found in the New Testament largely reflects the viewpoint of followers a half century after his death, it is difficult to determine the motives and teachings of the historical Jesus. Some experts believe that he was essentially a rabbi, or teacher. Offended by Jewish religious and political leaders' excessive concern with money and power and by the perfunctory nature of mainstream Jewish religious practice in his time, he prescribed a return to the personal faith and spirituality of an earlier age. Others stress his connections to the apocalyptic fervor found in certain circles of Judaism, such as John the Baptist and the community that authored the Dead Sea Scrolls. They view Jesus as a fiery prophet who urged people to prepare themselves for the imminent end of the world and God's ushering in of a blessed new age. Still others see him as a political revolutionary, upset by the downtrodden condition of the peasants in the countryside and the poor in the cities, who determined to drive out the Roman occupiers and their collaborators among the Jewish elite.

Whatever the real nature of his mission, the charismatic Jesus eventually attracted the attention of the Jewish authorities in Jerusalem, who regarded popular reformers as potential troublemakers. They turned him over to the Roman governor, Pontius Pilate. Jesus was imprisoned, condemned, and executed by crucifixion, a punishment usually reserved for common criminals. After his death his followers, the Apostles, sought to spread his teachings among their fellow Jews and persuade them that he was the Messiah and had been resurrected (returned from death to life).

Paul, a Jew from the Greek city of Tarsus in southeast Anatolia, converted to the new creed. Between 45 and 58 C.E. he threw his enormous talent and energy into spreading the word. Traveling throughout Syria-Palestine, Anatolia, and Greece, he became increasingly frustrated with the refusal of most Jews to accept that Jesus was the Messiah and had ushered in a new age. Many Jews, on the other hand, were appalled by the failure of the followers of Jesus to maintain traditional Jewish practices. Discovering a spiritual hunger among many non-Jews, Paul redirected his efforts toward them and set up a string of Christian (from the Greek name *christos*, meaning "anointed one," given to Jesus by his followers) communities in the eastern Mediterranean.

Paul's career exemplifies the cosmopolitan nature of the Roman Empire. Speaking both Greek and Aramaic, he moved comfortably between the Greco-Roman and Jewish worlds. He used Roman roads, depended on the peace guaranteed by Roman arms, called on his Roman citizenship to protect him from the arbitrary action of local authorities, and moved from city to city in his quest for converts. In 66 C.E. long-building tensions in Roman Judaea erupted into a full-scale revolt that lasted until 73. One of the casualties of the Roman reconquest of Judaea was the Jerusalem-based Christian community, which focused on converting the Jews. This left the field clear for Paul's non-Jewish converts, and Christianity began to diverge more and more from its Jewish roots.

For more than two centuries, the sect grew slowly but steadily. Many of the first converts were from disenfranchised groups—women, slaves, the urban poor. They received respect not accorded them in the larger society and obtained positions of responsibility when the members of early Christian communities democratically elected their leaders. However, as the religious movement grew and prospered, it developed a hierarchy of priests and bishops and became subject to bitter disputes over theological doctrine (see Chapter 11).

As monotheists forbidden to worship other gods, early Christians were persecuted by Roman officials, who regarded their refusal to worship the emperor as a sign of disloyalty. Despite occasional government-sponsored persecution and spontaneous mob attacks, or perhaps because of them, the young Christian movement continued to gain strength and attract converts. By the late third century C.E. its adherents were a sizable minority within the Roman Empire and included many educated and prosperous people with posts in the local and imperial governments.

The expansion of Christianity should be seen as part of a broader religious tendency. In the Hellenistic and Roman periods, a number of cults gained popularity by claiming to provide secret information about the nature of life and death and promising a blessed afterlife to their adherents. Arising in the eastern Mediterranean, they spread throughout the Greco-Roman lands in response to a growing spiritual and intellectual hunger not satisfied by traditional pagan practices. These included the worship of the mother-goddess Cybele in Anatolia, the Egyptian goddess Isis, and the Iranian sun-god Mithra. As we shall see, the ultimate victory of Christianity over these rivals had as much to do with historical circumstances as with its spiritual appeal.

Technology and Transformation   The relative safety and ease of travel brought by Roman arms and roads enabled merchants to sell their wares and early Christians to spread their faith. Surviving remnants of roads, fortification walls, aqueducts, and buildings testify to the engineering expertise of the ancient Romans. Using the labor of military personnel was one of the ways in which the Roman government kept large numbers of soldiers busy in peacetime. Some of the best engineers also served with the army, building bridges, siege works, and ballistic weapons that hurled stones and shafts.

Among the technological achievements of the Romans was the use of arches, which allow even distribution of great weights without thick supporting walls. With the invention of concrete—a mixture of lime powder, sand, and water that could be poured into molds—the Romans could create vast vaulted and domed interior spaces, unlike the rectilinear pillar-and-post construction of the Greeks. A third achievement was the **aqueduct**—a long elevated or underground conduit that carried water from a source to an urban center using only the force of gravity. Made of large cut stones closely fitted and held together by mortar, aqueducts were elevated atop walls or bridges, making it difficult for unauthorized parties to tap the water line for their own use. Sections of aqueduct that crossed rivers presented the same construction challenges as bridges. Roman engineers lowered prefabricated wooden cofferdams—large, hollow cylinders—into the riverbed and pumped out the water so workers could descend and construct cement piers to support the arched segments of the bridge. When an aqueduct reached the outskirts of a city, the water flowed into a reservoir, where it was stored. Pipes connected the reservoir to public fountains and the houses of the rich in different parts of the city.

Defending borders that stretched for thousands of miles was a major challenge. Augustus advised against further expanding the empire because the costs of administering and defending subsequent acquisitions would be greater than the revenues. The Roman army was then reorganized and redeployed to reflect the shift from an offensive to a defensive strategy. At most points the empire was protected by mountains, deserts, and seas. But the lengthy Rhine and Danube river frontiers in Germany and central Europe were vulnerable, guarded only by a string of forts with small garrisons adequate for dealing with raiders. On particularly desolate frontiers, such as in Britain and North Africa, the Romans built long walls to keep out intruders.

Most of Rome's neighbors were less technologically advanced and more loosely organized and so did not pose a serious threat to the security of the empire. The one exception was the Parthian kingdom, heir to the Mesopotamian and Persian Empires, which controlled the lands on the eastern frontier (today's Iran and Iraq). For centuries Rome and Parthia engaged in a rivalry that sapped both sides without any significant territorial gain by either party.

The Roman state prospered for two and a half centuries after Augustus's reforms, but in the third century C.E. cracks in the edifice became visible. Historians use the expression "**Third-Century Crisis**" to refer to the period from 235 to 284 C.E., when political, military, and economic problems beset and nearly destroyed the Roman Empire. The most visible symptom of the crisis was the frequent change of rulers: twenty or more men claimed the office of emperor during this period. Most reigned for only a few months or years before being overthrown by rivals or killed by their own troops. Germanic tribesmen on the Rhine/Danube frontier took advantage of the frequent civil wars and periods of anarchy to raid deep into the empire. For the first time in centuries, Roman cities began to erect walls for protection. Several regions, feeling that the central government was not adequately protecting them, broke away and turned power over to a leader who promised to put their interests first.

These crises had a devastating impact on the empire's economy. Buying the loyalty of the armies and defending the increasingly permeable frontiers drained the treasury. The unending demands of the central government for more tax revenues, as well as the interruption of commerce by fighting, eroded the towns' prosperity. Shortsighted emperors, desperate for cash, secretly reduced the amount of precious metal in coins and pocketed the excess. The public quickly caught on, and the devalued coinage became less and less acceptable in the marketplace. The empire reverted to a barter economy, a far less efficient system that further curtailed large-scale and long-distance commerce.

The municipal aristocracy, once the most vital and public-spirited class in the empire, was slowly crushed out of existence. As town councilors, its members were personally liable for shortfalls in taxes owed to the state. The decline in trade eroded their wealth, and many began to evade their civic duties and even went into hiding.

Population shifted out of the cities and into the countryside. Many sought employment and protection from both raiders and government officials on the estates of wealthy and powerful country landowners. The shrinking of cities and movement of the population to the country estates were the first steps in a demographic shift toward the social and economic structures of the European Middle Ages—roughly seven hundred years during which wealthy rural lords dominated a peasant population tied to the land (see Chapter 11).

Just when things looked bleakest, one man pulled the empire back from the brink of disaster. Like many rulers of that age, Diocletian came from one of the eastern European provinces most vulnerable to invasion. A commoner by birth, he had risen through the ranks of the army and gained power in 284. The proof of his success is that he ruled for more than twenty years and died in bed.

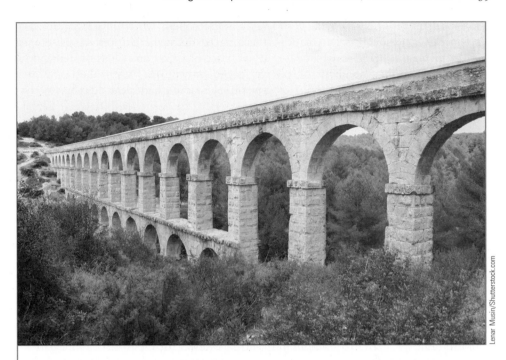

Lenar Musin/Shutterstock.com

Roman Aqueduct Near Tarragona, Spain *The growth of towns and cities challenged Roman officials to provide an adequate supply of water. Aqueducts channeled water from a source, sometimes many miles away, to an urban complex, using only the force of gravity. To bring an aqueduct from high ground into the city, Roman engineers designed long, continuous rows of arches that maintained a steady downhill slope. Scholars sometimes can roughly estimate the population of an ancient city by calculating the amount of water that was available to it.*

Diocletian implemented radical reforms that saved the Roman state by transforming it. To halt inflation (the process by which prices rise as money becomes worthless), Diocletian issued an edict specifying the maximum prices for various commodities and services. He froze many people into professions regarded as essential and required them to train their sons to succeed them. This unprecedented government regulation of prices and vocations had unforeseen consequences. A "black market" arose among buyers and sellers who ignored the government's price controls (and threats to impose the death penalty on violators). Many inhabitants of the empire began to see the government as an oppressive entity that no longer deserved their loyalty.

When Diocletian resigned in 305, the old divisiveness reemerged as various claimants battled for the throne. The eventual winner was **Constantine** (r. 306–337), who reunited the entire empire under his sole rule by 324.

In 312 Constantine won a key battle at the Milvian Bridge near Rome. He later claimed that he had seen a cross—the sign of the Christian God—superimposed on the sun before the battle. Believing that the Christian God had helped him achieve the victory, in the following year Constantine issued the Edict of Milan, ending the persecution of Christianity and guaranteeing freedom of worship to Christians and all others. Throughout his reign he supported the Christian church, although he tolerated other beliefs as well. Historians disagree about whether Constantine was spiritually motivated or pragmatically seeking to unify the peoples of the empire under a single religion. In either case, his embrace of Christianity was of tremendous significance. Large numbers of people began to convert when they saw that Christians seeking political office or government favors had clear advantages over non-Christians.

In 324 Constantine transferred the imperial capital from Rome to Byzantium, an ancient Greek city on the Bosporus (BAHS-puhr-uhs) strait leading from the Mediterranean into the Black Sea. The city was renamed Constantinople (cahn-stan-tih-NO-pul), "City of Constantine." This move both reflected and accelerated changes already taking place. Constantinople was closer than Rome to the most-threatened borders in eastern Europe. The urban centers and middle class in the eastern half of the empire had better withstood the Third-Century Crisis than those in the western half. In addition, more educated people and more Christians were living in the eastern provinces.

The conversion of Constantine and the transfer of the imperial capital are some-times seen as the end of Roman history. But many of the important changes that cul-minated during Constantine's reign had their roots in events of the previous two centuries, and the Roman Empire as a whole survived for at least another century. The eastern, or Byzantine, portion of the empire (discussed in Chapter 11) survived Constantine by more than a thousand years. Nevertheless, the Roman Empire of the fourth and fifth centuries C.E. was fundamentally different from the earlier empire, and it is convenient to see Constantine's reign as the beginning of a new epoch.

THE ORIGINS OF IMPERIAL CHINA, 221 B.C.E.–220 C.E.

The early history of China (described in Chapter 4) was characterized by the fragmen-tation that geography dictated. The Shang (ca. 1750–1045 B.C.E.) and Western Zhou (1045–771 B.C.E.) dynasties ruled over a compact zone in northeastern China. The last few centuries of nominal Zhou rule—the Warring States Period—saw frequent hostili-ties among a group of small states with somewhat different languages and cultures.

In the second half of the third century B.C.E. one of the warring states—the **Qin** (chin) state of the Wei (way) River Valley—rapidly conquered its rivals and created China's first empire (221–206 B.C.E.). Built at great cost in human lives and labor, the Qin Empire barely survived the death of its founder, **Shi Huangdi** (shih wahng-dee). Power soon passed to a new dynasty, the **Han**, which ruled China from 202 B.C.E. to 220 C.E. Thus began the long history of imperial China—a tradition of political and cultural unity and continuity that lasted into the early twentieth century and still has meaning for the very different China of our time.

The Qin Unification of China, 221–206 B.C.E. From the mid-third century B.C.E., Qin began to methodically conquer and incorporate the other Chinese states, and by 221 B.C.E. it had unified northern and central China in the first Chinese "empire." The name *China*, by which this land is known in the Western world, is probably derived from *Qin*. Qin emerged as the ultimate winner because of a combination of factors: the toughness and military preparedness of a frontier state long accustomed to defending itself against "barbarian" neighbors, the wholehearted adoption of severe Legalist methods for exploiting the natural and human resources of the kingdom (see Chapter 4), and the surpassing ambition of a ruthless and energetic young king.

The Qin monarch, Zheng (jahng), came to the throne at the age of thirteen in 246 B.C.E. Guided by a circle of Legalist advisers, he launched a series of wars of conquest. After defeating the last of his rivals in 221 B.C.E., he gave himself a title that symbolized the new state of affairs—Shi Huangdi, or "First Emperor"—and claimed that his dynasty would last ten thousand generations.

The new regime eliminated rival centers of authority. Its first target was the landowning aristocracy of the conquered states and the system on which aristocratic wealth and power had been based. The Qin government abolished primogeniture, the right of the eldest son to inherit all the landed property, requiring estates to be broken up and passed on to several heirs. A new, centrally controlled administrative structure was put in place, with district officials appointed by the king and watched over by his agents.

The Qin government's commitment to standardization helped create a unified Chinese civilization. A code of law, in force throughout the empire, applied punishments evenhandedly to all members of society. The Qin also imposed standardized weights and measures, a single coinage, a common system of writing, and even a specified axle-length for carts so that they would create a single set of ruts in the road.

Li Si (luh suh), the Legalist prime minister, persuaded Shi Huangdi that the scholars (primarily Confucian rivals of the Legalists; see Chapter 4) were subverting the goals of the regime. The Legalists viewed Confucian expectations of benevolent and nonviolent conduct from rulers as an intolerable check on the government's absolute power. Furthermore, the Confucians' appeal to the past impeded the new order being created by the Qin. A crackdown on the scholars ensued in which many Confucian books were publicly burned and many scholars brutally executed.

Shi Huangdi was determined to secure the northern border against nomadic raids on Chinese territory. Pastoralists and farmers had always exchanged goods on the frontier. Herders sought food and crafted goods produced by farmers and townsfolk, and farmers depended on the herders for animals and animal products. Sometimes, however, nomads raided the settled lands and took what they needed. For centuries the Chinese kingdoms had struggled with these tough, horse-riding warriors, building long walls along the frontier to keep them away from vulnerable farmlands (see Chapter 4). Shortly before the Qin unification of China, several states had begun to train soldiers on horseback to contend with the mobile nomads.

Shi Huangdi sent a large force to drive the nomads far north. His generals succeeded momentarily, extending Chinese territory beyond the great northern loop of the Yellow River. They also connected and extended earlier walls to create a continuous fortification, the ancestor of the Great Wall of China. A recent study concludes that, contrary to the common belief that the purpose of the wall was defensive—to keep the "barbarians" out of China—its primary function was offensive, to take in newly captured territory, to which large numbers of Chinese peasants were now dispatched and ordered to begin cultivation.[1]

---

[1] Nicola Di Cosmo, *Ancient China and Its Enemies: The Rise of Nomadic Power in East Asian History* (Cambridge: Cambridge University Press, 2002), 155–158.

Shi Huangdi's attack on the nomads had an unanticipated consequence. The threat to their way of life created by the Chinese invasion drove the normally fragmented and quarreling nomad groups to unite in a great confederacy under the dynamic leadership of Maodun (mow-doon). This **Xiongnu** (SHE-OONG-noo) Confederacy would pose a huge military threat to China for centuries, with frequent wars and high costs in lives and resources.

Needing many people to serve in the armies, construct roads and walls on the frontiers, and build new cities, palaces, and a monumental tomb for the ruler, the Qin government instituted an oppressive program of compulsory military and labor services and relocated large numbers of people. The recent discovery of a manual of Qin laws used by an administrator, with prescriptions less extreme than expected, suggests that the sins of the Qin may have been exaggerated by later sources. Nevertheless, the widespread uprisings that broke out after the death of Shi Huangdi attest to the harsh nature of the Qin regime.

When Shi Huangdi died in 210 B.C.E., several officials schemed with one of his sons to place him on the throne. The First Emperor was buried in a monumental tomb whose layout mirrored the geography of China, and the tomb was covered with a great mound of earth. Nearby were buried life-size sculptures of seven thousand soldiers to guard him in the afterlife, a more humane alternative to the human sacrifices of earlier eras. This terracotta (baked clay) army was discovered in the 1970s C.E., but the burial mound remains unexcavated.

The new emperor proved to be weak. Uprisings broke out on many fronts, reflecting both the resentment of the old aristocracies that had been deprived of wealth and privilege, and the anger of the commoners against excessive compulsory labor, forced relocations, and heavy taxation. By 206 B.C.E. Qin rule had been broken—the "ten-thousand-generation dynasty" had lasted only fifteen years. Nevertheless, the most important achievements of the Qin, the unification of China and the creation of a single, widely dispersed Chinese style of civilization, would endure.

The Long Reign of the Han, 202 B.C.E.–220 C.E.   Despite the overthrow of the Qin, fighting continued among various rebel groups. In 202 B.C.E. Liu Bang (le-oo bahng) prevailed and inaugurated a new dynasty, the Han, that would govern China for more than four centuries (202 B.C.E.– 220 C.E.). The Han created the machinery and ideology of imperial government that would prevail for two millennia, and Chinese people today refer to themselves ethnically as "Han."

The new emperor, generally known by the throne name **Gaozu** (gow-zoo), came from a modest background. Stories stress his peasant qualities: fondness for drink, blunt speech, and easy manner. Gaozu and his successors courted popularity and consolidated their rule by denouncing the harshness of the Qin and renouncing many Qin laws. In reality, however, they maintained—with sensible modifications— many Legalist-inspired institutions of the Qin to control far-flung territories and diverse populations.

The early Han rulers faced tough challenges. China had been badly damaged by the harsh exactions of the Qin and the widespread fighting in the period of rebellions. Because the economy needed time to recover, Gaozu and his immediate successors had to be frugal, keeping costs down to reduce taxes and undertaking measures to improve the state of agriculture. For instance, during prosperous times the government collected and stored surplus grain that could be sold at reasonable prices in times of shortage.

Gaozu reverted to the traditional feudal grants the Qin had abolished. The eastern parts of China were parceled out to relatives and major supporters, while the rest was divided into "commanderies" directly controlled by the central government. Over the next few reigns, these fiefs were reabsorbed as rebellions or deaths of the rulers provided the opportunity.

When Gaozu marched north to confront a Xiongnu incursion, he and his troops were trapped, and he had to negotiate a safe passage home for his army.

MAP 6.2 Han China

The Qin and Han rulers of northeast China extended their control over all of easternChina and extensive territories to the west. A series of walls in the north and northwest, built to check the incursions of nomadic peoples from the steppes, were joined together to form the ancestor of the present-day Great Wall of China. An extensive network of roads connecting towns, cities, and frontier forts promoted rapid communication and facilitated trade. The Silk Road carried China's most treasured products to Central, South, and West Asia and the Mediterranean lands.

Realizing the inferiority of Han troops and the limited funds for a military buildup, he adopted a policy of appeasing the Xiongnu. This essentially meant buying them off by dispatching annual "gifts" of rice, silk, and wine, as well as marrying a Han princess to the Xiongnu ruler.

While the throne passed to a young child when Gaozu died in 195 B.C.E., real power lay with Gaozu's formidable wife, Empress Lü (lyew). Throughout the Han era, empresses played a key role in determining which of the many sons (the emperors had multiple wives and concubines) would succeed to the throne, and they often chose minors or weak figures whom they and their male relatives could control. Under such circumstances Wu came to the throne as a teenager in 141 B.C.E. The deaths of his grandmother and uncle soon opened the way for him to rule in his own right, and thus began one of the longest and most eventful reigns in the history of the dynasty (141–87 B.C.E.).

We know much about the personality and policies of this emperor because of **Sima Qian** (sih-muh chyehn) (ca. 145–85 B.C.E.), who created the definitive form of historical writing in China. Serving as "chief astrologer" at the Han court, Sima Qian was castrated by Wu for defending a disgraced general. He therefore presents

Digital Vision/Getty Images

Terracotta Soldiers from the Tomb of Shi Huangdi, "First Emperor" of China, Late Third Century B.C.E. *Near the monumental tomb that he built for himself, the First Emperor filled a huge underground chamber with more than seven thousand life-sized baked-clay statues of soldiers. The terra-cotta army was unearthed in the 1970s.*

a generally negative view, portraying Wu as being manipulated by religious charlatans promising him magical powers, immortality, and séances with the dead. Reading his account critically, however, one could also conclude that Wu used religious pageantry to boost his own power.

Indeed, Wu did much to increase the power of the emperor. He launched military operations south as far as northern Vietnam, and north into Manchuria and North Korea. He abandoned the policy of appeasing the Xiongnu, concluding that this approach had failed since the nomads still made periodic attacks on the northern frontier. Wu built up his military, especially the cavalry, and went on the offensive. Thus began decades of bitter, costly fighting between China and the Xiongnu. In the long run Wu and his successors prevailed, and by the mid-first century C.E. the Xiongnu Confederacy had disintegrated, though nomad groups still threatened Chinese lands.

Wu dispatched forces to explore and conquer territories northwest of the Chinese heartland, essentially modern Gansu and Xinjiang (SHIN-jyahng). His goals were to improve access to large numbers of horses for his expanding cavalry and to pressure the Xiongnu on their western flank. Thus began the incorporation of this region into greater China. This expansion also brought new economic opportunities, laying the foundations for the Silk Road over which silk and other lucrative trade goods would be carried to Central, southern, and western Asia (see Chapter 9).

The military buildup and frequent wars with the Xiongnu were expensive, forcing Wu to find new revenues. One solution was government monopolies on several high-profit commodities: salt, iron, and alcoholic beverages. These measures were highly controversial.

Another momentous development was the adoption of Confucianism—modified to meet the circumstances of the era—as the official ideology of the imperial system. A university was opened on the outskirts of the capital city, Chang'an (chahng-ahn), and local officials were ordered to send a certain number of promising students from their districts each year. For two thousand years Chinese government would depend on scholar-officials promoted for their performance on exams probing their knowledge of Confucian texts. This alliance of Confucians and the imperial government, fraught with tensions, required compromises on both sides. The Confucians gained access to employment and power but had to accommodate ethical principles to the reality of far-from-perfect rulers. The emperors won the backing and services of a class of competent, educated people but had to deal with the Confucians' expectation that rulers should model ethical behavior and their insistence on giving often unwelcome advice.

Chinese Society   The Chinese government periodically conducted a census of inhabitants, and the results for 2 C.E. revealed 12 million households and 60 million people. Then, as now, the vast majority lived in the eastern river-valley regions where intensive agriculture could support a dense population.

The fundamental unit was the family, including not only the living but all previous generations. The Chinese believed their ancestors maintained an interest in the fortunes of living family members, so they consulted, appeased, and venerated them. Each generation must produce sons to perpetuate the family and maintain the ancestor cult that provided a kind of immortality to the deceased. In earlier times

Gold Belt Buckle, Xiongnu, Second Century B.C.E. *The Xiongnu, herders in the lands north of China, shared the artistic conventions of nomadic peoples across the steppes of Asia and eastern Europe, such as this fluid, twisting representation of the animals on which they depended for their livelihood. Shi Huangdi's military incursion into their pasturelands in the late third century* B.C.E. *catalyzed the formation of the Xiongnu Confederacy, whose horse-riding warriors challenged the Chinese for centuries.*

multiple generations and groups of families lived together, but by the imperial era independent nuclear families were the norm.

Within the family was a clear-cut hierarchy headed by the oldest male. Each person had a place and responsibilities, based on gender, age, and relationship to other family members, and people saw themselves as part of an interdependent unit rather than as individual agents. Parents' authority over children did not end with the passing of childhood, and parents occasionally took mature children to court for disobedience. The family inculcated the basic values of Chinese society: loyalty, obedience to authority, respect for elders and ancestors, and concern for honor and appropriate conduct. Because the hierarchy in the state mirrored the hierarchy in the family—peasants, soldiers, administrators, and rulers all made distinctive contributions to the welfare of society—these same attitudes carried over into the relationship between individuals and the state.

Traditional beliefs about conduct appropriate for women are preserved in a biography of the mother of the Confucian philosopher Mencius (Mengzi):

> *A woman's duties are to cook the five grains, heat the wine, look after her parents-in-law, make clothes, and that is all! ... [She] has no ambition to manage affairs outside the house.... She must follow the "three submissions." When she is young, she must submit to her parents. After her marriage, she must submit to her husband. When she is widowed, she must submit to her son.*[2]

In reality, a woman's status depended on her "location" within various social institutions. Women of the royal family, such as wives of the emperor or queen-mothers, could be influential political figures. A young bride, whose marriage had been arranged by her parents, would go to live with her husband's family, where she was, initially, a stranger who had to prove herself. Mothers-in-law had authority over their sons' wives, and mothers, sisters, and wives competed for influence with the men of the household and a larger share of the family's resources.

"Lessons for Women," written at the end of the first century C.E. by Ban Zhao (bahn jow), illuminates the unresolved tensions in Han society's attitudes toward women. Instructing her own daughters on how to conduct themselves as proper women, Zhao urges them to conform to traditional expectations by obeying males, maintaining their husbands' households, performing domestic chores, and raising the children. Yet she also makes an impassioned plea for the education of girls and urges husbands to respect and not beat their wives.

People lived in various milieus—cities, rural villages and farms, or military camps on the frontiers—and their activities and the quality of their lives were shaped by these contexts. From 202 B.C.E. to 25 C.E.—the period of the Early, or Western, Han—the capital was at **Chang'an** (modern Xi'an [shee-ahn]), in the Wei River Valley, an ancient seat of power from which the Zhou and Qin dynasties had emerged. Protected by a ring of hills but with ready access to the fertile plain, Chang'an was surrounded by a wall of pounded earth and brick 15 miles (24 kilometers) in circumference. In 2 C.E. its population was 246,000. Part of the city was carefully planned. Broad thoroughfares running north and south intersected with others running east and west. High walls protected the palaces, administrative offices, barracks, and storehouses of the imperial compound, to which access was restricted. Temples and marketplaces were scattered about the civic center. Chang'an became a model of urban planning, its main features imitated in cities and towns throughout China (it is estimated that between 10 and 30 percent of the population lived in urban centers). From 25 to 220 C.E. the Later, or Eastern, Han established its base farther east, in the more centrally located Luoyang (LWOE-yahng).

Han literature describes the appearance of the capitals and the activities taking place in the palace complexes, public areas, and residential streets. Moralizing writers criticized the excesses of the elite. Living in multistory houses, wearing fine silks, traveling in ornate horse-drawn carriages, well-to-do officials and merchants devoted their leisure time to art and literature, occult religious practices, elegant banquets, and various entertainments—music and dance, juggling and acrobatics,

---

[2]Patricia Buckley Ebrey, ed., *Chinese Civilization and Society: A Sourcebook* (New York: Free Press, 1981), 33–34.

dog and horse races, and cock and tiger fights. In stark contrast, the common people inhabited a sprawling warren of alleys, living in dwellings packed "as closely as the teeth of a comb."

While the upper echelons of scholar-officials resided in the capital, lower-level bureaucrats were scattered throughout smaller cities and towns serving as headquarters for regional governments. These scholar-officials shared a common Confucian culture and ideology. Exempt from taxes and compulsory military or labor services, they led comfortable lives by the standards of the time. While the granting of government jobs on the basis of performance on the exams theoretically should have given everyone an equal chance, in reality the sons of officials had distinct advantages in obtaining the requisite education in classical texts. Thus the scholar-officials became a self-perpetuating, privileged class. The Han depended on local officials for day-to-day administration of their far-flung territories. They collected taxes, regulated conscription for the army and labor projects, provided protection, and settled disputes.

Merchant families also were based in the cities, and some became very wealthy. However, ancient Chinese society viewed merchants with suspicion, accusing them of greedily driving prices up through speculation and being parasites who lived off the work of others. Advisers to the emperors periodically blamed merchants for the economic ills of China and proposed harsh measures, such as banning them and their children from holding government posts.

The Western Han state required two years of military service from able-bodied males, but by the Eastern Han period the military was staffed by professional soldiers. Large numbers of Chinese men spent long periods away from home in distant frontier posts, building walls and forts, keeping an eye on barbarian neighbors, fighting when necessary, and growing crops to support themselves. Poems written by soldiers complain of rough conditions in the camps, tyrannical officers, and the dangers of confrontations with enemy forces, but above all they are homesick, missing and worrying about aged parents and vulnerable wives and children.

New Forms of Thought and Belief   The Han period was rich in intellectual developments, thanks to the relative prosperity of the era, the growth of urban centers, and state support of scholars. In their leisure time scholar-officials read and wrote in a range of genres, including poetry, philosophy, history, and technical subjects.

The Chinese had been preserving historical records since the early Zhou period. However, Sima Qian, the aforementioned "chief astrologer" of Emperor Wu, is regarded as "the father of history" in China, both because he created an organizational framework that became the standard for subsequent historical writing and because he sought the causes of events. Sima's monumental history, covering 2,500 years from legendary early emperors to his own time, was organized in a very different way from Western historical writing. It was divided into five parts: dynastic histories, accounts of noble families, biographies of important individuals and groups (such as Confucian scholars, assassins, barbarian peoples), a chart of historical events, and essays on special topics such as the calendar, astrology, and religious ceremonies. The same event may be narrated in more than one section, sometimes in a different way, inviting the reader to compare and interpret the differences. Sima may have utilized this approach to offer carefully veiled interpretations of past and present. Historians and other scholars in Han China had the advantage, as compared to their Western counterparts, of being employed by the government, but the disadvantage of having to limit their criticism of that government.

There were advances in science and technology. Widespread belief in astrology engendered astronomical observation of planets, stars, and other celestial objects. The watermill, which harnessed the power of running water to turn a grindstone, was used in China long before it appeared in Europe. The development of a horse collar that did not constrict breathing allowed Chinese horses to pull heavier loads than European horses. The Chinese first made paper, perhaps as early as the second century B.C.E., replacing the awkward bamboo strips of earlier eras. Improvements in military technology included horse breeding techniques to supply the cavalry and a reliable crossbow trigger. One clever inventor even created an early seismometer to register earthquakes and indicate the direction where the event took place.

The Qin and Han built thousands of miles of roads—comparable in scale to the roads of the Roman Empire—to connect parts of the empire and move armies quickly. They also built a network of canals connecting the river systems of northern and southern China, at first for military purposes but eventually for transporting commercial goods as well. Ultimately, a network of waterways permitted continuous transport of goods between the latitudes of Beijing and Guangzhou (Canton), a distance of 1,250 miles (2,012 kilometers). Some of these canals are still in use.

Chinese religion encompassed a wide spectrum of beliefs. Like the early Romans, the Chinese believed that divinity resided within nature. Most people believed in ghosts and spirits. The state maintained shrines to the lords of rain, winds, and soil, as well as to certain great rivers and high mountains. Sima Qian devoted an essay to the connection between religion and power, showing how emperors used ancient ceremonies and new-fangled cults to secure their authority. Daoism (see Chapter 4) became popular with the common people, incorporating an array of mystical and magical practices, including alchemy (the art of turning common materials into precious metals such as gold) and the search for potions that would impart immortality. Because Daoism questioned tradition and rejected the hierarchy and rules of the Confucian elite classes, charismatic Daoist teachers led several popular uprisings in the unsettled last decades of the Han dynasty.

Perhaps as early as the first century C.E. Buddhism (BOOD-izm) began to trickle into China. Originating in northern India in the fifth century B.C.E. (see Chapter 7), it slowly spread through South Asia and into Central Asia, carried by merchants on the Silk Road. Certain aspects of Buddhism fit comfortably with Chinese values: reverence for classic texts was also a feature of Confucianism, and the emphasis on severing attachments to material goods and pleasures found echoes in Daoism. But in other ways the Chinese were initially put off by Buddhist practices. The fact that Buddhist monks withdrew from their families to live in monasteries, shaved off their hair, and abstained from sex and procreation of children was repugnant to traditional Chinese values, which emphasized the importance of family ties, the body as an inviolable gift from parents, and the need to produce children to maintain the ancestor cult. Gradually Buddhism gained acceptance and was reshaped to fit the Chinese context, a process accelerated by the non-Chinese dynasties that dominated the north after the fall of the Han.

Decline of the Han   A break in the long sequence of Han rulers occurred early in the first century C.E. when an ambitious official named Wang Mang (wahng mahng) seized power (9–23 C.E.). The new ruler implemented major reforms to address serious economic problems and to cement his popularity with the common people, including limiting the size of the estates of the rich and giving the surplus land to landless peasants. However, a cataclysmic flood that changed the course of the Yellow River caused large numbers of deaths and economic losses. Members of the Han family and other elements of the elite resisted their loss of status and property, and widespread poverty engendered a popular uprising of the "Red Eyebrows," as the insurgents were called. Wang Mang was besieged in his palace and killed, and a member of the Han royal family was soon installed as emperor. In 25 C.E. Guangwu, founder of the Eastern Han dynasty, moved the capital east to Luoyang.

The dynasty continued for another two centuries, but the imperial court was frequently plagued by weak leadership and court intrigue, with royal spouses and their families jockeying for power behind immature or ineffectual monarchs. Poems from this period complain of corrupt officials, unchecked attacks by barbarians, uprisings of desperate and hungry peasants, the spread of banditry, widespread poverty, and despair.

Several factors contributed to the fall of the Han. Continuous military vigilance along the frontier burdened Han finances and exacerbated the economic troubles of later Han times. Despite the earnest efforts of Qin and early Han emperors to reduce the power and wealth of the aristocracy and turn land over to a free peasantry, by the end of the first century B.C.E. nobles and successful merchants again controlled huge tracts of land. Many peasants sought their protection against the demands of the imperial government, which was thereby deprived of tax revenues and manpower. The Eastern Han rulers abandoned the system of military conscription and were forced to hire more and more foreign soldiers and officers, men willing to serve for pay but not necessarily loyal to the Han state. By the end of the second century the empire was convulsed by civil wars, and in 220 C.E., with the former empire broken up into three kingdoms ruled by warlords, the last Han emperor was forced to abdicate.

With the fall of the Han, China entered a period of political fragmentation that lasted until the rise of the Sui (sway) and Tang (tahng) dynasties in the late sixth and early seventh centuries C.E., a story we take up in Chapter 12. In this period the north was dominated by a series of barbarian peoples who combined elements of their own practices with the foundation of Chinese culture. Many ethnic Chinese migrated south into the Yangzi Valley, where Chinese rulers prevailed, and in this era the center of gravity of both the population and Chinese culture shifted to the south.

CONCLUSION

Both the Roman Empire and the first Chinese empire arose from relatively small states that, because of their discipline and military toughness, were initially able to subdue their neighbors. Ultimately they unified widespread territories under strong central governments.

Agriculture was the fundamental economic activity and source of wealth. Government revenues primarily derived from a percentage of the annual harvest. Both empires depended initially on sturdy independent farmers pressed into military service or other forms of compulsory labor, though later they came to rely on professional troops. Conflicts over who owned the land and how it was used were at the heart of political and social turmoil. The autocratic rulers of the Roman and Chinese states secured their positions by breaking the power of the old aristocratic families, seizing their excess land, and giving land to small farmers. The later reversal of this process, when wealthy noblemen again gained control of vast tracts of land and reduced the peasants to dependent tenant farmers, signaled the erosion of state authority.

Both empires spread out from an ethnically homogeneous core to encompass widespread territories containing diverse ecosystems, populations, and ways of life. Both brought those regions a cultural unity that has persisted, at least in part, to the present day. This development involved far more than military conquest and political domination. As the population of the core areas outstripped available resources, Italian and Han settlers moved into new regions, bringing their languages, beliefs, customs, and technologies. Many people in the conquered lands were attracted to the culture of the ruler nation and chose to adopt these practices and attach themselves to a "winning cause." Both empires found similar solutions to the problems of administering far-flung territories and large populations in an age when communication depended on men on horseback or on foot. The central government had to delegate considerable autonomy to local officials based in the cities and towns—in the Roman case local elites, in China officials dispatched by the central administration. In both empires a kind of civil service developed, staffed by educated and capable members of a prosperous middle class.

Technologies that facilitated imperial control also fostered cultural unification and improvements in the general standard of living. Roads built to expedite the movement of troops became the highways of commerce and the spread of imperial culture. A network of cities and towns linked the parts of the empire, providing local administrative bases, promoting commerce, and radiating imperial culture into the surrounding countryside. The majority of the population still resided in the countryside, but those living in urban centers enjoyed most of the advantages of empire. Cities and towns modeled themselves on the capital cities of Rome and Chang'an. Travelers found the same types of buildings and public spaces, and similar features of urban life, in outlying regions that they had seen in the capital.

The empires of Rome and Han China faced similar problems of defense: long borders located far from the administrative center and aggressive neighbors who coveted their prosperity. Both had to build walls and maintain chains of forts and garrisons to protect against incursions. The cost of frontier defense was staggering and eventually eroded the economic prosperity of the two empires. As imperial governments demanded more taxes and services from the hard-pressed civilian population, they lost the loyalty of their own people, many of whom sought protection on the estates of powerful rural landowners. As rough neighbors gradually learned the skills that had given the empires an initial advantage and were able to close the "technology gap," the Roman and Han governments eventually came to rely on soldiers hired from the same "barbarian" peoples who were pressing on the frontiers. Eventually, both empires were so weakened that their borders were overrun and their central governments collapsed. Ironically, the newly dominant immigrant groups were so deeply influenced by imperial culture that they maintained it to the best of their abilities.

In referring to the eventual failure of these two empires, we are brought up against important differences that led to different long-term outcomes. In China the imperial model was revived in subsequent eras, but the lands of the Roman Empire never again achieved the same level of unification. Several interrelated factors account for the different outcomes.

First, these cultures had different attitudes about the relationship of individuals to the state. In China the individual was more deeply embedded in the larger social group. The Chinese family, with its emphasis on a precisely defined hierarchy, unquestioning obedience, and solemn rituals of deference to elders and ancestors, served as the model for society and the state. Moreover, Confucianism, which sanctified hierarchy and provided a code of conduct for public officials, arose long before the imperial system and could be revived and tailored to fit changing political circumstances. Although the Roman family had its own hierarchy and traditions of obedience, the cult of ancestors was not as strong as among the Chinese, and the family was not the organizational model for Roman society and the Roman state. Also, there was no Roman equivalent of Confucianism—no ideology of political organization and social conduct that could survive the dissolution of the Roman state.

Another difference was that opportunities for economic and social mobility were greater in the Roman Empire than in ancient China. Whereas the merchant class in China was frequently disparaged and constrained by the government, the absence of government interference in the Roman Empire resulted in greater economic mobility and a thriving and influential middle class in the towns and cities. The Roman army, because it was composed of professional soldiers in service for decades and constituting a distinct and increasingly privileged group, frequently played a decisive role in political conflict. In China, on the other hand, the army was long drawn from draftees who served for two years and was much less likely to take the initiative in struggles for power.

Although Roman emperors tried to create an ideology to bolster their position, they were hampered by the persistence of Republican traditions and the ambiguities about the position of emperor deliberately cultivated by Augustus. As a result, Roman rulers were likely to be chosen by the army or by the Senate; the dynastic principle never took deep root; and the cult of the emperor had little spiritual content. This stands in sharp contrast to the unambiguous Chinese belief that the emperor was the divine Son of Heaven with privileged access to the beneficent power of the royal ancestors. Thus, in the lands that had once constituted the western part of the Roman Empire, there was no compelling basis for reviving the position of emperor and the territorial claims of empire in later ages.

Finally, Christianity, with its insistence on monotheism and one doctrine of truth, negated the Roman emperor's pretensions to divinity and was unwilling to compromise with pagan beliefs. The spread of Christianity through the provinces during the Late Roman Empire, and the decline of the western half of the empire in the fifth century C.E. (see Chapter 11), constituted an irreversible break with the past. On the other hand, Buddhism, which came to China in the early centuries C.E. and flourished in the post-Han era (see Chapter 12), was more easily reconciled with traditional Chinese values and beliefs.

IMPORTANT EVENTS 1000 B.C.E. TO 220 C.E.

1000 B.C.E.	First settlement on site of Rome
507 B.C.E.	Establishment of the Republic
480–221 B.C.E.	Warring States Period
290 B.C.E.	Defeat of tribes of Samnium gives Romans control of Italy
264–202 B.C.E.	Wars against Carthage guarantee Roman control of western Mediterranean
221 B.C.E.	Qin emperor unites eastern China
202 B.C.E.	Han dynasty succeeds Qin
200–146 B.C.E.	Wars against Hellenistic kingdoms lead to control of eastern Mediterranean
140–87 B.C.E.	Emperor Wu expands the Han Empire
109–91 B.C.E.	Sima Qian writes history of China
88–31 B.C.E.	Civil wars and failure of the Republic
31 B.C.E.–**14** C.E.	Augustus establishes the Principate
9–23 C.E.	Wang Mang usurps throne
23 C.E.	Han capital transferred from Chang'an to Luoyang
45–58 C.E.	Paul spreads Christianity in the eastern Mediterranean
99 C.E.	Ban Zhao composes "Lessons for Women"
220 C.E.	Fall of Han dynasty
235–284 C.E.	Third-Century Crisis
324 C.E.	Constantine moves capital to Constantinople

7

INDIA AND SOUTHEAST ASIA, 1500 B.C.E.–1025 C.E.

In the *Bhagavad-Gita* (BUH-guh-vahd GEE-tuh), the most renowned Indian sacred text, the legendary warrior Arjuna (AHR-joo-nuh) rides out in his chariot to the open space between two armies preparing for battle. Torn between his social duty to fight for his family's claim to the throne and his conscience, which balks at the prospect of killing relatives, friends, and former teachers in the enemy camp, Arjuna slumps down in his chariot and refuses to fight. But his driver, the god Krishna (KRISH-nuh) in disguise, persuades him, in a carefully structured dialogue, both of the necessity to fulfill his duty as a warrior and of the proper frame of mind for performing these acts. In the climactic moment of the dialogue Krishna endows Arjuna with a "divine eye" and permits him to see the true appearance of God:

> It was a multiform, wondrous vision,
> with countless mouths and eyes
> and celestial ornaments,
>
> Everywhere was boundless divinity
> containing all astonishing things,
> wearing divine garlands and garments,
> anointed with divine perfume.
>
> If the light of a thousand suns
> were to rise in the sky at once,
> it would be like the light
> of that great spirit.
>
> Arjuna saw all the universe
> in its many ways and parts,
> standing as one in the body
> of the god of gods.[1]

In all of world literature, this is one of the most compelling attempts to depict the nature of deity. Graphic images emphasize the vastness, diversity, and multiplicity of

---

[1]Barbara Stoler Miller, *The Bhagavad-Gita: Krishna's Counsel in Time of War* (New York: Bantam, 1986), 98–99.

the god, but in the end we learn that Krishna is the organizing principle behind all creation, that behind diversity and multiplicity lies a higher unity.

This is an apt metaphor for Indian civilization. The enormous variety of the Indian landscape is mirrored in the patchwork of ethnic and linguistic groups that occupy it, the political fragmentation that has marked most of Indian history, the elaborate hierarchy of social groups into which the Indian population is divided, and the thousands of deities who are worshiped at innumerable holy places that dot the subcontinent. Yet, in the end, one can speak of an Indian civilization united by shared views and values. The photograph shows the interior of a temple in the city of Madurai in southern India. Here the ten-day Chittarai Festival, the most important religious event of the year in that district, celebrates the wedding of a local goddess, Minakshi, and the great Hindu god Shiva, symbolizing the reconciliation of local and national deities, southern and northern cultural practices, and male and female potentialities.

This chapter surveys the history of South and Southeast Asia from approximately 1500 B.C.E. to 1025 C.E., highlighting the evolution of defining features of Indian civilization. Considerable attention is given to Indian religious conceptions, due both to religion's profound role in shaping Indian society and the sources of information available to historians. For reasons that will be explained below, writing came late to India, and ancient Indians did not develop the same kind of historical consciousness as other peoples of antiquity and took little interest in recording specific historical events.

FOUNDATIONS OF INDIAN CIVILIZATION, 1500 B.C.E.–300 C.E.

India is called a *subcontinent* because it is a large—roughly 2,000 miles (3,200 kilometers) in both length and breadth—and physically isolated landmass. It is set off from the rest of Asia to the north by the Himalayas (him-uh-LAY-uhs), the highest mountains on the planet, and by the Indian Ocean on its eastern, southern, and western sides. The most permeable frontier, used by invaders and migrating peoples, lies to the northwest, but people using this corridor must cross the mountain barrier of the Hindu Kush (HIHN-doo KOOSH) (via the Khyber [KIE-ber] Pass) and the Thar (tahr) Desert east of the Indus River.

The Indian Subcontinent   The subcontinent—which encompasses the modern nations of Pakistan, Nepal, Bhutan, Bangladesh, India, and the adjacent island of Sri Lanka—divides into three distinct topographical zones. The mountainous northern zone contains the heavily forested foothills and high meadows on the edge of the Hindu Kush and Himalaya ranges. Next come the great basins of the Indus and Ganges (GAHN-jeez) Rivers. Originating in the snow-clad Tibetan mountains to the north, these rivers have repeatedly overflowed their banks and deposited layer on layer of silt, creating large alluvial plains. Northern India is divided from the third zone, the peninsula proper, by the Vindhya range and the Deccan (de-KAN), an arid, rocky plateau. The tropical coastal strip of Kerala (Malabar) in the west, the Coromandel Coast in the east

MAP 7.1 Ancient India

Mountains and ocean largely separate the Indian subcontinent from the rest of Asia. Migrations and invasions usually came through the Khyber Pass in the northwest. Seaborne commerce with western Asia, Southeast Asia, and East Asia often flourished. Peoples speaking Indo-European languages migrated into the broad valleys of the Indus and Ganges Rivers in the north. Dravidian-speaking peoples remained the dominant population in the south. The diversity of the Indian landscape, the multiplicity of ethnic groups, and the primary identification of people with their class and caste lie behind the division into many small states that has characterized much of Indian political history.

with its web of rivers descending from the central plateau, the flatlands of Tamil Nadu on the southern tip of the peninsula, and the island of Sri Lanka often have followed paths of political and cultural development separate from those of northern India.

The northern rim of mountains shelters the subcontinent from cold Arctic winds and gives it a subtropical climate. The most dramatic source of moisture is the **monsoon** (seasonal wind). The Indian Ocean is slow to warm or cool, while the vast landmass of Asia swings between seasonal extremes of heat and cold. The temperature difference between water and land acts like a bellows, producing a great wind. The southwest monsoon begins in June, absorbing huge amounts of moisture from the Indian Ocean and dropping it over a swath of India that encompasses the rain forest belt on the western coast and the Ganges Basin. Three harvests a year are possible in some places. Rice is grown in the moist, flat Ganges Delta (modern Bengal). Elsewhere the staples are wheat, barley, and millet.

The Indus Valley, in contrast, gets little precipitation (see Chapter 2), and agriculture requires extensive irrigation.

Although invasions and migrations usually came by land through the northwest corridor, the ocean has not been a barrier to travel and trade. Mariners learned to ride the monsoon winds across open waters from northeast to southwest in January and to make the return voyage in July. Ships sailed west across the Arabian Sea to the Persian Gulf, the southern coast of Arabia, and East Africa, and east across the Bay of Bengal to Indochina and Indonesia (see Chapter 9).

Many characteristic features of later Indian civilization may derive from the Indus Valley civilization of the third and early second millennia B.C.E., but proof is hard to come by because writing from that period has not yet been deciphered. That society, with its advanced social organization and technology, succumbed around 1900 B.C.E. to some kind of environmental crisis (see Chapter 2).

The Vedic Age   Historians call the period from 1500 to 500 B.C.E. the Vedic Age, after the **Vedas** (VAY-duhs), religious texts that are our main source of information about the period. The foundations for Indian civilization were laid in the Vedic Age. Most historians believe that new groups of people—animal-herding warriors speaking Indo-European languages—migrated into northwest India around 1500 B.C.E. Some argue for a much earlier Indo-European presence in this region in conjunction with the spread of agriculture. In any case, in the mid-second millennium B.C.E. northern India entered a new historical period associated with the dominance of Indo-European groups.

After the collapse of the Indus Valley civilization there was no central authority to direct irrigation efforts, and the region became home to kinship groups that depended mostly on their herds of cattle for sustenance. These societies were patriarchal, with the father dominating the family as the king ruled the tribe. Members of the warrior class boasted of their martial skill and courage, relished combat, celebrated with lavish feasts of beef and rounds of heavy drinking, and filled their leisure time with chariot racing and gambling.

After 1000 B.C.E. some groups migrated east into the Ganges Plain. New technologies made this advance possible. Iron tools—harder than bronze and able to hold a sharper edge—allowed settlers to fell trees and work the newly cleared land with plows pulled by oxen. The soil of the Ganges Plain was fertile, well watered by the annual monsoon, and able to sustain two or three crops a year. As in Greece at roughly the same time (see Chapter 5), the use of iron tools to open new land for agriculture must have led to a significant increase in population.

Stories about this era, not written down until much later but long preserved by memorization and oral recitation, speak of bitter warfare between two groups of people: the Aryas, relatively light-skinned speakers of Indo-European languages, and the Dasas, dark-skinned speakers of Dravidian languages. It is possible that some Dasas were absorbed into Arya populations and that elites from both groups merged. For the most part, however, Aryas pushed the Dasas south into central and southern India, where their descendants still live. Today Indo-European languages are primarily spoken in northern India, while Dravidian speech prevails in the south.

Skin color has been a persistent concern of Indian society and is one of the bases for its historically sharp internal divisions. Over time there evolved a system of

varna—literally "color," though the word came to indicate something akin to "class." Individuals were born into one of four classes: *Brahmin*, comprising priests and scholars; *Kshatriya* (kshuh-TREE-yuh), warriors and officials; *Vaishya* (VIESH-yuh), merchants, artisans, and landowners; or *Shudra* (SHOOD-ra), peasants and laborers. The designation *Shudra* originally may have been reserved for Dasas, who were given the menial jobs in society. Indeed, the very term *dasa* came to mean "slave." Eventually a fifth group was marked off: the Untouchables. They were excluded from the class system, and members of the other groups literally avoided them because of the demeaning or polluting work to which they were relegated—such as leather tanning, which involved touching dead animals, and sweeping away ashes of the dead after cremations.

People at the top of the social pyramid could explain why this hierarchy existed. According to one creation myth, a primordial creature named Purusha allowed itself to be sacrificed. From its mouth sprang the class of Brahmin priests, the embodiment of intellect and knowledge. From its arms came the Kshatriya warrior class, from its thighs the Vaishya landowners and merchants, and from its feet the Shudra workers.

The varna system was just one of the mechanisms developed to regulate relations between different groups. Within the broad class divisions, the population was further subdivided into numerous **jati**, or birth groups (sometimes called *castes*, from a Portuguese term meaning "breed"). Each jati had its proper occupation, duties, and rituals. Individuals who belonged to a given jati lived with members of their group, married within the group, and ate only with members of the group. Elaborate rules governed their interactions with members of other groups. Members of higher-status groups feared pollution from contact with lower-caste individuals and had to undergo elaborate rituals of purification to remove any taint.

The class and caste systems came to be connected to a widespread belief in reincarnation. The Brahmin priests taught that every living creature had an immortal essence: the *atman*, or "breath." Separated from the body at death, the atman was later reborn in another body. Whether the new body was that of an insect, an animal, or a human depended on the **karma**, or deeds, of the atman in its previous incarnations. People who lived exemplary lives would be reborn into the higher classes. Those who misbehaved would be punished in the next life by being relegated to a lower class or even a lower life form. The underlying message was: You are where you deserve to be, and the only way to improve your lot in the next cycle of existence is to accept your current station and its attendant duties.

The dominant deities in Vedic religion were male and associated with the heavens. To release the dawn, Indra, god of war and master of the thunderbolt, daily slew the demon encasing the universe. Varuna, lord of the sky, maintained universal order and dispensed justice. Agni, the force of fire, consumed the sacrifice and bridged the spheres of gods and humans.

Sacrifice—the dedication to a god of a valued possession, often a living creature—was the essential ritual. The purpose of these offerings was to invigorate the gods and thereby sustain their creative powers and promote stability in the world.

Brahmin priests controlled the sacrifices, for only they knew the rituals and prayers. The *Rig Veda*, a collection of more than a thousand poetic hymns to various deities, and the *Brahmanas*, detailed prose descriptions of procedures for ritual and sacrifice, were collections of priestly lore couched in the Sanskrit language of the Arya upper classes. This information was handed down orally from one generation of priests to the next. The priests' "knowledge" (the term *veda* means just that) was the basis of their economic well-being. They were amply rewarded for officiating at sacrifices, and their knowledge gave them social and political power because they were the indispensable intermediaries between gods and humans. Some scholars hypothesize that the Brahmins resisted the introduction of writing in order to preserve their control of sacred knowledge. This might explain why writing came into widespread use in India later than in other societies of equivalent complexity. However, we may be unaware of earlier uses of writing because it involved perishable materials that have not survived in the archaeological record.

It is difficult to uncover the experiences of women in early India. Limited evidence indicates that women in the Vedic period studied sacred lore, composed religious hymns, and participated in the sacrificial ritual. They could own property and usually did not marry until reaching their middle or late teens. Strong and resourceful women appear in the Indian epic poems originating in this era.

The sharp internal divisions and complex hierarchy of Indian society served important social functions. They provided each individual with a clear identity and role and offered the benefits of group solidarity and support. Moreover, there is evidence that groups sometimes were able to upgrade their status. Thus the elaborate system of divisions was not static and provided a mechanism for working out social tensions. Many of these features have persisted into modern times.

Challenges to the Old Order: Jainism and Buddhism	After 700 B.C.E. various forms of reaction against Brahmin power and privilege emerged. People who objected to the rigid hierarchy of classes and castes or the community's demands on the individual could retreat to the nearby forest that still covered much of ancient India. These wild places

symbolized freedom from societal constraints.

Certain charismatic individuals who abandoned their town or village and moved to the forest attracted bands of followers. Calling into question the priests' exclusive claims to wisdom and the necessity of Vedic chants and sacrifices, they offered an alternate path to salvation: the individual pursuit of insight into the nature of the self and the universe through physical and mental discipline (*yoga*), special dietary practices, and meditation. They taught that by distancing oneself from desire for the things of this world, one could achieve **moksha**, or "liberation." This release from the cycle of reincarnations and union with the divine force that animates the universe sometimes was likened to "a deep, dreamless sleep." The *Upanishads* (ooh-PAH-nee-shad)—a collection of more than one hundred mystical dialogues between teachers and disciples—reflect this questioning of the foundations of Vedic religion.

The most serious threat to Vedic religion and Brahmin prerogatives came from two new religions that emerged around this time: Jainism and Buddhism. Mahavira (540–468 B.C.E.) was known to his followers as Jina, "the Conqueror," from which is derived *Jainism* (JINE-iz-uhm), the belief system that he established. Emphasizing the holiness of the life force animating all living creatures, Mahavira and his followers practiced strict nonviolence. They wore masks to prevent accidentally inhaling small insects, and they carefully brushed off a seat before sitting down. Those who gave themselves over completely to Jainism practiced extreme asceticism and nudity, ate only what they were given by others, and eventually starved themselves

akg-images/De Agostini Pict. Lib

Carved Stone Gateway Leading to the Great Stupa at Sanchi *Pilgrims traveled long distances to visit stupas, mounds containing relics of the Buddha. The complex at Sanchi, in central India, was begun by Ashoka in the third century B.C.E., though the gates probably date to the first century C.E. This relief shows a royal procession bringing the remains of the Buddha to the city of Kushinagara.*

to death. Less zealous Jainists, restricted from agricultural work by the injunction against killing, were city dwellers engaged in commerce and banking.

Far more significant for Indian and world history was the rise of Buddhism. So many stories were told about Siddhartha Gautama (563–483 B.C.E.), known as the **Buddha**, "the Enlightened One," that it is difficult to separate fact from legend. He came from a Kshatriya family of the Sakyas, a people in the foothills of the Himalayas. As a young man he enjoyed the princely lifestyle to which he had been born, but at some point he abandoned family and privilege to become a wandering ascetic. After six years of self-deprivation, he came to regard asceticism as no more likely to produce spiritual insight than the luxury of his previous life, and he decided to adhere to a "Middle Path" of moderation. Sitting under a tree in a deer park near Benares on the Ganges River, he gained a sudden and profound insight into the true nature of reality, which he set forth as "Four Noble Truths": (1) life is suffering; (2) suffering arises from desire; (3) the solution to suffering lies in curbing desire; and (4) desire can be curbed if a person follows the "Eightfold Path" of right views, aspirations, speech, conduct, livelihood, effort, mindfulness, and meditation. Rising up, the Buddha preached his First Sermon, a central text of Buddhism, and set into motion the "Wheel of the Law." He soon attracted followers, some of whom took vows of celibacy, nonviolence, and poverty.

In its original form, Buddhism centered on the individual. Although not quite rejecting the existence of gods, it denied their usefulness to a person seeking enlightenment. What mattered was living one's life with moderation, in order to minimize desire and suffering, and searching for spiritual truth through self-discipline and meditation. The ultimate reward was *nirvana*, literally "snuffing out the flame." With nirvana came release from the cycle of reincarnations and achievement of a state of perpetual tranquility. The Vedic tradition emphasized the eternal survival of the atman, the "breath" or nonmaterial essence of the individual. In contrast, Buddhism regarded the individual as a composite without any soul-like component that survived upon entering nirvana.

When the Buddha died, he left no final instructions, instead urging his disciples to "be their own lamp." As the Buddha's message—contained in philosophical discourses memorized by his followers—spread throughout India and into Central, Southeast, and East Asia, its very success began to subvert the individualistic and

Sculpture of the Buddha, Second or Third Century C.E.
This depiction of the Buddha, showing the effects of a protracted fast before he abandoned asceticism for the path of moderation, is from Gandhara in the northwest. It displays the influence of Greek artistic styles emanating from Greek settlements established in that region by Alexander the Great in the late fourth century B.C.E.

Robert Fisher

essentially atheistic tenets of the founder. Buddhist monasteries were established, and a hierarchy of Buddhist monks and nuns came into being. Worshipers erected *stupas* (STOO-puh) (large earthen mounds symbolizing the universe) over relics of the cremated founder. Believers began to worship the Buddha himself as a god. Many Buddhists also revered *bodhisattvas* (boe-dih-SUT-vuh), saintly men and women who had achieved enlightenment and were on the threshold of nirvana but chose to be reborn into mortal bodies to help others along the path to salvation.

The makers of early pictorial images refused to show the Buddha as a living person and represented him only indirectly, through symbols such as his footprints, his begging bowl, or the tree under which he achieved enlightenment, as if to emphasize his achievement of a state of nonexistence. From the second century C.E., however, statues of the Buddha and bodhisattvas began to proliferate, done in native sculptural styles and in a style that showed the influence of the Greek settlements established in Bactria (modern Afghanistan) by Alexander the Great (see Chapter 5). A schism emerged within Buddhism. Devotees of **Mahayana** (mah-huh-YAH-nuh) ("Great Vehicle") **Buddhism** embraced the popular new features, while practitioners of **Theravada** (there-uh-VAH-duh) ("Teachings of the Elders") **Buddhism** followed most of the original teachings of the founder.

The Evolution of Hinduism   Challenged by new, spiritually satisfying, and egalitarian movements, Vedic religion made important adjustments, evolving into **Hinduism**, the religion of hundreds of millions of people in South Asia today. The foundation of Hinduism is the Vedic religion of the Arya peoples of northern India. But Hinduism also incorporated elements drawn from the Dravidian cultures of the south, such as an emphasis on intense devotion to the deity and the prominence of fertility rituals. Also present are elements of Buddhism.

The process by which Vedic religion was transformed into Hinduism by the fourth century C.E. is largely hidden from us. The Brahmin priests maintained their high social status and influence. But sacrifice, though still part of traditional worship, was less central, and there was more opportunity for direct contact between gods and individual worshipers.

The gods were altered, both in identity and in their relationships with humanity. Two formerly minor deities, Vishnu (VIHSH-noo) and Shiva (SHEE-vuh), became preeminent. Hinduism emphasized the worshiper's personal devotion to a particular deity, usually Vishnu, Shiva, or Devi (DEH-vee) ("the Goddess"). Both Shiva and Devi appear to be derived from the Dravidian tradition, in which fertility cults and female deities played a prominent role. Vishnu, who has a clear Arya pedigree, remains more popular in northern India, while Shiva is dominant in the Dravidian south. These gods can appear in many guises. They are identified by various cult names and are represented by a complex symbolism of stories, companion animals, birds, and objects.

Vishnu, the preserver, is a benevolent deity who helps his devotees in time of need. Hindus believe that whenever demonic forces threaten the cosmic order, Vishnu appears on earth in one of a series of *avataras*, or incarnations. Among his incarnations are the legendary hero Rama, the popular cowherd-god Krishna, and the Buddha (a clear attempt to co-opt the rival religion's founder). Shiva, who lives in ascetic isolation on Mount Kailasa in the Himalayas, is a more ambivalent figure. He represents both creation and destruction, for both are part of a single, cyclical process. He often is represented performing dance steps that symbolize the acts of creation and destruction. Devi manifests herself in various ways—as a full-bodied mother-goddess who promotes fertility and procreation, as the docile and loving wife Parvati, and as the frightening deity who, under the name Kali or Durga, lets loose a torrent of violence and destruction.

The multiplicity of gods (330 million according to one tradition), sects, and local practices within Hinduism is dazzling, reflecting the ethnic, linguistic, and cultural diversity of India. Yet within this variety there is unity. Ultimately, all the gods and spirits are seen as manifestations of a single divine force that pervades the universe. This sense of underlying unity is expressed in texts, such as the passage from the *Bhagavad-Gita* quoted at the beginning of this chapter; in the different potentials of women represented in the various manifestations of Devi; and in composite statues that are split down the middle—half Shiva, half Vishnu—as if to say that they are complementary aspects of one cosmic principle.

Hinduism offers the worshiper a variety of ways to approach god and obtain divine favor—through special knowledge of sacred truths, mental and physical discipline, or extraordinary devotion to the deity. Worship centers on the temples, which range from humble village shrines to magnificent, richly decorated stone edifices built under royal patronage. Beautifully proportioned statues in which the deity may take up temporary residence are adored and beseeched by eager worshipers. A common form of worship is *puja*, service to the deity, which can take the form of bathing, clothing, or feeding the statue. Potent blessings are conferred on the man or woman who glimpses the divine image.

Pilgrimage to famous shrines and attendance at festivals offer worshipers additional opportunities to show devotion. The entire Indian subcontinent is dotted with sacred places where worshipers can directly sense and benefit from the inherent power of divinity. Mountains, caves, and certain trees, plants, and rocks are enveloped in an aura of mystery and sanctity. Hindus consider the Ganges River especially sacred, and each year millions of devoted worshipers bathe in its waters and receive their restorative and purifying power. The habit of pilgrimage has promoted contact and the exchange of ideas among people from different parts of India and has helped create a broad Hindu identity and the concept of India as a single civilization, despite enduring political fragmentation.

Religious duties may vary, depending not only on the worshiper's social standing and gender but also his or her stage of life. A young man from one of the three highest classes undergoes a ritual rebirth through the ceremony of the sacred thread, marking the attainment of manhood and readiness to receive religious knowledge. From this point, the ideal life cycle passes through four stages: (1) the young man becomes a student and studies the sacred texts; (2) he then becomes a householder, marries, has children, and acquires material wealth; (3) when his grandchildren are born, he gives up home and family and becomes a forest dweller, meditating on the nature and meaning of existence; (4) he abandons his personal identity altogether and becomes a wandering ascetic awaiting death. In the course of a virtuous life he has fulfilled first his duties to society and then his duties to himself, so that by the end he is so disconnected from the world that he can achieve *moksha* (liberation).

The successful transformation of a religion based on Vedic antecedents and the ultimate victory of Hinduism over Buddhism—Buddhism was driven from the land of its birth, though it maintains deep roots in Central, East, and Southeast Asia (see Chapters 9 and 11)—are remarkable phenomena. Hinduism responded to the needs of people for personal deities with whom they could establish direct connections. The austerity of Buddhism in its most authentic form, its denial of the importance of gods, and its expectation that individuals find their own path to enlightenment may have demanded too much of ordinary people. The very features that made Mahayana Buddhism more accessible to the populace—gods, saints, and myths—also made it more easily absorbed into the vast social and cultural fabric of Hinduism.

IMPERIAL EXPANSION AND COLLAPSE, 324 B.C.E.–650 C.E.

Political unity in India, on those rare occasions when it has been achieved, has not lasted long. A number of factors have contributed to India's habitual political fragmentation. Different terrains called forth varied forms of organization and economic activity, and peoples occupying diverse zones differed in language and cultural practices. Perhaps the most significant barrier to political unity lay in the complex social hierarchy. Individuals identified themselves primarily in terms of their class and caste; allegiance to a higher political authority was secondary.

Despite these divisive factors, two empires arose in the Ganges Plain in antiquity: the Mauryan (MORE-yuhn) Empire of the fourth to second centuries B.C.E. and the Gupta (GOOP-tuh) Empire of the fourth to sixth centuries C.E. Each extended political control over much of the subcontinent and fostered the formation of a common Indian civilization.

The Mauryan Empire, 324–184 B.C.E.   Around 600 B.C.E. independent kinship groups and states dotted the landscape of north India. The kingdom of Magadha, in eastern India south of the Ganges, began to play an increasingly influential role, however, thanks to wealth based on agriculture, iron mines, and its strategic location astride the trade routes of the eastern Ganges Basin. In the late fourth century B.C.E. Chandragupta Maurya (MORE-yuh), a young man from the Vaishya or Shudra class, gained control of Magadha and expanded it into the **Mauryan Empire**—India's first centralized empire. He may have been inspired by the example of Alexander the Great, who had followed up his conquest of the Persian Empire with a foray into the Punjab (northern Pakistan) in 326 B.C.E. (see Chapter 5). Chandragupta (r. 324–301 B.C.E.) and his successors Bindusara (r. 301–273 B.C.E.) and Ashoka (r. 273–232 B.C.E.) extended Mauryan control over the entire subcontinent except the southern tip. Not until the height of the Mughal Empire of the seventeenth century C.E. was so much of India again under the control of a single government.

Tradition holds that Kautilya, a crafty elderly Brahmin, guided Chandragupta in his conquests and consolidation of power. Kautilya is said to have written a surviving treatise on government, the *Arthashastra* (ahr-thuh-SHAHS-truh). Although recent studies have shown that the *Arthashastra* in its present form is a product of the third century C.E., its core text may well go back to Kautilya. This coldly pragmatic guide to political success and survival advocates the so-called *mandala* (man-DAH-luh) (circle) theory of foreign policy: "My enemy's enemy is my friend." It also presents schemes for enforcing and increasing the collection of tax revenues, and it prescribes the use of spies to keep watch on everyone in the kingdom.

A tax equivalent to as much as one-fourth the value of the harvest supported the Mauryan kings and government. Other revenues came from tolls on trade; government monopolies on mining, liquor sales, and the manufacture of weapons; and fees charged to those using the irrigation network. Close relatives and associates of the king governed administrative districts based on traditional ethnic boundaries. A large imperial army—with infantry, cavalry, and chariot divisions and the fearsome new element of war elephants—further secured power. Standard coinage issued throughout the empire was used to pay government and military personnel and promoted trade.

The Mauryan capital was at Pataliputra (modern Patna), where five tributaries join the Ganges. Surrounded by rivers and further protected by a timber wall and moat, the city extended along the riverbank for 8 miles (13 kilometers). Busy and crowded (the population has been estimated at 270,000), it was governed by six committees with responsibility for manufacturing, trade, sales, taxes, the welfare of foreigners, and the registration of births and deaths.

Ashoka, Chandragupta's grandson, is an outstanding figure in early Indian history. At the beginning of his reign he engaged in military campaigns that extended the boundaries of the empire. During his conquest of Kalinga, a coastal region southeast of Magadha, hundreds of thousands of people were killed, wounded, or deported. Overwhelmed by the brutality of this victory, the young monarch became a convert to Buddhism and preached nonviolence, morality, moderation, and religious tolerance in both government and private life.

Ashoka publicized this program by inscribing edicts on great rocks and polished pillars of sandstone scattered throughout his enormous empire. Among the inscriptions that have survived—they constitute the earliest decipherable Indian writing—is the following:

> *For a long time in the past, for many hundreds of years have increased the sacrificial slaughter of animals, violence toward creatures, unfilial conduct toward kinsmen, improper conduct toward Brahmins and ascetics. Now with the practice of morality by King [Ashoka], the sound of war drums has become the call to morality.... You [government officials] are appointed to rule over thousands of human beings in the expectation that you will win the affection of all men. All men are my children. Just as I desire that my children will fare well and be happy in this world and the next, I desire the same for all men.... King [Ashoka] ... desires that there should be the growth of the essential spirit of morality or holiness among all sects.... There should not be glorification of one's own sect and denunciation of the sect of others for little or no reason. For all the sects are worthy of reverence for one reason or another.*[2]

Ashoka, however, was not naive. Despite his commitment to peaceful means, he reminded potential transgressors that "the king, remorseful as he is, has the strength to punish the wrongdoers who do not repent."

Commerce and Culture in an Era of Political Fragmentation

The Mauryan Empire prospered for a time after Ashoka's death in 232 B.C.E. Then, weakened by dynastic disputes and the expense of maintaining a large army and administrative bureaucracy, it collapsed from the pressure of attacks in the northwest in 184 B.C.E. Five hundred years passed before another indigenous state exercised control over northern India.

---

[2]B. G. Gokhale, *Asoka Maurya* (New York: Twayne, 1966), 152–153, 156–157, 160.

In the meantime, a series of foreign powers dominated the northwest, present-day Afghanistan and Pakistan, and extended their influence east and south. The first was the Greco-Bactrian kingdom (180–50 B.C.E.), descended from troops and settlers left in Afghanistan by Alexander the Great. Greek influence is evident in the art of this period and in the designs of coins. Occupation by two nomadic groups from Central Asia followed, resulting from large-scale movements of peoples set off by the pressure of Han Chinese forces on the Xiongnu (see Chapter 6). The Shakas, an Iranian people driven southwest along the mountain barrier of the Pamirs and Himalayas, were dominant from 50 B.C.E. to 50 C.E. They were followed by the Kushans (KOO-shahn), originally from Xinjiang in northwest China, who were preeminent from 50 to 240 C.E. At its height the Kushan kingdom controlled much of present-day Uzbekistan, Afghanistan, Pakistan, and northwest India, fostering trade and prosperity by connecting to both the overland Silk Road and Arabian seaports (see Chapter 9). The eastern Ganges region reverted to a patchwork of small principalities, as it had been before the Mauryan era.

Despite political fragmentation in the five centuries after the Mauryan collapse, there were many signs of economic, cultural, and intellectual vitality. The network of roads and towns that had sprung up under the Mauryans fostered lively commerce within the subcontinent, and India was at the heart of international land and sea trade routes that linked China, Southeast Asia, Central Asia, the Middle East, East Africa, and the lands of the Mediterranean. The growth of crafts (metal-work, cloth making and dying, jewelry, perfume, glass, stone and terracotta sculpture), the increasing use of coins, and the development of local and long-distance commerce fostered the expansion and prosperity of urban centers. In the absence of a strong central authority, guilds of merchants and artisans became politically powerful in the towns. They were wealthy patrons of culture and endowed the religious sects to which they adhered—particularly Buddhism and Jainism—with richly decorated temples and monuments.

During the last centuries B.C.E. and first centuries C.E. the two greatest Indian epics, the *Ramayana* (ruh-muh-YAH-nuh) and the *Mahabharata* (muh-huh-BAH-ruh-tuh), based on oral predecessors dating back many centuries, achieved their final form. The events that both epics describe are said to have occurred several million years in the past, but the political forms, social organization, and other elements of cultural context—proud kings, beautiful queens, wars among kinship groups, heroic conduct, and chivalric values—seem to reflect the conditions of the early Vedic period, when Arya warrior societies were moving onto the Ganges Plain.

The vast pageant of the **Mahabharata** (it is eight times the length of the Greek *Iliad* and *Odyssey* combined) tells the story of two sets of cousins, the Pandavas and Kauravas, whose quarrel over succession to the throne leads them to a cataclysmic battle at the field of Kurukshetra. The battle is so destructive on all sides that the eventual winner, Yudhishthira, is reluctant to accept the fruits of so tragic a victory.

The **Bhagavad-Gita**, quoted at the beginning of this chapter, is a self-contained (and perhaps originally separate) episode set in the midst of those events. The great hero Arjuna, at first reluctant to fight his own kinsmen, is tutored by the god Krishna and learns the necessity of fulfilling his duty as a warrior. Death means nothing in a universe in which souls will be reborn again and again. The climactic moment comes when Krishna reveals his true appearance—awesome and overwhelmingly powerful—and his identity as time itself, the force behind all creation and destruction. The *Bhagavad-Gita* offers an attractive resolution to the tension in Indian civilization between duty to society and duty to one's own soul. Disciplined action—that is, action taken without regard for any personal benefits that might derive from it—is a form of service to the gods and will be rewarded by release from the cycle of rebirths.

This era also saw significant advances in science and linguistics. Indian doctors had a wide knowledge of herbal remedies. Panini (late fourth century B.C.E.) undertook a detailed analysis of Sanskrit word forms and grammar. His work led to the standardization of Sanskrit, arresting its natural development and turning it into a formal, literary, and administrative language. Prakrits—popular dialects—emerged to become the ancestors of the modern Indo-European languages of northern and central India.

This period of political fragmentation in the north also saw the rise of the Satavahana dynasty (also called Andhra) in the Deccan Plateau from the second century B.C.E. to the early third century C.E. Elements of north Indian technology and culture—including iron metallurgy, rice-paddy agriculture, urbanization, writing, coinage, and Brahmin religious authority—spread throughout central India, and indigenous kinship groups were absorbed into the Hindu system of class and caste.

In the southernmost parts of the peninsula were the three **Tamil kingdoms** of Cholas, Pandyas, and Cheras. While in frequent conflict with one another and experiencing periods of ascendancy and decline, they persisted in one form or another for over two thousand years. The period from the third century B.C.E. to the third century C.E. was a "classical" period of great literary and artistic productivity. Under the patronage of the Pandya kings and the intellectual leadership of an academy of five hundred authors, works of literature on a wide range of topics—grammatical treatises, collections of ethical proverbs, epics, and short poems about love, war, wealth, and the beauty of nature—were produced, and music, dance, and drama were performed.

The Gupta Empire, 320–550 C.E.
In the early fourth century C.E., following the decline of the Kushan and Satavahana regimes in northern and central India, a new imperial entity took shape in the north. Like its Mauryan predecessor, the **Gupta Empire** emerged from the Ganges Plain and had its capital at Pataliputra. The founder, consciously modeling himself on the first Mauryan king, called himself Chandra Gupta (r. 320–335). The monarchs of this dynasty never controlled territories as extensive as those of the Mauryans. Nevertheless, over the fifteen-year reign of Chandra Gupta and the forty-year reigns of his three successors—the war-loving Samudra Gupta, Chandra Gupta II, a famed patron of artists and scholars, and Kumara Gupta—Gupta power and influence reached across northern and central India, west to Punjab and east to Bengal, north to Kashmir, and south into the Deccan Plateau.

This new empire enjoyed the same strategic advantages as its Mauryan predecessor, sitting astride important trade routes, exploiting the agricultural productivity of the Ganges Plain, and controlling nearby iron deposits. Although similar methods for raising revenue and administering broad territories were adopted, Gupta control was never as effectively centralized as Mauryan authority, and the Gupta administrative bureaucracy and intelligence network were smaller and less pervasive. A standing army, whose strength lay in the excellent horsemanship (learned from the nomadic

Kushans) and skill with bow and arrow of its cavalry, maintained tight control and taxation in the core of the empire. Governors, whose position often passed from father to son, had a freer hand in the more outlying areas. Distant subordinate kingdoms and areas inhabited by kinship groups made annual donations of tribute, and garrisons were stationed at key frontier points. At the local level, villages were managed by a headman and council of elders, while the guilds of artisans and merchants had important administrative roles in the cities.

Limited in its ability to enforce its will on outlying areas, the empire found ways to "persuade" others to follow its lead. One medium of persuasion was the splendor, beauty, and orderliness of life at the capital and royal court. The Gupta Empire is a good example of a **"theater-state."** A constant round of solemn rituals, dramatic ceremonies, and exciting cultural events was a potent advertisement for the benefits of association with the empire. The center collected luxury goods and profits from trade and redistributed them to dependents through the exchange of gifts and other means. Subordinate princes gained prestige by emulating the Gupta center on whatever scale they could manage, and they maintained close ties through visits, gifts, and marriages to the Gupta royal family.

Astronomers, mathematicians, and other scientists received royal support. Indian mathematicians invented the concept of zero and developed the "Arabic" numerals and system of place-value notation used in most parts of the world today (see Environment and Technology: Indian Mathematics). The Gupta monarchs also supported poets and dramatists and the compilation of law codes and grammatical texts.

Because of the moist climate of the Ganges Plain, few archaeological remains from the Gupta era have survived. An eyewitness account, however, provides valuable information about Pataliputra, the capital city. A Chinese Buddhist monk named Faxian (fah-shee-en) made a pilgrimage to the homeland of his faith around 400 C.E. and left a record of his journey:

> The royal palace and halls in the midst of the city, which exist now as of old, were all made by spirits which [King Ashoka] employed, and which piled up the stones, reared the walls and gates, and executed the elegant carving and inlaid sculpture-work—in a way which no human hands of this world could accomplish.... By the side of the stupa of Ashoka, there has been made a Mahayana [Buddhist] monastery, very grand and beautiful; there is also a Hinayana [Theravada] one; the two together containing six hundred or seven hundred monks. The rules of demeanor and the scholastic arrangements in them are worthy of observation.[3]

There was a decline in the status of women in this period. As in Mesopotamia, Greece, and China, several factors—urbanization, increasingly complex political and social structures, and the emergence of a nonagricultural middle class that placed high value on the acquisition and inheritance of property—led to a loss of women's rights and an increase in male control over women's behavior.

Women in India lost the right to own or inherit property. They were also barred from studying sacred texts and participating in sacrificial rituals. In many respects, they were treated as equivalent to the lowest class, the Shudra. A woman

---

[3]James Legge, *The Travels of Fa-hien: Fa-hien's Record of Buddhistic Kingdoms* (Delhi: Oriental Publishers, 1971), 77–79.

was expected to obey first her father, then her husband, and finally her sons. Girls were married at an increasingly early age, sometimes as young as six or seven. This practice meant that the prospective husband could be sure of his wife's virginity and, by bringing her up in his own household, could train her to suit his purposes. The most extreme form of control took place in parts of India where a widow was expected to cremate herself on her husband's funeral pyre. This ritual, called *sati* (suh-TEE), was seen as a way of keeping a woman "pure." Women who declined to make this ultimate gesture of devotion were forbidden to remarry, shunned socially, and given little opportunity to earn a living.

Some women escaped male control by entering a Jainist or Buddhist religious community. Status also gave women more freedom. Women who belonged to powerful families and courtesans trained in poetry and music as well as ways of providing sexual pleasure had high social standing and sometimes gave money for the erection of religious shrines.

The Mauryans had been Buddhists, but the Gupta monarchs were Hindus. They revived ancient Vedic practices to bring an aura of sanctity to their position. This period also saw a reassertion of the importance of class and caste and the influence of Brahmin priests. In return for the religious validation of their rule given by the Brahmins, the Guptas gave the priests extensive grants of land. The Brahmins became wealthy from the revenues, which they collected directly from the peasants, and they even exercised administrative and judicial authority over the villages in their domains. Nevertheless, it was an era of religious tolerance. The Gupta kings were patrons for Hindu, Buddhist, and Jain endeavors. Buddhist monasteries with hundreds or even thousands of monks and nuns in residence flourished in the cities, and a Buddhist university was established at Nalanda. Northern India was the destination of Buddhist pilgrims from Southeast and East Asia, traveling to visit the birthplace of their faith.

The classic form of the Hindu temple evolved during the Gupta era. Sitting atop a raised platform surmounted by high towers, the temple was patterned on the sacred mountain or palace in which the gods of mythology resided and represented the inherent order of the universe. From an exterior courtyard worshipers approached the central shrine, where the statue of the deity stood. Paintings or sculptured depictions of gods and mythical events covered the walls of the best-endowed sanctuaries. Cave-temples carved out of rock were also richly adorned with frescoes or sculpture.

The vibrant commerce of the previous era continued into the Gupta period, with artisan guilds playing an influential role in the economic, political, and religious life of the towns. The Guptas sought control of the ports on the Arabian Sea but saw a decline in trade with the weakened Roman Empire. In compensation, trade with Southeast and East Asia was on the rise. Adventurous merchants from the ports of eastern and southern India made the sea voyage to the Malay (muh-LAY) Peninsula and islands of Indonesia to exchange Indian cotton cloth, ivory, metalwork, and animals for Chinese silk or Indonesian spices. The overland Silk Road from China was also in operation but was vulnerable to disruption by Central Asian nomads (see Chapter 9).

By the later fifth century C.E. the Gupta Empire was coming under pressure from the Huns, nomadic invaders from the steppes of Central Asia who poured into the northwest corridor. Defense of this distant frontier region eventually exhausted the imperial treasury, and the empire collapsed by 550.

ENVIRONMENT + TECHNOLOGY

Indian Mathematics

The so-called Arabic numerals used in most parts of the world today were developed in India. The Indian system of place-value notation was far more efficient than the unwieldy numerical systems of Egyptians, Greeks, and Romans, and the invention of zero was a profound intellectual achievement. This system is used even more widely than the alphabet derived from the Phoenicians (see Chapter 3) and is, in one sense, the only truly global language.

In its fully developed form the Indian method of arithmetic notation employed a base-ten system. It had separate columns for ones, tens, hundreds, and so forth, as well as a zero sign to indicate the absence of units in a given column. This system makes possible the economical expression of even very large numbers. It also allows for the performance of calculations not possible in a system like the numerals of the Romans, where any real calculation had to be done mentally or on a counting board.

A series of early Indian inscriptions using the numerals from 1 to 9 are deeds of property given to religious institutions by kings or other wealthy individuals. They were incised in the Sanskrit language on copper plates. The earliest known example has a date equivalent to 595 C.E. A sign for zero is attested by the eighth century, but textual evidence leads to the inference that a place-value system and the zero concept were already known in the fifth century.

This Indian system spread to the Middle East, Southeast Asia, and East Asia by the seventh century. Other peoples quickly recognized its capabilities and adopted it, sometimes using indigenous symbols. Europe received the new technology somewhat later. Gerbert of Aurillac, a French Christian monk, spent time in Spain between 967 and 970, where he was exposed to the mathematics of the Arabs. A great scholar and teacher who eventually became Pope Sylvester II (r. 999–1003), he spread word of the "Arabic" system in the Christian West.

Knowledge of the Indian system of mathematical notation eventually spread throughout Europe, partly through the use of a mechanical calculating device—an improved version of the Roman counting board, with counters inscribed with variants of the Indian numeral forms. Because the counters could be turned sideways or upside down, at first there was considerable variation in the forms. But by the twelfth century they had become standardized into forms close to those in use today. As the capabilities of the place-value system for calculations became clear, the counting

---

The early seventh century saw a brief revival of imperial unity. Harsha Vardhana (r. 606–647), ruler of the region around Delhi, extended his power over the northern plain and moved his capital to Kanauj on the Ganges River. By this time cities and commerce were in decline, much of the land had been given as grants to Brahmin priests and government officials, and the administration was decentralized, depending on the allegiance of largely autonomous vassal rulers. In many respects the situation was parallel to that of the later Roman Empire in Europe (see Chapter 6), as India moved toward a more feudal social and economic structure. After Harsha's death, northern India reverted to its customary state of political fragmentation and remained divided until the Islamic invasions of the eleventh and twelfth centuries (see Chapter 15).

board fell into disuse. This led to the adoption of the zero sign—not necessary on the counting board, where a column could be left empty—by the twelfth century. Leonardo Fibonacci, a thirteenth-century C.E. Italian who learned algebra in Muslim North Africa and employed the Arabic numeral system in his mathematical treatise, gave additional impetus to the movement to discard the traditional system of Roman numerals.

Why was this marvelous system of mathematical notation invented in ancient India? The answer may lie in the way its range and versatility correspond to elements of Indian cosmology. The Indians conceived of immense spans of time—trillions of years (far exceeding current scientific estimates of the age of the universe as approximately 14 billion years)—during which innumerable universes like our own were created, existed for a finite time, then were destroyed. In one popular creation myth, Vishnu is slumbering on the coils of a giant serpent at the bottom of the ocean, and worlds are being created and destroyed as he exhales and inhales. In Indian thought our world, like others, has existed for a series of epochs lasting more than 4 million years, yet the period of its existence is but a brief and insignificant moment in the vast sweep of time. The Indians developed a number system that allowed them to express concepts of this magnitude.

Facsimile by Georges Ifrah. Reproduced by permission of Georges Ifrah.

Copper Plate with Indian Numerals *This property deed from western India shows an early form of the symbol system for numbers that spread to the Middle East and Europe and today is used all over the world.*

During and after the centuries of Gupta ascendancy and decline in the north, the Deccan Plateau and the southern part of the peninsula followed an independent path. In this region, where the landscape is segmented by mountains, rocky plateaus, tropical forests, and sharply cut river courses, there were many small centers of power. From the sixth to twelfth centuries, the Pallavas, Chalukyas, and other warrior dynasties collected tribute and plundered as far as their strength permitted, storing their wealth in urban fortresses. These rulers sought legitimacy and fame as patrons of religion and culture, and much of the distinguished art and architecture of the period were produced in the kingdoms of the south. Many elements of northern Indian religion and culture spread in the south, including the class and caste system, Brahmin religious authority, and worship of Vishnu and Shiva. These king-doms also served as the conduit through which Indian religion and culture reached Southeast Asia.

SOUTHEAST ASIA, 50–1025 C.E.

Southeast Asia consists of three geographical zones: the Indochina mainland, the Malay Peninsula, and thousands of islands extending on an east-west axis far out into the Pacific Ocean. Encompassing a vast area of land and water, this region is now occupied by the countries of Myanmar (myahn-MAH) (Burma), Thailand, Laos, Cambodia, Vietnam, Malaysia, Singapore, Indonesia, Brunei (broo-NIE), and the Philippines. Poised between the ancient centers of China and India, South-east Asia has been influenced by the cultures of both civilizations. The region first rose to prominence and prosperity because of its intermediate role in the trade exchanges between southern and eastern Asia.

The strategic importance of Southeast Asia is enhanced by the region's natural resources. This is a geologically active zone; the islands are the tops of a chain of volcanoes. Lying along the equator, Southeast Asia has a tropical climate. The temperature hovers around 80 degrees Fahrenheit (30 degrees Celsius), and the monsoon winds provide dependable rainfall throughout the year. Thanks to several growing cycles each year, the region is capable of supporting a large human popu-lation. The most fertile agricultural lands lie along the floodplains of the largest silt-bearing rivers or contain rich volcanic soil deposited by ancient eruptions.

Early Civilization   Rain forest covers much of Southeast Asia. As early as 2000 B.C.E. people in this region practiced swidden agriculture, clearing land for farming by cutting and burning the vegeta-tion. The cleared land was farmed for several growing seasons. When the soil was exhausted, the farmers abandoned the patch, allowing the forest to reclaim it, while they cleared and cultivated other nearby fields in similar fashion. Rice was the sta-ple food—labor-intensive (see Chapter 4) but able to support a large population. A number of plant and animal species spread from Southeast Asia to other regions, including rice, soybeans, sugar cane, yams, bananas, coconuts, chickens, and pigs.

The Malay peoples who became the dominant population in this region were the product of several waves of migration from southern China beginning around 3000 B.C.E. Some indigenous peoples merged with the Malay newcomers; others retreated to remote mountain and forest zones. Subsequently (beginning, perhaps, around 1600 B.C.E.), rising population and disputes within communities prompted streams of people to leave the Southeast Asian mainland for the islands. By the first millennium B.C.E. Southeast Asians had developed impressive navigational skills. They knew how to ride the monsoon winds and interpret the patterns of swells, winds, clouds, and bird and sea life. Over a period of several thousand years groups of Malay peoples in large, double outrigger canoes spread out across the Pacific and Indian Oceans—half the circumference of the earth—to settle thousands of islands.

The inhabitants of Southeast Asia clustered along riverbanks or in fertile volca-nic plains. Their fields and villages were never far from the rain forest, with its wild animals and numerous plant species. Forest trees provided fruit, wood, and spices, and the shallow waters surrounding the islands teemed with fish. This region was also an early center of metallurgy. Metalsmiths heated copper and tin ore to the right temperature for producing and shaping bronze implements by using hollow bamboo tubes to funnel oxygen to the furnace.

Northern Indochina, by its geographic proximity, was vulnerable to Chinese pressure and cultural influences, and it was under Chinese political control for a thousand years (111 B.C.E.–939 C.E.). Farther south, larger states emerged in the early centuries C.E. in response to two powerful forces: commerce and Hindu-Buddhist culture.

Southeast Asia was situated along the trade routes that merchants used to carry Chinese silk westward to India and the Mediterranean. The movements of nomadic peoples had disrupted the old land route across Central Asia, but Indian demand for silk was increasing—both for domestic use and for transshipment to satisfy the fast-growing luxury market in the Roman Empire. Gradually merchants extended this exchange network to include goods from Southeast Asia, such as aromatic woods, resins, and cinnamon, pepper, cloves, nutmeg, and other spices. Southeast Asian centers rose to prominence by serving this trade network and controlling key points.

The other force leading to the rise of larger political entities was the influence of Hindu-Buddhist culture imported from India. Commerce brought Indian merchants and sailors into the ports of Southeast Asia. As Buddhism spread, Southeast Asia became a way station for Indian missionaries and East Asian pilgrims going to and coming from the birthplace of their faith. Shrewd Malay rulers looked to Indian traditions as a rich source of ideas and prestige. They borrowed Sanskrit terms such as *maharaja* (mah-huh-RAH-juh) (great king), utilized Indian models of bureaucracy, ceremonial practices, and forms of artistic representation, and employed priests, administrators, and scribes skilled in Sanskrit writing to expedite government business. Their special connection to powerful gods and higher knowledge raised them above their rivals.

However, the Southeast Asian kingdoms were not just passive recipients of Indian culture. They took what was useful to them and synthesized it with indigenous beliefs, values, and institutions—for example, local concepts of chiefship, ancestor worship, and forms of oaths. Moreover, they trained their own people in the new ways, so that the bureaucracy contained both foreign experts and native disciples. The whole process amounted to a cultural dialogue between India and Southeast Asia in which both were active participants.

The first major Southeast Asian center, called "**Funan**" (FOO-nahn) by Chinese visitors, flourished between the first and sixth centuries C.E., with its capital at the modern site of Oc-Eo in southern Vietnam. Funan occupied the delta of the Mekong (MAY-kawng) River, a "rice bowl" capable of supporting a large population, and its rulers mobilized large numbers of laborers to dig irrigation channels and prevent destructive floods. By extending its control over most of southern Indochina and the Malay Peninsula, Funan was able to dominate the trade route from India to China. The route began in the ports of northeast India, crossed the Bay of Bengal, continued by land over the Isthmus of Kra on the Malay Peninsula, and then continued across the South China Sea. Indian merchants found that offloading their goods from ships and carrying them across the narrow strip of land was safer than making the 1,000-mile (1,600-kilometer) voyage around the Malay Peninsula—a dangerous trip marked by treacherous currents, rocky shoals, and pirates. Once the portage across the isthmus was finished, the merchants needed food and lodging while waiting for the monsoon winds to shift so they could make the last leg of the voyage to China by sea. Funan stockpiled food and provided security for those engaged in this trade—in return for customs duties and other fees.

Chinese observers have left reports of the prosperity and sophistication of Funan, emphasizing the presence of walled cities, palaces, archives, systems of taxation, and state-organized agriculture. Nevertheless, Funan declined in the sixth century. The most likely explanation is that international trade routes changed and Funan no longer held a strategic position.

The Srivijayan Kingdom   By the sixth century a new, all-sea route had developed. Merchants and travelers from south India and Sri Lanka now sailed through the Strait of Malacca (between the west side of the Malay Peninsula and the northeast coast of the island of Sumatra) and into the South China Sea. Although presenting both human and navigational hazards, the new route significantly shortened the journey.

A new center of power, **Srivijaya** (sree-vih-JUH-yuh)—Sanskrit for "Great Conquest"—dominated the new southerly route by 683 C.E. The capital of the Srivijayan kingdom was at modern-day Palembang in southeastern Sumatra, 50 miles (80 kilometers) up the broad and navigable Musi River, with a good

Robert Harding Picture Library Ltd/Alamy

Aerial View of the Buddhist Monument at Borobodur, Java *This great monument of volcanic stone was more than 300 feet (90 meters) in length and over 100 feet (30 meters) high. Pilgrims made a 3-mile-long (nearly 5-kilometer-long) winding ascent through ten levels intended to represent the ideal Buddhist journey from ignorance to enlightenment. Numerous sculptured reliefs depicting Buddhist legends provide glimpses of daily life in early Java.*

natural harbor. The kingdom was well situated to control the southern part of the Malay Peninsula, Sumatra, parts of Java and Borneo, and the Malacca (muh-LAH-kuh) and Sunda straits—vital passageways for shipping.

The Srivijayan kingdom gained ascendancy over its rivals and assumed control of the international trade route by fusing four distinct ecological zones into an interdependent network. The core area was the productive agricultural plain along the Musi River. The king and his clerks, judges, and tax collectors controlled this zone directly. Control was less direct over the second zone, the upland regions of Sumatra's interior, with its commercially valuable forest products. Local rulers there were bound to the center by oaths of loyalty, elaborate court ceremonies, and the sharing of profits from trade. The third zone consisted of river ports that had been Srivijaya's main rivals. They were conquered and controlled thanks to an alliance between Srivijaya and neighboring sea nomads, pirates who served as a Srivijayan navy in return for a steady income.

The fourth zone was a fertile "rice bowl" on the central plain of the nearby island of Java—a region so productive, because of its volcanic soil, that it houses and feeds the majority of the population of present-day Indonesia. Srivijayan monarchs maintained alliances, cemented by intermarriage, with several ruling dynasties in this region, and the Srivijayan kings claimed descent from the main Javanese dynasty. These arrangements gave Srivijaya access to large quantities of foodstuffs that people living in the capital and merchants and sailors visiting the various ports needed.

The kings of Srivijaya who constructed and maintained this complex network of social, political, and economic relationships were men of energy and skill. Although their authority depended in part on force, it owed more to diplomatic and even theatrical talents. Like the Gupta monarchy, Srivijaya was a theater-state, securing its preeminence and binding dependents by its sheer splendor and its ability to attract labor, talent, and luxury products. The court was the scene of ceremonies designed to dazzle observers and reinforce an image of wealth, power, and sanctity. Subordinate rulers took oaths of loyalty carrying dire threats of punishment for violations, and in their home locales they imitated the splendid ceremonials of the capital.

The Srivijayan king, drawing upon Buddhist conceptions, presented himself as a bodhisattva, one who had achieved enlightenment and utilized his precious insights for the betterment of his subjects. The king was believed to have magical powers, controlling powerful forces of fertility associated with the rivers in flood and mediating between the spiritually potent realms of the mountains and the sea. He was also said to be so wealthy that he deposited bricks of gold in the river estuary to appease the local gods, and a hillside near town was covered with silver and gold images of the Buddha. The gold originated in East or West Africa and came to Southeast Asia through trade with the Muslim world (see Chapter 9).

The kings built and patronized Buddhist monasteries and schools. In central Java local dynasties allied with Srivijaya built magnificent temple complexes to advertise their glory. The most famous of these, **Borobodur** (booh-roe-boe-DOOR), built between 770 and 825 C.E., was the largest human construction in the Southern Hemisphere.

The kings of Srivijaya carried out this marvelous balancing act for centuries. But the system was vulnerable to shifts in the pattern of international trade. Some such change must have contributed to the decline of Srivijaya in the eleventh century, even though the immediate cause was a destructive raid on the capital Palembang by forces of the Chola kingdom of southeast India in 1025 C.E.

After the decline of Srivijaya, leadership passed to new, vigorous kingdoms on the eastern end of Java, and the maritime realm of Southeast Asia remained prosperous and connected to international trade networks. Through the ages Europeans remained dimly aware of this region as a source of spices and other luxury items. Some four centuries after the decline of Srivijaya, an Italian navigator serving under the flag of Spain—Christopher Columbus—sailed westward across the Atlantic Ocean, seeking to establish a direct route to the fabled "Indies" from which the spices came.

Conclusion

This chapter traces the emergence of complex societies in India and Southeast Asia between the second millennium B.C.E. and the first millennium C.E. Because of migrations, trade, and the spread of belief systems, an Indian style of civilization spread throughout the subcontinent and adjoining regions and eventually made its way to the mainland and island chains of Southeast Asia. In this period were laid cultural foundations that in large measure still endure.

The development and spread of belief systems—Vedism, Buddhism, Jainism, and Hinduism—have a central place in this chapter because nearly all the sources of information are religious. A museum visitor examining artifacts from ancient Mesopotamia, Egypt, the Greco-Roman Mediterranean, and China will find many objects of a religious nature. Only the Indian artifacts, however, will be almost exclusively from the religious sphere.

Writing came later to India than to other parts of the Eastern Hemisphere, for reasons particular to the Indian situation. Like Indian artifacts, most ancient Indian texts are of a religious nature. Ancient Indians did not develop a historical consciousness and generate historiographic texts like their Israelite, Greek, and Chinese contemporaries, primarily because they held a strikingly different view of time. The distinctive Indian conception—of vast epochs in which universes are created and destroyed again and again and the essential spirit of living creatures is reincarnated repeatedly—made the particulars of any brief moment seem relatively insignificant.

The tension between divisive and unifying forces can be seen in many aspects of Indian life. Political and social division has been the norm throughout much of the history of India, a consequence of the topographical and environmental diversity of the subcontinent and the complex mix of ethnic and linguistic groups inhabiting it. The elaborate structure of classes and castes was a response to this diversity—an attempt to organize the population and position individuals within an accepted hierarchy, as well as to regulate group interactions. Strong central governments, such as those of the Mauryan and Gupta kings, gained ascendancy for a time and promoted prosperity and development. They rose to dominance by gaining control of metal resources and important trade routes, developing effective military and administrative institutions, and creating cultural forms that inspired admiration and emulation. However, as in archaic Greece and Warring States China, the periods of fragmentation and multiple small centers of power seemed as economically and intellectually dynamic as the periods of unity.

Many distinctive social and intellectual features of Indian civilization—the class and caste system, models of kingship and statecraft, and Vedic, Jainist, and Buddhist belief systems—originated in the great river valleys of the north, where descendants of Indo-European immigrants predominated. Hinduism then embraced elements drawn from the Dravidian cultures of the south as well as from Buddhism. The capacity of the Hindu tradition to assimilate a wide range of popular beliefs facilitated the spread of a common Indian civilization across the subcontinent, although there was, and is, considerable variation from one region to another.

IMPORTANT EVENTS 1500 B.C.E. TO 1025 C.E.

ca. 1600 B.C.E.	Beginning of migrations from mainland Southeast Asia to islands in Pacific and Indian Oceans
ca. 1500 B.C.E.	Migration of Indo-European peoples into northwest India
ca. 1000 B.C.E.	Indo-European groups move into the Ganges Plain
ca. 500 B.C.E.	Siddhartha Gautama founds Buddhism; Mahavira founds Jainism
324 B.C.E.	Chandragupta Maurya becomes king of Magadha and lays foundation for Mauryan Empire
184 B.C.E.	Fall of Mauryan Empire
ca. 50–560 B.C.E.	Funan dominates southern Indochina and the Isthmus of Kra
320 C.E.	Chandra Gupta establishes Gupta Empire
ca. 500 C.E.	Trade route develops through Strait of Malacca
550 C.E.	Collapse of Gupta Empire
683 C.E.	Rise of Srivijaya in Sumatra
770–825 C.E.	Construction of Borobodur in Java
1025 C.E.	Chola attack on Palembang and decline of Srivijaya

8

PEOPLES AND CIVILIZATIONS OF THE AMERICAS, 1200 B.C.E.–1400 C.E.

The ancient Mesoamerican civilization of the Maya (MY-ah) developed a complex written language that enabled scribes like the one in this illustration to record the important actions of rulers and military events. Recent translations give us a glimpse into the life of a Maya princess. In late August 682 C.E. the Maya princess Lady Wac-Chanil-Ahau (wac-cha-NEEL-ah-HOW) walked down the steps from her family's residence and mounted a litter decorated with rich textiles and animal skins. As the procession exited from the urban center of Dos Pilas (dohs PEE-las), her military escort spread out through the fields and woods to prevent ambush by enemies. Lady Wac-Chanil-Ahau's destination was the Maya city of Naranjo (na-RAHN-hoe), where she was to marry a powerful nobleman. Her father had arranged her marriage to reestablish the royal dynasty of Naranjo, a dynasty eliminated when Caracol, the region's major military power, had conquered that city. Lady Wac-Chanil-Ahau's passage to Naranjo symbolized her father's desire to forge a military alliance that could resist Caracol. For us, the story of Lady Wac-Chanil-Ahau illustrates the importance of marriage and lineage in the politics of the classic-period Maya.

K'ak Tiliw Chan Chaak (kahk tee-lew CHAN cha-ahk), the son of Lady Wac-Chanil-Ahau, ascended the throne of Naranjo as a five-year-old in 693 C.E. During his long reign he proved to be a careful diplomat and formidable warrior. He was also a prodigious builder, leaving behind an expanded and beautified capital as part of his legacy. Mindful of the importance of his mother and her lineage from Dos Pilas, he erected numerous steles (carved stone monuments) that celebrated her life.[1]

The world of Wac-Chanil-Ahau was challenged by warfare and by dynastic crisis as population increased and competition for resources grew more violent. In this environment the rise of Caracol undermined long-standing commercial and political relations in much of southern Mesoamerica and led to more than a century of conflict. Eventually, the dynasty created at Dos Pilas by the heirs of Lady Wac-Chanil-Ahau challenged Caracol. Despite a shared culture and religion, the great Maya cities remained divided by the dynastic ambitions of their rulers.

---

[1]This summary closely follows the historical narrative and translation of names offered by Linda Schele and David Freidel in *A Forest of Kings: The Untold Story of the Ancient Maya* (New York: Morrow, 1990), 182–186.

As the story of Lady Wac-Chanil-Ahau's marriage and her role in the development of a Maya dynasty suggests, the peoples of the Americas were in constant competition for resources. Members of hereditary elites organized their societies to meet these challenges, even as their ambition for greater power predictably ignited new conflicts. No single set of political institutions or technologies worked in every environment, and enormous cultural diversity existed in the ancient Americas. In Mesoamerica (most of Mexico and Central America) and in the Andean region of South America, Amerindian peoples developed an extraordinarily productive and diversified agriculture. They also built great cities that rivaled the capitals of the Chinese and Roman Empires in size and beauty. The Olmec of Mesoamerica and Chavín (cha-VEEN) of the Andes were among the earliest civilizations of the Americas. In other regions of the hemisphere, indigenous peoples adapted combinations of hunting and agriculture to maintain a wide variety of settlement patterns, political forms, and cultural traditions. Despite differences, all the cultures and civilizations of the Americas experienced cycles of expansion and contraction as they struggled with the challenges of environmental change, population growth, and war.

FORMATIVE CIVILIZATIONS OF THE OLMEC AND CHAVÍN, 1200–200 B.C.E.

The domestication of new plant varieties, especially potatoes, corn, squash, and sweet potatoes, and a limited development of trade helped promote social stratification and the beginnings of urbanization in both Mesoamerica and the Andes. By 2000 B.C.E. a number of urban centers had begun to project their political and cultural power over neighboring territories, but very few of these early urban places had populations in excess of 2,500. Two of the hemisphere's most impressive cultural traditions, the Olmec of Mesoamerica (Mexico and northern Central America), and Chavín of the mountainous Andean region of South America, developed from these humble origins around 1200 B.C.E. Before their eclipse before 200 B.C.E., each had established a cultural legacy that would persist for more than a thousand years.

The Mesoamerican Olmec, 1200–400 B.C.E. Mesoamerica is a region of great geographic and climatic diversity. It is extremely active geologically, experiencing both earthquakes and volcanic eruptions. Mountain ranges break the region into microenvironments, including the temperate climates of the Valley of Mexico and the Guatemalan highlands, the tropical forests of the Petén and Gulf of Mexico coast, the rain forest of the southern Yucatán and Belize, and the drier scrub forest of the northern Yucatán.

Within each of these ecological niches, Amerindian peoples developed specialized technologies that exploited indigenous plants and animals, as well as minerals like obsidian, quartz, and jade. The ability of farmers to produce dependable surpluses of maize, beans, squash, and other locally domesticated plants permitted the first stages of craft specialization and urbanization. Eventually, contacts across environmental boundaries led to trade and cultural exchange with emerging centers across the region and ultimately with Central and South America. Enhanced trade, increasing agricultural productivity, and rising population created the conditions for social stratification.

Scholars refer to the period 1500 B.C.E. to 200 C.E. in Mesoamerica as the preclassic period. The most important civilization in this period was the **Olmec**, which flourished between 1200 and 400 B.C.E. near the tropical Atlantic coast of Mexico. It is unclear whether Olmec urban centers were rival city-states or were subject to a centralized political authority, but scholars agree that San Lorenzo (1200–900 B.C.E.), with a population of between 10,000 to 18,000, was the largest and most important Olmec center. San Lorenzo's cultural influence ultimately extended south and west to the Pacific coast of Central America and north to central Mexico, suggesting its ability to project political and military power. Also founded around 1200 B.C.E., La Venta (LA BEN-tah) became the preeminent Olmec center when San Lorenzo was abandoned or destroyed around 900 B.C.E. After La Venta's collapse around 600 B.C.E., Tres Zapotes (TRACE zah-POE-tace) survived as the largest Olmec center, although it was much smaller than either of its predecessors.

San Lorenzo and other Olmec cities served primarily as religious centers. The urban elite's power grew with the development of persuasive religious ideologies and compelling religious rituals that helped organize and subordinate neighboring rural populations. As a result, urban centers were dominated by religious architecture that included pyramids, monumental mounds, and raised platforms. Constructed by thousands of laborers recruited in surrounding agricultural zones, the massive urban architecture was embellished with religious symbols tied to the official cult. The elite dominated collective religious life and built their residences on raised platforms located near the most sacred ritual spaces.

The Olmec were polytheistic, and most of their deities had both male and female natures. The motifs found on ceramics, sculptures, and buildings also show that human and animal characteristics were blended. Rulers were especially associated with the jaguar. Priests and shamans who foretold the future, cured the sick, and led collective rituals claimed the ability to make direct contact with supernatural powers by transforming themselves into powerful animals, such as crocodiles, snakes, and sharks. These transformative powers were also associated with a ballgame played with a solid rubber ball in banked courts located near the center of temple precincts. Versions of this game survived until the arrival of Europeans in the sixteenth century.

Olmec religious practice included the close observation of the heavens, and all their major ceremonial centers were laid out in alignment with the paths of certain stars. This concern for astronomic observation led to the development of an accurate calendar that was used to predict seasonal rains and guide planting and harvesting. The Olmec also developed a form of writing (as yet undeciphered) that scholars believe influenced later innovations among the Maya.

Little is known about Olmec political structure, but it seems likely that the rise of major urban centers coincided with the appearance of a form of kingship that combined religious and secular roles. Rulers and their close kin came to be associated with the gods through bloodletting ceremonies and human sacrifice and through the staging of elaborate rituals that brought together urban and rural populations. The authority of the rulers is suggested by a series of colossal carved stone heads discovered buried near the major urban centers, especially San Lorenzo. These heads, some as large as 11 feet (3.4 meters) high, are the best-known monuments of Olmec culture. Archaeologists believe that they were carved to memorialize individual rulers. Some were depicted wearing the padded helmet used as protection in the sacred ballgame.

The first stage of urbanization was tied to the exploitation of products like salt, cacao (chocolate beans), and clay used for ceramics. Control of these resources led to the development of specialized crafts and to trade. In the largest urban centers, skilled artisans were full-time residents who decorated buildings with religious carvings and sculptures. They also produced high-quality crafts, such as exquisite carved jade figurines, necklaces, and ceremonial obsidian knives and axes. The diffusion of these Olmec products among distant locations suggests the existence of a specialized class of merchants.

The mounting wealth and power of the elite and the growing populations of Olmec cities depended on a bargain struck with the much larger populations of the surrounding countryside. The rural masses provided the labor that constructed the pyramids, platforms, and ball courts of the urban centers as well as the food that sustained urban populations, but they also received benefits. As a relief from their routines of heavy labor, they participated in awe-inspiring ceremonies at San Lorenzo and other centers. Here the official cult directed by the elite explained human origins and unforeseen natural events and helped to guide collective life. It provided practical benefits to the rural masses as well. The elite used its authority to organize labor to dig drainage canals and construct the raised fields that allowed agriculture in wetlands, thus expanding food production.

Georg Gerster/Photo Researchers, Inc.

Olmec Head *Giant heads sculpted from basalt are a widely recognized legacy of Olmec culture. Sixteen heads have been found, the largest approximately 11 feet (3.4 meters) tall. Experts in Olmec archaeology believe the heads are portraits of individual rulers, warriors, or ballplayers.*

Ultimately, every major Olmec center was abandoned, its monuments defaced and buried, and its buildings destroyed. Even the portrait heads were dragged from the centers, defaced, and buried. Archaeologists interpret these events differently; some see them as evidence of internal upheavals or military attacks by neighboring peoples, whereas others suggest that they were rituals associated with the death or overthrow of a ruler or evidence of social conflict. Regardless of the causes for Olmec decline, the influence of this civilization endured for centuries. Every subsequent Mesoamerican civilizations utilized the rich legacy of Olmec material culture, technology, religious belief and ritual, political organization, art, architecture, and sports.

Early South American Civilization: Chavín, 900–200 B.C.E.   Geography and environment played a critical role in the development of human society in the Andes. The region's diverse environments—a mountainous core, arid coastal plain, and dense interior tropical forests—challenged human populations, encouraging the development of specialized regional production as well as social institutions and cultural values that facilitated interregional exchanges and shared labor responsibilities.

Scholars use the term *Early Horizon* for the period 900 B.C.E. to 200 C.E. in Andean history. The earliest urban centers in this region were villages of a few hundred people built along the coastal plain or in the foothills near the coast, where an abundance of fish and mollusks provided a dependable food supply. The later introduction of corn (maize) cultivation from Mesoamerica increased the food supplies of the coast and interior foothills, allowing greater levels of urbanization. Trade between the peoples of the coastal region and Andean foothills also led to the exchange of ceremonial practices, religious motifs, and aesthetic ideas.

Between 900 and 250 B.C.E. **Chavín** dominated a densely populated region that included large areas of the Peruvian coastal plain and Andean foothills. The capital city of Chavín de Huantar (cha-BEAN day WAHN-tar) was located at 10,300 feet (3,139 meters) in the eastern range of the Andes north of the modern city of Lima. Its location facilitated exchanges among ecologically distinct zones, linking the coast to inland producers of quinoa (a local grain), maize, and potatoes, llama herders in high mountain valleys, and tropical producers of coca (the leaves were chewed, producing a mild narcotic effect) on the eastern flank of the Andes.

The development of these trade networks led to reciprocal labor obligations that permitted the construction and maintenance of roads, bridges, temples, palaces, and large irrigation and drainage projects, as well as textile production. These reciprocal labor obligations were organized initially by groups of related families who held land communally and claimed descent from a common ancestor. Group members thought of themselves as brothers and sisters and were obliged to aid one another. In the time of Chavín these groups were organized collectively by the state to provide labor to build temples, elite residences, and irrigation works.

Llamas, first bred in the mountainous interior of Peru, were the only domesticated beasts of burden in the Americas, and they played an important role in the integration of the Andean region. Llamas provided meat and wool and decreased the labor needed to transport goods. A single driver could control ten to thirty animals, each carrying up to 70 pounds (32 kilograms), while a human porter could carry only about 50 pounds (22.5 kilograms). By moving goods from one ecological zone to another, llamas promoted specialization of production and increased trade. Thus they were crucial to Chavín's development, not unlike the camel in the evolution of trans-Saharan trade (see Chapter 9).

Class distinctions appear to have increased in this period. Modern scholars see evidence that a powerful chief or king dominated Chavín's politics, while a class of priests directed religious life. The most common decorative motif in sculpture, pottery, and textiles was a jaguar-man similar in conception to the contemporary Olmec symbol. In both civilizations this powerful predator provided an enduring image of religious authority.

Chavín housed a large complex of multilevel platforms made of packed earth or rubble and faced with cut stone or adobe (sun-dried brick made of clay and straw). Small buildings used for ritual purposes or as elite residences were built on these platforms. Nearly all the structures were decorated with relief carvings of serpents, condors, jaguars, or human forms. The largest building at Chavín de Huantar measured 250 feet (76 meters) on each side and rose to a height of 50 feet (15 meters). Its hollow interior contained narrow galleries and small rooms that may have housed the remains of royal ancestors.

Metallurgy in the Western Hemisphere was first developed in the Andean region around 2000 B.C.E. The later introduction of metallurgy in Mesoamerica, like the appearance of maize agriculture in the Andes, suggests sustained trade and cultural contacts between the two regions. Archaeological investigations of Chavín de Huantar have uncovered remarkable silver, gold, and gold alloy ornaments that represent a clear advance over earlier technologies. Improvements in both the manufacture and decoration of textiles are also associated with the rise of Chavín.

Excavations of graves reveal that superior-quality textiles as well as gold crowns, breastplates, and jewelry distinguished rulers from commoners. These rich objects, the quality and abundance of pottery, and the monumental architecture of the major centers all indicate the presence of highly skilled artisans. The enormous scale of the capital and the dispersal of Chavín's pottery styles, religious motifs, and architectural forms over a wide area suggest that Chavín imposed political and economic control over its neighbors by military force. Most scholars believe, however, that, as in the case of the Olmec civilization, Chavín's influence depended more on the development of an attractive religious belief system and related rituals.

There is no convincing evidence, like defaced buildings or broken images, that the eclipse of Chavín (unlike the Olmec centers) was associated with conquest or rebellion. However, recent investigations have suggested that increased warfare throughout the region disrupted Chavín's trade and undermined the authority of the governing elite. Regardless of what caused the collapse of this powerful culture, the technologies, material culture, statecraft, architecture, and urban planning associated with Chavín influenced the Andean region for centuries.

CLASSIC-ERA CULTURE AND SOCIETY IN MESOAMERICA, 200–900

Between about 200 and 900 C.E. the peoples of Mesoamerica entered a period of remarkable cultural creativity. Despite enduring differences in language and the absence of regional political integration, Mesoamericans were unified by similarities in material culture, religious beliefs and practices, and social structures first forged in the Olmec era. Building on this legacy, the peoples of the area that is now Central America and south and central Mexico developed new forms of political organization, made great strides in astronomy and mathematics, and improved the productivity of their agriculture. Archaeologists call this mix of achievements the classic period. During this period, a growing population traded a greater variety of products over longer distances, and social hierarchies became more complex. Great cities were constructed that served as centers of political life and as arenas of religious ritual and spiritual experience. These political and cultural innovations did not result from the introduction of new technologies. Instead, the achievements of the classic era depended on the ability of increasingly powerful elites to organize and command growing numbers of laborers and soldiers.

Teotihuacan   Located about 30 miles (48 kilometers) northeast of modern Mexico City, **Teotihuacan** (teh-o-tee-WAH-kahn) (100–750 C.E.) was one of Mesoamerica's most important classic-period civilizations. At the height of its power around 450 C.E., it was the largest city in the Americas. With between 125,000 and 150,000 inhabitants, it was larger than all but a small number of contemporary European and Asian cities.

The city center was dominated by religious architecture that was situated to align with nearby sacred mountains and with the movement of the stars. The people of Teotihuacan recognized and worshiped many gods and lesser spirits. Enormous pyramids and more than twenty smaller temples devoted to these gods were arranged along a central avenue. The largest pyramids were dedicated to the Sun and the Moon and to Quetzalcoatl (kate-zahl-CO-ah-tal), the feathered serpent, a culture-god believed to be the originator of agriculture and the arts. Murals suggest that another pair of powerful gods, the storm-god Tlaloc and a powerful female god associated with fertility, were also central figures in the city's religious life. Like the earlier Olmec, Teotihuacan's population practiced human sacrifice, illustrated by the discovery of more than a hundred sacrificial victims during the modern excavation of the temple of Quetzalcoatl. Scholars believe that residents viewed sacrifice as a sacred duty to the gods and as essential to the well-being of society.

The rapid growth in urban population initially resulted from a series of volcanic eruptions that disrupted agriculture. Later, as the city elite increased their power, they forced farm families from the smaller villages in the region to relocate to the urban core. The elite organized these new labor resources to bring marginal lands into production, drain swamps, construct irrigation canals, and build terraces into hillsides. They also expanded the use of **chinampas** (chee-NAM-pahs), sometimes called "floating gardens." These were narrow artificial islands constructed along lakeshores or in marshes by heaping lake muck and waste material on beds of reeds and anchoring them to the shore. Chinampas permitted year-round agriculture—because of subsurface irrigation and resistance to frost—and thus played a crucial role in sustaining the region's growing population.

The city's role as a religious center and commercial power provided both divine approval of and a material basis for the elite's increased wealth and status. Members of the elite controlled the government, tax collection, and commerce. Their rich and ornate clothing, their abundant diet, and their large, well-made residences signaled the wealth and power of aristocratic families. Temple and palace murals make clear the authority and great prestige of the priestly class as well. Teotihuacan's wealth and religious influence drew pilgrims from distant regions, and many became permanent residents.

Unlike other classic-period civilizations, the people of Teotihuacan did not concentrate power in the hands of a single ruler. There is no clear evidence that individual rulers or a ruling dynasty gained overarching political power. In fact, some scholars suggest that allied elite families or weak kings who were the puppets of these powerful families ruled Teotihuacan.

Historians debate the role of the military in the development of Teotihuacan. The absence of walls and other defensive structures before 500 C.E. suggests that Teotihuacan enjoyed relative peace during its early development. Archaeological evidence, however, reveals that the city created a powerful military to protect long-distance trade and to compel peasant agriculturalists to transfer their surplus production to the city. Unlike later postclassic civilizations, however, Teotihuacan was not an imperial state controlled by a military elite.

It is unclear what forces brought about the collapse of Teotihuacan about 750 C.E. By 500 C.E. the urban population had declined to about 40,000 and the city's residents had begun to build defensive walls. Pictorial evidence from murals indicates that the city's final decades were violent. Scholars have uncovered evidence that the elite had mismanaged resources and then divided into competing factions, leading to class conflict and the breakdown of public order. In the final collapse the most important temples in the city center were destroyed and religious images defaced. Elite palaces were also systematically burned and many of their residents killed. Regardless of the causes, the eclipse of Teotihuacan was felt throughout Mexico and into Central America.

The Maya   During Teotihuacan's ascendancy in the north, the **Maya** developed an impressive civilization in the region that today includes Guatemala, Honduras, Belize, and southern Mexico. Given the difficulties imposed by a tropical climate and fragile soils, the cultural and architectural achievements of the Maya were remarkable. Although they shared a single culture, the Maya never created a single, unified state. Instead, rival kingdoms led by hereditary rulers struggled with each other for regional dominance, much like the Mycenaean-era Greeks (see Chapter 5).

Today Maya farmers prepare their fields by cutting down small trees and brush and then burning the dead vegetation to fertilize the land. Such swidden agriculture (also called shifting agriculture or slash and burn agriculture) can produce high yields for a few years. However, it uses up the soil's nutrients, eventually forcing farmers to move to more fertile land. The high population levels of the Maya classic period (200–900 C.E.) required more intensive forms of agriculture. Maya living near the major urban centers achieved high agricultural yields by draining swamps and building elevated fields. They used irrigation in areas with long dry seasons, and they terraced hillsides in the cooler highlands. Maya agriculturists also managed nearby forests, favoring the growth of the trees and shrubs that were most useful to them, as well as promoting the conservation of deer and other animals hunted for food.

During the classic period, Maya city-states proliferated. The most powerful cities controlled groups of smaller dependent cities and a broad agricultural zone by

Daniel Loncarevic/Shutterstock.com

The Great Plaza at Tikal *The impressive architectural and artistic achievements of the classic-era Maya are still visible in the ruins of Tikal, in modern Guatemala. Maya centers provided a dramatic setting for the rituals that dominated public life. Construction of Tikal began before 150 B.C.E.; the city was abandoned about 900 C.E. A ball court and residences for the elite were part of the Great Plaza.*

building impressive temples and by creating rituals that linked the power of kings to the gods. Open plazas were surrounded by high pyramids and by elaborately decorated palaces often built on high ground or on constructed mounds. The effect was to awe the masses drawn to the centers for religious and political rituals.

The Maya loved decoration. Carved decorations painted in bright colors covered nearly all public buildings. Religious allegories, the genealogies of rulers, and important historical events were the most common motifs. The Maya also erected beautifully carved altars and stone monoliths near major temples. As was true throughout the hemisphere, this rich legacy of monumental architecture was constructed without the aid of wheels—no pulleys, wheelbarrows, or carts—or metal tools. Masses of men and women aided only by levers and stone tools cut and carried construction materials and lifted them into place.

The Maya divided the cosmos into three layers connected along a vertical axis that traced the course of the sun. The earthly arena of human existence held an intermediate position between the heavens, conceptualized as a sky-monster, and a dark underworld. The Maya believed that a sacred tree rose through the three layers; its roots were in the underworld, and its branches reached into the heavens. The temple precincts of Maya cities physically represented essential elements of this religious cosmology. The pyramids were sacred mountains reaching to the heavens. The doorways of the pyramids were portals to the underworld.

The Mesoamerican Ball Game *From Guatemala to Arizona, archaeologists have found evidence of an ancient ball game played with a solid rubber ball on slope-sided courts shaped like a capital T. Among the Maya the game was associated with a creation myth and thus had deep religious meaning. Evidence suggests that some players were sacrificed. In this scene from a ceramic jar, players wearing elaborate ritual clothing—which includes heavy, protective pads around the chest and waist—play with a ball much larger than the ball actually used in such games. Some representations show balls drawn to suggest a human head.*

Rulers and other members of the elite served both priestly and political functions. They decorated their bodies with paint and tattoos and wore elaborate costumes of textiles, animal skins, and feathers to project both secular power and divine sanction. These lords communicated directly with the supernatural residents of the other worlds and with deified royal ancestors through bloodletting rituals and hallucinogenic trances.

The Maya infused warfare with religious meaning and celebrated it in elaborate rituals. Battle scenes and the depiction of the torture and sacrifice of captives were frequent decorative themes. Typically, Maya military forces fought to secure captives rather than territory. The king, his kinsmen, and other ranking nobles actively participated in war. Elite captives were nearly always sacrificed; captured commoners were more likely to be forced to labor for their captors.

Few women directly ruled Maya kingdoms, but Maya women of the ruling lineages did play important political and religious roles. The consorts of male rulers participated in bloodletting rituals and in other important public ceremonies, and their noble blood helped legitimate the power of their husbands. Although Maya society was patrilineal (tracing descent in the male line), there is clear evidence that some male rulers traced their lineages bilaterally (in both the male and female lines). Others, like Lady Wac-Chanil-Ahau's son discussed earlier, emphasized the female line if it held higher status. Little is known about the lives of poorer women, but scholars believe that women played a central role in the religious rituals of the home and some were healers and shamans. Women were essential to the household economy, maintaining essential garden plots and weaving, and in the management of family life.

Building on earlier Olmec achievements, the Maya made important contributions to the development of the Mesoamerican calendar and to mathematics and writing. Time was a central concern, and they developed an accurate calendar system that identified each day by three separate dating systems. The Maya calendar tracked a ritual cycle (260 days divided into thirteen months of 20 days). A second calendar tracked the solar year (365 days divided into eighteen months of 20 days, plus 5 unfavorable days at the end of the year). The Maya believed that the very survival of humanity was threatened every fifty-two years when the two calendars coincided. Alone among Mesoamerican peoples, the Maya also maintained a continuous "long count" calendar, which began with creation in 3114 B.C.E.

Maya mathematics and writing provided the foundations for both the calendars and the astronomical observations on which they were based. Their system of mathematics incorporated the concept of the zero and place value but had limited notational signs. Maya writing was a form of hieroglyphic inscription that signified whole words or concepts as well as phonetic cues or syllables. Scribes recorded aspects of public life, religious belief, and the biographies of rulers and their ancestors in books, on pottery, and on the stone columns and monumental buildings of the urban centers. In this sense every Maya city was a sacred text.

Between 800 and 900 C.E. the Maya abandoned many of their major urban centers. Many cities were destroyed by violence, although a small number of classic-period centers survived for centuries. Decades of urban decline, social conflict, and increased levels of warfare preceded this collapse in many areas. The earlier collapse of Teotihuacan around 750 had disrupted long-distance trade in ritual goods and may have begun to undermine the legitimacy of Maya rulers tied to that distant center. Certainly, rising regional population, climatic change, and environmental degradation undermined the fragile agricultural system that sustained Maya cities long before the collapse. But it was the growing scale and destructiveness of warfare that finally undermined the political legitimacy of ruling lineages and disrupted the web of economic relationships that tied rural agriculturalists to Maya cities.

THE POSTCLASSIC PERIOD IN MESOAMERICA TO 1400

The division between the classic and postclassic periods is somewhat arbitrary. Not only is there no single explanation for the collapse of Teotihuacan and the abandonment of many Maya centers, but these events occurred over more than a century and a half. While many smaller polities survived into the new period, the Mesoamerican world went through centuries of adjustment that ultimately led to the appearance of powerful new urban centers of culture and politics. Two of these, Tula and Cholula, had been deeply influenced by Teotihuacan before its eclipse.

Mesoamerican population expanded in the postclassic period. At the same time long-distance trade intensified, linking the producers of high-value goods like obsidian, cloth, and metal products to fast-growing cities. Resulting pressures on resources and competition for commercial advantage led to political instability and to increased warfare. The governing elites of major postclassic states, especially the Toltecs, responded to these harsh realities by increasing the size of their armies and by developing political institutions that facilitated their control of large and culturally diverse territories acquired through conquest.

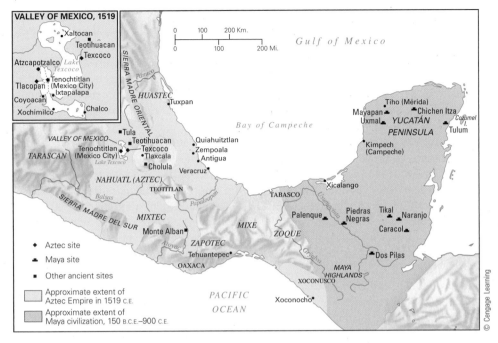

MAP 8.1   Major Mesoamerican Civilizations, 1000 B.C.E.–1519 C.E.

The Aztec Empire in 1518 was based on military conquest. The Aztec capital of Tenochtitlan was located near the classic era's largest city, Teotihuacan, and Tula, capital city of the postclassic Toltecs.

The Toltecs   While modern archaeology has revealed the civilizations of the Maya and Teotihuacan in previously unimaginable detail, the history of the **Toltecs** (TOLL-teks) remains in dispute. The Aztecs, the dominant late postclassic civilization (see Chapter 15), regarded the Toltecs as powerful and influential predecessors, much as the Romans regarded the Greeks. They erroneously believed that the Toltecs were the source of nearly all important cultural achievements. As one Aztec source later recalled:

> In truth [the Toltecs] invented all the precious and marvelous things…. All that now exists was their discovery…. And these Toltecs were very wise; they were thinkers, for they originated the year count, the day count. All their discoveries formed the book for interpreting dreams…. And so wise were they [that] they understood the stars which were in the heavens.[2]

In fact, all these contributions to Mesoamerican culture were in place long before Toltec power spread across central Mexico. Some scholars speculate that the Toltecs were originally a satellite population that Teotihuacan had placed on the northern frontier to protect against the incursions of nomads. Regardless of their origins, it is clear that Toltec culture was deeply influenced by Teotihuacan,

---

[2]From the Florentine Codex, quoted in Inga Clendinnen, *Aztecs* (New York: Cambridge University Press, 1991), 213.

including its preservation of the religious architecture and rituals associated with the feathered serpent god, Quetzalcoatl. It also utilized agricultural technologies, like irrigation and terraced hillsides, so important to Teotihuacan.

In this more violent era, the Toltecs created a state that depended on military power. This dependence was illustrated by the use of violent images, like impaled skulls, in the decoration of public buildings. The Toltecs' influence ultimately extended to distant Central America from their political capital at Tula (TOO-la), founded in 968 C.E. north of modern Mexico City. At its peak Tula covered 5.4 square miles (14 square kilometers) and had a population of approximately 60,000. The massive architecture of the city center featured impressive statues of warriors and serpents, colonnaded patios, raised stone platforms, and numerous temples.

Like the earlier Teotihuacan, Tula and its subject dependencies had a multiethnic character, hosting distinct cultural and language communities. The apex of Toltec power also coincided with the development of an alliance with another multiethnic state with historic ties to Teotihuacan located to the south, Culhuacán (kool whah KHAN). The exact nature of this alliance is unclear, but the presence of Toltec groups in Culhuacán is undeniable. Together the two cities benefited from a military alliance and from networks of tribute and trade established throughout the central Mexican region.

To understand the end of Toltec power, historians rely primarily on written sources from the era of the Spanish conquest, including accounts told to Catholic priests by native informants. According to most of these sources, two chieftains or kings shared power at Tula, and this division of responsibility eventually weakened Toltec power. Sometime around 1150 C.E. a struggle between elite groups identified with rival religious cults led to violent clashes within Toltec society and encouraged attacks by rival states. Legends that survived among the Aztecs claimed that Topiltzin (tow-PEELT-zeen)—one of the two rulers and a priest of the cult of Quetzalcoatl—and his followers were forced into exile in the east, "the land of the rising sun." One of the ancient texts relates these events in the following manner:

> Thereupon he [Topiltzin] looked toward Tula, and then wept.... And when he had done these things ... he went to reach the seacoast. Then he fashioned a raft of serpents. When he had arranged the raft, he placed himself as if it were his boat. Then he set off across the sea.[3]

Some scholars used this Aztec tale to suggest a Toltec conquest of the Maya region, an argument fortified by similarities in decorative motifs, architecture, and urban planning at Tula and at the Maya postclassic center of Chichen Itza (CHEECH-ehn EET-zah) in the Yucatán. Scholars now dispute this story, suggesting instead that these regions were linked by long-term cultural exchanges, not conquest.

Nevertheless, it is clear that Tula and the Toltec state entered a period of steep decline after 1150 C.E. that included internal power struggles and an external military threat from the north. The historical Topiltzin was closely linked to the fate of Tula, but his story was more complex than that indicated by Aztec legend. His father Mixcoatl (mish-coh-AHT-til) was a Toltec military leader active in Culhuacán and

---

[3] Quoted in Nigel Davies, *The Toltec Heritage: From the Fall of Tula to the Rise of Tenochtitlán* (Norman: University of Oklahoma Press, 1980), 3.

in Cholula, where another satellite Toltec population resided. Topiltzin was probably born in Culhuacán, not Tula. He attempted to save the beleaguered Toltec capital of Tula, but he ultimately failed and retired from power around 1175. While disaster then befell the once-dominant city of Tula, an independent Toltec legacy survived until at least 1300 C.E. in Culhuacán and in nearby Cholula.

Cholula   Located near the modern Mexican city of Puebla, Cholula developed at about the same time as Teotihuacan. It was situated to serve as a trade center and religious pilgrimage destination linking the Valley of Mexico with Maya regions to the southeast and with the Mixtec peoples to the southwest. Among the largest cities of postclassic Mesoamerica, Cholula had a large culturally and linguistically diverse population, including a large Toltec community. Cholula's original ties to the Toltecs is unclear, but sometime after 1000 C.E. the resident Toltec population appealed to Culhuacán for military assistance. Just as Topiltzin would later try to save Tula, his father, Mixcoatl, went to the aid Cholula. While the fate of this vulnerable Toltec community is not known, Cholula survived as an important regional power until the Spanish conquest, thus connecting the legacies of both Teotihuacan and the Toltecs to the later rise of the powerful Aztec Empire (see Chapter 15).

NORTHERN PEOPLES

By the end of the classic period in Mesoamerica, around 900 C.E., important cultural centers had appeared in the southwestern desert region and along the Ohio and Mississippi River Valleys of what is now the United States. The peoples of the Southwest benefited from the early introduction of maize and other Mesoamerican cultigens (before 1000 B.C.E.). The resulting improvement to agricultural productivity led before 500 C.E. to rising population, the beginnings of urbanization, and increased social stratification. Maize arrived among the Amerindian peoples of the Ohio Valley sometime after 200 C.E., but only became the region's chief staple after 800. Once widely adopted this useful crop accelerated the development of large population centers and new political institutions.

The two regions evolved different political traditions. The Anasazi (ah-nah-SAH-zee) and their neighbors in the Southwest maintained a relatively egalitarian social structure and retained collective forms of political organization based on kinship and age. The mound builders of the eastern river valleys evolved more hierarchical political institutions, which subordinated groups of small towns and villages to a political center ruled by a hereditary chief who wielded both secular and religious authority.

Southwestern   Around 300 B.C.E. in what is today Arizona, contacts with
Desert Cultures   Mesoamerica led to the introduction of agriculture based on
                         irrigation. Because irrigation allowed the planting of two maize crops per year, the population grew and settled village life soon appeared. Of all the southwestern cultures, the Hohokam of the Salt and Gila River Valleys show the strongest Mesoamerican influence. Hohokam sites have platform mounds and ball courts similar to those of Mesoamerica. Hohokam pottery, clay figurines, cast copper bells, and turquoise mosaics also reflect this influence. By 1000 C.E. the Hohokam had constructed an elaborate irrigation system. Hohokam agricultural

and ceramic technology then spread over to neighboring peoples, but it was the Anasazi to the north who left the most vivid legacy of these desert cultures.

Archaeologists use **Anasazi**, a Navajo word meaning "ancient ones," to identify a number of dispersed, though similar, desert cultures located in what is now the Four Corners region of Arizona, New Mexico, Colorado, and Utah. In the centuries before 700 C.E. the Anasazi developed an economy based on maize, beans, and squash. As irrigation and other technologies increased their productivity, they formed larger villages and evolved a much more complex cultural life centered on underground buildings called kivas. They produced pottery decorated with geometric patterns, learned to weave cotton cloth, and, after 900 C.E., began to construct large multistory residential and ritual centers.

One of the largest Anasazi communities was located in Chaco Canyon in what is now northwestern New Mexico. There were twelve towns in the canyon and surrounding mesas, suggesting a regional population of 15,000. Pueblo Bonito (founded in 919 C.E.) had more than 650 rooms arranged in a four-story block of residences and storage rooms; it also had thirty-eight kivas, including a great kiva more than 65 feet (19 meters) in diameter. Hunting, trade, and the need to maintain irrigation works often drew men away from the village. Women shared in agricultural tasks, were specialists in many crafts, and were responsible for food preparation and childcare. At Chaco Canyon the high-quality construction, the size and number of kivas, and the system of roads linking the canyon to outlying towns all suggest that Pueblo Bonito and its nearest neighbors exerted political and cultural dominance over a large region.

As had been the case with the Olmec center of San Lorenzo and Chavín de Huantar in Peru nearly a thousand years earlier, Pueblo Bonito's ascendancy depended on its identity as a sacred site and on the elaboration of an intense cycle of religious rituals that attracted pilgrims from distant locations.

Early archaeologists suggested that the Chaco Canyon culture originated as a colonial appendage of Mesoamerica, but the archaeological record provides little evidence for this theory. Merchants from Chaco did provide Toltec-period peoples of northern Mexico with turquoise in exchange for shell jewelry, copper bells, macaws, and trumpets, but these exchanges occurred late in Chaco's development. More importantly, the signature elements of Mesoamerican influence, such as pyramid-shaped mounds and ball courts, are missing at Chaco.

The abandonment of the major sites in Chaco Canyon in the twelfth century most likely resulted from a long drought that undermined the culture's fragile agricultural economy. Nevertheless, the Anasazi continued in the Four Corners region for more than a century after the abandonment of Chaco Canyon, with major centers at Mesa Verde in present-day Colorado and at Canyon de Chelly and Kiet Siel in Arizona. The construction of these settlements in large natural caves high above valley floors suggests increased levels of warfare, probably provoked by population pressure on the region's limited arable land.

Mound Builders: The Hopewell and Mississippian Cultures
From around 100 C.E. the Hopewell culture spread through the Ohio River Valley. Hopewell people constructed large villages and monumental earthworks. Once established, their influence spread west to Illinois, Michigan, and Wisconsin, east to New York and Ontario, and south to Alabama, Louisiana, Mississippi, and even Florida. For the necessities of daily life the Hopewell

Mesa Verde Cliff Dwelling *Located in southern Colorado, the Anasazi cliff dwellings of the Mesa Verde region hosted a population of about 7,000 in 1250 C.E. The construction of housing complexes and religious buildings in the area's large caves was prompted by increased warfare in the region.*

depended on hunting and gathering and on a limited agriculture. They are an early example of a North American **chiefdom**—populations as large as 10,000 and rule by a hereditary chief with both religious and secular responsibilities. Chiefs organized periodic rituals of feasting and gift giving to link diverse kinship groups and guarantee access to specialized crops and craft goods. They also managed long-distance trade for luxury goods and additional food supplies.

The largest Hopewell towns in the Ohio River Valley had several thousand inhabitants and served as ceremonial and political centers. Large mounds built to house burials and serve as platforms for religious rituals dominated major Hopewell centers. Some mounds were oriented to reflect sunrise and moonrise patterns. The abandonment of major sites around 400 C.E. marked the decline of Hopewell culture.

Hopewell influenced the development of the Mississippian culture (800–1500 C.E.). As in the case of the Anasazi, some experts have suggested that contacts with Mesoamerica influenced early Mississippian culture, but there is no convincing evidence to support this theory. It is true that maize, beans, and squash, all first domesticated in Mesoamerica, were crucial to the urbanized Mississippian culture. But these plants and related technologies were most likely acquired via intervening cultures.

The development of urbanized Mississippian chiefdoms resulted instead from the accumulated effects of small increases in agricultural productivity and the expansion of trade networks. An improved economy led to population growth, the building of cities, and social stratification. The largest towns shared a common urban plan based on a central plaza surrounded by large platform mounds.

The Mississippian culture reached its highest stage of evolution at the great urban center of Cahokia, located near the modern city of East St. Louis, Illinois. Cahokia, like Chavín de Huantar, the Olmec cities, and contemporary Pueblo Bonito served as a religious center and pilgrimage site. Subordinated rural populations were organized by the Cahokia elite through obligations of tribute, shared labor, and ritual. At the center of this site was the largest mound constructed in North America, a terraced structure 100 feet (30 meters) high and 1,037 by 790 feet (316 by 241 meters) at the base. Chunkey, a game infused with religious meaning and accompanied by gambling, helped establish Cahokia's cultural influence over a large region, as had the ballgame developed by the Olmec. Played with a stone disk and sticks, the game drew contestants and spectators from dependent towns and was used by the elite to organize tribute payments and labor for the construction of massive public works.

In this hierarchical society, commoners lived on the periphery of the ceremonial center where elite housing and temples were located. At its height in about 1200 C.E., Cahokia had a population of approximately 20,000—about the same as some of the postclassic Maya cities.

Cahokia controlled surrounding agricultural lands and a large number of secondary towns. Its political and economic influence depended on its location near the confluence of the Missouri, Mississippi, and Illinois Rivers, a location that facilitated commercial exchanges as far away as the coasts of the Atlantic and the Gulf of Mexico. Traders brought seashells, copper, mica, and flint to the city, where they were used in manufacture of ritual goods and tools. Burial evidence suggests that the rulers of Cahokia were rich and powerful. In one burial more than fifty young female and male retainers were sacrificed to accompany a ruler after death.

The construction of defensive walls around the ceremonial center and elite residences after 1250 C.E. provides some evidence that the decline and eventual abandonment of Cahokia were tied to the effects of military defeat or civil war, as had been true in Teotihuacan. There is also evidence that climate change and population pressures, exacerbated by environmental degradation caused by deforestation and more intensive farming practices, undermined Cahokia's viability. By 1300 Cahokia had lost control of its dependencies and its population was in precipitous decline. Despite its collapse, smaller Mississippian centers that preserved elements of Cahokian culture continued to flourish in the Southeast of the present-day United States until the arrival of Europeans.

ANDEAN CIVILIZATIONS, 200–1400

The Andean region of South America was an unlikely environment for the development of rich and powerful civilizations. Much of the region's mountainous zone is at altitudes that seem too high for agriculture and human habitation. Along the Pacific coast an arid climate posed a difficult challenge to the development of agriculture. To the east of the Andes Mountains, the hot and humid tropical

MAP 8.2 Andean Civilizations, 200 B.C.E.–1532 C.E.

In response to environmental challenges posed by an arid coastal plain and high interior mountain ranges, Andean peoples made complex social and technological adaptations. Irrigation systems, the domestication of the llama, metallurgy, and shared labor obligations helped provide a firm economic foundation for powerful, centralized states. In 1532 the Inca Empire's vast territory stretched from modern Chile in the south to Colombia in the north.

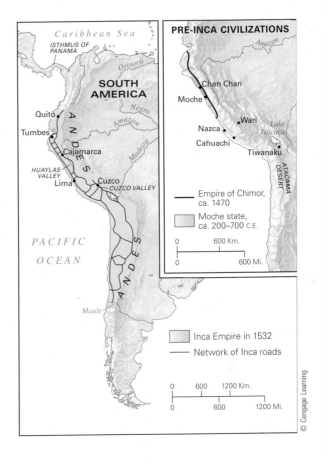

environment of the Amazon headwaters also offered formidable obstacles to the organization of complex societies. Yet the Amerindian peoples of the Andean area produced some of the most socially complex and politically advanced societies of the Western Hemisphere. The very harshness of the environment compelled the development of productive and reliable agricultural technologies and attached them to a complex fabric of administrative structures and social relationships that became the central features of Andean civilization.

Cultural Response to Environmental Challenge

From the time of Chavín all of the great Andean civilizations succeeded in connecting the distinctive resources of the coastal region, with its abundant fisheries and irrigated maize fields, to the mountainous interior with its herds of llamas and rich mix of grains and tubers. Both regions faced significant environmental challenges. Droughts and shifting sands that clogged irrigation works periodically overwhelmed the coastal region's fields, and the mountainous interior presented enormous environmental challenges, since it averaged between 250 and 300 frosts per year.

The development of compensating technologies required an accurate calendar to time planting and harvests and the domestication of frost-resistant varieties of potatoes and grains. Native peoples learned to practice dispersed farming at different altitudes to reduce risks from frosts, and they terraced hillsides to create micro environments within a single area. They also discovered how to use the cold, dry climate to produce freeze-dried vegetable and meat products that prevented famine when crops failed. The domestication of the llama and alpaca also proved crucial, providing meat, wool, and long-distance transportation that linked coastal and mountain economies.

It was the clan, or **ayllu** (aye-YOU), that provided the foundation for Andean achievement. Members of an ayllu held land communally. Ayllu members thought of each other as brothers and sisters and were obligated to aid each other in tasks that required more labor than a single household could provide. These reciprocal obligations provided the model for the organization of labor and the distribution of goods at every level of Andean society. Just as individuals and families were expected to provide labor to kinsmen, ayllus were collectively expected to provide labor and goods to their rulers.

With the development of territorial states ruled by hereditary aristocracies and kings after 1000 B.C.E., these obligations were organized on a larger scale. The **mita** (MEET-ah) was a rotational labor draft that organized members of ayllus to work the fields and care for the llama and alpaca herds owned by religious establishments, the royal court, and the aristocracy. Mita laborers built and maintained roads, bridges, temples, palaces, and large irrigation and drainage projects. They also produced textiles and goods essential to ritual life, such as beer made from maize and coca (dried leaves chewed as a stimulant and now also the source of cocaine).

The ayllu was intimately tied to a uniquely Andean system of production and exchange. Because the region's mountain ranges created a multitude of small ecological areas with specialized resources, each community sought to control a variety of environments so as to guarantee access to essential goods. Coastal regions produced maize, fish, and cotton. Mountain valleys contributed quinoa (the local grain) as well as potatoes and other tubers. Higher elevations contributed the wool and meat of llamas and alpacas, and the Amazonian region provided coca and fruits. Ayllus sent out colonists to exploit the resources of these distinct ecological niches, retaining the loyalty of the colonists by arranging marriages and coming together for rituals. Historians commonly refer to this system of controlled exchange across ecological boundaries as vertical integration, or verticality.

The Early Intermediate Period Moche   Scholars of the Andes call the period 200 to 600 C.E. the Early Intermediate period. The **Moche** (MO-che) were among the most influential and powerful Andean civilizations of this period, dominating the north coastal region of Peru. While they did not establish a formal empire or create unified political structures, they did exercise authority over a broad geographic region. The most powerful of the Moche urban centers, such as Cerro Blanco located near the modern Peruvian city of Trujillo, first established hegemony over neighboring towns and villages and then extended political and economic control over more distant neighbors militarily. Key to this expansion was the elaboration of a potent ideology that tied hereditary rulers to the gods through elaborate religious rituals in the major Moche cities.

Archaeological evidence indicates that the Moche cultivated maize, quinoa, beans, manioc, and sweet potatoes with the aid of massive irrigation works, a complex network of canals and aqueducts that connected fields with water sources as far away as 75 miles (121 kilometers). Moche rulers forced commoners and subject peoples to build and maintain these hydraulic works. The Moche also relied on large herds of alpacas and llamas to transport goods across the region's difficult terrain. Their wool, along with cotton provided by farmers, provided the raw material for the thriving Moche textile production.

Evidence from surviving murals and decorated ceramics suggests that Moche society was highly stratified and theocratic. Wealth and power were concentrated, along with political control, in the hands of priests and military leaders. The military conquest of neighboring regions reinforced this hierarchy. Because the elite constructed their residences atop large platforms at Moche ceremonial centers, the powerful literally looked down on the commoners whose labor supported them. Evidence, such as ceramic portrait vessels, suggests that the power of the elite was highly individualized and associated with divine sanction. Moche rulers and other members of the elite wore tall headdresses and rich garments as well as elaborate gold jewelry that reinforced their connections to the gods. Moche burial practices reflected these deep social distinctions. A recent excavation in the Lambeyeque Valley discovered the tomb of a warrior-priest buried with a rich treasure of gold, silver, and copper jewelry, textiles, feather ornaments, and shells (see Diversity and Dominance: Burials as Historical Texts). A group of retainers and servants were executed and then buried with this powerful man in order to serve him in the afterlife.

Most commoners, on the other hand, devoted their time to subsistence farming and to the payment of labor dues owed to their ayllu and to the elite. Both men and women were involved in agriculture, care of llama herds, and the household economy. They lived with their families in one-room buildings clustered in the outlying areas of cities and in surrounding agricultural zones.

The high quality of Moche textiles, ceramics, and metallurgy indicates the presence of numerous skilled artisans. Women had a special role in the production of textiles, and even elite women devoted time to weaving. Moche culture developed a brilliant representational art. Craftsmen produced highly individualized portrait vases and decorated other ceramics with representations of myths and rituals. They were also accomplished metal-smiths, producing beautiful gold and silver religious objects and jewelry for elite adornment. Metallurgy served more practical ends as well: artisans produced a range of tools made of heavy copper and copper alloy for agricultural and military purposes.

The archaeological record makes clear that the rapid decline of major Moche centers coincided with a succession of natural disasters in the sixth century as well as with long-term climate changes. A thirty-year drought expanded the area of coastal sand dunes during the sixth century, and powerful winds pushed sand onto fragile agricultural lands, overwhelming the irrigation system. As the land dried, periodic heavy rains caused erosion that damaged fields and weakened the economy that had sustained ceremonial and residential centers. Despite massive efforts to keep the irrigation canals open and despite the construction of new urban centers in less vulnerable valleys to the north, Moche civilization never fully recovered. In the eighth century, the rise of a new military power, the Wari (see below), also contributed to the disappearance of the Moche by putting pressure on trade routes that linked the coastal region with the highlands.

Tiwanaku and Wari

Between 500 and 1000 C.E., what Andean scholars call the Middle Horizon period, two powerful civilizations dominated the highlands. The ruins of **Tiwanaku** (tee-wah-NA-coo) stand

DIVERSITY + DOMINANCE

Burials as Historical Texts

Efforts to reveal the history of the Americas before the arrival of Europeans depend on the work of archaeologists. The burials of rulers and other members of elites can be viewed as historical texts that describe how textiles, precious metals, beautifully decorated ceramics, and other commodities were used to reinforce the political and cultural power of ruling lineages. In public, members of the elite were always surrounded by the most desirable goods and rarest products as well as by elaborate rituals and ceremonies. The effect was to create an aura of godlike power. The material elements of political and cultural power were also integrated into the experience of death and burial as members of the elite were sent into the afterlife.

The first photograph is of an excavated Moche tomb in Sipán, Peru. The Moche (200–ca. 700 C.E.) were one of the most important of the pre-Inka civilizations of the Andean region, masters of metallurgy, ceramics, and textiles. The excavations at Sipán revealed a "warrior-priest" buried with an amazing array of gold ornaments, jewels, textiles, and ceramics. Also buried with him were five human sacrifices, two

women, perhaps wives or concubines, two male servants, and a warrior. Three of these victims—the warrior, one woman, and a male servant—are each missing a foot, perhaps cut off to guarantee their continued faithfulness to the deceased ruler in the afterlife.

The second photograph shows the excavation of a classic-era (200–ca. 800 C.E.) Maya burial at Río Azul in Guatemala. After death this elite male was laid out on a carved wooden platform and cotton mattress and his body was painted with decorations. Mourners covered his body in rich textiles and surrounded him with valuable goods. These included a necklace of individual stones carved in the shape of heads, perhaps a symbol of his prowess in battle, and high-quality ceramics, some filled with foods consumed by the elite like cacao. The careful preparation of the burial chamber had required the work of numerous artisans and laborers, as was the case in the burial of the Moche warrior-priest. In death, as in life, these early American civilizations acknowledged the high status, political power, and religious authority of their elites.

at nearly 13,000 feet (3,962 meters) near Lake Titicaca in modern Bolivia. Tiwanaku's expansion depended on the adoption of technologies that increased agricultural productivity. Modern excavations provide the outline of vast drainage projects that reclaimed nearly 200,000 acres (80,000 hectares) of rich lakeside marshes for agriculture. This system of raised fields and ditches permitted intensive cultivation similar to that achieved by the use of chinampas in Mesoamerica. Fish from the nearby lake and llamas added protein to a diet largely dependent on potatoes and grains. Llamas were also crucial for the maintenance of long-distance trade relationships that brought in corn, coca, tropical fruits, and medicinal plants. The resulting abundance permitted a dense cycle of feasting and religious observance that fueled the rise of a powerful elite.

Tiwanaku was distinguished by the scale of its urban construction and by the high quality of its stone masonry. Thousands of laborers were mobilized to cut and move the large stones used to construct large terraced pyramids, sunken plazas,

Burials Reveal Ancient Civilizations *(Left) Buried around 300 C.E., this Moche warrior-priest was buried amid rich tribute at Sipán in Peru. Also buried were the bodies of retainers or kinsmen probably sacrificed to accompany this powerful man. The body lies with the head on the right and the feet on the left. (Right) Similarly, the burial of a member of the Maya elite at Río Azul in northern Guatemala indicates the care taken to surround the powerful with fine ceramics, jewelry, and other valuable goods.*

Questions for Analysis

1. If these burials are texts, what are stories?

2. Are there any visible differences in the two burials?

3. What questions might historians ask of these burials that cannot be answered?

4. Can modern burials be read as texts in similar ways to these ancient burials?

walled enclosures, and a reservoir. Despite a limited metallurgy that produced only tools of copper alloy, Tiwanaku's artisans built large structures of finely cut stone that required little mortar to fit the blocks. They also produced gigantic human statuary. The largest example, a stern figure with a military bearing, was cut from a single block of stone that measures 24 feet (7 meters) high. These sacred constructions were oriented to reflect celestial cycles and distant Andean peaks infused with religious significance. Collectively, they provided an awe-inspiring setting for the religious rituals that legitimized the city's control of distant territories and peoples and for the elite's domination of society.

Archaeological evidence suggests that Tiwanaku at its height around 800 C.E. had a full-time population of around 60,000, including communities attracted from distant regions by the city's religious rituals and trade. It is clear that Tiwanaku was a highly stratified society ruled by a hereditary elite. This elite initially organized and controlled the ayllus of the surrounding region, but, as their military power grew, eventually utilized drafted labor from conquered and incorporated populations as well. As Tiwanaku's power and wealth grew, thousands of skilled craftsmen constantly expanded and embellished the ceremonial architecture and produced the metal goods, textiles, and pottery consumed by the elite. Military conquests and the establishment of distant colonial populations provided dependable supplies of more exotic products from ecologically distinct zones, such as colorful shells, gold and copper, and fine textiles.

Sometime after 1000 C.E. urban Tiwanaku was abandoned. While the exact cause is uncertain, we know the eclipse of this great civilization took a long time. There is evidence that years of severe drought led to precipitous population loss and to the breakdown of the long-distance trade in elite goods. This period was associated with the destruction of monumental effigies and other religious symbols, suggesting that worsening material conditions undermined the legitimacy of the elite.

The contemporary site of **Wari** (WAH-ree) was located about 450 miles (751 kilometers) to the northwest of Tiwanaku, near the modern Peruvian city of Ayacucho. Wari clearly shared elements of the culture and technology of Tiwanaku, but the exact nature of the relationship between these civilizations remains unclear. Some scholars argue that Wari began as a dependency of Tiwanaku, while others suggest that they were joint capitals of a single empire. Most now argue that Wari was a distinct culture that evolved a politically centralized state and powerful military. Recent research indicates an aggressive imperial expansion lubricated by captive-taking and human sacrifice.

Urban Wari was larger than Tiwanaku, measuring nearly 4 square miles (10 square kilometers). A massive wall surrounded the city center, which was dominated by a large temple and multifamily housing for elites and artisans. Housing for commoners was located in a sprawling suburban zone. The small scale of its monumental architecture relative to Tiwanaku and the near absence of cut stone masonry in public and private buildings suggest either the weakness of the elite or the absence of specialized construction crafts compared with other Andean centers. A distinctive Wari ceramic style allows experts to trace Wari's influence to the coastal area and to the northern highlands. This expansion occurred at a time of climate change and increasing warfare throughout the Andes that led ultimately to the eclipse of both Tiwanaku and Wari after 1000 C.E. In the centuries that followed the collapse of these two powerful centers, the Andean highlands experienced increased levels of violence, as evidenced by the construction of numerous fortifications by the smaller polities and villages that now contended for power.

Chimú

On the north coast of Peru in the region previously dominated by the Moche, a powerful new imperial state appeared after 900 C.E., the period called Late Intermediate (1000–1476 C.E.) in Andean history. The **Chimú** Empire, or Chimor, with its capital of Chan Chan, eventually controlled more than 600 miles (966 kilometers) of the Pacific coast from Ecuador in the north to central Peru. Building upon the legacy of the Moche who earlier controlled this area, the Chimú depended on the abundant production of an irrigated agricultural hinterland and on the labor provided by conquered dependencies.

While the grandeur of Wari and Tiwanaku can still be seen in surviving monumental stone architecture, the once-great city of Chan Chan, built from adobe, has been much diminished by a thousand years of erosion. Nevertheless, the imperial character of the city remains clear. Nine large residential compounds provide the urban nucleus. Each one is believed to have housed a ruler and his family during his life and become his mausoleum upon his death. With each succession the new ruler would be forced to organize the labor and materials necessary to construct a new palace compound. In addition to the family residence of the ruler, each compound contained a U-shaped room used for official functions and numerous smaller rooms used to store food and other tribute items sent from dependent jurisdictions. This system depended ultimately on a potent military and a series of conquests that only ended in the fifteenth century with the appearance of a more powerful rival, the Inka (see Chapter 15).

While Chan Chan was the center of imperial government and hosted a large aristocratic population in addition to the reigning family, there was little urban planning. Elite residential compounds were separated by high walls from the humble habitations of commoners dispersed across the city. Chan Chan served primarily as the residential precinct of the elite and those who provided the elite with luxury goods like gold jewelry and high-quality textiles and pottery, rather than as a religious or even commercial center. These patterns were repeated on a modest scale in the regional political capitals that organized the labor necessary to maintain irrigation works and collect the tribute that sustained Chan Chan.

Both the urban architecture and the organization of labor expressed the profound social and economic distance that separated royalty and populace. With a population of only 25,000 to 30,000 at its peak, we know the massive Chimú capital city was built and maintained by labor tributes imposed on dependent rural populations. As the city grew, the construction of large structures like palaces and religious monuments was subdivided into multiple small tasks assigned to parties of tribute workers from distinct regions who made their own adobe bricks.

The Chimú Empire (Chimor) survived for over four centuries in the difficult arid environment of the Peruvian coast, expanding the scale of Moche irrigation works by developing a larger, more efficient bureaucracy that could organize thousands of conscripted laborers for ever more ambitious irrigation tasks. As this empire expanded, the improved agricultural productivity that resulted from these projects compensated dependent peoples for their labor and for their loss of autonomy. Unlike earlier Andean civilizations, the Chimú did not collapse because of environmental catastrophe or social unrest. Instead, in the 1470s, they fell victim to the rapid imperial expansion of the Inka, who then freely borrowed Chimú's technologies and political institutions.

CONCLUSION

The Toltec Empire and Cholula of Mesoamerica and Chimor of the Andean region were all powerful states that depended upon religious practices, technologies, political institutions, and social forms that had developed over nearly two thousand years. In some cases crucial elements of political life, culture, and economy dated from the era of the Olmec and Chavín. Despite these continuities, rising populations and competition for resources led inevitably to new cycles of violence in both regions. The survival of these states ultimately depended on the power of their armies as much as on the productivity of their economies or the wisdom of their rulers.

Mesoamerica and the Andean region were environmentally challenging regions where a succession of native states found ways to produce and distribute products from distinct ecological regions as well as ways to organize ethnically diverse populations into coherent polities. From the beginning rulers in both regions legitimized their authority religiously, serving as priestly intermediaries with the gods or claiming direct descent from them. The major cities of every important civilization from the time of the Olmec and Chavín to 1400 C.E. operated as religious as well as political centers. Their urban centers were dominated by monumental religious architecture decorated with symbols connecting elites to the gods through creation myths. Dense cycles of religious ritual conducted by priests and rulers in elaborate costumes legitimized the power of cities over the countryside and habituated rural populations to the transfer of goods and labor that made the achievements of these civilizations possible.

With the important exception of metallurgy developed in the Andes and transferred to Mesoamerica after 500 C.E., technology developed slowly in the Americas after the era of the Olmec and Chavín. The dominant powers of each successive era—Teotihuacan and the Moche and, ultimately, the Toltecs and Cholula and Chimú—all depended on the mobilization of ever-larger workforces to meet environmental challenges and support growing urbanization, rather than on new technologies. The construction of irrigation canals, raised fields, terraced hillsides, and, in the case of Mesoamerica, chinampas multiplied agricultural productivity, subsidized craft specialization, and, through trade, overcame environmental constraints, but all these technologies were in place for nearly a thousand years before the Toltec, Cholula, and Chimú periods. The growing size of cities, the mounting power of government, and the expanding scale of empire all depended on the refinement of ancient technologies and the mobilization of ever-larger workforces.

There were important differences between Mesoamerica and the Andean region. Mesoamerican cultures developed elementary markets to distribute specialized regional production, although the forced payment of goods as tribute remained important to sustain cities like Toltec Tula. In the postclassic period standardized quantities of cacao beans, metal goods, and cloth were being used as money in these markets. In the Andes reciprocal labor obligations and managed exchange relationships were used to allocate goods. There were important regional political differences as well. In Mesoamerica the Toltecs imposed tribute obligations on defeated peoples but left local hereditary elites in place. The Chimú of the Andes, in contrast, created a more centralized imperial administrative structure managed by a trained bureaucracy and used compulsory labor obligations to produce and distribute goods.

We can find similar patterns in North America. The transfer of agricultural technology from Mesoamerica, with its dependence on corn, beans, and squash, influenced the mound-building cultures of the Ohio and Mississippi River Valleys and the desert cultures of the Southwest. In the desert region of what is now the Southwest of the United States, the Anasazi and other peoples also utilized irrigated agriculture, a technology crucial to both Mesoamerican and Andean cultures. Both the desert and mound-building cultures of North America experienced cycles when powerful new political centers expanded the territories they controlled and consolidated their power until overwhelmed by environmental challenges or displaced by military rivals.

Beginning in the eleventh century the Toltec Empire weakened. The ultimate collapse of Tula left Culhuacán and Cholula as heirs of a much-diminished Toltec presence in central Mexico. Chimor persisted until the fifteenth century, when it also lost momentum and was militarily overwhelmed by the rising Inka Empire around 1470. Great civilizations in both Mesoamerica and the Andean region had risen and then been overwhelmed in earlier epochs as well, as had the major powers of the Four Corners desert region and the Ohio and Mississippi River Valleys. In all these cases, a long period of cultural and political adjustment led eventually to the creation of new indigenous institutions, the adoption of new technologies, and the appearance of new centers of power in new locations. With the appearance of the Aztec and Inka Empires in the fourteenth century, America would experience its final cycle of autonomous indigenous crisis and adjustment. At the end of that century the future of Amerindian peoples would become linked to the cultures of the Old World (See Chapter 15).

IMPORTANT EVENTS 1200 B.C.E. TO 1400 C.E.

1200–900 B.C.E.	Rise of Olmec civilization, centered on San Lorenzo
900–250 B.C.E.	Chavín civilization in the Andes
100 C.E.	Teotihuacan temple complex built
250	Maya early classic period begins
500–1000	Tiwanaku and Wari control Peruvian highlands
ca. 750	Teotihuacan destroyed
ca. 800	Chan Chan, capital of Chimor, built
800–900	Maya centers abandoned, end of classic period
ca. 900	beginnings of Mississippian Culture
968	Toltec capital of Tula founded
1050–1250	Cahokia reaches peak power
1150	Collapse of Anasazi centers begins
1175	Tula destroyed
1200	Chimu begin military expansion
1325	Aztec capital Tenochtitlan founded

Oral Societies and the Consequences of Literacy

The availability of written documents is a key factor used by historians to divide human prehistory from history. When we can read what people of the past thought and said about their lives, we begin to understand their cultures, institutions, values, and beliefs in ways that are not possible based only on the material remains unearthed by archaeologists.

Literacy and nonliteracy are not absolute alternatives. Personal literacy ranges from illiteracy through many shades of partial literacy (the ability to write one's name or to read simple texts with difficulty) to the fluent ability to read that is possessed by anyone reading this textbook. And there are degrees of societal literacy, ranging from nonliteracy through so-called craft literacy—in which a small specialized elite uses writing for limited purposes, such as administrative record keeping—up to the near-universal literacy and the use of writing for innumerable purposes that is the norm in the developed world in our times.

The vast majority of human beings of the last five to six thousand years, even those living in societies that possessed the technology of writing, were not themselves literate. If most people in a society rely on the spoken word and memory, that culture is essentially "oral" even if some members know how to write. The differences between oral and literate cultures are immense, affecting not only the kinds of knowledge that are valued and the forms in which information is preserved, but also the very use of language, the categories for conceptualizing the world, and ultimately the hard-wiring of the individual human brain (now recognized by neuroscientists to be strongly influenced by individual experience and mental activity).

Ancient Greece of the Archaic and Classical periods (ca. 800–323 B.C.E.) offers a particularly instructive case study because we can observe the process by which writing was introduced into an oral society as well as the far-reaching consequences. The Greeks of the Dark Age and early Archaic period lived in a purely oral society; all knowledge was preserved in human memory and passed on by telling it to others. The *Iliad* and the *Odyssey* (ca. 700 B.C.E.), Homer's epic poems, reflect this state of affairs. Scholars recognize that the creator of these poems was an oral poet, almost certainly not literate, who had heard and memorized the poems of predecessors and retold them his own way. The poems are treasuries of information that this society regarded as useful—events of the past; the conduct expected of warriors, kings, noblewomen, and servants; how to perform a sacrifice, build a raft, put on armor, and entertain guests; and much more.

Embedding this information in a story and using the colorful language, fixed phrases, and predictable rhythm of poetry made it easier for poet and audience to remember vast amounts of material. The early Greek poets, drawing on their strong memories, skill with words, and talent for dramatic performance, developed highly specialized techniques to assist them in memorizing and presenting their tales. They played a vital role in the preservation and transmission of information and thus enjoyed a relatively high social standing and comfortable standard of living. Analogous groups can be found in many other oral cultures of the past, including the bards of medieval Celtic lands, Norse *skalds*, west African *griots*, and the tribal historians of Native American peoples.

Nevertheless, human memory, however cleverly trained and well practiced, can only do so much. Oral societies must be extremely selective about what information to preserve in the limited storage medium of human memory, and they are slow to give up old information to make way for new.

Sometime in the eighth century B.C.E. the Greeks borrowed the system of writing used by the Phoenicians of Lebanon and, in adapting it to their language, created the first purely alphabetic writing, employing several dozen symbols to express the sounds of speech. The Greek alphabet, although relatively simple to learn as compared to the large and cumbersome sets of symbols in such craft literacy systems as cuneiform, hieroglyphics, or Linear B, was probably known at first only to a small number of people and used for restricted purposes. Scholars believe that it may have taken three or four centuries for knowledge of reading and writing to spread to large numbers of Greeks and for the written word to become the primary storage medium for the accumulated knowledge of Greek civilization. Throughout that time Greece was still primarily an oral society, even though some Greeks, mostly highly educated members of the upper classes, were beginning to write down poems, scientific speculations, stories about the past, philosophic musings, and the laws of their communities.

It is no accident that some of the most important intellectual and artistic achievements of the Greeks, including early science, history, drama, and rhetoric, developed in the period when oral and literate ways existed side by side. Scholars have persuasively argued that writing, by opening up a virtually limitless capacity to store information, released the human mind from the hard discipline of memorization and ended the need to be so painfully selective about what was preserved. This made previously unimaginable innovation and experimentation possible. The Greeks began to organize and categorize information in linear ways, perhaps inspired by the linear sequence of the alphabet; and they began to engage in abstract thinking now that it was no longer necessary to put everything in a story format. We can observe changes in the Greek language as it developed a vocabulary full of abstract nouns, accompanied by increasingly complex sentence structure now that the reader had time to go back over the text.

Nevertheless, all the developments associated with literacy were shaped by the deeply rooted oral habits of Greek culture. It is often said that Plato (ca. 429–347 B.C.E.) and his contemporaries of the later Classical Period may have been the first generation of Greeks who learned much of what they knew from books. Even so, Plato was a disciple of the philosopher Socrates, who wrote nothing, and Plato employed the oral form of the dialogue, a dramatized sequence of questions and answers, to convey his ideas in written form.

The transition from orality to literacy met stiff resistance in some quarters. Groups whose position in the oral culture was based on the special knowledge only they possessed—members of the elite who judged disputes, priests who knew the time-honored formulas and rituals for appeasing the gods, oral poets who preserved and performed the stories of a heroic past—resented the consequences of literacy. They did what they could to inflame the common people's suspicions of the impiety of literate men who sought scientific explanations for phenomena, such as lightning and eclipses, that had traditionally been attributed to the will and action of the gods. The elite attacked the so-called Sophists, or "wise men," who charged fees to teach what they claimed were the skills necessary for success, accusing them of subverting traditional morals and corrupting the young.

Other societies, ancient and modern, offer parallel examples of these processes.

Oral "specialists" in antiquity, including the Brahmin priests of India and the Celtic Druids, preserved in memory valuable religious information about how to win the favor of the gods. These groups jealously guarded their knowledge because it was the basis of their livelihood and social standing. In their determination to select and to maintain control over those who received this knowledge, they resisted committing it to writing, even after that technology was available. The ways in which oral authorities feel threatened by writing and resist it can be seen in the following quotation from a twentieth-century C.E. "griot," an oral rememberer and teller of the past in Mali in West Africa:

> We griots are depositories of the knowledge of the past.... Other peoples use writing to record the past, but this invention has killed the faculty of memory among them. They do not feel the past anymore, for writing lacks the warmth of the human voice. With them everybody thinks he knows, whereas learning should be a secret.... What paltry learning is that which is congealed in dumb books! ... For generations we have passed on the history of kings from father to son. The narrative was passed on to me without alteration, for I received it free from all untruth.[1]

This point of view is hard for us to grasp, living as we do in an intensely literate society in which the written word is often felt to be more authoritative and objective than the spoken word. It is important, in striving to understand societies of the past, not to superimpose our assumptions on them and to appreciate the complex interplay of oral and literate patterns in many of them.

Note

1. D. T. Niane, *Sundiata: An Epic of Old Mali* (Harlow, UK: Longman, 1986), 41.

PART THREE

GROWTH AND INTERACTION OF CULTURAL COMMUNITIES, 300 B.C.E.–1200 C.E.

CHAPTER 9
Networks of Communication and Exchange, 300 B.C.E.–1100 C.E.

CHAPTER 10
The Sasanid Empire and the Rise of Islam, 200–1200

CHAPTER 11
Christian Societies Emerge in Europe, 600–1200

CHAPTER 12
Inner and East Asia, 400–1200

In 300 B.C.E., societies had only limited contacts beyond their frontiers. By 1200 C.E., this situation had changed, as traders, migrating peoples, and missionaries brought peoples together. Products and technologies also moved along long-distance trade networks: the Silk Road across Asia, Saharan caravan routes, and sea-lanes connecting the Indian Ocean coastlands.

During this period migrating Bantu peoples from West Africa spread iron and new farming techniques through much of sub-Saharan Africa and helped foster a distinctive African culture. Conquering Arabs from the Arabian peninsula, inspired by the Prophet Muhammad, established Muslim rule from Spain to India, laying the foundation of a new culture.

In Asia, missionaries and pilgrims helped Buddhism spread from India to Sri Lanka, Tibet, Southeast Asia, and East Asia. The new faith interacted with older philosophies and religions to produce distinctive cultural patterns. Simultaneously, the Tang Empire in China disseminated Chinese culture and technologies throughout Inner and East Asia.

In Europe, monks and missionaries spread Christian beliefs that became enmeshed with new political and social structures: a struggle between royal and church authority in western Europe; a union of religious and imperial authority in the Byzantine east; and a similar but distinctive society in Kievan Russia. The Crusades reconnected western Europe with the lands of the east.

9

NETWORKS OF COMMUNICATION AND EXCHANGE, 300 B.C.E.–1100 C.E.

Inspired by the tradition of the Silk Road, a Chinese poet named Po Zhuyi (boh joo-yee) nostalgically wrote:

Iranian whirling girl, Iranian whirling girl—
Her heart answers to the strings,
Her hands answer to the drums.
At the sound of the strings and drums, she raises her arms,
Like whirling snowflakes tossed about, she turns in her twirling dance.
Iranian whirling girl,
You came from Sogdiana (sog-dee-A-nuh).
In vain did you labor to come east more than ten thousand tricents.
For in the central plains there were already some who could do the Iranian whirl,
And in a contest of wonderful abilities, you would not be their equal.[1]

The western part of Central Asia, the region around Samarkand (SAM-mar-kand) and Bukhara (boh-CAR-ruh) known in the eighth century C.E. as Sogdiana, was 2,500 miles (4,000 kilometers) from the Chinese capital of Chang'an (chahng-ahn). Caravans took more than four months to trek across the mostly unsettled deserts, mountains, and grasslands.

The Silk Road connecting China and the Middle East across Central Asia fostered the exchange of agricultural goods, manufactured products, and ideas. Musicians and dancing girls traveled, too—as did camel pullers, merchants, monks, and pilgrims. The Silk Road was not just a means of bringing peoples and parts of the world into contact; it was also a social system.

With every expansion of territory, the growing wealth of temples, kings, and emperors enticed traders to venture ever farther afield for precious goods. For the most part, the customers were wealthy elites. But the new products, agricultural and industrial processes, and foreign ideas and customs these long-distance traders brought with them sometimes affected an entire society.

Travelers and traders seldom owned much land or wielded political power. Socially isolated (sometimes by law) and secretive because any talk about markets,

---

[1]Victor H. Mair, ed., *The Columbia Anthology of Traditional Chinese Literature* (New York: Columbia University Press, 1994), 485; translated by Victor H. Mair.

products, routes, and travel conditions could help their competitors, they nevertheless contributed more to drawing the world together than did all but a few kings and emperors.

This chapter examines the social systems and historical impact of exchange networks that developed between 300 B.C.E. and 1100 C.E. in Europe, Asia, and Africa. The Silk Road and the Indian Ocean maritime system illustrate the nature of long-distance trade in this era.

Trading networks were not the only medium for the spread of new ideas, products, and customs. This chapter also compares developments along trade routes with folk migration by looking at the beginnings of contact across the Sahara and the simultaneous spread of Bantu-speaking peoples within sub-Saharan Africa. Chapter 6 discussed a third pattern of cultural contact and exchange, that taking place with the beginning of Christian missionary activity in the Roman Empire. This chapter further explores the process by examining the spread of Buddhism in Asia and Christianity in Africa and Asia.

THE SILK ROAD

Archaeology and linguistic studies show that the peoples of Central Asia engaged in long-distance movement and exchange from at least 1500 B.C.E. In Roman times Europeans became captivated by the idea of a trade route linking the lands of the Mediterranean with China by way of Mesopotamia, Iran, and Central Asia. The **Silk Road**, as it came to be called in modern times, experienced several periods of heavy use. The first began around 100 B.C.E.

Origins and Operations The Seleucid kings who succeeded to the eastern parts of Alexander the Great's empire in the third century B.C.E. focused their energies on Mesopotamia and Syria. This allowed an Iranian nomadic leader to establish an independent kingdom in northeastern Iran. The **Parthians**, a people originally from east of the Caspian Sea, had become a major force by 247 B.C.E. They left few written sources, and recurring wars with Greeks and Romans to the west prevented travelers from the Mediterranean region from gaining firm knowledge of their kingdom. It seems likely, however, that they helped foster the Silk Road by being located on the threshold of Central Asia and sharing customs with steppe nomads farther to the east.

In 128 B.C.E. a Chinese general named Zhang Jian (jahng jee-en) made his first exploratory journey across the deserts and mountains of Inner Asia on behalf of Emperor Wu of the Han dynasty. After crossing the broad and desolate Tarim Basin north of Tibet, he reached the fertile valley of Ferghana (fer-GAH-nuh) and for the first time encountered westward-flowing rivers. There he found horse breeders whose animals far outclassed any horses he had seen. Later Chinese historians looked on General Zhang, who ultimately led eighteen expeditions, as the originator of overland trade with the western lands, and they credited him with personally introducing a whole garden of new plants and trees to China.

Long-distance travel suited the people of the steppes more than the Chinese. The populations of Ferghana and neighboring regions included many nomads who followed their herds. Their migrations had little to do with trade, but they provided pack animals and controlled transit across their lands. The trading demands that brought the Silk Road into being were Chinese eagerness for western products, especially horses, and on the western end, the organized Parthian state, which had captured the flourishing markets of Mesopotamia from the Seleucids and maintained relations with other markets in India.

By 100 B.C.E., Greeks could buy Chinese silk from Parthian traders in Mesopotamian border entrepôts. Yet caravans also bought and sold goods along the way in prosperous Central Asian cities like Samarkand and Bukhara. These cities grew and flourished, often under the rule of local princes.

General Zhang definitely seems to have brought two plants to China: alfalfa and wine grapes. The former provided the best fodder for horses. In addition, Chinese farmers adopted pistachios, walnuts, pomegranates, sesame, coriander, spinach, and other new crops. Chinese artisans and physicians made good use of other trade products, such as jasmine oil, oak galls (used in tanning animal hides, dyeing, and making ink), sal ammoniac (for medicines), copper oxides, zinc, and precious stones.

Traders going west from China carried new fruits such as peaches and apricots, which the Romans mistakenly attributed to other eastern lands, calling them Persian plums and Armenian plums, respectively. They also carried cinnamon, ginger, and other spices that could not be grown in the West.

Nomadism in Central and Inner Asia   The Silk Road could not have functioned without pastoral nomads to provide animals, animal handlers, and protection. As discussed in Chapter 4, descriptions of steppe nomads known as Scythians appear in the sixth century B.C.E. in the history of the Greek writer Herodotus, who portrays them as superb riders, herdsmen, and hunters living in Central Asia, the lands to the north of the Black and Caspian Seas. Moving regularly and efficiently with flocks and herds of enormous size prevented overgrazing. Though the Scythians were fearsome horse archers, their homes, which were made of felt spread over a lightweight framework, were transported on two- or four-wheeled wagons drawn by oxen. This custom continued in some parts of Inner Asia, the grasslands and deserts extending eastward from Central Asia to the borders of China, for another two thousand years.

Nomads were not unfamiliar with agriculture or unwilling to use products grown by farmers, but their ideal was self-sufficiency. Since their wanderings with their herds normally took them far from any farming region, self-sufficiency dictated foods they could provide for themselves—primarily meat and milk—and clothing made from felt, leather, and furs. Women oversaw the breeding and birthing of livestock and the preparation of skins. They were also responsible for relocating the portable dwellings.

Nomads were most dependent on settled regions for the bronze or iron used in bridles, stirrups, cart fittings, and weapons. They acquired metal implements in trade and reworked them to suit their purposes. Scythians in the Ukraine worked extensively with iron as early as the fourth century B.C.E., and Turkic-speaking peoples had large ironworking stations south of the Altai Mountains in western Mongolia in the 600s C.E. Steppe nomads situated near settled areas also traded wool, leather, and horses for wood, silk, vegetables, and grain.

The Impact of the Silk Road   As trade became a more important part of Central Asian life, the Iranian-speaking peoples increasingly settled in trading cities and surrounding farm villages. By the sixth century C.E., nomads

MAP 9.1   Asian Trade and Communication Routes

The overland Silk Road was vulnerable to political disruption, but it was much shorter than the maritime route from the South China Sea to the Red Sea, and ships were more expensive than pack animals. Moreover, China's political centers were in the north.

originally from the Altai Mountains farther east had spread across the steppes and become the dominant pastoral group. These peoples spoke Turkic languages unrelated to the Iranian tongues. The nomads continued to live in the round, portable felt huts called yurts, or in Mongolia *gers*, that can still occasionally be seen in Central Asia, but prosperous individuals, both Turks and Iranians, built stately homes decorated with brightly colored wall paintings. The paintings show people wearing Chinese silks and Iranian brocades and riding on richly outfitted horses and camels. They also indicate an avid interest in Buddhism (discussed later in this chapter), which competed with Nestorian Christianity, Manichaeism, and Zoroastrianism in a lively and inquiring intellectual milieu.

Missionary influences exemplify the impact of foreign customs and beliefs on the peoples along the Silk Road. Military technology affords an example of the opposite phenomenon, steppe customs radiating into foreign lands. Chariot warfare and the use of mounted bowmen originated in Central Asia and spread eastward and westward through military campaigns and folk migrations that began in the second millennium B.C.E. and recurred throughout the period of the Silk Road.

Evidence of the **stirrup**, one of the most important inventions, comes first from the Kushan people who ruled northern Afghanistan in approximately the first century C.E. At first a solid bar, then a loop of leather to support the rider's big toe, and finally a device of leather and metal or wood supporting the ball of the foot, the stirrup gave riders far greater stability in the saddle—which itself was in all likelihood an earlier Central Asian invention.

Iranian Musicians from Silk Road *This three-color glazed pottery figurine, 23 inches (58.4 centimeters) high, comes from a northern Chinese tomb of the Tang era (sixth to ninth centuries C.E.) The musicians playing Iranian instruments confirm the migration of Iranian culture across the Silk Road. At the same time, dishes decorated by the Chinese three-color glaze technique were in vogue in northern Iran.*

© Cultural Relics Press

Using stirrups, a mounted warrior could supplement his bow and arrow with a long lance and charge his enemy at a gallop without fear that the impact of his attack would push him off his mount. Far to the west, the stirrup made possible the armored knights who dominated the battlefields of Europe (see Chapter 11), and it contributed to the superiority of the Tang cavalry in China (see Chapter 12).

THE INDIAN OCEAN MARITIME SYSTEM

While a land route was established in Central Asia, a multilingual, multiethnic society of seafarers established the **Indian Ocean Maritime System**, a trade network across the Indian Ocean and the South China Sea. Although these people left few records and seldom played a visible part in the rise and fall of kingdoms and empires, they forged increasingly strong economic and social ties between the coastal lands of East Africa, southern Arabia, the Persian Gulf, India, Southeast Asia, and southern China.

This trade took place in three distinct regions: (1) In the South China Sea, Chinese and Malays (including Indonesians) dominated trade. (2) From the east coast of India to the islands of Southeast Asia, Indians and Malays were the main traders. (3) From the west coast of India to the Persian Gulf and the east coast of Africa, merchants and sailors were predominantly Persians and Arabs. However, Chinese and Malay sailors could and did voyage to East Africa, and Arab and Persian traders reached southern China.

From the time of Herodotus in the fifth century B.C.E., Greek writers regaled their readers with stories of marvelous voyages down the Red Sea into the Indian Ocean or around Africa from the west. Most often, they attributed such trips to the Phoenicians, the most fearless of Mediterranean seafarers. Occasionally a Greek appears. One such was Hippalus, a Greek ship's pilot who was said to have discovered the seasonal monsoon winds that facilitate sailing across the Indian Ocean.

Of course, the regular, seasonal alternation of steady winds could not have remained unnoticed for thousands of years, waiting for an alert Greek to happen along. The great voyages and discoveries made before written records became common should surely be attributed to the peoples who lived around the Indian Ocean rather than to interlopers from the Mediterranean Sea. The story of Hippalus resembles the Chinese story of General Zhang Jian, whose role in opening trade with Central Asia overshadows the anonymous contributions made by the indigenous peoples. The Chinese may indeed have learned from General Zhang and the Greeks from Hippalus, but other people played important roles anonymously.

The ships used in the Indian Ocean differed from those used in the west. Whereas Mediterranean sailors of the time of Alexander used square sails and long banks of oars to maneuver among the sea's many islands and small harbors, Indian Ocean vessels relied on roughly triangular lateen sails and normally did without oars in running before the wind on long ocean stretches. Whereas Mediterranean shipbuilders nailed their vessels together, the planks of Indian Ocean ships were pierced, tied together with palm fiber, and caulked with bitumen. Mediterranean sailors rarely ventured out of sight of land. Indian Ocean sailors, thanks to the monsoon winds, could cover long reaches entirely at sea.

These technological differences prove that the world of the Indian Ocean developed differently than the world of the Mediterranean Sea, where the Phoenicians and Greeks established colonies that maintained contact with their home cities (see Chapters 3 and 5). The traders of the Indian Ocean, where distances were greater and contacts less frequent, seldom retained political ties with their home-lands. The colonies they established were sometimes socially distinctive but rarely independent of the local political powers.

Origins of Contact and Trade

By 2000 B.C.E. Sumerian records indicate regular trade between Mesopotamia, the islands of the Persian Gulf, Oman, and the Indus Valley. However, this early trading contact broke off, and later Mesopotamian trade references mention East Africa more often than India.

A similarly early chapter in Indian Ocean history concerns migrations from Southeast Asia to Madagascar, the world's fourth largest island, situated off the southeastern coast of Africa. About two thousand years ago, people from one of the many Indonesian islands of Southeast Asia established themselves in that for-ested, mountainous land 6,000 miles (9,500 kilometers) from home. They could not possibly have carried enough supplies for a direct voyage across the Indian Ocean, so their route must have touched the coasts of India and southern Arabia. No physical remains of their journeys have been discovered, however.

Apparently, the sailing canoes of these people plied the seas along the increas-ingly familiar route for several hundred years. Settlers farmed the new land and entered into relations with Africans who found their way across the 250-mile-wide (400-kilometer-wide) Mozambique (moe-zam-BEEK) Channel around the fifth cen-tury C.E. Descendants of the seafarers preserved the language of their homeland and some of its culture, such as the cultivation of bananas, yams, and other native Southeast Asian plants. These food crops spread to mainland Africa. But the mem-ory of their distant origins gradually faded, not to be recovered until modern times, when scholars unraveled the linguistic link between the two lands.

The Impact of Indian Ocean Trade

The demand for products from the coastal lands inspired mari-ners to persist in their long ocean voyages. Africa produced exotic animals, wood, and ivory. Since ivory also came from India, Mesopotamia, and North Africa, the extent of African ivory exports cannot be determined. The highlands of northern Somalia and southern Arabia grew the scrubby trees whose aromatic resins were valued as frankincense and myrrh. Pearls abounded in the Persian Gulf, and evidence of ancient copper mines has been found in Oman in southeastern Arabia. India shipped spices and manufactured goods, and more spices came from Southeast Asia, along with manufactured items, par-ticularly pottery, obtained in trade with China. In sum, the Indian Ocean trading region had a great variety of highly valued products. Given the long distances and the compar-ative lack of islands, however, the volume of trade there was undoubtedly much lower than in the Mediterranean Sea.

The culture of the Indian Ocean ports was often isolated from the hinterlands, particularly in the west. The coasts of the Arabian peninsula, the African side of the Red Sea, southern Iran, and northern India (today's Pakistan) were mostly barren desert. Ports in all these areas tended to be small, and many suffered from meager supplies of fresh water. Farther south in India, the monsoon provided ample water, but steep mountains cut off the coastal plain from the interior of the country. Thus few ports between Zanzibar and Sri Lanka had substantial inland populations within easy reach. The head of the Persian Gulf was one exception: ship-borne trade was possible from the port of Apologus (later called Ubulla, the precursor of modern Basra) as far north as Babylon and, from the eighth century C.E., nearby Baghdad.

By contrast, eastern India, the Malay Peninsula, and Indonesia afforded more hospitable and densely populated shores with easier access to inland populations. Though the fishers, sailors, and traders of the western Indian Ocean system supplied a long series of kingdoms and empires, none of these consumer societies became primarily maritime in orientation, as the Greeks and Phoenicians did in the Mediterranean. In contrast, seaborne trade and influence seem to have been important even to the earliest states of Southeast Asia.

In coastal areas throughout the Indian Ocean system, small groups of seafarers sometimes had a significant social impact despite their usual lack of political power. Women seldom accompanied the men on long sea voyages, so sailors and merchants often married local women in port cities. The families thus established were bilingual and bicultural. As in many other situations in world history, women played a crucial though not well-documented role as mediators between cultures. Not only did they raise their children to be more cosmopolitan than children from inland regions, but they also introduced the men to customs and attitudes that they carried with them when they returned to sea. As a consequence, the designation of specific seafarers as Persian, Arab, Indian, or Malay often conceals mixed heritages and a rich cultural diversity.

ROUTES ACROSS THE SAHARA

The windswept Sahara, a desert stretching from the Red Sea to the Atlantic Ocean and broken only by the Nile River, isolates sub-Saharan Africa from the Mediterranean world. The current dryness of the Sahara dates only to about 2500 B.C.E. The period of drying out that preceded that date lasted twenty-five centuries and encompassed several cultural changes. During that time, travel between a slowly shrinking number of grassy areas was comparatively easy. However, by 300 B.C.E., scarcity of water was restricting travel to a few difficult routes initially known only to desert nomads. Trade over **trans-Saharan caravan routes**, at first only a trickle, eventually expanded into a significant stream.

Early Saharan Cultures   Sprawling sand dunes, sandy plains, and vast expanses of exposed rock make up most of the great desert. Stark and rugged mountain and highland areas separate its northern and southern portions. The cliffs and caves of these highlands, the last spots where water and grassland could be found as the climate changed, preserve rock paintings and engravings that constitute the primary evidence for early Saharan history.

Though dating is difficult, what appear to be the earliest images, left by hunters in much wetter times, include elephants, giraffes, rhinoceroses, crocodiles, and other animals that have long been extinct in the region. Overlaps in the artwork indicate that the hunting societies were gradually joined by new cultures based on cattle breeding and well adapted to the sparse grazing that remained. Domestic cattle probably originated separately in northern Africa, western Asia, and southern Pakistan. They certainly reached the Sahara before it became completely dry. The beautiful paintings of cattle and scenes of daily

Henri Lhote

Cattle Herders in Saharan Rock Art *These paintings represent the most artistically accomplished type of Saharan art. Herding societies of modern times living in the Sahel region south of the Sahara strongly resemble the society depicted here.*

life seen in the Saharan rock art depict pastoral societies that bear little similarity to any in western Asia. The people seem physically akin to today's West Africans, and the customs depicted, such as dancing and wearing masks, as well as the breeds of cattle, particularly those with piebald coloring (splotches of black and white), strongly suggest later societies to the south of the Sahara. These factors support the hypothesis that some southern cultural patterns originated in the Sahara.

Overlaps in artwork also show that horse herders succeeded the cattle herders. The rock art changes dramatically in style, from the superb realism of the cattle pictures to sketchier images that are often strongly geometric. Moreover, the horses are frequently shown drawing light chariots. According to the most common theory, intrepid charioteers from the Mediterranean shore drove their flimsy vehicles across the desert and established societies in the few remaining grassy areas of the central Saharan highlands. Some scholars suggest possible chariot routes that refugees from the collapse of the Mycenaean and Minoan civilizations of Greece and Crete (see Chapter 5) might have followed deep into the desert around the twelfth century B.C.E. However, no archaeological evidence of actual chariot use in the Sahara has been discovered, and it is difficult to imagine large numbers of refugees from the politically chaotic Mediterranean region driving chariots into a waterless, trackless desert in search of a new homeland somewhere to the south.

ENVIRONMENT + TECHNOLOGY

Camel Saddles

As seemingly simple a technology as saddle design can indicate a society's economic structure. The south Arabian saddle, a Tunisian example of which is shown to the right, was good for riding, and baggage could easily be tied to the wooden arches at its front. It was militarily inefficient, however, because the rider knelt on the cushion behind the camel's hump, which made it difficult to use weapons.

The north Arabian saddle was a significant improvement that came into use in the first centuries B.C.E. The two arches anchoring the front end of the south Arabian saddle were separated and greatly enlarged, one arch going in front of the hump and the other behind. This formed a solid wooden framework to which loads could easily be attached, but the placement of the prominent front and back arches seated the rider on top of the camel's hump instead of behind it and thereby gave warriors a solid seat and the advantage of height over enemy horsemen. Arabs in northern Arabia used these

saddles to take control of the caravan trade through their lands.

The lightest and most efficient riding saddles, shown below, come from the southern Sahara, where personal travel and warfare took priority over trade. These excellent war saddles could not be used for baggage because they did not offer a convenient place to tie bundles.

Private collection

Camel Saddles *The militarily inefficient south Arabian saddle (above) seats the rider behind the animal's hump atop its hindquarters. The rider controls his mount by tapping its neck with a long camel stick. The Tuareg saddle (below) seats the rider over the animal's withers, leaving his hands free to wield a sword and letting him control his mount with his toes.*

Fred Bavendam/Minden Pictures

As with the cattle herders, therefore, the identity of the Saharan horse breeders and the source of their passion for drawing chariots remain a mystery. Only with the coming of the camel is it possible to make firm connections with the Saharan nomads of today through the depiction of objects and geometric patterns still used by the veiled, blue-robed Tuareg (TWAH-reg) people of the highlands in southern Algeria, Niger, and Mali.

Some historians maintain that the Romans inaugurated an important trans-Saharan trade, but they lack firm archaeological evidence. More plausibly, Saharan trade relates to the spread of camel domestication. Supporting evidence comes from rock art, where overlaps of images imply that camel riders in desert costume constitute the latest Saharan population. The camel-oriented images are decidedly the crudest to be found in the region.

The first mention of camels in North Africa comes in a Latin text of 46 B.C.E. Since the native camels of Africa probably died out before the era of domestication, the domestic animals most likely reached the Sahara from Arabia, probably by way of Egypt in the first millennium B.C.E. They could have been adopted by peoples farther and farther to the west, from one central Saharan highland to the next, only much later spreading northward and coming to the attention of the Romans. Camel herding made it easier for people to move away from the Saharan highlands and roam the deep desert (see Environment and Technology: Camel Saddles).

Trade Across the Sahara   Linkage between two different trading systems, one in the south, the other in the north, developed slowly. Southern traders concentrated on supplying salt from large deposits in the southern desert to the peoples of sub-Saharan Africa. Traders from the equatorial forest zone brought forest products, such as kola nuts (a condiment and source of caffeine) and edible palm oil, to trading centers near the desert's southern fringe. Each received the products they needed in their homelands from the other, or from the farming peoples of the **Sahel** (SAH-hel)—literally "the coast" in Arabic, the southern borderlands of the Sahara. Middlemen who were native to the Sahel played an important role in this trade, but precise historical details are lacking.

In the north, Roman colonists supplied Italy with agricultural products, primarily wheat and olives. Surviving mosaic pavements depicting scenes from daily life show that people living on the farms and in the towns of the interior consumed Roman manufactured goods and shared Roman styles. This northern pattern began to change only in the third century C.E. with the decline of the Roman Empire, the abandonment of many Roman farms, the growth of nomadism, and a lessening of trade across the Mediterranean.

SUB-SAHARAN AFRICA

The Indian Ocean network and later trade across the Sahara provided **sub-Saharan Africa**, the portion of Africa south of the Sahara, with a few external contacts. The most important African network of cultural exchange from 300 B.C.E. to 1100 C.E., however, arose within the region and took the form of folk migration. These migrations and exchanges put in place enduring characteristics of African culture.

A Challenging Geography   Many geographic obstacles impede access to and movement within sub-Saharan Africa. The Sahara, the Atlantic and Indian Oceans, and the Red Sea form the boundaries of the region. With the exception of the Nile, a ribbon of green traversing the Sahara from south to north, the major river systems empty into oceans: the Senegal, Niger, and Zaire (zah-EER) Rivers empty into the Atlantic, and the Zambezi River empties into the Mozambique Channel of the Indian Ocean. Rapids limit the use of these rivers for navigation.

Stretching over 50 degrees of latitude, sub-Saharan Africa encompasses dramatically different environments. A 4,000-mile (6,500-kilometer) trek from the southern edge of the Sahara to the Cape of Good Hope would take a traveler from the flat, semiarid **steppes** of the Sahel region to tropical **savanna** covered by long grasses and scattered forest, and then to **tropical rain forest** on the lower Niger and in the Zaire Basin. The rain forest gives way to another broad expanse of savanna, followed by more steppe and desert, and finally by a region of temperate highlands at the southern extremity, located as far south of the equator as Greece and Sicily are to its north. East-west travel is comparatively easy in the steppe and savanna regions—a caravan from Senegal to the Red Sea would have traversed a distance comparable to that of the Silk Road—but difficult in the equatorial rain-forest belt and across the mountains and deep rift valleys that abut the rain forest to the east and separate East from West Africa.

The Development of Cultural Unity   Cultural heritages shared by the educated elites within each region of the world—heritages that some anthropologists call **"great traditions"**—typically include a written language, common legal and belief systems, ethical codes, and other intellectual attitudes. They loom large in written records as traditions that rise above the diversity of local customs and beliefs commonly distinguished as **"small traditions."**

By the year 1 C.E. sub-Saharan Africa had become a distinct cultural region, though one not shaped by imperial conquest or characterized by a shared elite culture, a "great tradition." The cultural unity of sub-Saharan Africa rested on similar characteristics shared to varying degrees by many popular cultures, or "small traditions." These had developed during the region's long period of isolation from the rest of the world after the drying up of the Sahara and had been refined, renewed, and interwoven by repeated episodes of migration and social interaction. Historians know little about this complex prehistory beyond what archaeology indicates for the beginnings of ironworking and the spread of domesticated grains, such as pearl millet (from Mali) and teff (from Ethiopia), around the third millennium B.C.E. Thus, to a greater degree than in other regions, they call on anthropological descriptions, oral history, and comparatively late records of various "small traditions" to reconstruct the broad outlines of cultural formation.

Sub-Saharan Africa's cultural unity is less immediately apparent than its diversity. By one estimate, Africa is home to two thousand distinct languages, many corresponding to social and belief systems endowed with distinctive rituals and cosmologies. There are likewise numerous food production systems, ranging from hunting and gathering—very differently carried out by the Mbuti (m-BOO-tee) Pygmies of the equatorial rain forest and the Khoisan (KOI-sahn) peoples of the southwestern deserts—to the cultivation of bananas, yams, and other root crops in forest clearings and of sorghum, originally from Egypt, and millet in the savanna lands. Pastoral societies, particularly those depending on cattle, display somewhat less diversity across the Sahel and savanna belt from Senegal to Kenya. Equatorial regions have distinctive breeds of dwarf goats that are resistant to tsetse fly infection.

Sub-Saharan Africa covered a larger and more diverse area than any other cultural region in the first millennium C.E. and had a lower overall population density. Thus societies and polities had ample room to form and reform, and a substantial amount of space separated different groups. The contacts that did occur did not last long enough to produce rigid cultural uniformity.

In addition, for centuries external conquerors could not penetrate the region's natural barriers and impose a uniform culture. The Egyptians occupied Nubia, and some traces of Egyptian influence appear in Saharan rock art farther west, but the Nile cataracts and the vast swampland in the Nile's upper reaches blocked movement farther south. The Romans sent expeditions against pastoral peoples living in the Libyan Sahara but could not incorporate them into the Roman world. Not until the nineteenth century did outsiders gain control of the continent and begin the process of establishing an elite culture—that of European imperialism.

African Cultural Characteristics   European travelers who got to know the sub-Saharan region well in the nineteenth and twentieth centuries observed broad commonalities underlying African life and culture. In agriculture, the common technique was cultivation by hoe and digging stick. Plows were never used despite an abundance of cattle in the Sahel. Musically, different groups of Africans played many instruments, especially types of drums, but common features, particularly in rhythm, gave African music as a whole a distinctive character. Music played an important role in social rituals, as did dancing and wearing masks, which often showed great artistry in their design.

African kingdoms varied, but kingship displayed common features, most notably the ritual isolation of the king himself. Fixed social categories—age groupings, kinship divisions, distinct gender roles and relations, and occupational groupings—also show resemblances from one region to another, even in societies too small to organize themselves into kingdoms. Though not hierarchical, these categories played a role similar to the divisions between noble, commoner, and slave prevalent where kings ruled.

Some historians hypothesize that these common cultural features emanated from the peoples who once occupied the southern Sahara. In Paleolithic times, periods of dryness alternated with periods of wetness as the Ice Age that locked up much of the world's fresh water in glaciers and icecaps came and went. When European glaciers receded with the waning of the Ice Age, a storm belt brought increased wetness to the Saharan region. Rushing rivers scoured deep canyons. Now filled with fine sand, those canyons are easily visible on flights over the southern parts of the desert. As the glaciers receded farther, the storm belt moved northward to Europe, and dryness set in gradually after 5000 B.C.E. As a consequence, runs the hypothesis, the region's population migrated southward, becoming increasingly concentrated in the Sahel, which may have been the initial incubation center for Pan-African cultural patterns.

Increasing dryness and the resulting difficulty in supporting the population would have driven some people out of this core into more sparsely settled lands to the east, west, and south. In a parallel development farther to the east, migration away from the growing aridity of the desert seems to have contributed to the settling of the Nile Valley and the emergence of the Old Kingdom of Egypt (see Chapter 2). The archaeological site of Nabta Playa (NEB-tuh PLY-uh) in the totally barren desert west of the Nile in southern Egypt marks a stage in this process. Originally cattle herders around a lake in the tenth millennium B.C.E., the local population had developed large villages with deep wells, sorghum and millet cultivation, and sheep and goat herding by the seventh millennium. The fifth millennium witnessed their construction of an astronomically oriented ring of stones two thousand years older than Stonehenge, along with a cattle cult featuring animals buried in stone-built chambers. The excavators see a likely connection between that cult and later cattle worship in dynastic Egypt.

| **The Advent of Iron and the Bantu Migrations** | Archaeology confirms that agriculture had become common between the equator and the Sahara by the early second millennium B.C.E. It then spread southward, displacing hunting and gathering as a way of life. Moreover, botanical evidence |

indicates that banana trees, probably introduced to southeastern Africa from Southeast Asia, made their way north and west, retracing in the opposite direction the presumed migration routes of early agriculturists.

Traces of copper mining appear in the Sahara from the early first millennium B.C.E. Copper appears in the Niger Valley somewhat later and in the Central African copper belt after 400 C.E. Most important of all, iron smelting began in northern sub-Saharan Africa in the early first millennium C.E. and spread southward from there.

Many historians believe that the secret of smelting iron, which requires very high temperatures, was discovered only once, by the Hittites of Anatolia (modern Turkey) around 1500 B.C.E. (see Chapter 3). If that is the case, it is hard to explain how iron smelting reached sub-Saharan Africa. The earliest evidence of ironworking from the kingdom of Meroë, situated on the upper Nile and in cultural contact with Egypt, is no earlier than the evidence from West Africa (northern Nigeria). Even less plausible than the Nile Valley as a route of technological diffusion is the idea of a spread southward from Phoenician settlements in North Africa, since archaeological evidence has failed to substantiate the vague Greek and Latin accounts of Phoenician excursions to the south.

A more plausible scenario focuses on Africans' discovering for themselves how to smelt iron. Some historians suggest that they might have done so while firing pottery in kilns. No firm evidence exists to prove or disprove this theory.

Linguistic analysis provides the strongest evidence of extensive contacts among sub-Saharan Africans in the first millennium C.E.—and offers suggestions about the spread of iron. More than three hundred languages spoken south of the equator belong to the branch of the Niger-Congo family known as **Bantu**, after the word meaning "people" in most of the languages.

The distribution of the Bantu languages both north and south of the equator is consistent with a divergence beginning in the first millennium B.C.E. By comparing core words common to most of the languages, linguists have drawn some conclusions about the original Bantu-speakers, whom they call "proto-Bantu." These people engaged in fishing, using canoes, nets, lines, and hooks. They lived in permanent villages on the edge of the rain forest, where they grew yams and grains and harvested wild palm nuts from which they pressed oil. They possessed domesticated goats, dogs, and perhaps other animals. They made pottery and cloth. Linguists surmise that the proto-Bantu homeland was near the modern boundary of Nigeria and Cameroon.

Because the presumed home of the proto-Bantu lies near the known sites of early iron smelting, migration by Bantu-speakers seems a likely mechanism for the southward spread of iron. The migrants probably used iron axes and hoes to hack out forest clearings and plant crops. According to this scenario, their actions would have established an economic basis for new societies capable of sustaining much denser populations than could earlier societies dependent on hunting and gathering alone. Thus the period from 500 B.C.E. to 1000 C.E. saw a substantial transfer of Bantu traditions and practices southward, eastward, and westward and their transformation, through intermingling with preexisting societies, into Pan-African traditions and practices.

THE SPREAD OF IDEAS

Ideas, like social customs, religious attitudes, and artistic styles, can spread along trade routes and through folk migrations. In both cases, documenting the dissemination of ideas, particularly in preliterate societies, poses a difficult historical problem.

Ideas and Material Evidence   Historians know about some ideas only through the survival of written sources. Other ideas do not depend on writing but are inherent in material objects studied by archaeologists and anthropologists. Customs surrounding the eating of pork are a case in point. Scholars disagree about whether pigs became domestic in only one place, from which the practice of pig keeping spread elsewhere, or whether several peoples hit on the same idea at different times and in different places.

Southeast Asia was an important early center of pig domestication. Anthropological studies tell us that the eating of pork became highly ritualized in this area and that it was sometimes allowed only on ceremonial occasions. On the other side of the Indian Ocean, wild swine were common in the Nile swamps of ancient Egypt. There, too, pigs took on a sacred role, being associated with the evil god Set, and eating them was prohibited. The biblical prohibition on the Israelites' eating pork, echoed later by the Muslims, probably came from Egypt in the second millennium B.C.E.

In a third locale in eastern Iran, an archaeological site dating from the third millennium B.C.E. provides evidence of another religious taboo relating to pork. Although the area around the site was swampy and home to many wild pigs, not a single pig bone has been found. Yet small pig figurines seem to have been used as symbolic religious offerings, and the later Iranian religion associates the boar with an important god.

What accounts for the apparent connection between domestic pigs and religion in these far-flung areas? There is no way of knowing. It has been hypothesized that pigs were first domesticated in Southeast Asia by people who had no herd animals—sheep, goats, cattle, or horses—and who relied on fish for most of their animal protein. The pig therefore became a special animal to them. The practice of pig herding, along with religious beliefs and rituals associated with the consumption of pork, could conceivably have spread from Southeast Asia along the maritime routes of the Indian Ocean, eventually reaching Iran and Egypt. But no evidence survives to support this hypothesis. In this case, therefore, material evidence can only hint at the spread of religious ideas, leaving the door open for other explanations.

A more certain example of objects' indicating the spread of an idea is the practice of hammering a carved die onto a piece of precious metal and using the resulting coin as a medium of exchange. From its origin in the Lydian kingdom in Anatolia in the first millennium B.C.E. (see Chapter 5), the idea of trading by means of struck coinage spread rapidly to Europe, North Africa, and India. Was the low-value copper coinage of China, made by pouring molten metal into a mold, also inspired by this practice from far away? It may have been, but it might also derive from indigenous Chinese metalworking. There is no way to be sure.

The Spread of Buddhism

While material objects associated with religious beliefs and rituals are important indicators of the spread of spiritual ideas, written sources deal with the spread of today's major religions. Buddhism grew to become, with Christianity and Islam (see Chapter 10), one of the most popular and widespread religions in the world. In all three cases, the religious ideas spread without dependency on a single ethnic or kinship group.

King Ashoka, the Mauryan ruler of India, and Kanishka, the greatest king of the Kushans of northern Afghanistan, promoted Buddhism between the third century B.C.E. and the second century C.E. However, monks, missionaries, and pilgrims who crisscrossed India, followed the Silk Road, or took ships on the Indian Ocean brought the Buddha's teachings to Southeast Asia, China, Korea, and ultimately Japan.

The Chinese pilgrim Faxian (fah-shee-en) (died between 418 and 423 C.E.) left a written account of his travels. Faxian began his trip in the company of a Chinese envoy to an unspecified ruler or people in Central Asia. After traveling from one Buddhist site to another across Afghanistan and India, he reached Sri Lanka, a Buddhist land, where he lived for two years. He then embarked for China on a merchant ship with two hundred men aboard. A storm drove the ship to Java, which he chose not to describe since it was Hindu rather than Buddhist. After five months ashore, Faxian finally reached China on another ship.

Less reliable accounts make reference to missionaries traveling to Syria, Egypt, and Macedonia, as well as to Southeast Asia. One of Ashoka's sons allegedly led a band of missionaries to Sri Lanka. Later, his sister brought a company of nuns there, along with a branch of the sacred Bo tree under which the Buddha had received enlightenment. At the same time, there are reports of other monks traveling to Burma, Thailand, and Sumatra. Ashoka's missionaries may also have reached Tibet by way of trade routes across the Himalayas.

The different lands that received the story and teachings of the Buddha preserved or adapted them in different ways. Theravada Buddhism, "Teachings of the Elder," was centered in Sri Lanka. Holding closely to the Buddha's earliest teachings, it maintained that the goal of religion, available only to monks, is *nirvana*, the total absence of suffering and the end of the cycle of rebirth (see Chapter 7). This teaching contrasted with Mahayana, or "Great Vehicle" Buddhism, in later centuries the dominant form of the religion in East Asia, which stressed the goal of becoming a *bodhisattva*, a person who attains nirvana but chooses to remain in human company to help and guide others.

The Spread of Christianity   The post-Roman development of Christianity in Europe is discussed in Chapter 11. The Christian faith enjoyed an earlier spread in Asia and Africa before its confrontation with Islam (described in Chapter 10). Jerusalem in Palestine, Antioch in Syria, and Alexandria in Egypt became centers of Christian authority soon after the crucifixion, but the spread of Christianity to Armenia and Ethiopia illustrates the connections between religion, trade, and imperial politics.

Situated in eastern Anatolia (modern Turkey), **Armenia** served recurrently as a battleground between Iranian states to the south and east and Mediterranean states to the west. Each imperial power wanted to control this region so close to the frontier where Silk Road traders met their Mediterranean counterparts. In Parthian times, Armenia's kings favored Zoroastrianism. The invention of an Armenian alphabet in the early fifth century opened the way to a wider spread of Christianity. The Iranians did not give up domination easily, but within a century the Armenian Apostolic Church had become the center of Armenian cultural life.

Far to the south Christians similarly sought to outflank Iran. The Christian emperors in Constantinople (see Chapter 6) sent missionaries along the Red Sea trade route to seek converts in Yemen and **Ethiopia**. In the fourth century C.E. a Syrian philosopher traveling with two young relatives sailed to India. On the way back the ship docked at a Red Sea port occupied by Ethiopians from the prosperous kingdom of Aksum. Being then at odds with the Romans, the Ethiopians killed everyone on board except the two boys, Aedisius—who later narrated this story—and Frumentius. Impressed by their learning, the king made the former his cupbearer and the latter his treasurer and secretary.

When the king died, his wife urged Frumentius to govern Aksum on her behalf and that of her infant son, Ezana. As regent, Frumentius sought out Roman Christians among the merchants who visited the country and helped them establish Christian communities. When he became king, Ezana, who may have become a Christian, permitted Aedisius and Frumentius to return to Syria. The patriarch of Alexandria, on learning about the progress of Christianity in Aksum, elevated Frumentius to the rank of bishop, though he had not previously been a clergyman, and sent him back to Ethiopia as the first leader of its church.

The spread of Christianity into Nubia, the land south of Egypt along the Nile River, proceeded from Ethiopia rather than Egypt. Politically and economically,

Ethiopia became a power at the western end of the Indian Ocean trading system, occasionally even extending its influence across the Red Sea and asserting itself in Yemen.

CONCLUSION

Exchange facilitated by the early long-distance trading systems differed in many ways from the ebb and flow of culture, language, and custom that folk migrations brought about. Transportable goods and livestock and ideas about new technologies and agricultural products sometimes worked great changes on the landscape and in people's lives. But nothing resembling the commonality of African cultural features observed south of the Sahara can be attributed to the societies involved in the Silk Road, Indian Ocean, or trans-Saharan exchanges. Few people were directly involved in these complex social systems of travel and trade compared with the populations with whom they were brought into contact, and their lifestyles as pastoral nomads or seafarers isolated them still more. Communities of traders contributed to this isolation by their reluctance to share knowledge with people who might become commercial competitors.

The Bantu, however, if current theories are correct, spread far and wide in sub-Saharan Africa with the deliberate intent of settling and implanting a lifestyle based on iron implements and agriculture. The metallurgical skills and agricultural techniques they brought with them permitted much denser habitation and helped ensure that the languages of the immigrants would supplant those of their hunting and gathering predecessors. Where the trading systems encouraged diversity by introducing new products and ideas, the Bantu migrations brought a degree of cultural dominance that strongly affected later African history.

An apparent exception to the generalization that trading systems have less impact than folk migrations on patterns of dominance lies in the intangible area of ideas. Christianity and Buddhism both spread along trade routes, at least to some degree. Each instance of spread, however, gave rise to new forms of cultural diversity even as overall doctrinal unity made these religions dominant. As "great traditions," the new faiths based on conversion linked priests, monks, nuns, and religious scholars across vast distances. However, these same religions merged with myriad "small traditions" to provide for the social and spiritual needs of peoples living in many lands under widely varying circumstances.

IMPORTANT EVENTS 300 B.C.E. TO 1100 C.E.	
500 B.C.E.–ca. 1000 C.E.	Bantu migrations
247 B.C.E.	Parthian rule begins in Iran
ca. 200 B.C.E.	Camel nomads in southern Sahara
128 B.C.E.	General Zhang Jian reaches Ferghana
1st cent. C.E.–270 C.E.	Kushans rule northern Afghanistan and Sogdiana
1st cent. C.E.	*Periplus of the Erythraean Sea*; Indonesian migration to Madagascar

ca. 300	Beginning of camel nomadism in northern Sahara
ca. 400	Buddhist pilgrim Faxian travels Silk Road
ca. 630	Buddhist pilgrim Xuanzang travels Silk Road
639–642	Arabs conquer Egypt
683–1025	Srivijaya trading kingdom in Southeast Asia
711	Berbers and Arabs conquer Spain
711	Arabs conquer lower Indus Valley partially by sea
740	Berber revolts; independent states in North Africa; trade develops across Sahara
8th cent.	Kingdom of Ghana begins
ca. 900	Arab and Persian merchants in Canton
907	Collapse of Tang Empire
1076	Almoravids defeat ruler of Ghana

10

THE SASANID EMPIRE AND THE RISE OF ISLAM, 200–1200

Knowledge of papermaking, which spread from China to the Middle East after Arab conquests in the seventh century C.E. established an Islamic caliphate stretching from Spain to Central Asia, provided a medium that was superior to papyrus and parchment and well suited to a variety of purposes. Maps, miniature paintings, and, of course, books became increasingly common and inexpensive. With cheaper books came bookstores, and one of the most informative manuscripts of the period of the Islamic caliphate is a *Fihrist*, or descriptive catalogue, of the books sold at one bookstore in Baghdad.

Abu al-Faraj Muhammad al-Nadim, a man with good connections at the caliph's court, compiled the catalogue, though his father probably founded the bookstore. Its latest entry dates to ca. 990, al-Nadim's death date. Superbly educated, al-Nadim wrote such well-informed comments on books and authors that his catalogue presents a detailed survey of the intellectual world of Baghdad.

The first of the *Fihrist*'s ten books deals with Arabic language and sacred scriptures: the Quran, the Torah, and the Gospel. The second covers Arabic grammar, and the third writings from people connected with the caliph's court: historians, government officials, singers, jesters, and the ruler's boon companions. *Al-Nadim* means "book companion," so it is assumed that he knew this milieu well. After dealing with Arabic poetry, Muslim sects, and Islamic law in Books 3 through 6, he comes to Greek philosophy, science, and medicine in Book 7.

Most things we would find today in a bookstore are relegated to the final three chapters. Book 8 divides into three sections, the first being "Story Tellers and Stories." Here he lists a Persian book called *A Thousand Stories*, which in translation became *The Arabian Nights*. Al-Nadim's version no longer survives. The collection we have today comes from a manuscript written five hundred years later.

Then come books about "Exorcists, Jugglers, and Magicians," followed by "Miscellaneous Subjects and Fables." These include books on "Freckles, Twitching, Moles, and Shoulders," "Horsemanship, Bearing of Arms, the Implements of War," "Veterinary Surgery," "Birds of Prey, Sport with Them and Medical Care of Them," "Interpretation of Dreams," "Perfume," "Cooked Food," "Poisons," and "Amulets and Charms."

Non-Muslim sects and foreign lands—India, Indochina, and China—fill Book 9, leaving Book 10 for a few final notes on philosophers not mentioned previously.

All together, the thousands of titles and authors commented on by al-Nadim provide both a panorama of what interested book buyers in tenth-century Baghdad and a saddening picture of how profound the loss of knowledge has been since that glorious era.

THE SASANID EMPIRE, 224–651

The rise in the third century of a new Iranian state, the **Sasanid** (SAH-suh-nid) **Empire**, continued the old rivalry between Rome and the Parthians along the Euphrates frontier. However, behind this façade of continuity, a social and economic transformation took place that set the stage for a new and powerful religiopolitical movement: Islam.

Politics and Society   Ardashir, whose dynasty takes its name from an ancestor named Sasan, defeated the Parthians around 224 and established the Sasanid kingdom. To the west, the new rulers confronted the Romans, whom later historians frequently refer to as the Byzantines after about 330. Along their desert Euphrates frontier, the Sasanids subsidized nomadic Arab chieftains to protect their empire from invasion (the Byzantines did the same with Arabs on their Jordanian desert frontier). Arab pastoralists farther to the south remained isolated and independent. The rival empires launched numerous attacks on each other across that frontier between the 340s and 628. In times of peace, however, exchange between the empires flourished, allowing goods transported over the Silk Road to enter the zone of Mediterranean trade.

The mountains and plateaus of Iran proper formed the Sasanids' political hinterland, often ruled by the cousins of the shah (king) or by powerful families descending from the pre-Sasanid Parthian nobility. Cities there were small walled communities that served more as military strong-points than as centers of population and production. Society revolved around a local aristocracy that lived on rural estates and cultivated the arts of hunting, feasting, and war just like the warriors described in the sagas of ancient kings and heroes sung at their banquets.

Despite the dominance of powerful aristocratic families, long-lasting political fragmentation of the medieval European variety did not develop (see Chapter 11). Also, although many nomads lived in the mountain and desert regions, no folk migration took place comparable to that of the Germanic peoples who defeated Roman armies and established kingdoms in formerly Roman territory from about the third century C.E. onward. The Sasanid and Byzantine Empires generally maintained central control of imperial finances and military power and found effective ways of integrating frontier peoples as mercenaries or caravaneers.

The Silk Road brought new products to Mesopotamia, some of which became part of the agricultural landscape. Sasanid farmers pioneered in planting sugar cane, rice, citrus trees, eggplants, and other crops adopted from India and China. Although the acreage devoted to new crops increased slowly, these products became important consumption and trade items during the succeeding Islamic period.

Sasanid Silver Plate with Gold Decoration *The Sasanid aristocracy, based in the countryside, invested part of its wealth in silver plates and vessels. This image of a Sasanid king hunting on horseback also reflects a favorite aristocratic pastime.*

Religion and Empire

The Sasanids established their Zoroastrian faith (see Chapter 5), which the Parthians had not particularly stressed, as a state religion similar to Christianity in the Byzantine Empire (see Chapter 11), though other faiths may have competed effectively in eastern Iran. The proclamation of Christianity and Zoroastrianism as official faiths marked the fresh emergence of religion as an instrument of politics both within and between the empires, setting a precedent for the subsequent rise of Islam as the focus of a political empire.

Both Zoroastrianism and Christianity practiced intolerance. A late-third-century inscription in Iran boasts of the persecutions of Christians, Jews, and Buddhists carried out by the Zoroastrian high priest. Yet sizable Christian and Jewish communities remained, especially in Mesopotamia. Similarly, from the fourth century onward, councils of Christian bishops declared many theological beliefs heretical—so unacceptable that they were un-Christian.

Christians then became pawns in the political rivalry with the Byzantines and were sometimes persecuted, sometimes patronized, by the Sasanid kings. In 431 a council of bishops called by the Byzantine emperor declared the Nestorian Christians heretics for overemphasizing the humanness of Christ. The Nestorians believed that human characteristics and divinity coexisted in Jesus and that Mary was not the mother of God, as many other Christians maintained, but the mother of the human Jesus. After the bishops' ruling, the Nestorians sought refuge under the Sasanid shah and eventually extended their missionary activities along the Central Asian trade routes.

In the third century a preacher named Mani founded a new religion in Mesopotamia: Manichaeism. Mani preached a dualist faith—a struggle between Good and Evil— theologically derived from Zoroastrianism. Although at first he enjoyed the favor of the shah, he and many of his followers were martyred in 276. However, his religion survived and spread widely. Nestorian missionaries in Central Asia competed with Manichaean missionaries for converts. In later centuries, the term *Manichaean* was applied to all sorts of beliefs about a cosmic struggle between Good and Evil.

The Arabs became enmeshed in this web of religious conflict. The border protectors subsidized by the Byzantines adopted a Monophysite theology, which emphasized Christ's divine nature; the allies of the Sasanids, the Nestorian faith. Through them, knowledge of Christianity penetrated deeper into the Arabian peninsula during the fifth and sixth centuries.

Religion permeated all aspects of community life. Most subjects of the Byzantine emperors and Sasanid shahs identified themselves first and foremost as members of a religious community. Their schools and law courts were religious. They looked on priests, monks, rabbis, and the Zoroastrian mobads (priests officiating in fire temples) as moral guides in daily life. Most books discussed religious subjects. In some areas, religious leaders represented their flocks even in such secular matters as tax collection.

The Origins of Islam

The Arabs of 600 C.E. lived exclusively in the Arabian peninsula and on the desert fringes of Syria, Jordan, and Iraq. Along their Euphrates frontier, the Sasanids subsidized nomadic Arab chieftains to protect their empire from invasion. The Byzantines did the same with Arabs on their Jordanian frontier. Arab pastoralists farther to the south remained isolated and independent, seldom engaging the attention of the shahs and emperors. It was in these interior Arabian lands that the religion of Islam took form.

The Arabian Peninsula Before Muhammad   Throughout history more people living on the Arabian peninsula have subsisted as farmers than as pastoral nomads. Farming villages supported the comparatively dense population of Yemen, where abundant rainfall waters the highlands during the spring monsoon. Small inlets along the southern coast favored fishing and trading communities. The enormous sea of sand known as the "Empty Quarter" isolated many southern regions from the Arabian interior. In the seventh century, most people in southern Arabia knew more about Africa,

India, and the Persian Gulf than about the forbidding interior and the scattered camel- and sheep-herding nomads who lived there.

The Arab pastoralists inhabiting the desert between Syria and Mesopotamia supplied camels and guides and played a significant role as merchants and organizers of caravans. The militarily efficient North Arabian camel saddle, developed around the third century B.C.E., provided another key to Arab prosperity. The Arabs used it to take control of the caravan trade in their territories and thereby became so important as suppliers of animal power, even in agricultural districts, that wheeled vehicles—mostly ox carts and horse-drawn chariots—had all but disappeared by the sixth century C.E.

Caravan trading provided a rare link among peoples. Nomads derived income from providing camels, guides, and safe passage to merchants bringing the primary product of the south, the aromatic resins frankincense and myrrh, to northern customers. Return caravans brought manufactured products from Mesopotamia and Syria.

Arabs who accompanied the caravans became familiar with the cultures and lifestyles of the Sasanid and Byzantine Empires, and many of those who pastured their herds on the imperial frontiers adopted one form or another of Christianity. Even in the interior deserts, Semitic polytheism, with its worship of natural forces and celestial bodies, began to encounter more sophisticated religions.

Mecca, a late-blooming caravan city, occupies a barren mountain valley halfway between Yemen and Syria and somewhat inland from the Red Sea coast. A nomadic kin group known as the Quraysh (koo-RAYSH) settled in Mecca in the fifth century and assumed control of trade. Mecca rapidly achieved a measure of prosperity, partly because it was too far from Byzantine Syria, Sasanid Iraq, and Ethiopian-controlled Yemen for them to attack it.

A cubical shrine with idols inside called the Ka'ba (KAH-buh), a holy well called Zamzam, and a sacred precinct surrounding the two wherein killing was prohibited contributed to the emergence of Mecca as a pilgrimage site. Some Meccans associated the shrine with stories known to Jews and Christians. They regarded Abraham (Ibrahim in Arabic) as the builder of the Ka'ba, and they identified a site outside Mecca as the location where God asked Abraham to sacrifice his son. The son was not Isaac (Ishaq in Arabic), the son of Sarah, but Ishmael (Isma'il in Arabic), the son of Hagar, cited in the Bible as the forefather of the Arabs.

| Muhammad in Mecca and Medina | Born in Mecca in 570, **Muhammad** grew up an orphan in the house of his uncle. He engaged in trade and married a Quraysh widow named Khadija (kah-DEE-juh), whose caravan interests he superintended. Their son died in childhood, |

but several daughters survived. Around 610 Muhammad began meditating at night in the mountainous terrain around Mecca. During one night vigil, known to later tradition as the "Night of Power and Excellence," a being whom Muhammad later understood to be the angel Gabriel (Jibra'il in Arabic) spoke to him:

> Proclaim! In the name of your Lord who created. Created man from a clot of congealed blood. Proclaim! And your Lord is the Most Bountiful. He who has taught by the pen. Taught man that which he knew not.[1]

---

[1]Quran, Sura 96, verses 1–5.

For three years Muhammad shared this and subsequent revelations only with close friends and family members. This period culminated in his conviction that he was hearing the words of God (Allah [AH-luh] in Arabic). Khadija, his uncle's son Ali, his friend Abu Bakr (ah-boo BAK-uhr), and others close to him shared this conviction. The revelations continued until Muhammad's death in 632.

Like most people of the time, including Christians and Jews, the Arabs believed in unseen spirits: gods, demonic *shaitans*, and desert spirits called *jinns* who were thought to possess seers and poets. Therefore, when Muhammad recited his rhymed revelations in public, many people believed he was inspired by an unseen spirit, even if it was not, as Muhammad asserted, the one true god.

Muhammad's earliest revelations called on people to witness that one god had created the universe and everything in it, including themselves. At the end of time, their souls would be judged, their sins balanced against their good deeds. The blameless would go to paradise; the sinful would taste hellfire:

> *By the night as it conceals the light;*
> *By the day as it appears in glory;*
> *By the mystery of the creation of male and female;*
> *Verily, the ends ye strive for are diverse.*
> *So he who gives in charity and fears God,*
> *And in all sincerity testifies to the best,*
> *We will indeed make smooth for him the path to Bliss.*
> *But he who is a greedy miser and thinks himself self-sufficient,*
> *And gives the lie to the best,*
> *We will indeed make smooth for him the path to misery.*[2]

The revelation called all people to submit to God and accept Muhammad as the last of his messengers. Doing so made one a **Muslim**, meaning one who makes "submission," **Islam**, to the will of God.

Because earlier messengers mentioned in the revelations included Noah, Moses, and Jesus, Muhammad's hearers connected his message with Judaism and Christianity, religions they were already familiar with. Yet his revelations charged the Jews and Christians with being negligent in preserving God's revealed word. Thus, even though they identified Abraham/Ibrahim, whom Muslims consider the first Muslim, as the builder of the Ka'ba, which superseded Jerusalem as the focus of Muslim prayer in 624, Muhammad's followers considered his revelation more perfect than the Bible because it had not gone through an editing process.

Some scholars maintain that Muhammad appealed especially to people distressed over wealth replacing kinship as the most important aspect of social relations and over neglect of orphans and other powerless people. Most Muslims, however, put less emphasis on a social message than on the power and beauty of Muhammad's recitations.

Mecca's leaders feared that accepting Muhammad as the sole agent of the one true God would threaten their power and prosperity. They pressured his kin to disavow him and persecuted the weakest of his followers. Stymied by this hostility, Muhammad and his followers fled Mecca in 622 to take up residence in the agricultural community of **Medina** 215 miles (346 kilometers) to the north. This hijra (HIJ-ruh) marks the beginning of the Muslim calendar.

---

[2]Quran, Sura 92, verses 1–10.

**Formation of
the Umma**

Prior to the hijra, Medinan representatives had met with Muhammad and agreed to accept and protect him and his followers because they saw him as an inspired leader who could calm their perpetual feuding. Together, the Meccan migrants and major groups in Medina bound themselves into a single **umma** (UM-muh), a community defined by acceptance of Islam and of Muhammad as the "Messenger of God," his most common title. Partly because three Jewish kin groups chose to retain their own faith, the direction of prayer was changed from Jerusalem toward the Ka'ba in Mecca, now thought of as the "House of God."

Having left their Meccan kin groups, the immigrants in Medina felt vulnerable. During the last decade of his life, Muhammad took active responsibility for his umma. Fresh revelations provided a framework for regulating social and legal affairs and stirred the Muslims to fight against the still-unbelieving city of Mecca. At various points during the war, Muhammad charged the Jewish kin groups, whom he had initially hoped would recognize him as God's messenger, with disloyalty, and he finally expelled or eliminated them. The sporadic war, largely conducted by raiding and negotiating with desert nomads, sapped Mecca's strength and convinced many Meccans that God favored Muhammad. In 630 Mecca surrendered, and Muhammad and his followers made the pilgrimage to the Ka'ba unhindered.

Muhammad stayed in Medina, which had grown into a bustling city-state. Delegations came to him from all over Arabia and returned home with believers who could teach about Islam and collect alms. Muhammad's mission to bring God's message to humanity had brought him unchallenged control of a state that was coming to dominate the Arabian peninsula.

**Succession to
Muhammad**

In 632, after a brief illness, Muhammad died. Within twenty-four hours a group of Medinan leaders, along with three of Muhammad's close friends, determined that Abu Bakr, one of the earliest believers and the father of Muhammad's favorite wife A'isha (AH-ee-shah), should succeed him. They called him the *khalifa* (kah-LEE-fuh), or "successor," the English version of which is *caliph*. But calling Abu Bakr a successor did not clarify his powers. Everyone knew that neither Abu Bakr nor anyone else could receive revelations, and they likewise knew that Muhammad's revelations made no provision for succession or for any government purpose beyond maintaining the umma.

Abu Bakr continued and confirmed Muhammad's religious practices, notably the so-called Five Pillars of Islam: (1) avowal that there is only one god and Muhammad is his messenger, (2) prayer five times a day, (3) fasting during the lunar month of Ramadan, (4) paying alms, and (5) making the pilgrimage to Mecca at least once during one's lifetime. He also reestablished and expanded Muslim authority over Arabia's communities, some of which had abandoned their allegiance to Medina or followed various would-be prophets. Muslim armies fought hard to confirm the authority of the newborn **caliphate**. In the process, some fighting spilled over into non-Arab areas in Iraq.

Reportedly, Abu Bakr ordered the men who had written down Muhammad's revelations to collect them in a book. Hitherto written haphazardly on pieces of leather or bone, these now became a single document gathered into chapters. Muslims believe the **Quran** (kuh-RAHN), or the Recitation, acquired its final form around the year 650. They see it not as the words of Muhammad but as the unalterable word of God. Theologically, it compares not so much to the Bible, a book written by many hands over many centuries, as to the person of Jesus Christ, whom Christians consider an earthly manifestation of God.

Though united in accepting God's will, the umma soon disagreed over the succession to the caliphate. When rebels assassinated the third caliph, Uthman (ooth-MAHN), in 656, and the assassins nominated Ali, Muhammad's first cousin and the husband of his daughter Fatima, to succeed him, civil war broke out. Ali had been passed over three times previously, even though many people considered him to be the Prophet's natural heir. Those who believed Ali was the Prophet's heir came to be known as **Shi'ites**, after the Arabic term *Shi'at Ali* ("Party of Ali").

When Ali accepted the nomination to be caliph, two of Muhammad's close companions and his favorite wife A'isha challenged him. Ali defeated them in the Battle of the Camel (656), so called because the fighting raged around the camel on which A'isha was seated in an enclosed woman's saddle.

After the battle, the governor of Syria, Mu'awiya (moo-AH-we-yuh), a kinsman of the slain Uthman from the Umayya clan of the Quraysh, renewed the challenge. Inconclusive battle gave way to arbitration. The arbitrators decided that Uthman, whom his assassins considered corrupt, had not deserved death and that Ali had erred in accepting the caliphate. Ali rejected these findings, but before fighting could resume, one of his own supporters killed him for agreeing to the arbitration. Mu'awiya offered Ali's son Hasan a dignified retirement and thus emerged as caliph in 661.

Mu'awiya chose his own son, Yazid, to succeed him, thereby instituting the **Umayyad** (oo-MY-ad) **Caliphate**. When Hasan's brother Husayn revolted in 680 to reestablish the right of Ali's family to rule, Yazid ordered Husayn and his family killed. Sympathy for Husayn's martyrdom helped transform Shi'ism from a political movement into a religious sect.

Several variations in Shi'ite belief developed, but Shi'ites all agree that Ali was the rightful successor to Muhammad and that God's choice as Imam, leader of the Muslim community, has always been one or another of Ali's descendants. They see the caliphal office as more secular than religious. Because the Shi'ites seldom held power, their religious feelings came to focus on outpourings of sympathy for Husayn and other martyrs and on messianic dreams that one of their Imams would someday triumph.

Those Muslims who supported the first three caliphs gradually came to be called "People of Tradition and Community"—in Arabic, *Ahl al-Sunna wa'l-Jama'a*, **Sunnis** for short. Sunnis consider the caliphs to be Imams. As for Ali's followers who had abhorred his acceptance of arbitration, they evolved into small and rebellious Kharijite sects (from *kharaja*, meaning "to secede or rebel") claiming righteousness for themselves alone. These three divisions of Islam, the last now quite minor, still survive.

THE RISE AND FALL OF THE CALIPHATE, 632–1258

The Islamic caliphate built on the conquests the Arabs carried out after Muhammad's death gave birth to a dynamic and creative religious society. By the late 800s, however, one piece after another of this huge realm broke away. Yet the idea of a caliphate, however unrealistic, remains today a touchstone of Sunni belief in the unity of the umma.

Sunni Islam never gave a single person the power to define true belief, expel heretics, and discipline clergy. Thus, unlike Christian popes and patriarchs, the caliphs had little basis for reestablishing their universal authority once they lost political and military power.

The Islamic Conquests, 634–711

Arab conquests outside Arabia began under the second caliph, Umar (r. 634–644). Arab armies wrenched Syria (636) and Egypt (639–642) away from the Byzantine Empire and defeated the last Sasanid shah, Yazdigird III (r. 632–651). After a decade-long lull, expansion began again. Tunisia fell and became the governing center from which was organized, in 711, the conquest of Spain by an Arab-led army mostly composed of Berbers from North Africa. In the same year, Sind—the southern Indus Valley in today's Pakistan—succumbed to invaders from Iraq. The Muslim dominion remained roughly stable in size for three centuries until conquest began anew in the eleventh century. India and Anatolia experienced invasions; sub-Saharan Africa and other regions saw Islam expand peacefully by trade and conversion.

Muhammad's close companions, men of political and economic sophistication inspired by his charisma, guided the conquests. The social structure and hardy nature of Arab society lent itself to flexible military operations; and the authority of Medina, reconfirmed during the caliphate of Abu Bakr, ensured obedience.

The decision made during Umar's caliphate to prohibit Arabs from assuming ownership of conquered territory proved important. Umar tied army service, with its regular pay and windfalls of booty, to residence in military camps—two in Iraq (Kufa and Basra), one in Egypt (Fustat), and one in Tunisia (Qairawan). East of Iraq, Arabs settled around small garrison towns at strategic locations and in one large garrison at Marv in present-day Turkmenistan. This policy kept the armies together and ready for action and preserved normal life in the countryside, where some three-fourths of the population lived. Only a tiny proportion of the Syrian, Egyptian, Iranian, and Iraqi populations understood the Arabic language.

The million or so Arabs who participated in the conquests over several generations constituted a small, self-isolated ruling minority living on the taxes paid by a vastly larger non-Arab, non-Muslim subject population. The Arabs had little material incentive to encourage conversion, and there is no evidence of coherent missionary efforts to spread Islam during the conquest period.

The Umayyad and Early Abbasid Caliphates, 661–850

The Umayyad caliphs presided over an Arab realm rather than a religious empire. Ruling from Damascus, their armies consisted almost entirely of Muslim Arabs. Sasanid and Byzantine administrative practices continued in force. Only gradually did the caliphs replace non-Muslim secretaries and tax officials with Muslims and introduce Arabic as the language of government. Distinctively Muslim silver and gold coins introduced at the end of the seventh century symbolized the new order. Henceforward, silver dirhams and gold dinars bearing Arabic religious phrases circulated in monetary exchanges from Morocco to the frontiers of China.

The Umayyad dynasty fell in 750 after a decade of growing unrest. Converts to Islam numbered no more than 10 percent of the indigenous population, but they were still important because of the comparatively small number of Arab warriors. These converts resented Arab social domination. In addition, non-Syrian Arabs envied the Syrian domination of caliphal affairs, and pious Muslims looked askance at the secular and even irreligious behavior of the caliphs. Finally, Shi'ites and Kharijites attacked the Umayyad family's legitimacy as rulers, launching a number of rebellions.

In 750 one rebellion, begun in 747 in the region of Khurasan (kor-uh-SAHN) in what is today northeastern Iran, overthrew the last Umayyad caliph, though one family member escaped to Spain to found an Umayyad principality there in 755. Many Shi'ites supported the rebellion, thinking they were fighting for the family of Ali. As it turned out, the family of Abbas, one of Muhammad's uncles, controlled the secret organization that coordinated the revolt. Upon victory they established the **Abbasid** (ah-BASS-id) **Caliphate**. Some of the Abbasid caliphs who ruled after 750 befriended their relatives in Ali's family, and one even flirted with transferring the caliphate to them. The Abbasid family, however, held on to the caliphate until 1258, when Mongol invaders killed the last of them in Baghdad (see Chapter 13).

Initially, the Abbasid dynasty made a fine show of leadership and piety. Theology and religious law became preoccupations at court and among a growing community of scholars devoted to interpreting the Quran, collecting the sayings of the Prophet, and compiling Arabic grammar. (In recent years, some Western scholars have maintained that the Quran, the sayings of the Prophet, and the biography of the Prophet were all composed around this time to provide a foundation myth for the regime. This reinterpretation of Islamic origins has not been generally accepted either in the scholarly community or among Muslims.) Some caliphs sponsored ambitious projects to translate great works of Greek, Persian, and Indian thought into Arabic.

With its roots among the semi-Persianized Arabs of Khurasan, the new dynasty gradually adopted the ceremonies and customs of the Sasanid shahs. Government grew increasingly complex in Baghdad, the newly built capital city on the Tigris River. As more non-Arabs converted to Islam, the ruling elite became more cosmopolitan. Greek, Iranian, Central Asian, and African cultural currents met in the capital and gave rise to an abundance of literary works, a process facilitated by the introduction of papermaking from China. Arab poets neglected the traditional odes extolling life in the desert and wrote instead wine songs (despite Islam's prohibition of alcohol) or poems in praise of their patrons.

The translation of Aristotle into Arabic, the founding of the main currents of theology and law, and the splendor of the Abbasid court—reflected in stories of *The Arabian Nights* set in the time of the caliph Harun al-Rashid (hah-ROON al-rah-SHEED) (r. 776–809)—in some respects warrant calling the early Abbasid period a "golden age." Yet the refinement of Baghdad culture only slowly made its way into the provinces. Egypt remained predominantly Christian and Coptic-speaking in the early Abbasid period. Iran never adopted Arabic as a spoken tongue. Most of Berber-speaking North Africa rebelled and freed itself of direct caliphal rule after 740.

Gradual conversion to Islam among the conquered population accelerated in the second quarter of the ninth century. Social discrimination against non-Arab converts gradually faded, and the Arabs themselves—at least those living in cosmopolitan urban settings—lost their previously strong attachment to kinship and ethnic identity.

Political Fragmentation, 850–1050

Abbasid decline became evident in the second half of the ninth century as conversion to Islam accelerated. No government ruling so vast an empire could hold power easily. Caravans traveled only 20 miles (32 kilometers) a day, and the couriers of the caliphal post system usually did not exceed 100 miles (160 kilometers) a day. News of frontier revolts took weeks to reach Baghdad. Military responses might take months.

During the first two Islamic centuries, revolts against Muslim rule had been a concern. The Muslim umma had therefore clung together, despite the long distances. But with the growing conversion of the population to Islam, fears that Islamic dominion might be overthrown faded. Once they became the overwhelming majority, Muslims realized that a highly centralized empire did not necessarily serve the interests of all the people.

By the middle of the ninth century, revolts targeting Arab or Muslim domination gave way to movements within the Islamic community concentrating on seizure of territory and formation of principalities. None of the states carved out of the Abbasid Caliphate after that time repudiated or even threatened Islam. They did, however, cut the flow of tax revenues to Baghdad, thereby increasing local prosperity.

Increasingly starved for funds by breakaway provinces and by an unexplained fall in revenues from Iraq itself, the caliphate experienced a crisis in the late ninth century. Distrusting generals and troops from outlying areas, the caliphs purchased Turkic slaves, **mamluks** (MAM-luke), from Central Asia and established them as a standing army. Well trained and hardy, the Turks proved an effective but expensive military force. When the government could not pay them, the mamluks took it on themselves to seat and unseat caliphs, a process made easier by the construction of a new capital at Samarra, north of Baghdad on the Tigris River.

The Turks dominated Samarra without interference from an unruly Baghdad populace that regarded them as rude and highhanded. However, the money and effort that went into the huge city, which was occupied only from 835 to 892, further sapped the caliphs' financial strength and deflected labor from more productive pursuits.

In 945, after several attempts to find a strongman to save it, the Abbasid Caliphate fell under the control of rude mountain warriors from Daylam in northern Iran. Led by the Shi'ite Buyid (BOO-yid) family, they conquered western Iran as well as Iraq. Each Buyid commander ruled his own principality. After two centuries of glory, the sun began to set on Baghdad. The Abbasid caliph remained, but the Buyid princes controlled him. Being Shi'ites, the Buyids had no special reverence for the Sunni caliph. The Shi'ite teachings they followed held that the twelfth and last Imam had disappeared around 873 and would return as a messiah only at the end of time. Thus they had no Shi'ite Imam to defer to and retained the caliph only to help control their predominantly Sunni subjects.

Dynamic growth in outlying provinces paralleled the caliphate's gradual loss of temporal power. In the east in 875, the dynasty of the Samanids (sah-MAN-id), one of several Iranian families to achieve independence, established a glittering court in Bukhara, a major city on the Silk Road. Samanid princes patronized literature and learning, but the language they favored was Persian written in Arabic letters. For the first time, a non-Arabic literature rose to challenge the eminence of Arabic within the Islamic world.

In the west, the Berber revolts against Arab rule led to the appearance after 740 of the city-states of Sijilmasa (sih-jil-MAS-suh) and Tahert (TAH-hert) on the northern fringe of the Sahara. The Kharijite beliefs of these states' rulers interfered with their east-west overland trade and led them to develop the first regular trade across the Sahara desert (see Chapter 9). Once traders looked to the desert, they discovered that Berber speakers in the southern Sahara were already carrying salt from the desert into the Sahel region. The northern traders found that they could trade salt for gold by providing the southern nomads, who controlled the salt sources but had little use for gold, with more useful products, such as copper and manufactured goods. Sijilmasa and Tahert became wealthy cities, the former minting gold coins that circulated as far away as Egypt and Syria.

The earliest known sub-Saharan beneficiary of the new exchange system was the kingdom of **Ghana** (GAH-nuh). It first appears in an Arabic text of the late eighth century as the "land of gold." Few details survive about the early years of this realm, which was established by the Soninke (soh-NIN-kay) people and covered parts of Mali, Mauritania, and Senegal, but it prospered until 1076, when it was conquered by nomads from the desert. It was one of the first lands outside the orbit of the caliphate to experience a gradual and peaceful conversion to Islam.

MAP 10.1 Rise and Fall of the Abbasid Caliphate

Though Abbasid rulers occupied the caliphal seat in Iraq from 750 to 1258, when Mongol armies destroyed Baghdad, real political power waned sharply and steadily after 850. The rival caliphates of the Fatimids (909–1171) and Spanish Umayyads (929–976) were comparatively short-lived.

The North African city-states lost their independence after the Fatimid (FAH-tuh-mid) dynasty, whose members claimed (perhaps falsely) to be Shi'ite Imams descended from Ali, established itself in Tunisia in 909. After consolidating their hold on northwest Africa, the Fatimids culminated their rise to power by conquering Egypt in 969. Claiming the title of caliph in a direct challenge to the Abbasids, the Fatimid rulers governed from a palace complex outside the old conquest-era garrison city of Fustat (fuss-TAHT). They named the complex Cairo. For the first time Egypt became a major cultural, intellectual, and political center of Islam. The abundance of Fatimid gold coinage, now channeled to Egypt from West Africa, made the Fatimids an economic power in the Mediterranean.

Cut off from the rest of the Islamic world by the Strait of Gibraltar and, from 740 onward, by independent city-states in Morocco and Algeria, Umayyad Spain developed a distinctive Islamic culture blending Roman, Germanic, and Jewish traditions with those of the Arabs and Berbers. Historians disagree on how rapidly and completely the Spanish population converted to Islam. If we assume a process similar to that in the eastern regions, it seems likely that the most rapid surge in Islamization occurred in the middle of the tenth century.

As in the east, governing cities symbolized the Islamic presence in al-Andalus, as the Muslims called their Iberian territories. Cordoba, Seville, Toledo, and other cities grew substantially, becoming much larger and richer than contemporary cities in neighboring France. Converts to Islam and their descendants, unconverted Arabic-speaking Christians, and Jews joined with the comparatively few descendants of Arab settlers to create new architectural and literary styles. In the countryside, where the Berbers preferred to settle, a fusion of preexisting agricultural technologies with new crops, notably citrus fruits, and irrigation techniques from the east gave Spain the most diverse and sophisticated agricultural economy in Europe.

The rulers of al-Andalus took the title *caliph* only in 929, when Abd al-Rahman (AHB-d al–ruh-MAHN) III (r. 912–961) did so in response to a similar declaration by the newly established (909) Fatimid ruler in Tunisia. By the century's end, however, this caliphate encountered challenges from breakaway movements that eventually splintered al-Andalus into a number of small states. Political decay did not impede cultural growth. Some of the greatest writers and thinkers in Jewish history worked in Muslim Spain in the eleventh and twelfth centuries, sometimes writing in Arabic, sometimes in Hebrew. Judah Halevi (1075–1141) composed exquisite poetry and explored questions of religious philosophy. Maimonides (1135–1204) made a major compilation of Judaic law and expounded on Aristotelian philosophy. At the same time, Islamic thought in Spain attained its loftiest peaks in Ibn Hazm's (994–1064) treatises on love and other subjects, the Aristotelian philosophical writings of Ibn Rushd (IB-uhn RUSHED) (1126–1198, known in Latin as Averroës [uh-VERR-oh-eez]) and Ibn Tufayl (IB-uhn too-FILE) (d. 1185), and the mystic speculations of Ibn al-Arabi (IB-uhn ahl–AH-rah-bee) (1165–1240). Christians, too, shared in the intellectual and cultural dynamism of al-Andalus. Translations from Arabic to Latin made during this period had a profound effect on the later intellectual development of western Europe (see Chapter 11).

The Samanids, Fatimids, and Spanish Umayyads, three of many regional principalities, represent the political diversity and awakening of local awareness that coincided with Abbasid decline. Yet drawing and redrawing political boundaries did not result in the rigid division of the Islamic world into kingdoms. Religious and cultural developments, particularly the rise in cities of a social group of religious scholars known as the **ulama** (oo-leh-MAH)—Arabic for "people with (religious) knowledge"—worked against any permanent division of the Islamic umma.

Assault from Within and Without, 1050–1258   The role played by Turkish mamluks in the decline of Abbasid power established an enduring stereotype of the Turk as a ferocious, unsophisticated warrior. This image gained strength in the 1036 when the Seljuk (sel-JOOK) family established a Turkish Muslim state based on nomadic power. Taking the Arabic title *Sultan*, meaning "power," and the revived Persian title *Shahan-shah*, or King of Kings, the Seljuk ruler Tughril (TUUG-ruhl) Beg created a kingdom that stretched from northern Afghanistan to Baghdad, which he occupied in 1055. After a century under the thumb of the Shi'ite Buyids, the Abbasid caliph breathed easier under the slightly lighter thumb of the Sunni Turks. The Seljuks pressed on into Syria and Anatolia, administering a lethal blow to Byzantine power at the Battle of Manzikert (MANZ-ih-kuhrt) in 1071. The Byzantine army fell back on Constantinople, leaving Anatolia open to Turkish occupation.

Under Turkish rule, which coincided with a severe climatic cooling that reduced harvests in Iran, Iraq, and eastern Anatolia, cities shrank as pastoralists overran their agricultural hinterlands. Irrigation works suffered from lack of maintenance in the unsettled countryside. Tax revenues fell. Quarreling twelfth-century princes fought over cities, but few Turks participated in urban cultural and religious life.

Tomb of the Samanids in Bukhara *This early-tenth-century structure has the basic layout of a Zoroastrian fire temple: a dome on top of a cube. However, geometric ornamentation in baked brick marks it as an early masterpiece of Islamic architecture. The Samanid family achieved independence as rulers of northeastern Iran and western Central Asia in the tenth century.*

The gulf between a religiously based urban society and the culture and personnel of the government deepened. When factional riots broke out between Sunnis and Shi'ites, or between rival schools of Sunni law, rulers generally remained aloof, even as destruction and loss of life mounted.

By the early twelfth century, unrepaired damage from floods, fires, and civil disorder had reduced old Baghdad on the west side of the Tigris to ruins. The withering of Baghdad reflected a broader environmental problem: the collapse of the canal system on which agriculture in the Tigris and Euphrates Valley depended. For millennia a center of world civilization, Mesopotamia underwent substantial population loss and never again regained its geographical importance.

The Turks alone cannot be blamed for the demographic and economic misfortunes of Iran and Iraq. Too-robust urbanization, spurred largely by a boom in Iranian cotton production, resulted in strained food resources when the climate deteriorated after 1000. Baghdad, a city with a torrid climate today, experienced heavy winter snowfalls that killed date trees. In addition, the growing practice of paying soldiers and courtiers with land grants led to absentee landlords using agents to collect taxes. These agents gouged villagers to meet their quotas and took little interest in improving production, thus intensifying the agricultural crisis.

Internecine feuding was preoccupying the Seljuk family when the first Christian Crusaders reached the Holy Land and captured Jerusalem in 1099 (see Chapter 11). Though charged with the stuff of romance, the Crusades had little lasting impact on the Islamic lands. The four Crusader principalities of Edessa, Antioch, Tripoli, and Jerusalem simply became pawns in the shifting pattern of politics already in place. Newly arrived knights eagerly attacked the Muslim enemy, whom they called "Saracens" (SAR-uh-suhn); but veteran Crusaders recognized that practicing diplomacy and seeking partners of convenience among rival Muslim princes offered a sounder strategy.

The Muslims finally unified to face the European enemy in the mid-twelfth century. Nur al-Din ibn Zangi (NOOR uhd–DEEN ib-uhn ZAN-gee) established a strong state based in Damascus and sent an army to terminate the Fatimid Caliphate in Egypt. A nephew of the Kurdish commander of that expedition, Salah-al-Din, known in the West as Saladin, took advantage of Nur al-Din's timely death to seize power and unify Egypt and Syria. The Fatimid dynasty fell in 1171. In 1187 Saladin recaptured Jerusalem from the Europeans. He then took the title Khadim al-Haramain (KAH-dim al–ha-ra-MAYN), literally "Servant of the Two Holy Places," meaning Mecca and Medina, in a challenge to the caliph's claim to be the paramount Sunni potentate. Revitalizing the pilgrimage became a core concern for later rulers in Egypt and Syria, particularly after the termination of the Baghdad caliphate in 1258.

Saladin's descendants fought off subsequent Crusades. After one such battle, however, in 1250, Turkish mamluk troops seized control of the government in Cairo, ending Saladin's dynasty. In 1260 these mamluks rode east to confront a new invading force. At the Battle of Ain Jalut (ine jah-LOOT) (Spring of Goliath) in Syria, they met and defeated an army of Mongols from Central Asia (see Chapter 13), thus stemming an invasion that had begun several decades before and legitimizing their claim to dominion over Egypt and Syria.

During the ensuing Mamluk period a succession of slave-soldier sultans ruled Egypt and Syria until 1517. Fear of new Mongol attacks receded after 1300, but by then the new ruling system had become fixed. Young Turkish or Circassian slaves, the latter from the eastern end of the Black Sea, were imported from non-Muslim lands, raised in training barracks, and converted to Islam. Owing loyalty to the Mamluk officers who purchased them, they formed a military class that was socially disconnected from the Arabic-speaking native population.

The Mongol invasions, especially their destruction of the Abbasid Caliphate in Baghdad in 1258, shocked the world of Islam. The Mamluk sultan enthroned a relative of the last Baghdad caliph in Cairo, but the Egyptian Abbasids were mere puppets serving Mamluk interests. From Iraq eastward, non-Muslim rule lasted for much of the thirteenth century. Although the Mongols left few ethnic or linguistic traces in these lands, their initial destruction of cities and slaughter of civilian populations, their diversion of Silk Road trade from Baghdad to more northerly routes ending at Black Sea ports, and their casual disregard, even after conversion to Islam, for Muslim religious life and urban culture hastened currents of change already under way.

ISLAMIC CIVILIZATION

Though increasingly unsettled in its political dimension and subject to economic disruptions caused by war, the ever-expanding Islamic world underwent a fruitful evolution in law, social structure, and religious expression. Religious conversion and urbanization reinforced each other to create a distinct Islamic civilization. The immense geographical and human diversity of the Muslim lands allowed many "small traditions" to coexist with the developing "great tradition" of Islam.

Law and Dogma   The Shari'a, the law of Islam, provides the foundation of Islamic civilization. Yet aside from certain Quranic verses conveying specific divine ordinances—most pertaining to personal and family matters—Islam had no legal system in the time of Muhammad. Arab custom and the Prophet's own authority offered the only guidance. After Muhammad died, the umma tried to follow his example. This became harder and harder to do, however, as those who knew Muhammad best passed away and many Arabs found themselves living in far-off lands. Non-Arab converts to Islam, who at first tried to follow Arab customs they had little familiarity with, had an even harder time.

Islam slowly developed laws to govern social and religious life. The full sense of Islamic civilization, however, goes well beyond the basic Five Pillars mentioned earlier. Some Muslim thinkers felt that the reasoned consideration of a mature man offered the best resolution of issues not covered by Quranic revelation. Others argued for the sunna, or tradition, of the Prophet as the best guide. To understand that sunna they collected and studied thousands of reports, called **hadith** (hah-DEETH), purporting to convey the precise words or deeds of Muhammad. It became customary to precede each hadith with a chain of oral authorities leading back to the person who had direct acquaintance with the Prophet.

Many hadith dealt with ritual matters, such as how to wash before prayer. Others provided answers to legal questions not covered by Quranic revelation or suggested principles for deciding such matters. By the eleventh century most legal thinkers had accepted the idea that Muhammad's personal behavior provided the best role model and that the hadith constituted the most authoritative basis for law after the Quran itself.

Yet the hadith posed a problem because the tens of thousands of anecdotes included both genuine and invented reports, the latter sometimes politically motivated, as well as stories derived from non-Muslim religious traditions. Only a specialist could hope to separate a sound from a weak tradition. As the hadith grew in importance, so did the branch of learning devoted to their analysis. Scholars discarded thousands for having faulty chains of authority. The most reliable they collected into books that gradually achieved authoritative status. Sunnis placed six books in this category; Shi'ites, four.

As it gradually evolved, the Shari'a embodied a vision of an umma in which all subscribed to the same moral values and political and ethnic distinctions lost importance. Every Muslim ruler was expected to abide by and enforce the religious law. In practice, this expectation often lost out in the hurly-burly of political life. But the Shari'a proved an important basis for an urban lifestyle that varied surprisingly little from Morocco to India.

Converts and Cities

Conversion to Islam, more the outcome of people's learning about the new rulers' religion than an escape from the tax on non-Muslims, as some scholars have suggested, helped spur urbanization. Conversion did not require extensive knowledge of the faith. To become a Muslim, a person simply stated, in the presence of a Muslim: "There is no God but God, and Muhammad is the Messenger of God."

Few converts spoke Arabic, and fewer could read the Quran. Many converts knew no more of the Quran than the verses they memorized for daily prayers. Muhammad had established no priesthood to define and spread the faith. Thus new converts, whether Arab or non-Arab, faced the problem of finding out for themselves what Islam was about and how they should act as Muslims. This meant spending time with Muslims, learning their language, and imitating their practices.

In many areas, conversion involved migrating to an Arab governing center. The alternative, converting to Islam but remaining in one's home community, was difficult because religion had become the main component of social identity in Byzantine and Sasanid times. Converts to Islam thus encountered discrimination if they stayed in their Christian, Jewish, or Zoroastrian communities. Migration both averted discrimination and took advantage of the economic opportunities opened up by tax revenues flowing into the Arab governing centers.

The Arab military settlements of Kufa and Basra in Iraq blossomed into cities and became important centers for Muslim cultural activities. As conversion rapidly spread in the mid-ninth century, urbanization accelerated in other regions, most visibly in Iran, where most cities previously had been quite small. Nishapur in the northeast grew from fewer than 10,000 pre-Islamic inhabitants to between 100,000 and 200,000 by the year 1000. Other Iranian cities experienced similar growth. In Iraq, Baghdad and Mosul joined Kufa and Basra as major cities. In Syria, Aleppo and Damascus flourished under Muslim rule. Fustat in Egypt developed into Cairo, one of the largest and greatest Islamic cities. The primarily Christian patriarchal cities of Jerusalem, Antioch, and Alexandria, not being Muslim governing centers, shrank and stagnated.

Conversion-related migration meant that cities became heavily Muslim before the countryside did. This reinforced the urban orientation deriving from the fact that Muhammad and his first followers came from the commercial city of Mecca. Mosques in large cities served both as ritual centers and as places for learning and social activities.

Islam colored all aspects of urban social life (see Diversity and Dominance: Secretaries, Turks, and Beggars). Initially the new Muslims imitated Arab dress and customs, particularly favoring plain linen or cotton over the silk brocade of the non-Muslim Iranian elite, and emulated people they regarded as particularly pious. In the absence of a central religious authority, local variations developed in the way people practiced Islam and in the hadith they attributed to the Prophet. This gave the rapidly growing religion the flexibility to accommodate many different social situations.

By the tenth century, urban growth was affecting the countryside by expanding the consumer market. Citrus fruits, rice, and sugar cane, introduced by the Sasanids, increased in acreage and spread to new areas. Cotton became a major crop in Iran and elsewhere and stimulated textile production. Irrigation works expanded. Abundant coinage facilitated a flourishing intercity and long-distance trade that provided regular links between isolated districts and integrated the pastoral nomads, who provided pack animals, into the region's economy. Trade encouraged the manufacture of cloth, metal goods, and pottery.

Women Playing Chess in Muslim Spain *As shown in this thirteenth-century miniature, women in their own quarters, without men present, wore whatever clothes and jewels they liked. Notice the henna decorating the hands of the woman in the middle. The woman on the left, probably a slave, plays an oud.*

Album/Art Resource, NY

Science and technology also flourished. Building on Hellenistic traditions and their own observations and experience, Muslim doctors and astronomers developed skills and theories far in advance of their European counterparts. Working in Egypt in the eleventh century, the mathematician and physicist Ibn al-Haytham (IB-uhn al–HY-tham) wrote more than a hundred works. Among other things, he determined that the Milky Way lies far beyond earth's atmosphere, proved that light travels from a seen object to the eye and not the reverse, and explained why the sun and moon appear larger on the horizon than overhead.

Women and Islam   Women seldom traveled. Those living in rural areas worked in the fields and tended animals. Urban women, particularly members of the elite, lived in seclusion and did not leave their homes without covering themselves. Seclusion of women and veiling in public already existed in Byzantine and Sasanid times. Through interpretation of specific verses from the Quran, these practices now became fixtures of Muslim social life. Although women sometimes became literate and studied with relatives, they did so away from the gaze of unrelated men, and while they played influential roles within the family, public roles were generally barred. Only slave women could perform before unrelated men as musicians and dancers. A man could have sexual relations with as many slave concubines as he pleased, in addition to marrying as many as four wives.

Muslim women fared better legally under Islamic law than did Christian and Jewish women under their respective religious codes. Because Islamic law guaranteed daughters a share in inheritance equal to half that of a son, the majority of women inherited some amount of money or real estate. This remained their private property to keep or sell. Muslim law put the financial burden of supporting a family exclusively on the husband, who could not legally compel his wife to help out.

Women could also remarry if their husbands divorced them, and they received a cash payment upon divorce. Although a man could divorce his wife without stating a cause, a woman could initiate divorce under specified conditions. Women could also practice birth control. They could testify in court, although their testimony counted as half that of a man. They could go on pilgrimage. Nevertheless, a misogynistic tone sometimes appears in Islamic writings. One saying attributed to the Prophet observed: "I was raised up to heaven and saw that most of its denizens were poor people; I was raised into the hellfire and saw that most of its denizens were women."[3]

In the absence of writings by women about women from this period, the status of women must be deduced from the writings of men. Two episodes involving the Prophet's wife A'isha, the daughter of Abu Bakr, provide examples of how Muslim men appraised women in society. Only eighteen when Muhammad died, A'isha lived for another fifty years. Early reports stress her status as Muhammad's favorite, the only virgin he married and the only wife to see the angel Gabriel. These reports emanate from A'isha herself, who was an abundant source of hadith. As a fourteen-year-old she had become separated from a caravan and rejoined it only after traveling through the night with a man who found her alone in the desert. Gossips accused her of being untrue to the Prophet, but a revelation from God

---

[3]Richard W. Bulliet, *Islam: The View from the Edge* (New York: Columbia University Press, 1994), 87.

DIVERSITY + DOMINANCE

Secretaries, Turks, and Beggars

The passages below fall into the category of Arabic literature known as adab, or belles-lettres. The purpose of adab was to entertain and instruct through a succession of short anecdotes, verses, and expository discussions. It attracted the finest writers of the Abbasid era and affords one of the richest sources for looking at everyday life, always keeping in mind that the intended readers were a restricted class of educated men, including merchants, court and government officials, and even men of religion.

One of the greatest masters of Arabic prose, Jahiz (776–869), was a famously ugly man—his name means "Popeyed"— of Abyssinian family origin. Spending part of his life in his native Basra, in southern Iraq, and part in Baghdad, the Abbasid capital, he wrote voluminously on subjects ranging from theology to zoology to miserliness. These excerpts are from two of his short essays, "Censure of the Conduct of Secretaries" and "The Virtues of the Turks."

Censure of the Conduct of Secretaries

Furthermore, the foundation on which writing is based [is] that only a subordinate should take [it] up and only one who is in a sense a servant [can] master it. We have never seen an important person undertake it for its own sake or share in his secretary's work. Every secretary is required to be loyal and requested to bear hardship patiently. The most diverse conditions are imposed on him and he is sorely tried. The secretary has no right to set any of those conditions. On the contrary, he is thought slow at the first lapse even if exhausted and censured at the first error even if unintentional. A slave is entitled to many complaints against his master. He can request his sale to another if he wishes. The secretary has no way to lay claim to his late back

wages or to leave his patron if he acts unfairly. He is governed by the rules for slaves. His status is that of a dolt.

It should be enough for you to know of this group that the noblest of them is at the bottom of the pay scale. The most wealthy of them are the least regarded by the ruler. The head of the secretariat who acts as spokesman to the nation earns a tenth of the income of the head of land tax. The scribe whose handwriting lends beauty to the communications of the caliph earns a fraction of the income of the head copyist in the land tax bureau. The correspondence secretary is not fetched for a disaster nor is his aid sought in a crisis. When the ministers have settled on a course of action and agreed in their appraisal, a note is tossed him with the gist of the order. He prepares the text. When he has finished his editing and straightened out the words, he brings in his copyist. He sits as near as anyone to the caliph, in a restricted location away from visitors. Once that task is completed, however, there is no difference between those two scribes and the common people.

The Virtues of the Turks

The Turk has with him at the moment of attack everything he needs for himself, his weapons, his mount, and equipment for it. His endurance is quite amazing for long riding, continuous travel, lengthy night trips, and crossing a land.... The Turk is more skilled than the veterinarian and better at teaching his mount what he wants than trainers. He bred it and raised it as a foal. It followed him if he called and galloped behind him when he galloped.... If you sum up the life of the Turk and reckon his days you will find he sits longer on the back of his mount than on the face of the earth.

If he is unable to hunt people, he hunts wild animals. If he is unsuccessful in that or needs nourishment, he bleeds one of his riding animals. If thirsty he milks one of his mares. If he wants to rest the one under him he mounts another without touching the ground. There is no one on earth besides him whose body would not reel against eating only meat. His mount is likewise satisfied with stubble, grass, and shrubs. He does not shade it from the sun or cover it against the cold....

The Turk is a herdsman, groom, trainer, trader, veterinarian, and rider. A single Turk is a nation in himself.

Though rulers, warriors, and religious scholars dominate the traditional narratives, the society that developed over the early centuries of Islam was remarkably diverse. Beggars, tricksters, and street performers belonged to a single loose fraternity: the Banu Sasan, or Tribe of Sasan. Tales of their tricks and exploits amused staid, pious Muslims, who often encountered them in cities and on their scholarly travels. The tenth-century poet Abu Dulaf al-Khazraji, who lived in Iran, studied the jargon of the Banu Sasan and their way of life and composed a long poem in which he cast himself as one of the group. However, he added a commentary to each verse to explain the jargon words that his sophisticated court audience would have found unfamiliar.

We are the beggars' brotherhood, and no one can deny us our lofty pride....
And of our number is the feigned madman and mad woman, with metal charms strung from their necks.
And the ones with ornaments drooping from their ears, and with collars of leather or brass round their necks....
And the one who simulates a festering internal wound, and the people with false bandages round their heads and sickly, jaundiced faces.

And the one who slashes himself, alleging that he has been mutilated by assailants, or the one who darkens his skin artificially pretending that he has been beaten up and wounded....
And the one who practices as a manipulator and quack dentist, or who escapes from chains wound round his body, or the one who uses almost invisible silk thread mysteriously to draw off rings....
And of our number are those who claim to be refugees from the Byzantine frontier regions, those who go round begging on pretext of having left behind captive families....
And the one who feigns an internal discharge, or who showers the passers-by with his urine, or who farts in the mosque and makes a nuisance of himself, thus wheedling money out of people....
And of our number are the ones who purvey objects of veneration made from clay, and those who have their beards smeared with red dye.
And the one who brings up secret writing by immersing it in what looks like water, and the one who similarly brings up the writing by exposing it to burning embers.

Questions for Analysis

1. Why might the ruling elite have found the descriptions of diverse social groups entertaining?
2. What role does religion appear to play in the culture that patronized this type of literature?
3. How does the personality of the author show up in these passages?

Sources: First selection excerpts from *Nine Essays of al-Jahiz*, trans. William M. Hutchins, pp. 56, 64, 196. Copyright © 1989. Second selection excerpts from Clifford Edmund Bosworth, *The Mediaeval Islamic Underworld: The Banu Sasan in Arabic Society and Literature*, pp. 191–199. Copyright © 1976.

proved her innocence. The second event was her participation in the Battle of the Camel, fought to derail Ali's caliphate. These two episodes came to epitomize what Muslim men feared most about women: sexual infidelity and meddling in politics. Even though the earliest literature dealing with A'isha stresses her position as Muhammad's favorite, his first wife, Khadija, and his daughter, Ali's wife Fatima, eventually surpassed A'isha as ideal women. Both appear as model wives and mothers with no suspicion of sexual irregularity or political manipulation.

As the seclusion of women became commonplace in urban Muslim society, some writers extolled homosexual relationships, partly because a male lover could appear in public or go on a journey. Although Islam deplored homosexuality, one ruler wrote a book advising his son to follow moderation in all things and thus share his affections equally between men and women. Another ruler and his slave-boy became models of perfect love in the verses of mystic poets.

Islam allowed slavery but forbade Muslims from enslaving other Muslims or so-called People of the Book—Jews, Christians, and Zoroastrians, who revered holy books respected by the Muslims. Being enslaved as a prisoner of war, a fate that befell many women captured in the camps of defeated armies, constituted an exception. Later centuries saw a constant flow of slaves into Islamic territory from Africa and Central Asia. A hereditary slave society, however, did not develop. Usually slaves converted to Islam, and many masters then freed them as an act of piety. The offspring of slave women and Muslim men were born free.

The Recentering of Islam

Early Islam centered on the caliphate, the political expression of the unity of the umma. No formal organization or hierarchy, however, directed the process of conversion. Thus there emerged a multitude of local Islamic communities so disconnected from each other that numerous competing interpretations of the developing religion arose. Inevitably, the centrality of the caliphate diminished. The appearance of rival caliphates in Tunisia and Córdoba accentuated the problem of decentralization.

The rise of the ulama as community leaders did not prevent growing fragmentation because the ulama themselves divided into contentious factions. During the twelfth century factionalism began to abate, and new socioreligious institutions, including a revitalized pilgrimage to Mecca, emerged to provide the umma with a different sort of religious center. These new developments stemmed in part from an exodus of religious scholars from Iran in response to economic and political disintegration during the late eleventh and twelfth centuries. The flow of Iranians to the Arab lands and to newly conquered territories in India and Anatolia increased after the Mongol invasion.

Fully versed in Arabic as well as their native Persian, immigrant scholars were warmly received. They brought with them a view of religion developed in Iran's urban centers. A type of religious college, the *madrasa* (MAH-dras-uh), gained sudden popularity outside Iran, where madrasas had been known since the tenth century. Scores of madrasas, many founded by local rulers, appeared throughout the Islamic world. In the fourteenth century, Mecca became a major educational center for the first time since Muhammad's generation.

Iranians also contributed to the growth of mystic groups known as *Sufi* brotherhoods in the twelfth and thirteenth centuries. The doctrines and rituals of certain

Quran Page Printed from a Woodblock

Printing from woodblocks or tin plates existed in Islamic lands between approximately 800 and 1400. Most prints were narrow amulets designed to be rolled and worn around the neck in cylindrical cases. Less valued than handwritten amulets, many prints came from Banu Sasan con men. Why block-printing had so little effect on society in general and eventually disappeared is unknown.

By permission of the Syndics of Cambridge University Library

Sufis spread from city to city, giving rise to the first geographically extensive Islamic religious organizations. Sufi doctrines varied, but a quest for a sense of union with God through rituals and training was a common denominator. Sufism had begun in early Islamic times and had doubtless benefited from the ideas and beliefs of people from religions with mystic traditions who converted to Islam.

The early Sufis had been saintly individuals given to ecstatic and poetic utterances and wonder-working. They attracted disciples but did not try to organize them. The growth of brotherhoods, a less ecstatic form of Sufism, set a tone for society in general. It soon became common for most Muslim men, particularly in the cities, to belong to at least one brotherhood.

A sense of the social climate the Sufi brotherhoods fostered can be gained from a twelfth-century manual:

> Every limb has its own special ethics.... The ethics of the tongue. The tongue should always be busy in reciting God's names (dhikr) and in saying good things of the brethren, praying for them, and giving them counsel.... The ethics of hearing. One should

not listen to indecencies and slander.... The ethics of sight. One should lower one's eyes in order not to see forbidden things.[4]

Special dispensations allowed people who merely wanted to emulate the Sufis and enjoy their company to follow less demanding rules:

It is allowed by way of dispensation to possess an estate or to rely on a regular income. The Sufis' rule in this matter is that one should not use all of it for himself, but should dedicate this to public charities and should take from it only enough for one year for himself and his family....

There is a dispensation allowing one to watch all kinds of amusement. This is, however, limited by the rule: What you are forbidden from doing, you are also forbidden from watching.[5]

Some Sufi brotherhoods spread in the countryside, and local shrines and pilgrimages to the tombs of Muhammad's descendants and saintly Sufis became popular.

CONCLUSION

The Sasanid Empire that held sway in Iran and Iraq from the third to the seventh century resembled the contemporary realm of the eastern Roman emperors ruling from Constantinople. Both states forged strong relations between the ruler and the dominant religion, Zoroastrianism in the former empire, Christianity in the latter. Priestly hierarchies paralleled state administrative structures, and the citizenry came to think of themselves more as members of a faith community than as subjects of a ruler. This gave rise to conflict among religious sects and also raised the possibility of the founder of a new religion commanding both political and religious loyalty on an unprecedented scale. This possibility was realized in the career of the prophet Muhammad in the seventh century.

Islam culminated the trend toward identity based on religion. The concept of the umma united all Muslims in a universal community embracing enormous diversity of language, appearance, and social custom. Though Muslim communities adapted to local "small traditions," by the twelfth century a religious scholar could travel anywhere in the Islamic world and blend easily into the local Muslim community.

By the ninth century, the forces of conversion and urbanization fostered social and religious experimentation in urban settings. From the eleventh century onward, political disruption, the spread of pastoral nomadism, and climatic deterioration slowed this early economic and technological dynamism. Muslim communities then turned to new religious institutions, such as the madrasas and Sufi brotherhoods, to create the flexible and durable community structures that carried Islam into new regions and protected ordinary believers from capricious political rule.

---

[4]Abu Najib al-Suhrawardi, *A Sufi Rule for Novices*, trans. Menahem Milson (Cambridge, MA: Harvard University Press, 1975), 45–58.
[5]Ibid., 73–82.

IMPORTANT EVENTS 200–1200

224–651	Sasanid Empire
634	Conquests of Iraq and Syria commence
639–42	Conquest of Egypt by Arabs
656–61	Ali caliph; first civil war
661–750	Umayyad Caliphate rules from Damascus
711	Berbers and Arabs invade Spain from North Africa
711	Arabs capture Sind in India
747	Abbasid revolt begins in Khurasan
750	Beginning of Abbasid Caliphate
755	Umayyad state established in Spain
835–92	Abbasid capital moved from Baghdad to Samarra
875	Independent Samanid state founded in Bukhara
909	Fatimids seize North Africa, found Shi'ite Caliphate
929	Abd al-Rahman III declares himself caliph in Cordoba
945	Shi'ite Buyids take control in Baghdad
945	Buyids from northern Iran take control of Abbasid Caliphate
969	Fatimids conquer Egypt
1036	Beginning of Turkish Seljuk rule in Khurasan
1055	Seljuk Turks take control in Baghdad
1099	First Crusade captures Jerusalem
1171	Fall of Fatimid Egypt
1187	Saladin recaptures Jerusalem
1250	Mamluks control Egypt
1258	Mongols sack Baghdad and end Abbasid Caliphate
1260	Mamluks defeat Mongols at Ain Jalut

11

CHRISTIAN SOCIETIES EMERGE IN EUROPE, 600–1200

C hristmas Day in 800 found Charles, king of the Franks, in Rome instead of at his palace at Aachen in northwestern Germany. At six-foot-three, Charles towered over the average man of his time, and his royal career had been equally gargantuan. Crowned king in his mid-twenties in 768, he had crisscrossed Europe for three decades, waging war on Muslim invaders from Spain, Avar (ah-vahr) invaders from Hungary, and a number of German princes.

Charles had subdued many enemies and had become protector of the papacy. So not all historians believe the eyewitness report of his secretary and biographer that Charles was surprised when, as the king rose from his prayers, Pope Leo III placed a new crown on his head. "Life and victory to Charles the August, crowned by God the great and pacific Emperor of the Romans," proclaimed the pope.[1] Then, amid the cheers of the crowd, he humbly knelt before the new emperor.

Charlemagne (SHAHR-leh-mane) (from Latin *Carolus magnus,* "Charles the Great") was the first in western Europe to bear the title *emperor* in over three hundred years. Rome's decline and Charlemagne's rise marked a shift of focus for Europe—away from the Mediterranean and toward the north and west. German custom and Christian piety transformed the Roman heritage to create a new civilization. While the memory of Greek and Roman philosophy faded, Irish monks preaching in Latin became important intellectual influences in some parts of Europe. Urban life continued the decline that had begun in the later days of the Roman Empire. Historians originally called this era "**medieval**," literally "middle age," because it comes between the era of Greco-Roman civilization and the intellectual, artistic, and economic changes of the Renaissance in the fourteenth century; but research has uncovered many aspects of medieval culture that are as rich and creative as those that came earlier and later.

Charlemagne was not the only ruler in Europe to claim the title emperor. Another emperor held sway in the Greek-speaking east, where Rome's political and legal heritage continued. The Eastern Roman Empire was often called the **Byzantine Empire** after the seventh century, and it was known to the Muslims as

---

[1]Lewis G. M. Thorpe, *Two Lives of Charlemagne* (Harmondsworth, England: Penguin, 1969).

Rum (room). While western Europeans lived amid the ruins of empire, the Byzantines maintained and reinterpreted Roman traditions. The authority of the Byzantine emperors blended with the influence of the Christian church to form a cultural synthesis that helped shape the emerging kingdom of **Kievan Russia**. Byzantium's centuries-long conflict with Islam helped spur the crusading passion that overtook western Europe in the eleventh century.

The comparison between western and eastern Europe appears paradoxical. Byzantium inherited a robust and self-confident late Roman society and economy, while western Europe could not achieve political unity and suffered severe economic decline. Yet by 1200 western Europe was showing renewed vitality and flexing its military muscles, while Byzantium was showing signs of decline and military weakness. As we explore the causes and consequences of these different historical paths, we must remember that the emergence of Christian Europe included both developments.

THE BYZANTINE EMPIRE, 600–1200

The Byzantine emperors established Christianity as their official religion (see Chapter 6). They also represented a continuation of Roman imperial rule and tradition that was largely absent in the kingdoms that succeeded Rome in the west. Whereas only provincial forms of Roman law survived in the west, Byzantium inherited imperial law intact. Combining the imperial role with political oversight over the Christian church, the emperors made a comfortable transition into the role of all-powerful Christian monarchs. The Byzantine drama, however, played on a steadily shrinking stage. Territorial losses and almost constant military pressure from north and south deprived the empire of long periods of peace.

An Empire Beleaguered Having a single ruler endowed with supreme legal and religious authority prevented the breakup of the Eastern Empire into petty principalities, but a series of territorial losses sapped the empire's strength. Between 634 and 650, Arab armies destroyed the Sasanid Empire and captured Byzantine Egypt, Syria, and Tunisia (see Chapter 10). Islam posed a religious as well as a political challenge. By the end of the twelfth century, some two-thirds of the Christians in these former Byzantine territories had adopted the Muslim faith.

The loss of such populous and prosperous provinces shook the empire and reduced its power. Although it had largely recovered and reorganized militarily by the tenth century, it never regained the lost lands. Though Crusaders from western Europe established short-lived Christian principalities at the eastern end of the Mediterranean Sea at the very end of the eleventh century, the Byzantines found them almost as hostile as the Muslims (see the section below on the Crusades). Eventually the empire succumbed to Muslim conquest in 1453.

The later Byzantine emperors faced new enemies in the north and south. Following the wave of Germanic migrations (see Chapter 6), Slavic and Turkic peoples appeared on the northern frontiers as part of centuries-long and poorly understood population migrations in Eurasian steppe lands. Other Turks led by the Seljuk family became the primary foe in the south (see Chapter 10).

At the same time, relations with the popes and princes of western Europe steadily worsened. In the mid-ninth century the patriarchs of Constantinople (cahn-stan-tih-NO-pul) had challenged the territorial jurisdiction of the popes of Rome and some of the practices of the Latin Church. These arguments worsened over time and in 1054 culminated in a formal **schism** (SKIZ-uhm) between the Latin Church and the Orthodox Church—a break that has been only partially mended.

Society and Urban Life   Imperial authority and urban prosperity in the eastern provinces of the Late Roman Empire initially sheltered Byzantium from many of the economic reverses and population losses suffered by western Europe. However, the two regions shared a common demographic crisis during a sixth-century epidemic of bubonic plague known as "the plague of Justinian," named after the emperor who ruled from 527 to 565. A similar though gradual and less pronounced social transformation set in around the seventh century, possibly sparked by further epidemics and the loss of Egypt and Syria to the Muslims. Formal histories tell us little, but popular narratives of saints' lives show a transition from stories about educated saints hailing from cities to stories about saints who originated as peasants. In many areas, barter replaced money transactions; some cities declined in population and wealth; and the traditional class of local urban notables nearly disappeared.

As the urban elite class shrank, the importance of high-ranking aristocrats at the imperial court and of rural landowners increased. Power organized by family began to rival power from class-based officeholding. By the end of the eleventh century, a family-based military aristocracy had emerged. Of Byzantine emperor Alexius Comnenus (uh-LEX-see-uhs kom-NAY-nuhs) (r. 1081–1118) it was said: "He considered himself not a ruler, but a lord, conceiving and calling the empire his own house."[2] The situation of women changed, too. Although earlier Roman family life was centered on a legally all-powerful father, women had enjoyed comparative freedom in public. After the seventh century women increasingly found themselves confined to the home. Some sources indicate that when they went out, they concealed their faces behind veils. The only men they socialized with were family members. Paradoxically, however, from 1028 to 1056 women ruled the Byzantine Empire alongside their husbands. These social changes and the apparent increase in the seclusion of women resemble simultaneous developments in neighboring Islamic countries, but historians have not uncovered any firm linkage between them.

Economically, the Byzantine emperors continued the Late Roman inclination to set prices, organize grain shipments to the capital, and monopolize trade in luxury goods like Tyrian purple cloth. Such government intervention may have slowed technological development and economic innovation. So long as merchants and pilgrims hastened to Constantinople from all points of the compass, aristocrats could buy rare and costly goods. Just as the provisioning and physical improvement of Rome overshadowed the development of other cities at the height of the Roman Empire, so other Byzantine cities suffered from the intense focus on Constantinople. In the countryside, Byzantine farmers continued to use slow oxcarts and light

---

[2]A. P. Kazhdan and Ann Wharton Epstein, *Change in Byzantine Culture in the Eleventh and Twelfth Centuries* (Berkeley: University of California Press, 1985), 71.

scratch plows, which were efficient for many, but not all, soil types, long after farmers in western Europe had begun to adopt more efficient techniques (discussed later in this chapter).

Because Byzantium's Roman inheritance remained so much more intact than western Europe's, few people recognized the slow deterioration. Gradually, however, pilgrims and visitors from the west saw the reality beyond the awe-inspiring, incense-filled domes of cathedrals and beneath the glitter and silken garments of the royal court. An eleventh-century French visitor wrote:

> The city itself [Constantinople] is squalid and fetid and in many places harmed by permanent darkness, for the wealthy overshadow the streets with buildings and leave these dirty, dark places to the poor and to travelers; there murders and robberies and other crimes which love the darkness are committed. Moreover, since people live lawlessly in this city, which has as many lords as rich men and almost as many thieves as poor men, a criminal knows neither fear nor shame, because crime is not punished by law and never entirely comes to light. In every respect she exceeds moderation; for, just as she surpasses other cities in wealth, so too, does she surpass them in vice.[3]

A Byzantine contemporary, Anna Comnena, the brilliant daughter of Emperor Alexius Comnenus, expressed the view from the other side. She scornfully described a prominent churchman and philosopher who happened to be from Italy: "Italos ... was unable with his barbaric, stupid temperament to grasp the profound truths of philosophy; even in the act of learning he utterly rejected the teacher's guiding hand, and full of temerity and barbaric folly, [believed] even before study that he excelled all others."[4]

Cultural Achievements   Though the greatest Byzantine architectural monument, Constantinople's Hagia Sophia (AH-yah SOH-fee-uh) ("Sacred Wisdom") cathedral, dates to the reign of Justinian, artistic creativity continually manifested itself in the design and ornamentation of other churches and monasteries. Justinian also ordered the collection of all Roman imperial edicts in a massive law code known as the *Corpus Juris Civilis*, or Body of Civil Law. Byzantine religious art, featuring stiff but arresting images of holy figures against gold backgrounds, strongly influenced painting in western Europe down to the thirteenth century, and Byzantine musical traditions strongly affected the chanting employed in medieval Latin churches.

Another important Byzantine achievement dates to the empire's long period of political decline. In the ninth century brothers named Cyril and Methodius embarked on a highly successful mission to the Slavs of Moravia (part of the modern Czech Republic). They preached in the local language, and their followers perfected a writing system, called Cyrillic (sih-RIL-ik), that came to be used by Slavic Christians adhering to the Orthodox—that is, Byzantine—rite. Their careers also mark the beginning of a competition between the Greek and Latin forms of Christianity for the allegiance of the Slavs. The use today of the Cyrillic alphabet among the Russians and other Slavic peoples of Orthodox Christian faith, and of the Roman

---

[3]Ibid., 248.
[4]Ibid., 255.

alphabet among the Poles, Czechs, and Croatians, testifies to this competition (see the section on Kievan Russia).

EARLY MEDIEVAL EUROPE, 600–1000

The disappearance of the imperial legal framework that had persisted to the final days of the Western Roman Empire (see Chapter 6) and the rise of various kings, nobles, and chieftains changed the legal and political landscape of western Europe. In region after region, the family-based traditions of the Germanic peoples, which often fit local conditions better than previous practices, supplanted the edicts of the Roman emperors.

Fear and physical insecurity led communities to seek the protection of local strongmen. In places where looters and pillagers might appear at any moment, a local lord with a castle at which peasants could take refuge counted for more than a distant king. Dependency of weak people on strong people became a hallmark of the post-Roman period in western Europe.

The Time of Insecurity   In 711 a frontier raiding party of Arabs and Berbers, acting under the authority of the Umayyad caliph in Syria, crossed the Strait of Gibraltar and overturned the kingdom of the Visigoths in Spain (see Chapter 10). The disunited Europeans could not stop them from consolidating their hold on the Iberian Peninsula. After pushing the remaining Christian chieftains into the northern mountains, the Muslims moved on to France. They occupied much of the southern coast and penetrated as far north as Tours, less than 150 miles (240 kilometers) from the English Channel, before Charlemagne's grandfather, Charles Martel, stopped their most advanced raiding party in 732.

Military effectiveness was the key element in the rise of the Carolingian (kah-roe-LIN-gee-uhn) family (from Latin *Carolus*, "Charles"), first as protectors of the Frankish (French) kings, then as kings themselves under Charlemagne's father Pepin (r. 751–768), and finally, under Charlemagne, as emperors. At the peak of Charlemagne's power, the Carolingian Empire encompassed all of Gaul and parts of Germany and Italy, with the pope ruling part of the latter. When Charlemagne's son, Louis the Pious, died, the Germanic tradition of splitting property among sons led to the Treaty of Verdun (843), which split the empire into three parts. French-speaking in the west (France) and middle (Burgundy), and German-speaking in the east (Germany), the three regions never reunited. Nevertheless, the Carolingian economic system based on landed wealth and a brief intellectual revival sponsored personally by Charlemagne—though he himself was illiterate—provided a common heritage.

A new threat to western Europe appeared in 793, when the Vikings, sea raiders from Scandinavia, attacked and plundered a monastery on the English coast, the first of hundreds of such raids. Local sources from France, the British Isles, and Muslim Spain attest to widespread dread of Viking warriors descending from multi-oared, dragon-prowed boats to pillage monasteries, villages, and towns. Viking shipbuilders made versatile vessels that could brave the stormy North Atlantic and also maneuver up rivers to attack inland towns. As we shall see, in the ninth

© Cengage Learning

MAP 11.1 The Spread of Christianity

By the early eighth century, Christian areas around the southern Mediterranean from northern Syria to northern Spain, accounting for most of the Christian population, had fallen under Muslim rule; the slow process of conversion to Islam had begun. This accentuated the importance of the patriarchs of Constantinople, the popes in Rome, and the later converting regions of northern and eastern Europe.

Werner Forman/Art Resource, NY

Viking Runestone *Pre-Christian symbols and myths from northern Europe appear on stones like this one from Sweden. An inscription containing names written in the runic alphabet had elaborately intertwined ornaments at the ends, a feature that reappears in the Christian Book of Kells. The scene at the top is thought to depict Odin, the chief god of the Vikings.*

century raiders from Denmark and Norway harried the British and French coasts while Varangians (va-RAN-gee-anz) (Swedes) pursued raiding and trading interests, and eventually the building of kingdoms, along the rivers of eastern Europe and Russia. Although many Viking raiders sought booty and slaves, in the 800s and 900s Viking captains organized the settlement of Iceland, Greenland, and, around the year 1000, Vinland on the northern tip of Newfoundland.

Vikings long settled on lands they had seized in Normandy (in northwestern France) organized the most important and ambitious expeditions in terms of numbers of men and horses and long-lasting impact. William the Conqueror, the duke of Normandy, invaded England in 1066 and brought Anglo-Saxon domination of the island to an end. Other Normans (from "north men") attacked Muslim Sicily in the 1060s and, after thirty years of fighting, permanently severed it from the Muslim world.

A Self-Sufficient Economy   Archaeology and records kept by Christian monasteries and convents reveal a profound economic transformation that accompanied the new Germanic political order. The new rulers cared little for the urban-based civilization of the Romans, which accordingly shrank in importance. Though the pace of change differed from region to region, most cities lost population, in some cases becoming villages. Roman roads fell into disuse and disrepair. Small thatched houses sprang up beside abandoned villas, and public buildings made of marble became dilapidated in the absence of the laborers, money, and civic leadership needed to maintain them. Paying for purchases in coin largely gave way to bartering goods and services.

Trade across the Mediterranean did not entirely stop after the Muslim conquests. Archaeological investigations of sunken ships show a continuation of contact, but more with North African ports than with Egypt and Syria. Nevertheless, most of western Europe came to rely on meager local resources. These resources, moreover, underwent redistribution.

Roman centralization had channeled the wealth and production of the empire to the capital, which in turn radiated Roman cultural styles and tastes to the provinces. As Roman governors were replaced by Germanic territorial lords, who found the riches of their own culture more appealing than those of Rome, local self-sufficiency became more important. The decline of literacy and other aspects of Roman life made room for the growth of Germanic cultural traditions.

The diet in the northern countries featured beer, lard or butter, and bread made of barley, rye, or wheat, all supplemented by pork from herds of swine fed on forest acorns and beechnuts, and by game from the same forests. Nobles ate better than peasants, but even the peasant diet was reasonably balanced. The Roman diet based on wheat, wine, and olive oil persisted in the south. The average western European of the ninth century was probably better nourished than his or her descendants three hundred years later, when population was increasing and the nobility monopolized the resources of the forests.

In both north and south, self-sufficient farming estates known as **manors** became the primary centers of agricultural production. Fear of attack led many common farmers in the most vulnerable regions to give their lands to large landowners in return for political and physical protection. The warfare and instability of the post-Roman centuries made unprotected country houses especially vulnerable to pillaging. Isolated by poor communications and lack of organized government, landowners depended on their own resources for survival. Many became warriors or maintained a force of armed men. Others swore allegiance to landowners who had armed forces to protect them.

A well-appointed manor possessed fields, gardens, grazing lands, fishponds, a mill, a church, workshops for making farm and household implements, and a village where the farmers dependent on the lord of the manor lived. Depending on local conditions, protection ranged from a ditch and wooden stockade to a stone wall surrounding a fortified keep (a stone building). Fortification tended to increase until the twelfth century, when stronger monarchies made it less necessary.

Manor life reflected personal status. Nobles and their families exercised almost unlimited power over the **serfs**—agricultural workers who belonged to the manor, tilled its fields, and owed other dues and obligations. Serfs could not leave the manor where they were born and attach themselves to another lord. Most peasants in England, France, and western Germany were unfree serfs in the tenth and eleventh centuries. However, in Bordeaux (bore-DOE), Saxony, and a few other regions, free peasantry survived based on the egalitarian social structure of the Germanic peoples during their period of migration. Outright slavery, the mainstay of the Roman economy (see Chapter 6), diminished as more and more peasants became serfs in return for a lord's protection. At the same time, the enslavement of prisoners to serve as laborers became less important as an object of warfare.

Early Medieval Society in the West   Europe's reversion to a self-sufficient economy limited the freedom and potential for personal achievement of most people, but an emerging class of nobles reaped great benefits. During the Germanic migrations and later among the Vikings of Scandinavia, men regularly answered the call to arms issued by war chiefs, to whom they swore allegiance. All warriors shared in the booty gained from raiding. As settlement enhanced the importance of agricultural tasks, laying down the plow and picking up the sword at the chieftain's call became harder.

Those who, out of loyalty or desire for adventure, continued to join the war parties included a growing number of horsemen. Mounted warriors became the central force of the Carolingian army. At first, fighting from horseback did not make a person either a nobleman or a landowner. By the tenth century, however, nearly constant warfare to protect land rights or support the claims of a lord brought about a gradual transformation in the status of the mounted warrior, which led, at different rates in different areas, to landholding becoming almost inseparable from military service.

In trying to understand long-standing traditions of landholding and obligation, lawyers in the sixteenth century and later simplified thousands of individual agreements into a neat system they called "feudalism," from Latin *feodum*, meaning a land awarded for military service. It became common to refer to medieval Europe as a "feudal society" in which kings and lords gave land to "vassals" in return for sworn military support. By analyzing original records, more recent historians have discovered this to be an oversimplification. Relations between landholders and serfs and between lords and vassals differed too much from one place to another, and from one time to another, to fit together in anything resembling a regular system.

The German foes of the Roman legions had equipped themselves with helmets, shields, and swords, spears, or throwing axes. Some rode horses, but most fought on foot. Before the invention of the stirrup by Central Asian pastoralists in approximately the first century C.E., horsemen had gripped their mounts with their legs and fought with bows and arrows, throwing javelins, stabbing spears, and swords. Stirrups allowed a rider to stand in the saddle, lean forward, and absorb the impact when his lance struck an enemy at full gallop. This type of warfare required grain-fed horses that were larger and heavier than the small, grass-fed animals of the Central Asian nomads, though smaller and lighter than the draft horses bred in later times for hauling heavy loads. Thus agricultural Europe rather than the grassy steppes produced the charges of armored knights that came to dominate the battlefield.

By the eleventh century, the knight, called by different terms in different places, had emerged as the central figure in medieval warfare. He wore an open-faced helmet and a long linen shirt, or hauberk (HAW-berk), studded with small metal disks (see Environment and Technology: Iron Production). A century later, knightly equipment commonly included a visored helmet that covered the head and neck and a hauberk of chain mail.

Each increase in armor for knight and horse entailed a greater financial outlay. Since land was the basis of wealth, a knight needed financial support from land revenues. Accordingly, kings began to reward armed service with grants of land from their own property. Lesser nobles with extensive properties built their own military retinues the same way.

A grant of land in return for a pledge to provide military service was often called a **fief**. At first, kings granted fiefs to their noble followers, known as **vassals**, on a temporary basis. By the tenth century, most fiefs could be inherited as long as the specified military service continued to be provided. Though patterns varied greatly, the association of landholding with military service made the medieval society of western Europe quite different from the contemporary city-based societies of the Islamic world.

Kings and lords might be able to command the service of their vassals for only part of the year. Vassals could hold land from several different lords and owe loyalty to each one. Moreover, the allegiance that a vassal owed to one lord could entail military service to that lord's master in time of need.

A "typical" medieval realm—actual practices varied between and within realms—consisted of lands directly owned by a king or a count and administered by his royal officers. The king's or count's major vassals held and administered other lands, often the greater portion, in return for military service. These vassals, in turn, granted land to their own vassals.

The lord of a manor provided local governance and justice, direct royal government being quite limited. The king had few financial resources and seldom exercised legal jurisdiction at a local level. Members of the clergy, as well as the extensive agricultural lands owned by monasteries and nunneries, fell under the jurisdiction of the church, which further limited the reach and authority of the monarch.

Noblewomen became enmeshed in this tangle of obligations as heiresses and as candidates for marriage. A man who married the widow or daughter of a lord with no sons could gain control of that lord's property. Marriage alliances affected entire kingdoms. Noble daughters and sons had little say in marriage matters; issues of land, power, and military service took precedence. Noblemen guarded the women in their families as closely as their other valuables.

Nevertheless, women could own land. A noblewoman sometimes administered her husband's estates when he was away at war. Nonnoble women usually worked alongside their menfolk, performing agricultural tasks such as raking and stacking hay, shearing sheep, and picking vegetables. As artisans, women spun, wove, and sewed clothing. The Bayeux (bay-YUH) Tapestry, a piece of embroidery 230 feet (70 meters) long and 20 inches (51 centimeters) wide depicting William the Conqueror's invasion of England in 1066, was designed and executed entirely by women, though historians do not agree on who those women were.

THE WESTERN CHURCH

Just as the Christian populations in eastern Europe followed the religious guidance of the patriarch of Constantinople appointed by the Byzantine emperor, so the pope commanded similar authority over church affairs in western Europe. And just as missionaries in the east spread Christianity among the Slavs, so missionaries in the west added territory to Christendom with forays into the British Isles and the lands of the Germans. Throughout the period covered by this chapter, Christian society was emerging and changing in both areas.

In the west, Roman nobles lost control of the **papacy**—the office of the pope—and it became a more powerful international office after the tenth century. Councils of bishops—which normally set rules, called canons, to regulate the priests and laypeople (men and women who were not members of the clergy) under their jurisdiction—became increasingly responsive to papal direction.

Nevertheless, regional disagreements over church regulations, shortages of educated and trained clergy, difficult communications, political disorder, and the general insecurity of the period posed formidable obstacles to unifying church standards and practices. Clerics in some parts of western Europe were still issuing prohibitions against the worship of rivers, trees, and mountains as late as the eleventh century. Church problems included lingering polytheism, lax enforcement of prohibitions against marriage of clergy, nepotism (giving preferment to one's close kin), and simony (selling ecclesiastical appointments, often to people who were not members of the clergy). The persistence of the papacy in asserting its legal jurisdiction over clergy, combating polytheism and heretical beliefs, and calling on secular rulers to recognize the pope's authority, including unpopular rulings like a ban on first-cousin marriage, constituted a rare force for unity and order in a time of disunity and chaos.

Politics and the Church   In politically fragmented western Europe, the pope needed allies. Like his son, Charlemagne's father Pepin was a strong supporter of the papacy. The relationship between kings and popes was tense, however, since both thought of themselves as ultimate authorities. In 962 the pope crowned the first "Holy Roman Emperor" (Charlemagne never held this full title). This designation of a secular political authority as the guardian of general Christian interests proved more apparent than real. Essentially a loose confederation of German princes who named one of their own to the highest office, the **Holy Roman Empire** had little influence west of the Rhine River.

Although the pope crowned the early Holy Roman Emperors, this did not signify political superiority because the law of the church (known as canon law because each law was called a canon) gave the pope exclusive legal jurisdiction over all clergy and church property wherever located. However, since bishops who held land as vassals owed military support or other services and dues to kings and princes, the secular rulers argued that they should have the power to appoint those bishops because that was the only way to guarantee fulfillment of their duties as vassals. The popes disagreed.

In the eleventh century, this conflict over the control of ecclesiastical appointments came to a head. Hildebrand (HILL-de-brand), an Italian monk, capped a

Iron Production

Despite the collapse of the Roman economy, ironworking expanded throughout Europe. The iron swords of the Germans outperformed traditional Roman weapons, which became obsolete. The spreading use of armor also increased the demand for iron. Archaeologists have found extensive evidence of iron smelting well beyond the frontiers of the Roman Empire. Helg Island in a lake near Stockholm, Sweden, had a large walled settlement that relied entirely on iron trading. Discoveries of a Buddha from India and a christening spoon from Egypt, both datable to the sixth century C.E., indicate the range of these trade contacts. At Zelechovice in the Czech Republic, remains of fifty "slag-pit" furnaces have been dated to the ninth century.

Most iron smelting was done on a small scale. Ore containing iron oxide was shoveled onto a charcoal fire in an open-air hearth pit. The carbon in the charcoal combined with the oxygen in the ore to form carbon dioxide gas, leaving behind a soft glowing lump of iron called a "bloom." This bloom was then pounded on a stone to remove the remaining impurities, like sand and clay, before being turned over to the blacksmith for fabricating into swords or armor.

During the post-Roman centuries, smelters learned to build walls around the hearth pits and then to put domes and chimneys on them. The resulting "slag-pit" furnaces produced greater amounts of iron. They also consumed great amounts of wood. Twelve pounds of charcoal, made from about 25 pounds of wood, were needed to produce 1 pound of bloom iron, and about 3 pounds of useless slag. Though bellows were developed to force oxygen into the fire, temperatures in slag-pit furnaces never became high enough to produce molten metal.

Iron Smelting *Two bellows blowing alternately provide a constant stream of air to the furnace. The man on the right pounds the bloom into bars or plates that a blacksmith will reheat and shape.*

career of reorganizing church finances when the cardinals (a group of senior bishops) meeting in Rome selected him to be Pope Gregory VII in 1073. His personal notion of the papacy (preserved among his letters) represented an extreme position, stating among other claims, that

§ *The pope can be judged by no one;*
§ *The Roman church has never erred and never will err till the end of time;*
§ *The pope alone can depose and restore bishops;*
§ *He alone can call general councils and authorize canon law;*
§ *He can depose emperors;*
§ *He can absolve subjects from their allegiance;*
§ *All princes should kiss his feet.*[5]

Such claims antagonized lords and monarchs, who had become accustomed to *investing*—that is, conferring a ring and a staff as symbols of authority on bishops and abbots in their domains. Historians apply the term **investiture controversy** to the medieval struggle between the church and the lay lords to control ecclesiastical appointments; the term also refers to the broader conflict of popes versus emperors and kings. When Holy Roman Emperor Henry IV defied Gregory's reforms, Gregory excommunicated him in 1076, thereby cutting him off from church rituals. Stung by the resulting decline in his influence, Henry stood barefoot in the snow for three days outside a castle in northern Italy waiting for Gregory, a guest there, to receive him. Henry's formal act of penance induced Gregory to forgive him and restore him to the church; but the reconciliation, an apparent victory for the pope, did not last. In 1078 Gregory declared Henry deposed. The emperor then forced Gregory to flee from Rome to Salerno, where he died two years later.

The struggle between the popes and the emperors continued until 1122, when a compromise was reached at Worms, a town in Germany. In the Concordat of Worms, Emperor Henry V renounced his right to choose bishops and abbots or bestow spiritual symbols upon them. In return, Pope Calixtus II permitted the emperor to invest papally appointed bishops and abbots with any lay rights or obligations before their spiritual consecration. Such compromises did not fully solve the problem, but they reduced tensions between the two sides.

Assertions of royal authority triggered other conflicts as well. Though barely twenty when he became king of England in 1154, Henry II, a great-grandson of William the Conqueror, instituted reforms designed to strengthen the power of the Crown and weaken the nobility. He appointed traveling justices to enforce his laws and made juries, a holdover from traditional Germanic law, into powerful legal instruments. He also established the principle that criminal acts violated the "king's peace" and should be tried and punished in accordance with charges brought by the Crown instead of in response to charges brought by victims.

Henry had a harder time controlling the church. His closest friend and chancellor, or chief administrator, Thomas à Becket (ca. 1118–1170), lived the grand and luxurious life of a courtier. In 1162 Henry persuaded Becket to become a priest and

---

[5]R. W. Southern, *Western Society and the Church in the Middle Ages* (Harmondsworth, England: Penguin, 1970), 102.

assume the position of archbishop of Canterbury, the highest church office in England. Becket agreed but cautioned that from then on he would act solely in the interest of the church if it came into conflict with the Crown. When Henry sought to try clerics accused of crimes in royal instead of ecclesiastical courts, Archbishop Thomas, now leading an austere and pious life, resisted.

In 1170 four of Henry's knights, knowing that the king desired Becket's death, murdered the archbishop in Canterbury Cathedral. Their crime backfired, and an outpouring of sympathy caused Canterbury to become a major pilgrimage center. In 1173 the pope declared the martyred Becket a saint. Henry allowed himself to be publicly whipped twice in penance for the crime, but his authority had been badly damaged.

Henry II's conflict with Thomas à Becket, like the Concordat of Worms, yielded no clear victor. The problem of competing legal traditions made political life in western Europe more complicated than in Byzantium or the lands of Islam (see Chapter 10). Feudal law, rooted in Germanic custom, gave supreme power to the king. Canon law, based on Roman precedent, visualized a single hierarchical legal institution with jurisdiction over all of Western Christendom. In the eleventh century Roman imperial law, contained in the *Corpus Juris Civilis* (see above), added a third tradition.

Monasticism

Monasticism featured prominently in the religious life of almost all medieval Christian lands. The origins of group monasticism lay in the eastern lands of the Roman Empire. Pre-Christian practices such as celibacy, continual devotion to prayer, and living apart from society (alone or in small groups) came together in Christian form in Egypt.

The most important form of monasticism in western Europe, however, involved groups of monks or nuns living together in organized communities. The person most responsible for introducing this originally Egyptian practice in the Latin west was Benedict of Nursia (ca. 480–547) in Italy. Benedict began his pious career as a hermit in a cave but eventually organized several monasteries, each headed by an abbot. In the seventh century monasteries based on his model spread far beyond Italy. The Rule Benedict wrote to govern the monks' behavior envisions a balanced life of devotion and work, along with obligations of celibacy, poverty, and obedience to the abbot. Those who lived by this or other monastic rules became *regular clergy*, in contrast to *secular clergy*, priests who lived in society instead of in seclusion and did not follow a formal code of regulations. The Rule of Benedict was the starting point for most forms of western European monastic life and remains in force today in Benedictine monasteries.

Though monks and nuns, women who lived by monastic rules in convents, made up a small percentage of the total population, their secluded way of life reinforced the separation of religious affairs from ordinary politics and economics. Monasteries followed Jesus' axiom to "render unto Caesar what is Caesar's and unto God what is God's" better than the many town-based bishops who behaved like lords.

Although some rulers, like Charlemagne, encouraged scholarship at court, many illiterate lay nobles interested themselves only in warfare and hunting. Thus it was monasteries that preserved literacy and learning in the early medieval period. Monks (but seldom nuns) saw copying manuscripts and even writing books as a

Illustrated Manuscript from Monastic Library *This page from the Book of Kells, written around 800 in Ireland, combines an icon-like image of a gospel writer with complex interwoven patterns in the margin that derive from the pre-Christian art of northern Europe. Note the evangelist's blonde hair.*

Trinity College Library Dublin/The Bridgeman Art Library

religious calling, and monastic scribes preserved many ancient Latin works that would otherwise have disappeared. The survival of Greek works depended more on Byzantine and Muslim scribes in the east.

Monasteries and convents served other functions as well. A few planted Christianity in new lands, as Irish monks did in parts of Germany. Most serviced the needs of travelers, organized agricultural production on their lands, and took in infants abandoned by their parents. Convents provided refuge for widows and other women who lacked male protection in the harsh medieval world or who desired a spiritual life. These religious houses presented problems of oversight to the church, however. A bishop might have authority over an abbot or abbess (head of a convent), but he could not exercise constant vigilance over what went on behind monastery walls.

The failure of some abbots to maintain monastic discipline led to the growth of a reform movement centered on the Benedictine abbey of Cluny (KLOO-nee) in eastern France. Founded in 910 by William the Pious, the first duke of Aquitaine, who completely freed it of lay authority, Cluny gained similar freedom from the local bishop a century later. Its abbots pursued a vigorous campaign, eventually in alliance with reforming popes like Gregory VII, to improve monastic discipline and administration. A magnificent new abbey church symbolized Cluny's claims to eminence. With later additions, it became the largest church in the world.

At the peak of Cluny's influence, nearly a thousand Benedictine abbeys and priories (lower-level monastic houses) in various countries accepted the authority of its abbot. Whereas the Benedictine Rule had presumed that each monastery would be independent, the Cluniac reformers stipulated that every abbot and every prior (head of a priory) be appointed by the abbot of Cluny and have personal experience of the religious life of Cluny. Monastic reform also gained new impetus in the second half of the twelfth century with the rapid rise of the Cistercian order, which emphasized a life of asceticism and poverty. These movements set the pattern for the monasteries, cathedral clergy, and preaching friars that would dominate ecclesiastical life in the thirteenth century.

KIEVAN RUSSIA, 900–1200

Though Latin and Orthodox Christendom followed different paths in later centuries, which of them had a more promising future was not apparent in 900. The Poles and other Slavic peoples living in the north eventually accepted the Christianity of Rome as taught by German priests and missionaries. The Serbs and other southern Slavs took their faith from Constantinople.

The conversion of Kievan Russia, farther to the east, shows how economics, politics, and religious life were closely intertwined. The choice of orthodoxy over Catholicism had important consequences for later European history.

The Rise of the Kievan Empire   The territory between the Black and Caspian Seas in the south and the Baltic and White Seas in the north divides into a series of east-west zones. Frozen tundra in the far north gives way to a cold forest zone, then to a more temperate forest, then to a mix of forest and steppe grasslands, and finally to grassland only. Several navigable rivers, including the Volga, the Dnieper (d-NYEP-er), and the Don, run from north to south across these zones.

Early historical sources reflect repeated linguistic and territorial changes, seemingly under pressure from poorly understood population migrations. Most of the Germanic peoples, along with some Iranian and west Slavic peoples, migrated into eastern Europe from Ukraine and Russia in Roman times. The peoples who remained behind spoke eastern Slavic languages, except in the far north and south: Finns and related peoples lived in the former region, Turkic-speakers in the latter.

Forest dwellers, farmers, and steppe nomads complemented each other economically. Nomads traded animals for the farmers' grain; and honey, wax, and furs from the forests became important exchange items. Traders could travel east and west by steppe caravan (see Chapters 9 and 13), or they could use boats on the rivers to move north and south.

Hoards containing thousands of Byzantine and Islamic coins buried in Poland and on islands in the Baltic Sea where fairs were held attest to the trading activity of Varangians (Swedish Vikings) who sailed across the Baltic and down Russia's rivers. The Varangians exchanged forest products and slaves for manufactured goods and coins, which they may have used as jewelry rather than as money, at markets controlled by the Khazar Turks, a powerful kingdom centered around the mouth of the Volga River.

Historians debate the early meaning of the word *Rus* (from which *Russia* is derived), but at some point it came to refer to Slavic-speaking peoples ruled by Varangians. Unlike western European lords, the Varangian princes and their *druzhina* (military retainers) lived in cities, while the Slavs farmed. The princes occupied themselves with trade and fending off enemies. The Rus of the city of Kiev (KEE-yev), which was taken over by Varangians around 880, controlled trade on the Dnieper River and dealt more with Byzantium than with the Muslim world because the Dnieper flows into the Black Sea. The Rus of Novgorod (NOHV-goh-rod) played the same role on the Volga. The semilegendary account of the Kievan Rus conversion to Christianity must be seen against this background.

In 980 Vladimir (VLAD-ih-mir) I, a ruler of Novgorod who had fallen from power, returned from exile to Kiev with a band of Varangians and made himself the grand prince of Kievan Russia. Though his grandmother Olga had been a Christian, Vladimir built a temple on Kiev's heights and placed there the statues of the six gods his Slavic subjects worshiped. The earliest Russian chronicle reports that Vladimir and his advisers decided against Islam as the official religion because of its ban on alcohol, rejected Judaism (the religion to which the Khazars had converted) because they thought that a truly powerful god would not have let the ancient Jewish kingdom be destroyed, and even spoke with German emissaries advocating Latin Christianity. Why Vladimir chose Orthodox Christianity over the Latin version is not precisely known. The magnificence of Constantinople seems to have been a consideration. After visiting Byzantine churches, his agents reported: "We knew not whether we were in heaven or on earth, for on earth there is no such splendor of [sic] such beauty, and we are at a loss how to describe it. We know only that God dwells there among men, and their service is finer than the ceremonies of other nations."[6]

After choosing a reluctant bride from the Byzantine imperial family, Vladimir converted to Orthodox Christianity, probably in 988, and opened his lands to Orthodox clerics and missionaries. The patriarch of Constantinople appointed a metropolitan (chief bishop) at Kiev to govern ecclesiastical affairs; churches arose in Kiev, one of them on the ruins of Vladimir's earlier hilltop temple; and writing was introduced, using the Cyrillic alphabet devised earlier for the western Slavs. This extension of Orthodox Christendom northward provided a barrier against the eastward expansion of Latin Christianity. Kiev became firmly oriented toward trade with Byzantium and turned its back on the Muslim world, though the Volga trade continued through Novgorod.

Struggles within the ruling family and with other enemies, most notably the steppe peoples of the south, marked the later political history of Kievan Russia. But down to the time of the Mongols in the thirteenth century (see Chapter 13), the state remained and served as an instrument for the Christianization of the eastern Slavs.

---

[6]S. A. Zenkovsky, ed., *Medieval Russia's Epics, Chronicles, and Tales* (New York: New American Library, 1974), 67.

Society and Culture   The manorial agricultural system of western Europe never developed in Kievan Russia because its political power derived from trade rather than from landholding. Farmers practiced shifting cultivation of their own lands. They would burn a section of forest, then lightly scratch the ash-strewn surface with a plow. When fertility waned, they would move to another section of forest. Poor land and a short growing season in the most northerly latitudes made food scarce. Living on their own estates, the druzhina evolved from infantry into cavalry and focused their efforts more on horse breeding than on agriculture.

Large cities like Kiev and Novgorod may have reached thirty thousand or fifty thousand people—roughly the size of contemporary London or Paris, but far smaller than Constantinople or major Muslim metropolises like Baghdad and Nishapur. Many cities amounted to little more than fortified trading posts. Yet they served as centers for the development of crafts, some, such as glassmaking, based on skills imported from Byzantium. Artisans enjoyed higher status in society than peasant farmers. Construction relied on wood from the forests, although Christianity brought the building of stone cathedrals and churches on the Byzantine model.

Christianity penetrated the general population slowly. Several polytheist uprisings occurred in the eleventh century, particularly in times of famine, and passive resistance led some groups to reject Christian burial and persist in cremating the dead and keeping the bones of the deceased in urns. Women continued to use polytheist designs on their clothing and bracelets, and as late as the twelfth century they were still turning to polytheist priests for charms to cure sick children. Traditional Slavic marriage practices involving casual and polygamous relations particularly scandalized the clergy.

Christianity eventually triumphed, and its success led to increasing church engagement in political and economic affairs. In the twelfth century, Christian clergy became involved in government administration, some of them collecting fees and taxes related to trade. Direct and indirect revenue from trade provided the rulers with the money they needed to pay their soldiers. The rule of law also spread as Kievan Russia experienced its peak of culture and prosperity in the century before the Mongol invasion of 1237.

WESTERN EUROPE REVIVES, 1000–1200

Between 1000 and 1200 western Europe slowly emerged from nearly seven centuries of subsistence economy—in which most people who worked on the land could meet only their basic needs for food, clothing, and shelter. With the climate somewhat warmer than in previous centuries, population and agricultural production climbed, and a growing food surplus found its way to town markets, speeding the return of a money-based economy and providing support for larger numbers of craftspeople, construction workers, and traders.

Historians have attributed western Europe's revival to population growth spurred by new technologies and to the appearance in Italy and Flanders, on the coast of the North Sea, of self-governing cities devoted primarily to seaborne trade. For monarchs, the changes facilitated improvements in central administration, greater control over vassals, and consolidation of realms on the way to becoming stronger kingdoms.

The Role of Technology   A lack of concrete evidence confirming the spread of technological innovations frustrates efforts to relate the exact course of Europe's revival to technological change. Nevertheless, most historians agree that technology played a significant role in the near doubling of the population of western Europe between 1000 and 1200. The population of England seems to have risen from 1.1 million in 1086 to 1.9 million in 1200, and the population of the territory of modern France seems to have risen from 5.2 million to 9.2 million over the same period.

Examples that illustrate the difficulty of drawing historical conclusions from scattered evidence of technological change were a new type of plow and the use of efficient draft harnesses for pulling wagons. The Roman plow, which farmers in southern Europe and Byzantium continued to use, scratched shallow grooves, as was appropriate for loose, dry Mediterranean soils. The new plow cut deep into the soil with a knifelike blade, while a curved board mounted behind the blade lifted the cut layer and turned it over. This made it possible to farm the heavy, wet clays of the northern river valleys. Pulling the new plow took more energy, which could mean harnessing several teams of oxen or horses.

Horses plowed faster than oxen but were more delicate. Iron horseshoes, which were widely adopted in this period, helped protect their feet, but like the plow itself, they added to the farmer's expenses. Roman horse harnesses, inefficiently modeled on the yoke used for oxen, put such pressure on the animal's neck that a horse pulling a heavy load risked strangulation. A mystery surrounds the adoption of more efficient designs. The **horse collar**, which moves the point of traction from the animal's throat to its shoulders, first appeared around 800 in a miniature painting, and it is shown clearly as a harness for plow horses in the Bayeux Tapestry, embroidered after 1066. The breast-strap harness, which is not as well adapted for the heaviest work but was preferred in southern Europe, seems to have appeared around 500. In both cases, linguists have tried to trace key technical terms to Chinese or Turko-Mongol words and have argued for technological diffusion across Eurasia. Yet third-century Roman farmers in Tunisia and Libya used both types of harness to hitch horses and camels to plows and carts. This technology, which is still employed in Tunisia, appears clearly on Roman bas-reliefs and lamps; but there is no more concrete evidence of its movement northward into Europe than there is of similar harnessing moving across Asia. Thus the question of where efficient harnessing came from and whether it began in 500 or in 800, or was known even earlier but not extensively used, cannot be easily resolved.

Hinging on this problem is the question of when and why landowners in northern Europe began to use teams of horses to pull plows through moist, fertile river-valley soils that were too heavy for teams of oxen. Horses moved faster but cost more, particularly after the population increase raised the prices of the grain needed to feed them. Thus, it is difficult to say that one technology was always better: although agricultural surpluses did grow and better plowing did play a role in this growth, areas that continued to use oxen and even old-style plows seem to have shared in the general population growth of the period.

Cities and the Rebirth of the Trade   Independent cities governed and defended by communes appeared first in Italy and Flanders and then elsewhere. Communes were groups of leading citizens who banded together to defend their cities and demand the privilege of self-government from their lay or ecclesiastical lord. Lords who granted such privileges benefited from the commune's economic dynamism. Lacking extensive farmlands, these cities turned to manufacturing and trade, which they encouraged through the laws they enacted. Laws making serfs free once they came into the city, for example, attracted many workers from the countryside. Cities in Italy that had shrunk within walls built by the Romans now pressed against those walls, forcing the construction of new ones. Pisa built a new wall in 1000 and expanded it in 1156. Other twelfth-century cities that built new walls include Florence, Brescia (BREH-shee-uh), Pavia, and Siena (see-EN-uh).

The city of Venice was organized by settlers on a group of islands at the northern end of the Adriatic Sea that had been largely uninhabited in Roman times. In the eleventh century it became the dominant sea power in the Adriatic and competed with Pisa and Genoa, its rivals on the western side of Italy, for leadership in the trade with Muslim ports in North Africa and the eastern Mediterranean. A somewhat later merchant's list mentions trade in some three thousand "spices" (including dyestuffs, textile fibers, and raw materials), some of them products of Muslim lands and some coming via the Silk Road or the Indian Ocean Maritime System (see Chapter 9). Among them were eleven types of alum (for dyeing), eleven types of wax, eight types of cotton, four types of indigo, five types of ginger, four types of paper, and fifteen types of sugar, along with cloves, caraway, tamarind, and fresh oranges. By the time of the Crusades (see below), maritime commerce throughout the Mediterranean had come to depend heavily on ships from Genoa, Venice, and Pisa. At the same time, the climate-driven decline of agriculture in Iran and Iraq, which became colder while Europe enjoyed unusual warmth, caused more and more trade from the Indian Ocean and Asia to flow through Egypt and Syria.

Ghent, Bruges (broozh), and Ypres (EEP-r) in Flanders rivaled the Italian cities in prosperity, trade, and industry. Enjoying comparable independence based on privileges granted by the counts of Flanders, these cities centralized the fishing and wool trades of the North Sea region. Around 1200 raw wool from England began to be woven into woolen cloth for a very large market.

More abundant coinage also signaled the upturn in economic activity. In the ninth and tenth centuries most gold coins had come from Muslim lands and the Byzantine Empire. Being worth too much for most trading purposes, they seldom reached Germany, France, and England, where the widely imitated Carolingian silver penny sufficed. With the economic revival of the twelfth century, however, minting of silver coins began in Scandinavia, Poland, and other outlying regions, and in the following century the reinvigoration of Mediterranean trade made possible a new and abundant gold coinage.

THE CRUSADES, 1095–1204

Western European revival coincided with and contributed to the **Crusades**, a series of religiously inspired Christian military campaigns against Muslims in the eastern Mediterranean that dominated the politics of Europe from 1095 to 1204 (see Chapter 10). Four great expeditions, the last redirected against the Byzantines and resulting in the Latin capture of Constantinople, constituted the region's largest military undertakings since the fall of Rome. As a result of the Crusades, noble courts and burgeoning cities in western Europe consumed more goods from the east. This set the stage for the later adoption of ideas, artistic styles, and industrial processes from Byzantium and the lands of Islam.

The Roots of the Crusades   Several social and economic currents of the eleventh century contributed to the Crusades. First, reforming leaders of the Latin Church, seeking to soften the warlike tone of society, popularized the Truce of God. This movement limited fighting between Christian lords by specifying times of truce, such as during Lent (the forty days before Easter) and on Sundays. Many knights welcomed a religiously approved alternative to fighting other Christians. Second, ambitious rulers, like the Norman chieftains who invaded England and Sicily, were looking for new lands to conquer. Nobles, particularly younger sons in areas where the oldest son inherited everything, were hungry for land and titles to maintain their status. Third, Italian merchants wanted to increase trade in the eastern Mediterranean and acquire trading posts in Muslim territory. However, without the rivalry between popes and kings already discussed, and without the desire of the church to demonstrate political authority over western Christendom, the Crusades might never have occurred.

Several factors focused attention on the Holy Land, which had been under Muslim rule for four centuries. **Pilgrimages** played an important role in European religious life. In western Europe, pilgrims traveled under royal protection, with a few in their number actually being tramps, thieves, beggars, peddlers, and merchants for whom pilgrimage was a safe way of traveling. Genuinely pious pilgrims often journeyed to visit the old churches and sacred relics preserved in Rome or Constantinople. The most intrepid went to Jerusalem, Antioch, and other cities under Muslim control to fulfill a vow or to atone for a sin.

Knights who followed a popular pilgrimage route across northern Spain to pray at the shrine of Santiago de Compostela learned of the expanding efforts of Christian kings to dislodge the Muslims. The Umayyad Caliphate in al-Andalus had broken up in the eleventh century, leaving its smaller successor states prey to Christian attacks from the north (see Chapter 10). This was the beginning of a movement of reconquest that culminated in 1492 with the surrender of the last Muslim kingdom. The word *crusade*, taken from Latin *crux* for "cross," was first used in Spain. Stories also circulated of the war conducted by seafaring Normans against the Muslims in Sicily, whom they finally defeated in the 1090s after thirty years of fighting.

The tales of pilgrims returning from Palestine further induced both churchmen and nobles to consider the Muslims a proper target for Christian militancy. Muslim rulers, who had controlled Jerusalem, Antioch, and Alexandria since the seventh century, generally tolerated and protected Christian pilgrims. But after 1071, when a Seljuk army defeated the Byzantine emperor at the Battle of Manzikert (see Chapter 10), Turkish nomads spread throughout the region, and security along the pilgrimage route through Anatolia, already none too good, deteriorated further. The decline of Byzantine power threatened ancient centers of Christianity, such as Ephesus in Anatolia, previously under imperial control.

Despite the theological differences between the Orthodox and Roman churches, the Byzantine emperor Alexius Comnenus asked the pope and western European rulers to help him confront the Muslim threat and reconquer what the Christians termed the Holy Land, the early centers of Christianity in Palestine and Syria. Pope Urban II responded; at the Council of Clermont in 1095, he addressed a huge crowd of people gathered in a field and called on them, as Christians, to stop fighting one another and go to the Holy Land to fight Muslims.

"God wills it!" exclaimed voices in the crowd. People cut cloth into crosses and sewed them on their shirts to symbolize their willingness to march on Jerusalem. Thus began the holy war now known as the "First Crusade." People at the time more often used the word *peregrinatio*, "pilgrimage." Urban promised to free Crusaders who had committed sins from their normal penance, or acts of atonement, the usual reward for peaceful pilgrims to Jerusalem.

The First Crusade captured Jerusalem in 1099 and established four Crusader principalities, the most important being the Latin Kingdom of Jerusalem. The next two expeditions strove with diminishing success to protect these gains. Muslim forces retook Jerusalem in 1187. By the time of the Fourth Crusade in 1204, the original religious ardor had so diminished that the commanders agreed, at the urging of the Venetians, to sack Constantinople first to help pay the cost of transporting the army by ship.

The Impact of the Crusades   Exposure to Muslim culture in Spain, Sicily, Mediterranean seaports, and the Crusader principalities established in the Holy Land made many Europeans aware of things lacking in their own lives. Borrowings from Muslim society occurred gradually and are not always easy to date, but Europeans eventually learned how to manufacture pasta, paper, sugar, cotton cloth, colored glass, and many other items that had formerly been imported. Arabic translations of and commentaries on Greek philosophical, scientific, and medical works, and equally important original works by Arabs and Iranians, provided a vital stimulus to European thought.

Some works were brought directly into the Latin world through the conquests of Sicily, parts of Spain and the Holy Land, and Constantinople (for Greek texts). Others were rendered into Latin by translators who worked in parts of Spain that continued under Muslim rule. Generations passed before all these works were

Armored Knights in Battle *This painting from around 1135 shows the armament of knights at the time of the Crusades. Chain mail, a helmet, and a shield carried on the left side protect the rider. The lance carried underarm and the sword are the primary weapons. Notice that riders about to make contact with lances have their legs straight and braced in the stirrups, while riders with swords and in flight have bent legs.*

Pierpont Morgan Library/Art Resource, NY

studied and understood, but they eventually transformed the intellectual world of the western Europeans, who previously had had little familiarity with Greek writings. The works of Aristotle and the Muslim commentaries on them were of particular importance to theologians, but Muslim writers like Avicenna (Ibn Sina) (980–1037) were of parallel importance in medicine.

Changes affecting the lifestyle of the nobles took place more quickly. Eleanor of Aquitaine (1122?–1204), one of the most influential women of the crusading era, accompanied her husband, King Louis VII of France, on the Second Crusade (1147–1149). The court life of her uncle Raymond, ruler of the Crusader principality of Antioch, particularly appealed to her. After her return to France, a lack of male offspring led to an annulment of her marriage with Louis, and in 1151 she married Henry of Anjou, who inherited the throne of England as Henry II three years later. Eleanor's sons—Richard Lion-Heart, famed in romance as the chivalrous foe of Saladin during the Third Crusade (1189–1192), and John—rebelled against their father but eventually succeeded him as kings of England.

In Aquitaine, a powerful duchy in southern France, Eleanor maintained her own court for a time. The poet-singers called troubadours who enjoyed her favor made her court a center for new music based on the idea of "courtly love," an idealization of feminine beauty and grace that influenced later European ideas of romance. Thousands of troubadour melodies survive in manuscripts, and some show the influence of the poetry styles then current in Muslim Spain. The favorite troubadour instrument, moreover, was the lute, a guitarlike instrument with a bulging belly whose design and name (Arabic *al-ud*) come from Muslim Spain. In centuries to come the lute would become the mainstay of Renaissance music in Italy.

Conclusion

The legacy of Roman rule affected eastern and western Europe in different ways. Byzantium inherited the grandeur, pomp, and legal supremacy of the imperial office and merged it with leadership of the Christian church. Although it guarded its shrinking frontiers against foreign invasion, it gradually contracted around Constantinople, its imperial capital, as more and more territory was lost. By contrast, no Roman core survived in the west. The Germanic peoples overwhelmed the legions guarding the frontiers and established kingdoms based on their own traditions. The law of the king and the law of the church did not echo each other. Yet memories of Roman grandeur and territorial unity resurfaced with the idea of a Holy Roman Empire, however unworkable that empire proved to be.

The competition between the Orthodox and Catholic forms of Christianity complicated the role of religion in the emergence of medieval European society and culture. The Byzantine Empire, constructed on a Roman political and legal heritage that had largely passed away in the west, was generally more prosperous than the Germanic kingdoms of western Europe, and its arts and culture were initially more sophisticated. Furthermore, Byzantine society became deeply Christian well before a comparable degree of Christianization had been reached in western Europe. Yet despite their success in transmitting their version of Christianity and imperial rule to Kievan Russia, and in the process erecting a barrier between the Orthodox Russians and the Catholic Slavs to their west, the Byzantines failed to demonstrate the dynamism and ferment that characterized both the Europeans to their west and the Muslims to their south. Byzantine armies played only a supporting role in the Crusades, and the emperors lost their capital and their power, at least temporarily, to western Crusaders in 1204.

Technology and commerce deepened the political and religious gulf between the two Christian zones. Changes in military techniques in western Europe increased battlefield effectiveness, while new agricultural technologies accompanied population increases that revitalized urban life and contributed to the crusading movement by making the nobility hunger for new lands. At the same time, the need to import food for growing urban populations contributed to the growth of maritime commerce in the Mediterranean and North Seas. Culture and manufacturing benefited greatly from the increased pace of communication and exchange. Lacking parallel developments of a similar scale, the Byzantine Empire steadily lost the dynamism of its early centuries and by the end of the period had clearly fallen behind western Europe in prosperity and cultural innovation.

IMPORTANT EVENTS 300–1200

325	Constantine convenes Council of Nicaea; Arian heresy condemned
392	Emperor Theodosius bans paganism in Byzantine Empire
432	Saint Patrick begins missionary work in Ireland
476	Deposing of the last Roman emperor in the West
527–565	Justinian and Theodora rule Byzantine Empire; imperial edicts collected in single law code
ca. 547	Death of Saint Benedict
634–650	Muslims conquer Byzantine provinces of Syria, Egypt, and Tunisia
711	Muslim conquest of Spain
732	Battle of Tours
800	Coronation of Charlemagne
843	Treaty of Verdun divides Carolingian Empire among Charlemagne's grandsons
882	Varangians take control of Kiev
910	Monastery of Cluny founded
962	Beginning of Holy Roman Empire
980	Vladimir becomes grand prince of Kievan Russia
1054	Formal schism between Latin and Orthodox Churches
1066	Normans under William the Conqueror invade England
1077	Climax of investiture controversy
1081–1118	Alexius Comnenus rules Byzantine Empire, calls for western military aid against Muslims
1095	Pope Urban II preaches First Crusade
1204	Western knights sack Constantinople in Fourth Crusade

12

INNER AND EAST ASIA, 400–1200

After the Han Empire fell in 220 C.E. (see Chapter 6), China suffered four centuries of rule by short-lived and competing states. The powerful and expansive Tang Empire (618–907), discussed in this Chapter, finally brought that period of turmoil to an end. Tang rule also encouraged the spread of Buddhism, brought by missionaries from India and by Chinese pilgrims returning with sacred Sanskrit texts. The Tang left an indelible mark on the Chinese imagination long after it too fell.

The origins of East Asia, characterized by a shared writing system, political ideology, and culture, can also be traced to the Sui and Tang Empires. The Tang Empire in particular became a model for emerging regimes on the Korean Peninsula, in northeast Asia, on the Japanese islands, and, to a certain extent, in continental Southeast Asia. But the formation of East Asia did not occur in isolation. Travelers from as far as India and Persia traveled to Tang China, bringing with them their native religions, artistic aesthetic, popular entertainments, technology, and even cuisine. Foreigners worked in the Tang bureaucracy, served in the military, and maintained close ties to the royal family.

The Song Empire that eventually succeeded the Tang Empire never approached the Tang's dominance over East Asia, nor was it as globally connected. However, it was extraordinarily productive and advanced in terms of technology, economy, and government. The sustainable boom in population during the Song Dynasty that fostered urbanization, and the expansion of domestic markets and international trade, played a major role in these seemingly modern developments. However, these were not simply Chinese achievements, newly introduced grain from Southeast Asia pushed the Song agriculture revolution.

THE SUI AND TANG EMPIRES, 581–755

After the fall of the Han dynasty, China was fragmented for several centuries. It was reunified under the Sui (sway) dynasty, father and son rulers who held power from 581 until Turks from Inner Asia (the part of the Eurasian steppe east of the Pamir Mountains) defeated the son in 615. He was assassinated three years later, and the Tang filled the political vacuum.

The small kingdoms of northern China and Inner Asia that had come and gone during the centuries following the fall of the Han Empire had structured themselves around a variety of political ideas and institutions. Some favored the Chinese tradition, with an emperor, a bureaucracy using the Chinese language exclusively, and a Confucian state philosophy (see Chapter 6). Others reflected Tibetan, Turkic, or other regional cultures and depended on Buddhism to legitimate their rule. Throughout the period the relationship between northern China and the deserts and steppe of Inner Asia remained a central focus of political life, a key commercial linkage, and a source of new ideas and practices.

Though northern China constituted the Sui heartland, population centers along the Yangzi (yahng-zeh) River in the south grew steadily and pointed to what would be the future direction of Chinese expansion. To facilitate communication and trade with the south, the Sui built the 1,100-mile (1,771-kilometer) **Grand Canal** linking the Yellow River with the Yangzi, and they also constructed irrigation systems in the Yangzi Valley. On their northern frontier, the Sui also improved the Great Wall, the barrier against nomadic incursions that had been gradually constructed by several earlier states.

Sui military ambition, which extended to Korea and Vietnam as well as Inner Asia, required high levels of organization and mustering of resources—manpower, livestock, wood, iron, and food supplies. The same was true of their massive public works projects. These burdens proved more than the Sui could sustain. Overextension compounded the political dilemma stemming from the military defeat and subsequent assassination of the second Sui emperor. These circumstances opened the way for another strong leader to establish a new state.

In 618 the powerful Li family took advantage of Sui disorder to carve out an empire of similar scale and ambition. They adopted the dynastic name Tang. The brilliant emperor **Li Shimin** (lee shir-meen) (r. 626–649) extended his power primarily westward into Inner Asia. Though he and succeeding rulers of the **Tang Empire** retained many Sui governing practices, they avoided overcentralization by allowing local nobles, gentry, officials, and religious establishments to exercise significant power (see Diversity and Dominance: Law and Society in China and Japan).

The Tang emperors and nobility descended from the Turkic elites that built small states in northern China after the Han, as well as from Chinese officials and settlers who had moved there. They appreciated the pastoral nomadic culture of Inner Asia (see Chapter 9) as well as Chinese traditions. Some of the most impressive works of Tang art, for example, are large pottery figurines of the horses and two-humped camels used along the Silk Road, brilliantly colored with glazes devised by Chinese potters. In warfare, the Tang combined Chinese weapons—the crossbow and armored infantrymen—with Inner Asian expertise in horsemanship and the use of iron stirrups. At their peak, from about 650 to 751, when they were defeated in Central Asia (present-day Kyrgyzstan) by an Arab Muslim army at the Battle of Talas River, the Tang armies were a formidable force.

Chang'an: Metropolis at the Center of East Asia

Much of the global interaction in China during the Sui and Tang dynasties occurred in the capital Chang'an (chahng-ahn), named in honor of the old Han capital. With a population of nearly 2 million, Chang'an and its surrounding suburbs constituted the largest metropolitan area in the world at the time. Its sophisticated gridlike layout, with its palace located in the north Pole Star position to reflect the celestial order, was imitated by Korean and Japanese capitals.

Chang'an became the center of what is often called the **tributary system**, a type of political relationship dating from Han times by which independent countries acknowledged the Chinese emperor's supremacy. Each tributary state sent regular embassies to the capital to pay tribute. As symbols of China's political supremacy, these embassies sometimes meant more to the Chinese than to the tribute-payers, who might have seen them more as a means of accessing the vast Chinese market.

More than simply a political center, Chang'an was also the premier study-abroad destination in Asia. Rulers sent intellectuals to learn statecraft, the techniques of running a government, to bring back to their home governments. Nestorian Christian churches and even Jewish communities existed in Chang'an, as did many Daoist and Buddhist temples and monasteries. Monks from Korea and Japan could study with Chinese Buddhists and with Indian masters who taught there in Sanskrit. The diverse population also included Central Asian, Arab, and Persian merchants who became long-time residents of the city. So many Iranians lived in Chang'an, for example, that the government established a special office just to address Iranian-Tang affairs.

Buddhism and the Tang Empire

State cults based on Buddhism had flourished in Inner Asia and north China since the fall of the Han, and the Tang rulers followed these Inner Asian precedents in their political use of Buddhism. Some interpretations of Buddhist doctrine accorded kings and emperors the spiritual function of welding humankind into a harmonious Buddhist society. Protecting spirits were to help the ruler govern and prevent harm from coming to his people.

Mahayana (mah-HAH-YAH-nah), or "Great Vehicle," Buddhism predominated. Mahayana fostered faith in enlightened beings—bodhisattvas—who postpone nirvana (see Chapter 7) to help others achieve enlightenment. This permitted the absorption of local gods and goddesses into Mahayana sainthood and thereby made conversion more attractive to the common people. Mahayana also encouraged translating Buddhist scripture into local languages, and it accepted religious practices not based on written texts. The tremendous reach of Mahayana views, which proved adaptable to different societies and classes of people, invigorated travel, language learning, and cultural exchange.

Early Tang princes competing for political influence enlisted monastic leaders to pray for them, preach on their behalf, counsel aristocrats to support them, and—perhaps most important—contribute monastic wealth to their war chests. In return, the monasteries received tax exemptions, land privileges, and gifts.

As the Tang Empire expanded westward, contacts with Central Asia and India increased, and so did the complexity of Buddhist influence throughout China. The Mahayana network connecting Inner Asia and China intersected a vigorous commercial world in which material goods and cultural influences mixed. Though Buddhism and Confucianism proved attractive to many different peoples, regional cultures and identities remained strong, just as regional commitments to Tibetan, Uighur (WEE-ger), and other languages and writing systems coexisted with the widespread use of written Chinese. Textiles reflected Persian, Korean, and Vietnamese styles, while influences from every part of Asia appeared in sports, music, and painting. Many historians characterize the Tang Empire as "cosmopolitan" because of its breadth and diversity.

Upheavals and Repression, 750–879
The later years of the Tang Empire saw increasing turmoil as a result of conflict with Tibetans and Turkic Uighurs. One result was a backlash against "foreigners," which to Confucians included Buddhists. The Tang elites came to see Buddhism as undermining the Confucian idea of the family as the model for the state. The Confucian scholar Han Yu (768–824) spoke powerfully for a return to traditional Confucian practices. In "Memorial on the Bone of Buddha" written to the emperor in 819 on the occasion of ceremonies to receive a bone of the Buddha in the imperial palace, he scornfully disparages the Buddha and his followers:

> Now Buddha was a man of the barbarians who did not speak the language of China and wore clothes of a different fashion. His sayings did not concern the ways of our ancient kings, nor did his manner of dress conform to their laws. He understood neither the duties that bind sovereign and subject nor the affections of father and son. If he were still alive today and came to our court by order of his ruler, Your Majesty might condescend to receive him, but ... he would then be escorted to the borders of the state, dismissed, and not allowed to delude the masses. How then, when he has long been dead, could his rotten bones, the foul and unlucky remains of his body, be rightly admitted to the palace? Confucius said, "Respect spiritual beings, while keeping at a distance from them."[1]

Buddhism was also attacked for encouraging women in politics. Wu Zhao (woo jow), a woman who had married into the imperial family, seized control of the government in 690 and declared herself emperor. She based her legitimacy on claiming to be a bodhisattva, an enlightened soul who had chosen to remain on earth to lead others to salvation. She also favored Buddhists and Daoists over Confucians in her court and government.

Later Confucian writers expressed contempt for Wu Zhao and other powerful women, such as the concubine Yang Guifei (yahng gway-fay). Bo Zhuyi (baw joo-ee), in his poem "Everlasting Remorse," lamented the influence of women at the Tang court, which had caused "the hearts of fathers and mothers everywhere

---

[1]Theodore de Bary, ed., *Sources of Chinese Tradition*, vol. 1, 2nd ed. (New York: Columbia University Press, 1999), 584.

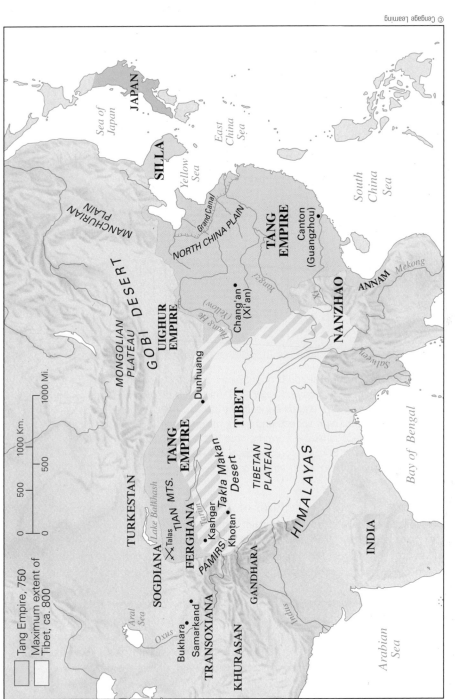

© Cengage Learning

MAP 12.1 The Tang Empire in Inner and Eastern Asia, 750

For over a century the Tang Empire controlled China and a very large part of Inner Asia. The defeat of Tang armies in 751 by a force of Arabs, Turks, and Tibetans at the Talas River in presentday Kyrgyzstan ended Tang westward expansion. To the east the Tang dominated Annam, and Japan and the Silla kingdom in Korea were leading tributary states of the Tang.

Horse figures, relief from Emperor T'ai Tsung's tomb in Hsi-An (Shensi). Chinese civilization, seventh century/De Agostini Picture Library/The Bridgeman Art Library

Iron Stirrups *This bas-relief from the tomb of Li Shimin depicts the type of horse on which the Tang armies conquered China and Inner Asia. Saddles with high supports in front and back, breastplates, and cruppers (straps beneath the tail that help keep the saddle in place) point to the importance of high speeds and quick maneuvering. Central and Inner Asian horsemen had iron stirrups available from the time of the Huns (fifth century). Earlier stirrups were of leather or wood. Stirrups could support the weight of shielded and well-armed soldiers rising in the saddle to shoot arrows or use lances.*

not to value the birth of boys, but the birth of girls."[2] Confucian elites heaped every possible charge on prominent women who offended them, accusing Emperor Wu of grotesque tortures and murders, including tossing the dismembered but still living bodies of enemies into wine vats and cauldrons. They blamed Yang Guifei for the outbreak of the An Lushan rebellion in 755 (see later in this Chapter).

Serious historians dismiss the stories about Wu Zhao as stereotypical characterizations of "evil" rulers. Eunuchs (castrated palace servants) charged by historians with controlling Chang'an and the Tang court and publicly executing rival bureaucrats represent a similar stereotype. In fact Wu seems to have ruled effectively and was not deposed until 705, when extreme old age (eighty-plus) incapacitated her. Nevertheless, traditional Chinese historians commonly

[2]Quoted in David Lattimore, "Allusion in T'ang Poetry," in *Perspectives on the T'ang*, ed. Arthur F. Wright and David Twitchett (New Haven, CT: Yale University Press, 1973), 436.

describe unorthodox rulers and all-powerful women as evil, and the truth about Wu will never be known.

Even Chinese gentry living in safe and prosperous localities associated Buddhism with social ills. People who worried about "barbarians" ruining their society pointed to Buddhism as evidence of the foreign evil, since it had such strong roots in Inner Asia and Tibet. Moreover, because Buddhism shunned earthly ties, monks and nuns severed relations with the secular world in search of enlightenment. They paid no taxes, served in no army. They deprived their families of advantageous marriage alliances and denied descendants to their ancestors. The Confucian elites saw all this as threatening to the family and to the family estates that underlay the Tang economic and political structure.

By the ninth century, hundreds of thousands of people had entered tax-exempt Buddhist institutions. In 840 the government moved to crush the monasteries whose tax exemption had allowed them to accumulate land, serfs, and precious objects, often as gifts. Within five years 4,600 temples had been destroyed. Now an enormous amount of land and 150,000 workers were returned to the tax rolls.

Buddhist centers like the cave monasteries at Dunhuang were protected by local warlords loyal to Buddhist rulers in Inner Asia. Nevertheless, China's cultural heritage suffered a great loss in the dissolution of the monasteries. Some sculptures and grottoes survived only in defaced form. Wooden temples and façades sheltering great stone carvings burned to the ground. Monasteries became legal again in later times, but Buddhism never recovered the influence of early Tang times.

The End of the Tang Empire, 879–907

The campaigns of expansion in the seventh century had left the empire dependent on local military commanders and a complex tax collection system. Reverses like the Battle of the Talas River in 751, where Arabs halted Chinese expansion into Central Asia, led to military demoralization and underfunding. In 755 An Lushan, a Tang general on the northeast frontier, led about 200,000 soldiers in rebellion. The emperor fled Chang'an and executed his favorite concubine, Yang Guifei, who was rumored to be An Lushan's lover. The rebellion lasted for eight years and resulted in new powers for the provincial military governors who helped suppress it. Even so, Chang'an never recovered, and during the eighth century, its decline symbolized Tang's waning influence over satellite states in Korea and Japan, which could no longer turn to China for support or inspiration.

A disgruntled member of the gentry, Huang Chao (wang show), led the most devastating uprising between 879 and 881. Despite his ruthless treatment of the villages he controlled, his rebellion attracted poor farmers and tenants who could not protect themselves from local bosses and oppressive landlords, or who simply did not know where else to turn in the deepening chaos. The new hatred of "barbarians" spurred the rebels to murder thousands of foreign residents in Canton and Beijing (bay-jeeng).

Local warlords finally wiped out the rebels, but Tang society did not find peace. Refugees, migrant workers, and homeless people became common sights.

Law and Society in China and Japan

The Tang law code, compiled in the early seventh century, served as the basis for the Tang legal system and as a model for later dynastic law codes. It combined the centralized authority of the imperial government, as visualized in the legalist tradition dating back to Han times, with Confucian concern for status distinctions and personal relationships. Like contemporary approaches to law in Christian Europe and the Islamic world, it did not fully distinguish between government as a structure of domination and law as an echo of religious and moral values.

Following a Preface, 502 articles, each with several parts, are divided into twelve books. Each article contains a basic ordinance with commentary, subcommentary, and sometimes additional questions. Excerpts from a single article from Book 1, General Principles, follow.

The Ten Abominations

Text: The first is called plotting rebellion
Subcommentary: The *Gongyang* (GON-gwang) *Commentary* states: "The ruler or parent has no harborers [of plots]. If he does have such harborers, he must put them to death." This means that if there are those who harbor rebellious hearts that would harm the ruler or father, he must then put them to death.

The king occupies the most honorable position and receives Heaven's precious decrees. Like Heaven and Earth, he acts to shelter and support, thus serving as the father and mother of the masses. As his children, as his subjects, they must be loyal and filial. Should they dare to cherish wickedness and have rebellious hearts, however, they will run counter to Heaven's constancy and violate human principle. Therefore this is called plotting rebellion.

Text: The second is called plotting great sedition
Subcommentary: This type of person breaks laws and destroys order, is against traditional norms, and goes contrary to virtue....

Commentary: Plotting great sedition means to plot to destroy the ancestral temples, tombs, or palaces of the reigning house.

Text: The third is called plotting treason
Subcommentary: The kindness of father and mother is like "great heaven, illimitable." ... Let one's heart be like the *xiao* bird or the *jing* beast, and then love and respect both cease. Those whose relationship is within the five degrees of mourning are the closest of kin. For them to kill each other is the extreme abomination and the utmost in rebellion, destroying and casting aside human principles. Therefore this is called contumacy.

Commentary: Contumacy means to beat or plot to kill [without actually killing] one's paternal grandparents or parents; or to kill one's paternal uncles or their wives, or one's elder brothers or sisters, or one's maternal grandparents, or one's husband, or one's husband's paternal grandparents, or his parents....

Text: The fifth is called depravity
Subcommentary: This article describes those who are cruel and malicious and who turn their backs on morality. Therefore it is called depravity.

Commentary: Depravity means to kill three members of a single household who have not committed a capital crime, or to dismember someone....

Commentary: The offense also includes the making or keeping of poison or sorcery.

Subcommentary: This means to prepare the poison oneself, or to keep it, or to give it to others in order to harm people. But if the preparation of the poison is not yet completed, this offense does not come under the ten abominations. As to sorcery, there are a great many methods, not all of which can be described.

Text: The tenth is called incest
Subcommentary: The *Zuo Commentary* states: "The woman has her husband's house; the man has his wife's chamber; and there must be no defilement on either side." If this is changed, then there is incest. If one behaves like birds and beasts and introduces licentious associates into one's family, the rules of morality are confused. Therefore this is called incest.

Commentary: This section includes having illicit sexual intercourse with relatives who are of the fourth degree of mourning or closer....

In Japan during the same period, there appeared a set of governing principles attributed to Prince Shotoku (573–621) called the "Seventeen-Article Constitution." These principles, which continued to influence Japanese government for many centuries, reflect Confucian ideals even though the prince was himself a devout Buddhist. The complete text of five of these principles follows:

I

Harmony is to be valued, and contentiousness avoided. All men are inclined to partisanship and few are truly discerning. Hence there are some who disobey their lords and fathers and who maintain feuds with the neighboring villages. But when those above are harmonious and those below are conciliatory and there is concord in the discussion of all matters, the disposition of affairs comes about naturally. Then what is there that cannot be accomplished?

VIII

Let ministers and functionaries attend the courts early in the morning, and retire late.

The business of the state does not admit of remissness, and the whole day is hardly enough for its accomplishment. If, therefore, the attendance at court is late, emergencies cannot be met; if officials retire soon, the work cannot be completed.

IX

Trustworthiness is the foundation of right. In everything let there be trustworthiness, for in this there surely consists the good and the bad, success and failure. If the lord and the vassal trust one another, what is there which cannot be accomplished? If the lord and the vassal do not trust one another, everything without exception ends in failure.

XIII

Let all persons entrusted with office attend equally to their functions. Owing to their illness or to their being sent on missions, their work may sometimes be neglected. But whenever they become able to attend to business, let them be as accommodating as if they had cognizance of it from before and not hinder public affairs on the score of their not having had to do with them.

XVII

Matters should not be decided by one person alone. They should be discussed with many others. In small matters, of less consequence, many others need not be consulted. It is only in considering weighty matters, where there is a suspicion that they might miscarry, that many others should be involved in debate and discussion so as to arrive at a reasonable conclusion.

Questions for Analysis
1. Why is one of these documents called a law code and the other a constitution?

2. How is the Confucian concern for family relations, duty, and social status differently manifested in the Chinese and Japanese documents?

3. Do these documents seem intended for government officials or for common people?

Sources: First selection from JOHNSON WALLACE; THE TANG CODE, VOL. I. © 1979 Princeton University Press. Reprinted by permission of Princeton University Press. Second selection from William Theodore de Bary et al., eds., *Sources of Japanese Tradition,* Vol. 1, *From Earliest Times to 1600* 2e, (New York: Columbia University Press, 2001), 50–54. Copyright © 2001 Columbia University Press. Reprinted with permission of the publisher.

Residents of northern China fled to the southern frontiers as groups from Inner Asia moved into localities in the north. Though Tang emperors continued in Chang'an until a warlord terminated their line in 907, they never regained power after Huang Chao's rebellion.

China and Its Rivals

In the aftermath of the Tang, three new states emerged and competed to inherit its legacy. The Liao (lee-OW) Empire of the Khitan (kee-THAN) people, pastoral nomads related to the Mongols living on the northeastern frontier, established their rule in the north. They centered their government on several cities, but the emperors preferred life in nomad encampments. On the Inner Asian frontier in northwestern China, the Minyak people (cousins of the Tibetans) established a state they called Tanggut (1038–1227) (TAHNG-gut) to show their connection with the fallen empire. The third state, the Chinese-speaking **Song Empire** came into being in 960 in central China.

These states embodied the political ambitions of peoples with different religious and philosophical systems—Mahayana Buddhism among the Liao, Tibetan Buddhism among the Tangguts, and Confucianism among the Song. Cut off from Inner Asia, the Song used advanced seafaring and sailing technologies to forge maritime connections with other states in East, West, and Southeast Asia. The Song elite shared the late Tang dislike of "barbaric" or "foreign" influences as they tried to cope with multiple enemies that heavily taxed their military capacities. Meanwhile, Korea, Japan, and some Southeast Asian states strengthened political and cultural ties with China.

The Liao and Jin Challenge   The Liao Empire of the Khitan people extended from Siberia to Inner Asia. Variations on the Khitan name became the name for China in these distant regions: "Kitai" for the Mongols, "Khitai" for the Russians, and "Cathay" for Italian merchants like Marco Polo who reported on China in Europe (see Chapter 13).

The Liao rulers prided themselves on their pastoral traditions as horse and cattle breeders, which were the continuing source of their military might, and they made no attempt to create a single elite culture. Instead they encouraged Chinese elites to use their own language, study their own classics, and see the emperor

Pierre Colombel/Corbis

Buddhist Cave Painting at Dunhuang *Hundreds of caves dating to the period when Buddhism enjoyed popularity and government favor in China survive in Gansu province, which was beyond the reach of the Tang rulers when they turned against Buddhism. This cave, dated to the period 565–576, depicts the historical Buddha flanked by bodhisattvas. Scenes of the Buddha preaching appear on the wall to the left.*

through Confucian eyes; and they encouraged other peoples to use their own languages and see the emperor as a champion of Buddhism or as a nomadic chieftain. On balance, Buddhism far outweighed Confucianism in this and other northern states, where rulers depended on their roles as bodhisattvas or as Buddhist kings to legitimate power. Liao rule lasted from 916 to 1125.

The Liao Empire was the most powerful East Asian empire at the time, with the largest army in East Asia. Superb horsemen and archers, the Khitans also challenged the Song with siege machines from China and Central Asia. A truce concluded in 1005 required the Song emperor to pay the Liao great quantities of cash and silk annually. A century later, the Song tired of paying tribute and secretly allied with the Jurchens of northeastern Asia, who also resented Liao rule. In 1115 the Jurchens first destroyed the Liao capital in Mongolia and proclaimed their own empire, the Jin, and then turned on the Song.

The Jurchens grew rice, millet, and wheat, but they also spent a good deal of time hunting, fishing, and tending livestock. Using Khitan military arts and political organization, they became formidable enemies in an all-out campaign against the Song in 1127, laying siege to the Song capital, Kaifeng (kie-fuhng), and capturing the Song emperor. Within a few years the Song withdrew south of the Yellow

River and established a new capital at Hangzhou (hahng-jo), leaving central as well as northern China in Jurchen control. Annual payments to the Jin Empire staved off further warfare. Historians generally refer to this period as the "Southern Song" (1127–1279).

Song Industries   The Southern Song came closer to initiating an industrial revolution than any other premodern state. Many Song advances in technology, medicine, astronomy, and mathematics had come to China in Tang times, sometimes from very distant places. Song officials, scholars, and businessmen had the motivation and resources to adapt this Tang lore to meet their military, agricultural, and administrative needs.

Song mathematicians introduced the use of fractions, first employing them to describe the phases of the moon. From lunar observations, Song astronomers constructed a very precise calendar and, alone among the world's astronomers, noted the explosion of the Crab Nebula in 1054. Song inventors drew on their knowledge of celestial coordinates, particularly the Pole Star, to refine compass design. The magnetic compass, an earlier Chinese invention, shrank in size in Song times and gained a fixed pivot point for the needle. With a protective glass cover, the compass now became suitable for seafaring, a use first attested in 1090.

Development of the seaworthy compass coincided with new techniques in building China's main oceangoing ship, the **junk**. A stern-mounted rudder improved the steering of the large ship in uneasy seas, and watertight bulkheads helped keep it afloat in emergencies. The shipwrights of the Persian Gulf soon copied these features in their ship designs.

Because they needed iron and steel to make weapons for their army of 1.25 million men, the Song rulers fought their northern rivals for control of mines in north China. Production of coal and iron soared. By the end of the eleventh century, cast iron production reached about 125,000 tons (113,700 metric tons) annually, putting it on a par with the output of eighteenth-century Britain. Engineers became skilled at high-temperature metallurgy using enormous bellows, often driven by water wheels, to superheat the molten ore. Military engineers used iron to buttress defensive works because it was impervious to fire or concussion. Armorers mass-produced body armor. Iron construction also appeared in bridges and small buildings. Mass-production techniques for bronze and ceramics in use in China for nearly two thousand years were adapted to iron casting and assembly.

To counter cavalry assaults, the Song experimented with **gunpowder**, which they initially used to propel clusters of flaming arrows. During the wars against the Jurchens in the 1100s, the Song introduced a new and terrifying weapon. Shells launched from Song fortifications exploded in the midst of the enemy, blowing out iron shrapnel and dismembering men and horses. The short range of these shells limited them to defensive uses.

Economy and Society in Song China   In a warlike era, Song elite culture idealized civil pursuits. Socially, the civil man outranked the military man. Private academies, designed to train young men for the official examinations, became influential in culture and politics. New

© Cengage Learning

MAP 12.2 Liao and Song Empires, ca. 1100

The states of Liao in the north and Song in the south generally ceased open hostilities after a treaty in 1005 stabilized the border and imposed an annual payment on Song China.

interpretations of Confucian teachings became so important and influential that the term **neo-Confucianism** is used for Song and later versions of Confucian thought.

Zhu Xi (jew she) (1130–1200), the most important early neo-Confucian thinker, wrote in reaction to the many centuries during which Buddhism and Daoism had over-shadowed the precepts of Confucius. He and others worked out a systematic approach to cosmology that focused on the central conception that human nature is moral, ratio-nal, and essentially good. To combat the Buddhist dismissal of worldly affairs as a transitory distraction, they reemphasized individual moral and social responsibility. Their human ideal was the sage, a person who could preserve mental stability and serenity while dealing conscientiously with troubling social problems. Whereas earlier Confucian thinkers had written about sage kings and political leaders, the neo-Confucians espoused the spiritual idea of universal sagehood, a state that could be achieved through proper study of the new Confucian principles and cosmology.

Popular Buddhist sects also persisted during the Song, demonstrating that anti-Buddhist feelings were not as ferocious as Confucian polemics against Buddhism might suggest. Some Buddhists elaborated on Tang-era folk practices derived from India and Tibet. The best known, Chan Buddhism (known as **Zen** in Japan and as Son in Korea), asserted that mental discipline alone could win salvation.

Meditation, a key Chan practice that was employed by Confucians as well as Buddhists, afforded prospective officials relief from studying for civil service exam-inations, which continued into the Song from the Tang period. Unlike the ancient Han policy of hiring and promoting on the basis of recommendations, Song-style examinations involved a large bureaucracy. Test questions, which changed each time the examinations were given, often related to economic management or foreign policy even though they were always based on Confucian classics.

Hereditary class distinctions meant less than they had in Tang times, when noble lineages played a greater role in the structure of power. The new system recruited the most talented men, whatever their origin. Yet men from wealthy fami-lies enjoyed an advantage. Preparation for the tests consumed so much time that peasant boys could rarely compete.

Success in the examinations brought good marriage prospects, the chance for a high salary, and enormous prestige. Failure could bankrupt a family and ruin a man both socially and psychologically. This put great pressure on candidates, who spent days writing essays in tiny, dim, airless examination cells.

During the Song era, a technical change from woodblock to an early form of **movable type** made printing cheaper. To promote its ideological goals, the Song government authorized the mass production of test preparation books in the years before 1000. Although a man had to be literate to read the preparation books and basic education was still rare, a growing number of candidates entered the Song bureaucracy without noble, gentry, or elite backgrounds.

The availability of printed books changed country life as well, since landlords gained access to expert advice on planting and irrigation techniques, harvesting, tree cultivation, threshing, and weaving. Landlords frequently gathered their tenants and workers to show them illustrated texts and explain their meaning. New agricultural land was developed south of the Yangtze River, and iron imple-ments such as plows and rakes, first used in the Tang era, were adapted to southern wet-rice cultivation.

From Joseph Needham, Science and Civilization in China, Vol. 4. After the original in Su Song's treatise Xinyi Xiangfayao, 1092

Su Song's Astronomical Clock *This gigantic clock built at Kaifeng between 1088 and 1092 combined mathematics, astronomy, and calendar making with skillful engineering. The team overseen by Su Song placed an armillary sphere on the observation platform and linked it with chains to the water-driven central mechanism shown in the cutaway view. The water wheel also rotated the Buddha statues in the multistory pagoda the spectators are looking at. Other devices displayed the time of the day, the month, and the year.*

The growing profitability of agriculture interested ambitious members of the gentry. Still a frontier for Chinese settlers under the Tang, the south saw increasing concentration of land in the hands of a few wealthy families. In the process, the indigenous inhabitants of the region, related to the modern-day populations of Malaysia, Thailand, and Laos, retreated into the mountains or southward toward Vietnam.

During the 1100s the total population of the Chinese territories, spurred by prosperity, rose above 100 million. The leading Song cities had fewer than a million inhabitants but were still among the largest cities in the world. Health and crowding posed problems in the Song capitals. Multistory wooden apartment houses fronted on narrow streets—sometimes only 4 or 5 feet (1.2 to 1.5 meters) wide—that were clogged by peddlers or families spending time outdoors. The crush of people called for new techniques in waste management, water supply, and firefighting.

In Hangzhou engineers diverted the nearby river to flow through the city, flushing away waste and disease. Arab and European travelers who had firsthand experience with the Song capital, and who were sensitive to urban conditions in their own societies, expressed amazement at Hangzhou's amenities: restaurants, parks, bookstores, wine shops, tea houses, theaters, and various entertainments.

The idea of credit, originating in the robust long-distance trade of the Tang period, spread widely under the Song. Intercity or interregional credit—what the Song called "flying money"—depended on the acceptance of guarantees that the paper could be redeemed for coinage at another location. The public accepted the practice because credit networks tended to be managed by families, so that brothers and cousins were usually honoring each other's certificates.

"Flying money" certificates differed from government-issued paper money, which the Song pioneered. In some years, military expenditures consumed 80 percent of the government budget. The state responded to this financial pressure by distributing paper money. But this made inflation so severe that by the beginning of the 1100s paper money was trading for only 1 percent of its face value. Eventually the government withdrew paper money and instead imposed new taxes, sold monopolies, and offered financial incentives to merchants.

The Night Revelry of Han Xizai, by Gu Hongzhong the court painter sent by his suspicious monarch to spy on Han and to make a record of Han's licentious behaviour/Werner Forman Archive/The Bridgeman Art Library

Female Musicians *A group of entertainers from a Song period copy of a lost Tang painting titled "Night Revels of Han Xizai." The emperor ordered the painter to document the lifestyle of a man who preferred music, dance, and poetry to accepting appointment as Prime Minister. The mood of genteel indulgence appealed to Song era elites. Chinese women were not veiled, but foot-binding became common under the Song.*

Hard-pressed for the revenue needed to maintain the army, canals, roads, waterworks, and other state functions, the government finally resorted to tax farming: selling the rights to tax collection to private individuals. Tax farmers made their profit by collecting the maximum amount and sending an agreed-upon smaller sum to the government. This meant exorbitant rates for taxable services, such as tolls, and much heavier tax burdens on the common people.

Rapid economic growth undermined the remaining government monopolies and the traditional strict regulation of business. Now merchants and artisans as well as gentry and officials could make fortunes. With land no longer the only source of wealth, the traditional social hierarchy common to an agricultural economy weakened, while cities, commerce, consumption, and the use of money and credit boomed. Urban life reflected the elite's growing taste for fine fabrics, porcelain, exotic foods, large houses, and exquisite paintings and books.

In conjunction with the backlash against Buddhism and revival of Confucianism that began under the Tang and intensified under the Song, women experienced subordination, legal disenfranchisement, and social restriction. Merchants spent long periods away from home, and many maintained several wives in different locations. Frequently they depended on wives to manage their homes and even their businesses in their absence. But though women took on responsibility for the management of their husbands' property, their own property rights suffered legal erosion. Under Song law, a woman's property automatically passed to her husband, and women could not remarry if their husbands divorced them or died.

The subordination of women proved compatible with Confucianism, and it became fashionable to educate girls just enough to read simplified versions of Confucian philosophy that emphasized the lowly role of women. Modest education made these young women more desirable as companions for the sons of gentry or noble families and as literate mothers in lower-ranking families aspiring to improve their status. The poet Li Qingzhao (lee CHING-jow) (1083–1141) acknowledged and made fun of her unusual status as a highly celebrated female writer:

> *Although I've studied poetry for thirty years*
> *I try to keep my mouth shut and avoid reputation.*
> *Now who is this nosy gentleman talking about my poetry*
> *Like Yang Ching-chih* (yahng SHING-she)
> *Who spoke of Hsiang Ssu* (sang sue) *everywhere he went.*[3]

Her reference is to a hermit poet of the ninth century who was continually and extravagantly praised by a court official, Yang Ching-chih.

Female footbinding first appeared among slave dancers at the Tang court, but it did not become widespread until the Song period. The bindings forced the toes under and toward the heel, so that the bones eventually broke and the woman could not walk on her own. In noble and gentry families, footbinding began between ages five and seven. In less wealthy families, girls worked until they were older, so footbinding began only in a girl's teens.

---

[3]Quoted at "Women's Early Music, Art, Poetry," http://music.acu.edu/www/iawm/pages/reference/tzusongs.html.

Many literate men condemned the maiming of innocent girls and the general uselessness of footbinding. Nevertheless, bound feet became a status symbol. By 1200 a woman with unbound feet had become undesirable in elite circles, and mothers of elite status, or aspiring to such status, almost without exception bound their daughters' feet. They knew that girls with unbound feet faced rejection. Working women and the indigenous peoples of the south, where northern practices took a longer time to penetrate, did not practice footbinding. Consequently they enjoyed considerably more mobility and economic independence than did elite Chinese women.

NEW KINGDOMS IN EAST ASIA

The best possibilities for expanding the Confucian worldview of the Song lay with newly emerging kingdoms to the east and south. Korea, Japan, and Vietnam, like Song China, devoted great effort to the cultivation of rice. This practice fit well with Confucian social ideas, as tending the young rice plants, irrigating the rice paddies, and managing the harvest required coordination among many village and kin groups and rewarded hierarchy, obedience, and self-discipline.

Confucianism also justified using agricultural profits to support the education, safety, and comfort of the literate elite. In each of these new kingdoms Song civilization melded with indigenous cultural and historical traditions to create a distinctive synthesis.

Chinese Influences   Korea, Japan, and Vietnam had first centralized power under ruling houses in the early Tang period, and their state ideologies continued to resemble that of the early Tang, when Buddhism and Confucianism seemed compatible. Government offices went to noble families and did not depend on passing examinations on Confucian texts. Landowning and agriculture remained the major sources of income, and landowners faced no challenges from a merchant class or urban elite.

Nevertheless, learned men prized literacy in classical Chinese and a good knowledge of Confucian texts. Though formal education was available to only a small number of people, the ruling and landholding elites sought to instill Confucian ideals of hierarchy and harmony among the general population (see Diversity and Dominance: Law and Society in China and Japan).

Korea   Our first knowledge of Korea, Japan, and Vietnam comes from early Chinese officials and travelers. When the Qin Empire established its first colony in the Korean peninsula in the third century B.C.E., Chinese bureaucrats began documenting Korean history and customs. Han writers noted the horse breeding, strong hereditary elites, and **shamanism** (belief in the ability of certain individuals to contact ancestors and the invisible spirit world) of Korea's small kingdoms. But Korea quickly absorbed Confucianism and Buddhism.

Mountainous in the east and north, Korea was heavily forested until modern times. The land that can be cultivated (less than 20 percent) lies mostly in the south, where a warm climate and monsoon rains support two crops per year. Population movements from Manchuria, Mongolia, and Siberia to the north and to Japan in the south promoted the spread of languages that were very different from Chinese but distantly related to the Turkic tongues of Inner Asia.

In the early 500s the dominant landholding families made inherited status—the "bone ranks"—permanent in Silla (SILL-ah or SHILL-ah), a kingdom in the southeast of the peninsula. In the early 660s, Silla defeated the southwestern kingdom of Paekche, which had played a major role as a maritime power in transmitting Chinese culture to Japan. Then in 668 the northern Koguryŏ kingdom came to an end after prolonged conflict with the Sui and Tang. Koguryŏ was so influential in Northeast Asia that the Liao and Jin Empires, and subsequent Korean kingdoms, claimed to inherit its legacy.

Supported by the Tang, Silla now took control of much of the Korean peninsula. The Silla rulers imitated Tang government and examined officials on the Confucian classics. They also sent Buddhist monks to China. But the intellectual exchange was not one-directional: writings by the monk Wonhyo, known as the "Korean Commentary," greatly influenced Buddhism in China. The fall of the Tang in the early 900s coincided with Silla's collapse and enabled the ruling house of **Koryo** (KAW-ree-oh), from which the modern name "Korea" derives, to rule a united peninsula for the next three centuries. Threatened constantly by the Liao and then the Jin in northern China, Koryo maintained amicable relations with Song China in the south. The Koryo kings supported Buddhism and made superb printed editions of Buddhist texts.

The oldest surviving woodblock print in Chinese characters comes from Korea in the middle 700s. Commonly used during the Tang period, woodblock printing required great technical skill. A calligrapher would write the text on thin paper, which would then be pasted upside down on a block of wood. Once wetted, the characters showed through from the back, and an artisan would carve away the wooden surface surrounding each character. A fresh block had to be carved for each printed page. Korean artisans developed their own advances in printing, including experiments with movable type. By Song times, Korean experiments reached China, where further improvements led to metal or porcelain type from which texts could be cheaply printed.

Japan

Japan consists of four main islands and many smaller ones stretching in an arc from as far south as Georgia to as far north as Maine. The nearest point of contact with the Asian mainland lies 100 miles away in southern Korea. In early times Japan was even more mountainous and heavily forested than Korea, with only 11 percent of its land area suitable for cultivation. Mild winters and monsoon rains supported the earliest population centers on the coastlands of the Inland Sea between Honshu and Shikoku Islands. The first rulers to extend their power broadly in the fourth and fifth centuries C.E. were based in the Yamato River Basin on the Kinai Plain at the eastern end of the sea.

The first Chinese description of Japan, dating from the fourth century, tells of an island at the eastern edge of the world that is divided into hundreds of small communities, with the largest one, called Yamatai, ruled over by a shamaness named Himiko or Pimiko. The location of the early Yamatai kingdom remains a source of debate and fascination in Japan, but archeological finds point to frequent interaction with China and Korea.

In the mid-600s the Yamatai rulers, acting on knowledge gained from Korean contacts and embassies to Chang'an sent by five different kings, implemented the Taika (TIE-kah) and other reforms, giving this regime the key features of Tang government. A legal code, an official variety of Confucianism, and an official reverence for Buddhism blended with the local recognition of indigenous and immigrant chieftains as territorial administrators. Within a century, a centralized government with a complex system of law had emerged, as attested by a massive history in the Confucian style.

Women from the aristocracy became royal consorts and thereby linked their kinsmen with the royal court. At the death of her husband in 592, Suiko, a woman from the immigrant aristocratic family of Soga, became empress. She occupied the throne until 628, enjoying a longer reign than any other ruler down to the nineteenth century. Asuka, her capital, saw a flowering of Buddhist art, and her nephew Shotoku opened relations with Sui China and is credited with promulgating a "Constitution" in 604 that had lasting influence on Japan's governing philosophy (see Diversity and Dominance: Law and Society in China and Japan).

The Japanese mastered Chinese building techniques so well that Nara (NAH-rah) (710-784) and Kyoto (794-1868), Japan's early capitals, provide invaluable evidence of the wooden architecture long since vanished from China. During the eighth century Japan in some ways surpassed China in Buddhist studies. In 752 dignitaries from all over Mahayana Buddhist Asia gathered at the enormous Todaiji temple, near Nara, to celebrate the "eye-opening" of the "Great Buddha" statue.

Though the Japanese adopted Chinese building styles and some street plans, Japanese cities were built without walls. One reason was that central Japan was not plagued by constant warfare. Also, the Confucian Mandate of Heaven, which justified dynastic changes, played no role in legitimating Japanese government. The *tenno*, or "heavenly sovereign"—often called "emperor" in English—belonged to a family believed to have ruled Japan since the beginning of history. The dynasty never changed. A prime minister and the leaders of the native religion, in later times called Shinto, the "way of the gods," exercised real control.

By 750 the government in Nara had reached its zenith. During the Nara and Early Heian periods, the rulers expanded their fledgling regime outward from central Japan. They did this by sending an army led by a "barbarian-subduing generalissimo," the shogun, into regions on the peripheries of the Japanese islands. The court extended Japanese rice-growing culture into the territory of the Hayato people of southern Kyushu and into northeastern Honshu, where the Emishi, a mixed indigenous population, practiced slash-and-burn agriculture. A collection of poems dating from the eight century, called *Ten Thousand Leaves*, records the hopes and fears of those engaged in expanding the sovereign's contact with China, the Korean peninsula, and Japanese islands distant from the capital city:

> *A frontier-guard when I set out, Oh what turmoil there was! Of the work my wife should do, I said not a word and came away.*[4]

In 794 the central government moved to Kyoto, usually called by its ancient name, Heian (hay-ahn). Legally centralized government lasted there until 1185,

---

[4]The Manyōshū: The Nippon Gakujutsu Shinkōkai translation of One Thousand poems, p. 254.

though power became decentralized toward the end. In Kyoto members of the **Fujiwara** (foo-jee-WAH-rah) clan—a family of priests, bureaucrats, and warriors who had succeeded the Soga clan in influence—controlled power and protected the emperor. Fujiwara dominance favored men of Confucian learning over the generally illiterate warriors, and noblemen of the Fujiwara period read the Chinese classics and appreciated painting and poetry.

Gradually, however, the Fujiwara nobles began to entrust responsibility for local government, policing, and tax collection to their warriors, who were known as *samurai*, literally "one who serves." Though often of humble origins, a small number of these warriors had achieved wealth and power by the late 1000s. By the middle 1100s the nobility had lost control, and civil war between rival warrior clans engulfed the capital.

Like other East Asian states influenced by Confucianism, the elite families of Fujiwara Japan did not encourage education for women. The hero of the celebrated Japanese novel about Fujiwara court culture, *The Tale of Genji*, written around the year 1000 and often regarded as the world's first novel, remarks: "Women should have a general knowledge of several subjects, but it gives a bad impression if they show themselves to be attached to a particular branch of learning."[5] However, within the marriage politics of the day, having interesting and talented women helped the Fujiwara monopolize the monarch's attention on their own women rather than those of other families.

Fujiwara noblewomen lived in near-total isolation, generally spending their time on cultural pursuits and the study of Buddhism. To communicate with their families or among themselves, they depended on writing. The simplified syllabic script that they used represented the Japanese language in its fully inflected form (the Chinese classical script used by Fujiwara men could not do so).

Sei Shonagon (SAY SHOH-nah-gohn), a lady attending one of the royal consorts, composed her *Pillow Book* between 996 and 1021. Most likely named for being kept by the author's pillow so she could jot down occasional thoughts, this famous work begins:

> Spring is best at dawn as gradually the hilltops lighten, while the light grows brighter until there are purple-tinged clouds trailing through the sky.
> Summer is best at night. That goes without saying when there is a full moon. But when fireflies flit here and there in a dark sky, that too is wonderful. It is even wonderful when it is raining.[6]

Military clans acquired increasing importance during the period 1156–1185, when warfare between rival families culminated in the establishment of the **Kamakura** (kah-mah-KOO-rah) **Shogunate** in eastern Honshu, far from the old religious and political center at Kyoto. The standing of the Fujiwara family fell as nobles and the emperor hurried to accommodate the new warlords. *The Tale of the Heike*, an anonymously composed thirteenth-century epic account of the clan war, reflects a Buddhist appreciation of the impermanence of worldly things, a view that became common among the new warrior class. This class eventually absorbed some

---

[5]Quoted in Ivan Morris, *The World of the Shining Prince: Court Life in Ancient Japan* (New York: Penguin Books, 1979), 221–222.

[6]Quoted in Ivan Morris, trans., *The Pillow Book of Sei Shonagon* (New York: Columbia University Press, 1991), section 1.

of the Fujiwara aristocratic values, but the monopoly of power by a nonmilitary civil elite had come to an end.

Vietnam   Not until Tang times did the relationship between Vietnam and China become close enough for economic and cultural interchange to play an important role. Occupying the coastal regions east of the mountainous spine of mainland Southeast Asia, Vietnam's economic and political life centered on two fertile river valleys, the Red River in the north and the Mekong (may-KONG) in the south. The rice-based agriculture of Vietnam made the region well suited for integration with southern China. In both regions the wet climate and hilly terrain demanded expertise in irrigation.

Early Vietnamese peoples may have preceded the Chinese in using draft animals in farming and working with metal. But in Tang and Song times the elites of Annam (ahn-nahm)—as the Chinese called early Vietnam—adopted Confucian bureaucratic training, Mahayana Buddhism, and other aspects of Chinese culture, and Annamese elites continued to rule in the Tang style after that dynasty's fall. In 936 Annam assumed the name Dai Viet (die vee-yet) and maintained good relations with Song China as an independent country.

Champa, located in what is now southern Vietnam, rivaled the Dai Viet state. The cultures of India and the Malay Peninsula strongly influenced Champa through maritime networks of trade and communication. During the Tang period, Champa fought with Dai Viet, but both kingdoms cooperated with the less threatening Song. Among the tribute gifts brought to the Song court by Champa emissaries was **Champa rice** (originally from India). Chinese farmers soon made use of this fast-maturing variety to improve their yields of the essential crop.

Vietnam shared the general Confucian interest in hierarchy, but attitudes toward women, like those in Korea and Japan, differed from the Chinese model. None of the societies adopted footbinding. In Korea strong family alliances that functioned like political and economic organizations allowed women a role in negotiating and disposing of property. Before the adoption of Confucianism, Annamese women had enjoyed higher status than women in China, perhaps because both women and men participated in wet-rice cultivation. The Trung sisters of Vietnam, who lived in the second century C.E. and led local farmers in resistance against the Han Empire, still serve as national symbols in Vietnam and as local heroes in southern China.

Conclusion

The Tang Empire put into place a solid system of travel, trade, and communications that allowed cultural and economic influences to move quickly from Inner Asia to Japan. In addition, diversity within the empire produced great wealth and new ideas. Eventually, however, tensions among rival groups weakened the political structure and led to great violence and misery.

The post-Tang fragmentation permitted regional cultures to emerge that experimented with and often improved on Tang military, architectural, and scientific technologies. In northern and Inner Asia, these refinements included state ideologies based on Buddhism, bureaucratic practices based on Chinese traditions, and military techniques combining nomadic horsemanship and strategies with Chinese armaments and weapons. In Song China, the spread of Tang technological knowledge resulted in the privatization of commerce, major advances in technology and industry, increased productivity in agriculture, and deeper exploration of ideas relating to time, cosmology, and mathematics.

The brilliant achievements of the Song period came from mutually reinforcing developments in economy and technology. Without the rampant warfare and exploitation of the economy in the mid to late Tang period, the Song economy, though much smaller than its predecessor, showed great productivity, circulating goods and money throughout East Asia and stimulating the economies of neighbors.

Korea, Japan, and Vietnam developed distinct social, economic, and political systems. Buddhism became the preferred religion in all three regions, but Chinese influences, largely deriving from a universal esteem for Confucian thought and writings, put down deep roots. All of these societies made advances in agricultural technology and productivity and raised their literacy rates as printing spread. In the absence of a land border with China, Japan retained greater political independence than Korea and Vietnam. The culture of its imperial center reached a high level of refinement, but the political system was ultimately based on a warrior aristocracy.

IMPORTANT EVENTS 200–1200

220–589	China disunited
552	Turkic Empire founded
581–618	Sui unification
618	Tang Empire founded
668	Silla victory in Korea
751	Battle of Talas River
752	"Eye-Opening" ceremony in Japan
755–763	An Lushan rebellion
840	Suppression of Buddhism
ca. 850	Buddhist political power secured in Tibet
879–881	Huang Chao rebellion
907	End of Tang Empire
916	Liao Empire founded
918	Koryo founded
960	Song Empire Founded
1115	Jin Empire founded
1185	Kamakura shogunate founded

PART FOUR

INTERREGIONAL PATTERNS OF CULTURE AND CONTACT, 1200–1550

CHAPTER 13
Mongol Eurasia and Its Aftermath, 1200–1500

CHAPTER 14
Latin Europe, 1200–1500

CHAPTER 15
Southern Empires, Southern Seas, 1200–1500

CHAPTER 16
The Maritime Revolution, to 1550

Part IV begins with the Mongol conquests under Chinggis Khan, whose empire made Mongolia the center of an administrative and trading system linking Europe, the Middle East, Russia, and East Asia. Some lands flourished; others groaned under tax burdens and physical devastation.

Societies that escaped conquest also felt the Mongol impact. Around the eastern Mediterranean coast and in eastern Europe, Southeast Asia, and Japan, fear of Mongol attack stimulated defense planning and accelerated processes of urbanization, technological development, and political centralization.

By 1500, Mongol dominance had waned. A new Chinese empire, the Ming, was expanding its influence in Southeast Asia. The Ottomans had overthrown the Byzantine Empire, and Christian monarchs in Spain and Portugal, victorious over Muslim enemies, were laying the foundations of new overseas empires.

As Eurasia's overland trade faded, merchants, soldiers, and explorers took to the seas. From China, the admiral Zheng He made state-sponsored long-distance voyages that were spectacular but without long-term results. Meanwhile, Africans explored the Atlantic, and Polynesians colonized the central and eastern Pacific in the 1300s and 1400s. By 1500 Christopher Columbus had reached the Americas; within twenty-five years a Portuguese ship would sail around the world.

The overland routes of Eurasia had generated massive wealth in East Asia and a growing hunger for commerce in Europe. These factors similarly spurred the development of maritime trade. Exposure to the achievements, wealth, and resources of the Americas, sub-Saharan Africa, and Asia guaranteed the further expansion of European exploration and maritime power.

13

MONGOL EURASIA AND ITS AFTERMATH, 1200–1500

When Temüjin (TEM-uh-jin) was a boy, a rival group murdered his father. Temüjin's mother tried to shelter him, but she could not find a safe haven. At fifteen Temüjin sought refuge with the leader of the Keraits (keh-rates), a warring confederation whose people spoke Turkic and respected both Christianity and Buddhism. Temüjin learned the importance of religious tolerance, the necessity of dealing harshly with enemies, and the variety of Inner Asia's cultural and economic traditions.

In 1206 the **Mongols** and their allies acknowledged Temüjin as **Chinggis Khan** (CHING-iz KAHN) (sometimes known as Genghis), or supreme leader. His advisers spoke many languages and belonged to different religions. His deathbed speech, which cannot be literally true even though a contemporary recorded it, captures the strategy behind Mongol success: "If you want to retain your possessions and conquer your enemies, you must make your subjects submit willingly and unite your diverse energies to a single end."[1] By implementing this strategy, Chinggis Khan became the most famous conqueror in history, initiating an expansion of Mongol dominion that by 1250 stretched from Poland to northern China.

Scholars today stress the positive developments that transpired under Mongol rule. European and Asian sources of the time, however, vilify the Mongols as agents of death, suffering, and conflagration, a still-common viewpoint based on reliable accounts of horrible massacres.

The tremendous extent of the Mongol Empire promoted the movement of people and ideas from one end of Eurasia to the other. Trade routes improved, markets expanded, and the demand for products grew. Trade on the Silk Road, which had declined with the fall of the Tang Empire (see Chapter 12), revived.

Between 1218 and about 1350 in western Eurasia and down to 1368 in China, the Mongols focused on specific economic and strategic interests, usually permitting local cultures to survive and develop. In some regions, local reactions to Mongol domination sowed seeds of regional and ethnic identity that blossomed in the period of Mongol decline. Regions as widely separated as Russia, Iran, China,

---

[1]Quotation adapted from Desmond Martin, *Chinggis Khan and His Conquest of North China* (Baltimore: The John Hopkins Press, 1950), 303.

Korea, and Japan benefited from the Mongol stimulation of economic and cultural exchange and also found in their opposition to the Mongols new bases for political consolidation and affirmation of cultural difference.

THE RISE OF THE MONGOLS, 1200–1260

The Mongol Empire owed much of its success to the cultural institutions and political traditions of the Eurasian steppes (prairies) and deserts. The pastoral way of life known as **nomadism** gives rise to imperial expansion only occasionally, and historians disagree about what triggers these episodes. In the case of the Mongols, a precise assessment of the personal contributions of Chinggis Khan and his successors remains uncertain.

Nomadism in Central and Inner Asia   The pastoral nomads of the Eurasian steppes played an on-again, off-again role in European, Middle Eastern, and Chinese history for hundreds of years before the rise of the Mongols (see Chapter 9). The Mongol way of life probably did not differ materially from that of those earlier peoples. Traditional accounts maintain that the Mongols put their infants on goats to accustom them to riding. Moving regularly and efficiently with flocks and herds and homes carried on two-wheeled vehicles required firm decision making, and the independence of individual Mongols and their families made this decision making public, with many voices being heard. A council with representatives from powerful families ratified the decisions of the leader, the *khan*. Yet people who disagreed with a decision could strike out on their own. Even during military campaigns, warriors moved with their families and possessions.

Menial work in camps fell to slaves—either prisoners of war or people who sought refuge in slavery to escape starvation. Weak groups secured land rights and protection from strong groups by providing them with slaves, livestock, weapons, silk, or cash. More powerful groups, such as Chinggis Khan's extended family and descendants, lived almost entirely off tribute, so they spent less time and fewer resources on herding and more on warfare designed to secure greater tribute.

Leading families combined resources and solidified intergroup alliances through arranged marriages and acts of allegiance, a process that helped generate political federations. Marriages were arranged in childhood—in Temüjin's case, at the age of eight—and children thus became pawns of diplomacy. Women from prestigious families could wield power in negotiation and management, though they ran the risk of assassination or execution just like men.

The wives and mothers of Mongol rulers traditionally managed state affairs during the interregnum between a ruler's death and the selection of a successor. Princes and heads of ministries treated such regents with great deference and obeyed their commands without question. Since a female regent could not herself succeed to the position of khan, her political machinations usually focused on gaining the succession for a son or other male relative.

Families often included believers in two or more religions, most commonly Buddhism, Christianity, or Islam. Virtually all Mongols observed the practices of traditional shamanism, rituals in which special individuals visited and influenced the supernatural world. Whatever their faith, the Mongols believed in world ruler-ship by a khan who, with the aid of his shamans, could speak to and for an ulti-mate god, represented as Sky or Heaven. This universal ruler transcended particular cultures and dominated them all.

The Mongol Conquests, 1215–1283   Shortly after his acclamation in 1206, Chinggis initiated two decades of Mongol aggression. By 1209 he had cowed the Tanggut (TAHNG-gut) rulers of northwest China, and in 1215 he captured the Jin capital of Yanjing, today known as Beijing (bay-jeeng). He turned westward in 1219 with an invasion of Khwarezm (kaw-REZM), a state east of the Caspian Sea that included much of Iran. After 1221, when most of Iran had fallen, Chinggis left the command of most campaigns to subordinate generals.

Ögödei (ERG-uh-day), Chinggis's son, became the Great Khan in 1227 after his father's death (see Figure 13.1). He completed the destruction of the Tanggut and the Jin and put their territories under Mongol governors. By 1234 he controlled most of northern China and was threatening the Southern Song (see Chapter 12). Two years later Chinggis's grandson Batu (BAH-too) (d. 1255) attacked Russian territories, took control of the towns along the Volga (VOHL-gah) River, and conquered Kievan Russia, Moscow, Poland, and Hungary in a five-year campaign. Only the death of Ögödei in 1241, which caused a suspension of campaigning, saved Europe from graver damage. With Chinggis's grandson Güyük (gi-yik) installed as the new Great Khan, the conquests resumed. In the Middle East a Mongol army sacked Baghdad in 1258 and executed the last Abbasid caliph (see Chapter 10).

Chinggis Khan's original objective had probably been collecting tribute, but the success of the Mongol conquests created a new situation. Ögödei unquestionably sought to rule a united empire based at his capital, Karakorum (kah-rah-KOR-um), and until his death he controlled the subordinate Mongol domains: the Golden Horde in Russia and the Chagatai (JAH-guh-die) domains in Central Asia. After Ögödei's death, however, family unity began to unravel; when Khubilai

FIGURE 13.1 Mongol Rulers, 1206–1260

The names of the Great Khans are shown in bold type. Those who founded the regional khanates are listed with their dates of rule.

(KOO-bih-lie) declared himself Great Khan in 1260, the descendants of Chinggis's son Chagatai (d. 1242) and other branches of the family refused to accept him. As Karakorum was destroyed in the ensuing fighting, Khubilai transferred his court to the old Jin capital now renamed Beijing. In 1271 he declared himself founder of the **Yuan Empire**.

Chagatai's descendants continued to dominate Central Asia and enjoyed close relations with the region's Turkic-speaking nomads. This, plus a continuing hatred of Khubilai, contributed to Central Asia becoming an independent Mongol center and to the spread of Islam there.

After the Yuan destroyed the Southern Song (see Chapter 12) in 1279, Mongol troops attacked Dai Viet—now northern Vietnam—and in 1283 invaded the kingdom of Champa in southern Vietnam. When the initially successful Mongols suffered a defeat, Khubilai was so infuriated that he postponed an invasion of Japan to focus on the Vietnamese kingdoms. In 1287, the Vietnamese troops, under the command of Tran Hung Dao, Vietnam's most famous military hero, defeated the Mongol forces in a final battle. A plan to invade Java by sea also failed, as did two invasions of Japan in 1274 and 1281.

Passport *The Mongol Empire facilitated the movement of products, merchants, and diplomats over long distances. Travelers frequently encountered new languages, laws, and customs. The* paisa *(from a Chinese word for "card" or "sign"), with its inscription in Mongolian, proclaimed that the traveler had the ruler's permission to travel through the region. Europeans later adopted the practice, thus making the* paisa *the ancestor of modern passports.*

The Metropolitan Museum of Art/Image source/Art Resource, NY

© Cengage Learning

MAP 13.1   The Mongol Domains in Eurasia in 1300

After the death of Genghis Khan in 1227, his empire was divided among his sons and grandsons. Son Ögödei succeeded Genghis as Great Khan. Grandson Khubilai expanded the domain of the Great Khan into southern China by 1279. Grandson Hülegü was the first Il-khan in the Middle East. Grandson Batu founded the Khanate of the Golden Horde in southern Russia. Son Jagadai ruled the Jagadai Khanate in Central Asia.

The Mongols seldom outnumbered their enemies, but they were extraordinary riders and utilized superior bows. The Central Asian bow, made by laminating layers of wood, leather, and bone, could shoot one-third farther (and was correspondingly more difficult to pull) than the bows used by sedentary enemies.

Rarely did an archer expend all of the five dozen arrows in his quiver. As the battle opened, arrows shot from a distance decimated enemy marksmen. Then the Mongols charged the enemy's infantry to fight with sword, lance, javelin, and mace. The Mongol cavalry met its match only at the Battle of Ain Jalut (ine jah-LOOT), where an under-strength force confronted Turkic-speaking Mamluks whose war techniques matched their own (see Chapter 10).

The Mongols also fired flaming arrows and hurled enormous projectiles—sometimes flaming—from catapults. The first Mongol catapults, built on Chinese models, transported easily but had short range and poor accuracy. During western campaigns in Central Asia, however, the Mongols encountered a design that was half again as powerful. They used it to hammer the cities of Iran and Iraq.

Cities that resisted faced siege and annihilation. Surrender was the only option. The slaughter the Mongols inflicted on Balkh (bahlk) (in present-day northern Afghanistan) and other cities spread terror and caused other cities to surrender. Each conquered area contributed men to the "Mongol" armies. In the Middle East, on the western fringe of their empire, a few Mongol officers commanded armies of recently recruited Turks and Iranians.

Overland Trade and Disease   Commercial integration under Mongol rule affected all parts of the empire. Like earlier nomad elites, Mongol nobles had the exclusive right to wear silk, almost all of which came from China. New styles and huge quantities of silk flowed westward to feed the luxury trade in the Middle East and Europe. Artistic motifs from Japan and Tibet reached as far as England and Morocco. Porcelain, another eastern luxury, became important in trade and strongly influenced later tastes in the Islamic world.

Merchants encountered ambassadors, scholars, and missionaries over the long routes to the Mongol courts. Some of the resulting travel literature, like the account of the Venetian Marco Polo (mar-koe POE-loe) (1254–1324), freely mixed the fantastic with the factual. Stories of immense wealth stimulated a European ambition to find easier routes to Asia.

Exchange also spread disease. In the mid-thirteenth century, marmots and other rodents became infected and passed their disease to dogs and people. Though other diseases contributed to the mortality of the resulting pandemic, **bubonic plague**, which probably originated in Central Asia, was certainly involved. An alternative theory sees southern China as the point of origin, but the great distances involved and the unusually cold winters experienced in China from 1344 to 1353, which would have impeded the reproduction of fleas, indicate otherwise. Plague incapacitated the Mongol army during its assault on the city of Kaffa (KAH-fah) in Crimea (cry-MEE-ah) in 1346. They withdrew, but the plague remained. From Kaffa flea-infested rats reached Europe and Egypt by ship (see Chapter 14).

Typhus, influenza, and smallpox traveled the same route. The combination of these and other diseases created the "great pandemic" of 1347–1352 and caused deaths far in excess of what the Mongol armies inflicted. Epidemics like this one

were exacerbated by the environmental devastation caused by the Mongol conquest. The Mongols destroyed dams, irrigation channels, farmland, and crops;
they also cut down trees that helped keep the desert at bay, with the effect of turning large portions of China into steppe.

THE MONGOLS AND ISLAM, 1260–1500

From the perspective of Mongol imperial history, the issue of which branches of the
family adopted Islam and which did not mostly concerns political rivalries. From the
standpoint of Islamic history, however, recovery from the devastation that culminated
in the destruction of the Abbasid Caliphate in Baghdad in 1258 attests to the vitality
of the faith and the ability of Muslims to overcome adversity. Within fifty years of its
darkest hour, Islam reemerged as a potent ideological and political force.

Mongol Rivalry   By 1260 the **Il-khan** (IL–con) state, established by Chinggis's
grandson Hülegü, controlled Iran, Azerbaijan, Mesopotamia,
and parts of Armenia. North of the Caspian Sea the Mongols who had conquered
southern Russia established the capital of their Khanate of the **Golden Horde** (also
called the Kipchak [KIP-chahk] Khanate) at Sarai (sah-RYE) on the Volga River.
Like the Il-khans, they ruled an indigenous, mostly Turkic-speaking, Muslim
population.

Some members of the Mongol imperial family professed Islam before the
Mongol assault on the Middle East, and Turkic Muslims served the family in various capacities. Hülegü himself, though a Buddhist, had a trusted Shi'ite adviser and
granted privileges to the Shi'ites. However, the Mongols under Hülegü's command
came only slowly to Islam.

Islamic doctrines clashed with Mongol ways. Muslims abhorred the Mongols'
worship of Buddhist and shamanist idols. Furthermore, Mongol law specified
slaughtering animals without spilling blood, which involved opening the chest and
stopping the heart. This horrified Muslims, who were forbidden to consume blood
and slaughtered animals by slitting their throats and draining the blood.

Islam became a point of inter-Mongol tension when Batu's successor as leader
of the Golden Horde declared himself a Muslim. He swore to avenge the murder of
the Abbasid caliph and laid claim to the Caucasus—the mountains between the
Black and Caspian Seas—which the Il-khans also claimed.

Some European leaders believed that if they helped the non-Muslim Il-khans
repel the Golden Horde from the Caucasus, the Il-khans would help them relieve
Muslim pressure on the Crusader principalities in Syria, Lebanon, and Palestine
(see Chapter 10). This resulted in a brief correspondence between the Il-khan
court and Pope Nicholas IV (r. 1288–1292) and a diplomatic mission that sent
two Christian Turks to western Europe as Il-khan ambassadors in the late 1200s.
The Golden Horde responded by seeking an alliance with the Muslim Mamluks in
Egypt (see Chapter 10) against both the Crusaders and the Il-khans. These complicated efforts extended the life of the Crusader principalities, but the Mamluks
finally ended their existence in the fifteenth century.

Before the Europeans' diplomatic efforts could bear fruit, a new Il-khan ruler,
Ghazan (gaz-ZAHN) (1271–1304), declared himself a Muslim in 1295. Conflicting

indications of Sunni and Shi'ite affiliation, such as divergent coin inscriptions, indicate that Ghazan had a casual attitude toward theological matters. It is similarly unclear whether the Muslim Turkic nomads who served in his army were Shi'ite or Sunni.

Islam and the State   The Il-khans gradually came to appreciate the traditional urban culture of the Muslim territories they ruled. Nevertheless, they used tax farming, a fiscal method developed earlier in the Middle East, to extract maximum wealth from their subjects. The government sold tax-collecting contracts to small partnerships, mostly consisting of merchants who might also finance caravans, small industries, or military expeditions. Whoever offered to collect the most revenue for the government won the contracts. They could collect by whatever methods they chose and keep anything in excess of the contracted amount.

Tax farming initially lowered administrative costs; but over the long term, the extortions of the tax farmers drove many landowners into debt and servitude. Agricultural productivity declined, making it hard to supply the army. So the government resorted to taking land to grow its own grain. Like property held by religious trusts, this land paid no taxes. Thus the tax base shrank even as the demands of the army and the Mongol nobility continued to grow.

Ghazan faced many economic problems. Citing Islam's humane values, he promised to reduce taxes. But the need for revenue kept the decrease from becoming permanent. The Chinese practice of printing paper money had been tried unsuccessfully by a predecessor. Now it was tried again. The experiment, to which the Il-khan's subjects responded negatively, pushed the economy into a depression that lasted beyond the end of the Il-khan state in 1349. Mongol nobles competed among themselves for the decreasing revenues, and fighting among Mongol factions destabilized the government.

While the Golden Horde and the Il-khan Empire quarreled, a new power was emerging in the Central Asian Khanate of Chagatai. The leader **Timur** (TEE-moor), known to Europeans as Tamerlane, maneuvered himself into command of the Chagatai forces and launched campaigns into western Eurasia, apparently seeing himself as a new Chinggis Khan. By ethnic background he was a Turk with only an in-law relationship to the family of the Mongol conqueror. This prevented him from assuming the title *khan*, but not from sacking the Muslim sultanate of Delhi in northern India in 1398 or defeating the sultan of the rising Ottoman Empire in Anatolia in 1402. He was reportedly preparing to march on China when he died in 1405. However, Timur's descendants could not hold the empire together.

Culture and Science in Islamic Eurasia   The Il-khans and Timurids (descendants of Timur) presided over a brilliant cultural flowering in Iran, Afghanistan, and Central Asia based on blending Iranian and Chinese artistic trends and cultural practices. The dominant cultural tendencies were Muslim, however. Timur died before he could reunite Iran and China, but by transplanting Middle Eastern scholars, artists, and craftsmen to his capital, Samarkand, he fostered the cultural achievements of his descendants.

The historian Juvaini (joo-VINE-nee) (d. 1283), who recorded Chinggis Khan's deathbed speech cited at the beginning of this chapter, came from the city of Balkh, which the Mongols had devastated in 1221. His family switched their allegiance to the Mongols, and both Juvaini and his older brother assumed high government posts. The Il-khan Hülegü, seeking to immortalize and justify his conquests, enthusiastically supported Juvaini's writing of the first comprehensive narrative of Chinggis Khan's empire.

Juvaini combined a florid style with historical objectivity, often criticizing the Mongols. This approach served as an inspiration to **Rashid al-Din** (ra-SHEED ad–DEEN), Ghazan's prime minister, when he attempted the first history of the world. Rashid al-Din's work included the earliest known general history of Europe, derived from conversations with European monks, and a detailed description of China based on information from an important Chinese Muslim official stationed in Iran. The miniature paintings that accompanied some copies of Rashid al-Din's work included depictions of European and Chinese people and events and reflected the artistic traditions of both cultures. The Chinese compositional techniques helped inaugurate the greatest period of Islamic miniature painting under the Timurids.

Rashid al-Din traveled widely and collaborated with administrators from other parts of the far-flung Mongol dominions. His idea that government should be in accord with the moral principles of the majority of the population buttressed Ghazan's adherence to Islam. Administratively, however, Ghazan did not restrict himself to Muslim precedents but employed financial and monetary techniques that roughly resembled those used in Russia and China.

Under the Timurids, the tradition of the Il-khan historians continued. After conquering Damascus, Timur himself met there with the greatest historian of the age, Ibn Khaldun (ee-bin hal-DOON) (1332–1406), a Tunisian. In a scene reminiscent of Ghazan's answering Rashid al-Din's questions on the history of the Mongols, Timur and Ibn Khaldun exchanged historical, philosophical, and geographical viewpoints. Like Chinggis, Timur saw himself as a world conqueror. At their capitals of Samarkand and Herat (in western Afghanistan), later Timurid rulers sponsored historical writing in both Persian and Chagatai Turkish.

A Shi'ite scholar named **Nasir al-Din Tusi** (nah-SEER ad–DEEN TOO-si) represents the beginning of Mongol interest in the scientific traditions of the Muslim lands. Nasir al-Din may have joined the entourage of Hülegü during a campaign in 1256 against the Assassins, a Shi'ite religious sect derived from the Fatimid dynasty in Egypt and at odds with his more mainstream Shi'ite views (see Chapter 10). Although Nasir al-Din wrote on history, poetry, ethics, and religion, he made his most outstanding contributions in mathematics and cosmology. Following Omar Khayyam (oh-mar kie-YAM) (1038?–1131), a poet and mathematician of the Seljuk (SEL-jook) period, he laid new foundations for algebra and trigonometry. Some followers working at an observatory built for Nasir al-Din at Maragheh (mah-RAH-gah), near the Il-khan capital of Tabriz, used the new mathematical techniques to reach a better understanding of celestial orbits.

Nasir al-Din's work led to major contributions in astronomy that had worldwide influence. Observational astronomy and calendar-making had engaged the interest of earlier Central Asian rulers, particularly the Uighurs (WEE-ger) and the Seljuks. Under the Il-khans, the astronomers of Maragheh excelled in predicting eclipses, and astrolabes, armillary spheres, three-dimensional quadrants, and other instruments acquired new precision. The remarkably accurate eclipse predictions and tables

Astronomy and Engineering

Observational astronomy went hand in hand not only with mathematics and calendrical science but also with engineering as the construction of platforms, instruments for celestial measurement, and armillary spheres became more sophisticated. This manual in Persian, completed in the 1500s but illustrating activities of the Il-khan period, illustrates the use of a plumb line with an enormous armillary sphere.

Science Source

prepared by Il-khan and Timurid astronomers reached the hostile Mamluk lands in Arabic translation; Byzantine monks took them to Constantinople and translated them into Greek; Christian scholars working in Muslim Spain rendered them into Latin; and in India the sultan of Delhi ordered Sanskrit versions of them.

Following one of these routes, the mathematical tables and geometric models of lunar motion devised by one of Nasir al-Din's students somehow became known to Nicholas Copernicus (1473–1543), a Polish monk and astronomer (see Chapter 14). Copernicus adopted this lunar model as his own, virtually without revision, and then proposed it as the proper model for planetary movement as well—but with the planets circling the sun.

The Great Khan Khubilai (discussed later in this chapter) summoned a team of Iranians to Beijing to build an observatory for him. Timur's grandson Ulugh Beg (oo-loog bek) (1394–1449), whose avocation was astronomy, constructed a great observatory in Samarkand and actively participated in compiling observational tables that were later translated into Latin and used by European astronomers.

A further advance made under Ulugh Beg came from the mathematician Ghiyas al-Din Jamshid al-Kashi (gee-YASS ad–DIN jam-SHEED al–KAH-shee), who noted that Chinese astronomers had long used one ten-thousandth of a day as a unit in calculating the occurrence of a new moon. This seems to have inspired him to employ decimal notation, by which quantities less than one could be represented by a marker to show place. Al-Kashi's proposed value for *pi* (π) was far more precise than any previously calculated. This innovation arrived in Europe by way of Constantinople, where a Greek translation of al-Kashi's work appeared in the fifteenth century.

REGIONAL RESPONSES IN WESTERN EURASIA

Safe, reliable overland trade benefited Mongol ruling centers and commercial cities along the Silk Road. But the countryside, ravaged by conquest, sporadic violence, and heavy taxes, suffered terribly. As Mongol control weakened, regional forces in Russia, eastern Europe, and Anatolia reasserted themselves. Sometimes this meant collaborating with the Mongols. At other times it meant using local ethnic or religious traditions to resist or roll back Mongol influence.

Russia and Rule from Afar   The Golden Horde, established after Chinggis's grandson Batu defeated a combined Russian and Kipchak (a Turkic people) army in 1223, started as a unified state but gradually lost unity as some districts crystallized into smaller khanates. The White Horde, for instance, ruled much of southeastern Russia in the fifteenth century, and the Crimean khanate on the northern shore of the Black Sea succumbed to Russian power only in 1783.

East-west routes across the steppe and north-south routes along the rivers of Russia and Ukraine (you-CRANE) conferred importance on certain trading entrepôts (places where goods are stored and from which they are distributed), as they had under Kievan Russia (see Chapter 11). The Golden Horde capital (Old) Sarai, just north of where the Volga flows into the Caspian Sea, ruled its Russian domains to the north and east from afar. To facilitate control, it granted privileges to the Orthodox Church, which then helped reconcile the Russian people to their distant masters.

The politics of language played a role in subsequent history. Old Church Slavonic, an ecclesiastical language, revived; but Russian steadily acquired greater importance and eventually became the dominant written language. Russian scholars shunned Byzantine Greek, previously the main written tongue, even after the Golden Horde permitted renewed contacts with Constantinople. The Golden Horde enlisted Russian princes to act as their agents, primarily as tax collectors and census takers.

The flow of silver and gold into Mongol hands starved the local economy of precious metal. Like the Il-khans, the Golden Horde attempted to introduce paper money as a response to the currency shortage. The unsuccessful experiment left such a vivid memory that the Russian word for money (*denga* [DENG-ah]) comes from the Mongolian word for the stamp (*tamga* [TAHM-gah]) used to create paper currency. In reality, commerce depended more on direct exchange of goods than on currency transactions.

Alexander Nevskii (nih-EFF-skee) (ca. 1220–1263), the prince of Novgorod, persuaded some fellow princes to submit to the Mongols. In return, the Mongols favored both Novgorod and the emerging town of Moscow, ruled by Alexander's

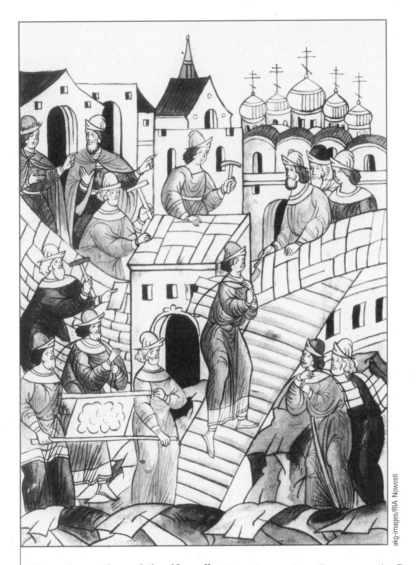

Transformation of the Kremlin *Like other northern Europeans, the Russians preferred to build in wood, which was easy to handle and comfortable to live in. But they fortified important political centers with stone ramparts. In the 1300s, the city of Moscow emerged as a new capital, and its old wooden palace, the Kremlin, was gradually transformed into a stone structure.*

son Daniel. As these towns eclipsed Kiev (earlier devastated by the Mongols) as political, cultural, and economic centers, they drew people northward to open new agricultural land far from the Mongol steppes. Decentralization continued in the 1300s, with Moscow only very gradually becoming Russia's dominant political center.

In appraising the Mongol era, some historians stress Mongol destructiveness and brutality in tax collecting. Ukraine, a fertile and well-populated region in the late Kievan period (1000–1230), suffered severe population loss from these sources.

Isolated from developments to the west, Russia and parts of eastern Europe are portrayed as suffering under the "Mongol yoke."

Other historians point out that even before the Mongols struck Kiev had declined economically and ceased to mint coins. Yet the Russian territories regularly paid the heavy Mongol taxes in silver, indicating both economic surpluses and an ability to convert goods into cash. The burdensome taxes stemmed less from the Mongols than from their tax collectors, Russian princes who often exempted their own lands and shifted the load to the peasants.

As for Russia's cultural isolation, skeptics observe that before the Mongol invasion, the powerful and constructive role played by the Orthodox Church oriented Russia primarily toward Byzantium (see Chapter 11). This situation discouraged but did not eliminate contacts with western Europe. But repeated wars with the expanding Catholic principality of Lithuania on Russia's western border discouraged extensive relations.

The traditional structure of local government survived Mongol rule, as did the Russian princely families, who continued to battle among themselves for dominance. The Mongols merely added a new player to those struggles.

In the late 1400s Ivan (ee-VAHN) III, the prince of Moscow (r. 1462–1505), established himself as an autocratic ruler. Before Ivan, the title **tsar** (from *caesar*), of Byzantine origin, applied only to foreign rulers, whether the emperors of Byzantium or the Turkic khans of the steppe. Ivan's use of the title probably represents an effort to establish a basis for legitimate rule with the decline of the Golden Horde and the disappearance of the Byzantine Empire.

New States in Eastern Europe and Anatolia   Anatolia and parts of Europe responded dynamically to the Mongol challenges. Raised in Sicily, the Holy Roman Emperor Frederick II (r. 1212–1250) appreciated Muslim culture and did not recoil from negotiating with Muslims. When the pope threatened to excommunicate him unless he waged a crusade, Frederick nominally regained Jerusalem through a flimsy treaty with the Mamluk sultan in Egypt. Dissatisfied, the pope continued to quarrel with the emperor, leaving Hungary, Poland, and Lithuania to deal with the Mongol onslaught on their own. Many princes capitulated and went to (Old) Sarai to offer their submission to Batu.

However, the Teutonic (two-TOHN-ik) Knights resisted. This German-speaking order of Christian warriors, originally organized in the Holy Land, sought to Christianize the pagan populations of northern Europe and colonize their territories with German settlers. They also fought against other Christians. To protect Slav territory, Alexander Nevskii joined the Mongols in fighting the Teutonic Knights and their Finnish allies. The latter suffered a catastrophe in 1242, when many broke through an icy northern lake and drowned. This event destroyed the power of the Knights, and the northern Crusades virtually ceased.

The "Mongol" armies encountered by the Europeans consisted mostly of Turks, Chinese, Iranians, a few Europeans, and at least one Englishman, who went to crusade in the Middle East but joined the Mongols and served in Hungary. But most commanders were Mongol.

Initial wild theories describing the Mongols as coming from Hell or from caves where Alexander the Great confined the monsters of antiquity gradually yielded to a more sophisticated understanding as European embassies to Mongol courts returned with reliable intelligence. In some quarters terror gave way to appreciation. Europeans learned about diplomatic passports, coal mining, movable type, high-temperature metallurgy, higher mathematics, gunpowder, and, in the fourteenth century, the casting and use of bronze cannon. Yet with the outbreak of bubonic plague in the late 1340s (see Chapter 14), the memory of Mongol terror helped ignite religious speculation that God might again be punishing the Christians.

In the fourteenth century several regions, most notably Lithuania (lith-oo-WAY-nee-ah), escaped the Mongol grip. When Russia fell to the Mongols, Lithuania had experienced an unprecedented centralization and military strengthening. Like Alexander Nevskii, the Lithuanian leaders maintained their independence by cooperating with the Mongols. In the late 1300s Lithuania capitalized on its privileged position to dominate Poland and ended the Teutonic Knights' hope of regaining power.

In the Balkans independent kingdoms separated themselves from the chaos of the Byzantine Empire and thrived amidst the political uncertainties of the Mongol period. The Serbian king Stephen Dushan (ca. 1308–1355) proved the most effective leader. Seizing power from his father in 1331, he took advantage of Byzantine weakness to turn the archbishop of Serbia into an independent patriarch. In 1346 the patriarch crowned him "tsar and autocrat of the Serbs, Greeks, Bulgarians, and Albanians," a title that fairly represents the wide extent of his rule. As in the case of Timur, however, his kingdom declined after his death in 1355 and disappeared entirely after a defeat by the Ottomans at the battle of Kosovo in 1389.

The Turkic nomads whose descendants established the **Ottoman Empire** came to Anatolia in the same wave of Turkic migrations as the Seljuks (see Chapter 10). Though Il-khan influence was strong in eastern Anatolia, a number of small Turkic principalities emerged in the west. The Ottoman principality was situated in the northwest, close to the Sea of Marmara. This not only put them in a position to cross into Europe and take part in the dynastic struggles of the declining Byzantine state, but it also attracted Muslim religious warriors who wished to do battle with Christians on the frontiers. The defeat of the Ottoman sultan by Timur in 1402 was only a temporary setback. In 1453 Sultan Mehmet II captured Constantinople and brought the Byzantine Empire to an end.

The Ottoman sultans, like the rulers of Russia, Lithuania, and Serbia, seized opportunities that arose with the decay of Mongol power. The powerful states they created put strong emphasis on religious and linguistic identity, factors that the Mongols themselves did not stress. As we shall see, Mongol rule stimulated similar reactions in the lands of East and Southeast Asia.

MONGOL DOMINATION IN CHINA, 1271–1368

After conquering northern China in the 1230s, Great Khan Ögödei told a Confucian adviser that he planned to turn the heavily populated North China Plain into a pasture for livestock. The adviser reacted calmly but argued that taxing the cities and villages would bring greater wealth. The Great Khan agreed, but he imposed an oppressive tax-farming system instead of the fixed-rate method traditional to China.

The Chinese suffered under this system during the early years, but the Yuan Empire, established by Chinggis Khan's grandson Khubilai in 1271, also brought benefits: secure trade routes; exchange of experts between eastern and western Eurasia; and transmission of information, ideas, and skills.

The Yuan Empire, 1271–1368   The Yuan sought a fruitful synthesis of the Mongol and Chinese traditions. **Khubilai Khan** gave his oldest son a Chinese name and had Confucianists participate in the boy's education. In public announcements and the crafting of laws, he took Confucian conventions into consideration. Buddhist and Daoist leaders who visited the Great Khan came away believing that they had all but convinced him of their beliefs.

Buddhist priests from Tibet called **lamas** (LAH-mah) became popular with some Mongol rulers. Their idea of a militant universal ruler bringing the whole world under control of the Buddha and thus pushing it nearer to salvation mirrored an ancient Inner Asian idea of universal rulership.

Beijing, the Yuan capital, became the center of cultural and economic life. Karakorum had been geographically remote, but Beijing served as the eastern terminus of caravan routes that began near Tabriz, the Il-khan capital, and (Old) Sarai, the Golden Horde capital. A horseback courier system utilizing hundreds of stations maintained communications along routes that were generally safe for travelers. Ambassadors and merchants arriving in Beijing found a city that was much more Chinese in character than Karakorum had been.

Called Great Capital (Dadu) or City of the Khan (*khan-balikh* [kahn-BAL-ik], Marco Polo's "Cambaluc"), Khubilai's capital included the Forbidden City, a closed imperial complex with wide streets and a network of linked lakes and artificial islands. In summer, Khubilai practiced riding and shooting at a palace and park in Inner Mongolia. This was Shangdu (shahng-DOO), the "Xanadu" (ZAH-nah-doo) with its "stately pleasure dome" celebrated by the English poet Samuel Taylor Coleridge.

Before the arrival of the Mongols, three separate states with different languages, writing systems, forms of government, and elite cultures competed in China (see Chapter 12), The Tanggut and Jin Empires controlled the north, and the Southern Song controlled most of the area south of the Yellow River. The Great Khans destroyed all three and encouraged the restoration or preservation of many features of Chinese government and society.

The Mongol-ruled Yuan state was cosmopolitan, attracting many non-Chinese who helped the Mongols govern China. By law, Mongols ranked highest. Below them came Central Asians and Middle Easterners, then northern Chinese, and finally southern Chinese. This ranking reflected a hierarchy of functions. The Mongols were the empire's warriors, the Central Asians and Middle Easterners its census takers and tax collectors. The northern Chinese outranked the southern Chinese because they came under Mongol control almost two generations earlier.

Though Khubilai included some "Confucians" (under the Yuan, a formal and hereditary status) in government, their position compared poorly with pre-Mongol times. The Confucians disparaged merchants, many of whom were from the Middle East or Central Asia, and physicians, whom they regarded as mere technicians or

Daoist mystics. But the Yuan encouraged doctors and began the process of integrating Chinese medical approaches with those contained in Muslim and Hellenistic sources.

A Muslim governor from Central Asia, Sayyid Ajall Shams al-Din (SAY-id a-JELL Shams ad–DEEN), exemplifies a non-Chinese person who helped the Mongols rule and yet still promoted Confucian culture. The Mongols appointed him governor of Yunnan (YOON-nahn), their newly acquired territory in the southwest that became a key transit area for trade between Tibet, Burma, the Vietnamese kingdoms, and China. Some scholars have called this area the Southwest Silk Road. Shams al-Din walked a fine line between connecting Yunnan with the imperial center and relying upon native chieftains to stabilize the area. Moreover, he promoted Confucian education, dress, and rituals and built schools and Confucian temples. Yunnan, once considered only a periphery to earlier Chinese rulers, became an integral part of China under the Mongol rule and remains so to the present.

Like the Il-khans, the Yuan rulers stressed census taking and tax collecting. Persian, Arab, and Uighur administrators staffed the offices of taxation and finance, and Muslim scholars worked at calendar-making and astronomy. The Mongols organized all of China into provinces. Central appointment of provincial governors, tax collectors, and garrison commanders marked a radical change by systematizing control in all parts of the country.

Many cities seem to have prospered: in north China by being on the caravan routes; in the interior by being on the Grand Canal; and along the coast by participation in maritime grain shipments from south China. The reintegration of East Asia (though not Japan) with the overland Eurasian trade, which had lapsed with the fall of the Tang (see Chapter 12), stimulated the urban economies.

With merchants a privileged group, life in the cities changed. So few government posts were open to the old Chinese elite that families that had previously spent fortunes on educating sons for government service sought other opportunities. Many gentry families chose commerce. Corporations—investor groups that behaved as single commercial and legal units and shared the risk of doing business—handled most economic activities, starting with financing caravans and expanding into tax farming and lending money to the Mongol aristocracy. Central Asians and Middle Easterners headed most corporations in the early Yuan period; but as Chinese bought shares, many acquired mixed membership, or even complete Chinese ownership.

The agricultural base, damaged by war, overtaxation, and the passage of armies, could not satisfy the financial needs of the Mongol aristocracy. Following earlier precedent, the imperial government made up the shortfall with paper money. But people doubted the value of the notes, which were unsecured. Copper coinage partially offset the failure of the paper currency. During the Song, exports of copper to Japan, where the metal was scarce, had caused a severe shortage in China, leading to a rise in the value of copper in relation to silver. By cutting off trade with Japan, the Mongols intentionally or unintentionally stabilized the value of copper coins.

As city life increasingly catered to the tastes of merchants instead of scholars, many gentry families moved from their traditional homes in the countryside to engage in urban commerce. Specialized shops selling clothing, grape wine, furniture, and religiously butchered meats became common. Teahouses offered sing-song girls, drum singers, operas, and other entertainments previously considered coarse. Writers published works in the style of everyday speech. And the increasing influence of the northern, Mongolian-influenced Chinese language, often called Mandarin in the West, resulted in lasting linguistic change.

Cottage industries linked to the urban economies dotted the countryside, where 90 percent of the people lived. Some villages cultivated mulberry trees and cotton using dams, water wheels, and irrigation systems patterned in part on Middle Eastern models. Treatises on planting, harvesting, threshing, and butchering were published. One technological innovator, Huang Dao Po (hwahng DOW poh), brought knowledge of cotton growing, spinning, and weaving from her native Hainan Island to the fertile Yangzi Delta.

Yet on the whole, the countryside did poorly during the Yuan period. Initially, the Mongol princes evicted many farmers and subjected the rest to brutal tax collection. By the time the Yuan shifted to lighter taxes and encouragement of farming at the end of the 1200s, it was too late. Servitude or homelessness had overtaken many farmers. Neglect of dams and dikes caused disastrous flooding, particularly on the Yellow River.

According to Song records from before the Mongol conquest and the Ming census taken after their overthrow—each, of course, subject to inaccuracy or exaggeration—China's population may have shrunk by 40 percent during eighty years of Mongol rule, with many localities in northern China losing up to five-sixths of their inhabitants. Scholars have suggested several causes: prolonged warfare, rural distress causing people to resort to female infanticide, epidemics, a southward flight of refugees, and flooding on the Yellow River. The last helps explain why losses in the north exceeded those in the south and why the population along the Yangzi River markedly increased.

The Fall of the Yuan Empire   In the 1340s strife broke out among the Mongol princes, and within twenty years farmer rebellions and inter-Mongol feuds engulfed the land. Amidst the chaos, in 1368 a charismatic Chinese leader, Zhu Yuanzhang (JOO yuwen-JAHNG), mounted a campaign that destroyed the Yuan Empire and brought China under control of his new empire, the Ming. Many Mongols—as well as the Muslims, Jews, and Christians who had come with them—remained in China. Most of their descendants took Chinese names and became part of the diverse cultural world of China.

Many other Mongols, however, had never moved out of their home territories in Mongolia. Now they welcomed back refugees from the Yuan collapse. Though Turkic peoples were becoming predominant in the steppe regions in the west, including territories still ruled by descendants of Chinggis Khan, Mongols continued to predominate in Inner Asia, the steppe regions bordering on Mongolia. Some Mongol groups adopted Islam; others favored Tibetan Buddhism. But religious affiliation proved less important than Mongol identity in fostering a renewed sense of unity.

The Ming thus fell short of dominating all the Mongols. The Mongols of Inner Asia paid tribute to the extent that doing so facilitated their trade. Other Mongols, however, remained a continuing threat on the northern Ming frontier.

THE EARLY MING EMPIRE, 1368–1500

Historians of China, like historians of Russia and Iran, divide over the overall impact of the Mongol era. Since the **Ming Empire** reestablished many practices that are seen as purely Chinese, it receives praise from people who ascribe central importance to Chinese traditions. On the other hand, historians who look upon the Mongol era as a pivotal historical moment when communication across the vast interior of Eurasia served to bring east and west together sometimes see the inward-looking Ming as less productive than the Yuan.

Ming China on a Mongol Foundation   Zhu Yuanzhang, a former monk, soldier, and bandit, had watched his parents and other family members die of famine and disease, conditions he blamed on Mongol misrule. During the Yuan Empire's chaotic last decades, he vanquished rival rebels and assumed imperial power under the name Hongwu (r. 1368–1398).

Hongwu moved the capital to Nanjing (nahn-JING) ("southern capital") on the Yangzi River, turning away from the Mongol's Beijing ("northern capital"). Though Zhu Yuanzhang the rebel had espoused a radical Buddhist belief in a coming age of salvation, once in power he used Confucianism to depict the emperor as the champion of civilization and virtue.

Hongwu choked off relations with Central Asia and the Middle East and imposed strict limits on imports and foreign visitors. Silver replaced paper money for tax payments and commerce. These practices, illustrative of an anti-Mongol ideology, proved as economically unwise as some of the Yuan economic policies and did not last. Eventually, the Ming government came to resemble the Yuan. Ming rulers retained the provincial structure and continued to observe the hereditary professional categories of the Yuan period. Muslims made calendars and astronomical calculations at a new observatory at Nanjing, a replica of Khubilai's at Beijing. The Mongol calendar continued in use.

Continuities with the Yuan became more evident after an imperial prince seized power through a coup d'état to rule as the emperor **Yongle** (yoong-LAW) (r. 1403–1424). Yongle returned the capital to Beijing and enlarged and improved Khubilai's Forbidden City, which now acquired its present features: moats, orange-red outer walls, golden roofs, and marble bridges. He intended this combination fortress, religious site, bureaucratic center, and imperial residential park to overshadow Nanjing, and it survives today as China's most imposing traditional architectural complex.

Yongle also restored commercial links with the Middle East. Because hostile Mongols still controlled much of the caravan route, Yongle explored maritime connections. In Southeast Asia, Vietnam became a Ming province as the early emperors continued the Mongol program of aggression. This focus on the southern frontier helped inspire the naval expeditions of the trusted imperial eunuch **Zheng He** (jehng huh) from 1405 to 1433.

A Muslim eunuch whose father and grandfather had made the pilgrimage to Mecca, Zheng He had a good knowledge of the Middle East; and his religion eased relations with the states of the Indian subcontinent, where he directed his first three voyages. Subsequent expeditions reached Hormuz on the Persian Gulf,

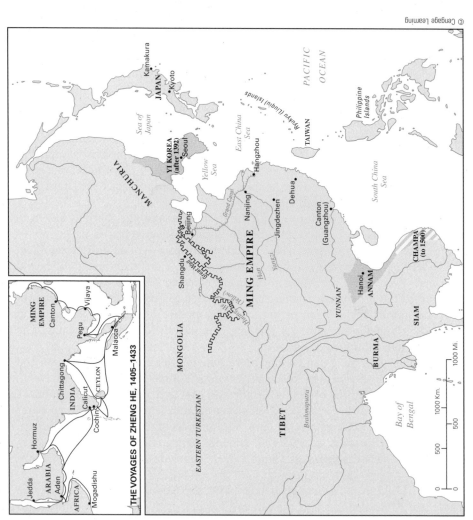

© Cengage Learning

MAP 13.2 The Ming Empire and Its Allies, 1368–1500

The Ming Empire controlled China but had a hostile relationship with peoples in Mongolia and Inner Asia who had been under the rule of the Mongol Yuan emperors. Mongol attempts at conquest by sea were continued by the Ming mariner Zheng He. Between 1405 and 1433 he sailed to Southeast Asia and then beyond, to India, the Persian Gulf, and East Africa.

sailed the southern coast of Arabia and the Horn of Africa (modern Somalia), and possibly reached as far south as the Strait of Madagascar.

On early voyages Zheng He visited long-established Chinese merchant communities in Southeast Asia to cement their allegiance to the Ming Empire and collect taxes. When a community on the island of Sumatra resisted, he slaughtered the men to set an example. The expeditions added some fifty new tributary states to the Ming imperial universe, but trade did not increase as dramatically. Sporadic embassies reached Beijing from rulers in India, the Middle East, Africa, and Southeast Asia. During one visit the ruler of Brunei (broo-NYE) died and received a grand burial at the Chinese capital. The expeditions stopped in the 1430s after the deaths of Yongle and Zheng He.

Why did the Chinese not develop seafaring for commercial and military gain? Contemporaries considered the voyages a personal project of Yongle, an upstart ruler who had always sought to prove his worthiness. Building the Forbidden City in Beijing and sponsoring gigantic encyclopedia projects might be taken to reflect a similar character. Yongle may also have been emulating Khubilai Khan's sea expeditions against Japan and Southeast Asia. This would fit with the rumor spread by Yongle's political enemies that he was actually a Mongol.

A less speculative approach starts with the fact that the new commercial opportunities fell short of expectations, despite bringing foreign nations into the Ming orbit. In the meantime, Japanese coastal piracy intensified, and Mongol threats in the north and west grew. The human and financial demands of fortifying the north, redesigning and strengthening Beijing, and outfitting campaigns against the Mongols ultimately took priority over the quest for maritime empire.

Technology and Population   The Ming government limited mining, partly to maintain the value of metal coins and partly to tax the industry. As a consequence, metal implements became more expensive for farmers. Techniques for making the high-quality bronze and steel used for weapons also declined. Japan quickly surpassed China in the production of extremely high-quality swords.

After the death of Emperor Yongle in 1424, shipbuilding skills deteriorated, and few advances occurred in printing, timekeeping, and agricultural technology. Agricultural production peaked around the mid-1400s and remained level for more than a century. New weaving techniques did appear, but technological development in this field had peaked by 1500.

Reactivation of the examination system for recruiting government officials (see Chapter 12) drew large numbers of ambitious men into a renewed study of the Confucian classics. This shift reduced the vitality of commerce, where they had previously been employed, just as population growth was creating a labor surplus. Records indicating a growth from 60 million at the end of the Yuan period in 1368 to nearly 100 million by 1400 may not be entirely reliable, but rapid population growth encouraged the production of staples—wheat, millet, and barley in the north and rice in the south—at the expense of commercial crops such as cotton that had stimulated many technological innovations under the Song. Staple crops yielded lower profits, which further discouraged capital improvements. New foods, such as sweet potatoes, became available but were little adopted. At the same time,

ENVIRONMENT + TECHNOLOGY

From Gunpowder to Guns

Long before the invention of guns, gunpowder was used in China and Korea to excavate mines, build canals, and channel irrigation. Alchemists in China used related formulas to make noxious gas pellets to paralyze enemies and expel evil spirits. A more realistic benefit was eliminating disease-carrying insects, a critical aid to the colonization of malarial regions in China and Southeast Asia. The Mongol Empire staged fireworks displays on ceremonial occasions, delighting European visitors to Karakorum who saw them for the first time.

Anecdotal evidence in Chinese records gives credit for the introduction of gunpowder to a Sogdian Buddhist monk of the 500s. The monk described the wondrous alchemical transformation of elements produced by a combination of charcoal and saltpeter. In this connection he also mentioned sulfur. The distillation of naphtha, a light, flammable derivative of oil or coal, seems also to have been first developed in Central Asia, the earliest evidence coming from the Gandhara region (in modern Pakistan).

By the eleventh century, the Chinese had developed flamethrowers powered by burning naphtha, sulfur, or gunpowder in a long tube. These weapons intimidated and injured foot soldiers and horses and also set fire to thatched roofs in hostile villages and, occasionally, the rigging of enemy ships.

In their long struggle against the Mongols, the Song learned to enrich saltpeter to increase the amount of nitrate in gunpowder. This produced forceful explosions rather than jets of fire. Launched from catapults, gunpowder-filled canisters could rupture fortifications and inflict mass casualties. Explosives hurled from a distance could sink or burn ships.

The Song also experimented with firing projectiles from metal gun barrels. The earliest gun barrels were broad and squat and were transported on special wagons to their emplacements. The

Launching Flaming Arrows *Song soldiers used gunpowder to launch flaming arrows.*

mouths of the barrels projected saltpeter mixed with scattershot minerals. The Chinese and then the Koreans adapted gunpowder to shooting masses of arrows—sometimes flaming—at enemy fortifications.

In 1280 weapons makers of the Yuan Empire produced the first device featuring a projectile that completely filled the mouth of the cannon and thus concentrated the explosive force. The Yuan used cast bronze for the barrel and iron for the cannonball. The new weapon shot farther and more accurately, and was much more destructive, than the earlier Song devices.

Knowledge of the cannon and cannonball moved westward across Eurasia. By the end of the thirteenth century cannon were being produced in the Middle East. By 1327 small, squat cannon called "bombards" were being used in Europe.

population growth in southern and central China caused deforestation and raised the price of wood.

Against the Mongol horsemen in the north the Ming used scattershot mortars and explosive canisters. They even used a few cannon, which they knew about from contacts with the Middle East and later with Europeans (see Environment and Technology: From Gunpowder to Guns). Fearing a loss of technological secrets, the government censored the chapters on gunpowder and guns in early Ming encyclopedias. Shipyards and ports shut down to avoid contact with Japanese pirates and to prevent Chinese from migrating to Southeast Asia.

A technology gap with Korea and Japan opened up nevertheless. When superior steel was needed, supplies came from Japan. Korea moved ahead of China in the design and production of firearms and ships, in printing techniques, and in the sciences of weather prediction and calendar-making. The desire to tap the wealthy Ming market spurred some of these advances.

| **The Ming Achievement** | In the late 1300s and the 1400s the wealth and consumerism of the early Ming stimulated high achievement in literature, the decorative arts, and painting. The plain writing of the |

Yuan period had produced some of the world's earliest novels. This genre flourished under the Ming. *Water Margin*, which originated in the raucous drum-song performances loosely related to Chinese opera, features dashing Chinese bandits who struggle against Mongol rule. Many authors had a hand in the final print version.

Luo Guanzhong (law gwahn-joong), one of the authors of *Water Margin*, is also credited with *Romance of the Three Kingdoms*, based on a much older series of stories that in some ways resemble the Arthurian legends. It describes the attempts of an upright but doomed war leader and his followers to restore the Han Empire of ancient times and resist the power of the cynical but brilliant villain. *Romance of the Three Kingdoms* and *Water Margin* express the militant but joyous pro-China sentiment of the early Ming era and remain among the most appreciated Chinese fictional works.

Probably the best-known product of Ming technological advance was porcelain. The imperial ceramic works at Jingdezhen (JING-deh-JUHN) experimented with new production techniques and new ways of organizing and rationalizing workers. "Ming ware," a blue-on-white style developed in the 1400s from Indian, Central Asian, and Middle Eastern motifs, became especially prized. Other Ming goods in high demand included furniture, lacquered screens, and silk, all of which found ready markets in Southeast Asia and the Pacific, India, the Middle East, and East Africa.

CENTRALIZATION AND MILITARISM IN EAST ASIA, 1200–1500

Korea, Japan, and the Vietnamese kingdoms, the other major states of East Asia, were all affected by confrontation with the Mongols, but with differing results. Japan and northern Vietnam escaped Mongol conquest but changed in response to the Mongol threat, becoming more effective and expansive regimes with enhanced commitments to independence.

As for Korea, just as the Ming stressed Chinese traditions and identity in the aftermath of Yuan rule, so Mongol domination contributed to revitalized interest in Korea's own language and history. The Mongols conquered Korea after a difficult war, and though Korea suffered socially and economically under Mongol rule, members of the elite associated closely with the Yuan Empire. After the fall of the Yuan, merchants continued the international connections established in the Mongol period, while Korean armies consolidated a new kingdom and fended off pirates.

Korea from the Mongols to the Choson Dynasty, 1231–1500   Korea was the answer to the Mongol search for coastal areas from which to launch naval expeditions and choke off the sea trade of their adversaries. By the time the Mongols attacked in 1231, the Choe family had assumed the role of military commander and protector of the Koryo (KAW-ree-oh) king (not unlike the shoguns of Japan). Four generations of Choe-led tyranny and years of defensive war left a ravaged countryside, exhausted armies, and burned treasure. The Choe's refusal to sue for peace, or emerge from their capital on Kanghwa Island to drive the Mongols from the Korean peninsula, led to widespread hardship among the populace and frustration among military men and nobles alike. The last of the Choe tyrants was killed by his underlings in 1258. Soon afterward the king surrendered to the Mongols and became a subject monarch by linking his family to the Great Khan by marriage.

By the mid-1300s the Koryo kings were of mostly Mongol descent and favored Mongol dress, customs, and language. The kings, their families, and their

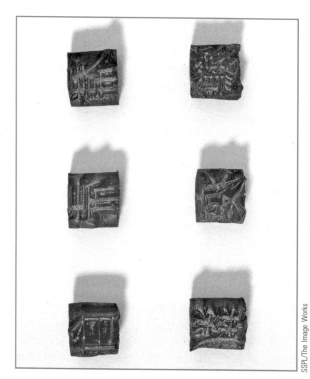

Movable Type *The improvement of cast bronze tiles, each showing a single character, eliminated the need to cast or carve whole pages. Individual tiles—the ones shown are Korean—could be moved from page frame to page frame and gave an even and pleasing appearance. All parts of East Asia eventually adopted this form of printing for cheap, popular books. In the mid-1400s Korea also experimented with a fully phonetic form of writing, which in combination with movable type allowed Koreans unprecedented levels of literacy and access to printed works.*

SSPL/The Image Works

entourages often traveled between China and Korea, thus exposing Korea to the philosophical and artistic styles of Yuan China: neo-Confucianism, Chan Buddhism (called Son in Korea), and celadon (light green) pottery.

Mongol control broke down centuries of comparative isolation. Cotton was introduced in southern Korea; gunpowder came into use; and the art of calendar-making stimulated astronomical observation and mathematics. Avenues of advancement opened for Korean scholars willing to learn Mongolian, landowners willing to open their lands to falconry and grazing, and merchants servicing the new royal exchanges with Beijing. These developments contributed to the rise of a new landed and educated class.

When the Yuan Empire fell in 1368, the Koryo ruling family remained loyal to the Mongols until a rebellious general, Yi Songgye (YEE SONG-gye), forced it to recognize the new Ming Empire. In 1392, Yi Songgye established a new kingdom called **Choson** (cho-sun) with a capital in Seoul and sought to reestablish a distinctive Korean identity. Like Russia and Ming China, the Choson regime publicly rejected the period of Mongol domination. Yet the Choson government continued to employ Mongol-style land surveys, taxation in kind, and military garrison techniques.

Like the Ming emperors, the Choson kings revived the study of the Confucian classics, an activity that required knowledge of Chinese and showed the dedication of the state to learning. This revival may have led to a key technological breakthrough in printing technology.

Koreans had begun using Chinese woodblock printing in the 700s. This technology worked well in China, where a large number of buyers wanted copies of a comparatively small number of texts. But in Korea, the comparatively few literate men had interests in a wide range of texts. Movable wooden or ceramic type appeared in Korea in the early thirteenth century and may have been invented there, but the texts were frequently inaccurate and difficult to read. In the 1400s Choson printers, working directly with the king, developed a reliable device to anchor the pieces of type to the printing plate. By replacing the old beeswax adhesive with solid copper frames, they improved the legibility of the printed page, and high-volume, accurate production became possible. Combined with the phonetic *han'gul* (HAHN-goor) writing system, this printing technology laid the foundation for a high literacy rate in Korea.

Choson publications told readers how to produce and use fertilizer, transplant rice seedlings, and engineer reservoirs. Building on Eurasian knowledge imported by the Mongols and introduced under the Koryo, Choson scholars developed a meteorological science of their own. They invented or redesigned instruments to measure wind speed and rainfall and perfected a calendar based on minute comparisons of the Chinese and Islamic systems.

In agriculture, farmers expanded the cultivation of cash crops, the reverse of what was happening in Ming China. Cotton, the primary crop, enjoyed such high value that the state accepted it for tax payments. The Choson army used cotton uniforms, and cotton became the favored fabric of the Korean elite. With cotton gins and spinning wheels powered by water, Korea advanced more rapidly than China in mechanization and began to export considerable amounts of cotton to China and Japan.

Although both the Yuan and the Ming withheld the formula for gunpowder from the Korean government, Korean officials acquired the information by subterfuge. By the later 1300s they had mounted cannon on ships that patrolled against pirates and used gunpowder-driven arrow launchers against enemy personnel and the rigging of enemy ships. Combined with skills in armoring ships, these techniques made the small Choson navy a formidable defense force.

Political Transformation in Japan, 1274–1500   Having secured Korea, the Mongols looked toward Japan, a target they could easily reach from Korea. Their first 30,000-man invasion force in 1274 included Mongol cavalry and archers and sailors from Korea and northeastern Asia. Its weaponry included light catapults and incendiary and explosive projectiles of Chinese manufacture. The Mongol forces landed successfully and decimated the Japanese cavalry, but a great storm on Hakata (HAH-kah-tah) Bay on the north side of Kyushu (KYOO-shoo) Island prevented the establishment of a beachhead and forced the Mongols to sail back to Korea.

The invasion hastened social and political changes that were already under way. Under the Kamakura (kah-mah-KOO-rah) Shogunate established in 1185—another powerful family actually exercised control—the shogun, or military leader, distributed land and privileges to his followers. In return they paid him tribute and supplied him with soldiers. This stable, but decentralized, system depended on balancing the power of regional warlords. Lords in the north and east of Japan's main island were remote from those in the south and west. Beyond devotion to the emperor and the shogun, little united them until the terrifying Mongol threat materialized.

After the return of his fleet, Khubilai sent envoys to Japan demanding submission. Japanese leaders executed them and prepared for war. The shogun then took steps to centralize his military government, effectively increasing the influence of warlords from the south and west of Honshu (Japan's main island) and from the island of Kyushu, where invasion seemed most likely. These local commanders acted under the shogun's orders.

Military planners studied Mongol tactics and retrained and outfitted Japanese warriors for defense against advanced weaponry, while farm laborers drafted from all over the country constructed defensive fortifications. This effort demanded, for the first time, a national system to move resources toward western points rather than toward the imperial or shogunal centers to the east.

The Mongols attacked again in 1281. They brought 140,000 warriors, including many non-Mongols, as well as thousands of horses, in hundreds of ships. However, the wall the Japanese had built to cut off Hakata Bay from the mainland deprived the Mongol forces of a reliable landing point. Japanese swordsmen rowed out and boarded the Mongol ships lingering offshore. Their superb steel swords shocked the invaders, while an epidemic decimated the Mongol troops. After a prolonged standoff, a typhoon struck and sank perhaps half of the Mongol ships. The remainder sailed away, never again to harass Japan. Religious institutions later claimed that their prayers for help brought a "divine wind"—**kamikaze** (kah-me-kah-zay)—that drove away the Mongols.

Nevertheless, the Mongol threat continued to influence Japanese development. Prior to his death in 1294, Khubilai had in mind a third invasion. Although his successors did not carry through with it, the shoguns did not know that the Mongols had given up the idea and rebuilt coastal defenses well into the fourteenth century, helping to consolidate the social position of Japan's warrior elite and stimulating the development of a national infrastructure for trade and communication. But the Kamakura Shogunate, based on regionally collected and regionally dispersed revenues, suffered financial strain in trying to pay for centralized road and defense systems.

Between 1333 and 1338 the emperor Go-Daigo (go-DIE-go) broke the centuries-old tradition of imperial seclusion and aloofness from government and tried to reclaim power from the shoguns. This effort ignited a civil war that destroyed the Kamakura system. In 1338, with the Mongol threat waning, the **Ashikaga** (ah-shee-KAH-gah) **Shogunate** took control at the imperial center of Kyoto.

Under the new shogunate, provincial warlords enjoyed renewed independence. Around their imposing castles, they sponsored the development of market towns, religious institutions, and schools, while the application of technologies imported in earlier periods, including water wheels, improved plows, and Champa rice, increased agricultural productivity.

Growing wealth and relative peace stimulated artistic creativity, mostly reflecting Zen Buddhist beliefs held by the warrior elite. In the simple elegance of architecture and gardens, in the contemplative landscapes of artists, and in the eerie, stylized performances of the Noh theater, the aesthetic code of Zen became established in the Ashikaga era.

Despite the technological advancement, artistic productivity, and rapid urbanization of this period, competition among warlords and their followers led to regional wars. By the later 1400s these conflicts resulted in the near destruction of the warlords. The great Onin War in 1477 left Kyoto devastated and the Ashikaga Shogunate a central government in name only. Ambitious but low-ranking warriors, some with links to trade with the continent, began to scramble for control of the provinces.

After the fall of the Yuan in 1368 Japan resumed overseas trade, exporting raw materials and swords, as well as folding fans, invented in Japan during the period of isolation. Japan's primary imports from China were books and porcelain. The volatile political environment in Japan gave rise to partnerships between warlords and local merchants. All worked to strengthen their own towns and treasuries through overseas commerce or, sometimes, through piracy.

The Emergence of Vietnam, 1200–1500

Before the first Mongol attack in 1257, the states of Dai Viet (northern Vietnam) and Champa (southern Vietnam) had clashed frequently. Dai Viet (once called Annam) looked toward China and had once been subject to the Tang. Chinese political ideas, social philosophies, dress, religion, and language heavily influenced its official culture. Champa related more closely to the trading networks of the Indian Ocean, and its official culture was strongly influenced by Indian religion, language, architecture, and dress. Champa's relationship with China depended in part on how close its enemy, Dai Viet, was to China at any particular time. During the Song period Dai Viet was neither formally subject to China nor particularly threatening to Champa militarily, so Champa inaugurated a trade and tribute relationship with China that spread fast-ripening Champa rice throughout East Asia.

The Mongols exacted tribute from both Dai Viet and Champa until the fall of the Yuan Empire in 1368. Mongol political and military ambitions were mostly focused elsewhere, however, which minimized their impact on politics and culture. The two Vietnamese kingdoms soon resumed their warfare. When Dai Viet moved its army to reinforce its southern border, Ming troops occupied the capital, Hanoi, and installed a puppet government. Almost thirty years elapsed before Dai Viet regained independence and resumed a tributary status. By then the Ming were turning to meet Mongol challenges to their north. In a series of ruthless campaigns, Dai Viet terminated Champa's independence, and by 1500 the ancestor of the modern state of Vietnam had been born.

The new state still relied on Confucian bureaucratic government and an examination system, but some practices differed from those in China. The Vietnamese legal code, for example, preserved group landowning and decision making within the villages, as well as women's property rights. Both developments probably had roots in an early rural culture based on the growing of rice in wet paddies; by this time the Dai Viet kingdom considered them distinctive features of its own culture.

CONCLUSION

Despite their brutality and devastation, the Mongol conquests brought a degree of unity to the lands between China and Europe that had never before been known. Nomadic mobility and expertise in military technology contributed to communication across vast spaces and initially, at least, an often-callous disregard for the welfare of farmers, as manifested in oppressive tax policies. By contrast, trade received active Mongol stimulation through the protection of routes and encouragement of industrial production.

The Mongols ruled with an unprecedented openness, employing talented people irrespective of their linguistic, ethnic, or religious affiliations. As a consequence, the period of comparative Mongol unity, which lasted less than a century, saw a remarkable exchange of ideas, techniques, and products across the breadth of Eurasia. Chinese gunpowder spurred the development of Ottoman and European cannon, while Muslim astronomers introduced new instruments and mathematical techniques to Chinese observatories.

However, rule over dozens of restive peoples could not endure. Where Mongol military enterprise reached its limit of expansion, it stimulated local aspirations for independence. Division and hostility among branches of Chinggis Khan's family— between the Yuan in China and the Chagatai in Central Asia or between the Golden Horde in Russia and the Il-khans in Iran—provided opportunities for achieving these aspirations. The Russians gained freedom from Mongol domination in western Eurasia, and the general political disruption and uncertainty of the Mongol era assisted the emergence of the Lithuanian, Serbian, and Ottoman states.

In the east, China, Korea, and Dai Viet similarly found renewed political identity in the aftermath of Mongol rule. The invasions expanded China's boundaries as never before, and they have changed little since. A resurgence of native Chinese culture blossomed in the following Ming dynasty. At the same time, Japan fought off two Mongol invasions and transformed its internal political and cultural identity in the process. In every case, the reality or threat of Mongol attack and domination encouraged centralization of government, improvement of military techniques, and renewed stress on local cultural identity. Thus, in retrospect, despite its traditional association with death and destruction, the Mongol period appears as a watershed, establishing new connections between widespread parts of Eurasia and leading to the development of strong, assertive, and culturally creative regional states.

IMPORTANT EVENTS 1200–1500

1219–1223	First Mongol attacks in Iran
1221–1223	First Mongol attacks on Russia
1227	Death of Genghis Khan
1234	Mongols conquer northern China
1240	Mongols sack Kiev
1242	Alexander Nevskii defeats Teutonic Knights
1258	Mongols conquer Koryo rulers in Korea
1258	Mongols sack Baghdad and kill the caliph
1260	War between Il-khans and Golden Horde
1260	Mamluks defeat Il-khans at Ain Jalut
1271	Founding of Yuan Empire
1274, 1281	Mongols attack Japan
1279	Mongol conquest of Southern Song
1283	Yuan invades Annam
1293	Yuan attacks Java
1333–1338	End of Kamakura Shogunate in Japan, beginning of Ashikaga
1346	Plague outbreak at Kaff a
1349	End of Il-khan rule
ca. 1350	Egypt infected by plague
1368	Ming Empire founded
1392	Founding of Yi kingdom in Korea
1402	Timur defeats Ottoman sultan
1405–1433	Voyages of Zheng He
1449	Mongol attack on Beijing
1453	Ottomans capture Constantinople
1462–1505	Ivan III establishes authority as tsar. Moscow emerges as major political center.
1471–1500	Annam conquers Champa

14

LATIN EUROPE, 1200–1500

In the summer of 1454, a year after the Ottoman Turks captured the Greek Christian city of Constantinople, Aeneas Sylvius Piccolomini (uh-NEE-uhs SIL-vee-uhs pee-kuh-lo-MEE-nee), destined in four years to become pope, expressed doubts as to whether anyone could persuade the rulers of Christian Europe to take up a new crusade against the Muslims: "Christendom has no head whom all will obey—neither the pope nor the emperor receives his due."

At the time, the Christian states thought more of fighting each other. French and English armies had been battling for over a century; the German emperor presided over dozens of states but did not really control them; and the numerous kingdoms and principalities of Spain and Italy could not unite. The Catholic rulers of Hungary, Poland, and Lithuania, on the front line against the Muslim Ottomans, seemed very far away from the western monarchs. With only slight exaggeration, Aeneas Sylvius moaned, "Every city has its own king, and there are as many princes as there are households." He attributed this lack of unity to European preoccupation with personal welfare and material gain. Both pessimism about human nature and materialism had increased during the previous century, after a devastating plague had carried off a third of Europe's population.

Yet despite all these divisions, disasters, and wars, historians now see the period from 1200 to 1500 (Europe's later Middle Ages) as a time of unusual progress. Prosperous cities adorned with splendid architecture, institutions of higher learning, and cultural achievements counterbalanced the avarice and greed that Aeneas Sylvius lamented. While frequent wars caused havoc and destruction, they also promoted the development of military technology and more unified monarchies.

Although their Muslim and Byzantine neighbors commonly called Catholic Europeans "Franks," they ordinarily referred to themselves as "Latins," underscoring their allegiance to the Roman Catholic church and the Latin language used in its rituals.

RURAL GROWTH AND CRISIS

Between 1200 and 1500, the countries of western Europe brought more land under cultivation using new farming techniques and made greater use of machinery and mechanical forms of energy. Yet for the nine out of ten people who lived in the countryside, hard labor brought meager returns, and famine, epidemics, and war struck often. After the devastation of the Black Death between 1347 and 1351, social changes speeded up by peasant revolts released many persons from serfdom and brought some improvements to rural life.

By contrast, eastern Europe, a region of vast open spaces and sparse population, saw in increase in serfdom. Faced with a labor shortage, nobles agreed to force farm workers to till their lands.

Peasants, Population, and Plague

In 1200, most western Europeans lived as serfs tilling the soil on large estates owned by the nobility and the church (see Chapter 11). They owed their lord both a share of their harvests and numerous labor services. These obligations combined with inefficient farming practices meant that peasants received meager returns for their hard work. Even with numerous religious holidays, peasants labored some fifty-four hours a week, more than half the time in support of the local nobility. Each noble family, housed in its stone castle, required the labor of fifteen to thirty peasant families living in one-room thatched cottage containing little furniture and no luxuries.

Scenes of rural life show both men and women at work in the fields, but equality of labor did not mean equality at home. In the peasant's hut as elsewhere in medieval Europe, women were subordinate to men. The influential theologian Thomas Aquinas (uh-KWY-nuhs) (1225–1274) spoke for his age when he argued that although both men and women were created in God's image, there was a sense in which "the image of God is found in man, and not in woman: for man is the beginning and end of woman; as God is the beginning and end of every creature."[1]

Rural poverty resulted partly from rapid population growth. In 1200, China's population may have exceeded Europe's by two to one; by 1300, the population of each was about 80 million. China's population fell because of the Mongol conquest (see Chapter 13), while Europe's more than doubled between 1100 and 1445. Some historians believe the reviving economy stimulated the increase. Others argue that severe epidemics were few, and warmer-than-usual temperatures after 950, referred to as the Medieval Warm Period by climate historians, reduced mortality from starvation and exposure.

More people required more productive farming and new agricultural settlements. One widespread new technique, the **three-field system**, replaced the custom of leaving half the land fallow (uncultivated) every year to regain its fertility. Farmers grew crops on two-thirds of their land each year, alternating wheat and rye with oats, barley, or legumes. The third field was left fallow. The oats restored nitrogen to the depleted soil and produced feed for plow horses. In much of Europe, however, farmers continued to let half of their land lie fallow and use oxen (less efficient but cheaper than horses) to pull their plows.

Population growth also encouraged new agricultural settlements. In the twelfth and thirteenth centuries, large numbers of Germans migrated into the fertile lands east of the Elbe River from the Baltic Sea in the north to Transylvania (part of

---

[1]Quoted in Marina Warner, *Alone of All Her Sex: The Myth and Cult of the Virgin Mary* (New York: Random House, 1983), 179.

Musée Condé, Chantilly, France/Bridgeman-Giraudon/ Art Resource, NY

Rural French Peasants *Many scenes of peasant life in winter are visible in this small painting by the Flemish Limbourg brothers from the 1410s. Above the snow-covered beehives one man chops firewood, while another drives a donkey loaded with firewood to a little village. At the lower right a woman, blowing on her frozen fingers, heads past the huddled sheep and hungry birds to join other women warming themselves in the cottage (whose outer wall the artists have cut away).*

modern Romania) in the south. The Order of Teutonic Knights, founded in the Holy Land but given a (temporary) European base of operations by the king of Hungary, slaughtered or drove away native inhabitants who had not yet adopted Christianity. During the thirteenth century, they conquered, resettled, and adminis-tered a vast area along the Baltic that later became Prussia.

Draining swamps and clearing forests also brought new land under cultivation. But as population continued to rise, some people had to farm lands with poor soils or vulnerability to flooding, frost, or drought. Average crop yields fell accordingly after 1250, and more people lived at the edge of starvation. According to one histo-rian, "By 1300, almost every child born in western Europe faced the probability of extreme hunger at least once or twice during his expected 30 to 35 years of life."[2] One unusually cold spell at the end of the Medieval Warm Period produced the Great Famine of 1315–1317, which affected much of Europe north of the Alps.

The **Black Death** reversed the population growth. This terrible plague originated in Inner Asia and spread westward with the Mongol armies (see Chapter 13). In 1346, the Mongols attacked the city of Kaffa (KAH-fah) on the Black Sea; a year later, Genoese (JEN-oh-eez) traders in Kaffa carried the disease to Italy and southern France. For two years, the Black Death spread across Europe, in some places carrying off two-thirds of the population. Average losses in western Europe amounted to one in three.

Victims developed boils the size of eggs in their groins and armpits, black blotches on their skin, foul body odors, and severe pain. In most cases, death came within a few days. Town officials closed their gates to people from infected areas and burned the victims' possessions. Such measures helped to spare some communities but could not halt the advance of the disease. Bubonic plague, the primary form of the Black Death, spreads from person to person and through the bites of fleas infesting the fur of certain rats. Even if the medieval doctors had understood the source of the disease, eliminating the rats that thrived on urban refuse would have been difficult.

The plague brought home to people how sudden and unexpected death could be. Some people became more religious, giving money to the church or lashing themselves with iron-tipped whips to atone for their sins. Others chose reckless enjoyment, spending their money on fancy clothes, feasts, and drinking.

Periodic returns of plague made recovery from population losses slow and uneven. Europe's population in 1400 equaled that in 1200. Not until after 1500 did it rise above its preplague level.

Social Rebellion   In addition to its demographic and psychological effects, the Black Death triggered social changes in western Europe. Workers who survived demanded higher pay for their services. When authorities tried to freeze wages at the old levels, peasants rose up against wealthy nobles and churchmen. During a widespread revolt in France in 1358, known as the Jacquerie, peasants looted castles and killed dozens of persons. In a large revolt in England in 1381 led by Wat Tyler, an estimated 50,000 peasants and craftsmen invaded London, calling for an end to serfdom and obligations to landowners and murdering the archbishop of Canterbury and other officials. Authorities put down these rebellions with great bloodshed and cruelty, but they could not stave off the higher wages and other social changes the rebels demanded.

Serfdom practically disappeared in western Europe as peasants bought their freedom or ran away. Some English landowners who could no longer hire enough fieldworkers began pasturing sheep for their wool. Others grew crops that required less care or made greater use of draft animals and laborsaving tools. Because the plague had not killed livestock and game, survivors had abundant meat and leather. Thus, the welfare of the rural masses generally improved after the Black Death, though the gap between rich and poor remained wide.

---

[2]Harry Miskimin, *The Economy of the Early Renaissance, 1300–1460* (Englewood Cliffs, NJ: Prentice Hall, 1969), 26–27.

In urban areas, employers raised wages to attract workers. Guilds (discussed later in this chapter) shortened the period of apprenticeship. Competition within crafts also became more common. Although the overall economy shrank with the decline in population, per capita production actually rose.

Mills and Mines   Mining, primarily in Germany and east-central Europe, and metalworking and craft mechanization everywhere expanded so greatly in the centuries before 1500 that some historians speak of an "industrial revolution" in medieval Europe. This is too strong a term, but the landscape fairly bristled with mechanical devices. Mills powered by water or wind ground grain, sawed logs, crushed olives, operated bellows, and pounded linen rags for making paper.

Watermills multiplied at a faster rate than the population. In 1086, 5,600 watermills flanked England's many rivers. After 1200, mills spread rapidly across the European mainland. By the early fourteenth century, entrepreneurs had crammed 68 watermills into a 1-mile section of the Seine (sen) River in Paris. Undershot wheels that depended on the river flowing beneath them were less efficient than overshot wheels where water channeled to fall over the top of the wheel combined the force of gravity with the water's current. Windmills multiplied in comparatively dry lands like Spain and in northern Europe, where water wheels froze in winter.

Designs for water mills dated back to Roman times, and the Islamic world, which inherited Hellenistic technologies, knew both water wheels and windmills. However, European-style heavy investment in water or wind power made no sense in Muslim lands because animal power from oxen and camels was so much cheaper where arid and semiarid wastes provided virtually free grazing. There comparatively cheap and simple single-animal mills and irrigation devices predominated. In Europe, by contrast, where grain farmers grew both human food and animal fodder, population growth increased the cost of animal energy, and of horsepower in particular. One result was that the family name *Miller* became very important in European languages but was rarely used in Arabic, Persian, or Turkish.

Owners invested heavily in building mills, but since nature furnished the energy to run them for free, they returned great profits. While individuals or monasteries constructed some mills, most were built by groups of investors. Rich millers often aroused the jealousy of their neighbors. In his *Canterbury Tales*, the English poet Geoffrey Chaucer (ca. 1340–1400) captured their unsavory reputation by portraying a miller as "a master-hand at stealing grain" by pushing down on the balance scale with his thumb.[3]

Waterpower aided the great expansion of iron making. Water powered the stamping mills that pulverized iron ore, the lifting devices that drained water from deep mines, and the bellows (first documented in the West in 1323) that raised temperatures to the point where liquid iron could be poured into molds. Blast furnaces producing high-quality iron are documented from 1380.

In addition to iron mines in many countries, new silver, lead, and copper mines in Austria and Hungary supplied metal for coins, church bells, cannon, and statues. Techniques of deep mining developed in central Europe spread west in the latter

---

[3]Quotations here and later in the chapter are from Geoffrey Chaucer, *The Canterbury Tales*, trans. Nevill Coghill (New York: Penguin Books, 1952), 25, 29, 32.

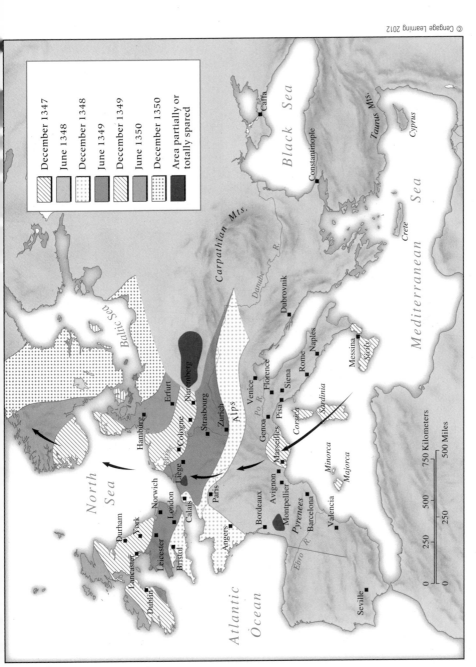

© Cengage Learning 2012

MAP 14.1   Spread of the Black Death

The plague entered Europe by way of Sicily in 1347 and within three years had killed between one-quarter and one-half of the population. Outbreaks continued into the early eighteenth century, and the European population took two hundred years to return to the level it had reached before the Black Death.

part of the fifteenth century. A building boom stimulated stone quarrying in France during the eleventh, twelfth, and thirteenth centuries.

Industrial growth changed the landscape. Towns grew outward and new ones were founded, dams and canals changed the flow of rivers, and quarries and mines scarred the hillsides. Urban tanneries (factories that cured and processed leather), the runoff from slaughterhouses, and human waste polluted streams. England's Parliament enacted the first recorded antipollution law in 1388, but enforcement proved difficult.

Deforestation accelerated. Trees provided timber for buildings and ships; tanneries stripped bark to make acid for tanning leather; and many forests gave way to farmland. The glass and iron industries used great quantities of charcoal, made by controlled burning of oak or other hardwood. A single iron furnace could consume all the trees within five-eighths of a mile (1 kilometer) in just forty days. Consequently, the later Middle Ages saw the end of many of western Europe's once-dense forests, except in places where powerful landowners established hunting preserves. Central and eastern Europe, being more lightly populated, experienced less environmental degradation.

Urban Revival

In the tenth century, no town in the Latin Europe could compete in size, wealth, or comfort with the cities of Byzantium and Islam. Yet by the later Middle Ages, the Mediterranean, Baltic, and Atlantic coasts boasted wealthy port cities, as did some major rivers draining into these seas. Some Byzantine and Muslim cities still exceeded those of the West in size, but not in commercial, cultural, and administrative dynamism, as marked by impressive new churches, guild halls, and residences.

Trading Cities   Most urban growth after 1200 resulted from manufacturing and trade, both between cities and their hinterlands and over long distances. Northern Italy particularly benefited from maritime trade with the port cities of the eastern Mediterranean and, through them, the markets of the Indian Ocean and East Asia. In northern Europe, commercial cities in the county of Flanders (roughly today's Belgium) and around the Baltic Sea profited from regional networks and from overland and sea routes to the Mediterranean.

A Venetian-inspired assault in 1204 against the city of Constantinople, misleadingly named the "Fourth Crusade," temporarily eliminated Byzantine control of the passage between the Mediterranean and the Black Sea and thereby allowed Venice to seize Crete and expand its trading colonies around the Black Sea. Another boon to Italian trade came from the westward expansion of the Mongol Empire, which opened trade routes from the Mediterranean to China that did not go through Iran and Iraq (see Chapter 13).

When Mongol decline interrupted the caravan trade in the fourteenth century, Venetian merchants purchased eastern silks and spices brought by other middlemen to Constantinople, Damascus, and Cairo. Three times a year, Venice dispatched convoys of two or three galleys, with sixty oarsmen each, capable of bringing back 2,000 tons of goods.

The sea trade of Genoa on northern Italy's west coast probably equaled that of Venice. Genoese merchants established colonies in the western and eastern Mediterranean and around the Black Sea. In northern Europe, an association of

Flemish Weavers, Ypres *The spread of textile weaving gave employment to many people in the Netherlands. The city of Ypres in Flanders (now northern Belgium) was an important textile center in the thirteenth century. This drawing from a fourteenth-century manuscript shows a man and a woman weaving cloth on a horizontal loom.*

trading cities known as the **Hanseatic** (han-see-AT-ik) **League** traded extensively in the Baltic, including the coasts of Prussia, newly conquered by German knights. Their merchants ranged eastward to Novgorod in Russia and westward across the North Sea to London.

In the late thirteenth century, Genoese galleys from the Mediterranean and Hanseatic ships from the Baltic were converging on the trading and manufacturing cities in Flanders. Artisans in the Flemish towns of Bruges (broozh), Ghent (gent [hard *g* as in *get*]), and Ypres (EE-pruh) transformed raw wool from England into a fine cloth that was softer and smoother than the coarse "homespuns" from simple village looms. Dyed in vivid hues, these Flemish textiles appealed to wealthy Europeans, who also appreciated fine textiles from Asia.

Along the overland route connecting Flanders and northern Italy, important trading fairs developed in the Champagne (sham-PAIN) region of Burgundy. The Champagne fairs began as regional markets, exchanging manufactured goods, livestock, and farm produce once or twice a year. When the king of France gained control of Champagne at the end of the twelfth century, royal guarantees of safe conduct to merchants turned these markets into international fairs that were important for currency exchange and other financial transactions as well. A century later, fifteen Italian cities had permanent consulates in Champagne to represent the interests of their citizens. During the fourteenth century, the large volume of trade made it cheaper to ship Flemish woolens to Italy by sea than to pack them overland on animal backs. Champagne's fairs consequently lost some international trade, but they remained important as regional markets.

In the late thirteenth century, the English monarchy raised taxes on exports of raw wool, making cloth manufacture in England more profitable than in Flanders. Flemish specialists crossed the English Channel and introduced the spinning wheel, perhaps invented in India, and other devices to England. Annual raw wool exports fell from 35,000 sacks of wool at the beginning of the fourteenth century to 8,000 in the mid-fifteenth century, while English wool cloth production rose from 4,000 pieces just before 1350 to 54,000 a century later.

Florence also replaced Flemish imports with its own woolens industry financed by local banking families. In 1338, Florence manufactured 80,000 pieces of cloth, while importing only 10,000. Elsewhere in northern Italy a new industry appeared to manufacture cotton cloth, which had previously been imported across the Mediterranean. These changes in the textile industry show how competition promoted the spread of manufacturing and encouraged new specialties. Other Italian industries that grew on the basis of techniques borrowed from the Muslim world were papermaking, glassblowing, ceramics, and sugar refining.

In the fifteenth century, Venice surpassed its European rivals in the volume of its trade in the Mediterranean as well as across the Alps into central Europe. Its craftspeople manufactured luxury goods once obtainable only from eastern sources, including cotton and sugar grown with slave labor on the islands of Crete, Cyprus, and Sicily. This enterprise later became the model for the slave-based sugar economy of the New World (see Chapter 16). Exports of Italian and northern European woolens to the eastern Mediterranean also rose. In the space of a few centuries, western European cities had used the eastern trade to increase their prosperity and then reduce their dependence on eastern goods.

Civic Life   Most northern Italian and German cities were independent states, much like the port cities of the Indian Ocean Basin (see Chapter 15). Other European cities held royal charters exempting them from the authority of local nobles. Their autonomy enabled them to adapt to changing market conditions more quickly than cities controlled by imperial authorities, as in China and the Islamic world. Since anyone who lived in a chartered city for over a year could claim freedom, urban life promoted social mobility.

Europe's Jews mostly lived in cities. Spain had the largest communities because of the tolerance of earlier Muslim rulers, but there were also sizable populations as far east as Magdeburg in Prussia. Commercial cities generally welcomed Jews with manufacturing and business skills. Despite official protection by certain Christian princes and kings, however, Jews endured violent religious persecutions or expulsions in times of crisis, such as during the Black Death (see Diversity and Dominance: Persecution and Protection of Jews, 1272–1349). In 1492, the Spanish monarchs expelled all Jews in the name of religious and ethnic purity. Only the papal city of Rome left its Jews undisturbed throughout the centuries before 1500.

Within most towns and cities, powerful associations known as guilds dominated civic life. **Guilds** brought together craft specialists, such as silversmiths, or merchants working in a particular trade, to regulate business practices and set prices. Guilds also trained apprentices and promoted members' interests with the city government. By denying membership to outsiders and Jews, guilds protected the interests of families that already belonged to them. They also perpetuated male dominance of most skilled jobs.

Nevertheless, in a few places, women could join guilds either on their own or as the wives, widows, or daughters of male guild members. Large numbers of poor women also toiled in nonguild jobs in urban textile industries and in the food and beverage trades, generally receiving lower wages than men.

Some women advanced socially through marriage to wealthy men. One of Chaucer's *Canterbury Tales* concerns a woman from Bath, a city in southern England, who became wealthy by marrying a succession of old men for their money (and then two other husbands for love), "aside from other company in youth." She was also a skilled weaver, Chaucer says: "In making cloth she showed so great a bent, / She bettered those of Ypres and of Ghent."

By the fifteenth century, a new class of wealthy merchant-bankers was operating on a vast scale and specializing in money changing and loans and making investments on behalf of other parties. Merchants great and small used their services. They also handled the financial transactions of ecclesiastical and secular officials and arranged for the transmission to the pope of funds known as Peter's pence, a collection taken up annually in every church in Latin Europe. Princes and kings supported their wars and lavish courts with credit. Some merchant-bankers even developed their own news services, gathering information on any topic that could affect business.

Florentine financiers offered checking accounts, organized private shareholding companies (the forerunners of modern corporations), and improved bookkeeping techniques. In the fifteenth century, the Medici (MED-ih-chee) family of Florence operated banks in Italy, Flanders, and London. Medicis also controlled the government of Florence and commissioned art works. The Fuggers (FOOG-uhrz) of Augsburg, who had ten times the Medici bank's lending capital, topped Europe's banking fraternity by 1500. Beginning as cloth merchants under Jacob "the Rich" (1459–1525), the family's many activities included the trade in Hungarian copper, essential for casting cannon.

Since Latin Christians generally considered charging interest (usury) sinful, Jews predominated in moneylending. Christian bankers devised ways to get around the condemnation of usury. Some borrowers repaid loans in a different currency at a rate of exchange favorable to the lender. Others added to their repayment a "gift" for the lender. For example, in 1501, church officials agreed to repay a Fugger loan of 6,000 gold ducats in five months along with a "gift" of 400 ducats, amounting to an effective interest rate of 16 percent a year. In fact, the return was less since the church failed to repay the loan on time.

Yet most residents of European cities suffered poverty and ill health. European cities generally lacked civic amenities such as public baths and water supply systems that had existed in Roman times and still survived in Islamic lands.

Gothic Cathedrals   Master builders and stone masons counted among the skilled people in greatest demand. Though cities competed with one another in the magnificence of their guild halls and town halls, **Gothic cathedrals**, first appearing about 1140 in France, cost the most and

Persecution and Protection of Jews, 1272–1349

Because they did not belong to the dominant Latin Christian faith, Jews suffered from periodic discrimination and persecution. For the most part, religious and secular authorities tried to curb such anti-Semitism. Jews, after all, were useful citizens who worshiped the same God as their Christian neighbors. Still, it was hard to know where to draw the line between justifiable and unjustifiable discrimination. The famous reviser of Catholic theology, St. Thomas Aquinas, made one such distinction in his Summa Theologica with regard to attempts at forced conversion.

Now, the practice of the Church never held that the children of Jews should be baptized against the will of their parents.... Therefore, it seems dangerous to bring forward this new view, that contrary to the previously established custom of the Church, the children of Jews should be baptized against the will of their parents.

There are two reasons for this position. One stems from danger to faith. For, if children without the use of reason were to receive baptism, then after reaching maturity they could easily be persuaded by their parents to relinquish what they had received in ignorance. This would tend to do harm to the faith.

The second reason is that it is opposed to natural justice ... it [is] a matter of natural right that a son, before he has the use of reason, is under the care of his father. Hence, it would be against natural justice for the boy, before he has the use of reason, to be removed from the care of his parents, or for anything to be arranged for him against the will of his parents.

The "new view" Aquinas opposed was much in the air, for in 1272 Pope Gregory X issued a decree condemning forced baptism. The pope's decree reviews the

history of papal protection given to the Jews, starting with a quotation from Pope Gregory I dating from 598, and decrees two new protections of Jews' legal rights.

Even as it is not allowed to the Jews in their assemblies presumptuously to undertake for themselves more than that which is permitted them by law, even so they ought not to suffer any disadvantage in those [privileges] which have been granted them.

Although they prefer to persist in their stubbornness rather than to recognize the words of their prophets and the mysteries of the Scriptures, and thus to arrive at a knowledge of Christian faith and salvation; nevertheless, inasmuch as they have made an appeal for our protection and help, we therefore admit their petition and offer them the shield of our protection through the clemency of Christian piety. In so doing we follow in the footsteps of our predecessors of happy memory, the popes of Rome—Calixtus, Eugene, Alexander, Clement, Celestine, Innocent, and Honorius.

We decree moreover that no Christian shall compel them or any one of their group to come to baptism unwillingly. But if any one of them shall take refuge of his own accord with Christians, because of conviction, then, after his intention will have been made manifest, he shall be made a Christian without any intrigue. For indeed that person who is known to come to Christian baptism not freely, but unwillingly, is not believed to possess the Christian faith.

Moreover, no Christian shall presume to seize, imprison, wound, torture, mutilate, kill, or inflict violence on them; furthermore no one shall presume, except by judicial action of the authorities of the country, to change the good customs in the land where they live for the purpose of taking their money or goods from them or from others.

In addition, no one shall disturb them in any way during the celebration of their festivals, whether by day or by night, with clubs or stones or anything else. Also no one shall exact any compulsory service of them unless it be that which they have been accustomed to render in previous times.

Inasmuch as the Jews are not able to bear witness against the Christians, we decree furthermore that the testimony of Christians against Jews shall not be valid unless there is among these Christians some Jew who is there for the purpose of offering testimony.

Since it occasionally happens that some Christians lose their Christian children, the Jews are accused by their enemies of secretly carrying off and killing these same Christian children, and of making sacrifices of the heart and blood of these very children. It happens, too, that the parents of these children, or some other Christian enemies of these Jews, secretly hide these very children in order that they may be able to injure these Jews, and in order that they may be able to extort from them a certain amount of money by redeeming them from their straits.

And most falsely do these Christians claim that the Jews have secretly and furtively carried away these children and killed them, and that the Jews offer sacrifice from the heart and the blood of these children, since their law in this matter precisely and expressly forbids Jews to sacrifice, eat, or drink the blood, or eat the flesh of animals having claws. This has been demonstrated many times at our court by Jews converted to the Christian faith: nevertheless very many Jews are often seized and detained unjustly because of this.

We decree, therefore, that Christians need not be obeyed against Jews in such a case or situation of this type, and we order that Jews seized under such a silly pretext be freed from imprisonment, and that they shall not be arrested henceforth on such a miserable pretext, unless—which we do not believe—they be caught in the commission of the crime. We decree that no Christian shall stir up anything against them, but that they should be maintained in that status and position in which they were from the time of our predecessors, from antiquity till now.

We decree, in order to stop the wickedness and avarice of bad men, that no one shall dare to devastate or to destroy a cemetery of the Jews or to dig up human bodies for the sake of getting money [by holding them for ransom]. Moreover, if anyone, after having known the content of this decree, should—which we hope will not happen—attempt audaciously to act contrary to it, then let him suffer punishment in his rank and position, or let him be punished by the penalty of excommunication, unless he makes amends for his boldness by proper recompense. Moreover, we wish that only those Jews who have not attempted to contrive anything toward the destruction of the Christian faith be fortified by the support of such protection....

Despite such decrees, violence against Jews might burst out when fears and emotions were running high. This selection is from the official chronicles of the upper-Rhineland towns.

In the year 1349 there occurred the greatest epidemic that ever happened. Death went from one end of the earth to the other, on that side and this side of the [Mediterranean] sea, and it was greater among the Saracens [Muslims] than among the Christians. In some lands everyone died so that no one was left.

Ships were also found on the sea laden with wares; the crew had all died and no one guided the ship. The Bishop of Marseilles and priests and monks and more than half of all the people there died with them. In other kingdoms and cities so many people perished that it would be horrible to describe. The pope at Avignon stopped all sessions of court, locked himself in a room, allowed no one to approach him and had a fire burning before him all the time. And from what this epidemic came, all wise teachers and physicians could only say that it was God's will. And the plague was now here, so it was in other places, and lasted more than a whole year. This epidemic also came to Strasbourg in the summer of the above mentioned year, and it is estimated about sixteen thousand people died.

In the matter of this plague the Jews throughout the world were reviled and accused in all lands of having caused it through the poison which they are said to have put into the water and the wells—that is what they were accused of—and for this reason the Jews were burnt all the way from the Mediterranean into Germany, but not in Avignon, for the pope protected them there.

Nevertheless they tortured a number of Jews in Berne and Zofingen who admitted they had put poison into many wells, and they found the poison in the wells. Thereupon they burnt the Jews in many towns and wrote of this affair to Strasbourg, Freibourg, and Basel in order that they too should burn their Jews.... The deputies of the city of Strasbourg were asked what they were going to do with their Jews. They answered and said that they knew no evil of them. Then ... there was a great indignation and clamor against the deputies from Strasbourg. So finally the Bishop and the lords and the Imperial Cities agreed to do away with the Jews. The result was that they were burnt in many cities, and wherever they were expelled they were caught by the peasants and stabbed to death or drowned....

On Saturday—that was St. Valentine's Day—they burnt the Jews on a wooden platform in their cemetery. There were about two thousand people of them. Those who wanted to baptize themselves were spared. Many small children were taken out of the fire and baptized against the will of their fathers and mothers. And everything that was owed to the Jews was cancelled, and the Jews had to surrender all pledges and notes that they had taken for debts. The council, however, took the cash that the Jews possessed and divided it among the working-men proportionately. The money was indeed the thing that killed the Jews. If they had been poor and if the feudal lords had not been in debt to them, they would not have been burnt.

Questions for Analysis

1. Why do Aquinas and Pope Gregory oppose prejudicial actions against Jews?

2. Why did prejudice increase at the time of the Black Death?

3. What factors account for the differences between the views of Christian leaders and the Christian masses?

Sources: First selection source is Pocket Books, a division of Simon & Schuster, Inc., and the Vernon & Janet Bourke Living Trust from The Pocket Aquinas, edited with translations by Vernon G. Bourke. Copyright © 1960 by Washington Square Press. Copyright renewed © 1988 by Simon & Schuster, Inc. Second and third selections from Jacob R. Marcus, ed., The Jew in the Medieval World: A Source Book, 315–1791 (Cincinnati: Union of American Hebrew Congregations, 1938), 152–154, 45–47. Reprinted with permission of the Hebrew Union College Press, Cincinnati.

brought the greatest prestige. The pointed, or Gothic, arch, replacing the older round, or Romanesque, arch, signaled the new design. External (flying) buttresses stabilizing the high, thin, stone columns below the arches constituted another distinctive feature. This design enabled master builders to push the Gothic cathedrals to great heights and fill the outside walls between the arches with giant windows depicting religious scenes in brilliantly colored stained glass. During the next four centuries, interior heights soared ever higher and walls became dazzling curtains of stained glass.

The men who designed and built the cathedrals had little or no formal education and limited understanding of the mathematical principles of civil engineering. Master masons sometimes miscalculated, causing parts of some overly ambitious cathedrals to collapse. The record-high choir vault of Beauvais Cathedral, for instance—154 feet (47 meters) in height—came tumbling down in 1284. But as builders gained experience and invented novel solutions to their problems, success rose from the rubble of their mistakes. The cathedral spire in Strasbourg reached 466 feet (142 meters) into the air—as high as a forty-story building. Such heights were unsurpassed until the nineteenth century.

LEARNING, LITERATURE, AND THE RENAISSANCE

Throughout the Middle Ages, people in the western Europe lived amid reminders of the achievements of the Romans. They wrote and worshiped in a version of their language, traveled their roads, and obeyed some of their laws. The vestments and robes of popes, kings, and emperors followed the designs of Roman officials. Yet the learning of Greco-Roman antiquity virtually disappeared outside of Byzantium and the Muslim world.

The Renaissance

A small revival of learning at the court of Charlemagne in the ninth century was followed by a larger renaissance (rebirth) in the twelfth century, when cities became centers of intellectual and artistic life. The universities established across Latin Europe after 1200 contributed to this cultural revival. In the mid-fourteenth century, the pace of intellectual and artistic life quickened in what is often called the **Renaissance**, which began in northern Italy and later spread to northern and eastern Europe. Some Italian authors saw the Italian Renaissance as a sharp break with an age of darkness.

Before 1100, Byzantine and Islamic scholarship generally surpassed scholarship in Latin Europe. But when Latin Christians wrested southern Italy from the Byzantines and Sicily and Toledo from the Muslims in the eleventh century, they acquired many manuscripts of Greek and Arabic works. These included works by Plato and Aristotle (AR-ih-stah-tahl) and Greek treatises on medicine, mathematics, and geography, as well as scientific and philosophical writings by Muslim writers. Latin translations of the Iranian philosopher Ibn Sina (IB-uhn SEE-nah) (980–1037), known in the West as Avicenna (av-uh-SEN-uh), had great influence because of their sophisticated blend of Aristotelian and Islamic philosophy. Jewish scholars contributed significantly to the translation and explication of Arabic and other manuscripts.

In a related development, the thirteenth century saw the foundation of two new religious orders, the Dominicans and the Franciscans. Living according to a rule but not confined to monasteries, these friars brought preaching to the common people and carried the Christian message abroad as missionaries. Some of their most talented members taught in the independent colleges that arose after 1200. Though some aspects of these institutions may derive from institutions of higher Islamic learning called *madrasas* that proliferated after 1100 (see Chapter 10), Latin Europe innovated the idea of **universities** as degree-granting corporations imparting both religious and nonreligious learning.

Between 1300 and 1500, sixty universities, from St. Andrews in Scotland to Krakow and Prague in eastern Europe, joined the twenty established before that time. Students banded together to start some of them; guilds of professors founded others. Teaching guilds, like crafts guilds, set standards for the profession, trained apprentices and masters, and defended their professional interests.

Universities set curricula and instituted final examinations for degrees. Students who passed the exams that ended their apprenticeship received a "license" to teach, while those who completed longer training and defended a masterwork of scholarship became "masters" and "doctors." The University of Paris gradually absorbed the city's various colleges, but the colleges of Oxford and Cambridge remained independent, self-governing organizations.

Since all universities used Latin, students and masters moved freely across political and linguistic borders, seeking the courses and professors they wanted. Some universities offered specialized training. Legal training centered on Bologna in Italy (buh-LOHN-yuh); Montpellier in southern France and Salerno in Sicily focused on medicine; Paris and Oxford excelled in theology.

Some topics, such as astronomy, were studied outside the university. Both Greek and Arabic traditions presumed that the planets traced circular orbits around the earth, the circle being a perfect geometrical figure. Celestial observations did not always fit this presumption, however. Fifteenth-century astronomers in both Europe and the lands of Islam theorized explanations for the observational deviations. At the very end of the fifteenth century, the Polish-German astronomer Nicolaus Copernicus (co-PER-ni-cus), basing his ideas mainly on the Greek Ptolemy but also aware of more recent writings in Arabic, hit on the idea of planets orbiting the sun instead of the earth. His work, finally published as he lay dying of a stroke in 1543, would pose a challenge to the church's assumption that the earth was the center of God's universe.

Though the new learning sometimes raised inconvenient questions, students aspiring to ecclesiastical careers, and their professors, conferred special prominence on theology, seen as the "queen of the sciences" encompassing all true knowledge. Hence, thirteenth-century theologians sought to synthesize the rediscovered philosophical works of Aristotle and the commentaries of Avicenna with the Bible's revealed truth. These efforts to synthesize reason and faith were known as **scholasticism** (skoh-LAS-tih-sizm).

Thomas Aquinas, a brilliant Dominican theology professor at the University of Paris, wrote the most notable scholastic work, the *Summa Theologica* (SOOM-uh thee-uh-LOH-jih-kuh), between 1267 and 1273. Although his exposition of Christian belief organized on Aristotelian principles came to be accepted as a masterly demonstration of the reasonableness of Christianity, scholasticism upset many traditional thinkers. Some church authorities tried to ban Aristotle from the curriculum. However, the considerable freedom of medieval universities from both secular and religious authorities enabled the new ideas to prevail over the fears of church administrators.

Humanists and Printers   This period also saw important literary contributions. The Italian Dante Alighieri (DAHN-tay ah-lee-GYEH-ree) (1265–1321) completed a long, elegant poem, the *Divine Comedy*, shortly before his death. This supreme expression of medieval preoccupations tells the allegorical story of Dante's journey through the nine circles of Hell and the seven terraces of Purgatory, followed by his entry into Paradise. The Roman poet Virgil guides him through Hell and Purgatory; Beatrice, a woman he had loved from afar since childhood and whose death inspired the poem, guides him to Paradise.

The *Divine Comedy* foreshadows the literary fashions of the later Italian Renaissance. Like Dante, later Italian writers made use of Greco-Roman classical themes and mythology and sometimes courted a broader audience by writing not in Latin but in their local language (Dante used the vernacular spoken in Tuscany [TUS-kuh-nee]).

The poet Geoffrey Chaucer (ca. 1343–1400), many of whose works show the influence of Dante, wrote in vernacular English. The *Canterbury Tales*, a lengthy poem written in the last dozen years of his life, contains often humorous and earthy tales told by fictional pilgrims on their way to the shrine of Thomas à Becket in Canterbury (see Chapter 11). They present a vivid cross-section of medieval people and attitudes.

Dante influenced a literary movement of the **humanists** that began in his native Florence in the mid-fourteenth century. The term refers to their interest in grammar, rhetoric, poetry, history, and moral philosophy (ethics)—subjects known collectively as the humanities, an ancient discipline. With the brash exaggeration characteristic of new intellectual fashions, humanist writers like the poet Francesco Petrarch (fran-CHES-koh PAY-trahrk) (1304–1374) and the poet and storyteller Giovanni Boccaccio (jo-VAH-nee boh-KAH-chee-oh) (1313–1375) proclaimed a revival of a Greco-Roman tradition they felt had for centuries lain buried under the rubble of post-Roman decay.

This idea of a rebirth of learning dismisses too readily the monastic and university scholars who for centuries had been recovering all sorts of Greco-Roman learning, as well as writers like Dante (whom the humanists revered), who anticipated humanist interests by a generation. Yet the humanists had a great impact as educators, advisers, and reformers. Their greatest influence came in reforming secondary education. They introduced a curriculum centered on the languages and literature of Greco-Roman antiquity, which they felt provided intellectual discipline, moral lessons, and refined tastes. This curriculum dominated European secondary schools well into the twentieth century.

Many humanists tried to duplicate the elegance of classical Latin and (to a lesser extent) Greek, which they revered as the pinnacle of learning, beauty, and wisdom. Boccaccio gained fame with his vernacular writings, which resemble

Dante's _Divine Comedy_ *This fifteenth-century painting by Domenico di Michelino shows Dante holding a copy of the Divine Comedy. Hell is depicted to the poet's left and the terraces of Purgatory behind him, surmounted by the earthly and heavenly Paradise. The city of Florence, with its recently completed cathedral, appears on the right.*

Dante's, and especially for the *Decameron*, an earthy work that has much in common with Chaucer's boisterous tales. Under Petrarch's influence, however, Boccaccio turned to writing in classical Latin.

As humanist scholars mastered Latin and Greek, they turned their language skills to restoring the original texts of Greco-Roman writers and of the Bible. By comparing different manuscripts, they eliminated errors introduced by generations of copyists. To aid in this task, Pope Nicholas V (r. 1447–1455) created the Vatican Library, buying scrolls of Greco-Roman writings and paying to have accurate copies and translations made. Working independently, the Dutch scholar Erasmus (uh-RAZ-muhs) of Rotterdam (ca. 1466–1536) produced a critical edition of the New Testament in Greek. Erasmus corrected many errors and mistranslations in the Latin text that had been in general use throughout the Middle Ages. Later, this humanist priest and theologian wrote—in classical Latin—influential moral guides, including the *Enchiridion militis christiani* (*The Manual of the Christian Knight*, 1503) and *The Education of a Christian Prince* (1515).

The influence of the humanists grew as the new technology of printing made their critical editions of ancient texts, literary works, and moral guides more available. The Chinese and the Arabs used carved woodblocks for printing, and block-printed playing cards circulated in Europe before 1450, but after that date three European improvements revolutionized printing: (1) movable pieces of type consisting of individual letters, independently invented in Korea (see Chapter 12); (2) walnut oil–based ink suitable for printing on paper without smearing; and (3) the **printing press**, a mechanical device that pressed sheets of paper onto inked type.

Johann Gutenberg (yoh-HAHN GOO-ten-burg) (ca. 1394–1468) of Mainz led the way. The Gutenberg Bible of 1454, the first book in the West printed from movable type, exhibited a beauty and craftsmanship testifying to the printer's years of experimentation. Humanists worked closely with the printers, who spread the new techniques to Italy and France. Erasmus did editing and proofreading for the Italian scholar-printer Aldo Manuzio (1449–1515) in Venice. Manuzio's press published many critical editions of classical Latin and Greek texts.

By 1500, at least 10 million printed volumes flowed from presses in 238 European towns, launching a revolution that affected students, scholars, and a growing literate population. These readers consumed unorthodox political and religious tracts along with ancient texts.

Renaissance Artists   Although the artists of the fourteenth and fifteenth centuries continued to depict biblical subjects, the Greco-Roman revival led some, especially in Italy, to portray ancient deities and myths. Another popular trend involved scenes of daily life.

Neither theme was entirely new, however. Renaissance art, like Renaissance scholarship, owed a debt to earlier generations. Italian painters of the fifteenth century credited the Florentine painter Giotto (JAW-toh) (ca. 1267–1337) with single-handedly reviving the "lost art of painting." In religious scenes, Giotto replaced the stiff, staring figures of the Byzantine style, which were intended to overawe viewers, with more natural and human portraits with whose depictions of grief and love viewers could identify. Rather than floating on backgrounds of gold leaf, his saints inhabit earthly landscapes.

North of the Alps, the Flemish painter Jan van Eyck (yahn vahn IKE) (ca. 1390–1441) mixed his pigments with linseed oil in place of the egg yolk of earlier centuries. Oil paints dried more slowly and gave pictures a superior luster. Italian painters quickly copied van Eyck's technique, though his own masterfully realistic paintings on religious and domestic themes remained distinctive.

Leonardo da Vinci (lay-own-AHR-doh dah-VIN-chee) (1452–1519) used oil paints for his *Mona Lisa*. Renaissance artists like Leonardo worked in many media, including bronze sculptures and frescos (painting on wet plaster) like *The Last Supper*. Leonardo's notebooks also contain imaginative designs for airplanes, submarines, and tanks. His younger contemporary Michelangelo (my-kuhl-AN-juh-low) (1472–1564) painted frescoes of biblical scenes on the ceiling of the Sistine Chapel in the Vatican, sculpted statues of David and Moses, and designed the dome for a new Saint Peter's Basilica in Rome.

The patronage of wealthy and educated merchants and prelates underlay the artistic blossoming in the cities of northern Italy and Flanders. The Florentine banker Cosimo de' Medici (1389–1464) and his grandson Lorenzo (1449–1492), known as "the Magnificent," spent immense sums on paintings, sculpture, and public buildings. In Rome, the papacy (PAY-puh-see) launched a building program that culminated in the construction of the new Saint Peter's Basilica and a residence for the pope.

These scholarly and artistic achievements exemplify the innovation and striving for excellence of the late Middle Ages. The new literary themes and artistic styles of this period had lasting influence on Western culture. But the innovations in the organization of universities, in printing, and in scientific thought had wider implications, for they were later adopted by cultures all over the world.

POLITICAL AND MILITARY TRANSFORMATIONS

Stronger and more unified states and armies developed in western Europe in parallel with the economic and cultural revivals. Crusades against Muslim states brought consolidation to Spain and Portugal. In Italy and Germany, however, political power remained in the hands of small states and loose alliances. Farther to the east, Lithuania, dynastically linked to Poland, became one of Europe's largest states, while Hungary confronted the Ottoman Empire.

Monarchs, Nobles, and the Church Thirteenth-century states continued early medieval state structures (see Chapter 11). Hereditary monarchs topped the political pyramid, but modest treasuries and the rights of nobles and the church limited their powers. Powerful noblemen who controlled vast estates had an important voice in matters of state. The church guarded closely its traditional rights and independence. Towns, too, had acquired rights and privileges. Towns in Flanders, the Hanseatic League, and Italy approached independence from royal interference. In theory the ruler's noble vassals owed military service in time of war. In practice, vassals sought to limit the monarch's power.

In the year 1200, knights still formed the backbone of western European armies, but changes in weaponry brought this into question. Improved crossbows could shoot metal-tipped arrows with enough force to pierce helmets and light body armor. Professional crossbowmen, hired for wages, became increasingly common and much feared. Indeed, a church council in 1139 outlawed the crossbow—ineffectively—as being too deadly for use against Christians. The arrival in Europe of firearms based on the Chinese invention of gunpowder (see Chapter 13) further transformed the medieval army, first on the Ottoman frontier and then farther west.

The church also resisted royal control. In 1302, the outraged Pope Boniface VIII (r. 1294–1303) asserted that divine law made the papacy superior to "every human creature," including monarchs. King Philip "the Fair" of France (r. 1285–1314) responded by sending an army to arrest the pope, a chastisement that hastened Pope Boniface's death. Philip then engineered the election of a French pope, who established a new papal residence at Avignon (ah-vee-NYON) in southern France in 1309.

A succession of French-dominated popes residing in Avignon improved church discipline but at the price of compromising their neutrality in the eyes of other rulers. The **Great Western Schism** between 1378 and 1415 saw rival papal claimants at Avignon and Rome vying for Christian loyalties. The papacy eventually regained its independence and returned to Rome, but the long crisis broke the

The Magna Carta

One of four extant copies, this document shows the ravages of time, but the symbolic importance of the charter King John of England signed under duress in 1215 for English constitutional history has not been diminished. Originally a guarantee of the barons' feudal rights, it came to be seen as a limit on the monarch's authority over all subjects.

The National Archives, Public Record Office and Historical Manuscripts Commission

pope's ability to challenge the rising power of monarchs like Philip, who had used the dispute to persuade his nobles to grant him a new tax.

The English monarchy wielded more centralized power as a result of consolidation that took place after the Norman conquest of 1066. Between 1200 and 1400, the Anglo-Norman kings incorporated Wales and reasserted control over most of Ireland. Nevertheless, under King John (r. 1199–1216), royal power suffered a severe setback. Forced to acknowledge the pope as his overlord in 1213, he lost his bid to reassert claims to Aquitaine in southern France the following year and then yielded to his nobles by signing the Magna Carta in 1215. This "Great Charter" affirmed that monarchs were subject to established law, confirmed the independence of the church and the city of London, and guaranteed the nobles' hereditary rights.

The Hundred Years' War   The conflict between the king of France and his vassals known as the **Hundred Years' War** (1337–1453) grew out of a marriage alliance. Marriage between Princess Isabella of France and King Edward II of England (r. 1307–1327) should have ensured the king's loyalty, as a vassal who had inherited French lands from his Norman ancestors. However, when the French royal line produced no other sons, Isabella's son, King Edward III of England (r. 1327–1377), laid claim to the French throne in 1337.

Early in the war, hired Italian crossbowmen reinforced the French cavalry, but the English longbow proved superior. Adopted from the Welsh, the 6-foot (1.8-meter) longbow could shoot farther and more rapidly than the crossbow. Its arrows could not pierce armor, but concentrated volleys found gaps in the knights' defenses or struck their less-protected horses. Heavier and more encompassing armor provided a defense but limited a knight's movements. Once pulled off his steed by a foot soldier armed with a pike (hooked pole), he could not get up.

Later in the Hundred Years' War, firearms gained prominence. The first cannon scared the horses with smoke and noise but did little damage. As they grew larger, however, they proved effective in battering the walls of castles and towns. The first artillery use against the French, at the Battle of Agincourt (1415), gave the English an important victory.

Faced with a young French peasant woman called Joan of Arc, subsequent English gains stalled. Acting, she believed, on God's instructions, she put on armor and rallied the French troops to defeat the English in 1429. Shortly afterward, she fell into English hands, and in 1431 she was tried by English churchmen and burned at the stake as a witch.

In the final battles, French cannon demolished the walls of once-secure castles held by the English and their allies. Armies now depended less on knights and more on bowmen, pikemen, musketeers, and artillerymen.

New Monarchies in France and England   The war proved a watershed in the rise of **new monarchies** in France and England, centralized states with fixed "national" boundaries and stronger representative institutions. English monarchs after 1453 consolidated control over territory within the British Isles, though the Scots defended their independence. The French monarchs also turned to consolidating control over powerful noble families in Burgundy and Brittany.

The new monarchies needed a way to finance their full-time armies. Some nobles agreed to money payments in place of military service and to additional taxes in time of war. For example, in 1439 and 1445, Charles VII of France (r. 1422–1461) successfully levied a new tax on his vassals' land. This not only paid the costs of the war with England but also provided the monarchy a financial base for the next 350 years.

Merchants' taxes also provided revenues. Taxes on the English wool trade, begun by King Edward III, paid most of the costs of the Hundred Years' War.

Some rulers taxed Jewish merchants or extorted large contributions from wealthy towns. Individual merchants sometimes curried royal favor with loans. The fifteenth-century French merchant Jacques Coeur (cur) gained many social and financial benefits for himself and his family by lending money to French courtiers, but his debtors accused him of murder and had his fortune confiscated.

In the west, the church provided a third source of revenue through voluntary contributions to support a war. English and French monarchs won the right to appoint important church officials in their realms in the fifteenth century. In the east, religion became increasingly a political issue as Catholic Lithuania fought a series of wars with Orthodox Russia with little regard for which faith the common people adhered to.

The shift in power to the monarchs and away from the nobility and the church did not deprive nobles of their social position and roles as government officials and military officers. Moreover, the kings of England and France in 1500 had to deal with representative institutions that had not existed in 1200. The English Parliament proved a permanent check on royal power: the House of Lords contained the great nobles and church officials; and the House of Commons represented the towns and the leading citizens of the counties. In France, the Estates General, a similar but less effective representative body, represented the church, the nobles, and the towns.

| **Iberian Unification** | Spain and Portugal's **reconquest of Iberia** from Muslim rule expanded the boundaries of Latin Christianity. The knights who pushed the borders of their kingdoms southward fur- |

thered both Christianity and their own interests. The spoils of victory included irrigated farmland, rich cities, and ports on the Mediterranean Sea and Atlantic Ocean. Serving God, growing rich, and living off the labor of others became a way of life for the Iberian nobility.

The reconquest took several centuries. In 1085 Toledo fell and became a Christian outpost. In 1147 English Crusaders bound for the Holy Land helped take Lisbon, which then displaced the older city of Oporto (meaning "the port"), from which Portugal took its name, as both capital and the kingdom's leading city. After a Christian victory in 1212 broke the back of Muslim power, the reconquest accelerated. Within decades, Portuguese and Castilian forces captured the prosperous cities of Cordova (1236) and Seville (1248) and drove the Muslims from the southwestern region known as Algarve (ahl-GAHRV) ("the west" in Arabic). Only the small kingdom of Granada hugging the Mediterranean coast remained in Muslim hands.

By incorporating Algarve in 1249, Portugal attained its modern territorial limits. After a pause to colonize, forcibly Christianize, and consolidate this land, Portugal took the crusade to North Africa. In 1415, Portuguese knights seized the port of Ceuta (say-OO-tuh) in Morocco, where they learned more about the Saharan caravan trade in gold and slaves. During the next few decades, Portuguese mariners sailed down the Atlantic coast of Africa seeking rumored African Christian allies and access to this trade (see Chapter 16).

Elsewhere in Iberia, the reconquest continued. Princess Isabella of Castile married Prince Ferdinand of Aragon in 1469. A decade later, when they inherited their respective thrones, the two kingdoms united to become Spain. Their conquest of Granada in 1492 secured the final piece of Muslim territory for the new kingdom.

Ferdinand and Isabella sponsored the first voyage of Christopher Columbus in 1492 (see Chapter 16). In a third momentous event of that year, the monarchs expelled the Jews from their kingdoms. Attempts to convert or expel the remaining Muslims led to a revolt at the end of 1499 that lasted until 1501, and in 1502 the Spanish rulers expelled the last Muslims. Portugal expelled the Jews in 1496, including 100,000 refugees from Spain. For some time afterward the Spanish Inquisition, a tribunal established by the two monarchs, exerted itself in identifying and punishing Jews, called Marranos, and Muslims, called Moriscos, who had nominally converted to Christianity but secretly retained their old, forbidden faiths.

The Ottoman Frontier   As Islam receded in the west, it advanced in the east as the Ottoman Empire (see Chapter 13) inflicted defeat after defeat on the Christian Balkan kingdoms. The Ottoman military was balanced between cavalry archers, primarily Turks, and slave infantrymen armed with hand-held firearms.

Slave soldiery had a long history in Islamic lands (see Chapter 10), but the conquest of the Balkans in the late fourteenth century gave the Ottomans access to a new military resource: Christian prisoners of war enslaved and converted to Islam. These "new troops," called *yeni cheri* in Turkish and *janissaries* (JAN-i-say-ree) in English, gave the Ottomans unusual military flexibility. Not coming from a nomadic background like the Turks, they readily accepted the idea of fighting on foot and learning to use guns, which at that time were still too heavy and awkward for a horseman to load and fire. The janissaries lived in barracks and trained all year round.

The process of selection for janissary training changed early in the fifteenth century. The new system, called the *devshirme*, imposed a regular levy of male children on Christian villages in the Balkans. Selected children were placed with Turkish families to learn their language and then sent to Istanbul for instruction in Islam, military training, and, for the most talented, opportunities to become senior military commanders and heads of government departments. The Christian European contest between nobles, monarchs, and church authorities scarcely existed in the Ottoman realm.

CONCLUSION

Ecologically, the peoples of Latin Europe harnessed the power of wind and water and mined and refined their mineral wealth at the cost of localized pollution and deforestation. However, inability to improve food production and distribution in response to population growth created a demographic crisis that climaxed with the Black Death that devastated Europe in the mid-fourteenth century.

Politically, basic features of the modern European state began to emerge. Frequent wars caused kingdoms of moderate size to develop exceptional military strength. The ruling class, seeing economic strength as the twin of political power, promoted the activities of commercial cities and taxed their profits.

Culturally, autonomous universities and printing supported the advance of knowledge, while art and architecture reached unsurpassed peaks in the Renaissance. Late medieval society also displayed a fundamental fascination with tools and techniques, many of them acquired from the Muslim world or farther east. European success, however, depended just as much on strong motives for expansion. From the eleventh century onward, population pressure, religious zeal, economic enterprise, and intellectual curiosity drove an expansion of territory and resources that took the Crusaders to the Holy Land, merchants to the eastern Mediterranean and Black Seas, German settlers across the Elbe River, and Iberian Christians into the Muslim south. The early voyages into the Atlantic, discussed in Chapter 16, extended these activities.

IMPORTANT EVENTS 1200–1500

1200s	Use of crossbows and longbows becomes widespread; windmills in increased use
1204	Fourth Crusade launched
1210s	Religious orders founded: Teutonic Knights, Franciscans, Dominicans
1215	Magna Carta issued
1225–1274	Thomas Aquinas, monk and philosopher
1300	First mechanical clocks in the West
1300–1500	Rise of universities
1315–1317	Great Famine
1337	Start of Hundred Years War
ca. 1340–1400	Geoffrey Chaucer, poet
1347–1351	Black Death
1381	Wat Tyler's Rebellion
1400s	Large cannon in use in warfare; hand-held firearms become prominent
1415	Portuguese take Ceuta
1431	Joan of Arc burned as witch
ca. 1450	First printing with movable type in the West
1452–1519	Leonardo da Vinci, artist
1453	End of Hundred Years War; Turks take Constantinople
1454	Gutenberg Bible printed
1469	Marriage of Ferdinand of Aragon and Isabella of Castile
1472–1564	Michelangelo, artist
1492	Expulsion of Jews from Spain
1492	Fall of Muslim state of Granada

15

SOUTHERN EMPIRES, SOUTHERN SEAS, 1200–1500

Sultan Abu Bakr (a-BOO BAK-uhr) customarily offered hospitality to distinguished visitors to his city of Mogadishu, an Indian Ocean port on the northeast coast of Africa. In 1331, he provided food and lodging for Muhammad ibn Abdullah **Ibn Battuta** (IB-uhn ba-TOO-tuh) (1304–1369), a young Muslim scholar from Morocco who had set out to explore the Islamic world. With a pilgrimage to Mecca and travel throughout the Middle East behind him, Ibn Battuta was touring the trading cities of the Red Sea and East Africa. Subsequent travels took him to Central Asia and India, China and Southeast Asia, Muslim Spain, and sub-Saharan West Africa. Recounting some 75,000 miles (120,000 kilometers) of travel over twenty-nine years, Ibn Battuta's journal provides invaluable information on these lands.

Hospitality being considered a noble virtue among Muslims, regardless of physical and cultural differences, the reception at Mogadishu mirrored that at other cities. Ibn Battuta noted that Sultan Abu Bakr had skin darker than his own and spoke a different native language (Somali), but as brothers in faith, they prayed together at Friday services, where the sultan greeted his foreign guest in Arabic, the common language of the Islamic world: "You are heartily welcome, and you have honored our land and given us pleasure." When Sultan Abu Bakr and his jurists heard and decided cases after the mosque service, they used the religious law familiar in all Muslim lands.

Islam aside, the most basic links among the diverse peoples of Africa and southern Asia derived from the tropical environment itself. A network of overland and maritime routes joined their lands, providing avenues for the spread of beliefs and technologies, as well as goods. Ibn Battuta sailed with merchants down the coast of East Africa and joined trading caravans across the Sahara from Morocco to West Africa. His path to India followed overland trade routes, and a merchant ship carried him on to China.

The tropics of the Western Hemisphere lay beyond even Ibn Battuta's prodigious itinerary. Nevertheless, their environmental features resembled those of tropical Africa and Asia and they witnessed the rise of the impressive empires of the Aztecs and Inkas.

TROPICAL AFRICA AND ASIA

The tropical regions of Africa and Asia shared environmental similarities, but they differed markedly in the extent of their interactions with other parts of the world (see Chapter 9). The western regions of Africa were semi-isolated by the Atlantic Ocean and Sahara Desert, while Africa's east coast was in maritime contact with the lands bordering the Indian Ocean. India had long been affected by overland routes through Afghanistan to the Middle East and Central Asia, and it in turn influenced cultural developments in both mainland and island Southeast Asia.

The Tropical Environment in Africa and Asia   Because of the angle of the earth's axis, the sun's rays warm the **tropics** year-round. The equator marks the center of the tropical zone, and the Tropic of Cancer and Tropic of Capricorn its outer limits. Africa lies almost entirely within the tropics, as do southern Arabia, most of India, and both mainland and island Southeast Asia. In the Western Hemisphere the regions that produced the earliest civilizations, Mesoamerica and the Andes and Pacific coast of South America, also lay in the tropics.

Lacking the hot and cold seasons of temperate lands, the rainy and dry seasons of the Afro-Asian tropics derive from atmospheric patterns across the surrounding oceans. Winds flow away from areas of high atmospheric pressure toward areas of low pressure. The earth's rotation causes these winds to move in a clockwise direction (anticyclone) north of the equator and a counterclockwise direction south of the equator. Thus a permanent high-pressure air mass over the South Atlantic delivers heavy rainfall to the western coast of Africa during much of the year. However, in December and January, large high-pressure zones over northern Africa and Arabia produce a southward movement of dry air that limits the inland penetration of the moist ocean winds.

In the lands around the Indian Ocean, the rainy and dry seasons reflect the influence of alternating winds known as **monsoons**. A gigantic high-pressure zone over the Himalaya (him-AH-la-yuh) Mountains that peaks from December to March produces southern Asia's dry season by forcing strong southward and westward air movements (the northeast monsoon) in the western Indian Ocean. Between April and August, a low-pressure zone over India reverses the process by drawing moist oceanic air from the south and west (the southwest monsoon). This brings southern Asia the heavy rains of its wet season, usually called the monsoon season.

Areas with the heaviest rainfall—the broad belt along the equator in coastal West Africa and West-Central Africa, parts of coastal India, and Southeast Asia—have dense rain forests. Lighter rains produce other forest patterns. The English word *jungle* comes from an Indian word for the tangled undergrowth in the forests that once covered most of tropical India.

Some other parts of the tropics rarely see rain at all. The world's largest desert, the Sahara, stretches across northern Africa and continues eastward across Arabia, southern Iran and Pakistan, and northwest India. Another desert occupies southwestern Africa. Tropical India and Africa fall mostly between the deserts and rain forests and experience moderate rainy seasons. These lands range from fairly wet woodlands to the much drier grasslands characteristic of much of East Africa.

Altitude produces other climatic variations. Thin atmospheres at high altitudes hold less heat than atmospheres at lower elevations. Snow covers some of the volcanic peaks of eastern Africa all or part of the year. The snowcapped Himalayas that form India's northern frontier rise so high that they block cold air from moving south and thus give northern India a more tropical climate than its latitude would suggest. The plateaus of inland Africa and the Deccan (DEK-uhn) Plateau of central India also enjoy cooler temperatures than the coastal plains.

Human Ecosystems   A careful observer touring the tropics in 1200 would have noticed many differences in societies deriving from their particular ecosystems—that is, from how human groups used the plants, animals, and other resources of their physical environments. These systems varied greatly in the density of population they could support.

Some peoples continued to rely primarily on hunting, fishing, and gathering and lived in small, mobile groups. For Pygmy (PIG-mee) hunters in the dense forests of Central Africa, small size permitted pursuit of prey through dense undergrowth. Hunting also prevailed among some inland groups in Borneo, New Guinea, and the Philippines. A Portuguese expedition led by Vasco da Gama visited the arid coast of southwestern Africa in 1497 and saw there a healthy group of people feeding themselves on "the flesh of seals, whales, and gazelles, and the roots of wild plants." Fishing, which was common along all the major lakes and rivers as well as in the oceans, could be combined with farming or with ocean trade, particularly in Southeast Asia.

Herding provided sustenance in areas too arid for agriculture. Pastoralists consumed milk and sometimes blood from their herds but did not eat a lot of meat since their animals were of greater value to them alive than dead. The deserts of northern Africa and Arabia had small populations that ranged widely with their camels, goats, and donkeys. Some, like the Tuareg (TWAH-reg) of the western Sahara, proved invaluable as caravan guides because of their intimate knowledge of the desert. Along the Sahara's southern edge the cattle-herding Fulani (foo-LAH-nee) gradually extended their range and by 1500 had spread throughout the western and central Sudan. Other cattle herders lived on either side of the Nile in Sudan and in Somalia.

Pastoral groups in India were less numerous and located mostly in the northwestern deserts. South and Southeast Asia, being generally wetter than tropical Africa outside the rain forest zone, did not favor pastoralism but did allow for intensive cultivation. High yields supported dense populations. In 1200, over 100 million people lived in South and Southeast Asia, more than four-fifths of them on the fertile Indian mainland. Though a little less than the population of China, this was triple the number of people living in all of Africa and nearly double the number in Europe.

Rice cultivation dominated in the fertile Ganges Plain of northeast India, mainland Southeast Asia, and southern China. In drier areas, farmers grew grains—wheat, sorghum, and millet—and legumes such as peas and beans whose ripening cycles matched the pattern of the rainy and dry seasons. Tree crops, such as kola nuts in West Africa, coconuts in Southeast Asia, and bananas everywhere, made major contributions to the diet, as did the root crops characteristic of rain forest clearings.

The spread of farming, including the movement to Africa of Indo-Malayan bananas and root crops like yams and cocoyams, also known as taro, did not necessarily change the natural environment. In most of sub-Saharan Africa and much of Southeast Asia, extensive rather than intensive cultivation prevailed. Instead of enriching fields with manure and vegetable compost so they could be cultivated year after year, farmers abandoned fields when the natural fertility of the soil fell and cleared new fields. Ashes from the brush, grasses, and tree limbs they cut down and burned boosted the new fields' fertility. Shifting to new land every few years made efficient use of labor in areas with comparatively poor soils and abundant space.

Water Systems and Irrigation   Though the inland delta of the Niger River in West Africa received naturally fertilizing annual floods and could grow rice for sale to the trading cities along the Niger bend, many tropical farmers in India and Southeast Asia had to bring water to their crops. Conserving some of the monsoon rainfall for use during the dry season helped in Vietnam, Java, Malaya, and Burma (now Myanmar), which had terraced hillsides with special water-control systems for growing rice. Villagers in southeast India built stone and earthen dams across rivers to store water for gradual release through elaborate irrigation canals. Similar dam and canal systems supplied water farther north.

As had been true since the first river-valley civilizations (see Chapter 2), governments built and controlled the largest irrigation systems. The **Delhi** (DEL-ee) **Sultanate** (1206–1526) in northern India developed extensive new water-control systems. One large reservoir that supplied Delhi in the first quarter of the thirteenth century had fields of sugar cane, cucumbers, and melons planted along its rim as the water level fell during the dry season. Irrigation canals built in the Ganges Plain in the fourteenth century remained unsurpassed for five hundred years. Such systems made it possible to grow crops throughout the year.

Since the tenth century, the island of Ceylon (ancient Serandip; modern Sri Lanka [sree LAHNG-kuh]) off India's southern tip possessed the world's greatest concentration of irrigation reservoirs and canals. These facilities supported the population of a large Sinhalese-speaking (sin-huh-LEEZ) kingdom in arid northern

Ceylon. In Southeast Asia, another impressive system of reservoirs and canals served Cambodia's capital city, Angkor (ANG-kor).

Between 1250 and 1400, however, the irrigation complex in Ceylon fell into ruin when invaders from south India disrupted the Sinhalese government. As a result, malaria spread by mosquitoes breeding in the irrigation canals ravaged the population. In the fifteenth century, the great Cambodian system fell into ruin when the government that maintained it collapsed. Neither system was ever rebuilt.

The vulnerability of complex irrigation systems built by powerful governments contrasts with village-based irrigation systems. Invasion and natural calamity might damage the latter, but they usually bounced back because they depended on local initiative and simpler technologies.

Mineral Resources   Throughout the tropics, ironworking provided the hoes, axes, and knives farmers used to clear and cultivate their fields. Between 1200 and 1500, the rain forests of coastal West Africa and Southeast Asia opened up for farming. Iron also supplied spear and arrow points, needles, and nails. Indian armorers became known for forging strong and beautiful swords. In Africa, many people attributed magical powers to iron smelters and blacksmiths.

King and Queen of Ife *This copper-alloy work shows the royal couple of the Yoruba kingdom of Ife, the oldest and most sacred of the Yoruba kingdoms of southwestern Nigeria. The casting dates to the period between 1100 and 1500, except for the reconstruction of the male's face, the original of which shattered in 1957 when the road builder who found it accidentally struck it with his pick.*

Andre Held Collection/akg-image

The Copperbelt of southeastern Africa came into prominence during the fourteenth and fifteenth centuries. Smelters cast the metal into large X-shaped ingots (metal castings) that local coppersmiths worked into wire and decorative objects.

A mining town in the western Sudan visited by Ibn Battuta produced two sizes of copper bars that served as currency in place of coins. Coppersmiths in the West African city of Ife (now in southern Nigeria) cast highly realistic copper and brass (an alloy of copper and zinc) statues and heads that now rank as masterpieces of world art. They utilized the "lost-wax" method, in which molten metal melts a thin layer of wax sandwiched between clay forms, replacing the "lost" wax with hard metal.

African gold moved in quantity across the Sahara and into the Indian Ocean and Red Sea trades. Some came from streambeds along the upper Niger River and farther south in modern Ghana (GAH-nuh). Far to the south, beyond the Zambezi (zam-BEE-zee) River (in modern Zimbabwe [zim-BAHB-way]), archaeologists have discovered thousands of mineshafts, dating from 1200, that were sunk up to 100 feet (30 meters) into the ground to get at gold ores. Although panning for gold remained important in the streams descending from the mountains of northern India, the gold and silver mines in India seem to have been exhausted by this period. Thus, Indians imported considerable quantities of gold for jewelry and temple decoration from Iran and the Ottoman Empire as well as from Southeast Asia and Africa.

New Islamic Empires

Paradoxically, given the Mongol destruction of the Baghdad caliphate in 1258 (see Chapter 13), the territorial expansion of Islam between 1200 and 1500 exceeded the Arab conquests of the seventh century. The Ottoman conquests in Europe extended Muslim domains in the Mediterranean heartland, but most of the expansion took place in the Muslim south in Africa, South Asia, and Southeast Asia.

The empires of Mali in West Africa and Delhi in northern India formed the largest and richest tropical states during Islam's second period of expansion. Both utilized administrative and military systems introduced from the Islamic heartland. Yet **Mali**, an indigenous African dynasty, grew out of the peaceful influence of Muslim merchants and scholars, while the Delhi Sultanate was founded and ruled by invading Turkish and Afghan Muslims.

Mali in the Western Sudan   Muslim rule in North Africa beginning in the seventh century (see Chapter 10) greatly stimulated trade across the Sahara.

In the centuries that followed, the faith of Muhammad spread slowly to the lands south of the desert, which the Arabs called the *bilad al-sudan* (bih-LAD uhs-soo-DAN), "land of the blacks."

Muslim Berbers invading out of the desert in 1076 caused the collapse of Ghana, the empire that preceded Mali in the western Sudan (see Chapter 10). Takrur (TAHK-roor), a kingdom on the Atlantic coast whose ruler had become the first sub-Saharan ruler to adopt Islam in the 1030s, allied with the invaders

MAP 15.1 Africa, 1200–1500

Many African states had beneficial links to the trade that crossed the Sahara and the Indian Ocean. Before 1500, sub-Saharan Africa's external ties were primarily with the Islamic world.

but remained a small state when the Berbers' interests in Morocco and Spain drew their attention away from the sub-Saharan region. Farther east, a truce that had endured since 652 between Christian Nubia along the Nile and Muslim Egypt fell apart in the thirteenth century as the Mamluks of Cairo (see Chapter 10) made repeated attacks. The small Christian kingdoms weakened and fell over the next two centuries, but Christian Ethiopia successfully withstood Muslim advances.

In general, however, Islam's spread south of the Sahara followed a pattern of gradual and peaceful conversion. The expansion of commercial contacts in the western Sudan and on the East African coast greatly promoted the conversion process.

Shortly after 1200, Takrur expanded under King Sumanguru (soo-muhn-GOO-roo), only to suffer a major defeat some thirty years later at the hands of Sundiata (soon-JAH-tuh), the upstart leader of the Malinke (muh-LING-kay) people. Though both leaders professed Islam, Malinke legends recall their battles as clashes between powerful magicians, suggesting how much old and new beliefs mingled. Sumanguru could reportedly appear and disappear at will, assume dozens of shapes, and catch arrows in midflight. Sundiata defeated Sumanguru's much larger forces through superior military maneuvers and by wounding his adversary with a special arrow that robbed him of his magical powers. Other victories followed and the Mali Empire was born.

Map of the Western Sudan (1375) *A Jewish geographer on the Mediterranean island of Majorca drew this lavish map in 1375, incorporating all that was known in Europe about the rest of the world. This portion of the Catalan Atlas shows a North African trader approaching the king of Mali, who holds a gold nugget in one hand and a golden scepter in the other. A caption identifies the black ruler as Mansa Musa, "the richest and noblest king in all the land."*

Sundiata's empire depended on a well-developed agricultural base and control of the regional and trans-Saharan trade routes, as had Ghana before it. Mali, however, controlled a greater area than Ghana, including not only the core trading area of the upper Niger but also the gold fields of the Niger headwaters to the southwest. Moreover, its rulers fostered the spread of Islam among the empire's political and trading elites. Control of the gold and copper trades and contacts with North African Muslim traders gave Mali unprecedented prosperity.

Under the ruler **Mansa Kankan Musa** (MAHN-suh KAHN-kahn MOO-suh) (r. 1312–1337), the empire's reputation for wealth spread far and wide. Mansa Musa's pilgrimage to Mecca in 1324–1325 fulfilled his personal duty as a Muslim and at the same time put on display his exceptional wealth. He traveled with a large entourage. Besides his senior wife and five hundred of her ladies in waiting and their slaves, one account says there were also sixty thousand porters and a vast caravan of camels carrying supplies and provisions. For purchases and gifts, he brought along eighty packages of gold, each weighing 122 ounces (3.8 kilograms). In addition, five hundred slaves each carried a golden staff. Mansa Musa dispersed so many gifts when he passed through Cairo that the value of gold was depressed for years. Obviously the days were past when caravan merchants could trade gold for an equal weight of salt because the value of the precious metal on north side of the Sahara was not known on the south side.

Two centuries after its founding, Mali began to disintegrate. Mansa Suleiman's successors could not prevent rebellions breaking out among the diverse peoples subjected to Malinke rule. Other groups attacked from without. The desert Tuareg retook their city of Timbuktu (tim-buk-TOO) in 1433. By 1500, the rulers of Mali had dominion over little more than the Malinke heartland.

The cities of the upper Niger survived Mali's collapse, but some trade and intellectual life moved east to the central Sudan. Shortly after 1450, the rulers of several Hausa city-states officially adopted Islam. These states took on importance as manufacturing and trading centers, becoming famous for cotton textiles and leather-working. The central Sudanic state of Kanem-Bornu (KAH-nuhm–BOR-noo) also expanded in the late fifteenth century from the ancient kingdom of Kanem, whose rulers had accepted Islam in about 1085. At its peak around 1250, Kanem had absorbed the state of Bornu south and west of Lake Chad and gained control of routes crossing the central Sahara. As Kanem-Bornu's armies conquered new territories, they also spread the rule of Islam.

The Delhi Sultanate in India

Having long ago lost the defensive unity of the Gupta Empire (see Chapter 7), the divided states of northwest India fell prey to raids by the powerful sultan Mahmud (mah-MOOD) based in Ghazna, Afghanistan, beginning in the early eleventh century. Repeated campaigns by successive rulers led to a series of Afghan and Turkic dynasties ruling from the city of Delhi from 1206 to 1526. One partisan Muslim chronicler wrote: "The city [Delhi] and its vicinity was freed from idols and idol-worship, and in the sanctuaries of the images of the [Hindu] Gods, mosques were raised by the worshippers of one God."[1] Turkish adventurers from Central Asia flocked to join the invading armies, overwhelming the small Indian states, which were often at war with one another.

Between 1206 and 1236, the Muslim invaders extended their rule over the Hindu princes and chiefs in much of northern India. Sultan Iltutmish (il-TOOT-mish) (r. 1211–1236) consolidated the conquest in a series of military expeditions that made his realm the largest in India. The caliph in Baghdad, soon to be killed by the Mongols, officially recognized the Delhi Sultanate as a Muslim realm. Incorporating north India into the Islamic world marked the beginning of the invaders' transformation from brutal conquerors to somewhat more benign rulers. Though doctrinally opposed to idol worship, they granted the Hindus freedom from persecution in return for paying the *jizya*, a tax required of Jews and Christians.

Iltutmish astonished his ministers by passing over his weak and pleasure-seeking sons and designating as his heir his beloved and talented daughter Raziya (RAH-zee-uh). He reportedly said, "My sons are devoted to the pleasures of youth: no one of them is qualified to be king.... There is no one more competent to guide the State than my daughter." Her brother, who was given to riding his elephant through the bazaar and showering the crowds with coins, ruled ineptly for seven months before the ministers relented and put Raziya on the throne.

A chronicler who knew her explained why this able ruler lasted less than four years (r. 1236–1240):

> *Sultan Raziya was a great monarch. She was wise, just, and generous, a benefactor to her kingdom, a dispenser of justice, the protector of her subjects, and the leader of her armies. She was endowed with all the qualities befitting a king, but she was not born of the right sex, and so in the estimation of men all these virtues were worthless. May God have mercy upon her!*[2]

Doing her best to prove herself a proper king, Raziya dressed like a man and led her troops atop an elephant. In the end, however, the Turkish chiefs imprisoned her; she escaped, but was killed by a robber soon afterward.

After a half century of stagnation and rebellion, the ruthless but efficient policies of Sultan Ala-ud-din Khalji (uh-LAH-uh–DEEN KAL-jee) (r. 1296–1316) increased control over the empire's outlying provinces. Successful frontier raids and high taxes filled his treasury, wage and price controls in Delhi kept down the cost of maintaining a large army, and a network of spies stifled intrigue. When a Mongol threat from Central Asia eased, Ala-ud-din's forces marched southward, capturing the rich trading state of **Gujarat** (goo-juh-RAHT) in 1298 and then briefly seizing the southern tip of the Indian peninsula.

Sultan Muhammad ibn Tughluq (TOOG-look) (r. 1325–1351) enlarged the sultanate to its greatest extent at the expense of the independent Indian states but balanced his aggressive policy with religious toleration. He even attended Hindu religious festivals. However, his successor, Firuz Shah (fuh-ROOZ shah) (r. 1351–1388),

---

[1] Hasan Nizami, Taju-l Ma-asir, in Henry M. Elliot, *The History of India as Told by Its Own Historians*, ed. John Dowson (London: Trübner and Co., 1869–1871), 2:219.

[2] Minhaju-s Siraj, Tabakat-i Nasiri, in ibid., 2:332–333.

alienated powerful Hindus by taxing the Brahmin elite. Muslim chroniclers praised him for constructing forty mosques, thirty colleges, and a hundred hospitals.

A small minority in a giant land, the Delhi sultans relied on force to keep their subjects submissive, on military reprisals to put down rebellion, and on pillage and high taxes to sustain the ruling elite in luxury and power. The sultanate never escaped the disadvantage of foreign origins and alien religious identity, but some sultans did incorporate a few Hindus into their administrations, and some members of the Muslim elite married women from prominent Hindu families, though the brides had to convert to Islam.

Personal and religious rivalries within the Muslim elite, along with Hindu discontent, threatened the Delhi Sultanate whenever it showed weakness and finally hastened its end. In the mid-fourteenth century, Muslim nobles challenged the sultan's dominion and established the independent Bahmani (bah-MAHN-ee) kingdom (1347–1482) on the Deccan Plateau. Defending against the southward push of Bahmani armies, the Hindu states of south India united to form the Vijayanagar (vee-JAY-yah-nah-GAR) Empire (1336–1565), which at its height controlled rich trading ports on both coasts of south India and held Ceylon as a tributary state.

Hindu Vijayanagar and the Muslim Bahmani state turned a blind eye to religious differences when doing so favored their interests. Bahmani rulers sought to balance Muslim domination by incorporating Hindu leaders into the government, marrying Hindu wives, and appointing Brahmins to high offices. Vijayanagar rulers hired Muslim horsemen and archers to strengthen their military forces and formed an alliance with the Muslim-ruled state of Gujarat.

By 1351, when all of south India had cast off Delhi's rule, much of north India rose in rebellion. In the east, Bengal broke away from the sultanate in 1338. In the west, Gujarat regained its independence by 1390. The weakening of Delhi's central authority tempted fresh Mongol interest in the area. In 1398, the Turko-Mongol leader Timur (see Chapter 13) captured the city of Delhi. When his armies withdrew the next year with vast quantities of loot and tens of thousands of captives, the largest city in southern Asia lay empty and in ruins. The Delhi Sultanate never recovered.

For all its shortcomings, the Delhi Sultanate triggered the development of centralized political authority in India. Prime ministers and provincial governors serving under the sultans established a bureaucracy, improved food production, promoted trade, and put in circulation a common coinage. Despite the many conflicts that Muslim conquest and rule provoked, Islam gradually acquired a permanent place in South Asia.

INDIAN OCEAN TRADE

When the collapse of the Mongol Empire in the fourteenth century disrupted overland routes across Central Asia, the Indian Ocean assumed greater strategic importance in tying together the peoples of Eurasia and Africa. Between 1200 and 1500,

The Indian Ocean Dhow

The sailing vessels that crossed the Indian Ocean shared the diversity of that trading area. The name by which we know them, *dhow*, comes from the Swahili language of the East African coast. The planks of teak from which their hulls were constructed were hewn from the tropical forests of south India and Southeast Asia. Their pilots, who navigated by stars at night, employed techniques that Arabs had used to find their way across the desert. Some pilots used a magnetic compass, which originated in China.

Dhows came in various sizes and designs, but all had two distinctive features in common. The first was hull construction. The hulls of dhows consisted of planks that were sewn together, not nailed. Cord made of fiber from the husk of coconuts or other materials was passed through rows of holes drilled in the planks. Because cord is weaker than nails, outsiders considered this shipbuild-ing technique strange. Marco Polo fanci-fully suggested that it indicated sailors' fear that large ocean magnets would pull any nails out of their ships. Better expla-nations observe that pliant sewn hulls were cheaper to build than rigid nailed hulls and were less likely to be damaged if the ships ran aground on coral reefs.

The second distinctive feature of dhows was their sails made of palm leaves or cotton. Sails that were either triangular (lateen) or had a very short leading edge were suspended from tall masts and could be turned to catch the wind.

Sewn hulls and lateen sails had appeared centuries earlier, but two innova-tions appeared between 1200 and 1500. First, a rudder positioned at the stern (rear end) of the ship replaced the large side oar that formerly had controlled steer-ing. Second, shipbuilders increased the size of dhows to accommodate bulkier cargoes.

SSPL/Getty Images

Dhow *This modern model shows the vessel's main features.*

the volume of trade in the Indian Ocean increased. The Indian Ocean routes also facilitated the spread of Islam.

Monsoon Mariners   The prosperity of Islamic and Mongol empires in Asia, cities in Europe, and new kingdoms in Africa and Southeast Asia stimulated and contributed to the vitality of the Indian Ocean network. The demand for luxuries—precious metals and jewels, rare spices, fine textiles, and other manufactures—rose. Larger ships made shipments of bulk cargoes of ordinary cotton textiles, pepper, food grains (rice, wheat, barley), timber, horses, and other goods profitable. Some goods were transported from one end of this trading network to the other, but few ships or crews made a complete circuit. Instead, the Indian Ocean trade divided into two legs: from the Middle East across the Arabian Sea to India and from India across the Bay of Bengal to Southeast Asia.

Shipyards in ports on the Malabar Coast (southwestern India) and in the Persian Gulf built large numbers of **dhows** (dow), the characteristic cargo and passenger ships of the Arabian Sea. They grew from an average capacity of 100 tons in 1200 to 400 tons in 1500. On a typical expedition, a dhow might sail west from India to Arabia and Africa on the northeast monsoon winds (December to March) and return on the southwest monsoons (April to August). Small dhows kept the coast in sight. Relying on the stars to guide them, skilled pilots steered large vessels by the quicker route straight across the water. A large dhow could sail from the Red Sea to mainland Southeast Asia in two to four months, but few did so. Eastbound cargoes and passengers from dhows reaching India were likely to be transferred to junks, which dominated the eastern half of the Indian Ocean and the South China Sea (see Environment and Technology: The Indian Ocean Dhow).

Junks, the largest, most technologically advanced, and most seaworthy vessels of the time, appeared first in China and spread as a part of Chinese overseas culture. Enormous nails held together hulls of heavy spruce or fir planks, in contrast with dhows, whose planks were sewn together with palm fiber. Below the deck, watertight compartments minimized flooding in case of damage to the ship's hull. The largest junks reportedly had twelve sails made of bamboo strips woven into mats and carried a crew of a thousand men, including four hundred soldiers. A large junk might accommodate a hundred passenger cabins and a cargo of over 1,000 tons. Junks dominated China's foreign shipping to Southeast Asia and India, but the Chinese did not control all of the junks that plied these waters. During the fifteenth century, similar vessels came out of shipyards in Bengal and Southeast Asia to be sailed by local crews.

Decentralized and cooperative commercial interests, rather than political authorities, connected the several regions that participated in the Indian Ocean trade. The **Swahili** (swah-HEE-lee) **Coast** supplied ivory, wood, and gold from inland areas of Africa, while ports around the Arabian peninsula supplied horses, incense, and manufactured goods from the Mediterranean region. Merchants in the cities of coastal India received goods from east and west, sold some locally, passed others along, and added Indian goods to the trade. The Strait of Malacca (meh-LAK-eh), between the eastern end of the Indian Ocean and the South China Sea, provided a meeting point for trade from Southeast Asia, China, and the Indian Ocean. In each region, certain ports functioned as giant emporia, consolidating goods from smaller ports and inland areas for transport across the seas.

Africa: The Swahili Coast and Zimbabwe   Trade expanded steadily along the East African coast from about 1250, giving rise to between thirty and forty separate city-states by 1500. After 1200, masonry buildings as much as four stories high replaced mud and thatch dwellings, and archaeological findings include Chinese porcelain, imported glass beads, and other exotic goods. Coastal and island peoples shared a common culture and a language built on African grammar and vocabulary but enriched with many Arabic and Persian terms and written in Arabic script. In time, these people became known as "Swahili," from the Arabic word *sawahil* (suh-WAH-hil), meaning "shores."

What attracted the Arab and Iranian merchants whom oral traditions associate with the Swahili Coast's commercial expansion? By the late fifteenth century, the

Royal Enclosure, Great Zimbabwe *Inside these oval stone walls the rulers of the trading state of Great Zimbabwe lived. Forced to enter the enclosure through a narrow corridor between two high walls, visitors were meant to be awestruck.*

major port of Kilwa, described by Ibn Battuta as "one of the most beautiful and well-constructed towns in the world," was annually exporting a ton of gold mined by inland Africans much farther south. Much of it came from or passed through a powerful state on the plateau south of the Zambezi River. At its peak in about 1400, its capital city, now known as **Great Zimbabwe**, occupied 193 acres (78 hectares) and had some eighteen thousand inhabitants.

Between about 1250 and 1450, local African craftsmen built stone structures for Great Zimbabwe's rulers, priests, and wealthy citizens. The largest structure, an enclosure the size and shape of a large football stadium with walls of unmortared stone 17 feet (5 meters) thick and 32 feet (10 meters) high, served as the king's court. A large conical stone tower was among the many buildings inside the walls.

As in Mali, mixed farming and cattle herding provided the economic basis of the Great Zimbabwe state, but long-distance trade brought added wealth. Trade began regionally with copper ingots from the upper Zambezi Valley, salt, and local manufactures. Gold exports to the coast expanded in the fourteenth and fifteenth centuries and brought Zimbabwe to its peak. However, historians suspect that the city's residents depleted nearby forests for firewood while their cattle overgrazed surrounding grasslands. The resulting ecological crisis hastened the empire's decline in the fifteenth century.

Arabia: Aden and the Red Sea   The city of **Aden** (ADD-en) near the southwestern tip of the Arabian peninsula had a double advantage in the Indian Ocean trade. Monsoon winds brought enough rainfall to supply drinking water to a large population and grow grain for export, and its location made it a convenient stopover for trade with India, the Persian Gulf, East Africa, and Egypt. Aden's merchants dealt in cotton cloth and beads from India; spices from Southeast Asia; horses from Arabia and Ethiopia; pearls from the Red Sea; manufactured luxuries from Cairo; slaves, gold, and ivory from Ethiopia; and grain, opium, and dyes from Aden's own hinterland.

Common commercial interests generally promoted good relations among the different religions and cultures of this region. For example, in the mid-thirteenth century, a wealthy Jew from Aden named Yosef settled in Christian Ethiopia, where he acted as an adviser. South Arabia had been trading with neighboring parts of Africa since before the time of King Solomon of Israel. The dynasty that ruled Ethiopia after 1270 boasted (legendary) descent from Solomon and the Queen of Sheba from across the Red Sea. Ethiopia's Solomonic dynasty greatly increased trade through the Red Sea port of Zeila (ZAY-luh), including slaves, amber, and animal pelts, which went to Aden and on to other destinations.

Friction sometimes arose, however. In the late fifteenth century, Ethiopia's territorial expansion and efforts to increase control over the trade provoked conflicts with Muslims who ruled the coastal states of the Red Sea.

India: Gujarat and the Malabar Coast

The state of Gujarat in western India prospered from the expanding trade of the Arabian Sea and the rise of the Delhi Sultanate. Blessed with a rich agricultural hinterland and a long coastline, Gujarat attracted new trade after the Mongol destruction of Baghdad in 1258 disrupted the northern land routes. Despite the violence of its forced incorporation into the Delhi Sultanate in 1298, Gujarat prospered from increased commercial interaction with Delhi's ruling class. Independent again after 1390, the Muslim rulers of Gujarat extended their control over neighboring Hindu states and regained their preeminent position in the Indian Ocean trade.

Gujaratis exported cotton textiles and indigo to the Middle East and Europe in return for gold and silver. They also shipped cotton cloth, carnelian beads, and foodstuffs to the Swahili Coast in exchange for ebony, slaves, ivory, and gold. During the fifteenth century, Gujarat's trade zone expanded eastward to the Strait of Malacca. There Gujarati merchants helped spread the Islamic faith among East Indian traders, some of whom even imported specially carved gravestones from Gujarat.

Unlike Kilwa and Aden, Gujarat manufactured goods for trade. According to the thirteenth-century Venetian traveler Marco Polo, Gujarat's leatherworkers dressed enough skins in a year to fill several ships to Arabia and other places. They made sleeping mats for export to the Middle East "in red and blue leather, exquisitely inlaid with figures of birds and beasts, and skillfully embroidered with gold and silver wire," as well as leather cushions embroidered in gold.

Later observers compared the Gujarati city of Cambay (modern name Khambhat) with cities in Flanders and northern Italy (see Chapter 14) in the scale, craftsmanship, and diversity of its textile industries. Cotton, linen, and silk cloth, along with carpets and quilts, found a large market in Europe, Africa, the Middle East, and Southeast Asia. Cambay also produced polished gemstones, gold jewelry, carved ivory, stone beads, and both pearls and mother of pearl. At the height of its prosperity in the fifteenth century, its well-laid-out streets and open places boasted fine stone houses with tiled roofs. Although Muslim residents controlled most Gujarati overseas trade, its Hindu merchant caste profited so much from related commercial activities that their wealth and luxurious lives became the envy of other Indians.

More southerly cities on the well-watered western coast of India, called the Malabar Coast, imitated Gujarat's success. Calicut (KAL-ih-cut) (modern name Kozhikode) and other coastal cities prospered from locally woven cotton textiles and locally grown grains and spices. They also served as clearing-houses for the long-distance trade of the Indian Ocean. The Zamorin (ZAH-much-ruhn) (ruler) of Calicut presided over a loose federation of its Hindu rulers that united the coastal region, but steep mountains known as the Western Ghats cut the coast off from the inland areas on the Deccan Plateau. As in eastern Africa and Arabia, rulers generally tolerated religious and ethnic groups who contributed to commercial profits. Most trading activity lay in the hands of Muslims, many originally from

Iran and Arabia, who intermarried with local Indian Muslims. Jewish merchants also operated from Malabar's trading cities.

Southeast Asia   At the eastern end of the Indian Ocean, the Strait of Malacca between the Malay Peninsula and the island of Sumatra provided the principal passage into the South China Sea. As trade increased in the fourteenth and fifteenth centuries, this commercial choke point became the site of political rivalry.

The mainland kingdom of Siam controlled most of the upper Malay Peninsula, while the Java-based kingdom of Majapahit (mah-jah-PAH-heet) extended its dominion over the lower Malay Peninsula and much of Sumatra. Majapahit, however, could not suppress a nest of Chinese pirates based at the Sumatran city of Palembang (pah-lem-BONG) who preyed on ships sailing through the strait. In 1407, a fleet from China commanded by the admiral Zheng He (see Chapter 13) smashed the pirates' power and took their chief back home for trial.

Majapahit, weakened by internal struggles, could not take advantage of China's intervention, making the chief beneficiary the newer port of **Malacca** (or Melaka), which dominated the narrowest part of the strait. Under a prince from Palembang, Malacca had grown from an obscure fishing village into an important port through a series of astute alliances. Nominally subject to the king of Siam, Malacca also secured an alliance with China that was sealed by the visit of the imperial fleet in 1407. The conversion of an early ruler from Hinduism to Islam helped promote trade with Muslim merchants from Gujarat and elsewhere. Merchants also appreciated Malacca's security and low taxes.

Malacca served not just as a meeting point but also as an emporium for Southeast Asian products: rubies and musk from Burma, tin from Malaya, gold from Sumatra, cloves and nutmeg from the Moluccas (or Spice Islands, as Europeans later dubbed them). Shortly after 1500, when Malacca was at its height, one resident counted eighty-four languages spoken among the merchants gathered there, who came from as far away as Turkey, Ethiopia, and the Swahili Coast. Four officials administered the foreign merchant communities: one for the Gujaratis, one for other Indians and Burmese, one for Southeast Asians, and one for the Chinese and Japanese. Malacca's wealth and its cosmopolitan residents set the standard for luxury in Malaya for centuries to come.

SOCIAL AND CULTURAL CHANGE

State growth, commercial expansion, and the spread of Islam between 1200 and 1500 led to changes in the society and cultural life of numerous peoples. Muslim political and commercial elites grew in numbers and power, and religious agents sought converts both within and beyond the boundaries of Muslim states. Yet Africa and India saw many and diverse instances of local art traditions, rituals, and even theological doctrines being combined with those of Islam to form syncretic religious formations, often in the guise of Sufi brotherhoods, reminiscent of the syncretism of the Hellenistic period (see Chapter 5).

Architecture, Learning, and Religion   Social and cultural changes typically affected cities more than rural areas. As travelers often observed, wealthy merchants and ruling elites spent lavishly on mansions, palaces, and places of worship while the lives of common people were less affected. Most mosques, local pilgrimage sites, and Sufi shrines surviving from this period blend older traditions and new influences. African Muslims produced Middle Eastern mosque designs in local building materials: sun-baked clay reinforced by wooden crossbeams in the western Sudan, masonry using blocks of coral on the Swahili Coast. Hindu temple architecture influenced, and sometimes provided material for, Muslim places of worship not only in newly Islamized regions like Gujarat, but also in older Muslim lands like Afghanistan and Iran that South Asian artisans were free to travel to once their homelands came under Muslim rule.

The congregational mosque at Cambay, built in 1325, utilized pillars, porches, and arches taken from sacked Hindu and Jain (jine) temples. The congregational mosque erected at the Gujarati capital of Ahmadabad (AH-muhd-ah-bahd) in 1423 had the open courtyard typical of mosques everywhere, but the surrounding verandas incorporated many Gujarati details and architectural conventions.

Mosques, churches, and temples were centers of education as well as prayer and ritual. Muslims promoted literacy among their sons (and sometimes their daughters) so that they could read sacred texts. In some lands south of the Sahara, Ethiopia excepted, Islam provided the first exposure to literate culture. In much of South Asia, literacy in Indo-European languages like Sanskrit and Dravidian languages like Tamil had been established many centuries before. Even there, however, a migration of Arabic and Persian vocabulary into local languages produced significant changes. Scholars adapted the Arabic alphabet to write local languages like Hausa in Mali and numerous tongues in the Malay Peninsula and island Southeast Asia.

Persian became the court language of the Delhi sultanate, but **Urdu** (ER-doo), a Persian-influenced form of the local Hindustani tongue of northern India, eventually became an important literary language written in Arabic characters. Muslims also introduced paper into their new lands. Although this was an improvement over palm leaves and other fragile materials, tropical humidity and insect life nevertheless made preservation of written knowledge difficult.

Muslim scholars everywhere studied the Quran along with Islamic law and theology. A few demonstrated a high level of interest in mathematics, medicine, science, and philosophy, partly derived from ancient Greek writings translated into Arabic (see Chapter 10). In sixteenth-century **Timbuktu**, over 150 schools taught the Quran while leading clerics taught advanced classes in mosques or homes. Books imported from North Africa brought high prices. Al-Hajj Ahmed, a scholar who died in Timbuktu in 1536, possessed some seven hundred volumes, an unusually large library for that time. In Southeast Asia, Malacca became a center of Islamic learning from which scholars spread Islam throughout the region. Some of the most influential scholars made the pilgrimage to Mecca and studied there before returning home to teach others. Other important centers of learning developed in Muslim India, particularly in Delhi, the capital.

Even in lands seized by conquest, Muslim rulers seldom required conversion. Example and persuasion by merchants and Sufis proved more effective in winning new believers. Muslim domination of long-distance trade assisted the adoption of Islam. Commercial transactions could take place across religious boundaries, but the common code of morality and law that Islam provided encouraged trust and drew many local merchants to Islam. From the major trading centers along the Swahili Coast, in the Sudan, in coastal India, and in Southeast Asia, Islam's influence spread along regional trade routes.

Islam also spread among rural peoples, such as the pastoral Fulani of West Africa and the Somali of northeastern Africa. In Bengal, Muslim religious figures working for state officials oversaw the conversion of jungle into rice paddies and thereby gained converts among the people who came to work the land and inhabit the new villages. At first the new converts melded Islamic beliefs with Hindu traditions, seeing Muhammad, for example, as a manifestation of the god Vishnu. Over time, however, more standard versions of Islam gained headway.

Marriage also played a role. Single Muslim men traveling to and settling in tropical Africa and Asia often married local women. Their children grew up in the paternal faith because Islamic doctrine specified the transmission of religious identity in the male line. Some wealthy men had dozens of children from up to four wives and additional slave concubines. Servants and slaves in such households normally professed Islam.

In India, Muslim invasions eliminated the last strongholds of long-declining Buddhism, including, in 1196, the great Buddhist center of study at Nalanda (nuh-LAN-duh) in Bihar (bee-HAHR). Its manuscripts were burned and thousands of monks killed or driven into exile in Nepal and Tibet. With Buddhism reduced to a minor faith in the land of its birth, Islam emerged as India's second most important religion. Islam displaced Hinduism as the elite religion in most of maritime Southeast Asia and slowly supplanted a variety of local cults. In mainland Southeast Asia, Buddhism and Islam vied for supremacy, with Islam prevailing in the south and Buddhism prevailing farther north in Thailand, Cambodia, and Burma (Myanmar).

Social and Gender Distinctions

A growth in slavery accompanied the rising prosperity of the elites. Military campaigns in India, according to Islamic sources, reduced hundreds of thousands of Hindu "infidels" to slavery. Delhi overflowed with slaves. Sultan Ala-ud-din owned 50,000 and Firuz Shah 180,000, including 12,000 skilled artisans. Sultan Tughluq sent 100 male slaves and 100 female slaves as a gift to the emperor of China in return for a similar gift.

When African awareness of the value of gold in Mediterranean lands cut into the profitability of trans-Saharan trade, Mali and Bornu sent slaves across the Sahara to North Africa. The expanding Ethiopian Empire regularly sent captives for sale to Aden traders at Zeila. Many eunuchs (castrated males) were included in this trade. According to modern estimates, Saharan and Red Sea traders sold about 2.5 million enslaved Africans between 1200 and 1500. African slaves from the Swahili Coast played conspicuous roles in the navies, armies, and administrations of some Indian states, especially in the fifteenth century. A few African slaves even reached China, where a source from about 1225 says rich families preferred gatekeepers with bodies "black as lacquer." Later Chinese paintings show Portuguese ships manned almost entirely by African seamen.

With "free" labor abundant and cheap, few slaves worked as farmers. In some places, hereditary castes of slaves dominated certain trades and military units. Indeed, the rulers of the Delhi Sultanate included a number of mamluks, or Turkic military slaves (see Chapter 10). A slave general in the western Sudan named Askia Muhammad seized control of the Songhai Empire (Mali's successor) in 1493. Less fortunate slaves, like the men and women who mined copper in Mali, did hard menial work.

Wealthy households used many slave servants. Eunuchs guarded the harems of wealthy Muslims, but women predominated as household slaves, serving also as entertainers and concubines. Some rich men aspired to having a concubine from every part of the world. One of Firuz Shah's nobles reportedly had two thousand harem slaves, including women from Turkey and China.

Hindu legal digests and commentaries suggest that the position of Hindu women may have improved somewhat compared to earlier periods. The ancient practice of sati (suh-TEE)—that is, of an upper-caste widow throwing herself on her husband's funeral pyre—remained a meritorious act strongly approved by social custom. But Ibn Battuta makes it clear that sati was strictly optional. Since the Hindu commentaries devote considerable attention to the rights of widows without sons to inherit their husbands' estates, one may even conclude that sati was exceptional.

Indian parents still gave their daughters in marriage before the age of puberty, but consummation of the marriage took place only when the young woman was ready. Wives faced far stricter rules of fidelity and chastity than their husbands and could be abandoned for any serious breach. But other offenses against law and custom usually brought lighter penalties than for men. A woman's male master—father, husband, or owner—determined her status. Women seldom played active roles in commerce, administration, or religion. Differences between Muslims and Hindus on matters relating to gender were not as great as the formal religious texts of the two religious traditions would suggest. South Asian tradition tended to outweigh Muslim practices imported from Arabia and Persia.

African Islam showed similar inclinations in the area of gender. In Mali's capital, Ibn Battuta was appalled that Muslim women both free and slave did not completely cover their bodies and veil their faces when appearing in public. He considered their nakedness an offense to women's (and men's) modesty. Elsewhere in Mali, he berated a Muslim merchant from Morocco for permitting his wife to sit on a couch and chat with her male friend. The husband replied, "The association of women with men is agreeable to us and part of good manners, to which no suspicion attaches." Ibn Battuta refused to visit the merchant again.

Besides child rearing, women involved themselves with food preparation and, when not prohibited by religious restrictions, brewing. In many parts of Africa, women commonly made beer from grains or bananas. These mildly alcoholic beverages played an important part in male rituals of hospitality and relaxation.

Throughout tropical Africa and Asia, women did much of the farm work. They also toted home heavy loads of food, firewood, and water balanced on their heads. Other common female activities included making clay pots for cooking and storage and making clothing. In India, the spinning wheel, possibly a local invention, sped up the process of making thread for weaving and thus reduced the cost. Women typically spun at home, leaving weaving to men. In West Africa, women often sold agricultural products, pottery, and other craftwork in the markets.

THE WESTERN HEMISPHERE

Though isolated from the Eastern Hemisphere by oceans that were not crossed until the end of the fifteenth century, the tropical regions of the Western Hemisphere shared many of the climatic characteristics of the Old World tropics (see Chapter 8). However, the region's two most powerful urbanized empires, the Aztec of Mexico and the Inka of Peru, developed at altitudes above 7,000 feet, thus experiencing lower average rainfall and temperature than is common across the tropics. They also differed in being themselves centers of civilization rather than subsidiary to dominating political and economic powers located in temperate lands to the north or south.

Mesoamerica had witnessed a series of urbanized societies—such as the Olmec, Maya, and Toltecs—from the second millennium B.C.E. onward, and the mountains and coastal deserts of the Andean region had an equally long sequence, including Moche, Tiwanaku, Wari, and Chimu. Apart from these advanced regions, which saw the rise of powerful empires between 1300 and 1500 C.E., most Western Hemisphere societies of the period subsisted at more basic levels as hunters and gatherers or village agriculturalists.

Mesoamerica: The Aztecs   The Mexica (meh-SHE-ca) were among the northern peoples who pushed into central Mexico in the wake of the Toltec collapse (see Chapter 8). As their power grew through political alliances and military conquest, they created a Mexica-dominated regional power called the Aztec Empire. At the time of their arrival the Mexica were organized as an **altepetl** (al-TEH-peh-tel), an ethnic state led by a tlatoani (tlah-toh-AHN-ee) or ruler. The altepetl, the common political building block across the region, directed the collective religious, social, and political obligations of the ethnic group. A group of **calpolli** (cal-POH-yee), each with up to a hundred families, served as the foundation of the altepetl, controlling land allocation, tax collection, and local religious life.

In their new environment the Mexica began to adopt the political and social practices that they found among the urbanized agriculturalists of the valley. At first, they served their more powerful neighbors as serfs and mercenaries. As their strength grew, they relocated to small islands near the shore of Lake Texcoco, and around 1325 C.E. they began the construction of their twin capitals, **Tenochtitlan** (teh-noch-TIT-lan) and Tlatelolco (tla-teh-LOHL-coh) (together the foundation for modern Mexico City).

Military successes allowed the Mexica to seize control of additional agricultural land along the lakeshore and to forge military alliances with neighboring altepetl. Once these more complex political and economic arrangements were in place, the Mexica-dominated alliance became the Aztec Empire. With increased economic independence, greater political security, and territorial expansion, the **Aztecs** transformed their political organization by introducing a monarchical system similar to that found in more powerful neighboring states and selecting a ruling dynasty with ties to the Toltecs (see Chapter 8). A council of powerful aristocrats selected new rulers from among male members of the ruling lineage. Once selected, the ruler had to renegotiate the submission of tribute dependencies and then demonstrate his divine mandate by undertaking a new round of military conquests. For the Aztecs war was infused with religious meaning, providing the ruler with legitimacy and increasing the prestige of successful warriors.

The Aztecs succeeded in developing a remarkable urban landscape. The population of Tenochtitlan and Tlatelolco combined with that of the cities and towns of the surrounding lakeshore was approximately 500,000 by 1500 C.E. Three causeways connected this island capital to the lakeshore. Planners laid out the urban center as a grid where canals and streets intersected at right angles to facilitate the movement of people and goods.

Although warfare gave increased power and privilege to males, women held substantial power and exercised broad influence in Aztec society. The roles of women and men were clearly distinguished, but women were held in high esteem. Scholars call this "gender complementarity." Following the birth of a boy, his umbilical cord was buried on the battlefield and he was given implements to signal his occupation or his role as a warrior. In the case of a girl, her umbilical cord was buried near the hearth and she was given weaving implements and female clothing. Women dominated the household and the markets, and they also served as teachers and priestesses. They were also seen as the founders of lineages, including the royal line.

Aztec military successes and territorial expansion allowed the warrior elite to seize land and peasant labor as spoils of war. In time, the royal family and highest-ranking members of the aristocracy possessed extensive estates that were cultivated by slaves and landless commoners. The lower classes received some material rewards from imperial expansion but lost most of their ability to influence or control decisions. Some commoners were able to achieve some social mobility through success on the battlefield.

However, by 1500 C.E. great inequalities in wealth and privilege characterized Aztec society. One of the Spaniards who participated in the conquest of the Aztec Empire remembered his first meeting with the Aztec ruler Moctezuma (mock-teh-ZU-ma) II (r. 1502–1520): "Many great lords walked before the great Montezuma [Moctezuma II], sweeping the ground on which he was to tread and laying down cloaks so that his feet should not touch the earth. Not one of these chieftains dared look him in the face."[3] While commoners lived in small dwellings and ate a limited diet of staples, members of the nobility lived in large, well-constructed, two-story houses and consumed a diet rich in animal protein.

A specialized class of merchants controlled long-distance trade. Given the absence of draft animals and wheeled vehicles, lightweight and valuable products like gold, jewels, feathered garments, cacao, and animal skins dominated this commerce. Merchants also provided essential political and military intelligence for the Aztec elite. But although merchants became wealthy and powerful as the Aztecs expanded their empire, they were denied the privileges of the high nobility, which was jealous of its power.

The Aztec state met the challenge of feeding an urban population of approximately 150,000 by efficiently organizing the labor of the calpolli and of additional laborers sent by defeated peoples to expand agricultural land. Aztec chinampas (artificial island gardens) contributed maize, fruits, and vegetables to the markets of Tenochtitlan. The imposition of a **tribute system** on conquered peoples also helped relieve some of the pressure of Tenochtitlan's growing population. Unlike the tribute system of Tang China, where tribute had a more symbolic character (see Chapter 12), one-quarter of the Aztec capital's food requirement was satisfied by tribute payments of maize, beans, and other foods sent by nearby political dependencies.

Like commerce throughout the Mesoamerican world, Aztec commerce was carried on without money and credit. Barter was facilitated by the use of cacao beans, quills filled with gold, and cotton cloth as standard units of value to compensate for differences in the value of bartered goods. Aztec expansion facilitated the integration of producers and consumers in the central Mexican economy. Hernán Cortés (1485–1547), the Spanish adventurer who eventually conquered the Aztecs, expressed his admiration for the abundance of the Aztec marketplace:

> One square in particular is twice as big as that of Salamanca and completely surrounded by arcades where there are daily more than sixty thousand folk buying and selling. Every kind of merchandise such as may be met with in every land is for sale...

---

[3] Bernal Díaz del Castillo, *The Conquest of New Spain*, trans. J. M. Cohen (London: Penguin Books, 1963), 217.

There is nothing to be found in all the land which is not sold in these markets, for over and above what I have mentioned there are so many and such various things that on account of their very number... I cannot detail them.[4]

Religious rituals dominated public life in Tenochtitlan. Like the other cultures of the Mesoamerican world, the Aztecs worshiped a large number of gods. Most of these gods had a dual nature—both male and female. The chief god of the Mexica was Huitzilopochtli (wheat-zeel-oh-POSHT-lee) or southern hummingbird. Originally associated with war, the Aztecs later identified this god with the Sun. Tenochtitlan was architecturally dominated by a great twin temple devoted to Huitzilopochtli and Tlaloc, the storm-god, symbolizing the two bases of the Aztec economy: war and agriculture.

The Andes: The Inka   In little more than a hundred years, the **Inka** developed a vast imperial state, which they called "Land of Four Corners." By 1525 the empire had a population of more than 6 million and stretched from the Maule River in Chile to northern Ecuador, conquered between 1500 and 1525, and from the Pacific coast across the Andes to the upper Amazon and, in the south, into Argentina. In the early fifteenth century the Inka were one of many competing military powers in the southern highlands, an area of limited political significance after the collapse of Wari (see Chapter 8). Centered in the valley of Cuzco, the Inka were initially organized as a chiefdom based on reciprocal gift giving and the redistribution of food and textiles. Strong and resourceful leaders consolidated political authority in the 1430s and undertook an ambitious campaign of military expansion.

The Inka state, like earlier highland powers, utilized traditional Andean social customs and economic practices. Tiwanaku had relied in part on the use of colonists to provide supplies of resources from distant, ecologically distinct zones. The Inka built on this legacy by conquering additional distant territories and increasing the scale of forced exchanges. Crucial to this process was the development of a large military. Unlike the peoples of Mesoamerica, who distributed specialized goods through markets and tribute relationships, Andean peoples used state power to broaden and expand the vertical exchange system that had permitted self-governing extended family groups called ayllus to exploit a range of ecological niches (see Chapter 8). Like earlier highland civilizations, the Inka were pastoralists, and their prosperity and military strength depended on vast herds of llamas and alpacas, which provided food and clothing as well as transport for goods. They gained access to corn, cotton, and other goods from the coastal region via forced exchanges.

Collective efforts by mita labor, a system of forced service to the ruler (see Chapter 8), made the Inka Empire possible. Cuzco, the imperial capital, and the provincial cities, the royal court, the imperial armies, and the state's religious cults all rested on this foundation. The mita system also created the material surplus that provided the bare necessities for the old, weak, and ill of Inka society. Each ayllu contributed approximately one-seventh of its adult male population to meet these collective obligations. These draft laborers served as soldiers, construction workers,

[4] Hernando Cortés, *Five Letters, 1519–1526*, trans. J. Bayard Morris (New York: Norton, 1991), 87.

craftsmen, and runners to carry messages along post roads. They also drained swamps, terraced mountainsides, filled in valley floors, built and maintained irrigation works, and built storage facilities and roads. Inka laborers constructed 13,000 miles (20,930 kilometers) of road, facilitating military troop movements, administration, and trade.

The hereditary chiefs of ayllus, a group that included women, carried out local administrative and judicial functions. As the Inka expanded, they generally left local rulers in place. By doing so they risked rebellion, but they controlled these risks by means of a thinly veiled system of hostage taking and the use of military garrisons. The rulers of defeated regions were required to send their heirs to live at the Inka royal court in Cuzco. Inka leaders even required that defeated peoples send representations of important local gods to Cuzco to be included in the imperial pantheon. These measures promoted imperial integration while at the same time providing hostages to ensure the good behavior of subject peoples.

Conquests magnified the authority of the Inka ruler and led to the creation of an imperial bureaucracy drawn from among his kinsmen. The royal family claimed descent from the Sun, the primary Inka god. Members of the royal family lived in palaces maintained by armies of servants, and their lives were dominated by political and religious rituals that helped legitimize their authority. Among the many obligations associated with kingship was the requirement to extend imperial boundaries by warfare. Thus each new ruler began his reign with conquest.

Tenochtitlan, the Aztec capital, had a population of about 150,000 in 1520. At the height of Inka power in 1530, Cuzco had a population of less than 30,000. Nevertheless, Cuzco was a remarkable place. The Inka were highly skilled stone craftsmen and constructed their most impressive buildings of carefully cut stones fitted together without mortar. Planners laid the city out in the shape of a giant puma (a mountain lion). At the city center were the palaces of rulers as well as the major temples. The richest was the Temple of the Sun, its interior lined with sheets of gold and its patio decorated with golden representations of llamas and corn. The ruler made every effort to awe and intimidate visitors and residents alike with a nearly continuous series of rituals, feasts, and sacrifices. Sacrifices of textiles, animals, and other goods sent as tribute dominated the city's calendar. The destruction of these valuable commodities, and a small number of human sacrifices, helped give the impression of splendor and sumptuous abundance that appeared to demonstrate the ruler's claimed descent from the Sun.

Inka cultural achievement rested on the strong foundation of earlier Andean civilizations. We know that astronomical observation was a central concern of the priestly class, as in Mesoamerica. The collective achievements of Andean peoples were accomplished with a limited record-keeping system adapted from earlier Andean civilizations. Administrators used knotted colored cords, called **khipus** (KEY-pooz), for public administration, population counts, and tribute obligations. Inka weaving and metallurgy, also based on earlier regional development, was more advanced than in Mesoamerica. Inka craftsmen produced utilitarian tools and weapons of copper and bronze as well as decorative objects of gold and silver. Inka women produced textiles of extraordinary beauty from cotton and the wool of llamas and alpacas.

Although the Inka did not introduce new technologies, they increased economic output and added to the region's prosperity. The conquest of large populations in environmentally distinct regions allowed the Inka to multiply the yields produced by the traditional exchanges between distinct ecological niches. This expansion of imperial economic and political power was purchased at the cost of reduced equality and diminished local autonomy. Members of the imperial elite, living in richly decorated palaces in Cuzco and other urban centers, were increasingly distant from the masses of Inka society. Even members of the provincial nobility were held at arm's length from the royal court, while commoners could be executed if they dared to look directly at the ruler's face.

After only a century of regional dominance, the Inka Empire faced a crisis in 1525. The death of the ruler Huayna Capac at the conclusion of the conquest of Ecuador initiated a bloody struggle for the throne. The rivalry of two sons compelled both the professional military and the hereditary Inka elite to choose sides. Civil war was the result. Regionalism and ethnic diversity had always posed a threat to the empire. Now civil war weakened the imperial state and ignited the resentments of conquered peoples on the eve of the arrival of Europeans.

Conclusion

Tropical Africa and Asia contained 40 percent of the world's population and over a quarter of its habitable land. Between 1200 and 1500, commercial, political, and cultural currents drew the region's peoples closer together. The Indian Ocean became the world's most important and richest trading area; the Delhi Sultanate brought the greatest political unity to India since the decline of the Guptas; and Mali extended the political and trading role pioneered by Ghana in the western Sudan. Trade and empire followed closely the enlargement of Islam's presence and the accompanying diversification of Islamic customs.

Yet many social and cultural practices remained stable. Most tropical Africans and Asians never ventured far outside the rural communities where their families had lived for generations. Their lives followed the patterns of agricultural or pastoral life, the cycle of religious observations, traditional occupational and kinship divisions, and the individual's passage through the stages of life from childhood to elder status. Village communities proved remarkably hardy. They might be ravaged by natural disaster or pillaged by advancing armies, but over time most recovered. Empires and kingdoms rose and fell, but village life endured.

In the Western Hemisphere the powerful empires of the Aztecs and Inka rose in Mesoamerica and the Andean region, respectively. Each was heir to a series of preceding cultures in their area, but they had in common an unprecedented territorial extent. Warfare and religious rituals were hallmarks of both empires, and their success depended on the economic subordination of conquered peoples as well as specialized production in a variety of environmentally distinct regions. The Aztecs excelled at irrigation and trade, the Inka at labor organization and road building.

IMPORTANT EVENTS 1200–1500

1206	Delhi Sultanate founded in India
1230s	Mali Empire founded
1270	Solomonic dynasty in Ethiopia founded
1298	Delhi Sultanate annexes Gujarat
1324–1325	Mansa Musa's pilgrimage to Mecca
1398	Timur sacks Delhi, Delhi Sultanate declines
1400s	Great Zimbabwe at its peak
1433	Tuareg retake Timbuktu, Mali declines
1500	Port of Malacca at its peak

16

THE MARITIME REVOLUTION, TO 1550

In 1511 young Ferdinand Magellan sailed from Europe around the southern tip of Africa and eastward across the Indian Ocean as a member of the first Portuguese expedition to explore the East Indies (maritime Southeast Asia). Eight years later, this time in the service of Spain, he led an expedition that sought to reach the East Indies by sailing westward. By the middle of 1521 Magellan's expedition had achieved its goal by sailing across the Atlantic, rounding the southern tip of South America, and crossing the Pacific Ocean—but at a high price.

Of the five ships that had set out from Spain in 1519, only three made the long passage across the vast Pacific. Dozens of sailors died from starvation and disease during the voyage. In the Philippines, Magellan, having survived numerous mutinies during the voyage, died in battle on April 27, 1521, while aiding a local ruler who had promised to become a Christian.

To consolidate their dwindling resources, the expedition's survivors burned the least seaworthy of their remaining three ships and consolidated men and supplies. In the end only the *Victoria* made it home across the Indian Ocean and back to Europe. Nevertheless, the *Victoria*'s return to Spain on September 8, 1522, was a crowning example of Europeans' determination to make themselves masters of the oceans. A century of daring and dangerous voyages backed by the Portuguese crown had opened new routes through the South Atlantic to Africa, Brazil, and the rich trade of the Indian Ocean. Rival voyages sponsored by Spain since 1492 opened new contacts with the American continents. A maritime revolution was under way that would change the course of history.

This new maritime era marked the end of a long period when Asia had initiated most overland and maritime expansion. Asia had been the source of the most useful technologies and the most influential systems of belief. It was also home to the most powerful states and the richest trading networks. The success of Iberian voyages of exploration in the following century would redirect the world's center of power, wealth, and innovation to the West.

This maritime revolution broadened and deepened contacts, alliances, and conflicts across ancient cultural boundaries. Some of these contacts ended tragically for individuals like Magellan. Some proved disastrous for entire populations: Amerindians, for instance, suffered conquest, colonization, and a rapid decline in numbers. And sometimes the results were mixed: Asians and Africans found both risks and opportunities in their new relations with Europe.

GLOBAL MARITIME EXPANSION BEFORE 1450

Since ancient times travel across the world's seas and oceans had been one of the great challenges to technological ingenuity. Ships had to be sturdy enough to survive heavy winds and seas, and pilots had to learn how to cross featureless expanses of water to reach their destinations. In time ships, sails, and navigational techniques perfected in the more protected seas were adapted to open oceans.

However complex the solutions and dangerous the voyages, the rewards of sea travel made them worthwhile. Ships could move goods and people more profitably than any form of overland travel then possible. Crossing unknown waters, finding new lands, developing new markets, and establishing new settlements attracted adventurers from every continent. By 1450 daring mariners had discovered and settled most of the islands of the Pacific, the Atlantic, and the Indian Ocean, but no one had yet crossed the Pacific in either direction. Even the smaller Atlantic remained a barrier to contact between the Americas, Europe, and Africa. The inhabitants of Australia were also nearly cut off from contact with the rest of humanity. All this was about to change.

The Indian Ocean   The archipelagos and coastal regions of Southeast Asia were connected in networks of trade and cultural exchange from an early date. While the region was divided politically, culturally, and religiously, the languages of Malaysia, Indonesia, and the Philippines—as well as coastal regions of Thailand, southern Vietnam, Cambodia, and Hainan, China—all originated from a common Austronesian linguistic root. Scholars often use the term *Malayo Indonesians* or *Malay* to describe the early peoples of this maritime realm.

The region's sailors were highly skilled navigators as well as innovative shipbuilders and sail makers who, in addition to their own achievements, influenced later Chinese and Arab maritime advances. Around 350 they discovered two direct sea routes between Sri Lanka and the South China Sea through the Straits of Malacca and Sunda, thus opening a profitable link to China's silk markets. They were also the first to use the seasonal monsoon winds of the Indian Ocean to extend their voyages for thousands of miles, ultimately reaching East Africa and settling in Madagascar.

By the first century C.E. the mariners and merchants of India and Southeast Asia were trading across the region for spices, gold, and aromatic woods, even sending spices as far west as Rome through Mediterranean intermediaries (see Chapter 7). Their success attracted African, Arab, and Chinese mariners and merchants into the region, creating a large, integrated, and highly profitable market in the centuries that followed. By 1000 the dhows (dow) of Arabs and Africans, as well as Malay *jongs* and Chinese junks, came together in the region's harbors for commerce.

The rise of medieval Islam (see Chapter 10) gave Indian Ocean trade an important boost. The great Muslim cities of the Middle East provided a demand for valuable commodities, and networks of Muslim traders were active across the region. These traders shared a common language, ethic, and law and actively spread their religion to distant trading cities. By 1400 there were Muslim trading communities all around the Indian Ocean. Chinese merchant communities were present as well.

Indian Ocean traders largely operated outside the control of the empires and states they served, but in East Asia imperial China's rulers were growing more and more interested in these wealthy ports of trade. In 1368 the Ming dynasty overthrew Mongol rule and began to reestablish China's predominance and prestige abroad. Having restored Chinese power and influence in East Asia, the Ming moved to establish direct contacts with the peoples around the Indian Ocean, sending out seven imperial fleets between 1405 and 1433 (see Chapter 13). The enormous size of these expeditions, far larger than needed for exploration or promoting trade, indicates that the Ming sought to inspire awe of their power and achievements. While curiosity about this prosperous region may have been a motive, the fact that the ports visited by the fleets were major commercial centers suggests that expanding China's trade was also an objective.

The scale of the Ming expeditions to the Indian Ocean Basin reflects imperial China's resources and importance. The first consisted of sixty-two specially built "treasure ships," large Chinese junks each about 300 feet long by 150 feet wide (90 by 45 meters). There were also at least a hundred smaller vessels. Each treasure ship had nine masts, twelve sails, many decks, and a carrying capacity of 3,000 tons (six times the capacity of Columbus's entire fleet). One expedition carried over 27,000 crew and passengers, including infantry and cavalry troops. The ships were armed with small cannon, but in most Chinese sea battles arrows from highly accurate crossbows dominated the fighting.

Admiral **Zheng He** (jung huh) (1371–1435) commanded the expeditions. A Chinese Muslim with ancestral connections to the Persian Gulf, Zheng was a fitting emissary to the increasingly Muslim-dominated Indian Ocean Basin. The expeditions carried other Arabic-speaking Chinese as interpreters. One of them recorded local customs and beliefs in a journal, observing new flora and fauna and noting exotic animals such as the black panther of Malaya and the tapir of Sumatra. In India he described the division of the coastal population into five classes, which correspond to the four Hindu varna and a separate Muslim class. He also recorded that traders in the rich Indian trading port of Calicut (KAL-ih-kut) could perform error-free calculations by counting on their fingers and toes rather than using the

Chinese Junk *This modern drawing shows how much larger one of Zheng He's ships was than one of Vasco da Gama's vessels. Watertight interior bulkheads made junks the most seaworthy large ships of the fifteenth century. Sails made of pleated bamboo matting hung from the junk's masts, and a stern rudder provided steering. European ships of exploration, though smaller, were faster and more maneuverable.*

Chinese abacus. After his return, the interpreter went on tour in China, telling of these exotic places and "how far the majestic virtue of [China's] imperial dynasty extended."[1]

The Chinese "treasure ships" carried rich silks and other valuable goods intended as gifts for distant rulers. In return those rulers sent back gifts of equal or greater value to the Chinese emperor. Although the main purpose of these exchanges was diplomatic, they also stimulated trade between China and its southern neighbors. Interest in new contacts was not limited to the Chinese.

At least three trading cities on the Swahili (swah-HEE-lee) Coast of East Africa sent delegations to China between 1415 and 1416. The delegates from one of them, Malindi, presented the emperor of China with a giraffe, creating quite a stir among normally reserved imperial officials. These African delegations may have encouraged more contacts because the next three of Zheng's voyages reached the African coast. Unfortunately, no documents record how Africans and Chinese reacted to each other during these historic meetings between 1417 and 1433, but it appears that China's lavish gifts stimulated the Swahili market for silk and porcelain.

---

[1]Ma Huan, *Ying-yai Sheng-lan: "The Overall Survey of the Ocean's Shores,"* ed. Feng Ch'eng-Chün, trans. J. V. G. Mills (Cambridge, England: Cambridge University Press, 1970), 180.

Had the Ming court wished to promote trade for the profit of its merchants, Chinese fleets might have come to play a dominant role in Indian Ocean trade. But some high Chinese officials opposed increased contact with peoples whom they regarded as barbarians incapable of making contributions to China. Such opposition caused a suspension in the voyages from 1424 to 1431. The final Chinese expedition sailed between 1432 and 1433.

While later Ming emperors would focus their attention on internal matters, long-established Chinese merchant communities continued as major participants in Indian Ocean trade, contributing to the rapid growth of prosperous commercial entrepôts (ON-truh-pohs) (places where goods are stored or deposited and from which they are distributed) throughout the region. As the sultan of one of the most prosperous trade centers, Melaka (in modern Malaysia), described the era in 1468, "We have learned that to master the blue oceans people must engage in commerce and trade. All the lands within the seas are united in one body. Life has never been so affluent in preceding generations as it is today."[2]

| The Pacific | Around 3000 B.C.E. seafaring peoples from Southeast Asia |
| Ocean | reached the island of New Guinea. Sustained contact between |

these Austronesian-speaking migrants and the island's original population accelerated agricultural development and led to population expansion and the settlement of nearby islands. The descendants these peoples eventually forged a new cultural identity, called Lapita by archaeologists, as they colonized the island chains of Melanesia (mel-uh-NEE-zhuh). Lapita settlers reached Tonga, Fiji, and Samoa around 1000 B.C.E.

By 500 B.C.E. a linguistically and culturally distinct Polynesian culture emerged from this Lapita origin. While the dates for Polynesian colonization of the remote islands of the Pacific are still debated, their mastery of long-distance maritime exploration in an era when European sailors still stayed close to shore is undeniable. Pushing east from Tonga, Samoa, and Fiji, Polynesians colonized the Marquesas (mar-KAY-suhs) and the Cook and Society archipelagos by approximately 300 B.C.E. Before 500 C.E. Polynesian colonies were established on the Hawaiian Islands 2,200 miles (3,541 kilometers) away, and Polynesian colonists settled Easter Island, 2,300 miles (3,702 kilometers) to the southeast, by 800 C.E. Finally, they established permanent colonies in New Zealand around 1000 C.E. Polynesian voyagers also made periodic contact with the mainland of South America after 1000 C.E., passing on the domesticated Asian chicken and returning with the sweet potato, an American domesticate that soon became a staple throughout the Pacific region.

Both DNA evidence and linguistic evidence make clear that the Polynesian settlement of the islands of the eastern Pacific was planned and not the result of accident. Following voyages of reconnaissance, Polynesian mariners carried colonizing expeditions in fleets of large double-hulled canoes that relied on scores of paddlers

---

[2]Quotation in Craig A. Lockard, "'The Sea Common to All': Maritime Frontiers, Port Cities, and Chinese Traders in the Southeast Asian Age of Commerce, ca. 1400–1750," *Journal of World History* 21, no. 2 (2010): 228.

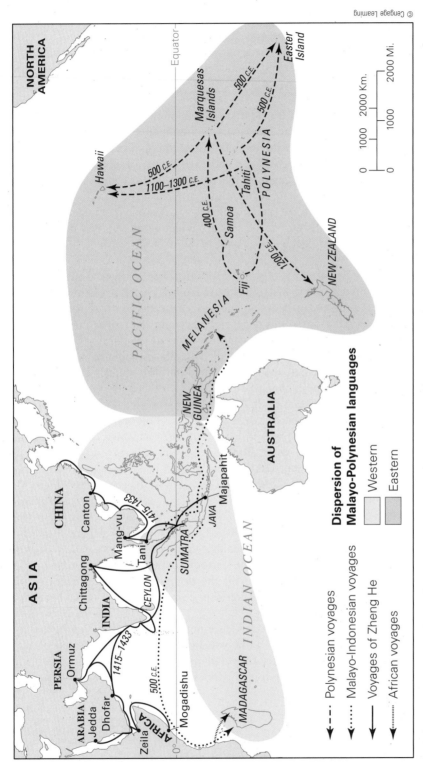

MAP 16.1 Exploration and Settlement in the Indian and Pacific Oceans Before 1500

Over many centuries, mariners originating in Southeast Asia gradually colonized the islands of the Pacific and Indian Oceans. The Chinese voyages led by Zheng He in the fifteenth century were lavish official expeditions.

as well as sails. Their largest canoes reached 120 feet (37 meters) in length and carried crews of fifty. A wide platform connected the two hulls of these crafts and permitted the transportation of animals and plants crucial to the success of distant and isolated settlements. Long-range expeditions took pigs, dogs, and chickens with them as well as domesticated plants such as taro, bananas, yams, and breadfruit. Their success depended upon reliably navigating across thousands of miles of ocean using careful observation of the currents and stars as the crews searched for evidence of land.

The most hierarchical social structures and political systems developed in the Hawaiian and Tongan archipelagos, where powerful hereditary chiefs controlled the lives of commoners and managed resources. Here, as well as in New Zealand, competition among chiefs led to chronic warfare.

While all Polynesian societies descended from the same originating culture and all began with the same tools and the same farming and fishing technologies, significant differences in the geography and climate led inexorably to the development of unique social, political, and economic systems. Most Polynesian communities depended on farming and fishing, but the intensity of these practices depended on local conditions. In Hawaii, for example, low-lying native forests were converted to farmland using controlled burns, and fishponds were built to increase fish yields. As a result, the Polynesian communities of this archipelago thrived into the era of European expansion. However, on Easter Island, among the most isolated of the Polynesian colonies, population growth led to total deforestation, soil erosion, intense resource competition, and, ultimately, to a brutal cycle of warfare that drastically reduced the population.

The Atlantic Ocean

The Vikings were the greatest mariners of the Atlantic in the early Middle Ages. These northern European raiders used their small, open ships to attack Europe's coastal settlements for several centuries. Like the Polynesians, the Vikings used their knowledge of the heavens and the seas rather than maps and other navigational devices to find their way over long distances.

The Vikings first settled Iceland in 770 and established a colony on Greenland in 982. By accident one group sighted North America in 986. Fifteen years later Leif Ericsson established a short-lived Viking settlement on the island of Newfoundland, which he called Vinland. When a colder climate returned after 1200, the northern settlements in Greenland went into decline and the Vikings abandoned Vinland.

Some southern Europeans applied maritime skills acquired in the Mediterranean and along the North Atlantic coast to explore to the south. Genoese and Portuguese expeditions pushed into the Atlantic in the fourteenth century, eventually exploring and settling the islands of Madeira (muh-DEER-uh), the Azores (A-zorz), and the Canaries.

There is some evidence of African voyages of exploration in this period. The celebrated Syrian geographer al-Umari (1301–1349) relates that when Mansa Kankan Musa (MAHN-suh KAHN-kahn MOO-suh), the ruler of the West African empire of Mali, passed through Egypt on his lavish pilgrimage to

Mecca in 1324, he told of voyages into the Atlantic undertaken by his predecessor, Mansa Muhammad. According to this source, Muhammad had sent out four hundred vessels with men and supplies, telling them, "Do not return until you have reached the other side of the ocean or if you have exhausted your food or water." After a long time one canoe returned, reporting that the others were lost in a "violent current in the middle of the sea." Muhammad himself then set out at the head of a second, even larger, expedition, from which no one returned.

In the Americas, early Amerindian voyagers from the Caribbean coast of South America colonized the West Indies. By the year 1000 Amerindians known as the **Arawak** (AR-uh-wahk) (also called Taino) had followed the small islands of the Lesser Antilles (Barbados, Martinique, and Guadeloupe) to the Greater Antilles (Cuba, Hispaniola, Jamaica, and Puerto Rico) as well as to the Bahamas. The Carib followed the same route in later centuries, and by the late fifteenth century they had overrun most Arawak settlements in the Lesser Antilles and were raiding parts of the Greater Antilles. Both Arawak and Carib peoples also made contact with the North American mainland.

The transfer of maize cultivation to South America after its domestication in Mesoamerica is suggestive of an early chain of contacts among Amerindian peoples, including the use of small boats along the Pacific coast. In the centuries after 100 there were significant ongoing maritime contacts between Pacific coast populations in South America and Mesoamerica. Mariners carried pottery, copper, gold and silver alloy jewelry, and textiles from the coast of Ecuador north in two-masted, balsa wood rafts that measured up to 36 feet (11 meters) in length. Rafts of this size could carry more than 20 metric tons of cargo and ten or more crew members. Travel north was facilitated by the favorable winds and currents of the Pacific, but these craft had the capacity to make the return trip carrying cargos of sacred spondylus shells as well. One important result of these contacts was the introduction of metallurgy to Mesoamerica after 500.

EUROPEAN EXPANSION, 1400–1550

While the pace and intensity of maritime contacts increased in many parts of the world before 1450, the epic sea voyages sponsored by the Iberian kingdoms of Portugal and Spain are of special interest because they began a maritime revolution that profoundly altered the course of world history. The Portuguese and Spanish expeditions ended the isolation of the Americas and increased the volume of global interaction.

Iberian overseas expansion was the product of two related phenomena. First, Iberian rulers had strong economic, religious, and political motives to expand their influence. And second, improvements in maritime and military technologies gave Iberians the means to master treacherous and unfamiliar ocean environments, seize control of existing maritime trade routes, and conquer new lands.

Motives for Exploration

The ambitions and adventurous personalities of the rulers of Portugal and Spain led them to sponsor voyages of exploration in the fifteenth century, but these voyages built upon four trends evident in Latin Europe since about the year 1000: (1) the revival of urban life and trade, (2) the unique alliance between merchants and rulers in Europe, (3) a struggle with Islamic powers for dominance of the Mediterranean that mixed religious motives with the desire for trade, and (4) growing intellectual curiosity about the outside world.

By 1450 the city-states of northern Italy had well-established trade links to northern Europe, the Indian Ocean, and the Black Sea, and their merchant princes had also sponsored an intellectual and artistic Renaissance. The Italian trading states of Venice and Genoa also maintained profitable commercial ties in the Mediterranean that depended on alliances with Muslims and gave their merchants privileged access to lucrative trade from the East. Even after the expansion of the Ottoman Empire disrupted their trade to the East, these cities did not take the lead in exploring the Atlantic. However, many individual Italians played leading roles in the Atlantic explorations.

In contrast, the history and geography of the Iberian kingdoms led them in a different direction. Muslim invaders from North Africa had conquered most of Iberia in the eighth century. Centuries of warfare between Christians and Muslims followed, and by 1250 the Iberian kingdoms of Portugal, Castile, and Aragon had reconquered all of Iberia except the southern Muslim kingdom of Granada (see Chapter 14). The dynastic marriage of Isabel of Castile and Ferdinand of Aragon in 1469 facilitated the conquest of Granada in 1492 and began the creation of Spain, sixteenth-century Europe's most powerful state.

Christian militancy continued to be an important motive for both Portugal and Spain in their overseas ventures. But the Iberian rulers and their adventurous subjects also sought material returns. With only a modest share of the Mediterranean trade, they were much more willing than the Italians to seek new routes to the rich trade of Africa and Asia via the Atlantic. Both kingdoms participated in the shipbuilding and the gunpowder revolutions that were under way in Atlantic Europe, and both were especially open to new geographical knowledge.

Portuguese Voyages

Portugal's decision to invest significant resources in new exploration rested on a well-established Atlantic fishing industry and a history of anti-Muslim warfare. When the Muslim government of Morocco in northwestern Africa showed weakness in the fifteenth century, the Portuguese attacked, conquering the city of Ceuta (say-OO-tuh) in 1415. The capture of this rich North African city gave the Portuguese better intelligence of the caravans bringing gold and slaves to Ceuta from African states south of the Sahara. Militarily unable to push inland and gain direct access to the gold trade, the Portuguese sought contact with the gold producers by sailing down the African coast.

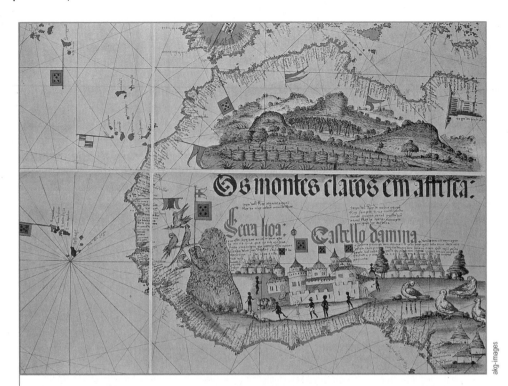

Portuguese Map of Western Africa, 1502 *This map shows in great detail a section of African coastline that Portuguese explorers charted and named in the fifteenth century. The cartographer illustrated the African interior, which was almost completely unknown to Europeans, with drawings of birds and views of coastal sights: Sierra Leone (Serra lioa), named for a mountain shaped like a lion, and the Portuguese Castle of the Mine (Castello damina) on the Gold Coast.*

Prince Henry (1394–1460), third son of the king of Portugal, had led the attack on Ceuta. Because he devoted the rest of his life to promoting exploration, he is known as **Henry the Navigator**. His official biographer emphasized Henry's mixed motives for exploration—converting Africans to Christianity, making contact with Christian rulers in Africa, and launching joint crusades with them against the Ottomans. Prince Henry also wished to discover new places and hoped that such new contacts would be profitable. Early explorations focused on Africa, but reaching India became the eventual goal of Portuguese explorers. While called "the Navigator," Henry himself never ventured far from home. Instead, he founded a center of research at Sagres (SAH-gresh) to study navigation that built on the pioneering efforts of Italian merchants and fourteenth-century Jewish cartographers. This center collected geographical information from sailors and travelers and sponsored new expeditions to explore the Atlantic. Henry's ships established permanent contact with the islands of Madeira in 1418 and the Azores in 1439.

Henry's staff also improved navigational instruments that had been first developed elsewhere. These instruments included the magnetic compass, first developed in China, and the astrolabe, an instrument of Arab or Greek invention that enabled mariners to determine their location at sea by measuring the position of the sun or the stars in the night sky. Even with such instruments, however, voyages still depended on the skill and experience of navigators.

Portuguese mariners also developed vessels appropriate for voyages of long-distance exploration. Neither the galleys in use in the Mediterranean, powered by large numbers of oarsmen, nor the three-masted ships of northern Europe with their square sails proved adequate for the Atlantic. The large crews of the galleys could not carry enough supplies for long voyages and the square-rigged northern vessels had trouble sailing at an angle to the wind. Instead, the voyages of exploration made use of a new vessel, the **caravel** (KAR-uh-vel), that was much smaller than either the largest European ships or the Chinese junks Zheng used to explore the Indian Ocean. Their size permitted them to enter shallow coastal waters and explore upriver, but they were strong enough to weather ocean storms. They could be equipped with triangular lateen sails that could take the wind on either side for enhanced maneuverability or fitted with square Atlantic sails for greater speed in a following wind. The addition of small cannon made them good fighting ships as well. The caravels' economy, speed, agility, and power justified a contemporary's claim that they were "the best ships that sailed the seas."[3]

Pioneering captains had to overcome the common fear that South Atlantic waters were boiling hot or contained ocean currents that would prevent any ship entering them from ever returning home. It took Prince Henry fourteen years—from 1420 to 1434—to coax an expedition to venture beyond southern Morocco. It would ultimately take the Portuguese four decades to cover the 1,500 miles (2,400 kilometers) from Lisbon to Sierra Leone (see-ER-uh lee-OWN); it then took only three additional decades to explore the remaining 4,000 miles (6,400 kilometers) to the southern tip of the African continent. With experience, navigators learned how to return home speedily by sailing northwest into the Atlantic to the latitude of the Azores, where they picked up prevailing westerly winds. The knowledge that ocean winds tend to form large circular patterns helped later explorers discover many other ocean routes.

During the 1440s Portuguese raids on the northwest coast of Africa and the Canary Islands began to return with slaves, finding a profitable market in an Iberia still recovering from the population losses of the Black Plague. The total number of Africans captured or purchased on voyages exceeded eighty thousand by the end of the century and rose steadily thereafter. However, the gold trade quickly became more important once the Portuguese contacted the trading networks that flourished in West Africa and reached across the Sahara. By 1457 enough African gold was coming back to Portugal for the kingdom to issue a new gold coin called the

---

[3]Alvise da Cadamosto in *The Voyages of Cadamosto and Other Documents*, ed. and trans. G. R. Crone (London: Hakluyt Society, 1937), 2.

cruzado (crusader), another reminder of how deeply the Portuguese entwined religious and secular motives.

While the Portuguese crown continued to sponsor voyages, the growing participation of private commercial interests accelerated the pace of exploration. In 1469 a prominent Lisbon merchant named Fernão Gomes purchased from the Crown the privilege of exploring 350 miles (550 kilometers) of African coast in return for a trade monopoly. He discovered the uninhabited island of São Tomé (sow toh-MAY) located on the equator and converted it to a major producer of sugar dependent on slaves imported from the African mainland. In the next century the island would serve as a model for the sugar plantations of Brazil and the Caribbean. Gomes also explored the **Gold Coast**, which became the headquarters of Portugal's West African trade.

The desire to find a passage around Africa to the rich spice trade of the Indian Ocean spurred the final thrust down the African coast. In 1488 **Bartolomeu Dias** became the first Portuguese explorer to round the southern tip of Africa and enter the Indian Ocean. In 1497–1498 **Vasco da Gama** sailed around Africa and reached India. Then, in 1500, ships on the way to India under the command of Pedro Alvares Cabral (kah-BRAHL) sailed too far west and reached the South American mainland. This discovery established Portugal's claim to Brazil, which would become one of the Western Hemisphere's richest colonies. The gamble that Prince Henry had begun eight decades earlier was about to pay off handsomely.

Spanish Voyages   In contrast to the persistence and planning behind Portugal's century-long exploration of the South Atlantic, haste and blind luck lay behind Spain's early discoveries. Throughout most of the fifteenth century, the Spanish kingdoms were preoccupied with internal affairs: completion of the reconquest of southern Iberia from the Muslims; consolidation of the territories of Isabel and Ferdinand; and the conversion or expulsion of religious minorities. The Portuguese had already found a new route to the Indian Ocean by the time the Spanish monarchs were ready to turn to overseas exploration.

The leader of the Spanish overseas mission was **Christopher Columbus** (1451–1506), a Genoese mariner. His four voyages between 1492 and 1504 established the existence of a vast new world across the Atlantic, whose existence few in "old world" Eurasia and Africa had ever suspected. But Columbus refused to accept that he had found unknown new continents and peoples, insisting that he had succeeded in finding a shorter route to the Indian Ocean.

As a young man Columbus gained considerable experience of the South Atlantic while participating in Portuguese explorations along the African coast, but he had become convinced there was a shorter way to reach the riches of the East than the route around Africa. By his reckoning (based on a serious misreading of a ninth-century Arab authority), the Canaries were a mere 2,400 nautical miles (4,450 kilometers) from Japan. The actual distance was five times as far.

Columbus proposed to reach Asia by sailing west, but Portuguese authorities twice rejected his plan. Columbus first proposed his expedition to Castile's able ruler Queen Isabel in 1486, but he was rejected. In 1492 his persistence was finally rewarded when the queen and her husband, King Ferdinand of Aragon, agreed to fund a modest expedition.

Columbus recorded in his log that he and his crew of ninety men "departed Friday the third day of August of the year 1492" toward "the regions of India." Their mission, the royal contract stated, was "to discover and acquire certain islands and mainland in the Ocean Sea." He carried letters of introduction from the Spanish sovereigns to Eastern rulers, including one to the "Grand Khan" (meaning the Chinese emperor), and brought along an Arabic interpreter to facilitate communication with the peoples of eastern Asia. The expedition traveled in three small ships, the *Santa María*, the *Niña*, and the *Pinta*. The *Niña* and the *Pinta* were caravels.

Unfavorable headwinds had impeded other attempts to explore the Atlantic west of the Azores, but Columbus chose a southern route because he had learned in his service with the Portuguese of west-blowing winds in the latitudes of the Canaries. In October 1492 the expedition reached the islands of the Caribbean. Columbus insisted on calling the inhabitants "Indians" because he believed that the islands were part of the East Indies. His second voyage to the Caribbean in 1493 did nothing to change his mind. Even when, two months after Vasco da Gama reached India in 1498, Columbus first sighted the mainland of South America on his third voyage, he stubbornly insisted it was part of Asia. But by then other Europeans were convinced that he had discovered islands and continents previously unknown to the Old World. Amerigo Vespucci's explorations, first on behalf of Spain and then for Portugal, led mapmakers to name the new continents "America" after him, rather than "Columbia" after Columbus.

To prevent disputes arising from their efforts to exploit their new discoveries and spread Christianity, Spain and Portugal agreed to split the world between them. The Treaty of Tordesillas (tor-duh-SEE-yuhs), negotiated by the pope in 1494, drew an imaginary line down the middle of the North Atlantic Ocean. The treaty allocated lands east of the line in Africa and southern Asia to Portugal; lands to the west in the Americas were reserved for Spain. Cabral's discovery of Brazil, however, gave Portugal a valid claim to the part of South America located east of the line.

Where would Spain's and Portugal's spheres of influence divide in the East? Given Europeans' ignorance of the earth's true size in 1494, it was not clear whether the Moluccas (muh-LOO-kuhz), whose valuable spices had been a goal of the Iberian voyages, were on Portugal's or Spain's side of the Tordesillas line. The size of the Pacific Ocean would determine the boundary. In the end, the Moluccas turned out to lie well within Portugal's sphere, as Spain formally acknowledged in 1529.

In 1519 **Ferdinand Magellan** (ca. 1480–1521) began his expedition to complete Columbus's interrupted westward voyage by sailing around the Americas and across the Pacific. Despite his death during this voyage on behalf of the king of Spain, Magellan was considered the first person to encircle the globe because a decade earlier he had sailed from Europe to the East Indies as part of an expedition sponsored by his native Portugal. His two voyages took him across the Tordesillas

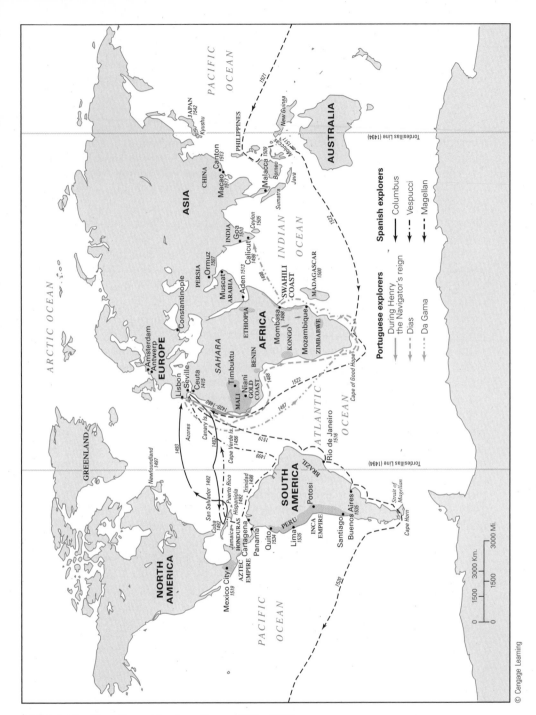

MAP 16.2 European Exploration, 1420–1542

Portuguese and Spanish explorers showed the possibility and practicality of intercontinental maritime trade. Before 1540 European trade with Africa and Asia was much more important than that with the Americas, but after the Spanish conquest of the Aztec and Inca Empires transatlantic trade began to increase. Notice the Tordesillas line, which in theory separated the Spanish and Portuguese spheres of activity.

line, through the separate spheres claimed by Portugal and Spain, and established the basis for Spanish colonization of the Philippines after 1564.

Although Columbus failed to find a new route to the East, the consequences of his voyages for European expansion were momentous. Those who followed in his wake laid the basis for Spain's large colonial empire in the Americas and for the empires of other European nations. In turn, these empires promoted the growth of a major new trading network whose importance rivaled and eventually surpassed the Indian Ocean network. Both the eastward and the westward voyages of exploration marked a tremendous expansion of Europe's role in world history.

ENCOUNTERS WITH EUROPE, 1450–1550

European actions alone did not determine the global consequences of these new contacts. The ways in which Africans, Asians, and Amerindians perceived these visitors and interacted with them influenced developments as well. Everywhere indigenous peoples evaluated the Europeans as potential allies or enemies, and everywhere Europeans attempted to insert themselves into existing commercial and geopolitical arrangements. In general, Europeans made slow progress in establishing colonies and asserting political influence in Africa and Asia, even while profiting from new commercial ties. In the Americas, however, Spain, Portugal, and later other European powers moved rapidly to create colonial empires. In this case the long isolation of the Amerindians from the rest of the world made them more vulnerable to the diseases that these outsiders introduced, limiting their potential for resistance and facilitating European settlement.

Western Africa Many along the West African coast were eager for trade with the Portuguese, since it offered new markets for exports and access to imports cheaper than those transported overland from the Mediterranean. This was evident along the Gold Coast of West Africa, first visited by the Portuguese in 1471. Miners in the hinterland had long sold their gold to traders, who took it to trading cities along the southern edge of the Sahara, where it was sold to traders who had crossed the desert from North Africa. Recognizing that they might get more favorable terms from the new visitors from the sea, coastal Africans were ready to negotiate with the royal representative of Portugal who arrived in 1482 to seek permission to erect a trading fort.

This Portuguese noble and his officers (likely including the young Christopher Columbus, who had entered Portuguese service in 1476) were eager to make a proper impression. They dressed in their best clothes, erected and decorated a reception platform, celebrated a Catholic Mass, and signaled the start of negotiations with trumpets, tambourines, and drums. The African king, Caramansa, staged his entrance with equal ceremony, arriving with a large retinue of attendants and musicians. Through an African interpreter, the two leaders exchanged flowery speeches pledging goodwill and mutual benefit. Caramansa then gave permission for a small trading fort, assured, he said, by the appearance of the Portuguese that they were honorable persons, unlike the "few, foul, and vile" Portuguese visitors of the previous decade.

Neither side made a show of force, but the Africans' upper hand was evident in Caramansa's warning that he and his people would move away, depriving their fort of food and trade, if the Portuguese acted aggressively. Trade at the post of Saint George of the Mine (later called Elmina) enriched both sides. The Portuguese crown had soon purchased gold equal to one-tenth of the world's production at the time. In return, Africans received large quantities of goods that Portuguese ships brought from Asia, Europe, and other parts of Africa.

After a century of aggressive expansion, the kingdom of Benin in the Niger Delta was near the peak of its power when it first encountered the Portuguese. Its oba (king) presided over an elaborate bureaucracy from a spacious palace in his large capital city, also known as Benin. In response to a Portuguese visit in 1486, the oba sent an ambassador to Portugal to learn more about these strangers. He then established a royal monopoly on trade with the Portuguese, selling pepper and ivory tusks (for export to Portugal) as well as stone beads, textiles, and prisoners of war (for resale as slaves at Elmina). In return, Portuguese merchants provided Benin with copper and brass, fine textiles, glass beads, and a horse for the king's royal procession. In the early sixteenth century, as the demand for slaves for the Portuguese sugar plantations on the nearby island of São Tomé grew, the oba first raised the price of slaves and then imposed restrictions that limited their sale.

Early contacts generally involved a mix of commercial, military, and religious exchanges. Some African rulers appreciated the advantage of European firearms over spears and arrows in conflicts with their enemies and actively sought them in trade. Because African religions were generally not exclusive, coastal rulers were also willing to test the value of the Christian practices promoted by the Portuguese. The rulers of Benin and Kongo, the two largest coastal kingdoms, accepted both Portuguese missionaries and soldiers as allies in battle to test the efficacy of the Christian religion and European weaponry.

However, Portuguese efforts to persuade the king and nobles of Benin to accept the Catholic faith ultimately failed. Early kings showed some interest, but after 1538 rulers declined to receive more missionaries. They also closed the market in male slaves for the rest of the sixteenth century. We do not know why Benin chose to limit its contacts with the Portuguese, but the result makes clear that these rulers had the power to control their contacts with Europeans.

Farther south, on the lower Congo River, relations between the kingdom of Kongo and the Portuguese began similarly but had a very different outcome. Like the oba of Benin, the manikongo (mah-NEE-KONG-goh) (king of Kongo) sent delegates to Portugal, established a royal monopoly on trade with the Portuguese, and expressed interest in Christian teachings. Deeply impressed with the new religion, the royal family made Catholicism the kingdom's official faith. But Kongo, lacking ivory and pepper, had less to trade than Benin. To acquire the goods brought by Portugal and to pay the costs of the missionaries, it had to sell more and more slaves.

Soon the manikongo began to lose his royal monopoly over the slave trade. In 1526 the Christian manikongo, Afonso I (r. 1506–ca. 1540), wrote to his royal "brother," the king of Portugal, begging for his help in stopping the trade because unauthorized Kongolese were kidnapping and selling people, even members of good families (see Diversity and Dominance: Kongo's Christian King). Alfonso's appeals for help received no reply from Portugal, whose interests were now concentrated in the Indian Ocean. Soon the effects of rebellion and the relocation of the slave trade from his kingdom to the south weakened the manikongo's authority.

Eastern Africa   Different still were the reactions of the Muslim rulers of the coastal trading states of eastern Africa. As Vasco da Gama's fleet sailed up the coast in 1498, most rulers gave the Portuguese a cool reception, suspicious of the intentions of visitors who painted Crusaders' crosses on their sails. But the ruler of one of the ports, Malindi, seeing the Portuguese as potential allies who could help him expand the city's trading position, provided da Gama with a pilot to guide him to India. The initial suspicions of the other rulers were proven correct seven years later when a Portuguese war fleet bombarded and looted most of the coastal cities of eastern Africa in the name of Christianity and commerce, while sparing Malindi.

Christian Ethiopia was another eastern African state that saw potential benefit in an alliance with the Portuguese. In the fourteenth and early fifteenth centuries, Ethiopia faced increasing conflict with Muslim states along the Red Sea. Emboldened by the rise of the Ottoman Turks, who had conquered Egypt in 1517 and launched a major fleet in the Indian Ocean to counter the Portuguese, the talented warlord of the Muslim state of Adal launched a furious assault on Ethiopia. Adal's decisive victory in 1529 reduced the Christian kingdom to a precarious state. At that point Ethiopia's contacts with the Portuguese became crucial.

For decades, delegations from Portugal and Ethiopia had explored a possible alliance based on their mutual adherence to Christianity. A key figure was Queen Helena of Ethiopia, who acted as regent for her young sons after her husband's death in 1478. In 1509 Helena sent a letter to "our very dear and well-beloved brother," the king of Portugal, along with a gift of two tiny crucifixes said to be made of wood from the cross on which Christ had died in Jerusalem. In her letter she proposed an alliance between her army and Portugal's fleet against the Turks; however, Helena's death in 1522 occurred before the alliance could be arranged. Ethiopia's situation then grew more desperate.

Finally, in 1539, when another woman ruler was holding what was left of the empire together, a small Portuguese force commanded by Vasco da Gama's son Christopher arrived to aid Ethiopia. With Portuguese help the Ethiopians renewed their struggle. While Muslim forces captured and tortured to death Christopher da Gama, their attack failed when their own leader was mortally wounded in battle.

DIVERSITY + DOMINANCE

Kongo's Christian King

The new overseas voyages brought conquest to some and opportunities for fruitful borrowings and exchanges to others. The decision of the ruler of the kingdom of Kongo to adopt Christianity in 1491 added cultural diversity to Kongolese society and in some ways strengthened the hand of the king. From then on Kongolese rulers sought to introduce Christian beliefs and rituals while at the same time Africanizing Christianity to make it more intelligible to their subjects. In addition, the kings of Kongo sought a variety of more secular aid from Portugal, including schools and medicine. But trade with the Portuguese introduced new social and political tensions, especially in the case of the export trade in slaves for the Portuguese sugar plantations on the island of São Tomé to the north.

Two letters sent to King João (zhwao) III of Portugal in 1526 illustrate how King Afonso of Kongo saw his kingdom's new relationship with Portugal and the problems that resulted from it. (Afonso adopted that name when baptized as a young prince.) After the death of his father in 1506, Afonso successfully claimed the throne and ruled until 1542. His son Henrique became the first Catholic bishop of the Kongo in 1521.

These letters were written in Portuguese and penned by the king's secretary, João Teixera (tay-SHER-uh), a Kongo Christian who, like Afonso, had been educated by Portuguese missionaries.

6 July 1526

To the very powerful and excellent prince Dom João, our brother:

On the 20th of June just past, we received word that a trading ship from your highness had just come to our port of Sonyo. We were greatly pleased by that arrival for it had been many days since a ship had come to our kingdom, for by it we would get news of your highness, which many times we had desired to know, ... and likewise as there was a great and dire need for wine and flour for the holy sacrament; and of this we had had no great hope for we have the same need frequently. And that, sir, arises from the great negligence of your highness's officials toward us and toward shipping us those things....

Sir, your highness should know how our kingdom is being lost in so many ways that we will need to provide the needed cure, since this is caused by the excessive license given by your agents and officials to the men and merchants who come to this kingdom to set up shops with goods and many things which have been prohibited by us, and which they spread throughout our kingdoms and domains in such abundance that many of our vassals, whose submission we could once rely on, now act independently so as to get the things in greater abundance than we ourselves; whom we had formerly held content and submissive and under our vassalage and jurisdiction, so it is doing a great harm not only to the service of God, but also to the security and peace of our kingdoms and state.

And we cannot reckon how great the damage is, since every day the mentioned merchants are taking our people, sons of the land and the sons of our noblemen and vassals and our relatives, because the thieves and men of bad conscience grab them so as to have the things and wares of this kingdom that they crave; they grab them and bring them to be sold. In such a manner, sir, has been the corruption and deprivation that our land is becoming completely depopulated, and your highness should not deem this good nor in your service. And to avoid this we need from these kingdoms [of yours] no more than priests and a few people to teach in schools, and no other goods except wine and flour for the holy sacrament, which is why we beg of your highness to help and assist us in this matter. Order your agents to send here neither merchants nor wares, because it is our will that in these kingdoms there should not be any dealing in slaves nor outlet for them, for the reasons stated above. Again we beg your highness's agreement, since otherwise we cannot cure such manifest harm. May Our Lord in His mercy have your highness always under His protection and may you always do the things of His holy service. I kiss your hands many times.

From our city of Kongo....

The King, Dom Afonso

18 October 1526

Very high and very powerful prince King of Portugal, our brother,

Sir, your highness has been so good as to promise us that anything we need we should ask for in our letters, and that everything will be provided. And so that there may be peace and health of our kingdoms, by God's will, in our lifetime. And as there are among us old folks and people who have lived for many days, many and different diseases happen so often that we are pushed to the ultimate extremes. And the same happens to our children, relatives, and people, because this country lacks physicians and surgeons who might know the proper cures for such diseases, as well as pharmacies and drugs to make them better. And for this reason many of those who had been already confirmed and instructed in the things of the holy faith of Our Lord Jesus Christ perish and die. And the rest of the people for the most part cure themselves with herbs and sticks and other ancient methods, so that they live putting

all their faith in these herbs and ceremonies, and die believing that they are saved; and this serves God poorly.

And to avoid such a great error, I think, and inconvenience, since it is from God and from your highness that all the good and the drugs and medicines have come to us for our salvation, we ask your merciful highness to send us two physicians and two pharmacists and one surgeon, so that they may come with their pharmacies and necessary things to be in our kingdoms, for we have extreme need of each and every one of them. We will be very good and merciful to them, since sent by your highness, their work and coming should be for good. We ask your highness as a great favor to do this for us, because besides being good in itself it is in the service of God as we have said above.

Moreover, sir, in our kingdoms there is another great inconvenience which is of little service to God, and this is that many of our people, out of great desire for the wares and things of your kingdoms, which are brought here by your people, and in order to satisfy their disordered appetite, seize many of our people, freed and exempt men. And many times noblemen and the sons of noblemen, and our relatives are stolen, and they take them to be sold to the white men who are in our kingdoms and take them hidden or by night, so that they are not recognized. And as soon as they are taken by the white men, they are immediately ironed and branded with fire. And when they are carried off to be embarked, if they are caught by our guards, the whites allege that they have bought them and cannot say from whom, so that it is our duty to do justice and to restore to the free their freedom. And so they went away offended.

And to avoid such a great evil we passed a law so that every white man living in our kingdoms and wanting to purchase slaves by whatever means should first inform three of our noblemen and officials of our court on whom we rely in this matter, namely Dom Pedro Manipunzo and Dom Manuel Manissaba, our head bailiff, and Gonçalo Pires, our chief supplier, who should investigate if the said slaves are captives or free men, and, if cleared with them, there will be no further doubt nor embargo and they can be taken and embarked. And if they reach the opposite conclusion, they will lose the aforementioned slaves. Whatever favor and license we give them [the white men] for the sake of your highness in this case is because we know that it is in your service too that these slaves are taken from our kingdom; otherwise we should not consent to this for the reasons stated above that we make known completely to your highness so that no one could say the contrary, as they said in many other cases to your highness, so that the care and remembrance that we and this kingdom have should not be withdrawn....

We kiss your hands of your highness many times.

From our city of Kongo, the 18th day of October,

The King, Dom Afonso

Questions for Analysis

1. What sorts of things does King Afonso desire from the Portuguese?
2. What is he willing and unwilling to do in return?
3. What problem with his own people has the slave trade created, and what has King Afonso done about it?
4. Does King Afonso see himself as an equal to King João or his subordinate? Do you agree with that analysis?

Source: From António Brásio, ed., *Monumenta Missionaria Africana: Africa Ocidental (1471–1531)* (Lisbon: Agência Geral do Ultramar, 1952), I: 468, 470–471, 488–491. Translated by David Northrup.

Portuguese aid helped the Ethiopian kingdom save itself from extinction, but a permanent alliance faltered because Ethiopian rulers refused to transfer their Christian affiliation from the patriarch of Alexandria to the Latin patriarch of Rome (the pope) as the Portuguese insisted.

As these examples illustrate, African encounters with the Portuguese before 1550 varied considerably, as much because of the strategies and leadership of particular African states as because of Portuguese policies. Africans and Portuguese might become royal brothers, bitter opponents, or partners in a mutually profitable trade, but Europeans remained a minor presence in most of Africa in 1550. By then the Portuguese had become far more interested in the Indian Ocean trade.

Indian Ocean States   Vasco da Gama did not make a great impression on the citizens of Calicut when he arrived on the Malabar Coast of India in May 1498. Da Gama's four small ships were far less imposing than the Chinese fleets that had called at Calicut sixty-five years earlier and no larger than many of the dhows that filled the harbor of this rich and important trading city. The samorin (ruler) of Calicut and his Muslim officials showed only mild interest in the Portuguese as new trading partners, since the gifts

Portuguese in India *In the sixteenth century Portuguese men moved to the Indian Ocean Basin to work as administrators and traders. This Indo-Portuguese drawing from about 1540 shows a Portuguese man speaking to an Indian woman, perhaps making a proposal of marriage.*

brought by da Gama had provoked derisive laughter. The twelve pieces of fairly ordinary striped cloth, four scarlet hoods, six hats, and six wash basins he presented had seemed inferior goods to those accustomed to the luxuries of the Indian Ocean trade. When da Gama tried to defend his gifts as those of an explorer, not a rich merchant, the samorin cut him short, asking whether he had come to discover men or stones: "If he had come to discover men, as he said, why had he brought nothing?"

Coastal rulers soon discovered that the Portuguese had no intention of remaining poor competitors in the rich trade of the Indian Ocean. Upon da Gama's return to Portugal in 1499, the jubilant King Manuel styled himself "Lord of the Conquest, Navigation, and Commerce of Ethiopia, Arabia, Persia, and India," thus setting forth the ambitious scope of his plans. Previously the Indian Ocean had been an open sea, used by merchants (and pirates) of all the surrounding coasts. Now the Portuguese crown intended to make it a Portuguese sea, the private property of Portugal alone.

The ability of little Portugal to assert control over the Indian Ocean stemmed from the superiority of its ships and weapons over those of the regional powers, especially the lightly armed merchant dhows. In 1505 a Portuguese fleet of eighty-one ships and some seven thousand men bombarded Swahili Coast cities. Indian ports were the next targets. Goa, on the west coast of India, fell to a well-armed fleet in 1510, becoming the base from which the Portuguese menaced the trading cities of Gujarat (goo-juh-RAHT) to the north and Calicut and other Malabar Coast cities to the south. The Portuguese also took the port of Hormuz, controlling entry to the Persian Gulf, in 1515, but Aden, at the entrance to the Red Sea, successfully resisted. The addition of the Gujarati port of Diu in 1535 consolidated Portuguese dominance of the western Indian Ocean.

Meanwhile, Portuguese explorers had reconnoitered the Bay of Bengal and the waters farther east. The city of Malacca (muh-LAH-kuh) on the strait between the Malay Peninsula and Sumatra became the focus of their attention. During the fifteenth century Malacca had become the main entrepôt for the trade from China, Japan, India, the Southeast Asian mainland, and the Moluccas. Among the city's more than 100,000 residents an early Portuguese visitor counted eighty-four different languages, including those of merchants from as far west as Cairo, Ethiopia, and the Swahili Coast of East Africa. Many non-Muslim residents of the city supported letting the Portuguese join its cosmopolitan trading community, perhaps hoping to offset the growing power of Muslim traders. In 1511, however, the Portuguese seized this strategic trading center outright with a force of a thousand fighting men, including three hundred recruited in southern India.

Force was not always necessary. On the China coast, local officials and merchants interested in profitable new trade with the Portuguese persuaded the imperial government to allow the Portuguese to establish a trading post at Macao (muh-COW) in 1557. Operating from Macao, Portuguese ships came to nearly monopolize trade between China and Japan.

In the Indian Ocean, the Portuguese used their control of major port cities to enforce an even larger trading monopoly. As their power grew, they required all spices, as well as goods carried between major ports like Goa and Macao, to be carried in Portuguese ships. In addition, the Portuguese tried to control and tax other Indian Ocean trade by requiring all merchant ships entering and leaving one of their ports to carry a Portuguese passport and pay customs duties. Portuguese patrols seized vessels that attempted to avoid these monopolies, confiscated their cargoes, and either killed the captain and crew or sentenced them to forced labor.

Reactions to this power grab varied. Like the emperors of China, the Mughal (MOO-gahl) emperors of India largely ignored Portugal's maritime intrusions, seeing their interests as maintaining control over their vast land possessions. The Ottomans responded more aggressively, supporting Egypt against the Christian intruders with a large fleet and fifteen thousand men between 1501 and 1509. Then, having absorbed Egypt into their empire, the Ottomans sent another large expedition against the Portuguese in 1538. Both expeditions failed because Ottoman galleys were no match for the faster, better-armed Portuguese vessels in the open ocean. However, the Ottomans continued to exercise control over the Red Sea and Persian Gulf.

The smaller trading states of the region were less capable of challenging Portuguese domination head-on, since rivalries among them impeded the formation of a common front. Some chose to cooperate with the Portuguese to maintain their prosperity and security. Others engaged in evasion and resistance. Two examples illustrate the range of responses among Indian Ocean peoples.

The merchants of Calicut put up some of the most sustained resistance. In retaliation, the Portuguese embargoed all trade with Aden, Calicut's principal trading partner, and centered their trade on the port of Cochin, which had once been a dependency of Calicut. Some Calicut merchants became adept at evading Portuguese naval patrols, but the price of resistance was the shrinking of Calicut's commercial importance as Cochin gradually became the major pepper-exporting port on the Malabar Coast.

The traders and rulers of the state of Gujarat farther north had less success in keeping the Portuguese at bay. At first they resisted Portuguese attempts at monopoly and in 1509 joined Egypt's failed effort to sweep the Portuguese from the Arabian Sea. But in 1535, finding his state at a military disadvantage due to Mughal attacks, the ruler of Gujarat made the fateful decision to allow the Portuguese to build a fort at Diu in return for their support. Once established, the Portuguese gradually extended their control, so that by midcentury they were licensing and taxing all Gujarati ships. Even after the Mughals (who were Muslims) took control of Gujarat in 1572, the Mughal emperor Akbar permitted the Portuguese to continue their maritime monopoly in return for allowing one ship a year to carry pilgrims to Mecca without paying the Portuguese any fee.

The Portuguese never gained complete control of the Indian Ocean trade, but their naval supremacy allowed them to dominate key ports and trade routes during the sixteenth century. The resulting profits from spices and other luxury goods had a dramatic effect. The Portuguese were now able to break the pepper monopoly long held by Venice and Genoa, who both depended on Egyptian middlemen, by selling at much lower prices. They were also able to fund a more aggressive colonization of Brazil.

In both Asia and Africa the consequences flowing from these events were startling. Asian and East African traders were now at the mercy of Portuguese warships, but their individual responses affected their fates. Some were devastated. Others prospered by meeting Portuguese demands or evading their patrols. Because the Portuguese sought to control trade routes, not occupy large territories, Portugal had little impact on the Asian and African mainlands, in sharp contrast to what was occurring in the Americas.

The Americas   In contrast to the trading empires the Portuguese created in Africa and Asia, the Spanish established a vast territorial empire in the Americas. This outcome had little to do with differences between the two kingdoms, even though Spain had a much larger population and greater resources. The Spanish and Portuguese monarchies had similar motives for expansion and used identical ships and weapons. Rather, the isolation of the Amerindian peoples made their responses to outside contacts different from those of African and Indian Ocean peoples. Isolation slowed the development of metallurgy and other militarily useful technologies in the Americas and also made these large populations more susceptible to new diseases introduced by Europeans. It was the spread of deadly new diseases, especially smallpox, among Amerindians after 1518 that weakened their ability to resist and facilitated Spanish and Portuguese occupation.

The first Amerindians to encounter Columbus were the Arawak of Hispaniola (modern Haiti and the Dominican Republic) in the Greater Antilles and the Bahamas to the north. They cultivated maize (corn), cassava (a tuber), sweet potatoes, and hot peppers, as well as cotton and tobacco. Although the islands did not have large gold deposits, and, unlike West Africans, the Arawak had not previously traded gold over long distances, the natives were skilled at working gold. While the Arawak at first extended a cautious welcome to the Spanish, they soon learned to tell exaggerated stories about gold deposits in other places to persuade them to move on.

When Columbus made his second trip to Hispaniola in 1493, he brought several hundred settlers who hoped to make their fortune, as well as missionaries who were eager to persuade the Amerindians to accept Christianity. The bad behavior of the settlers, including forced labor and sexual assaults on native women, provoked the Arawak to rebel in 1495. In this and later conflicts, steel swords, horses, and body armor led to Spanish victories and the slaughter of thousands. Thousands more were forced to labor for the Spanish. Meanwhile, cattle, pigs, and goats introduced by the settlers devoured the Arawak's food crops, causing deaths from famine and disease. A governor appointed by the Spanish crown in 1502 institutionalized these demands by dividing the surviving Arawak on Hispaniola among his allies as laborers.

The actions of the Spanish in the Antilles imitated Spanish actions and motives during the wars against the Muslims in Spain in previous centuries: they sought to serve God by defeating nonbelievers and placing them under Christian control—and to become rich in the process. Individual **conquistadors** (kon-KEY-stuh-dor) (conquerors) extended that pattern around the Caribbean as gold and indigenous labor became scarce on Hispaniola. New expeditions searched for gold and Amerindian laborers across the Caribbean region, capturing thousands of Amerindians and relocating them to Hispaniola as slaves. The island of Borinquen (Puerto Rico) was conquered in 1508 and Cuba between 1510 and 1511.

Following two failed expeditions to Mexico, Governor Velázquez of Cuba appointed an ambitious and ruthless nobleman, **Hernán Cortés** (kor-TEZ) (1485–1547), to undertake a new effort. Cortés left Cuba in 1519 with six hundred fighting men, including many who had sailed with the earlier expeditions, and most of the island's stock of weapons and horses. After demonstrating his military skills in a series of battles with the Maya, Cortés learned of the rich Aztec Empire in central Mexico.

The Aztecs (also called Mexica) had conquered their vast empire only during the previous century and a half, and many subject peoples were ready to embrace the Spanish as allies. They resented the tribute payments, forced labor, and large-scale human sacrifices demanded by the Aztecs. The Aztecs also had powerful native enemies, including the Tlaxcalans (thlash-KAH-lans), who became crucial allies of Cortés. Like the peoples of Africa and Asia when confronted by Europeans, Amerindian peoples, like the Tlaxcalans of Mexico, calculated as best they could the potential benefit or threat represented by these strange visitors. Individual Amerindians also made these calculations. Malintzin (mah-LEENT-zeen) (also called Malinche), a native woman given to Cortés shortly after his arrival in the Maya region, became his translator, key source of intelligence, and mistress. As peoples and as individuals, native allies were crucial to the Spanish campaign.

While the emperor **Moctezuma II** (mock-teh-ZOO-ma) (r. 1502–1520) hesitated to use force and attempted diplomacy instead, Cortés pushed toward the

The Execution of Inka Ruler Atahuallpa *Felipe Guaman Poma de Ayala, a native Andean from the area of Huamanga in Peru, drew this representation of the execution. While Pizarro sentenced Atahuallpa to death by strangulation, not beheading, Guaman Poma's illustration forcefully made the point that Spain had imposed an arbitrary and violent government on the Andean people.*

The Execution of the Inca King Atahualpa (woodcut), Poma de Ayala, Felipe Huaman (1526-1613)/Private Collection/The Bridgeman Art Library

Aztec capital of Tenochtitlan (teh-noch-TIT-lan). Spanish forces used firearms, cavalry tactics, and steel swords to great advantage in battles along their route. In the end Moctezuma agreed to welcome the Spaniards. As they approached his island capital, the emperor went out in a great procession, dressed in his finery, to welcome Cortés.

Despite Cortés's initial pledge that he came in friendship, Moctezuma was quickly imprisoned. The Spanish looted his treasury, interfered with the city's religious rituals, and eventually massacred hundreds during a festival. These actions provoked a mass rebellion directed against both the Spanish and Moctezuma. During the Spaniards' desperate escape, the Aztecs killed half the Spanish force and four thousand of Cortés's native allies. In the confusion Moctezuma also lost his life, either killed by the Spanish or in the Aztec attack.

The survivors, strengthened by Spanish reinforcements and aided by the Tlaxcalans, renewed their attack and captured Tenochtitlan in 1521. Their victory was aided by a smallpox epidemic that killed more of the city's defenders than did the fighting. One source remembered that the disease "spread over the people as a great destruction." Many Amerindians as well as Europeans blamed the devastating spread of this disease on supernatural forces. Cortés and other Spanish leaders then led expeditions to the north and south accompanied by the Tlaxcalans and other indigenous allies. Everywhere epidemic disease, especially smallpox, helped crush indigenous resistance.

Spanish settlers in Panama had heard tales of rich and powerful civilizations to the south even before the conquest of the Aztecs. During the previous century the Inka had built a vast empire along the Pacific coast of South America (see Chapter 15). As the empire expanded through conquest, the Inka enforced new labor demands and taxes and even exiled rebellious populations from their lands.

About 1525 the Inka ruler Huayna Capac (WHY-nah KAH-pak) died in Quito, where he had led a successful military campaign. Two of his sons then fought for the throne. In the end **Atahuallpa** (ah-tuh-WAHL-puh) (r. 1531–1533), the candidate of the northern army, defeated Huascar, the candidate of the royal court at Cuzco. As a result, the Inka military was decimated and the empire's political leadership weakened by the violence; at this critical time **Francisco Pizarro** (pih-ZAHR-oh) (ca. 1478–1541) and his force of 180 men, 37 horses, and two cannon entered the region.

Pizarro had come to the Americas in 1502 at the age of twenty-five to seek his fortune and had participated in the conquest of Hispaniola and in Balboa's expedition across the Isthmus of Panama to the Pacific. In the 1520s he gambled his fortune to finance the exploration of the Pacific south of the equator, where he learned of the riches of the Inka. With a license from the king of Spain, he set out from Panama in 1531 to conquer them.

Having seen signs of the civil war after landing, Pizarro arranged to meet the Inka emperor, Atahuallpa, near the Andean city of Cajamarca (kah-hah-MAHR-kah) in November 1532. With supreme boldness and brutality, Pizarro's small band of armed men attacked Atahuallpa and his followers as they entered an enclosed courtyard. Though surrounded by an Inka army of at least forty thousand, the Spaniards were able to use their cannon to create confusion while their swords brought down thousands of the emperor's lightly armed retainers and servants. Pizarro now replicated in Peru Cortés's strategy by capturing the Inka ruler.

Atahuallpa, seeking to guard his authority, quickly ordered the execution of his imprisoned brother Huascar. He also attempted to purchase his freedom. Having noted the glee with which the Spaniards seized gold and silver, Atahuallpa offered a ransom he thought would satisfy even the greediest among them: rooms filled to shoulder height with gold and silver. The Inka paid the ransom of 13,400 pounds (6,000 kilograms) of gold and 26,000 pounds (12,000 kilograms) of silver, but the Spaniards still executed Atahuallpa. With the unity of the Inka Empire already battered by the civil war and the death of the ruler, the Spanish occupied Cuzco, the capital city.

Nevertheless, Manco Inka, whom the Spanish had placed on the throne following the execution of his brother Atahuallpa, led a massive native rebellion in 1536. Although defeated by the Spanish, Manco Inka and his followers retreated to the interior and created a much-reduced independent kingdom that survived until 1572. The victorious Spaniards, now determined to settle their own rivalries, initiated a bloody civil war fueled by greed and jealousy. Before peace was established, this struggle took the lives of Francisco Pizarro and most of the other prominent conquistadors. Incited by the fabulous wealth of the Aztecs and Inka, conquistadors now extended their exploration and conquest of South and North America, dreaming of new treasures to loot.

CONCLUSION

The voyages of exploration undertaken by the Malays, Chinese, and Polynesians pursued diverse objectives. Malay voyagers were crucial participants in the development of the rich and varied commerce of Southeast Asia and initiated connections between these markets and Arabia and Africa. The great voyages of the Chinese in the early fifteenth century were motivated by an interest in trade, curiosity, and the desire to project imperial power. For the Polynesians, exploration opened the opportunity to both project power and demonstrate expertise while at the same time settling satellite populations that would relieve population pressures. The Vikings, Africans, and Amerindians all undertook long-distance explorations as well, although with fewer lasting consequences.

The projection of European influence between 1450 and 1550 was in some ways similar to that of other cultural regions in that it expanded commercial linkages, increased cross-cultural contacts, and served the ambitions of political leaders. But the result of their voyages proved to be a major turning point in world history. During those years European explorers opened new long-distance trade routes across the world's three major oceans, for the first time establishing regular contact among all the continents. As a result, a new balance of power arose in parts of Atlantic Africa, the Indian Ocean, and the Americas.

The rapid expansion of European empires and the projection of European military power around the world would have seemed unlikely in 1492. No European power matched the military and economic strength of China, and few could rival the Ottomans. Spain lacked strong national institutions, and Portugal had a small population; both had limited economic resources. Because of these limitations, the monarchs of Spain and Portugal allowed their subjects greater initiative as they engaged distant cultures.

The pace and character of European expansion in Africa and Asia were different than in the Americas. In Africa local rulers were generally able to limit European military power to coastal outposts and to control European trade. Only in the Kongo were the Portuguese able to project their power inland. In the Indian Ocean there were mature markets and specialized production for distant consumers when Europeans arrived. Here Portuguese (and later Dutch and British) naval power allowed Europeans to harvest large profits and influence regional commercial patterns, but most native populations continued to enjoy effective autonomy for centuries.

In the Americas, however, the terrible effects of epidemic disease and the destructiveness of the conquest led to the rapid creation of European settlements and the subordination of the surviving indigenous population. The Spanish and Portuguese found few long-distance markets and little large-scale production of goods that they could export profitably to Europe. The Americas would eventually produce great amounts of wealth, but this production of gold, silver, and sugar resulted from the introduction of new technologies, the imposition of oppressive new forms of labor, such as slavery, and the development of new roads and ports.

IMPORTANT EVENTS TO 1500

400–1300	Polynesian settlement of Pacific islands
770–1200	Viking voyages
Early 1300s	Mali voyages
1300s	Settlement of Madeira, Azores, Canaries
1405–1433	Voyages of Zheng He
1418–1460	Voyages of Henry the Navigator
1440s	First slaves from West Africa sent to Europe
1482	Portuguese at Gold Coast and Kongo
1486	Portuguese at Benin
1488	Bartolomeu Dias reaches Indian Ocean
1492	Columbus reaches Caribbean
1492–1500	Spanish conquer Hispaniola
1493	Columbus returns to Caribbean (second voyage)
1497–1498	Vasco da Gama reaches India
1498	Columbus reaches mainland of South America (third voyage)
1500	Cabral reaches Brazil
1505	Portuguese bombard Swahili Coast cities

1510	Portuguese take Goa
1511	Portuguese take Malacca
1513	Ponce de León explores Florida
1515	Portuguese take Hormuz
1519–1521	Cortés conquers Aztec Empire
1519–1522	Magellan expedition
1531–1533	Pizarro conquers Inca Empire
1535	Portuguese take Diu
1536	Rebellion of Maco Inca in Peru
1538	Portuguese defeat Ottoman fleet
1539	Portuguese aid Ethiopia

ISSUES IN WORLD HISTORY

Climate and Population to 1500

During the millennia before 1500, human populations expanded in three momentous surges. The first occurred after 50,000 B.C.E. when humans emigrated from their African homeland to all of the inhabitable continents. After that, the global population remained steady for several millennia. During the second expansion, between about 5000 and 500 B.C.E., population rose from about 5 million to 100 million as agricultural societies spread around the world (see Figure 1). Again population growth then slowed for several centuries before a third surge took world population to over 350 million by 1200 C.E. (Figure 2 shows population in China and Europe).

For a long time historians tended to attribute these population surges to cultural and technological advances. Indeed, a great many changes in culture and

technology are associated with adaptation to different climates and food supplies in the first surge and with the domestication of plants and animals in the second. However, historians have not found a cultural or technological change to explain the third surge, nor can they explain why creativity would have stagnated for long periods between the surges. Something else must have been at work.

Recently historians have begun to pay more attention to the impact of long-term variations in global climate. By examining ice cores drilled out of glaciers, scientists have been able to compile records of thousands of years of climate change. The comparative width of tree rings from ancient forests has provided additional data on periods of favorable and unfavorable growth. Such evidence shows that cycles of population growth

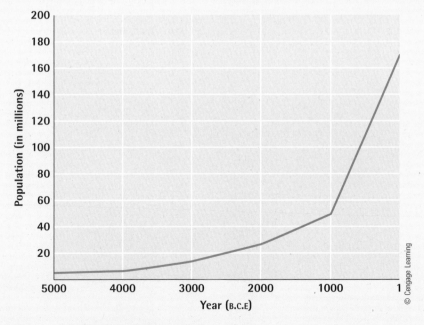

FIGURE 1   World Population, 5000–1 B.C.E.

and stagnation followed changes in global climate.

Historians now believe that global temperatures were above normal for extended periods from the late 1100s to the late 1200s c.e. In the temperate lands where most of the world's people lived, above-normal temperatures meant a longer growing season, more bountiful harvests, and thus a more adequate and reliable food supply. The ways in which societies responded to the medieval warm period are as important as the climate change, but it is unlikely that human agency alone would have produced the medieval surge. One notable response was that of the Vikings, who increased the size and range of their settlements in the North Atlantic, although their raids also caused death and destruction.

Some of the complexities involved in the interaction of human agency, climate, and other natural factors are also evident in the demographic changes that followed the medieval warm period. During the 1200s the Mongol invasions caused death and disruption of agriculture across Eurasia. China's population, which had been over 100 million in 1200, declined by a third or more by 1300. The Mongol invasions did not cause harm west of Russia, but climate changes in the 1300s resulted in population losses in Europe. Unusually heavy rains caused crop failures and a prolonged famine in northern Europe from 1315 to 1319.

The freer movement of merchants within the Mongol Empire also facilitated the spread of disease across Eurasia, culminating in the great pandemic known as the Black Death in Europe. The demographic recovery under way in China was reversed. The even larger population losses in Europe may have been affected by the decrease in global temperatures to their lowest point in many millennia between 1350 and 1375. After 1400 improving economic conditions enabled population to recover more rapidly in Europe than in China, where the conditions of rural life remained harsh.

Because many other historical circumstances interact with changing weather patterns, historians have a long way to go in deciphering the role of climate in history. Nevertheless, it is a factor that can no longer be ignored.

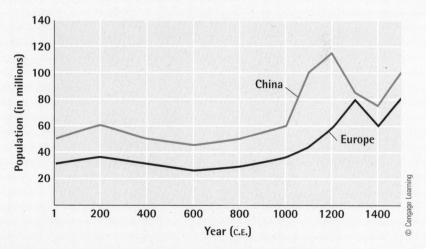

FIGURE 2 Population in China and Europe, 1–1500 c.e.

PART FIVE

◄——▼——►

THE GLOBE ENCOMPASSED, 1500–1750

CHAPTER 17
Transformations in Europe, 1500–1750

CHAPTER 18
The Diversity of American Colonial Societies, 1530–1770

CHAPTER 19
The Atlantic System and Africa, 1550–1800

CHAPTER 20
Between Europe and China, 1500–1750

CHAPTER 21
East Asia in Global Perspective

The decades between 1500 and 1750 witnessed a tremendous expansion of commercial, cultural, and biological exchanges around the world. New long-distance sea routes linked Europe with sub-Saharan Africa and the already established maritime networks of the Indian Ocean and East Asia. Spanish and Portuguese voyages ended the isolation of the Americas and created new webs of exchange in the Atlantic and Pacific. Overland expansion of Muslim, Russian, and Chinese empires also increased global interaction.

These expanding contacts had major demographic and cultural consequences. Domesticated animals and crops from the Old World transformed agriculture in the Americas, while Amerindian foods such as the potato became staples of the Old World diet. European diseases, meanwhile, devastated the Amerindian population, facilitating the establishment of large Spanish, Portuguese, French, and British empires. Europeans introduced enslaved Africans to relieve the labor shortage. Europe itself underwent significant change. The Protestant Reformation broke the hegemony of the Catholic Church and led to a long period of warfare. Nevertheless, Europe's population increased, its cities grew richer, and its economies gained strength. New colonial empires created by European powers in Africa, Asia, and the Americas contributed significantly to this mounting prosperity. While Spain, France, and England continued to dominate the continent, they faced stiff competition in distant markets from the Dutch, who had achieved independence and who introduced innovative economic institutions.

In Asia and Africa, unlike the Americas, the most important changes owed more to internal forces than to European actions. The Portuguese seized control of some important trading ports and networks in the Indian Ocean and pioneered new contacts with China and Japan. In time, the Dutch, French, and English expanded these profitable connections, but in 1750 Europeans were still primarily a maritime force. Asians and Africans generally retained control of their lands and participated freely in overseas trade.

The Islamic world saw the dramatic expansion of the Ottoman Empire in the Middle East and the establishment of the Safavid Empire in Iran and the Mughal Empire in South Asia. In northern Eurasia, Russia and China acquired vast new territories and populations, while a new national government in Japan promoted economic development and resisted foreign influence.

17

TRANSFORMATIONS IN EUROPE, 1500–1750

I n the late sixteenth century Dutch cities grew rich from long-distance trade routes that linked them to traditional markets of the Baltic and Mediterranean and to the newly opened markets of South Asia, Africa, and the Americas. Prosperity allowed the households of merchants, ship owners, and even artisans to consume luxuries with an extravagance previously limited to the nobility. They built substantial houses, wore rich clothing, and developed a taste for the exotic goods of distant lands.

By the 1570s tulips had been introduced from the Ottoman lands and were avidly collected by Dutch enthusiasts. Scarce and expensive, owning tulips became a sign of sophistication and wealth. The collectors and botanists who originally purchased tulips were joined by thousands of eager consumers who recognized potential profit in a rare commodity. As prices began to surge upward in the 1620s and then accelerated in the 1630s, a speculative market developed and ownership of tulip bulbs became a form of investment. Confident that prices would continue upward, individuals and partnerships paid extravagant amounts for bulbs. Between December 1636 and February 1637, for example, one of the most popular tulip varieties increased 12 times in value, becoming a speculative "bubble." At the peak of this frenzy the rarest bulbs sold for three times the annual income of a skilled carpenter. Then, in February 1637, the tulip market crashed as panicked investors rushed to unload their bulbs. If some had been made rich in this extraordinary trade, many of those who entered the market at the height of Tulipmania and paid peak prices were financially ruined.

While speculative bubbles roiled European economies throughout the early modern period, Europe was also growing richer and more powerful. The voyages of exploration and conquests of distant lands in the fifteenth and sixteenth centuries (see Chapter 16) had initiated a dramatic commercial expansion. Greater opportunities and accumulating wealth contributed to the growth of manufacturing and to the introduction of commercial and financial innovations such as stock markets, commercial insurance, and expanded property right protections. This was also an era of dramatic social and cultural change, as cities grew in power relative to the countryside and wealthy merchants, investors, and manufacturers grew in power relative to Europe's hereditary nobility.

During this period Europe also developed powerful and efficient armies and governments that large states elsewhere in the world feared, envied, and sometimes imitated. The balance of power was shifting slowly in Europe's favor. At the beginning of this era, the Ottomans threatened Europe, but by 1750, as the remaining chapters of Part V detail, Europeans had brought much of the world under their control. No single nation was responsible for this success. The Dutch eclipsed the pioneering Portuguese and Spanish; then the English and French bested the Dutch.

This was also a period of dynamic cultural change. At the beginning of this era a single Christian tradition dominated western Europe. By its end secular political institutions and economic interests had grown stronger, while Catholic and new Protestant churches were weakened by religious wars. Equally influential was the challenge to Christianity's long domination of European intellectual life posed by the Scientific Revolution and the first stages of the Enlightenment.

The years from 1500 to 1750 were not simply an age of progress for Europe. For many, the ferocious competition of European armies, merchants, and ideas was a wrenching experience. The growth of powerful states extracted a terrible price in death and destruction, and the Reformation brought widespread religious persecution and religious warfare as well as greater individual choice in religion. Women's fortunes remained closely tied to their social class, and few gained equality with men. The expanding economy benefited members of the emerging merchant elite and their political allies, but in an era of rising prices Europe's urban and rural poor struggled to survive.

CULTURE AND IDEAS

During the Reformation, theological controversies broke the religious unity of the Latin Church and contributed to long and violent wars. While the influence of classical ideas from Greco-Roman antiquity increased among better-educated Europeans, some bold thinkers challenged the authority of the ancients. They introduced new ideas about the motion of the planets and the natural world, encouraging others to challenge traditional social and political systems. Once in place, these new ideas would influence revolutionary political and social movements in the period after 1750. The transformative impact of these challenges to long-standing religious and intellectual beliefs was multiplied by the technology of the printing press and expanded European literacy.

Early Reformation   In 1500 the **papacy**, the central government of Latin Christianity, held an unrivaled position as Europe's preeminent religious and intellectual authority, although lax clerical standards and corruption were endemic. Recovered from a period when competing popes supported by rival secular rulers disputed control of the church, popes now exercised greater power, which was funded by larger donations and by income from the church's enormous real estate holdings. The construction of fifty-four new churches and other buildings in Rome demonstrated the church's power and showcased the artistic **Renaissance** then under way. The church leadership intended the size and splendor of the magnificent new Saint Peter's Basilica in Rome to glorify God, display the skill of Renaissance artists and builders, and enhance the standing of the papacy, but the vast expense of its construction and rich decoration also caused scandal.

The skillful overseer of the design and financing of the Saint Peter's Basilica was Pope Leo X (r. 1513–1521), a member of the wealthy Medici (MED-ih-chee) family of Florence, famous for its patronage of the arts. Pope Leo's artistic taste was superb and his personal life free from scandal, but he was more a man of action than a spiritual leader. During his papacy the church aggressively raised funds through the sale of **indulgences**—a forgiveness of the punishment due for past sins.

A young professor of sacred scripture, Martin Luther (1483–1546), saw this practice and other excesses as intolerably corrupt. As the result of a powerful religious experience, Luther had forsaken money and marriage for a monastic life of prayer, self-denial, and study. In his religious quest, he found personal consolation in a passage in Saint Paul's Epistle stating that salvation resulted from religious faith, not from "doing certain things." That passage led Luther to object to the way preachers emphasized giving money to the church more than they emphasized faith. He wrote to Pope Leo to complain of this abuse and challenged the preachers to a debate on the theology of indulgences.

This theological dispute was also a contest between two strong-willed men. Largely ignoring the theological objections, Pope Leo regarded Luther's letter as a challenge to papal power and moved to silence him. During a debate in 1519, a papal representative led Luther into open disagreement with church doctrines, for which the papacy condemned him. Blocked in his effort to reform the church from within, Luther burned the papal bull (document) of condemnation, rejected the pope's authority, and began the movement known as the **Protestant Reformation**.

Accusing those whom he called "Romanists" (Roman Catholics) of relying on "good works," Luther insisted that the only way to salvation was through faith in Jesus Christ. He further declared that Christian belief should be based on the word of God in the Bible and on Christian tradition, not on the authority of the pope. Luther's use of the printing press to spread his ideas won him the support of powerful Germans, who responded to his nationalist portrayal of an Italian pope seeking to beautify Rome with German funds.

Luther's denunciation of the ostentation and corruption of the church led others to call for a return to what they saw as authentic Christian practices and beliefs. John Calvin (1509–1564), a well-educated Frenchman who left the study of law for theology after experiencing a religious conversion, became an influential Protestant leader. Although Calvin agreed with Luther's emphasis on faith over works, he denied that human faith alone could merit salvation. Salvation, Calvin believed, was a gift God gave to those He "predestined." Calvin also went farther than Luther in curtailing the power of the clerical hierarchy and in simplifying religious rituals. Calvinist congregations elected their own governing committees and created regional and national synods (councils) to regulate doctrinal issues. Calvinists also displayed simplicity in dress, life, and worship, avoiding ostentatious living and stripping churches of statues, most musical instruments, stained-glass windows, incense, and vestments.

The Reformers appealed to genuine religious sentiments, but their successes and failures were also due to local political and economic conditions. It was no coincidence that German-born Luther had his greatest success among German speakers and linguistically related Scandinavians. Nor was it surprising that peasants and urban laborers sometimes defied their masters by adopting a different faith. Protestants were no more inclined than Roman Catholics to question male dominance in the church and the family, but most Protestants rejected the medieval tradition of celibate priests and nuns and advocated Christian marriage for all adults.

The Counter-Reformation and the Politics of Religion   Shaken by the intensity of the Protestant attack, the Catholic Church initiated a campaign of internal reforms. A church council meeting in Trent in northern Italy between 1545 and 1563 sought to distinguish Catholic doctrines from Protestant "errors" and reaffirmed the supremacy of the pope. It also reaffirmed traditional teaching, including salvation through both faith and good works, the importance of oral confession and penance, and the authority of ecclesiastical authorities in interpreting Scriptures. Bishops allied with the pope dominated the council and limited efforts to reform practices that Luther had condemned as corrupt. Seeking to address unpopular practices condemned by Protestants, the council called for bishops to reside in their dioceses and for dioceses to maintain a theological seminary to train priests.

The creation in 1540 of a new religious order, the Society of Jesus, or "Jesuits," by the Spanish nobleman Ignatius of Loyola (1491–1556) was among the most important events of the **Catholic Reformation** (also called the Counter-Reformation). Well-educated Jesuits helped stem the Protestant tide by their teaching and preaching, and they gained converts through missions in Asia, Africa, and the Americas (see Chapters 18 and Chapters 21).

Given the complexity and intensity stirred by the Protestant Reformation, it is not surprising that both sides persecuted and sometimes executed those of differing views. Bitter "wars of religion" would continue in parts of western Europe until 1648. The rulers of Spain and France were the chief defenders of the Catholic tradition against these Protestant challenges.

Charles V, Holy Roman Emperor and King of Spain, and his son, King Philip II, were the key political and military architects of the Counter-Reformation. To confront the Protestant threat in northern Europe, Charles V dialed back his campaign against the Ottoman Empire and North African Muslim states in the Mediterranean and sent large armies to central Europe and the low countries. As a result, Spain's enormous windfall of Western Hemisphere bullion went to subsidize this new military commitment rather than to develop its economy. Philip II continued his father's policies to their disastrous ends, the destruction of the Spanish Armada in 1588 and the recognition of effective Dutch independence in 1609.

In France the Calvinist opponents of the Valois dynasty gained the military advantage in the French Wars of Religion (1562–1598), but, in the interest of national unity, their leader Prince Henry of Navarre ultimately accepted the Catholic faith when he ruled as Henry IV of France. In pursuit of their objective of a union of church and state, Henry IV, his son King Louis XIII, and his grandson King Louis XIV supported the Catholic Church. Ultimately, Louis XIV revoked the Edict of Nantes (nahnt) by which his grandfather had granted religious freedom to his Protestant supporters in 1598.

In England King Henry VIII had initially been a strong defender of the papacy against Lutheran criticism. But when Henry failed to obtain a papal annulment of his marriage to Catherine of Aragon, who had not furnished him with a male heir, he challenged the papacy's authority over the English church. First the English archbishop of Canterbury annulled Henry's marriage in 1533 and then Parliament made the king head of an autonomous Church of England.

Like many Protestant rulers, Henry used this controversy to strengthen his authority and fatten his pocketbook by closing monasteries and convents and seizing their lands. He gave some land to his powerful allies and used profits from selling other land to pay for his new navy. While the king's power had grown at the expense of the Catholic Church, religious belief and practice were changing also. The new Anglican Church distanced itself from Catholic ritual and theology, but English Puritans (Calvinists who wanted to "purify" the church of all Catholic practices and beliefs) sought more. In 1603 they petitioned the first Stuart king, James I, to eliminate bishops.

Local Religion, Traditional Culture, and Witch-Hunts

Both in the Protestant north and the Catholic south the institutions that enforced religious orthodoxy were weakest in villages and small towns. In these settings, local religion commonly blended the rituals and beliefs of the established churches with local folk customs, pre-Christian beliefs, ancient curing practices, love magic, and the casting of spells. The vigor of these local religious traditions ebbed and flowed in response to the strength of national and regional religious institutions as well as to the experience of economic dislocations, famine, and epidemic. The widespread **witch-hunts** that Protestants and Catholics undertook in early modern Europe were linked to this widespread belief in white and black magic. Yet, these beliefs and fears would not have had such deadly consequences if many educated and powerful city dwellers did not believe in the Devil's power to affect society broadly.

Prevailing European ideas about the natural world blended two distinct traditions. One was an enduring belief in magic and spirits passed down orally from pre-Christian times. The second was the biblical teachings of the Christian and Jewish Scriptures, heard by all in church and read by growing numbers in vernacular translations. In the minds of most Europeans, Christian teachings about miracles, saints, and devils coincided easily with beliefs about magic, sorcery, and witchcraft rooted in the distant past.

It was widely assumed that some men and women possessed special powers derived from occult knowledge or, in some cases, from a compact with the Devil. In its benign version, practitioners could heal the sick, cause love to flourish, or guarantee good fortune. They could also solve disputes with masters or employers or punish enemies. The malevolent version was practiced by witches and warlocks who could cause infertility, illness, or death of loved ones and neighbors, cause crops or businesses to fail, or even provoke epidemics or droughts, sometimes in association with the Devil. While some theologians and jurists questioned the intellectual and religious underpinnings of these assumptions before the mid-sixteenth century, many European civil and ecclesiastical courts would continue to arrest and punish witches until the last decades of the seventeenth century.

Death to Witches *This woodcut from 1574 depicts three women convicted of witchcraft being burned alive in Baden, Switzerland. The scene on the left illustrates the purported witchcraft practiced by the three condemned women.*

The attribution of human triumphs and tragedies to supernatural causes persisted among Europeans long after the end of the witch hysteria. When an earthquake destroyed much of Lisbon, Portugal's capital city, in November 1755, for example, both educated and uneducated people saw the event as a punishment sent by God. A Jesuit stated that it was "scandalous to pretend that the earthquake was just a natural event." An English Protestant leader agreed, comparing Lisbon's fate with that of Sodom, the city that God destroyed because of the sinfulness of its citizens, according to the Hebrew Bible.

The extraordinary fear of witches that swept across Europe in the late sixteenth and seventeenth centuries was powerful testimony to the endurance of these beliefs among commoners and the governing class alike. The initial wave of mass witch-hunts began in Protestant regions of Germany in the last decades of the sixteenth century. They continued, and in some areas accelerated, during the Catholic Counter-Reformation. Before this hysteria ended, secular and church authorities had tried approximately 100,000 people and executed 60,000—some three-fourths of them women—for practicing witchcraft. The scale of these trials and executions reflected the participation of rulers and judicial authorities in this process. In German city-states like Würzburg and Bamberg, for example, local princes condoned and promoted the trials, thus contributing to hundreds of deaths, including scores of children, in the 1620s and 1630s.

Trial records make it clear that both the accusers and the accused believed that it was possible for angry, jealous, and evil individuals to use black magic in concert with the Devil to cause injury to others. Many, in fact, appear to have willingly admitted to having occult powers and even to consorting with the Devil, but some educated contemporaries wondered if these individuals were mentally unbalanced or simply very old. Clearly the common use of judicial torture by religious and secular authorities explains most of the confessions of accused witches.

The trials and executions transcended national and religious boundaries, but there were significant differences in regional and national practice, even in nations with similar religious traditions. While England's population was roughly five times larger than Scotland's, roughly three times as many witches were executed by the Scots, 120 in the two-year period 1661–1662 alone. The relatively strong Catholic states of France and Spain also had low numbers of executions relative to the German states. In Spain the Inquisition limited arrests of suspected witches based on testimony as early as 1526. The judges of the Parlement of Paris mandated appeals of convictions for witchcraft and began to overturn many before the wave of executions crested in northern Europe in the 1620s. Similarly, the more egalitarian and less centralized government of Holland also limited trials and executions. The death toll was highest in German states like Wurzburg and Bamberg, which executed 900 and 600, respectively, between 1626 and 1631. Sweden hosted one of the last mass campaigns of extirpation, executing 71 convicted witches on a single day in 1675. Even in Orthodox Russia, far from the center of this hysteria, 99 were accused of witchcraft and 10 were burned at the stake between 1622 and 1700.

While no single reason can explain the rise in witchcraft accusations and executions in early modern Europe, these events coincided with rising social tensions, growing rural poverty, and environmental strains. They also coincided with the violence of the wars in the Reformation period. While far from being a bizarre aberration, witch-hunts also reflected the tension between popular beliefs and practices and the ambitions of aggressive new religious and political institutions. The Reformation's focus on the Devil—the enemy of God—as the source of evil and the Catholic Counter-Reformation's effort to enforce orthodoxy both helped to propel the brutal persecutions of this period. In the eighteenth century the era of witchcraft persecutions effectively came to an end. The underlying beliefs were no longer credible among judges and rulers, while central governments were stronger and less willing to allow popular passions to sway the local administration of justice.

The Scientific Revolution   Europe's intellectual environment proved to be as tumultuous and unstable as its religious institutions and political organization in the early modern period. At the beginning of the period the writings of classic antiquity and the Bible were the most trusted guides to the natural world. The greatest authority on physics was Aristotle, a Greek philosopher who taught that the surface of the earth was composed of the two heavy elements, earth and water. The atmosphere was made up of two lighter elements, air and fire, which floated above the ground. Higher still were the sun, moon, planets, and stars, which, according to Aristotelian physics, were so light and pure that they floated in crystalline spheres. This division between the ponderous, heavy earth and airy, celestial bodies accorded perfectly with the commonsense perception that all heavenly bodies revolved around the earth.

Beginning in the sixteenth century, however, European understandings of the natural world were transformed by a new form of scientific inquiry that emphasized experimentation, careful observation, and mathematical calculations. While this period is often called the **Scientific Revolution**, many of the most influential intellectuals were committed Christians (both Catholic and Protestant) who sought to use science to reinforce religious beliefs. Nevertheless, as this movement gained momentum, and as the convincing results of the experimental method accumulated, European intellectual life became more secular and independent.

Nicholas Copernicus (1473–1543), a Polish monk and mathematician, helped initiate the new era when he proposed that the sun, not the earth, as taught by both religious and classical authorities, was the center of the universe (see Chapter 14). To escape anticipated controversies with church authorities, Copernicus delayed the publication of his heliocentric (sun-centered) theory until the end of his life. Once disseminated, his research began a revolution in the way human beings understood the structure of the heavens.

Other astronomers, including the Danish Tycho Brahe (1546–1601) and his German assistant Johannes Kepler (1571–1630), strengthened and improved on Copernicus's model, showing that planets actually move in elliptical, not circular, orbits. The most brilliant of the Copernicans was the Italian Galileo Galilei (gal-uh-LAY-oh gal-uh-LAY-ee) (1564–1642). In 1609 Galileo built a telescope through which he could look more closely at the heavens, thus confirming the speculations of other astronomers.

At first, those supporting the heliocentric universe faced formidable resistance because they directly challenged the intellectual synthesis of classical and biblical authorities. Many intellectual and religious leaders sought to suppress the new ideas. Most Protestant leaders, following the lead of Martin Luther, condemned the heliocentric universe as contrary to the Bible. Catholic authorities did not react immediately, but, when they did act, they proved more effective in suppressing the new scientific discoveries.

Copernicus died before his book was deemed heretical by Catholic authorities in 1616 and placed on the index of prohibited books. Yet his discoveries helped lead to a more accurate calendar issued in 1582 by Pope Gregory XIII and still used today. Galileo's empirical demonstration of the heliocentric theory led ultimately to a confrontation with the Inquisition. Galileo argued that the Bible was an inspired text, but, when science had established a demonstrable fact, the Bible should be interpreted to coincide with the evidence, since it could not be God's intention to mislead. Despite the controversial nature of his opinions, he continued to publish, pressing for a reliance on physical evidence and accurate measurement. Ordered before the Inquisition in 1633, Galileo was forced to recite and then sign a formal renunciation of his research. An apparent victory for tradition, this action put the Catholic Church in untenable opposition to a key early achievement of the new science.

Tycho Brahe at Work *Between 1576 and 1597, on the island of Ven between Denmark and Sweden, Tycho built the best observatory in Europe and set a new standard for accurate celestial observations before the invention of the telescope. This contemporary hand-colored engraving shows the Danish astronomer at work.*

Maritime Museum Kronberg Castle Denmark/ G.Dagli Orti/The Art Archive

Despite opposition from religious and secular authorities, printed books spread the new scientific ideas across Europe. Among the most influential intellectuals was the French philosopher and mathematician René Descartes (1595–1650), who furthered the development of physics and calculus when he demonstrated the usefulness of algebra to geometry. After hearing of Galileo's condemnation by the Inquisition in 1633, however, Descartes decided to delay publishing a potentially controversial work on optics and astronomy. In England, another intellectual, Robert Boyle (1627–1691), advocated tirelessly for the usefulness of the experimental method. One of the founders of modern chemistry, he developed an effective vacuum pump and demonstrated that air was necessary for the transmission of sound. He was also among the first to publish the details of experiments, including his failures. Boyle along with others became an enthusiastic missionary of mechanical science and played a key role in the 1662 founding of the Royal Society to promote science. Its motto is "Nullius in Verba" or "nothing in words," a demand that science should be based on experiments alone.

Another Englishman, the mathematician Isaac Newton (1642–1727), began his work in optics and mathematics, building on the work of Boyle and Descartes. He later carried Galileo's demonstration that the heavens and earth share a common physics to its logical conclusion by formulating mathematical laws that governed all physical objects. His Law of Gravity and his role in developing the calculus made him the most famous and influential man of his era, serving as president of the Royal Society from 1703 until his death.

As late as 1700 most religious and intellectual leaders viewed the new science with suspicion or hostility because it challenged long-established ways of thought. Yet most of the principal pioneers of the Scientific Revolution, including the Catholics Galileo and Descartes as well as the Protestant Boyle, were convinced that scientific discoveries and revealed religion could be reconciled. However, by showing that the Aristotelians and biblical writers held ideas about the natural world that were unsupportable in the face of scientific discovery, these pioneers opened the door to others who used reason and logic to challenge a broader range of unquestioned traditions and superstitions. The world of ideas was forever changed.

The Early Enlightenment   Advances in scientific thought inspired some to question the reasonableness of everything from agricultural methods to laws, religion, and social hierarchies. They believed that they could apply the scientific method to analyze economics, politics, and social organization and devise the best policies. This enthusiasm for an open and critical examination of human society energized a movement known as the **Enlightenment**. Like the Scientific Revolution, this movement was the work of a few "enlightened" individuals, who often faced bitter opposition from the political and religious establishments. Leading Enlightenment thinkers became accustomed to having their books burned or banned, and many spent long periods in exile to escape persecution.

Influences besides the Scientific Revolution affected the Enlightenment. The religious warfare and intolerance associated with the struggle between Catholicism and Protestantism undermined the moral authority of religion for many, and the efforts of church authorities to impugn the breakthroughs of science also pushed European intellectuals in a secular direction. The popular bigotry manifested in the brutal treatment of suspected witches also shocked many thoughtful people. The leading French thinker François-Marie d'Arouet, better known by his pen name Voltaire (1694–1778), declared: "No opinion is worth burning your neighbor for."

Although many circumstances shaped "enlightened" thinking, new scientific methods and discoveries provided the clearest model for changing European society. Accused of defamation by a powerful aristocrat, Voltaire fled to England, where he met many leading scientists as well as intellectual lights like Alexander Pope and Jonathan Swift. When he returned to France, he became a leading advocate for Newtonian physics in opposition to his countryman Descartes. In his publications he linked the prestige of the newly ascendant scientific method with his generation's mounting political and social concerns in these terms: "It would be very peculiar that all nature, all the planets, should obey eternal laws" but a human being, "in contempt of these laws, could act as he pleased solely according to his caprice." The English poet Alexander Pope (1688–1774) made a similar point in verse: "Nature and Nature's laws lay hidden in night; / God said, 'Let Newton be' and all was light."

The Enlightenment was more a frame of mind than a coherent movement. Individuals who embraced it drew inspiration from different sources and promoted different agendas. Its proponents were clearer about what they disliked than about what changes were necessary. Some thought an "enlightened" society could function with the mechanical orderliness of planets spinning in their orbits. Nearly all were optimistic that—at least in the long run—their discoveries would improve human beliefs and institutions. This faith in progress would help foster political and social revolutions after 1750, as Chapter 23 recounts.

While the Catholic Church and many Protestant clergymen opposed the Enlightenment, European monarchs selectively endorsed new ideas. Monarchs, ambitious to increase their power, found anticlerical intellectuals useful allies against church power and wealth. More predictably, monarchs and their reforming advisers discovered in the Enlightenment's demand for more rational and predictable policies justification for the expansion of royal authority and modern tax systems. Europe in 1750 was a place where political and religious divisions, growing literacy, and the printing press made it possible for these controversial and exciting new ideas to thrive despite opposition from ancient and powerful institutions.

SOCIAL AND ECONOMIC LIFE

There were large and important differences in the social structures of the major European nations, but there were many shared characteristics as well. European society was dominated by a small number of noble families who enjoyed privileged access to high offices in the church, government, and military and, in most cases, exemption from taxation. Below them was a much larger class of prosperous commoners that included many clergy, bureaucrats, professionals, and military officers as well as merchants, some artisans, and rural landowners. The vast majority of men and women were very poor. Laborers, journeymen, apprentices, and rural laborers struggled to earn their daily bread and often faced unemployment and privation. The poorest members of society lived truly desperate lives, surviving only through guile, begging, or crime. Women remained subordinated to men.

Some social mobility did occur, however, particularly in the middle. The principal engine of social change was an economy stimulated by long-distance trade and by access to the gold and silver of the Americas. Because cities enjoyed the benefits of this expansion disproportionally, they were the principal arenas of new opportunity and social mobility.

The Bourgeoisie   Europe's cities grew in response to expanding trade and rising commercial profits. In 1500 Paris was the only northern European city with over 100,000 inhabitants. By 1700 both Paris and London had populations over 500,000, and eleven other European cities contained over 100,000 people.

Urban wealth came from manufacturing and finance, but especially from trade, both within Europe and overseas. The French called the urban class that dominated

Iberfoto/The Image Works

The Fishwife, 1572 *Women were essential partners in most Dutch family businesses. This scene by the Dutch artist Adriaen van Ostade shows a woman preparing fish for retail sale.*

these activities the **bourgeoisie** (boor-zwah-ZEE) (burghers, town dwellers). Members of the bourgeoisie devoted long hours to their businesses and poured much of their profits back into them or into new ventures. Even so, most had enough money to live comfortably in large houses, and some had servants. In the seventeenth and eighteenth centuries wealthier consumers could buy exotic luxuries imported from the far corners of the earth—Caribbean and Brazilian sugar and rum, Mexican chocolate, Virginia tobacco, North American furs, East Indian cotton textiles and spices, and Chinese tea.

The Netherlands provides one of the best examples of this new bourgeois reality. The Dutch Republic was the most egalitarian European country in the early modern period. While it retained a nobility, wealthy commoners dominated its economy and politics. Manufacturers and craftsmen turned out a great variety of goods in their factories and workshops. The highly successful textile industry concentrated on the profitable weaving, finishing, and printing of cloth, leaving spinning to low-paid workers elsewhere. Along with fine woolens and linens, the Dutch also made cheaper textiles for mass markets. Factories in Holland refined

West Indian sugar, brewed beer made from Baltic grain, cut Virginia tobacco, and made imitations of Chinese ceramics (see Environment and Technology: East Asian Porcelain in Chapter 21). Free from the censorship and religious persecution imposed by political and religious authorities elsewhere, Holland's intellectuals were active in the Scientific Revolution and early Enlightenment, and its printers published books in many languages, including manuals with the latest advances in machinery, metallurgy, agriculture, and other technical areas. For a small nation that lacked timber and other natural resources, this was a remarkable achievement.

With a population of 200,000 in 1700, Amsterdam was Holland's largest city and Europe's major port. The Dutch developed huge commercial fleets that dominated sea trade in Europe and overseas. Around 1600 they introduced new ship designs, including the *fluit*, or "flyboat," a large-capacity cargo ship that was inexpensive to build and required only a small crew. As their trade with distant markets developed they introduced another successful type of merchant ship, the heavily armed "East Indiaman," that helped the Dutch establish their supremacy in the Indian Ocean. By one estimate, the Dutch conducted more than half of all the oceangoing commercial shipping in the world in the seventeenth century (for details see Chapters 20 and Chapters 21). Dutch mapmaking supported these distant commercial connections (see Environment and Technology: Mapping the World).

Amsterdam also served as Europe's financial center. Seventeenth-century Dutch banks had such a reputation for security that wealthy individuals and governments from all over western Europe entrusted them with their money. The banks in turn invested these funds in real estate, loaned money to factory owners and governments, and provided capital for commercial operations overseas.

Individuals seeking higher returns than those provided by banks could purchase shares in a **joint-stock company**, a sixteenth-century forerunner of the modern corporation. Individuals bought and sold shares in specialized financial markets called **stock exchanges**, an Italian innovation transferred to the cities of northwestern Europe in the sixteenth century. The lively Amsterdam Exchange, begun as an outdoor market around 1530, moved into impressive new quarters in 1611. It remained Europe's greatest stock market in the seventeenth and eighteenth centuries.

The Dutch government played a direct role in this process by pioneering the creation of monopoly commercial enterprises like the Dutch East and West India Companies, which were granted monopolies for trade with the East and West Indies. France and England soon chartered monopoly trading companies of their own. These companies then sold shares to individuals to raise large sums for overseas enterprises while spreading the risks (and profits) among many investors (see Chapter 19). In this same era insurance companies were developed to insure long-distance voyages against loss; by 1700, purchasing insurance had become standard commercial practice.

Governments also sought to promote trade by investing in infrastructure. The Dutch built numerous canals to speed transport, lower costs, and drain the lowlands for agriculture. Other governments financed canals as well, including systems of locks to raise barges up over hills. One of the most important was the 150-mile (240-kilometer) Canal du Midi built by the French government between 1661 and 1682 to link the Atlantic and the Mediterranean.

After 1650 the Dutch faced growing competition from the English, who were developing their own close association between business and government. With government support, the English merchant fleet doubled between 1660 and 1700, and foreign trade rose by 50 percent. As a result, state revenue from customs duties tripled. In a series of wars (1652–1678) the English government used its new naval might to break Dutch dominance in overseas trade and to extend England's colonial empire.

Some successful members of the bourgeoisie in England and France chose to use their wealth to raise their social status. By retiring from their businesses and buying country estates, they could become members of the **gentry**. They loaned money to impoverished peasants and to members of the nobility and in time increased their land ownership. Some sought aristocratic husbands for their daughters. The old nobility found such alliances attractive because of the large dowries that the bourgeoisie provided. Even in colonial settings, a small number of affluent and ambitious families purchased titles of nobility. While this kind of social mobility satisfied the desire for elevated status in hierarchical societies, it also removed the capital of the most successful bourgeoisie families from commerce and production.

Peasants and Laborers

Serfdom, which bound men and women to land owned by a local lord, had begun to decline after the great plague of the mid-fourteenth century. As population recovered in western Europe, the competition for work exerted a downward pressure on wages, reducing the usefulness of serfdom and other forms of forced labor to landowners. While there had been a brief expansion of slavery in southern Europe with the introduction of African slaves around 1500, Europeans shipped nearly all African slaves to the Americas after 1600. In eastern Europe, on the other hand, forced labor endured. Large-scale landowners in Russia and elsewhere who produced grains for growing urban markets continued to rely on the bound labor of serfs to ensure their profits.

There is much truth in the argument that western Europe continued to depend on unfree labor but kept it at a distance in its colonies rather than at home (see Chapters 18 and Chapters 19). In any event, legal freedom did little to make a peasant's life safer and more secure. The efficiency of European agriculture had improved little since 1300. As a result, bad years brought famine; good ones provided only small surpluses. Indeed, the material conditions experienced by the poor in western Europe may have worsened between 1500 and 1750 as the result of warfare, environmental degradation, and economic contractions. Europeans also felt the adverse effects of a century of relatively cool climate that began in the 1590s. During this **Little Ice Age** average temperatures fell only a few degrees, but the effects were startling (see Issues in World History: Climate and Population to 1500).

By 1700 high-yielding new crops from the Americas were helping the rural poor avoid starvation. Once grown only as famine foods, potatoes and maize (corn) became staples for the rural poor in the eighteenth century. Potatoes sustained life in northeastern and central Europe and in Ireland, while poor peasants in Italy subsisted on maize. The irony is that all of these lands were major exporters of wheat, but the laborers who planted and harvested this crop could not afford to eat it.

Other rural residents made their living as miners, lumber-jacks, and charcoal makers. The expanding iron industry in England provided work for all three, but the high consumption of wood fuel caused serious **deforestation**. One early-seventeenth-century observer lamented: "Within man's memory, it was held impossible to have any want of wood in England. But ... at present, through the great consuming of wood ... and the neglect of planting of woods, there is a great scarcity of wood throughout the whole kingdom."[1] Eventually, the high price of wood and charcoal encouraged smelters to use coal as an alternative fuel. England's coal mining increased twelvefold, from 210,000 tons in 1550 to 2,500,000 tons in 1700 and nearly 5 million tons by 1750.

France was more heavily forested than England, but increasing deforestation prompted Jean Baptiste Colbert, France's minister of finance, to predict that "France will perish for lack of wood." In Sweden and Russia, where wood fueled the furnaces of iron foundries, deforestation became an economic threat in the late eighteenth century as iron production rose.

Even in the prosperous Dutch towns, half of the population lived in acute poverty. Authorities estimated that permanent city residents who were too poor to tax, the "deserving poor," made up 10 to 20 percent of the population. That calculation did not include the large numbers of "unworthy poor"—recent migrants from impoverished rural areas, peddlers traveling from place to place, and beggars (many with horrible deformities and sores) who tried to survive on charity. The pervasive poverty of rural and urban Europe shocked those who were not hardened to it. In about 1580 the mayor of the French city of Bordeaux (bor-DOH) asked a group of visiting Amerindian chiefs what impressed them most about European cities. The chiefs are said to have expressed astonishment at the disparity between the fat, well-fed people and the poor, half-starved men and women in rags. Why, the visitors wondered, did the poor not grab the rich by the throat or set fire to their homes?[2]

In fact, misery provoked many rebellions in early modern Europe. For example, in 1525 peasant rebels in the Alps attacked both nobles and the clergy as representatives of the privileged and landowning classes. They had no love for merchants either, whom they denounced for lending at interest and charging high prices. Rebellions multiplied as rural conditions worsened. In southwestern France alone some 450 uprisings occurred between 1590 and 1715, many of them set off by food shortages and tax increases. A rebellion in southern France in 1670 began when a mob of townswomen attacked the tax collector. It quickly spread to the country, where peasant leaders cried, "Death to the people's oppressors!" Authorities dealt severely with such revolts and executed or maimed their leaders.

Women and the Family   Women's social and economic status was closely tied to that of their husbands. In some nations a woman could inherit a throne (see Table 17.1 on page 454 for examples)—in the absence of a male heir. These rare exceptions do not negate the rule that women everywhere ranked below men, but one should also not forget that class and wealth

---

[1]Quoted by Carlo M. Cipolla, "Introduction," *The Fontana Economic History of Europe*, vol. 2, *The Sixteenth and Seventeenth Centuries* (Glasgow: Collins/Fontana Books, 1976), 11–12.

[2]Michel de Montaigne, *Essais* (1588), ch. 31, "Des Cannibales."

ENVIRONMENT + TECHNOLOGY

Mapping the World

In 1602 in China the Jesuit missionary Matteo Ricci printed an elaborate map of the world. Working from maps produced in Europe and incorporating the latest knowledge gathered by European maritime explorers, Ricci introduced two changes to make the map more appealing to his Chinese hosts. He labeled it in Chinese characters, and he split his map down the middle of the Atlantic so that China lay in the center. This version pleased the Chinese elite, who considered China the "Middle Kingdom" surrounded by lesser states. A copy of Ricci's map in six large panels adorned the emperor's Beijing palace.

The stunningly beautiful maps and globes of sixteenth-century Europe were the most complete, detailed, and useful representations of the earth that any society had ever produced. The best mapmaker of the century was Gerhard Kremer, who is remembered as Mercator (the merchant) because his maps were so useful to European ocean traders. By incorporating the latest discoveries and scientific measurements, Mercator could depict the outlines of the major continents in painstaking detail, even if their interiors were still largely unknown to outsiders.

To represent the spherical globe on a flat map, Mercator drew the lines of longitude as parallel lines. Because such lines actually meet at the poles, Mercator's projection greatly exaggerated the size of every landmass and body of water distant from the equator. However, Mercator's rendering offered a very practical advantage: sailors could plot their course by drawing a straight line between their point of departure and their destination. Because of this useful feature, the Mercator projection of the world remained in common use until quite recently. To some extent, its popularity came from the exaggerated size this projection gave to Europe. Like the Chinese, Europeans liked to think of themselves as at the center of things. Europeans also understood their true geographical position better than people in any other part of the world.

---

defined a woman's position in life more than her sex. The wife or daughter of a rich man, for example, though often closely confined, had a materially better life than any poor man. Sometimes a single woman might secure a position of responsibility, as in the case of women from good families who headed convents in Catholic countries. But while unmarried women were routinely controlled by fathers and married women controlled by husbands, some widows independently controlled substantial properties and other assets.

In contrast to the arranged marriages that prevailed in much of the rest of the world, young men and women in early modern Europe often chose their own spouses, but privileged families were much more likely to arrange marriages than poor ones. Royal and noble families carefully plotted the suitability of their children's marriages in furthering family interests. Bourgeois parents were less likely to force their children into arranged marriages, but the fact that nearly all found spouses within their own social class strongly suggests that the bourgeoisie promoted marriages that advanced their social aspirations or furthered their business interests.

Dutch World Map, 1641 *It is easy to see why the Chinese would not have liked to see their empire at the far right edge of this widely printed map. Besides the distortions caused by the Mercator projection, geographical ignorance exaggerates the size of North America and Antarctica.*

World Map, from 'Le Theatre du Monde' or 'Nouvel Atlas', 1645 (coloured engraving), Blaeu, Willem (1571-1638)/ Bibliotheque des Arts Decoratifs, Paris, France/Archives Charmet/The Bridgeman Art Library

Europeans also married later than people in other cultural regions. Sons often put off marriage until they could live on their own. Many young women also had to work—helping their parents, as domestic servants, or in some other capacity—to save money for the dowry expected by potential husbands. A dowry was the money and household goods—the amount varied by social class—that enabled a young couple to begin marriage independent of their parents. As a result, the typical groom in western and central Europe could not hope to marry before his late twenties, and his bride would be a few years younger—in contrast to the rest of the world, where people usually married in their teens.

Besides enabling young people to be independent of their parents, the late age of marriage in early modern Europe also held down the birthrate and thus limited family size. Even so, about one-tenth of urban births were to unmarried women, often servants. Many mothers, unable to provide for these infants, left them on the doorsteps of churches, convents, or rich households to be raised as "orphans." Many neglected children perished; and many young women newly arrived in Europe's fast-growing cities from the countryside were forced into brothels or begging by their poverty.

POLITICAL INNOVATIONS

The monarchs of early modern Europe occupied the apex of the social order, were arbitrators of the intellectual and religious conflicts of their day, and exercised important influence on the economies of their realms. Many European monarchs introduced reforms that achieved a higher degree of political centralization and order in this era, but their ambitions and rivalries could also provoke destructive and costly conflicts. In some cases, civil and international conflicts forced monarchs to find common ground with potential enemies or introduce political innovations that strengthened their nations. During this period, political leadership in Europe passed from Spain to the Netherlands and then to England and France.

State   There was a great deal of political diversity in early modern
Development   Europe. City-states and principalities abounded, either inde-
                        pendently or bound together in federations, of which the
Holy Roman Empire of the German heartland was the most notable example. There were also a small number of republics. At the same time a number of strong monarchies emerged and developed national identities.

Dynastic ambitions and historical circumstances combined to favor and then block the creation of an integrated European empire in the early sixteenth century. Electors of the Holy Roman Empire chose Charles V (r. 1519–1556) to be emperor in 1519. Like his predecessors for three generations, Charles belonged to the powerful **Habsburg** (HABZ-berg) family of Austria. Three years earlier he had inherited the kingdoms of Castile and Aragon, becoming the first monarch of Spain as Charles I. With these vast resources, Charles sought to turn back the advance of Islam on Europe's Mediterranean flank while contending with France for dominance of Italy. Charles and his allies did stop the Ottomans at the gates of Vienna in 1529, but the Ottoman Empire as well as North African Muslim states continued to attack his territories in Italy and Spain, supported at times by the Christian king Francis I of France, who was more interested in defeating Charles's ambitions than in defending Christian Europe.

With the beginning of the Reformation, Charles redirected his attention and his resources northward in support of the Counter-Reformation. Charles's defense of Catholic doctrine in the imperial Diet (assembly) was opposed by German princes swayed by Luther's appeals to German nationalism. These disputes led to open warfare in 1546 (the German Wars of Religion). Even though Charles could rely on the great wealth transferred to Spain from the conquests of Mexico and Peru (see Chapter 18), these costly and destructive religious wars drained his treasury and forced him to accept a stalemate in the Mediterranean with the Ottomans.

In the end the ambitions of Charles V were overwhelmed by the scale of his challenges, despite his enormous resources. In the Peace of Augsburg (1555) he recognized the right of German princes to choose whether Catholicism or Lutheranism would prevail in their particular states. He also accepted that Protestant princes would keep any church lands they had seized. This triumph of religious diversity ended Charles's political ambitions and put off German political unification for three centuries. In poor health and exhausted by his efforts, Charles decided to abdicate both the Holy Roman and Spanish thrones and retire to a monastery in 1556.

Charles V's son, Philip II, inherited his father's European territories in the low countries and Italy. Defending these legacies would drain his resources for decades.

He also inherited the throne of Spain with its rich American empire. In 1580 Philip inherited the throne of Portugal as well, adding Brazil and Portuguese colonies in Africa and Asia to his Spanish possessions. Ruler of sixteenth-century Europe's mightiest state, Philip II aggressively pursued the geopolitical policies that had thwarted his father. For a time, an accelerating flow of silver and gold from American colonies filled his treasury, but Philip's ambitions outstripped the flow of treasure, and he followed his father's practice of borrowing against future bullion shipments.

In the end, Philip's wars against the Ottomans, northern European Protestants, and rebellious Dutch subjects squandered the great wealth flowing through Iberian ports from the colonial empire, leading to four bankruptcies during his reign. Philip's ambitious military campaigns also increased his dependence on the Spanish nobility, which directed his military forces. While Spain's aristocracy made up only 3 percent of the population, it controlled 97 percent of the land in 1600 and was exempt from normal taxation. The nation's commoners, on the other hand, faced high sales taxes on manufacturing and commerce. In the end, Philip's commitments consumed the great wealth of his empire, leaving Spain unprepared to maintain its early domination of the Atlantic when faced by sustained challenges from the Dutch, English, and French.

American bullion shipments dramatically increased the money supply in Europe. In Spain the effects of the resulting inflation (rising prices) made the nation's products uncompetitive, so that goods manufactured in France, Italy, or other European countries were cheaper than goods made in Spain. In this distorted market, Spanish guilds and merchants lost ground while the pace of technological innovation and commercial expansion grew across northern Europe. By 1700 most goods imported into Spain's colonies were of foreign origin. A Spanish saying captured the problem: American silver was like rain on the roof—it poured down and washed away.

Philip's effort to seal Spain off from the Protestant Reformation and the intellectual tumult of the Scientific Revolution also imposed economic costs. He ordered the borders closed to all foreign publications not licensed by the Catholic Church and commanded all Spanish students to leave foreign universities and return home. Spain had longsuffered from the negative intellectual and economic effects of the expulsions of Jews and Muslims in the period of Ferdinand and Isabel, and now Philip's commitment to the Counter-Reformation further isolated the nation's intellectuals from the debates and innovations of the era.

Despite Spain's problems, its rulers, like those of France and England, enjoyed some success promoting national political unification and religious unity. The most successful rulers reduced the autonomy of the church and the nobility by making them part of a unified national structure with the monarch at its head. The imposition of royal power over religious institutions in the sixteenth century was stormy, but the eventual outcome was clear. Bringing the nobles and other powerful interests into a centralized political system took longer and led to more diverse outcomes.

The Monarchies of England and France　　Over the course of the seventeenth century, the monarchs of England and France faced intense conflict with powerful rivals. Religion was never absent as an issue in these struggles, but the very different constitutional outcomes they produced in these two countries were of more significance in the long run.

To evade any check on his power, King Charles I of England (see Table 17.1) ruled for eleven years without summoning Parliament, his kingdom's representative

TABLE 17.1 │ RULERS IN EARLY MODERN WESTERN EUROPE

Spain	France	England/Great Britain
Habsburg Dynasty	**Valois Dynasty**	**Tudor Dynasty**
Charles I (1516–1556)	Francis I (1515–1547)	Henry VIII (1509–1547)
(Holy Roman Emperor	Henry II (1547–1559)	Edward VI (1547–1553)
Charles V)	Francis II (1559–1560)	Mary I (1553–1558)
Philip II (1556–1598)	Charles IX (1560–1574)	Elizabeth I (1558–1603)
	Henry III (1574–1589)	
	Bourbon Dynasty	**Stuart Dynasty**
Philip III (1598–1621)	Henry IV (1589–1610)[a]	James I (1603–1625)
Philip IV (1621–1665)	Louis XIII (1610–1643)	Charles I (1625–1649)[a,b]
Charles II (1665–1700)	Louis XIV (1643–1715)	(Puritan Republic,
		1649–1660)
		Charles II (1660–1685)
		James II (1685–1688)[b]
		William III (1689–1702)
		and Mary II
Bourbon Dynasty		(1689–1694)
Philip V (1700–1746)		Anne (1702–1714)
	Hanoverian Dynasty	
	Louis XV (1715–1774)	George I (1714–1727)
Ferdinand VI (1746–1759)		George II (1727–1760)

[a]Died a violent death.
[b]Was overthrown.

© Cengage Learning

body. Lacking Parliament's consent to new taxes, he raised funds by coercing "loans" from wealthy subjects and applying existing tax laws more broadly. In 1640 a rebellion in Scotland forced him to summon Parliament to approve new taxes to pay for an army. Noblemen and churchmen sat in the House of Lords while representatives from towns and counties sat in the House of Commons. Before it would authorize new taxes, Parliament insisted on strict guarantees that the king would never again ignore the body's traditional rights. King Charles refused and attempted to arrest his critics in the House of Commons in 1642, plunging the kingdom into the **English Civil War.**

Militarily defeated in 1648, Charles refused to compromise. A year later a "Rump" Parliament purged of his supporters ordered his execution. Parliament then replaced the monarchy with a republic led by the Puritan general Oliver Cromwell, who ruled until his death in 1658. Cromwell expanded England's presence overseas and imposed firm control over Ireland and Scotland, but he was also unwilling to share power with Parliament. With his death, Parliament restored the Stuart line in the person of the executed king's son, Charles II (r. 1660–1685). James II, his brother, then inherited the throne, but he provoked new conflict by again refusing to respect Parliament's rights and by baptizing his heir as a Roman Catholic. The leaders of Parliament forced him into exile in the bloodless Glorious Revolution of 1688. The Bill of Rights of 1689 formalized this new constitutional order by requiring the king to call Parliament frequently to consent to changes in laws or to raise an army in peacetime. Another law reaffirmed the official status of the Church of England but extended religious toleration to dissenting Puritans.

In France the Estates General, like the English Parliament, represented the traditional rights of the clergy, the nobility, and the towns (that is, the bourgeoisie). The Estates General was able to assert its rights during the sixteenth-century French Wars of Religion, when the monarchy was weak. Thereafter France's Bourbon monarchs generally ruled without calling it into session. They put off financial crises by more efficient tax collection and by selling appointments to high government offices, but by 1700 French debt levels challenged traditional fiscal practice. While some historians have used the term *absolutism* to describe the power of French monarchs in this era, even the most powerful, Louis XIV, carefully negotiated his policies with both the nobility and city authorities. While the king's power grew, long-established ways of governing like the sale of offices and reliance on patronage networks and personal relationships continued to frame decision making.

Louis XIV moved his court to a gigantic new palace at **Versailles** (vuhr-SIGH) in 1682. Capable of housing ten thousand people and surrounded by elaborately landscaped grounds and parks, the palace became an effective symbol of growing royal grandeur and power. The relocation of the court to this splendid palace created an arena where the high nobility and ecclesiastical hierarchy more intensely interacted with the monarch in a dense cycle of rituals and ceremonies that emphasized royal power.

Most contemporary European rulers admired and imitated the centralized powers and apparent absolutist authority of the French monarch. The checks and balances of the English model were more admired in later times and gained a favorable press with the beginnings of the Enlightenment. In his influential *Second Treatise of Civil Government* (1690), for example, the English political philosopher John Locke (1632–1704) disputed monarchial claims to absolute authority by divine right, arguing that rulers derived their authority from the consent of the governed and were subject to the law. If monarchs overstepped the law, Locke asserted, citizens had the right and the duty to rebel. The consequences of this idea are considered in Chapter 23.

Warfare and Diplomacy   In addition to the civil wars that afflicted the Holy Roman Empire, France, and England, European states fought numerous international conflicts provoked in part by efforts to protect or extend colonial empires. As a result, the major European nations were nearly always at war somewhere (see the Chronology at the beginning of the chapter). As the geographic scope of warfare and the size of armies and navies grew, monarchs expended ever-larger sums of money and caused widespread devastation and death. The worst of the international conflicts, the Thirty Years' War (1618–1648), caused long-lasting depopulation and economic decline in much of the Holy Roman Empire.

These wars led to dramatic improvements in the skill and weaponry of European armed forces, making them among the most powerful in the world. The numbers of men in arms increased steadily throughout the early modern period. French forces, for example, grew from 88 regiments of infantry and 72 of cavalry in 1691 to 238 regiments of infantry and 94 of cavalry in 1714. Even smaller European states built up impressive armies. Sweden, for example, with under a million people, had one of the finest and best-armed military forces in the seventeenth century, and Prussia, though it had fewer than 2 million inhabitants in 1700, boasted a large, well-disciplined army that made it one of Europe's major powers.

Larger armies required more effective command structures. But although some progress was made, the officer corps of the major powers was largely drawn from the nobility, and patronage, not skill, guided promotion and advancement. Training and battlefield control were marginally improved through more frequent drilling for professional troops and the introduction of new signaling techniques, but battlefields remained chaotic. Fortifications were expanded and improved in Europe and in colonial possessions, and even Spain, facing a deep fiscal crisis, borrowed to fortify Havana and Cartagena in the Americas. Paying for larger and better-armed fleets proved similarly expensive, but in the face of an intensifying competition for colonial wealth that stretched from the East Indies to the Caribbean and South Atlantic, no great power could afford to cut back.

Safe from the threat of direct invasion, only England among major European powers did not maintain a standing army. Its power depended on its navy. England's rise as a sea power had begun under King Henry VIII, who spent heavily on ships and promoted a domestic iron industry to supply cannon. The Royal Navy also copied innovative ship designs from the Dutch in the second half of the seventeenth century. The crushing defeat of the Spanish Armada in 1588 by Henry's daughter, Elizabeth I, demonstrated the usefulness of these decisions and accelerated Spain's decline under Philip II. By the early eighteenth century, the Royal Navy had surpassed the rival French fleet in numbers. Now more secure, England merged with Scotland to become Great Britain. It then annexed Ireland and built a North American empire.

As nations built up their strength, they also acted to preserve a **balance of power**. Although France was Europe's most powerful state, coalitions of the other great powers frustrated Louis XIV's efforts to expand its borders. In a series of costly eighteenth-century wars beginning with the War of the Spanish Succession (1701–1714), the combination of Britain's naval strength and the land armies of Austria and Prussia blocked French expansionist efforts and prevented the Bourbons from uniting the thrones of France and Spain.

Paying the Piper   European nations struggled to pay these heavy military costs while at the same time funding expanded bureaucracies, infrastructure improvements, and the growing extravagance of monarchs, but the obstacles were formidable. Governments collected taxes indirectly using **tax farmers**, private individuals who paid a flat rate to the government, typically less than 50 percent of the estimated tax obligation, for the right to collect the tax. This

MAP 17.1 Europe in 1740

By the middle of the eighteenth century the great powers of Europe were France, the Austrian Empire, Great Britain, Prussia, and Russia. Spain, the Holy Roman Empire, and the Ottoman Empire were far weaker in 1740 than they had been two centuries earlier.

system allowed governments to avoid creating expensive new bureaucracies, but it also guaranteed corruption and limited revenue growth. The tax exemptions enjoyed by the nobility and clergy were among the greatest obstacles to increasing revenues, since these sectors controlled most of Europe's wealth. In the case of France and Spain, this situation led to the imposition of regressive new taxes on peasants and on commerce. Desperate governments were therefore attracted to dangerous short-term fiscal expedients that included currency debasement and cynical defaults on debts like Philip II's four bankruptcies.

It was inevitable that the success of early capitalism's innovations—joint-stock companies and stock markets—would draw the attention of governments thwarted by the tax intransigence of the elite to look to these highly speculative and largely unregulated novelties to solve fiscal problems. The results were spectacularly visible in two nearly simultaneous speculative bubbles associated with the French Mississippi Company and the English South Sea Company.

After debasing the value of the nation's silver and gold coinage, the French government granted a license to create a bank to a fugitive Scottish nobleman, John Law, in 1716. The bank was allowed to issue paper money based on the promise to exchange these bills at face value for silver or gold coin. To everyone's surprise, the notes issued by Law's bank not only maintained their value but were preferred to coin for many transactions. As a result, the value of shares in the bank increased dramatically. Then in 1717 the French government allowed Law to create a monopoly company to develop French colonial territories along the Mississippi, a region erroneously believed to have rich mines. The value of the initial share offering soared and was supplemented by issues of additional shares that also quickly increased in value. In the midst of the bubble, prices for shares rose 10 or 20 percent in the course of a few hours. Stories of once-poor servants buying mansions and marrying their children into noble families abounded.

As the frenzy for shares mounted, the French government used Law's bank to print more paper money. After all, it was much easier to print money than collect taxes. The bank's apparent success fed a speculative bubble in Mississippi Company shares as well, even though the company never earned a profit. Then, in 1720, fears that the bank no longer had the resources to exchange coin for its paper bills put pressure on the entire edifice. Even though Law got the government to first discount gold and silver coin against the paper currency and then to restrict individual possession of coin, a nervous French public hoarded coins and avoided paper currency. This situation led to the panicked selling of shares in both the bank and the Mississippi Company. As huge amounts of paper wealth disappeared in a matter of days, Law was forced to run for his life, leaving the French government to face once again its structural fiscal crisis.

In the English example, in 1711 the English lord treasurer created the South Sea Company and granted it exclusive rights to trade with the Spanish colonies in the Americas. While the company issued stock that traded freely in the nation's nascent stock market, it was primarily a scheme to reduce the government's huge wartime debt. Holders of these debts were forced by statute to accept shares in the company to replace government debt obligations. Once in possession of the government bonds, the company borrowed new funds based on the supposed security of government debt. To individual investors, the South Sea Company seemed a profitable investment because it enjoyed both large annual interest payments from the government and a monopoly right to trade slaves to the Spanish colonies. In 1719, with news of the fast-rising share values of the French Mississippi Company on everyone's lips, the British government used the company to transform another £30,000,000 in debt into shares. When South Sea shares issued at £300 rose to £325, the company issued more stock, even though the company had almost no income from its commercial ventures.

In January 1720 share prices reached £1,050 before the inevitable crash dropped prices to £128 and thousands of investors found themselves ruined. Among the investors was the scientist Isaac Newton, who said, "I can calculate the motions of the heavenly bodies but not the madness of people." While financial markets would eventually recover from these crashes and grow stronger still, the governments of France and Britain would now be forced to pay their bills by imposing taxes on reluctant citizens (see Chapter 23).

The rise of the Netherlands as an economic power stemmed from very different policies. The Spanish crown had acquired these resource-poor but commercially successful provinces as part of Charles V's inheritance. The decision of his son, King Philip II, to impose Spain's ruinous sales tax and to enforce Catholic orthodoxy drove the Dutch to revolt in 1566 and again in 1572. If successful, those measures would have discouraged business and driven away the Calvinists, Jews, and others who were essential to Dutch prosperity. The Dutch fought with skill and ingenuity, raising and training an army and a navy that were among the most effective in Europe. Unable to bear the military costs any longer, Spain accepted a truce that recognized autonomy in the northern Netherlands in 1609. Finally, in 1648, the independence of the seven United Provinces of the Free Netherlands (their full name) became final.

Rather than being ruined by the long war, the Netherlands emerged as the world's greatest trading nation. This economic success owed much to a decentralized government. During the long struggle against Spain, the provinces united around the prince of Orange, their sovereign, who served as commander-in-chief of the armed forces. But in economic matters each province was free to pursue its own interests. The maritime province of Holland grew rich by favoring commercial interests.

After 1650 the Dutch faced growing competition from the English, who were developing their own close association of business and government. In a series of wars (1652–1678) England used its naval might to break Dutch dominance in overseas trade and extend its own colonial empire. With government support, the English merchant fleet doubled between 1660 and 1700, and foreign trade rose by 50 percent. As a result, state revenue from customs duties tripled. During the eighteenth century Britain's trading position strengthened still more.

The debts run up by the Anglo-Dutch Wars helped persuade the English monarchy to greatly enlarge the government's role in managing the economy. Instead of continuing to use tax farmers, the government increased revenues by taxing the formerly exempt landed estates of the aristocrats and by collecting taxes directly. To secure cash quickly for warfare and other emergencies and to reduce the burden of debts from earlier wars, England imitated the Dutch by creating a central bank that could issue long-term loans at low rates.

The French government also developed its national economy, especially under the royal adviser Jean Baptiste Colbert. He streamlined tax collection, promoted French manufacturing and shipping by imposing taxes on foreign goods, and improved transportation within France itself. Yet the power of the wealthy aristocrats kept the French government from following England's lead in taxing wealthy landowners, collecting taxes directly, and securing low-cost loans. Nor did France succeed in managing its debt as efficiently as England. (The role of governments in promoting overseas trade is also discussed in Chapter 19.)

CONCLUSION

Early modern Europe witnessed the weakening of the Catholic Church and the Protestant Reformation. Rejecting the authority of the pope and criticizing the institution of indulgences, Luther insisted on the moral primacy of faith over deeds; Calvin went further, holding that salvation was predestined by God. The pioneers of the Scientific Revolution such as Copernicus and Newton showed that they could explain the workings of the physical universe in natural terms. These scientists did not see any conflict between science and religion, but they paved the way for more secular thinkers of the Enlightenment, who believed that human reason was capable of—and responsible for—discovering the laws that govern social behavior.

Thanks to foreign and domestic trade, European cities in this period experienced rapid growth and the rise of a wealthy commercial class. It was also an era of growing speculative risk and market bubbles like Tulipmania and the Mississippi Company and South Sea bubbles. The Netherlands in particular prospered from expanded manufacturing and trade: with the formation of joint-stock companies and a powerful stock market, Amsterdam became Europe's major port and financial center. For peasants and laborers, however, life did not improve much, although serfdom was all but ended in western Europe. Rural poverty, coupled with the exemption from taxation enjoyed by wealthy landowners, sparked numerous armed rebellions. Women were dependent on their families' and husbands' wealth or lack of it and were barred from attending schools or joining guilds and professions.

Differing policies in the areas of religion, foreign relations, and economics explain the different histories of Europe's early modern states. Charles V, unable to reconcile the diverse interests of his Catholic and Protestant territories and their powerful local rulers, failed to create a unified Holy Roman Empire. Henry VIII, having failed to win an annulment of his marriage to Catherine of Aragon, severed all ties with the pope and led Parliament to accept him as head of the Church of England. Power struggles in England in the seventeenth century led to a stronger Parliament, while in contemporary France a stronger monarchy emerged, symbolized by Louis XIV's construction of the palace at Versailles. Spain was Europe's mightiest state in the sixteenth century, but its failure to suppress the Netherlands Revolt and the costs of other wars led to bankruptcy and decline. In the seventeenth century the United Netherlands became the dominant commercial power on the continent.

The growth of English naval power led to the defeat of the Dutch in the Anglo-Dutch Wars and of France in the early eighteenth century when it attempted to expand its own empire through a union with Spain. Unlike Spain and France, which maintained aristocrats' traditional exemption from taxation, England began to tax their estates, and this policy—together with the establishment of direct taxation and the creation of a central bank from which it could secure low-cost loans—gave England a stronger financial foundation than its rivals enjoyed.

IMPORTANT EVENTS 1500–1750

1519	Protestant Reformation begins
1526–1571	Ottoman wars
1540s	Scientific Revolution begins
1545	Catholic Reformation begins
1546–1555	German Wars of Religion
1562–1598	French Wars of Religion
1566–1648	Netherlands Revolt
1590s	Dutch develop flyboats; Little Ice Age begins
1609	Galileo's astronomical telescope
1618–1648	Thirty Years War
1642–1648	English Civil War
1652–1678	Anglo-Dutch Wars
1667–1697	Wars of Louis XIV
1682	Canal du Midi completed
1683–1697	Ottoman wars
1700s	The Enlightenment begins
1700–1721	Great Northern War
1701–1714	War of the Spanish Succession
1755	Lisbon Earthquake

18

THE DIVERSITY OF AMERICAN COLONIAL SOCIETIES, 1530–1770

S hulush Homa—an eighteenth-century Choctaw leader called "Red Shoes" by the English—faced a dilemma. For years he had befriended the French who had moved into the lower Mississippi Valley, protecting their outlying settlements from other indigenous groups and producing a steady flow of deerskins for trade. In return he received guns and gifts as well as honors previously given only to chiefs. Though born a commoner, he had parlayed his skillful politicking with the French—and the shrewd distribution of the gifts he received—to enhance his position in Choctaw society. Then his fortunes turned. In the course of yet another war between England and France, the English cut off French shipping. Faced with followers unhappy over his sudden inability to supply French guns, Red Shoes forged a dangerous new arrangement with the English that led his former allies, the French, to put a price on his head. His murder in 1747 launched a civil war among the Choctaw. By the end of this conflict both the French colonial population and the Choctaw people had suffered greatly.

The story of Red Shoes reveals a number of themes from the period of European colonization of the Americas. First, although the wars, epidemics, and territorial loss associated with European settlement threatened Amerindians, many adapted the new technologies and new political possibilities to their own purposes and thrived—at least for a time. In the end, though, the best that they could achieve was a holding action. The people of the Old World were coming to dominate the people of the New World.

Second, after centuries of isolation, the political and economic demands of European empires forced the Americas onto the global stage. The influx of Europeans and Africans resulted in a vast biological and cultural transformation, as new plants, animals, diseases, peoples, and technologies fundamentally altered the natural environment. This was not a one-way transfer, however. The technologies and resources of the New World also contributed to profound changes in the Old. Among them, American staple crops helped fuel a population spurt in Europe, Asia, and Africa while American riches altered European economic, social, and political relations.

Third, the story of Red Shoes and the Choctaw illustrates the complexity of colonial society, in which Amerindians, Europeans, and Africans all contributed to the creation of new cultures. Although similar processes took place throughout the

Americas, the particulars varied from place to place, creating a diverse range of cultures. The society that arose in each colony reflected the colony's mix of native peoples, its connections to the slave trade, and the characteristics of the European society establishing the colony. As the colonies matured, new concepts of identity developed, and those living in the Americas began to see themselves as distinct.

The Columbian Exchange

The term **Columbian Exchange** refers to the transfer of peoples, animals, plants, and diseases between the New and Old Worlds. The European invasion and settlement of the Western Hemisphere opened a long era of biological and technological transfers that altered American environments. Within a century of the first European settlement, the domesticated livestock and major agricultural crops of the Old World (the known world before Columbus's voyage) had spread over much of the Americas, and the New World's useful staple crops had enriched the agricultures of Europe, Asia, and Africa. Old World diseases that entered the Americas with European immigrants and African slaves devastated indigenous populations. These dramatic population changes weakened native peoples' capacity for resistance and accelerated the transfer of plants, animals, and related technologies. As a result, the colonies of Spain, Portugal, England, and France became vast arenas of cultural and social experimentation.

Demographic Changes Because of their long isolation from other continents (see Chapter 15), the peoples of the New World lacked immunity to diseases introduced from the Old World. As a result, death rates among Amerindian peoples during the epidemics of the early colonial period were very high. The lack of reliable estimates of the Amerindian population at the moment of contact has frustrated efforts to measure the deadly impact of these diseases, but scholars agree that Old World diseases had a terrible effect on native peoples. According to one estimate, the population of central Mexico fell from more than 13 million to approximately 700,000 in the century that followed 1521. In this same period the populations of the Maya and Inka regions declined by nearly 75 percent or more. Brazil's native population fell by more than 50 percent within a century of the arrival of the Portuguese.

Smallpox, which arrived in the Caribbean in 1518, was the most deadly of the early epidemics. In Mexico and Central America, 50 percent or more of the Amerindian population died during the first wave of smallpox epidemics. The disease then spread to South America with equally devastating effects. Measles arrived in the New World in the 1530s and was followed by diphtheria, typhus, influenza, and pulmonary plague. Mortality was often greatest when two or more diseases struck at the same time. Between 1520 and 1521 influenza and other ailments attacked the Cakchiquel of Guatemala. Their chronicle recalls:

> *Great was the stench of the dead. After our fathers and grandfathers succumbed, half the people fled to the fields. The dogs and vultures devoured the bodies.... So it was that we became orphans, oh my sons! ... We were born to die!*[1]

---

[1]Quoted in Alfred W. Crosby, Jr., *The Columbian Exchange: Biological and Cultural Consequences of 1492* (Westport, CT: Greenwood, 1972), 58.

By the mid-seventeenth century malaria and yellow fever were also present in tropical regions of the Americas. The deadliest form of malaria arrived with the African slave trade, ravaging the already reduced native populations and afflicting Europeans as well.

The development of English and French colonies in North America in the seventeenth century led to similar patterns of contagion and mortality. In 1616 and 1617 epidemics nearly exterminated New England's indigenous groups. Epidemics also followed French fur traders as far as Hudson Bay and the Great Lakes. Although there is very little evidence that Europeans consciously used disease as a tool of empire, the deadly results of contact clearly undermined the ability of native peoples to resist settlement.

Transfer of Plants and Animals

Even as epidemics swept through the indigenous population, the New and the Old Worlds were participating in a vast exchange of plants and animals that radically altered diet and lifestyles in both regions. Settlers brought all the staples of southern European agriculture—such as wheat, olives, grapes, and garden vegetables—to the Americas soon after contact. Colonization also introduced African and Asian crops such as rice, bananas, coconuts, breadfruit, and sugar. While natives remained loyal to their traditional staples, they added many foods like citrus fruits, melons, figs, and sugar as well as onions, radishes, and salad greens to their cuisines.

In return the Americas offered the Old World an abundance of useful plants. Maize, potatoes, and manioc revolutionized agriculture and diet in parts of Europe, Africa, and Asia. Many experts assert that the growth of world population after 1700 resulted from the spread of these useful crops, which provided more calories per acre than did most Old World staples. Beans, squash, tomatoes, sweet potatoes, peanuts, chilies, and chocolate also gained widespread acceptance in the Old World. In addition, the New World provided the Old with plants that provided dyes, medicine, varieties of cotton, and tobacco.

The introduction of European livestock had a dramatic impact on New World environments and cultures. Faced with few natural predators, cattle, pigs, horses, and sheep, as well as pests like rats and rabbits, multiplied rapidly in the Americas. On the vast plains of southern Brazil, Uruguay, and Argentina, for example, herds of wild cattle and horses exceeded 50 million by 1700.

Where Old World livestock spread most rapidly, environmental changes were dramatic. Many priests and colonial officials noted the destructive impact of marauding livestock on Amerindian agriculturists. The first viceroy of Mexico, Antonio de Mendoza, wrote to the Spanish king: "May your Lordship realize that if cattle are allowed, the Indians will be destroyed." Sheep, which grazed grasses close to the ground, were also an environmental threat.

Yet the viceroy's stark choice misrepresented the complex response of indigenous peoples to these new animals. For example, wild cattle on the plains of South America, northern Mexico, and Texas also provided indigenous peoples with abundant supplies of meat and hides. In the present-day southwestern United States, the Navajo became sheepherders and expert weavers. Even in the centers of European settlement, Amerindians turned European animals to their own advantage by becoming muleteers, cowboys, and sheepherders.

No animal had a more striking effect on the cultures of native peoples than the horse, which increased the efficiency of hunters and the military capacity of warriors on the plains. The horse permitted the Apache, Sioux, Blackfoot, Comanche, Assiniboine, and others to more efficiently hunt the vast herds of buffalo in North America. The horse also revolutionized the cultures of the Mapuche and Pampas peoples in South America.

Spanish America and Brazil

The frontiers of conquest and settlement expanded rapidly. Within one hundred years of Columbus's first voyage to the Western Hemisphere, the Spanish Empire in America included most of the islands of the Caribbean and a vast area that stretched from northern Mexico to the plains of the Rio de la Plata region (a region that includes the modern nations of Argentina, Uruguay, and Paraguay). Portuguese settlement developed more slowly, but before the end of the sixteenth century, Portugal had occupied most of the Brazilian coast.

Early settlers from Spain and Portugal sought to create colonial societies based on the institutions and customs of their homelands. They viewed society as a vertical hierarchy of estates (classes of society), as uniformly Catholic, and as an arrangement of patriarchal extended-family networks. They quickly moved to establish the religious, social, and administrative institutions that were familiar to them.

Despite the imposition of foreign institutions and loss of life caused by epidemics, indigenous peoples exercised a powerful influence on the development of colonial societies. Aztec and Inka elite families sought to protect their traditional privileges and rights through marriage or less formal alliances with Spanish settlers. They also used colonial courts to defend their claims to land. In Spanish and Portuguese colonies, indigenous military allies and laborers proved crucial to the development of European settlements. Nearly everywhere, Amerindian religious beliefs and practices survived beneath the surface of an imposed Christianity. Amerindian languages, cuisines, medical practices, and agricultural techniques also survived the conquest and influenced the development of Latin American culture.

The African slave trade added a third cultural stream to colonial Latin American society. At first, African slaves were concentrated in plantation regions of Brazil and the Caribbean (see Chapter 19), but by the end of the colonial era, Africans and their descendants were living throughout Spanish and Portuguese America, introducing elements of their agricultural practices, music, religious beliefs, cuisine, and social customs to colonial societies.

State and Church The Spanish crown moved quickly to curb the independent power of the conquistadors and to establish royal authority over both defeated native populations and European settlers, but geography and technology thwarted this ambition. European officials could not control the distant colonies too closely because it took a ship more than two hundred days to make a roundtrip voyage from Spain to Veracruz, Mexico. Additional months of travel were required to reach Lima, Peru.

As a result, the highest-ranking Spanish officials in the colonies, the viceroys of New Spain and Peru, enjoyed broad power, but they also faced obstacles to their authority in the vast territories they sought to control. Created in 1535, the Viceroyalty of New Spain, with its capital in Mexico City, included Mexico, the southwest of what is now the United States, Central America, and the islands of the

Caribbean. Created five years later, the Viceroyalty of Peru, with its capital in Lima, governed all of Spanish South America.

Until the seventeenth century, most colonial officials were born in Spain, but fiscal mismanagement eventually forced the Crown to sell appointments. As a result, local-born members of the colonial elite gained many offices.

In the sixteenth century Portugal concentrated its resources and energies on Asia and Africa. Because early settlers found neither mineral wealth nor rich native empires in Brazil, the Portuguese king was slow to create expensive mechanisms of colonial government in the New World, but mismanagement forced the king to appoint a governor-general in 1549 and make Salvador Brazil's capital. In 1720 the king named the first viceroy of Brazil.

The government institutions of the Spanish and Portuguese colonies had a more uniform character and were much more extensive and costly than those later established in North America by France and Great Britain. The enormous wealth produced in Spanish America by silver and gold mines and in Brazil by sugar plantations and, after 1690, gold mines financed these large and intrusive colonial bureaucracies. These institutions made the colonies more responsive to the initiatives of Spanish and Portuguese monarchs, but they also thwarted local economic initiative and political experimentation. More importantly, the heavy tax burden imposed by these two European states drained capital from the colonies, slowing investment and retarding economic growth.

In both Spanish America and Brazil, the Catholic Church became the primary agent for the introduction and transmission of Christian belief as well as European language and culture. The church undertook the conversion of Amerindians, ministered to the spiritual needs of European settlers, and promoted intellectual life through the introduction of the printing press and the founding of schools and universities.

Spain and Portugal justified their American conquests by assuming an obligation to convert native populations to Christianity. This effort to convert America's native peoples expanded Christianity on a scale similar to its earlier expansion in Europe at the time of Constantine in the fourth century. In New Spain alone hundreds of thousands of conversions and baptisms were achieved within a few years of the conquest. However, the small numbers of missionaries limited the quality of indoctrination. One Dominican claimed to the king that the rival Franciscans "have taken and occupied three fourths of the country, though they do not have enough friars for it. . . . In most places they are content to say a mass once a year; consider what sort of indoctrination they give them!"[2]

The Catholic clergy sought to achieve their evangelical ends by first converting members of the Amerindian elites, in the hope that they could persuade others to follow their example. To pursue this objective, Franciscan missionaries in Mexico created a seminary to train members of the indigenous elite to become priests, but they curtailed these idealistic efforts when church authorities discovered that many converts were secretly observing old beliefs and rituals. The trial and punishment of two converted Aztec nobles for heresy in the 1530s and the torture of hundreds of Maya in the 1560s repelled the church hierarchy and led it to end the violent

---

[2]Fray Andés de Moguer, 1554, quoted in James Lockhart and Enrique Otte, eds., *Letters and People of the Spanish Indies Sixteenth Century* (Cambridge, U.K. Cambridge University Press: 1976), 216.

Saint Martín de Porres (1579–1639)

Martín de Porres was the illegitimate son of a Spanish nobleman and a black servant. He entered the Dominican Order in Lima, Peru, where he was known for his generosity, his religious visions, and his ability to heal the sick. In this painting the artist celebrates Martín de Porres's spirituality while representing him doing the type of work presumed to be suitable for a person of mixed descent.

Private Collection

repression of native religious practice and limit the recruitment of an Amerindian clergy. In Peru a native millenarian movement sought to roll back the Christian evangelical effort in 1564, leading after 1609 to a focused effort by the Catholic Church to eradicate surviving indigenous belief and ritual.

Despite its failures, the Catholic clergy did provide native peoples with some protections against the abuse and exploitation of Spanish settlers. The priest **Bartolomé de Las Casas** (1474–1566) was the most influential defender of the Amerindians in the early colonial period. He arrived in Hispaniola in 1502 as a settler and initially lived from the forced labor of Amerindians. Deeply moved by the deaths of so many Amerindians and by the misdeeds of the Spanish, Las Casas entered the Dominican Order and later became the first bishop of Chiapas, in southern Mexico. For the remainder of his long life Las Casas served as the most important advocate for native peoples. His most important achievement was the enactment of the New Laws of 1542—reform legislation that outlawed the enslavement of Amerindians and limited other forms of forced labor.

European clergy had arrived in the Americas with the intention of transmitting Catholic Christian belief and ritual without alteration. The linguistic diversity of Amerindian populations and their geographic dispersal over a vast landscape defeated this ambition. The resulting slow progress and limited success of evangelization led to the appearance of a unique Amerindian Christianity that blended European Christian beliefs with important elements of traditional native cosmology and ritual. The Catholic clergy and most European settlers viewed this evolving mixture as the work of the Devil or as evidence of Amerindian inferiority. Instead, it was one component of the process of cultural borrowing and innovation that contributed to a distinct and original Latin American culture.

After 1600 the terrible loss of Amerindian population caused by epidemics and growing signs of resistance to conversion led the Catholic Church to redirect most of its resources from native regions in the countryside to growing colonial cities and towns with large European populations. One important outcome of this altered mission was the founding of universities and secondary schools and the stimulation of urban intellectual life. Over time, the church became the richest institution in the Spanish colonies, controlling ranches, plantations, and vineyards as well as serving as the society's banker.

Colonial Economies   The silver mines of Peru and Mexico and the sugar plantations of Brazil dominated the economic development of colonial Latin America. The mineral wealth of the New World fueled the early development of European capitalism and funded Europe's greatly expanded trade with Asia. Profits produced in these economic centers also promoted the growth of colonial cities, concentrated scarce investment capital and labor resources, and stimulated the development of livestock raising and agriculture in neighboring rural areas. Once established, this colonial dependence on mineral and agricultural exports left an enduring social and economic legacy in Latin America.

The Spanish and later the Portuguese produced gold worth millions of pesos, but silver mines in the Spanish colonies generated the most wealth and therefore exercised the greatest economic influence. The first important silver strikes occurred in Mexico in the 1530s and 1540s. In 1545 the Spanish discovered the single richest silver deposit in the Americas at **Potosí** (poh-toh-SEE) in Alto Peru (what is now Bolivia). The silver of Alto Peru and Peru dominated the Spanish colonial economy until 1680, when it was surpassed by Mexican silver production. At first, miners extracted silver ore by smelting, a process during which crushed ore, packed with charcoal, was fired in a furnace. But this wasteful use of forest resources led to deforestation near the mining centers. Faced with rising fuel costs, Mexican miners developed an efficient method of chemical extraction that relied on mixing mercury with the silver ore. Silver yields and profits increased with the use of mercury amalgamation, but this process, too, had severe environmental costs, since mercury is a poison that contaminated the environment and sickened the Amerindian workforce.

From the time of Columbus, indigenous populations had been compelled to provide labor for European settlers in the Americas. Until the 1540s in Spanish colonies, Spanish authorities divided Amerindians among settlers, who forced them to provide labor or goods. This form of forced labor was called **encomienda** (in-co-mee-EN-dah). As epidemics and mistreatment led to the decline in Amerindian population, reforms such as the New Laws sought to eliminate the encomienda. The discovery of silver, however, led to new forms of compulsory labor. In the mining region of Mexico, where epidemics had reduced Amerindian populations, silver miners came to rely on wage laborers. Peru's Amerindian population survived in larger numbers, allowing the Spanish to impose a form of labor called the mita (MEE-tah). Under this system, one-seventh of adult male Amerindians were compelled to work for two to four months each year in mines, farms, or textile factories.

As the Amerindian population declined with new epidemics, villages were forced to shorten the period between mita obligations. Instead of serving every seven years, many men returned to mines after only a year or two. Unwilling to accept mita service and the other tax burdens imposed on Amerindian villages, thousands abandoned traditional agriculture and moved permanently to Spanish mines and farms as laborers. The long-term result of these individual decisions weakened Amerindian village life and promoted the assimilation of Amerindians into Spanish-speaking Catholic colonial society.

Before the settlement of Brazil, the Portuguese had already developed sugar plantations using African slave labor on the Atlantic islands of Madeira, the Azores, the Cape Verdes, and São Tomé. Because of the success of these early experiences, they were able to quickly transfer this profitable form of agriculture to Brazil. After 1540 sugar production expanded rapidly, and by the seventeenth century it dominated the Brazilian economy.

At first the Portuguese sugar planters enslaved Amerindians captured in war or seized from their villages. As a result of the epidemics that raged across Brazil in the sixteenth and seventeenth centuries thousands of Amerindian slaves died, creating a labor shortage. Slave raiders then pushed into the interior, even attacking Amerindian populations in neighboring Spanish colonies.

Amerindian slaves remained an important source of labor and slave raiding a significant business in frontier regions into the eighteenth century. But sugar planters eventually came to rely more on African slaves. African slaves at first cost much more than Amerindian slaves, but planters found them more productive and more resistant to disease. As profits from the plantations increased, imports of African slaves rose from an average of two thousand per year in the late sixteenth century to approximately seven thousand per year a century later, outstripping the immigration of free Portuguese settlers. Between 1650 and 1750, for example, nearly five African slaves arrived in Brazil for every immigrant from Europe.

Within Spanish America, the mining centers of Mexico and Peru eventually exercised global economic influence. American silver increased the European money supply, promoting commercial expansion and, later, industrialization. Large amounts of silver also flowed to Asia. Both Europe and the Iberian colonies of Latin America ran chronic trade deficits with Asia. As a result, massive amounts of Peruvian and Mexican silver flowed to Asia via Middle Eastern middlemen or across the Pacific to the Spanish colony of the Philippines, where it paid for Asian spices, silks, and pottery.

The rich mines of Peru, Bolivia, and Mexico stimulated urban population growth as well as commercial links with distant agricultural and textile producers. The population of the city of Potosí, high in the Andes, reached 120,000 inhabitants by 1625. This rich mining town became the center of a vast regional market that depended on Chilean wheat, Argentine livestock, and Ecuadorian textiles.

Tobacco Factory Machinery in Colonial Mexico City *The tobacco factory in eighteenth-century Mexico City used a horse-driven mechanical shredder to produce snuff and cigarette tobacco.*

The sugar plantations of Brazil played a similar role in integrating the economy of the south Atlantic region. Brazil exchanged sugar, tobacco, and reexported slaves for yerba (Paraguayan tea), hides, livestock, and silver produced in neighboring Spanish colonies. Portugal's increasing openness to British trade also allowed Brazil to become a conduit for an illegal trade between Spanish colonies and Europe. At the end of the seventeenth century, the discovery of gold in Brazil promoted further regional and international economic integration.

Society in Colonial Latin America   With the exception of some early viceroys, few members of Spain's nobility came to the New World. *Hidalgos* (ee-DAHL-goes)—lesser nobles—were well represented, as were Spanish merchants, artisans, miners, priests, and lawyers. Small numbers of criminals, beggars, and prostitutes also found their way to the colonies. This flow of immigrants from Spain was never large, and Spanish settlers were always a tiny minority in a colonial society numerically dominated by Amerindians and rapidly growing populations of Africans, **creoles** (whites born in America to European parents), and people of mixed ancestry (see Diversity and Dominance: Race and Ethnicity in the Spanish Colonies: Negotiating Hierarchy).

The most powerful conquistadors and early settlers sought to create a hereditary social and political class comparable to the European nobility. But their systematic abuse of Amerindian communities and the catastrophic effects of the epidemics of the sixteenth century undermined their control of colonial society. With the passage of time colonial officials, the clergy, and the richest merchants came to dominate the social hierarchy. Europeans controlled the highest levels of the church and government as well as commerce, while wealthy American-born creoles exercised a similar role in colonial agriculture and mining. Although tensions between Spaniards and creoles were inevitable, most elite families included both groups.

Before the Europeans arrived in the Americas, the native peoples were members of a large number of distinct cultural and linguistic groups. The effects of conquest and epidemics undermined this rich social and cultural complexity, and the relocation of Amerindian peoples to promote conversion or provide labor further eroded ethnic boundaries among native peoples. Application of the racial label *Indian* by colonial administrators and settlers helped organize the tribute and labor demands imposed on native peoples, but it also registered the cultural costs of colonial rule.

Amerindian elites struggled to survive in the new political and economic environments created by military defeat and European settlement. Some sought to protect their positions by forging marriage or less formal relations with colonists. As a result, some indigenous and settler families were tied together by kinship in the decades after conquest, but these links weakened with the passage of time. Indigenous leaders also established political alliances with members of the colonial administrative classes. Hereditary native elites gained some security by becoming essential intermediaries between the indigenous masses and colonial administrators, collecting Spanish taxes and organizing the labor of their dependents for colonial enterprises.

Indigenous commoners suffered the heaviest burdens. Tribute payments, forced labor obligations, and the loss of traditional land rights were common. European domination dramatically changed the indigenous world by breaking the connections between peoples and places and transforming religious life, marriage practices, diet, and material culture. The survivors of these terrible shocks learned to adapt to the new colonial environment by embracing some elements of the dominant colonial culture or entering the market economies of the cities. They also learned new forms of resistance, like using colonial courts to protect community lands or to resist the abuses of corrupt officials.

Thousands of blacks, many born in Iberia or long resident there, participated in the conquest and settlement of Spanish America. Most of these were slaves; more than four hundred slaves participated in the conquests of Peru and Chile alone. In the fluid social environment of the conquest era, many were able to gain their freedom. Juan Valiente escaped from his master in Mexico and then participated in Francisco Pizarro's conquest of the Inka Empire. He later became one of the most prominent early settlers of Chile.

With the opening of a direct slave trade with Africa (for details, see Chapter 19), the cultural character of the black population of colonial Latin America was altered dramatically. While Afro-Iberians spoke Spanish or Portuguese and were Catholic, African slaves arrived in the colonies with different languages, religious beliefs, and cultural practices. European settlers viewed these differences as signs of inferiority that served as a justification for prejudice and discrimination.

A large percentage of slaves imported in the sixteenth century came from West Central Africa, where they had been exposed to elements of Iberian culture, including religion, language, and technology. The legacy of these shared African cultural

Race and Ethnicity in the Spanish Colonies: Negotiating Hierarchy

Many European visitors to colonial Latin America were interested in the mixing of Europeans, Amerindians, and Africans in the colonies. Many also commented on the treatment of slaves. The passages that follow allow us to examine these issues in two Spanish colonial societies.

Two young Spanish naval officers and scientists, Jorge Juan and Antonio de Ulloa, arrived in the colonies in 1735 as members of a scientific expedition. They later wrote the first selection after visiting the major cities of the Pacific coast of South America and traveling across some of the most difficult terrain in the hemisphere. In addition to their scientific chores, they described architecture, local customs, and the social order. In this section they describe the ethnic mix in Quito, now the capital of Ecuador.

The second selection was published in Lima under the pseudonym Concolorcorvo around 1776. We now know that the author was Alonso Carrío de la Vandera. Born in Spain, he traveled to the colonies as a young man. He served in many minor bureaucratic positions, one of which was the inspection of the postal route between Buenos Aires and Lima. Carrío used his experiences during this long and often uncomfortable trip as the basis of an insightful, and sometimes highly critical, examination of colonial society. The selection that follows describes Córdoba, Argentina.

Juan and Ulloa, as well as Carrío, were perplexed by colonial efforts to create and enforce a racial taxonomy that stipulated and named every possible mixture of European, Amerindian, and African. They were also critical of the vanity and social presumptions of the dominant white population. We are fortunate to have these contemporary descriptions of the diversity of colonial society, but it is important to remember that these authors were clearly rooted in their time and culture and were confident of European superiority. Although they noted many of the abuses suffered by the non-white population, their descriptions of these groups often reveal racial bias and the presumption of inferiority.

Quito

This city is very populous, and has, among its inhabitants, some families of high rank and distinction; though their number is but small considering its extent, the poorer class bearing here too great a proportion. The former are the descendants either of the original conquerors, or of presidents, auditors, or other persons of character [high rank], who at different times came over from Spain invested with some lucrative post, and have still preserved their luster, both of wealth and descent, by intermarriages, without intermixing with meaner families though famous for their riches. The commonalty may be divided into four classes; Spaniards or Whites, Mestizos, Indians or Natives, and Negroes, with their progeny.

The name of Spaniard here has a different meaning from that of Chapitone [sic] or European, as properly signifying a person descended from a Spaniard without a mixture of blood. Many Mestizos, from the advantage of a fresh complexion, appear to be Spaniards more than those who are so in reality; and from only this fortuitous advantage are accounted as such. The Whites, according to this construction of the word, may be considered as one sixth part of the inhabitants.

The Mestizos are the descendants of Spaniards and Indians.... Some are, however, equally tawny with the Indians themselves, though they are distinguished from them by their beards: while others, on the contrary, have so fine a complexion that they might pass for Whites, were it not for some signs which betray them, when viewed attentively. These marks... make it very difficult to conceal the fallacy of their complexion. The Mestizos may be reckoned a third part of the inhabitants.

The next class is the Indians, who form about another third; and the others, who are about one sixth, are the Castes [mixed]. These four classes...amount to between 50 and 60,000 persons, of all ages, sexes, and ranks. If among these classes the Spaniards, as is natural to think, are the most eminent for riches, rank, and power, it must at the same time be owned, however melancholy the truth may appear, they are in proportion the most poor, miserable and distressed; for they refuse to apply themselves to any mechanic business, considering it as a disgrace to that quality they so highly value themselves upon, which consists in not being black, brown, or of a copper color. The Mestizos, whose pride is regulated by prudence, readily apply themselves to arts and trades, but chose those of the greatest repute, as painting, sculpture, and the like, leaving the meaner sort to the Indians.

Córdoba

In my computation, there must be within the city and its limited common lands around 500 to 600 [property-owning] residents, but in the principal houses there are a very large number of slaves, most of them [native born blacks] of all conceivable classes, because in this city and in all of Tucumán there is no leniency about granting freedom to any of them.

As I was passing through Córdoba, they were selling 2,000 Negroes, all Creoles from Temporalidades [property confiscated from the Jesuit order in 1767].... Among this multitude of Negroes were many musicians and many of other crafts; they proceeded with the sale by families. I was assured that the nuns of Santa Teresa alone had a group of 300 slaves of both sexes, to whom they give their just ration of meat and dress in the coarse cloth which they make, while these good nuns content themselves with what is left from other ministrations. The number attached to other religious establishments is much smaller, but there is a private home which has 30 or 40, the majority of whom are engaged in various gainful activities. The result is a large number of excellent washerwomen whose accomplishments are valued so highly that they never mend their outer skirts in order that the whiteness of their undergarments may be seen. They do the laundry in the river, in water up to the waist, saying vaingloriously that she who is not soaked cannot wash well. They make ponchos [hand-woven capes], rugs, sashes, and sundries, and especially decorated leather cases which the men sell for 8 reales each, because the hides have no outlet due to the great distance to the port; the same thing happens on the banks of the Tercero and Cuarto rivers, where they are sold at 2 reales and frequently for less.

The principal men of the city wear very expensive clothes, but this is not true of the women, who are an exception in both Americas and even in the entire world, because they dress decorously in clothing of little cost. They are very tenacious in preserving the customs of their ancestors. They do not permit slaves, or even freedmen who have a mixture of Negro blood, to wear any cloth other than that made in this country, which is quite coarse. I was told recently that a certain bedecked mulatto [woman] who appeared in Córdoba was sent word by the ladies of the city that she should dress according to her station, but since she paid no attention to this reproach, they endured her negligence until one of the ladies, summoning her to her home under some other pretext, had the servants undress her, whip her, burn her finery before her eyes, and dress her in the clothes befitting her class; despite the fact that the [victim] was not lacking in persons to defend her, she disappeared lest the tragedy be repeated.

Questions for Analysis

1. What do the authors of these selections seem to think about the white elites of the colonies? Are there similarities in the ways that Juan and Ulloa and Carrío describe the mixed population of Quito and the slave population of Córdoba?

2. How do these depictions of mestizos and other mixtures compare with the image of the family represented in the painting of castas?

3. What does the humiliation of the mixed-race woman in Córdoba tell us about ideas of race and class in this Spanish colony?

Sources: Jorge Juan and Antonio de Ulloa, A Voyage to South America, The John Adams translation (abridged), Introduction by Irving A. Leonard (New York: Alfred A. Knopf, 1964), 135–137, copyright © 1964 by Alfred A. Knopf, a division of Random House, Inc.; Concolorcorvo, El Lazarillo, A Guide for Inexperienced Travelers Between Buenos Aires and Lima, 1773, translated by Walter D. Kline (Bloomington: Indiana University Press, 1965), 78–80.

elements became enduring components of the colonial cultures of Latin America. But significant differences were present as well, and in regions with large slave majorities, especially the sugar-producing regions of Brazil, these cultural and linguistic barriers often divided slaves and made resistance more difficult. Over time, elements from many African traditions blended and mixed with European (and in some cases Amerindian) language and beliefs to forge distinct local cultures.

Slave resistance took many forms, including sabotage, malingering, running away, and rebellion. Although many slave rebellions occurred, colonial authorities were always able to reestablish control. Groups of runaway slaves, however, were sometimes able to defend themselves for years. In both Spanish America and Brazil, communities of runaways (called quilombos [key-LOM-bos] in Brazil and palenques [pah-LEN-kays] in Spanish colonies) were common. The largest quilombo was Palmares in Brazil.

Slaves served as skilled artisans, musicians, servants, artists, cowboys, and even soldiers. However, the vast majority worked in agriculture. Conditions for slaves were worst on the sugar plantations of Brazil and the Caribbean, where harsh discipline, brutal punishments, and backbreaking labor were common. Because planters preferred to buy male slaves, there was nearly always a gender imbalance on plantations, proving a significant obstacle to the traditional marriage and family patterns of both Africa and Europe.

Brazil attracted smaller numbers of European immigrants than did Spanish America, and its native populations were smaller and less urbanized. It also came to depend on the African slave as a source of labor earlier than any other American colony. By the early seventeenth century, Africans and their American-born descendants were by far the largest racial group in Brazil. As a result, Brazilian colonial society (unlike Spanish Mexico and Peru) was more influenced by African culture than by Amerindian culture.

Both Spanish and Portuguese law provided for manumission, the granting of freedom to individual slaves, and colonial courts sometimes intervened to protect slaves from the worst physical abuse or to protect married couples from forced separation. The majority of those gaining their liberty had saved money and purchased their own freedom. This meant that manumission was more about the capacity of individual slaves and slave families to earn income and save than about the generosity of slave owners. Among the minority of slaves to be freed without compensation, household servants were the most likely beneficiaries. Slave women received the majority of manumissions, and because children born subsequently were considered free, the free black population grew rapidly.

Within a century of settlement, groups of mixed descent were in the majority in many regions. There were few marriages between Amerindian women and European men, but less formal relationships were common. Few European fathers recognized their mixed offspring, who were called **mestizos** (mess-TEE-zoh). Nevertheless, this rapidly expanding group came to occupy a middle position in colonial society, dominating urban artisan trades and small-scale agriculture and ranching. Many members of the elite in frontier regions were mestizos, some proudly asserting their descent from Amerindian noble families. The African slave trade also led to the appearance of new American ethnicities. Individuals of mixed European and African descent—called **mulattos**—came to occupy an intermediate position in the tropics similar to the social position of mestizos in Mesoamerica and the Andean region. In Spanish Mexico and Peru and in Brazil, mixtures of Amerindians and Africans were also common. These mixed-descent groups were called castas (CAZ-tahs) in Spanish America.

ENGLISH AND FRENCH COLONIES IN NORTH AMERICA

The North American empires of England and France had many characteristics in common with the colonial empires of Spain and Portugal. The governments of England and France hoped to find easily extracted forms of wealth like gold and silver or great indigenous empires like those of the Aztecs and Inka. Like the Spanish and Portuguese, English and French settlers responded to native peoples with a mixture of diplomacy and violence. All four colonial empires also imported large numbers of African slaves to spur the economic development of their colonies.

Important differences, however, distinguished North American colonial development from the Latin American model. The English and French colonies were developed nearly a century after Cortés's conquest of Mexico and the initial Portuguese settlement of Brazil. The intervening period had witnessed significant economic and demographic growth in Europe. By the time England and France secured a foothold in the Americas, increased trade had led to greater integration of world cultural regions. Distracted by ventures elsewhere and by increasing military confrontation in Europe, neither England nor France imitated the large and expensive colonial bureaucracies established by Spain and Portugal. As a result, private companies and individual proprietors played a much larger role in the development of English and French colonies. This period had also witnessed the Protestant Reformation, an event that helped frame the character of English and French settlement in the Americas.

Early English Experiments   England's effort to gain a foothold in the Americas in the late sixteenth century failed, but its effort to establish colonies in the seventeenth century proved more successful. The English relied on private capital to finance settlement and continued to hope that the colonies would become sources of high-value products such as silver, citrus, and wine. English experience in colonizing Ireland after 1566 also influenced these efforts. In Ireland land had been confiscated, cleared of its native population, and offered for sale to English investors. The city of London, English guilds, and wealthy private investors all purchased Irish "plantations" and then recruited "settlers." By 1650 investors had sent nearly 150,000 English and Scottish immigrants to Ireland. Indeed, Ireland attracted six times as many colonists in the early seventeenth century as did New England.

The South   In 1606 London investors organized as the Virginia Company took up the challenge of colonizing Virginia. A year later 144 settlers disembarked at Jamestown, an island 30 miles (48 kilometers) up the James River in the Chesapeake Bay region. Additional settlers arrived in 1609. The investors and settlers hoped for immediate profits, but the location was a swampy and unhealthy place where nearly 80 percent of the settlers died in the first fifteen years from disease or Amerindian attacks. There was no mineral wealth, no passage to Asia, and no docile and exploitable native population.

In 1624 the English crown dissolved the Virginia Company because of its mismanagement. Freed from the company's commitment to the original location, colonists pushed deeper into the interior and developed a sustainable economy based on furs, timber, and, increasingly, tobacco. The profits from tobacco soon attracted additional immigrants. Along the shoreline of Chesapeake Bay and the rivers that fed it, settlers spread out, developing plantations and farms. Colonial Virginia's dispersed population contrasted with the greater urbanization of Spanish and Portuguese America, where large and powerful cities and networks of secondary towns flourished. No city of any significant size developed in colonial Virginia.

From the beginning, colonists in Latin America had relied on forced labor of Amerindians to develop the region's resources. The African slave trade compelled the migration of millions of additional forced laborers to the colonies of Spain and Portugal. The English settlement of the Chesapeake Bay region added a new system of forced labor to the American landscape: indentured servitude. **Indentured servants** were racially and religiously indistinguishable from free settlers and eventually accounted for approximately 80 percent of all English immigrants to Virginia and the neighboring colony of Maryland. A young man or woman unable to pay for transportation to the New World accepted an indenture (contract) that bound him or her to a term ranging from four to seven years of labor in return for passage and, at the end of the contract, a small parcel of land, some tools, and clothes.

During the seventeenth century approximately fifteen hundred indentured servants, mostly male, arrived each year (see Chapter 19 for details on the indentured labor system). Planters were more likely to purchase the cheaper limited contracts of indentured servants rather than African slaves during the initial period of high mortality rates. As life expectancy improved, planters began to purchase more slaves because they believed they would earn greater profits from slaves owned for life than from indentured servants bound for short periods of time. As a result, Virginia's slave population grew rapidly from 950 in 1660 to 120,000 by 1756.

By the 1660s Virginia was administered by a Crown-appointed governor and by representatives of towns meeting together as the **House of Burgesses**. When elected representatives began to meet alone as a deliberative body, they initiated a form of democratic representation that distinguished the English colonies of North America from the colonies of other European powers. Ironically, this expansion in colonial liberties and political rights occurred along with the dramatic increase in the colony's slave population. The intertwined evolution of American freedom and American slavery gave England's southern colonies a unique and conflicted political character that endured after independence.

English settlement of the Carolinas initially relied on profits from the fur trade. English fur traders pushed into the interior to compete with French trading networks based in New Orleans and Mobile. Native peoples eventually provided over 100,000 deerskins annually to this profitable commerce, but at a high environmental and cultural cost. As Amerindian peoples hunted more intensely, they disrupted the natural balance of animals and plants in southern forests. The profits of the fur trade altered Amerindian culture as well, leading villages to place less emphasis on subsistence hunting, fishing, and traditional agriculture. Amerindian life was profoundly altered by deepening dependencies on European products, including firearms, metal tools, textiles, and alcohol.

While being increasingly tied to the commerce and culture of the Carolina colony, indigenous peoples were simultaneously weakened by epidemics, alcoholism, and a rising tide of ethnic conflicts generated by competition for hunting grounds. Conflicts among indigenous peoples—who now had firearms—became more deadly, and many captured Amerindians were sold as slaves to local colonists, who used them as agricultural workers or exported them to the sugar plantations of the Caribbean. Dissatisfied with the terms of trade imposed by fur traders and angered by this slave trade, Amerindians launched attacks on English settlements in the early 1700s. Their defeat by colonial military forces inevitably led to new seizures of Amerindian land by European settlers.

The northern part of the Carolinas, settled from Virginia, followed that colony's mixed economy of tobacco and forest products. Slavery expanded slowly in this region. Charleston and the interior of South Carolina followed a different path. Settled first by planters from Barbados in 1670, this colony developed an economy based on plantations and slavery in imitation of the colonies of the Caribbean and Brazil. In 1729 North and South Carolina became separate colonies.

Despite an unhealthy climate, the prosperous rice and indigo plantations near Charleston attracted both free immigrants and increasing numbers of African slaves. African slaves had been present from the founding of Charleston and were instrumental in introducing irrigated rice agriculture along the coastal lowlands. They were also crucial to developing plantations of indigo (a plant that produced a blue dye) at higher elevations away from the coast. Many slaves were given significant responsibilities. As one planter sending two slaves and their families to a frontier region put it: "[They] are likely young people, well acquainted with Rice & every kind of plantation business, and in short [are] capable of the management of a plantation themselves."[3]

As profits from rice and indigo rose, the importation of African slaves created a black majority in South Carolina. African languages, as well as African religious

---

[3]Crosby, *The Columbian Exchange*, 58.

beliefs and diet, strongly influenced this unique colonial culture. Gullah, a dialect with African and English roots, evolved as the common idiom of the Carolina coast. Africans played a major role in South Carolina's largest slave uprising, the Stono Rebellion of 1739. Twenty slaves, many of them African Catholics seeking to flee south to Spanish Florida, seized firearms and other weapons and then recruited about a hundred slaves from nearby plantations. Although the colonial militia defeated the rebels and executed many of them, the rebellion shocked slave owners throughout England's southern colonies and led to greater repression.

Colonial South Carolina was the most hierarchical society in British North America. Planters controlled the economy and political life. The richest families maintained impressive households in Charleston, the largest city in the southern colonies, as well as on their plantations in the countryside. Small farmers, cattlemen, artisans, merchants, and fur traders held an intermediate but clearly subordinate social position. Native peoples continued to participate in colonial society but lost ground from the effects of epidemic disease and warfare. As in colonial Latin America, a large mixed population blurred racial and cultural boundaries. On the frontier, the children of white men and Amerindian women held an important place in the fur trade. In the plantation regions and Charleston, the offspring of white men and black women often held preferred positions within the slave workforce or worked as free craftsmen.

New England   The colonization of New England by two separate groups of Protestant dissenters, Pilgrims and Puritans, put the settlement of this region on a different course. The **Pilgrims**, who came first, wished to break completely with the Church of England, which they believed was still essentially Catholic. As a result, in 1620 approximately one hundred settlers—men, women, and children—established the colony of Plymouth on the coast of present-day Massachusetts. Although nearly half of the settlers died during the first winter, the colony survived until 1691, when the larger Massachusetts Bay Colony of the Puritans absorbed Plymouth.

The **Puritans** wished to "purify" the Church of England, not break with it. They wanted to abolish its hierarchy of bishops and priests, free it from governmental interference, and limit membership to people who shared their beliefs. Subjected to increased discrimination in England for their efforts to transform the church, large numbers of Puritans began emigrating from England in 1630.

The Puritan leaders of the Massachusetts Bay Company—the joint-stock company that had received a royal charter to finance the Massachusetts Bay Colony—carried the company charter with them from England to Massachusetts. By bringing the charter, which spelled out company rights and obligations as well as the direction of company government, they limited Crown efforts to control them. By 1643 more than twenty thousand Puritans had settled in the Bay Colony.

Immigration to Massachusetts differed from immigration to the Chesapeake and to South Carolina. Most newcomers to Massachusetts arrived with their families. Whereas 84 percent of Virginia's white population in 1625 was male, Massachusetts had a normal gender balance in its population almost from the beginning. It was also the healthiest of England's colonies. The result was a rapid natural increase in population. The population of Massachusetts quickly became more "American" than the population of southern or Caribbean colonies, whose survival depended on a steady flow of

English immigrants and slaves to counter high mortality rates. Massachusetts also was more homogeneous and less hierarchical than the southern colonies.

Political institutions evolved from the terms of the company charter. Settlers elected a governor and a council of magistrates drawn from the board of directors of the Massachusetts Bay Company. By 1650, disagreements between this council and elected representatives of the towns led to the creation of a lower legislative house that selected its own speaker and developed procedures and rules similar to those of the House of Commons in England. The result was much greater autonomy and greater local political involvement than in the colonies of Latin America.

Economically, Massachusetts differed dramatically from the southern colonies. Agriculture met basic needs, but poor soils and harsh climate offered no opportunity to develop cash crops like tobacco or rice. To pay for imported tools, textiles, and other essentials, the colonists needed to discover some profit-making niche in the growing Atlantic market. Fur, timber, and fish provided the initial economic foundation, but New England's economic well-being soon depended on providing commercial and shipping services in a dynamic and far-flung commercial arena that included the southern colonies, the Caribbean islands, Africa, and Europe.

In Spanish and Portuguese America, heavily capitalized monopolies (companies or individuals given exclusive economic privileges) dominated international trade. In New England, by contrast, individual merchants survived by discovering smaller but more sustainable profits in diversified trade across the Atlantic. The colony's commercial success rested on market intelligence, flexibility, and streamlined organization. Urban population growth suggests the success of this development strategy. With sixteen thousand inhabitants in 1740, Boston, the capital of Massachusetts Bay Colony, was the largest city in British North America.

Lacking a profitable agricultural export like tobacco, New England did not develop the extreme social stratification of the southern plantation colonies. Slaves and indentured servants were present, but in very small numbers. While New England was ruled by the richest colonists and shared the racial attitudes of the southern colonies, it also was the colonial society with fewest differences in wealth and status and with the most uniformly British and Protestant population in the Americas.

The Middle Atlantic Region   Much of the future success of English-speaking America was rooted in the rapid economic development and remarkable cultural diversity that appeared in the Middle Atlantic colonies. In 1624 the Dutch West India Company established the colony of New Netherland and located its capital on Manhattan Island. Although poorly managed and underfinanced from the start, the colony commanded the potentially profitable and strategically important Hudson River. Dutch merchants established trading relationships with the **Iroquois Confederacy**—an alliance among the Mohawk, Oneida, Onondaga, Cayuga, and Seneca peoples—and with other native peoples that gave them access to the rich fur trade of Canada. When confronted by an English military expedition in 1664, the Dutch surrendered without a fight. James, duke of York and later King James II of England, became proprietor of the colony, which was renamed New York.

Tumultuous politics and corrupt public administration characterized colonial New York, but the development of New York City as a commercial and shipping center guaranteed the colony's success. Located at the mouth of the Hudson River, the city played an essential role in connecting the region's grain farmers to the booming markets of the Caribbean and southern Europe. By the early eighteenth century, this colony had a diverse population that included English, Dutch, German, and Swedish settlers as well as a large slave community.

Pennsylvania began as a proprietary colony and as a refuge for Quakers, a persecuted religious minority. The prominent Quaker William Penn secured an enormous grant of territory (nearly the size of England) in 1682 because the English king Charles II was indebted to his father. As proprietor (owner) of the land, Penn had sole right to establish a government, subject only to the requirement that he provide for an assembly of freemen.

Even though Penn quickly lost control of the colony's political life, the colony enjoyed remarkable success. By 1700 Pennsylvania had a population of more than 21,000, and Philadelphia, its capital, soon overtook Boston to become the largest city in the British colonies. Healthy climate, excellent land, relatively peaceful relations with native peoples (prompted by Penn's emphasis on negotiation rather than warfare), and access through Philadelphia to exterior markets led to rapid economic and demographic growth.

While both Pennsylvania and South Carolina were grain-exporting colonies, they were very different societies. South Carolina's rice plantations depended on the labor of large numbers of slaves. In Pennsylvania free workers produced the bulk of the colony's grain crops on family farms. As a result, Pennsylvania's economic expansion in the late seventeenth century occurred without reproducing South Carolina's hierarchical and repressive social order. By the early eighteenth century, however, a rich merchant elite was in place and the prosperous city of Philadelphia had a large population of black slaves and freedmen; the fast-growing economy continued to offer opportunities in skilled crafts, trade, and agriculture to free immigrants.

French America   Patterns of French colonial settlement more closely resembled those of Spain and Portugal than of England. The French were committed to missionary activity among Amerindian peoples and emphasized the extraction of natural resources—in this case furs rather than minerals. Between 1534 and 1542 the navigator and promoter Jacques Cartier explored the region of Newfoundland and the Gulf of St. Lawrence in three voyages. A contemporary of Cortés and Pizarro, Cartier hoped to find mineral wealth, but the stones he brought back to France turned out to be quartz and iron pyrite, "fool's gold."

The French waited more than fifty years before establishing settlements in North America. Coming to Canada after spending years in the West Indies, Samuel de Champlain founded the colony of **New France** at Quebec (kwuh-BEC), on the banks of the St. Lawrence River, in 1608. This location provided ready access to Amerindian trade routes, but it also compelled French settlers to take sides in the region's ongoing warfare. Champlain allied New France with the Huron and Algonquin peoples, traditional enemies of the powerful Iroquois Confederacy. Although French firearms and armor at first tipped the balance of power to France's native allies, the Iroquois Confederacy proved to be a resourceful and persistent enemy.

The European market for fur, especially beaver, fueled French settlement. Young Frenchmen were sent to live among native peoples to master their languages and customs. These **coureurs de bois** (koo-RUHR day BWA), or runners of the woods, often began families with indigenous women. Their mixed children, called

Frances Anne Hopkins, "Shooting the Rapids," Library and Archives Canada, Ref. # C-2774

Canadian Fur Traders *The fur trade provided the economic foundation of early Canadian settlement. Fur traders were cultural intermediaries. They brought European technologies and products like firearms and machine-made textiles to native peoples and native technologies and products like canoes and furs to European settlers. This canoe with sixteen paddlers was adapted from the native craft by fur traders to transport large cargoes.*

métis (may-TEES), helped direct the fur trade. Amerindians actively participated in the trade because they came to depend on the goods they received in exchange for furs—firearms, metal tools, textiles, and alcohol. This change in the material culture of native peoples led to overhunting, which rapidly transformed the environment and led to the depletion of beaver and deer populations. It also increased competition among native peoples for hunting grounds, thus promoting warfare.

The proliferation of firearms made indigenous warfare more deadly. The Iroquois Confederacy responded to the increased military strength of France's Algonquin allies by forging commercial and military links with Dutch and later English settlements along the Hudson River. Now well armed, the Iroquois Confederacy nearly eradicated the Huron in 1649 and inflicted a series of humiliating defeats on the French. At the high point of their power in the early 1680s, Iroquois hunters and military forces gained control of much of the Great Lakes region and the Ohio River Valley. A large French military expedition and a relentless attack focused on Iroquois villages and agriculture finally checked Iroquois power in 1701.

In French Canada, the Jesuits led the effort to convert native peoples to Christianity as they had in Brazil and Paraguay. Missionaries mastered native languages, created boarding schools for young boys and girls, and set up model agricultural communities for converted Amerindians. The Jesuits' greatest successes coincided with a destructive wave of epidemics and renewed warfare among native peoples in the 1630s. Eventually, they established churches throughout Huron and Algonquin territories. Nevertheless, native culture persisted. In 1688 a French nun who had devoted her life to instructing Amerindian girls expressed her frustration with the resilience of indigenous culture:

> We have observed that of a hundred that have passed through our hands we have scarcely civilized one.... When we are least expecting it, they clamber over our wall and go off to run with their kinsmen in the woods, finding more to please them there than in all the amenities of our French house.[4]

Even though the fur trade flourished, population growth was slow. Founded at about the same time as French Canada, Virginia had twenty times more European residents by 1627. Canada's small settler population and the fur trade's dependence on the voluntary participation of Amerindians allowed indigenous peoples to retain greater independence and more control over their traditional lands than was possible in the colonies of Spain, Portugal, or England. Unlike these colonial regimes, which sought to transform ancient ways of life or force the transfer of native lands, the French were compelled to treat indigenous peoples as allies and trading partners.

Despite Canada's small population and limited resources, the French aggressively expanded to the west and south. They founded Louisiana in 1699, but by 1708 there were fewer than three hundred soldiers, settlers, and slaves in this vast territory. Like Canada, Louisiana depended on the fur trade and on alliances with Amerindian peoples who in turn became dependent on European goods. In 1753 a French official reported a Choctaw leader as saying, "[The French] were the first ... who made [us] subject to the different needs that [we] can no longer now do without."[5]

France's North American colonies were threatened by wars between France and England and by the population growth and increasing prosperity of neighboring English colonies. The "French and Indian War" that began in 1754 led to the wider conflict called the Seven Years' War, 1756–1763, that determined the fate of French Canada. England committed a larger military force to the struggle and, despite early defeats, took the French capital of Quebec in 1759. The peace agreement forced France to yield Canada to the English and cede Louisiana to Spain. Amerindian populations soon recognized the difference between the English and the French. One Canadian indigenous leader commented to a British officer after the French surrender: "We learn that our lands are to be given away not only to trade thereon but also ... in full title to various [English] individuals.... We have always been a free nation, and now we will become slaves, which would be very difficult to accept after having enjoyed our liberty so long."[6] With the loss of Canada the French concentrated their efforts on their sugar-producing colonies in the Caribbean (see Chapter 19).

---

[4]Quoted in R. Douglas Francis, Richard Jones, and Donald B. Smith, *Origins: Canadian History to Confederation* (Toronto: Holt, Rinehart, and Winston of Canada, 1992), 52.

[5]Quoted in Daniel H. Usner, Jr., *Indians, Settlers and Slaves in a Frontier Exchange Economy: The Lower Mississippi Valley Before 1783*, Institute of Early American History and Culture Series (Chapel Hill: University of North Carolina Press, 1992), 96.

[6]Quoted in Cornelius J. Jaenen, "French and Native Peoples in New France," in *Interpreting Canada's Past*, ed. J. M. Bumsted, vol. 1, 2nd ed. (Toronto: Oxford University Press, 1993), 73.

© Cengage Learning

MAP 18.1   European Claims in North America, 1755–1763

The results of the French and Indian War dramatically altered the map of North America. France's losses precipitated conflicts between Amerindian peoples and the rapidly expanding population of the British colonies.

COLONIAL EXPANSION AND CONFLICT

Beginning in the last decades of the seventeenth century, nearly all the European colonies in the Americas experienced economic expansion and population growth. In the next century, the imperial powers responded by strengthening administrative and economic control of their colonies. They also sought to force colonial populations to pay a larger share of the costs of administration and defense. These efforts at reform and restructuring coincided with a series of imperial wars fought along Atlantic trade routes and in the Americas. France's loss of its North American colonies in 1763 was one of the most important results of these struggles. Equally significant, colonial populations throughout the Americas became more aware of separate national identities and more aggressive in asserting local interests against the will of distant monarchs.

Imperial Reform in Spanish America and Brazil Spain's Habsburg dynasty ended when Charles II died without an heir in 1700 (see Table 17.1 on page 454). After thirteen years of conflict involving the major European powers, Philip of Bourbon, grandson of Louis XIV of France, gained the Spanish throne. Under Philip V and his heirs, Spain reorganized its administration and tax collection and liberalized colonial trade policies. Spain also created new commercial monopolies and strengthened its navy to protect colonial trade.

For most of the Spanish Empire, the eighteenth century was a period of remarkable economic expansion associated with population growth. Amerindian populations began to recover from the early epidemics; the flow of Spanish immigrants increased; and the slave trade to plantation colonies was expanded. Mining production increased, with silver production rising steadily into the 1780s. Agricultural exports also expanded, especially exports of tobacco, dyes, hides, chocolate, cotton, and sugar.

The Spanish and Portuguese kings also sought to reduce the power of the Catholic Church while at the same time transferring some church wealth to their treasuries. These efforts led to a succession of confrontations between colonial officials and the church hierarchy. To the kings of Portugal and Spain, the Jesuits symbolized the independent power of the church. In 1759 the Portuguese king expelled this powerful order from his territories, and the Spanish king imitated this decision in 1767. In practice these actions forced many colonial-born Jesuits from their native lands and closed the schools that had educated many members of the colonial elite.

Bourbon political and fiscal reforms also contributed to a growing sense of colonial grievance by limiting creoles' access to colonial offices and by imposing new taxes and monopolies that transferred more colonial wealth to Spain. Consumer and producer resentment in the colonies led to a series of violent confrontations with Spanish administrators. Many colonials, including members of the elite, resented what they saw as the unilateral overturning of the arrangements and understandings that had governed these societies for centuries. However, the Spanish effort to recruit local elites as military officers to improve imperial defense offered some colonial residents a compensatory opportunity for higher social status and greater responsibility.

In addition to tax rebellions and urban riots, colonial reforms also provoked Amerindian uprisings. In 1780 the Peruvian Amerindian leader José Gabriel Condorcanqui began the largest rebellion. He assumed the name of his Inka ancestor

Tupac Amaru (TOO-pack a-MAH-roo), whom the Spanish executed in 1572. Although a hereditary Quechua leader, **Tupac Amaru II** received his education from the Jesuits and had close ties to the local bishop and other powerful colonial authorities. He was also actively involved in colonial trade. Tupac Amaru II did not clearly state whether he sought only to end local injustices or overthrow Spanish rule, but he clearly sought to redress the grievances of Amerindian communities who suffered from forced labor and from high taxes. As his rebellion spread, he attracted creoles, mestizos, and slaves as well as Amerindians to his cause. After his capture in 1781, the Spanish brutally executed Tupac Amaru II along with his wife and fifteen other family members and allies. By the time Spanish authority was firmly reestablished, more than 100,000 lives had been lost and enormous amounts of property destroyed.

Brazil also experienced a similar period of expansion and reform after 1700. Portugal created new administrative positions and gave monopoly companies exclusive rights to little-developed regions. As in Spanish America, a more intrusive colonial government that imposed new taxes led to rebellions and plots, including open warfare in 1707 between local-born "sons of the soil" and "outsiders" in São Paulo. The most aggressive period of reform occurred during the ministry of the marquis of Pombal (1750–1777). The discovery in Brazil of gold in the 1690s and diamonds after 1720 financed the reforms. Brazil's exports of minerals as well as coffee and cotton deepened dependence on the slave trade, and nearly 2 million African slaves were imported in the eighteenth century.

Reform and Reorganization in British America   England's efforts to reform and reorganize its North American colonies began earlier than the Bourbon initiative in Spanish America. After the period of Cromwell's Puritan Republic (see Chapter 17), the restored Stuart king, Charles II, undertook an ambitious campaign to establish greater control over the colonies. Between 1651 and 1673 a series of Navigation Acts sought to severely limit colonial trading and colonial production that competed directly with English manufacturers. England also attempted to increase royal control over colonial political life by replacing colonial charters and proprietorships. Because the king viewed the New England colonies as centers of smuggling, he temporarily suspended their elected assemblies while appointing colonial governors and granting them new fiscal and legislative powers.

James II's overthrow in the Glorious Revolution of 1688 ended this confrontation, but not before colonists were provoked to resist and, in some cases, rebel. Colonials overthrew the governors of New York and Massachusetts and removed the Catholic proprietor of Maryland. William and Mary restored relative peace, but these conflicts alerted colonials to the potential aggression of the English government. Colonial politics would remain confrontational until the American Revolution.

During the eighteenth century the English colonies experienced renewed economic growth and attracted a new wave of European immigration, but social divisions were increasingly evident. The colonial population in 1770 was more urban, more clearly divided by class and race, and more vulnerable to economic downturns. Crises were provoked when imperial wars with France and Spain disrupted trade in the Atlantic, increased tax burdens, forced military mobilizations, and

Sir Henry Chamberlain, *Views and Costumes of the City and Neighborhoods of Rio de Janeiro*, London, 1822

Market in Rio de Janeiro *In many of the cities of colonial Latin America, female slaves and black free women dominated retail markets. In this scene from late colonial Brazil, Afro-Brazilian women sell a variety of foods and crafts.*

provoked frontier conflicts with Amerindians. On the eve of the American Revolution, England defeated France and weakened Spain, but the cost was great. The administrative, military, and tax policies imposed to gain this empire-wide victory had also alienated much of the North American colonial population.

CONCLUSION

The New World colonial empires of Spain, Portugal, France, and England had many characteristics in common. All subjugated Amerindian peoples and introduced large numbers of enslaved Africans. Within all four empires European settlement and the introduction of Old World animals and plants also transformed the natural environment. Europeans introduced Old World diseases, such as smallpox, that had a devastating effect on the native populations. Settlers in all four colonial empires applied the technologies of the Old World to the resources of the New, producing mineral and agricultural wealth and exploiting the commercial possibilities of the emerging Atlantic market in ways that accelerated the integration of Europe, Asia, and America.

Each of the New World empires also reflected the distinctive cultural and institutional heritages of its colonizing power. Mineral wealth allowed Spain to develop the most centralized empire, with political and economic power concentrated in great cities like Mexico City and Lima. Portugal and France pursued objectives similar to Spain's, but neither Brazil's agricultural economy, based on sugar, nor France's Canadian fur trade produced the financial resources and levels of centralized control achieved by Spain. Nevertheless, unlike Britain, all three of these Catholic powers were able to impose and enforce significant levels of religious and cultural uniformity in their colonies.

Greater cultural and religious diversity characterized British North America. Immigrants came to the colonies from the British Isles, including all of Britain's religious traditions, as well as from Germany, Sweden, the Netherlands, and France. British colonial government varied somewhat from colony to colony and was much more responsive to local interests. Thus colonists in British North America were better able than those in the areas controlled by Spain, Portugal, and France to respond to changing economic and political circumstances and to influence government policies. Most importantly, the British colonies attracted many more European immigrants than did the other New World colonies. Between 1580 and 1760 French colonies received 60,000 European immigrants, Brazil 523,000, and the Spanish colonies 678,000. Within a shorter period—between 1600 and 1760—the British settlements welcomed 746,000. Population in British North America—free and slave combined—had reached an extraordinary 2.5 million by 1775.

IMPORTANT EVENTS 1500–1770	
1518	Smallpox arrives in Caribbean
1534–1542	Jacques Cartier's voyages to explore Newfoundland of St. Lawrence
1535	Creation of Vice royalty of New Spain
1540s	Creation of Viceroyalty of Peru
After 1540	Sugar begins to dominate the Brazilian economy
1607	Jamestown founded
1608	Quebec founded
1620	Plymouth founded
1630s	Quilombo of Palmares founded
1664	English take New York from Dutch
1699	Louisiana founded
1700	Last Habsburg ruler of Spain dies
1713	First Bourbon ruler of Spain crowned
1750–1777	Reforms of marquis de Pombal
1754–1763	French and Indian War
1760	English take Canada
1770s and 1780s	Amerindian revolts in Andean region

19

THE ATLANTIC SYSTEM AND AFRICA, 1550–1800

B y the eighteenth century, Caribbean colonies had become the largest producers of sugar in the world. Slaves represented about 90 percent of the
islands' population and provided nearly all the labor for harvesting and processing sugar cane. The profitable expansion of sugar agriculture in the seventeenth
century opened a new era in the African slave trade. As larger and faster ships carried growing numbers of slaves from Africa, the human cost escalated, as the following example demonstrates.

In 1694 the English ship *Hannibal* called at the West African port of Whydah
(WEE-duh) to purchase slaves. The king of Whydah invited the ship's captain and
officers to his residence, where they negotiated an agreement on the prices for
slaves. In all, the *Hannibal* purchased 692 slaves, of whom about a third were
women and girls. The ship's doctor then carefully inspected the naked captives to
be sure they were of sound body, young, and free of disease. After their purchase,
the slaves were branded with an H (for *Hannibal*) to establish ownership. Once
they were loaded on the ship, the crew put shackles on the men to prevent their
escape.

To keep the slaves healthy, the captain had the crew feed them twice a day on
boiled corn meal and beans brought from Europe and flavored with hot peppers
and palm oil purchased in Africa. Each slave received a pint (half a liter) of water
with every meal. In addition, the slaves were made to "jump and dance for an hour
or two to our bagpipe, harp, and fiddle" every evening to keep them fit. Despite the
incentives and precautions for keeping the cargo alive, deaths were common among
the hundreds of people crammed into every corner of a slave ship. The *Hannibal*'s
experience was worse than most; it lost 320 slaves and 14 crew members to smallpox and dysentery during the seven-week voyage to Barbados.

As the *Hannibal*'s experience suggests, the Atlantic slave trade took a devastating toll in African lives and was far from a sure-fire money maker for European
investors, who in this case lost more than £3,000 on the voyage. Nevertheless, the
slave trade and plantation slavery were crucial pieces of a booming new **Atlantic
system** that moved goods and wealth, as well as peoples and cultures, around the
Atlantic.

PLANTATIONS IN THE WEST INDIES

The West Indies was the first place in the Americas reached by Columbus, and it was also the first region in the Americas where native populations collapsed from epidemics. It took a long time to repopulate these islands and forge economic links with other parts of the Atlantic. But after 1650 sugar plantations, African slaves, and European capital made these islands a major center of the Atlantic economy.

Colonization Before 1650   Spanish settlers introduced sugar-cane cultivation into the West Indies shortly after 1500, but these colonies soon fell into neglect as attention shifted to colonizing the Western Hemisphere mainland. After 1600 the West Indies revived as a focus of colonization, this time by northern Europeans interested in growing tobacco and other crops. In the 1620s and 1630s, English and French colonists settled many islands of the Antilles. With greater government support, the English colonies prospered first, largely by producing tobacco.

Tobacco, a New World leaf long used by Amerindians for recreation and medicine, was finding a new market among seventeenth-century Europeans. Despite the opposition of individuals like King James I of England, who condemned tobacco smoke as "dangerous to the eye, hateful to the nose, harmful to the brain, and dangerous to the lungs," the habit spread. By 1614 seven thousand shops in and around London sold tobacco.

The first tobacco colonies suffered from diseases, hurricanes, and attacks by native Caribs and the Spanish (see Environment and Technology: Hurricanes and the Caribbean Plantation Economy). They also suffered from shortages of supplies from Europe and shortages of labor sufficient to clear land and plant tobacco. The governments of France and England controlled costs by allowing private investors organized as **chartered companies** to develop the colonies in exchange for monopoly control and annual fees. These companies provided passage to the colonies for poor Europeans who were obligated to work three or four years as indentured servants. As a result the French and English populations grew rapidly in the 1630s and 1640s. By the middle of the century, however, these Caribbean colonies were in crisis due to stiff competition from Virginia tobacco, also cultivated by indentured servants (see Chapter 18). As the English, French, and Dutch colonies of the Caribbean switched from tobacco to sugar cane and from European indentured laborers to the labor of African slaves, profits reached new heights.

The Portuguese first developed sugar plantations that relied on African slaves on islands along the African coast. They later introduced this complex in Brazil (see Chapter 18). By 1600 Brazil was the Atlantic world's greatest sugar producer. The Dutch were early participants in the Brazilian sugar business as investors, merchants, and processors.

Dramatic events in Europe overturned this prosperous alliance in the sugar business. Beginning in the 1560s, Dutch Protestants began a rebellion against their Spanish overlords. Then in 1580 the Spanish king Philip II inherited the throne of Portugal (see Chapter 17). As a result, Philip barred the rebellious Dutch from the rich sugar business of Brazil. Decades before formal independence in 1648, however, the Dutch were militarily and economically strong enough to extend their war against the king of Spain to the coast of Brazil. In 1621 the Dutch government chartered the **Dutch West India Company**, and in 1624 this commercial enterprise led an attack on Brazil's key sugar port, Salvador. The Dutch were soon forced to retreat in the face of local resistance. Then in 1628 a company fleet captured a Spanish treasure convoy in the Caribbean and used some of the windfall to finance an assault on Pernambuco, one of Brazil's valuable sugar-producing areas. Once established, the Dutch improved the efficiency of the Brazilian sugar industry and also profited from supplying African slaves and European goods to the region.

Once free of Spanish rule in 1640, the reestablished Portuguese crown turned its attention to reasserting its control in Brazil and by 1654 had driven the last of the Dutch from the colony. Some of the expelled planters transferred their capital and knowledge of sugar production to Dutch Caribbean colonies as well as to the English and French islands, modernizing the industry and dramatically expanding exports.

Like its assault on Brazil, the Dutch West India Company's entry into the African slave trade combined economic and political motives. It seized the important West African trading station of Elmina from the Portuguese in 1638 and took their port of Luanda (loo-AHN-duh) on the Angolan coast in 1641. From these coasts the Dutch shipped slaves to Brazil and the West Indies. Although the Portuguese were able to drive the Dutch out of Angola after a few years, Elmina remained the Dutch West India Company's headquarters in West Africa.

Sugar and Slaves   The infusion of Dutch expertise and money revived the French colonies of Guadeloupe and Martinique, but the English colony of Barbados best illustrates the dramatic transformation that sugar brought to the seventeenth-century Caribbean. In 1640 Barbados's economy depended largely on tobacco, mostly grown by European settlers, both free and indentured. By the 1680s sugar had become the principal crop and enslaved Africans were three times as numerous as Europeans. Exporting up to 15,000 tons of sugar a year, Barbados had become the wealthiest and most populous of England's American colonies. By 1700 Barbados and other West Indian colonies had collectively surpassed Brazil as the world's principal source of sugar.

This transformation was accomplished at a high environmental cost. Originally covered in tropical forest, Barbados was virtually deforested in a matter of decades. Forests were cut to provide fuel for the refineries and to make more land available for sugar. This deforestation led to soil erosion, silted rivers, and fields exhausted of nutrients. As colonists turned to sugar production, similar patterns appeared elsewhere in the Caribbean as well.

The expansion of sugar plantations in the West Indies required a sharp increase in the volume of the slave trade from Africa (see Figure 19.1). During the first half of the seventeenth century about ten thousand slaves a year had arrived from Africa. Most were destined for Brazil and the mainland Spanish colonies. In the second half of the century the trade averaged twenty thousand slaves annually, and more than half landed in the English, French, and Dutch West Indies. As sugar production surged between 1640 and 1807, more than 4 million slaves were imported into the Caribbean region, ten times the slave imports of British North America.

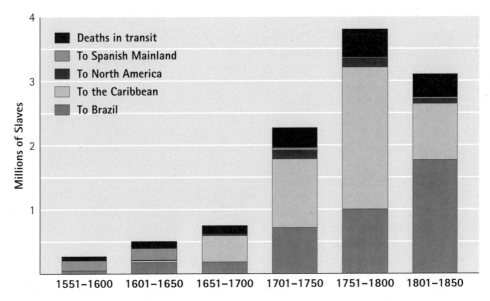

FIGURE 19.1 Transatlantic Slave Trade from Africa, 1551–1850

Source: Data from David Eltis, "The Volume and Structure of the Transatlantic Slave Trade: A Reassessment," *William and Mary* Quarterly, 3rd Series, 58 (2001), tables II and III.

Cash-short tobacco planters in the seventeenth century preferred indentured Europeans to African slaves because they cost half as much. Poor European men and women were willing to work for little in order to get to the Americas, where they could acquire their own land cheaply at the end of their term of service. However, as the cultivation of sugar spread after 1750, speculators drove land prices in the West Indies so high that former indentured servants could no longer afford to buy land. As a result, poor Europeans chose to indenture themselves in Britain's North American colonies, where cheap land was still available (see Chapter 18). Rather than raise wages to attract European laborers, Caribbean sugar planters switched to slaves.

Rising sugar prices allowed West Indian sugar planters to afford the higher cost of African slaves. The fact that slaves lived seven years on average after their arrival, while the typical indentured labor contract was for only three or four years, also made slaves a better investment. Dutch and other traders responded to rising labor demands by increasing the flow of slaves to meet the needs of the expanding plantations (see Figure 19.1), but slave prices rose throughout the eighteenth century. These high labor costs were one more factor favoring more-efficient large plantations over smaller operations.

PLANTATION LIFE IN THE EIGHTEENTH CENTURY

To find more land for sugar plantations, France and England expanded their Caribbean holdings by attacking older Spanish colonies. In 1655 the English seized Jamaica from the Spanish. They also took Havana, Cuba, in 1762 and held the

Plantation Scene, Antigua, British West Indies *The sugar made at the mill in the background was sealed in barrels and loaded on carts that oxen and horses drew to the beach. By means of a succession of vessels the barrels were taken to the ship that hauled the cargo to Europe. The importance of African labor is evident from the fact that only one white person appears in the painting.*

city for a year. By the time the occupation ended, English merchants had imported large numbers of slaves and Cuba had begun to switch from tobacco to sugar production. The French had seized the western half of the Spanish island of Hispaniola in the 1670s. During the eighteenth century this new French colony of Saint Domingue (san doh-MANGH) (present-day Haiti) became the greatest producer of sugar in the Atlantic world, while Jamaica surpassed Barbados as England's most important sugar colony. The technological, environmental, and social transformation of these island colonies illustrates the power of the new Atlantic system.

Technology and Environment   Sugar production had both an agricultural and an industrial character. On both small farms and large plantations, growing and harvesting sugar cane required only simple tools like spades, hoes, and machetes. Once the cane was cut, however, a more complex and expensive process was needed to produce sugar. Slaves rushed the cane to mills, where it was crushed and the juice extracted. Lead-lined wooden troughs carried cane juice to a series of large copper kettles where excess water was boiled off, leaving thick syrup. Placed in conical clay molds, the syrup turned to crystallized sugar as it dried. While small refiners used crushing mills powered by animals or even by laborers, large plantations used larger and more efficient mills that relied on wind or water power. The economies of scale generated by larger mills meant that over time the more-efficient, large-scale producers had lower costs and greater profits.

To make the operation more efficient and profitable, investors sought to utilize the costly crushing and refining machinery intensively. As a result, West Indian plantations expanded from an average of around 100 acres (40 hectares) in the seventeenth century to at least twice that size in the eighteenth century. Some plantations were even larger. In 1774 Jamaica's 680 sugar plantations averaged 441 acres (178 hectares), with the largest over 2,000 acres (800 hectares). By this date Jamaica was so specialized in sugar production that this agricultural colony had to import most of its food. Saint Domingue had a comparable number of plantations of smaller average size but generally higher productivity. This French colony was also more diverse in its economy. Although sugar production was paramount, some planters raised provisions for local consumption as well as crops such as coffee and cacao for export.

Sugar agriculture had a mixed environmental record. Some practices were not destructive. Planters powered their mills by water, wind, or animals and fueled their boilers by burning crushed cane. They fertilized their fields using manure from their livestock. Yet high profits led planters to exploit nature ruthlessly in other ways. Everywhere in the Caribbean, forests were cleared to plant sugar or other export crops. Repeated cultivation of a single crop was also damaging because it removed more nutrients from the soil than animal fertilizer and fallow periods could restore. Instead of rotating sugar with other crops to restore the nutrients naturally, planters found it more profitable to clear new lands when yields declined in the old fields. When land was finally exhausted, planters often moved on to new islands. Many of the English who settled Jamaica had been planters on Barbados. Similarly, the pioneer planters on Saint Domingue came from older French sugar colonies where production had begun to decline. As a result of these destructive practices, Jamaican sugar production began to fall behind Saint Domingue, which still had virgin land in the second half of the eighteenth century.

In addition to soil exhaustion and deforestation, the introduction of nonnative animals and cultivated plants transformed the Caribbean region. The Spanish brought cattle, pigs, and horses, which multiplied rapidly. They also introduced new plants. Bananas and plantains from the Canary Islands were a valuable addition to the food supply, and sugar and rice formed the basis of plantation agriculture, along with native tobacco. Other food crops arrived with the slaves from Africa, including okra, black-eyed peas, yams, grains such as millet and sorghum, and mangoes. Many of these new animals and plants were useful additions to the islands, but they crowded out indigenous species. The most tragic and dramatic transformation of the West Indies was demographic. Chapter 16 detailed how disease and abuse nearly eliminated the indigenous peoples of the large islands within fifty years of Columbus's first voyage. Far earlier and more completely than in any mainland colony, the West Indies were repeopled from across the Atlantic—first with thousands of free Europeans and then with millions of captive Africans.

Slaves' Lives   During the eighteenth century West Indian plantation colonies were the world's most polarized societies. On most islands 90 percent or more of the inhabitants were slaves. Power resided in the

ENVIRONMENT + TECHNOLOGY

Hurricanes and the Caribbean Plantation Economy

The European plantation colonies of the Caribbean produced prodigious amounts of wealth, but they were vulnerable to hurricanes and other natural disasters. By the middle of the eighteenth century this prosperous region was dominated by large sugar plantations and dependent on the labor of its fast-growing slave population. Between 1768 and 1786 alone the number of slaves in Jamaica increased from 168,900 to 255,700.

While Europe's growing demand for sugar created the potential for enormous profits in Caribbean plantation colonies,

Courtesy of the John Carter Brown Library at Brown University

Caribbean Hurricane *View of town of Léogane in French sugar colony of Saint Domingue (Haiti) during 1791 hurricane. Shipwreck with rescued passengers in foreground.*

hands of a **plantocracy**, a small number of very rich men who owned most of the slaves and most of the land. Between the slaves and the masters was a small middle group of estate managers, government officials, artisans, and small farmers, nearly all white. While some free blacks owned property or entered commerce, it is, nevertheless, only a slight simplification to describe eighteenth-century Caribbean society as being made up of a large, abject class of slaves and a small, powerful class of masters.

European planters and investors repeatedly faced the disastrous consequences of natural disasters, especially earthquakes and hurricanes. The 1692 earthquake that flattened Port Royal, Jamaica, was among the most destructive, but the Spanish colony of Puerto Rico also experienced powerful earthquakes in 1670 and 1787. Similarly, the French colony of Saint Domingue suffered four earthquakes in less than a century, with the 1751 quake causing the greatest loss of life and property destruction.

While earthquakes could be devastating, these geological events were typically separated by decades if not much longer time periods. The Caribbean hurricane season of the late summer and fall, however, routinely threatened this region annually. Hurricanes can also affect the Atlantic coast of North America, but they are much more frequent and generally more destructive in the Caribbean.

The prosperous British sugar colony of Jamaica, for example, experienced five hurricanes in a seven-year period in the late eighteenth century. One survivor of the October 1780 hurricane reported to readers in London that "every [sugar] cane, every plantain tree, every fruit-tree, every building [is] entirely blown down." This same storm ravaged Barbados, causing £1,000,000 sterling in damage. Slaves housed in the least substantial buildings in both colonies faced the greatest risks. More than two thousand slaves died in

Barbados, and more than five hundred more died in Jamaica in the same 1780 hurricane.

By the end of the eighteenth century the accumulated effects of hurricanes had played an important role in shaping the society and economy of the Caribbean. In an era without insurance for crops, homes, or refineries, planters attempted to reduce risk by bending every effort to harvest, process, and ship sugar before the hurricane season began, but this difficult schedule required ideal weather conditions, rapid refining, and the availability of shipping. Since these conditions were seldom present, nearly every planter was forced to absorb the disastrous costs of hurricane damage sooner or later. Following a hurricane, the poorest, most vulnerable planters were often compelled to sell land and slaves purchased with borrowed money at depreciated prices. Generally, the richest planters with the largest slaveholdings had the best chance to recover, since they could rebuild quickly and could absorb the steep short-term losses. But even the wealthiest planters were often forced to borrow at high interest rates for repairs, making them more vulnerable to ruin during the next hurricane season.

Source: This discussion relies in part on Matthew Mulcahy, "Weathering the Storms: Hurricanes and Risk in the British Greater Caribbean," *Business History Review* 78 (2004): 635–663.

The profitability of a Caribbean plantation depended on extracting as much work as possible from the slaves, and plantations achieved exceptional productivity through the threat and use of force. Slaves worked long hours in difficult conditions throughout the year, but, when the cane harvest and milling were in full swing, workdays might stretch to eighteen hours or more. As Table 19.1 shows, on a typical Jamaican plantation about 80 percent of the slaves were actively engaged in productive tasks; the only exceptions were infants, the seriously ill, and the very old.

TABLE 19.1 | SLAVE OCCUPATIONS ON A JAMAICAN SUGAR PLANTATION, 1788

Occupations and Conditions	Men	Women	Boys and Girls	Total
Field laborers	62	78		140
Tradesmen	29			29
Field drivers	4			4
Field cooks		4		4
Mule-, cattle-, and stablemen	12			12
Watchmen	18			18
Nurse		1		1
Midwife		1		1
Domestics and gardeners		5	3	8
Grass-gang			20	20
Total employed	125	89	23	237
Infants			23	23
Invalids (18 with yaws)				32
Absent on roads				5
Superannuated [elderly]				7
Overall total				304

Source: Adapted from "Edward Long to William Pitt," in Michael Craton, James Walvin, and David Wright, eds., *Slavery, Abolition, and Emancipation* (London: Longman, 1976), 103. © Michael Craton, James Walvin, and David Wright, reprinted by permission of Pearson Education Limited.

Table 19.1 also illustrates how planters organized slaves by age, sex, and ability. Only 2 or 3 percent of the slaves were house servants. About 70 percent of the able-bodied slaves worked in the fields, generally in one of three labor gangs. A "great gang," made up of the strongest slaves in the prime of life, did the heaviest work, such as breaking up the soil at the beginning of the planting season. A second gang of youths, elders, and less fit slaves did somewhat lighter work. A "grass gang," composed of children under the supervision of an elderly slave, was responsible for weeding and other simple work, such as collecting grass for the animals. Slaves too old for any field labor tended the toddlers. Women sometimes formed the majority of the field laborers, even in the great gang of some plantations. Owners seeking maximum profits even forced nursing mothers to take their babies with them to the fields.

Because the slave trade imported twice as many males as females, men outnumbered women on Caribbean plantations. As Table 19.1 shows, a little over half of adult males did nongang work. Some tended livestock, and others were skilled craftsmen, such as blacksmiths and carpenters. The most important artisan slave was the head boiler, who oversaw the delicate process of reducing the cane sap to crystallized sugar and molasses.

Planters often rewarded skilled slaves with better-quality food and clothing or with time off, but most field slaves were compelled to work without respite by fear of the lash. Slave gangs were led by a privileged male slave, appropriately called the **driver**, whose job was to ensure that the gang completed its work. Since production quotas were high, slaves toiled in the fields from sunup to sunset, except for meal breaks. Those who fell behind due to fatigue or illness soon felt the sting of the whip. Planters punished openly rebellious slaves who refused to work, disobeyed orders, or tried to escape with floggings, confinement in irons, or mutilation. While slaves usually did not work in the fields on Sunday, they could not rest, but had to use this time to farm their own provisioning grounds to supplement meager rations, maintain their dwellings, and do other chores, such as washing and mending their rough clothes.

Except for occasional holidays—including the Christmas-week revels in the British West Indies—there was little time for recreation and relaxation. Slaves might sing in the fields, but singing was simply a way to distract themselves from fatigue and the monotony of the work. There was certainly no time for schooling, nor were masters willing to educate slaves beyond the basic skills useful to the plantation.

Time for family life was also inadequate. Although the large proportion of young slaves in plantation colonies ought to have led to a high rate of natural increase, despite the sex imbalance that resulted from the slave trade, the opposite occurred. Poor nutrition and overwork led to lower fertility rates, but high mortality rates for infant slaves also limited population growth. The continuation of heavy fieldwork during the pregnancies of slave women made it difficult to carry a baby to term. Similarly, work demands limited a slave mother's ability to ensure her child's survival. As a result of these conditions, along with disease and accidents from dangerous mill equipment, deaths heavily outnumbered births on West Indian plantations (see Table 19.2). Life expectancy for slaves in nineteenth-century Brazil, for example, was only 23 years of age for males and 25.5 years for females. The figures were probably similar for the eighteenth-century Caribbean. A callous opinion, common among slave owners in

TABLE 19.2 | BIRTH AND DEATH ON A JAMAICAN SUGAR PLANTATION, 1779–1785

| Year | Born | | | Died | | |
	Males	Females	Purchased	Males	Females	Proportion of Deaths
1779	5	2	6	7	5	1 in 26
1780	4	3	—	3	2	1 in 62
1781	2	3	—	4	2	1 in 52
1782	1	3	9	4	5	1 in 35
1783	3	3	—	8	10	1 in 17
1784	2	1	12	9	10	1 in 17
1785	2	3	—	0	3	1 in 99
Total	19	18	27	35	37	
	Born 37			Died 72		

Source: From "Edward Long to William Pitt," in Michael Craton, James Walvin, and David Wright, eds., *Slavery, Abolition, and Emancipation* (London: Longman, 1976), 105. © Michael Craton, James Walvin, and David Wright, reprinted by permission of Pearson Education Limited.

the Caribbean and in parts of Brazil, held that it was cheaper to import a youthful new slave from Africa than to raise one to the same age on a plantation.

The harsh conditions of plantation life played a major role in shortening slaves' lives, but the greatest killer was disease. Dysentery caused by contaminated food and water was common. Slaves newly arrived from Africa went through the period of adjustment to a new environment known as **seasoning**, during which one-third, on average, died of unfamiliar diseases. Slaves also suffered from diseases brought with them, including malaria. On the plantation profiled in Table 19.1, for example, more than half of the slaves incapacitated by illness had yaws, a painful and debilitating skin disease common in Africa. As a consequence, only slave populations in the healthier temperate zones of North America experienced natural increase.

The combination of high mortality and low fertility among the slaves of the Caribbean plantation colonies led inexorably to an ever-larger African slave trade. Plantation owners had to continually purchase new slaves to replace those who died and to expand sugar production. As a result, the majority of slaves on most West Indian plantations were African-born, and African religious beliefs, patterns of speech, styles of dress and adornment, and music were prominent parts of West Indian life.

Alfredo Dagli Orti/The Art Archive at Art Resource

The Brutal Foundation of Plantation Prosperity *In Caribbean slave societies the punishment of slaves was often conducted in public places in order to intimidate other slaves. In this early nineteenth-century illustration, the slave in the foreground is whipped by two other slaves supervised by the owner. In the background a female slave is suspended by her wrists from a tree branch after being whipped.*

Given the harsh conditions of their lives, it is not surprising that slaves in the West Indies often sought to gain their freedom. Individual slaves often ran away, and sometimes large groups of plantation slaves rose in rebellion against their bondage and abuse. On Jamaica alone there were sixteen rebellions between 1655 and 1813. For example, a slave named Tacky, who had been a chief on the Gold Coast of Africa, led a large rebellion in Jamaica in 1760. After his followers broke into a fort and armed themselves, slaves from nearby plantations joined the rebellion. This force attacked several plantations, setting them on fire and killing the planter families. Tacky ultimately died in the fighting, and three of his lieutenants stoically endured cruel deaths by torture by colonial authorities who sought to deter others from rebellion.

Because European planters believed that slaves with the strongest African heritage led rebellions, they tried to curtail African cultural traditions. They required slaves to learn the colonial language and discouraged the use of African languages by deliberately mixing slaves from different parts of Africa. In French and Portuguese colonies, slaves were encouraged to adopt Catholic religious practices, though African deities, beliefs, and practices survived, serving as the foundation for modern African-derived religions like Brazilian candomblé. In the British West Indies, where only Quaker slave owners encouraged Christianity among their slaves before 1800, African herbal medicine remained strong, as did African beliefs concerning nature spirits and witchcraft.

Free Whites and Free Blacks   The lives of free men and women were very different from the lives of slaves. In the French colony of Saint Domingue, which had nearly half of all slaves in the Caribbean in the eighteenth century, there were three categories of free people. At the top were wealthy owners of large sugar plantations (the *grands blancs* [grawn blawnk], or "great whites"), mostly French nationals, who dominated the economy and society of the island. Second came less-well-off Europeans (*petits blancs* [pay-TEE blawnk], or "little whites"). Most served as colonial officials, retail merchants, or small-scale agriculturalists. Nearly all members of both groups owned slaves. Third came the free blacks. There were almost as many free blacks as free whites in Saint Domingue. While they ranked below whites socially, many free blacks owned property, and a surprising number also owned slaves.

The plantation elite was even more powerful in British colonies. Whereas sugar constituted about half of Saint Domingue's exports, in Jamaica the figure was over 80 percent. Such concentration on sugar crowded out small cultivators, white or black, and confined most landholding to a few larger owners. At midcentury three-quarters of the farmland in Jamaica belonged to individuals who owned 1,000 acres (400 hectares) or more.

One source estimated that a planter had to invest nearly £20,000 in 1774 (about £2,000,000 or $3,200,000 in 2012) to acquire a medium-size Jamaican plantation of 600 acres (240 hectares). A third of this money went for land on which to grow sugar and food crops, pasture animals, and cut timber and firewood. A quarter of the expense was for the mill and refinery. The largest expense was the purchase of 200 slaves at £40 (about £4,116 or $6,586 in 2012) each. In comparison, the wage of an English rural laborer at this time was about £10 (about £1,029 or $1,646 in 2012) a year (one-fourth the price of a slave), and the annual incomes of the ten wealthiest noble families in Britain in 1760 averaged only £20,000 each.

Reputedly the richest Englishmen of this time, West Indian planters often translated their wealth into political power and social prestige. The richest planters put their plantations under the direction of managers and lived in Britain. Between 1730 and 1775 seventy of these absentee planters secured election to the British Parliament, where they formed an influential voting bloc. Planters who continued to reside in the West Indies exercised political power through the control of colonial assemblies.

In most European plantation colonies it was possible to grant freedom to an individual slave or group of slaves. **Manumission** (the legal grant of freedom by an owner) was more common in Brazil and the Spanish and French colonies than in English colonies. Among English colonies, manumissions were more common in the Caribbean than in North American colonies like South Carolina. While some plantation owners in the Caribbean freed slave women with whom they had had sexual relationships or freed the children of their mistresses, the largest group of freed slaves across the Americas purchased their freedom from masters. Manumissions led to the development of a large free black population in many colonies. Since the legal condition of children followed that of the mother, slave families often struggled to free women in childbearing years first so that their children would be born free. By the late eighteenth century free blacks made up a large portion of the black populations of Brazil and the French colonies.

As in Brazil and Spanish colonies (see Chapter 18), escaped slaves constituted another part of the free black population. Communities of runaways, called **maroons**, were numerous in Jamaica and Hispaniola as well as in the Guianas (guy-AHN-uhs). Jamaican maroons, after withstanding several attacks by the colony's militia, signed a treaty in 1738 that recognized their independence in return for their cooperation in stopping new runaways and suppressing slave revolts. Unable to win decisive victories, colonial authorities in Spanish, Dutch, and Portuguese colonies signed similar treaties with runaway leaders as well.

CREATING THE ATLANTIC ECONOMY

At once archaic in their cruel system of slavery and oddly modern in their specialization in a single product for export and efforts to improve refining machinery, the West Indian plantation colonies were the bittersweet fruits of a new Atlantic trading system. Changes in the character of Atlantic commerce illustrate the rise of this new system. In the sixteenth century Spanish treasure fleets laden with silver and gold bullion had dominated Atlantic trade. In the late seventeenth and eighteenth centuries the Atlantic trade was dominated by sugar ships returning to Europe from the West Indies and Brazil and by slave ships transporting an average of 250 African captives each to the Americas.

In addition to the plantation system, new economic institutions, new partnerships between private investors and governments in Europe, and new working relationships between European and African merchants created the Atlantic economy. This new trading system is a prime example of how European capitalist relationships were reshaping the world.

Capitalism and Mercantilism   Many of the Spanish and Portuguese voyages of exploration in the fifteenth and sixteenth centuries were government ventures, and both Spain and Portugal tried to restrict the overseas trade of their colonies using royal monopolies (see Chapters 16 and 18). Monopoly control, however, proved both expensive and inefficient. The success of the Atlantic economy in the seventeenth and eighteenth centuries depended much more on private enterprise, which made trade more efficient and profitable and spread risk among a large number of participants. European private investors were attracted to colonial trade by the rich profits generated by New World agriculture and mining, but their success depended on new institutions and the continuation of government protection to reduce the possibility of catastrophic loss.

The growth of the Atlantic economy played an important role in the development of modern **capitalism**. The essence of this economic system was the expansion of credit and the development of large financial institutions—banks, stock exchanges, and chartered trading companies—that enabled merchants and investors to conduct business at great distances from their homes while reducing risks and increasing profits (see Chapter 17). Originally developed for business dealings within Europe, the capitalist system expanded overseas in the seventeenth century, when slow economic growth in Europe led many investors to seek profits in the production and export of colonial products and in satisfying the colonial demand for European products. Among the Western Hemisphere's exports after 1650, sugar yielded a far higher and more reliable profit than any other cash crop. These profits and the trade they lubricated proved crucial to linking Europe, Africa, and the Americas in the fast-growing Atlantic commercial region.

Europe reaped a far larger share of the wealth produced in this commercial expansion than American or African participants because it had developed institutions that facilitated investment and reduced commercial risks. Chief among these innovations were private banks, joint-stock companies, speculative markets in commodities and shares, and commercial insurance. It took more than a century for these novelties to take root across the continent, but the earliest adopters, especially the English and Dutch, led the commercial expansion and enjoyed most of the benefits. Spain, Portugal, and France changed more slowly, leaving intrusive state controls of commerce in place until the eighteenth century.

European empires sought to monopolize the profits produced in their colonies by controlling trade and accumulating capital in the form of gold and silver, a system called **mercantilism**. Mercantilist policies strongly discouraged trade with foreign merchants, especially in the colonies, because any balance of trade deficit would be paid in gold or silver. These commercial policies were enforced by customs authorities, navies, and coast guards when necessary to secure exclusive relations. The practical result of these policies was to make European goods imported into American colonies more expensive and the products of colonial planters and other exporters cheaper when purchased by European merchants.

Chartered companies were an important part of mercantilist capitalism. In 1602 the Netherlands gave the Dutch East India Company a monopoly over trade in the Indian Ocean. Private investors who bought shares in the company were amply rewarded when the Dutch East India Company captured control of long-distance trade in the Indian Ocean from the Portuguese (see Chapter 20). As we have seen, the Dutch West India Company, chartered in 1621, sought similar benefits in the Atlantic trade by seizing sugar-producing areas in Brazil and African slaving ports from the Portuguese.

These successes inspired other governments to set up their own chartered companies. In 1672 a royal charter placed all English trade with West Africa in the hands of the **Royal African Company** (RAC), which established its headquarters at Cape Coast Castle, just east of Elmina on the Gold Coast. The French government also chartered companies and promoted overseas trade and colonization. Jean Baptiste Colbert (kohl-BEAR), King Louis XIV's minister of finance from 1661 to 1683, chartered the French East India and French West India Companies to expel Dutch and English traders from French colonies.

French and English governments also used military force to gain trade advantages in the Americas. For example, restrictions on Dutch access to French and English colonies provoked a series of wars with the Netherlands between 1652 and 1678 (see Chapter 17). The larger English and French navies ultimately defeated the Dutch and drove the Dutch West India Company into bankruptcy. Military and diplomatic pressure also forced Spain after 1713 to grant England and later France monopoly rights to supply slaves to its colonies.

With Dutch competition in the Atlantic reduced, the French and English limited the privileges of their chartered companies. Such new mercantilist policies fostered competition among a nation's own citizens, while using high tariffs and restrictions to exclude foreigners. In the 1660s England passed a series of Navigation Acts that confined trade with its colonies to English ships and cargoes; it later opened trade in Africa to any English subject, claiming that competition would cut the cost of slaves to West Indian planters. The French called their mercantilist legislation, codified in 1698, the *Exclusif* (ek-skloo-SEEF), highlighting its exclusionary intentions. Other mercantilist laws sought to protect national manufacturing and agricultural interests from the competition of colonies, imposing prohibitively high taxes on their manufactured goods and products like refined sugar.

As a result of these mercantilist measures, the Atlantic became Britain, France, and Portugal's most important overseas trading area. The value of imports from West Indian colonies alone accounted for over one-fifth the value of total British imports, while French West Indian colonies played an even larger role in France's overseas trade. Only the Dutch, closed out of much of the American trade, depended more heavily on Asian trade (see Chapter 20). Profits from the Atlantic economy, in turn, promoted further economic expansion and increased the revenues of European governments.

The Atlantic Circuit   At the heart of this trading system was a clockwise network of sea routes known as the **Atlantic Circuit**. The first leg, from Europe to Africa, carried European manufactures—notably metals, hardware, and guns—as well as great quantities of cotton textiles brought from India. While some of these goods were exchanged for West African gold, ivory, timber, and other products, most goods went to purchase slaves, who were transported across the Atlantic to the plantation colonies in what was known as the **Middle Passage**. On the third leg, plantation goods from the colonies returned to Europe. Each leg carried goods from where they were abundant and

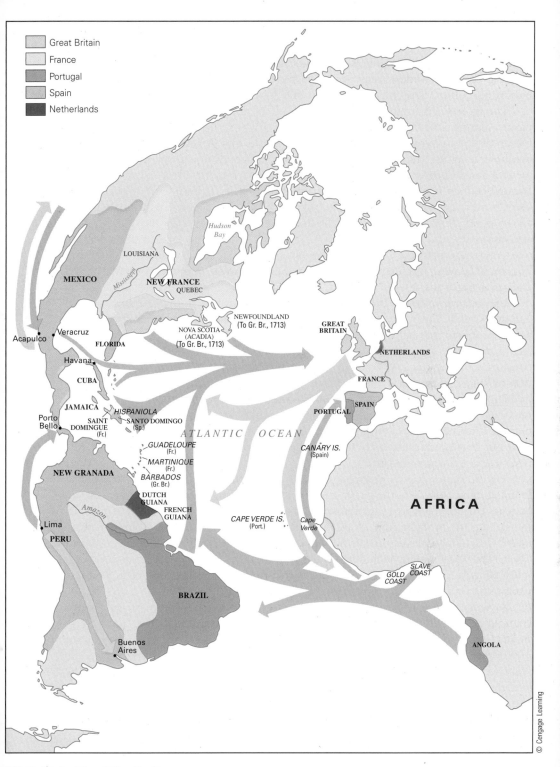

Legend:
- Great Britain
- France
- Portugal
- Spain
- Netherlands

Hudson Bay

LOUISIANA

MEXICO

NEW FRANCE
QUEBEC

Mississippi

NEWFOUNDLAND
(To Gr. Br., 1713)

NOVA SCOTIA
(ACADIA)
(To Gr. Br., 1713)

GREAT
BRITAIN

Acapulco

Veracruz

FLORIDA

Havana

CUBA

JAMAICA

NETHERLANDS

FRANCE

Porto
Bello

SAINT
DOMINGUE
(Fr.)

HISPANIOLA

SANTO DOMINGO
(Sp.)

PORTUGAL

SPAIN

ATLANTIC OCEAN

GUADELOUPE
(Fr.)

CANARY IS.
(Spain)

MARTINIQUE
(Fr.)

NEW GRANADA

BARBADOS
(Gr. Br.)

DUTCH
GUIANA

FRENCH
GUIANA

AFRICA

Amazon

Lima

PERU

CAPE VERDE IS.
(Port.)

Cape
Verde

BRAZIL

SLAVE
COAST

GOLD
COAST

Buenos
Aires

ANGOLA

© Cengage Learning

MAP 19.1 The Atlantic Economy

By 1700 the volume of maritime exchanges among the Atlantic continents had begun to rival the trade of the Indian Ocean Basin. Notice the trade in consumer products, slave labor, precious metals, and other goods. Silver trade to East Asia laid the basis for a Pacific Ocean economy.

relatively cheap to where they were scarce and therefore valuable. Thus, in theory, each leg of the Atlantic Circuit could earn profits. In practice, shipwrecks, deaths, piracy, and other risks could turn profit into loss.

The three-sided Atlantic Circuit is only one of many commercial routes that serviced Atlantic trade. Ships making the long voyage from Europe to the Indian Ocean and Asia typically exchanged African gold and American silver for cotton textiles and spices. Merchants then sold these Asian goods in Africa and the Americas as well as in Europe. Many commercial routes were more direct, carrying manufactured goods from Europe or foodstuffs and lumber from New England to the Caribbean. Some Rhode Island and Massachusetts merchants participated in a "Triangular Trade" that carried rum to West Africa, slaves to the West Indies, and molasses and rum back to New England. There was also a considerable two-way trade between Brazil and Angola that exchanged Brazilian tobacco and liquor for slaves. Brazilian tobacco also found its way north as a staple of the Canadian fur trade.

European investment capital, manufactured goods, and shipping dominated the Atlantic system. Europe was also the principal market for American plantation products, products that helped transform European material culture. Before the seventeenth century, sugar was scarce and expensive in Europe and was mostly consumed by the rich. As colonial production increased, prices fell and consumption of sugar in England rose to about 4 pounds (nearly 2 kilograms) per person in 1700. Europeans of modest means spooned sugar into popular new beverages imported from overseas—tea, coffee, and chocolate—to overcome the beverages' natural bitterness. Consumption increased to about 18 pounds (8 kilograms) by the early nineteenth century (well below the American average of about 152 pounds [69 kilograms] a year today).

The flow of sugar to Europe depended on the flow of slaves from Africa. The rising volume of the Middle Passage is one measure of the expansion of the Atlantic system. During the 150 years following the arrival of Europeans in the Americas, the slave trade brought some 800,000 Africans across the Atlantic. Volume rose to nearly 7.5 million slaves during the boom in sugar production between 1650 and 1800. The West Indies, including Cuba, imported nearly 50 percent of this total, while Brazil received nearly a third and North America another 5 percent. The rest went to Spain's mainland colonies (see Figure 19.1).

Seventeenth-century mercantilist policies placed much of the Atlantic slave trade in the hands of chartered companies. During their existence the Dutch West India Company and the English Royal African Company each carried about 100,000 slaves across the Atlantic. In the eighteenth century private English traders from Liverpool and Bristol controlled about 40 percent of the slave trade. The French, operating out of Nantes and Bordeaux, handled about 20 percent and the Dutch only 6 percent. The Portuguese supplying Brazil and other places had nearly 30 percent of the Atlantic slave trade, in contrast to the 3 percent carried in North American ships.

While the volume and duration of the slave trade indicate that it was profitable, the relative value of European goods and African slaves as well as slave prices in American ports determined the profit of individual voyages. Slave traders also had to deliver as many healthy slaves as possible for sale in the plantation colonies, but

© Cengage Learning

MAP 19.2   The African Slave Trade, 1500–1800

After 1500 a vast new trade in slaves from sub-Saharan Africa to the Americas joined the ongoing slave trade to the Islamic states of North Africa, the Middle East, and India. The West Indies were the major destination of the Atlantic slave trade, followed by Brazil.

the terrible conditions on slave ships and a long and treacherous voyage lasting from six to ten weeks led to high mortalities. Some ships arrived with all of their slaves alive, but large, even catastrophic, losses of life were common (see Figure 19.1). On average, however, slave traders succeeded in lowering mortality during the Middle Passage from about 23 percent on voyages before 1700 to half that in the last half of the eighteenth century.

Failed escapes and mutinies contributed to mortality. When opportunities presented themselves (nearness to land, illness among the crew), some enslaved Africans tried to overpower their captors and escape. As result, male slaves were routinely shackled together to prevent escapes while they were still in sight of land or when mutiny was feared while at sea. As an additional precaution, slave traders also commonly confined male slaves below deck during most of the voyage, except at mealtimes, when the crew brought them up in small groups under close supervision. In any event, "mutinies" were rarely successful and defeated mutineers were treated with brutality.

Mistreatment also contributed to the high mortality of the Middle Passage. Although it was in the interests of the captain and crew to deliver their slave cargo in good condition, slavers used whippings, beatings, and even executions to maintain order. Some slaves developed deep psychological depression, known to contemporaries as "fixed melancholy," and refused to eat. Crews attempted to force-feed these slaves, but some successfully willed themselves to death. The dangers and brutalities of the slave trade were so notorious that many ordinary seamen shunned such work. As a consequence, cruel and brutal officers and crews abounded on slave ships.

Although examples of unspeakable cruelties are common in the records, most deaths in the Middle Passage were the result of disease. Dysentery spread by contaminated food and water caused many deaths. Others died of contagious diseases such as smallpox carried on board by infected slaves or crew members. These maladies spread quickly in the crowded and unsanitary confines of the ships, claiming the lives of slaves already physically weakened and mentally traumatized by their ordeals. Crew members were exposed to the same epidemics. It is a measure of the callousness of the age, as well as the cheapness of European labor, that over the course of a round-trip voyage from Europe the proportion of crew deaths could be as high as the slave deaths.

AFRICA, THE ATLANTIC, AND ISLAM

The Atlantic system took a terrible toll in African lives both during the Middle Passage and under the harsh conditions of plantation slavery. Many other Africans died while being marched to African ports for sale. The overall effects on Africa of these losses and of other aspects of the slave trade have been the subject of considerable historical debate. It is clear that the trade's impact depended on the intensity and terms of different African regions' involvement.

Any assessment of the Atlantic system's effects in Africa must also take into consideration the fact that some Africans profited from the trade by capturing and selling slaves. They chained the slaves or bound them together using forked sticks fastened at the neck for the march to the coast. Once there, captives were bartered to the European slavers for trade goods. The effects on the enslaver were different from the effects on the enslaved. Finally, a broader understanding of the Atlantic system's effects in sub-Saharan Africa comes from comparisons with the effects of Islamic contacts.

The Gold Coast and the Slave Coast

As Chapter 16 showed, early European visitors to Africa's Atlantic coast were interested more in trading than in colonizing the continent. As the Africa trade mushroomed after 1650, this pattern continued. African kings and merchants sold slaves and other goods at many coastal sites, but the growing slave trade did not lead to substantial European colonization.

The transition to slave trading was not sudden. Even as slaves were becoming Atlantic Africa's most valuable export, goods such as gold, ivory, and timber remained important. For example, during its eight decades of operation from 1672 to 1752, the Royal African Company made 40 percent of its profits from gold, ivory, and forest products. In some parts of West Africa, such nonslave exports remained predominant even at the peak of the Atlantic trade.

African merchants were very discriminating about merchandise they took in exchange for slaves or other goods. A ship that arrived with goods of low quality or not suited to local tastes found it hard to purchase a cargo at a profitable price. European guidebooks to the African trade carefully noted the color and shape of beads, the pattern of textiles, the type of guns, and the sort of metals that were in demand on each section of the coast. Although African preferences for merchandise varied, textiles, hardware, and guns were in high demand. Of the goods the English Royal African Company traded in West Africa in the 1680s, over 60 percent were Indian and European textiles and 30 percent were hardware and weaponry. In the eighteenth century, tobacco and rum from the Americas became welcome imports.

Both Europeans and Africans sought to drive the best bargain for themselves and sometimes engaged in deceitful practices. The strength of the African bargaining position, however, may be inferred from the fact that as the demand for slaves rose, so too did their price in Africa. In the course of the eighteenth century the value of goods needed to purchase a slave on the Gold Coast doubled and in some places tripled or quadrupled.

African governments on the Gold and Slave Coasts forced Europeans to observe African trading customs and prevented them from taking control of African territory. Rivalry among European nations, each of which established its own trading "castles" along the Gold Coast, also reduced bargaining strength because Africans could shop for better deals among these competitors. In 1700 the head of the Dutch East India Company in West Africa, Willem Bosman (VIL-uhm boos-MAHN), bemoaned the fact that, to stay competitive against other European traders, his company had to include large quantities of muskets and gunpowder in the goods it exchanged, thereby adding to Africans' military power.

Bosman also related that his agents had to both pay the local king a substantial customs duty when buying slaves at Whydah and then pay a premium price for the slaves. By African standards, Whydah was a rather small kingdom controlling only the port and its immediate hinterland. In 1727, Dahomey (dah-HOH-mee), strengthened militarily by firearms acquired in the slave trade, annexed Whydah.

Two other regional powers, the kingdoms of Oyo (aw-YOH) and Asante (uh-SHAN-tee), also participated in the Atlantic trade, but neither kingdom was as dependent on it as Dahomey. Overseas trade formed a relatively modest part of the economies of these large and populous states, which maintained extensive overland trade with their northern neighbors and with states across the Sahara. Like the great medieval empires of the western Sudan, Oyo and Asante grew more powerful from external trade but were not dependent on it. In 1730, the Oyo kingdom over-ran Dahomey, forcing it to pay an annual tribute to keep its independence.

How did African kings and merchants obtain slaves for sale? Bosman dismissed misconceptions prevailing in Europe in his day. "Not a few in our country," he wrote to a friend in 1700, "fondly imagine that parents here sell their children, men their wives, and one brother the other. But those who think so, do deceive themselves; for this never happens on any other account but that of necessity, or some great crime; but most of the slaves that are offered to us are prisoners of war, which are sold by the victors as their booty."[1] His statement confirms other accounts claiming that prisoners of war were the most common source of slaves, but it is harder to prove that capturing slaves for export was a main cause of wars. "Here and there," conclude two respected historians of Africa, "there are indications that captives taken in the later and more peripheral stages of these wars were exported overseas, but it would seem that the main impetus of conquest was only incidentally concerned with the slave-trade."[2]

An early-nineteenth-century king of Asante had a similar view: "I cannot make war to catch slaves in the bush, like a thief. My ancestors never did so. But if I fight a king, and kill him when he is insolent, then certainly I must have his gold, and his slaves, and his people are mine too. Do not the white kings act like this?"[3] English rulers had indeed sentenced seventeenth-century Scottish and Irish prisoners to forced labor in the West Indies. One may imagine that neither African nor European prisoners shared their kings' view that such actions were legitimate.

The Bight of Biafra and Angola   In the eighteenth century the slave trade expanded eastward to the Bight (bite) of Biafra. In contrast to the Gold and Slave Coasts, where strong kingdoms predominated, the densely populated interior of the Bight of Biafra contained no large states. Even so, powerful merchant princes of the coastal ports made European traders give them rich presents.

Using a network of markets and inland routes, regional merchants supplied European slave traders at the coast with debtors, victims of kidnapping, and convicted criminals. As the volume of the Atlantic trade along the Bight of Biafra expanded in the late eighteenth century, some inland markets evolved into giant fairs with different sections specializing in slaves and imported goods. In the 1780s an English ship's doctor reported that African merchants collected slaves at fairs in the interior and that groups of twelve hundred to fifteen hundred enslaved men and women were then sent to the coast from a single fair.[4]

The local context of the Atlantic trade was different south of the Congo estuary at Angola, the greatest source of slaves for the Atlantic trade. This was also the one

---

[1]Willem Bosman, A New and Accurate Description of Guinea, etc. (London, 1705), quoted in David Northrup, ed., The Atlantic Slave Trade (Lexington, MA: D. C. Heath, 1994), 72.

[2]Roland Oliver and Anthony Atmore, The African Middle Ages, 1400–1800 (Cambridge, England: Cambridge University Press, 1981), 100.

[3]King Osei Bonsu, quoted in Northrup, ed., The Atlantic Slave Trade, 93.

[4]Alexander Falconbridge, Account of the Slave Trade on the Coast of Africa (London: J. Phillips, 1788), 12.

place along Africa's Atlantic coast where a single European nation, Portugal, controlled a significant amount of territory. Except for a brief period when the Dutch exercised control in the seventeenth century, Portuguese residents of the main ports of Luanda and Benguela (ben-GWAY-luh) served as middlemen between the caravans that arrived from the interior and the ships that crossed from Brazil. From these coastal cities Afro-Portuguese traders guided large caravans of trade goods inland to exchange for slaves at special markets.

Many of the slaves sold at these markets were prisoners of war captured by expanding African states. By the late eighteenth century prisoners captured in wars fought as far away as 600 to 800 miles (1,000 to 1,300 kilometers) were carried to the ports for transportation. Many were victims of wars of expansion fought by the giant federation of Lunda kingdoms. As elsewhere in Africa, prisoners sold as slaves seem to have been a byproduct of African wars, rather than the objective of the warring parties.

Research has identified a link between severe eighteenth-century droughts and the development of the Angolan slave trade. The environmental crisis in the hinterland drove famished refugees to better-watered areas.[5] Powerful African leaders gained control of these refugees in return for supplying them with food and water. These leaders valued refugee children, who would quickly assimilate, and adult women, who were valued as food producers and for reproduction. They often sold adult male refugees as slaves because they were more likely than women and children to escape or to challenge the ruler's authority. They used the textiles, weapons, and alcohol they received in return for slaves as gifts to attract new followers and to cement the loyalty of their established allies. The most successful became heads of powerful new states, stabilizing areas devastated by war and drought and repopulating them with the refugees and prisoners.

Although the organization of Atlantic trade varied from African region to region, it expanded and prospered because both European merchants and African elites benefited. African rulers and merchants exported slaves and other products to obtain foreign goods that made them wealthier and more powerful, and most of the exported slaves were prisoners taken in wars associated with African state growth. But strong African states or powerful merchant communities also proved better able to defend African territory and limit European economic advantages. The Africans who gained from this trade were the rich and powerful few. Many more Africans were losers in the exchanges.

Africa's European and Islamic Contacts   The ways in which sub-Saharan Africans established new contacts with Europe paralleled their much older pattern of relations with the Islamic world. But there were striking similarities and differences in Africans' political, commercial, and cultural interactions with these two external influences between 1500 and 1800.

During the three and a half centuries of contact up to 1800, Africans ceded very little territory to Europeans. Local African rulers kept close tabs on the European trading posts they permitted along the Gold and Slave Coasts and collected

---

[5] Joseph C. Miller, "The Significance of Drought, Disease, and Famine in the Agriculturally Marginal Zones of West-Central Africa," Journal of African History 23 (1982): 17–61.

lucrative rents and fees. Aside from some uninhabited islands off the Atlantic coast, Europeans established colonial beachheads in only two places, the Portuguese colony of Angola and the Dutch East India Company's Cape Colony at the southern tip of the continent. The Dutch colony was tied to Indian Ocean trade, not to the Atlantic trade, and, unlike Angola, did not export slaves. Most the Cape Colony's 25,750 slaves in 1793 were from Madagascar, South Asia, and the East Indies, not Africa.

North Africa had become a part of the Islamic world in the first century of Islamic expansion. Sub-Saharan Africans gradually learned of Muslim beliefs and practices from traders who crossed the Sahara from North Africa or who sailed from the Middle East to the Swahili trading cities of East Africa. In the sixteenth century the new Islamic Ottoman Empire annexed all of North Africa except Morocco, while Ethiopia lost extensive territory to other Muslim conquerors.

Until 1590 the Sahara remained an effective buttress against invasion from powerful northern states. The **Songhai** (song-GAH-ee) Empire of West Africa challenged the status quo when it pushed its frontier into the Sahara from the south. Ruled by an indigenous Muslim dynasty, Songhai drew its wealth from the trans-Saharan trade. This expansion led the kingdom of Morocco to challenge Songhai by sending a military expedition of four thousand men south across the desert. Although half the invading force perished, the survivors, armed with firearms, defeated Songhai's army of forty thousand in 1591. While Morocco was never able to annex the western Sudan, its forces extracted a massive tribute in slaves and goods from the local population and imposed tolls on trade for the next two centuries.

With Morocco's destruction of Songhai, the **Hausa** trading cities in the central Sudan attracted most of the caravans bringing textiles, hardware, and weapons across the Sahara. The goods the Hausa imported and distributed through their trading networks were similar to those that coastal African traders commanded from the Atlantic trade, except for the absence of alcohol, prohibited to Muslims. The goods they sent back in return also resembled the major African exports into the Atlantic: gold, textiles and leather goods, and slaves.

Few statistics of the slave trade to the Islamic north exist, but the size of the trade seems to have been substantial, if smaller than the transatlantic trade at its peak. Between 1600 and 1800 slave traders sent about 850,000 slaves to Muslim North Africa. A nearly equal number of slaves from sub-Saharan Africa entered the Islamic Middle East and India by way of the Red Sea and the Indian Ocean.

In contrast to the plantation slavery of the Americas, most African slaves in the Islamic world served as soldiers and servants. In the late seventeenth and eighteenth centuries Morocco's rulers employed an army of 150,000 African slaves, trusting their loyalty more than that of recruits from their own lands. Moroccans also used slaves on sugar plantations, as servants, and as artisans. Unlike in the Americas, the majority of African slaves in the Islamic world were women who served wealthy households as concubines, servants, and entertainers. The trans-Saharan slave trade also included a much higher proportion of children than the Atlantic trade.

The central Sudanese kingdom of **Bornu** illustrates several aspects of trans-Saharan contacts. Ruled by the same dynasty since the ninth century, this Muslim state had grown and expanded in the sixteenth century as the result of guns

Entrance of Heinrich Barth's (1821–65) Caravan into Timbuktu in 1853, from "Travels and Discoveries in North and Central Africa" by Barth, engraved by Eberhard Emminger (1808–85) published 1857 (colour engraving), Bernatz, Johann Martin (1802–1878) (after)/Bibliotheque Nationale, Paris, France/Archives Charmet/The Bridgeman Art Library

Traders Approaching Timbuktu *As they had done for centuries, traders brought their wares to this ancient desert-edge city. Timbuktu's mosques tower above the ordinary dwellings of the fabled city.*

imported from the Ottoman Empire. Bornu retained many captives from its wars or sold them as slaves to the north in return for the firearms and horses that underpinned the kingdom's military power. One Bornu king, Mai Ali, conspicuously displayed his kingdom's new power and wealth while on four pilgrimages to Mecca between 1642 and 1667. On the last, an enormous entourage of slaves—said to number fifteen thousand—accompanied him.

Like Christians of this period, Muslims saw no moral impediment to owning or trading in slaves. Indeed, Islam considered enslaving "pagans" to be a meritorious act because it brought them into the faith. Although Islam forbade the enslavement of Muslims, Muslim rulers in Bornu, Hausaland, and elsewhere were not strict observers of that rule.

Sub-Saharan Africans had much longer exposure to Islamic cultural influences than to European cultural influences. Scholars and merchants learned to use the Arabic language to communicate with visiting North Africans and to read the Quran. Islamic beliefs and practices as well as Islamic legal and administrative systems were influential in African trading cities on the southern edge of the Sahara and on the Swahili coast. In some places Islam had extended its influence among rural people, but in 1750 it was still very much an urban religion.

European cultural influence in Africa was more limited. Some coastal Africans had shown an interest in Western Christianity after contacts with the Portuguese, but in the 1700s only Angola had a significant number of Christians. Coastal African traders found it useful to learn European languages, but African languages continued to dominate inland trade routes. A few African merchants sent their sons to Europe to learn European ways. One of these young men, Philip Quaque (KWAH-kay), who was educated in England, was ordained as a priest in the Church of England and became the official chaplain of the Cape Coast Castle from 1766 until his death in 1816.

Overall, how different and similar were the material effects of Islam and Europe in sub-Saharan Africa by 1800? While Muslims and Europeans obtained slaves from sub-Saharan Africa, the European trade was larger. The Atlantic trade carried about 8 million Africans to the Americas between 1550 and 1800. During this period the Islamic trade to North Africa and the Middle East transported perhaps 2 million African captives. What were the effects on Africa's population? Scholars generally agree on three points: (1) even at the peak of the trade in the 1700s, sub-Saharan Africa's overall population remained very large; (2) localities that contributed heavily to the slave trade, such as lands near the Slave Coast, suffered acute losses; (3) the ability of a population to recover from losses was related to the proportion of fertile women who were shipped away. The fact that Africans sold fewer women than men into the larger Atlantic trade somewhat reduced the long-term demographic effects of this larger trade.

The slave trade had a mixed impact on sub-Saharan economies. Africans were very particular about what they received in exchange for slaves, and their imports reflected their tastes and needs. The limited volume of manufactured imports could not overwhelm established African weavers, metalworkers, and other producers, and some imported products like textiles and metal bars actually stimulated the local production of tools and clothing. However, while African as well as European states benefited by taxing this trade, most of the economic benefits went to European nations and to their American colonies.

Profits from transporting and selling slaves mostly went to European merchants and ship owners. European manufacturers, like the producers of textiles and metal goods, profited as well. But Europe's American colonies were the major beneficiaries of the African slave trade. With Amerindian population diminished by epidemics and European immigration inadequate to develop American resources, it was the forced labor of African slaves that made possible the enormous wealth produced in a vast region that spread from the Chesapeake to the Río de la Plata. This wealth accelerated the rapid expansion of Western capitalism in the seventeenth and eighteenth centuries, a period that witnessed the political and economic decline of the Ottoman Empire, the dominant state of the Middle East, and other Muslim kingdoms (see Chapter 20).

Conclusion

European merchants and investors played a central role in the creation of the Atlantic system. European merchants had expanded trade in the century before Columbus, trading over longer distances and using new credit mechanisms to facilitate transactions. They had engaged the markets of Asia through Muslim middlemen and initiated the first tentative contacts with African markets. By the seventeenth century a more confident and adventurous European investor class was ready to promote colonial production and long-distance trade in a much more aggressive way. The development of banks, stock exchanges, maritime insurance, and chartered companies supported these new ambitions.

The new Atlantic trading system had great importance in world history. In the first phase of their expansion Europeans conquered and colonized the Americas and captured major Indian Ocean trade routes. The development of the Atlantic system showed their ability to move beyond capturing the benefits of existing systems to create a major new trading network. Beginning in the seventeenth century, the English, Dutch, and French created new colonies in the Caribbean to compete with earlier colonies created by the Spanish and Portuguese (see Chapter 18). While these colonies remained fragile for decades, settlers found ways to profitably produce goods sought by European consumers. Tobacco was the first, but sugar soon supplanted it.

The establishment of plantation societies was not just a matter of replacing native vegetation with alien plants and native peoples with Europeans and Africans. More fundamentally, it made these once-isolated islands part of a dynamic trading system controlled from Europe. The West Indies was not the only place affected. Brazil, large parts of Spanish Central and South America, and the southern region of British North America developed similar linkages, producing sugar, cacao, cotton, coffee, and indigo and using slave labor.

Despite the central importance of their shared dependence on export markets and African slaves, there were important differences among Europe's American tropical colonies. Only the English experimented with indentured labor on a large scale. But like the colonies of the Portuguese, Dutch, and French, they soon depended on African slave labor. Joint-stock companies and individual investors were crucial to the English colonies. The French entered the process late, but the French state and French monopoly companies quickly developed a massive flow of slaves while securing a profitable home market for the sugar of Saint Domingue and other colonies. After the Dutch attacked but failed to hold Portugal's sugar-producing colony of Brazil and the slave-exporting colony of Angola, they became influential in the transfer of sugar technology and the expansion of the slave trade. While Spain had introduced sugar to the Caribbean and imported African slaves in the early sixteenth century, its most important Caribbean colony, Cuba, joined the sugar revolution late, becoming the major destination for the slave trade and the major producer of sugar by 1820.

While Africa played an essential role in the Atlantic system, importing trade goods and exporting slaves to the Americas, the Atlantic system dominated Europe's American colonies much more comprehensively. Africans remained in control of their continent and interacted culturally and politically more with the Islamic world than with the Atlantic.

Sub-Saharan Africa had long-established trade connections with the Islamic world that included the sale of slaves. These trade relationships facilitated the spread of Islam to sub-Saharan Africa and the creation of Islamic states like Mali and Songhai (see Chapter 15). The volume of the Atlantic trade was much larger than the Islamic slave trade, but the Islamic trade persisted after European reformers ended the Atlantic trade (see Chapter 25). Between 1550 and 1800 four slaves crossed the Atlantic to European colonies for every slave carried across the Sahara. While more males were carried across the Atlantic, the Islamic trade took more women and children, and few slaves in the Islamic region were subjected to the brutal labor conditions of the West Indian plantations.

IMPORTANT EVENTS 1500–1800

ca. 1500	Spanish settlers introduce sugar-cane cultivation to West Indies
1500–1700	Gold trade predominates in Africa
1530	Amsterdam Exchange opens
1591	Morocco conquers Songhai
1620s and 1630s	English and French colonies in Caribbean
1621	Dutch West India Company chartered
1638	Dutch take Elmina
1640s	Dutch bring sugar plantation system from Brazil
1654	Dutch expelled from Brazil
1655	English take Jamaica
1660s	English Navigation Acts
1670s	French occupy western half of Hispaniola (modern Haiti)
1672	Royal African Company chartered
1698	French Exclusif
1700	West Indies surpass Brazil in sugar production
1700–1830	Slave trade predominates in Africa
1713	English receive slave trade monopoly from Spanish Empire
1760	Tacky's rebellion in Jamaica

20

BETWEEN EUROPE AND CHINA, 1500–1750

In 1667, Stenka Razin, the leader of a robber band camped on a tributary of the Don River in southern Russia, pillaged a rich convoy of government and merchant barges on the Volga River and sailed southward toward the trading city of Astrakhan. The city's governor was unable to stop their progress, and they established a new camp by the Caspian Sea at the mouth of the Ural River. From there Razin raided across the sea and down into Iran, defeating both Iranian and Russian armies. In 1670, his forces swollen to 20,000, Razin moved up the Volga, threatening to take Moscow and overthrow the tsar. There a tsarist army finally stopped him, and he was executed in the following year.

Razin's followers were Cossacks, people of various ethnic origins who made their way to southern Russia, many of them escaping serfdom in the north, to live as social equals in societies with minimal government and the power to maintain their independence. Modern Russian culture has glorified Razin in music and poetry as a defender of the poor and foe of noble privilege. A famous folksong portrays him sacrificing his bride for the sake of leading his warriors.

> So that peace may reign forever
> In this band so free and brave
> Volga, Volga, Mother Volga
> Make this lovely girl a grave.

A less lurid historical understanding of his revolt focuses on the unsettled state of the lands north of the Caspian Sea that had once been the center of the Mongol Golden Horde (see Chapter 13). Muslim Tartars, Buddhist Kalmyks from western Mongolia, and Orthodox Christian Ukrainians and Russians mingled in the sparsely populated frontier between the tsars, the Ottoman sultans, and the Iranian shahs.

But this zone was also becoming a trading nexus. The old Silk Road traversing Central and Inner Asia from East to West had faded, but a new axis was in the process of opening, one that linked the Ottoman, Safavid, and Mughal Empires to the south with a growing Russian Empire to the north. Few Russian merchants traveled beyond the tsarist frontiers, but Indian and Armenian traders abounded. Twenty-seven Indians resided on the outskirts of Moscow in 1684, along with various Armenian, Iranian, and Bukharan merchants. Ten times that number lived in Astrakhan, which Ivan IV, "The Terrible," had added to his domains in 1556 and defended against Ottoman attack in 1569.

Russia imported cotton and silk textiles from Iran and India and exported furs, leather goods, walrus tusks, and some woolens. In their business organization, the Indian family firms closely resembled the Italian merchant enterprises of the Renaissance era.

Thus a pattern was set that would last into the twentieth century: while western Europe maintained rigid religious boundaries with very few Muslims living under Christian monarchs, Russia more closely resembled the Muslim empires to its south in tolerating the ethnic and religious diversity that had been a hallmark of Mongol rule. This pattern of various religious groups living together extended into the maritime states of the period as well.

THE OTTOMAN EMPIRE, TO 1750

The most durable of the post-Mongol Muslim realms was the **Ottoman Empire**, founded around 1300. By extending Islamic conquests into eastern Europe starting in the late fourteenth century, and by taking Syria and Egypt from the Mamluk rulers in the early sixteenth, the Ottomans seemed to re-create the might of the medieval Islamic caliphate. However, the empire more closely resembled the new centralized monarchies of Europe (see Chapter 17) than any medieval model.

Enduring until 1922, the Ottoman Empire survived several periods of wrenching change, some caused by economic and political problems and others by military innovations. These periods of change reveal the problems faced by the land-based empires situated between Europe and China.

Expansion and Frontiers   The Ottoman Empire grew from a tiny state in northwestern Anatolia because of three factors: (1) the shrewdness of its founder, Osman (from which the name *Ottoman* comes), and his descendants, (2) control of a strategic link between Europe and Asia on the Dardanelles strait, and (3) the creation of an army that took advantage of the traditional skills of the Turkish cavalryman and the new military possibilities presented by gunpowder.

Ottoman armies attacked Christian enemies in Greece and the Balkans before conquering neighboring Muslim principalities. In 1389 a strong Serbian kingdom was defeated at the Battle of Kosovo (KO-so-vo), and by 1402 the sultans ruled much of southeastern Europe and Anatolia. In 1453, Sultan Mehmed II, "the Conqueror," laid siege to Constantinople. His forces used enormous cannon to crush the city's walls, dragged warships over a high hill from the Bosporus strait to the city's inner harbor to get around its sea defenses, and finally overcame the city's land walls with direct infantry assaults. The fall of Constantinople—henceforward commonly known as Istanbul—brought to an end over eleven hundred years of Byzantine rule and made the Ottomans seem invincible.

Selim (seh-LEEM) I, "the Grim," conquered Egypt and Syria in 1516 and 1517, making the Red Sea the Ottomans' southern frontier. His son, **Suleiman** (SOO-lay-man) **the Magnificent** (r. 1520–1566), presided over the greatest Ottoman assault on Christian Europe. Seemingly unstoppable, he conquered Belgrade in 1521, expelled the Knights of the Hospital of St. John from the island of Rhodes the following year, and laid siege to Vienna in 1529. Vienna was saved by the need to retreat before the onset of winter more than by military action. Later Ottoman historians looked back on the reign of Suleiman as the period when the imperial system worked to perfection, and they spoke of it as the golden age of Ottoman greatness.

While Ottoman armies pressed deeper and deeper into eastern Europe, the sultans also sought to control the Mediterranean. Between 1453 and 1502, the Ottomans fought the opening rounds of a two-century war with Venice, the most powerful of Italy's commercial city-states. The initial fighting left Venice in control of its lucrative islands like Crete and Cyprus for another century. But it also left Venice a reduced military power compelled to pay tribute to the Ottomans.

In the early sixteenth century, merchants from southern India and Sumatra sent emissaries to Istanbul requesting naval support against the Portuguese. The Ottomans responded vigorously to Portuguese threats close to their territories, such as at Aden at the southern entrance to the Red Sea, and seemed to have a coherent policy for defending Muslim lands bordering the Indian Ocean. By century's end, however, they had pulled back from major maritime commitments outside the Mediterranean Sea. Since eastern luxury products still flowed to Ottoman markets and Portuguese power was territorially limited to fortified coastal points, such as Hormuz at the entrance to the Persian Gulf, Goa in western India, and Malacca in Malaya, it seemed wiser to concentrate the state's resources on defending territory in Europe.

Aya Sofya Mosque in Istanbul *Originally a Byzantine cathedral, Aya Sofya (in Greek, Hagia Sophia) was transformed into a mosque after 1453, and four minarets were added. It then became a model for subsequent Ottoman mosques. To the right behind it is the Bosporus strait dividing Europe and Asia, to the left the Golden Horn inlet separating the old city of Istanbul from the newer parts. The gate to the Ottoman sultan's palace is to the right of the mosque. The pointed tower to the left of the dome is part of the palace.*

MAP 20.1 Muslim Empires in the Sixteenth and Seventeenth Centuries

Iran, a Shi'ite state flanked by Sunni Ottomans on the west and Sunni Mughals on the east, had the least exposure to European influences. Ottoman expansion across the southern Mediterranean Sea intensified European fears of Islam. The areas of strongest Mughal control dictated that Islam's spread into Southeast Asia would be heavily influenced by merchants and religious figures from Gujarat instead of from eastern India.

**Central
Institutions**

By the 1520s, the Ottoman Empire was the most powerful and best-organized state in either Europe or the Islamic world. Its military was balanced between cavalry archers, primarily Turks, and military slaves known as **Janissaries** (JAN-nih-say-rees).

Slave soldiery had a long history in Islamic lands, but the conquest of Christian territories in the Balkans in the late fourteenth century gave the Ottomans access to a new military resource. Originating as Christian prisoners of war converted to Islam, these "new troops," called *yeni cheri* in Turkish and *Janissaries* in English, gave the Ottomans unusual military flexibility. Since horseback riding and bowmanship were not part of their cultural backgrounds, they readily accepted the idea of fighting on foot and learning to use guns, which at that time were still too heavy and awkward for a horseman to load and fire. The Janissaries lived in barracks and trained all year round.

The recruitment of Janissaries from prisoners changed early in the fifteenth century. A new system, called the *devshirme*, imposed a levy of male children on Christian villages in the Balkans and occasionally elsewhere. Selected children were placed with Turkish families for language learning and then sent to Istanbul for an education that included instruction in Islam, military training, and, for the top 10 percent, skills that could be used in government administration. Senior military commanders and heads of government departments up to the rank of grand vizier were commonly drawn from among the chosen few who received special training.

The cavalrymen were supported by land grants and administered most rural areas in Anatolia and the Balkans. They maintained order, collected taxes, and reported for each summer's campaign with their horses, retainers, and supplies, all paid for from the taxes they collected. When not campaigning, they stayed at home.

The Ottoman galley-equipped navy was manned by Greek, Turkish, Algerian, and Tunisian sailors, usually under the command of an admiral from one of the North African ports. The balance of the Ottoman land forces brought success to Ottoman arms in recurrent wars with the Safavids of Iran, who were slower to adopt firearms, and in the inexorable conquest of the Balkans. Expansion by sea was less dramatic. A major expedition against Malta in the western Mediterranean failed in 1565. Combined Christian forces also achieved a massive naval victory at the Battle of Lepanto, off Greece, in 1571. But the Ottomans' resources were so extensive that in a year's time they had replaced all of the galleys sunk in that battle.

The Ottoman Empire became cosmopolitan in character. The sophisticated court language, Osmanli (os-MAHN-lih) (the Turkish form of *Ottoman*), shared basic grammar and vocabulary with Turkish, but Arabic and Persian elements made it distinct from the Turkish spoken by Anatolia's nomads and villagers. Everyone who served in the military or the bureaucracy and conversed in Osmanli was considered to belong to the *askeri* (AS-keh-ree), or "military," class. Members of this class were exempt from taxes and owed their positions to the sultan.

The Ottomans saw the sultan as providing justice for his "flock of sheep" (*raya* [RAH-yah]) and military forces to protect that flock. In return, the raya paid the

DIVERSITY + DOMINANCE

Islamic Law and Ottoman Rule

Ebu's-Su'ud was the Mufti of Istanbul from 1545 to 1574, serving under the sultans Suleiman the Magnificent (1520–1566) and his son Selim II (1566–1574). Originally one of many city-based religious scholars giving opinions on matters of law, the mufti of Istanbul by Ebu's-Su'ud's time had become the top religious official in the empire and the personal adviser to the sultan on religious and legal matters. The position would later acquire the title Shaikh al-Islam.

Historians debate the degree of independence these muftis had. Since the ruler, as a Muslim, was subject to the Shari'a, the mufti could theoretically veto his policies. On important matters, however, the mufti more often seemed to come up with the answer that best suited the sultan who appointed him. This bias is not apparent in more mundane areas of the law.

The collection of Ebu's-Su'ud's fatwas, or legal opinions, from which the examples below are drawn shows the range of matters that came to his attention. They are also an excellent source for understanding the problems of his time, the relationship between Islamic law and imperial governance, and the means by which the state asserted its dominance over the common people. Some opinions respond directly to questions posed by the sultan. Others are hypothetical, using the names Zeyd, 'Amr, and Hind the way police today use John Doe and Jane Doe. While qadis, or Islamic judges, made findings of fact in specific cases on trial, muftis issued only opinions on matters of law. A qadi as well as a plaintiff or defendant might ask a question of a mufti. Later jurists consulted collections of fatwas for precedents, but the fatwas had no permanent binding power.

On the plan of Selim II to attack the Venetians in Crete in 1570

A land was previously in the realm of Islam. After a while, the abject infidels overran it, destroyed the colleges and mosques, and left them vacant. They filled the pulpits and the galleries with the tokens of infidelity and error, intending to insult the religion of Islam with all kinds of vile deeds, and by spreading their ugly acts to all corners of the earth.

His Excellency the Sultan, the Refuge of Religion, has, as zeal for Islam requires, determined to take the aforementioned land from the possession of the shameful infidels and to annex it to the realm of Islam.

When peace was previously concluded with the other lands in the possession of the said infidels, the aforenamed land was included. An explanation is sought as to whether, in accordance with the pure shari'a, this is an impediment to the Sultan's determining to break the treaty.

Answer: There is no possibility that it could ever be an impediment. For the Sultan of the People of Islam (may God glorify his victories) to make peace with the infidels is legal only when there is a benefit to all Muslims. When there is no benefit, peace is never legal. When a benefit has been seen, and it is then observed to be more beneficial to break it, then to break it becomes absolutely obligatory and binding.

His Excellency [Muhammad] the Apostle of God (may God bless him and give him peace) made a ten-year truce with the Meccan infidels in the sixth year of the Hegira. His Excellency 'Ali (may God ennoble his face) wrote a document that was corroborated and confirmed. Then, in the following year, it was considered more beneficial to break it and, in the eighth year of the Hegira, [the Prophet] attacked [the Meccans], and conquered Mecca the Mighty.

On war against the Shi'ite Muslim Safavids of Iran

Is it licit according to the shari'a to fight the followers of the Safavids? Is the person who kills them a holy warrior, and the person who dies at their hands a martyr?

Answer: Yes, it is a great holy war and a glorious martyrdom.

Assuming that it is licit to fight them, is this simply because of their rebellion and enmity against the [Ottoman] Sultan of the People of Islam, because they drew the sword against the troops of Islam, or what?

Answer: They are both rebels and, from many points of view, infidels.

Can the children of Safavid subjects captured in the Nakhichevan campaign be enslaved?

Answer: No.

The followers of the Safavids are killed by order of the Sultan. If it turns out that some of the prisoners, young and old, are [Christian] Armenian[s], are they set free?

Answer: Yes. So long as the Armenians have not joined the Safavid troops in attacking and fighting against the troops of Islam, it is illegal to take them prisoner.

On the Holy Land

Are all the Arab realms Holy Land, or does it have specific boundaries, and what is the difference between the Holy Land and other lands?

Answer: Syria is certainly called the Holy Land. Jerusalem, Aleppo and its surroundings, and Damascus belong to it.

On land-grants

What lands are private property, and what lands are held by feudal tenure [i.e., assignment in exchange for military service]?

Answer: Plots of land within towns are private property. Their owners may sell them, donate them or convert them to trust. When [the owner] dies, [the land] passes to all the heirs. Lands held by feudal tenure are cultivated lands around villages, whose occupants bear the burden of their services and pay a portion of their [produce in tax]. They cannot sell the land, donate it or convert it to trust. When they die, if they have sons, these have the use [of the land]. Otherwise, the cavalryman gives [it to someone else] by *tapu* [title deed].

On the consumption of coffee

Zeyd drinks coffee to aid concentration or digestion. Is this licit?

Answer: How can anyone consume this reprehensible [substance], which dissolute men drink when engaged in games and debauchery?

The Sultan, the Refuge of Religion, has on many occasions banned coffee-houses. However, a group of ruffians take no notice, but keep coffee-houses for a living. In order to draw the crowds, they take on unbearded apprentices, and have ready instruments of entertainment and play, such as chess and backgammon. The city's rakes, rogues and vagabond boys gather there to consume opium and hashish. On top of this, they drink coffee and, when they are high, engage in games and false sciences, and neglect the prescribed prayers. In law, what should happen to a judge who is able to prevent the said coffee-sellers and drinkers, but does not do so?

Answer: Those who perpetrate these ugly deeds should be prevented and deterred by severe chastisement and long imprisonment. Judges who neglect to deter them should be dismissed.

On matters of theft

How are thieves to be "carefully examined"?

Answer: His Excellency 'Ali (may God ennoble his face) appointed Imam Shuraih as judge. It so happened that, at that time, several people took a Muslim's son to another district. The boy disappeared and, when the people came back, the missing boy's father brought them before Judge Shuraih. [When he brought] a claim [against them on account of the loss of his son], they denied it, saying: "No harm came to him from us." Judge Shuraih thought deeply and was perplexed.

When the man told his tale to His Excellency 'Ali, [the latter] summoned Judge Shuraih and questioned him. When Shuraih said; "Nothing came to light by the shari'a," ['Ali] summoned all the people who had taken the man's son, separated them from one another, and questioned them separately. For each of their stopping places, he asked: "What was the boy wearing in that place? What did you eat? And where did he disappear?" In short, he made each of them give a detailed account, and when their words contradicted each other, each of their statements was written down separately. Then he brought them all together, and when the contradictions became apparent, they were no longer able to deny [their guilt] and confessed to what had happened.

This kind of ingenuity is a requirement of the case. [This fatwa appears to justify investigation of crimes by the state instead of by the qadi. Judging from court records, which contain very few criminal cases, it seems likely that in practice, many criminal cases were dealt with outside the jurisdiction of the qadi's court.]

Zeyd takes 'Amr's donkey without his knowledge and sells it. Is he a thief?

Answer: His hand is not cut off.

Zeyd mounts 'Amr's horse as a courier and loses it. Is compensation necessary?

Answer: Yes.

In which case: What if Zeyd has a Sultanic decree [authorizing him] to take horses for courier service?

Answer: Compensation is required in any case. He was not commanded to lose [the horse]. Even if he were commanded, it is the person who loses it who is liable.

On homicides

Zeyd enters Hind's house and tries to have intercourse forcibly. Since Hind can repel him by no other means, she strikes and wounds him with an axe. If Zeyd dies of the wound, is Hind liable for anything?

Answer: She has performed an act of Holy War [*jihad*].

Questions for Analysis

1. What do these fatwas indicate with regard to the balance between practical legal reasoning and religious dictates?

2. How much was the Ottoman government constrained by the Shari'a?

3. What can be learned about day-to-day life from materials of this sort?

Source: Excerpts from Colin Imper, *Ebu's-Su'ud: The Islamic Legal Tradition*. Copyright © 1997 Colin Imber, originating publisher Edinburgh University Press. All rights reserved. Used with permission of Stanford University Press: www.sup.org, and Edinburgh University Press, www.euppublishing.com.

taxes that supported both the sultan and the military. In reality, the sultan's government remained comparatively isolated from the lives of most subjects. As Islam gradually became the majority religion in some Balkan regions, Islamic law (the Shari'a [sha-REE-ah]) conditioned urban institutions and social life (see Diversity and Dominance: Islamic Law and Ottoman Rule). Local customs prevailed among non-Muslims and in many rural areas, and non-Muslims looked to their own religious leaders for guidance in family and spiritual matters.

Crisis of the Military State, 1585–1650

As military technology evolved, cannon and lighter-weight firearms played an ever-larger role on the battlefield. Accordingly, the size of the Janissary corps—and its cost to the government—grew steadily, and the role of the Turkish cavalry diminished. To pay the Janissaries, the sultan started reducing the number of landholding cavalrymen. Revenues previously spent on their living expenses and military equipment went directly into the imperial treasury. Inflation caused by a flood of cheap silver from the New World bankrupted many of the remaining landholders, who were restricted by law to collecting a fixed amount of taxes. Their land was returned to the state. Displaced cavalrymen, armed and unhappy, became a restive element in rural Anatolia.

This complicated situation, exacerbated after 1600 by the climatic deterioration known as the Little Ice Age (see p. 559), resulted in revolts that devastated Anatolia between 1590 and 1610. Former landholding cavalrymen, short-term soldiers released at the end of the campaign season, peasants overburdened by emergency

Topkapi Palace Museum

Ottoman Glassmakers on Parade *Celebrations of the circumcisions of the sultan's sons featured parades organized by the craft guilds of Istanbul. This float features glassmaking, a common craft in Islamic realms. The most elaborate glasswork included oil lamps for mosques and colored glass for the small stained-glass windows below mosque domes.*

taxes, and even impoverished students of religion formed bands of marauders. Anatolia experienced the worst of the rebellions and suffered greatly from emigration and the loss of agricultural production. But an increase in banditry, made worse by the government's inability to stem the spread of muskets among the general public, beset other parts of the empire as well.

In the meantime, the Janissaries took advantage of their growing influence to gain relief from prohibitions on their marrying and engaging in business. Janissaries who involved themselves in commerce lessened the burden on the state budget, and married Janissaries who enrolled sons or relatives in the corps made it possible in the seventeenth century for the government to save state funds by abolishing forced recruitment. These savings, however, were more than offset by the increase in the total number of Janissaries and in their steady deterioration as a military force, which necessitated the hiring of more and more supplemental troops.

Economic Change and Growing Weakness   A very different Ottoman Empire emerged from this crisis. Sultans once had led armies. Now they mostly resided in palaces and had little experience of the real world. The affairs of government were overseen more and more by the chief administrators—the grand viziers.

Involvement in business and transmission of corps membership by heredity did not prevent the Janissaries from becoming a powerful faction in urban politics. Tax farming created other new pressures. Tax farmers paid specific taxes, such as customs duties, in advance in return for the privilege of collecting a greater amount from the actual taxpayers.

Rural administration, already disrupted by the rebellions, suffered from the transition to tax farms. The former military landholders had kept order on their lands in order to maintain their incomes. Tax farmers were less likely to live on the land. The imperial government therefore faced greater administrative burdens and came to rely heavily on powerful provincial governors or on wealthy men who purchased lifelong tax collection rights and behaved more or less like private landowners.

Military power slowly ebbed. The ill-trained Janissaries sometimes resorted to hiring substitutes to go on campaign, and the sultans relied on partially trained seasonal recruits and on armies raised by the governors of frontier provinces. A second mighty siege of Vienna failed in 1683, and by the middle of the eighteenth century it was obvious to the Austrians and Russians that the Ottoman Empire was weakening. On the eastern front, however, Ottoman exhaustion after many wars was matched by the demise in 1722 of their perennial adversary, the Safavid state of Iran.

The Ottoman Empire lacked both the wealth and the inclination to match western European economic advances, but it remained much more prosperous than the Russian Empire. While overland trade from the East dwindled as political disorder in Safavid Iran cut deeply into Iranian silk production, new products also came into vogue. Farmers in Greece, Macedonia, Bulgaria, and Anatolia grew mild-flavored, low-nicotine tobacco; and coffee, a Yemeni product, rose from obscurity in the fifteenth century to become the rage first in the Ottoman Empire and then in Europe.

By 1770, Muslim merchants trading in the Yemeni port of Mocha (MOH-kuh) (literally "the coffee place") were charged 15 percent in duties and fees, while European traders, benefiting from long-standing trade agreements with the Ottoman Empire, paid little more than 3 percent.

Such trade agreements, called capitulations, from Latin *capitula*, or "chapter," were first granted as favors by powerful sultans, but they eventually led to European domination of Ottoman seaborne trade. Nevertheless, the Europeans did not control strategic ports in the Mediterranean comparable to Malacca in the Indian Ocean and Hormuz on the Persian Gulf, so their economic power stopped short of colonial settlement or direct control in Ottoman territories.

A few astute Ottoman statesmen observed the growing disarray of the empire and advised the sultans to re-establish the land-grant and devshirme systems of Suleiman's reign. Most people, however, could not perceive the downward course of imperial power, much less the reasons behind it. Far from seeing Europe as the enemy that would eventually dismantle the empire, the Istanbul elite experimented with European clothing and furniture styles and purchased printed books from the empire's first (and short-lived) press. Ottoman historians named the period between 1718 and 1730 when European fashions were in favor the "**Tulip Period**" because of the craze for high-priced tulip bulbs that swept Ottoman ruling circles. The craze echoed a Dutch tulip mania that had begun in the mid-sixteenth century, when the flower was introduced into Holland from Istanbul. The mania peaked in 1636 with particularly rare bulbs going for 2,500 florins apiece—the value of twenty-two oxen.

In 1730, however, gala soirees at which guests watched turtles with candles on their backs wander in the dark through massive tulip beds gave way to a conservative Janissary revolt with strong religious overtones. Sultan Ahmed III abdicated, and the leader of the revolt, Patrona Halil (pa-TROH-nuh ha-LEEL), an Albanian former seaman and stoker of the public baths, swaggered around the capital for several months dictating government policies before he was seized and executed.

The Patrona Halil rebellion confirmed the perceptions of a few that the Ottoman Empire was facing severe difficulties. Yet decay at the center spelled benefit elsewhere. In the provinces, ambitious and competent governors, wealthy landholders, urban notables, and nomad chieftains took advantage of the central government's weakness. By the middle of the eighteenth century groups of mamluks had regained a dominant position in Egypt. Though Selim I had defeated the mamluk sultanate in the early sixteenth century, the practice of buying slaves in the Caucasus and training them as soldiers reappeared by the end of the century in several Arab cities. In Baghdad, Janissary commanders and Georgian mamluks competed for power, with the latter emerging triumphant by the mid-eighteenth century.

In Aleppo and Damascus, however, the Janissaries came out on top. Meanwhile, in central Arabia, a puritanical Sunni movement inspired by Muhammad ibn Abd al-Wahhab began a remarkable rise beyond the reach of Ottoman power. Although no region declared full independence, the sultan's power was slipping away to the advantage of a broad array of lower officials and upstart chieftains in all parts of the empire while the Ottoman economy was reorienting itself toward Europe.

THE SAFAVID EMPIRE, 1502–1722

The **Safavid Empire** of Iran resembled its long-time Ottoman foe in many ways: it initially relied militarily on cavalry paid through land grants, and its population spoke several languages and included many non-Muslims. It also had distinct qualities that to this day set Iran off from its neighbors: it derived part of its legitimacy from the pre-Islamic dynasties of ancient Iran, and it adopted the Shi'ite form of Islam.

Safavid Society and Religion   The ultimate victor in a complicated struggle for power among Turkish chieftains east of the Ottoman lands was Ismail (IS-ma-eel), a boy of Kurdish, Iranian, and Greek ancestry. In 1502, at age sixteen, Ismail proclaimed himself Shah of Iran and declared that from that time forward his realm would be devoted to **Shi'ite** Islam, which revered the family of Muhammad's cousin and son-in-law Ali. Although Ismail's reasons for compelling Iran's conversion to Shi'ism are unknown, the effect of this radical act was to create a deep chasm between Iran and its Sunni Muslim neighbors. For the first time since its incorporation into the Islamic caliphate in the seventh century, Iran became a truly separate country.

The imposition of Shi'ite belief confirmed differences between Iran and its neighbors that had been long in the making. Persian, written in the Arabic script from the tenth century onward, had emerged as the second language of Islam. Iranian scholars and writers normally read Arabic as well as Persian and sprinkled their writings with Arabic phrases, but their Arab counterparts were much less inclined to learn Persian. After the Mongols destroyed Baghdad, the capital of the Islamic caliphate, in 1258, Iran developed largely on its own, having more extensive contacts with India—where Muslim rulers favored the Persian language—than with the Arabs.

In the post-Mongol period, artistic styles in Iran, Afghanistan, and Central Asia also went their own way. Painted and molded tiles and tile mosaics, often in vivid turquoise blue, became the standard exterior decoration of mosques in Iran but never were used in Syria and Egypt. Persian poets raised verse to peaks of perfection that had no counterpart in Arabic poetry, generally considered to be in a state of decline.

To be sure, Islam itself provided a tradition of belief, learning, and law that crossed ethnic and linguistic borders, but Shah Ismail's imposition of Shi'ism set Iran significantly apart. Shi'ite doctrine says that all temporal rulers, regardless of title, are temporary stand-ins for the **Hidden Imam**, the twelfth descendant of Ali, who disappeared as a child in the ninth century. Some Shi'ite scholars taught the faithful to calmly accept the world as it was and wait quietly for the Hidden Imam's return. Others maintained that they themselves should play a stronger role in political affairs because they were best qualified to know the Hidden Imam's wishes. These two positions, which still play a role in Iranian Shi'ism, enhanced the self-image of religious scholars as independent of imperial authority and stood in the way of their becoming subordinate government functionaries, as happened in the Ottoman Empire.

Shi'ism also affected popular psychology. Annual commemoration of the martyrdom of Imam Husayn (d. 680), Ali's son and third Imam, regularized an emotional outpouring with no parallel in Sunni lands. Day after day for two weeks, preachers recited the woeful tale to crowds of weeping believers, and elaborate street processions, often organized by craft guilds, paraded chanting and self-flagellating men past crowds of reverent onlookers. Of course, Shi'ites elsewhere observed rites of mourning for Imam Husayn, but the impact of these rites was especially great in Iran, where 90 percent of the population was Shi'ite. Over time, the subjects of the Safavid shahs came to feel more than ever a people apart.

A Tale of Two Cities: Isfahan and Istanbul   Outwardly, Ottoman Istanbul looked quite different from Isfahan (is-fah-HAHN), which became Iran's capital in 1598 by decree of **Shah Abbas I** (r. 1587–1629). Built on seven hills beside the narrow Golden Horn inlet, Istanbul boasted a skyline punctuated by the gray stone domes and thin, pointed minarets of the great imperial mosques. The mosques surrounding the royal plaza in Isfahan, in contrast, had unobtrusive minarets and brightly tiled domes. High walls surrounded the sultan's palace in Istanbul. Shah Abbas in Isfahan focused his capital on the giant royal plaza, which was large enough for his army to play polo, and he used an airy palace overlooking the plaza to receive dignitaries and review his troops.

Istanbul's harbor teemed with sailing ships and smaller craft, many of them belonging to a colony of European merchants perched on a hilltop on the other side of the Golden Horn. Isfahan, far from the sea, was only occasionally visited by Europeans. Trade was mostly in the hands of Jews, Hindus and Jains from India, and especially a colony of Armenian Christians brought in by Shah Abbas.

Beneath these superficial differences, the two capitals had much in common. Wheeled vehicles were scarce in hilly Istanbul and nonexistent in Isfahan. Both cities were built for walking and lacked the open spaces common in contemporary European cities. Streets were narrow and irregular. Houses crowded against each other in dead-end lanes. Residents enjoyed their privacy in interior courtyards. Artisans and merchants organized themselves into guilds that had strong social and religious bonds. The shops of each guild adjoined one another in the markets.

Women seldom appeared in public, even in Istanbul's mazelike covered market or in Isfahan's long, serpentine bazaar. At home, the women's quarters—called *anderun* (an-deh-ROON), or "interior," in Iran and *harem*, or "forbidden area,"

Istanbul Family on the Way to a Bath House *Public baths, an important feature of Islamic cities, set different hours for men and women. Young boys, such as the lad in the turban shown here, went with their mothers and sisters. Notice that the children wear the same styles as the adults.*

Austrian National Library, picture archive

in Istanbul—were separate from the public rooms where the men of the family received visitors. In both areas, low cushions, charcoal braziers for warmth, carpets, and small tables constituted most of the furnishings.

The private side of family life has left few traces, but women's society—consisting of wives, children, female servants, and sometimes one or more eunuchs—was not entirely cut off from the outside world. Ottoman court records reveal that women, using male agents, were very active in the urban real estate market. Often they were selling inherited shares of their father's estate, but some both bought and sold real estate on a regular basis and even established religious endowments for pious purposes.

The fact that Islamic law, unlike European codes, permitted a wife to retain her property after marriage gave some women a stake in the general economy and a degree of independence from their spouses. Women also appeared in other types of court cases, where they often testified for themselves, for Islamic courts did not recognize the role of attorney. Although comparable Safavid court records do not survive, historians assume that a parallel situation prevailed in Iran.

European travelers commented on the veiling of women outside the home, but the norm for both sexes was complete coverage of arms, legs, and hair. Miniature paintings indicate that ordinary female garb consisted of a long, ample dress with a scarf or shawl pulled tight over the forehead to conceal the hair. Lightweight baggy trousers were worn under the dress. This mode of dress differed little from that of men. Poor men wore light trousers, a long shirt, a jacket, and a hat or turban. Wealthier men wore over their trousers ankle-length caftans, often closely fitted around the chest.

Public life was a male domain. Poetry and art, both more elegantly developed in Isfahan than in Istanbul, were as likely to extol the charms of beardless boys as pretty women. Despite religious disapproval of homosexuality, attachments to adolescent boys were neither unusual nor hidden. Women who appeared in public—aside from non-Muslims, the aged, and the very poor—were usually slaves. Miniature paintings frequently depict female dancers, musicians, and even acrobats in attitudes and costumes that range from decorous to decidedly erotic.

Despite social similarities, the overall flavors of Isfahan and Istanbul were not the same. Isfahan had its prosperous Armenian quarter across the river from the city's center, but it was not as cosmopolitan as Istanbul. Shah Abbas located his capital toward the center of his domain away from any unstable frontier. Istanbul, in contrast, was a great seaport and a crossroads located on the straits separating the sultan's European and Asian possessions.

People of all sorts lived or spent time in Istanbul: Venetians, Genoese, Arabs, Turks, Greeks, Armenians, Albanians, Serbs, Jews, Bulgarians, and more. In this respect, Istanbul conveyed the cosmopolitan character of major seaports from Venice to Canton (Guangzhou), though its prosperity rested on the vast reach of the sultan's territories rather than on the voyages of Muslim merchants.

Economic Crisis and Political Collapse   The Safavid Empire's foreign trade rested on the silk fabrics of northern Iran. However, the products that eventually became most powerfully associated with Iran were deep-pile carpets made by knotting colored yarns around stretched warp threads. Different cities produced distinctive carpet designs. Women and girls did much of the actual knotting work.

Overall, Iran's manufacturing sector was neither large nor notably productive. Most of the shah's subjects, whether Iranians, Turks, Kurds, or Arabs, lived by subsistence farming or herding. Neither area of activity recorded significant technological advances during the Safavid period.

The Safavids, like the Ottomans, had difficulty finding the money to pay troops armed with firearms. By the end of the sixteenth century, it was evident that a more systematic adoption of cannon and firearms in the Safavid Empire would be needed to hold off the Ottomans and the Uzbeks (UHZ-bek) (Turkish rulers who had succeeded the Timurids on Iran's Central Asian frontier. Like the Ottoman cavalry a century earlier, warriors from nomadic groups were not inclined to trade their bows for firearms. Shah Abbas responded by establishing a slave corps of year-round soldiers and arming them with guns. The Christian converts to Islam who initially provided the manpower for the new corps were mostly captives taken in raids on Georgia in the Caucasus (CAW-kuh-suhs).

In the late sixteenth century, the inflation caused by cheap silver spread into Iran; then overland trade through Safavid territory declined because of mismanagement of the silk monopoly after Shah Abbas's death in 1629. As a result, the later shahs could not afford to pay their army and bureaucracy. Trying to unseat the nomads from their lands to regain control of taxes was more difficult and more disruptive militarily than the piecemeal dismantlement of the land-grant system in the Ottoman Empire. The nomads remained cohesive military forces, and pressure from the center simply caused them to withdraw to their mountain pastures. By 1722, the government had become so weak and commanded so little support from the nomadic groups that an army of marauding Afghans was able to capture Isfahan and effectively end Safavid rule.

THE MUGHAL EMPIRE, 1526–1739

What distinguished the Indian empire of the Mughal (MOH-guhl) sultans from the empires of the Ottomans and Safavids was the fact that India was a land of Hindus ruled by a Muslim minority. Repeated military campaigns from the early eleventh century onward had established Muslim dominion, but five centuries later the Mughals still had to contend with the Hindus' long-standing resentment. Thus, the challenge facing the Mughals was not just conquering and organizing a large territorial state but also finding a formula for Hindu-Muslim coexistence.

Political Foundations   Babur (BAH-bur) (1483–1530), the founder of the **Mughal Empire**, was a Muslim descendant of both Timur and Chinggis Khan (*Mughal* is Persian for "Mongol"). Invading from Central Asia, Babur defeated the last Muslim sultan of Delhi (DEL-ee) in 1526. Babur's grandson **Akbar** (r. 1556–1605), a brilliant but mercurial man, established the central administration of the expanding state. Under him and his three successors—the last of whom died in 1707—all but the southern tip of India fell under Mughal rule, administered first from Agra and then from Delhi.

Akbar granted land revenues to military officers and government officials in return for their service. Grants were called *mansabs* (MAN-sab) and their holders *mansabdars* (man-sab-DAHR). As in the other Islamic empires, revenue grants were not considered hereditary, and the central government kept careful track of them.

With a population of 100 million, a thriving trading economy based on cotton cloth, and a generally efficient administration, India under Akbar was probably the most prosperous empire of the sixteenth century. He and his successors faced few external threats and experienced generally peaceful conditions in their northern Indian heartland.

European trade boomed at the port of Surat in the northwest, but merchants from Multan, today on the Indus River in Pakistan, did more business with Iran and Russia. Lacking a regular navy, the rulers saw the Europeans—after Akbar's time, primarily Dutch and English, the Portuguese having lost most of their Indian ports—less as enemies than as shipmasters whose support could be procured as needed in return for trading privileges.

Hindus and Muslims
The Mughal state inherited traditions of religious tolerance from both the Islamic caliphate and the Mongols. Seventy percent of the *mansabdars* appointed under Akbar were Muslim soldiers born outside India, but 15 percent were Hindus. Most of the Hindu appointees were warriors from the north called **Rajputs** (RAHJ-put), one of whom rose to be a powerful revenue minister.

Akbar differed from his Ottoman and Safavid counterparts—Suleiman the Magnificent and Shah Abbas the Great—in his striving for social harmony and not just for territory and revenue. His marriage to a Rajput princess encouraged reconciliation and even intermarriage between Muslims and Hindus. The birth of a son in 1569 ensured that future rulers would have both Muslim and Hindu ancestry.

Akbar ruled that in legal disputes between two Hindus, decisions would be made according to village custom or Hindu law as interpreted by local Hindu scholars, while Shari'a law was for Muslims. Akbar made himself the legal court of last resort.

Akbar also made himself the center of a new "Divine Faith" incorporating Muslim, Hindu, Zoroastrian, Sikh (sick), and Christian beliefs. He liked Sufi ideas, which permeated the religious rituals he instituted at court. To promote serious consideration of his religious doctrines, he personally oversaw, from an elevated catwalk, debates among scholars of all religions assembled in his octagonal audience chamber. When courtiers uttered the Muslim exclamation "Allahu Akbar"—"God is great"—they also understood it in its second grammatical meaning: "God is Akbar."

Akbar's religious views did not survive him, but the court culture he fostered, reflecting a mixture of Muslim and Hindu traditions, flourished until his zealous great-grandson Aurangzeb (ow-rang-ZEB) (r. 1658–1707) reinstituted many restrictions on Hindus. Mughal and Rajput miniature paintings reveled in realistic portraits of political figures and depictions of scantily clad women, even though they brought frowns to the faces of pious Muslims, who deplored the representation of human beings. Most of the leading painters were Hindus. In addition to the florid style of Persian verse favored at court, a new taste developed for poetry and prose in the popular language of the Delhi region. The modern descendant of this language is called *Urdu* in Pakistan and *Hindi* in India.

Central Decay and Regional Challenges Mughal power did not long survive Aurangzeb's death in 1707. Aurangzeb's additions to Mughal territory in southern India were not all well integrated into the imperial structure, and strong regional powers arose to challenge Mughal military supremacy. A climax came in 1739 when Nadir Shah, a warlord who had seized power in Iran after the fall of the Safavids, invaded the Mughal capital and carried off to Iran the "peacock throne," the priceless jewel-encrusted symbol of Mughal grandeur. Another throne was found for the later Mughals to sit on; but their empire, which survived in name to 1858, was finished.

In 1723, Nizam al-Mulk (nee-ZAHM al-MULK), the sultan's powerful vizier, gave up on the central government and established his own nearly independent state at Hyderabad in the eastern Deccan. Other officials bearing the title *nawab* (nah-WAHB) became similarly independent in Bengal and Oudh (OW-ad) in the northeast, as did the militant Hindu Marathas in the center. In the northwest, simultaneous Iranian and Mughal weakness allowed the Afghans to establish an independent kingdom.

Some of the new regional powers were prosperous and benefited from the removal of the sultan's heavy hand. Linguistic and religious communities, freed from Aurangzeb's religious intolerance, similarly enjoyed greater opportunity for political expression. However, this disintegration of central power favored the intrusion of European adventurers.

In 1741 Joseph François Dupleix (doo-PLAY) took over the presidency of the French stronghold of Pondicherry (pon-dih-CHER-ree) and began a new phase of European involvement in India. He captured the English trading center of Madras and used his small contingent of European and European-trained Indian troops to become a power broker in southern India. Though offered the title *nawab*, Dupleix preferred to operate behind the scenes, using Indian princes as puppets. His career ended in 1754 when he was called home. Deeply involved in European wars, the French government declined further adventures in India. Dupleix's departure opened the way for the British, whose exploits in India are described in Chapter 26.

THE RUSSIAN EMPIRE, 1500–1725

Though it was Christian rather than Muslim, the Russian Empire encountered problems and opportunities not unlike the large territorial empires discussed above. Before 1500, the Russian principalities had been dominated by steppe nomads (see Chapter 13). During the next three centuries, however, the rulers of **Muscovy** (MUSS-koe-vee), the principality based on Moscow, forged an empire that stretched from eastern Europe across northern Asia and into North America. Moscow lay in the forest zone north of the treeless steppe (grasslands) favored by Mongol horse nomads (also known as Tatars or, in western European languages, Tartars). The princes of Muscovy led the movement against the Golden Horde and ruthlessly annexed the territories of the neighboring Russian state of Novgorod in 1478. Prince Ivan IV (r. 1533–1584), known as "the Terrible" (meaning the fearsome), pushed Muscovy's conquests south and east at the expense of the Tatar Khanates of Kazan and Astrakhan.

Since 1547 the Russian ruler used the title **tsar** (zahr) (from the Roman imperial title *caesar*), the term Russians had earlier used for the rulers of the Mongol Empire. The

Russian church called Moscow the "third Rome," successor to the Roman Empire's second capital, Constantinople, which had fallen to the Ottoman Turks in 1453.

Yet Russian claims to greatness were exaggerated: in 1600 the empire was poor, backward, and landlocked. Only one seaport—Arkhangelsk near the Arctic circle—connected to the world's oceans. The Crimean Tatars to the south were powerful enough to sack Moscow in 1571, just as Stenka Razin's Cossacks from a nearby region threatened to do a century later. Beyond them, the Ottoman Empire controlled access to the Black Sea, while trade with India had to go through Iran. The kingdoms of Sweden and Poland-Lithuania to the west similarly blocked Russian access to the Baltic Sea.

The Drive Across Northern Asia   The one route open to expansion, **Siberia**, turned out to be Russia's version of the New World, an immense region of little-known peoples and untapped resources. The Russians and their trading partners particularly prized the soft, dense fur that sables and other forest animals grew to survive the long northern winters. The Strogonovs, a wealthy Russian trading family, led the early Russian exploration of Siberia. The small bands of foragers and reindeer herders already living there could not resist the armed adventurers the Strogonovs hired. Using rifles, their troops destroyed the only political power in the region, the Khanate of Sibir, in 1582. Moving through the dense forests by river, Russian fur trappers reached the Pacific Ocean during the seventeenth century and soon crossed over into Alaska. Russian political control followed more slowly into what was more a frontier zone with widely scattered forts than a province under full control. Beginning in the early seventeenth century the tsars also used Siberia as a penal colony for criminals and political prisoners. In the 1640s Russian settlers began to grow grain in the Amur River Valley east of Mongolia, where they came into contact with Chinese authorities (see Chapter 21).

Russian Society and Politics to 1725   As the empire expanded, it incorporated people with different languages, religious beliefs, and ethnic identities. Orthodox missionaries strove to Christianize the peoples of Siberia, but among the relatively more populous steppe peoples, Islam prevailed as the dominant religion. Differences in how people outside of cities made their living were equally fundamental. Russians tended to live as farmers and hunters, while the peoples newly incorporated into the empire were either herders and caravan workers or hunters and fishers living along the Siberian rivers.

Diversity arose even among Russian speakers of Orthodox faith. The name *Cossack*, referring to bands of people living on the steppe between Moscovy and the Caspian and Black Seas, probably comes from a Turkic word for a warrior or mercenary soldier. Actually, Cossacks had diverse origins and beliefs, but they all belonged to close-knit bands, fought superbly from the saddle, and terrified both villagers and legal authorities. Cossack allegiances with rulers were temporary; loyalty to the chiefs of their bands was paramount. Cossacks provided most of the soldiers and settlers employed by the Strogonovs, and they founded every major town in Russian Siberia. They also manned the Russian camps on the Amur River. West of the Urals the Cossacks defended Russia against Swedish and Ottoman incursions, but they also preserved their political autonomy (see beginning of this chapter).

The early seventeenth century was a "Time of Troubles" marking the end of the old line of Muscovite rulers. During this era, which coincided with the beginning of the Little Ice Age and a similar period of internal disorder in the Ottoman Empire, Swedish and Polish forces briefly occupied Moscow on separate occasions. Eventually the Russian aristocracy—the boyars (BOY-ar)—allowed one of their own, Mikhail Romanov (ROH-man-off or roh-MAN-off) (r. 1613–1645), to inaugurate a dynasty that would soon consolidate its own authority while successfully competing with neighboring powers. The Romanovs often represented conflicts between Slavic Russians and Turkic steppe peoples as being between Christians and "infidels" or between the civilized and the "barbaric." Despite this rhetoric, there were many similarities between their empire and those of their Muslim neighbors to the south.

As centralized tsarist power rose, the freedom of the peasants who tilled the land in European Russia fell. The Moscovy rulers and early tsars, like the sultans and shahs, rewarded the loyal nobles who dominated the military with grants of land that obliged the local peasants to work for the lords. Law and custom permitted peasants to change masters during a two-week period each year, which encouraged lords to treat their peasants well; but the rising commercialization of agriculture also raised the value of these labor obligations.

Long periods of warfare in the late sixteenth and early seventeenth centuries disrupted peasant life and caused many to flee to the Cossacks or into Siberia. Some who couldn't flee sold themselves into slavery to keep from starving. When peace returned, landlords sought to recover the runaways and bind them more tightly to their land. A law change in 1649 finally transformed the peasants into **serfs** by eliminating the period when they could change masters and ordering runaways to return to their masters.

Like slavery, serfdom was hereditary. In theory the serf was tied to a piece of land, not owned by a master. In practice, strict laws narrowed the difference between serf and slave. In the Russian census of 1795, serfs made up over half the population: landowners made up only 2 percent.

Peter the Great   The greatest of the Romanovs, Tsar **Peter the Great** (r. 1689–1725), came to the throne a century or so later than the eminent Muslim potentates Suleiman the Magnificent, the Safavid Shah Abbas, and the Mughal sultan Akbar. Whereas Suleiman fought wars with Europeans, and Abbas and Akbar knew them as merchant adventurers, Peter was aware that Europe's wealth and military power had increased enormously during the intervening period. Some Ottoman officials shared this awareness, as evidenced by the vogue for European styles during the "Tulip Period" that coincided with Peter's reign. But no Muslim notable could safely sojourn in Christian Europe long enough to master the new techniques of ruling and acquiring power.

When Peter ascended the throne, there were already hundreds of foreign merchants in Moscow, as there were in Istanbul. Military officers from western Europe, who were parelleled by European converts to Islam in the Ottoman Empire, had already introduced new weapons and techniques, and Italian builders were already influencing church and palace architecture.

Peter the Great *This portrait from his time as a student in Holland in 1697 shows Peter as ruggedly masculine and practical, quite unlike most royal portraits of the day that posed rulers in foppish elegance and haughty majesty. Peter was a popular military leader as well as an autocratic ruler.*

UniversalImagesGroup/Getty Images

Peter accelerated these tendencies in unprecedented fashion. While his half-sister Sophia governed as regent for him and her sickly brother Ivan, he lived on an estate near the foreigners' quarter outside Moscow, where he busied himself gaining practical skills in blacksmithing, carpentry, shipbuilding, and the arts of war. When Princess Sophia tried to take complete control of the government in 1689, Peter rallied enough support to send her to a monastery, secure the abdication of Ivan, and take charge of Russia. He was still in his teens.

To secure a port on the Black Sea, he constructed a small but formidable navy. Describing his wars with the Ottoman Empire as a new crusade to liberate Constantinople from the Muslim sultans, Peter fancied himself the legal protector of Orthodox Christians living under Ottoman rule. His forces seized the port of Azov in 1696 but lost it again in 1713, thus calling a halt to southward expansion.

In the winter of 1697–1698, after his Black Sea campaign, Peter traveled in disguise across Europe to discover how western European societies were becoming so powerful and wealthy. He paid special attention to ships and weapons, even working for a time as a ship's carpenter in the Netherlands. Upon his return to Russia, Peter resolved to expand and reform his vast but backward empire.

In the long and costly Great Northern War (1700–1721), Peter's modernized armies broke Swedish control of the Baltic Sea, making possible more direct contacts between Russia and Europe. This victory forced the European powers to recognize Russia as a major power for the first time, just as the Ottoman Empire was then being viewed as past its prime.

On land captured from Sweden at the eastern end of the Baltic, Peter built St. Petersburg, his window on the West. In 1712 the city became Russia's capital. To demonstrate Russia's new sophistication, Peter ordered architects to build St. Petersburg's houses and public buildings in the baroque style then fashionable in France.

Peter also pushed the Russian elite to imitate European fashions. He personally shaved off his noblemen's long beards to conform to Western styles. To end the traditional seclusion of upper-class Russian women, Peter required officials, military officers, and merchants to bring their wives to the social gatherings he organized in the capital. He also directed the nobles to educate their children.

A decree of 1716 proclaimed that the tsar "is not obliged to answer to anyone in the world for his doings, but possesses power and authority over his kingdom and land, to rule them at his will and pleasure as a Christian ruler." Under this expansive definition of his role, Peter sharply reduced the traditional roles of the boyars in government and the army, brought the Russian Orthodox Church more firmly under state control, built factories and foundries to provide supplies for the military, increased taxes, and imposed more forced labor on the serfs. Peter was an absolutist ruler of the sort then common in western Europe, but he is equally comparable to the most authoritarian rulers in the contemporary Muslim empires.

THE MARITIME WORLDS OF ISLAM, 1500–1750

As land powers, the Mughal, Safavid, Ottoman, and Russian Empires faced similar problems in the seventeenth and eighteenth centuries. Complex changes in military technology and in the world economy, along with the increasing difficulty of basing an extensive land empire on military forces paid through land grants, affected them all adversely.

The new pressures faced by land powers were less important to seafaring countries intent on turning trade networks into maritime empires. Improvements in ship design, navigation accuracy, and the use of cannon gave an ever-increasing edge to European powers competing with local seafaring peoples. Moreover, the development of joint-stock companies, in which many merchants pooled their capital, provided a flexible and efficient financial instrument for exploiting new possibilities. The English East India Company was founded in 1600, the Dutch East India Company in 1602.

Although the Ottomans, Safavids, and Mughals did not effectively contest the growth of Portuguese and then Dutch, English, and French maritime power, the majority of non-European shipbuilders, captains, sailors, and traders were Muslim. The sizable groups of Armenian, Jewish, and Hindu traders remained almost as aloof from the Europeans as the Muslims did. The presence in every port of Muslims following the same legal traditions and practicing their faith in similar ways cemented the Muslims' trading network, and conversion to Islam encouraged the growth of coastal Muslim communities.

Although European missionaries, particularly the Jesuits, tried to extend Christianity into Asia and Africa (see Chapters 16 and 21), most Europeans, the Portuguese excepted, did not treat local converts or the offspring of mixed marriages as full members of their communities. Islam was generally more welcoming. As a consequence, Islam spread extensively into East Africa and Southeast Asia during precisely the same time as rapid European commercial expansion.

Muslims in Southeast Asia   Historians disagree about the chronology and manner of Islam's spread in Southeast Asia. Arab traders appeared in southern China as early as the eighth century, so Muslims probably reached the East Indies (the island portions of Southeast Asia) at a similarly early date. Nevertheless, the continuing dominance of Indian cultural influences in the area indicates that early Muslim visitors had little impact on local beliefs. Clearer indications of the formation of Muslim communities date from roughly the fourteenth century, with the strongest overseas linkage being to the port of Cambay in India rather than to the Arab world. Islam first took root in port cities and in some royal courts and spread inland only slowly, possibly transmitted by itinerant Sufis.

Although appeals to the Ottoman sultan for support against the Europeans ultimately proved futile, Islam strengthened resistance to Portuguese, Spanish, and Dutch intruders. When the Spaniards conquered the Philippines during the decades following the establishment of their first fort in 1565, they encountered Muslims on the southern island of Mindanao (min-duh-NOW) and the nearby Sulu archipelago. They called them "Moros," the Spanish term for their old enemies, the Muslims of North Africa. In the ensuing Moro wars, the Spaniards portrayed the Moros as greedy pirates who raided non-Muslim territories for slaves. In fact, they were political, religious, and commercial competitors whose perseverance enabled them to establish the Sulu Empire based in the southern Philippines, one of the strongest states in Southeast Asia from 1768 to 1848.

Other local kingdoms that looked on Islam as a force to counter the aggressive Christianity of the Europeans included the actively proselytizing Brunei (BROO-neye) Sultanate in northern Borneo and the **Acheh** (AH-cheh) **Sultanate** in northern Sumatra. At its peak in the early seventeenth century, Acheh succeeded Malacca as the main center of Islamic expansion in Southeast Asia, prospering by trading pepper for cotton cloth from Gujarat in India. Acheh declined after the Dutch seized Malacca from Portugal in 1641.

How well Islam was understood in these Muslim kingdoms is open to question. In Acheh, for example, a series of women ruled between 1641 and 1699. This practice ended when local Muslim scholars obtained a ruling from scholars in Mecca and Medina that Islam did not approve of female rulers. After this ruling, scholarly understandings of Islam gained greater prominence in the East Indies.

Historians have looked at merchants, Sufi preachers, or both as the first propagators of Islam in Southeast Asia. The scholarly vision of Islam, however, took root in the sixteenth century by way of pilgrims returning from years of study in Mecca and Medina. Islam promoted the dissemination of writing in the region. Some of the returning pilgrims wrote in Arabic, others in Malay or Javanese. As Islam continued to spread, *adat* ("custom"), a form of Islam rooted in pre-Muslim religious and social practices, retained its preeminence in rural areas over practices centered on the Shari'a, the religious law. But the royal courts in the port cities began to heed the views of the pilgrim teachers.

Muslims in Coastal Africa   Muslim rulers also governed the East African ports that the Portuguese began to visit in the fifteenth century. People living in the millet and rice lands of the Swahili Coast—from the Arabic *sawahil* (suh-WAH-hil) meaning "coasts"—had little contact with those in the dry hinterlands. Throughout this period, the East African lakes region and the highlands of Kenya witnessed unprecedented migration and relocation of peoples because of drought conditions that persisted from the late sixteenth through most of the seventeenth century.

Cooperation among the trading ports of Kilwa, Mombasa, and Malindi was hindered by the thick bush country that separated the cultivated tracts of coastal land and by the fact that the ports competed with one another in the export of ivory, ambergris (AM-ber-grees) (a whale byproduct used in perfumes), and forest products such as beeswax, copal tree resin, and wood. Kilwa also exported gold. In the eighteenth century slave trading, primarily to Arabian ports but also to India, increased in importance. Because Europeans—the only peoples who kept consistent records of slave-trading activities—played a minor role in this slave trade, few records have survived to indicate its extent. Perhaps the best estimate is that 2.1 million slaves were exported between 1500 and 1890, a little over 12.5 percent of the total traffic in African slaves during that period (see Chapter 19).

Initially, the Portuguese favored the port of Malindi, which caused the decline of Kilwa and Mombasa. Repeatedly plagued by local rebellion, Portuguese power suffered severe blows when the Arabs of **Oman** in southeastern Arabia captured their south Arabian stronghold at Musqat (1650) and then went on to seize Mombasa (1698), which had become the Portuguese capital in East Africa. The Portuguese briefly retook Mombasa but lost control permanently in 1729. From then on, the Portuguese had to content themselves with Mozambique in East Africa and a few remaining ports in India (Goa) and farther east (Macao and Timor).

The Omanis created a maritime empire of their own, one that worked in greater cooperation with the African populations. The Bantu language of the coast, broadened by the absorption of Arabic, Persian, and Portuguese loanwords, developed into **Swahili** (swah-HEE-lee), which was spoken throughout the region. Arabs and other Muslims who settled in the region intermarried with local families, giving rise to a mixed population that played an important role in developing a distinctive Swahili culture.

In Northwest Africa the seizure by Portugal and Spain of coastal strongholds in Morocco provoked a militant response. The Sa'adi family, which claimed descent from the Prophet Muhammad, led a resistance to Portuguese aggression that climaxed in victory at the battle of al-Qasr al-Kabir (Ksar el Kebir) in 1578. The triumphant Moroccan sultan, Ahmad al-Mansur, restored his country's strength and independence. By the early seventeenth century naval expeditions from the port of Salé, referred to in British records as "the Sally Rovers," raided European shipping as far as Britain itself.

Corsairs, or sea raiders, working out of Algerian, Tunisian, and Libyan ports brought the same sort of warfare to the Mediterranean. European governments called these Muslim raiders pirates and slave-takers, and they leveled the same charges against other Muslim mariners in the Persian Gulf and the Sulu Sea. But there was little distinction between the actions of the Muslims and of their European adversaries.

European Powers in Southern Seas   Through their well-organized Dutch East India Company, the Dutch played a major role in driving the Portuguese from their possessions in the East Indies. Just as the Portuguese had tried to dominate the trade in spices, so the Dutch concentrated at first on the spice-producing islands of Southeast Asia. The Portuguese had seized Malacca, a strategic town on the narrow strait at the end of the Malay Peninsula, from a local Malay ruler in 1511 (see Chapter 16). The Dutch took it away from them in 1641, leaving Portugal little foothold in the East Indies except the islands of Ambon (am-BOHN) and Timor.

Although the United Netherlands was one of the least autocratic countries of Europe, the governors-general appointed by the Dutch East India Company deployed almost unlimited powers in their efforts to maintain their trade monopoly. They could even order the execution of their own employees for "smuggling"—that is, trading on their own. Under strong governors-general, the Dutch fought a series of wars against Acheh and other local kingdoms on Sumatra and Java. In 1628 and 1629 their new capital at **Batavia**, now the city of Jakarta on Java, was besieged by a fleet of fifty ships belonging to the sultan of Mataram (MAH-tah-ram), a Javanese kingdom. The Dutch held out with difficulty and eventually prevailed when the sultan was unable to get effective help from the English.

In the course of the eighteenth century, the Dutch gradually turned from being middlemen between Southeast Asian producers and European buyers to producing crops in areas they controlled, notably in Java. Javanese teak forests yielded high-quality lumber, and coffee, transplanted from Yemen, grew well in the western hilly regions. In this new phase of colonial export production, Batavia developed from being the headquarters town of a far-flung enterprise to being the administrative capital of a conquered land.

CONCLUSION

The complex changes in military technology and economic organization that were under way in smaller European countries in the seventeenth and eighteenth centuries affected the Ottoman, Safavid, and Mughal Empires adversely. Only Russia, by virtue of a single ruler who was able to learn western European techniques at first hand, found success in adopting some of the changes. By western European standards, however, Russia was still a poor and backward country when Peter's reign ended in 1725 while the Muslims ruled rich lands that were ripe for European exploitation.

Improvements in ship design, navigation accuracy, and the use of cannon gave an ever-increasing edge to European powers competing with local seafaring peoples. In contrast to the age-old Eurasian belief that imperial wealth came from controlling broad expanses of land, western European rulers promoted joint-stock companies and luxuriated in the prosperity gained from their ever-increasing control of Indian Ocean commerce. Eighteenth-century European observers marveled no less at the riches and industry of these eastern lands than at the fundamental weakness of their political and military systems. Yet they persistently underestimated the importance of Islam as a focus of local allegiance and political opposition.

IMPORTANT EVENTS 1500–1750	
1502–1524	Shah Ismail establishes Safavid rule in Iran
1511	Portuguese seize Malacca from local Malay ruler
1514	Selim I defeats Safavid Shah at Chaldiran; conquers Egypt and Syria (1516–1517)

1514	Defeat by Ottomans at Chaldiran limits Safavid growth
1520–1566	Reign of Suleiman the Magnificent; peak of Ottoman Empire
1526	Babur defeats last sultan of Delhi at Panipat
1529	First Ottoman siege of Vienna
1533–1584	Rule of Prince Ivan IV
1556–1605	Akbar rules in Agra; peak of Mughal Empire
1565	Spanish establish their first fort in the Philippines
1571	Ottoman naval defeat at Lepanto
1582	Russians conquer Khanate of Sibir
1587–1629	Reign of Shah Abbas the Great; peak of Safavid Empire
1600	English East India company founded
1602	Dutch East India Company founded
1606	Dutch reach Australia
1610	End of Anatolian revolts
1613–1645	Rule of Mikhail, the first Romanov tsar
1622	Iranians oust Portuguese from Hormuz after 108 years
1641	Dutch seize Malacca from Portuguese
1650	Omani Arabs capture Musqat from Portuguese
1658–1707	Aurangzeb imposes conservative Islamic regime
1689–1725	Rule of Peter the Great
1698	Omani Arabs seize Mombasa from Portuguese
1712	St. Petersburg becomes Russia's capital
1718–1730	Tulip Period
1722	Afghan invaders topple last Safavid Shah
1736–1747	Nadir Shah temporarily reunites Iran; invades India (1739)
1739	Iranians under Nadir Shah sack Delhi
1741	Expansion of French Power in India

21

EAST ASIA IN GLOBAL PERSPECTIVE

I n the sixteenth century Ming China became a driving force in the first truly global economy, one that joined together Asia, Europe, the Americas, and, to a lesser extent, Africa. To meet China's skyrocketing demand for silver, European traders imported American silver and in return shipped silk, spices, tea, and other precious goods back to Europe. Christian missionaries joined European merchants as intellectual middlemen in this global interaction.

At century's end, however, from 1592 to 1598, the Imjin War, a conflict surpassed in violence only by the wars of the nineteenth and twentieth centuries, embroiled Korea, Japan, and China. After attempting to conquer China, the Japanese finally returned to their islands, leaving the weakened Ming to face other foes. Korea, the devastated battleground, did not recover for centuries.

In the seventeenth century, **Manchu** armies from Manchuria on China's northeast frontier succeeded where Japan had failed. The Ming emperor had slashed the government payroll to pay the army defending Beijing (**bay-JING**) against the Manchu. Among those losing his job was an apprentice ironworker named Li Zicheng (**lee ZUH-cheng**). By 1630 Li Zicheng had found work as a soldier, but he and his fellow soldiers mutinied when the government failed to provide needed supplies. A natural leader, Li soon headed several thousand Chinese rebels, and in 1635 he and other rebel leaders gained control over much of north-central China.

Wedged between the Manchu armies to the north and the rebels south of Beijing, the Ming government tottered. Li Zicheng's forces moved on Beijing, promising an end to Ming abuses and a restoration of peace and prosperity. In April 1644 Li's forces took the city without a fight. The last Ming emperor hanged himself in the palace garden, bringing to an end the dynasty that had ruled China since 1368.

Li's victory was short-lived, however. Preferring the Manchus to an uneducated warlord, the Ming general Wu Sangui and his new northern allies retook Beijing in June. Li's forces scattered, and a year later he was dead, either a suicide or beaten to death by peasants whose food he tried to steal.[1] Now the new masters of China, the Manchus installed their young sovereign as emperor, declared the beginning of a new dynasty called "Qing" (**ching**), and over the next two decades hunted down the last of the Ming loyalists and heirs to the throne.

---

[1]Adapted from Jonathan D. Spence, *The Search for Modern China* (New York: W. W. Norton, 1990), 21–25.

These centuries may be referred to as the early modern period, a time of greater cultural, commercial, and military connectivity within East Asia. Maritime networks replaced the land-based Silk Road trade. This led to increased presence of Europeans. Some people in China, Korea, and Japan welcomed the European presence, but rulers in Korea and Japan eventually sought to curb foreign influence. Japan and Korea would eventually experience relative peace during the early modern period, while China suffered from large-scale warfare, rebellions, and natural disasters at the beginning and end of the early modern period. Each country, however, at its peak generated commercial and cultural developments that rivaled achievements in Europe.

EAST ASIA AND EUROPE

In the sixteenth century, European merchant adventurers traveling from Southeast Asia helped build thriving trade networks in East Asia. Because of changes in the Ming fiscal system that required taxes to be paid in cash, China had an urgent demand for silver. Prior to 1500, Japan had supplied much of the foreign silver China needed, as much as 30 percent of the world's total output. This was replaced by American silver, however, mostly from the mines at Potosí in Bolivia (see Chapter 18). European ships transported the bullion with their masters also acting as middlemen in Asian trade routes, sometimes operating as privateers and even pirates.

Trading Companies and Missionaries   For European merchants, the China trade was second in importance only to the spice trade of Southeast Asia. China's vast population and manufacturing skills drew a steady stream of would-be merchants from western Europe; however, enthusiasm for the trade developed only slowly at the Ming court.

In late 1513 a Portuguese ship reached China but was not permitted to trade. A formal Portuguese embassy in 1517 got bogged down in Chinese protocol and procrastination, and China expelled the Portuguese in 1522. Finally, in 1557, the Portuguese gained permission to trade from a base in Macao (**muh-KOW**) on the southern coast. Spain's China trade was conducted from Manila in the Philippines, where silver-laden galleons arrived from South America. For a time, the Spanish and the Dutch both maintained trading outposts on the island of Taiwan (then called Formosa), but in 1662 they were forced to concede control to the Qing, who for the first time incorporated Taiwan into China.

By then, the Dutch East India Company (VOC for Vereenigde Oost-Indische Compagnie) (see Chapter 19) had displaced the Portuguese as the paramount European traders in the Indian Ocean. The Portuguese had tried to dominate the trade in spices by seizing Malacca, a strategic town on the narrow strait at the end of the Malay Peninsula, from a local Malay ruler in 1511. The Dutch took it away from them in 1641, leaving Portugal little foothold in the East Indies except the Islands of Ambon (**am-BOHN**) and Timor.

The governors-general appointed by the VOC deployed almost unlimited authority in their efforts to maintain their trade monopoly. They could even order the execution of their own employees for "smuggling"—that is, trading on their own. Under strong governors-general, the Dutch fought a series of wars against

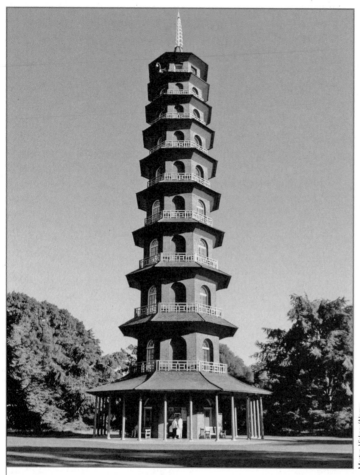

Martyn Vickery/Alamy

Great Pagoda at Kew Gardens *A testament to Europeans' fascination with Chinese culture is the towering Pagoda at the Royal Botanic Gardens in London. Completed in 1762, it was designed by Sir William Chambers as the principal ornament in the pleasure grounds of the White House at Kew, residence of Augusta, the mother of King George III.*

local rulers in Southeast Asia, such as the sultan of a Javanese kingdom called Mataram (**MAH-tah-ram**). Suppressing local rulers, however, was not enough to control the spice trade once other Europeans countries adopted Dutch methods, learned where goods could be acquired, and started to send ships into eastern waters.

In East Asia as well, the VOC established itself as the main European trader. VOC representatives courted official favor in China by acknowledging the moral superiority of the emperor. This meant performing the ritual kowtow (in which the visitor knocked his head on the floor while crawling toward the throne) to the Ming emperor.

Along with trade came missionaries. Catholic missionaries accompanied the Portuguese and Spanish merchants to China. While the Franciscans and Dominicans pursued the conversion efforts at the bottom of society, a strategy pioneered in Japan, the Jesuits (members of the Catholic religious order the Society of Jesus) focused on China's intellectual and political elite.

The outstanding Jesuit of late Ming China, Matteo Ricci (**mah-TAY-oh REE-chee**) (1552–1610), became expert in the Chinese language and an accomplished scholar of the Confucian classics. Under Ricci's leadership, the Jesuits adapted Catholicism to Chinese cultural traditions while introducing the Chinese to the latest science and technology from Europe. After 1601 Ricci resided in Beijing on an imperial stipend as a Western scholar. Later Jesuits headed the office of astronomy that issued the official calendar.

Jesuits helped create maps in the European style as practical guides to newly conquered regions and as symbols of Qing dominance. One Chinese emperor, Kangxi, considered introducing the European calendar, but protests from the Confucian elite caused him to drop the plan. When he fell ill with malaria in the 1690s, Jesuit medical treatment (in this case, South American quinine) aided his recovery. Kangxi also ordered the creation of illustrated books in Manchu detailing European anatomical and pharmaceutical knowledge.

To gain converts, the Jesuits made important compromises in their religious teaching. Most importantly, they tolerated Confucian ancestor worship. This excited controversy between the Jesuits and their Catholic rivals in China, the Franciscans and Dominicans, and also between the Jesuits and the pope. In 1690 the disagreement reached a high pitch. Kangxi wrote to Rome supporting the Jesuit position and after further dispute ordered the expulsion of all missionaries who refused to sign a certificate accepting his position. The Jesuit presence in China declined in the eighteenth century, and later Chinese emperors persecuted Christians rather than naming them to high office.

Chinese Influences on Europe

The exchange of information between Chinese and Europeans was never one-way. While the Jesuits brought forward new knowledge of anatomy, for example, the Chinese demonstrated an early form of inoculation, called "variolation," that had helped curtail smallpox after the conquest of Beijing. The technique inspired Europeans to develop other vaccines.

Similarly, Jesuit writings about China excited admiration in Europe. The wealthy and the aspiring middle classes demanded Chinese things, or at least "chinoiserie," that is, things that looked Chinese. Silk, porcelain, and tea were avidly sought, along with cloisonné jewelry, jade, lacquered and jeweled room dividers, painted fans, and carved ivory (which originated in Africa and was finished in China). Wallpaper began as an adaptation of the Chinese practice of covering walls with enormous loose-hanging watercolors or calligraphy scrolls. By the mid-1700s special workshops throughout China were producing wallpaper and other items according to the specifications of European merchants. The items were exported to Europe via Canton.

Chinese political philosophy impressed Europeans, too. In the late 1770s poems supposedly written by Emperor Qianlong were translated into French and disseminated in intellectual circles. In these poems the Chinese emperors rule as benevolent despots campaigning against superstition and ignorance, curbing aristocratic excesses, and patronizing science and the arts. This image of a practical, secular, compassionate ruler impressed the French thinker Voltaire, who proclaimed that Chinese emperors were model philosopher-kings and advocated such rulership as a protection against the growth of aristocratic privilege.

Japan and the Europeans   European contacts with Japan also presented that country with new opportunities and problems. Within thirty years of the arrival of the first Portuguese in 1543, warlords known as *daimyo* (**DIE-mee-oh**) were fighting with Western-style firearms, copied and improved upon by Japanese armorers.

The Japanese welcomed but closely regulated traders from Portugal, Spain, the Netherlands, and England. Aside from a brief boom in porcelain exports in the seventeenth century, few Japanese goods went to Europe, and not much from Europe found a market in Japan. The Japanese sold the Dutch copper and silver, which the Dutch exchanged in China for silks that they then resold in Japan. The Japanese, of course, had their own trade with China.

Portuguese and Spanish merchant ships also brought Catholic missionaries. One of the first, Francis Xavier, a co-founder of the Jesuit Order, went to India in the mid-sixteenth century looking for converts and later traveled throughout Southeast and East Asia. He spent two years in Japan, where he died in 1552, hoping to gain entry to China.

Japanese responses to Xavier and other Jesuits were mixed. Many ordinary Japanese found the new faith deeply meaningful, but the Japanese elite more often opposed it as disruptive and foreign. By 1580 more than 100,000 Japanese had become Christians, and one daimyo gave Jesuit missionaries the port city of Nagasaki (**NAH-guh-SAHK-kee**). In 1613 Date Masamune (**DAH-tay ´mah-suh-MOO-nay**), the fierce and independent daimyo of northern Honshu (**HOHN-shoo**), sent his own embassy to the Vatican, by way of the Philippines (where there were significant communities of Japanese merchants and pirates) and Mexico City. Some daimyo converts ordered their subjects to become Christians as well.

By the early seventeenth century there were some 300,000 Japanese Christians and even some Japanese priests. However, suspicions about the intentions of the Europeans turned the shogunal regime against Christianity. A decree issued in 1614 banned Christianity and charged its adherents with seeking to overthrow true doctrine, change the government, and seize the country. Some missionaries left Japan; others worked underground. In 1617 the government began persecutions in earnest, and the beheadings, crucifixions, and forced recantations over the next several decades destroyed almost the entire Christian community. Small groups of Christians practiced their religion in secret, but missionary efforts were generally far less successful than in China, at least until the modern era.

To keep Christianity from resurfacing, a series of decrees issued between 1633 and 1639 sharply curtailed trade with Europe. Europeans who entered the country illegally faced the death penalty, and Japanese subjects were required to produce certificates from Buddhist temples attesting to their religious orthodoxy and loyalty to the regime.

The exclusion of Europe was not total, however. A few Dutch were permitted to reside on a small artificial island in Nagasaki's harbor, and a few Japanese were licensed to supply their needs. What these intermediaries learned about European weapons technology, shipbuilding, mathematics and astronomy, anatomy and medicine, and geography was termed "Dutch studies."

Japanese restrictions on the number of Chinese ships that could trade in Japan were harder to enforce. Regional lords in northern and southern Japan not only pursued overseas trade and piracy but also claimed dominion over islands between Japan and Korea and southward toward Taiwan, including present-day Okinawa. Despite such evasions, the new shogunate achieved substantial success in exercising its authority, keeping most daimyo from forming their own relations with European interests.

THE IMJIN WAR AND JAPANESE UNIFICATION

The Imjin War, the largest pre-twentieth-century conflict in East Asian history, had no European involvement. Named in Korean for the year of the water dragon (Imjin), it also has many Chinese names, including "the Korean campaign." In Japan today, it is called "Hideyoshi's invasions." Seven years long (1592–1598), the war had lasting effects in Korea, facilitated the demise of the Ming dynasty in China, and produced bad feelings between Japan and Korea that have lasted down to the present.

Japan changed in three different dimensions between 1500 and 1800: internal and external military conflicts, political growth and strengthening, and expanded commercial and cultural contacts. Along with its relatively homogeneous population and natural boundaries, Japan's smaller size made political unification more achievable than in the great empire of China.

The Ashikaga Shogunate had weakened after the Onin War (see Chapter 13), opening opportunities for daimyo across Japan to fight for land and influence. Warfare among the different daimyo was common, and in the late 1500s it culminated in a prolonged civil war. Each daimyo had a castle town, a small bureaucracy, and a band of warriors, their *samurai*. Daimyo pledged a loose allegiance to the Japanese emperor and to the shogun residing in the capital city of Kyoto (**KYOH-toh**), but neither figure wielded significant political power. Three warlords, often referred to as the "three unifiers," gradually consolidated control over parts of Japan, ending in full unification in the early seventeenth century. First, Oda Nobunaga succeeded in unifying the central part of Japan, including the influential area around Kyoto. When he was betrayed by one of his generals, the second of the unifiers, Hideyoshi Toyotomi, avenged his death, taking control of Nobunaga's forces.

Although born a lowly peasant, Hideyoshi (**HEE-day-YOH-shee**) rose through the warrior ranks and eventually unified the country. Even as he was consolidating his control over Japan, he planned to invade Korea in order to conquer China. In addition, he dispatched retainers to meet officials as far away as the Spanish governor in the Philippines and the Portuguese viceroy in Goa (western India), demanding that they submit to him and send tribute. In 1592, buoyed with his progress in unifying Japan, the supremely confident Hideyoshi sent a 160,000-man invasion force to the Asian mainland. Various reasons are given for his decision to invade: to impress domestic rivals, to keep major daimyo busy fighting outside of Japan so they could not rebel, to push out Christian daimyo (who provided a sizable portion of the forces sent to Korea), to dominate East Asian trade networks. His sights were set on China, however.

Several centuries of peace and court factionalism had left the Koreans ill prepared to handle the battle-tested samurai-led armies. But although the Koreans failed to implement large-scale musket manufacturing or training, a policy that changed after the war began, they did possess cannon. After initial disastrous defeats, what eventually saved them was assistance from the Ming Chinese and their own advanced naval strategy.

While daimyo armies sent to Korea were skilled at land-based fighting, the Japanese navy was unprepared for serious combat. To intercept a portion of the Japanese fleet, Korean admiral Yi Sunshin successfully deployed "turtle ships," highly maneuverable vessels with large cannon and completely covered decks. All told, Yi won some twenty-three consecutive naval battles. On land, the Koreans called upon China for help. Regarding Korea as one of its client states, China obliged. At first the Ming sent only a few thousand troops to Korea, but Hideyoshi's military successes and the fear that his armies might actually reach China convinced the emperor to send more soldiers, eventually totaling some 100,000.

After 1593, the Chinese negotiated a peace with the Japanese, but after a short time Hideyoshi decided that the terms of the peace were inadequate. His forces invaded again in 1597, employing brutal punitive measures as they advanced through the Korean peninsula. However, many daimyo were losing interest in Hideyoshi's dream of defeating China and hoped instead to secure a few provinces in southern Korea for Japan. In poor health, Hideyoshi too grew tired of the war. On his deathbed he gave an order to withdraw all troops from Korea, an order that was followed after his passing in 1598. It still took many years, however, for Japan to conclude peace with Korea. Formal relations did not resume until 1617.

The invasion devastated Korea. In the turmoil after the Japanese withdrawal, the Korean ruling class of nobles laid claim to so much taxpaying land that royal revenues may have fallen by two-thirds. Roughly 80 percent of the arable land was devastated, and nearly 20 percent of the population lost, either killed in the fighting or taken as slaves to Japan. Confucian scholars and artisans were included in that number. The occasionally used phrase "pottery wars" refers to the fact that Korean pottery technology, in particular, was so advanced that transplanted Korean specialists transformed Japanese ceramics production in the postwar period.

China also suffered dire consequences. Fighting in Korea depleted the Ming coffers at a time when the empire was also battling peoples to the north. When the emperor established a new tax to recover revenue, protests erupted in the provinces. The battles in Manchuria weakened the Chinese garrisons there, permitting Manchu opposition to consolidate. Manchu forces invaded Korea in the 1620s and eventually compelled Korea to become a tributary state. By 1644 the Manchus would be in possession of Beijing, China's capital.

TOKUGAWA JAPAN AND CHOSON KOREA TO 1800

Japanese Reunification and Economic Growth

Despite wartime losses, Japan flourished in the postwar era. After Hideyoshi's demise, the last of the three unifiers, Tokugawa Ieyasu (**TOH-koo-GAH-wah ee-ay-YAH-soo**) (1543–1616), asserted his domination over other daimyo and in 1603 established a new military regime known as the **Tokugawa Shogunate**. The shoguns also created a new administrative capital at

Edo (**EH-doh**) (now Tokyo). Trade along the well-maintained road between Edo and the imperial capital of Kyoto promoted the development of the Japanese economy and the formation of other trading centers.

Although the Tokugawa Shogunate gave Japan more political unity than the islands had seen in centuries, the regionally based daimyo retained a great deal of power and autonomy. Ieyasu and his successors struggled for political centralization, but economic integration proved to be a more important feature of Tokugawa Japan. Because the shoguns required the daimyo to visit Edo frequently, good roads and maritime transport linked the city to the castle towns on three of Japan's four main islands. Commercial traffic developed along these routes. Lords received their incomes locally in rice, and they paid their followers in rice. Recipients converted much of this rice into cash, a practice that led to the development of rice exchanges at Edo and at Osaka (**OH-sah-kah**), where merchants speculated in rice prices. By the late seventeenth century Edo was one of the largest cities in the world, with nearly a million inhabitants.

The domestic peace of the Tokugawa era forced the warrior class to adapt to the growing bureaucratic needs of the state. As the samurai became better educated and more attuned to the tastes of the civil elite, they became important customers for merchants dealing in silks, *sake* (**SAH-kay**) (rice wine), fans, porcelain, lacquer ware, books, and moneylending. The state attempted—unsuccessfully—to curb the independence of the merchants when the economic well-being of the samurai was threatened by low rice prices or high interest rates.

The 1600s and 1700s were centuries of high achievement in artisanship. Japanese skills in steel making, pottery, and lacquer ware were joined by excellence in the production of porcelain (see Environment and Technology: East Asian Porcelain), thanks in no small part to Korean experts brought back to Japan after the invasion of 1592. In the early 1600s manufacturers and merchants amassed enormous family fortunes. Several of the most important industrial and financial enterprises of the twentieth century—for instance, the Mitsui (**MIT-sue-ee**) companies—had their origins in sake breweries of the early Tokugawa period and then branched out into manufacturing, finance, and transport.

Wealthy merchants weakened the Tokugawa policy of controlling commerce by cultivating close alliances with their regional daimyo and, when possible, with the shogun himself. By the end of the 1700s the merchant families of Tokugawa Japan held the key to future modernization and the development of heavy industry.

| **Japanese Elite Decline and Social Crisis** | During the 1700s population growth put a great strain on the well-developed lands of central Japan. In more remote provinces, where the lords promoted new settlements and agricultural expansion, the rate of economic growth was |

significantly greater.

Also troubling the Tokugawa government in the 1700s was the shogunate's inability to stabilize rice prices and halt the economic decline of the samurai. The Tokugawa government realized that the rice brokers could manipulate prices and interest rates to enrich themselves at the expense of the samurai, who had to convert their rice allotments into cash. Early Tokugawa laws designed to regulate interest and prices were later supplemented by laws requiring moneylenders to forgive

ENVIRONMENT + TECHNOLOGY

East Asian Porcelain

By the 1400s artisans in China, Korea, and Japan were all producing high-quality pottery with lustrous surface glazes. The best-quality pottery, intended for the homes of the wealthy and powerful, was made of pure white clay and covered with a hard translucent glaze. Artisans often added intricate decorations in cobalt blue and other colors. Cheaper pottery found a huge market in East Asia.

Such pottery was also exported to Southeast Asia, the Indian Ocean, and the Middle East. Little found its way to Europe before 1600, but imports soared once the Dutch established trading bases in East Asia. Europeans called the high-quality ware "china" or "porcelain." Blue and white designs were especially popular.

One of the great centers of Chinese production was at the large artisan factory at Jingdezhen (**JING-deh-JUHN**). No sooner had the Dutch tapped into this source than the civil wars and Manchu conquests disrupted production in the middle 1600s. Desperate for a substitute source, the Dutch turned to porcelain from Japanese producers at Arita and Imari, near Nagasaki. Despite Japan's restriction of European trade, the Dutch East India Company transported some 190,000 pieces of Japanese ceramic ware to the Netherlands between 1653 and 1682.

In addition to a wide range of Asian designs, Chinese and Japanese artisans made all sorts of porcelain for the European market. These included purely decorative pottery birds, vases, and pots as well as utilitarian vessels and dishes intended for table use. The serving dish illustrated here came from dinnerware sets the Japanese made especially for the Dutch East India Company. The VOC logo is the acronym of the company's name in Dutch. It is surrounded by Asian design motifs.

After peace returned in China, the VOC imported tens of thousands of Chinese porcelain pieces a year. The Chinese artisans sometimes produced imitations of Japanese designs that had become popular

samurai debts. But these laws were not always enforced. By the early 1700s many lords and samurai were dependent on the willingness of merchants to provide credit.

The legitimacy of the Tokugawa shoguns rested on their ability to reward and protect the interests of the lords and samurai who had supported their rise to power. Moreover, the Tokugawa government, like the governments of China, Korea, and Vietnam, accepted the Confucian idea that agriculture should be the basis of state wealth and that merchants, who were considered morally weak, should occupy lowly positions in society. Tokugawa decentralization, however, not only failed to hinder but actually stimulated the growth of commercial activities.

From the founding of the Tokugawa Shogunate in 1603 until 1800, the economy grew faster than the population. Household amenities and cultural resources that in China appeared only in the cities were common in the Japanese countryside. Despite official disapproval, merchants enjoyed relative freedom and influence in in Europe. Meanwhile, the Dutch were experimenting with making their own imitations of East Asian porcelain, right down to the Asian motifs and colors that had become so fashionable in Europe.

Photograph courtesy Peabody Essex Museum, #83830

Japanese Export Porcelain *Part of a larger set made for the Dutch East India Company.*

eighteenth-century Japan. They produced a vivid culture of their own, fostering the development of *kabuki* theater, colorful woodblock prints and silk-screened fabrics, and restaurants.

The "Forty-Seven Ronin" (**ROH-neen**) incident of 1701–1703 exemplified the ideological and social crisis of Japan's transformation from a military to a civil society. A senior minister provoked a young daimyo into drawing his sword at the shogun's court. For this offense the young lord was sentenced to commit *seppuku* (**SEP-poo-koo**), the ritual suicide of the samurai. His own followers then became *ronin*, "masterless samurai," obliged by the traditional code of the warrior to avenge their deceased master. They broke into the house of the senior minister and killed him and others in his household. Then they withdrew to a temple in Edo and notified the shogun of what they had done out of loyalty to their lord and to avenge his death.

A legal debate ensued. To deny the righteousness of the ronin would be to deny samurai values. But to approve their actions would create social chaos, undermine

Woodblock Print of the "Forty-Seven Ronin" Story *The saga of the forty-seven ronin and the avenging of their fallen leader has fascinated the Japanese public since the event occurred in 1702. This watercolor from the Tokugawa period shows the leaders of the group pausing on the snowy banks of the Sumida River in Edo (Tokyo) before storming their enemy's residence.*

Archives Charmet/The Bridgeman Art Library

laws against murder, and deny the shogunal government the right to try cases of samurai violence. The shogun ruled that the ronin had to die but would be permitted to die honorably by committing seppuku. Traditional samurai values had to surrender to the supremacy of law. The purity of purpose of the ronin is still celebrated in Japan, but since then Japanese writers, historians, and teachers have recognized that the self-sacrifice of the ronin for the sake of upholding civil law was necessary.

Choson Korea Recovery after the Imjin War was hindered by Manchu invasions that lasted until the late 1630s. Even after the Korean king submitted to the new Qing dynasty, factionalism broke out among the officials that turned violent, an on-again, off-again problem throughout the Choson dynasty (1392–1910). Despite these challenges, the Choson dynasty proved to be the longest-lasting state in East Asian history (see Chapter 13). The dominant influence on Korean culture had long been China, to which Korean rulers generally paid tribute. Thus, although the Korean and Japanese languages are closely related, and although Korea had developed its own system of writing in 1443 and made extensive use of printing with movable type from the fifteenth century on, most printing continued to use Chinese characters.

In many ways the Choson dynasty was also a model Confucian state. The government was staffed by men who passed the civil examination system, modeled on the Chinese institution of the same name. But there was one important difference. In theory, if not in practice, anyone could sit for the civil examinations in China, but by the sixteenth century in Choson Korea, one had to be born into the *yangban* (**YAHNG-bahn**) class to take an examination and work in any position of real influence in government. The yangban, literally "two orders," were a hereditary status group who dominated the civil and military examinations, filling nearly all of the official positions in the national and local governments. Only occasionally was social mobility possible for commoners who tested into the military yangban group, a status typically disdained by the civil yangban. This played a role in stifling recovery from the devastation of war.

The growing influence of Confucianism throughout the Choson dynasty affected attitudes toward women, as it did throughout East Asia. In the previous Koryo period, and early Choson, women were listed in family genealogies alongside their brothers, even after marriage. By the latter part of the Choson dynasty, however, when a woman married, she was removed from her natal family's register. As in China, Confucian teachings discouraged widows from remarrying. Like China and Japan however, Korean women negotiated Confucian dogma toward women. Women dominated shaman positions, influencing royalty, while some women even became philosophers.

Unlike the majority of commoners, the yangban did not have to pay a household tax, nor did they have to serve in the military (unless they were military yangban). During the Choson period they also owned most of the slaves, which at one point made up nearly 30 percent of the population. In addition to privately owned slaves, local governments also maintained slaves for a variety of clerical and labor jobs. Even Buddhist temples owned slaves. The slave population dropped to about 10 percent in the eighteenth century, when runaway slaves increased and the poor economy meant that most yangban simply hired poor commoners to work in agriculture.

FROM MING TO QING

The internal and external forces at work in China were different from those in Japan and operated on a much larger scale, but they led in similar directions. By 1800 China had a greatly enhanced empire, an expanding economy, and growing doubts about the importance of European trade and Christianity.

Ming Economic Growth, 1500–1644   The economic and cultural achievements of the early **Ming Empire** (see Chapter 13) continued during the 1500s. But this productive period was followed by many decades of political weakness, warfare, and rural woes until a new dynasty, the Qing from Manchuria, guided China back to peace and prosperity.

European accounts from the early sixteenth century express astonishment at the power, exquisite manufactures, and vast population of Ming China, where cities had long been culturally and commercially vibrant. Many large landowners and absentee landlords lived in town, as did officials, artists, and rich merchants who had purchased ranks or prepared their sons for the examinations. The elite classes had created a brilliant culture in which novels, operas, poetry, porcelain, and painting were all closely interwoven. Catering to these urban elites were many small businesses that prospered through printing, tailoring, running restaurants, or selling paper, ink, ink-stones, and writing brushes. The imperial government operated factories for the production of ceramics and silks, and enormous government complexes at Jingdezhen and elsewhere invented assembly-line techniques and produced large quantities of high-quality ceramics for sale in China and abroad.

Despite these achievements, serious problems developed that left the Ming Empire economically and politically exhausted. There is evidence that the climate changes known as the Little Ice Age in seventeenth-century Europe affected the climate in China as well (see Issues in World History: The Little Ice Age). Annual temperatures dropped, reached a low point around 1645, and remained low until the early 1700s. The resulting agricultural distress and famine fueled large uprisings that hastened the end of the Ming Empire. The devastation caused by these uprisings and the spread of epidemic disease resulted in steep declines in local populations.

The rapid urban growth and business speculation that were part of the burgeoning trading economy also produced problems. Some provinces suffered from price inflation caused by the flood of silver from America. In contrast to the growing involvement of European governments in promoting economic growth, the Ming government pursued some policies that hindered growth. Ming governments persisted, despite earlier failed experiments, in issuing new paper money and copper coinage, even after silver had won the approval of the markets. Corruption compounded government problems. Disorder and inefficiency came to plague the imperial factories, touching off strikes in the late sixteenth and seventeenth centuries. During a labor protest at Jingdezhen in 1601, workers threw themselves into the kilns to protest working conditions.

Yet the urban and industrial sectors of later Ming society fared much better than the agricultural sector. Despite knowledge of new African and American crops gained from European traders, farmers were slow to change their ways. Neither the rice-growing regions in southern China nor the wheat-growing regions in northern China experienced a meaningful increase in productivity under the later Ming. After 1500 economic depression in the countryside, combined with recurring epidemics in central and southern China, kept rural population growth in check.

Ming Collapse and the Rise of the Qing

Environmental, economic, and administrative problems aside, the primary reasons for the fall of the Ming Empire were internal rebellion and threats on the borders. Powerful Mongol federations in the north and west had long exerted pressure on the frontiers. In the late 1500s large numbers of Mongols were unified by their devotion to the Dalai Lama (**DAH-lie LAH-mah**), or universal teacher of Tibetan Buddhism. Building on this spiritual unity, a brilliant leader named Galdan restored Mongolia as a regional military power around 1600. At the same time, the Manchus, an agricultural people who controlled the region north of Korea, grew stronger in the northeast (see chapter opening).

Pirates based in southwest Japan, Okinawa, and Taiwan, many of them Japanese, frequently looted the southeast coast. Ming military resources, concentrated against

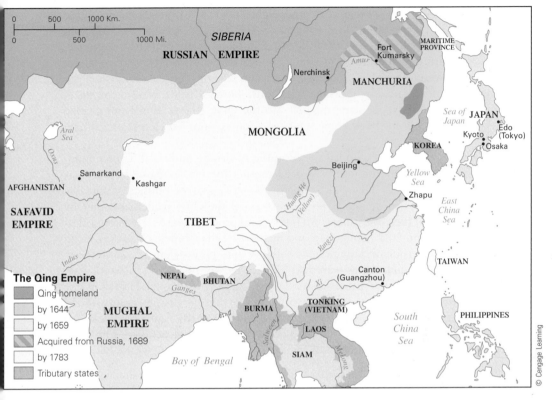

MAP 21.1   The Qing Empire, 1644–1783

The Qing Empire began in Manchuria and captured north China in 1644. Between 1644 and 1783 the Qing conquered all the former Ming territories and added Taiwan, the lower Amur River basin, Inner Mongolia, eastern Turkestan, and Tibet. The resulting state was more than twice the size of the Ming Empire.

the Mongols and the Manchus in the north, could not be deployed to defend the coasts. As a result, many southern Chinese migrated to Southeast Asia to profit from the sea-trading networks of the Indian Ocean.

The Imjin War had prompted the Ming to seek the assistance of Manchu troops that then became enemies after the war. With the rebel leader Li Zicheng in possession of Beijing (see the beginning of this chapter) and the emperor dead by his own hand, a Ming general joined forces with the Manchu leaders in the summer of 1644. Instead of restoring the Ming, however, the Manchus claimed China for their own and began a forty-year conquest of the rest of the Ming territories, as well as Taiwan and parts of Mongolia and Central Asia.

A Manchu family headed the new **Qing Empire**, and Manchu generals commanded the military forces. But Manchus made up a very small portion of the population. Most Qing officials, soldiers, merchants, and farmers were ethnic Chinese. Like other successful invaders of China, the Qing soon adopted Chinese institutions and policies.

Emperor Kangxi   The seventeenth and eighteenth centuries—particularly the reigns of the **Kangxi** (KAHNG-shee) (r. 1662–1722) and Qianlong (**chee-YEN-loong**) (r. 1736–1796) emperors—saw renewed economic, military, and cultural achievement in China. Roads and waterworks were repaired, transit taxes lowered, rents and interest rates cut, and incentives established for resettling areas devastated by peasant rebellions. Foreign trade was encouraged. Vietnam, Burma, and Nepal sent embassies to the Qing tribute court and carried the latest Chinese fashions back home. Overland routes from Korea to Central Asia revived.

The Manchu aristocrats who led the conquest of Beijing and north China dominated the first Qing emperor and served as regents for his young son, who was declared emperor in 1662. This child-emperor, Kangxi, sparred politically with the regents until 1669, when at age sixteen he executed the chief regent and thereby gained real control of the government. An intellectual prodigy who had mastered classical Chinese, Manchu, and Mongolian and memorized the Chinese classics, Kangxi guided imperial expansion and maintained stability until his death in 1722.

In the north, the Qing rulers feared an alliance between Galdan's Mongol state and the expanding Russian presence along the **Amur** (AH-moor) **River**. In the 1680s Qing forces attacked the wooden forts built by hardy Russian scouts on the river's northern bank. Neither empire sent large forces into the Amur territories, so the contest was partly a struggle for the goodwill of the local peoples. The Qing emperor emphasized the importance of treading lightly in the struggle:

> Upon reaching the lands of the Evenks and the Dagurs you will send to announce that you have come to hunt deer. Meanwhile, keep a careful record of the distance and go, while hunting, along the northern bank of the Amur until you come by the shortest route to the town of Russian settlement at Albazin. Thoroughly reconnoiter its location and situation. I don't think the Russians will take a chance on attacking you. If they offer you food, accept it and show your gratitude. If they do attack you, don't fight back. In that case, lead your people and withdraw into our own territories.[2]

Qing forces twice attacked Albazin. The Qing were worried about Russian alliances with other frontier peoples, while Russia wished to protect its access to the furs, timber, and metals concentrated in Siberia and Manchuria. The Qing and Russians were also rivals for control of northern Asia's Pacific coast. Seeing little benefit in continued conflict, in 1689 the two empires negotiated the Treaty of Nerchinsk, using Jesuit missionaries as interpreters. The treaty fixed the border along the Amur River and regulated trade across it. Although this was a thinly settled area, the treaty proved important, and the frontier it demarcated has long endured.

The next step was to settle the Mongolian frontier. Kangxi personally led troops in the great campaigns that defeated Galdan, and by 1691 he had brought Inner Mongolia under Qing control.

Tea and   Like the Ming before them, the Qing were reluctant to grant
Diplomacy   too much access to Europeans. To maintain control over trade, facilitate tax collection, and suppress piracy, the Qing

---

[2]Adapted from G. V. Melikhov, "Manzhou Penetration into the Basin of the Upper Amur in the 1680s," in *Manzhou Rule in China*, ed. S. L. Tikhvinshii (Moscow: Progress Publishers, 1983).

permitted only one market point for each foreign sector. Thus Europeans could trade only at Canton.

This system worked well enough until the late 1700s, when Britain became worried about its massive trade deficit with China. From bases in India and Singapore, British traders moved eastward and by the early 1700s dominated European trading in Canton, displacing the Dutch. The directors of the East India Company (EIC) anticipated limitless profits from China's gigantic markets and advanced technologies.

One item of interest was tea. In medieval and early modern times, tea from China had spread overland to Russia, Central Asia, and the Middle East to become a prized import. Consumers knew it by its northern Chinese name, *cha*—as did the Portuguese. Other western Europeans acquired tea from the sea routes and with it the name used in the Fujian province of coastal China and Taiwan: *te*. In much of Europe, tea competed with chocolate and coffee as a fashionable drink by the mid-1600s.

Emperor Kangxi *In a portrait from about 1690, the young Manchu ruler is portrayed as a refined scholar in the Confucian tradition. He was a scholar and had great intellectual curiosity, but this portrait would not suggest that he was also capable of leading troops in battle.*

British tea importers accumulated great fortunes. However, the Qing Empire took payment in silver and rarely bought anything from Britain. With domestic revenues declining in the later 1700s, the Qing government needed the silver and was disinclined to loosen import restrictions. To make matters worse, the East India Company (EIC) had managed its worldwide holdings badly. As it teetered on bankruptcy, its attempts to manipulate Parliament became increasingly intrusive. In 1792 the British government dispatched Lord George Macartney, a well-connected peer with practical experience in Russia and India, to China. Staffed by scientists, artists, and translators as well as guards and diplomats, the **Macartney mission** showed Britain's great interest in the Qing Empire as well as the EIC's desire to revise the trade system.

To fit Chinese traditions, Macartney portrayed himself as a "tribute emissary" come to salute the Qianlong emperor's eightieth birthday. However, he refused to perform the kowtow, though he did agree to bow on one knee as he would to King George III. The Qianlong emperor received Macartney courteously in September 1793 but refused to alter the Canton trading system, open new ports of trade, or allow the British to establish a permanent mission in Beijing. The emperor sent a letter to King George explaining that China had no need to increase its foreign trade, had no use for Britain's ingenious devices and manufacturers, and set no value on closer diplomatic ties.

Dutch, French, and Russian missions to achieve what Macartney could not do also failed. European frustration mounted while admiration for China faded. The Qing court would not communicate with foreign envoys or observe the simplest rules of the European diplomatic system. In Macartney's view, China was like a venerable old warship, well maintained and splendid to look at, but obsolete and no longer up to the task.

Population Growth and Environmental Stress   The Chinese who escorted Macartney and his entourage in 1792–1793 took them through China's prosperous cities and productive farmland. They did not see, however, the economic and environmental decline that had set in during the last decades of the 1700s.

Population growth—a tripling in size since 1500—had intensified demand for food and for more intensive agriculture. With an estimated 350 million people in the late 1700s, China had twice the population of all of Europe. Despite efficient farming and the gradual adoption of New World crops like corn and sweet potatoes, population pressure touched off social and environmental problems. Increased demand for building materials and firewood shrank woodlands. Deforestation, in turn, accelerated wind and water erosion and increased flooding. Dams and dikes were not maintained, and silted-up river channels were not dredged. By the end of the eighteenth century parts of the thousand-year-old Grand Canal linking the rivers of north and south China were nearly unusable, and the towns that bordered it were starved for commerce.

Some interior districts responded to this misery by increasing their output of export goods like tea, cotton, and silk. Some peasants sought seasonal jobs in better-off agricultural areas or worked in low-status jobs as barge pullers, charcoal burners, or night soil (human waste) carriers. Begging, prostitution, and theft increased in the cities. Rebellions broke out in flood-ravaged central and southwestern China. Indigenous peoples concentrated in the less fertile lands in the south and in the northern and western borderlands of the empire often joined in revolts.

The Qing government was not up to controlling its vast empire. It was twice the size of the Ming geographically, but it employed about the same number of officials. The government's dependence on working alliances with local elites had led to widespread corruption and shrinking government revenues. The Qing's spectacular rise had ended, and decline had set in.

CONCLUSION

It would be a mistake to think of early modern East Asia as three strictly defined countries filled with people who invariably acted on behalf of their homelands in trade or warfare. During the Imjin War, some Japanese grew tired of fighting in Korea, decided to join the Ming military, and were promoted to high posts by the Chinese. Similarly, some Chinese troops remained in Korea, married local women, and became part of local Korean communities.

Trade and warfare also presented opportunities for groups of people who did not identify with any one country. For example, the Ming-Qing transition and growth in sea trade spurred an increase in piracy during the seventeenth century. The Zheng family dominated piracy in East Asia, defeated the Dutch bases in Taiwan, and eventually worked for the Ming regime to battle the Manchu. The most prominent Zheng pirate-merchant was the half Japanese, half Chinese, Zheng Chenggong. An enemy of the Qing, he continued to expand the Zheng enterprise and was well-known even among Europeans in Asia, who called him Koxinga, the European pronunciation for the name given to him by the Ming loyalists. Even early modern Japanese knew of his exploits through puppet plays. The Zheng also pursued state-building activities, such as establishing an office to collect taxes and regulating trade in the South China Sea.

China is one example of the flourishing of empires in Eurasia between 1500 and 1800. Already a vast empire under the Ming, China doubled in size under the Qing, mostly through westward expansion into less densely populated areas. Like the Russian, Ottoman, and Mughal Empires, it had the strengths and problems of administrative control and tax collection that characterized a large land-based state. The expansion of China incorporated not just new lands but also new peoples. Chinese society had long been diverse, and its geographical, occupational, linguistic, and religious differences grew as the Qing expanded. China had also long used Confucian models, imperial customs, and a common system of writing to transcend such differences and to assimilate elites.

Japan was different. Though it was nominally headed by an emperor, real power lay with the successive shoguns. However, Japan lacked a centralizing, common political philosophy like China's Confucianism, which became a common denominator for a wide variety of elites from different cultures, ethnicities, and regions. Tokugawa Japan was similar in size and population to France, the most powerful state of western Europe, but its political system was much more decentralized. As the chapter has shown, Japan's efforts to add colonies on the East Asian mainland failed.

By the late eighteenth century, the weaknesses in China and Japan were becoming more evident to Europeans and would ultimately make these countries vulnerable to Western penetration. China had once led the world in military innovation, including the first uses of gunpowder, but Chinese armies continued to depend on superior numbers and tactics for their success rather than on new technology. Infantrymen armed with guns served alongside others armed with bows and arrows, swords, and spears. The military forces of Japan underwent more innovative changes than those of China and Korea, in part through Western contacts, and in the course of its sixteenth-century wars of unification, Japan produced its own gunpowder revolution. Thereafter, however, it lacked the means to stay abreast of the world's most advanced military technology.

Finally, neither China nor Japan developed navies commensurate with their size and coastlines. Korea had a small but effective navy during the Imjin War, but it could not match China's or Russia's in strength or size. China's defenses against pirates and other sea invaders were left to the small war junks of its maritime provinces, and Japan's naval capacity was similarly decentralized. In 1792, when Russian ships exploring the North Pacific turned toward the Japanese coast, the local daimyo used his own forces to chase them away. All Japanese daimyo understood that they would be on their own if and when foreign incursions increased. As later chapters show, these foreign incursions became reality in the nineteenth century.

IMPORTANT EVENTS 1500–1800	
1517	Portuguese embassy to China
1543	First Portuguese contacts
1592	Japanese invasion of Korea
1601	Matteo Ricci allowed to reside in Beijing
1603	Tokugawa Shogunate formed
1633–1639	Edicts close down trade with Europe
1644	Qing conquest of Beijing
1662–1722	Rule of Emperor Kangxi
1689	Treaty of Nerchinsk with Russia
1691	Qing control of Inner Mongolia
1702	Trial of the Forty-Seven Ronin
1736–1795	Rule of Emperor Qianlong
1762–1796	Rule of Catherine the Great
1792	Russian ships first spotted off the coast of Japan

The Little Ice Age

A giant volcanic eruption in the Peruvian Andes in 1600 affected the weather in many parts of the world for several years. When volcanic ash from the eruption of Mount Huanyaputina (hoo-AHN-yah-poo-TEE-nuh) shot into the upper atmosphere and spread around the world, it screened out sunlight. As a result, the summer of 1601 was the coldest in two hundred years in the Northern Hemisphere.

Archaeologist Brian Fagan has pointed out that Mount Huanyaputina's chilling effects were a spectacular event in a much longer pattern of climate change that has been called the Little Ice Age.[1] Although global climate had been cooling since the late 1200s, in the northern temperate regions the 1590s had been exceptionally cold. Temperatures remained cooler than normal throughout the seventeenth century.

The most detailed information on the Little Ice Age comes from Europe. Glaciers in the Alps grew much larger. Trade became difficult when rivers and canals that had once been navigable in winter froze solid from bank to bank. In the coldest years, the growing season in some places was as much as two months shorter than normal. Unexpectedly late frosts withered the tender shoots of newly planted crops in spring. Wheat and barley ripened more slowly during cooler summers and were often damaged by early fall frosts.

People could survive a smaller-than-average harvest in one year by drawing on food reserves, but when cold weather damaged crops in two or more successive years, the consequences were devastating. Deaths due to malnutrition and cold increased sharply when summer temperatures in northern Europe registered 2.7°F (1.5°C) lower than average in 1674 and 1675 and again in 1694 and 1695. The cold spell of 1694 and 1695 caused a famine in Finland that carried off a quarter to a third of the population.

At the time people had no idea what was causing the unusual cold of the Little Ice Age. Advances in climate history make it clear that the cause was not a single terrestrial event such as the eruption of Mount Huanyaputina. Nor was the Little Ice Age the product of human actions, unlike some climate changes such as today's global warming.

Ultimately, the earth's weather is governed by the sun. In the seventeenth century astronomers in Europe reported seeing fewer sunspots, dark spots on the sun's surface that are indicative of solar activity and thus the sun's warming power. Diminished activity in the sun was primarily responsible for the Little Ice Age.

If the sun was the root cause, the effects of global cooling should not have been confined to northern Europe. Although contemporary accounts are much scarcer in other parts of the world, there is evidence of climate changes around the world in this period. Observations of sunspots in China, Korea, and Japan drop to zero between 1639 and 1700. China experienced unusually cool weather in the seventeenth century, but the warfare and disruption accompanying the fall of the Ming and the rise of the Qing probably were much more to blame for the famines and rural distress of that period. The Ottoman Empire also experienced rural unrest during the coldest years.

By itself, a relatively slight decrease in average annual temperature would not have a significant effect on human life outside the northern temperate areas. However, evidence suggests that there was also a significant rise in humidity in this period in other parts of the world. Ice cores drilled into ancient glaciers in the Arctic and Antarctic show increased snowfall. Information compiled by historian James L. A. Webb, Jr., shows that lands south of the Sahara received more rainfall between 1550 and 1750 than they had during the previous era.[2] Increased rainfall would have been favorable for pastoral people, whose herds found new pasture in what had once been desert, and for the farmers farther south whose crops got more rain.

In the eighteenth century the sun's activity began to return to normal. Rising temperatures led to milder winters and better harvests in northern Eurasia. Falling rainfall allowed the Sahara to advance again southward, forcing the agricultural frontier to retreat.

[1]Brian Fagan, *The Littlest Ice Age: How Climate Made History, 1300–1850* (New York: Basic Books, 2000).

[2]James L. A. Webb, Jr., *Desert Frontier: Ecological Change Along the Western Sahel, 1600–1850* (Madison: University of Wisconsin Press, 1995).

PART SIX

REVOLUTIONS RESHAPE THE WORLD, 1750–1870

CHAPTER 22
The Early Industrial Revolution, 1760–1851

CHAPTER 23
Revolutionary Changes in the Atlantic World, 1750–1850

CHAPTER 24
Land Empires in the Age of Imperialism, 1800–1870

CHAPTER 25
Nation Building and Economic Transformation in the Americas, 1800–1890

Between 1750 and 1870, nearly every part of the world experienced dramatic political, economic, and social change. The beginnings of industrialization and the American, French, and Haitian revolutions, as well as the revolutions for independence in Latin America, transformed political and economic life. European nations expanded into Africa, Asia, and the Middle East, while Russia and the United States acquired vast new territories.

The Industrial Revolution introduced new technologies and patterns of work that made these societies wealthier and militarily more powerful. Western intellectual life became more secular. The Atlantic slave trade and later slavery itself were abolished, and the first efforts to improve the status of women were initiated.

The Industrial Revolution also led to a new wave of imperialism. France conquered Algeria, and Great Britain expanded its colonial rule in India and established colonies in Australia and New Zealand. European political and economic influence also expanded in Africa and Asia. The Ottoman Empire and the Qing Empire met this challenge by implementing reform programs that preserved traditional structures while adopting elements of Western technology and organization. Though lagging behind western Europe in transforming its economy and political institutions, Russia attempted modernization efforts, including the abolition of serfdom.

The economic, political, and social revolutions that began in the mid-eighteenth century shook the foundations of European culture and led to the expansion of Western power around the globe. Some of the nations of Asia, Africa, and Latin America reformed and strengthened their own institutions and economies, while others pushed for more radical change. After 1870 Western imperialism became more aggressive, and few parts of the world were able to resist it.

22

THE EARLY INDUSTRIAL REVOLUTION, 1760–1851

Manchester was just a small town in northern England in the early eighteenth century. A hundred years later, it had turned into the fastest-growing city in history. To contemporaries, it was both a marvel and a horror. Prosperous cotton mills were interspersed with workers' housing, built as cheaply as possible. The economist Nassau Senior described these workers' quarters:

> But when I went through their habitations ... my only wonder was that tolerable health could be maintained by the inmates of such houses. These towns ... have been erected by small speculators with an utter disregard to everything except immediate profit.... In one place we saw a whole street following the course of a ditch, in order to have deeper cellars (cellars for people, not for lumber) without the expense of excavation. Not a house in this street escaped cholera.... the streets are unpaved, with a dunghill or a pond in the middle; the houses built back to back, without ventilation or drainage, and whole families occupy each a corner of a cellar or of a garret.[1]

Not everyone deplored the living conditions in the new industrial city. Friedrich Engels, both a factory owner and critic of capitalism, recounted a meeting with a well-to-do citizen:

> One day I walked with one of these middle-class gentlemen into Manchester. I spoke to him about the disgraceful unhealthy slums and drew his attention to the disgusting condition of that part of the town in which the factory workers lived. I declared that I had never seen so badly built a town in my life. He listened patiently and at the corner of the street at which we parted company, he remarked: "And yet there is a great deal of money made here. Good morning, Sir!"[2]

Manchester's rise as a large, industrial city was a result of what historians call the **Industrial Revolution**, the most profound transformation in human life since the beginnings of agriculture. This revolution involved dramatic innovations in

---

[1] Nassau W. Senior, *Letters on the Factory Act, as it affects the cotton manufacture, addressed to the Right Honourable, the President of the Board of Trade*, 2d ed. (London: Fellows, 1844), 20.

[2] Friedrich Engels, *Condition of the Working Class in England*, trans. and ed. by W. O. Henderson and W. H. Chaloner (Oxford: Blackwell, 1958), 312.

manufacturing, mining, transportation, and communications and equally rapid changes in society and commerce, as new relationships between social groups created an environment that was conducive to technical innovation and economic growth. These changes allowed the industrializing countries—first Britain, then western Europe and the United States—to unleash massive increases in production and productivity, exploit the world's natural resources as never before, and transform the environment and human life in unprecedented ways.

Industrialization widened the gap between rich and poor. The people who owned and controlled industrial innovations amassed wealth and power over nature as well as over other people. While some lived in spectacular luxury, workers, including large numbers of children, worked long hours in dangerous factories and lived crowded together in unsanitary tenements. At the same time, the middle class of industrializing nations grew rapidly, exercising increased influence in politics and culture.

The effect of the Industrial Revolution around the world was also very uneven. The first countries to industrialize grew rich and powerful, facilitating a second great wave of European imperialism in the nineteenth century. In Egypt and India, the economic and military power of Europe stifled the tentative beginnings of industrialization. The disparity in wealth and power between the industrial and the developing countries that exists today has its origins in the early nineteenth century.

Causes of the Industrial Revolution

What caused the Industrial Revolution, and why did it develop so rapidly in England in the eighteenth century? These are two of the great questions of history. The basic preconditions of this momentous event seem to have been population growth that increased demand for goods, an agricultural revolution, the expansion of trade, and an openness to experimentation and innovation.

Population Growth   Population growth helped fuel the Industrial Revolution by increasing the demand for goods and by lowering labor costs. Between 1650 and 1850 Europe's population grew from 100 million to 266 million. Simultaneously, Europe became more urban, with the number of city dwellers more than doubling in this same period. This pattern was clearest in England and Wales, where population increased from about 6 million in 1700 to 9 million in 1800 and 18 million by 1850—increases never before experienced in European history. As the pace of manufacturing mounted in the eighteenth century, rural laborers and their families moved to cities in hope of higher earnings and better lives.

The growth of population resulted from more widespread resistance to disease and from more abundant and reliable food supplies, thanks to the new crops that originated in the Americas (see Chapter 18). Gradual improvements in income allowed Europeans to marry at earlier ages and have more children. As a result, roughly 40 percent of the population of Britain was under fifteen years of age in the nineteenth century. This high proportion of youths explains the vitality of the British people in that period as well as the widespread use of child labor. People also migrated at an unprecedented rate—not only from the countryside to the cities, but also from Ireland to England and, more generally, from Europe to the Americas. Thanks to immigration, the population of the United States rose from 4 million in 1791 to 9.6 million in 1820 and 31.5 million in 1860—faster than in any other part of the world at the time.

The Agricultural Revolution   A revolution in farming provided an increased food supply to fast-growing urban populations and at the same time forced many peasants off the land. This **agricultural revolution** had begun long before the eighteenth century. One important aspect was the introduction of new crops like the potato, introduced from South America in the sixteenth century. In the cool and humid regions of Europe, potatoes yielded two or three times more calories per acre than did the wheat, rye, and oats they replaced. Maize (American corn) was also grown across Europe from northern Iberia to the Balkans, adding substantially to the food supply.

Prosperous landowners with secure titles to their land could afford to bear the risk of trying new methods and new crops. In Great Britain rich landowners "enclosed" the land—that is, consolidated their holdings—and got Parliament to give them title to the commons that in the past had been open to all. Once in control of the land, they could drain and improve the soil, breed better livestock, and introduce crop rotation. This "enclosure movement" further impoverished the rural poor by turning tenants and sharecroppers into landless farm laborers. Many of the displaced rural poor moved to the cities to seek work; others became vagrants; still others emigrated to Canada, Australia, and the United States.

Trade and Inventiveness   The Industrial Revolution was preceded by a long period of commercial expansion based on growing population and on a much deeper engagement with colonial possessions and with other foreign markets. The innovations of the industrial age came about in part as manufacturers sought to meet increased domestic and foreign demand for textiles and other products through improved efficiency and productivity.

Traditionally, European textiles were produced by skilled artisans organized in guilds using centuries-old technologies. In this system increasing production meant training more artisans, an expensive process that took years. Beginning in the seventeenth century, merchant investors began to relocate some basic textile production away from guild-dominated cities to benefit from lower-cost rural labor, especially during the period between harvesting and planting. Called proto-industrialization, merchant investors delivered raw materials and supplied simple machinery, like looms and spinning wheels, to the homes of farm families and to rural jobbers who organized groups of laborers. In this system the complex tasks associated with artisan production were subdivided into simple procedures that allowed rural workers to quickly gain competence and become productive. Unlike urban artisans, who typically earned daily wages, these proto-industrial workers were only paid for what they produced thus reducing labor costs. Skilled manufacturers then transformed the spun wool and rough cloth produced by rural laborers into finished goods for domestic and foreign consumers. While proto-industrialization increased cloth production and lowered labor costs, there were chronic problems with quality control and inefficiencies that resulted from the dispersal of production.

In the eighteenth century a dramatic expansion of European commerce with markets in the Americas, Africa, and Asia reinforced the economic effects of the fast-growing European population. Nearly all the European powers profited from plantation colonies in the Americas. As Europeans of even modest means consumed ever-growing quantities of sugar to sweeten their tea, coffee, cocoa, pastries, and candies, the demand for manufactures like porcelain cups and dinnerware increased as well. At the same time planters in the Caribbean imported a steeply rising volume of cotton textiles to clothe themselves and their slaves. Initially, these cotton textiles were imported from Asia, but increasing demand led to the creation of domestic cotton textile industries, the first truly modern mechanized industry.

European governments played a key role in this economic expansion. Governments across Europe sponsored improvements in road networks, but maintenance was often inadequate. In Britain local governments' neglect of the roads that served long-distance traffic led to the formation of private "turnpike trusts" that built numerous toll roads. As the volume of commerce increased, canal-building booms occurred in Britain, France, and the low countries in the late eighteenth century. Governments also directly invested in skills and new technologies by creating royal manufacturers that produced fine china, silks, and carpets. Authorities in England, France, Prussia, and Spain, among other European nations, recruited skilled artisans from rival nations, subsidized periodicals that disseminated new technologies, and expanded their navies to better protect foreign trade.

Beginning in the seventeenth century, educated people throughout Europe and the Americas were increasingly fascinated by technology and innovation (see Chapter 17). Across Europe inexpensive periodicals informed the general public of new technologies and scientific discoveries. But it was the *Encyclopédie*, published in France over a period of more than twenty years, that most influenced the dissemination of useful technologies by providing detailed diagrams of everything from printing and textile machinery to canal locks and foundry equipment. During the eighteenth century the French, Spanish, and British governments also sought to promote economic growth by sending expeditions around the world to collect plants that could profitably be grown domestically or in their colonies. They also offered prizes for scientific discoveries, like determining the longitude of a ship at sea and the accurate measurement of the earth's circumference. It was an era when innovators and scientists were celebrities.

Britain and Continental Europe   Industrialization did not take place everywhere at once. Great Britain took the lead in introducing new technologies and maintained its place as Europe's major industrial power to the end of the nineteenth century. It is useful to divide the British experience into two phases. In the eighteenth century inventors developed machines that multiplied the productive capacities of individual workers, especially in the textile industry. While production increased dramatically, British industry continued to rely on traditional sources of energy, particularly wind, water, and animal power. Then early in the nineteenth century the development of efficient steam engines allowed British entrepreneurs to apply this potent source of energy to industrial machinery.

The technologies associated with both stages of this revolution spread rapidly to continental Europe and the United States. British engineers and skilled machinists were the most active agents in the dissemination of the new technologies. European and American investors quickly recognized the advantages of the new technologies and provided high salaries and other inducements to skilled British workers willing to immigrate and introduce the newest technologies. Belgium had the earliest successes in imitating the British industrial model, becoming the continent's most industrialized economy by 1840. While slower to embrace the new technologies, Germany after 1850 became the continent's major producer of coal, iron, and steel. The United States was well established as a major industrial power by 1860, having quickly adopted textile and metallurgical technologies developed first in Great Britain.

Historians disagree about why Britain played such an important role in the introduction of industrial technologies in the eighteenth and nineteenth centuries. It is clear that Britain enjoyed a rising standard of living, thanks to good harvests and a booming overseas trade, and that this prosperity increased consumption and stimulated innovation in manufacturing. Britain was already the world's leading exporter of tools, guns, hardware, clocks, and other manufactured goods, and it had a strong craft tradition that trained a large number of skilled mechanics. At the same time, its mining and metal industries employed engineers with a tradition of experimentation and innovation. British commercial culture was also among Europe's most modern, having long enjoyed the benefits of strong banks, joint-stock companies, a stock market, and commercial insurance. In addition, its patent system offered inventors the hope of rich rewards by protecting their intellectual property rights. Growing public awareness of early innovators who became wealthy and respected for their inventions stimulated others to experiment.

At the dawn of the industrial age, Britain had one of the most fluid societies in Europe. The court was less ostentatious, its aristocracy was less powerful, and the lines separating the social classes were not as sharply drawn as elsewhere in Europe, with the exception of the Netherlands. Compared to France or Spain, the two most important continental powers, British political power was not as centralized or intrusive. There were fewer bureaucrats and officials and fewer obstacles to commerce and manufacturing than in most continental nations. As commoners grew wealthy in trade and manufacturing, society became less hierarchical and more fluid.

At a time when transportation by land was very costly, Great Britain had good water transportation thanks to its long coastline, navigable rivers, and growing network of canals. It also had a unified internal market with none of the duties and tolls that goods had to pay every few miles in France or Spain. This advantage facilitated a growing trade between regions. More important still, Britain had abundant supplies of coal and iron ore, two key ingredients in the Industrial Revolution.

In contrast to Britain, the economies of continental Europe were hampered by high transportation costs, misguided government regulations, and rigid social structures. As a result, attempts to import British techniques and organize factory production elsewhere often foundered for lack of markets or management skills. Nevertheless, British textile machinery was introduced in France and Spain before the French Revolution (see Chapter 23). From then until the end of the Napoleonic wars in 1815, Europe's economies were distorted by the effects of mass military mobilizations and warfare. Although war created opportunities for suppliers of weapons and uniforms, the interruption of trade between Britain and continental Europe slowed the diffusion of new technologies, and the insecurity of countries at war discouraged businessmen from investing in factories and machinery.

Once revolutions had swept away most of the restrictions of Europe's old regimes, both private investors and European governments acted to import new technologies and adapt them to local conditions. Acutely aware of Britain's head start and the need to stimulate their own industries, continental governments sponsored efforts to imitate or steal British industrial secrets. They recruited British engineers and artisans, created technical schools, and eliminated internal tariff barriers, tolls, and other hindrances to trade. By the 1820s there were several thousand Britons working on the continent, setting up machines, training workers in the new methods, and even starting their own businesses. European governments also encouraged the formation of joint-stock companies and banks to channel private savings into industrial investments. By 1830 the political climate in western Europe had become as favorable to business as Britain's had been a half century earlier. First Belgium and then, after 1850, Germany and France enjoyed industrial booms based on iron, cotton, steam engines, and railroads. Key to the success of Belgium and Germany was the existence of abundant coal and iron-ore deposits. Without abundant coal, France retained a more traditional manufacturing economy until the introduction of electricity late in the nineteenth century.

THE TECHNOLOGICAL REVOLUTION

Five innovations spurred industrialization: (1) mass production through the division of labor, (2) new machines and mechanization, (3) a great increase in the manufacture of iron, (4) the steam engine, and (5) the electric telegraph. While the full realization of these innovations occurred first in Great Britain and then spread to the United States and continental Europe in the nineteenth century, China had achieved the first three during the Song dynasty (960–1279). But China did not develop the steam engine or electricity, innovations that dramatically multiplied human productivity. The transformation of Western economies through industrialization depended on the full integration of these new forms of energy with the process of mechanical innovation.

Mass Production: Pottery   The pottery industry offers a good example of **mass production**, the making of many identical items by breaking the process into simple repetitive tasks. Before the mid-eighteenth century, only the wealthy could afford imported Chinese porcelain. Middle-class people used pewter tableware, and the poor ate from wooden or earthenware bowls. Royal manufacturers produced exquisite handmade products for the courts and aristocracy, but their products were much too expensive for mass consumption. As more and more Europeans acquired a taste for tea, cocoa, and coffee, they wanted porcelain that would not spoil the flavor of hot beverages. This demand created opportunities for inventive entrepreneurs.

DIVERSITY + DOMINANCE

Adam Smith and the Division of Labor

Adam Smith (1723–1790), a Scottish philosopher, is famous for his book An Inquiry into the Nature *and Causes of the Wealth of* Nations, *first published in 1776. It was the first work to explain the economy of a nation as a system. Smith criticized the notion, common in the eighteenth century, that a nation's wealth was synonymous with the amount of gold and silver in the government's coffers. Instead, he defined wealth as the amount of goods and services produced by a nation's people. By this definition, labor and its products are an essential element in a nation's prosperity.*

In the passage that follows, Smith contrasts two methods of making pins. In one a team of workers divided up the job of making pins and produced a great many every day; in the other pin workers "wrought separately and independently" and produced very few pins per day. It is clear that the division of labor produced more pins per worker per day. But who benefited? Left unsaid is that a pin factory had to be owned and operated by a manufacturer who hired workers and assigned a task to each one.

The illustration shows a pin-maker's workshop in late-eighteenth-century France. Each worker is performing a specific task on a few pins at once, and all the energy comes from human muscles. These are the characteristics of a proto-industrial workshop.

To take an example, therefore, from a very trifling manufacture—but one in which the division of labour has been very often taken notice of—the trade of the pin-maker: a workman not educated to this business (which the division of labour has rendered a distinct trade), nor acquainted with the use of machinery employed in it (to the invention of which the same division of labour has probably given occasion), could scarce, perhaps, with his utmost industry, make one pin in a day, and certainly could not make twenty. But in the way in which this business is now carried on, not only the whole work is a peculiar trade, but it is divided into a number of branches, of which the greater part are likewise peculiar trades. One man draws out the wire, another straights it, a third cuts it, a fourth points it, a fifth grinds it at the top for receiving the head; to make the head requires two or three distinct operations, to put it on, is a peculiar business, to whiten the pins is another; it is even a trade by itself to put them into the paper; and the important business of making a pin is, in this manner, divided into about eighteen distinct operations, which, in some manufactories, are all performed by distinct hands, though in others the same man will sometimes perform two or three of them. I have seen a small manufactory of this kind where ten men only were employed, and where some of them, consequently, performed two or three distinct operations. But though they were very poor, and therefore but indifferently accommodated with the necessary machinery, they could, when they exerted themselves, make among them about twelve pounds of pins in a day. There are in a pound upwards of four thousand pins of a middling size. Those ten persons, therefore, could make among them upwards of forty-eight thousand pins in a

Britain had many small pottery workshops where craftsmen made a few plates and cups at a time. Much of this activity took place in a part of the Midlands that possessed good clay, coal for firing, and lead for glazing. In 1759, **Josiah Wedgwood**, the son of a potter, started his own pottery business. Today the name *Wedgwood* is associated with expensive, highly decorated china. But Wedgwood's day. Each person, therefore, making a tenth part of forty-eight thousand pins, might be considered as making four thousand eight hundred pins a day. But if they had all wrought separately and independently, and without any of them having been educated to this peculiar business, they certainly could not each of them have made twenty, perhaps not one pin in a day; that is, certainly, not the two hundred and fortieth, perhaps not the four thousand eight hundredth part of what they are at present capable of performing, in consequence of a proper division and combination of their different operations.

Questions for Analysis

1. Why does dividing the job of pin-making into ten or more operations result in the production of more pins per worker? How much more productive are these workers than if each one made complete pins from start to finish?

2. How closely does the picture of a pin-maker's workshop illustrate Smith's verbal description?

3. What disadvantage would there be to working in a pin factory where the job was divided as in Smith's example, compared to making entire pins from start to finish?

4. What other examples can you think of, from Adam Smith's day or from more recent times, of the advantages of the division of labor?

Source: Adam Smith, *An Inquiry into the Nature and Causes of the Wealth of Nations,* ed. Edward Gibbon Wakefield (London: Charles Knight and Co., 1843), 7–9.

A Pin-Maker's Workshop *The man in the middle (Fig. 2) is pulling wire off a spindle (G) and through a series of posts. This ensures that the wire will be perfectly straight. The worker seated on the lower right (Fig. 3) takes the long pieces of straightened wire and cuts them into shorter lengths. The man in the lower left-hand corner (Fig. 5) sharpens twelve to fifteen wires at a time by holding them against a grindstone turned by the worker in Fig. 6. The men in Figs. 4 and 7 put the finishing touches on the points. Other operations—such as forming the wire to the proper thickness, cleaning and coating it with tin, and attaching the heads—are depicted in other engravings in the same encyclopedia.*

The Pin Factory, plate 2 from Volume IV of the Encyclopedia of Denis Diderot (1713–84) and Jean le Rond d'Alembert (1717–83), 1751–52 (engraving), French School, (18th century) / Private Collection/The Bridgeman Art Library

most important contribution lay in producing ordinary porcelain cheaply by means of the **division of labor** (see Diversity and Dominance: Adam Smith and the Division of Labor).

Wedgwood subdivided the work into simple repetitive tasks, such as unloading the clay, mixing it, pressing flat pieces, dipping the pieces in glaze, putting handles on cups, packing kilns, and carrying things from one part of his plant to another. To prevent interruptions, he instituted strict discipline among his workers. He substituted molds for the potter's wheel whenever possible, a change that not only saved labor but also created uniform plates and bowls that could be stacked. The end result was that while workers became more productive, they had fewer skills and were paid less.

Wedgwood's interest in applying technology to manufacturing was sparked by his membership in the Lunar Society, a group of businessmen, scientists, and craftsmen that met each month when the moon was full to discuss the practical application of knowledge. In 1782, the naturalist Erasmus Darwin encouraged him to purchase a steam engine from Boulton and Watt, a firm founded by two other members of the society. The engine that Wedgwood bought to mix clay and grind flint was one of the first to be installed in a factory. The division of labor and new steam-driven machinery allowed Wedgwood to lower the cost of his products while improving their quality, and to offer his wares for sale at lower prices.

Mechanization: The Cotton Industry   The cotton industry, the largest industry in this period, illustrates the role of **mechanization**, the use of machines to do work previously done by hand. Cotton had long been grown in China, India, and the Middle East, where it was spun and woven by hand. The cloth was so much cooler, softer, and cleaner than wool that wealthy Europeans developed a liking for the costly import. When the powerful English woolen industry persuaded Parliament to forbid the import of cotton cloth, that prohibition stimulated attempts to import cotton fiber and make the cloth domestically. Here was an opportunity for enterprising inventors to reduce costs with laborsaving machinery.

Beginning in the 1760s a series of inventions revolutionized the spinning of cotton thread. The first was the jenny, invented in 1764, which mechanically drew out the cotton fibers and twisted them into thread. The jenny was simple, cheap to build, and easy for one person to operate. Early models permitted a single worker to spin six or seven threads at once, later ones up to eighty. The thread, however, was soft and irregular and could be used only in combination with linen, a strong yarn derived from the flax plant.

In 1769, **Richard Arkwright** invented another spinning machine, the water frame, which produced thread strong enough to be used without linen. Arkwright was both a gifted inventor and a successful businessman. His machine was larger and more complex than the jenny and required a source of power such as a water wheel, hence the name "water frame." To obtain the necessary energy, he installed dozens of machines in a building next to a fast-flowing river. The resemblance to a flour mill gave such enterprises the name *cotton mill*. Within a few decades of the introduction of the jenny and water frame, these technologies were imported and adapted to local conditions elsewhere. The skilled mechanics who built British machines served as vectors for this dissemination as they moved to France, Belgium, and the United States to seek higher wages.

In 1785, British inventor Samuel Crompton patented a machine that combined the best features of the jenny and the water frame. This device, called a mule, produced a strong thread that was thin enough to be used to make a high-quality cotton cloth called muslin. The mule could make a finer, more even thread than could any human being, and at a lower cost. At last British industry could undersell high-quality handmade cotton cloth from India. With these innovations in place, British cotton output increased tenfold between 1770 and 1790, despite the fact that these large-scale producers still depended on waterpower.

The boom in thread production and the soaring demand for cloth encouraged inventors to mechanize the rest of textile manufacturing. Power looms were perfected after 1815. Other inventions of the period included carding machines, chlorine bleach, and cylindrical presses to print designs on fabric. By the 1830s large textile mills powered by steam engines were performing all the steps necessary to turn raw cotton into printed cloth.

Mechanization offered two advantages: increased productivity for the manufacturer and lower prices for the consumer. Whereas in India it took five hundred hours to spin a pound of cotton, the mule of 1790 could do so in three person-hours, and the self-acting mule—an improved version introduced in 1830—required only eighty minutes. Cotton mills needed very few skilled workers, and managers often hired children to tend the spinning machines. The same was true of power looms, which gradually replaced handloom weaving: the number of power looms rose from 2,400 in 1813 to 500,000 by 1850. Meanwhile, the price of cloth fell by 90 percent between 1782 and 1812 and kept on dropping.

The industrialization of Britain made cotton America's most valuable crop (see Chapter 25). In the 1790s most of Britain's cotton came from India. But in 1793 the American Eli Whitney patented his cotton gin, a simple device that separated the bolls or seedpods from the fiber and made cotton growing economical. This invention permitted the spread of cotton farming into Georgia, then into Alabama, Mississippi, and Louisiana, and finally as far west as Texas. By the late 1850s the southern states were producing a million tons of cotton a year, five-sixths of the world's total.

With the help of British craftsmen who introduced jennies, mules, and power looms, Americans developed their own cotton industry in the 1820s. Immigrants from Great Britain played a key role in this process, as did the willingness of American investors to ignore the patent rights of British inventors. By 1840, the United States had twelve hundred cotton mills that served the booming domestic market, two-thirds of them in New England.

While the resistance of long-established artisan guilds to the introduction of new technologies slowed technological innovation in the wool textile industry in Britain and elsewhere, machinery adapted from cotton production quickly transformed the spinning of woolen thread by the 1830s. Steam-driven looms soon followed. In Belgium in 1810, only 5 of 144 woolen factories were mechanized, but they produced more than 50 percent of total production.

The Iron Industry   Iron making also was transformed during the Industrial Revolution. Throughout Eurasia and Africa, iron had long been used for tools, weapons, and household items. During the Song period, Chinese forges had produced cast iron in large quantities. Although production declined after the Song, iron continued to be common and inexpensive in China. Wherever iron was produced, however, deforestation eventually drove up the cost of charcoal (used for smelting) and restricted output. Furthermore, iron had to be repeatedly heated and hammered to drive out impurities, a difficult and costly process. Because of limited wood supplies and the high cost of skilled labor, iron was a rare and valuable metal outside China before the eighteenth century.

A first breakthrough occurred in 1709 when Abraham Darby discovered that coke (coal from which the impurities have been cooked out) could be used in place of charcoal. The resulting metal was of lower quality than charcoal-smelted iron but much cheaper to produce, for coal was plentiful. In 1784, British inventor Henry Cort found a way to remove some of the impurities in coke-iron by puddling—stirring the molten iron with long rods. Cort's process made it possible to turn coal into coke to produce wrought iron (a soft and malleable form of iron) very cheaply. By 1790 four-fifths of Britain's iron was made with coke, while other countries still used charcoal. Coke-iron allowed a great expansion in the size of individual blast furnaces. As a result, Britain's iron production rose fast, from 17,000 tons in 1740 to 3 million tons in 1844, as much as in the rest of the world put together. As in Britain, the existence of large supplies of coal and iron ore largely explains the fast pace of industrialization of Belgium and Germany after 1820.

In turn, there seemed no limit to the novel applications for this cheap and useful material. In 1779, Abraham Darby III (grandson of the first Abraham Darby) built a bridge of iron across the Severn River. In 1851 Londoners marveled at the **Crystal Palace**, a huge exhibition hall made entirely of iron and glass. The Great Exhibition showcased British industry and power but included exhibits from the colonies and from other nations.

The availability of cheap iron made the mass production of objects such as guns, hardware, and tools appealing. However, fitting together the parts of these products required a great deal of labor. To reduce labor costs, manufacturers, like the Americans Eli Whitney (firearms) and Eli Terry (clocks), contributed to the development of standardized interchangeable parts. By the mid-nineteenth century, interchangeable-parts manufacturing had been widely adopted, including the manufacture of farm equipment and sewing machines. By the 1850s Europeans had begun to call this the "American system of manufactures."

The Steam Engine   In the history of the world, there had been a number of periods of great technological inventiveness and economic growth. But in all previous cases, the dynamism eventually faltered. The Industrial Revolution, in contrast, has only accelerated. One reason has been increased interactions between scientists, technicians, and businesspeople. Another has been access to a source of cheap energy, namely fossil fuels. The first machine to transform fossil fuel into mechanical energy was the **steam engine**, a device that set the Industrial Revolution apart from all previous periods of growth and innovation.

Before the eighteenth century, deep mines filled with water faster than pumps powered by horses could lift it out. Then, between 1702 and 1712, Thomas Newcomen developed the first practical steam engine, a crude but effective device that could clear water from mines much faster than earlier pumps. The Newcomen engine's voracious appetite for fuel mattered little in coal mines, where fuel was cheap, but it made the engine too costly for other uses. In 1764 another Briton, **James Watt**, a maker of scientific instruments at Glasgow University in Scotland, was asked to repair the university's model Newcomen engine. Watt realized that the engine wasted fuel because the cylinder had to be alternately heated and cooled. He developed a separate condenser—a vessel into which the steam was allowed to escape, leaving the cylinder always hot and the condenser always cold. Watt patented his idea in 1769 and enlisted the help of the iron manufacturer Matthew Boulton to turn his invention into a commercial product. Their first engines were sold to pump water out of copper and tin mines, where fuel was too costly for Newcomen engines. In 1781, Watt invented the sun-and-planet gear, which turned the back-and-forth action of the piston into rotary motion. This allowed steam engines to power machinery in flour and cotton mills, pottery manufactures, and other industries as well. Because there seemed almost no limit to the amount of coal in the ground, steam-generated energy appeared to be an inexhaustible source of power, and steam engines could be used where animal, wind, and water power were lacking. By the 1820s steam engines were powering textile machinery in Belgium and the United States as well as in Great Britain. In places where coal supplies were limited, like France, the application of steam power to manufacturing developed slowly.

Science & Society Picture Library/Contributo/Getty Images

Transatlantic Steamship Race *In 1838, two ships equipped with steam engines, the* Sirius *and the* Great Western, *steamed from England to New York. Although the* Sirius *left a few days earlier, the* Great Western—*shown here arriving in New York harbor*—*almost caught up with it, arriving just four hours after the* Sirius. *This race inaugurated regular transatlantic steamship service.*

Inspired by the success of Watt's engine, several inventors put steam engines on boats. The first commercially successful steamboat was Robert Fulton's *North River*, which sailed the Hudson River between New York City and Albany, New York, in 1807. Soon steamboats were launched on the Ohio and the Mississippi, gateways to the Midwest. By 1830, some three hundred steamboats plied the Mississippi and its tributaries. The United States was fast becoming a nation that moved by water.

Oceangoing steam-powered ships were much more difficult to build than river boats, for the first steam engines used so much coal that no ship could carry more than a few days' supply. The *Savannah*, which crossed the Atlantic in 1819, was a sailing ship with an auxiliary steam engine that was used for only ninety hours of its twenty-nine-day trip. Engineers soon developed more efficient engines, and in 1838 two steamers, the *Great Western* and the *Sirius*, crossed the Atlantic on steam power alone.

Railroads

After Watt's patent expired in 1800, inventors experimented with lighter, more powerful high-pressure engines—an idea Watt had rejected as too dangerous. In 1804, Richard Trevithick built an engine that consumed only one-third the coal used by Watt's design and then created several steam-powered vehicles able to travel on roads or rails.

By the 1820s England had many railways on which horses pulled heavy wagons. In 1829, the owners of the Liverpool and Manchester Railway organized a contest between steam-powered locomotives and horse-drawn wagons. George Stephenson and his son Robert won the contest with their locomotive *Rocket*, which pulled a 20-ton train at up to 30 miles (48 kilometers) per hour. After that triumph, a railroad-building mania swept Britain. In the late 1830s, as passenger traffic soared, entrepreneurs built lines between the major cities and even to small towns. Railroads were far cheaper, faster, and more comfortable than stagecoaches, and millions of people got in the habit of traveling. By 1850 Great Britain had 6,087 miles (9,797 kilometers) of railroad line.

The introduction of railroads had their most transformative effects in the United States. By the 1840s, 6,000 miles (10,000 kilometers) of track radiated from Boston, New York, Philadelphia, and Baltimore. In the 1850s, 21,000 miles (34,000 kilometers) of additional track were laid, much of it westward across the Appalachians to Memphis, St. Louis, and Chicago. After 1856 the trip from New York to Chicago, which had once taken three weeks by boat and on horseback, could be made in forty-eight hours. This rapid expansion of railroads opened up the Midwest, dispersing the waves of immigrants, turning the vast prairie into farms to feed the industrial cities of the eastern United States, and creating a vast internal market for manufactures.

Railways also accelerated the industrialization of Europe. Belgium, independent since 1830, quickly copied the British railways. In France and Prussia, construction was delayed until the mid-1840s. When it began, however, it not only satisfied the long-standing need for transportation in those countries but also stimulated the iron, machinery, and construction industries. By 1850 Germany had built 3,639 miles (5,856 kilometers) of railroad line and France 1,811 miles (2,915 kilometers).

Bettmann/Corbis

The *De Witt Clinton* Locomotive, 1835–1840 *The* De Witt Clinton *was the first steam locomotive built in the United States. The high smokestack let the hot cinders cool so they would not set fire to nearby trees, an important consideration at a time when eastern North America was still covered with forest. The three passenger cars are clearly horse carriages fitted with railroad wheels.*

Communication over Wires   After the Italian scientist Alessandro Volta invented the battery in 1800, making it possible to produce an electric current, many inventors tried to apply electricity to communication. The first practical **electric telegraph** systems were developed almost simultaneously in England and America. In 1837, in England, Charles Wheatstone and William Cooke introduced a five-wire telegraph, while the American Samuel Morse introduced a code of dots and dashes that could be transmitted with a single wire. Morse convinced the Congress to provide $30,000 (nearly $800,000 in 2012) to "wire" America in 1842 and built a telegraph line connecting Baltimore and Washington D.C. a year later.

The railroad companies allowed telegraph companies to string wires along the tracks in exchange for the right to send telegrams from station to station announcing the departure and arrival of trains. Such messages made railroads much safer as well as more efficient. By the late 1840s telegraph wires crisscrossed the eastern United States and western Europe. In 1851, the first submarine telegraph cable was laid across the English Channel from England to France (cutting the transmission of news from up to four days to minutes); it was the beginning of a network that eventually connected the entire globe. No longer were communications limited to the speed of a sailing ship, a galloping horse, or a fast-moving train. Together railroads and telegraphs had an enormous economic impact. While railroads could move bulk goods more rapidly and at lower cost than other forms of land transportation, telegraphs dramatically transformed market intelligence by making it possible for producers to keep track of distant consumer needs and prices, thus making markets more efficient and profits more dependable.

THE IMPACT OF THE EARLY INDUSTRIAL REVOLUTION

The Industrial Revolution led to profound changes in society, politics, and the economy. At first, the changes were local. Some people became wealthy and built mansions, while others lived in slums with polluted water and air. By the mid-nineteenth century, the worst local effects were being alleviated and cities had become cleaner and healthier. Industrial nations then faced more complex problems: business cycles, labor conflicts, and the degradation of entire regions by mining and industrial pollution. At the global level, industrialization empowered the nations of western Europe and North America to impose themselves on less developed nations.

The New Industrial Cities   The most dramatic environmental changes brought about by industrialization occurred in the towns. Towns had never before grown so fast. London, one of the largest cities in Europe in 1700 with 500,000 inhabitants, grew to 1,117,000 by 1800 and to 2,685,000 by 1850; it was then the largest city the world had ever known. Manchester, a small town of 20,000 in 1758, reached 303,000 a century later, a fifteenfold increase. New York City, already 100,000 strong in 1815, reached 600,000 (including Brooklyn) in 1850. In some areas, towns merged and formed megalopolises, such as Greater London, the English Midlands, central Belgium, and the Ruhr district of Germany.

A great deal of money went into the building of fine homes, churches, museums, and theaters in wealthy neighborhoods. Much of the beauty of London dates from the time of the Industrial Revolution. Yet, by all accounts, industrial cities grew much too fast, and much of the growth occurred in the poorest neighborhoods. As poor migrants streamed in from the countryside, developers built the cheap, shoddy row houses for them to rent that Nassau Senior described.

Sudden population growth caused serious urban environmental problems. Town dwellers recently arrived from the country brought country ways with them. People threw their sewage and trash out the windows to be washed down the gutters in the streets. The poor kept pigs and chickens; the rich kept horses; and pedestrians stepped into the street at their own risk. Air pollution from burning coal, a problem since the sixteenth century, got steadily worse. People drank water drawn from wells and rivers contaminated by sewage and industrial runoff. The River Irwell, which ran through Manchester, was, in the words of one visitor, "considerably less a river than a flood of liquid manure."[3] "Every day that I live," wrote an American visitor to Manchester, "I thank Heaven that I am not a poor man with a family in England."[4] At the same time, railroads invaded the towns, bringing noise

---

[3] Quoted in Lewis Mumford, *The City in History* (New York: Harcourt Brace, 1961), 460.

[4] Quoted in F. Roy Willis, *Western Civilization: An Urban Perspective*, vol. II (Lexington, MA: D.C. Heath, 1973), 675.

MAP 22.1 Industrialization in Europe, ca. 1850

In 1850, industrialization was in its early stages on the European continent. The first industrial regions were comparatively close to England and possessed rich coal deposits: Belgium and the Ruhr district of Germany. Politics determined the location of railroads. Notice the star-shaped French network of rail lines emanating from Paris and the lines linking the different parts of the German Confederation.

and smoke into densely populated neighborhoods. On the outskirts of cities, railroad yards, sidings, and repair shops covered acres of land, surrounded by miles of warehouses and workers' housing.

Under these conditions, diseases proliferated. To the long list of preindustrial diseases, industrialization added new ailments. Rickets, a bone disease caused by lack of sunshine, became endemic in dark and smoky industrial cities. Steamships brought cholera from India, causing great epidemics that struck poor neighborhoods especially hard. Observers documented the horrors of slum life in vivid detail. Their shocking reports led to municipal reforms, such as garbage removal, water and sewage systems, and parks and schools. These measures began to alleviate the ills of urban life after the mid-nineteenth century.

Rural Environments

Long before the Industrial Revolution began, practically no wilderness areas were left in Britain and very few in western Europe. Almost every piece of land was covered with fields, forests, or pastures shaped by human activity, or by towns; yet humans continued to alter the environment. As they had been doing for centuries, people cut timber to build ships and houses, to heat homes, and to manufacture bricks, iron, glass, beer, bread, and many other items.

North Americans transformed their environment on a vast scale. The Canadian and American governments seized land from the Indians and made it available at low cost to farmers and logging companies. Settlers viewed forests not as a valuable resource but as a hindrance to development. In their haste to "open up the wilderness," pioneers felled trees and burned them, built houses and abandoned them, and moved on. The cultivation of cotton in the South was especially harmful. Planters cut down forests, grew cotton for a few years until the soil was depleted, and then moved west, abandoning the land to scrub pines (see Chapter 25).

In industrializing Europe, raw materials once grown on the land—such as wood, hay, and wool—were replaced by materials found underground, like iron ore and coal, or obtained overseas, like cotton. Across Europe the expansion of coal and iron mining had dramatic effects on the environment. As the population increased and land grew scarcer, the cost of growing feed for horses rose, creating incentives to find new, less land-hungry means of transportation. Likewise, as iron became cheaper and wood more expensive, ships and many other objects formerly made of wood began to be made of iron.

Working Conditions

Industrialization offered new opportunities to the enterprising. Carpenters, metalworkers, and machinists were in great demand. Some workers became engineers or went into business for themselves. The boldest Britons moved to the European continent, the Americas, or India, using their skills to establish new industries.

The successful, however, were a minority. Most industrial jobs were unskilled, repetitive, and boring. Factory work did not vary with the seasons or the time of day but began and ended by the clock. Gas lighting expanded the working day past sunset. Workdays were long, there were few breaks, and foremen watched constantly. Workers who performed one simple task over and over had little sense of

Section of a Parisian building, illustration from 'Le Magasin Pittoresque', engraved by John Quartley (fl.1835–67) 1847 (engraving) (b/w photo), Girardet, Karl (1813–71) (after) / Bibliotheque des Arts Decoratifs, Paris, France / Archives Charmet / The Bridgeman Art Library

Paris Apartment at Night *This cutaway drawing in a French magazine shows the vertical segregation by social class that prevailed in the 1840s. The lower level is occupied by the concierge and her family. The first floor belongs to a wealthy family throwing a party for high-society friends. Middle-class people living on the next floor seem annoyed by the noise coming from below. Above them, a thief has entered an artist's studio. A poor seamstress and her child live in the garret under the roof. When elevators were introduced in the late nineteenth century, people of different income levels were more likely segregated by neighborhoods instead of by floors.*

achievement or connection to the final product. Industrial accidents were common and could ruin a family. Unlike the artisans they replaced, factory workers had no control over their tools, jobs, or working hours.

Industrial work had a major impact on women and family life. Women who could not afford servants had always worked, but mostly within the family: spinning and weaving, sewing hats and clothes, preparing food, washing, and doing a myriad other household chores. In rural areas, women also did farm work, especially caring for gardens and small animals.

In the early years of industrialization, even where factory work was available, it was never the main occupation of working women. Most young women who sought paid employment became domestic servants in spite of the low pay, drudgery, and risk of sexual abuse by male employers. Women with small children tried hard to find work they could do at home, such as laundry, sewing, embroidery, millinery, or taking in lodgers. Those who worked in factories were concentrated in textile mills, because textile work required less strength than metalworking, construction, or hauling. On average, women earned one-third to one-half as much as men. The economist Andrew Ure wrote in 1835: "It is in fact the constant aim and tendency of every improvement in machinery to supersede human labour altogether or to diminish its cost, by substituting the industry of women and children for that of men."[5] Young unmarried women worked to support themselves or to save for marriage. Married women took factory jobs when their husbands were unable to support the family. Mothers of infants faced a hard choice: whether to leave their babies with wet nurses at great expense or bring them to the factory and keep them drugged. Husbands and wives increasingly worked in different places.

As in preindustrial societies, parents thought children should contribute to their upkeep as soon as they were able to. The first generation of industrial workers brought children as young as five or six with them to the factories and mines, since there were no public schools or day-care centers. Employers preferred child workers because they were cheaper and more docile than adults and because they were better able to tie broken threads or crawl under machines to sweep the dust. In Arkwright's cotton mills, for example, two-thirds of the workers were children. Mine operators used children to pull coal carts along the low passageways from the coal face to the mine shaft. Nearly all these children worked fourteen to sixteen hours a day and were beaten if they made mistakes or fell asleep. Some manufacturers tried to provide more humane environments. When Francis Cabot Lowell built a cotton mill in Massachusetts, he hired the unmarried daughters of New England farmers, promising them decent wages and housing in dormitories under careful moral supervision. Other manufacturers eager to combine profits with morality followed his example. But soon these early social experiments were overwhelmed by the profit motive, and manufacturers, especially in highly competitive industries, imposed longer hours, harsher working conditions, and lower wages. When young women in New England factories went on strike, the mill owners replaced them with impoverished Irish immigrants willing to accept lower pay and worse conditions.

The cotton boom enriched planters, merchants, and manufacturers and also reinforced and expanded the institution of slavery in the Americas. In the 1790s, there were 700,000 slaves of African descent in the United States. As the "Cotton Kingdom" expanded, the number of slaves increased, reaching 3.2 million by 1850,

---

[5] Quoted in Joan W. Scott, "The Mechanization of Women's Work," *Scientific American* 247, no. 3 (September 1982): 171.

"Love Conquers Fear" *This is a sentimental Victorian drawing of children in a textile mill. Child labor was common in the first half of the nineteenth century, and workers were exposed to dangerous machines and moving belts, as well as to dust and dirt.*

From William Playfair, The Commercial and Political Atlas, 1801. Visual Connection Archive

60 percent located in the cotton region. While cotton profits soared, the lives of slaves grew more oppressive. Thousands of slave families were broken up by the internal slave trade that moved slaves from tobacco regions to the cotton frontier. At the same time, slave states also limited or outlawed manumissions, closing the door on slave families' hopes for freedom. Similarly, European demand for sugar prolonged plantation slavery in the West Indies and spread it to the coffee-growing regions of southern Brazil. Slavery was not, as white American southerners maintained, a "peculiar institution," a consequence of biological differences or biblical injunctions, but an integral part of both commercial capitalism and the Industrial Revolution.

Changes in Society

In his novel *Sybil, or, The Two Nations*, the British politician Benjamin Disraeli (**diz-RAY-lee**) (1804–1881) spoke of "two nations between whom there is no intercourse and no sympathy, who are as ignorant of each other's habits, thoughts, and feelings as if they were dwellers in different zones, or inhabitants of different planets ... the rich and the poor."[6]

In Britain the worst-off were those who clung to an obsolete skill or craft. The high wages and low productivity of handloom weavers in the 1790s induced inventors to develop power looms. As a result, by 1811 handloom weavers' wages had fallen by a third; by 1832, by two-thirds. Even by working longer hours, they could not escape destitution. The standard of living of factory workers did not decline steadily like those of handloom weavers but fluctuated wildly.

During the war years of 1792 to 1815, the price of food, on which the poor spent most of their income, rose faster than wages, causing widespread hardship. Then, in the 1820s real wages and public health began to improve. Prices for food, housing, and clothing fell and wages rose. Even the poor could afford comfortable, washable cotton clothes and underwear. But hard times returned in the "hungry forties." In 1847–1848 the potato crop failed in Ireland. One-quarter of the Irish population died in the resulting famine, and another quarter emigrated to England and North America. As these desperate men and women entered the workforce, wages fell.

The real beneficiaries of the early Industrial Revolution were the middle class. In Britain landowning gentry and merchants had long shared wealth and influence. In the late eighteenth century a new group arose: entrepreneurs whose money came from manufacturing. Most, like Arkwright and Wedgwood, were the sons of middling shopkeepers, craftsmen, or farmers. Their enterprises were usually self-financed, for little capital was needed to start a cotton-spinning or machine-building business. A generation later, in the nineteenth century, some newly rich industrialists bought their way into high society. The same happened in western Europe and the United States after 1815.

Before the Industrial Revolution, wives of merchants had often participated in the family business, and widows occasionally managed sizable businesses on their own. With industrialization came a "cult of domesticity" to justify removing middle-class women from contact with the business world. Instead, they became responsible for the home, the servants, the education of children, and the family's social life (see Chapter 27). Not all women accepted the change; in response Mary Wollstonecraft (1759–1797) wrote the first feminist manifesto, *Vindication of the Rights of Woman*, in 1792.

Middle-class people who attributed their success to their own efforts and virtues believed that if some people could succeed through hard work, thrift, and temperance, then those who did not succeed had no one but themselves to blame. Many workers, however, were newly arrived from rural districts and earned too little to save for the long stretches of unemployment they experienced. The moral position of the middle class mingled condemnation with concern, coupled with feelings of helplessness in the face of terrible social problems, such as drunkenness, prostitution, and child abandonment.

New Economic and Political Ideas

The profound changes unleashed by the Industrial Revolution triggered political ferment and ideological conflict. So many wars and revolutions took place during those years that we cannot neatly separate out the consequences of industrialization from the rest (see Chapter 23). But it is clear that by undermining social traditions and causing a growing gap between rich and poor, the Industrial Revolution strengthened the ideas of laissez faire (**LAY-say fair**) and socialism and sparked workers' protests.

Laissez Faire and Its Critics

The most celebrated exponent of **laissez faire** ("let them do") was Adam Smith (1723–1790), a Scottish economist. In *The Wealth of Nations* (1776) Smith argued that if individuals were allowed to seek personal gain, the effect, as though guided by an "invisible hand," would be to increase the general welfare. The government should refrain from interfering in business, except to protect private property; it should even allow duty-free trade with foreign countries. By advocating free-market capitalism, Smith was challenging the prevailing economic doctrine, **mercantilism**, which argued that governments should regulate trade in order to maximize their hoard of precious metals (Chapter 19).

Persuaded by Adam Smith's arguments, governments after 1815 dismantled many of their regulations, but no major power opened its economy to foreign competitors. Nonetheless, it was obvious that industrialization was causing widespread misery. Two other British thinkers, Thomas Malthus (1766–1834) and David Ricardo (1772–1832), attempted to explain the poverty they saw without challenging the basic premises of laissez faire. The cause of the workers' plight, they said, was the population boom, which outstripped the food supply and led to falling wages. The workers' poverty, they claimed, was as much a result of "natural law" as was the wealth of successful businessmen. For them the only way for the working class to avoid mass famine was to delay marriage and practice self-restraint and sexual abstinence.

Businesspeople in Britain eagerly adopted laissez-faire ideas that justified their activities and kept the government at bay. But not everyone accepted the grim conclusions of the "dismal science," as economics was then known. The British philosopher Jeremy Bentham (1748–1832) believed that it was possible to maximize "the greatest happiness of the greatest number," if only Parliament would study the social problems of the day and pass appropriate legislation. The German economist Friedrich List (1789–1846) rejected laissez faire and free trade as a British trick "to make the rest of the world, like the Hindus, its serfs in all industrial and commercial relations." To protect their "infant industries" from British competition, he argued, the German states had to erect high tariff barriers against imports from Britain. On the European continent, List's ideas helped lead to the formation of the Zollverein (**TSOLL-feh-rine**), a customs union of most of the German states, in 1834.

French social thinkers, moved by sincere concern for the poor, offered a radically new vision of a just civilization. Espousing a philosophy called **positivism**, the count of Saint-Simon (1760–1825) and his disciple Auguste Comte (**COMB-tuh**) (1798–1857) argued that the scientific method could solve social as well as technical problems. They recommended that the poor, guided by scientists and artists, form workers' communities under the protection of benevolent business leaders. These ideas attracted the enthusiastic support of bankers and entrepreneurs, for whom positivism provided a rationale for investing in railroads, canals, and other symbols of modernity. Positivism was most influential in Latin America, where the political elites of Brazil and Mexico pursued a top-down program of economic development reinforced by harsh police controls and the manipulation of political institutions. Its chief tenets are emblazed on the Brazilian flag: Order and Progress.

As numerous protest organizations formed across Europe in the wake of the Industrial Revolution, a minority sought to overthrow the new industrial order. Groups calling themselves communists were the most prominent of these radical groups. Two German-born intellectuals, Karl Marx (1818–1883) and his long-time collaborator and benefactor Friedrich Engels (1820–1895), played key roles in formulating this movement's criticism of industrial capitalism. They argued that the concentration of wealth and power associated with industrialization had led to the unbearable oppression of industrial workers (what they called the **proletariat**) and justified revolution. While the monumental work *Das Kapital* (Capital) was Marx's major intellectual achievement, it was *The Communist Manifesto*, published in 1848 with Engels, that proved most influential in spreading his radical critique of capitalism and urging the mobilization of the working class. This short, powerful book argued that history was dominated by class struggle and that proletarians would inevitably come together to overthrow the bourgeoisie, the modern class that controlled industry. The book's final words were "Proletarians of all countries unite!"

Protests and Reforms   Workers benefited little from the ideas of these middle-class philosophers. Instead, they resisted harsh working conditions in their own ways. Periodically, they rioted or went on strike, especially when food prices were high or when downturns in the business cycle left many unemployed. In some places, craftsmen broke into factories and destroyed the machines that threatened their livelihoods. Such acts of resistance did little to change the nature of industrial work.

From the beginnings of the Industrial Revolution workers resisted the introduction of new technologies. They believed that mechanized production would diminish the value of their skills and force them into poverty. As early as 1767, disgruntled textile workers mobilized to destroy one of the first innovations, James Hargreaves' spinning jenny. Subsequent innovations in both the cotton and woolen industries were also attacked by angry crowds of workers. In 1779, for example, workers destroyed nearly every machine driven by waterpower in Blackburn, England. Then in 1811 angry workers in the lace and stocking industries began a campaign of systematic machine breaking. Calling themselves Luddites, they attacked more than one hundred businesses and destroyed nearly every machine in the district. Machine breaking in France was even more violent. As French entrepreneurs began introducing British industrial technologies in textiles and metallurgy in the late 1770s, workers organized protests against these "foreign" innovations, attacking British craftsmen and destroying the new machines. In the early stages of the French Revolution (see Chapter 23), popular revolutionary sentiment reinforced the resistance of workers to new machinery and undermined the ability of the government to protect factories. The result was that French artisans retained traditional control of production and France fell decades behind Britain in industrializing.

Mechanization was also resisted in rural areas. The effects of enclosure (described earlier in this chapter) and rural population growth combined to force many rural families in Great Britain into poverty. Thousands of tenants and small farmers lost their land, becoming seasonal labors or migrating to industrial cities. This impoverished class of rural workers rose up when wealthy farmers began to introduce reapers and other machines. Often called the "Captain Swing" riots, rural laborers organized against mechanization, setting fires, threatening landlords, demanding higher wages, and breaking machines. This popular movement culminated after 1830 when widespread rural riots forced the British government to mobilize troops and militia in defense of property. In the end, thousands of protestors were arrested and either imprisoned in Britain or transported to Australia as convict laborers.

These violent efforts to block innovation and protect long-established customs in manufacturing and agriculture were superseded by laboring class organizations focused on workplace reform, higher wages, and expanded political rights. Gradually, workers organized to demand universal male suffrage and shorter workdays. In 1834, Robert Owen founded the Grand National Consolidated Trade Union to lobby for an eight-hour workday; it quickly gained half a million members but collapsed a few months later in the face of government prosecution. A new movement called Chartism arose soon thereafter, led by William Lovett and Fergus O'Connor, that appealed to miners and industrial workers. It demanded universal male suffrage, the secret ballot, salaries for members of Parliament, and annual elections. Chartism collapsed in 1848, but it left a legacy of labor organizing (see Chapter 23). By 1850 the beginnings of the modern union movement were in place in Europe's most industrialized nations.

Eventually, mass movements persuaded the British Parliament to investigate conditions in factories and mines and initiate some reforms. The Factory Act of 1833 prohibited the employment of children younger than nine in textile mills. It also limited the working hours of children between the ages of nine and thirteen to eight hours a day and of fourteen- to eighteen-year-olds to twelve hours. The Mines Act of 1842 prohibited the employment of women and boys under age ten underground. Belgium and other European nations were slower to introduce workplace reforms. The British learned to seek reform through accommodation. On the European continent, in contrast, the revolutions of 1848 revealed widespread discontent with repressive governments but failed to soften the hardships of industrialization (see Chapter 27).

THE LIMITS OF INDUSTRIALIZATION OUTSIDE THE WEST

Egypt   The spread of the Industrial Revolution in the early nineteenth century transformed the relations of western Europe and North America with the rest of the world. Egypt, strongly influenced by European ideas since the French invasion of 1798, began to industrialize in the early nineteenth century. The driving force was its ruler, **Muhammad Ali** (1769–1849), a man who was to play a major role in the history of the Middle East and East Africa (see Chapters 24 and 26). Muhammad Ali wanted to build up the Egyptian economy and military in order to become less dependent on the Ottoman sultan, his nominal overlord. To do so, he imported advisers and technicians from Europe and built cotton mills, foundries, shipyards, weapons factories, and other industrial enterprises. To pay for all this, he made the peasants grow wheat and cotton, which the government bought at a low price and exported at a profit. He also imposed high tariffs on imported goods to force the pace of industrialization.

Muhammad Ali's efforts fell afoul of the British, who did not want a powerful country threatening to interrupt the flow of travelers and mail across Egypt, the shortest route between Europe and India. When Egypt went to war against the Ottoman Empire in 1839, Britain intervened and forced Muhammad Ali to eliminate all import duties in the name of free trade. Unprotected, Egypt's fledgling industries could not compete with the flood of cheap British products. Thereafter, Egypt exported raw cotton, imported manufactured goods, and became an economic dependency of Britain.

India

Until the late eighteenth century, India had been the world's largest producer and exporter of cotton textiles, handmade by skilled spinners and weavers. The British East India Company took over large parts of India just as the Industrial Revolution was beginning in Britain. It then allowed cheap British factory-made yarn and cloth to flood the Indian market duty-free, putting spinners and handloom weavers out of work. Unlike Britain, India had no factories to which displaced handicraft workers could turn for work and most of them became landless peasants, eking out a precarious living.

Like other tropical regions, India became an exporter of raw materials and an importer of British industrial goods. To hasten the process, British entrepreneurs and colonial officials introduced railroads into the subcontinent. The construction of India's railroad network began in the mid-1850s, along with coal mining to fuel the locomotives and the installation of telegraph lines to connect the major cities.

Some Indian entrepreneurs saw opportunities in the atmosphere of change that the British created. In 1854, the Bombay merchant Cowasjee Nanabhoy Davar imported an engineer, four skilled workers, and several textile machines from Britain and started India's first textile mill. This was the beginning of India's mechanized cotton industry. Despite many gifted entrepreneurs, however, India's industrialization proceeded at a snail's pace, for the government was in British hands and the British did nothing to encourage Indian industry.

China

In the eighteenth century, the Chinese economy benefited from a long period of relative political stability and from population growth and commercial expansion. During the Qing dynasty, specialized market towns devoted to cotton textiles, silk, and staples developed in east-central China. At the same time, China developed markets in land and labor as well as rudimentary banking and credit mechanisms that facilitated long-distance trade. There were few direct threats to either Chinese borders or Chinese trade. This situation changed as European powers, first the Portuguese and Dutch and then the British and French, established highly militarized commercial presences in Asia. Nevertheless, even as European power grew, China continued to play a major role in the major markets of Asia, maintaining a favorable balance of trade with Europe that was financed by silver from European colonies.

China, however, remained an agrarian empire much less dependent on foreign trade than the major European powers, especially Great Britain. As a result, the Chinese government focused its attention and resources on the production and distribution of food, an effective guarantee of social peace, rather than on trade. While Britain and its European rivals viewed foreign trade as crucial to national well-being and as inherently competitive, the Chinese government saw foreign trade as narrowly supplemental to the domestic economy.

With inexpensive and abundant labor, the absence of a true national market, and limited engagement in foreign markets, the Chinese government did not see a clear need to subsidize or promote technology transfers as new machine technologies rapidly transformed the European economy in the first half of the nineteenth century. This situation began to rapidly change when Great Britain, its military transformed by the Industrial Revolution, pressed to reverse the steep trade imbalance long enjoyed by China. Compelled now to recognize the economic and military transformations wrought by industrial innovation in Europe, China faced a succession of internal and foreign threats to stability before its own reforms could begin to take hold.

In January 1840, a shipyard in Britain launched a radically new ship. The *Nemesis* had an iron hull, a flat bottom that allowed it to navigate in shallow waters, and a steam engine to power it upriver and against the wind. In November it arrived off the coast of China, heavily armed. Though ships from Europe had been sailing to China for three hundred years, the *Nemesis* was the first steam-powered iron gunboat in Asian waters. It was soon joined by other steam-powered warships that collectively established European control of Chinese rivers, bombarding forts and cities and transporting troops and supplies far more quickly than Chinese soldiers could move on foot. With this new weapon, Britain, a small island nation half a world away, was able to defeat the largest and most populated country in the world (see Chapter 24). The cases of Egypt, India, and China show how the demands of Western nations and the military advantage they gained from industrialization led them to interfere in the internal affairs of nonindustrial societies. As we shall see in Chapter 27, this was the start of a new age of Western dominance.

CONCLUSION

The Industrial Revolution was the most momentous transformation in history since the beginning of agriculture. The steam engine and other new machines greatly lowered the cost and increased the production of goods like cotton and iron, as well as increased the speed of transportation and communication.

The process caused social upheavals and environmental problems, however. Many entrepreneurs and businesspeople became very wealthy, while industrial workers—many of them children—worked under appalling conditions and lived in overcrowded tenements in badly polluted cities. Economists and philosophers proposed many theories and offered many solutions to the radical problems of industrial societies.

Industrialization had political consequences on a global scale. A small number of industrializing nations—first Great Britain, then those of western Europe and

North America—grew more powerful. Other parts of the world were left behind to become political or economic dependencies of these powerful nations.

Eventually the industrial nations learned to alleviate their social problems, but the disparity between the rich and poor nations persisted for two centuries or more, and the environmental effects of industrialization have changed from local to global.

IMPORTANT EVENTS 1750–1854

1702–1712	Thomas Newcomen builds first steam engine
1776	Adam Smith's *Wealth of Nations*
1776–1783	American Revolution
1779	First iron bridge
1789–1799	French Revolution
1792	Mary Wollstonecraft's *A Vindication of the Rights of Woman*
1793	Eli Whitney's cotton gin
1804–1815	Napoleonic Wars
1820s	Construction of Erie Canal
1820s	U.S. cotton industry begins
1829	*Rocket*, first prize-winning locomotive
1833	Factory Act in Britain
1834	German Zollverein; Robert Owen's Grand National Consolidated Trade Union
1837	Wheatstone and Cooke's telegraph
1838	First ships steam across the Atlantic
1840	*Nemesis* sails to China
1843	Samuel Morse's Baltimore-to-Washington telegraph
1846	Repeal of British Corn Laws
1847–1848	Irish famine
1848	Collapse of Chartist movement; revolutions in Europe
1851	Crystal Palace opens in London
1854	First cotton mill in India

23

REVOLUTIONARY CHANGES IN THE ATLANTIC WORLD, 1750–1850

In August 1791, slaves and free blacks began an insurrection in the plantation district of northern Saint Domingue (san doe-MANG) (present-day Haiti). During the following decade and a half, Haitian revolutionaries abolished slavery; defeated military forces from Britain and France; and achieved independence.

News and rumors about revolutionary events in France had helped move the island's slave community to rebel. These same events had divided the island's white population into royalists (supporters of France's King Louis XVI) and republicans (who sought an end to monarchy). The large free mixed-race population had secured some political rights from the French Assembly but was forced into rebellion by the violent resistance of the slave-owning elite to these reforms.

A black freedman, François Dominique Toussaint, led the insurrection. Taking the name Toussaint L'Ouverture (too-SAN loo-ver-CHORE), he became one of the most remarkable representatives of the revolutionary era. He organized the rebels militarily, negotiated with the island's competing factions and with representatives of Britain and France, and wrote his nation's first constitution. Commonly portrayed as a fiend by slave owners, Toussaint became a towering symbol of resistance to oppression to slaves everywhere.

The Haitian slave rebellion was an important event in the political and cultural transformation of the Western world. Profound changes to the economy, politics, and intellectual life occurred as well. The Industrial Revolution (see Chapter 22) increased manufacturing productivity and led to greater global interdependence, new patterns of consumerism, and altered social structures. At the same time, intellectuals questioned the traditional place of monarchy and religion in Western society. Enriched by the economic dynamism of this period, merchants, professionals, and manufacturers provided an audience for the new intellectual currents as they pressed for a larger political role.

This revolutionary era turned the Western world "upside down." The *ancien régime* (ahn-see-EN ray-ZHEEM), the French term for Europe's old order, rested on medieval principles: politics dominated by powerful monarchs, intellectual and cultural life dominated by religion, and economics dominated by hereditary agricultural elites. In the West's new order, commoners entered political life; science took the place of religion in intellectual life; and economies opened to competition.

This radical transformation did not take place without false starts or setbacks. Imperial powers resisted the loss of colonies; monarchs and nobles struggled to retain their ancient privileges; and church authorities fought against the claims of science. While the liberal and nationalist ideals of the eighteenth-century revolutionary movements were sometimes thwarted in Europe and the Americas, belief in national self-determination and universal suffrage and a passion for social justice continued to animate reformers into the twentieth century.

PRELUDE TO REVOLUTION: THE EIGHTEENTH-CENTURY CRISIS

The cost of wars fought among Europe's major powers over colonies and trade helped precipitate the revolutionary era that began in 1775 with the American Revolution. Britain, France, and Spain were the central actors in these global struggles, but other imperial powers participated as well. While these nations had previously fought unpopular and costly wars and paid for them with new taxes, changes in Western intellectual and political environments now produced a much more critical response. Any effort to extend monarchical power or impose new taxes now raised questions about the rights of individuals and the legitimacy of political institutions.

Colonial Wars and Fiscal Crises   In the seventeenth century competition among European powers became global in character. The newly independent Netherlands attacked the trade routes that linked Spain and Portugal to their American and Asian colonies, even seizing parts of Portugal's colonial empire in Brazil and Angola. Europe's other emerging sea power, Great Britain, also attacked Spanish fleets and seaports in the Americas. These rivalries made the defense of trade routes and distant colonies more expensive and difficult.

The eighteenth century further tested the ability of European powers to pay for their imperial ambitions. As Dutch power ebbed, Britain and France began a long struggle for political preeminence in western Europe and for territory and trade outlets in the Americas and Asia as the older empires of Spain and Portugal struggled to hang on. Nearly all of Europe's great powers participated in the War of the Spanish Succession (1701–1714). A few decades later war between Britain and Spain over smuggling broadened into a generalized European conflict, the War of Austrian Succession (1740–1748). Less than two decades later a frontier conflict between French and British forces and their Amerindian allies then led to a wider struggle, the Seven Years' War (1756–1763). With peace Britain emerged with undisputed control of North America east of the Mississippi River while France had been forced to surrender Canada and its holdings in India.

The enormous cost of these conflicts distinguished them from earlier wars. Traditional taxes collected in traditional ways no longer covered the obligations of governments. While Britain's total budget before the Seven Years' War had averaged only £8 million, in 1763 its war debt had reached £137 million and interest payments alone exceeded £5 million. Even as European economies expanded, fiscal crises overtook one European government after another. In an intellectual environment transformed by the Enlightenment, the need for new revenues provoked debate and confrontation within a vastly expanded and more critical public.

**The
Enlightenment
and the Old
Order**

The complex and diverse intellectual movement called the **Enlightenment** applied the methods and questions of the Scientific Revolution of the seventeenth century to the study of human society as well as to the natural world (see Chapter 17). Some European intellectuals sought to systematize knowledge and organize reference materials. For example, the Swedish botanist Carolus Linnaeus (kar-ROLL-uhs lin-NEE-uhs) sought to categorize all living organisms, and Samuel Johnson published a comprehensive English dictionary. In France Denis Diderot (duh-nee DEE-duh-roe) worked with other thinkers to create a compendium of human knowledge, the thirty-five-volume *Encyclopédie*.

Other thinkers pursued lines of inquiry that more directly challenged long-established religious and political institutions. Some argued that if scientists could understand the laws of nature, then surely similar forms of disciplined investigation might reveal laws of human nature. The most radical wondered whether society and government could be better regulated and more productive if guided by science rather than by hereditary rulers and the church. These new perspectives and the intellectual optimism that fed them helped guide the revolutionary movements of the late eighteenth century.

The English political philosopher John Locke (1632–1704) argued in 1690 that governments were created to protect life, liberty, and property and that the people had a right to rebel when a monarch violated these natural rights. Locke's closely reasoned theory began with the assumption that individual rights were the foundation of civil government. In *The Social Contract*, published in 1762, the French-Swiss intellectual Jean-Jacques Rousseau (zhan-zhock roo-SOE) (1712–1778) asserted that the will of the people was sacred and that the legitimacy of monarchs depended on the consent of the people. Although both men believed that government rested on the will of the people, Locke emphasized the importance of individual rights secured institutionally while Rousseau, much more distrustful of society and government, envisioned the people acting collectively as a result of their shared historical experience.

All Enlightenment thinkers were not radicals like Rousseau. There was never a uniform program for political and social reform, and the era's intellectuals often disagreed about principles and objectives. While the Enlightenment is commonly associated with hostility toward religion and monarchy, few intellectuals openly expressed republican or atheist sentiments. Even Voltaire, one of the Enlightenment's most critical intellects and great celebrities, believed that Europe's monarchs were likely agents of political and economic reform.

Indeed, sympathetic members of the nobility and reforming European monarchs such as Charles III of Spain (r. 1759–1788), Catherine the Great of Russia (r. 1762–1796), and Frederick the Great of Prussia (r. 1740–1786) actively sponsored and promoted the dissemination of new ideas, providing patronage for many intellectuals. They recognized that elements of the Enlightenment buttressed their own efforts to expand royal authority at the expense of religious institutions, the nobility, and regional autonomy. Goals such as the development of national bureaucracies staffed by civil servants selected on merit, the creation of national legal systems, and the modernization of tax systems united many of Europe's monarchs and intellectuals. Monarchs also understood that the era's passion for science and technology held the potential of fattening national treasuries and improving economic performance.

Though willing to embrace reform proposals when they served royal interests, Europe's monarchs moved quickly to suppress or ban radical ideas that promoted republicanism or directly attacked religion. However, too many channels of communication were open to permit a thoroughgoing suppression of ideas. In fact, censorship tended to enhance intellectual reputations, and persecuted intellectuals generally found patronage in the courts of foreign rivals.

Many of the major intellectuals of the Enlightenment corresponded with each other as well as with political leaders. This communication led to numerous first-hand contacts among the intellectuals of different nations and helped create a more coherent assault on what they saw as ignorance—beliefs and values associated with the ancien régime. Rousseau met the Scottish philosopher David Hume in Paris. Later, when Rousseau feared arrest, Hume helped him seek refuge in Britain. Similarly, Voltaire sought patronage and protection in England and later in Prussia when facing threats in France.

Women were instrumental in the dissemination of these new ideas. In England large numbers of educated middle-class women purchased and discussed books and pamphlets. Some, like Mary Wollstonecraft, were important contributors to intellectual life as writers and commentators, raising by example and in argument the issue of the rights of women. In Paris wealthy women made their homes centers of debate, intellectual speculation, and free inquiry. Their salons brought together philosophers, social critics, artists, members of the aristocracy, and the commercial elite.

The intellectual ferment of the era deeply influenced the expanding middle class in Europe and the Western Hemisphere. Members of this class were eager consumers of books and inexpensive newspapers and journals, which were widely available. This broadening of the intellectual audience overwhelmed traditional institutions of censorship. New public venues like the thousands of coffeehouses and teashops of cities and market towns also became locations to discuss scientific discoveries, new technologies, and controversial works on human nature and politics, expanding the Enlightenment's influence beyond the literate minority.

Many European intellectuals were interested in the Americas. Some continued to dismiss the region as barbaric and inferior, but others used idealized accounts of the New World to support their critiques of European society. Many looked to Britain's North American colonies for confirmation of their belief that human nature unconstrained by the corrupted practices of Europe's old order would quickly produce material abundance and social justice. More than any other American, the writer and inventor **Benjamin Franklin** came to symbolize the vast potential of America to Europe's intellectuals.

Born in Boston in 1706, the young Franklin trained as a printer. In Philadelphia he succeeded in business and became famous for his *Poor Richard's Almanac*. At forty-two he retired to pursue writing, science, and public affairs. Franklin was instrumental in the creation of the Philadelphia Free Library, the American Philosophical Society, and the University of Pennsylvania. His contributions were both practical and theoretical. The inventor of bifocal glasses, the lightning rod, and an efficient wood-burning stove, he also contributed to scientific knowledge with publications like his 1751 paper, *Experiments and Observations on Electricity*, which won him acclaim from European intellectuals.

Franklin was also an important political figure. He served in many capacities in the colonies and was selected as a delegate to the Continental Congress that issued the Declaration of Independence in 1776. He later became ambassador to Paris, where his achievements, witty conversation, and careful self-promotion made him the symbol of the era. His life seemed to confirm the Enlightenment's most radical objective, the freeing of human potential from the effects of inherited privilege.

As Franklin demonstrates, the Western Hemisphere shared in Europe's intellectual ferment. As the Enlightenment penetrated the New World, intellectuals actively debated the legitimacy of colonialism itself. European efforts to reform colonial policies by unilaterally altering colonial institutions and overturning long-established political practices further radicalized colonial intellectuals. Among peoples compelled to accept the dependence and inferiority explicit in colonial rule, the idea that government authority rested on the consent of the governed proved explosive.

Many intellectuals resisted the Enlightenment, seeing it as a dangerous assault on the authority of the church and monarchy. This Counter Enlightenment was most influential in France and other Catholic nations. Its adherents emphasized the importance of faith to human happiness and social well-being. They also emphasized duty and obligation to the community of believers in opposition to the concern for individual rights and individual fulfillment common in the works of the Enlightenment. Most importantly for the politics of the era, they rejected their enemies' enthusiasm for change and utopianism, reminding their readers of human fallibility and the importance of history and tradition. While the central ideas of the Enlightenment gained strength across the nineteenth century, the Counter Enlightenment provided ideological support for the era's conservatism and later popular antidemocratic movements.

Folk Cultures and Popular Protest   While intellectuals and the reforming royal courts of Europe debated the rational and secular enthusiasms of the Enlightenment, most people in Western society remained loyal to competing cultural values grounded in the preindustrial past. Regional folk cultures were rooted in the memory of shared experience and nourished by religious practices that encouraged emotional release. These cultural traditions included coherent expressions of the rights and obligations that connected people with their rulers. Authorities who violated these understandings were likely to face violent opposition.

In the eighteenth century, European monarchs sought to increase their authority and to centralize power by reforming tax collection, judicial practice, and public administration. Although monarchs viewed these changes as reforms, common people often saw them as violations of sacred customs and responded with bread riots, tax protests, and attacks on royal officials. These violent actions sought to preserve custom and precedent rather than overturn traditional authority. In Spain and the Spanish colonies, protesting mobs often expressed love for their monarch while at the same time assaulting his officials and preventing the implementation of reforms, shouting "Long Live the King! Death to Bad Government!"

Enlightenment-era reformers sought to bring order and discipline to the citizenry by banning or altering numerous popular traditions—such as harvest festivals, religious holidays, and country fairs—that enlivened the drudgery of

The Art Archive

Beer Street (1751) *William Hogarth's engraving shows an idealized London street scene where beer drinking is associated with manly strength, good humor, and prosperity. The self-satisfied corpulent figure in the left foreground reads a copy of the king's speech to Parliament. We can imagine him offering a running commentary to his drinking companions as he reads.*

everyday life. These events were popular celebrations of sexuality and individuality as well as opportunities for masked and costumed celebrants to mock the greed, pretension, and foolishness of government officials, the wealthy, and the clergy. Hard drinking, gambling, and blood sports like cockfighting and bearbaiting were popular in preindustrial mass culture, but reformers viewed them as corrupt and decadent. As reforming governments undertook to substitute civic rituals, patriotic anniversaries, and institutions of self-improvement for older customs, they often provoked protests and riots.

The efforts of ordinary men and women to resist the growth of government power and the imposition of new cultural forms provide an important political undercurrent to much of the revolutionary agitation and conflict between 1750 and 1850.

Spontaneous popular uprisings and protests punctuated nearly every effort at reform in the eighteenth century. But popular protest gained revolutionary potential only when it coincided with ideological division and conflict within the governing class.

THE AMERICAN REVOLUTION, 1775–1800

In British North America, clumsy efforts to increase colonial taxes to cover rising defense expenditures and to diminish the power of elected colonial legislatures outraged a populace accustomed to local autonomy. Once begun, the American Revolution ushered in a century-long process of political and cultural transformation in Europe and the Americas. By the end of this revolutionary century, constitutions had limited or overturned the authority of monarchs, and religion had lost its dominance of Western intellectual life. At the same time revolutionary changes in manufacturing and commerce replaced the long-established social order determined by birth with a new social ideal emphasizing competition and social mobility.

Frontiers and Taxes   After defeating the French in 1763, the British government faced two related problems in its North American colonies. As settlers pushed west into Amerindian lands, Britain feared the likelihood of renewed conflict and rising military expenses. Already burdened with heavy debts, Britain tried to limit settler pressure on Amerindian lands and get colonists to shoulder more of the costs of colonial defense and administration.

In the Great Lakes region the British tried to contain costs by reducing fur prices and by refusing to continue the French practice of giving gifts and paying rent for frontier forts to Amerindian peoples. But lower fur prices forced native peoples to hunt more aggressively, putting pressure on the environment and endangering some species. The situation got worse as settlers and white trappers pushed across the Appalachians to compete directly with native hunters. The predictable result was renewed violence along the frontier led by Pontiac, an Ottawa chief. His broad alliance of native peoples forged in 1763 drove the British military from some western outposts but was unable to take Fort Detroit. Failure led to disaffection among the Amerindian allies and finally to a peace treaty in 1766.

With the outbreak of this conflict the British government reacted by publishing the Proclamation of 1763. This policy established a western limit for settlement, thus undermining the claims of thousands of established farmers without effectively protecting Amerindian land. No one was satisfied. In 1774, Britain tried again to slow the movement of settlers onto Amerindian lands by annexing western territories to the province of Quebec. Like the 1763 proclamation, this action provoked bitter resentment in the colonies.

In comparison with the French, Spanish, and Portuguese colonies of the Americas, the settlers of the British colonies enjoyed substantial political autonomy, exercising effective local control through elected legislatures and courts. Even as slavery expanded in the southern colonies, free settlers prospered. One measure of this mounting, broadly distributed wealth was the rising tide of imported British consumer goods. While enriching metropolitan producers and merchants, colonial consumption of British cloth, porcelains, tea, and other imports also played a key role in forging a unified colonial culture that transcended regional economic, social, and even religious differences.

When the British government sought to assert greater political control and force the colonies to pay a much larger share of the costs of defense and governance in the wake of the French and Indian War, colonial settlers would use consumer boycotts to great effect. While frontier policies imposed following Pontiac's rebellion led to colonial hostility and suspicion, they did not lead to a breach. British fiscal reforms and new taxes, however, sparked a series of political confrontations that led to political mobilizations and popular protests across the colonies and, ultimately, to rebellion. For example, British regulations imposed in 1764 threatened New England's profitable trade with Spanish and French Caribbean sugar colonies and more effectively policed colonial smuggling. More disruptive still was Britain's outlawing of colonial issues of paper money, a custom made necessary by the colonies' chronic balance-of-payments deficits. Each of these measures met with the protests of colonial legislatures and popular assemblies.

The Stamp Act of 1765—a tax on all legal documents, newspapers, pamphlets, and nearly all printed material—caused especially deep resentment. Propertied colonists, including holders of high office and members of the colonial elite, assumed leading roles in protests and used fiery political language, identifying Britain's rulers as "parricides" and "tyrants" and suggesting that a dependence on British imports threatened traditional liberties. Women from prominent colonial families played a crucial role in organizing boycotts of British goods. For them and for poorer women as well, producing and wearing homespun textiles was increasingly seen as a patriotic obligation. Organizations such as the Sons of Liberty were more confrontational, holding public meetings, intimidating royal officials, and organizing committees to enforce the boycotts. Although this combination of protest and boycott forced the repeal of the Stamp Act, Britain imposed new taxes and duties in 1767. Parliament also sent British troops to quell colonial riots. While the boycotts against the Stamp Act were mostly confined to cities, these new taxes ignited protests across the colonies. Legislatures, town governments, and *ad hoc* committees mobilized the colonists to boycott British goods. One indignant woman expressed her anger to a British officer:

> [T]he most ignorant peasant knows ... that no man has the right to take their money without their consent. The supposition is ridiculous and absurd, as none but highwaymen and robbers attempt it. Can you, my friend, reconcile it with your own good sense, that a body of men in Great Britain, who have little intercourse with America ... shall invest themselves with a power to command our lives and properties [?][1]

British authorities reacted to boycotts and attacks on royal officials by threatening colonial liberties. They dissolved the colonial legislature of Massachusetts and sent two regiments of soldiers to re-establish control of Boston's streets. Popular support for a complete break with Britain grew after March 5, 1770, when British soldiers fired at an angry Boston crowd, killing five civilians. The "Boston Massacre" exposed the naked force on which colonial rule rested and radicalized public opinion throughout the colonies.

Parliament attempted to calm colonial opinion by repealing some taxes and duties, but it stumbled into another crisis when it granted the East India Company

---

[1] Quoted in Ray Raphael, *A People's History of the American Revolution* (New York: Perennial, 2001), 141.

a monopoly to import tea to the colonies. This decision raised again the constitutional issue of Parliament's right to tax the colonies. It also provided the perfect target for colonial dissidents seeking to organize protest on a broad scale. Since tea was consumed by nearly everyone, its boycott would potentially unite nearly every class and region. In the heated language of protest, buying and drinking tea was acquiescing to British tyranny. The crisis came to a head when protesters dumped tea worth £10,000 (about £1.3 million or $1.9 million in 2012) into Boston harbor. As news of this act spread, tea was surrendered or, in some cases, seized and burned in innumerable towns and villages across the colonies. Britain responded by appointing a military man, Thomas Gage, as governor of Massachusetts and by closing the port of Boston. British troops now enforced public order in Boston, and public administration was in the hands of a general. This militarization of colonial government undermined Britain's constitutional authority and made rebellion inevitable.

The Course of Revolution, 1775–1783   In 1775 representatives from the colonies met in Philadelphia to discuss the situation. Most of the representatives elected to this Continental Congress had been active in the boycotts and protests of the previous decade, and they again used nonimportation as a political weapon. But events were moving quickly toward armed confrontation and revolution. Patriot militias had already fought British troops at Lexington and Concord, Massachusetts, and few thought compromise possible. The Congress now assumed the powers of government, created a currency, and organized an army led by **George Washington** (1732–1799), a Virginia planter who had served in the French and Indian War.

The angry rhetoric of thousands of street-corner speakers and the inflammatory pamphlet *Common Sense*, written by Thomas Paine, a recent immigrant from England, propelled popular support for independence. On July 4, 1776, Congress approved the Declaration of Independence, the document that proved to be the most enduring statement of the revolutionary era's ideology:

> We hold these truths to be self evident: That all men are created equal; that they are endowed by their creator with certain unalienable rights; that among these are life, liberty and the pursuit of happiness; that, to secure these rights, governments are instituted among men, deriving their just powers from the consent of the governed.

The Declaration's affirmation of popular sovereignty and individual rights would influence the language of revolution and popular protest around the world.

Great Britain reacted by sending additional military forces to pacify the colonies. By 1778 Britain had 50,000 British troops and 30,000 German mercenaries in the colonies. Despite the existence of a large loyalist community, the British army found it difficult to control the countryside. Although British forces won most of the battles, Washington slowly built a competent Continental army as well as civilian support networks that provided supplies and financial resources.

The British government also tried to find a political compromise that would satisfy colonial grievances. Half-hearted efforts to resolve the conflict over taxes failed, and an offer to roll back the clock and re-establish the administrative arrangements of 1763 made little headway. Overconfidence in its military and poor leadership kept the British from finding a political solution before revolutionary institutions were in place and the armies engaged. By allowing confrontation to occur, the British government lost the opportunity to mobilize and give direction to the large numbers of loyalists and pacifists in the colonies.

Along the Canadian border, both sides solicited Amerindians as allies and feared them as potential enemies. For over a hundred years, members of the powerful Iroquois Confederacy—Mohawk, Oneida, Onondaga, Cayuga, Seneca, and (after 1722) Tuscarora—had protected their traditional lands with a combination of diplomacy and warfare. Just as the American Revolution forced settler families to join the rebels or remain loyal, it divided the Iroquois, who fought on both sides.

The Mohawk proved to be valuable British allies. Their loyalist leader **Joseph Brant** (Thayendanegea [ta-YEHN-dah-NEY-geh-ah]) organized Britain's most potent fighting force along the Canadian border. His raids along the northern frontier earned him the title "Monster" Brant, but he was actually a man who moved easily between European and Amerindian cultures. Educated by missionaries, he was fluent in English and helped translate Protestant religious tracts into Mohawk. He was friendly with many loyalist families and British officials and had traveled to London for an audience with George III (r. 1760–1820).

The defeat in late 1777 of Britain's general John Burgoyne by General Horatio Gates at Saratoga, New York, put the future of the Mohawk at risk. American forces followed this victory with destructive attacks on Iroquois villages that reduced their political and military power. After Britain's defeat, Brant and the Mohawk joined the loyalist exodus to Canada.

The British defeat at Saratoga also convinced France to enter the war as an ally of the United States in 1778. French military help proved crucial, supplying American forces and forcing the British to defend their colonies in the Caribbean. The French contribution was most clear in the final battle, fought at Yorktown, Virginia, in 1781. With the American army supported by French soldiers and a French fleet, General Charles Cornwallis surrendered to Washington as the British military band played "The World Turned Upside-Down."

This victory effectively ended the war, and the Continental Congress sent representatives to the peace conference with instructions to work in tandem with the French. Believing that France was more concerned with containing British power than with guaranteeing a strong United States, America's peace delegation chose to negotiate directly with Britain and gained a generous settlement. The Treaty of Paris (1783) granted unconditional independence and established generous boundaries for the former colonies. In return the United States promised to repay prewar debts due to British merchants and to allow loyalists to recover property confiscated by patriot forces. In the end, loyalists were badly treated, and thousands left for Canada.

The Construction of Republican Institutions, to 1800

Even before the Declaration of Independence, many colonies had created new governments and summoned constitutional conventions to draft formal charters. Europeans were fascinated by the drafting of written constitutions and by their ratification by popular vote. Many early state constitutions were translated and published in Europe. Remembering colonial conflicts with royal governors, state constitutions placed severe limits on executive authority and granted broad powers to legislatures. Many also included bills of rights to provide further protection against tyranny.

It proved more difficult to frame a national constitution. The Second Continental Congress sent the Articles of Confederation—the first constitution of the United States—to the states for approval in 1777, but it was not accepted until 1781. It created a one-house legislature in which each state had a single vote. While a simple majority of the thirteen states was sufficient to pass minor legislation, nine votes were necessary for declaring war, imposing taxes, and coining or borrowing money. A committee, not a president, exercised executive power. Given the intended weakness of this government, it is remarkable that it defeated Great Britain.

Many of the most powerful political figures in the United States recognized that the Confederation was unable to enforce unpopular requirements of the peace treaty such as the recognition of loyalist property claims, the payment of prewar debts, and even the payment of military salaries and pensions due veterans. As a result, in September 1786 Virginia invited the other states to discuss the government's failure to deal with trade issues. This assembly called for a new convention to meet in Philadelphia. A rebellion led by Revolutionary War veterans in western Massachusetts gave the assembling delegates a sense of urgency.

The **Constitutional Convention**, which met in May 1787, achieved a nonviolent second American Revolution. The delegates pushed aside the announced purpose of the convention—"to render the constitution of the federal government adequate to the exigencies of the union"—and secretly undertook to write a new constitution with George Washington serving as presiding officer.

Debate focused on representation, electoral procedures, executive powers, and the relationship between the federal government and the states. The final compromise distributed political power among executive, legislative, and judicial branches and divided authority between the federal government and the states. The chief executive—the president—was to be elected indirectly by "electors" selected by ballot in the states.

Although this constitution created the most democratic government of the era, only a minority of the adult population had full political rights. While some northern states were hostile to slavery, southern leaders protected the institution. Slaves were denied participation in the political process, but slave states were permitted to count three-fifths of the slave population to allocate the number of congressional representatives, thus multiplying the political power of the slave-owning class. Southern delegates also gained a twenty-year continuation of the slave trade to 1808 and a fugitive slave clause that required all states to return runaway slaves to masters.

During the war, women had led prewar boycotts and organized relief and charitable organizations. Some had also served in the military as nurses, and a smaller number had joined the ranks disguised as men. Nevertheless, women were denied political rights in the new republic. Only New Jersey granted the vote to women and African Americans who met property requirements, and in 1807 state lawmakers eliminated this right.

THE FRENCH REVOLUTION, 1789–1815

The French Revolution undermined traditional monarchy and hereditary aristocracy as well as the power of the Catholic Church but, unlike the American Revolution, did not create enduring representative institutions. The colonial revolution in North America, however, did not confront so directly the entrenched privileges of an established church, monarchy, and aristocracy. Among its achievements, the French Revolution expanded mass participation in political life and radicalized the democratic tradition inherited from the English and American experiences. The political passions unleashed by revolutionary events in France also ultimately led to rule by popular demagogues and the dictatorship of Napoleon.

French Society and Fiscal Crisis   French society was divided in three estates. The clergy, called the First Estate, numbered about 130,000 in a nation of 28 million. The Catholic clergy was organized hierarchically, and priests from noble families held almost all top positions in the church. The church owned about 10 percent of the nation's land and extracted substantial amounts of wealth from the economy in the form of tithes and ecclesiastical fees, but it paid few taxes.

The 300,000 members of the nobility, the Second Estate, controlled about 30 percent of the land and retained ancient rights on much of the rest. Nobles held most high administrative, judicial, military, and church positions. Though barred from some types of commercial activity, nobles were important participants

Parisian Stocking Mender *The poor lived very difficult lives. This woman uses a discarded wine barrel as a shop where she mends socks.*

in wholesale trade, banking, manufacturing, and mining. Like the clergy, this estate was hierarchical: important differences in wealth, power, and outlook separated the higher from the lower nobility. In the eighteenth century many wealthy commoners who purchased administrative and judicial offices claimed noble status.

The Third Estate included everyone else, from wealthy financiers to beggars. The number of propertied and successful commoners grew rapidly in the eighteenth century. Commerce, finance, and manufacturing accounted for much of the wealth of the Third Estate. Wealthy commoners also owned nearly a third of the nation's land. This literate and socially ambitious group supported an expanding publishing industry, subsidized the fine arts, and purchased many of the extravagant new homes built in Paris and other cities.

Artisans, shopkeepers, and small landowners owned property and lived decently when crops were good and prices stable, but by 1780 poor harvests had increased their cost of living and led to a decline in consumer demand for their products. They were rich enough to fear the loss of their property and status and well educated enough to be aware of the growing criticism of the king, but they lacked the means to influence policy.

Poverty was common. Among peasants, who accounted for 80 percent of the French population, family poverty and vulnerability forced young children to seek seasonal work and led many to crime and beggary. In Paris and other French cities the vile living conditions and unhealthy diet of the urban poor were startling to visitors from other European nations. City streets swarmed with beggars and prostitutes. The problem of child abandonment suggests the wretchedness of the French poor: on the eve of the French Revolution French parents gave up at least 40,000 children per year. Their belief that these children would be adopted was no more than a convenient fiction; in reality the majority died of neglect.

Unable to afford decent housing, obtain steady employment, or protect their children, the poor periodically erupted in violent protest and rage. In the countryside the decisions of the nobility or clergy to increase taxes and other burdens often led to violence. In towns and cities any increase in the price of bread could spark a riot, since bread prices determined the quality of life of the poor. These explosive episodes, however, were not revolutionary in character; rioters sought immediate relief rather than structural change. That was to change when the Crown tried to solve its fiscal crisis.

The cost of the War of the Austrian Succession (1740–1748) began the crisis. When Louis XV (r. 1715–1774) tried to impose new taxes on the nobility and other privileged groups, widespread protests erupted. New debt from the Seven Years' War deepened the crisis and compelled the king to impose emergency fiscal measures, but the Parlement of Paris, an appeal court, resisted these measures. Frustrated by these actions, French authorities exiled members of the Parlement and pushed through a series of unpopular fiscal measures.

When the twenty-two-year-old Louis XVI assumed the throne in 1774, he faced a desperate fiscal situation compounded by the growing opposition of French courts to new taxes. In 1774 his chief financial adviser warned that the government could barely afford to operate; as he put it, "the first gunshot [act of war] will drive the state to bankruptcy." Despite this warning, the king decided to support the American Revolution, delaying financial collapse by borrowing enormous sums and disguising the growing debt in misleading fiscal accounts. By the end of the war, more than half of France's national budget was required to pay the interest on its debt.

In 1787, the desperate king called an Assembly of Notables to approve a radical and comprehensive reform of economic and fiscal policy. Despite the fact that the king's advisers selected this assembly from the high nobility, the judiciary, and the clergy, these representatives of privilege proved unwilling to support the proposed reforms and new taxes.

Protest Turns to Revolution, 1789–1792   In frustration, the king dismissed the Notables and attempted to implement reforms on his own, but his effort was met by an increasingly hostile judiciary and by popular demonstrations. The refusal of the elite to grant needed tax concessions forced the king to call the **Estates General**, a customary consultative body representing the three estates that had not met since 1614. The narrow self-interest and greed of the rich—who would not tolerate an increase in their own taxes—rather than the grinding poverty of the common people had created the conditions for revolution.

In late 1788 and early 1789 members of the three estates came together throughout the nation to discuss grievances and elect representatives to meet at Versailles (vuhr-SIGH). The Third Estate's representatives were mostly men of substantial property, but some were angry with the king's ministers and inclined to move France toward constitutional monarchy with an elected legislature. Many nobles and members of the clergy sympathized with the reform agenda of the Third Estate, but deep internal divisions over procedural and policy issues limited the power of the First and the Second Estates. Nevertheless, some clergy, and eventually nobles, joined the debates of the Third Estate, beginning a transition toward an assembly that could claim to represent the nation.

After six weeks of deadlock, the Third Estate, with allies from the other estates, signaled its ambitions by calling itself the National Assembly. Fearful of the growing assertiveness of these representatives, the king locked them out of their meeting place. They then moved to an indoor tennis court and pledged to write a constitution. The ascendant ideas of the era, that the people are sovereign and the legitimacy of rulers depends on their fulfilling the people's will, now swept away the king's narrow desire to solve the nation's fiscal crisis. Louis prepared for a confrontation with the National Assembly by moving military forces to Versailles. Before he could act, the people of Paris intervened.

A succession of bad harvests beginning in 1785 had propelled bread prices upward throughout France and provoked an economic depression as demand for nonessential goods collapsed. By the time the Estates General met, nearly a third of the Parisian workforce was unemployed. Hunger and anger marched hand in hand through working-class neighborhoods.

When the people of Paris heard that the king was massing troops in Versailles to arrest the representatives, crowds of common people began to seize arms and mobilize. On July 14, 1789, a crowd attacked the Bastille (bass-TEEL), a medieval fortress used as a prison. The futile defense of the Bastille cost ninety-eight lives before its garrison surrendered. Enraged, the attackers hacked the commander to death and then paraded through the city with his head and that of Paris's chief magistrate stuck on pikes.

These events coincided with uprisings by peasants in the country. Peasants sacked manor houses and destroyed documents that recorded their traditional labor and tax obligations. They then refused to pay taxes and dues to landowners and seized common lands. Forced to recognize the fury raging through rural areas, the National Assembly voted to end traditional obligations and the privileges of the nobility and church, essentially ending the feudal system. Having won this victory, peasants ceased their revolt.

These popular uprisings strengthened the hand of the National Assembly in its dealings with the king and led to passage of the **Declaration of the Rights of Man and the Citizen**, which stated the principles for a future constitution. Similarities between the language of this declaration and the U.S. Declaration of Independence resulted in part from the limited participation of Thomas Jefferson, author of the American document, who was U.S. ambassador to Paris. The French declaration, however, was more sweeping in its language. Among the enumerated natural rights were "liberty, property, security, and resistance to oppression." The Declaration of the Rights of Man and the Citizen also guaranteed free expression of ideas, equality before the law, and representative government.

While delegates debated political issues in Versailles, the economic crisis worsened in Paris. Women employed in the garment industry and small shopkeepers were particularly hard hit. Because the working women of Paris faced high food prices every day as they struggled to feed their families, their anger had a hard edge. Public markets became political arenas where the urban poor met daily in angry assembly. Here the revolutionary link between the material deprivation of the French poor and the political aspirations of the French bourgeoisie was forged.

On October 5, thousands of market women marched the 12 miles (19 kilometers) to Versailles and forced their way into the National Assembly, shouting "the point is that we want bread." The crowd then entered the royal apartments, killed some of the king's guards, and searched for Queen Marie Antoinette (ann-twah-NET), whom they hated as a symbol of extravagance. They then forced the royal family to relocate to Paris.

With the king's ability to resist democratic change overcome by the Paris crowd, the National Assembly achieved a radically restructured French society in the next two years. A new constitution dramatically limited monarchial power and abolished the nobility as a hereditary class. Economic reforms swept away monopolies and trade barriers within France. Renamed the Legislative Assembly, legislators took on the church, seizing its lands to use as collateral for a new paper currency; they also mandated the election of priests and placed them on the public payroll. When the Assembly forced priests to take a loyalty oath, however, many Catholics joined a growing counterrevolutionary movement.

At first, many European monarchs welcomed the weakening of the French king, but by 1791 Austria and Prussia threatened to intervene in support of the monarchy. The Legislative Assembly responded by declaring war. Although the war went badly at first for French forces, people across France responded patriotically to foreign invasions, forming huge new volunteer armies and mobilizing national resources to meet the challenge.

**The Terror,
1793–1794**

In this period of national crisis and foreign threat, the French Revolution entered its most radical phase. A failed effort by the king and queen to escape from Paris cost the king his remaining popular support. On August 10, 1792, a crowd invaded his palace in Paris, forcing the king to seek protection in the Legislative Assembly, which suspended his authority and ordered his imprisonment. These actions helped lead to the formation of a new legislative and executive body, the National Convention. They also created a political environment where competing political factions used rumors of plots and conspiracies to justify the use of violence against their enemies.

Rumors of counterrevolutionary plots also kept working-class neighborhoods in an uproar, and in September a mob surged through the city's prisons, killing nearly half the prisoners. Swept along by popular passion and fear of conspiracy, the newly elected National Convention convicted Louis XVI of treason, sentenced him to death, and proclaimed France a republic. The guillotine ended the king's life in January 1793 (see Environment and Technology: The Guillotine). These events precipitated a wider war with nearly all of Europe's powers allied against France.

The National Convention—the new legislature of the French Republic—convened in September. Almost all its members were from the middle class, and nearly all were **Jacobins** (JAK-uh-bin)—the most uncompromising democrats. Deep political differences, however, separated moderate Jacobins—called "Girondists (juh-RON-dist)," after a region in southern France—and radicals known as "the Mountain." Members of the Mountain—so named because their seats were on the highest level in the assembly hall—were more sympathetic than the Girondists to the demands of the Parisian working class and less patient with parliamentary procedure. **Maximilien Robespierre** (ROBES-pee-air), a young, little-known lawyer influenced by Rousseau's ideas, dominated the Mountain.

With the French economy in crisis and Paris suffering from inflation, high unemployment, and scarcity, Robespierre used the popular press and political clubs to forge an alliance with the volatile Parisian working class. His growing strength in the streets allowed him to purge and execute many of his enemies in the National Convention and to restructure the government. He placed executive power in the hands of the newly formed Committee of Public Safety, which created special courts to seek out and punish enemies of the Revolution.

Among the groups that lost influence were the active feminists of the Parisian middle class and the working-class women who had sought the right to bear arms in defense of the Revolution. These women had provided decisive leadership at crucial times, helping propel the Revolution toward widened suffrage and a more democratic structure. Armed women had actively participated in every confrontation with conservative forces. It is ironic that the National Convention—the revolutionary era's most radical legislative body—chose to repress the militant feminist forces that had prepared the ground for its creation.

Faced with rebellion in the provinces and foreign invasion, Robespierre and his allies unleashed a period of repression called the Reign of Terror (1793–1794). During the Terror, executions and deaths in prison claimed 40,000 lives while another 300,000 suffered imprisonment. In the Vendée region as many as 170,000 died as the government in Paris asserted control. One general stated, "I crushed the children under the feet of the horses, massacred the women who, at least for these,

ENVIRONMENT + TECHNOLOGY

The Guillotine

No machine more powerfully symbolizes the revolutionary era than the guillotine. The machine immortalizes Joseph Ignace Guillotin (1738–1814), a physician and member of the French Constituent Assembly. In 1789, Guillotin recommended that executions be made more humane by use of a beheading device. He sought to replace hangings, used for commoners, and beheadings by axe, used for the nobility. Both forms of execution were often conducted with little skill, leading to gruesome and painful deaths. Guillotin believed that a properly designed machine would produce predictable, nearly painless deaths and remove the social distinction between commoners and nobles, seen as embarrassing in a more egalitarian age.

After 1791 execution by beheading became the common sentence for all capital crimes. Another physician, Antoine Louis, secretary of the College of Surgeons, designed the actual machine. Once directed to produce a suitable device, Louis, in many ways a typical technician of his time, systematically examined devices used elsewhere and experimented until satisfied with his results. Praised by contemporaries because it seemed to remove human agency, and therefore revenge, from the death penalty, the guillotine became the physical symbol of the Terror.

The Guillotine *The guillotine, introduced as a more humane and democratic alternative to traditional executions, came to symbolize the arbitrary violence of the French Revolution. In this contemporary cartoon Robespierre, the architect of the Terror, serves as executioner while surrounded by guillotines.*

The Art Archive

will not give birth to any more brigands. I do not have a prisoner to reproach me. I have exterminated all."[2]

The revolutionary government also took new actions against the clergy as well, including the provocative measure of forcing priests to marry. Even time was subject to revolutionary change. A new republican calendar created twelve 30-day months divided into 10-day weeks. Sunday, with its Christian meanings, was removed from this revolutionary calendar.

By spring 1794 the Revolution was secure from foreign and domestic enemies, but repression continued. Among the victims were some of Robespierre's closest political collaborators during the Terror. The execution of these former allies prepared the way for Robespierre's own fall by undermining the sense of invulnerability that had secured the loyalty of his remaining partisans. After French victories eliminated the immediate foreign threat in 1794, conservatives in the Convention voted to arrest Robespierre and then ordered his execution along with that of nearly a hundred of his allies in July.

Reaction and the Rise of Napoleon, 1795–1815   Purged of Robespierre's collaborators, the Convention began to undo the radical reforms. It removed emergency economic controls that held down prices and protected the working class. Gone also was toleration for violent popular demonstrations. When the Paris working class rose in protest in 1795, the Convention reacted with overwhelming military force. It allowed the Catholic Church to regain much of its former influence, but it did not return the church's confiscated wealth. It also put in place a more conservative constitution that protected property, established a voting process that reduced the power of the masses, and created a new executive authority, the Directory.

After losing the election of 1797, the Directory refused to give up power, effectively ending the republican phase of the Revolution. Political authority now depended on coercive force rather than elections. Two years later, a brilliant young general in the French army, **Napoleon Bonaparte** (1769–1821), seized power. Just as the American and French Revolutions had been the start of the modern democratic tradition, the military intervention that brought Napoleon to power in 1799 marked the advent of another modern form of government: popular authoritarianism.

The American and French Revolutions resulted in part from conflicts over representation. If the people were sovereign, what institutions best expressed popular will? In the United States the answer was the expansion of the right to vote and creation of representative institutions. The French Revolution took a different direction with the Reign of Terror. Interventions on the floor of the National Convention by market women and soldiers, the presence of common people at revolutionary tribunals and at public executions, and the expansion of military service were all forms of political communication that temporarily satisfied the French people's desire to influence their government. Napoleon tamed these forms of political expression to organize Europe's

---

[2] Quoted in David A. Bell, *The First Total War: Napoleon's Europe and the Birth of Warfare as We Know It* (Boston: Houghton Mifflin, 2007), 173.

Playing Cards from the French Revolution *Even playing cards could be used to attack the aristocracy and Catholic Church. In this pack of cards, "Equality" and "Liberty" replaced kings and queens.*

New Playing card designs dating from the French Revolution, 1793 (coloured engraving), French School, (18th century)/Private Collection/Archives Charmet/The Bridgeman Art Library

first popular dictatorship. He succeeded because his military reputation promised order to a society exhausted by a decade of crisis, turmoil, and bloodshed.

Napoleon sought to realize France's dream of dominating Europe while providing effective protection for persons and property at home. Negotiations with the Catholic Church led to the Concordat of 1801. This agreement gave French Catholics the right to freely practice their religion, but it also recognized the French government's authority to nominate bishops and retain priests on the state payroll. In his comprehensive rewriting of French law, the Civil Code of 1804, Napoleon won the support of the peasantry and the middle class by asserting two basic principles inherited from the moderate first stage of the French Revolution: equality in law and protection of property. Some members of the nobility were won over when Napoleon declared himself emperor and France an empire in 1804. Despite his willingness to make dramatic changes, however, Napoleon continued the denial of political rights for women begun during the Terror. The Civil Code denied women basic political rights and only allowed them to participate in the economy with the guidance and supervision of fathers and husbands.

While it re-established order, the Napoleonic system denied or restricted many individual rights. Free speech was limited. Criticism of the government, viewed as subversive, was proscribed, and most opposition newspapers disappeared. Spies and informers directed by the minister of police enforced these draconian policies.

Ultimately, the Napoleonic system depended on the success of French arms. From Napoleon's assumption of power until his fall, no single European state could defeat the French military. Austria and Prussia suffered humiliating defeats and became allies of France. Only Britain, protected by its powerful navy, remained able to thwart Napoleon's plans to dominate Europe.

Desiring to again extend French power to the Americas, Napoleon invaded Portugal in 1807 and Spain in 1808. Despite early French victories, Spanish and

Portuguese patriots supported by Great Britain eventually tied French armies down in a costly conflict. Frustrated by events on the Iberian Peninsula and faced with a faltering economy, Napoleon made the fateful decision to invade Russia. In June 1812, he began his campaign with the largest army ever assembled in Europe, approximately 600,000 men. His army took Moscow but after five weeks abandoned the city. During the retreat, the brutal Russian winter and attacks by Russian forces destroyed Napoleon's army. A broken and battered remnant of 30,000 men made it back to France.

After the debacle in Russia, Austria and Prussia deserted Napoleon and entered an alliance with England and Russia against France. Unable to defend Paris, Napoleon abdicated the throne in April 1814 and was exiled to the island of Elba off the coast of Italy. The victorious allies then restored the French monarchy. The following year Napoleon escaped from Elba and returned to France, but an allied army defeated his forces in 1815 at Waterloo, in Belgium. His final exile was on the distant island of St. Helena in the South Atlantic, where he died in 1821.

REVOLUTION SPREADS, CONSERVATIVES RESPOND, 1789–1850

Even as the dictatorship of Napoleon tamed the democratic legacy of the French Revolution, revolutionary ideology was spreading and taking hold in Europe and the Americas. In Europe the French Revolution promoted nationalism and republicanism. In the Americas the legacies of the American and French Revolutions led to a new round of struggles for independence. News of revolutionary events in France destabilized the colonial regime in Saint Domingue (present-day Haiti), a small French colony on the western half of the island of Hispaniola, and helped initiate the first successful slave rebellion. In Europe, however, the spread of revolutionary fervor was met by the concerted reaction of an alliance of conservative monarchs committed to extinguishing further revolutionary outbreaks.

The Haitian Revolution, 1789–1804
In 1789, the French colony of Saint Domingue was among the richest colonies in the Americas. Its production of sugar, cotton, indigo, and coffee accounted for two-thirds of France's tropical imports and generated nearly one-third of all French foreign trade. This wealth depended on a brutal slave regime. The harsh punishments and poor living conditions experienced by Saint Domingue's slaves were notorious throughout the Caribbean. The resulting high mortality and low fertility rates created an insatiable demand for African slaves. As a result, in 1790 the majority of the colony's 500,000 slaves were African-born.

When news of the meeting of the Estates General arrived on the island in 1789, wealthy planters sent a delegation to Paris to seek more home rule and greater economic freedom for Saint Domingue. The free mixed-race population, the **gens de couleur** (zhahn deh koo-LUHR), also sent representatives. Representing a large class of free black planters and urban merchants who owned slaves, they sought political rights and a limit to race discrimination, not an end to slavery. As the French Revolution became more radical, the gens de couleur forged an alliance with sympathetic French radicals, who saw the colony's wealthy planters as royalists and aristocrats.

© Cengage Learning

MAP 23.1 Napoleon's Europe, 1810

By 1810, Great Britain was the only remaining European power at war with Napoleon. Because of the loss of the French fleet at the Battle of Trafalgar in 1805, Napoleon was unable to threaten Britain with invasion, and Britain was able to actively assist the resistance movements in Spain and Portugal, thereby helping weaken French power.

The political turmoil in France weakened the authority of colonial administrators in Saint Domingue. In the vacuum that resulted, rich planters, poor whites, and the gens de couleur all pursued their narrow interests, engendering an increasingly bitter and confrontational struggle. Given the slaves' hatred of the brutal regime that oppressed them and the accumulated grievances of the free people of color, there was no way to limit the violence once the control of the slave owners slipped. When Vincent Ogé (oh-ZHAY), a leader of the gens de couleur mission to France, returned to Saint Domingue in 1790, the planters captured him and ordered his torture and execution. The free black and slave populations soon repaid this cruelty in kind.

By 1791 whites, led by the planter elite, and the gens de couleur were engaged in open warfare. This conflict was transformed when a slave rebellion began on the plantations of the north. Rebelling slaves destroyed plantations, killed masters and overseers, and burned crops. A leadership emerged among the rebellious slaves that relied on elements of African political practice and revolutionary ideology from France to mobilize and direct their supporters. With the colony in flames, the French Assembly finally granted political rights to the gens de couleur in April 1792.

The rebellious slaves gained the upper hand under the command of **François Dominique Toussaint L'Ouverture**, a former domestic slave, who created a disciplined military force. While some French radicals had attacked the institution of slavery from the early days of the Revolution, the radical National Convention in Paris only abolished slavery in all French possessions in 1794. This was not narrowly the triumph of idealism over greed. With France at war with Britain and other European powers and Saint Domingue threatened by a British military force, the French government realized that its control of its colony could only be salvaged by acknowledging Toussaint's political and military dominance. Legitimized by the French government's decision, Toussaint swept aside his local rivals, defeated the British expeditionary force in 1798, and then led an invasion of the neighboring Spanish colony of Santo Domingo, freeing slaves there. While Toussaint asserted his loyalty to France, he gave the French government no effective role in local affairs.

As reaction overtook revolution in France, both the abolition of slavery and Toussaint's political position were threatened. When the Directory contemplated the re-establishment of slavery, Toussaint protested:

> Do they think that men who have been able to enjoy the blessing of liberty will calmly see it snatched away? They supported their chains only so long as they did not know any condition of life more happy than slavery. But today when they have left it, if they had a thousand lives they would sacrifice them all rather than be forced into slavery again.[3]

In 1802, Napoleon sent a large military force to re-establish both French colonial authority and slavery in Saint Domingue, as well as in Guadeloupe. At first French forces were successful, capturing Toussaint and sending him to France, where he died in prison. Eventually, however, the loss of thousands of lives to yellow fever and the resistance of the revolutionaries turned the tide. In 1804

---

[3] Quoted in C. L. R. James, *The Black Jacobins*, 2d ed. (New York: Vintage Books, 1963), 196.

Toussaint's successors declared independence, and the free republic of Haiti joined the United States as the second independent nation in the Western Hemisphere.

The Congress of Vienna and Conservative Retrenchment, 1815–1820

In 1814–1815 representatives of Britain, Russia, Austria, Prussia, and other European nations met as the **Congress of Vienna** to re-establish political order in Europe. The French Revolution and Napoleon's imperial ambitions had threatened the survival of Europe's old order. The very existence of the nobility and church had seemed at risk at the height of the revolutionary era. Ancient monarchies had been overturned and dynasties had been replaced with interlopers, often relatives of Napoleon. International borders were redrawn or ignored, while long-established political institutions were threatened or overturned. Responding to more than two decades of revolution and war, the Austrian foreign minister, Prince Klemens von Metternich (MET-uhr-nik) (1773–1859), provided key leadership as the victorious allies sought to create a comprehensive peace settlement that would safeguard the conservative order.

The central objective of the Congress of Vienna was to create a strong and stable France as the best guarantee of future peace. To this end it re-established the French monarchy and recognized France's 1792 borders, although most of the allies received some territorial gains. Metternich believed that a strong and stable France had to be offset by a balance of power. Austria, Russia, and Prussia therefore formed a separate alliance to repress revolutionary and nationalist movements that sought to imitate the French Revolution. In 1820 this "Holy Alliance" used military force to defeat liberal revolutions in Spain and Italy. The Holy Alliance also attempted to blunt the force of revolutionary ideas by repressing republican and nationalist ideas in universities and the press.

Nationalism, Reform, and Revolution, 1821–1850

While Metternich's program of conservative retrenchment succeeded in the short term, the powerful ideas associated with liberalism and nationalism remained a vital part of European political life throughout the nineteenth century. Despite the power of the conservative monarchs, popular support for national self-determination and democratic reform grew throughout Europe.

Greece had been under Ottoman control since the fifteenth century. In 1821 Greek patriots launched an independence movement. While Metternich and other conservatives opposed Greek independence, European artists and writers enamored with the cultural legacy of ancient Greece rallied political support for intervention. After years of struggle, Russia, France, and Great Britain forced the Ottoman Empire to recognize Greek independence in 1830.

In 1814 the victorious allies placed Louis XVIII, brother of the executed Louis XVI, on the throne of France. Unlike his ancestors, he ruled as a constitutional monarch until his death in 1824, when his brother, the conservative Charles X, inherited the throne. In 1830 Charles decided to repudiate the constitution, provoking a mass uprising in Paris that forced him to abdicate. The crown then went to the king's cousin, Louis Philippe (loo-EE fee-LEEP) (r. 1830–1848), who agreed to accept the constitution and extended voting privileges.

Revolutionary violence in France made the British aristocracy and the conservative Tory Party fearful of democracy and mass movements of any kind. In 1815 the British government passed the Corn Laws, which limited the importation of foreign grains. The laws favored the profits of wealthy landowners who produced grain, rather than the poor who would now be forced to pay more for their bread. When poor consumers organized to overturn these laws, the government outlawed public meetings and used troops to crush protest in Manchester. Reacting against these policies, English reformers increased the power of the House of Commons, redistributed votes from agricultural to industrial districts, and increased the number of voters by nearly 50 percent. Although the most radical demands of reformers, called Chartists, were defeated, new labor and economic reforms addressing the grievances of workers were put in place (see Chapter 22).

Despite the achievement of Greek independence and limited political reform in France and Great Britain, conservatives continued to hold the upper hand. In 1848, the desire for democratic reform and national self-determination led to upheavals across Europe. The **Revolutions of 1848** began in Paris, where members of the middle class and workers united to overthrow the regime of Louis Philippe and create the Second French Republic. Reformers gave adult men voting rights, abolished slavery in French colonies, ended the death penalty, and legislated the ten-hour workday. But Parisian workers' demands for programs to reduce unemployment and prices provoked conflicts with the middle class, which wanted to protect property rights. When workers rose up against the government, French troops crushed them. Desiring the re-establishment of order, the French elected Louis Napoleon, nephew of the former emperor, president in December 1848. Three years later, he overturned the constitution and, after ruling briefly as dictator, proclaimed himself Emperor Napoleon III.

In 1848, reformers in Hungary, Italy, Bohemia, and elsewhere pressed for greater national self-determination from the Austro-Hungarian Empire. When the monarchy did not meet their demands, students and workers in Vienna took to the streets to force political reforms similar to those sought in Paris. With revolution spreading throughout the empire, Metternich, the symbol of reaction, fled Vienna in disguise. Little lasting change occurred, however, because the new Austrian emperor, Franz Joseph (r. 1848–1916), used Russian military assistance and loyal Austrian troops to re-establish his authority.

Similarly, middle-class reformers and workers in Berlin joined forces to force the Prussian king to accept a liberal constitution and seek German unification. But the Constituent Assembly called to write a constitution and negotiate national integration was diverted to deal with diplomatic conflicts with Austria and Denmark. As a result, Frederick William IV (r. 1840–1861) reasserted his authority and thwarted constitutional reform and unification.

Despite their heroism on the barricades of Paris, Vienna, Rome, and Berlin, the revolutionaries of 1848 failed to gain their nationalist and republican objectives. Monarchs retained the support not only of aristocrats but also of professional militaries, largely recruited from among peasants who had little sympathy for urban workers. Revolutionary coalitions, in contrast, proved fragile, as when workers' demands for higher wages and labor reform drove their middle-class allies into the arms of the reactionaries.

CONCLUSION

The last decades of the eighteenth century began a long period of revolutionary upheaval in the Atlantic world. Costly wars in Europe and along Europe's colonial frontiers in the Americas and Asia helped to provoke change, forcing European monarchs to impose new and unpopular taxes. The American Revolution initiated these transformations. Having defeated Britain, the citizens of this new American republic created the most democratic government of the time. While full rights were limited and slavery persisted, many Europeans saw this experiment as demonstrating the efficacy of the Enlightenment's most revolutionary political ideas. In the end, however, the compromises over slavery that had made a new Constitution possible in 1787 failed, and, as discussed in Chapter 25, the new nation nearly disintegrated after 1860.

The French Revolution led temporarily to a more radical formulation of representative democracy, but it also led to the Terror, which cost tens of thousands of lives, the militarization of western Europe, and a destructive cycle of wars. Yet, despite these terrible costs, the French Revolution propelled the idea of democracy and the ideal of equality far beyond the boundaries established by the American Revolution. The Haitian Revolution, set in motion by events in France, not only created the second independent nation of the Western Hemisphere but also delivered a powerful blow to the institution of slavery. In Europe, the excesses of the French Revolution and the wars that followed in its wake promoted the political ascent of Napoleon Bonaparte and democracy's modern nemesis, popular authoritarianism.

Each revolution had its own character. The revolutions in France and Haiti proved to be more violent and destructive than the American Revolution. American revolutionaries defeated Great Britain and established independence without overturning a colonial social and political order that depended on slavery in most of the southern colonies. Revolutionaries in France and Haiti faced more strongly entrenched and more powerful oppositions as well as greater social inequalities than American revolutionaries. The resistance of entrenched and privileged elites led inexorably to greater violence. Both French and Haitian revolutionaries also faced powerful foreign interventions that intensified the bloodshed and destructiveness of these revolutions.

The conservative retrenchment that followed the defeat of Napoleon succeeded in the short term. Monarchy, multinational empires, and the established church retained the loyalty of millions of Europeans and could count on the support of many of Europe's wealthiest and most powerful individuals. But liberalism and nationalism continued to stir revolutionary sentiment. The contest between adherents of the old order and partisans of change was to continue well into the nineteenth century. In the end, the nation-state, the Enlightenment legacy of rational inquiry, broadened political participation, and secular intellectual culture prevailed. This outcome was determined in large measure by the old order's inability to satisfy the demands of new social classes tied to an emerging industrial economy. The narrow confines of a hereditary social system could not contain the material transformations generated by industrial capitalism, and the doctrines of traditional religion could not contain the rapid expansion of scientific learning.

These revolutions began the transformation of Western society, but they did not complete it. Only a minority gained full political rights. Women did not achieve full political rights until the twentieth century. Democratic institutions, as in revolutionary France, often failed. Moreover, as Chapter 25 discusses, slavery endured in the Americas past the mid-1800s, despite the revolutionary era's enthusiasm for individual liberty.

IMPORTANT EVENTS 1750–1850	
1754–1763	French and Indian War
1756–1763	Seven Years War
1770	Boston Massacre
1776	American Declaration of Independence
1778	United States alliance with France
1778	Death of Voltaire and Rousseau
1781	British surrender at Yorktown
1783	Treaty of Paris ends American Revolution
1789	Storming of Bastille begins French Revolution; Declaration of Rights of Man and Citizen in France
1791	Slaves revolt in Saint Domingue (Haiti)
1793–1794	Reign of Terror in France
1795–1799	The Directory rules France
1798	Toussaint L'Ouverture defeats British in Haiti
1799	Napoleon overthrows the Directory
1804	Haitians defeat French invasion and declare independence
1804	Napoleon crowns himself emperor
1814	Napoleon abdicates; Congress of Vienna opens
1815	Napoleon defeated at Waterloo
1830	Greece gains independence; revolution in France overthrows Charles X
1848	Revolutions in France, Austria, Germany, Hungary, and Italy

24

LAND EMPIRES IN THE AGE OF IMPERIALISM, 1800–1870

During the late 1860s, a little-known warlord named Yaqub Beg unified several Muslim uprisings in Central Asia against a foreign occupier, the Qing Empire. Only a hundred years earlier, in 1759, Qing armies had successfully conquered a vast region of Central Asia and called it Xinjiang, meaning "new territory." Despite attempts to work with local leaders, tensions between locals and Chinese never eased, and the natives rebelled.

Yaqub took full diplomatic advantage of the empires surrounding him. To his south lay India, under control of an expanding British Empire. To his north was the Russian Empire, Britain's rival in the quest to gain territory in Central Asia. Yaqub sent emissaries to both empires in 1868 and signed commercial treaties in 1872 in exchange for their recognition of his rule over Xinjiang. He even received military support from the distant Ottoman Empire, whose ruler bestowed upon him the title *Commander of the Faithful.* For a time it seemed that the Qing might not try to retake Xinjiang. It would be an expensive venture for a government that was looking to spend money modernizing its army and navy. But fears that Russia might take over neighboring Mongolia drove the Chinese back into Xinjiang, and Yaqub's regime collapsed in 1877.

Yaqub's story illustrates the challenges facing Eurasian empires as they overextended themselves. The largest problem, common to all the land-based empires of Eurasia, was the old and inefficient ways of governing that put states at risk. While the international climate was increasingly dominated by industrializing European economies drawing on the wealth of their overseas colonies, during the early 1800s rapid population growth and slow agricultural growth affected much of Eurasia. In addition, earlier military expansion had stretched the resources of imperial treasuries (see Chapter 21), leaving the land-based empires vulnerable to European military pressure. Responses to this pressure varied, with reform and adaptation gaining headway in some lands and tradition being reasserted in others. In the long run, attempts to meet western Europe's economic and political demands produced financial indebtedness to France, Britain, and other Western powers.

This chapter contrasts the experiences of the Qing Empire with those of the Russian and Ottoman Empires. Whereas the Qing opted for resistance, the others made varying attempts to adapt and reform. Russia eventually became part of Europe and shared in many aspects of European culture, while the Ottomans and the Qing became subject to ever-greater imperialist pressure. These different responses raise the question of the role of culture in shaping western Europe's relations with the rest of the world in the nineteenth century.

THE OTTOMAN EMPIRE

During the eighteenth century the central government of the Ottoman Empire lost much of its power to provincial governors, military commanders, ethnic leaders, and bandit chiefs. In several parts of the empire local officials and large landholders tried to increase their independence and divert imperial funds into their own coffers.

A kingdom in Arabia led by the Saud family, following the puritanical and fundamentalist religious views of an eighteenth-century leader named Muhammad ibn Abd al-Wahhab (moo-HAH-muhd ib-uhn ab-dahl-wa-HAHB), took control of the holy cities of Mecca and Medina and deprived the sultan of the honor of organizing the annual pilgrimage. Meanwhile, in Egypt factions of mamluk slave-soldiers purchased as boys in Georgia and nearby parts of the Caucasus and educated for war reasserted their influence. Such soldiers had ruled Egypt between 1260 and 1517, when they were defeated by the Ottomans. Now Ottoman weakness allowed mamluk factions based on a revival of the slave-soldier tradition to re-emerge as local military forces.

For the sultans, the outlook was bleak. At the end of the eighteenth century, the inefficient Janissary corps used the political power it enjoyed in Istanbul to force Sultan Selim III to abandon efforts to train a modern, European-style army. This situation unexpectedly changed when France invaded Egypt.

Egypt and the Napoleonic Example   Napoleon Bonaparte and an invasion force of 36,000 men and four hundred ships invaded Egypt in May 1798. The French quickly defeated the mamluk forces that for several decades had dominated the country under the loose jurisdiction of the Ottoman sultan in Istanbul. Fifteen months later, after being stopped by Ottoman land and British naval forces in an attempted invasion of Syria, Napoleon secretly left Cairo and returned to France. Three months later he seized power and made himself emperor.

Back in Egypt, his generals tried to administer a country that they only poorly understood. Cut off from France by British ships in the Mediterranean, they had little hope of remaining in power and agreed to withdraw in 1801. For the second time in three years, a collapse of military power produced a power vacuum in Egypt. The winner of the ensuing contest was **Muhammad Ali** (moo-HAM-mad AH-lee), the commander of a contingent of Albanian soldiers sent by the sultan to restore imperial control. By 1805 he had taken the place of the official Ottoman governor, and by 1811 he had dispossessed the mamluks of their lands and privileges.

Muhammad Ali's rise to power coincided with the meteoric career of Emperor Napoleon I. It is not surprising, therefore, that he adopted many French practices in rebuilding the Egyptian state. Militarily, he established special schools for training artillery and cavalry officers, army surgeons, military bandmasters, and others. The curricula of these schools featured European skills and sciences, and Muhammad Ali began to send promising officer trainees to France for education. In 1824 he started a gazette devoted to official affairs, the first newspaper in the Islamic world.

As discussed in Chapter 22, Muhammad Ali built all sorts of factories to outfit his new army. These did not prove efficient enough to survive, but they showed a determination to achieve independence and parity with the European powers.

In the 1830s Muhammad Ali's son Ibrahim invaded Syria and instituted some of the changes already under way in Egypt. The improved quality of the new Egyptian army had been proven during the Greek war of independence (see below), when Ibrahim had commanded an expeditionary force to help the sultan. In response, the sultan embarked on building his own new army in 1826. The two armies met when Ibrahim attacked northward into Anatolia in 1839 and defeated the army of his suzerain, the Ottoman sultan. The road to Istanbul seemed open until the European powers intervened and forced a withdrawal to the present-day border between Egypt and Israel.

Muhammad Ali remained Egypt's ruler, under the suzerainty of the sultan, until his death in 1849; and his family continued to rule the country until 1952. But his dream of making Egypt a mighty country capable of standing up to Europe faded. What survived was the example he had set for the sultans in Istanbul.

Ottoman Reform and the European Model, 1807–1853   At the end of the eighteenth century Sultan Selim (seh-LEEM) III (r. 1789–1807), a forward-looking ruler who stayed abreast of events in Europe, introduced reforms to create European-style military units, bring provincial governors under central government control, and standardize taxation. The rise in government expenditures to implement the reforms was supposed to be offset by taxes on selected items, primarily tobacco and coffee.

The reforms failed for political more than economic reasons. The most violent and persistent opposition came from the **Janissary** (JAN-nih-say-ree) military corps (see Chapter 20). In the eighteenth century the Janissaries became a significant political force in Istanbul and in provincial capitals like Damascus and Aleppo. Their interest in preserving special economic privileges made them resist the creation of new military units.

At times, Janissary power produced military uprisings. In the Ottoman territory of **Serbia**, local residents intensely resented the control exercised by Janissary governors. The Orthodox Christians claimed that the Janissaries abused them. In response, Selim threatened to reassign the Janissaries to Istanbul. Suspecting that the sultan wanted to curb their political power, in 1805 the Janissaries revolted and massacred Christians in Serbia. Unable to re-establish central Ottoman rule over Serbia, the sultan had to rely on the ruler of Bosnia, another Balkan province, who joined his troops with the peasants of Serbia to suppress the Janissary uprising. The threat of Russian intervention prevented the Ottomans from disarming the victorious Serbians, so Serbia became effectively independent.

Other opponents of reform included ulama, or Muslim religious scholars, who distrusted the secularization of law and taxation that Selim proposed. In the face of widespread rejection of his reforms, Selim suspended his program in 1806. Nevertheless, a massive military uprising occurred at Istanbul, and the sultan was deposed and imprisoned. Reform forces recaptured the capital, but not before Selim had been executed.

Selim's cousin, Sultan Mahmud (mah-MOOD) II (r. 1808–1839), cautiously revived Selim's program, but he realized that reforms needed to be more systematic and imposed more forcefully. The effectiveness of radical reform in Muhammad Ali's Egypt drove this lesson home, as did the insurrection in Greece, during which the Egyptian military performed much better than the main Ottoman army.

Greek independence in 1830 had dramatic international significance. A combination of Greek nationalist organizations and interlopers from Albania formed the independence movement. Europe's interest in the classical age of Greece and Rome led many Europeans to consider the Greeks' struggle for independence a campaign to recapture their classical glory from Muslim oppression. Some—including the "mad, bad and dangerous to know" English poet Lord Byron, who lost his life in the war—went to Greece to fight as volunteers. When the combined squadrons of the British, French, and Russian fleets, under orders to observe but not intervene in the war, made an unauthorized attack that sank the Ottoman fleet at the Battle of Navarino, Greek victory was assured.

Mahmud II concurred with the pro-Greek Europeans in viewing Ottoman military reversals in Greece as a sign of profound weakness. With popular outrage over the military setbacks strong, the sultan made his move in 1826. First he announced the creation of a new artillery unit, which he had secretly been training. When the Janissaries rose in revolt, he ordered the new unit to bombard the Janissary barracks. The Janissary corps was officially dissolved.

Like Muhammad Ali, Mahmud felt he could not implement major changes without reducing the political power of the religious elite. He visualized restructuring the bureaucracy and the educational and legal systems, where ulama power was strongest. Before such strong measures could be undertaken, however, Ibrahim attacked from Syria in 1839. Battlefield defeat, the decision of the rebuilt Ottoman navy to switch sides and support Egypt, and the death of Mahmud, all in the same year, left the empire completely dependent on the European powers for survival.

Mahmud's reforming ideas received their widest expression in the **Tanzimat** (TAHNZ-ee-MAT) ("reorganization"), a series of reforms announced by his sixteen-year-old son and successor, Abdul Mejid (ab-dul meh-JEED), in 1839 and strongly endorsed by the European ambassadors. One proclamation called for public trials and equal protection under the law for all, whether Muslim, Christian, or Jew. It also guaranteed some rights of privacy, equalized the eligibility of men for conscription into the army (a practice copied from Egypt), and provided for a new, formalized method of tax collection that legally ended tax farming in the Ottoman Empire. It took many years and strenuous efforts by reforming bureaucrats, known as the "men of the Tanzimat," to give substance to these reforms.

Over time, one legal code after another—commercial, criminal, civil procedure—was introduced to take the place of the corresponding areas of religious legal jurisdiction. All the codes were modeled closely on those of Europe. The Shari'a, or Islamic law, gradually became restricted to matters of family law such as marriage and inheritance. As the Shari'a was displaced, job opportunities for the ulama shrank.

European observers praised the reforms for their noble principles and rejection of religious influence. Ottoman citizens were more divided; the Christians and Jews, for whom the Europeans showed the greatest concern, were generally more enthusiastic than the Muslims. Many historians see the Tanzimat as the dawn of modern

© Cengage Learning

MAP 24.1   The Ottoman and Russian Empires, 1829–1914

At its height the Ottoman Empire controlled most of the perimeter of the Mediterranean Sea. But in the 1800s Ottoman territory shrank as many countries gained their independence. The Black Sea, where the Turkish coast was vulnerable to assault, became a weak spot as Russian naval power grew. Russian challenges to the Ottomans at the eastern end of the Black Sea and to the Persians east and west of the Caspian aroused fears in Europe that Russia was trying to reach the Indian Ocean.

thought and enlightened government in the Middle East. Others point out that removing the religious elite from influence in government also removed the one remaining check on authoritarian rule.

Like Muhammad Ali, Sultan Mahmud sent military cadets to France and the German states for training. In the 1830s an Ottoman imperial school of military sciences, later to become Istanbul University, was established in which instructors from western Europe taught chemistry, engineering, mathematics, and physics in addition to military history. Military education became the model for more general educational reforms. In 1838 the first medical school was established to train army doctors and surgeons. Later, a national system of preparatory schools was created to feed graduates into the military schools. The subjects that were taught and many of the teachers were foreign, raising the issue of whether Turkish should be a language of instruction. Because it was easier to import and use foreign textbooks than to write new ones in Turkish, French became the preferred language in all advanced professional and scientific training. In numerical terms, however, the great majority of students still learned to read and write in Quran schools down to the twentieth century.

In the capital city of Istanbul, the reforms stimulated the growth of a small but cosmopolitan milieu embracing European language and culture. The first Turkish newspaper, a government gazette modeled on that of Muhammad Ali, appeared in 1831. Other newspapers followed, many written in French. Travel to Europe—particularly to England and France—became popular among wealthy Turks. Interest in importing European military, industrial, and communications technology remained strong through the 1800s.

Changes in military practice had unforeseen cultural and social effects. Accepting the European notion that modern weapons and drill required modern military dress, beards were deemed unhygienic and, in artillery units, a fire hazard. Military headgear also became controversial. European military caps, which had leather bills on the front to protect against the glare of the sun, were not acceptable because they interfered with Muslim soldiers' touching their foreheads to the ground in prayer. The compromise was the brimless cap now called the *fez*, which was adopted by the military and then by Ottoman civil officials in the early years of Mahmud II's reign.

The empire's new orientation spread beyond the military. Government ministries that normally recruited from traditional bureaucratic families and relied on on-the-job training were gradually transformed into formal civil services hiring men educated in the new schools. Among self-consciously progressive men, particularly those in government service, European dress became the fashion in the Ottoman cities of the later 1800s, while traditional dress became a symbol of the religious, the rural, and the parochial.

Secularization of the legal code particularly affected non-Muslim Ottoman subjects. Islamic law had required non-Muslims to pay a special head tax that was sometimes explained as a substitute for military service. Under the Tanzimat, the tax was abolished and non-Muslims became liable for military service—unless they bought their way out by paying a new military exemption tax. The new law codes gave all male subjects equal access to the civil courts, while the operations of the Islamic law courts shrank. What enhanced the status of non-Muslims most, however, was the strong concern for their welfare consistently expressed by the European powers. The Ottoman Empire became a rich field of operation for

Christian missionaries and European supporters of Jewish community life in the Muslim world.

The public rights and political participation granted during the Tanzimat applied specifically to men. Private life, including everything connected to marriage and divorce, remained within the sphere of religious law, and at no time was there a question of political participation or reformed education for women. Indeed, the reforms may have decreased the influence of women. The political changes ran parallel to economic changes that also narrowed women's opportunities.

After silver from the Americas began to flood the empire in the 1600s, workers were increasingly paid in cash rather than in goods, and businesses associated with banking and finance developed. But women were barred from the early industrial labor and the professions, and traditional "woman's work" such as weaving was increasingly mechanized and done by men.

Nevertheless, in the early 1800s women retained considerable power in the management and disposal of their own property, gained mostly through fixed shares of inheritance. After marriage a woman was often pressured to convert her landholdings to cash in order to transfer her personal wealth to her husband's family, with whom she and her husband would reside. However, this was not a requirement, since men were legally obligated to support their families single-handedly. Until the 1820s many wealthy women retained their say in the distribution of property through the creation of charitable trusts for their offspring. Because these trusts were set up in the religious courts, they could be designed to conform to the wishes

From Ignatius Mouradgea d'Ohsson, *Tableau General de l'Empire Ottoman*, large folio edition, Paris, 1787–1820, pl. 178, following p. 340

Interior of the Ottoman Financial Bureau *This engraving from the eighteenth century depicts the governing style of the Ottoman Empire before the era of westernizing reforms. By the end of the Tanzimat period in 1876, government offices and the costumes of officials looked much more like those in contemporary European capitals.*

Street Scene in Cairo *This engraving from Edward William Lane's influential travel book,* Account of the Manners and Customs of the Modern Egyptians Written in Egypt During the Years 1833–1835 *conveys the image of narrow lanes and small stores that became stock features of European thinking about Middle Eastern cities.*

From Edward William Lane, *The Manners and Customs of the Modern Egyptians* (London: J. M. D & Co. 1860)

of family members. Then, in the 1820s and 1830s the secularizing reforms of Mahmud II, which did not always produce happy results, transferred jurisdiction over the charitable trusts from religious courts to the state and ended women's control over this form of property.

The Crimean War and Its Aftermath   Since the reign of Peter the Great (r. 1689–1725), the Russian Empire had been attempting to expand southward at the Ottomans' expense (see the section on Russia and Asia). His successor, Catherine the Great (r. 1762–1796), had captured control of the north shore of the Black Sea by 1783, and by 1815 Russia had pried the Georgian region of the Caucasus away from the Ottomans. Moreover, the threat of Russian intervention had prevented the Ottomans from crushing Serbian independence. When Muhammad Ali's Egyptian army invaded Syria in 1833, Russia signed a treaty in support of the Ottomans. In return, the sultan recognized Russia's claim to being the protector of all of the empire's Orthodox subjects. This set the stage for an obscure dispute that resulted in war.

Bowing to British and French pressure, the sultan named France Protector of the Holy Sepulchre in Jerusalem in 1852. Russia protested, but the sultan held firm. So Russia invaded Ottoman territories in what is today Romania, and Britain and France went to war as allies of the sultan. The real causes of the war went beyond church quarrels in Jerusalem and involved diplomatic maneuvering among European powers over whether the Ottoman Empire should continue to exist and, if not, who should take over its territory. The *Eastern Question* was the simple name given to this complex issue. Though the powers, including Russia, had agreed to save the empire in 1839, Britain subsequently became suspicious of Russian ambitions. Prominent anti-Russian politicians in Britain feared that Russia would threaten the British hold on India.

Between 1853 and 1856 the **Crimean** (cry-ME-uhn) **War** raged in Romania, on the Black Sea, and on the Crimean peninsula. Britain, France, and the Italian kingdom of Sardinia-Piedmont sided with the Ottomans. Britain and France trapped the Russian fleet in the Black Sea, where its commanders decided to sink the ships to protect the approaches to Sevastopol, their main base in Crimea. However, an army largely made up of British and French troops landed and laid siege to the city. Official corruption and lack of railways hampered the Russians' attempts to supply their forces. On the Romanian front, the Ottomans resisted effectively. At Sevastopol, the Russians were outmatched militarily and suffered badly from disease. Tsar Nicholas died as defeat loomed, leaving his successor, Alexander II (r. 1855–1881), to sue for peace when Sevastopol finally fell three months later.

The Crimean War brought significant changes to all the combatants. The tsar and his government, already beset by demands for the reform of serfdom, education, and the military (discussed later), were further discredited. In Britain and France, the conflict was accompanied by massive propaganda campaigns. For the first time newspapers effectively mobilized public support for a war. British press accounts so glamorized British participation that the false impression has lingered that Ottoman troops played a negligible role in the conflict. At the time, however, British and French commanders noted the massive losses among Turkish troops in particular. The French press, dominant in Istanbul, promoted a sense of unity between Turkish and French society that continued to influence many aspects of Turkish urban culture.

The larger significance of the Crimean War was that it marked the transition from traditional to modern warfare. All the combatants had previously prided themselves on the use of highly trained cavalry to smash through the front lines of infantry. Cavalry coexisted with firearms until the early 1800s, primarily because early rifles were awkward to load and not very accurate. Cavalry could attack during the intervals between volleys. Then in the 1830s and 1840s, percussion caps that did away with pouring gunpowder into the barrel of a musket came into use. In Crimean War battles many cavalry units were destroyed by the rapid fire of rifles that loaded at the breech rather than down the barrel. That was the fate of the famed British Light Brigade, which was sent to relieve an Ottoman unit surrounded by Russian troops.

After the Crimean War, the Ottoman Empire increased its involvement with European commerce. The Ottoman imperial bank was founded in 1840, and a few years later currency reform pegged the value of Ottoman gold coins to the British pound. Sweeping changes in the 1850s expedited the creation of banks, insurance companies, and legal firms throughout the empire. Bustling trade also encouraged a migration from country to city between about 1850 and 1880. Many of the major cities of the empire—Istanbul, Damascus, Beirut, Alexandria,

Cairo—expanded. A small but influential urban professional class emerged, as did a considerable class of wage laborers. Other demographic shifts involved refugees from Poland and Hungary, where rivalry between the European powers and the Russian Empire caused political tension and sporadic warfare, and from Georgia and other parts of the Caucasus, where Russian expansion forced many Muslims to emigrate (discussed later).

However, commercial vigor and urbanization could not make up for declining revenues and the chronic insolvency and corruption of the imperial government. From the conclusion of the Crimean War in 1856 on, the Ottoman government became heavily dependent on foreign loans. In return it lowered tariffs to favor European imports and allowed European banks to open in Ottoman cities. Europeans living in Istanbul and other commercial centers enjoyed **extraterritoriality**, the right to be subject to their own laws and exempt from Ottoman jurisdiction.

As the result of these measures, imported goods multiplied, but—apart from tobacco and the Turkish opium that American traders took to China to compete against British opium from India—Anatolia produced few exports. As foreign debt grew, so did inflationary trends that left urban populations in a precarious position. By contrast, Egyptian cotton exports soared during the American Civil War, when American cotton exports plummeted; but the profits benefited Muhammad Ali's descendants, who had become the hereditary governors of Egypt, rather than the Ottoman government. The Suez Canal, which was partly financed by cotton profits, opened in 1869, and Cairo was redesigned and beautified. Eventually overexpenditure on such projects plunged Egypt into the same debt crisis that plagued the empire as a whole.

The decline of Ottoman power and prosperity had a strong impact on a group of well-educated young urban men who aspired to wealth and influence. They doubted that the empire's rulers and the Tanzimat officials who worked for them would ever stand up to European domination. Though lacking a sophisticated organization, these Young Ottomans (sometimes called Young Turks, though that term properly applies to a later movement) promoted a mixture of liberal ideas derived from Europe, national pride in Ottoman independence, and modernist views of Islam. Prominent Young Ottomans helped draft a constitution that was promulgated in 1876 by a new and as yet untried sultan, Abdul Hamid II. This apparent triumph of liberal reform was short-lived. With war against Russia again threatening in the Balkans in 1877, Abdul Hamid suspended the constitution and the parliament that had been elected that year. Though he ruthlessly opposed further political reforms, the Tanzimat programs of extending modern schooling, utilizing European military practices and advisers, and making the government bureaucracy more orderly continued during his reign.

THE RUSSIAN EMPIRE

In 1812, when Napoleon's march on Moscow ended in a disastrous retreat brought on more by what a later tsar called "Generals January and February" than by Russian military action, the European image of Russia changed. Just as Napoleon's withdrawal from Egypt led to Muhammad Ali briefly becoming a political power, so his withdrawal from Russia conferred status on Tsar Alexander I (r. 1801–1825). Conservative Europeans still saw Russia as alien, backward, and oppressive, but they acknowledged its immensity and potential and included the tsar in efforts to suppress revolutionary tendencies throughout Europe.

In several important respects Russia resembled the Ottoman Empire more than the conservative kingdoms of Europe whose autocratic practices it so staunchly supported. Socially dominated by nobles whose country estates were worked by unfree serfs, Russia had almost no middle class. Industry was still at the threshold of development by the standards of the rapidly industrializing European powers, though it was somewhat more dynamic than Ottoman industry. Like Egypt and the Ottoman Empire, Russia engaged in reforms from the top down under Alexander I, but when his conservative brother Nicholas I (r. 1825–1855) succeeded to the throne, iron discipline and suspicion of modern ideas took priority over reform.

Russia and Europe   In 1700 only three Russians out of a hundred lived in cities, two-thirds of them in Moscow alone. By the mid-1800s the town population had grown tenfold, though it still accounted for only 6 percent of the total because the territories of the tsars had grown greatly through wars and colonization (see Chapter 21). These figures demonstrate that, like the Ottoman Empire, Russia was an overwhelmingly agricultural land. However, it had poorer transportation than the Ottoman Empire, since many Ottoman cities were seaports. Both empires encompassed peoples speaking many different languages.

Well-engineered roads did not begin to appear until 1817, and steam navigation commenced on the Volga in 1843. Tsar Nicholas I built the first railroad from St. Petersburg, the Russian capital, to his summer palace in 1837. A few years later his commitment to strict discipline led him to insist that the trunk line from St. Petersburg to Moscow run in a perfectly straight line. American engineers, among them the father of the painter James McNeill Whistler, who learned to paint in St. Petersburg, oversaw the laying of track and built locomotive workshops. Industrialization projects depended heavily on foreign expertise. British engineers set up the textile mills that gave woolens and cottons a prominent place among Russia's industries.

Until the late nineteenth century the Russian government's interest in industry was limited. An industrial revolution required educated and independent-minded artisans and entrepreneurs, but Nicholas feared the spread of literacy and modern education—especially anything smacking of liberalism, socialism, or revolution—beyond the minimum needed to train the officer corps and the bureaucracy. He preferred serfs to factory workers, and he paid for imported industrial goods with exports of grain and timber.

Like Egypt and the Ottoman Empire, Russia aspired to Western-style economic development. But when France and Britain entered the Crimean War, they faced a Russian army equipped with obsolete weapons and bogged down by lack of transportation. At a time when European engineers were making major breakthroughs in loading cannon through an opening at the breech end, muzzle-loading artillery remained the Russian standard.

Yet in some ways Russia bore a closer resemblance to other European countries than the Ottoman Empire did. From the point of view of the French and the British, the Cyrillic alphabet and the Russian Orthodox form of Christianity seemed foreign, but they were not nearly as foreign as the Arabic alphabet and the Muslim faith. Britain and France feared Russia as a rival for power in the east, but they increasingly accepted Tsar Nicholas's view of the Ottoman Empire as "the sick man of Europe," capable of surviving only so long as the European powers permitted.

From the Russian point of view, kinship with western Europe was of questionable value. Westernizers, like the men of the Tanzimat in the Ottoman Empire, put their trust in technical advances and governmental reform. Opposing them were intellectuals known as **Slavophiles**, who considered the Orthodox faith, the solidity of peasant life, and the tsar's absolute rule to be the proper bases of Russian civilization. After Russia's humiliation in the Crimea, the Slavophile tendency gave rise to **Pan-Slavism**, a militant political doctrine advocating unity of all the Slavic peoples, including those living under Austrian and Ottoman rule.

On the diplomatic front, the tsar's inclusion as a major European ruler contrasted sharply with the sultan's exclusion. However, this did not prevent a powerful sense of Russophobia from developing in the West. Britain in particular saw Russia as a threat to India and despised the subjection of the serfs, who gained their freedom from Tsar Alexander II only in 1861, twenty-seven years after the British had abolished slavery. In addition, the passions generated by the Crimean War and its outcome affected the relations of Russia, Europe, and the Ottoman Empire for the remainder of the nineteenth century.

Russia and Asia   The Russian drive to the east in the eighteenth century brought the tsar's empire to the Pacific Ocean and the frontiers of China by century's end. In the nineteenth century Russian expansionism focused on the south. There the backwardness of the Russian military did not matter since the peoples they faced were even less industrialized and technologically advanced. In 1860, Russia established a military outpost on the Pacific coast that would eventually grow into the great naval port of Vladivostok, today Russia's most southerly city. In Central Asia the steppe lands of the Kazakh nomads came under Russian control early in the century, setting the stage for a confrontation with three Uzbek states farther south. They succumbed one by one, beginning in 1865, giving rise to the new province of Turkestan, with its capital at Tashkent in present-day Uzbekistan.

In the region of the Caucasus Mountains, the third area of southward expansion, Russia first took over Christian Georgia (1786), Muslim Azerbaijan (ah-zer-by-JAHN) (1801), and Christian Armenia (1813) before gobbling up the many small principalities in the heart of the mountains. Between 1829 and 1864 Dagestan, Chechnya (CHECH-nee-yah), Abkhazia (ab-KAH-zee-yah), and other regions that would one day gain political prominence after the breakup of the Soviet Union became parts of the Russian Empire.

The drive to the south intensified political friction with Russia's new neighbors: Qing China and Japan in the east, Iran on the Central Asian and Caucasus frontiers, and the Ottoman Empire at the eastern end of the Black Sea. In the latter two instances, Muslim refugees from the territories newly absorbed by Russia spread anti-Russian feelings, though some of them brought with them modern skills and ideas gained from exposure to Russian administration and education.

The Russian drive to the south added a new element to the Eastern Question. Many British statesmen and strategists reckoned that a warlike Russia would press on until it had conquered all the lands separating it from British India, a prospect that made them shudder, given India's enormous contribution to Britain's prosperity. The competition that ensued over which power would control southern Central Asia resulted in a standoff in Afghanistan, which became a buffer zone under the control of neither. In Iran, the standoff between the powers helped preserve the weak Qajar dynasty of shahs.

Cultural Trends   Unlike Egypt and the Ottoman Empire, which began to send students to Europe for training only in the nineteenth century, Russia had been in cultural contact with western Europe since the time of Peter the Great (r. 1689–1725). Members of the Russian court knew Western languages, and the tsars employed officials and advisers from Western countries. Peter had also enlisted the well-educated Ukrainian clerics who headed the Russian Orthodox Church to help spread a Western spirit of education. As a result, Alexander I's reforms met a more positive reception than those of Muhammad Ali and Mahmud II. However, his reforms promised more on paper than they brought about in practice. It took many years to develop a sufficient pool of trained bureaucrats to make the reforms effective.

Ironically, much of the opposition to Alexander's reforms came from well-established families that were not at all unfriendly to Western ideas. Their fear was that the new government bureaucrats, who often came from humbler social origins, would act as agents of imperial tyranny. This fear was realized during the conservative reign of Nicholas I in the same way that the Tanzimat-inspired bureaucracy of the Ottoman Empire served the despotic purposes of Sultan Abdul Hamid II after 1877. Individuals favoring more liberal reforms, including military officers who had served in western Europe, intellectuals who read Western political tracts,

Raising of the Alexander Monument in St. Petersburg *The death of Alexander I in 1825 brought to power his conservative brother Nicholas I. Yet Alexander remained a heroic figure for his resistance to Napoleon. This monument in Winter Palace Square was erected in 1829.*

Visual Connection Archive

and members of Masonic lodges who exchanged views with Freemasons in the West, formed secret societies of opposition. Some placed their highest priority on freeing the serfs; others advocated a constitution and a republican form of government. When Alexander I died in December 1825, confusion over who was to succeed him encouraged a group of reform-minded army officers to try to take over the government and provoke an uprising. This so-called **Decembrist revolt** failed, and many of the participants were severely punished. These events ensured that the new tsar, Nicholas I, would pay little heed to calls for reform over the next thirty years.

The great powers meeting in Paris to settle the Crimean War in 1856 forced Russia to return land to the Ottomans in both Europe and Asia. This humiliation spurred Nicholas's son and successor, Alexander II (r. 1855–1881), to institute major new reforms to reinvigorate the country. The greatest of his reforms was the emancipation of the serfs in 1861. He also authorized new joint-stock companies, projected a railroad network to tie the country together, and modernized the legal and administrative arms of government.

Earlier intellectual and cultural trends flourished under Alexander II. More and more people became involved in intellectual, artistic, and professional life. Most prominent intellectuals received some amount of instruction at Moscow University or some German university. Universities also appeared in provincial cities like Kharkov in Ukraine and Kazan on the Volga River. Student clubs, along with Masonic lodges, became places for discussing new ideas. As Russian scholars and scientists began to achieve recognition for their contributions to European thought, scholarly careers attracted young men from clerical families, who in turn helped stimulate reforms in religious education.

Just as the Tanzimat reforms of the Ottoman Empire preceded the emergence of the Young Ottomans as a new and assertive political and intellectual force in the second half of the nineteenth century, so the initially ineffective reforms of Alexander I set in motion cultural currents that would make Russia a dynamic center of intellectual, artistic, and political life under his nephew Alexander II. Thus Russia belonged to two different spheres of development. It entered the nineteenth century a recognized force in European politics, but in other ways it resembled the Ottoman Empire. Rulers in both empires instituted reforms, overcame opposition, and increased the power of their governments. These activities stimulated intellectual and political trends that would ultimately work against the absolute rule of tsar and sultan. Yet Russia would eventually develop much closer relations with western Europe and become an arena for every sort of European intellectual, artistic, and political tendency, while the Ottoman Empire would ultimately succumb to European imperialism.

THE QING EMPIRE

In 1800 the Qing Empire faced many problems, but no reform movement of the kind initiated by Sultan Selim III emerged in China. The reasons are not difficult to understand. The Qing emperors had skillfully countered Russian strategic and diplomatic moves in the 1600s. Instead of having a Napoleon threatening them with invasion, they enjoyed the admiration of Jesuit priests, who likened them to enlightened philosopher-kings. In 1793, however, a British attempt to establish diplomatic and trade relations—the Macartney mission—turned European opinion against China (see Chapter 21).

China's most serious crises were domestic, not foreign: rebellions by displaced indigenous peoples and the poor, and protests against the injustice of the local magistrates. The Qing dealt with these problems by suppressing rebels and dismissing incompetent or untrustworthy officials. They also brushed aside the complaints from European merchants who chafed against the restrictions of the "Canton system" by which the Qing limited and controlled foreign trade.

Economic and Social Disorder   Early Qing successes and territorial expansion sowed the seeds of the domestic and political chaos of the later period. The early emperors encouraged the recovery of farmland, the opening of previously uncultivated areas, and the restoration and expansion of the road and canal systems. These measures expanded the agricultural base and supported a doubling of the population between about 1650 and 1800. Enormous numbers of farmers, merchants, and day laborers migrated in search of less crowded conditions, and a permanent floating population of the unemployed and homeless emerged. By 1800, population strain had caused serious environmental damage in some parts of central and western China.

While farmers tried to cope with agricultural deterioration, other groups vented grievances against the government: minority peoples in central and southwestern China complained about being driven off their lands during the boom of the 1700s; Mongols resented appropriation of their grazing lands and the displacement of their traditional elites. In some regions, village vigilante organizations took over policing and governing functions from Qing officials who had lost control. Growing numbers of people mistrusted the government, suspecting that all officials were corrupt. The increasing presence of foreign merchants and missionaries in Canton and in the Portuguese colony of Macao aggravated discontent in neighboring districts.

In some parts of China the Qing were hated as foreign conquerors and were suspected of sympathy with the Europeans. In 1794 the White Lotus Rebellion—partly inspired by a messianic ideology that predicted the restoration of the Chinese Ming dynasty and the coming of the Buddha—raged across central China and was not suppressed until 1804. It initiated a series of internal conflicts that continued through the 1800s (see discussion of Yaqub Beg's revolt at the beginning of this chapter). Ignited by deepening social instabilities, these movements were sometimes intensified by local ethnic conflicts and by unapproved religions. The ability of some village militias to defend themselves and attack others intensified the conflicts, though the same techniques proved useful to southern coastal populations attempting to fend off British invasion.

The Opium War and Its Aftermath, 1839–1850   Unlike the Ottomans, the Qing knew little about the enormous fortunes being made in the early 1800s by European and American merchants smuggling opium into China. They did not know that silver gained in this illegal trade was helping finance the industrial transformation of England and the United States. Only slowly did Qing officials become aware of British colonies in

India that grew and exported opium, and of the major naval base at Singapore through which British opium reached East Asia.

In 1729, the first Qing law banning opium imports was promulgated. By 1800, however, opium smuggling had swelled the annual import level to as many as four thousand chests. Though British merchants had pioneered this profitable trade, Chinese merchants likewise profited from distributing the drugs. A price war in the early 1820s stemming from competition between British and American importers raised demand so sharply that as many as thirty thousand chests were being imported by the 1830s. Addiction spread to people at all levels of Qing society, including high-ranking officials. The Qing emperor and his officials debated whether to legalize and tax opium or to enforce the existing ban more strictly. Having decided to root out the use and importation of opium, in 1839 they sent a high official to Canton to deal with the matter.

Britain considered the ban on opium importation an intolerable limitation on trade, a direct threat to Britain's economic health, and a cause for war. British naval and marine forces arrived on the south China coast in late 1839. The **Opium War** (1839–1842) broke out when negotiations between the Qing official and British representatives reached a stalemate. The war exposed the fact that the traditional, hereditary soldiers of the Qing Empire—the **Bannermen**—were, like the Janissaries of the Ottoman Empire, hopelessly obsolete. As in the Crimean War, the British excelled at sea, where they deployed superior technology. British ships landed marines who pillaged coastal cities and then sailed to new destinations. The Qing lacked a navy powerful enough to deal with the British. Thus until they were able to engage the British in prolonged fighting on land, they were unable to defend themselves against British attacks. Even in the land engagements, Qing resources proved woefully inadequate. The British could quickly transport their forces by sea along the coast, whereas Qing troops moved primarily on foot. Moving Qing reinforcements from central to eastern China took more than three months; and when the defense forces arrived, they were exhausted and basically without weapons.

The Bannermen used the few muskets the Qing had imported during the 1700s. The weapons were matchlocks, which required the soldiers to ignite the load of gunpowder in them by hand. Firing the weapons was dangerous, and the canisters of gunpowder that each musketeer carried on his belt were likely to explode if a fire broke out nearby—a frequent occurrence in encounters with British artillery. Most of the Bannermen, however, had no guns at all and fought with swords, knives, spears, and clubs. They were greatly outmatched by the soldiers under British command—many of them Indians—who carried percussion-cap rifles, which were far quicker, safer, and more accurate than the matchlocks. In addition, the long-range British artillery could be moved from place to place and proved deadly in the cities and villages of eastern China.

Qing commanders thought that British gunboats rode so low in the water that they could not sail up the Chinese rivers. So they evacuated the coastal areas to counter the British threat. But the British deployed new gunboats for shallow waters and moved without difficulty up the Yangzi River (see Chapter 22).

When the invaders approached Nanjing, the former Ming capital, the Qing decided to negotiate. In 1842 the terms of the **Treaty of Nanking** (the British name for Nanjing) dismantled the old Canton system. The number of **treaty ports**—cities opened to foreign residents—increased from one (Canton) to five (Canton, Xiamen, Fuzhou, Ningbo, and Shanghai [shahng-hie]). The island of Hong Kong became a British colony, and British residents in China gained extraterritorial rights. The Qing government agreed to set a low tariff of 5 percent on imports and to pay Britain an indemnity of 21 million ounces of silver as a penalty for having started the war. A supplementary treaty the following year guaranteed **most-favored-nation status** to Britain: any privileges that China granted to another country would be automatically extended to Britain as well. This provision effectively prevented the colonization of China, because giving land to one country would have necessitated giving it to all.

With each round of treaties came a new round of privileges for foreigners. In 1860 a new treaty legalized their right to import opium. Later, French treaties established the rights of foreign missionaries to travel in the Chinese countryside and preach their religion. The number of treaty ports grew, too; by 1900 they numbered more than ninety.

The treaty system and the principle of extraterritoriality resulted in the colonization of small pockets of Qing territory, where foreign merchants lived at ease. Greater territorial losses resulted when outlying regions gained independence or were ceded to neighboring countries. Districts north and south of the Amur River in the northeast fell to Russia by treaty in 1858 and 1860; parts of modern Kazakhstan and Kyrgyzstan in the northwest met the same fate in 1864. From 1865 onward the British gradually gained control of territories on China's Indian frontier. In the late 1800s France forced the court of Vietnam to end its tribute relationship to the Qing, while Britain encouraged Tibetan independence.

In Canton, Shanghai, and other coastal cities, Europeans and Americans maintained offices and factories that employed local Chinese as menial laborers. The foreigners built comfortable housing in zones where Chinese were not permitted to live, and they entertained themselves in exclusive restaurants and bars. Around the foreign establishments, gambling and prostitution offered employment to part of the local urban population.

Whether in town or in the countryside, Christian missionaries whose congregations sponsored hospitals, shelters, and soup kitchens or gave stipends to Chinese who attended church enjoyed a good reputation. But just as often the missionaries themselves were regarded as another evil. They seemed to subvert Confucian beliefs by condemning ancestor worship, pressuring poor families to put their children into orphanages, or fulminating against footbinding. The growing numbers of foreigners, and their growing privileges, became targets of resentment for a deeply dissatisfied, daily more impoverished, and increasingly militarized society.

The Taiping Rebellion, 1850–1864   The inflammatory mixture of social unhappiness and foreign intrusion exploded in the great civil war usually called the **Taiping** (tie-PING) **Rebellion**. In Guangxi, where the Taiping movement originated, entrenched social problems had been generating disorders for half a century. Agriculture in the region was unstable, and many people made their living from arduous and despised trades such as disposing of human waste, making charcoal, and mining. Ethnic divisions complicated economic distress. The lowliest trades frequently involved a minority group, the Hakkas, and tensions between them and the majority were rising. Problems may have been intensified by sharp fluctuations in the opium trade and reactions to the cultural and economic impact of the Europeans and Americans in Canton.

Hong Xiuquan (hoong shee-OH-chew-an), the founder of the Taiping movement, experienced all of these influences. Hong came from a humble Hakka background. After years of study, he competed in the provincial Confucian examinations, hoping for a post in government. He failed the examinations repeatedly, and it appears that he suffered a nervous breakdown in his late thirties. Afterward he spent some time in Canton, where he met both Chinese and American Protestant missionaries, who inspired him with their teachings. Hong had his own interpretation of the Christian message. He saw himself as the younger brother of Jesus, commissioned by God to found a new kingdom on earth and drive the Manchu conquerors, the Qing, out of China. The result would be universal peace. Hong called his new religious movement the "Heavenly Kingdom of Great Peace."

Hong quickly attracted a community of believers, primarily Hakkas like himself. They believed in the prophecy of dreams and claimed they could walk on air. Hong and his rivals for leadership in the movement went in and out of ecstatic trances. They denounced the Manchus as creatures of Satan. News of the sect reached the government, and Qing troops arrived to arrest the Taiping leaders. But the Taipings soundly repelled the imperial troops. Local loyalty to the Taipings spread quickly; their numbers multiplied; and they began to enlarge their domain.

The Taipings relied at first on Hakka sympathy and the charismatic appeal of their religious doctrine to attract followers. But as their numbers and power grew, they altered their methods of preaching and governing, replacing the anti-Chinese appeals used to enlist Hakkas with anti-Manchu rhetoric designed to enlist Chinese. They forced captured villages to join their movement. Once people were absorbed, the Taipings strictly monitored their activities. They also segregated men and women and organized them into work and military teams. Women were forbidden to bind their feet (the Hakkas had never practiced footbinding) and participated fully in farming and labor. Brigades of women soldiers took to the field against Qing forces.

As the movement grew, it began to move toward eastern and northern China. Panic preceded the Taipings. Villagers feared being forced into Taiping units, and Confucian elites recoiled in horror from the bizarre ideology of foreign gods, totalitarian rule, and walking, working, warring women. But the huge numbers the Taipings were able to muster overwhelmed attempts at local defense. The tremendous growth in the number of Taiping followers required the movement to establish a permanent base. When the rebel army conquered Nanjing in 1853, the Taiping leaders decided to settle there and make it the capital of the new "Heavenly Kingdom of Great Peace."

Qing forces attempting to defend north China became more successful as problems of organization and growing numbers slowed Taiping momentum. Increasing Qing military success resulted mainly from the flexibility of the imperial military commanders in the face of an unprecedented challenge. In addition, the military commanders received strong backing from a group of civilian provincial governors who had studied the techniques developed by local militia forces for self-defense.

Certain provincial governors combined their knowledge of civilian self-defense and local terrain with more efficient organization and the use of modern weaponry. The result was the formation of new military units, in which many of the Bannermen voluntarily served under civilian governors. The Qing court agreed to special taxes to fund the new armies and acknowledged the new combined leadership.

When the Taipings settled into Nanjing, the new Qing armies surrounded the city, hoping to starve out the rebels. The Taipings, however, had provisioned and fortified themselves well. They also had the services of several brilliant young military commanders, who mobilized enormous campaigns in nearby parts of eastern China, scavenging supplies and attempting to break the encirclement of Nanjing. For more than a decade the Taiping leadership remained ensconced at Nanjing, and the "Heavenly Kingdom" endured.

In 1856 Britain and France, freed from their preoccupation with the Crimean War, turned their attention to China. European and American missionaries had visited Nanjing, curious to see what their fellow Christians were up to. Their reports were discouraging. Hong Xiuquan and the other leaders appeared to lead lives of indulgence and abandon, and more than one missionary accused them of homosexual practices. Relieved of the possible accusation of quashing a pious Christian movement, the British and French surveyed the situation. Though the Taipings were not going to topple the Qing, rebellious Nian ("Bands") in northern China added a new threat in the 1850s. A series of simultaneous large insurrections might indeed destroy the empire. Moreover, since the Qing had not observed all the provisions of the treaties signed after the Opium War, Britain and France were now considering renewing war on the Qing themselves.

In 1856 the British and French launched a series of swift, brutal coastal attacks—a second opium war, called the Arrow War (1856–1860)—that culminated in a British and French invasion of Beijing and the sacking of the Summer Palace in 1860. A new round of treaties punished the Qing for not enacting all the provisions of the Treaty of Nanking. Having secured their principal objective, the British and French forces then joined the Qing campaign against the Taipings. Attempts to coordinate the international forces were sometimes riotous and sometimes tragic, but the injection of European weaponry and money helped quell both the Taiping and the Nian rebellions during the 1860s.

The Taiping Rebellion ranks as the world's bloodiest civil war and the greatest armed conflict before the twentieth century. Estimates of deaths range from 20 million to 30 million. The loss of life came primarily from starvation and disease, for most engagements consisted of surrounding fortified cities and waiting until the enemy forces died, surrendered, or were so weakened that they could be easily defeated. Many sieges continued for months. Reports of people eating grass, leather, hemp, and human flesh were widespread. The dead were rarely buried properly, and epidemic disease was common.

The area of early Taiping fighting was close to the regions of southwest China in which bubonic plague had been lingering for centuries. When the rebellion was suppressed, many Taiping followers sought safety in the highlands of Laos and Vietnam, which soon showed infestation by plague. Within a few years the disease reached Hong Kong. From there it spread to Singapore, San Francisco, Calcutta, and London. In the late 1800s there was intense apprehension over the possibility of a worldwide outbreak, and Chinese immigrants were regarded as likely carriers. This fear became a contributing factor in the passage of discriminatory immigration bans on Chinese in the United States in 1882.

The Taiping Rebellion devastated the agricultural centers of China. Many of the most intensely cultivated regions of central and eastern China were depopulated. Some were still uninhabited decades later, and major portions of the country did not recover until the twentieth century.

Cities, too, were hard hit. Shanghai, a treaty port of modest size before the rebellion, saw its population multiplied many times by the arrival of refugees from war-blasted neighboring provinces. The city then endured months of siege by the Taipings. Major cultural centers in eastern China lost masterpieces of art and architecture; imperial libraries were burned or their collections exposed to the weather; and the printing blocks used to make books were destroyed. While the empire faced the mountainous challenge of dealing with the material and cultural destruction of the war, it also was burdened by a major ecological disaster in the north.

Tz'u Hsi (1835–1908) Empress Dowager of China, 1903 (b/w photo), French Photographer, (20th century)/Private Collection/The Bridgeman Art Library

Cixi's Allies *In the 1860s and 1870s, Cixi was a supporter of reform. In later years she was widely regarded as corrupt and self-centered and as an obstacle to reform. Her greatest allies were the court eunuchs. Introduced to palace life in early China as managers of the imperial harems, eunuchs became powerful political parties at court. The first Qing emperors refused to allow the eunuchs any political influence, but by Cixi's time the eunuchs once again were a political factor.*

The Yellow River changed course in 1855, destroying the southern part of impoverished Shandong province with flood and initiating decades of drought along the former riverbed in northern Shandong.

Decentralization at the End of the Qing Empire, 1864–1875   The Qing government emerged from the 1850s with no hope of achieving solvency. The corruption of the 1700s, attempts in the very early 1800s to restore waterworks and roads, and declining yields from land taxes had bankrupted the treasury. By 1850, before the Taiping Rebellion, Qing government expenditures were ten times revenues. The indemnities demanded by Europeans after the Opium and Arrow Wars compounded the problem. Vast stretches of formerly productive rice land were devastated, and the population was dispersed. Refugees pleaded for relief, and the imperial, volunteer, foreign, and mercenary troops that had suppressed the Taipings demanded unpaid wages.

Britain and France became active participants in the period of recovery that followed the rebellion (see Diversity and Dominance: Chinese Responses to Imperialism). To ensure repayment of the debt to Britain, Robert Hart was installed as inspector-general of a newly created Imperial Maritime Customs Service. Britain and the Qing split the revenues he collected. Britons and Americans worked for the Qing government as advisers and ambassadors, attempting to smooth communications between the Qing, Europe, and the United States.

The real work of the recovery, however, was managed by provincial governors who had come to the forefront in the struggle against the Taipings. To prosecute the war, they had won the right to levy their own taxes, raise their own troops, and run their own bureaucracies. These special powers were not entirely canceled when the war ended. Chief among these governors was Zeng Guofan (zung gwoh-FAN), who oversaw programs to restore agriculture, communications, education, and publishing, as well as efforts to reform the military and industrialize armaments manufacture.

Like many provincial governors, Zeng preferred to look to the United States rather than to Britain for models and aid. He therefore hired American advisers to run his weapons factories, shipyards, and military academies. He also sponsored a daring program in which promising Chinese boys were sent to Hartford, Connecticut, a center of missionary activity, to learn English, science, mathematics, engineering, and history. They returned to China to assume some of the positions previously held by foreign advisers. Though Zeng was never an advocate of participation in public life by women, his Confucian convictions taught him that educated mothers were more than ever a necessity. He not only encouraged but also partly oversaw the advanced classical education of his own daughters. Zeng's death in 1872 deprived the empire of a major force for reform.

The period of recovery marked a fundamental structural change in the Qing Empire. Although the emperors after 1850 were ineffective rulers, a coalition of aristocrats supported the reform and recovery programs. Without their legitimization of the new powers of provincial governors like Zeng Guofan, the empire might have evaporated within a generation. A crucial member of this alliance was Cixi (TSUH-shee), who was known as the "Empress Dowager" after the 1880s.

DIVERSITY + DOMINANCE

Chinese Responses to Imperialism

The Opium War, followed by the Taiping Rebellion, revealed China's weakness for all to see, but there was no agreement on what should be done to restore its strength. A few provincial officials were able to take effective action, but the competing ideas that were heard at the imperial court tended to cancel each other out.

Feng Guifen, an official and a scholar, came into contact with Westerners defending Shanghai when he took refuge there from the Taipings. The following is from a book of essays he published in 1861.

According to a general geography compiled by an Englishman, the territory of China is eight times that of Russia, ten times that of the United States, one hundred times that of France, and two hundred times that of Great Britain.... Yet we are shamefully humiliated by the four nations, not because our climate, soil, or resources are inferior to theirs, but because our people are inferior.... Now, our inferiority is not due to our allotment from Heaven [i.e., our inherent nature], but is rather due to ourselves....

Why are the Western nations small and yet strong? Why are we large and yet weak? We must search for the means to become their equal, and that depends solely upon human effort....

We have only one thing to learn from the barbarians, and that is strong ships and effective guns.... Funds should be allotted to establish a shipyard and arsenal in each trading port. A few barbarians should be employed, and Chinese who are good in using their minds should be selected to receive instruction so that in turn they may teach many craftsmen. When a piece of work is finished and is as good as that made by the barbarians, the makers should be rewarded with an

official *juren* degree and be permitted to participate in the metropolitan examinations on the same basis as other scholars. Those whose products are of superior quality should be rewarded with the *jinshi* degree [ordinarily conferred in the metropolitan examinations] and be permitted to participate in the palace examinations like others. The workers should be paid double so that they will not quit their jobs.

Our nation's emphasis on civil service examinations has sunk deep into people's minds for a long time. Intelligent and brilliant scholars have exhausted their time and energy in such useless things as the stereotyped examination essays, examination papers, and formal calligraphy.... We should now order one-half of them to apply themselves to the manufacturing of instruments and weapons and to the promotion of physical studies.... The intelligence and ingenuity of the Chinese are certainly superior to those of the various barbarians; it is only that hitherto we have not made use of them. When the government above takes delight in something, the people below will pursue it further: their response will be like an echo carried by the wind. There ought to be some people of extraordinary intelligence who can have new ideas and improve on Western methods. At first they may take the foreigners as their teachers and models; then they may come to the same level and be their equals; finally they may move ahead and surpass them. Herein lies the way to self-strengthening.

In 1867 the debate over how to resist foreign military pressure surged through the imperial court. Woren, a Mongol who held the rank of grand secretary, spoke for the conservatives.

Mathematics, one of the six arts, should indeed be learned by scholars as indicated in the imperial decree, and it should not be considered an unworthy subject. But according to the viewpoint of your servant, astronomy and mathematics are of very little use. If these subjects are going to be taught by Westerners as regular studies, the damage will be great. . . . Your servant has learned that the way to establish a nation is to lay emphasis on rites and rightness, not on power and plotting. The fundamental effort lies in the minds of people, not in techniques. Now, if we seek trifling arts and respect barbarians as teachers .... all that can be accomplished is the training of mathematicians. From ancient down to modern times, your servant has never heard of anyone who could use mathematics to raise the nation from a state of decline or to strengthen it in time of weakness....

Since the conclusion of the peace, Christianity has been prevalent, and half of our ignorant people have been fooled by it. The only thing we can rely on is that our scholars should clearly explain to the people the Confucian tenets, which may be able to sustain the minds of the ignorant populace. Now if these brilliant and talented scholars, who have been trained by the nation and reserved for great future usefulness, have to change from their regular course of study to follow the barbarians, then the correct spirit will not be developed, and accordingly the evil spirit will become stronger. After several years it will end in nothing less than driving the multitudes of the Chinese people into allegiance to the barbarians.

The opposing group of ministers who backed the idea of "self-strengthening" responded.

Your ministers have examined the memorial of Woren: the principles he presents are very lofty and the opinion he maintains is very orthodox. Your ministers' point of view was also like that before they began to manage foreign affairs; and yet today they do not presume to insist on such ideas, because of actual difficulties that they cannot help....

From the beginning of foreign relations to the present there have been twenty or thirty years. At first the officials inside and outside the capital did not grasp the crux of the matter, and whether they negotiated peace or discussed war, generally these were empty words without effect.... Therefore your ministers have pondered a long-term policy and discussed the situation thoroughly with all the provincial officials. Proposals to learn the written and spoken languages of foreign countries, the various methods of making machines, the training of troops with foreign guns, the dispatching of officials to travel in all countries, the investigation of their local customs and social conditions ... all these painstaking and special decisions represent nothing other than a struggle for self-strengthening....

We too are afraid that the people who are learning these things will have no power of discrimination and are likely to be led astray by foreigners, as Woren fears. Therefore we have deliberated and decided that those who participate in these examinations must be persons from regular scholastic channels. It is indeed those students who have read widely and who understand right principles and have their minds set upon upright and grand purposes—and the present situation is just what causes the scholars and officials to feel pain in heart and head—who would certainly be able to lie on faggots and taste gall [i.e., nurse vengeance] in order to encourage each other vigorously to seek the actual achievement of self-strengthening. They are different from those who have vague, easygoing, or indifferent ideas.

Questions for Analysis
1. How do the views of the writers reflect their own backgrounds as officials who achieved their offices through the traditional examination system?
2. In what ways do these passages indicate a deep or a shallow understanding of the West?
3. How do the ideas expressed here compare with the attitudes toward reform in the Ottoman and Russian Empires as discussed elsewhere in this chapter?

Source: Essays of Feng Tuifen published in 1861 in Jiaobinlu kangyi (Personal Protests from the Study of Jiaobin). English translations from Chester Tan, published in Wm. Theodore de Bary and Richard Lafrano, *Sources of Chinese Tradition*, vol. 2, 2d ed. pp. 235–236, 238–239. Copyright © 2000 Columbia University Press. Reprinted with permission of the publisher.

Later observers, both Chinese and foreign, reviled her as a monster of corruption and arrogance. But in the 1860s and 1870s Cixi supported the provincial governors, some of whom became so powerful that they were managing Qing foreign policy as well as domestic affairs.

No longer a conquest regime dominated by a Manchu military caste and its Chinese civilian appointees, the empire came under the control of a group of reformist aristocrats and military men, independently powerful civilian governors, and a small number of foreign advisers. The Qing lacked strong, central, unified leadership and could not recover their powers of taxation, legislation, and military command once these had been granted to the provincial governors. From the 1860s forward, the Qing Empire disintegrated into a number of large power zones in which provincial governors handed over leadership to their protégés in a pattern that the Qing court eventually could only ritually legitimate.

CONCLUSION

The Ottoman, Qing, and Russian Empires shared several characteristics both in their early successes and late-stage challenges. All three maintained a flexible approach when incorporating a diverse group of peoples and cultures into their growing empires. Around the mid-eighteenth century, however, the need to maintain order and increase tax revenues pushed rulers to differentiate groups of people and create stricter hierarchies within each empire, leading to conflict between the minority rulers and the ruled. In addition, population growth that began in the sixteenth century throughout Eurasia, which had been sustainable and beneficial in the expanding territories of Russia and the Qing, eventually became unsupportable. By the nineteenth century, even the Qing Empire, the largest and most advanced Eurasian empire in terms of commercial economy and efficient bureaucratic structures, could no longer effectively deal with the increasing demographic pressures, regional conflict, and political dysfunctions.

Most of the subjects of the Ottoman, Russian, and Qing rulers did not think of European pressure or competition as determining factors in their lives during the first half of the nineteenth century. They continued to live according to the social and economic institutions they inherited from previous generations. By the 1870s, however, the challenge of Europe had become widely realized. The Crimean War, where European allies achieved a hollow victory for the Ottomans and then pressured the sultan for more reforms, confirmed both Ottoman and Russian military weakness. The Opium War did the same for China. But China, unlike the other empires, was also stricken by rampaging civil war and regional uprisings.

In analyzing the crises of the three empires, historians today stress European economic pressures and observe that all three empires ultimately became insolvent and saw the overthrow of their ruling dynasties. However, at the time what most impressed the Ottomans, Russians, and Chinese was European military superiority, as demonstrated in the Greek war of independence, the Crimean War, and the Opium War. Thus for all three empires, dealing with military emergency took priority over deeper reforms throughout most of the time period of this chapter.

IMPORTANT EVENTS 1800–1908	
1794–1804	White Lotus Rebellion
1801–1825	Reign of Alexander I
1805–1849	Muhammad Ali governs Egypt
1808–1839	Rule of Mahmud II
1812	Napoleon's retreat from Moscow
1825	Decembrist revolt
1825–1855	Reign of Nicholas I
1826	Janissary corps dissolved
1829	Greek independence
1839	Abdul Mejid begins Tanzimat reforms
1839–1842	Opium War
1850–1864	Taiping Rebellion
1853–1856	Crimean War
1855–1881	Reign of Alexander II
1856–1860	Arrow War
1860	Sack of Beijing
1861	Emancipation of the serfs
1861–1873	Empress Dowager Cixi wields power during her son's minority
1875–1908	After her son's death, Empress Dowager Cixi resumes power behalf of minor successors
1876	First constitution by an Islamic government

25

NATION BUILDING AND ECONOMIC TRANSFORMATION IN THE AMERICAS, 1800–1890

During the nineteenth century the newly independent nations of the Western Hemisphere sought to emulate the rapid economic progress of Europe under the influence of the Industrial Revolution. No technology seemed to represent that progress better than railroads. Everywhere from Argentina to Canada, governments sponsored railroad development. By 1850 there were 9,000 miles (14,480 kilometers) of track in the United States, as much as in the rest of the world. Latin American nations committed to this technology later than the United States, but railroads there also soon proved important to exports, to new industries, and to political and cultural integration.

Mexico granted the first concession for railroad construction in 1837, but the first significant rail line was completed in 1873. Few new projects were begun until the presidency of Porfirio Díaz (1876–1880 and 1884–1911), who promoted railroad construction. By the time revolutionaries forced him from office, Mexico had 12,000 miles (19,300 kilometers) of track. Although railroads proved crucial to Mexican economic growth, there was a downside. Foreign investment helped pay for new railroads, but this dependence on foreign capital led to political protests and economic nationalism. Railroad development also had a powerful effect on native peoples, who still controlled large areas of rural Mexico. Because railroads made their lands more valuable, powerful landed families used their political influence to strip this land from indigenous subsistence farmers and use it to produce export crops. As Amerindian villagers lost their traditional lands, the number of rural uprisings increased.

In the nineteenth century the Western Hemisphere witnessed radical political and social changes in addition to technological innovations and economic expansion. Brazil and nearly all of Spain's American colonies achieved independence by 1825. As was true in the earlier American and French Revolutions (see Chapter 23), rising nationalism and the ideal of political freedom promoted these changes. Despite the achievement of independence, however, Mexico and other nations in the hemisphere faced foreign interventions and other threats to sovereignty, including regionalism and civil war.

The new nations of the Western Hemisphere faced difficult questions. If colonies could reject submission to imperial powers, could not regions with distinct cultures, social structures, and economies refuse to accept the political authority of newly formed national governments? How could nations born in revolution accept the political strictures of written constitutions—even those they wrote themselves? How could the ideals of liberty and freedom expressed in those constitutions be reconciled with the denial of rights to Amerindians, slaves, recent immigrants, and women?

While trying to resolve these political questions, the new nations also attempted to promote economic growth. They imported new technologies like railroads, opened new areas to settlement, and promoted immigration. But the legacy of colonial economic development, with its emphasis on agricultural and mining exports, inhibited efforts to promote diversification and industrialization, just as the legacy of class and racial division thwarted the realization of political ideals.

INDEPENDENCE IN LATIN AMERICA, 1800–1830

As the eighteenth century drew to a close, Spain and Portugal held vast colonial possessions in the Western Hemisphere, although their power had declined relative to that of their British and French rivals. Both Iberian empires had reformed their colonial administration and strengthened their military forces in the eighteenth century (see Chapter 18). Despite these efforts, the same economic and political forces that had undermined Britain's rule in its colonies were present in Spanish America and Brazil.

Roots of Revolution, to 1810

The great works of the Enlightenment as well as revolutionary documents like the American Declaration of Independence and the French Declaration of the Rights of Man and the Citizen circulated widely in Latin America, but few colonial residents wanted revolutionary change. While colonial elites and middle classes were frustrated by imperial policies, it was events in Europe that propelled the colonies toward independence. Napoleon's decision to invade Portugal (1807) and Spain (1808), not revolutionary ideas, created a crisis of legitimacy that undermined the authority of colonial officials and ignited Latin America's struggle for independence.

As a French army neared Lisbon in 1808, the Portuguese royal family fled to Brazil. Once arrived, King John VI would maintain his court there for over a decade. Soon Napoleon forced King Ferdinand VII of Spain to abdicate and placed his own brother, Joseph Bonaparte, on the throne. Spanish patriots fighting against the French created a new political body, the Junta (HUN-tah) Central, to administer the areas they controlled. The junta claimed authority over Spain's colonies, inviting the election of colonial deputies to help write the nation's first written constitution.

Most residents of colonial Spanish America favored obedience to the Junta Central and many colonies elected deputies, but a vocal minority, including some members of the elite, objected. These dissenters argued that they were subjects of the king, not dependents of the Spanish nation. They wanted to create local juntas and govern their own affairs until Ferdinand regained the throne. Spanish loyalists resisted this assertion of local autonomy, provoking armed uprisings. In late 1808 and 1809 popular movements overthrew Spanish colonial officials in Venezuela, Mexico, and Alto Peru (modern Bolivia) and created local juntas. In each case, Spanish officials quickly reasserted control and punished the leaders. This harsh repression, however, further polarized public opinion in the colonies and gave rise to a greater sense of a separate American nationality. By 1810 Spanish colonial authorities were facing a new round of revolutions now focused on independence.

Spanish South America, 1810–1825   In Caracas (the capital city of modern Venezuela) a revolutionary junta led by creoles (colonial-born whites) declared independence in 1811. Although this group espoused representative democracy, its leaders were landowners who defended slavery and opposed full citizenship for the black and mixed-race majority. Their aim was to expand their own privileges by eliminating Spaniards from the upper levels of government and the church. The junta's narrow agenda spurred Spanish loyalists to rally thousands of free blacks and slaves to defend the Spanish Empire. Faced with this determined resistance, the revolutionary movement placed overwhelming political authority in the hands of its military leader **Simón Bolívar** (see-MOAN bow-LEE-varh) (1783–1830), who would become the preeminent leader of the independence movement.

The son of wealthy Venezuelan planters, Bolívar had traveled in Europe and studied the works of the Enlightenment. He was a charismatic personality who effectively mobilized political support and held the loyalty of his troops. Defeated on many occasions, Bolívar successfully adapted his objectives and policies to attract new allies and build coalitions. Although initially opposed to the abolition of slavery, for example, he agreed to support emancipation in order to draw slaves and freemen to his cause and to gain military supplies from Haiti. Bolívar was also capable of using harsh methods to ensure victory, proclaiming in 1813 that "any Spaniard who does not … work against tyranny in behalf of this just cause will be considered an enemy and punished; as a traitor to the nation, he will inevitably be shot by a firing squad."[1]

Military advantage shifted back and forth between the patriots and loyalists until Bolívar enlisted demobilized English and French veterans of the Napoleonic Wars. Spanish resolve was then fatally weakened by a military revolt in Spain in 1820. The European veterans, hardened by combat, improved the battlefield performance of Bolívar's army, while the revolt in Spain in 1820 forced Ferdinand VII— restored to power in 1814—to accept a constitution that limited the powers of both the monarch and the church. Colonial loyalists who for a decade had fought to maintain the authority of monarch and church viewed these reforms as unacceptably liberal.

---

[1] Quoted in Lyman L. Johnson, "Spanish American Independence and Its Consequences," in *Problems in Modern Latin American History: A Reader*, ed. John Charles Chasteen and Joseph S. Tulchin (Wilmington, DE: Scholarly Resources, 1994), 21.

With the king's supporters now divided, momentum swung to the patriots. After liberating present-day Venezuela, Colombia, and Ecuador, Bolívar's army entered Peru and Bolivia and defeated the last Spanish armies in 1824. Bolívar and his supporters then attempted to create a confederation of the former Spanish colonies. The first steps were the creation of Gran Colombia (now Venezuela, Colombia, and Ecuador) and the unification of Peru and Bolivia, but these initiatives had failed by 1830.

Buenos Aires (the capital city of modern Argentina) was the second important center of revolutionary activity in Spanish South America. In Buenos Aires news of French victories in Spain led to the creation of a junta organized by militia commanders, merchants, and ranchers, which overthrew the viceroy in 1810. To deflect the opposition of Spanish loyalists, the junta claimed loyalty to the imprisoned king. Two years after Ferdinand regained the Spanish throne in 1814, junta leaders declared independence as the United Provinces of the Río de la Plata.

Patriot leaders in Buenos Aires at first sought to retain control over the territory of the Viceroyalty of Río de la Plata, but Spanish loyalists in Uruguay and Bolivia and a separatist movement in Paraguay defeated these ambitions. Even within the territory of Argentina, the government in Buenos Aires was unable to control regional rivalries and political differences. As a result, the region rapidly descended into political chaos.

A weak succession of juntas, collective presidencies, and dictators lost control over much of the interior of Argentina. But the government in Buenos Aires did manage to support a mixed force of Chileans and Argentines led by José de San Martín (hoe-SAY deh san mar-TEEN) (1778–1850), who crossed the Andes Mountains to attack Spanish forces in Chile and Peru. During this campaign San Martín's most effective troops were former slaves, who had gained their freedom by enlisting in the army. After gaining victory in Chile, San Martín pushed on to Peru in 1820, but he failed to gain a clear victory there. Unable to make progress, San Martín surrendered command of patriot forces in Peru to Simón Bolívar, who overcame final Spanish resistance in 1824.

Mexico,
1810–1823

In 1810 Mexico was Spain's wealthiest and most populous colony. Its silver mines were the richest in the world, and the colony's capital, Mexico City, was larger than any city in Spain. Mexico also had the largest population of Spanish immigrants among the colonies. When news of Napoleon's invasion of Spain reached Mexico, conservative Spaniards in Mexico City overthrew the local viceroy, thinking him too sympathetic to the creoles. This action by Spanish loyalists underlined the new reality: with the king removed from his throne by the French, colonial authority now rested on brute force.

The first stage of the revolution against Spain occurred in central Mexico, where ranchers and farmers had aggressively forced Amerindian communities from their traditional agricultural lands. Crop failures and epidemics afflicted the region's rural poor, while miners and the urban poor faced higher food prices and rising unemployment as well. With the power of colonial authorities weakened by events in Spain, anger and fear spread through towns and villages in central Mexico.

MAP 25.1 Latin America by 1830

By 1830 patriot forces had overturned the Spanish and Portuguese Empires of the Western Hemisphere. Regional conflicts, local wars, and foreign interventions challenged the survival of many of these new nations following independence.

On September 16, 1810, the parish priest of the small town of Dolores, **Miguel Hidalgo y Costilla** (mee-GEHL ee-DAHL-go ee cos-TEA-ah), rang the church bells and attracted a crowd. In a fiery speech he urged the crowd to rise up against the oppression of Spanish officials. Tens of thousands of the rural and urban poor soon joined his movement. While they lacked military discipline and weapons, they knew who their oppressors were, the Spanish and colonial-born whites who owned the ranches and mines. Recognizing the threat posed by the angry masses following Hidalgo, most wealthy Mexicans supported the Spanish authorities. The military tide quickly turned, and Spanish forces captured and executed Hidalgo in 1811.

The revolution continued under the leadership of another priest, **José María Morelos** (hoe-SAY mah-REE-ah moh-RAY-los), a former student of Hidalgo's. A more adept military and political leader than his mentor, Morelos created a formidable fighting force and, in 1813, convened a congress that declared independence and drafted a constitution. Despite these achievements, loyalist forces defeated and executed Morelos in 1815. Although small numbers of insurgents continued to fight Spanish forces, colonial rule seemed secure in 1820, but news of the military revolt in Spain unsettled the conservative groups who had opposed Hidalgo and Morelos. In 1821, Colonel Agustín de Iturbide (ah-goos-TEEN deh ee-tur-BEE-deh) and other loyalist commanders forged an alliance with insurgents to declare Mexico's independence. The conservative origins of Mexico's independence were made clear by the decision to create a monarchial government and crown Iturbide emperor. In early 1823, however, the army overthrew Iturbide and Mexico became a republic. When Iturbide returned to Mexico from exile in 1824, he was captured and, like Hidalgo and Morelos, was executed by a firing squad.

Brazil, to 1831   The arrival of the Portuguese royal family in Brazil in 1808 helped maintain the loyalty of the colonial elite. With Napoleon's defeat, the Portuguese government called for King John VI to return to Portugal. At first he resisted, but a liberal revolt in Portugal forced the king to return to Portugal in 1821 to protect his throne. He left his son Pedro in Brazil as regent.

By this date the Spanish colonies along Brazil's borders had experienced ten years of revolution and civil war, and some, like Argentina and Paraguay, had gained independence. Unable to ignore these struggles, some Brazilians began to reevaluate Brazil's relationship with Portugal. Many resented their homeland's economic subordination to Portugal, while the arrogance of Portuguese soldiers and bureaucrats led others to talk openly of independence.

Unwilling to return to Portugal and committed to maintaining his family's hold on Brazil, Pedro aligned himself with rising separatist sentiment, and in 1822 declared Brazilian independence. Pedro's decision launched Brazil on a unique political trajectory. Unlike its neighbors, which became constitutional republics, Brazil gained independence as a constitutional monarchy with Pedro I, son of the king of Portugal, as emperor.

Pedro I was committed to both monarchy and to liberal principles. The constitution of 1824 provided for an elected assembly and granted rights to the

Padre Hidalgo *Padre Miguel Hidalgo y Costilla led the first stage of Mexico's revolution for independence by rallying the rural masses. His defeat, trial, and execution made him one of Mexico's most important political martyrs.*

Schaalkwijk/Art Resource, NY

political opposition, but Pedro made enemies by protecting the Portuguese who remained in Brazil from arrest and seizure of property. Pedro I also opposed slavery, even though the slave-owning class dominated Brazil. In 1823, he anonymously published an article that characterized slavery as a "cancer eating away at Brazil." His decision in 1831 to ratify a treaty with Great Britain ending Brazilian participation in the slave trade provoked opposition, as did his use of military force to control neighboring Uruguay. As military losses and costs rose, the Brazilian public grew impatient. A vocal minority that sought the creation of a democracy used these issues to rally public opinion against the emperor. Confronted by street demonstrations, Pedro I abdicated the throne in 1831 in favor of his five-year-old son Pedro II. After a nine-year regency, Pedro II assumed full powers as emperor of Brazil and reigned until overthrown by republicans in 1889.

THE PROBLEM OF ORDER, 1825–1890

All the newly independent nations of the Western Hemisphere encountered difficulties establishing stable political institutions. Popular sovereignty found broad support across the hemisphere as all the new nations sought to establish constitutions and elected assemblies. However, this widespread support for constitutional order and for representative government failed to prevent bitter factional conflict, regionalism, and the threats posed by charismatic political leaders and military uprisings.

Constitutional Experiments   In reaction to what they saw as arbitrary and tyrannical rule by colonial authorities, revolutionary leaders in the United States and Latin America espoused constitutionalism. They believed that the careful description of political powers in written constitutions offered the best protection for individual rights and liberties. In practice, however, many new constitutions proved unworkable. In the United States, George Washington, James Madison, and other leaders became dissatisfied with the first constitution, the Articles of Confederation, and helped write a new constitution. In Latin America few constitutions survived the rough-and-tumble of national politics. For example, Venezuela and Chile ratified and then rejected a combined total of nine constitutions between 1811 and 1833.

Important differences in colonial political experience influenced later political developments in the Americas. The ratification of a new constitution in the United States was the culmination of a long historical process that had begun with the development of English constitutional law and continued under colonial charters. The British colonies provided many opportunities for holding elective offices, and, by the time of independence, citizens had grown accustomed to elections, political parties, and factions. In contrast, neither Brazil nor Spanish America had significant experience with elections and representative institutions prior to independence.

Democratic passions and the desire for effective self-rule led to significant political reform in the Americas, even in regions that remained colonies. British Canada included a number of separate colonies and territories, each with a discrete government. A provincial governor and appointed advisory council drawn from the local elite dominated political life in each colony, while elected assemblies exercised limited power. The desire to make government responsive to the will of the assemblies led to armed rebellion in 1837. Britain responded by establishing limited self-rule in each of the Canadian provinces. By the 1860s regional political leaders realized that economic development required a government with a "national" character. Negotiations between Canadian leaders and the British government led to a union of Canadian provinces, the **Confederation of 1867**, and to the creation of the Dominion of Canada with a central government in Ottawa.

The path to effective constitutional government was rockier to the south. Because neither Spain nor Portugal had permitted anything like the elected legislatures and municipal governments of colonial British America, the drafters of Latin American constitutions were less constrained by practical political experience. As a result, many of the new Latin American nations experimented with untested political institutions.

Latin American nations found it particularly difficult to define the role of the Catholic Church after independence. In the colonial period the Catholic Church was a religious monopoly that controlled all levels of education and dominated intellectual life. Many early constitutions aimed to reduce this power by making education secular and by permitting other religions. The church reacted by organizing and financing conservative movements. Conflicts between liberals who sought the separation of church and state and conservatives who supported the church's traditional powers dominated political life in the nineteenth century.

Limiting the power of the military was another obstacle to the creation of constitutional governments in Latin America. The wars for independence elevated the prestige of military leaders, and, when the wars were over, military commanders seldom proved willing to subordinate themselves to civilian authorities. Frustrated by the chaotic workings of democracy, many citizens saw dictatorships led by the heroes of independence as better protection for their lives and property.

Personalist Leaders   Patriot leaders in both the United States and Latin America gained mass followings during the wars for independence, and some used these followings to gain political power. George Washington's ability to dominate early republican politics in the United States anticipated the later political ascendancy of revolutionary heroes such as Iturbide in Mexico and Bolívar in Gran Colombia. In each case, military reputation provided the foundation for personal political power. Washington was distinguished from most other military leaders by his willingness to surrender power at the end of a term determined by a constitution. More commonly, **personalist leaders** relied on their mass followings rather than on constitutions and laws to govern. In Latin America, a personalist leader who gained and held political power without constitutional sanction was called a *caudillo* (kouh-DEE-yoh).

Powerful personal followings allowed **Andrew Jackson** of the United States and **José Antonio Páez** (hoe-SAY an-TOE-nee-oh PAH-ays) of Venezuela to challenge constitutional limits to their authority. During the independence wars in Venezuela and Colombia, Páez (1790–1873) was one of Bolívar's most successful generals. Like most of his followers, Páez was uneducated and poor, but his physical strength, courage, and guile made him a natural guerrilla leader and helped him build a powerful political base. Páez described his authority in the following manner: "[The soldiers] resolved to confer on me the supreme command and blindly to obey my will, confident ... that I was the only one who could save them."[2] Able to count on the personal loyalty of his followers, Páez was seldom willing to accept the constitutional authority of a distant president.

After defeating the Spanish, Bolívar pursued his dream of forging a union of former Spanish colonies modeled on the United States. But he underestimated the strength of nationalist sentiment unleashed by the independence wars. Páez and other Venezuelan leaders resisted the surrender of their hard-won power to Bolívar's Gran Colombian government in distant Bogotá. When political opponents challenged Bolívar in 1829, Páez declared Venezuela's independence. Merciless to his enemies and indulgent with his followers, Páez ruled the country as president or dictator for the next eighteen years. Despite implementing an economic program favorable to the elite, Páez remained popular with the masses. Even as his personal wealth grew, he took care to present himself as a common man.

Andrew Jackson (1767–1845) was the first U.S. president born in humble circumstances. A self-made man who eventually acquired substantial property and

---

[2] José Antonio Páez, *Autobiografía del General José Antonio Páez*, vol. 1 (New York: Hallety Breen, 1869), 83.

owned over a hundred slaves, Jackson was extremely popular among frontier residents, urban workers, and small farmers. Although he was notorious for his untidy personal life as well as for dueling, his courage, individualism, and willingness to challenge authority helped him attain political success as judge, general, congressman, senator, and president.

During his military career, Jackson proved to be impatient with civilian authorities. Widely known because of his victories over the Creek and Seminole peoples, he was elevated to the pinnacle of American politics by his celebrated defeat of the British at the Battle of New Orleans in 1815 and by his seizure of Florida from the Spanish in 1818. In 1824 he received a plurality of the popular votes for president but failed to win a majority of electoral votes. His followers were embittered when the House of Representatives chose John Quincy Adams as president.

Jackson's followers viewed his landslide election victory in 1828 and reelection in 1832 as the triumph of democracy over entrenched aristocracy. In office Jackson challenged constitutional limits on his authority, increasing presidential power at the expense of Congress and the Supreme Court. Like Páez, Jackson was able to dominate national politics by blending a populist political style that celebrated the virtues and cultural enthusiasms of common people with support for policies that promoted the economic interests of powerful propertied groups.

Personalist leaders were common in both Latin America and the United States, but Latin America's weaker constitutional tradition, more limited protection of property rights, lower literacy levels, and less-developed communications systems facilitated the ambitions of popular politicians. Latin America's personalist leaders often ignored constitutional restraints on their authority, and election results seldom determined access to presidential power. As a result, by 1900 every independent Latin American nation had experienced periods of dictatorship.

The Threat of Regionalism	After independence, national governments were generally weaker than the colonial governments they replaced. Debates over tariffs, tax and monetary policies, and, in many nations,

slavery and the slave trade led regional elites to attempt secession. Some of the hemisphere's newly independent nations did not survive these struggles, while others lost territories to aggressive neighbors.

In Spanish America all efforts to forge large multistate federations after independence failed. The Viceroyalty of New Spain had included Central America and Mexico, but after independence this union failed when in 1823 local elites broke with Mexico to form the Republic of Central America. A new round of regional disputes and civil wars led to the creation of five separate nations during the 1820s and 1830s. In South America, Bolívar attempted to maintain the colonial unity of Venezuela, Colombia, and Ecuador by creating Gran Colombia with its capital in Bogotá. But even before his death in 1830, Venezuela and Ecuador had become independent states. In the colonial era Argentina, Uruguay, Paraguay, and Bolivia were organized as a single viceroyalty with its capital in Buenos Aires. After the defeat of Spain, the leaders in Paraguay, Uruguay, and Bolivia declared their independence from Argentina.

Regionalism threatened the United States as well. The defense of state and regional interests played an important role in the framing of the U.S. Constitution.

MAP 25.2 Territorial Growth of the United States, 1783–1853

The rapid western expansion of the United States resulted from aggressive diplomacy and warfare against Mexico and Amerindian peoples. Railroad development helped integrate the trans-Mississippi west and promote economic expansion.

Many important constitutional provisions represented compromises forged among competing state and regional leaders. Yet, despite these constitutional compromises, regional rivalries still threatened the nation.

Slavery divided the nation into two separate and competitive societies. A rising tide of immigration to the northern states in the 1830s and 1840s began to move the center of political power away from the South. Southern leaders sought to protect slavery by expanding into new territories. They supported the Louisiana Purchase in 1803, which transferred to the United States a vast French territory extending from the Gulf of Mexico to Canada, and the Mexican-American War in 1846, which added nearly half of Mexico to the United States. However, this territorial expansion forced a national debate about slavery that contributed to the election of Abraham Lincoln as president in 1860.

Lincoln was committed to checking the spread of slavery, and his election provoked the southern planter elite to choose the dangerous course of secession from the Union. The seceding states formed a new government, the Confederate States of America, known as the Confederacy. Lincoln preserved the Union but at an enormous cost. The U.S. Civil War (1861–1865) was the most destructive conflict in the history of the Western Hemisphere. Up to 750,000 lives were lost before the Confederacy surrendered in 1865. The Union victory led to the abolition of slavery and also transferred national political power to a northern elite committed to industrial expansion and federal support for the construction of railroads and other internal improvements.

The Confederate States of America was better prepared politically and economically for independence than were the successful secessionist movements that broke up Gran Colombia and other Spanish American federations. Nevertheless, the Confederacy failed, in part because of poor timing. The new nations of the Western Hemisphere were most vulnerable to secessionist movements in the early years of their existence; indeed, all the successful secessions occurred shortly after independence. In the case of the United States, an experienced national government legitimated and strengthened by more than seven decades of relative stability and reinforced by dramatic economic and population growth defeated secession only with enormous effort.

Foreign Interventions and Regional Wars   Wars often determined national borders, access to natural resources, and control of markets in the Western Hemisphere. Even after the achievement of independence, Mexico and other Western Hemisphere nations were forced to defend themselves against Europe's great powers. Contested national borders and regional rivalries also led to wars between Western Hemisphere nations. By the end of the nineteenth century the United States, Brazil, Argentina, and Chile had all successfully waged wars against their neighbors and established themselves as regional powers.

Within thirty years of independence, the United States fought a second war with England—the War of 1812. The burning of the White House and Capitol by British troops in 1814 symbolized the weakness of the new republic. By the end of the nineteenth century, however, the United States was the hemisphere's greatest military power. Its war against Spain in 1898–1899 created an American empire that reached from the Philippines in the Pacific Ocean to Puerto Rico in the Caribbean (see Chapter 26).

European powers challenged the sovereignty of Latin American nations as well. Following independence Argentina faced British and French naval blockades, and British naval forces systematically violated Brazil's territorial waters to stop the importation of slaves. Mexico faced the most serious threats to sovereignty, defeating a weak Spanish invasion in 1829, a French assault on the city of Veracruz in 1838, and a large-scale French invasion in 1862.

Mexico also faced a grave threat from the United States. In the 1820s Mexico had encouraged Americans to immigrate to its northern province of Texas. By the early 1830s Americans outnumbered Mexican nationals in Texas and were aggressively challenging Mexican laws such as the prohibition of slavery. An alliance of Mexican liberals and American settlers rebelled in 1835 and gained independence for Texas in 1836. In 1845 the United States made Texas a state, provoking war with Mexico a year later. The surrender of Mexico City in 1848 to American forces compelled Mexico to accept a harsh treaty that forced it to cede vast territories to the United States, including present-day New Mexico, Arizona, and California.

Erich Lessing/Art Resource, NY

Execution of Emperor Maximilian of Mexico *This painting by Edouard Manet shows the 1867 execution by firing squad of Maximilian and two of his Mexican generals. The defeat of the French intervention was a great triumph for Mexican patriots led by Benito Juárez.*

In return Mexico received $15 million. When gold was discovered in California in 1848, the magnitude of Mexico's loss became clear.

With the very survival of the nation at stake, Mexico's liberals took power and imposed sweeping reforms, including a new constitution in 1857 that limited the power of the Catholic Church and military. This provoked a civil war with conservatives (1858–1861). **Benito Juárez** (beh-NEE-toh WAH-rez) assumed the presidency and defeated the conservatives, who then turned to Napoleon III of France for assistance. In 1862, French forces invaded Mexico, forced Juárez to flee Mexico City, and installed the Austrian Habsburg Maximilian as emperor of Mexico. After years of warfare, Juárez drove the French army out of Mexico in 1867, aided by U.S. diplomatic pressure. After capturing Maximilian, Juárez ordered his execution.

This victory over a powerful foreign enemy redeemed a nation humiliated two decades earlier by the United States. But the creation of democracy proved more elusive than the protection of Mexican sovereignty. Despite the Mexican constitution's prohibition of presidential reelection, Juárez would serve as president until his death in 1872.

As was clear in the Mexican-American War, wars between Western Hemisphere nations could lead to dramatic territorial changes. Chile established itself as the leading military and economic power on the west coast of South America when it fought two successful wars against an alliance of Peru and Bolivia (1836–1839 and 1879–1883). The second contest, the War of the Pacific, forced Bolivia to cede its only outlet to the sea and Peru to yield rich mining districts.

Argentina and Brazil fought for control of Uruguay in the 1820s, but a military stalemate eventually forced them to recognize Uruguayan independence. Then, in 1865, Argentina and Uruguay joined Brazil to wage war against Paraguay (War of the Triple Alliance). After five years of warfare, the Paraguayan dictator Francisco Solano López (fran-CEES-co so-LAN-oh LOH-pehz) and more than 20 percent of the nation's population had died. Paraguay then experienced military occupation, loss of territory, and economic penalties.

Native Peoples and the Nation-State   Both diplomacy and war shaped relations between the Western Hemisphere's new nation-states and indigenous peoples. During late colonial times, Spanish, Portuguese, and British colonial governments attempted to restrict the expansion of settlements into territories occupied by Amerindians. With independence, the colonial powers' role as mediator and protector ended.

Still-independent Amerindian peoples posed a significant military challenge to many Western Hemisphere republics. Weakened by civil wars and constitutional crises, new nations were less able to maintain frontier peace than the colonial governments they replaced. After independence Amerindian peoples in Argentina, the United States, Chile, and Mexico succeeded in pushing back frontier settlements. But despite early victories, native military resistance was overcome in most of the hemisphere by 1890.

After the American Revolution, tens of thousands of settlers entered territories previously guaranteed to Amerindians by treaties with Britain. Indigenous leaders responded by forging military alliances with British officials in Canada and with other native peoples. In the Ohio River Valley two Shawnee brothers, **Tecumseh** (teh-CUM-sah) and the Prophet (Tenskwatawa), created a broad, well-organized alliance among Amerindian peoples that gained British support. During the War of 1812, American military forces defeated the alliance. Tecumseh died in battle fighting alongside his British allies.

Throughout the 1820s native peoples lost lands to settlers across the Midwest and Southeast. The 1828 presidential election of Andrew Jackson, a veteran of earlier wars against native peoples, brought matters to a head. The Indian Removal Act of 1830 forced the resettlement of Cherokee, Creek, Choctaw, and other eastern peoples to land west of the Mississippi River. Nearly half these forced migrants died on this journey, known as the Trail of Tears.

The native peoples of the Great Plains offered formidable resistance to the expansion of white settlement. By the time substantial numbers of white buffalo hunters, cattlemen, and settlers reached the American west, indigenous peoples were skilled in the use of horses and firearms. These technologies allowed the Sioux, Comanche, Pawnee, Kiowa, and other plains peoples to hunt more efficiently and develop potent military capacities.

After the Civil War, however, a new wave of settlers pushed onto the plains. Buffalo herds were hunted to near extinction and native lands were appropriated by farmers and ranchers. Amerindian resistance to these assaults on their way of life led to four decades of armed conflict with the United States Army. The U.S. government forced the Comanche, who had long dominated the southern plains, to cede their traditional lands in Texas in 1865. The Sioux and their allies held

National Anthropological Archives, Smithsonian Institution, SPC-BAE-4420 Vol. 6 01007800

Navajo Leaders Gathered in Washington to Negotiate *As settlers pushed west in the nineteenth century, Amerindian peoples were forced to negotiate territorial concessions with the U.S. government. This photo shows Navajo leaders and their Anglo translators in Washington, D.C., in 1874.*

out longer, overwhelming General George Armstrong Custer and the Seventh Cavalry in the Battle of Little Bighorn in 1876, but they were also soon forced to accept reservation life. Military campaigns in the 1870s and 1880s then broke the resistance of the Apache.

The indigenous peoples of Argentina and Chile experienced a similar trajectory of adaptation, resistance, and defeat. Herds of wild cattle provided these peoples with a limitless food supply, and their mastery of the horse increased their military capacities. For a while the natives of Argentina and Chile were able to check the southern expansion of agriculture and ranching. Unable to defeat these resourceful enemies, the governments of Argentina and Chile relied on an elaborate system of gift giving and prisoner exchanges to maintain peace on the frontier.

By the 1860s, however, population increase, political stability, and military modernization allowed Argentina and Chile to take the offensive. In the 1870s the government of Argentina used a large military force armed with modern weapons to crush native resistance on the pampas. In the 1850s, civil war and an economic depression weakened the Chilean government, and the Mapuches (mah-POO-chez) (also called "Araucanians") pushed back frontier settlements, but by the 1870s Chilean forces had overwhelmed Amerindian resistance.

In Chile, Argentina, and the United States, national governments justified military campaigns by demonizing native peoples. Newspaper editorials and the speeches of politicians portrayed Amerindians as brutal and cruel and as obstacles to progress. In April 1859 a Chilean newspaper commented:

> *The necessity, not only to punish the Araucanian [Mapuche] race, but also to make it impotent to harm us, is well recognized ... as the only way to rid the country of a million evils. It is well understood that they are odious and prejudicial guests in Chile ... conciliatory measures have accomplished nothing with this stupid race—the infamy and disgrace of the Chilean nation.*[3]

The author of this racist pronouncement apparently felt no obligation to explain how his nation's original inhabitants had become "guests."

Political divisions and civil wars within the new nations also provided opportunities for some long-pacified native peoples to rebel. In the Yucatán region of Mexico, large landowners forced many Maya (MY-ah) communities from traditional agricultural lands, reducing thousands to peonage. Weakened by internal rebellions and by the American invasion, the Mexican government faced a mass rebellion by the Maya in 1847. This well-organized and popular uprising, known as the **Caste War,** nearly returned the Yucatán to native control. Grievances accumulated over more than three hundred years led to great violence and property destruction. The end of the war with the United States allowed the government of Mexico to regain control of major towns. Even then, some Maya rebels retreated to unoccupied territories and created an independent state, which they called the "Empire of the Cross." Organized around a mix of traditional beliefs and Christian symbols, this indigenous state resisted Mexican forces until 1870. A few Maya strongholds survived until 1901.

---

[3] Quoted in Brian Loveman, *Chile: The Legacy of Hispanic Capitalism* (New York: Oxford University Press, 1979), 170.

THE CHALLENGE OF SOCIAL AND ECONOMIC CHANGE

During the nineteenth century the newly independent nations of the Western Hemisphere struggled to realize the Enlightenment ideals of freedom and individual liberty that had helped ignite the revolutions for independence. The persistence of slavery and other oppressive colonial-era institutions slowed this process. Nevertheless, by century's end reform movements had ended the slave trade, abolished slavery, expanded voting rights, and assimilated immigrants from Asia and Europe.

Industrialization and integration in the world economy sometimes challenged political stability and social arrangements. While a small number of Western Hemisphere nations embraced industrialization, most were dependent on the export of agricultural and mining production. By the end of the century it was clear that the industrializing nations had grown richer than the nations that remained exporters of raw materials. All the region's economies, regardless of development path, had become more vulnerable and volatile as a result of greater dependence on foreign markets. Like contemporary movements for social reform, efforts to assert economic sovereignty produced powerful new political forces.

The Abolition of Slavery   Leaders of the independence movements of the United States and Latin America asserted ideals of universal freedom and citizenship that contrasted sharply with the reality of slavery. Those who sought to end the institution were called **abolitionists**. Despite their efforts, slavery survived in most of the hemisphere until the 1850s. It proved especially difficult to eradicate in regions where the export of plantation products was most important—such as the United States, Brazil, and Cuba.

Slavery in the United States was weakened first by the abolition of slavery in some northern states and by the end of the African slave trade in 1808. But the profitable expansion of cotton agriculture after the War of 1812 stalled further progress. In Spanish America tens of thousands of slaves gained freedom by joining revolutionary armies during the wars for independence (see Chapter 23). After independence, most Spanish American republics prohibited the slave trade, but growing international demand for sugar and coffee slowed the achievement of abolition. As prices rose for plantation products, Brazil and Cuba increased their imports of slaves.

During the long struggle to end slavery in the United States, American abolitionists argued that slavery offended Christian morality and the universal rights asserted in the Declaration of Independence. Abolitionist Theodore Weld articulated the religious objection to slavery in 1834:

> No condition of birth, no shade of color, no mere misfortune of circumstance, can annul the birth-right charter, which God has bequeathed to every being upon whom he has stamped his own image, by making him a free moral agent [emphasis in original], and that he who robs his fellow man of this tramples upon right, subverts justice, outrages humanity ... and sacrilegiously assumes the prerogative of God.[4]

---

[4] Quoted in Bernard Bailyn, David Brion Davis, David Herbert Donald, John L. Thomas, Robert H. Wiebe, and Gordon S. Wood, *The Great Republic: A History of the American People* (Lexington, MA: D. C. Heath, 1981), 398.

Two groups denied full rights under the Constitution, women and free African Americans, played important roles in the abolition of slavery. Women were among the leaders of the American Anti-Slavery Society and produced effective propaganda against slavery. Eventually, thousands of women joined the abolitionist cause. Social conservatives attacked their highly visible public role, leading many women to become public advocates of female suffrage as well. Frederick Douglass, a former slave, was one of the most visible and effective leaders of the abolitionist movement. Some black leaders, believing that peaceful means would fail, pushed the abolitionist movement to accept the inevitability of violence. In 1843 Henry Highland Garnet stirred the National Colored Convention when he demanded, "Brethren, arise, arise, arise! ... Let every slave in the land do this and the days of slavery are numbered."[5]

In the 1850s the electoral strength of the newly formed Republican Party forced a confrontation between slave and free states. Following the election of Abraham Lincoln in 1860, eleven southern states seceded from the Union. During the Civil War pressure for emancipation rose as tens of thousands of black freemen and escaped slaves joined the Union army. In 1863, in the midst of the Civil War and two years after the abolition of serfdom in Russia (see Chapter 27), Lincoln issued the Emancipation Proclamation, ending slavery in rebel states not occupied by the Union army. In 1865 the Thirteenth Amendment to the Constitution abolished slavery completely, but most African Americans continued to live in harsh conditions. By the end of the century southern states had instituted "Jim Crow" laws that segregated blacks in public transportation, jobs, and schools. The implementation of these laws coincided with increased racial violence that saw an average of fifty African Americans lynched each year.

In Brazil slavery survived for more than two decades after abolition in the United States. Britain, Brazil's major trading partner, pressed for an end to the slave trade after prohibiting this trade to its own colonies. Despite agreeing to end the trade in 1830, Brazil imported another half-million African slaves before the British navy forced compliance in the 1850s. The Brazilian emperor, Pedro II, and many liberals worked to abolish slavery, but their effort to find a form of gradual emancipation acceptable to slave owners failed.

During Brazil's war with Paraguay (1865–1870), large numbers of slaves joined the Brazilian army in exchange for freedom. Their patriotism and heroism convinced many Brazilians of the injustice of slavery. Educated Brazilians had also come to view slavery as an obstacle to economic development and as an impediment to democratic reform. As political support for slavery weakened in the 1880s, growing numbers of slaves fled their masters and army officers resisted demands to capture and return the runaways. Brazil finally abolished slavery in 1888. A year later a rebellion ended the Brazilian monarchy.

The Caribbean received almost 40 percent of all African slaves shipped to the New World. Throughout the region, tiny white minorities lived surrounded by slave and free colored majorities. In the eighteenth century the slave rebellion in Saint Domingue (see Chapter 23) spread terror among slave owners across the

---

[5] Quoted in Mary Beth Norton et al., *A People and a Nation: A History of the United States*, 6th ed. (Boston: Houghton Mifflin, 2001), 284.

Caribbean, convincing slave owners that any effort to overthrow colonial rule would unleash new insurrections. As a result, there was little local support for abolition in the Caribbean. In these colonies abolition would result from decisions made in Europe by imperial governments.

In the Caribbean, as in Brazil and other plantation economies, slaves helped to force abolition by rebelling, running away, and resisting in more subtle ways. Although slave rebellions in Jamaica and Cuba and other Caribbean colonies failed to achieve the success of the Haitian Revolution (1791–1804), they made clear that slaves would never accept their condition.

After 1800, when the profitability of sugar plantations in the British West Indian colonies declined, a coalition of British labor unions, Protestant ministers, and free traders pushed for the abolition of slavery. Britain, the major participant in the eighteenth-century expansion of slavery in the Americas, ended its participation in the slave trade in 1807. It then negotiated treaties with Spain, Brazil, and other importers of slaves to eliminate the slave trade and used its naval forces to force compliance.

Abolition in British colonies occurred in 1834, but "freed" slaves were compelled to remain with former masters as "apprentices." Abuses by planters and resistance to apprenticeship by former slaves led to complete abolition in 1838. A decade later, France abolished slavery in its Caribbean colonies. The decision to abolish slavery in the Dutch Empire in 1863 freed 33,000 slaves in Surinam and 12,000 in the Antilles.

In the Caribbean, slavery lasted longest in Spain's remaining colonies of Cuba and Puerto Rico. Britain used diplomatic pressure and naval force to undermine the slave trade after 1820, but local support for abolition appeared as well. Both Cuba and Puerto Rico had larger white and free colored populations than did the Caribbean colonies of Britain and France, and there was little fear that abolition would lead to the political ascendancy of former slaves. In Puerto Rico, where slaves numbered approximately 30,000, local reformers secured the abolition of slavery in 1873. In Cuba, where slavery was much more important because of a booming sugar industry, forces supporting independence helped propel the Spanish colonial government toward abolition (see Environment and Technology: Industrializing Sugar Agriculture in Cuba). Beginning in the 1870s, Spain passed a series of laws promoting gradual abolition but requiring long periods of service to former masters. Spain finally abolished slavery in 1886.

Immigration

During the colonial period free Europeans were a minority among immigrants to the Western Hemisphere. From 1500 to 1760 imported African slaves outnumbered European immigrants in the Western Hemisphere by nearly two to one. Another 4 million African slaves were then imported before the end of the slave trade in the 1850s. After the African slave trade came to an end, millions of Europeans and Asians arrived in the Western Hemisphere as immigrants. This new flood of immigrants in the nineteenth century helped foster the rapid economic growth and territorial occupation of frontier regions in the United States, Canada, Argentina, Chile, and Brazil. By century's end nearly all of the hemisphere's fastest-growing cities (Buenos Aires, Chicago, New York, and São Paulo, for example) had large immigrant populations.

In general, European immigrants avoided regions that had depended on slavery with their traditions of oppressive labor conditions and low wages. At the same time, tens of thousands of immigrants from China and India arrived with indenture contracts that directed them to plantation zones in the Caribbean region.

Europe provided the majority of immigrants to the Western Hemisphere in the nineteenth century. Initially, most came from western Europe, but after 1870 most immigrants were southern or eastern Europeans. The United States received approximately 600,000 European immigrants in the 1830s, 1.5 million in the 1840s, and then 2.5 million per decade until 1880. In the 1890s an astonishing total of 5.2 million immigrants arrived. Immigration helped push the national population from 39 million in 1871 to 63 million in 1891. Most of these immigrants settled in cities. Chicago, for example, grew from 444,000 in 1870 to 1.7 million in 1900.

European immigration to Latin America also increased dramatically. Combined immigration to Argentina and Brazil rose from under 130,000 in the 1860s to 1.7 million in the 1890s. By 1910, 30 percent of the Argentine population was foreign-born, more than twice the proportion in the U.S. population. Argentina was an extremely attractive destination for European immigrants, receiving more than twice as many immigrants as Canada between 1870 and 1930. Even so, immigration to Canada increased tenfold during this period.

Asian immigration to the Western Hemisphere also increased after 1850. Between 1849 and 1875, approximately 100,000 Chinese immigrants arrived in Peru and another 120,000 entered Cuba. Canada attracted about 50,000 Chinese immigrants in the second half of the century, and the United States received 300,000 Chinese immigrants between 1854 and 1882. India also contributed to the social transformation of the Western Hemisphere, sending more than a half-million immigrants to the Caribbean region. British Guiana alone received 238,000 immigrants, mostly indentured laborers, from the Asian subcontinent.

Despite the obvious economic benefits that accompanied this inflow of people, hostility to immigration mounted in many nations. Nativist political movements argued that it was impossible to integrate large numbers of foreigners into national political cultures. By the end of the century, fear and prejudice led many governments in the Western Hemisphere to limit immigration or to distinguish between "desirable" and "undesirable" immigrants, commonly favoring Europeans over Asians.

Asians faced more obstacles than did Europeans and were more often victims of violence and discrimination. In the 1870s and 1880s anti-Chinese riots erupted in many western cities in the United States. Congress responded to this wave of racism by passing the Chinese Exclusion Act in 1882, which eliminated most Chinese immigration. In 1886, popular fears that "inferior races" threatened Canada led that government to impose a head tax, making immigration more difficult for Chinese families. During this same period strong anti-Chinese prejudice surfaced in Peru, Mexico, and Cuba. Japanese immigrants in Brazil and East Indians in the English-speaking Caribbean faced similar prejudice.

European immigrants faced prejudice and discrimination as well. Popular opinion portrayed Italians as criminals or anarchists. In Argentina and the United States, some social scientists argued that Italian immigrants were more violent and less honest than the native-born population. Immigrants from Spain were widely stereotyped in Argentina as miserly and dishonest. Eastern European Jews seeking to

Archivo General de la Nación, Buenos Aires

Arrest of Labor Activist in Buenos Aires *The labor movement in Buenos Aires grew in numbers and became more radical with the arrival of tens of thousands of Italian and Spanish immigrants. Fearful of socialist and anarchist unions, the government of Argentina used an expanded police force to break strikes.*

escape pogroms and discrimination at home found themselves barred from many educational institutions and professional careers in both the United States and Latin America. Irish, German, Swedish, Polish, and Middle Eastern immigrants were branded with negative stereotypes as well. The justifications for these prejudices were remarkably similar from Canada to Argentina. Immigrants, critics claimed, threatened the well-being of native-born workers by accepting low wages and threatened national culture by resisting assimilation.

Many intellectuals and political leaders wondered if the evolving mix of culturally diverse populations could sustain a common citizenship. This concern led to efforts to compel immigrants to assimilate. Schools became cultural battlegrounds where language, cultural values, and patriotic attitudes were transmitted to the children of immigrants. Ignoring Canada's large French-speaking population, an English-speaking Canadian reformer commented on recent immigration: "If Canada is to become in a real sense a nation, if our people are to become one people, we must have one language."[6] These fears and prejudices promoted the singing of patriotic songs, the veneration of national flags and other symbols, and the writing of national histories that emphasized patriotism and civic virtue.

---

[6] J. S. Woodsworth in 1909, quoted in R. Douglas Francis, Richard Jones, and Donald B. Smith, *Destinies: Canadian History Since Confederation*, 2d ed. (Toronto: Holt, Rinehart and Winston, 1992), 141.

American Cultures

Despite discrimination, immigrants continued to stream into the Western Hemisphere, where they introduced new languages, living arrangements, technologies, and customs. Immigrants also altered politics in many of the hemisphere's nations as they sought to influence government policies and gain access to power. To compensate for their isolation from home, language, and culture, most immigrant groups created ethnically based mutual aid societies, sports and leisure clubs, and neighborhoods. These organizations provided valuable social and economic support for recent arrivals while sometimes worsening the fears of the native-born that immigration posed a threat to national culture. At the same time, shared experiences in their adopted nations as workers, neighbors, or soldiers changed immigrants individually and collectively. The modification of language, customs, values, and behaviors as a result of contact with people from another culture is called **acculturation**.

Immigrants and their children, in turn, made their mark on the cultures of their adopted nations. They learned the language spoken in their adopted countries as fast as possible in order to improve their earning capacity, while words and phrases from their languages entered the vocabularies of their adoptive nations. Languages as diverse as Yiddish and Italian strongly influenced American English, Argentine Spanish, and Brazilian Portuguese. Dietary practices introduced from Europe and Asia altered the cuisine of nearly every American nation. In popular music, the Argentine tango, based on African rhythms, was transformed by new instrumentation and orchestral arrangements brought by Italian immigrants. Mexican ballads blended with English folk music in the U.S. Southwest, and Italian operas played to packed houses in Buenos Aires.

Union movements and electoral politics in the hemisphere also felt the influence of new arrivals who aggressively sought to influence politics and improve working conditions. The anarchist and socialist beliefs of European immigrants influenced the labor movements of Mexico, Argentina, and the United States. Immigrants also helped form new political movements. Their mutual benevolent societies and less formal ethnic associations pooled resources to help immigrants open businesses, aid the immigration of relatives, or bury family members.

Women's Rights and the Struggle for Social Justice

In 1848, a group of women angered by their exclusion from an international antislavery meeting issued a call for a conference to discuss women's rights. The resulting **Women's Rights Convention** at Seneca Falls, New York, issued a statement that said, in part, "We hold these truths to be self-evident: that all men and women are equal." While moderates focused on the issues of economic independence and legal rights, increasing numbers of women demanded the right to vote. Others lobbied to provide better conditions for women working outside the home, especially in textile factories. Sarah Grimké responded to criticism of women's activism:

> This has been the language of man since he laid aside the whip as a means to keep woman in subjection. He spares her body, but the war he has waged against her mind, her heart, and her soul, has been no less destructive to her as a moral being. How monstrous is the doctrine that woman is to be dependent on man![7]

---

[7] Sarah Grimké, "Reply to the Massachusetts Clergy," in *Early American Women: A Documentary History*, 1600–1900, ed. Nancy Woloch (Belmont, CA: Wadsworth, 1992), 343.

Progress toward equality between men and women was equally slow in Canada and in Latin America. Canada's first women doctors received their training in the United States because women could not receive medical degrees until 1895. Argentina and Uruguay were among the first Latin American nations to provide public education for women, introducing coeducation in the 1870s. Chilean women gained access to some careers in medicine and law in the 1870s, while in Brazil the first women graduated in medicine in 1882. In Argentina the first woman doctor graduated from medical school in 1899.

Throughout the hemisphere more rapid progress occurred in lower-status careers that threatened male economic power less directly, and, by the end of the century, women dominated elementary school teaching. From Canada to Argentina and Chile, the majority of working-class women, although having no direct involvement in reform movements, succeeded in transforming gender relations in their daily lives. By the end of the nineteenth century, large numbers of poor women worked outside the home on farms, in markets, and, increasingly, in factories. Many bore full responsibility for providing for their children. Whether men thought women should remain in the home or not, by the end of the century women were unambiguously present in the economy (see also Chapter 27).

There was little progress toward eliminating racial discrimination in the nineteenth century. Blacks were denied the vote throughout the southern United States and were subjected to the indignity of segregation—consigned to separate schools, hotels, restaurants, seats in public transportation, and even water fountains. Racial discrimination against men and women of African descent was also common in Latin America. Unlike the southern states of the United States, however, Latin American nations did not insist on formal racial segregation or permit lynching. Nor did they enforce a strict color line. Many men and women of mixed background were able to enter the skilled working class or middle class, and some rose to political prominence. Latin Americans tended to view racial identity across a continuum of physical characteristics rather than in the narrow terms of black and white that defined race relations in the United States.

The abolition of slavery in Latin America did not end discrimination. Some leaders of the abolition struggles later organized to promote racial integration. They demanded access to education, the right to vote, and greater economic opportunity, pointing out the economic and political costs of denying full rights to all citizens. Their success depended on effective political organization and on forging alliances with sympathetic white politicians. Black intellectuals also struggled to overturn racist stereotypes. In Brazil, Argentina, and Cuba, as in the United States, political and literary magazines celebrating black cultural achievement became powerful weapons in the struggle against racial discrimination. While men and women of African descent continued to experience prejudice and discrimination everywhere in the Americas, successful men and women of mixed descent in Latin America confronted fewer obstacles to advancement than did similar groups in the United States.

Development and Underdevelopment   While the Atlantic economy experienced three periods of severe economic contraction during the nineteenth century, nearly all the nations of the Western Hemisphere were richer in 1900 than in 1800. The effects of the Industrial Revolution, worldwide population growth, and an increasingly integrated world market combined to stimulate economic expansion (see Environment and Technology: Industrializing Sugar Agriculture in Cuba). Wheat, corn, wool, meats, and nonprecious minerals joined the region's earlier exports of silver, sugar, dyes, coffee, and cotton. The United States was the only Western Hemisphere nation to industrialize, but nearly every government promoted new industries and technologies. Governments invested in roads, railroads, canals, and telegraph systems to better serve distant markets, while adopting tariff and monetary policies to foster economic diversification and growth. Despite these efforts, by 1900 only three Western Hemisphere nations—the United States, Canada, and Argentina—achieved individual income levels similar to those of western Europe. All three nations had open land, temperate climates, diverse resources, and large inflows of immigrants.

New demands for copper, zinc, lead, coal, and tin unleashed by the Industrial Revolution led to mining booms in the western United States, Mexico, and Chile. The mining companies of the late nineteenth century were heavily capitalized international corporations that could bully governments and buy political favors. By 1900 European and North American corporations owned nearly all the largest mining enterprises in Latin America. Petroleum development, which occurred at the end of the century in Mexico and elsewhere, followed this pattern as well (see the discussion of the Mexican economy during the Díaz dictatorship in Chapter 26).

New technology accelerated economic integration, but the high cost of this technology often increased dependence on foreign capital. Many governments promoted railroads by granting tax benefits, free land, and monopoly rights to both domestic and foreign investors. As a result, by 1890 vast areas of the Great Plains in the United States, the Canadian prairie, the Argentine pampas, and parts of northern Mexico were producing grain and livestock for foreign markets opened by the development of railroads. Steamships also lowered the cost of transportation to distant markets, and the telegraph stimulated expansion by speeding information about the demand for and availability of products.

The simultaneous acquisition of several new technologies could have a dramatic effect on a nation's economy. In Argentina, for example, the railroad, the telegraph, barbed wire, and refrigeration were all introduced in the 1870s and 1880s. Although Argentina had had abundant livestock herds since the colonial period, the distance from Europe's markets prevented Argentine cattle raisers from exporting fresh meat or live animals. Technology overcame these obstacles. The combination of railroads and the telegraph lowered freight costs and improved information about markets, steamships shortened the time needed for transatlantic crossings, and refrigerated ships made it possible to sell meat in distant markets. As land values rose and livestock breeding improved, ranchers protected new investments with barbed wire, the first inexpensive fencing available on the nearly treeless plains.

Growing interdependence and increased competition produced deep structural differences among Western Hemisphere economies by 1900. Two distinct economic tracks became visible. One led to industrialization and prosperity: **development**. The other continued colonial dependence on exporting raw materials and on low-wage industries: **underdevelopment**. By 1900 prosperity was greater and economic development more diversified in English-speaking North America than in the nations of Latin America. With a temperate climate, vast fertile prairies, and an influx of European immigrants, Argentina was the only Latin American nation to approach the prosperity of the United States and Canada in 1900.

ENVIRONMENT + TECHNOLOGY

Industrializing Sugar Agriculture in Cuba

Sugar played a key role in the development of the Western Hemisphere, with the profits of sugar plantations rivaling the vast wealth in silver and gold extracted from Spain's colonial empire. The expansion of sugar agriculture from Brazil to the Caribbean was the major driving force in the African slave trade until its effective end in the 1850s. The fact that 70 percent of all African slaves brought to the Americas were distributed to sugar-producing regions is one measure

Library of Congress Prints and Photographs Division [LC-D4-9223]

Cuban Sugar Refinery Showing Mix of Traditional and Modern Technologies *Sugar cane was delivered to the crushing mill by both ox carts and railroad lines. In the background, steam-driven machinery moves cane to a crusher.*

Changes in the performance of international markets helped determine the trajectory of Western Hemisphere economies as new nations promoted economic development. When the United States gained independence, the world economy enjoyed rapid growth. With a large merchant fleet, a diversified economy that included some manufacturing, and adequate banking and insurance services, the United States benefited from this expansion. Rapid population growth due in large measure to immigration, high levels of individual wealth, widespread landownership, and of sugar's influence in the hemisphere. When most of Haiti's sugar plantations were destroyed by revolutionary violence, world sugar prices shot upward in the early nineteenth century. Cuban planters jumped into the vacuum, importing tens of thousands of slaves and opening new lands to sugar production. Within two decades, Cuba had become the world's largest sugar producer.

Cuba's sugar industry soon confronted two challenges to its ascendency. Having already ended the slave trade to its own sugar islands in 1807, Great Britain pushed Spain to end the slave trade to Cuba, ultimately using its navy to reduce imports to a trickle. Almost simultaneously, new technologies were introduced in Europe that permitted the profitable extraction of sugar from beets. As a result, labor became more expensive for Cuban planters at the same time that sugar prices fell internationally. To remain profitable, the Cuban sugar industry embraced technological innovations that had earlier revolutionized manufacturing.

Planters with the largest estates and the largest numbers of slaves had always enjoyed a competitive advantage over smaller producers because they could afford the most efficient crushing and refining technologies, benefiting from what economists call economies of scale (see Chapter 19). With beet sugar production driving prices lower, Cuba's large-scale producers displaced their less efficient competitors while at the same opening virgin land to sugar production.

Between 1878 and 1900 alone, more than 1.4 million acres of forest were lost to the expanding sugar plantations. As lower prices increased competition and as the volume of sugar production soared in Cuba, the number of sugar producers steadily decreased, a pattern that neither political violence nor the abolition of slavery (1886) could alter.

Concentration was also promoted by the high cost of mechanization. The most heavily capitalized producers imported steam engines to replace the animal traction and water power previously used to crush cane and then introduced new, more efficient refining technologies. As crushing and refining capacities expanded in the modern mills, called *centrales* in Spanish, small-scale producers closed their expensive and inefficient mills to concentrate on growing sugar cane. Railroad construction multiplied the effects of these innovations, tying distant sugar growers to the mechanized refiners, many of them foreign owned. As had happened in English textile manufacturing during the Industrial Revolution (see Chapter 22), technological innovation in Cuba's sugar industry had concentrated the control of production and wealth in the hands of a new elite. The centrales were truly factories in the fields. As Cuba neared independence in the 1890s, the island's modernized sugar sector consisted of a relatively small number of industrialized refiners and a mass of increasingly vulnerable and dependent cane farmers.

relatively high literacy rates also fostered rapid economic development. By 1865 the United States had already established the world's largest railroad network, but by 1915 railroad mileage had multiplied elevenfold. Steel production grew rapidly as well, with the United States overtaking world leaders Britain and Germany in the 1890s.

Canada's achievement of greater political autonomy, the Confederation of 1867, coincided with a second period of global economic expansion. Canada also benefited from a special trading relationship with Britain, the world's preeminent industrial nation, and from a rising tide of immigrants after 1850. Nevertheless, some regions within each of these prosperous North American nations—Canada's Maritime Provinces and the southern part of the United States—demonstrated the same patterns of underdevelopment found in Latin America.

Most Latin American nations gained independence in the 1820s when the global economy contracted. In the colonial period, Spain and Portugal had promoted the production of agricultural and mining exports in their colonies. After independence these exports faced increased competition. Although these sectors experienced periods of great prosperity in the nineteenth century, they also faced stiff competition and falling prices as new regions began production or competing products captured markets.

The history of the Latin American economies, subject to periodic problems of oversupply and low prices, was one of boom and bust. Many Latin American governments sought to promote exports in the face of increased competition and falling prices by resisting union activity and demands for higher wages and by opening domestic markets to foreign manufactures. The resulting low wages and an abundance of foreign manufactured goods, in turn, undermined efforts to promote industrialization in Latin America.

Weak governments, political instability, and, in some cases, civil war also slowed Latin American economic development. Because Latin America was also dependent on importing foreign capital and technology, Great Britain and, by the end of the century, the United States often imposed unfavorable trade conditions or even intervened militarily to protect their investments. The combined impact of these domestic and international impediments to development became clear when Mexico, Chile, and Argentina failed to achieve high levels of domestic investment in manufacturing late in the nineteenth century, despite a rapid accumulation of wealth derived from traditional exports.

Altered Environments   Population growth, economic expansion, new technologies, and the introduction of foreign plants and animals dramatically altered American environments in the nineteenth century. Cuba's planters cut down the island's forests in the early nineteenth century to expand sugar production. Growing demand for meat led ranchers to expand livestock-raising into fragile environments in Argentina, Uruguay, southern Brazil, and the southwestern United States. Other forms of commercial agriculture also threatened the environment. Farmers in South Carolina and Georgia gained a short-term increase in cotton production by abandoning crop rotation after 1870, but this practice quickly led to soil exhaustion and erosion. Similarly, coffee planters in Brazil exhausted fertility with a destructive cycle of overplanting followed by expansion onto forest reserves cleared by cutting and burning. The transfers of land from public to private ownership in order to promote livestock-raising and agriculture also altered landscapes. Finally, new technologies had environmental effects. For example, the use of steel plows on North American prairies and Argentine pampas eliminated many native grasses and increased the threat of soil erosion.

Rapid urbanization also imposed environmental costs. New York, Chicago, Rio de Janeiro, Buenos Aires, and Mexico City were among the world's fastest-growing cities in the nineteenth century, and governments strained to provide sewers, clean water, and garbage disposal. Timber companies clear-cut large areas of Michigan, Wisconsin, and the Appalachian Mountains in the United States to provide lumber for railroad ties and housing, pulp for paper, and fuel for locomotives and foundries. At the same time, the forest industries of British Honduras (now Belize), Nicaragua, and Guatemala grew rapidly in response to demand in Europe and North America for tropical hardwoods like mahogany. As forests throughout the hemisphere were cleared, animal habitats and native plant species disappeared.

The scale of mining in Nevada, Montana, and California accelerated erosion and pollution. Similar results occurred in other mining areas as well. Nitrate mining and open-pit copper mining in Chile scarred and polluted the environment. The state of Minas Gerais (ME-nas JER-aize) in Brazil experienced a series of mining booms that began with gold in the late seventeenth century and continued with iron ore in the nineteenth. By the end of the nineteenth century, its red soil had been ripped open, its forests were depleted, and erosion was uncontrolled. Similar devastation afflicted parts of Bolivia and Mexico.

By the end of the nineteenth century, small-scale conservation efforts were under way in many nations, and the first national parks and nature reserves were created. In the United States large areas remained undeveloped. In 1872 Yellowstone in Wyoming became the first national park. President Theodore Roosevelt (1901–1909) and the naturalist John Muir played major roles in preserving large areas of the western states. Canada created its first national park in Banff in 1885 and expanded it from 10 to 260 square miles (26 to 673 square kilometers) two years later. When confronted with a choice between economic growth and environmental protection, however, the hemisphere's nations embraced growth.

CONCLUSION

While the new nations of the Western Hemisphere faced similar challenges in the nineteenth century, they had developed from different colonial traditions. The effort to establish stable constitutional systems proved difficult nearly everywhere. While the constitution of the United States endured, conflict over slavery led to a civil war that threatened the nation's survival. Elsewhere most new constitutions failed within a generation. In Argentina, for example, fifty years passed before a stable national government was in place. Personalist political leaders with large followings, like José Antonio Páez and Andrew Jackson, resisted the constraints of constitutions. Regionalism, ideological confrontations, racial divisions, and conflict with native peoples all threatened stability as well.

New nations also faced foreign interventions and local wars with regional powers. By 1850, Mexico had lost 50 percent of its territory to the United States and then faced a French invasion in 1862. Bolivia and Peru lost territory to an expansive Chile, while Paraguay lost a disastrous war to an alliance of Argentina, Brazil, and Uruguay. American nations also fought numerous wars with indigenous peoples, crushing resistance by the 1890s.

The nations of the hemisphere also experienced a series of dramatic social and economic changes in this period. The slave trade and slavery persisted long after independence (see Chapter 19), but after a century of protest and political mobilization, the hemisphere's last slave state, Brazil, freed its slaves in 1888. Slavery left a legacy of racism and discrimination across the Americas. In places where the institution was most important—the plantation regions of Brazil, the Caribbean, and the American South—racial prejudice, discrimination, and persistent low levels of investment in education and internal improvements slowed economic growth and weakened democracy. By 1890 many of the hemisphere's poorest nations or poorest regions within nations were those that had depended on slavery.

Amerindian populations experienced centuries of exploitation, forced integration in market economies, and compulsory removal to marginal lands. In most of Latin America, Amerindians had been subjected to exploitation for centuries when the Spanish and Portuguese empires finally fell. Once in place, forced labor and other abuses persisted into the twentieth century in nations like Guatemala and Bolivia. With independence, new national governments undertook the pacification of the hemisphere's remaining independent native peoples. By the 1890s nearly all were reduced to reservations or forced onto marginal lands. As a result, Amerindians were among the poorest peoples in the hemisphere, suffering oppression, poverty, and disenfranchisement.

Immigration transformed many Western Hemisphere nations. As a general rule, the millions of European immigrants that entered the Western Hemisphere in the nineteenth century avoided regions where slavery dominated or where indigenous populations were compelled to labor. Argentina, Brazil, Canada, and the United States were the most popular destinations, and immigrants to Brazil and the United States avoided the former plantation zones. Instead, hundreds of thousands of Chinese and East Indians, migrating as indentured laborers, were directed to plantation regions, especially in the Caribbean, where they faced racism and discrimination.

Industrialization had a transforming effect on the hemisphere. Wealth, political power, and population were increasingly concentrated in urban areas, and bankers and manufacturers, rather than farmers and plantation owners, increasingly directed national destinies. Industrialization altered the natural environment in dramatic ways. Modern factories consumed huge amounts of raw materials and energy. Copper mines in Chile and Mexico, Cuban sugar plantations, Brazilian coffee plantations, and Canadian lumber companies all left their mark on the natural environment, and all had ties to markets in the United States.

In 1900 nearly every American nation was wealthier, better educated, more democratic, and more populous than at independence. But most of these new nations were also more vulnerable to distant economic forces and more profoundly split between haves and have-nots. The hemisphere was also more clearly divided into a rich north and a poorer south. A small number of nations located in the temperate regions—Canada, the United States, Argentina, and Chile—had become prosperous regional powers relative to their neighbors. While most of the hemisphere's growth continued to depend on the export of agricultural goods and raw materials—sugar, cotton, grains, minerals, and livestock products—the United States had become one of the world's richest industrial nations by 1890.

IMPORTANT EVENTS 1800–1890

1789	U.S. Constitution ratified
1803	Louisiana Purchase
1808	Portuguese royal family arrives in Brazil
1808–1809	Revolutions for independence begin in Spanish South America
1810–1821	Mexican movement for independence
1812–1815	War of 1812
1822	Brazil gains independence
1831	Brazil signs treaty with Great Britain to end slave trade. Illegal trade continues.
1836	Texas gains independence from Mexico
1845	Texas admitted as a state
1846–1848	War between Mexico and the United States
1847–1870	Caste War
1848	Women's Rights Convention in Seneca Falls, New York
1850	Brazilian illegal slave trade suppressed
1857	Mexico's new constitution limits power of Catholic Church and military
1861–1865	Civil War
1862–1867	French invade Mexico
1865–1870	Argentina, Uruguay, and Brazil wage war against Paraguay
1867	Creation of Dominion of Canada
1867	Emperor Maximilian executed
1870s	Governments of Argentina and Chile begin final campaigns against indigenous peoples
1876	Sioux and allies defeat U.S. Army in Battle of Little Bighorn
1879–1881	Chile wages war against Peru and Bolivia; telegraph, refrigeration, and barbed wire introduced in Argentina
1888	Abolition of slavery in Brazil
1890	"Jim Crow" laws enforce segregation in South
1890s	United States becomes world's leading steel producer

ISSUES IN WORLD HISTORY

State Power, the Census, and the Question of Identity

Between the American Revolution and the last decades of the nineteenth century, Europe and the Americas were transformed. The ancient power of kings and the authority of religion were eclipsed by muscular new ways of organizing political, economic, and intellectual life. The Western world was vastly different in 1870 than it had been a century earlier. One of the less heralded but enduringly significant changes was the huge expansion of government statistical services.

The rise of the nation-state was associated with the development of modern bureaucratic departments that depended on reliable statistics to measure the nation's achievements and discover its failures. The nation-state, whether democratic or not, mobilized resources on a previously unimaginable scale. Modern states were more powerful and wealthier, and they were also more ambitious and more intrusive. The growth of their power can be seen in the modernization of militaries, the commitment to internal improvements such as railroads, and the growth in state revenues. In recent years historians have begun to examine a less visible but equally important manifestation of growing state power: census taking.

Governments and religious authorities have counted people since early times. Our best estimates of the Amerindian population of the Western Hemisphere in 1500 rest almost entirely on what were little more than missionaries' guesses about the numbers of people they baptized. Spanish and Portuguese kings were eager to count native populations, since "indios" (adult male Amerindians) were subject to special labor obligations and tribute payments. So, from the mid-sixteenth century onward, imperial officials conducted regular censuses of Amerindians, adapting practices already in place in Europe.

The effort to measure and categorize populations was transformed in the last decades of the eighteenth century when the nature of European governments began to change. The Enlightenment belief that the scientific method could be applied to human society proved to be attractive both to political radicals, like the French revolutionaries, and to reforming monarchs like Maria Theresa of Austria. Enlightenment philosophers had argued that a science of government could remove the inefficiencies and irrationalities that had long subverted the human potential for prosperity and happiness. The French intellectual Condorcet wrote in 1782:

Those sciences, created almost in our own days, the object of which is man himself, the direct goal of which is the happiness of man, will enjoy a progress no less sure than that of the physical sciences. . . . In meditating on the nature of the moral sciences [what we now call the social sciences], one cannot help seeing that, as they are based like the physical sciences on the observation of fact, they must follow the method, acquire a language equally exact and precise, attaining the same degree of certainty.[1]

As confidence in this new "science" grew, the term previously used to describe the collection of numbers about society, *political arithmetic*, was abandoned by governments and practitioners in favor of *statistics*, a term that clearly suggests its close ties to the "state." In the nineteenth century the new objectives set out by Condorcet and others led to both the formal university training of statisticians and the creation of government statistical services.

The ambitions of governments in this new era were great. Nation-states self-consciously sought to transform society, sponsoring economic development, education, and improvements in health and welfare. They depended on statistics to measure the effectiveness of their policies and, as a result, were interested in nearly everything. They counted taverns, urban buildings, births and deaths, and arrests and convictions. They also counted their populations with a thoroughness never before seen. As statistical reporting became more uniform across Europe and the Americas, governments could measure not only their own progress but also that of their neighbors and rivals.

The revolutionary governments of France modernized the census practices of the overthrown monarchy. They spent much more money, hired many more census takers, and devoted much more energy to training the staff that designed censuses and analyzed results. Great Britain set up an official census in 1801, but it established a special administrative structure only in the 1830s. In the Western Hemisphere nearly every independent nation provided for "scientific" censuses. In the United States the federal constitution required that a census be taken every ten years. Latin American nations, often torn by civil war in the nineteenth century, took censuses less regularly, but even the poorest nations took censuses when they could. It was as if the census itself confirmed the existence of the government, demonstrating its modernity and seriousness.

Until recently, historians who relied on these documents in their research on economic performance, issues of race and ethnicity, family life, and fertility and mortality asked few questions about the politics of census design. What could be more objective than rows of numbers? But the advocates of statistics who managed census taking were uninhibited in advertising the usefulness of reliable numbers to the governments that employed them. At the 1860 International Statistical Congress held in London, one speaker said, "I think the true meaning to be attached to 'statistics' is not every collection of figures, but figures collected with the sole purpose of applying the principles deduced from them to questions of importance to the state."[2] The desire to be useful meant that statistics could not be fully objective.

Subjectivity was an unavoidable problem with censuses. Censuses identified citizens and foreign residents by place of residence, sex, age, and family relationships within households as well as profession and literacy. These determinations were sometimes subjective. Modern scholars have demonstrated that census takers also routinely undercounted the poor and those living in rural areas.

Because census takers, as agents of nation-states, were determined to be useful, they were necessarily concerned with issues of nationality and, in the Americas, with race because these characteristics commonly determined political rights and citizenship. The assessment and recording of nationality and race would prove to be among the most politically dubious objectives of the new social sciences.

Nationality had not been a central question for traditional monarchies. For the emerging nation-state, however, nationality was central. A nation's strength was assumed to depend in large measure on the growth of its population, a standard that, once articulated, suggested that the growth of minority populations was dangerous. Who was French? Who was Austrian or Hungarian? European statisticians relied on both *language of use* and *mother tongue* as proxies for *nationality*, the first term being flexible enough to recognize the assimilation of minorities, the second suggesting a more permanent identity based on a person's original language. Both terms forced bilingual populations to simplify their more complex identities. Ethnic minorities, once identified, were sometimes subject to discrimination such as exclusion from military careers or from universities. In parts of Spanish America, *language* was used as a proxy for *race*. Those who spoke Spanish were citizens in the full sense, even if they were indistinguishable from Amerindians in appearance. Those who spoke indigenous languages were "indios" and therefore subject to special taxes and labor obligations and effectively denied the right to vote.

Beyond providing a justification for continuing discrimination, census categories compressed and distorted the complexity and variety of human society to fit the preconceptions of bureaucrats and politicians. Large percentages of the residents of Mexico, Peru, and Bolivia, among other parts of the Americas, were descended from both Europeans and Amerindians and, in the Caribbean region, from Europeans and Africans. Census categories never adequately captured the complexities of these biological and cultural mixtures. We now know that the poor were often identified as "indios" or "blacks" and the better-off were often called something else—"Americanos," "criollos" (creoles), or even whites. Since this process flattened and streamlined the complexities of identity, censuses on their own are not reliable guides to the distribution of ethnicity and race in a population.

In Europe, the issue of nationality proved similarly perplexing for census takers and similarly dangerous to those identified as minorities. Linguistic and ethnic minorities had always lived among the politically dominant majorities: Jewish and Polish minorities in areas controlled by German speakers, German speakers among the French, and Serbo-Croatian speakers among Hungarians, for example. The frontiers between these minority populations and their neighbors were always porous. Sexual unions and marriages were common, and two or more generations of a family often lived together in the same household, with the elder members speaking one language and the younger members another. Who was what? In a very real sense, nationality, like race in the Americas, was ultimately fixed by the census process, as the nation-state forced a limited array of politically utilitarian categories onto the rich diversity of ethnicity and culture.

[1]Quoted in James C. Scott, *Seeing like a State. How Certain Schemes to Improve the Human Condition Have Failed* (New Haven: Yale University Press, 1998), 91.

[2]This discussion relies heavily on Eliza Johnson (now Ablovatski), "Counting and Categorizing: The Hungarian Gypsy Census of 1893" (M.A. Thesis, Columbia University, 1996), especially Chapter III. She quotes from the *Proceedings of the Sixth International Statistical Congress Held in London, 1860*, 379.

Part Seven

Global Diversity and Dominance, 1750–1945

CHAPTER 26
Varieties of Imperialism in Africa, India, Southeast Asia, and Latin America, 1750–1914

CHAPTER 27
The New Power Balance, 1850–1900

CHAPTER 28
The Crisis of the Imperial Order, 1900–1929

CHAPTER 29
Revolutions in Living, 1900–1950

CHAPTER 30
The Collapse of the Old Order, 1929–1949

During the century that preceded 1830, European imperialism gained new footholds, sometimes against intense resistance, in parts of Africa and Asia. Most expansion continued earlier patterns in which European trading companies rather than governments took the initiative.

From roughly 1830 onward, formal colonies governed by state-appointed administrators and supported by European armies came to the fore in a scramble for territory in Africa and the Pacific region. By World War I Europe, the United States, and Japan collectively dominated much of the world and tried to convert other peoples to their own cultures and ways of life.

In Europe, mounting tensions led to the Great War of 1914–1918. Russia and China erupted in revolution. Soon after, the heartland of the Ottoman Empire became modern Turkey, while its Arab provinces were taken over by France and Britain.

Amidst a worldwide transformation of lifestyles brought on by new technologies, the political and economic system the European powers crafted after the war fell apart in the 1930s. While the capitalist nations fell into a depression, the Soviet Union industrialized at breakneck speed. In Germany and Japan, extremists sought to solve their countries' grievances by military conquest.

As World War II loomed, nationalists in India yearned for independence while nationalists in Latin America sought an end to foreign military interventions, increasing global economic and political tensions.

The war caused the death of millions of people and the destruction of countless cities. It also weakened Europe's overseas empires. India gained its independence in 1947. Two years later, Mao Zedong led the Chinese communists to victory. Latin American leaders embraced nationalist economic and social policies that challenged the traditional role of foreign investors. Of all the once great powers, only the United States and the Soviet Union remained to compete for global dominance.

26

VARIETIES OF IMPERIALISM IN AFRICA, INDIA, SOUTHEAST ASIA, AND LATIN AMERICA, 1750–1914

L ike many regions that looked to be coherent countries on the maps drawn by imperialism, Algeria was not a unified realm in 1830 when France landed 35,000 troops outside of Algiers. Five days later, at a cost of 6,000 dead and wounded Frenchmen, the *dey* (ruler) of Algiers, an autonomous governor ruling under Ottoman suzerainty, surrendered the city. French nationalists called the invasion a defense of French honor because three years earlier the dey had struck a French diplomat with a fly whisk during an argument over debts lingering from the Napoleonic wars, which had ended more than a decade earlier. Actually the invasion plan had been drawn up by Napoleon himself in 1808 in response to commercial interests in southern France that sought to acquire new land in North Africa.

Control of Algiers, however, did not prevent the king of Morocco from pressing a claim to rule Algeria's western region, nor did it fit the political interests of the country's five major Sufi brotherhoods, which had earlier staged revolts against Ottoman imperialism. The brotherhood that would prove the hardest for the French to defeat was the Qadiriya, which waged a sixteen-year *jihad* (holy war) that only ended in 1847 with the surrender of its leader Abd al-Qadir.

Abd al-Qadir (AHB-dahl-KAH-deer) was only twenty-five when he took over from his father as head of the brotherhood, but he had spent three years traveling in the Middle East, making the pilgrimage to Mecca, getting to know other Qadiriya leaders, and studying at famous institutions of learning in Tunis and Cairo. He had also observed the efforts of Muhammad Ali in Egypt to build a modern army and state.

The key to Abd al-Qadir's success was a network of religious centers (*zawiyas*) that trained judges and administrators and disseminated his vision of an egalitarian society that would observe Islamic law and be dominated by neither Ottoman officials nor French generals. Other Sufi brotherhoods fought separately against the French, but not as successfully.

Though Abd al-Qadir was allowed to settle in Damascus after his defeat and there pursued an eminent career as a leader of the Muslim community, his historical image is primarily one of resistance to imperialism. Like most movements elsewhere opposing imperialist aggression, Abd al-Qadir's Sufi followers could not prevail against European firepower. In the long run, however, such histories of resistance laid the ideological, if sometimes semilegendary, groundwork for anticolonial movements that would gain momentum after World War II.

Defenders of imperialism often cite the benefits of European rule in terms of railroad construction, orderly governance, integration of local production with currents of international trade, and similar economic and administrative factors. But the reputations or legends of leaders like Abd al-Qadir would eventually eclipse the memory of some of the generals and administrators who oversaw a massive increase in European imperialism starting in the late eighteenth century.

CHANGES AND EXCHANGES IN AFRICA

In the century before 1870, Africa underwent dynamic political changes and a great expansion of foreign trade. While a few indigenous African leaders held out against European imperialism, maps of Africa became increasingly tinted with pink and green, the conventional colors of British and French colonies, respectively. On the economic plane, however, as the slave trade died under British pressure, trade in other goods grew sharply. Africans consumed large quantities of machine-made textiles, and those rulers who retained a measure of independence purchased European firearms.

Southern Africa   For many centuries the Nguni (ng-GOO-nee) peoples had farmed and raised cattle in the fertile coast-lands of southeastern Africa. When drought hit the region at the beginning of the nineteenth century, an upstart military leader named Shaka (r. 1818–1828) created the **Zulu** kingdom. Strict military drill and close-combat tactics featuring ox-hide shields and lethal stabbing spears made the Zulu the most powerful and most feared fighters in southern Africa.

Shaka expanded his kingdom by raiding his African neighbors, seizing their cattle, and capturing their women and children. Breakaway military bands spread this system of warfare and state building inland to the high plateau country as far north as Lake Victoria. As the power and population of these new kingdoms increased, so too did the number of displaced and demoralized refugees around them.

To protect themselves from the Zulu, some neighboring Africans created their own states. The Swazi kingdom consolidated north of the Zulu, and the kingdom of Lesotho (luh-SOO-too) grew by attracting refugees to strongholds in southern Africa's highest mountains. Both Lesotho and Swaziland survive as independent states to this day.

Although Shaka ruled for little more than a decade, he left behind a mythic identity as well as a new kingdom. These were destined to conflict, however, with southern Africa's attractiveness to European settlers. The Cape Colony, first a Dutch possession but definitively under British rule after 1806, flourished because of Cape Town's strategic importance as a supply station for ships making the long voyages between Europe and India. With the port city came some twenty thousand descendants of Dutch and French settlers who occupied farms and ranches in its hinterland. Despite their European origins, these people thought of themselves as permanent residents of Africa and were beginning to refer to themselves as **Afrikaners** (af-rih-KAHN-uhr). British governors prohibited any expansion of the white settler frontier because such expansion invariably led to wars with indigenous Africans. This decision, along with the

Zulu in Battle Dress, 1838 *Elaborate costumes helped impress opponents with the Zulus' strength. Shown here are long-handled spears and thick leather shields.*

imposition of laws protecting African rights within Cape Colony (including the emancipation of slaves in 1834), alienated many Afrikaners.

Between 1836 and 1839 parties of Afrikaners embarked on a "Great Trek," leaving British-ruled Cape Colony for the fertile high *veld* (plateau) to the north that two decades of Zulu wars had depopulated. The Great Trek laid the foundation of three new settler colonies in southern Africa: the Afrikaners' Orange Free State and Transvaal on the high veld and the British colony of Natal on the Indian Ocean coast. Although firearms enabled the settlers to win some important battles against the Zulu and other Africans, they were still a tiny minority surrounded by the populous and powerful independent African kingdoms.

Phenomenal deposits of diamonds, gold, and copper, as well as coal and iron ore, soon added to the appeal of good pasture and farmland. The discovery of diamonds at Kimberley in 1868 lured thousands of European prospectors as well as Africans looking for work. Great Britain annexed the diamond area in 1871, angering the Afrikaners. Once in the interior, the British defeated the Xhosa (KOH-sah) people in 1877 and 1878. Then in 1879 they confronted the Zulu, militarily the most powerful of the African peoples in the region.

The Zulu, led by their king Cetshwayo (set-SHWAH-yo), resented their encirclement by Afrikaners and British, and their proud military tradition led them into a war with the British in 1879. They defeated the British at Isandhlwana (ee-sawn-dull-WAH-nuh), but a few months later they were in turn defeated. Cetshwayo was captured and sent into exile, and the Zulu lands were given to white ranchers.

Relations between the British and the Afrikaners, already tense as a result of British encroachment, took a turn for the worse when gold was discovered in the Afrikaner republic of Transvaal (trans-VAHL) in 1886. In the gold rush that ensued, the British soon outnumbered the Afrikaners.

Britain's invasion of southern Africa was driven in part by the ambition of **Cecil Rhodes** (1853–1902), who once declared that he would "annex the stars" if he could. Rhodes made his fortune in the Kimberley diamond fields, founding De Beers Consolidated, a company that has dominated the world's diamond trade ever since. He then turned to politics. He encouraged a concession company, the British South Africa Company, to push north into Central Africa, where he named two new colonies after himself: Southern Rhodesia (now Zimbabwe) and Northern Rhodesia (now Zambia). The Ndebele (en-duh-BELL-ay) and Shona peoples, who inhabited the region, resisted this invasion, but the machine guns of the British finally defeated them (see Diversity and Dominance: Two Africans Recall the Arrival of the Europeans).

The inflow of English-speaking whites into the gold- and diamond-mining areas and British attempts to annex the two Afrikaner, also called Boer, republics, Transvaal and Orange Free State, led to the South African or Boer War, which lasted from 1899 to 1902. At first the Afrikaners had the upper hand, for they were highly motivated, possessed modern rifles, and knew the land. In 1901, however, Great Britain brought in 450,000 troops and crushed the Afrikaner armies. Ironically, the Afrikaners' defeat in 1902 led to their ultimate victory. Wary of costly commitments overseas, the British government expected European settlers in Africa to manage their own affairs, as they were doing in Canada, Australia, and New Zealand. Thus, in 1910 the European settlers created the Union of South Africa, in which the Afrikaners eventually emerged as the ruling element.

Unlike Canada, Australia, and New Zealand, South Africa had a majority of indigenous inhabitants and substantial numbers of Indians and "Cape Coloureds" (people of mixed ancestry). Yet the Europeans were both numerous enough to demand self-rule and powerful enough to deny the vote and other civil rights to the majority. In 1913 the South African parliament passed the Natives Land Act, assigning Africans to reservations and forbidding them to own land elsewhere. This and other racial policies turned South Africa into a land of segregation and oppression.

West and Equatorial Africa

Simultaneous with the formation of Shaka's Zulu kingdom, Islamic reform movements were creating another cluster of powerful states in the savannas of West Africa. Islam had long been a force in the politics and cities of this region, but most Muslim rulers had found it prudent to tolerate the older religious practices of their subjects. In the 1770s, however, Muslim scholars began preaching the need to reform Islamic practices. They condemned the accommodations Muslim rulers had made with older traditions and called for a forcible conquest of rural "pagans." Their jihad added new lands where governments enforced Islamic laws and promoted the religion's spread.

The largest of the new Muslim reform movements occurred in the Hausa (HOW-suh) states (in northern Nigeria) under the leadership of Usuman dan Fodio (OO-soo-mahn dahn FOH-dee-oh) (1745–1817). He charged that the Hausa kings, despite their official profession of Islam, were "undoubtedly unbelievers … because they practice polytheistic rituals and turn people away from the path of God." Muslims unhappy with their social or religious position spread the movement to other Hausa states. The successful armies united the conquered Hausa states and neighboring areas under a caliph who ruled from the city of Sokoto.

These new Muslim states became centers of Islamic learning and reform. Schools for training boys in Quranic subjects spread rapidly, and the great library at Sokoto attracted many scholars. Officials permitted non-Muslims within the empire to follow their religions in exchange for paying a special tax, but they suppressed dances and ceremonies associated with traditional religions. The **Sokoto Caliphate** (1809–1906) was the largest state in West Africa since the sixteenth century.

In coastal West Africa, however, the French, who had maintained a foothold in Senegal for centuries, envisioned building a railroad from the upper Senegal River to the upper Niger in order to open the interior to French merchants. This in turn led the French military to undertake the conquest of the interior. Sokoto remained independent, but after 1890 it was embattled both by neighboring rulers and European encroachment. In 1906 the empire came to an end with France, Britain, and Germany gobbling up various portions.

Farther south, **King Leopold II** of Belgium, following the advice of an American journalist and explorer, **Henry Morton Stanley**, invested his personal fortune in "opening up"—that is, occupying—the Congo Basin, an enormous forested region in the heart of equatorial Africa. With Leopold's money, Stanley returned to Africa from 1879 to 1884 to establish trading posts along the southern bank of the Congo River. At the same time, **Savorgnan de Brazza**, an Italian officer serving in the French army, obtained from an African ruler living on the opposite bank a treaty that placed the area under the "protection" of France.

The Berlin Conference   These events sparked a flurry of diplomatic activity. German chancellor Bismarck called the **Berlin Conference** on Africa of 1884 and 1885. There the major powers agreed that henceforth "effective occupation" would replace the former trading relations between Africans and Europeans. Every country with colonial ambitions had to send troops into Africa and participate in the division of the spoils. As a reward for triggering the "scramble" for Africa, Leopold II acquired a personal domain under the name *Congo Free State*, while France and Portugal took most of the rest of equatorial Africa. In this manner, the European powers and King Leopold managed to divide Africa among themselves, at least on paper.

Except in Kenya, Northern Rhodesia, and South Africa, where Europeans found the land and climate to their liking and forced Africans to become squatters, sharecroppers, or ranch hands on land they had farmed for generations, the colonial rulers declared any land that was not farmed to be "vacant" and gave it to

DIVERSITY + DOMINANCE

Two Africans Recall the Arrival of the Europeans

We know a great deal about the arrival of the Europeans into the interior of Africa from the perspective of the conquerors, but very little about how the events were experienced by Africans. Here are two accounts by African women, one from northern Nigeria whose land was occupied by the British, the other from the Congo Free State, a colony of King Leopold II of Belgium. They show not only how Africans experienced European colonial dominance but also how diverse these African experiences were.

Baba of Karo, a Nigerian Woman, Remembers Her Childhood

When I was a maiden the Europeans first arrived. Ever since we were quite small the *malams* had been saying that the Europeans would come with a thing called a train, they would come with a thing called a motor-car, in them you would go and come back in a trice. They would stop wars, they would repair the world, they would stop oppression and lawlessness, we should live at peace with them. We used to go and sit quietly and listen to the prophecies.

I remember when a European came to Karo on a horse, and some of his foot soldiers went into the town. Everyone came out to look at them, but in Zerewa they didn't see the European. Everyone at Karo ran away—"There's a European, there's a European!"

At that time Yusufu was the king of Karo. He did not like the Europeans, he did not wish them, he would not sign their treaty. Then he say that perforce he would have to agree, so he did. We Habe wanted them to come, it was the Fulani who did not like it. When the Europeans came the Habe saw that if you worked for them they paid you for it, they didn't say, like the Fulani, "Commoner, give me this! Commoner, bring me that!" Yes, the Habe wanted them; they saw no harm in them.

The Europeans said that there were to be no more slaves; if someone said "Slave!" you could complain to the *alkali* who would punish the master who said it, the judge said, "That is what the Europeans have decreed." The first order said that any slave, if he was younger than you, was your younger brother, if he was older than you was your elder brother— they were all brothers of their master's family. No one used the word "slave" any more. When slavery was stopped, nothing much happened at our *rinji* except that some slaves whom we had bought in the market ran away. Our own father went to his farm and worked, he and his son took up their large hoes; they loaned out their spare farms. Tsoho our father and Kadiri my brother with whom I live now and Babambo worked, they farmed guineacorn and millet and groundnuts and everything; before this they had supervised the slaves' work— now they did their own.

In the old days if the chief liked the look of your daughter he would take her and put her in his house; you could do nothing about it. Now they don't do that.

Ilanga, a Congolese Woman, Recounts Her Capture by Agents of the Congo Free State

… we were all busy in the fields hoeing our plantations, for it was the rainy season, and the weeds sprang quickly up, when a runner came to the village saying that a large band of men was coming, that they all wore red caps and blue cloth, and carried guns and long knives, and that many white men were with them, the chief of whom was *Kibalanga* (Michaux). Niendo at once called all the chief men to his house, while the drums were beaten to summon the people to the village. A long consultation was held, and finally we were all told to go quietly to the fields and bring in ground-nuts, plantains, and cassava for the warriors who were coming, and goats and fowl for the white men. The women all went with baskets and filled them, and put them in the road, which was blocked up, so many were there. Niendo then commanded everyone to go and sit quietly in the houses until he gave other orders. This we did, everyone remaining quietly seated while Niendo went up the road with the head men to meet the white chief. We did not know what to think, for most of us feared that so many armed men coming boded evil; but Niendo thought that, by giving presents of much food, he would induce the strangers to pass on without harming us. And so it proved, for the soldiers took the baskets, and were then ordered by the white men to move off through the village. Many of the soldiers looked into the houses and shouted at us words we did not understand. We were glad when they were all gone, for we were much in fear of the white men and the strange warriors, who are known to all the people as being great fighters, bringing war wherever they go....

When the white men and their warriors had gone, we went again to our work, and were hoping that they would not return; but this they did in a very short time. As before, we brought in great heaps of food; but this time *Kibalanga* did not move away directly, but camped near our village, and his soldiers came and stole all our fowl and goats and

tore up our cassava; but we did not mind as long as they did not harm us. The next morning it was reported that the white men were going away; but soon after the sun rose over the hill, a large band of soldiers came into the village, and we all went into the houses and sat down. We were not long seated when the soldiers came rushing in shouting, and threatening Niendo with their guns. They rushed into the houses and dragged the people out. Three or four came to our house and caught hold of me, also my husband Oleka and my sister Katinga. We were dragged into the road, and were tied together with cords about our necks, so that we could not escape. We were all crying, for now we knew that we were to be taken away to be slaves. The soldiers beat us with the iron sticks from their guns, and compelled us to march to the camp of *Kibalanga*, who ordered the women to be tied up separately, ten to each cord, and the men in the same way. When we were all collected—and there were many from other villages whom we now saw, and many from Waniendo—the soldiers brought baskets of food for us to carry, in some of which was smoked human flesh (*niama na nitu*).

We then set off marching very quickly. My sister Katinga had her baby in her arms, and was not compelled to carry a basket; but my husband Oleka was made to carry a goat. We marched until the afternoon, when we camped near a stream, where we were glad to drink, for we were much athirst. We had nothing to eat, for the soldiers would give us nothing, so we lay upon the ground, and at night went to sleep. The next day we continued the march, and when we camped at noon were given some maize and plantains, which were gathered near a village from which the people had run away. So it continued each day until the fifth day, when the soldiers took my sister's baby and threw it in the grass, leaving it to die, and made her carry some cooking pots which they found in the deserted village. On the sixth day we became very weak from lack of food and from constant marching and sleeping in the damp grass, and my husband, who marched behind us with the goat, could not stand up longer, and so he sat down beside the path and refused to walk more. The soldiers beat him, but still he refused to move. Then one of them struck him on the head with the end of his gun, and he fell upon the ground. One of the soldiers caught the goat, while two or three others stuck the long knives they put on the ends of their guns into my husband. I saw the blood spurt out, and then saw him no more, for we passed over the brow of a hill and he was out of sight. Many of the young men were killed the same way, and many babies thrown into the grass to die. A few escaped; but we were so well guarded that it was almost impossible.

Questions for Analysis

1. How do Baba and Ilanga recall their existence before the Europeans came?
2. What did they expect when they first heard of the arrival of Europeans? Instead, what happened to them, their relatives, and their towns?
3. How do you explain the difference between these two accounts?

Sources: From M. F. Smith, ed., *Baba of Karo: A Woman of the Muslim Hausa* (New York: Philosophical Library, 1955), 66–68. Edgar Canisius, *A Campaign Amongst Cannibals* (London: R. A. Everett & Co., 1903), 250–256.

private concession companies. In the Gold Coast (now Ghana), British trading companies bought the cocoa grown by African farmers at low prices and resold it for large profits. The interior of French West Africa lagged behind. Although the region could produce cotton, peanuts, and other crops, the difficulties of transportation limited its development before 1914.

Compared to West Africa, equatorial Africa had few inhabitants and little trade. Rather than try to govern these vast territories directly, authorities in the Congo Free State, the French Congo, and the Portuguese colonies of Angola and Mozambique farmed out huge pieces of land to private concession companies, offering them monopolies on the natural resources and trade of their territories and the right to employ soldiers and tax the inhabitants. Freed from outside supervision, the companies forced the African inhabitants at gunpoint to produce cash crops and carry them, on their heads or backs, to the nearest railroad or navigable river. The worst abuses took place in the Congo Free State, where a rubber boom made it profitable for private companies to brutalize Africans collecting latex from vines that grew in the forests. After 1906 the British press began publicizing the horrors. The public outcry that followed, coinciding with the end of the rubber boom, convinced the Belgian government to take over Leopold's private empire in 1908.

Modernization in Egypt and Ethiopia   While colonial states were arising elsewhere, in northeastern Africa Egypt and Ethiopia retained their independence and experimented with **modernization**. Muhammad Ali, who ruled Egypt from 1805 to 1849, began a series of reforms aimed at creating a modern Egypt (see Chapter 24). European pressure sharply curtailed these efforts after 1839, but by the end of his reign Egypt's population had nearly doubled; trade with Europe had expanded by almost 600 percent; and a new class of educated Egyptians was beginning to wield some influence.

Muhammad Ali's grandson Ismail (is-mah-EEL) (r. 1863–1879) focused on westernizing Egypt rather than confronting Europe militarily. "My country is no longer in Africa," Ismail declared, "it is in Europe."[1] His efforts increased the number of European advisers in Egypt, as well as Egypt's debts to French and British banks. In the first decade of his reign, revenues increased thirtyfold and exports doubled (largely because of a huge increase in cotton exports during the American Civil War). By 1870 Egypt had a network of new irrigation canals, 800 miles (1,300 kilometers) of railroads, a postal service, and a few dazzling modernization projects in the capital city of Cairo. It also had the **Suez Canal**, which opened in 1969 and immediately affected communications between Europe and Asia.

Ambitions like the canal and Ismail's dream of an Egyptian empire extending south into Sudan and Ethiopia cost vast sums of money, which the khedives borrowed from European creditors at high interest rates. When the market for Egyptian cotton collapsed after the American Civil War, these debts became a problem. By 1876 foreign debt had risen to £100 million sterling, and the interest payments alone consumed one-third of Egypt's foreign export earnings. To avoid bankruptcy the Egyptian government sold its shares in the Suez Canal to Great Britain and accepted four foreign "commissioners of the debt" to oversee its finances. French and British bankers, still not satisfied, lobbied their governments to secure the loans by stronger measures. In 1878 the two governments obliged Ismail to appoint a Frenchman as minister of public works and a Briton as minister of finance. When high taxes caused hardship and popular discontent, the French and British persuaded the Ottoman sultan to depose Ismail. This foreign intervention provoked a military uprising under Egyptian army colonel Arabi Pasha, which threatened the Suez Canal.

Fearing for their investments, the British sent an army into Egypt in 1882. So important was the Suez Canal to Britain's maritime supremacy that they stayed for seventy years. During those years the British ruled Egypt "indirectly"—that is, they maintained the Egyptian government and the fiction of Egyptian sovereignty but retained real power in their own hands.

Eager to develop Egyptian cotton production, the British brought in engineers and contractors to build the first dam across the Nile, at Aswan in Upper Egypt. When completed in 1902, it captured the annual Nile flood and released its waters throughout the year, allowing farmers to grow two, sometimes three, crops a year. The economic development of Egypt by the British enriched a small elite of landowners and merchants, many of them foreigners. Egyptian peasants got little relief from the heavy taxes collected to pay for their country's crushing foreign debt and the expenses of the British army of occupation. Most Egyptians found British rule more onerous than that of the Ottomans. By the 1890s Egyptian politicians and intellectuals were demanding that the British leave.

State building and reform were also under way in Christian Ethiopia. Beginning in the 1840s, Ethiopian rulers purchased modern weapons from European sources and

---

[1]Quoted in P. J. Vatikiotis, *The History of Modern Egypt: From Muhammad Ali to Mubarak*, 4th ed. (Baltimore: Johns Hopkins University Press, 1991), 74.

created strong armies loyal to the ruler. Emperor Téwodros (tay-WOH-druhs) II (r. 1833–1868) also encouraged the manufacture of weapons locally. However, his efforts to coerce more technical aid by holding some British officials captive backfired when the British invaded instead. As the British forces advanced, Téwodros committed suicide to avoid being taken prisoner. Satisfied that their honor was avenged, the British withdrew. Téwodros's successor Yohannes (yoh-HAHN-nehs) IV (r. 1872–1889) continued to bring most highland regions under imperial rule. The only large part of ancient Ethiopia that remained outside Emperor Yohannes's rule was the independent Shoa kingdom, ruled by **Menelik II** (MEN-uh-lik) from 1865.

In 1889 Menelik II became emperor of Ethiopia, at a time when his country was threatened by Sudanese Muslims to the west and by France and Italy, which controlled the coast of the Red Sea to the east. As already stated, Ethiopia had been purchasing European and American weapons for many years. When Italians attempted to establish a protectorate over Ethiopia, they found the Ethiopians armed with thousands of rifles and even machine guns and artillery pieces. Although Italy sent twenty thousand troops to attack Ethiopia, in 1896 they were defeated at Adowa (AH-do-ah) by a larger and better-trained Ethiopian army.

Transition from the Slave Trade   The successful slave revolt in Saint Domingue in the 1790s (see Chapter 23) ended slavery in the largest plantation colony in the West Indies. Elsewhere in the Americas, however, slave revolts were brutally repressed. As news of the slave revolts and their repression spread, humanitarians and religious reformers called for an end to the trade. Support for abolition of the trade was found even among Americans wanting to preserve slavery. In 1807 both Great Britain and the United States made importing slaves from Africa illegal for their citizens. Most other Western countries followed suit by 1850, but few enforced abolition with the vigor of the British.

Once the world's greatest slave traders, the British became the most aggressive abolitionists. Britain sent a naval patrol to enforce the ban along the African coast and negotiated treaties allowing the patrol to search other nations' vessels suspected of carrying slaves. Although British patrols captured 1,635 slave ships and liberated over 160,000 enslaved Africans, the trade proved difficult to stop. Cuba and Brazil continued to import huge numbers of slaves, which drove prices up and persuaded some African rulers and merchants to continue to sell slaves and to help foreign slavers evade the British patrols. Because the slave trade moved to other parts of Africa, the transatlantic slave trade did not end until 1867.

In exchange for slaves, Africans purchased cloth, metals, and other goods. To continue those imports, Africans expanded their **"legitimate" trade** (exports other than slaves). As the Atlantic slave trade was shut down, they revived old exports or developed new ones. The most successful of the new exports from West Africa was palm oil, used by British manufacturers for soap, candles, and lubricants. Though still a major source of slaves until the mid-1830s, the trading states of the Niger Delta emerged as the premier exporters of palm oil. Coastal African traders bought the palm oil at inland markets and delivered it to European ships at the coast.

The dramatic increase in palm-oil exports—from a few hundred tons at the beginning of the century to tens of thousands of tons by midcentury—altered the social structure of the coastal trading communities. Coastal traders used their

Hulton Archive/Getty Images

King Jaja of Opobo *This talented man rose from slavery in the Niger Delta port of Bonny to head one of the town's major palm-oil trading firms, the Anna Pepple House, in 1863. Six years later, Jaja founded and ruled his own trading port of Opobo.*

wealth to buy slaves to paddle the giant dugout canoes that transported palm oil from inland markets along the narrow delta creeks to the trading ports. Niger Delta slavery could be as harsh and brutal as slavery on New World plantations, but it offered some slaves a chance to gain wealth and power. Male slaves who supervised canoe fleets were well compensated, and a few even became wealthy enough to take over the leadership of coastal "canoe houses" (companies). The most famous, known as "Jaja" (ca. 1821–1891), rose from canoe slave to become the head of a major canoe house. In 1869, to escape discrimination by free-born Africans, he founded the new port of Opobo, which he ruled as king. In the 1870s Jaja of Opobo was the greatest palm-oil trader in the Niger Delta.

Another effect of the suppression of the slave trade was the spread of Western cultural influences in West Africa. To serve as a base for their anti-slave-trade naval squadron, the British had taken over the small colony of Sierra Leone (see-AIR-uh lee-OWN) in 1808. Over the next several years, 130,000 men, women, and children taken from "captured" vessels were liberated in Sierra Leone. Christian missionaries helped settle these **recaptives** in and around Freetown, the capital. Mission churches and schools made many converts among such men and women.

Sierra Leone's schools also produced a number of distinguished graduates. Samuel Adjai Crowther (1808–1891), freed from a slave ship in 1821, became the first Anglican bishop in West Africa in 1864, administering a pioneering diocese along the lower Niger River. James Africanus Horton (1835–1882), the son of slaves liberated in Sierra Leone, became a doctor and the author of many studies of West Africa.

Other Western cultural influences came from people of African birth or descent returning to their ancestral homeland. In 1821, free black Americans founded a settlement that grew into the Republic of Liberia, a place of liberty at a time when slavery was legal and flourishing in the United States. After their emancipation in 1865 other African Americans moved to Liberia. Emma White, a literate black woman from Kentucky, moved from Liberia to Opobo in 1875, where King Jaja employed her to write his commercial correspondence and run a school for his children. Edward Wilmot Blyden (1832–1912), born in the West Indies and proud of his West African parentage, emigrated to Liberia in 1851 and became a professor of Greek, Latin, and Arabic at the fledgling Liberia College.

Secondary Empire in Eastern Africa   When British patrols hampered the slave trade in West Africa, slavers moved to eastern Africa. There the Atlantic slave trade joined an existing trade in slaves to the Islamic world that also was expanding. Two-thirds of the 1.2 million slaves exported from eastern Africa in the nineteenth century went to markets in North Africa and the Middle East; the other third went to plantations in the Americas and to European-controlled Indian Ocean islands.

Slavery also became more prominent within eastern Africa itself. Between 1800 and 1873 Arab and Swahili (swah-HEE-lee) owners of clove plantations along the coast purchased some 700,000 slaves to do the hard work of harvesting this spice. The plantations were on Zanzibar Island and in neighboring territories belonging to the Sultanate of Oman, an Arabian kingdom on the Persian Gulf that had been expanding its control over the East African coast since 1698. The sultan had even moved his court to Zanzibar in 1840 to take advantage of the burgeoning trade in cloves. Zanzibar also was an important center of ivory and slaves until British pressure induced the sultan to ban the export of slaves in 1857 and their import in 1873.

INDIA UNDER BRITISH RULE

The might of the Mughal Empire did not long outlast the reign of Aurangzeb, who died in 1707 (see Chapter 20). In 1739 Iranian invaders sacked Delhi and carried off vast amounts of booty. Indian states also took advantage of Mughal weakness to assert their independence. By midcentury, the Maratha (muh-RAH-tuh) Confederation, a coalition of states in central India, controlled more land than the Mughals did. Several **nawabs** (NAH-wab), a term used for Muslim princes who were nominally deputies of the Mughal emperor, carved out powerful states of their own.

Ambitious young "company men" employed by British, French, and Dutch trading companies used hard bargaining, and hard fighting when necessary, to persuade Indian rulers to allow them to establish coastal trading posts protected by Indian troops known as **sepoys** (SEE-poy). In divided India these private armies came to hold the balance of power.

East India
Company

In 1691, Great Britain's East India Company (EIC) had persuaded the nawab of Bengal in northeast India to allow a company trading post at the fishing port of Calcutta. In 1756, a new nawab overran the post and imprisoned a group of EIC men in a cell so small that many died of suffocation. To avenge their deaths in this "Black Hole of Calcutta," a large EIC force from Madras, led by Robert Clive, overthrew the nawab. The weak Mughal emperor was persuaded to acknowledge the East India Company's right to rule Bengal in 1765. By 1788, Calcutta had grown into a city of 250,000.

Bombay was the third major center of British power in India. There, in 1818, the East India Company annexed large territories to form the core of what was called the "Bombay Presidency." This gave the East India Company an empire more populous than western Europe and with fifty times the population of the colonies the British had lost in North America. One goal of the **British raj** (regime) was to remake India on a British model through administrative and social reform, economic development, and the introduction of new technology. Yet the company men—like the Mughals before them—had to temper their interference with Indian social and religious customs lest they provoke rebellion or lose the support of their Indian princely allies.

Another British policy was to substitute private property for India's complex and overlapping patterns of landholding. In Bengal this reform worked to the advantage of large landowners, but in Mysore the peasantry gained. Private ownership made it easier for the state to collect the taxes that were needed to pay for administration, the army, and economic reform.

Such policies of "westernization, Anglicization, and modernization," as they have been called, were only one side of British rule. The other side was the bolstering of "traditions"—both real and newly invented. In the name of tradition the Indian princes who ruled nearly half of British India were frequently endowed by their British overlords with greater power and splendor and longer tenure than their predecessors had ever had. Likewise, Hindu and Muslim holy men were able to expand their "traditional" power over property and people far beyond what had been the case in earlier times. At the same time, princes, holy men, and other Indians frequently used claims of tradition to resist British rule as well as to turn it to their advantage. The British rulers themselves invented many "traditions"—including elaborate parades and displays—half borrowed from European royal pomp, half from Mughal ceremonies.

The British and Indian elites worked sometimes in close partnership, sometimes in opposition, but always at the expense of the ordinary people of India. Women of every status, members of subordinate Hindu castes, the "untouchables" and "tribals" outside the caste system, and the poor experienced few benefits from the British reforms and much new oppression from the taxes and "traditions" that exalted their superiors' status.

The transformation of British India's economy was also doubled-edged. On the one hand, the raj created many new jobs as a result of the growth of trade and expanded crop production, such as opium in Bengal, largely for export to

China (see Chapter 24); coffee in Ceylon; and tea in Assam in northeastern India. On the other hand, competition from cheap cotton goods produced in Britain's industrial mills drove many Indians out of the handicraft textile industry. In the eighteenth century India had been the world's greatest exporter of cotton textiles; in the nineteenth century India increasingly shipped raw cotton fiber to Britain.

During the first half of the nineteenth century, British rulers readily handled these isolated local rebellions, but they were more concerned about the loyalty of their Indian sepoys. The EIC employed 200,000 sepoys in 1857, along with 38,000 British troops. Armed with modern rifles and disciplined in fighting methods, the sepoys had a potential for successful rebellion that other groups lacked.

In the early decades of EIC rule, most sepoys came from Bengal. The Bengali sepoys resented the active recruitment of other ethnic groups into the army after 1848, such as Sikhs (sick) from Punjab and Gurkhas from Nepal. In addition, many high-caste Hindus objected to a new law in 1856 requiring new recruits to be available for service overseas in the growing British empire, for their religion prohibited ocean travel. Finally, the replacement of the standard military musket by the more accurate Enfield rifle in 1857 required soldiers to use their teeth to tear open the ammunition cartridges, which were greased with animal fat. Hindus were offended by this order if the fat came from cattle, which they considered sacred. Muslims were offended if the fat came from pigs, which they considered unclean.

Although the cartridge-opening procedure was quickly changed, the initial discontent grew into rebellion by Hindu sepoys in May 1857. British troubles mushroomed when Muslim sepoys, peasants, and discontented elites joined in. The rebellion was put down ten months later, but it shook this empire to its core.

Historians have attached different names and meanings to the events of 1857 and 1858. Nineteenth-century British historians labeled it the "**Sepoy Rebellion**" or "Mutiny." Seeing in these events the beginnings of the later movement for independence, some modern Indian historians have termed it the "Revolution of 1857."

Political Reform and Industrial Impact
Regardless of label, the events of 1857–1858 marked a turning point in the history of modern India. In their wake Indians gained a new centralized government, entered a period of rapid economic growth, and began to develop a new national consciousness.

In 1858, Britain eliminated the last traces of Mughal and Company rule. In their place, a new secretary of state for India in London oversaw Indian policy, and a new governor-general in Delhi acted as the British monarch's viceroy. In November 1858, Queen Victoria guaranteed all Indians equal protection of the law and the freedom to practice their religions and social customs; she also assured Indian princes that so long as they were loyal to the queen British India would respect their control of territories and "their rights, dignity and honour."[2]

---

[2]Quoted by Bernard S. Cohn, "Representing Authority in Victorian India," in *The Invention of Tradition*, ed. Eric Hobsbawm and Terence Ranger (Cambridge, England: Cambridge University Press, 1983), 165.

Legend

- Northern limit of Mughal Empire in 1707
- Muslim land in 1765
- Muslim land in 1805
- Area controlled by Hindus in 1805
- Land under British East India Company rule in 1805
- ✕ Site of important battle

MAP 26.1   India, 1707–1805

As Mughal power weakened during the eighteenth century, other Indian states and the East India Company expanded their territories.

British rule continued to emphasize both tradition and reform after 1857. At the top, the British viceroys lived in enormous palaces amid hundreds of servants and gaudy displays of luxury meant to convince Indians that the British viceroys were legitimate successors to the Mughal emperors. They treated the quasi-independent Indian princes with elaborate ceremonial courtesy and maintained them in splendor. When Queen Victoria was proclaimed "Empress of India" in 1877 and periodically thereafter, the viceroys put on great pageants known as **durbars**. At the durbar in Delhi in 1902–1903 to celebrate the coronation of King Edward VII, Viceroy Lord

Curzon honored himself with a 101-gun salute and a parade of 34,000 troops in front of 50 princes and 173,000 visitors.

Meanwhile, a powerful and efficient bureaucracy controlled India. Members of the elite **Indian Civil Service** (ICS) held the senior administrative and judicial posts. Numbering only a thousand at the end of the nineteenth century, these men visited the villages in their districts, heard lawsuits and complaints, and passed judgments.

Recruitment into the ICS was by open examinations. In theory any British subject could take these exams; since they were given in England, however, in practice the system worked to exclude Indians. In 1870 only one Indian was a member of the ICS. Subsequent reforms led to fifty-seven Indian appointments by 1887, but there the process stalled. Working under the ICS were thousands of lesser Indian officials.

The reason qualified Indians were denied entry into the upper administration of their country was the racist contempt most British officials felt for the people they ruled. When he became commander-in-chief of the Indian army in 1892, Lord Kitchener declared:

> It is this consciousness of the inherent superiority of the European which had won for us India. However well educated and clever a native may be, and however brave he may have proved himself, I believe that no rank we can bestow on him would cause him to be considered an equal of the British officer.[3]

After 1857 the government invested millions of pounds sterling in harbors, cities, irrigation canals, and other public works. Forests were felled to make way for tea plantations. Indian farmers were persuaded to grow cotton and jute for export. Engineers built great irrigation systems to alleviate the famines that periodically decimated whole provinces. As a result, India's trade expanded rapidly.

Most of the exports were agricultural commodities: cotton fiber, opium, tea, silk, and sugar. In return India imported manufactured goods from Britain, including machine-made cotton textiles that undercut Indian hand-loom weavers. Some women found jobs at very low pay on plantations or in the growing cities, where prostitution flourished. Everywhere in India poverty remained the norm.

The Indian government also promoted the introduction of new technologies into India. Earlier in the century there were steamboats on the rivers and a massive program of canal building for irrigation. Beginning in the 1840s a railroad boom gave India its first national transportation network, followed by telegraph lines, and by 1870 India had the fifth largest rail network in the world. Originally designed to serve British commerce, the railroads were owned by British companies, constructed with British rails and equipment, and paid dividends to British investors. Ninety-nine percent of the railroad employees were Indians, but Europeans occupied all the top positions—"like a thin film of oil on top of a glass of water, resting upon but hardly mixing with [those] below," as one official report put it.

Although some Indians opposed the railroads at first because the trains mixed people of different castes, faiths, and sexes, the Indian people took to rail travel with great enthusiasm. Indians rode trains on business, on pilgrimage, and in search of work. In 1870 over 18 million passengers traveled along the network's

---

[3]James Truslow, *Empire of the Seven Seas: The British Empire 1784–1939* (New York: Charles Scribners Sons, 2007), 268.

4,775 miles (7,685 kilometers) of track, and more than half a million messages were sent up and down the 14,000 miles (22,500 kilometers) of telegraph wires.

But the freer movement of Indian pilgrims and the flood of poor Indians into the cities also promoted the spread of cholera (KAHL-uhr-uh), a disease transmitted through water contaminated by human feces. Cholera deaths rose rapidly during the nineteenth century, and eventually the disease spread to Europe. In many Indian minds *kala mari* ("the black death") was a divine punishment for failing to prevent the British takeover. This chastisement also fell heavily on British residents, who died in large numbers. In 1867, officials demonstrated the close connection between cholera and pilgrims who bathed in and drank from sacred pools and rivers. The installation of a new sewerage system and a filtered water supply (1869) in Calcutta dramatically reduced cholera deaths there. Similar measures in Bombay and Madras also led to great reductions, but most Indians lived in small villages where famine and lack of sanitation kept cholera deaths high.

Indian Nationalism   After the failure of the rebellion of 1857 to overthrow British rule, some Indians argued that the only way for Indians to regain control of their destiny was to reduce their country's social and ethnic divisions and promote Pan-Indian nationalism.

Individuals such as Rammohun Roy (1772–1833) had promoted development along these lines a generation earlier. A Western-educated Bengali from a Brahmin family, Roy was a successful administrator for the East India Company and a student of comparative religion. His Brahmo Samaj (BRAH-moh suh-MAHJ) (Divine Society), founded in 1828, attracted Indians who sought to reconcile the values of the West with the religious traditions of India. They advocated reforming some Hindu customs, such as the caste system and child marriage, and urged a return to the founding principles of the *Upanishads*, ancient sacred writings of Hinduism. They also backed British efforts to ban practices they found repugnant. Widow burning (*sati* [suh-TEE]) was outlawed in 1829 and slavery in 1843. Reformers sought to correct other abuses of women: prohibitions against widows remarrying were revoked in 1856, and female infanticide was made a crime in 1870.

Although Brahmo Samaj remained influential after the rebellion of 1857, many Indian intellectuals turned to Western secular values and nationalism as the way to reclaim India. In this process the spread of Western education played an important role, a process aided by European and American missionaries. Roy had studied both Indian and Western subjects and helped found the Hindu College in Calcutta in 1816. Other Western-curriculum schools quickly followed, including Bethune College in Calcutta, the first secular school for Indian women, in 1849. India's three universities were established in 1857. In 1870 there were over 24,000 elementary and secondary schools, whose graduates articulated a new Pan-Indian nationalism that transcended regional and religious differences.

Many of the new nationalists came from the Indian middle class, which had prospered from the increase of trade and manufacturing. Educated people were angered by the obstacles that British rules and prejudices put in the way of their advancement. Hoping to increase their influence and improve their employment opportunities in the Indian government, they convened the first **Indian National Congress** in 1885. The members sought a larger role for Indians in the Civil Service.

They also called for reductions in military expenditures, which consumed 40 percent of the government's budget, so that more could be spent on alleviating the poverty of the Indian masses. But although the Indian National Congress promoted unity among the country's many religions and social groups, most early members were upper-caste Western-educated Hindus and Parsis. Until it attracted the support of the masses, it could not hope to challenge British rule.

SOUTHEAST ASIA AND THE PACIFIC

Different parts of Southeast Asia and the Pacific region had differing histories, yet all came under intense imperialist pressure during the nineteenth century. Thomas Stamford Raffles had governed Java from 1811 to 1814, when the politics of Napoleon's wars in Europe allowed the English to displace the Dutch. After a peace treaty in Europe dictated Java's return to the Dutch, Raffles helped establish, in 1824, a new free port at Singapore on the site of a small Malay fishing village with a superb harbor. British merchants and Chinese businessmen and laborers soon made Singapore the paramount center of trade and shipping between the Indian Ocean and China. Along with Malacca and other possessions on the strait, Singapore formed the "Straits Settlements," which British India administered until 1867.

British expansion came more quickly in neighboring Burma, which had emerged as a powerful kingdom by 1750. In 1785 Burma tried to annex neighboring territories of Siam (now Thailand) to the east, but a coalition of Thai leaders thwarted Burmese advances by 1802. Burma next attacked Assam to the west, but this provoked a war with British India. After a two-year war, India annexed Assam in 1826 and occupied two coastal provinces of northern Burma. As the rice and timber trade from these provinces grew important, the occupation became permanent, and in 1852 British India annexed the rest of coastal Burma. The last piece of the country was annexed in 1885, but Thailand remained an independent kingdom.

Indochina fell under French control piece by piece until it was finally subdued in 1895. Similarly, Malaya (now Malaysia) came under British rule in stages during the 1870s and 1880s. In northern Sumatra, however, a region that supplied half the world's production of black pepper, the Dutch fought a ferocious war between 1873 and 1913 against the rulers of Acheh. The Achehnese warriors were inspired, in part, by the mystique of an Islamic jihad, thus creating a tradition of resistance that would continue to resonate throughout the twentieth century.

Australia   In the once-remote South Pacific, British settlers displaced the indigenous populations of Australia and New Zealand, just as they had done in North America. Portuguese mariners had sighted Australia in the early seventeenth century, but it was too remote to be of much interest to Europeans. However, after the English captain James Cook explored New Zealand and the eastern coast of Australia between 1769 and 1778, expanding shipping networks brought in growing numbers of visitors and settlers.

At the time of Cook's visits, Australia was the home of about 650,000 hunting-and-gathering people, whose Melanesian (mel-uh-NEE-zhuhn) ancestors had settled there some forty thousand years earlier. New Zealand was inhabited by about 250,000 Maori (MOW-ree [ow as in cow]), who practiced hunting, fishing, and simple forms of agriculture, which their Polynesian ancestors had introduced around 1200. Because of their long isolation from the rest of humanity, the populations of Australia and New Zealand were as vulnerable as the Amerindians had been to unfamiliar diseases introduced by new overseas contacts. By the 1890s, only 93,000 aboriginal Australians and 42,000 Maori survived, and British settler populations outnumbered and dominated the indigenous peoples.

The first permanent British settlers in Australia were 736 convicts, of whom 188 were women, sent into exile in 1788. Over the next few decades, Australian penal colonies grew slowly and had only slight contact with the indigenous population, whom the British called "Aborigines." However, the discovery of gold in 1851 brought a flood of free European settlers (and some Chinese) and hastened the end of the penal colonies. When the gold rush subsided, government subsidies enabled tens of thousands of British settlers to settle "down under." Though it still took more than three months to reach Australia from Britain, by 1860 Australia had a million immigrants, and the settler population doubled during the next fifteen years.

New Zealand　　British settlers were drawn more slowly to New Zealand. Some of the first were temporary residents along the coast who slaughtered seals and exported pelts to Western countries to be made into men's felt hats. A single ship in 1806 took away sixty thousand sealskins. By the early 1820s overhunting had nearly exterminated the seal population. Special ships also hunted sperm whales extensively near New Zealand for their oil, used for lubrication, soap,

Bettmann/CORBIS

Emilio Aguinaldo *In 1896, a revolt led by Emilio Aguinaldo attempted to expel Spaniards from the Philippines. When the United States purchased the Philippines from Spain two years later, the Filipino people were not consulted. Aguinaldo continued his campaign, this time against the American occupation forces, until his capture in 1901. In this picture, he appears on horseback, surrounded by some of his troops.*

and lamps; ambergris (AM-ber-grees), an ingredient in perfume; and whalebone (actually baleen, feeding bristles made like fingernails of keratin), used as stays in women's corsets. A brief gold rush and faster ships and subsidized passages attracted more British immigrants after 1860. The colony especially courted women immigrants to offset the preponderance of single men. By the early 1880s this most distant frontier of the British Empire had a settler population of 500,000. Britain encouraged the settlers in Australia and New Zealand to become self-governing, following the 1867 model that had formed the Dominion of Canada out of the diverse and thinly settled colonies of British North America. By gradually turning over governing power to the colonies' inhabitants, Britain satisfied the settlers' desire for greater control over their own territories, muted demands for independence, and made the colonial governments responsible for most of their own expenses.

North American patterns also shaped the indigenous peoples' fate. Aborigines lacked the rights of Australian citizens. The requirement that voters had to be able to read and write English kept Maori from voting in early New Zealand elections, but four seats in the lower house of the legislature were reserved for Maori from 1867 on.

Hawaii and the Philippines, 1878–1902   The United States was a latecomer in the race for colonial territories. However, by the 1890s it had a fast-growing population and industries that produced more manufactured goods than they could sell at home. This growth contributed to economic depressions in 1893 and 1896 and led merchants and bankers to look to China as a new export market. Guam, Hawaii, and the Philippines being naval stations on the route to China, the new expansionism looked in that direction. China was in the minds of those who agreed with the naval strategist Alfred T. Mahan (mah-HAHN): "Whether they will or no, Americans must now begin to look outward. The growing production of the country requires it."

This was not the beginning of American interest in the Pacific. In 1878 the United States obtained the harbor of Pago Pago in Samoa as a coaling and naval station, and in 1887 it secured the use of Pearl Harbor in Hawaii for the same purpose. By 1898, the United States under President William McKinley (1897–1901) had become openly imperialistic and annexed Hawaii as a steppingstone to Asia. As the United States became ever more involved in Asian affairs, Hawaii's strategic location brought an inflow of U.S. military personnel, and its fertile land caused planters to import laborers from Japan, China, and the Philippines. These immigrants soon outnumbered the native Hawaiians.

While large parts of Asia were falling under colonial domination, the people of the Philippines were chafing under their Spanish rulers. **Emilio Aguinaldo**, leader of a secret society, rose in revolt and proclaimed a republic in 1899. The revolutionaries had a good chance of winning independence, for Spain had its hands full with a revolution in Cuba. Unfortunately for Aguinaldo and his followers, the United States declared war against Spain in April 1898 and quickly overcame Spanish forces in the Philippines and Cuba. After the Spanish defeat, President McKinley realized that a weakened Spain might lose the islands to another imperialist power. Japan, having recently defeated China in the Sino-Japanese War (1894–1895) and annexed Taiwan (see Chapter 27), was eager to expand its empire. So was Germany, which had taken over parts of New Guinea and Samoa and several

Pacific archipelagoes during the 1880s. To forestall them, McKinley purchased the Philippines from Spain for $20 million.

The Filipinos were not eager to trade one master for another. For a while, Aguinaldo cooperated with the Americans in the hope of achieving full independence. When his plan was rejected, he rose up again in 1899 and proclaimed the independence of his country. In spite of protests by anti-imperialists in the United States, the U.S. government decided that its global interests outweighed the interests of the Filipino people. In rebel areas, a U.S. army of occupation tortured prisoners, burned villages and crops, and forced the inhabitants into "reconcentration camps." By the end of the insurrection in 1902, the war had cost the lives of 5,000 Americans and 200,000 Filipinos.

After the insurrection ended, the United States attempted to soften its rule with public works and economic development projects. New buildings went up in the city of Manila; roads, harbors, and railroads were built; and the Philippine economy was tied ever more closely to that of the United States. In 1907 Filipinos were allowed to elect representatives to a legislative assembly, but ultimate authority remained in the hands of a governor appointed by the president of the United States. In 1916 the Philippines were the first U.S. colony to be promised independence, a promise fulfilled only thirty years later.

IMPERIALISM IN LATIN AMERICA

The United States played a lesser role than Britain and other European countries in the economic dominance that characterized imperialism in Latin America, and business played a more important role than military intervention. But America's clash with Spain over control of the Philippines carried over into Spanish possessions closer to home.

American Expansionism and the Spanish-American War, 1898   The United States had long had interests in Cuba, the closest and richest of the Caribbean islands and a Spanish colony. American businesses had invested great sums of money in Cuba's sugar and tobacco industries, and thousands of Cubans had migrated to the United States. In 1895, the Cuban nationalist José Martí started a revolution against Spanish rule. American newspapers thrilled readers with lurid stories of Spanish atrocities; businessmen worried about their investments; and politicians demanded that the U.S. government help liberate Cuba.

On February 15, 1898, the U.S. battleship *Maine* accidentally blew up in Havana harbor, killing 266 American sailors. The U.S. government immediately blamed Spain and issued an ultimatum that the Spanish evacuate Cuba. Spain agreed to the ultimatum, but the American press and Congress were eager for war, and President McKinley did not restrain them.

The **Spanish-American War** was over quickly. On May 1, 1898, U.S. warships destroyed the Spanish fleet at Manila in the Philippines. Two months later the United States Navy sank the Spanish Atlantic fleet off Santiago, Cuba. By mid-August Spain was suing for peace. U.S. Secretary of State John Hay called it "a splendid little war." The United States purchased the Philippines from Spain but took over Puerto Rico and Guam as war booty. The two islands remain American possessions to this day. Cuba became an independent republic, subject to interference by the United States.

Economic Imperialism

Latin America achieved independence from Spain and Portugal in the nineteenth century but did not industrialize. Most Latin American republics, suffering from ideological divisions, unstable governments, and violent upheavals, traded their commodities for foreign manufactured goods and investments and became economically dependent on Great Britain or other foreign countries. A traumatic social revolution and civil war shook Mexico, but even there the region-wide deep split between wealthy landowners and desperately poor peasants persisted.

Yet Latin America's economic potential was huge, for the region could produce many agricultural and mineral products in demand in the industrial countries. What was needed was a means of opening the interior to development. Railroads seemed the perfect answer.

Foreign merchants and bankers and Latin American landowners and politicians embraced the new technology. Starting in the 1870s, almost every country in Latin America acquired railroads, usually connecting mines or agricultural regions with the nearest port rather than linking up the different parts of the interior. All the equipment and building material came from Britain or the United States. So did the money to build the networks, the engineers who designed and maintained them, and the managers who ran them.

Argentina, a land of rich soil that produced wheat, beef, and hides, gained the longest and best-developed rail network south of the United States. By 1914, 86 percent of the railroads in Argentina were owned by British firms; 40 percent of the employees were British; and the official language of the railroads was not Spanish but English. The same was true of mining and industrial enterprises and public utilities throughout Latin America.

In many ways, the situation resembled those of India and Ireland, which also obtained rail networks in exchange for raw materials and agricultural products. The difference was that the Indians and Irish had little say in the matter because they were under British rule. But in Latin America the political elites encouraged foreign companies with generous concessions as the most rapid way to modernize their countries and enrich the property owners. The majority were neither consulted nor allowed to benefit from the railroad boom.

Revolution and Civil War in Mexico

At the beginning of the twentieth century Mexican society was divided into rich and poor and into populations of Spanish, Indian, and mixed ancestry. A few very wealthy families of Spanish origin, less than 1 percent of the population, owned 85 percent of Mexico's land, mostly in huge *haciendas* (estates). A handful of American and British companies controlled most of Mexico's railroads, silver mines, plantations, and other productive enterprises. At the other end of the social scale were Indians, many of whom did not speak Spanish. *Mestizos* (mess-TEE-so), people of mixed Indian and European ancestry, were only slightly better off; most of them were peasants who worked on the haciendas or farmed small communal plots near their ancestral villages.

After independence in 1821 wealthy Mexican families and American companies used bribery and force to acquire millions of acres of good agricultural land from villages in southern Mexico. Peasants lost not only their fields but also their access to firewood and pasture and had little choice but to work on haciendas. To survive, they had to buy food and other necessities on credit from the landowner's store; eventually, they fell permanently into debt.

For thirty-four years General Porfirio Díaz (DEE-as) (1830–1915) had ruled Mexico under the motto "Liberty, Order, Progress." To Díaz "liberty" meant freedom for rich hacienda owners and foreign investors to acquire more land. The government imposed "order" through rigged elections, bribes to Díaz's supporters, and summary justice for those who opposed him. "Progress" meant mainly the importing of foreign capital, machinery, and technicians to take advantage of Mexico's labor, soil, and natural resources.

During the Díaz years (1876–1910) Mexico City became a showplace with paved streets, streetcar lines, electric street lighting, and public parks. New telegraph and railroad lines connected cities and towns throughout Mexico. But this material progress benefited only a handful of well-connected businessmen and lowered the average Mexican's standard of living.

Though a mestizo himself, Díaz discriminated against the nonwhite majority of Mexicans. He and his supporters tried to eradicate what they saw as Mexico's rustic traditions. On many middle- and upper-class tables French cuisine replaced traditional Mexican dishes, and the wealthy traded sombreros and ponchos for European garments. To the educated middle class—the only group with a strong sense of Mexican nationhood—this devaluation of Mexican culture became a symbol of the Díaz regime's failure to defend national interests against foreign influences.

The **Mexican Revolution** was a social revolution that developed haphazardly under ambitious but limited leaders, each representing a different segment of Mexican society. The first was American-educated Francisco I. Madero (1873–1913), the son of a wealthy landowning and mining family. Strongly opposed to Díaz, he called on his fellow citizens to oppose electing him for a sixth term. This sparked a revolution in 1910 and the election of Madero as Díaz's successor. While the Madero presidency was welcomed in some quarters, it was opposed in others. The American ambassador Henry Lane Wilson helped General Victoriano Huerta, one of Madero's former supporters, engineer a coup d'état in 1913, and Madero was assassinated after only two years in the presidency. President Woodrow Wilson then disavowed American support of Huerta, recalled Ambassador Wilson, and, as a token of American concern with Mexican unrest, sent United States Marines to seize the port city of Veracruz, which they occupied for six months.

The inequities of Mexican society and foreign intervention angered Mexico's middle class and industrial workers. They found leaders in Venustiano Carranza, a landowner, and in Alvaro Obregón (oh-bray-GAWN), a schoolteacher. Calling themselves Constitutionalists, Carranza and Obregón organized private armies and overthrew Huerta in 1914. By then, the revolution had spread to the countryside.

Madero's key "popular" ally in 1910–1911 had been **Emiliano Zapata** (sah-PAH-tah) (1879–1919), but the two parted ways on the issue of land reform. Himself an Indian farmer, Zapata had led a revolt against the haciendas in the mountains of Morelos, south of Mexico City. His soldiers were peasants mounted on horseback and armed with pistols and rifles. For several years they periodically came down from the mountains, burned hacienda buildings, and returned land to the Indian villages to which it had once belonged.

Another leader appeared in Chihuahua, a northern state where seventeen individuals owned two-fifths of the land and 95 percent of the people had no land at all. Starting in 1913, **Francisco "Pancho" Villa** (1877–1923), a former ranch hand, mule driver, and bandit, organized an army of three thousand men, most of them cowboys, and divided large haciendas into family ranches. After a failed and unexplained attack on the town of Columbus, New Mexico, the U.S. Army sent General John Pershing on a nine-month mission to hunt Villa down. The mission was cut short by American entry into World War I, but, like the occupation of Veracruz, it demonstrated increasing American concern for protecting land and business interests in Mexico.

Zapata and Villa enjoyed tremendous popular support but could never rise above their regional and peasant origins and lead a national revolution. The Constitutionalists had fewer soldiers than Zapata and Villa, but they held the major cities and used the proceeds of oil sales to buy modern weapons. Gradually the Constitutionalists took over most of Mexico. In 1919 they defeated and killed Zapata; Villa was given a large estate to retire to but was assassinated in 1923 after resuming political activity. An estimated 2 million people lost their lives in the civil war, and much of Mexico lay in ruins.

During their struggle to win support against Zapata and Villa, the Constitutionalists adopted many of their rivals' agrarian reforms, such as restoring communal lands to the Indians of Morelos. They also proposed social programs designed to appeal to workers and the middle class. The Constitution of 1917 set out first principles: a one-term limit on presidential power; economic nationalism (recapturing subsoil rights from foreigners, land reform, and the right of labor to organize); and severe constraints on the church. However, powerful Mexican forces and the United States sought to prevent full implementation of the constitution. By 1928 the Mexican government had made more progress against the church than in the implementation of either political or economic reform.

By the early 1920s a decade of violence had drained the country without resolving the question of who would rule. Carranza, elected president in 1917, did not wish Obregón to succeed him. In response, Obregón allied with two other ambitious leaders and marched on Mexico City. Carranza was killed as he fled. Following the constitution, Obregón served one four-year term as president. He then managed the election of Plutarco Elías Calles (KAH-yace), his colleague in the anti-Carranza plot, who served one term with the understanding that Obregón would return to the presidency in 1928. A Catholic militant put a stop to this arrangement by assassinating Obregón before he could take office.

American Intervention in the Caribbean and Central America, 1901–1914

American intervention in the Western Hemisphere was not limited to Mexico. The nations of the Caribbean and Central America were small and poor, and their governments were corrupt, unstable, and often bankrupt. They seemed to offer an open invitation to foreign interference. A government would borrow money to pay for railroads, harbors, electric power, and other symbols of modernity. When it could not repay the loan, the lending banks in Europe or the United States would ask for assistance from their home governments, which sometimes threatened to intervene. To ward off European intervention, the United States sent in the marines on more than one occasion.

Presidents Theodore Roosevelt (1901–1909), William Taft (1909–1913), and Woodrow Wilson (1913–1921) felt impelled to intervene in the region, though they differed sharply on the proper policy the United States should follow toward the small nations to the south. Roosevelt encouraged regimes friendly to the United States; Taft sought to influence them through loans from American banks; and the moralist Wilson tried to impose clean governments by military means.

Having "liberated" Cuba from Spain, in 1901 the United States forced the Cuban government to accept the Platt Amendment, which gave the United States the "right to intervene" to maintain order on the island. The United States used this excuse to occupy Cuba militarily from 1906 to 1909, in 1912, and again from 1917 to 1922. In all but name Cuba became an American protectorate. U.S. troops also occupied the Dominican Republic from 1904 to 1907 and again in 1916, Nicaragua and Honduras in 1912, and Haiti in 1915. They brought sanitation and material progress but no political improvements.

The United States was especially forceful in Panama, which was a province of Colombia. Here the issue was not corruption or debts but a more vital interest. When the United States acquired Hawaii and the Philippines, it recognized the need for a canal that would allow warships to move quickly between the Atlantic and Pacific Oceans. The main obstacle was Colombia, which refused to give the United States a piece of its territory. In 1903 the U.S. government supported a Panamanian rebellion against Colombia and quickly recognized the independence of Panama. In exchange, it obtained the right to build a canal and to occupy a zone 5 miles (8 kilometers) wide on either side of it. Work began in 1904, and the **Panama Canal** opened on August 15, 1914.

THE WORLD ECONOMY AND THE GLOBAL ENVIRONMENT

The nineteenth-century imperialists were not traditional conquerors or empire builders like the Spanish conquistadors. They expressed their belief in progress and their good intentions in the clichés of the time: "the conquest of nature," "the annihilation of time and space," "the taming of the wilderness," and "our civilizing mission."

Expansion of the World Economy   For centuries Europe had been a ready market for spices, sugar, silk, and other imported products. The Industrial Revolution expanded this demand, especially for stimulants such as tea, coffee, and chocolate. The trade in industrial raw materials grew even faster, as well as trade in agricultural products like cotton, jute for bags, palm oil for soap and lubricants, and minerals like diamonds, gold, and copper. Some wild forest products eventually came to be cultivated: timber for buildings and railroad ties, cinchona bark, rubber for rainwear and tires, and gutta-percha (guttah-PER-cha) (the sap of a Southeast Asian tree) to insulate electric cables.

Economic botany and agricultural science were applied to every promising plant species. European botanists had long collected and classified exotic plants

A Rubber Plantation

As bicycles and automobiles proliferated in the early twentieth century, the demand for rubber outstripped the supply available from wild rubber trees in the Amazon forest. Rubber grown on plantations in Southeast Asia came on the market from 1910 on. The rubber trees had to be tapped very carefully and on a regular schedule to obtain the latex or sap from which rubber was extracted. In this picture a woman and a boy perform this operation on a plantation in British Malaya.

Mary Evans Picture Library/The Image Works

from around the world. In the nineteenth century they founded botanical gardens in Java, India, Mauritius (maw-REE-shuss), Ceylon, Jamaica, and other tropical colonies. These gardens not only collected local plants but also transferred commercially valuable plant species from one tropical region to another. Cinchona (sin-CHO-nah) (the source of the antimalarial drug quinine), tobacco, sugar, coffee, tea, and other crops were introduced, improved, and vastly expanded in the colonies of Southeast Asia and Indonesia. Cacao and coffee growing spread over large areas of Brazil and Africa; oil-palm plantations were established in Nigeria and the Congo Basin. After 1910, rubber, used to make waterproof garments and bicycle tires, came from plantations in Southeast Asia.

Throughout the tropics, land once covered with forests or devoted to slash-and-burn agriculture was transformed into permanent farms and plantations. In Java and India farmers felled trees to obtain arable land and firewood, terraced hillsides, drained swamps, and dug wells. Colonial rule also fostered population growth. Even in areas not developed to export crops, growing populations put pressure on the land. For example, the population of Java, an island the size of Pennsylvania, doubled from 16 million in 1870 to over 30 million in 1914.

Free Trade   By 1870, Britain had added several dozen colonies to the twenty-six colonies it had in 1792. The underlying goal of most British imperial expansion during these decades was trade rather than territory. Most of the new colonies were meant to serve as ports in the growing network of shipping that encircled the globe or as centers of production and distribution for those networks.

This new commercial expansion was closely tied to the needs of Britain's growing industrial economy and reflected a new philosophy of overseas trade. Rather than rebuilding the closed mercantilist network of trade with its colonies, Britain sought to trade freely with all parts of the world. Free trade was also a wise policy in light of the independence of so many former colonies in the Americas (see Chapter 23).

Whether colonized or not, more and more lands were being drawn into the commercial networks created by British expansion and industrialization. Uncolonized parts of West Africa became major exporters to Britain of vegetable oils and forest products, while areas of eastern Africa free of European control exported ivory that ended up as piano keys and decorations in the homes of the middle and upper classes.

In return for the foodstuffs and industrial raw materials that flowed toward Europe and the United States, the factories of the industrialized nations supplied manufactured goods at very attractive prices. By the mid-nineteenth century a major part of their textile production was destined for overseas markets. Sales of cotton cloth to Africa increased 950 percent from the 1820s to the 1860s. British trade to India grew 350 percent between 1841 and 1870, while India's exports increased 400 percent. Trade with other regions also expanded rapidly. In most cases such trade benefited both sides, but there is no question that the industrial nations were the dominant partners.

New Labor   Between 1834 and 1870 many thousands of Indians, Chinese,
Migrations   and Africans went overseas to work, especially on sugar plantations. In the half century after 1870, tens of thousands of Asians and Pacific islanders made similar voyages.

In part these migrations were linked to the end of slavery. After their emancipation in British colonies in 1834, many slaves left the plantations. To compete with sugar plantations in Cuba, Brazil, and the French Caribbean that were still using slave labor, British colonies had to recruit new laborers.

India's impoverished people seemed one obvious alternative. After planters on Mauritius successfully introduced Indian laborers, the Indian labor trade moved to the British Caribbean in 1838. In 1841, the British government also allowed Caribbean planters to recruit Africans whom British patrols had rescued from slave ships and liberated in Sierra Leone and elsewhere. By 1870 nearly 40,000 Africans had settled in British colonies, along with over a half-million Indians and over 18,000 Chinese. After the French and Dutch abolished slavery in 1848, their colonies also recruited new laborers from Asia and Africa.

Slavery was not abolished in Cuba until 1886, but the rising cost of slaves led the burgeoning sugar plantations to recruit 138,000 new laborers from China between 1847 and 1873. Indentured labor recruits also became the mainstay of new sugar plantations in places that had never known slave labor. After 1850 American planters in Hawaii recruited labor from China and Japan; British planters in Natal (in South Africa) recruited from India; and those in Queensland (in northeastern Australia) relied on laborers from neighboring South Pacific islands.

Larger, faster ships (see Chapter 27) made transporting laborers halfway around the world affordable, though voyages from Asia to the Caribbean still took an average of three months. Despite close regulation and supervision of shipboard conditions, the crowded accommodations encouraged the spread of cholera and other contagious diseases that took many migrants' lives.

All of these laborers served under **contracts of indenture**, which bound them to work for a specified period (usually from five to seven years) in return for free passage to their overseas destination. They were paid a small salary and were provided with housing, clothing, and medical care. Indian indentured laborers also received the right to a free passage home if they worked a second five-year contract. British Caribbean colonies required forty women to be recruited for every hundred men as a way to promote family life. So many Indians chose to stay in Mauritius, Trinidad, British Guiana, and Fiji that they constituted a third or more of the total population of these colonies by the early twentieth century.

The indentured labor trade reflected the unequal commercial and industrial power of the West, but it was not an entirely one-sided creation. The men and women who signed indentured contracts were trying to improve their lives by emigrating, and many succeeded. Whether for good or ill, more and more of the world's peoples saw their lives being influenced by the existence of Western colonies, Western ships, and Western markets.

Conclusion

What is the global significance of these complex political and economic changes in southern Asia, Africa, the South Pacific, and Latin America? One perspective stresses the continuing and growing imperialist exploitation of non-Europeans. From another perspective what was most important about this period was not the political and military strength of the Europeans but their growing domination of the world's commerce, especially investment in plantations, railroads, mines, and long-distance ocean shipping. Motives differed somewhat from region to region. Imperialists were drawn to Africa and Southeast Asia by a desire for tropical foodstuffs and industrial raw materials. Land for settlement was the attraction in Australia, New Zealand, and South Africa, as it earlier had been for European settlers in the New World. India and Latin America, having more prosperous middle classes, provided markets for European and American manufactures.

The growing exchanges could be mutually beneficial. As in Europe itself, overseas consumers found industrially produced goods far cheaper and sometimes better than the handicrafts they replaced. Industrialization also created new markets for African and Asian goods, as in the case of palm oil from West Africa or rubber from Malaya. There were also negative impacts, as in the case of weavers thrown out of work in India and the beginnings of deforestation in Southeast Asia.

Imperialist military and commercial strength did not reduce Africa, Asia, Latin America, and the Pacific to mere appendages of Europe. While the balance of power shifted in the Europeans' favor between 1750 and 1914, other cultures were still vibrant and local initiatives often dominant. Islamic reform movements, the rise of the Zulu nation, and the Mexican revolution had greater significance for their respective regions than did Western forces. Despite European power, Latin Americans and Southeast Asians were still largely in control of their own destinies. Even in India, most people's lives and beliefs maintained continuity with the past.

IMPORTANT EVENTS 1750–1914	
1756	Black Hole of Calcutta
1765	East India Company (EIC) rule of Bengal begins
1807	Britain outlaws slave trade
1808	Britain takes over Sierra Leone
1809	Sokoto Caliphate founded
1818	Shaka founds Zulu kingdom
1818	EIC creates Bombay Presidency
1821	Foundation of Republic of Liberia
1826	EIC annexes Assam and northern Burma
1828	Brahmo Samaj founded
1831–1847	Algerians resist French takeover
1834	Indentured labor migrations begin
1834	Britain frees slaves in its colonies
1836–1839	Afrikaners' Great Trek
1840	Omani sultan moves capital to Zanzibar
1848	France abolishes slaves in its colonies
1857–1858	Sepoy Rebellion leads to end of EIC rule and Mughal rule
1867	End of Atlantic slave trade
1869	Jaja founds Opobo
1876–1910	Porfirio Díaz, dictator of Mexico
1877	Queen Victoria becomes Empress of India
1885	First Indian National Congress formed
1898	Spanish-American War. U.S. takes over Cuba and Philippines
1899–1902	Boer War
1900s	Railroads connect ports to the interior of Africa
1910	Mexican Revolution begins
1917	New constitution proclaimed in Mexico

27

THE NEW POWER BALANCE, 1850–1900

O n July 8, 1853, four American warships, two of them steam-powered, appeared in Edo Bay, close to the capital of Japan. The commander of the fleet, **Commodore Matthew Perry**, delivered a letter from the president of the United States, demanding that Japan open its ports to foreign trade. Japan had had contact with Europe since the sixteenth century, when Portuguese mariners and Jesuit missionaries arrived. The Dutch followed in the seventeenth century. Worried by the disruptive effects of this Western presence, Japan suppressed Christian conversion efforts and then "excluded" European merchants in 1639, although limited contact was permitted at the port of Nagasaki.

While Japan had rejected a similar request delivered by a smaller U.S. naval force in 1845, Perry's modern, well-armed fleet and a series of threatening military maneuvers made clear the dangers associated with refusing his demand to open Japanese markets. When he returned the following year, the Japanese agreed to end the exclusion policies that had kept the nation isolated for two and a half centuries. If his display of military force had compelled change, Perry's visit also served to introduce a compelling array of the Industrial Revolution's technological and scientific triumphs to Japan, including a miniature railroad, a short telegraph line, and other marvels. For the next twenty years, Japanese society was torn between those who wanted to retreat into isolation and those who wished to embrace the foreign ways and acquire modern machines. For it was now clear that only by industrializing could Japan escape the fate of weaker nations then being taken over by Europe and the United States.

In the late nineteenth century a very small number of states, known as "great powers," dominated the world. Great Britain and France had been recognized as great powers long before the industrial age. Russia achieved that status as an ally against Napoleon and began industrializing in the late nineteenth century, as did Germany, the United States, and Japan. At the dawn of the twentieth century the economic and military capacities of these rapidly industrializing powers had dramatically altered long-standing political and cultural arrangements globally. Each had extended its territorial reach by establishing new colonies and also by creating informal empires where weak local authorities were compelled to grant preferable trade concessions. While rivalries among these powers could lead to conflict and competition, they collectively exercised a world-wide ascendancy never previously witnessed.

NEW TECHNOLOGIES AND THE WORLD ECONOMY

The Industrial Revolution marked the beginning of a massive transformation of the world. In the nineteenth century the technologies discussed in Chapter 22—textile mills, railroads, steamships, the telegraph, and others—spread from Britain to other parts of the world. By 1890, Germany and the United States had surpassed Great Britain as the world's leading industrial powers. Industrialization also introduced entirely new technologies, notably electricity and the steel and chemical industries, which revolutionized everyday life and transformed the world economy. The motive force behind this second phase of industrialization consisted of potent combinations of business, engineering, and science. By the mid-nineteenth century this combination was institutionalized in engineering schools and research laboratories, first in Germany and then in the United States.

Railroads   By the mid-nineteenth century, steam engines had become the prime mover of industry and commerce. Nowhere was this more evident than in the spread of **railroads**. By 1850 the first railroads had proved so successful that every industrializing country, and many that aspired to become industrial, began to build lines. The next fifty years saw a tremendous expansion of the world's rail networks. After a rapid spurt of building new lines, British railroad mileage leveled off in the 1870s at around 20,000 miles (over 32,000 kilometers). France and Germany ultimately built networks larger than Britain's, as did Canada and Russia. The nation with the largest railroad network in 1865, the United States, then increased its mileage eleven times by 1917.

Railroads were not confined to the industrialized nations; they could be constructed almost anywhere they would be of value to business or government. That included regions with abundant raw materials or agricultural products, like South Africa, Mexico, and Argentina, or densely populated countries like Egypt. Great Britain built the fourth largest rail network in the world in its largest colony, India, to reinforce political control and develop new trade opportunities.

With the exception of Japan, European or American engineers built the railroads of Africa, Asia, and Latin America with equipment imported from the West. In 1855, barely a year after Commodore Perry's visit, the Japanese instrument maker Tanaka Hisashige built a model steam train that he demonstrated to an admiring audience. In the 1870s, the Japanese government hired British engineers to build the first line from Tokyo to Yokohama and then sent them home in the 1880s once they had trained Japanese engineers. Within a few years, Japan began manufacturing its own railroad equipment.

Railroads consumed huge amounts of land. Many old cities doubled in size to accommodate railroad stations, sidings, tracks, warehouses, and repair shops. In the countryside, railroads required bridges, tunnels, and embankments. They also consumed vast quantities of timber, initially for fuel and then for ties to support the rails and for bridges. As railroads pushed across the landscape, they often left miles of deforested land on either side of their tracks. At the same time, railroads opened new land to agriculture, mining, and other human exploitation of natural resources wherever they were built, becoming major engines of global economic development.

Steamships and Telegraph Cables

In the mid-nineteenth century, a series of developments radically transformed ocean shipping. First iron, then steel, replaced the wood that had been used for hulls since shipbuilding began. Paddle wheels replaced sails and then were replaced by propellers as engineers built more powerful and fuel-efficient engines. The average size of freighters also increased, growing from an average of 200 tons in 1850 to 7,500 tons in 1900. As both the size of ships and the number of ships grew, coaling stations and ports able to handle large ships were built around the world. For example, the Suez Canal, constructed in 1869, shortened the distance between Europe and Asia and triggered a massive switch from sail power to steam (see Chapter 26).

These modern shipping lines offered fast, punctual, and reliable service on a fixed schedule for passengers, mail, and perishable freight as the world's fleet of merchant ships grew from 9 million tons in 1850 to 35 million tons in 1910. The result was falling freight costs and greater commercial integration, changes that benefited not only the exporters of industrial products in Europe and North America but also the Asian, African, and Latin American exporters of agricultural and mining products.

At the same time, shipping companies and commercial firms were able to use a new medium of communication, **submarine telegraph cables**, to respond to changing conditions in distant markets. The early development of this technology depended on the financial support of the French and British governments, which sought to improve communication with distant colonies. European businesses were more interested in laying a cable across the Atlantic to further develop commercial linkages. The initial efforts of the 1850s failed, but an improved transatlantic cable was successfully laid in 1866. By the turn of the century, cables connected every country and almost every inhabited island. As they became the indispensable tools of modern shipping and business, the public and the press extolled this "annihilation of time and space."

The Steel and Chemical Industries

Until the nineteenth century **steel** could be made only by skilled blacksmiths in very small quantities and was reserved for swords, knives, axes, and watch springs. Then came a series of inventions that made it the cheapest and most versatile metal ever known. In the 1850s, the American William Kelly and the Englishman Henry Bessemer discovered that air forced through molten pig iron by powerful pumps turned it into steel without additional fuel. Other new processes permitted steel to be made from scrap iron, an increasingly important raw material, and from the phosphoric iron ores common in western Europe. Following these discoveries, steel became cheap and abundant enough to make rails, bridges, ships, and even "tin" cans meant to be used once and thrown away.

The chemical industry followed a similar pattern of innovation. In 1856 the Englishman William Perkin created the first synthetic dye, aniline purple, from coal tar; the next few years were known in Europe as the "mauve decade" from the color of fashionable women's clothes. Industry began mass-producing other organic chemicals—compounds containing carbon atoms. Toward the end of the century German chemists synthesized red, violet, blue, brown, and black dyes as well. These bright, long-lasting colors were cheaper to manufacture and could be produced in much greater quantities and at much lower prices than natural dyes. They delighted consumers but ruined the indigo plantations of India and Latin America. Chemistry also made important advances in the manufacture of explosives. The first of these, nitroglycerin, was so dangerous that it exploded when shaken. In 1866, the Swedish scientist Alfred Nobel found a way to turn nitroglycerin into a stable solid—dynamite. This and other new explosives were useful in mining and were critical in the construction of railroads and canals. They also enabled the armies and navies of the great powers to arm themselves with increasingly accurate and powerful rifles and cannon.

The growing complexity of industrial chemistry made it one of the first fields where science and technology interacted on a daily basis. This development gave a great advantage to Germany, which had the most advanced engineering schools and scientific institutes of the time and whose government funded research and encouraged cooperation between universities and industries. By the end of the nineteenth century, Germany was the world's leading producer of dyes, drugs, synthetic fertilizers, ammonia, and nitrates used in making explosives.

Environmental Problems   Industrialization and rapid urbanization powerfully affected entire regions such as the English Midlands, the German Ruhr, parts of Pennsylvania in the United States, and the regions around Tokyo and Osaka in Japan. The new steel mills took up as much space as whole towns, belched smoke and particulates, and left behind huge hills of slag and other waste products. Coal-burning steam engines powered the new machine age and, along with mounting domestic coal consumption for cooking and heating, also filled the skies of Manchester, England, and the world's other manufacturing centers with dense smog.

Rapidly growing urban populations in industrializing European and American cities overwhelmed primitive sanitation systems until the last decades of the nineteenth century. When a drought lowered water levels in Britain's Thames River in 1858, Londoners experienced what they called the Big Stink caused by the vast quantities of untreated human and industrial waste long dumped into the river. More threatening still were pollution-related diseases like typhoid and cholera.

The coal smoke of railroad locomotives and other steam engines contributed to air pollution as well. The chemical industries also produced tons of toxic effluents that were dumped into rivers. Thus while industrialization brought vast amounts of wealth, without environmental regulations it also caused considerable damage to nature and to the health of nearby human populations.

Electricity   No innovation of the late nineteenth century changed people's lives as radically as **electricity**. As an energy source, electricity was more flexible and much easier to use than water power or stationary steam engines. At first, producing electric current was so costly that it was used only for electroplating and telegraphy. Then in 1831, the Englishman Michael Faraday showed that the motion of a copper wire through a magnetic field induced an electric current in the wire. Based on this discovery, inventors in the 1870s devised generators that turned mechanical energy into electric current.

Electricity now had a host of new applications. Initially, arc lamps lit up public squares, theaters, and stores, while homes continued to rely on gas lamps, which produced a softer light. Then in 1879, in the United States, **Thomas Edison** developed an incandescent lamp well suited to lighting small rooms. In 1882, Edison created the world's first electrical distribution network in New York City. By the turn of the century electric lighting was rapidly replacing gas lamps in the cities of Europe and North America.

Other uses of electricity quickly appeared. Electric streetcars and subways transported people throughout the cities of Europe and North America. Electric motors replaced steam engines and power belts, increasing productivity and improving workers' safety. Commonly dependent on coal-fired generators, electric energy production contributed to air pollution as well. As demand for electricity grew, engineers built hydroelectric plants. The plant at Niagara Falls, on the border between Ontario, Canada, and New York State, produced an incredible 11,000 horsepower when it opened in 1895. At the newly created Imperial College of

akg-images/Newscom

Paris Lit Up by Electricity, 1900 *The electric light bulb was invented in the United States and Britain, but Paris made such extensive use of the new technology that it was nicknamed "city of lights." To mark the Paris Exposition of 1900, the Eiffel Tower and all the surrounding buildings were illuminated with strings of light bulbs while powerful spotlights swept the sky.*

Engineering in Japan, an Englishman, William Ayrton, became the first professor of electrical engineering anywhere in the world; his students later went on to found major corporations and government research institutes.

World Trade and Finance

Improvements in transportation and communication, along with rising world population, led to a tenfold increase in international trade between 1850 and 1913. Europe imported wheat from Canada, the United States, and India, wool from Australia, and beef from Argentina, while it exported coal, railroad equipment, textiles, and machinery to Asia, Africa, and the Americas. Because steamships were much more efficient and faster than sailing ships, the cost of freight dropped dramatically, intensifying long-distance commercial links.

The growth of world trade transformed different parts of the world in different ways. The economies of western Europe and North America, the first to industrialize and the prime beneficiaries, grew more diversified and prosperous. Industries mass-produced consumer goods for a growing number of middle-class and even working-class customers: soap, canned and packaged foods, ready-made clothes, household items, and small luxuries like cosmetics and engravings. This revolution in consumption occurred at a much slower pace in the developing world and the benefits were more narrowly limited to elites and the middleclass. These privileged sectors often paid for imported novelties by imposing harsh conditions on the masses who labored in plantations and mines.

Even growing capitalist economies were prey to sudden swings in the business cycle—booms followed by deep depressions, or busts, in which workers lost their jobs and investors their fortunes. Because of the close connections among the industrial economies, the collapse of a bank in Austria in 1873 triggered a depression that spread to the United States, causing mass unemployment. Destabilizing worldwide recessions also occurred in the mid-1880s and mid-1890s. Many contemporaries feared that industrial production was growing faster than the capacity of traditional markets to consume goods, leading to falling prices and recession. The perceived solution, to expand markets and gain protected access to raw materials, helped propel the United States and the European powers to undertake a new wave of imperialist adventures in Asia, Africa, and Latin America (see Chapter 26). Tariffs could not insulate countries from the business cycle, for money continued to flow almost unhindered around the world. One of the main causes of the growing interdependence of the global economy was the financial power of Great Britain, which dominated the flow of trade, finance, and information. In 1900, two-thirds of the world's submarine cables were British owned or passed through Britain, and over half of the world's shipping was British owned. Britain invested one-fourth of its national wealth overseas, much of it in India, the United States, and Argentina. British money financed many of the railroads, harbors, mines, and other big projects outside Europe. While other currencies fluctuated, the pound sterling was as good as gold, and nine-tenths of international transactions used sterling.

Nonindustrial areas also were tied to the world economy as never before. Because many of them produced raw materials that could be replaced by synthetic substitutes (like dyestuffs) or alternative sources of supply, they were more vulnerable to changes in price and demand than were the industrialized nations. Developing regions that produced sugar, cotton, and dyes all experienced these upsets in the nineteenth century. Nevertheless, until 1913 the value of exports from the tropical countries generally kept up with the growth of their populations.

SOCIAL CHANGES

As fast-growing populations swelled Europe's cities to unprecedented size, millions of other Europeans emigrated to the Americas. At the same time, strained relations between industrial employers and workers spawned labor movements and new forms of radical politics. Women as well found their lives dramatically altered by economic and technological change, both in the home and in the public sphere.

Population and Migrations
The population of Europe grew faster from 1850 to 1914 than ever before or since, almost doubling from 265 million to 468 million. In non-European countries with predominantly white populations—the United States, Canada, Australia, New Zealand, and Argentina—the increase was even greater because of the inflow of European immigrants. There were many reasons for the mass migrations of this period: the Irish famine of 1847–1848; the persecution of Jews in Russia; poverty and population growth in Italy, Spain, Poland, and Scandinavia; and the cultural ties between Great Britain and English-speaking countries overseas. Equally important was the attraction of enhanced opportunities in places like Argentina, Australia, Canada, and the United States. The availability to travelers of cheap and rapid steamship and railroad transportation at both ends of immigration pathways also contributed to the scale of this massive population transfer (see Environment and Technology: Railroads and Immigration).

Between 1850 and 1900, on average, over 1 million Europeans migrated overseas every year; then, between 1900 and 1914, the flood rose to over 3 million a year. Over this same fifty-year period the population of the United States and Canada rose from 25 million to 98 million, and the proportion of people of European ancestry in the world's population rose from one-fifth to one-third. Great Britain was the most important source of immigrants by far, but very large numbers of Germans, Italians, and Spaniards joined the swelling ranks.

Why did the number of Europeans and their descendants overseas jump so dramatically? Much of the increase came from a drop in mortality, as epidemics and starvation became less common. The Irish famine of the 1840s was the last peacetime famine in European history. As farmers plowed up the plains of North America and planted wheat, much of which was shipped to Europe, food supplies increased faster than population. New technologies like canning and refrigeration also made food more abundant year-round, facilitating the export of Argentine beef and mutton to Europe. The diet of Europeans and North Americans also improved as meat, fruit, vegetables, and oils became part of the daily fare of city dwellers in winter as well as in summer.

During this period Asians also migrated in large numbers as indentured laborers who were recruited to work on distant plantations, in mines, and on railroads (see Chapter 26). Indians went to Africa, Southeast Asia, and other tropical colonies of Great Britain. Along with Chinese, Indians also emigrated to the East

ENVIRONMENT + TECHNOLOGY

Railroads and Immigration

Why did so many Europeans emigrate to North America in the late nineteenth and early twentieth centuries? The quick answer is that millions of people longed to escape the poverty or tyranny of their home countries and start new lives in a land of freedom and opportunity. Personal desire alone, however, does not account for the migrations. After all, poverty and tyranny existed long before the late nineteenth century. Two other factors helped determine when and where people migrated: whether they were allowed to migrate, and whether they were able to.

In the nineteenth century Asians were recruited to build railroads and work on farms. But from the 1890s on, the United States and Canada closed their doors to non-Europeans, so regardless of what they wanted, they could not move to North America. In contrast, emigrants from Europe were admitted almost without restriction until after the First World War.

The ability to travel was a result of improvements in transportation. Until the 1890s most immigrants came from Ireland, England, or Germany—countries with good rail transportation to their own harbors and low steamship fares to North America. As rail lines were extended into eastern and southern Europe, more and more immigrants came from Italy, Austria-Hungary, and Russia.

Similarly, until the 1870s most European immigrants to North America settled on the east coast. Then, as the railroads pushed west, more of them settled on farms in the central and western parts of the continent. The power of railroads moved people as much as their desires did.

Emigrant Waiting Room *The opening of the western region of the United States attracted settlers from the east coast and from Europe. These migrants are waiting for a train to take them to the Black Hills of Dakota during one of the gold rushes of the late nineteenth century.*

Library of Congress

Indies and the Caribbean to work on sugar plantations. At the same time, Japanese migrated in large numbers to Brazil and other parts of Latin America. Many Japanese, as well as Chinese and Filipinos, also went to work in agriculture and menial trade in Hawaii and California, where they encountered growing hostility from European–Americans.

Urbanization and Urban Environments   In 1851, Britain became the first nation with a majority of its population living in towns and cities. By 1914, 80 percent of Britain's population was urban, as were 60 percent of the German population and 45 percent of the French. Cities grew to unprecedented size. London grew from 2.7 million in 1850 to 6.6 million in 1900. New York, a small town of 64,000 people in 1800, reached 3.4 million by 1900, more than a fiftyfold increase. In 1800 New York had covered only the southernmost quarter of Manhattan Island, some 3 square miles (nearly 8 square kilometers); by 1900 it covered 150 square miles (390 square kilometers). In the English Midlands, in the German Ruhr, and around Tokyo Bay, fast-growing towns fused into one another, filling in the fields and woods that had once separated them.

As cities grew, they changed in character. Newly built railroads not only brought goods into the cities on a predictable schedule but also allowed people to live farther apart. At first, only the well-to-do could afford to commute by train; by the end of the century, electric streetcars and subways allowed working-class people to live miles from their workplaces.

In preindustrial and early industrial cities, the poor crowded together in tenements; sanitation was bad; water was often contaminated with sewage; and darkness made life dangerous. New urban technologies and the growing powers and responsibilities of governments transformed city life for all but the poorest residents. The most important change was the installation of pipes to bring in clean water and to carry away sewage. At the same time, gas lighting and then electric lighting made cities safer at night. By the turn of the twentieth century municipal governments in Europe and North America provided police and fire protection, sanitation and garbage removal, building and health inspection, schools, parks, and other amenities unheard of a century earlier.

As sanitation improved, epidemics became rare. For the first time, urban death rates fell below birthrates. The decline in infant mortality was an especially significant indicator of improved hygiene and medical care. Confident that their children would survive infancy, couples began to limit the number of children they had, and ancient scourges like infanticide and child abandonment became less frequent.

To accommodate the growing population, builders created new neighborhoods, from crowded tenements for the poor to opulent mansions for the newly rich. In the United States urban planners laid out new cities, such as Chicago, on rectangular grids, and middle-class families moved to new developments on the edges of cities, the suburbs. In Paris older neighborhoods with narrow crooked streets and rickety tenements were torn down to make room for broad boulevards and modern apartment buildings. Brilliantly lit by gas and electricity, Paris became the "city of lights," a model for city planners from New Delhi to Buenos Aires. The rich continued to live in inner cities that contained the monuments, churches, and palaces of preindustrial times, while workers often moved to the outskirts.

Lower population densities and better transportation divided cities into industrial, commercial, and residential zones occupied by different social classes. Improvements such as water and sewerage, electricity, and streetcars always benefited the wealthy first, then the middle class, and finally the working class. In the complex of urban life, businesses of all kinds arose, and the professions—engineering, accounting, research, journalism, and the law, among others—took on increased importance. The new middle class exhibited its wealth in fine houses with servants and in elegant entertainment.

While urban environments improved in many ways, air quality worsened. Coal, burned to power steam engines and heat buildings, polluted the air, creating unpleasant and sometimes dangerous "pea-soup" fog and coating everything with a film of grimy dust. The thousands of horses that pulled carts and carriages covered the streets with their wastes, causing a terrible stench. The introduction of electricity helped alleviate some of these environmental problems. Electric motors and lamps did not pollute the air, and coal-burning power plants were built at a distance from cities. As electric trains and streetcars began replacing horse-drawn trolleys and coal-burning locomotives, cities became cleaner and healthier. However, most of the environmental benefits of electricity were to come in the twentieth century.

Middle-Class Women's "Separate Sphere" In English-speaking countries the period from about 1850 to 1901 is known as the **Victorian Age**. The expression refers not only to the reign of Queen Victoria of England (r. 1837–1901) but also to rules of behavior and to an ideology surrounding the family and the relations between men and women. The Victorians contrasted the masculine ideals of strength and courage with the feminine virtues of beauty and kindness, and they idealized the home as a peaceful and loving refuge from the dog-eat-dog world of competitive capitalism.

Victorian morality claimed to be universal, yet it best fit upper- and middle-class European families. Men and women were thought to belong in **"separate spheres."** Successful businessmen spent their time at work or relaxing in men's clubs. They put their wives in charge of rearing the children, running the household, and spending the family money to enhance the family's social status. The majority of women from the less privileged classes, however, lived constantly with financial pressures. Many worked outside the home for wages. Others took in laundry or did low-wage piecework, like sewing for garment companies to supplement household income.

Before electric appliances, maintaining a middle-class home involved enormous amounts of work. Not only were families larger, but middle-class couples entertained often and lavishly. Carrying out these tasks required servants. A family's status and the activities and lifestyle of the "mistress of the house" depended on the availability of servants to help with household tasks. Only families that employed at least one full-time servant were considered middle class.

Toward the turn of the century modern technology began to transform middle-class homes. Plumbing eliminated the pump and the outhouse. Central heating replaced fireplaces, stoves, trips to the basement for coal, and endless dusting. Gas and electricity lit houses and cooked food without soot, smoke, and ashes. In the early twentieth century wealthy families acquired the first vacuum cleaners and washing machines. However, these technological advances did not mean less housework for women. As families acquired new household appliances, they raised their standards of cleanliness, thus demanding just as much labor as before.

The most important duty of middle-class women was raising children. Victorian mothers nursed their own babies and showered their children with love and attention. Even those who could afford governesses remained personally involved in their children's education. Girls' education was very different from that of boys. While boys were being prepared for the business world or the professions, girls were taught embroidery, drawing, and music, skills that enhanced their social graces and marriage prospects.

Young middle-class women could work until they got married, but only in genteel places like stores and offices, never in factories. When the typewriter and telephone were introduced into the business world in the 1880s, businessmen found that they could get better work at lower wages from educated young women than from men, and operating these machines was stereotyped as women's work.

Most professional careers were closed to women, and few universities granted women degrees. In the United States, higher education was available to women only at elite colleges in the East and teachers' colleges in the Midwest. European women had fewer opportunities. Before 1914 very few women became doctors, lawyers, or professional musicians. Instead, women were considered well suited to teaching young children and girls—an extension of the duties of Victorian mothers—but only until marriage. A married woman was expected to become pregnant right away and to stay home taking care of her own children rather than other people's.

A home life, no matter how busy, did not satisfy all middle-class women. Some became volunteer nurses or social workers, receiving little or no pay. Others organized to fight prostitution, alcohol, and child labor. By the turn of the century a few challenged male domination of politics and the law. Suffragists, led in Britain by Emmeline Pankhurst and in the United States by Elizabeth Cady Stanton and Susan B. Anthony, demanded the right to vote. By 1914 U.S. women had won the right to vote in twelve states. British women did not gain the right to vote until 1918.

Working-Class Women   In the new industrial cities, men and women no longer worked together at home or in the fields, a separation of work and home that affected women even more than men. While working-class women formed a majority of the workers in the textile industries and in domestic service, they also needed to keep homes and raise children. As a result, they led lives of toil and pain. Parents expected girls as young as ten to contribute to the household. In Japan, as in Ireland and New England, tenant farmers, squeezed by rising taxes and rents, were forced to send their daughters to work in textile mills. Others became domestic servants, commonly working sixteen or more hours a day, six and a half days a week, for little more than room and board, usually in attics or basements. Without appliances, much of their work was physically hard: hauling coal and water up stairs, washing laundry by hand.

Young women often preferred factory work to domestic service. Men worked in construction, iron and steel, heavy machinery, or on railroads; women worked

Jimmy Sime/Hulton Archive/Getty Images

Emmeline Pankhurst Under Arrest *The leader of the British women's suffrage movement frequently called attention to her cause by breaking the law to protest discrimination against women. Here she is being arrested and carried off to jail by the police.*

in textiles and the clothing trades, extensions of traditional women's household work. Appalled by the abuses of women and children in the early years of industrialization, most industrial countries eventually passed protective legislation limiting hours worked or forbidding the employment of women in the hardest and most dangerous occupations, such as mining and foundry work. While the stated intention was to protect women, such legislation reinforced gender divisions in industry, keeping women in low-paid, subordinate positions. Even where women worked alongside men, in factories, for example, they earned between one-third and two-thirds of the wages paid men.

Married women with children were expected to stay home, even if their husbands did not make enough to support the family. Yet they had to contribute to the family's income. Families who had room to spare, even a bed or a corner in the kitchen, took in boarders. Many women did piecework such as sewing dresses, making hats or gloves, or weaving baskets at home. The hardest and worst-paid work was washing other people's clothes. Overall, many poor women worked at home ten to twelve hours a day and enlisted the help of their small children, perpetuating practices long outlawed in factories. Without electric lighting and indoor plumbing, even ordinary household duties like cooking and washing remained heavy burdens.

SOCIALISM AND LABOR MOVEMENTS

The experience of industrialization combined with the revolutionary ideas of the late eighteenth century to produce two kinds of movements that demanded economic and political reforms: socialism and labor unions. **Socialism** was an ideology developed by radical thinkers who questioned the sanctity of private property and argued in support of industrial workers against their employers. **Labor unions** were organizations formed by industrial workers to defend their interests in negotiations with employers. The socialist and labor movements were never identical. Most of the time they were allies; occasionally they competed for the support of workers.

Revolutionary Alternatives   The growing wealth and power of new industrial elites and the harsh living and working conditions experienced by industrial workers led to the formation of labor unions, the creation of the first social welfare policies, demands for voting rights, and, for some, the dream of revolutionary transformation. Those seeking a revolution were divided among numerous parties and factions. Within the diverse and contentious world of left-leaning politics (see Chapter 22), **Karl Marx** was a formidable theorist of revolution as well as a major contestant for power. Marx shared the Enlightenment's enthusiasm for reason and logic and identified his revolutionary ideal as "scientific socialism." His adherents generally referred to themselves as communists or Marxists. Marx believed that the relentless competition inherent in industrial capitalism would lead ultimately to a social order divided between a wealthy powerful few and a mass of exploited and impoverished workers. This division, once in place, would inevitably lead in Marx's view to revolutions that would end capitalism and create a dictatorship of the proletariat (industrial workers). Once accomplished, this revolution by workers would distribute the material benefits and scientific progress achieved by the Industrial Revolution to society in general. With private property abolished, Marx asserted, the resources of government and industry could be harnessed to end poverty and injustice.

Many of those committed to revolutionary change rejected Marx's insistence that revolutionary action, violent resistance to the status quo, wait for the full development of industrial capitalism and the appearance of the proletariat. Although in broad agreement with Marx's critique of capitalism, they believed that the levels of injustice and inequality already present in society justified revolutionary violence immediately. Some of the revolutionaries rejected Marx's belief that his proposed dictatorship of the proletariat, or, indeed, any form of government, could avoid recreating the inequality and injustice that already oppressed the poor. The Russian intellectual Mikhail Bakunin (1814–1876) argued forcibly that peasants, displaced and unemployed artisans, and other exploited groups also had revolutionary potential and, consequently, that many unindustrialized regions of Europe were ready for revolution. He also dismissed Marx's faith in a future worker's government as naive.

Bakunin exercised a powerful influence over the development of anarchism, the chief revolutionary alternative to communism. Anarchists believed that revolution could be achieved through direct action by individuals and small groups, what they called "propaganda of the deed." The result of this movement's development was a series of assassinations and bombings that shook the political structures of Europe and the Americas. These attacks included the bombings of the opera (1893) and Corpus

Christi celebration (1896) in Spain and the Haymarket bombing in Chicago (1896). They also included the assassinations of President Carnot of France (1894), Prime Minister Cánovas del Castillo of Spain (1897), Empress Elizabeth of Austria (1898), King Umberto of Italy (1900), and President McKinley of the United States (1901).

The conflict between Marx and Bakunin culminated in 1872 when Bakunin and his adherents were expelled from the revolutionary umbrella organization, the International Workingman's Association. While the followers of Marx forced Bakunin from the center of revolutionary activity, his followers remained a potent source of political violence and working-class mobilization in Italy, Spain, and Argentina well into the twentieth century.

Labor Unions and Movements Since the beginning of the nineteenth century, workers had united to create "friendly societies" for mutual assistance in times of illness, unemployment, or disability. Laws that forbade workers to strike were abolished in Britain in the 1850s and in the rest of Europe soon thereafter. Labor unions sought not only better wages but also improved working conditions and insurance against illness, accidents, disability, and old age. They grew slowly because they required a permanent staff as well as a great deal of money to sustain their members during strikes. Nevertheless, by the end of the century, British labor unions counted 2 million members, and German and American unions had 1 million members each. Once organized, unions became a political force in all democratic countries, advocating for improved wages and working conditions.

Just as labor unions strove to share in the benefits of a capitalist economy, so did electoral politics persuade workers to become part of the existing political system. The nineteenth century saw a gradual extension of the right to vote throughout Europe and North America. Universal male suffrage became law in the United States in 1870, in France and Germany in 1871, in Britain in 1885, and in the rest of Europe soon thereafter. With so many newly enfranchised workers, many socialist politicians hoped to capture seats in their nations' parliaments. Rather than seize power through revolution, these democratic socialists expected to obtain concessions from government and eventually even to form a government.

Working-class women, burdened with both job and family responsibilities, found little time for politics and were not welcome in the male-dominated trade unions or radical political parties. A few radicals such as the German socialist Rosa Luxemburg and the American **anarchist** Emma Goldman became famous but did not have a large following. It was never easy to reconcile the demands of male workers with those of women. In 1889 the German socialist Clara Zetkin wrote: "Just as the male worker is subjected by the capitalist, so is the woman by the man, and she will always remain in subjugation until she is economically independent. Work is the indispensable condition for economic independence." Six years later, she recognized that the liberation of women would have to await a change in the position of the working class as a whole: "The proletarian woman cannot attain her highest ideal through a movement for the equality of the female sex, she attains salvation only through the fight for the emancipation of labor."[1]

---

[1]Quoted in Bonnie S. Anderson and Judith P. Zinsser, *A History of Their Own: Women in Europe from Prehistory to the Present*, vol. 2 (New York: Harper & Row, 1988), 372, 387.

Nationalism and the Rise of Italy, Germany, and Japan

The most influential idea of the nineteenth century was **nationalism**. Whereas people had previously been considered the subjects of a sovereign, French revolutionaries defined people as the citizens of a *nation*—a concept identified with a territory, the state that ruled it, and the culture of its people.

Language and National Identity in Europe before 1871

Language was usually the crucial element in creating a feeling of national unity. It was important both as a way to unite the people of a nation and as the means of persuasion by which political leaders could inspire their followers. Language was the tool of the new generation of political activists, most of them lawyers, teachers, students, and journalists. Yet language and citizenship seldom coincided perfectly.

The fit between France and the French language was closer than in most large countries, though some French-speakers lived outside of France and some French people spoke other languages. Italian- and German-speaking people, however, were divided among many small states. Living in the Austrian Empire were peoples who spoke German, Czech, Slovak, Hungarian, Polish, and other languages. Even where people spoke a common language, they could be divided by religion or institutions. The Irish, though English-speaking, were mostly Catholic, whereas the English were primarily Protestant.

The idea of redrawing the boundaries of states to accommodate linguistic, religious, or cultural differences was revolutionary. In Italy and Germany, it led to the forging of large new states out of many small ones in 1871. In central and eastern Europe, nationalism threatened to break up large states into smaller ones.

Until the 1860s nationalism was associated with **liberalism**, the revolutionary middle-class ideology that emerged from the French Revolution, asserted the sovereignty of the people, and demanded constitutional government, a national parliament, and freedom of expression (see Chapter 23). The most famous nationalist of the early nineteenth century was the Italian liberal Giuseppe Mazzini (jew-SEP-pay mots-EE-nee) (1805–1872), the leader of the failed revolution of 1848 in Italy. Mazzini sought to unify the Italian peninsula into one nation and associated with revolutionaries elsewhere to bring nationhood and liberty to all peoples oppressed by tyrants and foreigners. The governments of Russia, Prussia, and Austria censored the new ideas but could not quash them.

The revolutions of 1848 convinced conservatives that governments could not forever keep their citizens out of politics and that mass politics, if properly managed, could strengthen rather than weaken the state (see Chapter 23). A new generation of conservative political leaders learned how to preserve the status quo through public education, universal military service, and colonial conquests, all of which built a sense of national unity.

The Unification of Italy, 1860–1870

By midcentury, popular sentiment was building throughout Italy for unification. Opposing it were Pope Pius IX, who abhorred everything modern, and Austria, which controlled two Italian provinces, Lombardy and Venetia. The prime minister of

Piedmont-Sardinia, Count Camillo Benso di Cavour, saw the rivalry between France and Austria as an opportunity to unify Italy. He secretly formed an alliance with France and then instigated a war with Austria in 1858. The war was followed by uprisings throughout northern and central Italy in favor of joining Piedmont-Sardinia, a moderate constitutional monarchy under King Victor Emmanuel.

MAP 27.1   Unification of Italy, 1859–1870

The unification of Italy was achieved by the expansion of the kingdom of Piedmont-Sardinia, with the help of France.

If Cavour's conservative, top-down approach to unification prevailed in the north, a more radical approach was still possible in the south. In 1860 the fiery revolutionary **Giuseppe Garibaldi** (jew-SEP-pay gary-BAHL-dee) and a small band of followers landed in Sicily and then in southern Italy, overthrew the Kingdom of the Two Sicilies, and prepared to found a democratic republic. The royalist Cavour, however, took advantage of the unsettled situation to sideline Garibaldi and transform Piedmont-Sardinia into a new Kingdom of Italy. Unification was completed with the addition of Venetia in 1866 and the Papal States in 1870.

The process of Italian unification illustrates the shift of nationalism from a radical democratic idea to a conservative method of building popular support for a strong centralized government, even an aristocratic and monarchical one.

The Unification of Germany, 1866–1871

The unification of most German-speaking people into a single state in 1871 had momentous consequences for the world. Until the 1860s the region of central Europe where people spoke German consisted of Prussia, the western half of the Austrian Empire, and numerous smaller states. Some German nationalists wanted to unite all Germans under the Austrian throne. Others wanted to exclude Austria with its many non-Germanic peoples and unite all other German-speaking areas under Prussia. The divisions were also religious: Austria and southwestern Germany were Catholic; Prussia and the northeast were Lutheran. The Prussian state had two advantages: (1) the newly developed industries of the Rhineland, and (2) the first European army to make use of railroads, telegraphs, breechloading rifles, steel artillery, and other products of modern industry.

During the reign of King Wilhelm I (r. 1861–1888), Prussia was ruled by a brilliant and authoritarian aristocrat, Chancellor **Otto von Bismarck** (UTT-oh von BIS-mark) (1815–1898). Bismarck was determined to use Prussian industry and German nationalism to make his state the dominant power in Germany. In 1866, Prussia attacked and defeated Austria. To everyone's surprise, Prussia took no Austrian territory. Instead, Prussia and some smaller states formed the North German Confederation, the nucleus of a future Germany. Then in 1870 Bismarck attacked France. Prussian armies, joined by troops from other German states, used their superior firepower and tactics to achieve a quick victory. "Blood and iron" were the foundation of the new German Empire.

The spoils of victory included a large indemnity and two provinces of France bordering on Germany: Alsace and Lorraine. The French paid the indemnity easily enough but resented the loss of their provinces. To the Germans, this region was German because a majority of its inhabitants spoke German. To the French, it was French because most of its inhabitants considered themselves French. These two conflicting definitions of nationalism kept enmity between France and Germany smoldering for decades. In this case, nationalism turned out to be a divisive rather than a unifying force.

The West Challenges Japan

In Japan the emperor was revered but had no power. Instead, Japan was governed by the Tokugawa Shogunate—a secular government under a military leader, or *shogun*, that had come to power in 1600 (see Chapter 21). Local lords, called

MAP 27.2   Unification of Germany, 1866–1871

Germany was united after a series of short, successful wars by the kingdom of Prussia against Austria in 1866 and against France in 1871.

daimyos, were permitted to control their lands and populations with very little interference from the shogunate.

When threatened from outside, this system showed many weaknesses. For one thing, it did not permit the coordination of resources necessary to resist major political or military challenges. Attempting to minimize exposure to Christianity and other threats to traditional culture, the shoguns prohibited foreigners from entering Japan and Japanese from going abroad in the early 1600s. They did permit the Dutch to retain a small commercial outpost at Nagasaki. While the penalty for breaking these laws was death, many Japanese ignored them. The most flagrant violators were powerful lords in southern Japan who ran large and very successful pirate or black-market operations and benefited from the decentralization of the shogunal political system in their entrepreneurial activities. But when a genuine foreign threat was suggested—as when, in 1792, Russian and British ships were spotted off the Japanese coast—the local lords realized that Japan was too weak and decentralized to resist a foreign invasion. As a result, a few of the regional lords began to develop their own reformed armies, arsenals, and shipyards. At the same time a small number of Japanese intellectuals engaged European culture, what they called Dutch learning.

By the 1800s Satsuma (SAT-soo-mah) and Choshu (CHOE-shoo), two large domains in southern Japan, had become wealthy and ambitious, enjoying high rates of revenue and population growth. Their remoteness from the capital Edo (now Tokyo) and their economic vigor also fostered a strong sense of local self-reliance.

When Commodore Matthew C. Perry, backed by a powerful fleet, demanded that Japan open its ports to trade and allow American ships to refuel and take on supplies during their voyages between China and California in 1853, he precipitated a political crisis. After consultation with the provincial daimyos, the shogun's advisers advocated capitulation to Perry, pointing to China's humiliating defeats in the Opium and Arrow Wars. As a result, when Perry returned in 1854, representatives of the shogun indicated their willingness to sign the Treaty of Kanagawa (KAH-nah-GAH-wah), modeled on the unequal treaties between China and the Western powers. Angry and disappointed, some provincial governors began to encourage an underground movement calling for the destruction of the Tokugawa regime and the banning of foreigners from Japan.

Tensions between the shogunate and some provincial leaders, particularly in Choshu and Satsuma, increased in the early 1860s. Young, ambitious, educated men who faced mediocre prospects under the rigid Tokugawa class system emerged as provincial leaders. When British and French ships shelled the southwestern coasts in 1864 to protest the treatment of foreigners, the action enraged the provincial samurai who rejected the Treaty of Kanagawa and resented the shogunate's inability to protect the country. In 1867, the Choshu leaders Yamagata Aritomo and Ito Hirobumi finally realized that they should stop warring with their rival province, Satsuma, and join forces to lead a rebellion against the shogunate.

The Meiji Restoration and the Modernization of Japan, 1868–1894

The civil war was intense but brief. In 1868, provincial rebels overthrew the Tokugawa Shogunate and declared young emperor Mutsuhito (moo-tsoo-HEE-toe) (r. 1868–1912) "restored." The new leaders called their regime the "**Meiji** (MAY-gee) **Restoration**" after Mutsuhito's reign name (*Meiji* means "enlightened rule"). The "Meiji oligarchs," as the new rulers were known, were extraordinarily talented and far-sighted. Determined to protect their country from Western imperialism, they encouraged its transformation into "a rich country with a strong army" with world-class industries. Though imposed from above, the Meiji Restoration marked as profound a change as the French Revolution.

The oligarchs were under no illusion that they could fend off the Westerners without changing their institutions and their society. In the Charter Oath issued in

1868, the young emperor included a prophetic phrase: "Knowledge shall be sought throughout the world and thus shall be strengthened the foundation of the imperial polity." It was to be the motto of a new Japan, which embraced all foreign ideas, institutions, and techniques that could strengthen the nation. The literacy rate in Japan was the highest in Asia at the time, and the oligarchs shrewdly exploited it in their introduction of new educational systems, a conscript army, and new communications. The government was able to establish heavy industry, thanks to decades of industrial development and financing in the provinces in the earlier

MAP 27.3 Expansion and Modernization of Japan, 1868–1918

As Japan acquired modern industry, it followed the example of the European powers in seeking overseas colonies. Its colonial empire grew at the expense of its neighbors: Taiwan was taken from China in 1895; Karafutu (Sakhalin) from Russia in 1905; and all of Korea became a colony in 1910.

1800s. With a conscript army and a revamped educational system, the oligarchs attempted to create a new citizenry that was literate and competent but also loyal and obedient.

The Meiji leaders copied the government structure of imperial Germany and modeled the new Japanese navy on the British and the army on the Prussian. They also introduced Western-style postal and telegraph services, railroads and harbors, banking, clocks, and calendars. To learn the secrets of Western strength, they sent hundreds of students to Britain, Germany, and the United States. Western-style clothing and hairstyles and garden parties as well as formal dances became popular.

The government was especially interested in Western technology. It opened vocational, technical, and agricultural schools, founded four imperial universities, and brought in foreign experts to advise on medicine, science, and engineering. To encourage industrialization, the government set up state-owned enterprises to manufacture cloth and inexpensive consumer goods for sale abroad. The first Japanese industries exploited their workers ruthlessly, just as the first industries in Europe and America had done. In 1881 the government sold these enterprises to private investors, mainly large *zaibatsu* (zye-BOT-soo), or conglomerates, and also encouraged individual technological innovation. Thus the carpenter Toyoda Sakichi founded the Toyoda Loom Works (now Toyota Motor Company) in 1906; ten years later he patented the world's most advanced automatic loom.

Nationalism and Social Darwinism   The Franco-Prussian War of 1870–1871 changed the political climate of Europe, making France more liberal. Germany, Austria-Hungary (as the Austrian Empire had renamed itself in 1867), and Russia remained conservative and used nationalism to maintain the status quo. The kingdom of Italy completed the unification of the peninsula begun decades earlier.

Nationalism and parliamentary elections made politicians of all parties appeal to public opinion. They were greatly aided by the press, especially cheap daily newspapers that sought to increase circulation by publishing sensational articles about overseas conquests and foreign threats. As governments increasingly came to recognize the advantages of an educated population in the competition between states, they opened public schools in every town and admitted women into public-service jobs for the first time. Politicians and journalists appealed to the emotions of the poor, diverting their anger from their employers to foreigners and their votes from socialist to nationalist parties.

In many countries the dominant group used nationalism to impose its language, religion, or customs on minority populations. The Russian Empire attempted to "Russify" its diverse ethnic populations. The Spanish government made Spanish compulsory in the schools, newspapers, and courts of its Basque- and Catalan-speaking provinces. Similarly, immigrants to the United States were expected to learn English.

Western culture in the late nineteenth century exalted the powerful over the weak, men over women, rich over poor, Europeans over other races, and humans over nature. Some people attempted to use science to justify the harsh inequalities of gender, ethnicity, and class that were common across Europe and the Americas.

One of the most influential scientists of the century, and the one whose ideas were most widely appropriated and misinterpreted, was the English biologist Charles Darwin (1809–1882).

In his 1859 book *On the Origin of the Species*, Darwin challenged common assumptions derived from religious beliefs by arguing that the earth was much older than previously believed. Based on years of research of the fossil record and careful observation of nature, he proposed that all forms of life had either evolved in the struggle for survival or become extinct over the course of hundreds of thousands of years. While controversial initially, Darwin's discoveries led to a revolution in the life sciences.

The philosopher Herbert Spencer (1820–1903) and others took up Darwin's ideas of "natural selection" and "survival of the fittest" and applied them to human society. These Social Darwinists developed elaborate pseudo-scientific theories of racial and ethnic differences, claiming that they were the result not of history but of biology. They saw social and racial differences as resulting from natural processes and opposed state intervention to alleviate inequities. Although not based on any research, these ideas gave a scientific-sounding justification for the power of the privileged and for imperialism.

THE GREAT POWERS OF EUROPE, 1871–1900

After the middle of the century, politicians and journalists discovered that minor incidents involving foreigners could be used to stir up popular indignation against neighboring countries. Military officers, impressed by the awesome power of the weapons that modern industry provided, began to think that the weapons were invincible. As a result, rivalries over colonial territories, ideological differences, and even minor border incidents or trade disagreements contributed to growing international tensions and, ultimately, to war.

Germany at the Center of Europe International relations revolved around Germany because it was located in the center of Europe and had the most powerful army on the European continent. After creating a unified Germany in 1871, Bismarck declared that his country had no further territorial ambitions, and he put his efforts into maintaining the peace in Europe. To isolate France, he forged a loose coalition with Austria-Hungary and Russia, the other two conservative monarchical powers. Despite their competing ambitions in the Balkans, he was able to keep his coalition together for twenty years.

Bismarck proved equally adept at strengthening German unity at home. To weaken the influence of middle-class liberals, he extended the vote to all adult men, thereby allowing Socialists to win seats in the *Reichstag* or parliament. By imposing high tariffs on manufactured goods and wheat, he gained the support of both the wealthy industrialists of the Rhineland and the great landowners of eastern Germany, traditional rivals for power. His government supported public and technical education as a means to stimulate industrial expansion. Bismarck also introduced path-breaking social legislation—medical, unemployment, and disability insurance as well as old age pensions—long before other industrial countries.

Under his leadership, the German people developed a strong sense of national unity and pride in their industrial and military power.

In 1888 Wilhelm I was succeeded by his grandson Wilhelm II (r. 1888–1918), an insecure and arrogant man who tried to gain respect by making belligerent speeches. Within two years he had dismissed Chancellor Bismarck and surrounded himself with yes men. He talked about his "global policy" and demanded the creation of a colonial empire. Ruler of the nation with the mightiest army and the largest industrial economy in Europe, he felt that Germany deserved "a place in the sun."

The Liberal Powers: France and Great Britain   France, once the dominant nation in Europe, had difficulty reconciling itself to being in second place. Though a prosperous country with flourishing agriculture and a large colonial empire, the French republic had some serious weaknesses. France trailed Great Britain and Germany in the development of modern heavy industry. Also troubling was the fact that France's population was scarcely growing; in 1911 France had only 39 million people compared to Germany's 64 million. In an age when the power of nations was roughly proportional to the size of their armies, France could field an army only two-thirds the size of Germany's.

The French people were also deeply divided over the very nature of the state: some were monarchists and Catholic, but a growing number held republican and anticlerical views. Yet if French political life seemed fragile and frequently in crisis, a long tradition of popular participation in politics and a strong sense of nationhood, reinforced by a fine system of public education, gave the French people a deeper cohesion than appeared on the surface.

Great Britain had a long experience with parliamentary elections and competing parties. The British government alternated smoothly between the Liberal and Conservative Parties, and the income gap between rich and poor gradually narrowed. Nevertheless, Britain had problems that grew more apparent as time went on. One was Irish resentment of English rule. Nationalism had strengthened the allegiance of the English, Scots, and Welsh to the British state. But the Irish, excluded from meaningful participation in government because they were Catholic and predominantly poor, saw the British as a foreign occupying force.

Another problem was the British economy. By the last decades of the nineteenth century, Great Britain had fallen behind the United States and Germany in such important industries as steel, chemicals, electricity, and textiles. Even in shipbuilding and shipping, Britain's traditional specialty, Germany was catching up.

Britain was also preoccupied with its enormous and fast-growing empire. A source of wealth for investors and the envy of other imperialist nations, the empire was a constant drain on Britain's finances, for it required Britain to maintain costly fleets of warships throughout the world.

For most of the nineteenth century Britain pursued a policy of "splendid isolation." Britain's preoccupation with India led British statesmen to exaggerate the Russian threat to the Ottoman Empire and to the Central Asian approaches to India. Periodic "Russian scares" and Britain's age-old rivalry with France for overseas colonies diverted the attention of British politicians from the potent threat posed by the rise of Germany.

The Conserva-
tive Powers:
Russia and
Austria-Hungary

The forces of nationalism weakened rather than strengthened Russia and Austria-Hungary. Their populations were far more divided, socially and ethnically, than were the German, French, or British peoples.

Nationalism was most divisive in south-central Europe, where many different language groups lived in close proximity. In 1867, the Austrian Empire renamed itself the Austro-Hungarian Empire to appease its Hungarian critics. Although its attempts to promote the cultures of its Slavic-speaking minorities failed to gain their political allegiance, it still thought of itself as a great power and attempted to dominate the Balkans. This strategy irritated Russia, which thought of itself as the protector of Slavic peoples everywhere.

Ethnic diversity also contributed to the instability of imperial Russia. The Polish people rebelled in 1830 and again in 1863–1864. The tsarist empire also included Finland, Estonia, Latvia, Lithuania, and Ukraine; the Caucasus; and the Muslim population of Central Asia conquered between 1865 and 1881. Furthermore, Russia had the largest Jewish population in Europe, and the harshness of its anti-Semitic laws and periodic *pogroms* (massacres) prompted many Jews to flee to America. Given this ethnic complexity, the state's attempts to impose the Russian language on its subjects were divisive instead of unifying.

In 1861, the moderate conservative Tsar Alexander II (r. 1855–1881) emancipated the peasants from serfdom. He did so partly out of a genuine desire to strengthen the bonds between the monarchy and the Russian people, and partly to promote industrialization by enlarging the labor pool. That half-hearted measure, however, only turned serfs into farm workers with few skills and little capital. Though "emancipated," the great majority of Russians had little education, few legal rights, and no say in the government. After Alexander's assassination in 1881, his successors Alexander III (r. 1881–1894) and Nicholas II (r. 1894–1917) reluctantly permitted limited attempts at social change. The Russian commercial middle class was small and had little influence. Industrialization consisted largely of state-sponsored projects, such as railroads, iron foundries, and armament factories, and led to social unrest among urban workers. Wealthy landowning aristocrats continued to dominate the Russian court and administration and blocked most reforms.

The weaknesses in Russia's society and government became glaringly obvious during a war with the rapidly industrializing Japan in 1904 and 1905. The fighting took place in Manchuria, a province in northern China far from European Russia and both armies suffered large losses. Ultimately, the Russian army, which received all its supplies by means of the inefficient Trans-Siberian Railway, was defeated by the better-trained and better-equipped Japanese. When the Russian navy finally arrived in Asian waters in 1905 after its long voyage around Eurasia and Africa, it was destroyed by the Japanese fleet at Tsushima Strait, validating the Meiji commitment to military modernization.

The shock of defeat caused a revolution in 1905 that forced Tsar Nicholas II to grant a constitution and permit an elected Duma (parliament). But as soon as he was able to rebuild the army and the police, he reverted to the traditional despotism of his forefathers. In response, small groups of radical intellectuals, angered by the contrast between the wealth of the elite and the poverty of the common people, began plotting the violent overthrow of the tsarist autocracy.

CHINA, JAPAN, AND THE WESTERN POWERS

After 1850, China and Japan—the two largest countries in East Asia—felt the influence of the Western powers as never before, but their responses were completely opposite. China resisted Western influence and became weaker, while Japan transformed itself into a major industrial and military power. One reason for this difference was the Western powers' already deep involvement in China and the distance to Japan, the nation most remote from Europe by ship. More important was the difference between the Chinese and Japanese elites' attitudes toward foreign cultures.

China in Turmoil   China had been devastated by the Taiping (tie-PING) Rebellion that raged from 1850 to 1864 (see Chapter 24). The French and British took advantage of China's weakness to demand the establishment of treaty ports where they could trade at will. In addition, the British took over China's customs enforcement and allowed the free import of opium until 1917. In response a Chinese "self-strengthening movement" tried in vain to bring about significant reforms by

The Boxer Uprising
In 1900 a Chinese secret society, the Righteous Fists, rose up with the encouragement of the Empress Dowager Cixi and attacked foreigners and their establishments. In the Western press they were known as "Boxers." These men are putting up a poster that reads "Death to Foreigners!"

Mary Evans Picture Library/The Image Works

reducing government expenditures and eliminating corruption. While Meiji reformers in Japan sought foreign technologies to defend against imperialist aggressions, the **Empress Dowager Cixi** (TSUH-shee) (r. 1862–1908) of China opposed railways and other foreign technologies that could carry foreign influences to the interior. Government officials, who did not dare resist the Westerners outright, secretly encouraged crowds to attack and destroy the intrusive devices. They were thus able to slow the foreign intrusion, but in doing so, they denied themselves the best means of defense against foreign pressure.

Japan Confronts China

The late nineteenth century marked the high point of European power and arrogance, as the nations of Europe, in a frenzy known as the "New Imperialism," rushed to gobble up the last remaining unclaimed pieces of the world. Yet at that very moment two nations outside Europe were becoming great powers. One of them, the United States, was inhabited mainly by people of European origin. Its rise to great-power status had been predicted early in the nineteenth century by astute observers like the French statesman Alexis de Tocqueville. The other one, Japan, seemed so distant and exotic in 1850 that no European guessed that it would join the ranks of the great powers.

The motive for the transformation of Japan was to protect the nation from the Western powers, but the methods that strengthened Japan against the imperial ambitions of others could also be used to carry out its own conquests. Japan's path to imperialism was laid out by **Yamagata Aritomo**, a leader of the Meiji oligarchs. He believed that to be independent Japan had to define a "sphere of influence" that included Korea, Manchuria, and part of China. If other countries controlled this sphere, Japan would be at risk. To protect this sphere of influence, Yamagata insisted, Japan must sustain a vigorous program of military industrialization, culminating in the building of battleships.

As Japan grew stronger, China was growing weaker. In 1894 the two nations went to war over Korea. The Sino-Japanese War lasted less than six months, and it forced China to evacuate Korea, cede Taiwan and the Liaodong (li-AH-oh-dong) Peninsula, and pay a heavy indemnity. France, Germany, Britain, Russia, and the United States, upset at seeing a newcomer join the ranks of the imperialists, made Japan give up Liaodong in the name of the "territorial integrity" of China. In exchange for their "protection," the Western powers then made China grant them additional territorial and trade concessions, including ninety treaty ports.

In 1900, Chinese officials around the Empress Dowager Cixi encouraged a series of antiforeign riots known as the Boxer Uprising. Military forces from the European powers, Japan, and the United States put down the riots and occupied Beijing. Emboldened by China's obvious weakness, Japan and Russia competed for possession of the mineral-rich Chinese province of Manchuria.

Japan's participation in the suppression of the Boxer Uprising demonstrated its military power in East Asia. Then in 1905 Japan surprised the world by defeating Russia in the Russo-Japanese War. By the Treaty of Portsmouth that ended the war, Japan established a protectorate over Korea. In spite of Western attempts to restrict it to the role of junior partner, Japan continued to increase its influence. It gained control of southern Manchuria, with its industries and railroads, and in 1910 it finally annexed Korea, joining the ranks of the world's colonial powers.

CONCLUSION

After World War I broke out in 1914, many people, especially in Europe, looked back on the period from 1850 to 1914 as a golden age. For some, and in certain ways, it was. Industrialization was a powerful torrent changing Europe, North America, and East Asia. While shipping and railroads increased their global reach, new technologies—electricity, the steel and chemical industries, and the global telegraph network—contributed to the enrichment and empowerment of the industrial nations.

With these new technologies, memories of the great scourges—famines, wars, and epidemics—faded. Clean water, electric lights, and railways began to improve the lives of city dwellers, even the poor. Municipal services made city life less dangerous and chaotic. Goods from distant lands, even travel to other continents, came within the reach of millions. Middle-class women continued to focus on domestic pursuits and lived in a "separate sphere" from men, but access to education and professional careers initiated a long cycle of change. Many working-class women took jobs in the textile industry, yet their work outside the home paid less that similar jobs held by men and their traditional domestic and child-rearing responsibilities continued.

Though Karl Marx predicted a class struggle between workers and employers, socialism became more an intellectual current than a revolutionary movement. Workers achieved improvements in wages, job security, and workplace safety through labor unions, not revolutions. By the turn of the century, liberal political reforms had taken hold in western Europe. Universal male suffrage became law in the United States in 1870 and in various parts of Europe by the 1880s. At the same time women mobilized in large numbers to demand political rights, an objective not attained in Europe or North America until the twentieth century.

The framework for all these changes was the nation-state. Until the 1860s nationalism was associated with liberalism, but later generations of conservatives used public education, military service, and colonial conquests to build a sense of national unity. By 1871 both Italy and Germany had become unified states. In Japan, the Meiji Restoration restored power to the emperor and ushered in a period of Western influences and rapid economic growth.

The world economy, international politics, and even cultural and social issues revolved around a handful of countries—the great powers—that believed they controlled the destiny of the world. These included the most powerful European nations of the previous century, as well as three newcomers—Germany, the United States, and Japan.

IMPORTANT EVENTS 1850–1910	
1851	Majority of British population living in cities
1853–1854	Commodore Matthew Perry visits Japan
1856	Bessemer converter; first synthetic dye
1859	Charles Darwin, *On the Origin of Species*
1860–1870	Unification of Italy
1861	Emancipation of serfs (Russia)

1861–1865	American Civil War
1862–1908	Rule of Empress Dowager Cixi (China)
1866	Alfred Nobel develops dynamite
1867	Karl Marx, *Das Kapital*
1868	Meiji Restoration begins modernization drive in Japan
1868–1894	Japan undergoes Western-style industrialization and societal changes
1870–1871	Franco-Prussian War
1871	Unification of Germany
1875	Social Democratic Party founded in Germany
1879	Thomas Edison develops incandescent lamp
1894	Sino-Japanese War
1894–1906	Dreyfus affair (France)
1900	Boxer Uprising (China)
1904–1905	Russo-Japanese War
1905	Revolution of 1905 (Russia)
1910	Japan annexes Korea

28

THE CRISIS OF THE IMPERIAL ORDER,
1900–1929

O n June 28, 1914, Archduke Franz Ferdinand, heir to the throne of
Austria-Hungary, was riding in an open carriage through Sarajevo, a city
Austria had annexed six years earlier. When the carriage stopped momentarily, Gavrilo Princip, member of a pro-Serbian conspiracy, fired his pistol twice,
killing the archduke and his wife.

Those shots ignited a global conflict. All previous wars had caused death and
destruction, but they were also marked by heroism and glory. In this new war,
four years of bitter fighting produced no victories, no gains, and no glory, only
death for millions of soldiers. The war became global as the Ottoman Empire
fought against Britain and Japan attacked German positions in China. France and
Britain involved their empires in the war and brought Africans, Indians, Australians, and Canadians to Europe to fight and labor on the front lines. Finally, in
1917, the United States entered the fray.

In this chapter, we will look at the causes of war between the great powers, the
consequences of that conflict in Europe, the Middle East, and Russia, and the
upheavals in China and Japan. We will also look at the more indirect impact of
the war on noncombatant states in Latin America.

ORIGINS OF THE CRISIS IN EUROPE
AND THE MIDDLE EAST

When the twentieth century opened, the world seemed firmly under the control of
the great powers (see Chapter 27). The first decade of the twentieth century was a
period of relative peace and economic growth in most of the world. Several new
technologies—airplanes, automobiles, radio, and cinema—aroused much excitement (see Chapter 29). The great powers consolidated their colonial conquests of
the previous decades, and their alliances were evenly matched. The only international war of the period, the Russo-Japanese War (1904–1905), ended quickly
with a decisive Japanese victory.

However, two major changes undermined the apparent stability. In Europe,
tensions mounted as Germany, with its growing industrial and military might,

challenged Britain at sea and France in Morocco. And the Ottoman Empire grew weaker, leaving a dangerous power vacuum. The resulting chaos in the Balkans gradually drew the European powers into a web of hostilities.

The Ottoman Empire and the Balkans

From the fifteenth to the nineteenth centuries the Ottoman Empire was one of the most powerful states. By the late nineteenth century, however, it had fallen behind economically, technologically, and militarily. Europeans referred to it as the "sick man of Europe."

As the Ottoman Empire weakened, it began losing European provinces: Macedonia in 1902–1903, Bosnia in 1908, Crete in 1909, Albania in 1910. In 1912 Italy conquered Libya, the Ottomans' last foothold in Africa. In 1912–1913 Serbia, Bulgaria, Romania, and Greece chased the Ottomans out of Europe, except for a small enclave around Constantinople.

In reaction, the Turks began to assert themselves against rebellious minorities and meddling foreigners. Many officers in the army, the most Europeanized segment of Turkish society, blamed Sultan Abdul Hamid II (r. 1876–1909) for the decline of the empire. A group known as "Young Turks" plotted to force the sultan to reinstate a stillborn constitution that he had suspended in 1876 before it could have an impact. They alienated other anti-Ottoman groups by advocating centralized rule and the Turkification of ethnic minorities.

In 1909 the parliament, dominated by Young Turks, overthrew Abdul Hamid. The new regime reinvigorated the Tanzimat reform movement (see Chapter 24) that had begun in the early nineteenth century. At the same time, it cracked down on Greek and Armenian minorities. Galvanized by their defeat in the Balkan Wars, the Turks hired a German general to modernize their armed forces. The dangerous mixture of modern armies and nationalism was not limited to the Ottoman Empire, however.

Nationalism, Alliances, and Military Strategy

The assassination of Franz Ferdinand triggered a chain of events over which military and political leaders lost control. The escalation from assassination to global war had causes that went back many years. One was nationalism, which bound citizens to their ethnic group and led them, when called upon, to kill people they viewed as enemies. Another was the system of alliances and military plans that the great powers had devised to protect themselves from their rivals. A third was Germany's yearning to dominate Europe.

Nationalism united the citizens of France, Britain, and Germany behind their respective governments and gave them tremendous cohesion and strength of purpose. Only the most powerful feelings could inspire millions of men to march into battle and sustain civilian populations through years of hardship.

Nationalism could also be a dividing force. The Russian, Austro-Hungarian, and Ottoman Empires, large but fragile, contained numerous ethnic and religious minorities. Having repressed some minorities for centuries, the governments could never count on their full support. The very existence of an independent Serbia threatened Austria-Hungary by stirring up the hopes and resentments of its Slavic populations.

Imbued with nationalism, most people viewed war as a crusade for liberty or as long-overdue revenge for past injustices. During the nineteenth century, as memories of the misery and carnage caused by the Napoleonic Wars faded, revulsion against war gradually weakened. The Crimean War of 1853–1856 and the Franco-Prussian War of 1871 had caused few casualties or long-term consequences. And in the imperialist wars in Africa and Asia (see Chapter 26), Europeans almost always had been victorious at a small cost in money and manpower.

What turned an incident in the Balkans into a conflict involving all the great powers was the system of alliances. At the center of Europe stood Germany, the most heavily industrialized country in Europe. Its army was the best trained and equipped, and it challenged Great Britain's naval supremacy by building "dreadnoughts"—heavily armed battleships. In 1882 it joined Austria-Hungary and Italy in the Triple Alliance, while France allied itself with Russia. In 1904 Britain and France reached an Entente (on-TONT) ("understanding"), joined by Russia in 1907. Europe was thus divided into two blocs of roughly equal power.

The alliance system was cursed by inflexible military planning. In 1914, western and central Europe had highly developed railroad networks but very few motor vehicles, and European armies had grown to include millions of soldiers and reservists. To mobilize these forces and transport them to battle would require thousands of trains running on precise schedules. Once under way, a country's mobilization could not be canceled or postponed without causing chaos.

In the years before World War I, military planners in France and Germany had worked out elaborate railroad timetables to mobilize their respective armies in a few days. Russia, a large country with an underdeveloped rail system, needed several weeks to mobilize its forces. Britain, with a tiny volunteer army, had no mobilization plans, and German planners believed that the British would stay out of a war on the European continent. So that Germany could avoid having to fight France and Russia at the same time, German war planners expected to defeat France in a matter of days, then transport the entire army across Germany to the Russian border by train before Russia could fully mobilize.

On July 28, Austria-Hungary declared war on Serbia. The declaration of war triggered the general mobilization plans of Russia, France, and Germany. On July 29 the Russian government ordered general mobilization to force Austria to back down. On August 1 France ordered general mobilization. Minutes later Germany did likewise. Because of the rigid railroad timetables, war was now automatic.

The German plan was to wheel around through neutral Belgium and into northwestern France. The German General Staff expected France to capitulate before the British could get involved. But on August 3, when German troops entered Belgium, Britain demanded their withdrawal. When Germany refused, Britain declared war on Germany.

THE "GREAT WAR" AND THE RUSSIAN REVOLUTIONS, 1914–1918

Throughout Europe, people greeted the outbreak of war with parades and flags, expecting a quick victory. German troops marched off to the front shouting "To Paris!" Spectators in France encouraged marching French troops with shouts of

"Send me the Kaiser's moustache!" The German sociologist Max Weber wrote: "This war, with all its ghastliness, is nevertheless grand and wonderful. It is worth experiencing."[1]

When the war began, very few imagined that their side might not win. No one foresaw that everyone would lose.

Stalemate, 1914–1917

The war that erupted in 1914 was known as the "Great War" until the 1940s, when a far greater one overshadowed it. Its form came as a surprise to all belligerents, from the generals on down. In the classic battles that every officer studied, the advantage always went to the fastest-moving army led by the boldest general. In 1914 the generals' carefully drawn plans went awry from the start. Believing that a spirited attack would always prevail, French generals hurled their troops, dressed in bright blue-and-red uniforms, against the well-defended German border and suffered a crushing defeat. In battle after battle the much larger German armies defeated the French and the British. By early September the Germans held Belgium and northern France and were fast approaching Paris.

German victory seemed assured. But German troops, who had marched and fought for a month, were exhausted, and their generals wavered. A gap opened between two German armies along the Marne River, into which General Joseph Joffre moved France's last reserves. At the Battle of the Marne (September 5–12, 1914), the Germans were thrown back several miles.

During the next month, both sides spread out until they formed an unbroken line extending over 300 miles (some 500 kilometers) from the North Sea to the border of Switzerland. All along this **Western Front**, the opposing troops prepared their defenses. Their most potent weapons were machine guns, which provided an almost impenetrable defense against advancing infantry but were useless for the offensive because they were too heavy for one man to carry and took too much time to set up.

To escape the deadly streams of bullets, soldiers dug holes in the ground, connected the holes to form shallow trenches, then dug communications trenches to the rear. Within weeks, the battlefields were scarred by lines of trenches several feet deep, their tops protected by sandbags and their floors covered with planks. Trenches were nothing new. What was extraordinary was that the trenches along the entire Western Front were connected, leaving no gaps through which armies could advance. How, then, could either side ever hope to win?

For four years, generals on each side again and again ordered their troops to attack. In battle after battle, thousands of young men on one side climbed out of their trenches, raced across the open fields, and were mowed down by enemy machine-gun fire. Hoping to destroy the machine guns, the attacking force would saturate the entrenched enemy lines with artillery barrages. But this tactic alerted the defenders to an impending attack and allowed them to rush in reinforcements and set up new machine guns.

The year 1916 saw the bloodiest and most futile battles of the war. The Germans attacked French forts at Verdun, losing 281,000 men and causing 315,000 French

---

[1]Frank B. Tipton, *A History of Modern Germany since 1815* (Berkeley: University of California Press, 2003), 295.

casualties. In retaliation, the British attacked the Germans at the Somme River and suffered 420,000 casualties—60,000 on the first day alone—while the Germans lost 450,000 and the French 200,000.

Warfare had never been waged this way before. It was mass slaughter in a moonscape of mud, steel, and flesh. Both sides attacked and defended, but neither side could win, for the armies were stalemated by trenches and machine guns. During four years of the bloodiest fighting the world had ever seen, the Western Front moved no more than a few miles one way or another.

At sea, the war was just as inconclusive. As soon as war broke out, the British cut the German overseas telegraph cables, blockaded the coasts of Germany and Austria-Hungary, and set out to capture or sink all enemy ships still at sea. The German High Seas Fleet, built at enormous cost but mostly coal-fueled, seldom left port. Only once, in May 1916, did it confront the oil-fueled and thus more efficient British Grand Fleet. At the Battle of Jutland, off the coast of Denmark, the two fleets lost roughly equal numbers of ships, and the Germans escaped back to their harbors.

Women in World War I *Women played a more important role in World War I than in previous wars. As the armies drafted millions of men, employers hired women for essential war work. This poster extolls the importance of women workers in supplying munitions.*

ON HER THEIR LIVES DEPEND

WOMEN MUNITION WORKERS   Enrol at once

Imperial War Museum/The Art Archive

In early 1915, in retaliation for the British naval blockade, Germany announced a blockade of Britain by submarines. German submarines attacked every vessel they could. One of their victims was the British ocean liner *Lusitania*. The death toll from that attack was 1,198 people, 139 of them Americans. When the United States protested, Germany ceased its submarine campaign, hoping to keep America neutral.

Airplanes were used for reconnaissance and engaged in spectacular but inconsequential dogfights above the trenches. Poison gas, introduced on the Western Front in 1915, killed and wounded attacking soldiers as well as their intended victims, adding to the horror of battle. Primitive tanks aided, but did not cause, the collapse of the German army in the last weeks of the war. Although these weapons were of limited effectiveness in World War I, they offered an insight into the future of warfare.

The Home Front and the War Economy   Trench-bound armies demanded ever more weapons, ammunition, and food, so civilians had to work harder, eat less, and pay higher taxes. Textiles, coal, meat, fats, and imported products such as tea and sugar were strictly rationed. Governments gradually imposed stringent controls over all aspects of their economies.

The war economy transformed civilian life. In France and Britain food rations were allocated according to need, improving nutrition among the poor. Unemployment vanished. Thousands of Africans, Indians, and Chinese were recruited for heavy labor in Europe. Employers hired women to fill jobs vacated by men off to war. Some women became streetcar drivers, mail carriers, and police officers. Others found work in the burgeoning government bureaucracies. Many joined auxiliary military services as doctors, nurses, mechanics, and ambulance drivers; after 1917, as the war took its toll of young men, the British government established women's auxiliary units for the army, navy, and air force. These positions gave thousands of women a sense of participation in the war effort and a taste of personal and financial independence.

German civilians paid an especially high price for the war, for the British naval blockade severed their overseas trade. Wheat flour disappeared, replaced first by rye, then by potatoes and turnips, then by acorns and chestnuts, and finally by sawdust. After the failure of the potato crop in 1916 came the "turnip winter," when people had to survive on 1,000 calories per day, half the normal amount that an active adult needed. Women, children, and the elderly were especially hard hit. Soldiers at the front raided enemy lines to scavenge food.

The war also brought hardships to Europe's African colonies. When the war began, the British and French overran German Togo on the West African coast. The much larger German colonies of Southwest Africa and German Cameroon were conquered in 1915. In German East Africa, the Germans remained undefeated until the end of the war. The Europeans requisitioned foodstuffs, imposed heavy taxes, and forced Africans to grow export crops and sell them at low prices. As Europeans stationed in Africa joined the war, the combination of increased demands on Africans and fewer European officials led to uprisings that lasted for several years. Over a million Africans served in the various armies, and perhaps three times that number were drafted as porters to carry army equipment. Faced with a shortage of young Frenchmen, France drafted Africans into its army, where many fought side by side with Europeans.

One country grew rich during the war: the United States. For two and a half years the United States stayed technically neutral but did a roaring business supplying France and Britain. When the United States entered the war in 1917, businesses engaging in war production made spectacular profits. Civilians were exhorted to help the war effort by investing their savings in war bonds and growing food in backyard "victory gardens." Employment opportunities created by the war played a major role in the migration of African Americans from the rural South to the cities of the North.

The Ottoman   On August 2, 1914, the Turks signed a secret alliance with
Empire at War   Germany. In November they joined the fighting, hoping to
                     gain land at Russia's expense. During the campaign in the
Caucasus the Turks expelled the Armenians, whom they suspected of being pro-Russian, from their homelands in eastern Anatolia. Hunger and exposure killed hundreds of thousands during the forced march to Syria across the mountains in the winter. Many others were killed by regular and irregular Ottoman military forces.

The Turks also closed the Dardanelles, the strait between the Mediterranean and Black Seas. Seeing little hope of victory on the Western Front, Britain tried to open the Dardanelles by landing troops on the nearby Gallipoli Peninsula in 1915. Turkish troops pushed the invaders back into the sea. The British then promised the emir (hereditary governor) of Mecca, Hussein ibn Ali, a kingdom of his own if he would lead an Arab revolt against the Turks. In 1916 Hussein rose up and was proclaimed king of Hejaz (heh-JAHZ) (western Arabia). His son **Faisal** (FIE-sahl) then led an Arab army in support of the British advance from Egypt into Palestine and Syria. The Arab Revolt of 1916 did not affect the struggle in Europe, but it did contribute to the defeat of the Ottoman Empire.

The British made promises to Jews as well as Arabs. For centuries, Jewish minorities in eastern and central Europe had developed a thriving culture despite frequent persecutions. By the early twentieth century a nationalist movement called Zionism, led by **Theodore Herzl**, arose among those who wanted to return to their ancestral homeland in Palestine. The concept of a Jewish homeland appealed to many Europeans as a humanitarian solution to the problem of anti-Semitism.

By 1917 Chaim Weizmann (hi-um VITES-mun), leader of the British Zionists, had persuaded several British politicians that a Jewish homeland in Palestine should be carved out of the Ottoman Empire and placed under British protection, thereby strengthening the Allied cause. In November, as British armies were advancing on Jerusalem, Foreign Secretary Sir Arthur Balfour wrote:

His Majesty's Government view with favor the establishment in Palestine of a national home for the Jewish people and will use their best endeavours to facilitate the achievement of that object, it being clearly understood that nothing shall be done which may prejudice the civil and religious rights of existing non-Jewish communities in Palestine.[2]

---

[2]Walter Z. Laqueur and Barry Rubin, eds., *The Arab-Israeli Reader: A Documentary History of the Middle East Conflict*, 4th ed. (New York: Penguin Books, 1984), 18.

The British did not foresee that this statement, known as the **Balfour Declaration**, would lead to conflicts between Arabs living in Palestine and Jewish settlers.

**Double
Revolution
in Russia**

At the beginning of the war Russia had the largest army in the world, but its generals were incompetent, supplies were lacking, and soldiers were poorly trained and equipped. In August 1914 two Russian armies invaded eastern Germany but were thrown back.

In 1916, after a string of defeats, the Russian army ran out of ammunition and other essential supplies. Soldiers were ordered into battle unarmed and told to pick up the rifles of fallen comrades. Railroads broke down for lack of fuel and parts, and crops rotted in the fields. Civilians faced shortages and widespread hunger, and food and fuel became scarce in the cities. During the bitterly cold winter of 1916–1917, factory workers and housewives had to line up in front of grocery stores before dawn to get food. The court of Tsar Nicholas II, however, remained as extravagant and corrupt as ever.

In early March 1917 (February by the old Russian calendar), food ran out in Petrograd (St. Petersburg), the capital. Women staged mass demonstrations, and soldiers mutinied and joined striking workers to form soviets (councils) to take over factories and barracks. A few days later the tsar abdicated, and leaders of the parliamentary parties, led by Alexander Kerensky, formed a Provisional Government. Thus began what Russians called the "February Revolution."

Revolutionaries formerly hunted by the tsar's police came out of hiding. Most numerous were the Social Revolutionaries, who advocated the redistribution of land to the peasants. The Mensheviks advocated electoral politics and reform in the tradition of European socialists and had a large following among intellectuals and factory workers. The **Bolsheviks**, their rivals, were a small but tightly disciplined group of radicals obedient to the will of their leader, **Vladimir Lenin** (1870–1924).

Lenin, the son of a government official, became a revolutionary in his teens when his older brother was executed for plotting to kill the tsar. He spent years in exile, first in Siberia and later in Switzerland, where he devoted his full attention to organizing his followers. His goal was to create a party that would lead the revolution rather than wait for it. He explained: "The will of a class is sometimes fulfilled by a dictator.... Soviet socialist democracy is not in the least incompatible with individual rule and dictatorship."[3]

In early April 1917 the German government, hoping to destabilize Russia, allowed Lenin to travel from Switzerland to Russia in a sealed railway car. As soon as he arrived in Petrograd, he announced his program: immediate peace, all power to the soviets, and transfers of land to the peasants and factories to the workers. This plan proved immensely popular among soldiers and workers exhausted by the war.

The next few months witnessed a tug-of-war between the Provisional Government and the various revolutionary factions in Petrograd. When Kerensky ordered another offensive against the Germans, Russian soldiers began to desert by the

---

[3]David Shub, *Lenin: A Biography* (Garden City, NY: Doubleday, 1948), 257.

hundreds of thousands, throwing away their rifles and walking back to their villages. As the Germans advanced, the government lost the little support it had.

Meanwhile, the Bolsheviks were gaining support among the workers of Petrograd and the soldiers and sailors stationed there. On November 6, 1917 (October 24 in the Russian calendar), they rose up and took over the city, calling their action the "October Revolution." Their sudden move surprised rival revolutionary groups that believed that a "socialist" revolution could happen only after many years of "bourgeois" rule. Lenin, more interested in power than in the fine points of Marxist doctrine, overthrew the Provisional Government and arrested Mensheviks, Social Revolutionaries, and other rivals.

Seizing Petrograd was only the first step, for the rest of Russia was in chaos. The Bolsheviks nationalized all private land and ordered the peasants to hand over their crops without compensation. The peasants, having seized their landlords' estates, resisted. In the cities the Bolsheviks took over the factories and drafted the workers into compulsory labor brigades. To enforce his rule Lenin created the Cheka, a secret police force with powers to arrest and execute opponents.

The Bolsheviks also sued for peace with Germany and Austria-Hungary. By the Treaty of Brest-Litovsk, signed on March 3, 1918, Russia lost territories containing a third of its population and wealth. Poland, Finland, and the Baltic states (Estonia, Latvia, and Lithuania) became independent republics. Russian colonies in Central Asia and the Caucasus broke away temporarily.

The End of the War in Western Europe, 1917–1918

Like many Americans, President **Woodrow Wilson** wanted to stay out of the European conflict. For nearly three years he kept the United States neutral and tried to persuade the belligerents to compromise. But in late 1916, German leaders decided to starve the British into submission by using submarines to sink ships carrying food supplies to Great Britain. The Germans knew that unrestricted submarine warfare was likely to bring the United States into the war, but they were willing to gamble that Britain and France would collapse before the United States could send enough troops to help them.

The submarine campaign resumed on February 1, 1917, and the German gamble failed. The British organized their merchant ships into convoys protected by destroyers, and on April 6 President Wilson asked the United States Congress to declare war on Germany.

In January 1918, President Wilson presented his **Fourteen Points**, a peace plan that called for the German evacuation of occupied lands, the settling of territorial disputes by the decisions of the local populations, and the formation of an association of nations to guarantee the independence and territorial integrity of all states. In response, General Erich von Ludendorff launched a series of surprise attacks that pushed to within 40 miles (64 kilometers) of Paris, but victory eluded him. Meanwhile, every month brought another 250,000 American troops to the front. In August the Allies counterattacked, and the Germans began a retreat that could not be halted.

In late October Ludendorff resigned, and sailors in the German fleet mutinied. Two weeks later, a new German government signed an armistice. At 11 A.M. on November 11, the guns on the Western Front went silent.

PEACE AND DISLOCATION IN EUROPE, 1919–1929

The Great War lasted four years. Millions of people had died or been disabled; political tensions and resentments lingered; and national economies remained depressed until the mid-1920s. In the late 1920s peace and prosperity finally seemed assured, but this hope proved to be illusory.

The Impact of the War   Between 9 million and 10 million soldiers died in the war, almost all of them young men. Among the dead were about 2 million Germans, 1.7 million Russians, and 1.7 million Frenchmen. Austria-Hungary lost 1.5 million, the British Empire a million, the Ottoman Empire half a million, Italy 460,000, and the United States 115,000. Perhaps twice that many returned home wounded, gassed, or shell-shocked, many of them injured for life.

War and revolution forced almost 2 million Russians, 750,000 Germans, and 400,000 Hungarians to flee their homes. Postwar conflicts also led to the expulsion of hundreds of thousands of Greeks from Anatolia and Muslims from Greece. Many refugees found shelter in France, which welcomed 1.5 million people to bolster its declining population. About 800,000 immigrants reached the United States before immigration laws passed in 1921 and 1924 closed the door to eastern and southern Europeans. Canada, Australia, and New Zealand adopted similar restrictions on immigration. The Latin American republics welcomed European refugees, but their poverty discouraged potential immigrants.

One unexpected byproduct of the war was the great influenza epidemic of 1918–1919, which started among soldiers heading for the Western Front. This virulent strain infected almost everyone on earth and killed one person in every forty. Half a million Americans perished in the epidemic—five times as many as died in the war. Worldwide, some 20 million people died.

The war also caused serious damage to the environment. No place was ever so completely devastated as the scar across France and Belgium known as the Western Front. The fighting ravaged forests and demolished towns. The earth was gouged by trenches, pitted with craters, and littered with ammunition, broken weapons, chunks of concrete, and the bones of countless soldiers. After the war, it took a decade to clear away the debris, rebuild the towns, and create dozens of military cemeteries with neat rows of crosses stretching for miles.

The Peace Treaties   In early 1919 delegates of the victorious powers met in Paris. The defeated powers were kept out until the treaties were ready for signing. Russia was not invited.

From the start, three men dominated the Paris Peace Conference: U.S. president Wilson, British prime minister David Lloyd George, and French premier Georges Clemenceau (zhorzh cluh-mon-SO). They ignored the Italians, who had joined the Allies in 1915, and paid even less attention to the delegates of smaller European nations. They rejected the Japanese proposal that all races be treated equally. They ignored the Pan-African Congress organized by the African American W. E. B. Du Bois to call attention to the concerns of African peoples around the world. They also ignored the ten thousand other delegates of various nationalities that did not

MAP 28.1 Territorial Changes in Europe After World War I

Although the heaviest fighting took place in western Europe, the territorial changes there were relatively minor. In eastern Europe, in contrast, the changes were enormous. The disintegration of the Austro-Hungary Empire and the defeat of Russia allowed a belt of new countries to arise, stretching from Finland in the north to Yugoslavia in the south.

represent sovereign states—the Arab leader Faisal, the Zionist Chaim Weizmann, and several Armenian delegations—but came to Paris to lobby for their causes. They were, in the words of Britain's Foreign Secretary Balfour, "three all-powerful, all-ignorant men, sitting there and carving up continents"[4]

Wilson, a high-minded idealist, wanted to apply the principle of self-determination to European affairs, by which he meant creating nations that reflected

---

[4]David Vital, *A People Apart: The Jews of Europe, 1789–1939* (Oxford: Oxford University Press, 1999), 756.

ethnic or linguistic divisions. He proposed a **League of Nations**, a world organization to safeguard the peace and foster international cooperation. His idealism clashed with the more hardheaded and self-serving nationalism of the Europeans. Lloyd George insisted that Germany pay a heavy indemnity, while Clemenceau wanted Germany to return Alsace and Lorraine, provinces France had lost in the Franco-Prussian War of 1870–1871.

The result was a series of compromises that satisfied no one. The European powers formed a League of Nations, but the U.S. Congress refused to let the United States join. France recovered Alsace and Lorraine but had to content itself with vague promises of British and American protection if Germany ever rebuilt its army. Britain acquired new territories in Africa and the Middle East but was greatly weakened by human losses and the disruption of its trade.

On June 28, 1919, the German delegates reluctantly signed the **Treaty of Versailles** (vuhr-SIGH). Germany was forbidden to have an air force and was permitted only a token army and navy. It also gave up large parts of its eastern territory to a newly reconstituted Poland. The Allies made Germany promise to pay reparations to compensate the victors for their losses, but they did not set a figure or a period of time for payment. A "guilt clause," which was to rankle for years to come, obliged the Germans to accept "responsibility for causing all the loss and damage" of the war. The treaty left Germany humiliated but largely intact. Establishing a peace neither of punishment nor of reconciliation, it was one of the great failures in history.

Meanwhile, the Austro-Hungarian Empire fell apart. New countries appeared in the lands lost by Russia, Germany, and Austria-Hungary: Poland, resurrected after over a century; Czechoslovakia, created from the northern third of Austria-Hungary; and Yugoslavia, combining Serbia and the former south Slav provinces of Austria-Hungary. The new boundaries coincided with the major linguistic groups of eastern Europe, but they all contained disaffected minorities. These small nations were safe only as long as Germany and Russia lay defeated and prostrate.

Russian Civil War and the New Economic Policy

In December 1918, civil war broke out in Russia. The Communists—as the Bolsheviks called themselves after March 1918—held central Russia, but all the surrounding provinces rose up against them. Counter-revolutionary armies led by former tsarist officers obtained weapons and supplies from the Allies. For three years the two sides burned farms and confiscated crops, causing a famine that claimed 3 million victims, more than had died in Russia in seven years of fighting. By 1921 the Communists had defeated most of their enemies.

Finland, the Baltic states, and Poland remained independent, but the Red Army reconquered other parts of the tsar's empire one by one. In 1922, Ukraine merged with Russia to create the Union of Soviet Socialist Republics (USSR), or Soviet Union. In 1920–1921 the Red Army reconquered the Caucasus and replaced the indigenous leaders with Russians. In 1922 the new Soviet republics of Georgia, Armenia, and Azerbaijan joined the USSR. In this way the Bolsheviks retained control over lands and peoples that had been part of the tsar's empire.

Years of warfare, revolution, and mismanagement had ruined the Russian economy. Factories and railroads had shut down for lack of fuel, raw materials, and parts. Farmland had been devastated and livestock killed, causing hunger in the cities. Finding himself master of a country in ruin, Lenin announced the **New Economic Policy** (NEP) in 1923. It allowed peasants to own land and sell their crops, private merchants to trade, and private workshops to produce goods and sell them on the free market. Only the biggest businesses, such as banks, railroads, and factories, remained under government ownership.

The relaxation of controls had an immediate effect. Production began to climb, and food and other goods became available. But the NEP reflected no change in the ultimate goals of the Communist Party. It merely provided breathing space, what Lenin called "two steps back to advance one step forward." The Communists had every intention of creating a modern industrial economy without private property. This meant investing in heavy industry and electrification and moving farmers to the cities to work in the new industries. It also meant providing food for the urban workers without spending scarce resources to purchase it from the peasants. In other words, it meant making the peasants, the great majority of the Soviet people, pay for the industrialization of Russia. This policy turned them into bitter enemies of the Communists.

When Lenin died in January 1924, his associates jockeyed for power. The leading contenders were Leon Trotsky, commander of the Red Army, and Joseph Stalin, general secretary of the Communist Party. Trotsky had the support of many "Old Bolsheviks" who had joined the party before the revolution. Having spent years in exile, he saw the revolution as a spark that would ignite a world revolution of the working class. Stalin, the only leading Communist who had never lived abroad, insisted that socialism could survive "in one country."

Stalin filled the party bureaucracy with individuals loyal to himself. In 1926–1927 he had Trotsky expelled for "deviation from the party line," and in January 1929 he forced Trotsky to flee the country. Then, as absolute master of the party, he prepared to industrialize the Soviet Union at breakneck speed.

An Ephemeral Peace   After the enormous sacrifices made during the war, the survivors developed hugely unrealistic expectations and were soon disillusioned. Conservatives in Britain and France longed for a return to the stability of the prewar era—the hierarchy of social classes, prosperous world trade, and European dominance over the rest of the world. All over the rest of the world, people's hopes had been raised by the rhetoric of the war, then dashed by its outcome. In Europe, Germans felt cheated out of a victory that had seemed within their grasp, and Italians were disappointed that their sacrifices had not been rewarded with large territorial gains. Arabs and Indians longed for independence; the Chinese looked for social justice and a lessening of foreign intrusion; and the Japanese hoped to expand their influence in China. In Russia, the Communists were eager to consolidate their power and export their revolution to the rest of the world.

In 1923 Germany suspended reparations payments. In retaliation for the French occupation of the Ruhr, the German government began printing money recklessly, causing the most severe inflation the world had ever seen. Soon German money was worth so little that it took a wheel-barrow full of it to buy a loaf of bread. As Germany teetered on the brink of civil war, radical nationalists tried to overthrow the government. Finally, the German government issued a new currency and promised to resume reparations payments, and the French agreed to withdraw their troops from the Ruhr.

Beginning in 1924 the world enjoyed a few years of calm and prosperity. After the end of the German crisis of 1923, the western European nations became less confrontational, and Germany joined the League of Nations. The vexed issue of reparations also seemed to vanish, as Germany borrowed money from New York banks to make its payments to France and Britain, which used the money to repay their wartime loans from the United States. This triangular flow of money, based on credit, stimulated the rapid recovery of the European economies. France began rebuilding its war-torn northern zone; Germany recovered from its hyperinflation; and a boom began in the United States that was to last for five years.

While their economies flourished, governments grew more cautious and businesslike. Even the Communists, after Lenin's death, seemed to give up their attempts to spread revolution abroad. Yet neither Germany nor the Soviet Union accepted its borders with the small nations that had arisen between them. In 1922, they signed a secret pact allowing the German army to conduct maneuvers in Russia (in violation of the Versailles treaty) in exchange for German help in building up Russian industry and military potential.

The League of Nations proved adept at resolving numerous technical issues pertaining to health, labor relations, and postal and telegraph communications. Without U.S. participation, however, sanctions against states that violated League rules carried little weight.

CHINA AND JAPAN: CONTRASTING DESTINIES

China and Japan were both subject to Western pressures, but their modern histories have been strikingly opposite. China clung much longer than Japan to a traditional social structure and economy, then collapsed into chaos and revolution. Japan experienced reform from above (see Chapter 27), acquiring industry and a powerful military, which it used to take advantage of China's weakness. Their different reactions to the pressures of the West put these two great nations on a collision course.

Social and Economic Change

China's population—about 400 million in 1900—was the largest of any country in the world and growing fast. In 1900 peasant plots averaged between 1 and 4 acres (less than 2 hectares) apiece, half as large as they had been two generations earlier. Farming methods had not changed in centuries, and landlords and tax collectors took more than half of the harvest. Most Chinese worked incessantly, survived on a diet of grain and vegetables, and spent their lives in fear of floods, bandits, and tax collectors.

Above the peasantry, Chinese society was divided into many groups and strata. Landowners lived off the rents of their tenants. Officials, chosen through an elaborate examination system, enriched themselves from taxes and the

Bettmann/Corbis

The Bund in Shanghai *On the Bund, the most important street in Shanghai, banks, corporate headquarters, and luxury hotels faced the waterfront where ships from around the world docked. Although Shanghai was China's industrial and commercial center, many of its workers loaded and unloaded ships by hand or pulled wealthy customers in rickshaws.*

government's monopolies on salt, iron, and other products. Shanghai, China's financial and commercial center, was famous for its wealthy foreigners and its opium addicts, prostitutes, and gangsters.

Although foreign trade represented only a small part of China's economy, contact with the outside world had a tremendous impact on Chinese politics. Young men living in the treaty ports saw no chance for advancement in the old system of examinations and official positions. Some learned foreign ideas in Christian mission schools or abroad. The contrast between the squalor in which most urban residents lived and the luxury of the foreigners' enclaves in the treaty ports sharpened the resentment of educated Chinese.

Japan had few natural resources and very little arable land on which to grow food for its rising population. Typhoons regularly hit its southern regions, and earthquakes periodically shook the country, which lies on the great ring of tectonic fault lines that surround the Pacific Ocean. The Kanto earthquake of 1923 destroyed all of Yokohama and half of Tokyo and killed some 200,000 people.

Japan's population reached 60 million in 1925 and was increasing by a million a year. The crash program of industrialization begun in 1868 by the Meiji oligarchs (see Chapter 27) accelerated during the First World War, when Japan's economy grew four times as fast as western Europe's and eight times faster than China's.

Economic growth aggravated social tensions. The *narikin* ("new rich") affected Western ways and lifestyles that clashed with the austerity of earlier times. In the big cities *mobos* (modern boys) and *mogas* (modern girls) shocked traditionalists with their foreign ways: dancing together, wearing short skirts and tight pants, and behaving like Americans. Students who flirted with dangerous thoughts were called "Marx boys."

The main beneficiaries of prosperity were the *zaibatsu* (zie-BOT-soo), or conglomerates, four of which—Mitsubishi, Sumitomo, Yasuda, and Mitsui—controlled most of Japan's industry and commerce. Farmers, who constituted half of the population, remained poor; in desperation some sold their daughters to textile mills or into domestic service. Labor unions were weak and repressed by the police.

Japanese prosperity depended on foreign trade. The country exported silk and light manufactures and imported almost all its fuel, raw materials, and machine tools, and even some of its food. Though less at the mercy of the weather than China, Japan was much more vulnerable to swings in the world economy.

Revolution and War, 1900–1918   In 1900 China's Empress Dowager Cixi (TSUH-shee), who had seized power in a palace coup two years earlier, encouraged a secret society, the Righteous Fists, or Boxers, to rise up and expel all the foreigners from China. When the Boxers threatened the foreign legation in Beijing, an international force from the Western powers and Japan captured the city and forced China to pay a huge indemnity. Shocked by these events, many Chinese students became convinced that China needed a revolution to get rid of the Qing dynasty and modernize their country.

When Cixi died in 1908, the Revolutionary Alliance led by **Sun Yat-sen** (soon yot-SEN) (1866–1925) prepared to take over. Sun had spent much of his life in Japan, England, and the United States, plotting the overthrow of the Qing dynasty. His ideas were a mixture of nationalism, socialism, and Confucian philosophy. His patriotism, his powerful ambition, and his tenacious spirit attracted a large following.

The military thwarted Sun's plans. After China's defeat in the war with Japan in 1895, the government had agreed to equip the army with modern rifles and machine guns. This, combined with the fact that local armies were beholden to warlords rather than to the central government, created a threatening situation for the Qing. When a regional army mutinied in October 1911, **Yuan Shikai** (you-AHN she-KIE), the most powerful of the regional generals, refused to defend the Qing. A revolutionary assembly at Nanjing elected Sun Yat-sen president of China in December 1911, but he had no military forces at his command. To avoid a clash with the army, he resigned after a few weeks, and a new national assembly elected Yuan president of the new Chinese republic.

Yuan was an able military leader, but he had no political program. When Sun reorganized his followers into a political party called the **Guomindang** (gwo-min-dong) (National People's Party), Yuan quashed every attempt at creating a Western-style government and harassed Sun's followers. Victory in the first round of the struggle to create a new China went to the military.

Meanwhile, the Japanese were quick to join the Allied side in World War I, since they saw the war as an opportunity to advance their interests while the Europeans were occupied elsewhere. They quickly conquered the German colonies in the northern Pacific and on the coast of China, then turned their attention to the rest of China. In 1915 Japan presented China with Twenty-One Demands, which would have turned it into a virtual protectorate. Britain and the United States persuaded Japan to soften the demands but could not prevent it from keeping the German coastal enclaves and extracting railroad and mining concessions at China's expense. In protest, anti-Japanese riots and boycotts broke out throughout China. Thus began a bitter struggle between the two countries that was to last for thirty years.

Chinese Warlords and the Guomindang, 1919–1929   At the Paris Peace Conference, the great powers accepted Japan's seizure of the German enclaves in China. To many Chinese, this decision was a cruel insult. On May 4, 1919, students demonstrated in front of the Forbidden City of Beijing. Despite a government ban, the May Fourth Movement spread to other parts of China. A new generation was growing up to challenge the old officials, the regional generals, and the foreigners.

Sun Yat-sen tried to make a comeback in Guangzhou (Canton) in the early 1920s. Though not a Communist, he was impressed with the efficiency of Lenin's revolutionary tactics and let a Soviet adviser reorganize the Guomindang along Leninist lines. He also welcomed members of the newly created Chinese Communist Party into the Guomindang.

When Sun died in 1925, the leadership of his party passed to Jiang Jieshi, known in the West as **Chiang Kai-shek** (chang kie-shek) (1887–1975). An officer and director of the military academy, Chiang trained several hundred young officers who remained loyal to him thereafter. In 1927 he determined to defeat the regional warlords. As his army moved north from its base in Canton, he briefly formed an alliance with the Communists. Once his troops occupied Shanghai, however, he crushed the labor unions and decimated the Communists, whom he considered a threat. He then defeated or co-opted most of the other warlords and established a dictatorship.

Chiang's government issued ambitious plans to build railroads, develop agriculture and industry, and modernize China from the top down. However, his followers were neither competent administrators nor ruthless modernizers. Instead, his government attracted thousands of opportunists whose goals were to "become officials and get rich" by taxing and plundering businesses. In the countryside tax collectors and landowners squeezed the peasants ever harder, even in times of natural disasters. What little money reached the government's coffers went to the military. Thus for twenty years after the fall of the Qing, China remained mired in poverty, subject to corrupt officials and the whims of nature.

THE NEW MIDDLE EAST

After the war, the Arab peoples expected to have a say in the outcome of the Great War. But the victorious French and British planned to treat the Middle East like a territory open to colonial rule. The result was a legacy of instability that has persisted to this day.

The Mandate System   At the Paris Peace Conference, France, Britain, Italy, and Japan proposed to divide the former German colonies and the territories of the Ottoman Empire among themselves, but their ambitions clashed with President Wilson's ideal of national self-determination. Eventually, the victors arrived at a compromise solution called the **mandate system**: colonial rulers would administer the territories but would be accountable to the League of Nations for "the material and moral well-being and the social progress of the inhabitants."

Class C Mandates—those with the smallest populations—were treated as colonies by their conquerors. South Africa replaced Germany in Southwest Africa (now Namibia); Britain, Australia, New Zealand, and Japan took over the German islands in the Pacific. Class B Mandates, larger than Class C but still underdeveloped, were to be ruled for the benefit of their inhabitants under League of Nations supervision. Most of Germany's African colonies, including Tanganyika, Cameroon, and Togo, fell into this category.

The Arab-speaking territories of the old Ottoman Empire were Class A Mandates. The League of Nations declared that they had "reached a state of development where their existence as independent nations can be provisionally recognized subject to the rendering of administrative advice and assistance by a Mandatory, until such time as they are able to stand alone." While Arabs interpreted this ambiguous wording as a promise of independence, Britain and France sent troops into the region "for the benefit of its inhabitants." Palestine (divided now into Israel in the west, Jordan in the east, and the Occupied West Bank in between) and Iraq (formerly Mesopotamia) became British mandates; France claimed Syria and Lebanon. (See Diversity and Dominance: The Middle East After World War I.)

The Rise of Modern Turkey   At the end of the war, as the Ottoman Empire teetered on the brink of collapse, France, Britain, and Italy saw an opportunity to expand their empires, and Greece eyed those parts of Anatolia inhabited by Greeks. In 1919 French, British, Italian, and Greek forces occupied Constantinople and parts of Anatolia. By the Treaty of Sèvres (1920) the Allies made the sultan give up most of his lands.

In 1919, Mustafa Kemal had formed a nationalist government in central Anatolia with the backing of fellow army officers. In 1922, after a short but fierce war against invading Greeks, his armies reconquered Anatolia and the area around Constantinople. The victorious Turks forced hundreds of thousands of Greeks from their ancestral homes in Anatolia. In response the Greek government expelled all Muslims from Greece. A Turkish Republic was proclaimed in 1923.

As a war hero and proclaimed savior of his country, Mustafa Kemal was able to impose wrenching changes on his people. An outspoken modernizer, he was

The Middle East After World War I

During the First World War, Entente forces invaded and occupied Palestine, Mesopotamia, and Syria. This raised the question of what to do with these territories after the war. Would they be returned to the Ottoman Empire? Would they simply be added to the colonial empires of Britain and France? Or would they become independent Arab states?

The following documents illustrate the diversity of opinions among various groups planning the postwar settlement: Great Britain, concerned with defeating Germany and maintaining its empire; the United States, basing its policies on lofty principles; and Arab delegates from the Middle East, seeking self-determination.

In the early twentieth century, in response to the rise of anti-Semitism in Europe, a movement called Zionism had arisen among European Jews. Zionists, led by Theodore Herzl, hoped for a return to Israel, the ancestral homeland of the Jewish people. For two thousand years this land had been a province of various empires—the Roman, Byzantine, Arab, and Ottoman—and was inhabited by Arabic-speaking people, most of whom practiced the Islamic religion.

During the war the British government was receptive to the idea of establishing a Jewish homeland in Palestine. It was motivated by the need to win the war, but it also considered the more distant future. The result was a policy statement, sent by Foreign Secretary Arthur James Balfour to Baron Rothschild, a prominent supporter of the Zionist movement in England. This statement, called the "Balfour Declaration," has haunted the Middle East ever since.

The Balfour Declaration of 1917

Foreign Office
November 2nd, 1917

Dear Lord Rothschild:

I have much pleasure in conveying to you, on behalf of His Majesty's Government, the following declaration of sympathy with Jewish Zionist aspirations which have been submitted to, and approved by, the Cabinet:

> His Majesty's Government view with favor the establishment in Palestine of a national home for the Jewish people, and will use their best endeavors to facilitate the achievement of this object, it being clearly understood that nothing shall be done which may prejudice the civil and religious rights of existing non-Jewish communities in Palestine, or the rights and political status enjoyed by Jews in any other country.

I should be grateful if you would bring this declaration to the knowledge of the Zionist Federation.

Yours,
Arthur James Balfour

On January 8, 1918, the American president Woodrow Wilson issued his famous Fourteen Points proposal to end the war. Much of his speech was devoted to European affairs or to international relations in general, but two of his fourteen points referred to the Arab world.

Woodrow Wilson's Fourteen Points

What we demand in this war ... is that the world be made fit and safe to live in; and particularly that it be made safe for every peace-loving nation which, like our own, wishes to live its own life, determine its own institutions, be assured of justice and fair dealing by the other peoples of the world as against force and selfish aggression. All the peoples of the world are in effect partners in this interest, and for our own part we see very clearly that unless justice be done to others it will not be done to us. The programme of the world's peace, therefore, is our programme; and that programme, the only possible programme, as we see it, is this:

XII. The Turkish portions of the present Ottoman Empire should be assured a secure sovereignty, but the other nationalities which are now under Turkish rule should be assured an undoubted security of life and an absolutely unmolested opportunity of autonomous development....

When the war ended, the victorious Allies assembled in Paris to determine, among other things, the fate of the former Arab provinces of the Ottoman Empire. Arab leaders had reason to doubt the intentions of the great powers, especially Britain and France. When the Allies decided to create mandates in the Arab territories on the grounds that the Arab peoples were not ready for independence, Arab leaders expressed their misgivings, as in the following statement:

Memorandum of the General Syrian Congress, July 2, 1919

We the undersigned members of the General Syrian Congress, meeting in Damascus on Wednesday, July 2nd, 1919, made up of representatives from the three Zones, viz., The Southern, Eastern, and Western, provided with credentials and authorizations by the inhabitants of our various districts, Moslems, Christians, and Jews, have agreed upon the following statement of the desires of the people of the country who have elected us....

1. We ask absolutely complete political independence for Syria....

3. Considering the fact that the Arabs inhabiting the Syrian area are not naturally less gifted than other more advanced races and that they are by no means less developed than the Bulgarians, Serbians, Greeks, and Roumanians at the beginning of their independence, we protest against Article 22 of the Covenant of the League of Nations, placing us among the nations in their middle stage of development which stand in need of a mandatory power.

4. ... relying on the declarations of President Wilson that his object in waging war was to put an end to the ambition of conquest and colonization, ... and believing that the American Nation is furthest from any thought of colonization and has no political ambition in our country, we will seek the technical and economic assistance from the United States of America, provided that such assistance does not exceed 20 years.

5. In the event of America not finding herself in a position to accept our desire for assistance, we will seek this assistance from Great Britain, also provided that such does not prejudice our complete independence and unity of our country and that the duration of such assistance does not exceed that mentioned in the previous article.

6. We do not acknowledge any right claimed by the French Government in any part whatever of our Syrian country and refuse that she should assist us or have a hand in our country under any circumstances and in any place.

7. We opposed the pretensions of the Zionists to create a Jewish

commonwealth in the southern part of Syria, known as Palestine, and oppose Zionist migration to any part of our country; for we do not acknowledge their title but consider them a grave peril to our people from the national, economical, and political points of view. Our Jewish compatriots shall enjoy our common rights and assume our common responsibilities.

Questions for Analysis

1. Was there a contradiction between Balfour's proposal to establish "a national home for the Jewish people" and the promise "that nothing shall be done which may prejudice the civil and religious rights of existing non-Jewish communities in Palestine"? If so, why did he make two contradictory promises?

2. How would Woodrow Wilson's statements about "an absolutely unmolested opportunity of autonomous development" apply to Palestine?

3. Why did the delegates to the General Syrian Congress object to the plan to create mandates in the former Ottoman provinces? What alternatives did they offer?

4. Why did the delegates object to the creation of a Jewish commonwealth?

Sources: The Balfour Declaration, *The Times* (London), November 9, 1917. Memorandum of the General Syrian Congress, *Foreign Relations of the United States: Paris Peace Conference,* vol. 12 (Washington, DC: Government Printing Office, 1919), 780–781.

---

eager to bring Turkey closer to Europe as quickly as possible. He abolished the sultanate, declared Turkey a secular republic, and introduced European laws. In a radical break with Islamic tradition, he suppressed Muslim courts, schools, and religious orders and replaced the Arabic alphabet with the Latin alphabet.

He also attempted to westernize the traditional Turkish family. Women received civil equality, including the right to vote and to be elected to the national assembly. Kemal forbade polygamy and instituted civil marriage and divorce. He even changed people's clothing, strongly discouraging women from veiling their faces, and replacing the fez, a men's hat adopted as a symbol of reform in the nineteenth century, with the European brimmed hat. He ordered everyone to take a family name, choosing the name **Atatürk** ("father of the Turks") for himself. His reforms spread quickly in the cities; but in rural areas, where Islamic traditions remained strong, resistance continued.

Arab Lands and the Question of Palestine   Among the Arab people, the thinly disguised colonialism of the mandate system set off protests and rebellions. Arabs viewed the European presence not as liberation from Ottoman oppression, but as foreign occupation, such as fellow Arabs in Algeria, Tunisia, and Morocco were experiencing under French rule.

After World War I, which had left enormous numbers dead from violence and famine, Middle Eastern society underwent dramatic changes. Trucks replaced camel caravans, and landless peasants migrated to the swelling cities. The population of the region is estimated to have bounced back by 50 percent between 1914 and 1939, while that of large cities such as Constantinople, Baghdad, and Cairo doubled.

The urban and mercantile middle class, encouraged by the transformation of Turkey, adopted Western ideas, customs, and styles of housing and clothing. To prepare their sons for jobs in government and business, some families sent them to European secular or mission schools, then to Western colleges in Istanbul, Cairo, or Beirut or to universities abroad. A few women became schoolteachers or nurses. Secular educational opportunities varied widely from Lebanon, where French influence was strong; to Iran, whose first university was established in 1933; to Saudi Arabia, which strongly resisted Western influences.

The region in closest contact with Europe was the Maghrib—Algeria, Tunisia, and Morocco—which the French army considered its private domain. Alongside the old native quarters, the French built modern neighborhoods inhabited mainly by Europeans. France had occupied Algeria since 1830 and had encouraged European immigration. The settlers owned the best lands and monopolized government jobs and businesses, while Arabs and Berbers remained poor and suffered intense discrimination.

The British attempted to control the Middle East with a mixture of bribery and intimidation. They made Faisal, leader of the Arab Revolt, king of Iraq and used aerial bombing of rebellious nomads to enforce their will. In 1931 they reached an agreement with King Faisal's government: official independence for Iraq in exchange for the right to keep two air bases, a military alliance, and an assured flow of petroleum. France, meanwhile, sent thousands of troops to Syria and Lebanon to crush nationalist uprisings.

In Egypt, as in Iraq, the British substituted a phony independence for official colonialism. They declared Egypt independent in 1922 but reserved the right to station troops along the Suez Canal to secure their link with India in the event of war. Most galling to the Wafd (Nationalist) Party was the British attempt to remove Egyptian troops from Sudan, a land many Egyptians considered a colony of Egypt. Britain was successful in keeping Egypt in limbo—neither independent nor a colony—thanks to an alliance with King Fuad and conservative Egyptian politicians who feared both secular and religious radicalism.

Before the war, a Jewish minority lived in Palestine, as in other Arab countries. Small numbers of Jews had immigrated to Palestine following their expulsion from Spain in 1492, and a trickle continued into the nineteenth century. As soon as Palestine became a British mandate in 1920, however, many more came from Europe, encouraged by the Balfour Declaration of 1917. Those supporting a socialist version of Zionism established *kibbutzim*, or communal farms, while nonsocialists belonging to the Revisionist wing of the Zionist movement preferred to settle in the cities. But purchases of land by Jewish agencies angered the indigenous Arabs, especially tenant farmers who were evicted to make room for settlers, and in 1920–1921 riots erupted between Jews and Arabs. When far more Jewish immigrants arrived than they had anticipated, the British tried to limit immigration, thereby alienating the Jews without mollifying the Arabs. Increasingly, Jews arrived without papers, smuggled in by militant Zionist organizations. In the 1930s the country was torn by strikes and guerrilla warfare that the British could not control. In the process, Britain earned the hatred of both sides.

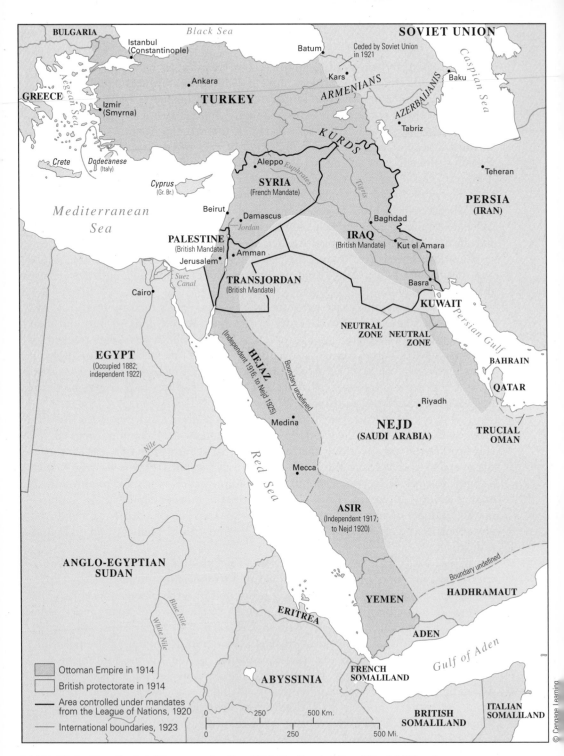

MAP 28.2   Territorial Changes in the Middle East After World War I

The defeat and dismemberment of the Ottoman Empire at the end of World War I resulted in an entirely new political map of the region. The Turkish Republic inherited Anatolia and a small piece of the Balkans, while the Ottoman Empire's Arab provinces were divided between France and Great Britain. Only Iran and Egypt did not change.

Hulton Archive/Getty Images

The Jewish Settlement of Palestine *Thousands of Jews fleeing persecution and discrimination in Europe settled on the land and founded kibbutzim, or collective farms. In this picture taken in 1912, an eighty-four-year-old immigrant from Russia learns to plow the land.*

CONCLUSION

In the late 1920s it seemed as though the victors in the Great War might reestablish the prewar prosperity and European dominance of the globe. But the spirit of the 1920s was not real peace; instead it was the eye of a hurricane. The Great Depression and World War II were in the offing.

The Great War caused a major realignment among the nations of the world. France and Britain, the two leading colonial powers, emerged economically weakened despite their victory. The war brought defeat and humiliation to Germany but did not reduce its military or industrial potential. It destroyed the old regime of Russia, leading to civil war and revolution from which the victorious powers sought to isolate themselves. Two other old empires—the Austro-Hungarian and the Ottoman—were divided into many smaller and weaker nations.

Japan took advantage of the European conflict to develop its industries and press its demands on a China weakened by domestic turmoil and social unrest. The United States emerged as the most prosperous and potentially most powerful nation, restrained only by the isolationist sentiments of many Americans.

In the Middle East, the fall of the Ottoman Empire awakened aspirations of nationhood among the Turkish, Arab, Armenian, and Kurdish inhabitants and

Jewish immigrants. These aspirations were thwarted when France and Great Britain succeeded in imposing their rule upon the former Ottoman lands, giving rise to conflicts and bitter enmities.

IMPORTANT EVENTS 1900–1929	
1900	Boxer uprising in China
1904	British-French Entente
1904–1905	Russo-Japanese War
1907	British-Russian Entente
1909	Young Turks overthrow Sultan Abdul Hamid
1911	Chinese revolutionaries led by Sun Yat-sen overthrow Qing dynasty
1912	Italy conquers Libya, last Ottoman territory in Africa
1912–1913	Balkan Wars
1914	Assassination of Archduke Franz Ferdinand sparks World War I
1915	British defeat at Gallipoli
1915	Japan presents Twenty-One Demands to China
1916	Battles of Verdun and the Somme
1916	Arab Revolt in Arabia
1917	Russian Revolutions; United States enters the war
1917	Balfour Declaration
1918	Armistice ends World War I
1918–1921	Civil war in Russia
1919	Treaty of Versailles
1919	May Fourth Movement in China
1919–1922	War between Turkey and Greece
1922	Egypt nominally independent
1923	Mustafa Kemal proclaims Turkey a republic
1923–1928	New Economic Policy in Russia
1927	Guomindang forces occupy Shanghai and expel Communists

29

REVOLUTIONS IN LIVING, 1900–1950

In 1869 three Japanese businessmen—an entrepreneurial former cook, a greengrocer, and a wagon builder—responded to government concerns about urban congestion and applied for a license to build a *jinriksha* ("man-power-vehicle"). They described it as "a little seat in the Western style, mounted on wheels so that it can be pulled about. It does not shake as much as the usual cart, and it is easy to turn round. It will not hinder other traffic, and since it can be pulled by one person, it is very cheap."[1] Their first vehicles, which quickly came to be called rickshaws, appeared a year later. A year after that, in 1871, Japan enacted its first patent law, and the three applied for exclusive manufacturing rights. However, so many workshops were by then turning out rickshaws that their application was denied.

An alternative claim of invention arose when an irascible American Baptist missionary named Jonathan Goble petitioned the Tokyo Metropolitan Government to grant him a share of the tax levied on the thirty thousand rickshaws then officially registered. He claimed to be the inventor, and a number of Westerners living in Japan supported him, some stating that Goble had built the first rickshaw for his ailing wife, and others that he had designed it at the request of a Japanese officer for use in the "imperial pleasure gardens."

The Japanese version of the story, which was reinforced in 1900 by government cash awards to the three businessmen, is highly credible since two-wheeled carts with a similar arrangement of shafts for pulling were in use on Japanese farms and for transporting loads well before European carriages came to be known through the "opening of Japan" in the 1850s (see Chapter 27). Moreover, Japan became the export source for rickshaws throughout Asia and the Indian Ocean region. The Goble story, however, made better sense to Westerners, who had a hard time crediting non-Europeans with inventiveness.

People today often look back and marvel at the incredible material changes their parents and grandparents lived through in the twentieth century. Movies, radio, television, telephones, automobiles, and airplanes all developed during the

---

[1]F. Calvin Parker, *Jonathan Goble of Japan: Marine, Missionary, Maverick* (Lanham, MD: University Press of America, 1990), 222.

first half of the century. Norms of daily life rooted in the nineteenth century gave way to new assumptions about many aspects of human life.

Yet many of these assumptions applied more to the industrialized countries of Europe and North America than to those parts of the world that before World War II consisted mostly of imperial possessions or, in the case of Latin America, politically independent countries whose economies were dominated by European or American businesses and investors. Automobiles may have changed dating habits in the United States, but not in China or India, where few private individuals owned cars. Telephones may have put people in easy contact with family and friends in Europe, but not in Africa, where imperialist economic interests saw no profit in stringing copper wire throughout the land.

Changes in the way people lived in the West between 1900 and 1950 will be discussed later in this chapter. First we will consider how other parts of the world experienced change in more limited ways, often incorporating local cultural traditions that took their societies in distinctive directions.

NEW TECHNOLOGY OUTSIDE THE INDUSTRIALIZED WORLD

Urbanization   According to one estimate, Constantinople, the capital of the Byzantine Empire, had a population of 200,000 in 1000 C.E. and was the only European city to be ranked among the world's ten largest cities. By 1500 Paris had joined Constantinople on the list, and by 1800 so had London. Beijing, the most populous city, then had over 1 million inhabitants, about twice as many as the largest city in 1000.

Industrialization deeply affected population distribution in the course of the nineteenth century. By 1900 all of the world's top ten cities were European or American except for Tokyo. The largest, London, had 6.4 million inhabitants. European dominance waned in the first half of the twentieth century. In 1950 Shanghai, Buenos Aires, Tokyo, and Calcutta (now Kolkata) were on the list, and 12.4 million people resided in the largest city, New York. Today, two European cities, Moscow and Istanbul (formerly Constantinople), make the top ten. Of the rest, four are in China and two in South Asia. Tehran (Iran) and Sao Paulo (Brazil) round out the list. New York is nineteenth. The largest city, Shanghai, has a population of 17.8 million.

In Asia and the Indian Ocean basin, the rickshaw (see chapter opening) contributed to this transformation of urban life just as streetcars had earlier done in Europe and America. Before 1850, Japanese civilians either walked or were carried in plain (*kago*) or fancy (*norimono*) palanquins, small seats or cabins suspended from poles carried on the shoulders of bearers. A palanquin required a minimum of two men, or more if the trip was long or the rider wanted to display his or her wealth. The rickshaw cut the expense of personal transport in half and doubled its speed because a rickshaw puller, unlike palanquin bearers, usually ran rather than walked. Rickshaw transport effectively enlarged the area of cities that had previously been scaled for pedestrian access, just as public transport made it possible for Bostonians and Londoners to live away from the city center. Rickshaws also avoided the plague of Western cities: horse manure.

The technical specifications of the first rickshaws have not survived, but the claim that "it does not shake as much as the usual cart" suggests that what made the vehicle a sensational success from the very start was the provision of leaf springs (arced steel strips bound at the ends to form an ellipse). The first leaf spring design had been patented in England in 1804 and was probably in use on carriages imported into Japan in the 1850s. Early drawings and photographs of rickshaws consistently show them with leaf springs.

Japanese-made rickshaws stimulated the growth of big Asian cities like Shanghai, Beijing, Singapore, Calcutta, and Bombay and reached across the Indian Ocean to Madagascar and South Africa. Tens of thousands of unskilled workers flocked to these cities to become rickshaw pullers in the way that European villagers entered the urban economy by way of unskilled manufacturing jobs. Like European mill-hands, rickshaw pullers endured miserable living conditions and occasionally banded together in strikes, particularly in opposition to streetcar companies that threatened their livelihoods. However, streetcars could not deliver passengers directly to their homes or take children safely to school, so the rickshaws survived and evolved into the pedicabs and auto-rickshaws that are still common today.

The rickshaw provides a rare example of an Asian invention transforming urban life in ways unfamiliar to Europeans and Americans. The more frequently told stories focus on Western inventions like railroads and automobiles transforming the non-Western world. Yet even there, the innovations of the Industrial Revolution (see Chapter 22) that imperialist governments and businesses exported to their colonies affected the non-Western world differently than later innovations that spread worldwide in the first half of the twentieth century. Whereas railroads and automobiles required steel mills and factories, other new inventions were comparatively inexpensive and adaptable to local customs.

Electricity   Electricity, produced in industrial quantities since the 1890s (see Chapter 27), transformed home life in Europe and North America by attracting private customers. Middle-class homeowners wanted to replace their gas lamps with tungsten filament incandescent bulbs, which improved greatly in brightness and durability between 1904 and World War I. Household items like electric irons, fans, washing machines, and hot plates followed.

Outside of Europe and North America, however, the small size of the middle class made private subscription a poor business model. Electrical generators might be acquired to run factories or light a ruler's palace, but an appliance-oriented lifestyle was slow to develop. Consequently the foot-operated sewing machine, which had undergone a long development in America and Europe in the nineteenth century, had a wider global spread before World War II than any other appliance. The enormous Japanese electronics company Brother Industries, Ltd. began in 1908 as the Yasui Sewing Machine Company.

New Media   **Auguste and Louis Lumière** projected the first motion pictures in Paris in 1895. The following year the brothers held demonstrations in Bombay, London, Montreal, New York, and Buenos Aires. Other exhibitors soon showed off the new medium in Johannesburg, Alexandria, and Tokyo. Unlike expensive innovations like automobiles and airplanes, motion pictures could be made cheaply using fairly inexpensive equipment. The idea of moving images appealed just as much to non-European audiences as it did to Europeans.

The first experiments with film in India appeared two years after the Lumières' visit. The first full-length feature, screening in 1912, told the story of a legendary Indian king from the classical Sanskrit epics. Movies also caught on quickly in

Japan, which had a tradition of magic lantern displays. Local theatrical traditions like *kabuki* and *bunraku* influenced the style and content of the earliest films just as early European film makers concentrated on reproducing stage plays. Japanese films of the silent era were usually accompanied by spoken narration, as were the films the Japanese exported to Formosa (now Taiwan), a Chinese-speaking island that came under Japanese control in 1895.

American and European silent films found ready markets around the world, but non-Western film making flourished in some countries. Moreover, the impact of film was not limited to entertainment. Documentary films and especially newsreels became major sources of information. Filmed news coverage of key political figures like Mahatma Gandhi in India played a major role in their success, especially after the advent of sound in the late 1920s.

Practical photography began in Europe in 1839, and forty years later an efficient way was developed for printing photographs in newspapers. Photographic images soon became common throughout the world, often as picture postcards. European photographers, however, tended to look upon Asians and Africans, particularly seminude women, as exotic subjects and thereby catered to common European assumptions about racial superiority.

Non-European photographers rarely became known outside their home countries. Nevertheless, they produced thousands of images that are now used to reconstruct history. Chinese newspapers and magazines usually published images without naming the photographers. A dozen early photographers became famous in Japan, however, possibly because popular woodblock prints had created an audience for artistic images of everyday scenes. In Iran, the most avid photographer was the ruler Naser al-Din Shah (r. 1848–1896). Despite Muslim clerical disapproval of making images of human beings, the shah shot some forty-eight thousand pictures, including members of his own family and even nudes and prisoners.

Photography enabled newspapers, magazines, and advertisements to inform even illiterate people about what their country and their fellow citizens looked like, who was ruling them, and how traditional elites and prosperous Europeanized families lived. Thus photography contributed to feelings of national identity and common experience even in lands that were internally divided by language and ethnicity.

Radio had served ships and the military during the Great War as a means of point-to-point telecommunication. After the war, amateurs used surplus radio equipment to talk to one another. The first commercial station began broadcasting in Pittsburgh in 1920. By 1924 six hundred stations were broadcasting news, sports, soap operas, and advertising to homes throughout North America. By 1930, 12 million families owned radio receivers. In Europe radio spread more slowly because governments reserved the airwaves for cultural and official programs and taxed radio owners to pay for the service.

Japan followed the North American model of commercial radio. The first AM station began broadcasting in 1925, and by 1941 there were almost fifty stations organized in two networks covering both the home islands and imperial possessions in Formosa (Taiwan), Korea, and Manchuria. Programming increasingly reflected the militarist tendencies of the government, but it also included Japanese and classical Western music, English lessons, exercise programs, and tips for urban gardeners.

Radio development in Shanghai was also robust, with 100,000 receivers in use by 1936. Most were imported, but small local manufacturers contributed to the new fad. British authorities in India and Africa, on the other hand, established central control of radio transmissions and programming. French colonial administrations did likewise.

NEW WAYS OF LIVING IN THE INDUSTRIALIZED WORLD

World War I left a deep imprint on European society and culture. After the war, class and gender distinctions began to fade. Many European aristocrats had died on the battlefields, and with them went their class's long domination of the army, the diplomatic corps, and other elite sectors of society. The United States and Canada had never had as rigidly defined a class structure as European societies or as elaborate a set of traditions and manners. On both sides of the Atlantic, engineers, businessmen, lawyers, and other professionals rose to prominence while department stores, banks, insurance companies, and other businesses increased their white-collar workforce. At the same time government administrative jobs expanded in the areas of housing, transportation, schools, public health, and other services. The ambitions and tastes of the rapidly expanding middle class became increasingly evident in the postwar period, while the role of the working class remained about the same.

Identity   As the centuries-old European distinction between aristocrats and commoners faded in significance, standardized forms of identity became more common. An American passport issued in 1905 was a single 12- by 17-inch piece of paper bearing the seal of the State Department, the secretary of state's signature in facsimile, and in lieu of a photograph, one- or two-word descriptions of the holder's forehead, eyes, nose, mouth, chin, complexion, and facial shape. A Chinese passport of the same period was entirely in Chinese. Crossing international borders became a more complicated process during World War I, and in 1920 the League of Nations held the first of several conferences that standardized the now familiar photograph-and-booklet design.

Prussia in 1910 was the first country to require every automobile operator to have a driver's license, and the practice spread rapidly. In 1913 New Jersey was the first American state to institute such a requirement. These documents eventually became standard proofs of identity in countries that did not issue identity cards to their citizens. Social Security cards began to be issued in the United States in the 1930s, and they too acquired some of the functions of identity cards. In other countries, such as Germany, Great Britain, and Japan, national health system documents took on similar roles.

Hereditary titles and listings of noble lineages in reference books like *Burke's Peerage* continued in use among the nobility. However, the idea increasingly spread that a person's identity was tied to his or her name (without title), a photograph, and one or more official numbers issued by government agencies. This idea spread much more slowly outside of Europe and North America.

An additional form of personal identification came forth in 1897 when the world's first fingerprint bureau opened under British auspices in Calcutta (Kolkata). Two Indians, Azizul Haque and Hem Chandra Bose, devised the system of determining every human being's unique identity, but it became known as the Henry System from the name of their British supervisor. Scotland Yard adopted the system in 1901, and the New York Police Department did so in 1906.

Women's Lives   Women's lives changed more rapidly in the 1920s than ever before. Although the end of the war saw the end of wartime job opportunities, some women remained in the workforce. The young and wealthy enjoyed more personal freedoms than their mothers had before the war; they drove cars, played sports, traveled alone, and smoked in public. For others, the upheavals of war brought more suffering than liberation. Millions of women had lost their male kin in the war or in the great influenza epidemic. After the war many single women led lives of loneliness and destitution.

In Europe and North America advocates of women's rights had been demanding the vote for women since the 1890s. New Zealand was the only nation to grant women the vote before the twentieth century. Women in Norway were the first to obtain it in Europe, in 1915. Russian women followed in 1917, and Canadians and Germans in 1918. Britain gave women over age thirty the vote in 1918 and later extended it to younger women. The Nineteenth Amendment to the U.S. Constitution granted suffrage to American women in 1920. Women in Turkey began voting in 1934. Everywhere, their influence on politics was less radical than feminists had hoped and conservatives had feared. Even when it did not transform politics and government, however, the right to vote was a potent symbol.

Women were active in many other areas besides the suffrage movement. On both sides of the Atlantic women participated in social reform movements to prevent mistreatment of women and children and of industrial workers. In the United States such reforms were championed by Progressives like Jane Addams (1860–1935), who founded a settlement house in a poor neighborhood and received the Nobel Peace Prize in 1931. In Europe reformers were generally aligned with Socialist or Labour Parties.

Among the most controversial, and eventually most effective, of the reformers were those who advocated contraception, such as the American **Margaret Sanger** (1883–1966). Her campaign brought her into conflict with many authorities, who equated birth control with pornography. Finally, in 1923 she was able to found a birth control clinic in New York. In France, the government prohibited contraception and abortion in 1920 in an effort to increase the birthrate and make up for the loss of so many young men in the war.

Revolution in the Sciences: The New Physics   The word *progress*, as much associated with extending "modern civilization" to the non-Western world as with technological developments such as railroads and undersea cables, had been a hallmark of most nineteenth-century Euro–American ideologies. After 1900 the word *science* increasingly took its place as a signifier of Western self-esteem. At the end of the nineteenth century, a revolution in physics undermined the old certainties about nature that had already been shaken by Darwinism. Physicists discovered that atoms, the building blocks of matter, are not indivisible, but consist of far smaller subatomic particles. In 1900, the German physicist **Max Planck** (1858–1947) found that atoms emit or absorb energy in discrete amounts called *quanta*.

Few people understood these findings at the time, much less **Albert Einstein's** (1879–1955) pronouncement in 1916 that time, space, energy, and mass are not fixed but are relative to one another. But scientific discovery, punctuated by prestigious Nobel prizes that began to be awarded in 1901, excited pride and wonder in nations that contributed to such advances.

The New Social Sciences   The new social sciences were more understandable, and thus more unsettling, than the new physics, for they challenged Victorian morality and middle-class values. **Sigmund Freud** (1856–1939), a Viennese physician, developed the technique of psychoanalysis to probe the minds of his patients. His technique uncovered hidden layers of emotion and desire repressed by social restraints. "It is during this [childhood] period of . . . latency that the psychic forces develop which later act as inhibitions on the sexual life, and narrow its direction like dams. These psychic forces are loathing, shame, and moral and esthetic ideal demands,"[2] he declared. Meanwhile, sociologists and anthropologists had begun the empirical study of societies, both Western and non-Western. Before the war the French sociologist Emile Durkheim (1858–1917) had come to the then shocking conclusion that "there are no religions that are false. All are true after their own fashion."[3]

If the words *primitive* and *savage* applied to Europeans as well as to other peoples, and if religions were all equally "true," then what remained of the superiority of Western civilization? Cultural relativism, as the new approach to human societies was called, could be as unnerving as relativity in physics; but for many it stimulated a tenacious desire to cling to the old truths.

The arts became a battlefield for confronting traditional values with new images and rhythms. Cubism, an approach to painting and sculpture that sought to go beyond realism and depict many aspects of an image simultaneously, aroused lively debates in the 1910s. A painter like the Spaniard **Pablo Picasso** (1881–1973) changed his nonrealistic style of painting time and again over his long career. Paralleling his audacity in the field of music, the Russian composer **Igor Stravinsky** (1882–1971) incorporated so-called primitive rhythms in his ballet *The Rite of Spring*, which debuted in 1913.

The incredible human losses experienced during the Great War shook many artists' and intellectuals' faith in reason and progress. Some poets and artists joined the **Dada** movement, which abandoned rationality and relied instead on intuition, randomness, and nonsense—*dada* stood for the use of meaningless syllables in poetry. Others became Surrealists and produced dreamlike images incorporating what they considered to be symbols of the unconscious mind. Some people accepted the new ideas with enthusiasm. Others condemned and rejected them, particularly in the United States, and clung to the sense of order and faith in progress that had energized Western culture before the war.

New Technologies and Activities   Some people viewed the sciences with mixed feelings, but new technologies aroused almost universal excitement. In North America even working-class people could afford some of the new products of inventors' ingenuity (see Environment and Technology: New Materials). Mass consumption in Europe lagged behind the United States, but science and technology were just as advanced, and public fascination with the latest inventions—the cult of the modern—was just as strong.

---

[2]Sigmund Freud, *Three Contributions to the Theory of Sex*, tr. A. A. Brill, 2 ed. (Washington: Nervous and Mental Health Disease Publishing Company, 1920), 40.

[3]Emile Durkheim, *The Elementary Forms of Religious Life*, trans. by Karen Elise Fields (New York: Free Press, 1995), 2.

67

Museum of Flight/Corbis

First Aluminum Airplane *From the Wright Brothers' first aircraft in 1903 down to the air battles of World War I, wood, cloth, and wire made up the wings and bodies of airplanes. Metals were too heavy for anything but engines and weapons until the German manufacturer Hugo Junkers designed the first aluminum flying machine, shown here, in 1917.*

Of all the innovations of the time, none attracted public interest more than airplanes. In 1903 two young American mechanics, **Wilbur and Orville Wright**, built the first aircraft that was heavier than air and could be maneuvered in flight. From that moment on, airplanes fascinated people. In 1911 a French pilot flew 6,500 letters from one city in British India to another 8.1 miles (13 kilometers) away, thus inaugurating the first important use of air transport. Military observation and aerial warfare came second. During the Great War the exploits of air aces relieved the tedium of news from the front.

The first flight of **KLM Royal Dutch Airlines**, the oldest continuously operating airline, took off in 1920. That year it carried 440 passengers and 22 tons of cargo. Scheduled service to a number of northern European cities soon followed. Its most important service, as an air link to the Dutch East Indies (now Indonesia), began in 1929. Every country with imperial possessions saw international air service as a political necessity. Two of the oldest airlines, however, Qantas in Australia and the German-owned precursor of Avianca in Colombia, functioned entirely outside of Europe.

Health and hygiene were part of the cult of modernity. Advances in medicine—some learned on the battlefield—saved many lives. Wounds were regularly disinfected, and **Marie Curie** (1867–1934), the French discoverer of x-rays, organized radiology vans to help army doctors diagnose fractures during the Great War. Cities built costly water supply and sewage treatment systems. By the 1920s indoor plumbing and flush toilets were becoming common even in working-class neighborhoods.

Interest in cleanliness entered private life. Doctors and home economists bombarded women with warnings and advice on how to banish germs. Soap and appliance manufacturers filled women's magazines with advertisements for products to help keep homes and clothing spotless and meals fresh and wholesome. The decline in infant mortality and improvements in general health and life expectancy in this period owe as much to the cult of cleanliness as to advances in medicine.

Organized baseball leagues arose in America after the Civil War. Football found favor as a college sport around the same time, while basketball originated in 1891 as a YMCA activity. In Britain soccer (football) and rugby leagues formed in the 1880s. All of these sports flourished as spectator activities in the early twentieth century and gave rise to lively press coverage in newspapers. Soccer and rugby, along with the much older sport of cricket, spread readily into Europe's colonies, while baseball found limited favor overseas, primarily in Japan, Cuba, and the Dominican Republic.

Internationally, the upsurge in the role of sports and spectating was closely tied to the revival of the Olympic Games. The ancient Greek games had been discontinued in 393 C.E. The inspiration to create a modern form came from **Baron Pierre de Coubertin** (1863–1937), a French educator who was impressed by the sports played at English private schools like Eton and Rugby. He concluded that "organised sport can create moral and social strength."

Coubertin's aristocratic vision of purely amateur international competition came to fruition in Athens in 1896 when fourteen countries, all of them European except Australia and Chile, sent athletes to compete in nonteam sports like tennis, fencing, shooting, cycling, and gymnastics. Women were not included, nor did Coubertin realize his idea that medals should also be given for sports-themed art and architecture. The male-only rule was dropped starting with the Paris Olympics of 1900, where women competed in tennis and golf. The role of women increased steadily after that, though the arts medals were only given seven times between Stockholm in 1912 and London in 1948.

Individual excellence was the touchstone of Olympic competition, but nationalistic pride increasingly marked the quadrennial events. The Berlin Olympics of 1936 thus became a showcase for Nazi ideology and spectacle.

Technology and the Environment

Two new technologies—the skyscraper and the automobile—transformed the urban environment even more radically than the railroad had done. At the end of the nineteenth century architects had begun to design ever-higher buildings using load-bearing steel frames and elevators. Major corporations in Chicago and New York competed to build the most daring buildings in the world, such as New York's fifty-five-story Woolworth Building (1912). A building boom in the late

ENVIRONMENT + TECHNOLOGY

New Materials

Nineteenth-century commerce brought many raw materials from European colonies and other faraway places into industrial use. Examples include rubber, a Southeast Asian tree sap called gutta-percha used for electrical insulation, Central Asian camel's hair used for transmission belts, and whale oil for lighting. These exotic materials were valuable, but they did not change the age-old pattern of almost every useful item being manufactured from natural substances.

The first half of the twentieth century saw a revolutionary change in this

imagebroker/Alamy

Bakelite Jewelry *This pioneering plastic was so attractive that it was made into jewelry. However, its ease of manufacture, hardness, and resistance to electricity, heat, and chemicals suited it to thousands of other uses from clarinets to wire insulation to kitchenware. During World War II it was even considered as a replacement for the copper penny.*

1920s produced dozens of skyscrapers, culminating with the eighty-six-story Empire State Building in New York in 1932.

European cities restricted the height of buildings to protect their architectural heritage; Paris forbade buildings over 56 feet (17 meters) high. In the 1920s the Swiss architect Charles Edouard Jeanneret (1887–1965), known as **Le Corbusier** (luh cor-booz-YEH), outlined a new approach to architecture that featured pattern. Metallurgists and chemists led the way in creating new materials that wrought permanent changes in the look and feel of everyday life. Materials science would go on to become one of the most important areas of technical innovation in later decades.

Though aluminum follows oxygen and silicon as the third most abundant element, it combines so readily with other elements that it was not discovered until 1827. Initially as precious as silver, a 2.4-kilogram piece was installed as the capstone of the Washington Monument in 1884. Four years later, however, almost simultaneously in the United States and France, an inexpensive electrolytic method of extracting the metal from bauxite ore was discovered. The lightweight, noncorrosive metal now became available for all manner of uses, from airplanes, beginning with a design by the German Hugo Junkers in 1917, to aluminum foil, which was invented in 1910.

Stainless steel, made by combining noncorrosive chromium with steel, was invented in 1912, and its many uses accustomed people to thinking of metal products as shiny. Electroplating with chromium came into use in 1924 in Germany and two years later in the United States. The shiny, rust-free metal, which could be deposited as a thin film on either a metallic or plastic base, found numerous uses from musical instruments to automobiles.

Plastics were invented at about the same time. Alexander Parkes invented celluloid, a stable form of explosive guncotton—itself made by soaking fine cotton in sulfuric and nitric acids—and exhibited it at London's Great Exhibition in 1862. The first thermoplastic, it could be molded above a certain temperature but became solid when it cooled. It was used for detachable men's shirt collars, ping-pong balls, and photographic film, but it was both fragile and flammable.

Belgian-born Leo Hendrik Baekeland invented Bakelite, a more durable plastic that was also attractive enough to be used for jewelry in 1907. Five years later the Swiss chemist Jacques E. Brandenberger, trying to discover a way of waterproofing cloth, experimented with a cellulose-based coating that failed to stick to the cloth and instead peeled off in a clear sheet. Thus was cellophane invented. In the 1930s an American, Richard Drew, coated cellophane with adhesive and Scotch tape was born.

And there were others. Silklike rayon, 1904; isoprene synthetic rubber, 1909; vinyl, 1926; neoprene synthetic rubber, 1931; plexiglass, 1933; nylon, 1935; Lucite, 1936; fiberglass, 1938—the list goes on, with even more new materials being developed in the later decades of the century.

Questions for Analysis

1. Why do we take for granted a material environment constructed from manufactured substances that did not even exist before 1900?

2. What are the objects we use every day made of?

3. Why did new materials find such broad acceptance?

---

simplicity of form, absence of surface ornamentation, easy manufacture, and inexpensive materials such as concrete and glass. Other architects—including the Finn Eero Saarinen, the Germans Ludwig Mies van der Rohe (LOOD-vig MEES fon der ROW-uh) and Walter Gropius, and the American Frank Lloyd Wright—also contributed to what became known as the International Style.

Meanwhile, outlying areas were spreading far into the countryside, thanks to the automobile. The assembly line pioneered by Henry Ford mass-produced vehicles in ever-greater volume and at falling prices. By 1929 the United States had one car for every five people, five-sixths of the world's automobiles. Automobiles were praised as the solution to urban pollution; as they replaced carts and carriages, horses disappeared from city streets, as did tons of manure.

The most important environmental effect of automobiles was suburban sprawl. Middle-class families could now live in single-family homes too far apart to be served by public transportation. As middle- and working-class families bought cars, cities acquired rings of automobile suburbs. Los Angeles, the first true automobile city, consisted of suburbs spread over hundreds of square miles and linked together by broad avenues. Many Americans saw Los Angeles as the portent of a glorious future in which everyone would have a car.

European cities that had inherited narrow streets from the premodern past adapted less easily to passenger automobiles. In the countryside, however, high-speed, limited-access expressways, called *autostrada* in Italy and *autobahn* in Germany, became sources of national pride for the regimes of Benito Mussolini and Adolf Hitler. Yet compared with the United States, private automobile ownership remained uncommon.

Technological advances also transformed rural economies. In 1915 Ford introduced a gasoline-powered tractor, and by the mid-1920s these versatile machines began replacing horses. Larger farms profited most from this innovation, while small farmers sold their land and moved to the cities. Tractors and other expensive equipment hastened the transformation of agriculture from family enterprises to larger businesses, or in the USSR to collective farms with state-owned tractor stations (see Chapter 30).

In India, Australia, and the western United States, engineers built dams and canals to irrigate dry lands. Dams offered the added advantage of producing electricity, for which there was a booming demand. The immediate benefits of water control—irrigated land, prevention of floods, and generation of electricity—far outweighed such distant negative consequences as salt deposits on irrigated fields and harm to wildlife.

A New India, 1905–1947

Some parts of the world, such as India, became much more involved in the emerging technologically oriented culture than others, such as sub-Saharan Africa (see below). The consequences of this inequality of access to "modern" developments are still felt today.

Under British rule India acquired railroads, harbors, modern cities, and cotton and steel mills, as well as an active and worldly middle class. The economic transformation of the region awakened in this educated middle class a sense of national dignity that demanded political fulfillment. In response, the British gradually granted India a limited amount of political autonomy while maintaining overall control. Religious and communal tensions among the Indian peoples were carefully papered over, and when the British, exhausted by World War II (see Chapter 30), withdrew in 1947, violent conflicts tore India apart.

The Land and the People   Much of India is fertile land, but it is vulnerable to droughts caused by the periodic failure of the monsoons. When the rains failed from 1896 to 1900, 2 million people died of starvation.

Despite periodic famines, the Indian population grew from 250 million in 1900 to 319 million in 1921 and 389 million in 1941. This growth created pressures in many areas. Landless young men converged on the cities, exceeding the number of jobs available in the slowly expanding industries. Many of them entered the urban economy as rickshaw pullers. To produce timber for construction and railroad ties and to clear land for tea and rubber plantations, foresters cut down most of the tropical hardwood forests that had covered the subcontinent in the nineteenth century. But in spite of deforestation and extensive irrigation, the amount of land available to peasant families shrank with each successive generation. Economic development hardly touched the average Indian.

Indians were divided into many classes. Peasants, always the great majority, paid rents to landowners, interest to village moneylenders, and taxes to the government and had little left to improve their land or raise their standard of living. The government protected property owners, from village moneylenders all the way up to the maharajahs (mah-huh-RAH-juh) or ruling princes, who owned huge tracts of land. The cities were crowded with craftsmen, traders, and workers of all sorts, most very poor. Although the British had banned the burning of widows on their husbands' funeral pyres, in other respects women's lives changed little under British rule.

Indians also spoke many different languages. As a result of British rule, increasing trade and travel, and newspapers like *The Times of India*, established under that name in 1861, English became the common medium of communication for the Western-educated middle class. This new class of English-speaking bureaucrats, professionals, and merchants was to play a leading role in the independence movement.

The majority of Indians who practiced Hinduism were subdivided into hundreds of castes (*jati*), each affiliated with a particular occupation or kinship group. Hinduism discouraged intermarriage and other social interactions among the castes and with non-Hindus. Until displaced by the British in the eighteenth century, Muslim rulers had dominated northern and central India, and Muslims now constituted one-quarter of the Indian population while forming a majority in the northwest and in eastern Bengal. They felt discriminated against by both British and Hindus.

British Rule and Indian Nationalism   Colonial India was ruled by a viceroy appointed by the British government and administered by a few thousand members of the Indian Civil Service. These men, drawn mostly from the English gentry, believed it was their duty to protect the Indian people from the dangers of industrialization and to defend their own positions from Indian nationalists.

As Europeans they admired modern technology. They encouraged railroads, harbors, telegraphs, and other communications technologies, as well as irrigation and plantations, because these increased India's foreign trade and strengthened British control. Yet, they discouraged the cotton and steel industries and limited the training of Indian engineers, to spare India the social upheavals that had accompanied the Industrial Revolution in Europe while protecting British industry from Indian competition.

At the turn of the century most Indians—especially peasants, landowners, and princes—accepted British rule. But the Europeans' racist attitude toward dark-skinned people increasingly offended Indians who had learned English and absorbed English ideas of freedom and representative government, only to discover that racial quotas excluded them from the Indian Civil Service, the officer corps, and prestigious sporting clubs.

In 1885, a small group of English-speaking Hindu professionals founded a political organization called the **Indian National Congress**. For twenty years its members respectfully petitioned the government for access to higher administrative positions and for a voice in official decisions, but they had little influence. Then, in 1905, Viceroy Lord Curzon divided the province of **Bengal** in two to improve the efficiency of its administration. This decision, made without consulting anyone, angered not only educated Indians, who saw it as a way to lessen their influence, but also millions of uneducated Hindu Bengalis, who found themselves outnumbered by Muslims in East Bengal. Soon Bengal was the scene of demonstrations, boycotts of British goods, and even incidents of violence against the British.

In 1906, while the Hindus of Bengal were protesting the partition of their province, Muslims, fearful of Hindu dominance elsewhere in India, founded the **All-India Muslim League**. (Note the English names of these political groups.) The government responded by granting Indians a limited franchise based on wealth. Muslims, however, were on average poorer than Hindus, possibly because many poor and low-caste Hindus had converted to Islam to escape caste discrimination. Taking advantage of these religious divisions, the British instituted separate representation and different voting qualifications for Hindus and Muslims. Then, in 1911, the British transferred the capital of India from Calcutta (Kolkata) to Delhi (DEL-ee), the former capital of the Mughal (MOO-guhl) emperors. These changes disturbed Indians of all classes and religions and raised their political consciousness. Politics, once primarily the concern of westernized intellectuals, turned into two mass movements: one by Hindus and one by Muslims.

British geologists looked for minerals like coal and manganese that British industry required. However, when the only Indian member of the Indian Geological Service, Pramatha Nath Bose, wanted to prospect for iron ore, he had to resign because the government wanted no part of an Indian steel industry that might compete with that of Britain. Bose joined forces with Jamsetji Tata, a Bombay textile magnate who decided to produce steel in spite of British opposition. With the help of German and American engineers and equipment, Tata's son Dorabji opened the first steel mill in India in 1911, in a town called Jamshedpur in honor of his father.

Although it produced only a fraction of the steel that India required, Jamshedpur became a powerful symbol of Indian national pride. It also prompted Indian nationalists to ask why a country that could produce its own steel needed foreigners to run its government.

During World War I Indians supported Britain enthusiastically; 1.2 million men volunteered for the army, and millions more voluntarily contributed money to the government. Many expected the British to reward their loyalty with political concessions. Others organized to demand a voice in the government. In 1917, in response to the agitation, the British government announced "the gradual development of self-governing institutions with a view to the progressive realization of responsible government in India as an integral part of the British Empire." This sounded like a promise of self-government, but the timetable was so vague that nationalists denounced it as a devious maneuver to postpone India's independence.

On April 13, 1919, in the city of Amritsar, General Reginald Dyer ordered his troops to fire into a peaceful crowd of some 10,000 demonstrators, killing at least 379 and wounding 1,200. While waves of angry demonstrations swept over India, the British House of Lords voted to approve Dyer's actions, and a fund was raised in appreciation of his services. Indians interpreted these gestures as showing British contempt for their colonial subjects. In the charged atmosphere of the time, the period of gradual accommodation between the British and the Indians came to a close.

Mahatma Gandhi and Militant Nonviolence

For the next twenty years India teetered on the edge of violent uprisings and harsh repression. That it did not succumb was due to **Mohandas K. Gandhi** (GAHN-dee) (1869–1948), a man known to his followers as "Mahatma," the "great soul."

Gandhi began life with every advantage. His family was wealthy enough to send him to England for his education. After his studies he lived in South Africa and practiced law for the small Indian community there. During World War I he returned to India and was one of many Western-educated Hindu intellectuals who joined the Indian National Congress.

Unlike many radical political thinkers of his time, Gandhi denounced the popular ideals of power, struggle, and combat. Instead, inspired by both Hindu and Christian ideals, he preached the saintly virtues of *ahimsa* (uh-HIM-sah) (nonviolence) and *satyagraha* (suh-TYAH-gruh-huh) (the search for truth). He refused to countenance violence among his followers and called off several demonstrations when they turned violent.

In 1921, Gandhi gave up the Western-style suits worn by lawyers and the fine raiment of wealthy Indians and henceforth wore simple peasant garb: a length of homespun cloth below his waist (*dhoti*) and a shawl to cover his torso. He spoke for the farmers and the outcasts, whom he called *harijan* (HAH-ree-jahn), "children of God." He attracted ever-larger numbers of followers among the poor and the illiterate, who soon began to revere him; and he transformed the cause of Indian independence from an elite movement of the educated into a mass movement with a quasi-religious aura.

Gandhi was a brilliant political tactician and a master of public relations gestures. In 1929, for instance, he led a few followers on an 80-mile (129-kilometer) walk, camped on a beach, and gathered salt from the sea in a blatant and well-publicized act of civil disregard for the government's monopoly on salt. But he discovered that unleashing the power of popular participation was one thing and controlling its direction was quite another. Within days of his "Walk to the Sea," demonstrations of support broke out all over India, in which the police killed a hundred demonstrators and arrested over sixty thousand.

Many times during the 1930s Gandhi threatened to fast "unto death," and several times he came close to death, to protest the violence of both the police and his followers and to demand independence. He was repeatedly arrested and spent a total of six years in jail. But every arrest made him more popular. He became a figure of adulation not only in his own country but also in the Western media. In the words of historian Percival Spear, he made the British "uncomfortable in their cherished field of moral rectitude," and he gave Indians the feeling that theirs was the ethically superior cause.

Gandhi's Salt March to the Sea *Mohandas Gandhi, bareheaded and more simply dressed than his followers, led a march of 80 miles to collect sea salt in an act of civil disobedience. News photographs like this played a key role in popularizing his cause and displaying his saintly habits. To his left one man carries a sitar and another has a drum hanging from his shoulder.*

Dinodia Photos/Alamy

India Moves Toward Independence

In the 1920s, slowly and reluctantly, the British handed over control of "national" areas such as education, the economy, and public works to Indians. They also gradually admitted more Indians into the Civil Service and the officer corps.

In the years before the Second World War, Indian politicians obtained the right to erect high tariff barriers against imports to protect India's infant industries from foreign competition. Behind these barriers, Indian entrepreneurs built plants to manufacture iron and steel, cement, paper, textiles, sugar, and other products. This early industrialization did not provide enough jobs to improve the lives of the Indian peasants or urban poor, but it created a class of wealthy Indian businessmen who supported the Indian National Congress and its demands for independence. Though paying homage to Gandhi, they preferred his designated successor as leader of the Indian National Congress, **Jawaharlal Nehru** (NAY-roo) (1889–1964). Unlike Gandhi, Nehru looked forward to creating a modern industrial India.

Congress politicians won regional elections but continued to be excluded from the viceroy's cabinet, the true center of power. When World War II began (see Chapter 30), Viceroy Lord Linlithgow declared war without consulting a single Indian. The Congress-dominated provincial governments resigned in protest and found that boycotting government office increased their popular support. When the British offered to give India its independence once the war ended, Gandhi demanded full independence immediately. His "Quit India" campaign aroused popular demonstrations against the British and provoked a wave of arrests, including his own. The Second World War divided the Indian people. Most Indian soldiers felt they were fighting to defend their country rather than to support the British Empire. As in World War I, Indians contributed heavily to the Allied war effort, supplying 2 million soldiers and enormous amounts of resources, especially the timber needed for emergency construction. A small number of Indians were so anti-British that they joined the Japanese side.

Partition and Independence

When the war ended, Britain's new Labour Party government prepared for Indian independence, but deep suspicions between Hindus and Muslims complicated the process. The break between the two communities had started in 1937, when the Indian National Congress won provincial elections and refused to share power with the Muslim League. In 1940 the leader of the League, **Muhammad Ali Jinnah** (JIH-nah) (1876–1948), demanded what many Muslims had been dreaming of for years: a country of their own, to be called Pakistan.

As independence approached, talks between Jinnah and Nehru broke down and battle lines were drawn. Violent rioting between Hindus and Muslims broke out. Gandhi's appeals for tolerance and cooperation fell on deaf ears. The British made frantic proposals to keep India united, but their authority was waning fast.

In early 1947 the Indian National Congress accepted the partition of India into two states, one secular but dominated by Hindus, the other Muslim. On August 15

British India gave way to a new India and Pakistan. The Indian National Congress, led by Nehru, formed the first government of India; Jinnah and the Muslim League established a government for the provinces that made up Pakistan.

The rejoicing over independence was marred by violent outbreaks between Muslims and Hindus. In protest against the mounting chaos, Gandhi refused to attend the independence day celebration. Throughout the land, Muslim and Hindu neighbors turned on one another, and armed members of one faith hunted down people of the other faith. Leaving most of their possessions behind, Hindus fled from predominantly Muslim areas, and Muslims fled from Hindu areas. Trainloads of desperate refugees of one faith were attacked and massacred by members of the other or were left stranded in the middle of deserts. Within a few months some 12 million people had abandoned their ancestral homes and a half-million lay dead. In January 1948 Gandhi died too, gunned down by an angry Hindu refugee.

After the sectarian massacres and flights of refugees, Muslims were a minority in all but one state of India. That state was Kashmir, a strategically important region in the foothills of the Himalayas. India annexed Kashmir because the local maharajah was Hindu and because the state held the headwaters of the rivers that irrigated millions of acres of farmland. Most inhabitants would have joined Pakistan if they had been allowed to vote on the matter. The annexation of Kashmir turned India and Pakistan into bitter enemies that fought several wars over the next half century.

MEXICO, ARGENTINA, AND BRAZIL, 1917–1949

Though some parts of the world, notably Latin America, were untouched by the Great War, they still experienced the disruptions and new ways of life of the post-war period. In the early 1920s, after a decade of violence that exhausted all classes (see Chapter 26), the Mexican Revolution lost momentum. President Obregón and his closest associates made all the important decisions, and his successor, Plutarco Elías Calles (KAH-yace), founded the National Revolutionary Party, or PNR (the abbreviation of its name in Spanish). The PNR was a forum where all the pressure groups and vested interests—labor, peasants, businessmen, landowners, the military, and others—worked out compromises. The establishment of the PNR gave the Mexican Revolution a second wind.

The Cárdenas Reforms   **Lázaro Cárdenas** (LAH-sah-roe KAHR-dih-nahs), chosen by Calles to be president in 1934, brought peasants' and workers' organizations into the party, removed generals from government positions, and implemented the reforms promised in the Constitution of 1917.

In 1938 Cárdenas seized the foreign-owned oil industry, which had gained importance with the wartime recognition that modern navies needed petroleum. The American and British oil companies expected their governments to come to their rescue, perhaps with military force. But Mexico and the United States chose to resolve the issue through negotiation, and Mexico retained control of its oil.

The Transformation of Argentina

Most of Argentina consists of *pampas* (POM-pus), flat, fertile land that is easy to till, much like the prairies of the midwestern United States and Canada. At the end of the nineteenth century railroads and refrigerator ships changed Argentina's exports and land use. In the 1920s, European consumers, freed from wartime rationing, savored fresh meat. To safeguard valuable herds, the pampas were divided, cultivated, and fenced with barbed wire. Wheat- and grain-fed beef and mutton replaced the lean free-range cattle of earlier generations. Soon the pampas became one of the world's great centers of wheat and meat production.

Argentina's government represented the interests of the *oligarquía* (oh-lee-gar-KEE-ah), a small group of wealthy landowners and exporters. They owned fine homes in Buenos Aires (BWAY-nos EYE-res), a city that was built to resemble Paris, traveled frequently to Europe, and spent lavishly. However, they were content to let British companies build Argentina's railroads, processing plants, and public utilities. Argentina imported almost all its manufactured goods from Europe and the United States. So important were British interests in the Argentinean economy that English, not Spanish, was used on the railroads.

Brazil and Argentina, to 1929

Before the First World War, Brazil produced most of the world's coffee and cacao, grown on vast estates. Natural rubber came from rubber trees growing wild in the Amazon rain forest but had not yet been recognized as a key strategic commodity. Like their Argentinean counterparts, Brazil's elite built palaces in Rio de Janeiro (REE-oh day zhuh-NAIR-oh) and even an opera house deep in the Amazon. British companies build railroads, harbors, and other infrastructure and imported most manufactured goods.

Both Argentina and Brazil had small but outspoken middle classes that demanded a share in government and looked to European models. The poor, at the bottom of the social pyramid, were mainly Spanish and Italian immigrants turned landless laborers and meat processors in Argentina or sharecroppers and plantation workers, many descended from slaves, in Brazil.

Rubber exports collapsed after 1912, replaced by cheaper plantation rubber from Southeast Asia. Two years later the outbreak of war put an end to imports from Europe as Britain and France focused all their industries on war production and Germany was cut off entirely. The disruption of the old trade patterns weakened the landowning class. In Argentina the urban middle class obtained the secret ballot and universal male suffrage in 1916 and elected a liberal politician, **Hipólito Irigoyen** (ee-POH-lee-toe ee-ree-GO-yen), as president. To a certain extent, the United States replaced the European countries as suppliers of machinery and consumers of coffee. European immigrants built factories to manufacture textiles and household goods.

The postwar years were a period of prosperity in South America. Trade with Europe resumed; prices for agricultural exports remained high; and both Argentina and Brazil used profits accumulated during the war to industrialize and improve their transportation systems and public utilities. Yet it was also a time of social turmoil, as workers and middle-class professionals demanded the same social reforms and enhanced voice in politics as their European counterparts. In Argentina students' and workers' demonstrations were brutally crushed. In Brazil junior officers faced off several times against the government. Though they accomplished little, these demonstrations laid the groundwork for later reformist movements.

Yet as Argentina and Brazil prospered, new technologies again left them dependent on the advanced industrial countries. Aviation reached Latin America after World War I, when European and American companies such as Aéropostale and Pan American Airways introduced airmail service between cities and linked Latin America with the United States and Europe.

Before and during World War I, radio was used only for point-to-point communications. Transmitters powerful enough to send messages across oceans or continents were complex and expensive, with antennas covering many acres. They used as much electricity as a small town. Right after the war, no Latin American country possessed the knowledge or funds to build its own transmitters. Four powerful radio companies—one British, one French, one German, and one American—formed a cartel to control all radio communications in Latin America. Thus, even as Brazil and Argentina were asserting state control over their railroads and older industries, as Mexico had done with its oil industry, the major industrial countries controlled the diffusion of the newer aviation and radio technologies.

The Depression and the Vargas Regime in Brazil   The Great Depression (see Chapter 30) hit Latin America as hard as it hit Europe and the United States and proved a more important turning point for the region than either world war. As long-term customers cut back orders, the value of agricultural and mineral exports fell by two-thirds between 1929 and 1932. Argentina and Brazil could no longer afford imported manufactured goods. An imploding economy also undermined their shaky political systems. Like European countries, Argentina and Brazil veered toward authoritarian regimes that promised to solve their economic problems.

In 1930 **Getulio Vargas** (jay-TOO-lee-oh VAR-gus) (1883–1954), a state governor, staged a coup and proclaimed himself president of Brazil. He proved to be a masterful politician. He wrote a new constitution that broadened the franchise and limited the president to one term. He also raised import duties and promoted national firms and state-owned enterprises. By 1936 industrial production had doubled, especially in textiles and small manufactures. Under his guidance, Brazil was on its way to becoming an industrial country, as well as a model for other Latin American countries attempting to break away from neocolonial dependency.

The industrialization of Brazil brought the familiar environmental consequences. Powerful new machines allowed the reopening of old mines and the digging of new ones. Cities grew as poor peasants looking for work arrived from the countryside. In Rio de Janeiro and São Paulo (sow PAL-oh), the poor turned steep hillsides and vacant lands into immense *favelas* (feh-VEL-luhs) (slums) of makeshift shacks.

The countryside also was transformed. Scrubland was turned into pasture or planted in wheat, corn, and sugar cane. Even the Amazon rain forest—half of the

Juan and Eva Perón

Juan Perón's presidency of Argentina (1946–1955) relied on his, and especially on his wife Eva's, popularity with the working class. To sustain their popularity, they often organized parades and demonstrations in imitation of the fascist dictators of Europe. This picture shows them riding in a procession in Buenos Aires in 1952.

Brown Brothers

land area of Brazil—was affected. In 1930, American industrialist Henry Ford invested $8 million to clear land along the Tapajós River and prepare it to become the site of the world's largest rubber plantation. Ford encountered opposition from Brazilian workers and politicians; the rubber trees proved vulnerable to diseases; and he had to abandon the project—but not before leaving 3 million acres (1.2 million hectares) denuded of trees.

Although Vargas instituted many reforms favorable to urban workers, he refused to help the millions of landless peasants or challenge the great landowners. In 1938, prohibited by his own constitution from being reelected, Vargas staged another coup, abolished the constitution, and instituted the Estado Novo (esh-TAH-doe NO-vo), or "New State," with himself as supreme leader. He abolished political parties, jailed opposition leaders, and turned Brazil into a fascist state, though one that contributed troops and ships to the Allied war effort once the Second World War broke out.

Argentina After 1930   Economically, the depression hurt Argentina almost as badly as it hurt Brazil. Politically, however, the consequences were delayed. In 1930 General José Uriburu (hoe-SAY oo-ree-BOO-roo) overthrew the popularly elected President Irigoyen. For thirteen years the generals and the oligarchy ruled, doing nothing to lessen the poverty of the workers or the frustrations of the middle class. When World War II broke out, Argentina remained officially neutral.

In 1943 another military revolt flared, this one among junior officers led by Colonel **Juan Perón** (hoo-AHN pair-OWN) (1895–1974). The intentions of the rebels were clear:

> Civilians will never understand the greatness of our ideal; we shall therefore have to eliminate them from the government and give them the only mission which corresponds to them: work and obedience.[4]

Once in power the officers took over the highest positions in government and business and began to lavish money on military equipment and their own salaries. Their goal, inspired by Nazi victories (see Chapter 30), was nothing less than the conquest of South America.

As the war turned against the Nazis, the officers saw their popularity collapse. Perón, however, had other plans. Inspired by his charismatic wife **Eva Duarte Perón** (AY-vuy doo-AR-tay pair-OWN) (1919–1952), he appealed to the urban workers. Eva Perón became the champion of the *descamisados* (des-cah-mee-SAH-dohs), or "shirtless ones," and campaigned tirelessly for social benefits and for the cause of women and children. With his wife's help, Perón won the presidency in 1946 and created a populist dictatorship in imitation of the Vargas regime in Brazil. When Eva died in 1952, however, he lost his political skills (or perhaps they were hers), and soon thereafter was overthrown in yet another military coup.

SUB-SAHARAN AFRICA, 1900–1945

In contrast with India and Latin America, sub-Saharan Africa experienced very few of the transformations that marked the first half of the twentieth century. Africa was the last continent to come under European rule (see Chapter 26), and it was still being subjected to the economic and political organizational forces of imperialism when territories that had been colonized longer were already in the beginning stages of political awakening. After World War I Britain, France, Belgium, and South Africa divided Germany's African colonies among themselves. Then in the 1930s Italy invaded Ethiopia. The colonial empires reached their peak shortly before World War II.

Yet it would be a mistake to conclude that developments in Africa would have resembled those elsewhere if imperialism had started sooner. European attitudes toward sub-Saharan African peoples were affected by a long history of racism. One economic theory, for example, "the backward bending supply curve of labor," maintained that people who were accustomed to living at a bare subsistence level would work fewer hours if their pay was raised above what little was needed to maintain that level. They would prefer to idle their lives away sitting around the village rather than striving to better their standard of living the way European workers theoretically would. This theory was used to stigmatize African workers and justify paying them very low wages.

---

[4]George Blankstein, *Perón's Argentina* (Chicago: University of Chicago Press, 1953), 37.

Colonial Africa: Economic and Social Changes   Outside of Algeria, Kenya, and South Africa, few Europeans lived in Africa, and they variously spoke Portuguese, Spanish, German, French, English, or Afrikaans. In 1930 Nigeria, with a population of 20 million, was ruled by 386 British officials and by 8,000 policemen and military personnel, of whom 150 were European. Yet even such a small presence stimulated deep social and economic changes.

The colonial powers had built railroads from coastal cities to mines and plantations in the interior to transport raw materials to the industrial world, but few Africans benefited from these changes. Colonial governments took lands from Africans and sold or leased them to European companies or to white settlers. Large European companies dominated wholesale commerce, while Indians, Greeks, and Syrians handled much of the retail trade.

Where land was divided into small farms, some Africans benefited from the boom. Farmers in the Gold Coast (now Ghana [GAH-nuh]) profited from the high price of cacao, as did palm oil producers in Nigeria and coffee growers in East Africa. In most of Africa women played a major role in the retail trades, selling cloth, food, pots and pans, and other items in the markets. Many maintained their economic independence and kept their household finances separate from those of their husbands, following a custom that predated the colonial period.

For many Africans, however, economic development meant working in European-owned mines and plantations, often under compulsion. Colonial governments were eager to develop the resources of the territories under their control but would not pay wages high enough to attract workers. Instead, they used their police powers to force Africans to work under harsh conditions for little or no pay. In the 1920s, when the government of French Equatorial Africa decided to build a railroad from Brazzaville to the Atlantic coast, a distance of 312 miles (502 kilometers), it drafted 127,000 men to carve a roadbed across mountains and through rain forests. For lack of food, clothing, and medical care, 20,000 of them died, an average of 64 deaths per mile of track.

Europeans prided themselves on bringing modern health care to Africa; yet before the 1930s other aspects of colonialism actually worsened public health. Migrants and soldiers spread syphilis, gonorrhea, tuberculosis, and malaria. Sleeping sickness and smallpox epidemics raged throughout Central Africa. In recruiting men to work, colonial governments also depleted rural areas of farmers needed to plant and harvest crops. Forced requisitions of food to feed the workers left the remaining populations undernourished and vulnerable to diseases. Not until the 1930s did colonial governments realize the negative consequences of their labor policies and begin to invest in agricultural development and health care for Africans.

In 1900 Ibadan (ee-BAH-dahn) in Nigeria was the only city in sub-Saharan Africa with more than 100,000 inhabitants; fifty years later, dozens of cities had reached that size. Africans migrated to cities because they offered hope of jobs and excitement and, for a few, the chance to become wealthy.

However, migrations damaged the family life of those involved, for almost all the migrants were men leaving women in the countryside to farm and raise children. Reflecting the colonialists' attitudes, cities built during the colonial period had racially segregated housing, clubs, restaurants, hospitals, and other institutions.

Patterns of racial discrimination were most rigid in the white-settler colonies of eastern and southern Africa.

Religious and Political Changes   Traditional religious belief could not explain the dislocations that foreign rule, migrations, and sudden economic changes brought to the lives of Africans. Many therefore turned to Christianity or Islam.

Christianity was introduced into Africa by Western missionaries, except in Ethiopia, where it was indigenous. It was most successful in West and South Africa, where the European influence was strongest. A major attraction of the Christian denominations was their mission schools, which taught both craft skills and basic literacy, providing access to employment as minor functionaries, teachers, and shopkeepers. These schools educated a new elite, many of whom learned not only skills and literacy but Western political ideas as well. Yet very few students continued their education to the university level. Many Africans accepted Christianity enthusiastically, reading the suffering of their own peoples into the biblical stories of Moses and the parables of Jesus. The churches trained some pupils to become catechists, teachers, and clergymen. Independent Christian churches associated Christian beliefs with radical ideas of racial equality and participation in politics.

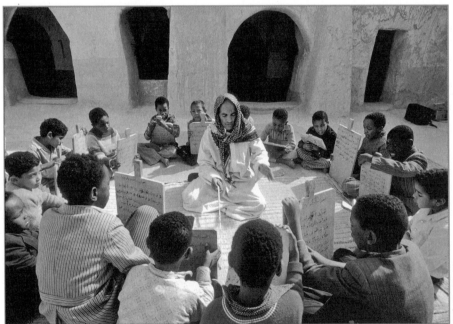

Olivier Martel/Corbis

A Quranic School *In Muslim countries, religious education is centered on learning to read, write, and recite the Quran, the sacred book of the Islamic religion, in the original Arabic. This picture shows boys in a Libyan madrasa (Quranic school) studying writing and religion.*

Islam spread inland from the East African coast and southward from the Sahel (SAH-hel) through the influence and example of Arab and African merchants. Islam also emphasized literacy—in Arabic rather than a European language—and was less disruptive of traditional African customs such as polygamy. In some areas, such as Somalia, Sudan, and Mali, certain Muslim Sufi brotherhoods became associated with resistance to European imperialism.

In Dakar in Senegal and Cape Town in South Africa, small numbers of Africans could obtain secondary education. Even smaller numbers went on to college in Europe or America. Though few in number, they became the leaders of political movements. The contrast between the liberal ideas imparted by Western education and the realities of racial discrimination under colonial rule contributed to the rise of nationalism among educated Africans. In Senegal **Blaise Diagne** (dee-AHN-yuh) agitated for African participation in politics and fair treatment in the French army during World War I, and in the 1920s J. E. Casely Hayford began organizing a movement for greater autonomy in British West Africa. These nationalist movements were inspired by the ideas of Pan-Africanists from America such as W. E. B. Du Bois and Marcus Garvey, who advocated the unity of African peoples around the world, as well as by European ideas of liberty and nationhood. To defend the interests of Africans, Western-educated lawyers and journalists in South Africa founded the **African National Congress** in 1912. Before World War II, however, these nationalist movements were small and had little influence.

The Second World War had a profound effect on the peoples of Africa, even those far removed from the theaters of war. The war brought hardships, such as increased forced labor, inflation, and requisitions of raw materials. Yet it also brought hope. During the campaign to oust the Italians from Ethiopia, Emperor **Haile Selassie** (HI-lee seh-LASS-ee) (r. 1930–1974) led his own troops into Addis Ababa, his capital, and reclaimed his title. A million Africans served as soldiers and carriers in Burma, North Africa, and Europe, where many became aware of Africa's role in helping the Allied war effort. They listened to Allied propaganda in favor of European liberation movements and against Nazi racism and returned to their countries with new and radical ideas.

Africa and the New Media   South Africa saw the first tries at radio broadcasting in 1924, but these enjoyed very little success until the South African Broadcasting Corporation was established with monopolistic control over the medium in 1936. Down to World War II it broadcast only in English and Afrikaans. Most efforts in other colonies, such as Mozambique and Kenya, likewise targeted European listeners. The exception was British West Africa—Sierra Leone, Ghana, and Nigeria—where African languages were used. Rather than wireless service, subscribers had loudspeakers in their homes that were connected by wire to the radio station. After 1936 the British authorities generally began to see radio as a medium for reaching Africans who did not understand English.

Africa had almost no cinematic presence prior to World War II, apart from fourteen stereotype-filled Tarzan films made in Hollywood between 1918 and 1949. A few films were made for British and Afrikaner audiences in South Africa, but the French issued a decree in 1934 prohibiting the shooting of movies.

CONCLUSION

The First and Second World Wars and the intervening period of economic depression, fascism, and militarism constituted the great dramas of the first half of the twentieth century. But not all parts of the world experienced these convulsions to the same degree. Moreover, these narratives of world war, global depression, and varying regional development do not incorporate the profound changes in ways of living that affected most parts of the world between 1900 and 1950.

While participating in many of these changes, the nonindustrialized nations also had their own technological breakthroughs, such as the rickshaw, and did not use some inventions, such as electricity, in the same way as the West. New media such as cinema and radio were used in different ways as well and sometimes perpetuated themes and images from local cultural sources. At the same time, traditional patterns of village life began to erode as cities grew and urban life, at least for the privileged classes, took on the demeanor and attitudes of Europe. But becoming like Europe did not mean coming to like Europe.

To a much greater degree, the industrialized world experienced a flood of new inventions—automobiles, electric lights, radios, movies, airplanes—that stimulated not only a broader respect for science, but also an expectation that science would continue indefinitely to improve human lives. This was the cult of the modern. Technology even affected the arts, providing new materials for architecture and furniture design, new electronic means of amplifying and distributing music, and an ever-expanding array of tools for making and reproducing images, both still and moving. Yet the devastating human tragedies of war and depression also encouraged currents of nihilism, despair, and questioning of faith.

Imperialism being focused, as always, on benefits for the home country and disdain for native peoples with darker skins, colonial administrators in different parts of the world tried to control the flow of global technological and ideological changes. Having a larger and better-educated middle class than many other non-European lands, India entered more fully into the new ways of living than did sub-Saharan Africa. Latin America, with many European immigrants, was closer economically and ideologically to Europe. Political and cultural independence became a realizable goal in India, where Mahatma Gandhi's nonviolent movement pioneered an entirely new form of political activism. In sub-Saharan Africa, however, European racism and the unwavering favoritism shown to European settlers stifled almost all attempts at change.

IMPORTANT EVENTS 1900–1950	
1903	Wright brothers fly first airplane
1905	Viceroy Curzon splits Bengal; mass demonstrations
1906	Muslims found All-India Muslim League
1911	British transfer capital from Calcutta to Delhi
1912	African National Congress founded

1912	First feature-length movie in India
1913	Henry Ford introduces assembly-line production
1915–1920	Women gain vote in Norway, Russia, Canada, Germany, Britain, and the United States
1919	Amritsar Massacre
1920	Commercial radio begins in United States
1920s	J. E. Casely Hayford organizes political movement in British West Africa
1923	Margaret Sanger opens first birth control clinic
1925	Commercial radio begins in Japan
1928	Plutarco Elías Calles founds Mexico's National Revolutionary Party
1929	Gandhi leads March to the Sea
1930s	Gandhi calls for independence; he is repeatedly arrested
1930–1945	Getulio Vargas, dictator of Brazil
1932	Empire State Building opens
1934–1940	Lázaro Cárdenas, president of Mexico
1936	Olympic games in Berlin
1938	Cárdenas nationalizes Mexican oil industry; Vargas proclaims Estado Novo in Brazil
1939	British bring India into World War II
1939–1945	A million Africans serve in World War II
1940	Muhammad Ali Jinnah demands a separate nation for Muslims
1943	Juan Perón leads military coup in Argentina
1946	Perón elected president of Argentina
1947	Partition and independence of India and Pakistan

30

◆

THE COLLAPSE OF THE OLD ORDER, 1929–1949

Before the First World War the Italian poet Filippo Marinetti exalted violence as noble and manly: "We want to glorify war, the world's only hygiene—militarism, deed, destroyer of anarchisms, the beautiful ideas that are death-bringing, and the subordination of women."[1] His friend Gabriele d'Annunzio added: "If it is a crime to incite citizens to violence, I shall boast of this crime."[2] Poets are sometimes more prescient than they imagine.

In the nineteenth century the governments of the great powers were manipulated by politicians through appeals to popular nationalism. Internationally, the world order relied on the maintenance of empires by military or economic means. And the global economy was based on free-market capitalism in which the industrial countries exchanged manufactured goods for the agricultural and mineral products of the nonindustrial world.

After the trauma of World War I the world seemed to return to what U.S. president Warren Harding called "normalcy": prosperity in Europe and America, European colonialism in Asia and Africa, American domination of Latin America, and peace almost everywhere. But in 1929 normalcy vanished. As the Great Depression spread around the world, governments turned against one another in desperate attempts to protect their people's livelihood.

Most survivors of the war had learned to abhor violence. For a few, however, war and domination became a creed, a goal, and a solution to their problems. The Japanese military tried to save their country from the depression by conquering China, which erupted in revolution. In Germany many blamed their troubles on communists and Jews and turned to the Nazis, who promised to save German society by crushing others. In the Soviet Union, Stalin used energetic and murderous means to force his country into a communist version of the Industrial Revolution.

As the old order collapsed, the world was engulfed by a second Great War, one far more global and destructive than the first. Unlike World War I, this was a war

---

[1]Apollonio Umbro, ed., *Documents of Twentieth Century Art: Futurist Manifestos* (New York: Viking Press, 1973), 23.

[2]Richard F. Hamilton and Holger H. Herwig, *Decisions for War, 1914–1917* (Cambridge: Cambridge University Press, 2004), 199.

of movement in which entire countries were conquered in a matter of weeks. It was also a war of machines: fighter planes and bombers that targeted civilians, tanks, aircraft carriers, and, finally, atomic bombs that obliterated entire cities.

At the end of World War II much of Europe and East Asia lay in ruins, and millions of destitute refugees sought safety in other lands. The colonial powers were either defeated or so weakened that they could no longer prevent their Asian and African subjects from demanding independence.

THE STALIN REVOLUTION

During the 1920s the Soviet Union recovered from the Revolutions of 1917 and the civil war that followed (see Chapter 28). After Stalin achieved total mastery over this huge nation in 1929, he led it through an economic and social transformation that turned it into a great industrial and military power and intensified both admiration for and fear of communism throughout the world.

Five-Year Plans   **Joseph Stalin** (1879–1953) was the son of a poor shoemaker. Before becoming a revolutionary, he studied for the priesthood. Under the name *Stalin* (Russian for "man of steel"), he played a small part in the Revolutions of 1917. He was a hard-working and skillful administrator who rose within the party bureaucracy and filled its upper ranks with men loyal to himself. He then proceeded to make himself absolute dictator and transform Soviet society.

Stalin's ambition was to turn the USSR into an industrial nation. However, industrialization was to serve a different purpose than in other countries. It was not expected to produce consumer goods for a mass market or to enrich individuals. Instead, its aim was to increase the power of the Communist Party domestically and that of the Soviet Union in relation to other countries.

Stalin was determined to prevent a repetition of the humiliating defeat Russia had suffered at the hands of Germany in 1917. His goal was to quintuple the output of electricity and double that of heavy industry—iron, steel, coal, and machinery—in five years. To do so, he devised the first of a series of **Five-Year Plans**. Beginning in October 1928, the Communist Party and government created whole industries and cities from scratch, then trained millions of peasants to work in the new factories, mines, and offices. In every way except actual fighting, Stalin's Russia resembled a nation at war.

Rapid industrialization hastened environmental changes. Hydroelectric dams turned rivers into strings of reservoirs. Roads, canals, and railroad tracks cut the landscape. Forests and grassland were turned into farmland. From an environmental perspective, the Five-Year Plans resembled the transformation that had occurred in the United States and Canada a few decades earlier.

Collectivization   Since the Soviet Union was still a predominantly agrarian
of Agriculture   country, the only way to pay for these massive investments, provide the labor, and feed the millions of new industrial workers was to squeeze the peasantry. Stalin therefore proceeded with the most radical social experiment conceived up to that time: the collectivization of agriculture.

Collectivization meant consolidating small private farms into vast collectives and making the farmers work together in commonly owned fields. Each collective was expected to supply the government with a fixed amount of food and distribute what was left among its members. Collectives were to become outdoor factories where food was manufactured through the techniques of mass production and the application of machinery. The purpose of this collectivization was to bring the peasants under government control so they never again could withhold food supplies, as they had done during the Russian civil war of 1918–1921.

When collectivization was announced, the government mounted a massive propaganda campaign and sent party members into the countryside to enlist the farmers' support. At first all seemed to go well, but soon *kulaks* (COO-lock) ("fists"), the better-off peasants, began to resist giving up all their property. When soldiers came to force them into collectives at gunpoint, they burned their crops, smashed their equipment, and slaughtered their livestock. Within a few months they slaughtered half of the Soviet Union's horses and cattle and two-thirds of the sheep and goats. In retaliation, Stalin ruthlessly ordered the "liquidation of kulaks as a class" and incited the poor peasants to attack their wealthier neighbors. Over 8 million kulaks were arrested. Many were executed, and the rest were sent to slave labor camps, where most starved to death.

The peasants who were left had been the least successful before collectivization and proved to be the least competent after. Many were sent to work in factories. The rest were forbidden to leave their farms. With half of their draft animals gone, they could not plant or harvest enough to meet the swelling demands of the cities. Yet government agents took whatever they could find, leaving little or nothing for the farmers themselves. After bad harvests in 1933 and 1934, a famine swept through the countryside, killing some 5 million people, about one in every twenty farmers.

Stalin's second Five-Year Plan, designed to run from 1933 to 1937, was originally intended to produce consumer goods. But when the Nazis took over Germany in 1933 (see below), Stalin changed the plan to emphasize heavy industries that could produce armaments. Between 1927 and 1937 the Soviet output of metals and machines increased fourteen-fold while consumer goods became scarce and food was rationed. After a decade of Stalinism, the Soviet people were more poorly clothed, fed, and housed than they had been before the war.

Terror and Opportunities

The 1930s brought both terror and opportunities to the Soviet people. The forced pace of industrialization, the collectivization of agriculture, and the uprooting of millions of people could be accomplished only under duress. To prevent any possible resistance or rebellion, the NKVD, Stalin's secret police force, created a climate of suspicion and fear.

As early as 1930 Stalin had hundreds of engineers and technicians arrested on trumped-up charges of counterrevolutionary ideas and sabotage. Three years later, he expelled a million members of the Communist Party—one-third of the membership—on similar charges. He then turned on his most trusted associates.

In December 1934 Sergei Kirov, the party boss of Leningrad (now St. Petersburg), was assassinated, perhaps on Stalin's orders. Stalin made a public display of mourning Kirov while blaming others for the crime. He then ordered a series of spectacular purge trials in which he accused most of Lenin's associates of treason. In 1937 he had his eight top generals and many lower officers executed, leaving the Red Army dangerously weakened. Under torture or psychological pressure, almost all the accused confessed to the "crimes" they were charged with.

While "Old Bolsheviks" and high officials were being put on trial, terror spread steadily downward. The government regularly made demands that people could not meet, so everyone was guilty of breaking some regulation or other. People from all walks of life were arrested, some on mere suspicion or because of a false accusation by a jealous coworker or neighbor, some for expressing a doubt or working too hard or not hard enough, some for being related to someone previously arrested, some for no reason at all. Millions of people were sentenced without trials. At the height of the terror, some 8 million were sent to *gulags* (GOO-log) (labor camps), where perhaps a million died each year of exposure or malnutrition. To its victims the terror seemed capricious and random. Yet it turned a sullen and resentful people into docile hard-working subjects of the party.

In spite of the fear and hardships, many Soviet citizens supported Stalin's regime. Suddenly, with so many people gone and new industries and cities being built everywhere, there were opportunities for those who remained, especially the poor and the young. Women entered careers and jobs previously closed to them, becoming steelworkers, physicians, and office managers; but they retained their household and child-rearing duties, receiving little help from men (see Diversity and Dominance: Women, Family Values, and the Russian Revolution). People who moved to the cities, worked enthusiastically, and asked no questions could hope to rise into the upper ranks of the Communist Party, the military, the government, or the professions—where the privileges and rewards were many.

Stalin's brutal methods helped the Soviet Union industrialize faster than any country had ever done. By the late 1930s the USSR was the world's third largest industrial power, after the United States and Germany. To foreign observers it seemed to be booming with construction projects and labor shortages. Even anti-Communist observers admitted that government planning worked. To millions of Soviet citizens who took pride in the new strength of their country and to many foreigners who contrasted conditions in the Soviet Union with the unemployment and despair in the West, Stalin's achievement seemed worth any price.

THE DEPRESSION

On October 24, 1929—"Black Thursday"—the New York stock market went into a dive. Within days stocks had lost half their value. The fall continued for three years, ruining millions of investors. People with bank accounts rushed to make withdrawals, causing thousands of banks to collapse.

Economic Crisis   What began as a stock market crash soon turned into the deepest depression in history. As consumers reduced their purchases, businesses cut production, laying off thousands of workers. Female employees were the first laid off on the grounds that men had to support families while women worked only for "pin money." Jobless men deserted their families. Small farmers went bankrupt and lost their land. By mid-1932 the American economy had shrunk by half, and unemployment had risen to an unprecedented 25 percent of the workforce. Many observers thought that free-enterprise capitalism was doomed.

In 1930 the U.S. government, hoping to protect American industries from foreign competition, imposed the Smoot-Hawley tariff, the highest in American history. In retaliation, other countries raised their tariffs in a wave of "beggar thy neighbor" protectionism. The result was crippled export industries and shrinking world trade. While global industrial production declined by 36 percent between 1929 and 1932, world trade dropped by a breathtaking 62 percent.

Depression in Industrial Nations   By 1931 the depression had spread to Europe. Governments canceled reparations payments and war loans, but it was too late to save the world economy. Though their economies stagnated, France and Britain weathered the depression by making their colonial empires purchase their products rather than the products of other countries. Nations that relied on exports to pay for imported food and fuel suffered much more. In Germany unemployment reached 6 million by 1932, twice as high as in Britain. Half the German population lived in poverty, while those who kept their jobs saw their salaries cut and their living standards fall. In Japan the burden of the depression fell hardest on the farmers and fishermen.

This massive economic upheaval had profound political repercussions. Nationalists everywhere called for autarchy, or independence from the world economy. In the United States Franklin D. Roosevelt was elected president in 1932 on a "New Deal" platform of government programs to stimulate and revitalize the economy. Although the American, British, and French governments intervened in their economies, they remained democratic. In Germany and Japan, as economic grievances worsened long-festering political resentments, radical leaders came to power and turned their nations into military machines, hoping to acquire, by war if necessary, empires large enough to support self-sufficient economies and at the same time provide employment in arms factories.

Depression in Nonindustrial Regions   The depression also spread to Asia, Africa, and Latin America, but very unevenly. In 1930 India erected a wall of import duties to protect its infant industries from foreign competition; its living standards stagnated but did not drop. China was little affected by trade with other countries; its problems were more political than economic.

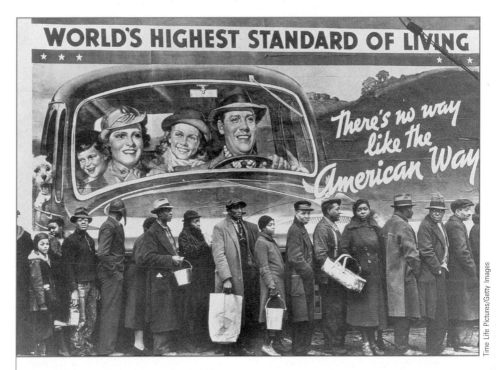

Two Views of the American Way *In this classic photograph,* Life *magazine photographer Margaret Bourke-White captured the contrast between advertisers' view of the ideal American family and the reality of bread lines for the poor.*

Countries that depended on exports were hard hit by the depression. Malaya, Indochina, and the Dutch East Indies produced most of the world's natural rubber; when automobile production in the United States and Europe dropped by half, so did imports of rubber, devastating their economies. Egypt, dependent on cotton exports, was also affected, and in the resulting political strife, the government became autocratic and unpopular.

Throughout Latin America unemployment and homelessness increased markedly. The industrialization of Argentina and Brazil was set back a decade or more. Disenchanted with liberal politics, military officers seized power in several Latin American countries (see Chapter 29). Consciously imitating dictatorships emerging in Europe, they imposed authoritarian control over their economies, hoping to stimulate local industries and curb imports.

Other than the USSR, only southern Africa boomed during the 1930s. As other prices dropped, gold became relatively more valuable. Copper deposits, found in Northern Rhodesia (now Zambia) and the Belgian Congo (now Democratic Republic of the Congo), proved to be cheaper to mine than Chilean copper. But this mining boom benefited only a small number of European and white South African mine owners. For Africans it was a mixed blessing; mining provided jobs and cash wages to men while women stayed behind in the villages, farming, herding, and raising children without their husbands' help.

Women, Family Values, and the Russian Revolution

The Bolsheviks were of two minds on the subject of women. They were opposed to bourgeois morality and to the oppression of women, especially working-class women, under capitalism. But what to put in its place?

Alexandra Kollontai was the most out-spoken of the Bolsheviks on the subject of women's rights. She advocated the liberation of women, the replacement of housework by communal kitchens and laundries, and divorce on demand. Under socialism, love, sex, and marriage would be entirely equal, reciprocal, and free of economic obligations. Childbearing would be encouraged, but children would be raised communally: "The worker mother ... must remember that there are henceforth only our children, those of the communist state, the common possession of all workers."

In a lecture she gave at Sverdlov University in 1921, Kollontai declared:

... it is important to preserve not only the interests of the woman but also the life of the child, and this is to be done by giving the woman the opportunity to combine labour and maternity. Soviet power tries to create a situation where a woman does not have to cling to a man she has learned to loathe only because she has nowhere else to go with her children, and where a woman alone does not have to fear for her life and the life of her child. In the labour republic it is not the philanthropists with their humiliating charity but the workers and peasants, fellow-creators of the new society, who hasten to help the working woman and strive to lighten the burden of motherhood.... I would like to say a few words about ... the question of abortion, and Soviet Russia's attitude toward it. On 20 November 1920 the labour republic issued a law abolishing the penalties that had been attached to abortion. What is the reason behind this new attitude? Russia after all suffers not from an overproduction of living labour but rather from a lack of it. Russia is thinly, not densely populated. Every unit of labour power is precious. Why then have we declared abortion to be no longer a criminal offence? ...

Abortion exists and flourishes every-where, and no laws or punitive measures have succeeded in rooting it out. A way round the law is always found. But "secret help" only cripples women; they become a burden on the labour government, and the size of the labour force is reduced. Abor-tion, when carried out under proper medi-cal conditions, is less harmful and dangerous, and the woman can get back to work quicker. Soviet power realizes that the need for abortion will only disap-pear on the one hand when Russia has a broad and developed network of institu-tions protecting motherhood and provid-ing social education, and on the other hand when women understand that *child-birth is a social obligation*; Soviet power has therefore allowed abortion to be per-formed openly and in clinical conditions.

Besides the large-scale development of motherhood protection, the task of labour Russia is to strengthen in women the healthy instinct of motherhood, to make motherhood and labour for the collective compatible and thus do away with the need for abortion. This is the approach of the labour republic to the question of abortion, which still faces women in the bourgeois countries in all its magnitude. In these countries women are exhausted by the dual burden of hired labour for cap-ital and motherhood. In Soviet Russia the working woman and peasant woman are helping the Communist Party to build a new society and to undermine the old way of life that has enslaved women. As soon as woman is viewed as being essen-tially a labour unit, the key to the solution of the complex question of maternity can be found.

Fifteen years later Joseph Stalin reversed the Soviet policy on abortion.

The published draft of the law prohibiting abortion and providing material assistance to mothers has provoked a lively reaction throughout the country. It is being heatedly discussed by tens of millions of people and there is no doubt that it will serve as a further strengthening of the Soviet family....

When we speak of strengthening the Soviet family, we are speaking precisely of the struggle against the survivals of a bourgeois attitude towards marriage, women, and children. So-called "free love" and all disorderly sex life are bourgeois through and through, and have nothing to do with either socialist principles or the ethics and standards of conduct of the Soviet citizens. Socialist doctrine shows this, and it is proved by life itself.

The elite of our country, the best of the Soviet youth, are as a rule also excellent family men who dearly love their children. And vice versa: the man who does not take marriage seriously, and abandons his children to the whims of fate, is usually also a bad worker and a poor member of society....

It is impossible even to compare the present state of the family with that which obtained before the Soviet regime—so great has been the improvement towards greater stability and, above all, greater humanity and goodness. The single fact that millions of women have become economically independent and are no longer at the mercy of men's whims, speaks volumes. Compare, for instance, the modern woman collective farmer who sometimes earns more than her husband, with the pre-revolutionary peasant woman who completely depended on her husband and was a slave in the household. Has not this fundamentally changed family relations, has it not rationalized and strengthened the family? The very motives for setting up a family, for getting married, have changed for the better, have been cleansed of atavistic and barbaric elements. Marriage has ceased to be a matter of sell-and-buy. Nowadays a girl from a collective farm is not given away (or should we say "sold away"?) by her father, for now she is her own mistress, and no one can give her away. She will marry the man she loves....

We alone have all the conditions under which a working woman can fulfill her duties as a citizen and as a mother responsible for the birth and early upbringing of her children.

A woman without children merits our pity, for she does not know the full joy of life. Our Soviet women, full-blooded citizens of the freest country in the world, have been given the bliss of motherhood. We must safeguard the family and raise and rear healthy Soviet heroes!

Questions for Analysis

1. How does Kollontai expect women to be both workers and mothers without depending on a man? How would Soviet society make this possible?

2. Why does Alexandra Kollontai advocate the legalization of abortion in Soviet Russia? Does she view abortion as a permanent right or as a temporary necessity?

3. Why does Stalin characterize a "light-hearted, negligent attitude toward marriage" and "all disorderly sex life" as "bourgeois through and through"?

4. How does Stalin's image of the Soviet family differ from Kollontai's? Are his views a variation of her views, or the opposite?

Sources: First selection from Alexandra Kollontai, "The Labour of Women in the Revolution of the Economy," in *Selected Writings of Alexandra Kollontai*, translated by Alix Holt (Lawrence Hill & Company, 1978), pp. 148–149. Second selection from Discussion of the Law on Abolition of Legal Abortion, Pravda, Editorials of May 28 and June 9, 1936 (English translation in Rudolf Schlesinger, ed., Changing Attitudes in Soviet Russia: The Family in the USSR, London, Routledge & Kegan Paul, 1949, pp. 251–54, 268–69.

THE RISE OF FASCISM

The Russian Revolution and its Stalinist aftermath frightened property owners in Europe and North America. In western Europe and North America, middle- and upper-income voters took refuge in conservative politics. In southern and central Europe, the war had turned people's hopes of victory to bitter disappointment. Many blamed ethnic minorities, especially Jews, for their troubles. In their yearning for a mythical past of family farms and small shops, increasing numbers rejected representative government and sought more dramatic solutions.

Radical politicians applied wartime propaganda techniques to appeal to a confused citizenry. They promised to use any means necessary to bring back full employment, stop the spread of communism, and achieve the territorial conquests that World War I had denied them. While defending private property from communism, they borrowed the communist model of politics: a single party and a secret police that ruled by terror and intimidation.

Mussolini's Italy   The first country to seek radical answers was Italy. World War I, which had never been popular, left thousands of veterans who found neither pride in their victory nor jobs in the postwar economy. Unemployed veterans and violent youths banded together into *fasci di combattimento* (fighting units) to demand action and intimidate politicians. When workers threatened to strike, factory and property owners hired gangs of these *fascisti* to defend them.

Benito Mussolini (1883–1945) had supported Italy's entry into the war. A spellbinding orator, he quickly became the leader of the **Fascist Party**, which glorified warfare and the Italian nation. By 1921 the party had 300,000 members, many of whom used violent methods to repress strikes, intimidate voters, and seize municipal governments. A year later Mussolini threatened to march on Rome if he was not appointed prime minister. The government, composed of timid parliamentarians, gave in.

Mussolini proceeded to install Fascist Party members in all government jobs, crush all opposition parties, and jail anyone who criticized him. The party took over the press, public education, and youth activities and gave employers control over their workers. The Fascists lowered living standards but reduced unemployment and provided social security and public services. They proved to be neither ruthless radicals nor competent administrators.

What Mussolini and the Fascist movement really excelled at was bombastic speeches, spectacular parades, and signs everywhere proclaiming "Il Duce (eel DOO-chay) [the Leader] is always right!" Mussolini's genius was to apply the techniques of modern mass communications and advertisement to political life. Movie footage and radio news bulletins galvanized the masses in ways never before done in peacetime. His techniques of whipping up public enthusiasm were not lost on other radicals. By the 1930s fascist movements had appeared in most European countries, as well as in Latin America, China, and Japan. Fascism appealed to many people who were frightened by rapid changes and placed their hopes in charismatic leaders. Of all of Mussolini's imitators, none was as sinister as Adolf Hitler.

**Hitler's
Germany**

Germany had lost the First World War after coming very close to winning. The hyperinflation of 1923 wiped out the savings of middle-class families. Less than ten years later the depression caused more unemployment and misery than in any other country. Millions of Germans blamed Socialists, Jews, and foreigners for their troubles.

Adolf Hitler (1889–1945) joined the German army in 1914 and was wounded at the front. He later looked back fondly on the clear lines of authority and the camaraderie he had experienced in battle. After the war he used his gifts as an orator to lead a political splinter group called the National Socialist German Workers' Party—**Nazis** for short. While serving a brief jail sentence he wrote *Mein Kampf* (mine compf) (*My Struggle*), in which he outlined his goals and beliefs.

When it was published in 1925, *Mein Kampf* attracted little notice. Its ideas seemed so insane that almost no one took it, or its author, seriously. Hitler's ideas went far beyond ordinary nationalism. He believed that Germany should incorporate all German-speaking areas, even those in neighboring countries. He distinguished among a "master race" of Aryans (he meant Germans, Scandinavians, and Britons), a degenerate "Alpine" race of French and Italians, and an inferior race of Russian and eastern European Slavs, fit only to be slaves of the master race. He reserved his most intense hatred for Jews, on whom he blamed every disaster that had befallen Germany, especially the defeat of 1918. He glorified violence and looked forward to a future war in which the "master race" would defeat and subjugate all others.

Hitler's first goal was to reverse the humiliation and repeal the military restrictions of the Treaty of Versailles. Next he planned to annex all German-speaking territories to a greater Germany, then gain *Lebensraum* (LAY-bens-rowm) (room to live) at the expense of Poland and the USSR. Finally, he planned to eliminate all Jews from Europe.

From 1924 to 1930 Hitler's followers remained a tiny minority, for most Germans found his ideas too extreme. But when the depression hit, the Nazis gained supporters among the unemployed, who believed their promises of jobs for all, and among property owners frightened by the growing popularity of communists.

In March 1933 Hitler became chancellor of Germany. Once in office, he quickly assumed dictatorial powers. He put Nazis in charge of all government agencies, educational institutions, and professional organizations; banned all other political parties; and threw their leaders into concentration camps. The Nazis deprived Jews of their citizenship and civil rights, prohibited them from marrying "Aryans," ousted them from the professions, and confiscated their property. In August 1934 Hitler proclaimed himself *Führer* (FEW-rer) ("leader") and called Germany the "Third Reich," the third German empire after the Holy Roman Empire of medieval times and the German Empire of 1871 to 1918.

The Nazis' economic and social policies were spectacularly effective. The government undertook massive public works projects. Businesses got contracts to manufacture weapons. Women who had entered the workforce were urged to release their jobs to men. By 1936 business was booming; unemployment was at its lowest level since the 1920s; and living standards were rising. Most Germans believed that their economic well-being outweighed the loss of liberty.

The Road to War, 1933–1939

However, Hitler's goal was not prosperity or popularity, but conquest. As soon as he came to office, he began to build up the armed forces. Meanwhile, he tested the reactions of the other powers through a series of surprise moves followed by protestations of peace.

In 1933 Hitler withdrew Germany from the League of Nations. Two years later he announced that Germany was going to introduce conscription, build up its army, and create an air force—in violation of the Versailles treaty. Neither Britain nor France was willing to risk war by standing up to Germany.

In 1935, emboldened by the weakness of the democracies, Italy invaded Ethiopia, the last independent state in Africa and a member of the League of Nations. The League and the democracies protested but refused to close the Suez Canal to Italian ships or impose an oil embargo. The following year, when Hitler sent troops into the Rhineland on the borders of France and Belgium, the other powers merely protested.

By 1938 Hitler decided that his rearmament plans were far enough advanced that he could afford to escalate his demands. In March Germany invaded Austria. Most Austrians were German-speakers and accepted the annexation of their country without protest. Then came Czechoslovakia, where a German-speaking minority lived along the German border. Hitler first demanded their autonomy from Czech rule, then their annexation to Germany. Throughout the summer he threatened to

AP/Wide World Photos

A Nazi Rally *Hitler organized mass rallies at Nuremberg to whip up popular support for his regime and to indoctrinate young Germans with a martial spirit. Thousands of men in uniform marched in torch-lit parades before Hitler and his top officials.*

go to war. At the Munich Conference of September 1938, the leaders of France, Britain, and Italy gave him everything he wanted without consulting Czechoslovakia. Once again, Hitler learned that aggression paid off.

The weakness of the democracies—now called "appeasement"—had three causes. The first was the deep-seated fear of war among people who had lived through World War I. Unlike the dictators, politicians in the democracies could not ignore their constituents' yearnings for peace. Most people believed that the threat of war might go away if they wished for peace fervently enough. The second cause of appeasement was fear of communism among conservatives, who feared Stalin more than Hitler because Hitler claimed to respect Christianity and private property. The third cause was the very novelty of fascist tactics. Britain's prime minister Neville Chamberlain assumed that political leaders (other than the Bolsheviks) were honorable men and that an agreement was as valid as a business contract. Thus, when Hitler promised to incorporate only German-speaking people into Germany and said he had "no further territorial demands," Chamberlain believed him.

After Munich it was too late to stop Hitler, short of war. Germany and Italy signed an alliance called the Axis, and in March 1939 Germany invaded what was left of Czechoslovakia. Belatedly realizing that Hitler could not be trusted, France and Britain sought Soviet help. Stalin, however, distrusted the "capitalists" as much as they distrusted him. When Hitler offered to divide Poland between Germany and the Soviet Union, Stalin accepted. The Nazi-Soviet Pact of August 23, 1939, freed Hitler from the fear of a two-front war and gave Stalin time to build up his armies. One week later, on September 1, German forces swept into Poland, and the war was on.

EAST ASIA, 1931–1945

When the depression hit, the collapse of demand for silk and rice ruined thousands of Japanese farmers; to survive, some even sold their daughters into prostitution, while many poor young men flocked to the military. Ultranationalists resented their country's dependence on foreign trade and what they believed was unnecessary party politics that sullied the righteousness of the divine imperial will. If only Japan had a colonial empire, they thought, it would not be beholden to the rest of the world. But Europeans and Americans had already taken most potential colonies in Asia. Japanese nationalists saw the conquest of China, with its vast population and resources, as the solution to their country's problems.

The Manchurian Incident of 1931   Meanwhile, in China the Guomindang (gwo-min-dong) (see Chapter 28) was becoming stronger and preparing to challenge the Japanese presence in Manchuria, a province rich in coal and iron ore. Junior officers in the Japanese army, frustrated by the caution of their superiors, took action. In September 1931 they blew up part of a railroad track as a pretext for invading the entire province. This invasion was promoted as achieving the "independence" of Manchuria under the name *Manchukuo* (man-CHEW-coo-oh), but in reality, Manchukuo remained under Japanese control. Many civilian officials and military leaders back in Tokyo had not approved of the attack, but they soon joined the overwhelming positive reaction to the incident expressed by the public, press, and even leftist critics.

The U.S. government condemned the Japanese conquest, and the League of Nations refused to recognize Manchukuo and urged the Japanese to remove their troops from China. Persuaded that the Western powers would not fight, Japan resigned from the League.

During the next few years the Japanese built railways and heavy industries in Manchuria and northeastern China and sped up their rearmament. At home, production was diverted to the military, especially to building warships. The government grew more authoritarian, jailing thousands of dissidents. On several occasions, ultranationalists, many of them junior officers, mutinied or assassinated leading political figures. The mutineers received mild punishments, and generals and admirals sympathetic to their views replaced more moderate civilian politicians.

The Long March   Until the Japanese seized Manchuria, the Chinese government seemed to be creating conditions for a national recovery. The main challenge to the government of **Chiang Kai-shek** (chang kie-shek) came from the Communists. The Chinese Communist Party had been founded in 1921 by a handful of intellectuals, and for several years it lived in the shadow of the Guomindang. Its efforts to recruit members among industrial workers came to naught in 1927, when Chiang Kai-shek arrested and executed Communists and labor leaders alike. The few Communists who escaped the mass arrests fled to the remote mountains of Jiangxi (jang-she), in southeastern China.

Among them was **Mao Zedong** (ma-oh zay-dong) (1893–1976), a farmer's son who had left home to study philosophy. Mao was a man of action whose first impulse was to call for violent effort: "To be able to leap on horseback and to shoot at the same time; to go from battle to battle; to shake the mountains by one's cries, and the colors of the sky by one's roars of anger." In the early 1920s Mao discovered the works of Karl Marx, joined the Communist Party, and soon became one of its leaders.

In Jiangxi Mao began studying conditions among the peasants, in whom Communists had previously shown no interest. He planned to redistribute land from the wealthier to the poorer peasants, thereby gaining adherents for the coming struggle with the Guomindang army. His goal was a complete social revolution from the bottom up. Mao's reliance on the peasantry was a radical departure from Marxist-Leninist ideology, which stressed the backwardness of the peasants and pinned its hopes on industrial workers. Mao therefore had to be careful to cloak his pragmatic tactics in communist rhetoric to allay the suspicions of Stalin and his agents.

Mao was an advocate of women's equality. Before 1927 the Communists had organized the women who worked in Shanghai's textile mills, the most exploited of all Chinese workers. Later, in their mountain stronghold in Jiangxi, they organized women farmers, allowed divorce, and banned arranged marriages and footbinding. But the party was still run by men whose primary task was warfare.

The Guomindang army pursued the Communists into the mountains, building small forts throughout the countryside. Rather than risk direct confrontations, Mao responded with guerrilla warfare. He harassed the army at its weak points with hit-and-run tactics, relying on the terrain and the support of the peasantry. Whereas government troops often mistreated civilians, Mao insisted that his soldiers help the peasants, pay a fair price for food and supplies, and treat women with respect.

In spite of their good relations with the peasants of Jiangxi, the Communists gradually found themselves encircled by government forces. In 1934 Mao and his followers decided to break out of the southern mountains and trek to Shaanxi (SHAWN-she), an even more remote province in northwestern China. The so-called **Long March** took them 6,000 miles (nearly 9,700 kilometers) in one year over desolate mountains and through swamps and deserts, pursued by the army and bombed by Chiang's aircraft. Of the 100,000 Communists who left Jiangxi in October 1934, only 4,000 reached Shaanxi a year later. Chiang's government thought it was finally rid of the Communists.

| The Sino-Japanese War, 1937–1945 | In Japan politicians, senior officers, and business leaders disagreed on how to solve their country's economic problems. Some proposed a quick conquest of China; others advocated war with the Soviet Union. While their superiors |

hesitated, junior officers decided to take matters into their own hands.

On July 7, 1937, Japanese troops attacked Chinese forces near Beijing. The junior officers who ordered the attack quickly obtained the support of their commanders and then, reluctantly, of the government. Within weeks Japanese troops seized Beijing, Tianjin, Shanghai, and other coastal cities, and the Japanese navy blockaded the entire coast of China.

Once again, the United States and the League of Nations denounced the Japanese aggression. Yet the Western powers were too preoccupied with events in Europe and with their own economic problems to risk a military confrontation in Asia. When the Japanese sank a U.S. gunboat and shelled a British ship on the Yangzi River, the U.S. and British governments responded only with righteous indignation and pious resolutions.

The Chinese armies were large and fought bravely, but they were poorly led and armed and lost every battle. Japanese planes bombed cities while soldiers broke dikes and burned villages, killing thousands of civilians. Within a year Japan controlled the coastal provinces of China and the lower Yangzi and Yellow River Valleys, China's richest and most populated regions.

In spite of Japanese organizational and fighting skills, the attack on China did not bring the victory Japan had hoped for. The Chinese people continued to resist, either in the army or with the Communist guerrilla forces. As Japan sank deeper into the Chinese quagmire, life became harsher and more repressive for the Japanese people, as taxes rose, food and fuel became scarce, and more and more young men were drafted.

Warfare between the Chinese and Japanese was incredibly violent. In the winter of 1937–1938 Japanese troops took Nanjing, raped 20,000 women, killed roughly 200,000 prisoners and civilians, and looted and burned the city. To slow them down, Chiang ordered the Yellow River dikes blasted open, causing a flood that destroyed four thousand villages, killed 890,000 people, and made millions homeless. Two years later, when the Communists ordered a massive offensive, the

Japanese retaliated with a "kill all, burn all, loot all" campaign, destroying hundreds of villages down to the last person, building, and farm animal.

The Chinese government, led by Chiang Kai-shek, escaped to the mountains of Sichuan in the center of the country. There Chiang built up a huge army, not to fight Japan but to prepare for a future confrontation with the Communists. The army drafted over 3 million men, even though it had only a million rifles and could not provide food or clothing for all its soldiers. The Guomindang raised farmers' taxes, even when famine forced farmers to eat the bark of trees. Such taxes were not enough to support both a large army and the thousands of government officials and hangers-on who had fled to Sichuan. To avoid taxing its wealthy supporters the government printed money, causing inflation, hoarding, and corruption.

From his capital of Yan'an in Shaanxi province, Mao also built up his army and formed a government. Unlike the Guomindang, the Communists listened to the grievances of the peasants, especially the poor, to whom they distributed land confiscated from wealthy landowners. They imposed rigid discipline on their officials and soldiers and tolerated no dissent or criticism from intellectuals. Though they had few weapons, the Communists obtained support and intelligence from farmers in Japanese-occupied territory. They turned military reversals into propaganda victories, presenting themselves as the only group in China that was serious about fighting the Japanese.

THE SECOND WORLD WAR

Many people feared that the Second World War would be a repetition of the First. Instead, it was much bigger in every way. It was fought around the world, from Norway to New Guinea and from Hawaii to Egypt, and on every ocean. It killed far more people than World War I, involved all civilians and productive forces, and showed how effectively industry, science, and nationalism could be channeled into mass destruction.

The War of Movement   In World War II motorized weapons gave back the advantage to the offensive. Opposing forces moved fast, their victories hinging as much on the aggressive spirit of their commanders and the military intelligence they obtained as on numbers of troops and firepower.

The Wehrmacht (VAIR-mokt), or German army, was the first to learn this lesson. It not only had tanks, trucks, and fighter planes but had also perfected their combined use in a tactic called *Blitzkrieg* (BLITS-creeg) (lightning war): fighter planes scattered enemy troops and disrupted communications, tanks punctured the enemy's defenses, and then, with the help of the infantry, they encircled and captured enemy troops. At sea, both Japan and the United States had developed aircraft carriers that could launch planes against targets hundreds of miles away.

Armies ranged over vast theaters of operation, and countries were conquered in days or weeks. The belligerents mobilized the economies of entire continents, squeezing them for every possible resource. They tried not only to defeat their enemies' armed forces but—by blockades, submarine attacks, and bombing raids—to damage the economies that supported those armed forces. They thought of civilians as legitimate targets and, later, as vermin to be exterminated.

War in Europe and North Africa   It took less than a month for the Wehrmacht to conquer Poland. Britain and France declared war on Germany but took no military action. Meanwhile, the Soviet Union invaded eastern Poland and the Baltic republics. Although the Poles fought bravely, their infantry and cavalry were no match for German and Russian tanks. During the winter of 1939–1940 Germany and the Western democracies faced each other in what soldiers called a "phony war."

In March 1940 Hitler went on the offensive again, conquering Denmark, Norway, the Netherlands, and Belgium in less than two months. In May he attacked France. Although the French army had as many soldiers, tanks, and aircraft as the Wehrmacht, its morale was low and it quickly collapsed. By the end of June Hitler was master of all of Europe between Russia and Spain.

MAP 30.1   World War II in Europe and North Africa

In a series of quick and decisive campaigns from September 1939 to December 1941, German forces overran much of Europe and North Africa. There followed three years of bitter fighting as the Allies slowly pushed the Germans back.

Germany still had to face Britain. The British had no army to speak of, but they had other assets: the English Channel, the Royal Navy and Air Force, and a tough new prime minister, Winston Churchill. The Germans knew they could invade Britain only by gaining control of the airspace over the Channel, so they launched a massive air attack—the Battle of Britain—lasting from June through September. The attack failed because the Royal Air Force used radar and code-breaking to detect approaching German planes.

Frustrated in the west, Hitler turned his attention eastward, even though it meant fighting a two-front war. So far he had gotten the utmost cooperation from Stalin, who supplied Germany with grain, oil, and strategic raw materials. Yet he had always wanted to conquer Lebensraum in the east and enslave the Slavic peoples who lived there, and he feared that if he waited, Stalin would build a dangerously strong army. In June 1941 Hitler launched the largest attack in history, with 3 million soldiers and thousands of planes and tanks. Within five months the Wehrmacht conquered the Baltic states, Ukraine, and half of European Russia, captured a million prisoners of war, and reached the very gates of Moscow and Leningrad. The USSR seemed on the verge of collapse. Then the weather turned cold, machines froze, and the fighting came to a halt. Like Napoleon, Hitler had ignored the environment of Russia to his peril.

The next spring the Wehrmacht renewed its offensive. It surrounded Leningrad in a siege that was to cost a million lives. Leaving Moscow aside, it turned toward the Caucasus and its oil wells. In August the Germans attacked **Stalingrad** (now Volgograd), the key to the Volga River and the supply of oil. For months German and Soviet soldiers fought over every street and every house. When winter came, the Red Army counterattacked and encircled the city. In February 1943 the remnants of the German army in Stalingrad surrendered. Hitler had lost an army of 200,000 men and his last chance of defeating the Soviet Union and of winning the war.

From Europe the war spread to Africa. When France fell in 1940, Mussolini decided that the time had come to realize his imperial ambitions. Italian forces quickly overran British Somaliland, then invaded Egypt. Their victories were ephemeral, however, for when the British counterattacked, Italian resistance crumbled. During 1941 British forces conquered Italian East Africa and invaded Libya as well. The Italian rout in North Africa brought the Germans to their rescue, and during 1942 the German army and the forces of the British Commonwealth seesawed back and forth across the deserts of Libya and Egypt. At **El Alamein** in northern Egypt the British prevailed because they had more weapons and supplies and were better informed about their enemies' plans. The Germans were finally expelled from Africa in May 1943.

War in Asia and the Pacific   The fall of France and the involvement of Britain and the USSR against Germany presented Japan with the opportunity it had been looking for. Suddenly the European colonies in Southeast Asia, with their abundant oil, rubber, and other strategic materials, seemed ripe for the taking. In July 1941, when the French government, then under German control, allowed Japanese forces to occupy Indochina, the United States stopped shipments of steel, scrap iron, oil, and other products that

Japan desperately needed. This left Japan with three alternatives: giving up its conquests, as the Americans insisted; facing economic ruin; or widening the war. Japan chose war.

Admiral Isoroku Yamamoto, commander of the Japanese fleet, told Prime Minister Fumimaro Konoye: "If I am told to fight regardless of the consequences, I shall run wild for the first six months or a year, but I have utterly no confidence for the second or third year.... . I hope that you will endeavor to avoid a Japanese-American war." Ignoring his advice, the war cabinet made plans for a surprise

MAP 30.2 World War II in Asia and the Pacific

Having conquered much of China between 1937 and 1941, Japanese forces launched a sudden attack on Southeast Asia and the Pacific in late 1941 and early 1942. American forces slowly reconquered the Pacific islands and the Philippines. In August 1945, the atomic bombing of Hiroshima and Nagasaki forced Japan's surrender.

attack on the United States Navy, followed by an invasion of Southeast Asia. They knew they could not hope to defeat the United States, but they calculated that the shock of the attack would be so great that isolationist Americans would accept the Japanese conquest of Southeast Asia as readily as they had acquiesced to Hitler's conquests in Europe.

On December 7, 1941, Japanese planes bombed the U.S. naval base at **Pearl Harbor**, sinking or damaging scores of warships but missing the aircraft carriers, which were at sea. Then, in early 1942, the Japanese conquered all of Southeast Asia and the Dutch East Indies. They soon began to confiscate food and raw materials and demand heavy labor from the inhabitants.

Japan's dream of an East Asian empire seemed within reach, for its victories surpassed even Hitler's in Europe. The United States, however, quickly began preparing for war. In April 1942 American planes bombed Tokyo. In May the United States Navy defeated a Japanese fleet in the Coral Sea, ending Japanese plans to conquer Australia. A month later, at the **Battle of Midway**, Japan lost four of its six largest aircraft carriers. Without them, Japan faced a long and hopeless war.

The End of War   After the Battle of Stalingrad the advantage on the Eastern Front shifted to the Soviet Union. By 1943 the Red Army was receiving a growing stream of supplies from factories in Russia and the United States. Slowly at first and then with increasing vigor, it pushed the Wehrmacht back toward Germany.

The Western powers, meanwhile, staged two invasions of Europe. Beginning in July 1943 they captured Sicily and invaded Italy. Italy signed an armistice, but German troops held off the Allied advance for two years. On June 6, 1944—forever after known as D-day—156,000 British, American, and Canadian troops landed on the coast of Normandy in western France—the largest shipborne assault ever staged. Within a week the Allies had more troops in France than Germany did, and by September Germany faced an Allied army of over 2 million men and half a million vehicles.

Although the Red Army was on the eastern border of Germany, ready for the final push, Hitler transferred part of the Wehrmacht westward. Despite overwhelming odds, Germany held out for almost a year, a result of the fighting qualities of its soldiers and the terror inspired by the Nazi regime, which commanded obedience to the end. On May 7, 1945, a week after Hitler committed suicide, German military leaders surrendered.

Japan fought on a while longer because the United States had aimed most of its war effort at Germany. Pacific islands had to be captured by amphibious landings, with high casualty rates on both sides. In June 1944, U.S. bombers began attacking Japan and American submarines sank many Japanese merchant ships, cutting Japan off from its sources of oil and other raw materials. After May 1945, with Japanese fighters grounded for lack of fuel, U.S. planes began destroying Japanese shipping, industries, and cities at will.

Even as their homeland was being pounded, the Japanese still held strong positions in Asia. Despite its name, "Greater East Asian Co-Prosperity Sphere," the Japanese occupation was harsh and brutal. By 1945 Asians were eager to see the Japanese leave, but not to welcome back the Europeans. Instead, they looked forward to independence (see Chapters 29 and 32).

Hiroshima After the Atomic Bomb *On August 6, 1945, an atomic bomb destroyed the city, killing some eighty thousand people. This fire truck, stationed at the Hiroshima Fire Department, is one of the few identifiable objects in the photo. It was located 4,000 feet from ground zero.*

On August 6, 1945, the United States dropped an atomic bomb on **Hiroshima**, killing some 80,000 people in a flash and leaving about 120,000 more to die in agony from burns and radiation. Three days later another atomic bomb destroyed Nagasaki. On August 14 Emperor Hirohito gave the order to lay down arms. Two weeks later Japanese leaders signed the terms of surrender. The war was officially over.

Were these atomic weapons necessary? At the time, Americans believed that the conquest of the Japanese homeland would take more than a year and cost the lives of hundreds of thousands of American soldiers. Although some believed the Japanese were determined to fight to the bitter end, others thought they would surrender if they could retain their emperor. Winston Churchill wrote: "It would be a mistake to suppose that the fate of Japan was settled by the atomic bomb. Her defeat was certain before the first bomb fell."[3]

Collapse of the Guomindang and Communist Victory

The formal Japanese surrender in September 1945 surprised the Guomindang. The United States gave millions of dollars of aid and weapons to the Guomindang, all the while urging "national unity" and a "coalition government" with the Communists. But Chiang used all means available to prepare for a civil war. By late 1945 he had U.S. support, control of China's cities, and an

---

[3]Gar Alperowitz, *Atomic Diplomacy: Hiroshima and Potsdam* (New York: Simon & Schuster, 1965), 176–181 and 236–242.

Henri Cartier-Bresson/Magnum Photos

Sale of Gold in the Last Days of the Guomindang *This picture was taken by famed French photojournalist Henri Cartier-Bresson in Shanghai just before the arrival of the Communist-led People's Liberation Army in 1949. It shows people desperate to buy gold before their Guomindang currency becomes worthless.*

army of 2.7 million, more than twice the size of the Communist forces. But the Guomindang's behavior eroded whatever popular support they had. As they moved into formerly Japanese-held territory, they acted like an occupation force. They taxed the people they "liberated" more heavily than the Japanese had, confiscated supplies, and enriched themselves at the expense of the population. Chiang's government printed money so fast that it soon lost all its value. In the countryside the Guomindang's brutality alienated the peasants.

Meanwhile, the Communists obtained Japanese equipment seized by the Soviets in the last weeks of the war and American weapons brought over by deserting Guomindang soldiers. In Manchuria, where they were strongest, they pushed through a radical land reform program, distributing the properties of wealthy landowners among the poorest peasants. In battles against government forces, the higher morale and popular support they enjoyed outweighed the heavy equipment of the Guomindang, whose soldiers began deserting by the thousands.

By 1949 the Guomindang armies were collapsing everywhere, defeated more by their own greed and ineptness than by the Communists. As the Communists advanced, high-ranking members of the Guomindang fled to Taiwan, protected from the mainland by the U.S. Navy. On October 1, 1949, Mao Zedong announced the founding of the People's Republic of China.

THE CHARACTER OF WARFARE

The war left an enormous death toll. Recent estimates place the figure at close to 60 million deaths, six to eight times more than in World War I. Over half of the dead were civilian victims of massacres, famines, and bombs. The Soviet Union lost between 20 million and 25 million people, more than any other country. China suffered 15 million deaths; Poland lost some 6 million, of whom half were Jewish; the Jewish people lost another 3 million outside Poland. Over 4 million Germans and over 2 million Japanese died. Great Britain lost 400,000 people, and the United States 300,000. In much of the world, families mourned one or more of their members.

Many parts of the world were flooded with refugees. Some 90 million Chinese fled the Japanese advance. In Europe millions fled from the Nazis or the Red Army or were herded back and forth on government orders. Many refugees never returned to their homes.

Belligerents identified not just soldiers but entire peoples as enemies. Some even labeled their own ethnic minorities as "enemies." Another reason for the devastation was the appearance of new technologies that carried destruction deep into enemy territory, far beyond the traditional battlefields. New technologies of warfare and changes in morality formed a lethal combination.

The Science and Technology of War

As fighting spread around the world, the mobilization of manpower and economies and the mobility of the armed forces grew increasingly crucial, while new aspects of war took on a growing importance. Chemists found ways to make synthetic rubber from coal or oil. Physicists perfected radar, which warned of approaching enemy aircraft and submarines. Cryptanalysts broke enemy codes and were able to penetrate secret military communications. Pharmacologists developed antibiotics that saved the lives of wounded soldiers, who in any earlier war would have died of infections. The war also brought new inventions in media technology.

Aircraft development was especially striking. As war approached, German, British, and Japanese aircraft manufacturers developed fast, maneuverable fighter planes. U.S. industry was especially noted for heavy bombers designed to fly in huge formations and drop tons of bombs on enemy cities. Germany responded with radically new designs, including the first jet fighters, low-flying unmanned buzz bombs, and, finally, V-2 missiles against which there was no warning or defense.

Military planners expected scientists to furnish secret weapons that could doom the enemy. In October 1939 President Roosevelt received a letter from physicist Albert Einstein, a Jewish refugee from Nazism, warning of the dangers of nuclear power: "There is no doubt that sub-atomic energy is available all around us, and that one day man will release and control its almost infinite power. We cannot prevent him from doing so and can only hope that he will not use it exclusively in blowing up his next door neighbor." Roosevelt placed the vast resources of the U.S. government at the disposal of physicists and engineers. By 1945 they had built two atomic bombs, each one powerful enough to annihilate an entire city.

U.S. Army Medics and Holocaust Victims *When Allied troops entered the Nazi concentration camps, they found the bodies of thousands of victims of the Holocaust. In Dachau in southern Germany, two U.S. Army medics are overseeing a truckload of corpses to be taken to a burial site.*

Hulton Deutsch Collection/Corbis

Bombing Raids   Since it was very hard to pinpoint individual buildings, especially at night, British air chief marshal Arthur "Bomber" Harris decided that "operations should now be focused on the morale of the enemy civilian population and in particular the industrial workers."

In May 1942, 1,000 British planes dropped incendiary bombs on Cologne, setting fire to the old city. Between July 24 and August 2, 1943, 3,330 British and American planes fire-bombed Hamburg, killing 50,000 people, mostly women and children. Later raids destroyed Berlin, Dresden, and other German cities. The bombing raids against Germany killed 600,000 people—more than half of them women and children—and injured 800,000, but they failed to break the morale of the German people. German armament production continued to increase until late 1944, and the population remained obedient and hard-working. However, bombing raids against oil depots and synthetic fuel plants almost brought the German war effort to a standstill by early 1945.

Japanese cities were also the targets of American bombing raids. As early as April 1942 sixteen planes launched from an aircraft carrier bombed Tokyo. Later, as American forces captured islands close to Japan, the raids intensified. Their effect was even more devastating than the fire-bombing of German cities, for Japanese cities were made mostly of wood. In March 1945 bombs set Tokyo ablaze, killing 80,000 people and leaving a million homeless.

The Holocaust   In World War II, for the first time, more civilians than soldiers were deliberately put to death. The champions in the art of killing defenseless civilians were the Nazis. Their murders were not the accidental byproducts of some military goal but a calculated policy of exterminating whole races of people.

Their first targets were Jews. Soon after Hitler came to power, he deprived German Jews of their citizenship and legal rights. When eastern Europe fell under Nazi rule, the Nazis herded its large Jewish population into ghettos in the major cities, where many died of starvation and disease. Then, in early 1942, the Nazis decided to carry out Hitler's "final solution to the Jewish problem" by applying modern industrial methods to the slaughter of human beings. Thousands of ordinary German citizens supported and aided the genocide. Every day trainloads of cattle cars arrived at the extermination camps in eastern Europe and disgorged thousands of captives and the corpses of those who had died along the way. The strongest survivors were put to work and fed almost nothing until they died. Women, children, the elderly, and the sick were shoved into gas chambers and asphyxiated with poison gas. **Auschwitz**, the biggest camp, was a giant industrial complex designed to kill up to twelve thousand people a day. This mass extermination, now called the **Holocaust** ("burning"), claimed some 6 million Jewish lives.

Besides the Jews, the Nazis also killed 3 million Polish Catholics—especially professionals, army officers, and the educated—in an effort to reduce the Polish people to slavery. They also exterminated homosexuals, Jehovah's Witnesses, Gypsies, the disabled, and the mentally ill—all in the interests of "racial purity." Whenever a German was killed in an occupied country, the Nazis retaliated by burning a village and all its inhabitants. After the invasion of Russia the Wehrmacht was given orders to execute all captured communists, government employees, and officers. They also worked millions of prisoners of war to death or let them die of starvation.

The Home Front in Europe and Asia   In the First World War there had been a clear distinction between the "front" and the "home front." Not so in World War II, where rapid military movements and air power carried the war into people's homes. For the civilian populations of China, Japan, Southeast Asia, and Europe, the war was far more terrifying than their worst nightmares. Armies swept through the land, confiscating food, fuel, and anything else of value. Bombers and heavy artillery pounded cities into rubble, leaving only the skeletons of buildings, while survivors cowered in cellars. Even when a city was not targeted, air-raid sirens awakened people throughout the night. In countries occupied by the Germans, the police arrested civilians, deporting many to die in concentration camps or to work as slave laborers in armaments factories. Millions fled their homes in terror, losing their families and friends. Even in Britain, children and the elderly were sent to live in the countryside.

The war demanded an enormous and sustained effort from all civilians, but more so in some countries than in others. In 1941, the Soviets dismantled over fifteen hundred factories and rebuilt them in the Ural Mountains and Siberia, where they soon turned out more tanks and artillery than the Axis.

Half of the ships afloat in 1939 were sunk during the war, but the Allied losses were more than made up for by American shipyards, while Axis shipping was reduced to nothing by 1945. The production of aircraft, trucks, tanks, and other materiel showed a similar imbalance. Although the Axis powers made strenuous efforts to increase their production, they could not compete with the vast outpouring of Soviet tanks and American materiel.

The Red Army eventually mobilized 22 million men; Soviet women took over half of all industrial and three-quarters of all agricultural jobs. In the other Allied countries, women also played major roles in the war effort, replacing men in fields, factories, and offices. The Nazis, in contrast, believed that German women should stay home and bear children, and they imported 7 million "guest workers"—a euphemism for captured foreigners.

The Home Front in the United States The United States flourished during the war. Safe behind their oceans, Americans felt no bombs, saw no enemy soldiers, had almost no civilian casualties, and suffered fewer military casualties than other countries. The economy went into a prolonged boom after 1940. By 1944 the United States was producing twice as much as all the Axis powers combined. Thanks to huge military orders, jobs were plentiful, bread lines disappeared, and nutrition and health improved. Most Americans saved part of their paychecks, laying the basis for a phenomenal postwar consumer boom. Many Americans later looked back on the conflict as the "good war."

World War II also did much to weaken the hold of traditional ideas, as employers recruited women and members of racial minorities to work in jobs once reserved for white men. Six million women entered the labor force during the war, 2.5 million of them in manufacturing jobs previously considered "men's work." In a book entitled *Shipyard Diary of a Woman Welder* (1944), Augusta Clawson recalled her experiences in a shipyard in Oregon:

> *The job confirmed my strong conviction—I have stated it before—what exhausts the woman welder is not the work, not the heat, nor the demands upon physical strength. It is the apprehension that arises from inadequate skill and consequent lack of confidence; and this can be overcome by the right kind of training. . . . And so, in spite of the discomforts of climbing, heavy equipment, and heat, I enjoyed the work today because I could do it.*[4]

Many men opposed women doing work that would take them away from their families. As the labor shortage got worse, however, employers and politicians grudgingly admitted that the government ought to help provide day care for the children of working mothers. The entry of women into the labor force proved to be one of the most significant consequences of the war.

---

[4]Rosalyn Fraad Baxandall, Linda Gordon, and Susan Reverby, eds., *America's Working Women* (New York: Random House, 1976), 253.

The war loosened racial bonds as well. Seeking work in war industries, 1.2 million African Americans migrated to the north and west. In the southwest Mexican immigrants took jobs in agriculture and war industries. But no new housing was built to accommodate the influx of migrants to the industrial cities, and many suffered from overcrowding and discrimination. In addition, 112,000 Japanese Americans living on the west coast of the United States were arrested and herded into remote interior internment camps until the war was over, ostensibly for fear of spying and sabotage, but actually because of their race.

War and the Environment   During the depression, construction and industry had slowed to a crawl, reducing environmental stress. The war reversed this trend, sharply accelerating pressures on the environment.

One reason for the change was the fighting itself. Battles scarred the landscape, leaving behind spent ammunition and damaged equipment. Retreating armies flooded large areas of China and the Netherlands. The bombing of cities left ruins that remained visible for a generation or more.

The main cause of environmental stress, however, was not the fighting but the economic development that sustained it. The war's half-million aircraft required thousands of air bases, many of them in the Pacific, China, Africa, and other parts of the world that had seldom seen an airplane before. Barracks, shipyards, docks, warehouses, and other military construction sprouted on every continent.

As war industries boomed, so did the demand for raw materials. Mining companies opened new mines and towns in Africa to supply strategic minerals. Latin American countries deprived of manufactured imports began building their own steel mills, factories, and shipyards. In India, China, and Europe, timber felling accelerated far beyond the reproduction rate of trees, replacing forests with denuded land. In a few instances, however, the war was good for the environment. For example, submarine warfare made fishing and whaling so dangerous that fish and whale populations had a few years in which to increase.

CONCLUSION

After the Great War ended, the world seemed to return to its prewar state, but it was an illusion. In the Soviet Union, Joseph Stalin was determined to turn his country into a modern industrial state at breakneck speed, regardless of the human cost. Several million people—most of them peasants—died, and millions more were enslaved during the Five-Year Plans and the collectivization of agriculture. By 1941 the USSR was much better prepared for a war with Germany than Russia had been in 1914–1917.

In 1929, after a few years of prosperity, the New York stock market collapsed. Within a few months, the world economy fell into the Great Depression, throwing millions out of work throughout the world. France and Britain survived the depression by making their colonial empires purchase their products. Countries that were dependent on exports, such as Germany and Japan, suffered more until they turned their economies toward arms production. Only the USSR and southern Africa boomed during the 1930s.

In Italy, Mussolini installed Fascist Party members in all government jobs and jailed anyone who criticized him. In Germany, economic collapse led people to entrust their government to Adolf Hitler and his Nazi followers, who quickly set to work establishing a totalitarian government. Nazi Germany's rebuilding of its military and its invasion of Austria and Czechoslovakia were greeted with a policy of appeasement by Western democracies, until finally they could no longer overlook Germany's intentions.

Hard hit by the depression, Japan saw China as a potential colony with resources to help solve its economic problems. In 1931, Japan conquered Manchuria. The United States and the League of Nations protested but did little else. Starting in 1937, a long and brutal war with China became a drain on the Japanese economy and resources. Meanwhile, the Communists, led by Mao Zedong, were slowly gaining support in the Chinese countryside.

The war spread to Europe in 1939 when Germany conquered Poland, then Denmark, Norway, the low countries, and France in 1940. The war turned global in 1941 when Germany invaded the Soviet Union and Japan attacked the United States. In 1943, the Red Army began to push the Germans back. Beginning in June 1944, Anglo-American forces, backed by the overwhelming industrial resources of the United States, drove German forces back from the west. U.S. naval victories in the Pacific and atomic weapons defeated Japan and ended the war in 1945.

The Second World War was by far the deadliest in history. Modern mechanized forces swept across entire nations and oceans. Their targets were not only each other's armed forces, but their civilian populations as well. Though Germany had considerable scientific and technical talent, the war favored the nations with the most heavy industries, namely, the United States and the Soviet Union. The Allies destroyed German and Japanese cities with fire-bombs, and the United States dropped atomic bombs on Hiroshima and Nagasaki. Of the roughly 60 million people who died in the war, most were civilians.

IMPORTANT EVENTS 1920s–1949	
1928	Stalin introduces Five Year Plans and the collectivization of agriculture
1929	Great Depression begins in United States
1931	Great Depression reaches Europe
1931	Japanese forces occupy Manchuria
1933	Hitler comes to power in Germany
1934–1935	Mao leads Communists on Long March
1936	Hitler invades the Rhineland
1937	Japanese troops invade China, conquer coastal provinces; Chiang Kai-shek flees to Sichuan
1937–1938	Japanese troops take Nanjing
1939 (Sept. 1)	German forces invade Poland

1940 (March–April)	German forces conquer Denmark, Norway, the Netherlands, and Belgium
1940 (May–June)	German forces conquer France
1940 (June–Sept.)	Battle of Britain
1941 (June 21)	German forces invade USSR
1941 (Dec. 7)	Japanese aircraft bomb Pearl Harbor
1942 (Jan.–March)	Japanese conquer Thailand, Philippines, and Malaya
1942 (June)	United States Navy defeats Japan at Battle of Midway
1942–1943	Allies and Germany battle for control of North Africa
1943	Soviet victory in Battle of Stalingrad
1943–1944	Red Army slowly pushes Wehrmacht back to Germany
1944 (June 6)	D-day: U.S., British, and Canadian troops land in Normandy
1945 (May 7)	Germany surrenders
1945 (Aug. 6)	United States drops atomic bomb on Hiroshima
1945 (Aug. 14)	Japan surrenders
1945–1949	Civil war in China
1949 (Oct. 1)	Communist defeat Guomindang; Mao proclaims People's Republic

Famines and Politics

Human history is filled with tales of famines—times when crops failed, food supplies ran out, and people starved.

Natural Famines

India, dependent on the monsoon rains, has been particularly prone to such calamities, with famines striking two to four times a century, whenever the rains fail for several years in succession. Three times in the eighteenth century famines killed several million people. The nineteenth century was worse, with famines in 1803–1804, 1837–1838, 1868–1870, and 1876–1878. The famine of 1876–1878 also afflicted northern China, causing between 9 and 13 million deaths from hunger and from the diseases of malnutrition. There were even incidents of cannibalism, as starving adults ate starving children.

When drought hit a region, it decimated not only the human population but also the animals they relied on to transport crops or plow the land. When water levels dropped in rivers and canals, food could not be transported by boat to areas where people were starving.

Commercial Famines

That all changed in the nineteenth century. Railroads and steamships could transport foodstuffs quickly across great distances, regardless of the weather. Great Britain, for example, became dependent on imports of wheat and beef. Yet the global death toll from starvation has been far higher since the mid-nineteenth century than ever before. Why?

Consider Ireland. By the early nineteenth century the potato had become the main source of nutrition for the Irish people. Potatoes grew abundantly and produced more calories per acre than any other crop, allowing the population to increase dramatically.

In 1845 a blight turned the potatoes in the fields black, mushy, and inedible. The harvest was ruined the following year as well. It recovered slightly in 1847 but was bad again in 1848. Tens of thousands died of starvation, while hundreds of thousands died from dysentery, typhus, or cholera. Travelers saw corpses rotting in their hovels or on the sides of roads. Altogether, a million or more people died, while another million emigrated, reducing the population of Ireland by half.

Throughout those years, Ireland exported wheat to England, where people had money to pay for it. Food cost money, and the Irish, poor even before the famines, were destitute and could not afford to buy wheat or bread. The British government was convinced that interfering with the free market would only make things worse. Relief efforts were half-hearted at best; the official responsible for Irish affairs preferred to leave the situation to "the operation of natural causes."

The same held true in India, like Ireland a colony of Great Britain. The drought of 1876–1878 killed over 5 million Indians in the Deccan region, while British officials stood by helpless or indifferent. Part of the problem was transportation. In the 1870s most goods were still transported in bullock carts, but the bullocks starved during the drought. Another obstacle was political. The idea that a government should be responsible for feeding the population was unthinkable at the time. And so, while millions were starving in the Deccan, the Punjab was exporting wheat to Britain.

Over the next twenty years, so-called famine railways were built in the regions historically most affected by the failures of the monsoon. When drought struck again at the end of the century, the railways were ready to transport food to areas that had previously been accessible only by bullock carts. However, the inhabitants of the affected regions had no money with which to buy what little food there was, and the government was still reluctant to interfere with free enterprise. Grain merchants bought all the stocks, hoarded them until the price rose, then used the railways to transport them out of the famine regions to regions where the harvests were better and people had more money.

In the twentieth century, commercial famines became rare as governments realized that they had a responsibility to provide food not only for their own people but also for people in other countries. Yet commercial famines have not entirely disappeared. In 1974, when a catastrophic flood covered half of Bangladesh, the government was too disorganized to distribute its stocks of rice, while merchants bought what they could and exported it to India. Thousands died, and thousands more survived only because of belated shipments of food from donor countries.

Political Famines

To say that governments are responsible for food supplies does not mean that they exercise that responsibility for the good of the people. Some do, but in many instances food is used as a weapon. In the twentieth century, global food supplies were always adequate for the population of the world, and transportation was seldom a problem. Yet the century witnessed the most murderous famines ever recorded.

As commercial famines declined, war famines became common. The destruction or requisitioning of crops caused famines in the Russian civil war of 1921–1922, the Japanese occupation of Indochina in 1942–1945, and the Biafran war in Nigeria in 1967–1969.

In 1942 the Japanese army had conquered Burma, a rich rice-producing colony. Food supplies in Bengal, which imported rice from Burma, dropped by 5 percent. As prices began to rise, merchants bought stocks of rice and held them in the hope that prices would continue to increase. Sharecroppers sold their stocks to pay off their debts to landlords and village moneylenders. Meanwhile, the railroads that in peacetime would have carried food from other parts of India were fully occupied with military traffic. By the time Viceroy Lord Wavell ordered the army to transport food to Bengal in October 1943, between 1.5 and 2 million Bengalis had died.

Worst of all were the famines caused by deliberate government policies. The most famous was the famine of 1932–1933 caused by Stalin's collectivization of agriculture. The Communists tried to force the peasants to give up their land and livestock and join collectives, where they could be made to work harder and provide food for the growing cities and industries. When the peasants resisted, their crops were seized. Millions were sent to prison camps, and millions of others died of starvation.

An even worse famine took place in China from 1958 to 1961 during the "Great Leap Forward" (see Chapter 32). Communist Party Chairman Mao Zedong decided to hasten the transformation of China into a communist state by relying not on the expertise of economists and technocrats but on the enthusiasm of the masses. Farms were consolidated into huge communes. Peasants were told to make steel out of household utensils in backyard furnaces. The harvest of 1959 was poor, and later ones were even worse. The amount of grain per person declined from 452 pounds (205 kilograms) in 1957 to 340 pounds (154 kilograms) in 1961. Since the Central Statistical Bureau had been shut down, the central government was unaware of the shortages and demanded ever higher requisitions of food to feed the army and urban and industrial workers and to export to the Soviet Union to pay off China's debts. The amount of food left to the farmers was between one-fifth and one-half of their usual subsistence diet. From 1958 to 1961 between 20 and 30 million Chinese are estimated to have starved or died of the diseases of malnutrition. It was the worst famine in the history of the world. Mao denied its existence.

Nothing quite as horrible has happened since the Great Leap Forward. During the droughts in Africa in the 1970s and 1980s, most people in the affected regions received international food aid. However, to crush rebellions, the governments of Ethiopia and Sudan denied that their people were hungry and prevented food shipments from reaching drought victims.

In the world today, natural disasters are as frequent as ever, and many countries are vulnerable to food shortages. No one now claims that governments have no business providing food to the starving. Though food is not equitably distributed, there is enough for all human beings now, and there will be enough for the foreseeable future. However, humanitarian feelings compete with other political agendas, and the specter of politically motivated famines still stalks the world.

PART EIGHT

PERILS AND PROMISES OF A GLOBAL COMMUNITY, 1945 TO THE PRESENT

CHAPTER 31
The Cold War and Decolonization, 1945–1975

CHAPTER 32
The End of the Cold War and the Challenge of Economic Development and Immigration, 1975–2000

CHAPTER 33
New Challenges in a New Millennium

After World War II an increasingly interconnected world faced new hopes and fears. The United Nations promoted peace, international cooperation, and human rights. Colonized peoples gained independence, and global trade expanded. At the same time the United States and the Soviet Union, victorious former Allies in the war against the Axis, mobilized every resource in a global contest for economic and political influence. This "Cold War" led to nuclear stalemate as well as a new round of warfare, dispelling dreams of world peace. Wars in Korea and Vietnam, as well as proxy conflicts from Nicaragua to Afghanistan, pitted the United States against communist regimes. Following the Cold War, nuclear proliferation and terrorism became top concerns. The 9/11 attacks by Muslim extremists on the World Trade Center and the Pentagon triggered an American-led "global war on terrorism." The ensuing invasions of Afghanistan and Iraq made the Middle East a top danger spot.

The industrialized nations, including Germany and Japan, recovered quickly from World War II. Elsewhere economic development came slowly, except in a handful of countries: South Korea, Taiwan, Brazil, Argentina, and, after 2000, China and India. In Africa and other poor regions, population growth usually offset economic gains.

Although the Green Revolution of the 1960s and the fruits of genetic engineering thirty years later alleviated much world hunger, industrial growth and automobile use increased pollution and competition for petroleum supplies. Global warming became an international concern, along with overfishing, deforestation, and endangerment of wild species.

Globalization affected culture as well. Transnational corporations selling uniform products threatened localized economic enterprises, and Western popular culture aroused fears of cultural imperialism, fear offset in part by the rise of Asian economic powers. The Internet and the emergence of English as the global language improved international communication but also stimulated fears that cultural diversity could be lost.

31

THE COLD WAR AND
DECOLONIZATION, 1945–1975

O
n January 1, 1959, the thirty-two-year-old Fidel Castro entered Havana, Cuba, after having successfully defeated the dictatorship of Fulgencio Batista (ful-HEHN-see-oh bah-TEES-tah). Castro had initiated his revolution in 1953 with an attack on a military barracks, but the attack failed. At his trial, Castro put on a spirited defense that he later published as *History Will Absolve Me*. He proclaimed his objectives as the restoration of Cuban democracy and an ambitious program of social and economic reforms designed to ameliorate the effects of underdevelopment.

On September 26, 1960, Castro addressed the United Nations General Assembly. Relations between the Castro government and the United States were already heading toward confrontation as a result of Castro's policies. In his speech, Castro offered a broad internationalist and anti-imperialist criticism of the world's developed nations and of the United Nations. He criticized the role of the United Nations in the Congo, suggesting that it had supported Colonel Mobutu Sese Seko, a client of imperialism, rather than Patrice Lumumba, identified by the United States as a dangerous radical. He also strongly supported the independence struggle of the Algerians against the French.

In this speech, Castro outlined an ambitious program of new revolutionary reforms in Cuba, claiming that the United States had supported the Batista dictatorship to protect American investors. Once back in Cuba, Castro pressed ahead with economic reforms that included concentrating power in the hands of his closest allies and nationalizing most American investments. Cuba became a flash point in the Cold War when the United States tried and failed to overthrow Castro in 1961. Castro declared himself to be a socialist and forged an economic and military alliance with the Soviet Union that led in 1962 to the Cuban missile crisis.

The intensity of the Cold War, with its accompanying threat of nuclear destruction, obscured a postwar phenomenon of more enduring importance. The colonial empires were overthrown, and Western power and influence declined in Asia, Africa, and Latin America. The leaders who headed these new nations were sometimes able to use Cold War antagonisms to their own advantage when they sought economic or military assistance. Some, like Castro, became frontline participants in this struggle, but most focused on nation building.

Each former colony had its own history and followed its own route to independence. Thus these new nations had difficulty finding a collective voice in a world increasingly oriented toward two superpowers, the United States and the Soviet Union. Some former colonies sided openly with one or the other, while others banded together in a posture of neutrality. All spoke with one voice about their need for economic and technical assistance and the obligation of the wealthy nations to satisfy those needs.

The Cold War military rivalry led to extraordinary advances in weaponry and associated technologies, but many new nations faced basic problems of educating their citizens, nurturing industry, and escaping the economic constraints imposed by their former imperialist masters. The environment suffered severe pressures from oil exploration and transport to support the growing economies of the wealthy nations and from deforestation and urbanization in poor regions. Neither rich nor poor nations fully anticipated the ultimate costs that would be associated with these environmental changes.

THE COLD WAR

For more than a century, political and economic leaders in the industrialized West had viewed socialism as a threat to free markets and private property. The Russian Revolution as well as the destabilizing economic effects of the Great Depression heightened these fears. The wartime alliance between the United States, Great Britain, and the Soviet Union had therefore succeeded despite these antagonisms and fears. With the defeat of Germany, however, growing Soviet assertiveness in Europe and communist insurgencies in China and elsewhere confirmed to Western leaders the threat of worldwide revolution.

Western leaders identified the Soviet Union as the sponsor of world revolution and as a military power capable of launching a war as destructive and terrible as the one recently ended. As early as 1946 Great Britain's wartime leader, Winston Churchill, said in a speech in Missouri, "From Stettin in the Baltic to Trieste in the Adriatic, an iron curtain has descended across the Continent.... I am convinced there is nothing they [the communists] so much admire as strength, and there is nothing for which they have less respect than weakness, especially military weakness." The phrase "**iron curtain**" became a watchword of the **Cold War**, the state of political tension and military rivalry then beginning between the United States and its allies and the Soviet Union and its allies.

Each side viewed every action by its rival a direct threat. Fearful of growing Soviet power, the United States and the nations of western Europe established a military alliance in 1949, the **North Atlantic Treaty Organization (NATO)**. Soviet leaders, struggling to recover from the terrible losses sustained in the war against the Axis, responded by creating their own military alliance, the **Warsaw Pact**, in 1955. The distrust and suspicion of the two alliances would now play out on a worldwide stage.

The United Nations   In 1944 representatives from the United States, Great Britain, the Soviet Union, and China drafted proposals that led to a treaty called the United Nations Charter, ratified on October 24, 1945.

Like the earlier League of Nations, the **United Nations** had two main bodies: the General Assembly, with representatives from all member states; and the Security Council, with five permanent members—China (the anticommunist Chinese government based in Taiwan until 1971), France, Great Britain, the United States, and the Soviet Union—and seven rotating members. A full-time bureaucracy headed by a Secretary General carried out the organization's day-to-day business and directed agencies focused on specialized international problems—for example, UNICEF (United Nations Children's Emergency Fund), FAO (Food and Agriculture Organization), and UNESCO (United Nations Educational, Scientific and Cultural Organization) (see Environment and Technology: The Green Revolution). Unlike the League of Nations, which required unanimous agreement in both deliberative bodies, the United Nations operated by majority vote, except that the five permanent members of the Security Council had veto power in that chamber.

All signatories to the United Nations Charter renounced war and territorial conquest. Nevertheless, peacekeeping, the sole preserve of the Security Council, became a vexing problem as permanent members exercised their vetoes to protect their allies and interests. Throughout the Cold War the United Nations was seldom able to forestall or quell international conflicts, though from time to time it sent observers or peacekeeping forces to monitor truces or other international agreements.

The decolonization of Africa and Asia greatly swelled the size of the General Assembly but not the Security Council. Many newly independent countries looked to the United Nations for material assistance and access to a wider political world. While the rivalry of the Security Council's permanent members stymied actions that even indirectly touched on Cold War concerns, the General Assembly became an arena for debates over issues like decolonization and development.

In the early years of the United Nations, General Assembly resolutions carried great weight. An example is a 1947 resolution that sought to divide Palestine into sovereign Jewish and Arab states. Gradually, though, the flood of new members produced a voting majority concerned more with poverty, racial discrimination, and the struggle against imperialism than with the Cold War. As a result, Western powers increasingly disregarded the General Assembly, allowing new countries to have their say but effectively preventing any collective action contrary to their interests.

Capitalism and Communism In July 1944, with Allied victory inevitable, economic specialists representing over forty countries met at Bretton Woods, a New Hampshire resort, to devise a new international monetary system. The signatories eventually agreed to fix exchange rates and to create the International Monetary Fund (IMF) and World Bank. The IMF used currency reserves from member nations to finance temporary trade deficits, while the **World Bank** provided funds for reconstructing Europe and helping needy countries after the war.

The Soviet Union attended the Bretton Woods Conference and signed the agreements that went into effect in 1946. But growing hostility between the Soviet Union and the United States and Britain undermined cooperation. While the United States held reserves of gold and the rest of the world held reserves of dollars to maintain the stability of the monetary system, the Soviet Union established a closed monetary system for itself and for allied communist regimes in eastern Europe. In Western countries, supply and demand determined production priorities and prices; in the Soviet command economy, government agencies allocated resources, labor, and goods and even set prices according to governmental priorities, irrespective of market forces.

Many leaders of newly independent states, having won their nation's independence from European colonial powers, preferred the Soviet Union's socialist example to the capitalism of their former masters. Thus, the relative success of economies patterned on Eastern or Western models became part of the Cold War argument. Each side trumpeted economic successes measured by industrial output, changes in per capita income, and productivity gains.

During World War II the U.S. economy escaped the lingering effects of the Great Depression (see Chapter 30) as increased military spending and the military draft raised employment and wages. During the war, U.S. factories were converted from the production of consumer goods to weapons. With peace, the pent-up demand for consumer goods led to a period of rapid economic growth and prosperity. Europe, still rebuilding from the destruction of the war, at first lagged behind.

World War II had heavily damaged the economy of western Europe. Bombs had flattened cities and destroyed railroads, port facilities, and communication networks. Populations had lost their savings and struggled to find employment. Seeking to forestall the radicalization of European politics and the potential expansion of Soviet influence, the United States decided to financially support the reconstruction of Europe. The **Marshall Plan** and other aid programs provided more than $20 billion to Europe by 1961 (about $155 billion in 2013). European determination backed by American aid spurred recovery, and by 1963 the resurgent European economies had doubled their total 1940 output.

Given that public funds played a significant role in this process, recovering western European governments sought a greater role in economic management than was common in the United States. In Great Britain, for example, the Labour Party government of the early 1950s nationalized coal, steel, railroads, and health care. Similarly, the French government nationalized public utilities; the auto, banking, and insurance industries; and parts of the mining industry. These steps provided large infusions of capital for rebuilding and acquiring new technologies and enhanced economic planning.

In 1948 European nations initiated a process of economic cooperation and integration with the creation of the Organisation for European Economic Co-operation (OEEC). They began by cooperating on coal and steel production. Located in disputed border areas, these industries had previously been flash points that led to war. With success in these areas, some OEEC countries lowered tariffs to encourage trade. Then in 1957 France, West Germany, Italy, the Netherlands, Belgium, and Luxembourg signed a treaty creating the **European Economic Community**, also known as the **Common Market**. By the 1970s this economic alliance had nearly overtaken the United States in industrial production. Then between 1973 and 1995, Great Britain, Denmark, Greece, Ireland, Spain, Portugal, Finland, Sweden, and Austria joined the alliance, renamed the European Union (EU) in 1993 to reflect growing political integration.

ENVIRONMENT + TECHNOLOGY

The Green Revolution

Concern about world food supplies appeared with the serious shortages caused by the devastation and trade disruptions of World War II. Feeding the world's fast-growing population also provided an immediate challenge to long-established agricultural practices. The Food and Agriculture Organization of the United Nations, the Rockefeller Foundation, and the Ford Foundation took leading roles in fostering crop research and agricultural education. In 1966 the International Rice Research Institute (established in 1960–1962) began distributing seeds for an improved rice variety known as IR-8. Crop yields from this and other new varieties, along with improved farming techniques, were initially so impressive, especially in Asia, that a hoped-for new era in agriculture was called the Green Revolution.

After the successful introduction of new rice strains, scientists developed new varieties of corn and wheat. Building on twenty years of Rockefeller-funded research in Mexico, the Centro Internacional de Mejoramiento de Maíz y Trigo (International Center for the Improvement of Maize and Wheat) was established in 1966. This organization distributed new varieties of wheat that were resistant to disease and responsive to fertilizer. By 1970 other centers for research on tropical agriculture were established.

Despite these advances, experts believed that the success of the Green Revolution required a more comprehensive effort that would mobilize government, foundation, and private-sector resources. The Consultative Group on International Agricultural Research brought together World Bank expertise, private foundations, international organizations, and national foreign aid agencies to undertake worldwide support of efforts to increase food productivity and improve natural resource management. Soon 25 percent of U.S. development assistance and 30 percent of World Bank lending went to agriculture. The combination of innovation and investment led to approximately 2 percent per year in increased productivity in the 1970s.

Early optimism about these innovations is now muted. Although crop yields often improved as a result of new seeds, improved fertilizers, and irrigation, these improvements were too expensive for poor farmers to employ. While both Asian and Latin American agriculture became much more productive, small farmers were often sacrificed. Africa was little affected by these changes, and only today, as Africa faces deepening cycles of famine, is an

The resulting prosperity brought dramatic changes to the societies of western Europe. Wages increased and social welfare benefits expanded. Governments increased spending on health care, unemployment benefits, old-age pensions, public housing, and grants to poor families, with richer nations like Germany subsidizing the mounting prosperity of poorer nations like Ireland, Spain, Portugal, and Greece. The combination of economic growth and income redistribution raised living standards and fueled demand for consumer goods, leading to the development of a mass consumer society. These benefits would be threatened by the growing health-care and retirement needs of Europe's rapidly aging populations after 2000 (see Chapter 32).

international effort under way to introduce reforms. Where the Green Revolution's innovations have been the most successful, dependence on patented, costly seed varieties, chemical fertilizers, and irrigation has promoted agricultural consolidation and rewarded large investors. This has meant in practice that, as agricultural production has risen, land has been increasingly concentrated in the hands of the rich and the rural poor have been forced to become laborers or migrate to cities.

Miracle Rice *New strains of so-called miracle rice made many nations in South and Southeast Asia self-sufficient in food production. Genetically altered rice is now planted in the Ivory Coast and other African nations.*

The Soviet experience was dramatically different. The rapid growth of the Soviet state after 1917 had challenged traditional Western assumptions about economic development and social policy. From the 1920s the Soviet state relied on bureaucratic agencies and political processes to determine the production, distribution, and price of goods. The government regulated and administered nearly every area of the society, including housing, medical services, retail shops, factories, and the land. Despite many problems, the Soviet state achieved a dramatic expansion in basic industrial production.

As in western Europe, the economies of the Soviet Union and its eastern European allies were devastated at the end of the Second World War, but they took a different path to reconstruction. The Soviet command economy had enormous natural resources, a large population, and abundant energy at its disposal. It also benefited from the state's large investments in technical and scientific education and heavy industries during the 1930s and war years.

As a result, recovery was rapid at first, creating the structural basis for modernization and growth. However, as industrial production throughout the world refocused on consumer goods such as television sets and automobiles rather than coal and steel, the inefficiencies of bureaucratic control became obvious. By the 1970s the economic gap with the West had widened. Soviet industry failed to meet domestic demand for clothing, housing, food, automobiles, and consumer electronics, while Soviet agricultural production failed to meet even domestic needs. More significant still, the Soviet Union fell behind the West in civilian sector technological innovation.

West Versus East in Europe and Korea   In Germany, Austria, and Japan, the end of the war meant foreign military occupation and governments controlled by the victors. The Soviet Union initially seemed willing to accept governments in neighboring states that included a mix of parties as long as they were not hostile to local communist groups or to the Soviets. In the nations of central and eastern Europe, many remembered the Soviets as enemies of the fascists and were eager to support local communist parties. As relations between the Soviets and the West worsened in the late 1940s, communists gained a series of political victories across eastern Europe. Western leaders saw the emergence of communist regimes in Poland, Czechoslovakia, Hungary, Bulgaria, Romania, Yugoslavia, and Albania as a sign of growing Soviet aggressiveness.

By 1948 the United States viewed the Soviet Union as an adversary and threat. While the United States had seemed amenable to the Soviet desire for access to the Mediterranean through the Bosporus and Dardanelles straits at war's end, by 1947 it acted to strengthen Turkey and Greece to resist Soviet military pressure and local communist subversion. This decision to hold the line against further Soviet expansion led to the admission of Turkey and Greece to NATO and to the decision to allow West Germany to rearm. The Soviets created the Warsaw Pact in 1955 as a strategic counterweight to NATO.

Increased hostility did not lead to a direct military confrontation between the two powerful alliances. But the Soviet Union did test Western resolve, first by blockading the British, French, and American zones of Berlin (located in Soviet-controlled East Germany) in 1947–1948 and then in 1961 by building the Berlin Wall to prevent East Germans from fleeing to West Berlin.

In turn, the West tested the East by encouraging divisions within the Warsaw Pact. This policy contributed to an armed anti-Soviet revolt in Hungary that Soviet troops crushed in 1956. Then, in 1968, Soviet troops repressed a peaceful democratic reform effort in Czechoslovakia, making clear that, like the West, it would defend its sphere of influence. By failing to support either of these challenges to Soviet control, the West effectively accepted the political and ideological boundaries established by the Cold War. In 1968 Leonid Brezhnev, general secretary of the Soviet Union (1964–1982), asserted that all communist countries would be defended if they "fell to 'bourgeois forces,'" meaning, in effect, that any country in

MAP 31.1   Cold War Confrontation

A polar projection is shown on this map because Soviet and U.S. strategists planned to attack one another by missile in the polar region; hence the Canadian-American radar lines.

communist eastern Europe would be invaded if it decided to embrace western-style democracy and capitalism.

By the end of the Second World War, Soviet troops controlled the Korean peninsula north of the thirty-eighth parallel, while American troops controlled the south. When these two powers could not reach an agreement to hold countrywide elections, a communist North Korea and a noncommunist South Korea emerged as independent states in 1948. Two years later North Korea invaded South Korea. The United Nations Security Council, in the absence of the Soviet delegation, condemned the invasion and called on its members to come to the defense of South Korea. In the ensuing **Korean War**, which lasted until 1953, the United States was the primary military ally of South Korea. Victories by American and South Korean forces forced North Korean forces north until the People's Republic of China entered the war in support of North Korea's communist regime.

Because the United States feared that launching attacks into China might prompt China's ally, the Soviet Union, to retaliate, the conflict remained limited to the Korean peninsula. When the contending armies eventually reached a stalemate along the thirty-eighth parallel, the two sides agreed to a truce but could not agree to a formal peace treaty. As a result, fear of renewed warfare between the two Koreas has lingered until the present.

The United States and Vietnam

The most important postwar communist movement arose in French Indochina in Southeast Asia. The Vietnamese leader Ho Chi Minh (hoe chee min) (1890–1969) had spent several years in France during World War I and helped form the French Communist Party. In 1930, after training in Moscow, he returned to Vietnam to found the Indochina Communist Party. Forced to take refuge in China during World War II, Ho cooperated with the United States while Japan controlled Vietnam.

At war's end the French government was determined to keep its colonial possessions. Ho Chi Minh's nationalist coalition, called the Viet Minh, fought the French with help from the People's Republic of China. After a brutal struggle, the French stronghold of Dienbienphu (dee-yen-bee-yen-FOO) fell in 1954, marking the end of France's colonial enterprise. Ho's Viet Minh government took over in the north, and a noncommunist nationalist government ruled in the south.

Under President Dwight D. Eisenhower (1953–1961), the United States provided limited support to the French but ultimately decided not to prop up French

The Vietnamese People at War

American and South Vietnamese troops burned many villages to deprive the enemy of civilian refuges. This policy undermined support for the South Vietnamese government in the countryside.

Dana Stone/Black Star

colonial rule in Vietnam, perceiving that the European colonial empires were doomed (see Chapter 32). After winning independence, communist North Vietnam supported a communist guerrilla movement—the Viet Cong—against the noncommunist government of South Vietnam. At issue was the ideological and economic orientation of an independent Vietnam.

As President John F. Kennedy (served 1961–1963) changed American policy to support the South Vietnamese government of President Ngo Dinh Diem (dee-YEM), North Vietnam committed its military forces more directly to the war with support from the Soviet Union and the Republic of China. Although he knew that the Diem government was corrupt and unpopular, Kennedy feared that a communist victory would encourage communist movements throughout Southeast Asia and alter the Cold War balance of power. He therefore significantly increased the number of American military advisers and also encouraged South Vietnamese military officers to overthrow their government. After Diem was overthrown and assassinated in early November 1963, American military involvement grew. On November 22, 1963, the unrelated assassination of President Kennedy in Dallas, Texas, elevated Lyndon B. Johnson (served 1963–1969) to the American presidency. He gained congressional support for an unlimited U.S. military deployment that eventually reached 500,000 troops. Because South Vietnam's new rulers proved to be as corrupt and unpopular as the earlier Diem government, many South Vietnamese supported the Viet Cong and Hanoi's drive for national reunification. Despite battlefield success in the **Vietnam War**, the United States failed to achieve a comprehensive victory. In the massive 1968 Tet Offensive, the Viet Cong guerrillas and their North Vietnamese allies gained significant military credibility while suffering significant losses. With a clear victory now unlikely, the antiwar movement in the United States grew in strength (see below).

In 1973 a treaty between North Vietnam and the United States ended U.S. involvement in the war and promised future elections. Two years later, in violation of the treaty, Viet Cong and North Vietnamese troops overran the South Vietnamese army and captured the southern capital of Saigon, renaming it Ho Chi Minh City. They then united the two Vietnams in a single state ruled from the north. Over a million Vietnamese and 58,000 Americans had died during the war. As the victors imposed a new economic and political order, hundreds of thousands of refugees from South Vietnam left for the United States and other Western nations.

While the United States had rationalized its military involvement in South Vietnam as part of its global confrontation with communism, the communist-led government of a newly reunited Vietnam soon found itself at war with its communist neighbors, rather than with U.S. allies in the region. In 1975 communist revolutionaries (the Khmer Rouge) gained power in Cambodia, Vietnam's western neighbor. Not only did this brutal regime led by Pol Pot execute more than 1 million of their fellow citizens, but they also provoked a war with the communist government of Vietnam in 1978. A Vietnamese force of more than 150,000 defeated the Khmer Rouge and set up an occupation government that lasted a decade. During this occupation, the Vietnamese found themselves facing a resilient guerrilla force that eventually compelled them to withdraw. The Vietnamese invasion of Cambodia also led the Vietnamese into a two-month-long war with the Republic of China, which favored the Cambodians.

President Johnson began his administration committed to a broad program of social reforms and civil rights initiatives, called the Great Society, and was instrumental in passing major civil rights legislation that responded to the heroic campaign for voting rights and integration led by Martin Luther King, Jr. As the commitment of U.S. troops in Vietnam grew, a massive antiwar movement applied the tactics of the civil rights movement to end the war. Growing economic problems and a rising tide of antiwar rallies, soon international in character, undermined support for Johnson, who declined to seek reelection.

The Race for Nuclear Supremacy   The terrible devastation of Hiroshima and Nagasaki by atomic weapons (see Chapter 30) framed the strategic decisions in the Korean and Vietnamese Wars. The Soviet Union had exploded its first nuclear device in 1949. The United States claimed a new advantage when it exploded a more powerful hydrogen bomb in 1952, but the Soviet Union followed suit less than a year later. As a result, the United States took care not to directly challenge the Soviet Union or China (a nuclear power from 1964) during the Korean or Vietnamese conflicts. But while the Cold War rivals avoided a direct confrontation, the use of threats and the proliferation of small conflicts frightened a world deeply scarred by two world wars.

In 1954 President Eisenhower warned Soviet leaders against attacking western Europe. In response to such an attack, he said, the United States would reduce the Soviet Union to "a smoking, radiating ruin at the end of two hours." A few years later the Soviet leader Nikita Khrushchev (KROOSH-chef) made an equally stark promise: "We will bury you." He was referring to economic competition, but Americans interpreted the statement to mean literal burial. Rhetoric aside, both men—and their successors—had the capacity to deliver on their threats, and everyone in the world knew that all-out war with nuclear weapons would produce the greatest global devastation in human history.

The Soviet Union's deployment of nuclear missiles to Cuba in 1962 pushed the two sides to the brink of war. Reacting to U.S. efforts to overthrow the Cuban government, Khrushchev and Fidel Castro decided that the deployment of nuclear weapons in Cuba would force the United States to accept the island's status quo. When the missiles were discovered, the United States declared a naval blockade and prepared to invade Cuba, forcing Khrushchev to remove the missiles. As frightening as the **Cuban missile crisis** was, the fact that the superpowers chose diplomacy over war gave reason to hope that nuclear weapons might be contained.

Fear of a nuclear holocaust produced an international effort to limit proliferation. In 1963 Great Britain, the United States, and the Soviet Union agreed to ban the testing of nuclear weapons in the atmosphere, in space, and under water, thus reducing the danger of radioactive fallout. In 1968 the United States and the Soviet Union together proposed a world treaty against further proliferation, leading ultimately to the Nuclear Non-Proliferation Treaty (NPT) signed by 137 countries. Not until 1972, however, did the two superpowers begin the arduous and extremely slow process of negotiating weapons limits.

The atomic powers France and Britain were economically unable to keep up with the Soviet–American arms race. Instead, they led the European states in an effort to relax tensions. Between 1972 and 1975 the Conference on Security and Cooperation in Europe (CSCE) brought delegates from thirty-seven European states, the United States, and Canada to Helsinki. The Soviet Union's chief objective was European acceptance of the political boundaries of the Warsaw Pact nations as a condition for broad cooperation. In the end, the **Helsinki Accords** affirmed these boundaries and also called for economic, social, and governmental contacts and for cooperation in humanitarian fields between the rival alliances.

Space exploration was another offshoot of the nuclear arms race. The contest to build larger and more accurate missiles prompted the superpowers to prove their skills in rocketry by launching space satellites. The Soviet Union placed a small *Sputnik* satellite into orbit around the earth in October 1957, and the United States responded with its own satellite three months later. The space race was on, a contest in which accomplishments in space were understood to signify equivalent achievements in the military sphere. In 1969, when Neil A. Armstrong and Edwin E. ("Buzz") Aldrin became the first humans to walk on the moon, America had demonstrated its technological superiority.

Decolonization and Nation Building

After World War I Germany, Austria-Hungary, and the Ottoman Empire lost their empires, and many colonies and dependencies were transferred to the victors, especially to Great Britain and France. In the two decades following World War II, nearly all remaining colonies gained independence. Circumstances differed profoundly from place to place. In some Asian countries, where colonial rule was of long standing, new states possessed viable industries, communications networks, and education systems. In other countries, notably in Africa, decolonized nations faced dire economic problems and disunity resulting from language and ethnic differences.

Most Latin American nations had achieved political independence in the nineteenth century (see Chapter 25). Following World War II, mass political movements in this region focused on the related issue of economic sovereignty—freedom from growing American economic domination. Great Britain and other European nations still retained colonies in the Caribbean after World War II. In the 1960s Barbados, Guyana, Jamaica, and Trinidad Tobago gained independence from Britain, and the smaller British colonies followed in the 1970s and 1980s, as did Surinam, which gained independence from the Netherlands.

Despite their differences, a sense of kinship arose among the nations of Latin America, Africa, and Asia. All shared feelings of excitement and rebirth. As North Americans, Europeans, and the Chinese settled into the exhausting deadlock of the Cold War, visions of independence and national development captivated the rest of the world.

New Nations in South and Southeast Asia After partition in 1947 the independent states of India and Pakistan were strikingly dissimilar. Muslim Pakistan defined itself according to religion and quickly fell under the control of military leaders. India, a secular republic led by Prime

Minister Jawaharlal Nehru, was much larger and inherited the considerable industrial and educational resources developed by the British, along with a large share of trained civil servants and military officers. Ninety percent of its population was Hindu and most of the rest Muslim.

Adding to the tensions of independence (see Chapter 29) was the decision by the Hindu ruler of the northwestern state Jammu and Kashmir, now commonly called Kashmir, to join India without consulting his overwhelmingly Muslim subjects. As a result, war between India and Pakistan over Kashmir broke out in 1947 and ended with an uneasy truce. In 1965 war broke out again, this time involving large military forces and the use of air power by both sides. Kashmir has remained a flash point, with new clashes in 1999 and 2000.

Despite early predictions that multilingual India might break up into a number of linguistically homogeneous states, most Indians recognized that unity benefited everyone; and the country pursued a generally democratic and socialist line of development. Pakistan, in contrast, did break up. In 1971 the Bengali-speaking eastern section seceded to become the independent country of Bangladesh. During the fighting Indian military forces again struck against Pakistan. Despite their shared political heritage, India, Pakistan, and Bangladesh have found cooperation difficult and have pursued markedly different economic, political, religious, and social paths.

During the war the Japanese supported anti-British Indian nationalists as a way to weaken their enemy; they also encouraged the aspirations of nationalists in the countries they occupied in Southeast Asia. Many Asian nationalists saw Japanese victories over British, French, and Dutch colonial armies as a demonstration of the political and military capacities of Asian peoples. In the Dutch East Indies, Achmad Sukarno (1901–1970) cooperated with the Japanese in the hope that the Dutch, who had dominated the region economically since the seventeenth century, could be expelled. The Dutch finally negotiated withdrawal in 1949, and Sukarno became dictator of the resource-rich but underdeveloped nation of Indonesia. He ruled until 1965, when a military coup ousted him and brutally eliminated the nation's once-powerful Communist Party. The nation's large Chinese ethnic community was the target of violence during this period, and the new Indonesian government attempted to compel its assimilation, leading to decades of ethnic tension and discrimination.

In 1946 the United States kept its promise of postwar independence for the Philippine Islands but retained close economic ties and leases on military bases, later renegotiated. Britain granted independence to Burma (now Myanmar [my-ahn-MAR]) in 1948 and established the Malay Federation the same year. Singapore, once a member of the federation, became an independent city-state in 1965.

The Struggle for Independence in Africa   Between 1952 and 1956 France granted independence to Tunisia and Morocco, but it sought to retain Algeria. France had controlled this colony for nearly 150 years and had encouraged settlement; in 1950, 10 percent of the Algerian population was of French or other European origin. France also granted political rights to the settler population and asserted the fiction of Algeria's political and economic integration in the French nation. In reality few Algerians benefited from this arrangement, and most resented their continued colonial status.

The Vietnamese military victory over France in 1954 helped provoke a nationalist uprising in Algeria, during which both sides acted brutally. The Algerian revolutionary organization, the Front de Libération National (FLN), was supported by Egypt and other Arab countries who sought the emancipation of all Arab peoples. French colonists considered the country theirs and fought to the bitter end. When Algeria finally won independence in 1962, a flood of angry colonists returned to France. Since few Arabs had received technical training, this departure undermined the economy. Despite harsh feelings left by the war, Algeria retained close and seemingly indissoluble economic ties to France, and Algerians in large numbers emigrated to France in the decades that followed.

Independence was achieved in most of sub-Saharan Africa through negotiation, not revolution. In colonies with significant white settler minorities, however, the path to independence followed the violent experience of Algeria. African nationalists were forced to overcome many obstacles, but they were also able to take advantage of many consequential changes put in place during colonial rule. In the 1950s and 1960s world economic expansion and growing popular support for liberation overcame African worries about potential economic and political problems that

Bettmann/CORBIS

Jomo Kenyatta *Kenya's newly elected premier, Jomo Kenyatta, cheered by crowds in Nairobi in 1963. Kenyatta (waving ceremonial "wisk") had led the struggle to end British colonial rule in Kenya.*

might follow independence. Moreover, improvements in medical care and public health had led to rapid population growth in Africa, and the continent's young population embraced the idea of independence.

Western nationalist and egalitarian ideals also helped fuel resistance to colonialism. Most of the leaders of African independence movements were among the most westernized members of these societies. African veterans of Allied armies during World War II had exposure to Allied propaganda that emphasized ideas of popular sovereignty and self-determination. In addition, many leaders were recent graduates of educational institutions created by colonial governments, and a minority had obtained advanced education in Europe and the United States.

African nationalists were able to take advantage of other legacies of colonial rule as well. Schools, labor associations, and the colonial bureaucracy itself proved to be fertile nationalist recruiting centers. Languages introduced by colonial governments were useful in building multiethnic coalitions, while networks of roads and railroads built to promote colonial exports forged new national identities and a new political consciousness.

The young politicians who led the nationalist movements devoted their lives to ridding their homelands of foreign occupation. An example is Kwame Nkrumah (KWAH-mee nn-KROO-muh) (1909–1972), who in 1957 became prime minister of Ghana (formerly the Gold Coast), the first British colony in West Africa to achieve independence. After graduating from a Catholic mission school and a government teacher-training college, Nkrumah spent a decade studying philosophy and theology in the United States, where he absorbed ideas about black pride and independence propounded by W. E. B. Du Bois and Marcus Garvey.

During a brief stay in Britain, Nkrumah joined Kenyan nationalist Jomo Kenyatta, a Ph.D. in anthropology, to found an organization devoted to African freedom. In 1947 Nkrumah returned to the Gold Coast to work for independence. The time was right. There was no longer strong public support in Britain for colonialism, and Britain's political leadership was not enthusiastic about investing resources to hold restive colonies. When Nkrumah's party won a decisive election victory in 1951, the British Gold Coast governor appointed him prime minister. Full independence came in 1957. Although Nkrumah remained an effective international spokesman for colonized peoples, he was overthrown in 1966 by a disaffected group of army officers.

Britain soon granted independence to its other West African colonies, including large, populous, and resource-rich Nigeria in 1960. In some British colonies in eastern and southern Africa, however, long-established white settler populations resisted independence. In Kenya a small but influential group of wealthy coffee planters claimed that a protest movement among the Kikuyu (kih-KOO-you) people was proof that Africans were not ready for self-government. The settlers called the movement "Mau Mau," a made-up name meant to evoke an image of primitive savagery. When violence between settlers and anticolonial fighters escalated after 1952, British troops hunted down movement leaders and resettled the Kikuyu in fortified villages. They also declared a state of emergency, banned all African political protest, and imprisoned Kenyatta and other nationalists. Released in 1961, Kenyatta negotiated with the British to write a constitution for an independent Kenya, and in 1964 he was elected the nation's first president. Kenyatta proved to be an effective, though autocratic, ruler, and Kenya benefited from greater stability and prosperity than Ghana and many other former colonies.

African leaders in the sub-Saharan French colonies were more reluctant than their counterparts in British colonies to call for full independence. Promises made during World War II by the Free French movement of General Charles de Gaulle at a conference in Brazzaville, in French Equatorial Africa, seemed to offer dramatic changes without independence. Dependent on the troops and supplies of French African colonies, de Gaulle had promised Africans a more democratic government, broader suffrage, and greater access to employment in the colonial government. He had also promised better education and health services and an end to many abuses in the colonial system. He had not promised independence, but the politics of post-war colonial self-government ultimately proved irresistible.

Most Africans elected to office following the reforms were trained civil servants. Because of the French policy of job rotation, they had typically served in a number of different colonies and thus had a broad regional outlook. They realized that some colonies—such as Ivory Coast, with coffee and cacao exports, fishing, and hardwood forests—had good economic prospects, while others, such as landlocked, desert Niger, did not. Furthermore, they recognized the importance of French public investment in the region—a billion dollars between 1947 and 1956—and their own dependence on colonial civil service salaries. As a result, they generally looked to achieve greater self-government incrementally.

When Charles de Gaulle returned to power in France in 1958, at the height of the Algerian war, he warned that a rush to independence would have costs, saying, "One cannot conceive of both an independent territory and a France which continues to aid it." Ultimately, however, African patriotism prevailed in all of France's West African and Equatorial African colonies. Guinea, under the dynamic leadership of Sékou Touré (SAY-koo too-RAY), gained full independence in 1958 and the others in 1960.

Independence in the Belgian Congo was chaotic and violent. Contending political and ethnic groups found external allies; some were supported by Cuba and the Soviet Union, while others were supported by the West or by business groups tied to the rich mines. Civil war, the introduction of foreign mercenaries, and the rhetoric of Cold War confrontation roiled the waters and led to a heavy loss of life and great property destruction. In 1965 Mobuto Sese Seko seized power in a military coup that included the assassination of Patrice Lumumba, the nation's first prime minister. Once in power, Mobuto maintained one of the region's most corrupt governments until driven from power in 1997.

The opposition of European settler communities delayed decolonization in southern Africa. While the settler minority tried to defend white supremacy, African-led liberation movements were committed to the creation of nonracial societies and majority rule. In the 1960s African guerrilla movements successfully fought to end Portuguese rule in Angola and Mozambique. Their efforts led to both the overthrow of the antidemocratic government of Portugal in 1974 and independence the following year. After a ten-year fight, European settlers in the British colony of Southern Rhodesia accepted African majority rule in 1980. The new government changed the country's name to Zimbabwe, the name of a great stone city built by Africans long before the arrival of European settlers.

South Africa and neighboring Namibia remained in the hands of European minorities much longer. The large white settler population of South Africa achieved effective independence from Britain in 1961 but kept the black and mixed-race majority in colonial-era subjection, separating the races in a system they called *apartheid* (a-PART-hite). Descendents of Dutch and English settlers made up 13 percent of the population but controlled the productive land, the industrial, mining, and commercial enterprises, and the government. Meanwhile, discrimination and segregation in housing, education, and employment confined the lives of people of mixed parentage (10 percent of the population) and South Asians (less than 3 percent).

Indigenous Africans, 74 percent of the population, were subjected to even stricter limitations on housing, freedom of movement, and access to jobs and public facilities. The government created fictional African "homelands" as a way of denying the African majority citizenship and political rights. Not unlike Amerindian reservations, these "homelands" were located in poor regions far from the more dynamic and prosperous urban and industrial areas. Overcrowded and lacking investment, they were impoverished and lacking in services and opportunities.

The African National Congress (ANC), formed in 1912, led opposition to apartheid. After police fired on demonstrators in the African town of Sharpeville in 1960 and banned all peaceful political protest by Africans, a lawyer named Nelson Mandela 1918–2013 organized guerrilla resistance by the ANC. The government sentenced Mandela to life in prison in 1964 and persecuted the ANC, but it was unable to defeat the movement. Facing growing opposition internationally, South Africa freed Mandela from prison in 1990 and began the transition to majority rule (see Chapters 32 and 33).

The Quest for Economic Freedom in Latin America

Although Latin America had achieved independence from colonial rule more than a hundred years earlier, European and American economic domination of the region created a semicolonial order (see Chapters 26 and 29). Foreigners controlled Chile's copper, Cuba's sugar, Colombia's coffee, and Guatemala's bananas, leading by the 1930s to growing support for economic nationalism. During the 1930s and 1940s populist political leaders experimented with programs that would constrain foreign investors or, alternatively, promote local efforts to industrialize (see discussion of Getulio Vargas and Juan Perón in Chapter 29).

In Mexico the revolutionary constitution of 1917 began an era of economic nationalism that culminated in the expropriation of foreign oil interests, mostly American, in 1938. The Institutional Revolutionary Party, or PRI (the abbreviation of its name in Spanish), controlled Mexico until the 1990s and had overseen a period of economic expansion during World War II. But a yawning gulf between rich and poor persisted. Although the government dominated important industries like petroleum and restricted foreign investment, rapid population growth, uncontrolled migration to Mexico City and other urban areas, and political corruption undermined efforts to lift the nation's poor. Economic power was concentrated at the top of society, with two thousand elite families controlling much of the nation's wealth. At the other end of the economic scale were the millions of poor Mexicans struggling to survive. Thwarted by limited opportunities at home, millions of Mexicans migrated to the United States.

Guatemala's situation was more representative of Latin America in 1950. An American corporation, the United Fruit Company, was Guatemala's largest landowner; it also controlled much of the nation's infrastructure, including port facilities and railroads. To limit banana production and keep international prices high, United Fruit kept much of its Guatemalan lands fallow. Jacobo Arbenz Guzmán, elected in 1951, advocated positions broadly similar to those of leaders like Perón of Argentina and Vargas of Brazil (see Chapter 29), who confronted powerful foreign interests. He advocated land reform, which would have transferred these fallow lands to the nation's rural poor. The threatened expropriation angered the United Fruit Company. Simultaneously, Arbenz tried to reduce U.S. political influence, raising fears in Washington that he sought closer ties to the Soviet Union. Reacting to the land reform efforts and to reports that Arbenz was becoming friendly to communism, the U.S. Central Intelligence Agency (CIA), in one of its first major overseas operations, sponsored a takeover by the Guatemalan military in 1954. CIA intervention removed Arbenz, but it also condemned Guatemala to decades of governmental instability and violence.

By the 1950s American companies dominated the Cuban economy. They controlled sugar production, the nation's most important industry, as well as banking, transportation, tourism, and public utilities. The United States was also the most important market for Cuba's exports and the most important source of Cuba's imports. Thus the performance of the U.S. economy largely determined the ebb and flow of Cuban foreign trade. By 1956 sugar accounted for 80 percent of Cuba's exports and 25 percent of Cuba's national income. But demand in the United States dictated keeping only 39 percent of the land owned by the sugar companies in production, while Cuba experienced chronic underemployment. Similarly, immense deposits of nickel in Cuba went untapped because the U.S. government, which owned them, considered them to be a strategic reserve.

While high unemployment and slow growth afflicted the nation, profits went north to the United States or to a small class of wealthy Cubans. Cuba's government was also notoriously corrupt and subservient to the wishes of American interests. As reform-minded young Cubans organized for a national election, Fulgencio Batista, a former military leader and president, illegally seized power in a coup in 1953. Hostility to Batista and anger with the corruption, repression, and foreign economic domination of his government gave rise to the revolution led by Fidel Castro.

Fidel Castro (b. 1927), a young lawyer who had played a prominent role in left-wing politics while at university, led a failed uprising in 1953. Convicted, jailed, and then sent into exile, Castro returned to Cuba in 1956 to establish a successful revolutionary movement in the countryside. His supporters included student groups, labor unions, and adherents of Cuba's traditional parties. When he and his youthful followers took power in 1959, they vowed not to suffer the fate of Arbenz and the Guatemalan reformers. Ernesto ("Che") Guevara (CHAY-guh-VAHR-uh), Castro's Argentine-born chief lieutenant who became the main theorist of communist revolution in Latin America, had witnessed the CIA coup in Guatemala firsthand. He and Castro believed that confrontation with the United

States was inevitable and moved quickly to remove the existing military leadership and begin revolutionary changes in the economy.

Within a year Castro's government seized and redistributed land, lowered urban rents, and raised wages, effectively transferring 15 percent of the national income from the rich to the poor. Within two years the Castro government had nationalized the property of almost all U.S. corporations in Cuba as well as the wealth of Cuba's elite. To achieve his revolutionary objectives, Castro sought economic support from the Soviet Union. He also consolidated his personal political power, putting aside promises of democratic reform made when fighting Batista.

The United States responded by seeking to destabilize the Cuban economy and undermine the Castro government. These punitive measures by the United States, the nationalization of so much of the economy, and the punishment of Batista supporters caused tens of thousands of Cubans to leave, including some who had opposed Batista. Initially, most emigrants were from wealthy families and the middle class, but when the economic failures of the regime became clear, many poor Cubans fled to the United States or to other Latin American nations.

There is little evidence that Castro was committed to communism before the revolution, but his commitment to break the economic and political power of the United States in Cuba and undertake dramatic social reforms led inevitably to conflict with the United States and to reliance on the Soviet Union. In April 1961, in an attempt to apply the strategy that had removed Arbenz from power in Guatemala, an army of Cuban exiles trained and armed by the CIA landed at the Bay of Pigs in an effort to overthrow Castro. The Cuban army defeated the attempted invasion in a matter of days. The Eisenhower administration had planned the invasion, but the newly elected U.S. president, John F. Kennedy, agreed to carry it out and lived with the embarrassment. This failure helped precipitate the Cuban missile crisis. Fearful of a new invasion, Castro and Khrushchev placed nuclear weapons as well as missiles and bombers in Cuba to forestall an anticipated second attack.

The failure of the Bay of Pigs tarnished the reputation of the United States and the CIA and gave heart to revolutionaries all over Latin America. But the armed revolutionary movements that imitated the tactics and objectives of Cuba's bearded revolutionaries experienced little success. Among the thousands to lose their lives was Che Guevara, captured and executed in 1967 by Bolivian troops trained by the United States. Nevertheless, Castro had demonstrated that revolutionaries could successfully challenge American power and put in place a radical program of economic and social reform in the Western Hemisphere.

Beyond a Bipolar World

Although no one doubted the dominating role of the East-West superpower rivalry in world affairs, newly independent nations had concerns that were primarily domestic and regional. Their challenge was to pursue their ends within the bipolar structure of the Cold War—and when possible to take advantage of the East–West rivalry. Where nationalist forces sought to assert political or economic independence, Cold War antagonists provided arms and political support even when the nationalist goals were quite different from those of the supporting superpower. For other nations, the ruinously expensive superpower arms race opened opportunities to expand industries and exports. In short, the superpowers dominated the world but did not control it.

The Third World   As a leader of the decolonization movement, Indonesia's president Sukarno was an appropriate figure to host a 1955 meeting of twenty-nine African and Asian countries at Bandung, Indonesia, that proclaimed solidarity among those fighting against colonial rule. This conference marked the beginning of an effort by the many new, poor, mostly non-European nations emerging from colonialism to gain more influence in world affairs. The terms *nonaligned nations* and *Third World*, which became commonplace in the following years, signaled these countries' collective stance toward the rival sides in the Cold War. If the West, led by the United States, and the East, led by the Soviet Union, represented two worlds locked in mortal struggle, the Third World consisted of everyone else.

Leaders of so-called Third World countries preferred the label *nonaligned*, which signaled their independence from Soviet or U.S. control. Leaders in the West noted that the Soviet Union supported many national liberation movements

Bandung Conference, 1955 *India's Jawaharlal Nehru (in white hat) was a central figure at the conference held in Indonesia to promote solidarity among nonaligned developing nations.*

and that the nonaligned movement included communist countries such as China and Yugoslavia. As a result, they refused to take the term *nonaligned* seriously. In a polarized world, they saw Sukarno, Nehru, Nkrumah, and Egypt's Gamal Abd al-Nasir (gah-MAHL AHB-d al–NAH-suhr) as stalking horses for an ambitious campaign to extend Soviet influence globally. This may have been the view of some Soviet leaders as well, since they were quick to offer military and financial aid to many nonaligned countries.

For the movement's leaders, however, nonalignment was primarily a way to extract money and support from one or both superpowers. By flirting with the Soviet Union or its ally, the People's Republic of China, a country could get weapons, training, and barter agreements that offered an alternative to selling agricultural or mineral products on Western-dominated world markets. The same flirtation might also prompt the United States and its allies to proffer grants and loans, cheap or free surplus grain, and investments in new industries or in infrastructure development.

Nonaligned countries could sometimes play the Cold War rivals against each other. Nasir, who had led a military coup against the Egyptian monarchy in 1952, and his successor Anwar al-Sadat (al-seh-DAT) played this game skillfully. The United States offered to build a dam at Aswan (AS-wahn), on the Nile River, to increase Egypt's electrical generating and irrigation capacity, but it withdrew the offer when Egypt turned to the Warsaw Pact for armaments in 1956. Worsened relations with the West then led Nasir to nationalize the Suez Canal and the Soviet Union to commit to building the dam. Later that same year Israel, Great Britain, and France allied to invade Egypt, aiming to overthrow Nasir, regain the Suez Canal, and secure Israel from any Egyptian threat. The invasion succeeded militarily, but the United States and the Soviet Union both pressured the invaders to withdraw, thus saving Nasir's government. In 1972 Sadat evicted Soviet military advisers, but a year later he used his Soviet weapons to attack Israel. After he lost that war, he disengaged from the Soviets; he then improved relations with, and sought increased aid from, the United States.

Other nations adopted similar balancing strategies. In each case, local leaders sought to develop their nations' economies and assert or preserve their nations' interests. Manipulating the superpowers was a means toward those ends and implied very little about true ideological orientation.

Japan and China   No countries took more effective advantage of opportunities presented by the superpowers' preoccupations than Japan and China. Japan signed a peace treaty with most of its former enemies in 1951 and regained independence from American occupation the following year. Renouncing militarism and its imperialist past (see Chapter 30), Japan remained on the sidelines throughout the Korean War. Its new constitution, written under American supervision in 1946, allowed only a limited self-defense force, banned the deployment of Japanese troops abroad, and gave the vote to women.

Like the Europeans, the Japanese had suffered high levels of population loss and property destruction in the war. With peace restored, they focused their resources on rebuilding industries and expanding trade. Peace treaties with countries in Southeast

Asia specified reparations payable in the form of goods and services, thus reintroducing Japan to that region as a force for economic development rather than as a military occupier. Beginning during the U.S. occupation, Japan had become closely tied to the West by trade and soon benefited from the postwar recovery. At the same time, controls placed on Japan by peace conditions kept its military expenditures low during the Cold War, providing an exceptional environment to invest in economic development and infrastructure.

Three industries that took advantage of government aid and new technologies were key to Japan's emergence as an economic superpower after 1975. Electricity was in short supply in 1950, and Tokyo suffered from chronic power outages. Japan responded by constructing a power grid between 1951 and 1970 that produced 60 million kilowatts of electricity. Most of this new capacity came from hydroelectric sources. At the same time steel production and shipbuilding developed rapidly, placing Japan among world leaders in both industries.

While Japan benefited from avoiding the heavy defense costs associated with the Cold War, China was at the center of Cold War politics. When Mao Zedong (maow dzuh-dong) and the communists defeated the nationalists in 1949 and established the People's Republic of China (PRC), their main ally and source of arms was the Soviet Union. By 1956, however, the PRC and the Soviet Union were beginning to diverge politically, partly in reaction to the Soviet rejection of Stalinism and partly because of China's reluctance to accept the role of subordinate. Mao had his own notions of communism that focused strongly on the peasantry, which the Soviets had ignored in favor of the industrial working class.

Mao's Great Leap Forward in 1958 was intended to propel China into the ranks of world industrial powers by maximizing the output of small-scale, village-level industries and by instituting mass collectivization in agriculture. These untested policies demonstrated Mao's willingness to carry out massive economic and social experiments of his own devising in the face of criticism by the Soviets as well as by traditional economists. By 1962 the revolutionary reforms had failed comprehensively, leading to an estimated 20 to 30 million deaths.

In 1966 Mao instituted another radical program, the **Cultural Revolution**, that ordered the mass mobilization of Chinese youth into Red Guard units. His goal was to kindle revolutionary fervor in a new generation to ward off the stagnation and bureaucratization he saw in the Soviet Union, as well as to increase his own power within the Communist Party. Red Guard units criticized and purged teachers, party officials, and intellectuals for "bourgeois values." Executions, beatings, and incarcerations were widespread, leading to a half-million deaths and 3 million purged by 1971. Finally, Mao admitted that attacks on individuals had gotten out of hand and intervened to reestablish order. Mao's wife Jiang Qing (jyahn ching) and radical allies dominated the last years of the Cultural Revolution, harshly restricting artistic and intellectual activity.

The rift between the PRC and the Soviet Union allowed U.S. president Richard Nixon (served 1969–1974) to revive relations with China. In 1971 the United States agreed to allow the PRC to join the United Nations and occupy China's permanent seat on the Security Council. This decision necessitated the expulsion of the Chinese nationalist government based on the island of Taiwan, which had previously claimed to be the only legal Chinese authority. The following year, Nixon visited

Beijing, initiating a new era of enhanced cooperation between the People's Republic of China and the United States.

The Middle East   Independence came gradually to the Arab countries of the Middle East. Britain granted Syria and Lebanon independence after World War II. Iraq, Egypt, and Jordan enjoyed nominal independence between the two world wars but remained under indirect British control until the 1950s. Military coups overthrew King Faruq (fuh-ROOK) of Egypt in 1952 and King Faisal (FIE-suhl) II of Iraq in 1958. King Husayn (hoo-SANE) of Jordan dismissed his British military commander in 1956 in response to the Suez crisis, but his poor desert country remained dependent on British and later American financial aid.

Overshadowing all Arab politics, however, was the struggle with Israel, a clear illustration that the superpowers could not control all dangerous international disputes. British policy on Palestine between the wars oscillated between favoring Zionist Jews—who emigrated to Palestine, encouraged by the Balfour Declaration—and support for the indigenous Palestinian Arabs, who suspected that the Zionists were aiming at an independent state. As more and more Jews sought a safe haven from persecution by the Nazis, Arabs felt more and more threatened. The Arabs unleashed a guerrilla uprising against the British in 1936, and Jewish groups turned to militant tactics a few years later. Occasionally, Arabs and Jews confronted each other in riots or killings, making it clear that peaceful coexistence in Palestine would be difficult or impossible to achieve.

After the war, under intense pressure to resettle European Jewish refugees, Britain turned the Palestine problem over to the United Nations. In November 1947 the General Assembly voted in favor of partitioning Palestine into two states, one Jewish and one Arab. The Jewish community made plans to declare independence, while the Palestinians, who felt that the proposed land division was unfair, took up arms. When Israel declared its independence in May 1948, neighboring Arab countries sent armies to help the Palestinians crush the newborn state.

Israel prevailed and some 700,000 Palestinians became refugees, finding shelter in United Nations refugee camps in Jordan, Syria, Lebanon, and the Gaza Strip (a bit of coastal land on the Egyptian-Israeli border). The right of these refugees to return home remains a focal point of Arab politics today. In 1967 Israel responded to threatening military moves by Egypt's Nasir by preemptively attacking Egyptian and Syrian air bases. In six days Israel won a smashing victory. When Jordan entered the war, Israel took control of Jerusalem, which it had previously split with Jordan, and the West Bank. Acquiring all of Jerusalem satisfied Jews' deep longing to return to their holiest city, but Palestinians continued to regard Jerusalem as their destined capital, and Muslims in many countries protested Israeli control of the Dome of the Rock, a revered Islamic shrine located in the city. Israel also occupied the Gaza Strip, the strategic Golan Heights in southern Syria, and the entire Sinai Peninsula. These acquisitions resulted in a new wave of Palestinian refugees.

The rival claims to Palestine continued to plague Middle Eastern politics. The Palestine Liberation Organization (PLO), headed by Yasir Arafat (AR-uh-fat), waged guerrilla war against Israel, frequently engaging in acts of terrorism. The

James Pozarik/Getty Images

Shortage at the Pumps *As prices rose in the late 1970s, consumers tried to hoard supplies by filling gas cans at neighborhood stations. For the first time gas prices exceeded $1 a gallon.*

Israelis were able to blunt or absorb these attacks and launch counterstrikes that likewise involved assassinations and bombings. Though the United States was a firm friend to Israel and the Soviet Union armed the Arab states, neither super-power saw the struggle between Zionism and Palestinian nationalism as a vital concern—until oil became a political issue.

The phenomenal concentration of oil wealth in the Middle East—Saudi Arabia, Iran, Iraq, Kuwait, Libya, Qatar, Bahrain, and the United Arab Emirates—was not fully realized until after World War II, when demand for oil rose sharply as civilian economies recovered. In 1960, as world demand rose, oil-producing states formed the **Organization of Petroleum Exporting Countries (OPEC)** to promote their collective interest in higher revenues.

Oil politics and the Arab-Israeli conflict intersected in October 1973 during the Yom Kippur War. Surprise attacks by Syria and Egypt threw the Israelis into temporary disarray, but Israel won a clear military victory in the end. Supported by military supplies from the United States, it drove back Syrian forces and trapped an Egyptian army at the Suez Canal's southern end. The United States then arranged a ceasefire and the disengagement of forces. But before that could happen, the Arab oil-producing countries voted to embargo oil shipments to the United States and the Netherlands as punishment for their support of Israel.

The implications of using oil as an economic weapon profoundly disturbed the worldwide oil industry. Prices rose—along with feelings of insecurity. In 1974 OPEC responded to the turmoil in the oil market by quadrupling prices, setting the stage for massive transfers of wealth to the producing countries and provoking a feeling of crisis throughout the consuming countries.

The Emergence of Environmental Concerns

The Cold War and the massive investments made in postwar economic recovery focused public and governmental attention on technological innovations and enormous projects such as hydroelectric dams and nuclear power stations. Only a few people warned that untested technologies and industrial expansion were degrading the environment. The superpowers were particularly negligent of the environmental impact of pesticide and herbicide use, automobile exhaust, industrial waste disposal, and radiation.

The wave of student unrest that swept many parts of the world in 1968 and the early 1970s created a new awareness of environmental issues and a new constituency for environmental action. As youth activism grew, governments in the West began to pass new environmental regulations. Among them was the Clean Air Act of 1970. Earth Day, a benchmark of the new awareness, was also first celebrated in 1970, the year in which the United States also established its Environmental Protection Agency.

When oil prices skyrocketed, the problem of finite natural resources became more broadly recognized. Making gasoline engines and home heating systems more efficient and lowering highway speed limits to conserve fuel became matters of national debate in the United States, while poorer countries struggled to find the money to import oil. A widely read 1972 study called *The Limits of Growth* forecast a need to cut back on consumption of natural resources in the twenty-first century. Ecological and environmental problems now vied for public attention with superpower rivalry and Third World nation building.

CONCLUSION

The alliance between the Soviet Union and the Western democracies led by the United States did not survive into the post–World War II era. Shortly after the war, both sides began to prepare for a new round of hostilities, establishing competing military alliances and attempting to influence the new governments of nations formerly occupied by the Axis. In the end this confrontation was projected into space, as each side sought to advertise its technological capacity through satellite launches and finally a moon landing.

Each side portrayed this tension as a struggle between irreconcilably different social and economic systems, and each side emphasized the corruption, injustice, and unfairness of its opponent. When Winston Churchill spoke in 1946 of Soviet control in eastern Europe as an iron curtain, he suggested that the Soviet system was, in effect, a prison.

Massive armies armed with increasingly sophisticated weapons, including nuclear weapons far more destructive than those dropped on Japan, defended the boundary that separated the United States and its allies and the Soviet Union and its allies. This Cold War quickly became global in character as distant civil wars, regional conflicts, and nationalist revolutions were transformed by support provided by these rivals for global ascendancy.

The desire of colonized peoples to throw off imperial controls and establish independent nations provided many of the era's flash points. The Western nations had defined World War II as a war for freedom and self-determination. The Free

French had promised greater autonomy to African colonies, the United States had used nationalist forces to fight against the Japanese in the Philippines and in Vietnam, and Britain also had used forces recruited throughout its empire to fight the war. Once organized and set in motion, these nationalist energies eventually overwhelmed colonial rule. The most powerful force in the postwar era was nationalism, the desire of peoples to control their own destinies.

In Africa, the Middle East, South Asia, and Latin America, this desire to throw off foreign controls led to the creation of scores of new nations by the 1970s. Each nation's struggle had its own character. While in India these passions led to independence, similar sentiments led in China to the overthrow of a government seen as weak and subordinate to foreign powers and to the creation of a communist dictatorship. In much of Africa, the Middle East, and the Caribbean, nationalism overturned colonial rule. In the Middle East the desire for self-government was complicated by the creation of the state of Israel. In Latin America, where most nations had been independent for well over a century, nationalist passions focused on a desire for economic independence and an end to foreign military interventions.

The end of Japanese control in Korea and Vietnam led to territorial partitions that separated Soviet-leaning and Western-allied polities. Civil war and foreign interventions soon followed. In both cases the Soviet Union and China supported communist forces. The United States committed large military forces to protect the anticommunist governments, gaining a stalemate in Korea and eventually failing in Vietnam. While these outcomes were mixed for the superpowers, the wars were contained and managed so as to prevent direct engagement and nuclear conflict.

This period also witnessed the beginning of the international environmental movement. Public attention increasingly focused on resource management, pollution, and the preservation of endangered species. In response, the United States and governments in western Europe put in place the first generation of environmental laws. The Clean Air Act in the United States and other measures had an immediate impact, but both policymakers and the public grew aware of ever more serious challenges. The gas crisis of the 1970s gave these efforts a sense of urgency.

IMPORTANT EVENTS 1945–1975

1947	Partition of India
1949	NATO formed
1949	Dutch withdraw from Indonesia
1950–1953	Korean War
1952	United States detonates first hydrogen bomb
1954	CIA intervention in Guatemala; defeat at Dienbienphu ends French hold on Vietnam
1954	Jacobo Arbenz overthrown in Guatemala, supported by CIA
1955	Warsaw Pact created
1955	Bandung Conference

1956	Soviet Union suppresses Hungarian revolt
1957	Soviet Union launches first artificial satellite into earth orbit
1957	Ghana becomes first British colony in Africa to gain independence
1959	Triumph of Fidel Castro's revolution Cuba
1960	Shootings in Sharpeville intensify South African struggle against apartheid; Nigeria becomes independent
1961	East Germany builds Berlin Wall
1961	Bay of Pigs (Cuba)
1962	Cuban missile crisis
1962	Algeria wins independence
1968	Nuclear Non-Proliferation Treaty
1971	Bangladesh secedes from Pakistan
1975	Helsinki Accords; end of Vietnam War

32

⬥

THE END OF THE COLD WAR AND THE CHALLENGE OF ECONOMIC DEVELOPMENT AND IMMIGRATION, 1975–2000

At the end of the 1970s China began an ambitious program of economic reforms. Until then China, with the world's largest population, was a very poor nation with a gross domestic product (GDP) per capita of approximately $110.00 per year (total goods and services produced divided by population). It lagged far behind the mature industrialized nations of Europe and North America in economic performance, as well as behind more dynamic neighboring nations like Japan and South Korea. Since the reforms, China has experienced rapid economic growth and has become one of the few socialist nations to successfully make the transition to a market economy, reaching a GDP per capita of $5,413.57 in 2010. Despite this remarkable expansion, millions of Chinese still live in poverty. As is indicated in the opening illustration, ancient technology and poverty can exist in close proximity with modernity and affluence in China. These same problems of poverty and inequality exist across the globe. In an era of astounding technological change and, until the recession of 2008, spreading prosperity, more than a billion of the world's population still live on less than $1.25 a day.

At the end of the twentieth century, population growth continued to outstrip economic resources in many of the nations of the developing world. Since the deep recession that began in 2008, politicians as well as social reformers in the wealthy industrialized nations have criticized the effects of high levels of unemployment, family breakdown, substance abuse, and homelessness. At the start of the twenty-first century, as in the Industrial Revolution (see Chapter 22), an era of relative affluence, increased global economic integration, and rapid technological progress coincided with problems of social dislocation and inequality. Among the most important events of the period were the emergence of new industrial powers in Asia, the precipitous demise of the Soviet Union and its socialist allies, and the migration of tens of millions of people from poor to rich nations.

POSTCOLONIAL CRISES AND ASIAN ECONOMIC EXPANSION

Between 1975 and the end of the century, wars and revolutions spread death and destruction through many of the world's least-developed regions. In most cases the origins of conflict were found in the experience of colonialism and foreign intervention, but each conflict also had a unique historical character. Throughout these decades of conflict the two superpowers sought to avoid direct military confrontation while working to gain strategic advantages. The United States and the Soviet Union each supplied arms and financial assistance to nations or insurgent forces hostile to the other. Once linked to superpower rivalries, local conflicts became deadlier. Conflicts where the rival superpowers financed and armed competing factions or parties are called **proxy wars**.

In Latin America superpower rivalry transformed limited conflicts over political rights, social justice, and economic policies into a violent cycle of revolution, military dictatorship, and foreign meddling. In Iran and Afghanistan resentment against foreign intrusion and a growing religious hostility to secular culture led to revolutionary transformations. Here again, superpower ambitions and regional political instability helped provoke war and economic decline. These experiences were not universal, however. During this period some Asian nations experienced rapid economic transformation. Japan emerged as one of the world's leading industrial powers, and a small number of other Asian economies entered the ranks of industrial and commercial powers. Socialist China joined this group of fast-developing Asian nations after initiating market-based economic reforms.

At the end of the 1980s the Cold War ended with the collapse of the Soviet system in eastern Europe, but the transition to democracy and market economy proved difficult. As both developing and former socialist nations opened their markets to foreign investment and competition, they experienced wrenching social change. Increased globalization coincided with increased inequality in many nations, but some developing nations also attained substantial benefits from rapid technological change and world economic integration.

This period also witnessed a great increase in world population and international immigration. Population growth and increased levels of industrialization had a dramatic impact on the global environment, with every continent feeling the destructive effects of forest depletion, soil erosion, and pollution. Wealthy nations with slow population growth found it easier to respond to these environmental challenges than did poor nations experiencing rapid population growth.

Revolutions, Repression, and Democratic Reform in Latin America   In the 1970s Latin America entered a dark era of political violence. When revolutionary movements challenged the established order, militaries in many countries overturned constitutional governments and instituted repressive measures. A region of weak democracies in 1960 became a region dominated by military dictatorships with little patience for civil liberties and human rights fifteen years later.

The ongoing confrontation between Fidel Castro and the government of the United States (see Chapter 31) helped propel the region toward crisis. The fact that the Cuban communist government survived efforts by the United States to overthrow it energized the revolutionary left throughout Latin America. Fearful that revolution would spread across Latin America, the United States increased support for its political and military allies in that region, training many of the military leaders who led coups during this period.

Brazil was the first nation to experience the region-wide conservative reaction to the Cuban Revolution. Claiming that Brazil's civilian political leaders could not protect the nation from communist subversion, the army overthrew the constitutional government of President João Goulart (ju-wow go-LARHT) in 1964. Once in power, the military suspended the constitution, outlawed all existing political parties, and exiled former presidents and opposition leaders. Death squads—illegal paramilitary organizations sanctioned by the government—detained, tortured, and executed thousands of citizens. The dictatorship also undertook an ambitious economic program that promoted industrialization through import substitution, using tax and tariff policies to successfully compel foreign-owned companies to increase investment in manufacturing, especially the auto industry.

This combination of dictatorship, violent repression, and government promotion of industrialization came to be called the "Brazilian Solution." Elements of this "solution" were later imposed across much of the region. In 1970 Chile's newly elected president, **Salvador Allende** (sal-VAH-dor ah-YEHN-day), undertook an ambitious program of socialist reforms and nationalized Chile's heavy industry and mines, including the American-owned copper companies that dominated the economy. From the beginning of Allende's presidency the administration of President Richard Nixon (served 1969–1973) sought to undermine the Chilean government. Afflicted by inflation, mass consumer protests, and declining foreign trade, a military uprising led by General Augusto Pinochet (ah-GOOS-toh pin-oh-CHET) and supported by the United States overthrew Allende in 1973. President Allende and thousands of Chileans died in the uprising, and thousands more were jailed, tortured, and imprisoned without trial. Once in power Pinochet rolled back Allende's socialist innovations, dramatically reducing state participation in the economy and encouraging foreign investment.

In 1976 Argentina followed Brazil and Chile into dictatorship. Juan Perón had been exiled in 1955 after a military uprising, but with Argentina torn by rising levels of political violence he was allowed to return and was then elected president in 1973 (see Chapter 29). Perón had insisted that his third wife, Isabel Martínez de Perón (EES-ah-bell mar-TEEN-ehz deh pair-OWN), be elected vice president, and she inherited the presidency after his death in 1974. Her weak administration faced a potent guerrilla insurgency, a wave of kidnappings, high inflation, and labor protests. Impatient with the policies of the president, the military seized power and suspended the constitution in 1976. During the next seven years it fought what it called the **Dirty War** against terrorism. More than nine thousand Argentines lost their lives, and thousands of others endured arrest and torture before democracy was restored.

While the left suffered these reverses in South America, a revolutionary movement came to power in Nicaragua in 1979, overthrowing the corrupt dictatorship of Anastasio Somoza. This broad alliance of revolutionaries and reformers called themselves **Sandinistas** (sahn-din-EES-tahs). They took their name from Augusto César Sandino, who had led Nicaraguan opposition to U.S. military intervention between 1927 and 1932. Once in power, the Sandinistas moved leftward, seeking to imitate the command economies of Cuba and the Soviet Union and nationalizing properties owned by members of the Nicaraguan elite and U.S. companies.

U.S. president Jimmy Carter (served 1977–1980) championed human rights in the hemisphere and stopped the flow of U.S. arms to military regimes with the worst records, like Argentina. Carter also agreed to the reestablishment of Panamanian sovereignty in the Canal Zone at the end of 1999, but his effort to find common ground with the Sandinistas failed due to their intransigence.

Carter was defeated in the next election by Ronald Reagan, who was committed to overturning the Nicaraguan Revolution and defeating a revolutionary movement in neighboring El Salvador. With the memory of the Vietnam War still strong (see Chapter 31), the U.S. Congress resisted any use of U.S. combat forces in Nicaragua and El Salvador and put strict limits on military aid. As a result, the Reagan administration tried to roll back the Nicaraguan Revolution through punitive economic measures and the recruitment and arming of a proxy force of anti-Sandinista Nicaraguans, called Contras (counter-revolutionaries).

Confident that they were supported by the majority of Nicaraguans and assured that the U.S. Congress was close to cutting off aid to the Contras, the Sandinistas called for free elections in 1990. But they had miscalculated politically. Exhausted by more than a decade of violence, a majority of Nicaraguan voters rejected the Sandinistas and elected a middle-of-the-road coalition led by Violeta Chamorro (vee-oh-LET-ah cha-MOR-roe).

In neighboring El Salvador another guerrilla movement, the Farabundo Martí (fah-rah-BOON-doh mar-TEE) National Liberation Front, or FMLN (acronym for Spanish name), seemed on the verge of taking power. The Reagan administration responded by providing hundreds of millions of dollars in military assistance and by training units of the El Salvadoran army. The assassination of Archbishop Oscar Romero and other members of the Catholic clergy by death squads tied to the Salvadoran government as well as the murder of thousands of noncombatants by military units trained by the United States undermined this effort. However, the electoral defeat of the Sandinistas in Nicaragua and the collapse of the Soviet Union (see below) finally forced the FMLN rebels to negotiate peace, transforming themselves into a civilian political party.

During this same period, the violent political confrontation of right and left abated in South America as well. The right-wing military dictatorships established in Brazil, Chile, and Argentina all came to an end between 1983 and 1990, brought down by their own excesses and by popular desires for a return to constitutional government. By 2000, with the Cold War ended, 95 percent of Latin America's population lived again under civilian rule.

At the same time, the influence of the United States grew substantially. The United States had thwarted the left in Nicaragua and El Salvador by funding military proxies. It used its own military in a 1983 invasion of the tiny Caribbean nation of Grenada and again in 1989 to overthrow and arrest dictator General Manuel Noriega (MAN-wel no-ree-EGG-ah) of Panama. These actions were powerful reminders to Latin Americans of prior interventions (see Chapter 26), but they also served as reminders of American power at a time when socialism was discredited by the collapse of the Soviet bloc.

From this position of strength the United States pushed Latin American nations to reform their economies by removing limitations on foreign investment, eliminating many social welfare programs, and reducing public-sector employment. Latin American governments responded by selling public-sector industries, like national airlines, manufacturing facilities, and public utilities, to foreign corporations. But popular support for these policies, what Latin Americans called neo-liberalism, eroded quickly due to political scandals and a slowing world economy. A catastrophic economic and political meltdown in Argentina between 2001 and 2002 contributed to the appearance of a reinvigorated nationalist left in Latin America that sought to roll back neo-liberal reforms (see Diversity and Dominance: The Struggle for Women's Rights in an Era of Global Political and Economic Change). Among the most vocal critic of neo-liberalism and American influence was Hugo Chávez (HUGH-go SHAH-vez), elected president of Venezuela in 1998 and serving as the region's chief critic of U.S. policy until his death in 2013. Left-of-center presidents were later elected in Brazil (Luiz Inácio Lula da Silva, 2002), Argentina (Néstor Kirchner, 2003), Bolivia (Evo Morales, 2005), and Ecuador (Rafael Correa, 2007).

Islamic Revolutions in Iran and Afghanistan

Although the Arab–Israel conflict and the oil crisis (see Chapter 31) concerned both superpowers, the prospect of direct military involvement remained remote. When unexpected crises developed in Iran and Afghanistan, however, significant strategic issues for the superpowers came to the foreground. Both countries adjoined Soviet territory, making Soviet military intervention more likely. Exercising post–Vietnam War caution, the United States reacted with restraint in Iran. The Soviet Union chose a bolder and ultimately disastrous course in Afghanistan.

Muhammad Reza Pahlavi (REH-zah PAH-lah-vee) succeeded his father as shah of Iran in 1941. In 1953 covert intervention by the U.S. Central Intelligence Agency (CIA) helped the shah retain his throne in the face of a movement to overturn royal power. Even when he finally nationalized the foreign-owned oil industry, the shah continued to enjoy American support. As oil revenues increased following the price increases of the 1970s, the United States encouraged the shah to spend his nation's growing wealth on equipping the Iranian army with American weaponry. By the 1970s popular resentment against the ballooning wealth of the elite families that supported the shah and the brutality, inefficiency, malfeasance, and corruption of his government led to mass opposition.

Ayatollah Ruhollah Khomeini (A-yat-ol-LAH ROOH-ol-LAH ko-MAY-nee), a Shi'ite (SHE-ite) philosopher-cleric who had spent most of his eighty-plus years in religious and academic pursuits, became the leader of the opposition. Massive protests forced the shah to flee Iran and ended the monarchy in 1979. In the Islamic Republic of Iran, which replaced the monarchy, Ayatollah Khomeini was supreme arbiter of disputes and guarantor of the government's religious legitimacy. He oversaw a parliamentary regime based on European models but imposed religious control over legislation and public behavior. The electoral process was not open to monarchists, communists, and other opposition groups. Shi'ite clerics with little training for government service held many of the highest posts, and stringent

Mohsen Shandiz/Sygma/Corbis

Muslim Women Mourning the Death of Ayatollah Khomeini in 1989 *An Islamic revolution overthrew the shah of Iran in 1979. Ayatollah Khomeini sought to lead Iran away from the influences of Western culture and challenged the power of the United States in the Persian Gulf.*

measures were taken to combat Western styles and culture. Universities were temporarily closed, and their faculties were purged of secularists and monarchists. Women were compelled to wear modest Islamic garments outside the house, and semiofficial vigilante committees policed public morals and cast a pall over entertainment and social life. Many sectors of the Iranian economy were also placed under the direction of clerically controlled foundations, leading to massive capital flight. Clerical mismanagement and inflation have contributed to decades of economic stagnation in Iran.

President Carter had criticized the shah's repressive regime, but the overthrow of a long-standing ally and the creation of the Islamic Republic were blows to American prestige. The new Iranian regime was anti-Israeli and anti-American. Seeing the United States as a "Great Satan" opposed to Islam, Khomeini fostered Islamic revolutionary movements that threatened the United States and Israel. In November 1979 Iranian radicals seized the U.S. embassy in Tehran and held fifty-two diplomats hostage for 444 days. Americans felt humiliated by their inability to rescue the hostages or negotiate their release.

In the fall of 1980, shortly after negotiations for the release of the hostages began, **Saddam Hussein** (sah-DAHM hoo-SANE), the ruler of neighboring Iraq, invaded Iran to topple the Islamic Republic. His own dictatorial rule rested on a secular, Arab-nationalist philosophy and long-standing friendship with the Soviet

Union, which had provided him with advanced weaponry. He feared that the fervor of Iran's revolutionary Shi'ite leaders would infect his own country's Shi'ite majority and threaten his power. The war pitted American weapons in the hands of the Iranians against Soviet weapons in the hands of the Iraqis, but the superpowers avoided overt involvement during eight years of bloodshed. Covertly, however, the United States used Israel to transfer arms to Iran, hoping to gain the release of other American hostages held by radical Islamic groups in Lebanon and to help finance the Contra war against the Sandinista government of Nicaragua. When this deal came to light in 1986, the resulting political scandal intensified American hostility to Iran. Openly tilting toward Iraq, President Reagan sent the United States Navy to the Persian Gulf, ostensibly to protect nonbelligerent shipping. The move helped force Iran to accept a cease-fire in 1988.

While the United States dealt with Iran, the Soviet Union faced even more serious problems in neighboring Afghanistan. In 1978 a Marxist party with a secular agenda seized power. Offended by the new regime's efforts to reform education and grant rights to women, traditional Afghan ethnic and religious leaders led a successful rebellion. The Soviet Union responded by sending its army into Afghanistan to install a communist regime. With the United States, Saudi Arabia, and Pakistan paying, equipping, and training Afghan rebels, the Soviet Union found itself in an unwinnable war like the one the United States had stumbled into in Vietnam. Facing growing economic problems and widespread domestic discontent over the war, Soviet leaders withdrew their troops in 1989. Three years later rebel groups took control of the entire country and then began to fight among themselves over who should rule. In this chaotic situation a radical Islamic party with close ties to Pakistan, the Taliban, took power in 1996. They installed a harsh religious regime and soon faced armed opposition. The Taliban had received financial support from the Saudi Arabian Usama bin Laden during their rise to power and later provided him with protection as he organized the militant organization al-Qaeda that later attacked the United States (see Chapter 33).

Asian Transformation

Although Japan has few mineral resources and is dependent on oil imports, the Japanese economy weathered the oil price shocks of the 1970s much better than did the economies of Europe and the United States. In fact, Japan experienced a faster rate of economic growth in the 1970s and 1980s than did any other major developed economy, growing at about 10 percent a year and becoming the world's second largest economy. Average income also increased rapidly, overtaking that of the United States in 1986.

There were major differences between the Japanese and U.S. industrial models. During the American occupation, Japanese industrial conglomerates known as *zaibatsu* (see Chapter 27) were broken up. Although ownership of major industries became less concentrated, business leaders created new industrial alliances to control competition and facilitate the allocation of resources. During the period of dramatic growth there were six major **keiretsu** (kay-REHT-soo), each of which included a major bank as well as firms in industry, commerce, and construction tied together in an interlocking ownership structure. There were also minor keiretsu dominated by major industrial corporations, like Toyota.

The Struggle for Women's Rights in an Era of Global Political and Economic Change

The struggle for women's rights has been one of the most important social movements of the twentieth and twenty-first centuries. Although we can identify fundamental similarities in objectives across cultural and political boundaries, women in less developed nations are forced to recognize that their objectives and strategies must take into account international inequalities in power and wealth.

In this section Gladys Acosta, a militant Peruvian feminist, discusses the appropriate agenda for this struggle in the era after the fall of the Soviet Union and the rise of **neo-liberalism,** *the term used in Latin America to identify the free-market economic policies advocated by the United States. Among its chief characteristics are an end to the protection of local industries, a reduction in government social welfare policies, a reduction in public-sector employment, a commitment to paying debts to international creditors, and the removal of impediments to foreign investment. Many Latin Americans believe that neoliberalism is a new form of imperialism. While written in the 1990s, this political manifesto deals directly with issues of great relevance today: international indebtedness, the social costs of austerity, and gender inequality.*

Neo-Liberalism in Action

When I talk of neo-liberalism, I mean austerity measures, foreign debts, and increased liberties for all those who have the power of money at their disposal and the power of repression over those who make demands. We have now reached a new form of capitalist accumulation. The world's economic system is in a state of change and capital has become more concentrated and centralised. I would not go as far as to say countries don't exist anymore but national identities do certainly play a different role now.... If we look at the bare face of neo-liberalism from a woman's point of view, we cannot fail to notice its murderous consequences.... At the moment we're experiencing capitalism's greatest ideological offensive. It's all business: everything is bought and sold and everything has its price.

The Consequences of Neo-Liberal Politics

[W]omen play an important role in this ever-more internationalized economy because we represent, as ever, a particularly exploitable workforce. A number of studies have revealed the existence of

Tariffs and import regulations inhibiting foreign competition were crucial to the early stages of development of Japan's major industries. These restrictions and Japanese success at exporting manufactured goods through the 1970s and 1980s produced huge trade surpluses with other nations. Although the United States and the European Community engaged in tough negotiations to try to force open the Japanese market, these efforts had only limited success, and by 1990 Japan's trade surplus with the rest of the world was double that of 1985.

subcontractor chains who work for transnational companies "informally" and mainly employ women. Basically we are dealing with a kind of integration into the world market which often uses our own homes as its outlet. Obviously, this work is badly paid and completely unprotected and has to be done without any of those social rights which were formerly achieved by trade union struggles.... As it advances worldwide, this capitalism also encourages the expansion of certain kinds of tourism. A visible increase in prostitution is part of this, whereby women from poor countries are smuggled into large, internationally operated rings which exploit them. The reports of Filipina women traded on the West German market send shivers down our spines....

How the Adoption of Austerity Measures Affects Women's Lives

It is obvious that foreign debt is one of the most inhuman forms of exploitation in our countries when one considers the ratio between work necessary for workers' needs and work producing profit for employers. The experts have already explained how the prevailing exchange and investment structures have created international finance systems which keep whole populations in inhuman conditions.... Women in every household are suffering every day as a result of impoverished economies and those who

are most exposed to the effects of foreign debt are women.

When it comes to shopping, caring for sick children or the impossibility of meeting their schooling costs, the illusion of "leaving poverty behind" evaporates. Yet the problem is not only of an economic nature because under such circumstances the constant tension leads to grave, often lasting exhaustion. The psychosocial damage is alarming. The adoption of austerity measures means a curtailment of the state's commitment to social services with a direct effect on women. Daily life becomes hell for them. The lack of even minimal state welfare presents women (and obviously children too) with crushing working days.

Questions for Analysis

1. What is neo-liberalism?
2. According to Acosta, how does global economic integration fostered by neo-liberalism affect the lives of women as workers?
3. Acosta claims that indebtedness to foreign lenders leads to austerity measures. How do these measures impact families in poor countries?

Source: From Gladys Acosta, "The View of a Peruvian Militant," in Compañeras. Voices from the Latin American Women's Movement, *edited by Gaby Küppers (London: Latin American Bureau, 1994). Reprinted with permission of the publisher.*

Many experts assumed that Japan's competitive advantages would propel it past the United States as the world's preeminent industrial economy, but during the 1990s Japan entered what would become a two-decade-long crisis that dramatically slowed the growth of both GDP (gross domestic product) and average income. In the thirty months between January 1990 and July 1992, Japanese stocks and real estate markets lost $2.5 trillion in market value, while the national growth rate fell from 3.1 percent a year to 0.2 percent.

Before the crisis, Japanese real estate and stock markets had become highly overvalued as the nation's huge trade imbalances with the United States and other trading partners flooded the economy with cash and fueled speculation. As the crisis deepened and prices collapsed, the close relationships between industry, government, and banks proved to be a liability, as these powerful institutions acted to prop up inefficient companies and support unsustainable market values. By the end of the 1990s Japan's GDP had suffered a loss greater than that suffered by the United States in the Great Depression, leaving the nation with a crushing debt burden. Despite government efforts to promote recovery with public works projects and low interest rates, Japan's economy has grown very slowly to the present.

Other Asian states imitated the Japanese model of development in the 1970s and 1980s. These nations protected new industries from foreign competition while encouraging close alliances among industries and banks. The largest and most successful of them, the Republic of Korea, commonly called South Korea, used a combination of inexpensive labor, strong technical education, and substantial domestic capital reserves to support a massive industrialization effort. Success in heavy industries such as steel and shipbuilding as well as in consumer industries such as automobiles and consumer electronics soon made it a global economic power.

The small nations of Taiwan and Singapore, along with Hong Kong, a British colony until 1997, also became industrial powerhouses. As a result of their rapid development, these three economies along with South Korea were called the **Asian Tigers**. While Taiwan suffered a number of political reverses, including the loss of its United Nations seat to the People's Republic of China in 1971 and the withdrawal of diplomatic recognition by the United States, it achieved remarkable economic progress, based in large part on investment in the economy of the People's Republic of China. Hong Kong and Singapore—long British colonies with extremely limited natural resources—also enjoyed rapid economic development. Both were historically important Asian ports and commercial centers that later developed successful manufacturing, banking, and commercial sectors.

These **newly industrialized economies (NIEs)** shared many characteristics that help explain their rapid industrialization. All had disciplined and hard-working labor forces, and all invested heavily in education. For example, as early as 1980 South Korea had as many engineering graduates as Germany, Britain, and Sweden combined. All had very high rates of personal saving, about 35 percent of GDP, that funded new technologies, and all emphasized outward-looking export strategies. And, like Japan, all benefited from government sponsorship and protection. Despite this momentum, the region was deeply shaken by a financial crisis that began in 1997. Like the recession that afflicted Japan in 1990, a combination of bad loans, weak banks, and the international effects of currency speculation led to a deep regional crisis that was stabilized only by the efforts of the United States, Japan, and international institutions like the International Monetary Fund.

China Rejoins the World Economy

After Mao Zedong's death in 1976, the Chinese communist leadership began economic reforms that relaxed state control, allowing more initiative and permitting individuals to accumulate wealth. The results were remarkable. Under China's leader **Deng Xiaoping** (dung shee-yao-ping) China permitted foreign investment for the first time since the communists came to power in 1949. Between 1979 and 2005 foreign direct investment in China grew to more than $600 billion as McDonald's, General Motors, Coca-Cola, Airbus, Toyota, and many other foreign companies began doing business. As a result, by 2010 China had become a major industrial power and the world's most important exporting nation. Despite these changes, state-owned enterprises still employed more than 100 million workers, and most foreign-owned companies were limited to special economic zones. The result was a dual industrial sector—one modern, efficient, and connected to international markets, the other directed by political decisions. While the Chinese have not yet privatized land, by 1990 over 90 percent of China's agricultural land was in the hands of farmers permitted to sell what they produced.

In 2010 China became the world's second largest economy, surpassing Japan. The scale of this achievement can be represented by the remarkable growth of China's GDP, the total value of all goods and services produced by the nation. In 1970 China, with a population of nearly 1 billion, had a GDP of $56 billion, smaller than the GDP of Italy ($111 billion), which had a population of 55 million people. By 2010 China's GDP had increased eighty-one times, surpassing $4,520 billion. Other developing countries grew substantially in this period as well. India's economy, for example, was larger than China's in 1970 ($66 billion) and increased nineteen times by 2010, to $1,251 billion.

Despite its enormous achievement, China, with a per capita GDP of $5,413.57, has remained substantially poorer than mature industrial economies, which have an average per capita GDP of $42,063. However, China is now richer than much of the developing world. Latin America has a per capita GDP of $4,299, the Middle East $2,329, and sub-Saharan Africa $940. While poverty levels in China have fallen swiftly during this period of rapid development, inequality, especially between rural and urban dwellers, has increased.

The combination of economic reforms, high levels of foreign investment, and technology transfers from developed industrial nations has helped make China one of the world's major industrial powers. As was true earlier with Japan and the Asian Tigers, China's expansion has depended heavily on exports, which accounted for over 40 percent of GPD in 2008. Success in foreign markets produced a large foreign trade surplus. As was the case with Japan three decades ago, these cash surpluses paid for the government's massive investments in infrastructure, promoted speculation in real estate and stocks, and propped up a weak banking sector. While the Chinese economy continued to grow at a healthy rate during the worldwide recession that began in 2008, some economists wonder if the speculative excesses can be overcome without a deep contraction similar to that experienced by Japan in the 1990s.

Deng Xiaoping's strategy of balancing change and continuity avoided some of the social and political costs experienced by Russia and other socialist countries that abruptly embraced capitalism and democracy (see next section), but he faced a major challenge in 1989. Responding to inflation and to worldwide mass movements in favor of democracy, Chinese students and intellectuals led a series of protests demanding more democracy and an end to corruption. This movement culminated in **Tiananmen** (tee-yehn-ahn-men) **Square**, in the heart of Beijing, where hundreds of thousands of protesters gathered and refused to leave. After weeks of standoff, tanks pushed into the square, killing hundreds and arresting thousands. The Communist Party has not faced another direct challenge to its power since then, but growing levels of labor unrest, protests in favor of political rights, corruption scandals, and ethnic confrontations continue to challenge this one-party dictatorship.

THE END OF THE BIPOLAR WORLD

After the end of World War II, competition between the alliances led by the United States and the Soviet Union created a bipolar world (see Chapter 31). Every conflict, no matter how local its origins, had the potential of engaging the attention of one or both of the superpowers. The Korean War, decolonization in Africa, the Vietnam War, the Cuban Revolution, and hostilities between Israel and its neighbors increased tension between the nuclear-armed superpowers. Given this succession of provocations, politics everywhere was dominated by arguments over the relative merits of the competing systems.

Few in 1980 predicted the startling collapse of the Soviet Union. Western observers tended to see communist nations as both more uniform in character and more subservient to the Soviet Union than was true. Long before the 1980s, deep divisions had appeared among communist states. Similarly, nationalism had reappeared as a powerful force among the once-independent nations and ethnic groups brought together within the Soviet Union. By the late 1980s these forces threatened the survival of this communist world power.

Crisis in the Soviet Union   Under U.S. president Ronald Reagan and the Soviet Union's general secretary Leonid Brezhnev (leh-oh-NEED BREZ-nef), Cold War rhetoric remained intense. Massive new U.S. investments in armaments placed heavy competitive burdens on a Soviet economy already suffering from shortages and mismanagement. Obsolete industrial plants and centralized planning stifled initiative in the Soviet Union and led to a declining standard of living relative to the West, while the arbitrariness of the bureaucracy, the manipulation of information, and material deprivations created a crisis in morale.

Despite the unpopularity of the war in Afghanistan and growing discontent, Brezhnev refused to modify his unsuccessful policies, but he could not escape criticism. Self-published underground writings (*samizdat* [sah-meez-DAHT]) by critics of the regime circulated widely despite government efforts to suppress them. In a series of powerful books, the writer Alexander Solzhenitzyn (sol-zhuh-NEET-sin) castigated the Soviet system. Although he won a Nobel Prize in literature, authorities charged him with treason and expelled him in 1974.

By the time **Mikhail Gorbachev** (GORE-beh-CHOF) came to power in 1985, weariness with war in Afghanistan, economic decay, and vocal protest had reached critical levels. Casting aside Brezhnev's hard line, Gorbachev authorized major reforms in an attempt to stave off total collapse. His policy of political openness (*glasnost*) permitted criticism of the government and the Communist Party. His policy of **perestroika** (per-ih-STROY-kuh) ("restructuring") was an attempt to address long-suppressed economic problems by moving away from central state planning. In 1989 he ended the unpopular war in Afghanistan.

The Collapse of the Socialist Bloc   In 1980 protests by Polish shipyard workers in the city of Gdansk led to the formation of **Solidarity**, a labor union that grew to 9 million members. The Roman Catholic Church in Poland, strengthened by the elevation of a Pole, Karol Wojtyla (KAH-rol voy-TIL-ah), to the papacy as John Paul II in 1978, gave strong moral support to the protest movement.

The Polish government imposed martial law in 1981 in response to the growing power of Solidarity and its allies, giving the army effective political control. Seeing Solidarity under tight controls and many of its leaders in prison, the Soviet Union decided not to intervene. But Solidarity remained a potent force with a strong institutional structure and nationally recognized leaders. As Gorbachev loosened political controls in the Soviet Union after 1985, communist leaders elsewhere lost confidence in Soviet resolve, and critics and reformers in Poland and throughout eastern Europe were emboldened.

Beleaguered Warsaw Pact governments vacillated between relaxation of control and suppression of dissent. Just as the Catholic clergy in Poland had supported Solidarity, Protestant and Orthodox religious leaders aided the rise of opposition groups elsewhere. This combination of nationalism and religion provided a powerful base for opponents of the communist regimes. Communist governments sought to quiet the opposition by turning to the West for trade and financial assistance. They also opened their nations to travelers, ideas, styles, and money from Western countries, all of which accelerated the demand for change.

By the end of 1989 communist governments across eastern Europe had fallen. The dismantling of the Berlin Wall vividly represented this transformation. While communist leaders in Poland, Hungary, Czechoslovakia, and Bulgaria decided that change was inevitable, the dictator Nicolae Ceausescu (nehk-oh-LIE chow-SHES-koo) of Romania refused to surrender power and was overthrown and executed. The comprehensiveness of these changes became clear in 1990, when the Polish people elected Solidarity leader Lech Walesa (leck wah-LEN-sah) as president and the people of Czechoslovakia elected dissident playwright Vaclav Havel (vah-SLAV hah-VEL) as president.

Following the fall of the Berlin Wall, a tidal wave of patriotic enthusiasm swept aside the once-formidable communist government of East Germany. In the chaotic months that followed, East Germans crossed to West Germany in large numbers, and government services in the eastern sector nearly disappeared. The collapse of the East German government led quickly in 1990 to reunification.

Soviet leaders knew that similarly powerful nationalist sentiments existed within the Soviet Union as well. The year 1990 brought declarations of independence by Lithuania, Estonia, and Latvia, three small states on the Baltic Sea that the Soviet Union had annexed in 1939. The end of the Soviet Union then came suddenly in 1991. After communist hardliners botched a coup against Gorbachev, disgust with communism boiled over. Boris Yeltsin, the president of the Russian Republic, emerged as the most powerful leader in the country. Russia, the largest republic in the Soviet Union, was effectively taking the place of the disintegrating

Bossu Regis/Corbis Sygma

The Fall of the Berlin Wall *The Berlin Wall was the most important symbol of the Cold War. Constructed to keep residents of East Germany from fleeing to the West and defended by armed guards and barbed wire, it was the public face of communism. As the Soviet system fell apart, the residents of East and West Berlin broke down sections of the wall.*

USSR. In September 1991 the Congress of People's Deputies—the central legislature of the USSR—voted to dissolve the union. Then in December a weak successor state with little central control, the Commonwealth of Independent States (CIS), was created and Gorbachev resigned.

The ethnic and religious passions that fueled the breakup of the Soviet Union also overwhelmed the Balkan nation of Yugoslavia. In 1991 it dissolved into a morass of separatism and warring ethnic and religious groups. Slovenia and Croatia, the most westerly provinces, both heavily Roman Catholic, became independent states in 1992. The population of Bosnia and Herzegovina was more mixed: 40 percent were Muslims, 30 percent Serbian Orthodox, and 18 percent Catholics. Following the declaration of Bosnian national independence in 1992, the nation's Orthodox Serbs attempted to rid the state of Muslims in a violent process called **ethnic cleansing**. After extensive television coverage of atrocities and wanton destruction, the United States intervened and eventually brokered a settlement in 1995 that effectively created two ethnically separate political entities.

In 1999 new fighting and a new round of ethnic cleansing occurred in the southernmost Yugoslavian province of Kosovo. Seen by Serbs as their homeland, Kosovo had a predominantly Muslim and Albanian population. When Serbia refused to stop military action, the United States, Britain, and France acted on behalf of NATO by launching an aerial war on Serbian targets in Kosovo and in Serbia itself that forced the withdrawal of Serbian forces from Kosovo. Serbia's president during this violent period, Slobodan Milosevic, was forced from power and turned over to a war crimes tribunal in The Hague, where he died in prison.

Africa in the Era of Global Political Change   Sub-Saharan Africa has experienced political instability, military coups, civil wars, and conflicts over resources since independence. It has also remained among the poorest regions in the world. Southern Africa, however, has seen democratic progress and a steady decline in armed conflicts since 1991. A key change came in South Africa in 1994, when long-time political prisoner Nelson Mandela and his African National Congress (ANC) won the first national elections in which the African majority could participate equally. Also hopeful has been the return to democracy of Nigeria, Africa's most populous state, after decades of military rulers. In 1999, after a succession of military governments, Nigerians elected President Olusegun Obasanjo (oh-LOO-she-gun oh-BAH-san-jo) (a former coup leader), and a 2003 vote gave him a second term, despite serious voting irregularities. Similarly, in 2002 Kenyans voted out the Kenya African National Union Party that had held power for thirty-nine years.

Africa was also a scene of ethnic cleansing. In 1994 the political leaders of the Central African nation of Rwanda incited the Hutu people to massacre their Tutsi neighbors. Although the major powers had earlier promised to intervene in genocides, they sought to avoid military involvement in Rwanda by not using the word *genocide* to describe the slaughter. Without foreign intervention, the carnage claimed 750,000 lives, with millions more becoming refugees. Finally, the United States and other powers intervened and the United Nations set up a tribunal to try those responsible for the genocide. In 1998 violence spread from Rwanda to neighboring Congo, where growing opposition and ill health had forced President Joseph Mobutu from office after over three decades of dictatorial misrule. Various peacemaking attempts failed to restore order, and by mid-2003 more than 3 million Congolese had died from disease, malnutrition, and injuries related to the fighting.

The Persian Gulf War

The Persian Gulf War was the first significant military conflict to occur after the breakup of the Soviet Union and the end of the Cold War. Iraq's ruler, Saddam Hussein, had borrowed a great deal of money from neighboring Kuwait and failed to get Kuwait's royal family to reduce this debt. He was also eager to control Kuwait's oil fields. Hussein believed that the smaller and militarily weaker nation could be quickly defeated, and he suspected that the United States would not react. The invasion occurred in August 1990.

The United States decided to react. Saudi Arabia, an important ally of the United States and a major oil producer, also supported intervention. With his intention to use force endorsed by the United Nations and with many Islamic nations supporting military action, President George H. W. Bush ordered an attack in early 1991. Iraq's military defeat was comprehensive, but Hussein remained in power, crushing an uprising just months following his defeat. The United States imposed various conditions on Iraq that kept tensions high, helping create the conditions for a new, larger, war in 2003 (see Chapter 33).

MAP 32.1   The End of the Soviet Union

When communist hardliners failed to overthrow Gorbachev in 1991, popular anticommunist sentiment swept the Soviet Union. Following Boris Yeltsin's lead in Russia, the republics that constituted the Soviet Union declared their independence.

THE CHALLENGE OF POPULATION GROWTH

For most of human history, governments viewed population growth as beneficial, a source of national wealth and power. Since the late eighteenth century, however, many intellectuals and politicians have viewed population increases with alarm, fearing that the production of food and other essential resources could not keep up with population growth. Late in the nineteenth century some social critics expressed concern that growing populations would lead to class and ethnic struggle. By the second half of the twentieth century, fears of population growth were primarily attached to environmental concerns. Are urban sprawl, pollution, and soil erosion the inevitable results of population growth? The questions and debates continue today, but clearly population growth is both a cause and a result of increased global interdependency.

Demographic Transition The population of Europe almost doubled between 1850 and 1914, putting enormous pressure on rural land and urban housing and overwhelming fragile public institutions that provided crisis assistance (see Chapter 27). This dramatic growth forced a large wave of immigration across the Atlantic, helping to develop the Western Hemisphere and invigorating the Atlantic economy (see Chapter 25). Population growth also contributed to Europe's Industrial Revolution by lowering labor costs and increasing consumer demand.

While some Europeans saw the rapid increase in human population as a blessing, others warned of disaster. The best-known pessimist was the English cleric **Thomas Malthus**, who in 1798 argued that unchecked population growth would outstrip food production. When Malthus looked at Europe's future, he used a prejudiced image of China to terrify his readers. A visitor to China, he claimed, "will not be surprised that mothers destroy or expose many of their children; that parents sell their daughters for a trifle; ... and that there should be such a number of robbers. The surprise is that nothing still more dreadful should happen."[1]

The generation that came of age in the years after World War II lived in a world where Malthus seemed to have little relevance. Industrial and agricultural productivity had multiplied supplies of food and other necessities. At the same time, cultural changes associated with expanded female employment, older age at marriage, and more effective family planning had slowed the rate of population increase. By the 1960s Europe and other industrial societies had made the **demographic transition** to lower fertility rates (average number of births per woman) and reduced mortality. This meant that populations would age quickly. In the world's most developed nations, for example, median age rose from twenty-nine years in 1950 and to thirty-seven years by 2000.

By the late 1970s, the developing world had still not experienced the demographic transition and the global discussion of population growth became politicized. Leaders in some developing nations actively promoted large families, arguing that larger populations increased national power. When industrialized

---

[1] Quoted in Antony Flew, "Introduction," in Thomas Robert Malthus, *An Essay on the Principle of Population and a Summary View of the Principle of Population* (New York: Penguin Books, 1970), 30.

Chinese Family-Planning Campaign *To slow population growth, the Chinese government has sought to limit parents to a single child. Billboards and other forms of mass advertising have been an essential part of the campaign.*

nations, mostly white, raised concerns about rapid population growth in Asia, Africa, and Latin America, populist political leaders in these regions responded by asking whether these concerns were racist.

This question exposed the influence of racism in the population debate and temporarily disarmed Western advocates of birth control. However, once the economic shocks of the 1970s and 1980s had revealed the vulnerability of poor nations, governments in the developing world jettisoned policies that promoted population growth. Mexico is a good example. In the 1970s the government had encouraged high fertility, and population grew an average of 3 percent per year. In the 1980s Mexico rejected these policies and began to promote birth control, leading by the 1990s to an annual population growth of 1.7 percent.

World population exploded in the twentieth century, more than doubling between 1950 and 2000 (see Table 32.1). Although the rate of growth has slowed since the 1980s, world population still increases by a number equal to the total population of the United States roughly every three years. If fertility were to remain constant from today, with a world average of 2.5 children per woman, population would reach nearly 27 billion in 2100. This will not happen, however, because fertility is declining in most developing nations and is at less than replacement levels in most industrialized countries. As a result, most experts estimate a world population in 2100 of around 10 billion.

TABLE 32.1 | POPULATION FOR WORLD AND MAJOR AREAS, 1750–2050

Major Area	Population Size (Millions)						
	1750	1800	1850	1900	1950	1995	2050*
World	791	978	1,262	1,650	2,521	5,666	8,909
Africa	106	107	111	133	221	697	1,766
Asia	502	635	809	947	1,402	3,437	5,268
Europe	163	203	276	408	547	728	628
Latin America and the Caribbean	16	24	38	74	167	480	809
North America	2	7	26	82	172	297	398
Oceania	2	2	2	6	13	28	46

Major Area	Percentage Distribution						
	1750	1800	1850	1900	1950	1995	2050*
World	100	100	100	100	100	100	100
Africa	13.4	10.9	8.8	8.1	8.8	12	23.7
Asia	63.5	64.9	64.1	57.4	55.6	61	57.1
Europe	20.6	20.8	21.9	24.7	21.7	13	5.3
Latin America and the Caribbean	2.0	2.5	3.0	4.5	6.6	8	9.4
North America	0.3	0.7	2.1	5.0	6.8	5	4.1
Oceania	0.3	0.2	0.2	0.4	0.5	1	0.5

*Estimated

Source: J. D. Durand, "Historical Estimates of World Population: An Evaluation" (Philadelphia: University of Pennsylvania, Population Studies Center, 1974, mimeographed); United Nations, The Determinants and Consequences of Population Trends, vol. 1 (New York: United Nations, 1973); United Nations, World Population Prospects as Assessed in 1963 (New York: United Nations, 1966); United Nations, World Population Prospects: The 1998 Revision (New York: United Nations, forthcoming); United Nations Population Division, Department of Economic and Social Affairs, World Population to 2300. (2004.), http://www.un.org/esa/population/publications/longrange2/World Pop2300final.pdf.

At the same time mortality rates have increased in some areas as immigration, commercial expansion, and improved transportation have facilitated the transmission of disease. The rapid spread of HIV/AIDS is an example of this phenomenon. Less developed regions with poorly funded public health institutions and with few resources to invest in prevention and treatment experience the highest rates of infection and the greatest mortality. Of the countries with the highest HIV/AIDS rates in 2010, thirty-seven are in Africa, three in Asia, and six in Latin America and the Caribbean. These countries are home to 87 percent of all HIV/AIDS infections. By 2007 approximately 25 million people had died of AIDS and another 33 million were infected worldwide. In recent years prevention programs and improved drug therapies have slowed both mortality and infection rates, with the greatest successes registered in rich countries with the greatest medical resources.

The Industrialized Nations   In the developed industrial nations of western Europe and in Japan, fertility levels are so low that population would fall without immigration. Japanese women have an average of 1.4 children, while Italian women have 1.2. Although Sweden tries to promote fertility with cash payments, tax incentives, and job leaves to families with children, the average number of births per woman is 1.4. By comparison, the average African woman now has 4.6 children. Higher levels of female education and employment, the material values of consumer culture, and access to contraception and abortion explain the low fertility of mature industrial nations. An Italian woman in Bologna, the city with the lowest fertility in the world, put it this way: "I'm an only child and if I could, I'd have more than one child. But most couples I know wait until their 30's to have children. People want to have their own life, they want to have a successful career. When you see life in these terms, children are an impediment."[2]

In industrialized nations life expectancy improved as fertility declined. The combination of abundant food, improved hygiene, and more effective medicines and medical care has lengthened human lives. In 2000 about 20 percent of the population in Europe was sixty-five or over. By 2050 this proportion will rise to over one-third. Italy soon will have more than twenty adults fifty years old or over for each five-year-old child. Because of higher fertility and greater levels of immigration, the United States is moving in this direction more slowly than western Europe; by 2050 the median age in Europe will be fifty-two, while it will be thirty-nine in the United States.

The combination of falling fertility and rising life expectancy in the industrialized nations presents a challenge very different from the one foreseen by Malthus. These nations generally offer a broad array of social services, including retirement income, medical services, and housing supplements for the elderly. As the number of retirees increases relative to the number of employed people, the cost of these programs may become unsustainable. Economists track this problem by using the PSR (potential support ratio): the ratio of persons fifteen to sixty-four years old (likely workers) to persons sixty-five or older (likely retirees). Between 1950 and 2000 the world's PSR fell from 12 to 9. In mature industrial countries the PSR fell from 8 to 5. By 2050 it will fall to 4 for the world's population and to an unsustainable 2 in mature industrial countries.

The Developing Nations   At current rates, 95 percent of all future population growth will be in developing nations (see Table 32.1). A comparison between Europe and Africa illustrates these changes. In 1950 Europe had more than twice the population of Africa. By 1985 Africa's population

---

[2]"Population Implosion Worries a Graying Europe," *New York Times*, July 10, 1998.

had drawn even with Europe, and, according to United Nations projections, its population will be three times larger than Europe's by 2050.

Rapid population growth continued after 2000 in the developing world even as birthrates fell. Among all developing nations, average birthrates fell from 44 births per thousand inhabitants in 1950 to 22 today. Birthrates fell most steeply in countries experiencing the most rapid economic development. In China the birthrate fell from 42 births per thousand in 1950 to a First World level of 13 today. In this same period birthrates declined from 43 per thousand to 23 in India, another fast-growing economy. Change occurred much more slowly in sub-Saharan Africa, where the birthrates fell from 47 per thousand to 38, and in Muslim countries like Pakistan and Afghanistan, where birthrates declined from 42 to 28 and 53 to 45 per thousand, respectively. The populations of Latin America were also expanding, but at rates much slower than in sub-Saharan Africa and the Muslim nations. In this same period, Latin America's birthrate declined from 43 per thousand in 1950 to 19 in 2010. Regardless of these changes, birthrates remain more than twice as high in the developing world as in the mature industrial nations, with the highest levels in the poorest countries.

Old and Young Populations   Population pyramids generated by demographers clearly illustrate the profound transformation in human reproductive patterns and life expectancy since World War II. Figure 32.1 shows the 2001 age distributions in Pakistan, South Korea, and Sweden—nations at three different stages of economic development. Sweden is a mature industrial nation. South Korea is rapidly industrializing and has surpassed many European nations in both industrial output and per capita wealth. Pakistan is a poor, traditional Muslim nation with rudimentary industrialization, low educational levels, and little effective family planning.

In 2001 nearly 50 percent of Pakistan's population was under age sixteen. The resulting pressures on the economy have been extraordinary. Every year

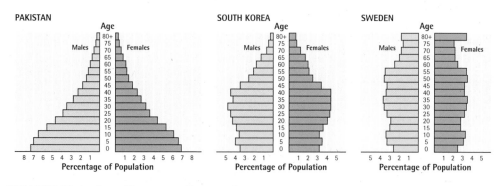

FIGURE 32.1 Age Structure Comparison

Islamic Nation (Pakistan), Non-Islamic Developing Nation (South Korea), and Developed Nation (Sweden), 2001.

Source: U.S. Bureau of the Census, *International Database*, 2001.

approximately 150,000 men reach age sixty-five—and another 1.2 million turn sixteen. Pakistan, therefore, has to create more than a million new jobs a year or face growing unemployment and declining wages. Sweden confronts a different problem. Sweden's aging population, growing demand for social welfare benefits, and declining labor pool means that its industries may become less competitive and living standards may decline. In South Korea, a decline in fertility dramatically altered the ratio of children to adults, creating an age distribution similar to that of western Europe.

Unequal Development and the Movement of Peoples

Two characteristics of the postwar world should now be clear. First, despite decades of experimentation with state-directed economic development, most nations that were poor in 1960 are still poor today. There are notable exceptions. In Asia, first Japan, then the Asian Tigers (Taiwan, Singapore, South Korea, and Hong Kong), and more recently China have generated high rates of growth and are now among the world's most competitive industrial powers. In recent years Brazil, Mexico, and India have also experienced significant growth. This industrial transformation has increased world demand for raw materials, which in turn has elevated the wealth of an equally small number of oil-exporting nations. Second, world population has increased to startlingly high levels, and much of the increase was, and will continue to be, in the poorest nations.

The combination of intractable poverty and growing population has generated a surge in international immigration. Few issues have stirred more controversy. Even moderate voices have sometimes framed this discussion of immigration as a competition among peoples. Large numbers of legal and illegal immigrants from poor nations with growing populations are entering the developed industrial nations, with the exception of Japan. Large-scale migrations within developing countries are a related phenomenon. The movement of impoverished rural residents to the cities of Asia, Africa, and Latin America (see Table 32.2) has increased steadily since the 1970s. This internal migration often serves as the first step toward migration abroad.

The Problem of Inequality   Since 1945 the global economy has expanded more rapidly than at any time in the past. Faster, cheaper communications and transportation have combined with improvements in industrial and agricultural technologies to create material abundance that would have amazed those who experienced the first Industrial Revolution (see Chapter 22). Despite this remarkable economic expansion, the differences between rich and poor nations remain stark.

The gap between rich and poor nations has grown wider since 1945, although the 2008 recession has had a powerful negative effect on many advanced industrial economies. China's spectacular rise as an industrial power since 1980 is a strong indicator that some once-poor countries can modernize and become competitive industrial nations. Nevertheless, the vast majority of the world's population continues to live in

TABLE 32.2 | THE WORLD'S LARGEST CITIES (URBAN AGGLOMERATIONS OF 13 MILLION OR MORE)

City	1970	City	1990	City	2011	City	2025
1 Tokyo	23.3	1 Tokyo	32.5	1 Tokyo	37.2	1 Tokyo	38.7
2 New York	16.2	2 New York	16.1	2 Delhi	22.7	2 Delhi	32.9
		3 Mexico City	15.3	3 Mexico City	20.4	3 Shanghai	28.4
		4 São Paulo	14.8	4 New York	20.4	4 Mumbai	26.6
		5 Mumbai	12.4	5 Shanghai	20.2	5 Mexico City	24.6
		6 Osaka-Kobe	11.0	6 São Paulo	19.9	6 New York	23.6
		7 Calcutta	10.9	7 Mumbai	19.7	7 São Paulo	23.2
		8 Los Angeles	10.9	8 Beijing	15.6	8 Dhaka	22.9
		9 Seoul	10.5	9 Dhaka	15.4	9 Beijing	22.6
		10 Buenos Aires	10.5	10 Calcutta	14.4	10 Karachi	20.2
				11 Karachi	13.9	11 Lagos	18.9
				12 Buenos Aires	13.5	12 Calcutta	18.7
				13 Los Angeles	13.4	13 Manila	16.3
						14 Los Angeles	15.7
						15 Shenzhen	15.5
						16 Buenos Aires	15.5
						17 Guangzhou	15.5
						18 Istanbul	14.9
						19 Cairo	14.7
						20 Kinshasa	14.5
						21 Chongqing	13.6
						22 Rio de Janeiro	13.6
						23 Bangalore	13.2

Source: United Nations, Economic and Social Affairs, World Urbanization Prospects: The 2011 Revision Highlights, 6-7.

poverty. There are many measures of the relative wealth of nations; GDP (gross domestic product) per capita measured in U.S. dollars is among the most common.

In 2010 the per capita GDP of Luxembourg was the highest in the world, $104,512; the U.S. figure was $46,702, and the Japanese figure was $43,063. The countries of the European Union were generally rich, but some of the former Soviet satellites recently admitted to the European Union have the GDP per capita of developing nations. France and Germany have per capita GDPs of $39,170 and $39,852, respectively. The poorest countries in the European Union, Bulgaria and Romania, have per capita GDPs similar to Russia's ($6,335)—$7,539 and $10,481, respectively.

Many countries in the developing world now approach the poorest tier of European countries in per capita GDP. Per capita GDP for Mexico is $9,133, Brazil $10,993, Chile $12,640, South Africa $7,272, and Gabon $8,768. But many more countries, especially in Asia and Africa, remain very poor: the Philippines, $2,140; India, $1,375; Pakistan, $1,019; Nigeria, $1,242; and Sudan, $1,538. The poorest, like Haiti, Kenya, and Bangladesh, have per capita GDP levels under $1,000.

Internal Migration: The Growth of Cities   In developing nations migration from rural areas to urban centers increased threefold between 1925 and 1950; the pace of migration then accelerated (see Table 32.2). While slums around the major cities of developing nations are seen as signs of social breakdown and economic failure, life in these urban slums was generally better than life in the countryside. A World Bank study estimated that three out of four rural-to-urban migrants made economic gains. Residents of cities in sub-Saharan Africa, for example, were six times more likely than rural residents to have safe water. An unskilled migrant from the depressed northeast of Brazil could triple his or her income by moving to Rio de Janeiro.

Eco Images/Universal Images Group/Getty Images

Garbage Dump in Manila, Philippines *In Third World nations thousands of poor families live by sorting and selling bottles, aluminum cans, plastic, and newspapers in urban landfills.*

As the scale of rural-to-urban migration grew, these benefits became more elusive. In the cities of the developing world basic services have been crumbling under the pressure of rapid population growth. In cities like Mexico City and Manila, which are among the world's largest cities, tens of thousands live in garbage dumps, scavenging for food. In Rio de Janeiro alone an estimated 350,000 abandoned children live in the streets and parks, begging, selling drugs, stealing, and engaging in prostitution to survive. Some nations have tried to relocate migrants back to the countryside. Indonesia, for example, has relocated more than a half-million urban residents since 1969.

Global Migration   Each year hundreds of thousands of men and women leave developing nations to go to industrialized nations. Dramatically rising numbers after 1960 have led to increased ethnic and racial tensions. Political refugees and immigrants have faced murderous violence in Germany; growing anti-immigrant sentiment has strengthened right-wing political movements and led to riots in cities with large immigrant populations in France and Greece; and in the United States the government has dramatically expanded its effort to control its southern border.

Immigrants from developing nations have brought host nations many of the same benefits that the great migration of Europeans to the Americas provided a century earlier (see Chapter 25). The United States actively recruited Mexican workers during World War II, and many European nations promoted guest worker programs and other inducements to immigration in the 1960s, when an expanding European economy experienced labor shortages. However, attitudes toward immigrants have changed as the size of immigrant populations has grown, particularly during periods of economic contraction like the recession that began in 2008. Under intense pressure, native-born workers demanded an end to immigration, seeing immigrants as competitors willing to work for lower wages and less likely to support labor unions.

High fertility among immigrants contributes to these tensions. Most immigrants are young adults who retain the positive attitudes toward early marriage and large families of their native cultures in Latin America, Africa, and the Middle East and have higher fertility rates than do host populations. Spain provides a useful example. In 2000 Spain had one of the world's lowest fertility rates, 1.2 births per woman. A member of the European Union, its economy was growing and employment opportunities were available to immigrants from Latin America, North Africa, and elsewhere. As a result, Spain briefly became the major immigrant-receiving nation in the European Union, and the immigrant component of Spain's population rose from 2.1 to 14.1 percent between 1990 and 2010. Because the birthrate of the immigrant population is twice as high as that of the native-born population, the effect of this trend has been multiplied, with foreign-born mothers accounting for 20 percent of all births. Since the beginning of the recession in 2008, immigration to Spain has slowed and birthrates of both native-born and foreign-born have fallen. But even in this altered context, immigrant groups continue to grow much faster than the native-born population. Similarly, as immigrant populations have increased across Europe and in the

United States in the twenty-first century, the resulting cultural conflicts have tested definitions of citizenship and nationality.

TECHNOLOGICAL AND ENVIRONMENTAL CHANGE

Technological innovation powered the economic expansion that began after World War II. New technologies increased productivity and disseminated human creativity. They also altered the way people lived, worked, and played. Because most of the economic benefits were initially concentrated in the advanced industrialized nations, technology increased the power of those nations relative to the developing world. This has changed in the last decade with globalization and the rising industrial role of China. Even within developed nations, postwar technological innovations did not benefit all classes, industries, and regions equally. There were losers as well as winners.

Population growth and increased levels of migration and urbanization multiplied the numbers of acres farmed and factories, intensifying environmental threats. In the early twenty-first century, loss of rain forest, soil erosion, global warming, air and water pollution, and extinction of species threatened the quality of life and the survival of human societies. Environmental protection, like the acquisition of new technology, had progressed most in societies with the greatest economic resources.

New Technologies and the World Economy

Nuclear energy, jet engines, radar, and tape recording were among the many World War II developments that later had an impact on consumers' lives. New technology increased industrial productivity, reduced labor requirements, and improved the flow of information that made markets more efficient. The consumer electronics industry rapidly developed new products, changes seen in the music industry's movement from vinyl records to 8-track tapes, CDs, and then MP3 technologies. Computers became faster and less expensive, cell phones were transformed into smartphones, and the speed of news and data accelerated at an unanticipated rate, transforming business, education, and politics globally.

Improvements in existing technologies accounted for much of the developed world's productivity increases during the 1950s and 1960s, as faster, more efficient transportation and communication cut costs and expanded markets. But new technologies were important as well. Governments bore much of the cost of developing and constructing nuclear power plants and sponsored research into new technologies. None has proved more influential in the last four decades than the computer, which transformed both work and leisure. The first computers were expensive, large, and slow, and only corporations, governments, and universities could afford them. Each new generation of computer has been smaller, faster, and less expensive. As a result, the serial utilization of desktops, laptops, tablets, and smartphones transformed commerce, education, and government. Today the computational capacity of a 1970s university mainframe computer can be found in the affordable and portable laptops of individual university students. The modern smartphone continues this pattern, serving as a platform for basic computing, search functions, and gaming as well as a sophisticated means of communication.

Computers also altered manufacturing. Small dedicated computers now control and monitor machinery in most modern industries. In the developed world, as well as in China and other fast-growing developing economies, factories forced by global competition to improve efficiency and product quality increasingly depend on robots. Japan's early lead in robotics in the 1990s has been reduced as Europe, the United States, and China have all raced to introduce robotics across their economies.

The transnational corporation became the primary agent for these technological changes. By the twentieth century the growing economic power of corporations in industrialized nations allowed them to invest directly in the mines, plantations, and public utilities of less developed regions. In the post–World War II years many of these companies became truly transnational, having multinational ownership and management. International trade agreements and open markets furthered the process. Ford, Nissan, BMW, and other car companies not only produced and sold cars internationally, but their shareholders, workers, and managers also came from numerous nations.

The location of manufacturing plants overseas and the acquisition of corporate operations by foreign buyers rendered such global firms as transnational as the products they sold. In the 1970s and 1980s American brand names like Levi's, Coca-Cola, Marlboro, Gillette, McDonald's, and Kentucky Fried Chicken were global phenomena. But in time Asian names—Honda, Hitachi, Sony, Sanyo, and Mitsubishi—were blazoned in neon and on giant video screens on the sides of skyscrapers, along with European brands such as Nestlé, Mercedes, Pirelli, and Benetton. Since 1979, China's emergence as a global industrial power has accelerated this process of integration and diffusion.

As transnational manufacturers, agricultural conglomerates, and financial giants became wealthier and more powerful, they increasingly escaped the controls imposed by national governments. If labor costs were too high in Japan, antipollution measures too intrusive in the United States, or taxes too high in Great Britain, transnational companies relocated—or threatened to do so. In 1945, for example, the U.S. textile industry was located in low-wage southern states, dominating the American market and exporting to the world. As wages in the American South rose and global competition increased, producers began relocating plants to Puerto Rico in the 1980s and to Mexico after NAFTA went into effect in 1994 (see Chapter 33). Now China is the primary manufacturer of textiles.

Conserving and Sharing Resources   In the 1960s environmental activists and political leaders began warning about the devastating environmental consequences of population growth, industrialization, and the expansion of agriculture onto marginal lands. Assaults on rain forests, the disappearance of species, and the poisoning of streams and rivers raised public consciousness, as did the depletion and pollution of the world's oceans. Environmental damage occurred both in the advanced industrial economies and in developing nations. The former Soviet Union, where industrial and nuclear wastes were routinely dumped with little concern for environmental consequences, had the worst environmental record.

In the developed world, industrial activity increased much more rapidly than the population grew, and the consumption of energy (coal, electricity, and petroleum) rose proportionally. This pattern is now clear in India, China, and other industrializing nations as well. Indeed, the consumer-driven economic expansion of the post–World War II years became an obstacle to addressing environmental problems, since modern economies depend on a profligate consumption of goods and resources. When consumption slows, industrial nations enter a recession, as recently demonstrated in 2008. How could the United States, Germany, Japan, or China change consumption patterns to protect the environment without endangering corporate profits, wages, and employment levels?

Since 1945 population growth has been most dramatic in the developing countries, where environmental pressures have also been extreme. In Brazil, India, and China, for example, the need to expand food production led to rapid deforestation and the extension of farming and grazing onto marginal lands. The results were predictable: erosion and water pollution. These and many other poor nations sought to stimulate industrialization because they believed that the transition from agriculture to manufacturing was the only way to provide for their rapidly growing populations. The argument was compelling: Why should Indians or Brazilians remain poor while Americans, Europeans, and Japanese grew rich?

Responding to Environmental Threats   Despite the gravity of environmental threats, there were many successful efforts to preserve and protect the environment. The Clean Air Act, the Clean Water Act, and the Endangered Species Act were passed in the United States in the 1970s as part of an environmental effort that included the nations of the European Community and Japan. Grassroots political movements and the media encouraged environmental awareness, and most nations in the developed world enforced strict antipollution laws and sponsored massive recycling efforts. Many also encouraged resource conservation by rewarding energy-efficient factories and manufacturers of fuel-efficient cars and by promoting the use of alternative energy sources such as solar and wind power.

Environmental efforts produced significant results. In western Europe and the United States, air quality improved dramatically. Smog levels in the United States fell nearly a third from 1970 to 2000, even though the number of automobiles increased more than 80 percent. Emissions of lead and sulfur dioxide were down as well. The Great Lakes, Long Island Sound, and Chesapeake Bay were all much cleaner at the beginning of the new century than they had been in 1970.

New technologies made much of the improvement possible; for example, pollution controls on automobiles, planes, and factory smokestacks reduced harmful emissions. At the same time, the desire to preserve the natural environment was growing around the world. In developed nations continued political organization and enhanced awareness of environmental issues seemed likely to lead to step-by-step improvements in environmental policy. In the developing world and most of the former Soviet bloc, however, population pressures and weak governments were major obstacles to effective environmental policies. Since the 1990s the rapid expansion of China's industrial sector as well as industrial growth in other developing nations like India and Brazil has put additional pressure on the environment.

It now seems likely that industrialized nations will have to fund global improvements and that the cost will be high. Slow growth and fiscal crises in the mature industrial economies after the 2008 recession have politicized and slowed the progress of environmental reform. Nevertheless, growing evidence of environmental degradation and global warming have continued to propel popular reform efforts, as when the media drew attention to the precipitous shrinkage of Peru's Andean glaciers and to loss of rain forest in Brazil. Yet, without broad agreement among the rich nations, the economic and political power necessary for environmental protections on a global scale will be very difficult to institute. When representatives from around the world negotiated a far-reaching treaty to reduce greenhouse gases in Kyoto, Japan, in 1997, President George W. Bush refused American participation even though the treaty was affirmed by nearly all other industrial nations. Canada subsequently withdrew from the agreement, and China and other rapidly industrializing nations were largely exempted from the treaty's limits. This agreement, as a result, has had a limited effect on greenhouse gas emissions.

CONCLUSION

The world was profoundly altered between 1975 and the first decade of the twenty-first century. Both the United States and the Soviet Union feared that every conflict and every regime change represented a potential threat to their strategic interests, and every conflict threatened to provoke confrontation between them. As a result, the superpowers inserted themselves into a succession of civil wars and revolutions. The costs in lives and property were terrible, the gains small. As defense costs escalated, the Soviet system crumbled. By 1991 the Soviet Union and the socialist Warsaw Pact had disappeared, transforming the international stage.

The world was also altered by economic growth and globalization, by population growth and movement, and by technological and environmental change. Led by the postwar recovery of the industrial powers and the remarkable economic expansion of Japan, the Asian Tigers, and more recently China, the world economy grew dramatically until the global recession of 2008. The development and application of new technology contributed significantly to this process. International markets were more open and integrated than at any other time. However, not all the nations of the world benefited from the new wealth and exciting technologies of the postwar era. The capitalist West and a handful of Asian nations grew richer and more powerful, while most of the world's nations remained poor.

Population growth in the developing world was one reason for this divided experience. Despite falling birthrates in many poor countries, most of the world's population growth in recent decades is in developing nations with limited economic growth. Unable to find adequate employment or, in many cases, bare subsistence, people in developing nations have migrated across international borders, hoping to improve their lives. These movements have often provided valuable labor in the factories and farms of the developed world, but they have also provoked cultural, racial, and ethnic tension. Problems of inequality, population growth, and international migration will continue to challenge the global community in the coming decades.

Growing population and the development process have forced marginal lands into production and stimulated the exploitation of new resources. The need to feed a rapidly growing world population has also pressured ocean resources. As the world's population surpassed 6 billion and the largest cities reached 20 million, the need to produce and deliver raw materials and finished goods has put tremendous stress on the environment. In the 1990s the rapid development of the Chinese and Indian economies compounded these pressures.

At the same time, new technologies and the wealth produced by economic expansion have allowed the world's richest nations to implement ambitious programs of environmental protection. As a result, pollution produced by automobiles and factories has actually declined in the richest nations. The question that remains is whether rapidly developing nations, such as Brazil, China, and India, will move more quickly than the mature industrial nations did to introduce these new technologies.

IMPORTANT EVENTS 1970–2000

1970	Salvador Allende elected president of Chile
1973	Allende overthrown
1975	Vietnam War ends
1976	Military takeover in Argentina
1978	USSR sends troops to Afghanistan
1979	Sandinistas overthrow Anastasio Somoza in Nicaragua
1979	Shah of Iran overthrown in Islamic Revolution
1979	China begins economic reforms
1980–1988	Iran-Iraq War
1983–1990	Democracy returns in Argentina, Brazil, and Chile
1985	Mikhail Gorbachev becomes Soviet head of state
1986	Average Japanese income overtakes income in United States
1989	United States invades Panama
1989	USSR withdraws from Afghanistan
1989	Tiananmen Square confrontation
1989	Berlin Wall falls

1989–1991	Communism ends in eastern Europe
1990	Sandinistas defeated in elections in Nicaragua
1990	Iraq invades Kuwait
1990	Reunification of Germany
1990s	Japanese recession
1991	Persian Gulf War
1992	Yugoslavia disintegrates; Croatia and Slovenia become independent nations

33

▼

New Challenges
in a New Millennium

The workday began normally at the World Trade Center in lower Manhattan on the morning of September 11, 2001. The 50,000 people who worked there were making their way to the two 110-story towers. Suddenly, at 8:46 A.M., an American Airlines Boeing 767 with 92 people on board, traveling at a speed of 470 miles per hour (756 kilometers per hour), crashed into floors 94 to 98 of the north tower, igniting the 10,000 gallons (38,000 liters) of fuel in its tanks. Just before 9:03 A.M. a United Airlines flight with 65 people on board and a similar fuel load hit floors 78 to 84 of the south tower.

As the burning jet fuel engulfed the collision areas, the buildings' occupants struggled through smoke-filled corridors and down dozens of flights of stairs. Many of those trapped above the crash sites used cell phones to say good-bye to loved ones. Rather than endure the flames and fumes, a few jumped to their deaths.

Just before 10 o'clock, temperatures that had risen to 2,3008 Fahrenheit (1,2608 Celsius) caused the steel girders in the impacted area of the south tower to give way. The collapsing upper floors crushed the floors underneath one by one, engulfing lower Manhattan in a dense cloud of dust. Twenty-eight minutes later the north tower pancaked in a similar manner. Miraculously, most of the buildings' occupants had escaped before the towers collapsed. Besides the people on the planes, nearly 2,600 lost their lives, including some 400 police officers and firefighters helping in the evacuation.

That same morning another American Airlines jet crashed into the Pentagon, killing all 64 people on board and 125 others inside the military complex near Washington, D.C. Passengers on a fourth plane managed to overpower their hijackers, and the plane crashed in rural Pennsylvania, killing all 45 on board.

The four planes had been hijacked by teams of Middle Eastern men who slit the throats of service and flight personnel and seized control. Of the nineteen hijackers, fifteen were from Saudi Arabia. All had links to an extremist Islamic organization, al-Qaeda (ahl–KAW-eh-duh) (the base or foundation), commanded by a rich Saudi named Usama bin Laden (oo-SAH-mah bin LAH-din), who was incensed with American political, military, and cultural influence in the Middle East. The men were educated and well traveled, had lived in the United States, and spoke English. Some had trained as pilots so that they could fly the hijacked aircraft.

The hijackers left few records of their motives, but the acts spoke for themselves. The World Trade Center was a focal point of international business, the Pentagon the headquarters of the American military. The fourth plane was probably meant to hit the Capitol or the White House, the legislative and executive centers of the world's only superpower.

The events of September 11, which became commonly referred to as 9/11, can be understood on many levels. The hijackers and those who sympathized with them saw themselves as engaged in a holy struggle against economic, political, and military institutions they believed to be evil. People directly affected, political leaders around the world, and most television watchers described the attacks as evil deeds against innocent victims.

To understand why the nineteen attackers were heroes to some and terrorists to others, one needs to explore the historical context of global changes at the turn of the millennium and the ideological tensions they have generated. The unique prominence of the United States in every major aspect of global integration, as well as its support for pro-American governments overseas, also elicits sharply divergent views.

GLOBALIZATION AND ECONOMIC CRISIS

The turn of the millennium saw the intensification of **globalization** trends that had been building since the 1970s. Growing trade and travel and new technologies were bringing all parts of the world into closer economic, political, and cultural integration and interaction. The collapse of the Soviet Union had completed the dissolution of territorial empires that had been under way throughout the twentieth century. Autonomous national states (numbering about two hundred) became an almost universal norm, and a growing number of them had embraced democratic institutions. However, increasing interdependency would also facilitate a global economic crisis that exploded in 2008 when the massive accumulation of debt in American financial institutions became unsustainable.

An Interconnected Economy
The expansion of trade, global interconnections, and privatization of government enterprises that gained momentum with the dismantling of Soviet-style socialist economies in the 1990s cooled abruptly in the wake of 9/11. The rate of growth in world trade fell from 13 percent in 2000 to only 1 percent in 2001.

Growth in China and India resumed quickly, however, and the large populations of these two countries marked them as future world economic powers. Their growth increased pressure on world energy supplies, though the United States continued to consume a quarter of the world's petroleum production and by

2013 had resumed its position of world's largest producer through the production of oil derived from shale deposits. OPEC's manipulation of world oil prices, combined with political instability in the Middle East, had caused crude oil prices to soar between 1973 and 1985. But aside from those years, the average price of oil remained consistently below $20 per barrel (adjusted for inflation) throughout the second half of the twentieth century. In the year 2000, however, oil prices began a new period of increase caused not by OPEC but by rising demand and confidence in the fevered pace of world economic expansion. By the middle of 2006, the price of a barrel of crude had crept past $70, and in 2008 it spiked to $145 a barrel. This increase fueled ambitious economic programs in producing countries like Russia, Venezuela, Iran, Saudi Arabia, and the small sheikhdoms of the Persian Gulf, as well as in the newer OPEC states Ecuador, Nigeria, and Angola. With the economic crisis of 2008, prices fell abruptly, but by 2013 the price per barrel was back in the $90–$100 range.

Regional trade associations came into being to promote growth, reduce the economic vulnerability of member states, and, less explicitly, balance American economic dominance. The twenty-seven-member European Union (EU) was the most successful. The euro, a common currency inaugurated in 2002 and used in twelve member states, competed with the U.S. dollar for investment and banking. However, unequal levels of development among members became a source of crisis in 2009 as the world economic downturn devastated stock markets and increased rates of unemployment. Countries like Greece that had taken on more debt than the revenues produced by their shrunken economies could cover sought assistance from the rest of the EU, but the wealthier countries, led by Germany, proved reluctant to rescue them. Instead they urged an austerity program of radical cutbacks in public expenditures, which increased unemployment and popular discontent. The idea of the euro, a common currency that symbolized Europe's progress toward unity, also came into question because countries belonging to the euro zone were not at liberty to devalue their currency and thereby reduce their debt burdens. In an increasingly globalized network of financial markets and institutions, Europe's recurrent debt crises generated economic anxiety from Japan to New York City.

Despite the EU's expansion, the North American Free Trade Agreement (NAFTA), which eliminated tariffs among the United States, Canada, and Mexico in 1994, governed the world's largest free-trade zone. Yet heated debate in the United States over illegal immigration across the Mexican border, as well anti-Hispanic prejudice, limited popular enthusiasm for the agreement. The third largest free-trade zone, Mercosur, created by Argentina, Brazil, Paraguay (now suspended), and Uruguay in 1991 and subsequently expanded to include Venezuela and Bolivia,, visualized a parliament consisting of eighteen representatives from each member state. Other free-trade associations operated in West Africa, southern Africa, Southeast Asia, Central America, the Pacific Basin, and the Caribbean.

The Shanghai Cooperation Organization (SCO), formed in 2001 with China, Russia, and four former Soviet Central Asian republics as members, originally pursued common security interests, such as combating separatist movements and terrorism. But the organization's five observer members—Iran, India, Pakistan,

Palm Island, Dubai *The seemingly unlimited wealth of the oil producing states of the Persian Gulf spurred ambitious development plans like this one in Dubai, one of the United Arab Emirates. Its publicists proclaimed that "Palm Island" would include 2,000 villas, up to 40 luxury hotels, shopping complexes, cinemas, and the Middle East's "first marine park" and would be "visible from the moon."*

Afghanistan, and Mongolia—the first a major oil exporter and the last two possessing huge unexploited mineral deposits, also lent credence to its twenty-year-plan for reducing barriers to trade and population movement. Iran's application for membership, formally made in 2008, has been held up by international pressure. U.S.-led international sanctions designed to curb Iran's nuclear program have encountered resistance from both Russia and China, but the SCO has a rule barring countries subjected to sanctions from membership.

In 1995 the world's major traders established the **World Trade Organization (WTO)**, dedicated to reducing barriers and enforcing international agreements. With the accession of Russia as its 157th member in 2012, the largest economy not to be included was Iran. The WTO had many critics and regularly encountered street protests during its ministerial meetings. Some protesters claimed that the organization's idea of free trade enabled low-cost foreign manufacturers to attract business and shrink the job opportunities in richer states; others demanded continuing tariff protection for local farmers.

Global Financial Crisis   The global financial crisis that began in 2008 had complicated roots. During an Asian financial crisis a decade earlier, vast amounts of European and American investment in Thailand, Indonesia, South Korea, and other East Asian countries had

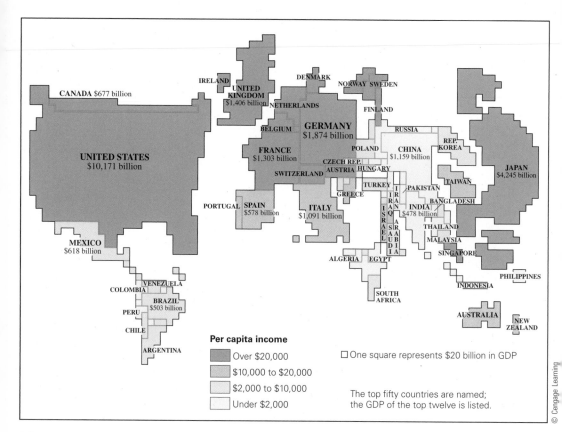

MAP 33.1 Global Distribution of Wealth

Early industrialization and efficient investment contributed to individual prosperity to the citizens of Japan and Western countries by the 1990s. However, economic dynamism in late-industrializing countries like China and India began to change the world balance of economic power in the early twenty-first century. In nearly all countries the distribution of wealth among individuals varies tremendously, with the gap between rich and poor generally increasing.

created an illusion of great economic dynamism. However, in 1997 the invest-ment boom burst, leading to a severe economic downturn in the region. When economic stability returned, greater investor caution reversed the flow of money. The United States in particular became a favorite place to invest, help-ing spur a rapid increase in stock market and housing prices and massive growth in the purchase of imported goods. Seeing the value their houses increase at an unprecedented rate, Americans became wedded to borrowing money with their homes as collateral. Money from overseas invested in the U.S. treasury also made it possible for the United States to fight wars in Afghanistan and Iraq (see below) while lowering taxes. The American national debt climbed dramatically.

In 2008 the fevered boom in housing prices collapsed, leaving many home-owners so deeply in debt on their mortgages that they lost their homes. Their mortgage debts, however, were no longer being held by a local bank in the traditional fashion. New and risky lending techniques based on homeowners' assumptions that home prices would continue to rise indefinitely had caused the bad debts to be distributed throughout the banking system, not just in the United States but around the world. Similar housing speculation occurred in Spain and other countries. When Lehman Brothers, one of the country's foremost financial firms, declared bankruptcy in September, a recession turned into a catastrophic economic downturn. Stock prices fell, banks teetered on the brink of collapse, and unemployment climbed as employers laid off workers they could no longer afford or did not need as consumer demand plummeted. The effects spread worldwide. Knowledgeable political leaders and economists proclaimed it the worst economic crisis since the Great Depression of the 1930s.

The sense that Barack Obama had a firm understanding of the crisis and the ability to lead the country out of it contributed to his election as president. During the first weeks after he took office in January 2009, he proposed a series of steps, including massive increases in government spending, to jolt the economy back to health. Some of the plans yielded fruit, such as a rescue of

ZUMA Wire Service/Alamy

Unemployment Protest *Recovery from the job losses of the economic recession of 2008 proved particularly slow. In the United States, banks and businesses returned to profitability but found they did not need so many workers. In Spain, Greece, and other parts of Europe, the unemployment rate was triple that of the United States in 2013, sometimes fueling the growth of radical and anti-immigrant political movements.*

the American automobile industry. Others were stymied after 2010, however, when Republicans who felt national debt and government budget deficits were more important than unemployment took over the House of Representatives. The legislative deadlock that ensued curbed administration plans to address unemployment through increased government spending, but Republican sponsorship of tax and governmental budget cuts failed to attract enough voters to prevent Barack Obama from being reelected in 2012. Economic recovery remained slow and fragile. In both the United States and the European Union, the trade expansion that had signaled the promise of globalization at the beginning of the century faded from memory, and the interdependence that had bound the world's economies in a cycle of growth became a dead weight that dragged many countries down.

Globalization and Democracy   The last decades of the twentieth century saw expansions of democratic institutions and personal freedom. People in many countries recognized that elections offered a peaceful way to settle differences among a country's social classes, cultural groups, and regions. Although majority votes could swing from one part of the political spectrum to another, democracies tended to encourage political moderation. Moreover, wars between fully democratic states were extremely rare.

The nations of eastern Europe embraced democracy after the fall of the Soviet Union, though some newly democratic states became subject to great mood swings among the electorate. The shift to private ownership of businesses after decades of rigid state control brought riches to a select few, and the removal of trade barriers characteristic of Cold War rivalry opened up new markets and fostered investment from the West.

By 2008, however, rising unemployment and falling export levels and stock prices threatened these experiments in free elections and free markets. In Russia, the popular but somewhat authoritarian leader Vladimir Putin followed his country's constitution by stepping down in 2008 after two terms as president. However, he engineered the election of his protégé Dimitri Medvedev as his successor, took the office of prime minister for himself, and then was elected to a new presidential term in 2012. These moves led some political thinkers to fear a possible return to Soviet-era Russian domination.

Asian democracies proved somewhat more stable. Beginning with free parliamentary elections in 1999, the populous state of Indonesia moved from years of authoritarian and corrupt rule toward more open political institutions. The following years saw a violent independence movement of the Acheh (ah-CHEH) district of northern Sumatra, the secession in 2002 of East Timor after years of brutal Indonesian military occupation, terrorist bombings on the island of Bali in 2004, and a devastating earthquake and tsunami in the same year. But democratic elections were regularly held. The losing candidates left office peacefully, and the populace at large accepted the results.

Myanmar (formerly Burma), where stifling military governments had held sway since 1962, experienced a rapid move toward democracy after free elections were held in 2010. The following year the military junta was dissolved, and the formerly banned opposition party led by the female Nobel Peace Prize winner Aung San Suu Kyi (owng SAHN soo chi) gained a significant role in parliament.

In India a major political shift seemed to be at hand in 1998 when the Bharatiya Janata Party (BJP) secured an electoral victory that interrupted four decades of Congress Party rule. The BJP success came through blatant appeals to Hindu nationalism, the condoning of violence against India's Muslims, and opposition to the social and economic progress of the Untouchables (those traditionally confined to the dirtiest jobs). In 2004, however, the Congress Party returned to power and governmental stability proved strong even in the face of sensational terrorist attacks in Mumbai by Pakistani gunmen in 2008.

Democracy in Pakistan itself proved more uncertain. President and former military commander Pervez Musharraf's (pair-VEZ moo-SHAH-ref) abrupt firing of the country's chief justice, combined with his unpopular support of the Bush administration's war policies, sparked protests and calls for impeachment. He resigned the presidency in 2008. Asif Ali Zardari (AH-sef AH-lee zar-DAH-ree), who succeeded him, had inherited the leadership of the majority Pakistan People's Party after the assassination the year before of his charismatic wife Benazir Bhutto, the daughter of a popular earlier prime minister. Zardari faced difficulties forming a strong government because of the growing movement of the Pakistani Taliban to impose their own governance and a rigid Muslim behavioral code in outlying districts, as well as popular opposition to American antiterrorist attacks launched from Afghanistan. In 2013 he was succeeded by his long-time rival Nawaz Sharif.

In sub-Saharan Africa, democracy had mixed results. Nelson Mandela, the leader of the African National Congress (ANC) who had become the first post-apartheid president of South Africa in 1994 (see Chapters 31 and 32), left office in 1999 and was succeeded by the deputy president and ANC leader Thabo Mbeki (TAA-boh um-BEH-kee). Mbeki stepped down in 2008 amidst turmoil in the leadership of the ANC. But the democratic system did not seem threatened. Elsewhere some elected leaders, such as Robert Mugabe (moo-GAH-bay) in Zimbabwe, used violence and intimidation to hold on to power, and other states, such as Congo, were plagued with internal revolts and civil wars. Liberians emerged from fourteen years of civil war in 2003 and two years later chose Ellen Johnson-Sirleaf (SUHR-leef) to be Africa's first elected female head of state. In Sudan, the general who had led a military coup in 1989, Omar al-Bashir, became the first sitting head of state to be charged with genocide and crimes against humanity by the International Criminal Court in 2009. A festering conflict in Darfur in western Sudan, which had then cost hundreds of thousands of lives and displaced over 2 million people, was at the heart of the charges. However, a long rebellion in the south finally came to an end in 2011 with the creation of a new country with a democratic constitution, the Republic of South Sudan.

In the Arab world, a rash of popular demonstrations starting at the end of 2010 led to the "Arab Spring," an anti-authoritarian political current that toppled the rulers of Tunisia, Libya, Egypt, and Yemen and plunged Syria into a grinding civil war. Though not the instigators of the demonstrations, previously suppressed Muslim political parties like Egypt's Muslim Brotherhood emerged as the best-organized contenders as shaky democratic regimes struggled into being.

Regime Change in Iraq and Afghanistan   The most closely watched experiments in democratization took place in Iraq and Afghanistan, countries that the United States invaded after the terrorist attacks of 9/11. Afghanistan's provision of a safe haven for Usama bin Laden and his al-Qaeda organization gave clear justification for the overthrow in December 2001 of the militantly religious Taliban regime. However, the rationale for invading Iraq was less persuasive. Leading up to the war the American government contended that Iraq was a clear and present danger to the United States because it possessed **weapons of mass destruction** (WMDs): nuclear, chemical, and biological weapons that it might supply to terrorists like bin Laden.

When United Nations inspectors failed to find any banned weapons, a split widened between those nations wanting to continue inspections and those, led by the United States, wanting to intervene militarily. Deciding to go it alone, an American-led "coalition of the willing" opened the invasion of Iraq with a spectacular aerial bombardment of Baghdad on March 20, 2003. Twenty-five days later the United States declared that "major fighting" had ended, little realizing that guerrilla insurgency, sectarian violence, and economic devastation would continue for years.

AP Photos/Khalil Hamra

Arab Spring Demonstrators *Part of the enormous crowds that unseated the rulers of Egypt, Tunisia, Libya, and Yemen, these women in Cairo's Tahrir Square wear the colorful head scarves that are commonplace in Egypt, sometimes to demonstrate allegiance to Islam and sometimes because they are stylish.*

Though Iraq fell into a state of turmoil because the coalition army was too small or otherwise unprepared to prevent the looting and destruction of government facilities and other lawlessness, a thorough search was launched for WMDs. The search came up empty, and intelligence analyses failed to uncover any evidence that Saddam Hussein, Iraq's fallen dictator, had played a role in the 9/11 attacks. American troops finally withdrew from the country in 2010, leaving behind a government elected under a new constitution adopted in 2006 but nevertheless divided by strong animosity between a Shi'ite majority and separate Arab and Kurdish Sunni minorities.

American concern for WMDs was not confined to Iraq. North Korea had an open program to build nuclear weapons, and Iran was suspected of having a covert plan based in part on technological aid secretly given by the head of Pakistan's successful nuclear program. Iran's outspokenly anti-American and anti-Israeli president, Mahmoud Ahmedinejad, who served from 2005 to 2013, and North Korea's dictator Kim Jong-il (kim jong-ill) presented the United States with difficult challenges. But the military invasion option chosen for Iraq, though favored by some Bush advisers, was held in abeyance in favor of diplomatic initiatives that continued into Obama's second term in office.

Iran's challenge to America's hopes for a democratic reshaping of the Middle East took a step forward in 2005 when the Lebanese Shi'ite movement Hezbollah captured 23 out of 128 seats in the Lebanese parliament; then in 2006 the militantly anti-Israeli Hamas movement won an absolute majority of the vote in elections for the Palestine Governing Authority. Both groups were firmly allied with Iran. Attacks launched by Israel against both Hamas and Hezbollah in response to kidnappings of Israeli soldiers in 2006 suggested that Israeli fear of Islamic movements, and of Iran, might someday become more consequential than Arab world democratization, particularly if Iran should acquire a nuclear weapon.

In 2007 the elected Hamas government succeeded in driving its Palestinian rivals out of the Gaza Strip. During the following months, largely inaccurate rocket barrages launched from there against Israel became a major factor in Israeli politics. A security barrier built on the West Bank had almost eliminated attacks by Palestinian suicide bombers, but the rockets provoked public outrage even though the number of casualties was very small. During the final month of the manifestly pro-Israeli Bush administration, the Israel Defense Force undertook to deal once and for all with Hamas in the Gaza Strip. Aerial bombardments and ground force incursions left well over a thousand Palestinians dead, while Israeli casualties were negligible. However, there was no sign that Hamas had been seriously harmed as a political organization. Indeed, in 2012 a renewed exchange of Hamas rockets and Israeli air strikes showed the persistence of the stalemate in Gaza. Worldwide reactions to these events engendered sufficient criticism of Israel that a resolution in the United Nations General Assembly to grant the Palestinian Governing Authority enhanced observer status saw only one major nation, Canada, vote no along with the United States and Israel.

American hopes for democratization also were disappointed in Afghanistan. The Afghan government elected with enthusiastic American support in 2004 proved corrupt and uncooperative and did not extend over the entire country. By 2008 the Taliban were again a serious threat, and opium production, the key to the country's unrest, was higher than ever. Though the United States was able to enlist the participation of NATO forces in helping to police Afghanistan, the prospects for the country were so dim that President Barack Obama made intensification of efforts to bring peace and stability and suppress terrorism a key part of his foreign policy while at the same time promising to withdraw American troops by the end of 2014.

The Question of Values

As people around the world first faced the opportunities of globalization and then the fear of global recession, they tried to make sense of these changes in terms of their own value systems. With 7 billion people, the world was big enough to include many different approaches, whether religious or secular, local or international, traditional or visionary. In some cases, however, conflicting visions fed violence.

Faith and Politics
Religious beliefs increasingly inspired political actions during the second half of the twentieth century, and the trend intensified in the new century. Though for Americans this change reversed two centuries of growing secularism, Western analysts did not agree on the cause of the religious revival.

Evangelical Protestants became a powerful conservative political force in the United States, particularly during the Bush presidency. Around the world, Catholic conservatives led by Pope John Paul II, Pope Benedict XVI, and Pope Francis who succeeded to the post in 2013 after Benedict's retirement, forcefully reiterated politically sensitive teachings: opposition to abortion, homosexuality, marriage of priests, and admission of women to the priesthood. In Israel, hyperorthodox Jews known as *haredim* played a leading role in settling the Palestinian territories captured by Israel in 1967 and vehemently resisted both Israel's unilateral withdrawal from Gaza in 2005 and subsequent plans for withdrawal from the West Bank. And in India, Hindu zealots made the BJP party a powerful political force.

Yet most discussions of faith and politics focused on Islam. The birth of the Islamic Republic of Iran in the revolution of 1979 made visible a current of Muslim political assertiveness that had been building there for twenty-five years. By the year 2000, however, non-Iranian Muslim groups claiming to be acting for religious reasons were capturing the headlines with acts of **terrorism**.

Terrorism is a political tactic by which comparatively weak militants use grotesquely inhumane and lethal acts to convince a frightened public that danger is everywhere and their government is incapable of protecting them. Although terrorism has a long history, the instantaneous media links made possible by satellite communications, and the tradition in the news business of publicizing violence, increased its effectiveness from the 1980s onward.

Bombings, kidnappings, and assassinations made political sense to all sorts of political groups: secular Palestinians confronting Israel; national separatists like the Tamils in Sri Lanka, Basques in Spain, and Chechens in Russia; and Catholic and Protestant extremists in Northern Ireland, to name a few. But Muslim groups gained the lion's share of attention when they targeted the United States and Europe, recruited from Muslim populations all over the world, and made effective use of news coverage and audiovisual communications.

Their media star and ideological spokesman was **Usama bin Laden**. Born into a wealthy Saudi family and educated as an engineer, bin Laden fought against the Soviet Union in Afghanistan and there recruited and trained a core group of fighters called al-Qaeda. Though his family disowned him and Saudi Arabia stripped him of his citizenship, his calls for holy war (*jihad*) and his portrayal of the United States as a puppet-master manipulating both non-Muslim (e.g., Israel, India, Russia) and Muslim (e.g., Egypt, Algeria, Saudi Arabia) governments to murder and oppress innocent Muslims made sense to millions of Muslims, even if only a very few committed themselves to follow him into battle.

Al-Qaeda blew up American embassies in Kenya and Tanzania in 1998, crippled the U.S. Navy destroyer *Cole* during a port call in Yemen in 2000, and then capped everything by attacking the World Trade Center and the Pentagon on 9/11. When the "global war on terrorism" declared by President Bush failed to eliminate bin Laden, his mystique grew. Further terrorist attacks—by Indonesians on tourists on the island of Bali in 2002, by North Africans on commuter trains servicing Madrid in 2004, by English-born Muslims on the London transit system in 2005, and by Pakistanis on luxury hotels in Mumbai, India, in 2008—made it clear that the current of violence unleashed by al-Qaeda had become decentralized and that recruits and cells might no longer be taking orders from bin Laden. Even after an American commando operation killed bin Laden in his hideout in Pakistan in 2011, groups affiliated with al-Qaeda continued to operate in Yemen, Libya, and Mali. In response, the United States expanded its use of pilotless drone aircraft to kill suspected terrorists from afar.

In trying to explain a current of violence that could strike anywhere in the world but seemed to be centered on Muslims, some analysts argued that Islam itself encouraged violence against non-Muslims. The counterargument pointed out that terrorists came from many backgrounds and that the vast majority of Muslims saw their religion as one of peace. Others maintained that rigidly conservative Muslims were blindly opposed to freedom and modernity. The counterargument pointed out that al-Qaeda used modern military and propaganda techniques and that many of its operatives, like bin Laden himself, graduated from modern technical programs. A third school of thought felt that the United States instigated al-Qaeda's wrath by supporting Israel and stationing troops in Saudi Arabia. The counterargument pointed out that the United

States had also championed the Muslim cause in Bosnia, driven the secular dictator Saddam Hussein out of Kuwait, and supported the popular uprisings of the Arab Spring.

Universal Rights and Values   Alongside the growing influence of religion on politics, efforts to promote adherence to universal human rights also expanded. The modern human rights movement grew out of secular statements like the French Declaration of the Rights of Man (1789) and the U.S. Constitution (1788) and Bill of Rights (1791). The **Universal Declaration of Human Rights**, passed by the United Nations General Assembly in 1948, culminated this movement by proclaiming itself "a common standard of achievement for all peoples and nations." Its thirty articles condemned slavery, torture, cruel and inhuman punishment, and arbitrary arrest, detention, and exile. The Declaration called for freedom of movement, assembly, and thought. It asserted rights to life, liberty, and security of person; to impartial public trials; and to education, employment, and leisure. The principle of equality was most fully articulated in Article 2:

> *Everyone is entitled to all the rights and freedoms set forth in this Declaration, without distinction of any kind, such as race, color, sex, language, religion, or political or other opinion, national or social origin, property, birth or other status.*[1]

This passage reflected an international consensus against racism and imperialism and a growing acceptance of the importance of social and economic equality. Most newly independent countries joining the United Nations willingly signed the Declaration because it implicitly condemned European colonial regimes.

Besides the official actions of the United Nations and various national governments, individual human rights activists, often working through philanthropic bodies known as **nongovernmental organizations (NGOs)**, have been important forces promoting human rights. Amnesty International, founded in 1961, concentrates on gaining the freedom of people who have been tortured or imprisoned without trial and campaigns against summary execution by government death squads or other gross violations of rights. Arguing that no right is more fundamental than the right to life, other NGOs have devoted themselves to famine relief, refugee assistance, and health care around the world. Médecins Sans Frontières (Doctors Without Borders), founded in 1971, was awarded the Nobel Peace Prize in 1999 for offering medical assistance in scores of crises.

While NGOs often worked in specific countries, other universal goals became enshrined in international agreements. Such agreements made genocide a crime

---

[1]"Universal Declaration of Human Rights," in *Twenty-five Human Rights Documents* (New York: Center for the Study of Human Rights, Columbia University, 1994), 6.

and promoted environmental protection of the seas, of Antarctica, and of the atmosphere (see Environment and Technology: Global Warming). The United States and a few other nations were greatly concerned that such treaties would limit their sovereignty or threaten their national interests. For this reason the U.S. Congress delayed ratifying the 1949 convention on genocide until 1986. More recently the United States drew widespread criticism for demanding exemption for Americans from the jurisdiction of the International Criminal Court, created in 2002 to try international criminals, and for declaring that "enemy combatants" taken prisoner during the "global war on terrorism" should not be treated in accordance with the Third Geneva Convention (1950) on humane treatment of prisoners of war.

Women's Rights   The women's rights movement, which began on both sides of the North Atlantic in the nineteenth century, became an important human rights issue in the twentieth century. Rights for women became accepted in Western countries and were enshrined in the constitutions of many nations newly freed from colonial rule. In 1979 the United Nations General Assembly adopted the Convention on the Elimination of All Forms of Discrimination Against Women, and in 1985 the first international conference on the status of women, sponsored by the United Nations Division for the Advancement of Women, was held in Nairobi, Kenya. A second conference in Beijing ten years later added momentum to the movement. By 2012, all but seven UN member countries—Iran, Palau, Somalia, Sudan, South Sudan, Tonga, and the United States—had ratified the convention, though the United States and Palau had signed it without ratification.

Besides highlighting the problems women face around the world, international conferences have also revealed great variety in the views and concerns of women. Feminists from the West, who had been accustomed to dictating the agenda and who had pushed for the liberation of women in other parts of the world, sometimes found themselves accused of having narrow concerns and condescending attitudes. Some non-Western women complained about Western feminists' endorsement of sexual liberation and about the deterioration of family life in the West. They found Western feminists' concern with matters such as comfortable clothing misplaced and trivial compared to the issues of poverty and disease.

Other cultures came in for their share of criticism. Western women and many secular leaders in Muslim countries protested Islam's requirement that a woman cover her head and wear loose-fitting garments to conceal the shape of her body, practices enforced by law in countries such as Iran and Saudi Arabia. Nevertheless, many outspoken Muslim women voluntarily donned concealing garments as expressions of personal belief, statements of resistance to secular dictatorship, or defense against coarse male behavior.

The conferences were more important for the attention they focused on women's issues than for the solutions they generated. Such efforts raised the

ENVIRONMENT + TECHNOLOGY

Global Warming

Until the 1980s environmental alarms focused mainly on localized episodes of air and water pollution, exposure to toxic substances, waste management, and the disappearance of wilderness. The development of increasingly powerful computers and complex models of ecological interactions in the 1990s, however, made people aware of the global scope of certain environmental problems.

Many scientists and policymakers came to perceive global warming, the slow increase of the temperature of the earth's lower atmosphere, as an environmental threat requiring preventive action on an international scale. The warming is caused by a layer of atmospheric gases (carbon dioxide, methane, nitrous oxide, and ozone) that allow solar radiation to reach earth and warm it but that keep infrared energy (heat) from radiating from earth's surface back into space. Called the *greenhouse effect*, this process normally keeps the earth's temperature at a level suitable for life. However, increases in greenhouse-gas emissions—particularly from the burning of fossil fuels in industry and transportation—have added to this insulating atmospheric layer.

Recent events have confirmed predictions of global temperature increases and melting glaciers and icecaps. Greenland glaciers and Arctic Ocean sea ice are melting at record rates, and huge sections of the Antarctic ice shelf are breaking off and floating away. Andean glaciers are shrinking so fast they could disappear in a decade, imperiling water supplies for drinking, irrigation, and hydroelectric production. Drought has affected much of the United States in recent years, and Australia has experienced the "Big Dry," its worst drought in a century.

Despite this evidence, governments of the industrialized countries that produce the most greenhouse gasses have been slow to adopt measures stringent enough to reduce emissions. They cite the negative effects they believe this could have on their economies. Because of these fears, many nations hesitated to sign the 1997 Kyoto Protocol, the first international agreement to impose penalties on countries that failed to cut greenhouse-gas emissions. It was a major environmental victory when Japan added its signature in March 2001, but to the consternation of many world leaders President George W. Bush rejected the agreement.

Shortly after being elected in 2008, Barack Obama announced to an audience of scientists and citizens concerned

prominence of human rights as a global concern and put pressure on governments to consider human rights when making foreign policy decisions. Skeptics observed, however, that a Western country might successfully prod a non-Western country to improve its human rights performance—for example, by granting women better access to education and careers—but that reverse criticism of a Western country often fell on deaf ears—for example, condemnation of the death penalty in the United States. For such critics the human rights movement was seen not as an effort to make the world more humane but as another form of Western cultural imperialism.

with climate matters: "You can be sure that the United States will once again engage vigorously in these negotiations, and help lead the world toward a new era of global cooperation on climate change." Yet when he ran for reelection in 2012, the issue of global warming, which his Republican opponents denied was a real phenomenon, played no role in his campaign. Ironically, a tropical superstorm named Sandy that dealt a devastating blow to New York and New Jersey just before the election seemed to vindicate the prediction that the increased energy in the atmosphere caused by global warming would produce severe weather anomalies around the world.

Flooding in Bangladesh *Typhoon-driven floods submerge the low-lying farmlands of Bangladesh with tragic regularity. Any significant rise in the sea level will make parts of the country nearly uninhabitable.*

GLOBAL CULTURE

Because of changes in electronic technology, today political and economic events have almost instantaneous impact in all parts of the world. A global language, a global educational system, and global forms of artistic expression have all come into being. Trade, travel, and migration have made a common popular culture unavoidable. These changes have delighted and enriched some but angered others.

The Media and the Message   The fact that the most pervasive elements of global culture have their origins in the West raised concerns in many quarters about **cultural imperialism**. Critics complained that entertainment conglomerates were flooding the world's movie theaters and television screens with Western images and that goods catering to Western tastes but manufactured in countries with low labor costs, like China and Indonesia, were flooding world markets. In this view, global marketing was especially insidious in trying to shape a world with a single Western outlook based on capitalist ideology, and at the same time suppressing or devaluing traditional cultures and alternative ideologies. As the leader of the capitalist world, the United States was seen as the primary culprit.

The pace of cultural globalization began to quicken during the economic recovery after World War II. The Hollywood films and American jazz recordings that had become popular in Europe and parts of Asia before the war (see Chapter 29) continued to spread. But the birth of electronic technology opened contacts with large numbers of people who could never have afforded to go to a movie or buy a record.

The first step was the development of cheap transistor radios that could run on a couple of small batteries. Perfected by American scientists at Bell Telephone Laboratories in 1948, solid-state electronic transistors replaced power-hungry and less reliable glass tubes in radios and other devices. Tube radios, which in some countries required a license to own, had spread worldwide in the decades before the war, but small portable transistor radios reached parts of the world where homes lacked electricity.

Television, made possible by the electron-scanning gun invented in 1928, became widely available to Western consumers in the 1950s. In poorer parts of the world TVs were not common until the 1980s and 1990s, after mass production and cheap transistors made sets more affordable. Outside the United States, television broadcasting was usually a government monopoly at first, following the pattern of telegraph and postal service and radio broadcasting. Governments expected news reports and other programming to disseminate a unified national viewpoint.

However, government monopolies eroded as the high cost of television production opened up global markets for rebroadcasts of American, Indian, and Mexican soap operas and dramas. By the 1990s a global network of satellites brought privately owned television broadcasting to even remote areas of the world, and the VCR (videocassette recorder) provided an even greater variety of programs. In the following decade DVD players continued the trend. As a result of wider circulation of programming, people often became familiar with different dialects of English and other languages. People in Portugal who in the 1960s had found it difficult to understand Brazilian Portuguese became avid fans of Brazilian soap operas. And immigrants from Albania and North Africa often arrived in Italy with a command of Italian learned from Italian stations whose signals they could pick up at home.

CNN (Cable News Network) expanded its international market after becoming the most-viewed and informative news source during the 1991 Persian Gulf War, when it broadcast live from Baghdad. Other 24-hour news broadcasters followed this lead. Some, like CNN and the British Broadcasting Corporation (BBC), reflected the outlook of their home audiences. In response, Al-Jazeera, based in the Persian Gulf emirate of Qatar, broadcast statements by Usama bin Laden from 2001 onward and offered video footage and interpretation that differed greatly from American coverage of the war in Iraq in 2003. It gradually gained a reputation for vivid and generally reliable coverage of news events in the Muslim world.

The Internet, a linkage of academic, government, and business computers developed by the American Department of Defense in the 1960s, began to transform world culture in the early years of the twenty-first century. Personal computers proliferated in the 1980s, and with the establishment of the easy-to-use graphic interface of the World Wide Web in 1994, the number of Internet users skyrocketed. Myriad new companies formed to exploit "e-commerce," the commercial dimension of the Internet, and students were soon spending less time studying conventional books and more exploring the Web for information and entertainment. Blogs, or weblogs, offered a vehicle for anyone in the world to place his or her opinions, experiences, and creative efforts before anyone with access to a computer. Easy access to the Internet took a step forward with the establishment of "social media" sites like Facebook (2004) and Twitter (2006). Initially these were mainly means of keeping in touch with friends, but the Arab Spring of 2011 saw them develop as tools for communication among antiregime protesters.

As had happened so often throughout history, technological developments had unanticipated consequences. Although the new telecommunications and entertainment technologies derived disproportionately from American invention, industry, and cultural creativity, Japan and other East Asian nations took the lead in manufacturing and refining electronic devices. Cellular mobile phones became increasingly used for taking and transmitting pictures and connecting to the Internet. Non-Western countries that had adopted telephones late and had limited networks of copper wire benefited most from the improved communication. In 2012 the United States ranked 114th in per capita cellular phone use, sandwiched between the Congo Republic and the Dominican Republic. Qatar topped the list as the country with the highest per capita use.

The Spread of Pop Culture   For most of history, popular culture consisted of folk tales and highly localized styles of dress, cooking, music, and visual expression. Only the literate few had full access to the riches of a broader "great tradition," such as Confucianism, Islam, or Buddhism. In modern times, government school systems increased literacy rates but also promoted specifically national values and cultural tastes. Prescribed languages of

Japanese Comic Books *After World War II comic magazines emerged as a major form of publication and a distinctive product of culture in Japan. Different series are directed to different age and gender groups. Issued weekly and running to some three hundred pages in black and white, the most popular magazines sell as many copies as do major newsmagazines in the United States.*

instruction eroded the use and memory of local languages and traditions. In their place there arose **global pop culture**.

Initially, the content was heavily American. Singer Michael Jackson was almost as well known to the youth of Dar-es-Salaam (Tanzania) and Bangkok (Thailand) as to American fans. Businesses sought out worldwide celebrities like basketball star Michael Jordan and championship golfer Tiger Woods to endorse their products. American television programs, following in the path of American movies, acquired immense followings and inspired local imitations.

But the United States had no monopoly on global pop culture. Rap music showed up in almost every language. Latin American soap operas, *telenovelas*, had a vast following in the Americas, eastern Europe, and elsewhere. Mumbai, India, long the world's largest producer of films, made or inspired more films for international audiences, like the 2009 Academy Award–winning *Slumdog Millionaire*. And the martial arts film makers of Hong Kong saw their style flourish in high-budget international spectaculars like director Ang Lee's *Crouching Tiger, Hidden Dragon* (2000) and the *Matrix* trilogy (1999–2003), which relied heavily on Hong Kong fight choreographers.

Emerging Global Elite Culture

While the globalization of popular culture has been criticized, cultural links across national and ethnic boundaries at a more elite level have generated little controversy. The end of the Cold War reopened intellectual and cultural contacts between former adversaries, making possible such things as Russian-American collaboration on space missions and extensive business contacts among former rivals. The English language, modern science, and higher education became the key elements of this **global elite culture**.

The emergence of English as the first global language began with the British Empire's introduction of the language to its far-flung colonies. After achieving independence in the wake of World War II, most former colonies chose to continue using English as an official language because it provided national unity and a link to the outside world that local languages could not. Countries that chose instead to make a local language official often found the decision counterproductive. Indian nationalists had pushed for Hindi to be India's official language, but they found that students taught in Hindi were unable to compete internationally because of poor knowledge of English. Sri Lanka, which had made Sinhala its official language in 1956, reversed itself after local reporters revealed in 1989 that prominent officials were sending their children to English-medium private schools.

While similar postcolonial language developments extended the reach of French, Spanish, and other European tongues, the use of English as a second language was greatly stimulated by the importance of the United States in postwar world affairs. After the collapse of Soviet domination, students in eastern Europe flocked to study English instead of Russian. Ninety percent of students in Cambodia (a former French colony) chose to study English, even though a Canadian agency offered a sizable cash bonus if they would study French. In the 1990s China made the study of English as a second language nearly universal from junior high school onwards.

English has become the language of choice for most international academic conferences, business meetings, and diplomatic gatherings. International organizations that provide equal status to many languages, such as the United Nations and the European Union, often conduct informal committee meetings in English. In cities throughout the world, signs and notices are commonly posted in the local language and in English. Writers from Africa and India have received high honors for novels written in English, as have Arab and Caribbean authors for works written in French. Nevertheless, world literature remains highly diverse in form and language.

By contrast, science and technology have become standardized components of global culture. Though imperialism helped spread the Western disciplines of biology, chemistry, and physics around the world, their importance expanded even further after decolonization as students from newly independent nations sought to compete at an international level. Standardization of scientific terms, weights and measures, and computer codes underlay the worldwide expansion of commerce.

The third pillar of global elite culture, along with science and globalized languages, is the university. The structure and curricula of modern universities are nearly indistinguishable around the world, making student experiences similar across national boundaries. Instruction in the pure sciences varies little from place to place. Some doctoral science programs in American universities now enroll mostly students from non-Western countries. Standardization is nearly as common in applied sciences such as engineering and medicine and only slightly less so in the social sciences. Although the humanities preserve greater diversity in subject matter and approach, professors and students around the world pay attention to the latest literary theories and topics of historical interest.

New universities, many of them privately funded, have mushroomed in many parts of the world as young people increasingly strive for learning that will improve their employment opportunities. Some American universities have contributed to this educational expansion by opening branches or research centers in foreign countries.

While university subjects are taught in many languages, instruction in English is spreading rapidly. Because discoveries are often first published in English, advanced students in science, business, and international relations need to know that language to keep up with the latest developments. Many courses in northern European countries have long been offered in English, and elsewhere in Europe courses taught in English have facilitated the EU's efforts to encourage students to study outside their home countries.

Enduring Cultural Diversity

Although protesters regularly denounce the "Americanization" of the world, a closer look suggests that cultural globalization is more complex. Just as English has spread widely as a second language, so global culture is primarily a second culture that dominates some contexts but does not displace other traditions. From this perspective, American music, fast food, and fashions are more likely to add to a society's options than to displace local culture.

Japan might appear to be the most "westernized" country in Asia. Japan was one of the first countries in Asia to adopt and adapt political, educational, military, and even corporate institutions from western Europe and the United States during the late nineteenth and early twentieth centuries. Those institutions promoted what many believed to be traditional Japanese cultural characteristics, such as respect for hierarchy, the importance of the group over the individual, and solid work ethic. Such traits, observers argued, contributed to Japan's rapid economic recovery and global eminence since the end of World War II. While culture may have played some role in Japan's economic success story, structural problems led to the bursting of the economic bubble during the 1990s. Those so-called traditional values were rejected by young people who could no longer find secure employment. Instead of touting business culture, then, the Japanese government promoted Japan's popular culture—graphic novels (manga), anime, and J-pop music—as its unique cultural contribution to the world.

As awareness of the economic impact of Japanese culture and society began to spread, it became apparent that Taiwan and South Korea, along with Singapore and Hong Kong (a British colony before being reunited with China in 1997), were developing dynamic industrial economies of their own. Today India, Brazil, Turkey, and the People's Republic of China are following the same path without forsaking their national tastes and heritages.

This does not mean that the world's cultural diversity is secure. Every decade a number of minority languages cease to be spoken. Televised national ceremonies or performances for tourists may prevent folk customs and costumes from dying out, but they also tend to devitalize rituals that once had many local variations. While a century ago it was possible to recognize the nationality of people from their clothing and grooming, today most urban men dress the same the world over, although women's clothing shows greater variety. As much as one may regret the disappearance or commercialization of some folkways, most anthropologists would agree that change is characteristic of all healthy cultures. What doesn't change risks extinction.

IMPORTANT EVENTS 2000–2012

2000	Al-Qaeda attacks American destroyer USS *Cole* in Yemen
2001	George W. Bush becomes president of the United States
2001	Terrorists destroy the World Trade Center and damage the Pentagon on September 11
2001–2003	Terrorist attacks trigger global recession
2001	Shanghai Cooperation Organization formed
2001	United States armed forces overthrow Taliban regime in Afghanistan
2002	Euro currency adopted in twelve European countries
2003	United States and Britain invade and occupy Iraq
2004	Terrorists bomb Spanish trains
2004	Facebook popularizes Internet social media
2004–2009	Genocidal conflict ongoing in Darfur region of Sudan
2005	Terrorists bomb London transport system
2005	Mahmoud Ahmedinejad elected president of Iran
2006	Iraqis elect a government under a new constitution
2006	Hamas movement defeats PLO in Palestinian election
2006	Israel attacks Hezbollah in Lebanon in response to its seizure of Israeli soldiers

2007	Assassination of Benazir Bhutto deepens political crisis in Pakistan
2008	Barack Obama elected president of the United States
2008	Collapse of mortgage debt bubble in United States triggers global recession
2010	American forces withdraw from Iraq
2011	Arab Spring demonstrators topple authoritarian governments
2011	American raiders kill Usama bin Laden in Pakistan
2011	Muslim Brotherhood emerges as a powerful force in Egypt
2012	Barack Obama reelected president of the United States
2012	Vladimir Putin returns to the presidency in Russia

Index

Abbas I, Shah, 527, 528, 529, 530, 533

Abbasid Caliphate, 255–256, 257, 258(*map*), 262; literature of, 266–267

Abbas (uncle of Muhammad), 256

Abbots, 284, 286. *See also* Monasteries (monks and nuns)

Abd al-Qadir, 675–676

Abd al-Rahman, Caliph, 259

Abdul Hamid II, Sultan, 624, 627, 733

Abdul Mejid, Sultan, 618

Abkhazia, 626

Abolition (abolitionist movement): in Brazil, 657; British navy and, 657, 658, 684; in Caribbean colonies, 657–658; in Cuba and Puerto Rico, 658, 701; in Dutch colonies, 658, 701; in French colonies, 589, 610, 658, 701; legitimate trade with Africa and, 684; in United States, 657; in Americas, 656–658

Aborigines, Australian, 693, 694

Abortion, 762, 862; Soviet policy on, 790–791

Abraham (Ibrahim), 64, 251, 252

Absolutism. *See also* Authoritarianism; of French kings, 455; of Russian tsars, 535

Abu Bakr, Caliph, 253, 254

Abu Bakr, Sultan, 374

Academies: in Assyria, 62–63; in Athens, 131; Tamil, in India, 187; in Song China, 308, 310

Acculturation, of immigrants, 661

Achaean League, 137

Achaeans, 58. *See also* Greece

Achaemenids, 114, 135. *See also* Persia

Acheh, 538, 692, 880; sultanate in, 536

Acosta, Gladys, 850–851

Acropolis, 122, 128, 131

Adal, 401

Adam and Eve story, 2

Addams, Jane, 762

Aden, 388, 393; Portuguese and, 422, 517

Administration (administrators). *See also* Bureaucracy; Civil Service; Mesopotamian,

26–27, 30; Egyptian, 40, 41; Mycenaean Greek, 57, 59; Assyrian Empire, 61–62; colonial Latin America, 465, 471, 484, 485; colonial North America, 477, 479–480; Dutch East Indies, 538; early China, 83, 84; Persian Empire, 115–116, 135, 140; Hellenistic kingdoms, 136; Roman Empire, 149, 155, 171–172; imperial China, 161, 168, 171–172; imperial India, 185, 187–188; Andean peoples, 215; Islamic caliphate, 255; Christian monasteries, 286–287; Russian clergy and, 289; Japan, 316; Mughal Empire, 529; Il-khanate, 329; Yuan China, 337; Ottoman, 519, 524; in British India, 690, 769; Russian, 727; in industrialized world, 761; fascist Italy, 792; Soviet Union, 821

Adowa, Battle of (1896), 684

Aedisius, 244

Aegean world, 49, 56–59, 120(*map*). *See also* Greece; Minoan Crete, 56, 58

Aéropostale, 776

Afghanistan (Afghans), 55, 391, 531, 863, 877; Bactrian kingdom in, 186; Kushans in, 186, 232, 243; Timurids in, 330; India and, 382; Safavid Iran and, 529; Russia and, 627; Soviet war in, 847, 849, 854; Taliban in, 849, 882, 883–884; Islamic Revolution in, 849; NATO war in, 884

Afonso I (Kongo), 417, 418–420

Africa (Africans). *See also* East Africa; North Africa; South Africa; Sub-Saharan Africa; West Africa; *and specific countries and peoples*; agriculture in, 15; human origins in, 2–8, 21; migration out of, 4, 6–8, 7(*map*); pastoralism in, 16–17; foraging in, 17–18; Bantu migrations in, 227, 245; cultural unity in, 239–240; chronology

(1230s–1433), 400; ivory trade in, 92, 234; Asian food crops in, 234; gold trade, 195, 258, 409, 411, 415; Portuguese in, 410(*illus.*), 411, 414(*map*), 415–416, 417; chronology (1500–1730), 514; Berlin Conference on, 679, 682; changes and exchanges in, 676–686; as laborers in British colonies, 701; cotton cloth sales to, 701; chronology (1808–1900s), 703; German colonies in, 737, 749; in World War I armies, 737–738; chronology (1900s–1945), 782–783; Depression (1930s) in, 789; World War II and, 800, 809, 830; famine in, 820–821; decolonization of, 818, 828–832; HIV/AIDS in, 861; fertility in, 862; population in (1750–2050), 861(*table*)

African-Americans: as abolitionists, 657; racial discrimination and, 662; in Liberia, 686; World War I and, 737; World War II and, 809; Pan-Africanist, 781

African National Congress (ANC), 781; Mandela and, 832, 857, 881

African slaves. *See* Slaves (slavery), African; Slave trade, African

Afrikaners (South Africa), 676–678; Great Trek of, 677; war with Britain, 678

Afro-Asiatic languages, 19

Afro-Brazilians, 486(*illus.*), 662

Afterlife, belief in: Stone Age, 14; Egyptian, 38, 43, 44, 48; Kushite, 94; Celtic, 103; Zoroastrian, 117; Chinese, 81, 162

Agincourt, Battle of (1415), 370

Agriculture. *See also* Farmers; Irrigation; Landowners; Peasants; Plows; Rural societies; Sugar plantations; *and specific crops*; transition from food gathering, 14–16; Neolithic revolution in, 14–18, 95–96;

Mesopotamian, 25; population growth and, 17, 18, 22, 177, 430; Egyptian, 42; Chinese, 80, 83; Nubian, 92; Assyrian Empire, 62; Greek, 120(*map*), 123; Indian, 177, 187; Mesoamerica, 202, 204, 210; Chavín, 203; Roman, 144, 171; Chinese, 163, 171, 310–311, 341; swidden (shifting), 15, 192, 205, 289, 316, 377; Northern Amerindian, 211, 215; Andean civilizations, 215, 217–218; sub-Saharan Africa, 245; Muslim Spain, 259; Kievan Russia, 289; medieval European, 280, 290, 295, 351; East Asian, 314; Il-khanate, 329; Aztec, 395, 396; Korean, 345; Japanese, 347; population and, 430, 464; European, 448; Columbian exchange and, 464; Chinese, 551–552, 629, 634, 837; colonial Latin America, 484; Japanese, 548; revolution in, 564; economic botany and, 699–700; Soviet collectivization of, 768, 785–786, 813; tractors for, 768; Green Revolution, 820–821 *and illus.*; Chinese collectivization of, 837

Aguinaldo, Emilio, 693(*illus.*), 694–695

Ahhijawa, 58. *See also* Greece

Ahmadabad, 391

Ahmed III, Sultan, 525

Ahmedinejad, Mahmoud, 883

Ahmose (Egypt), 52

Ahuramazda, 117

AIDS/HIV, 861–862

Ain Jalut, Battle of (1260), 261, 327

Airbus corporation, 853

Aircraft (aviation): aluminum for, 764(*illus.*), 767; invention of, 764; World War I, 737, 764; commercial airlines, 764; World War II, 798, 806, 809; Latin American, 775–776; in September 11 (2001) terrorism, 874; pilotless (drone), 885

Aircraft carriers (ships), 798

Air pollution (air quality), 870; from coal burning, 576, 707, 713

A'isha (wife of Muhammad), 253, 254, 265, 268

Akbar, Sultan, 423, 529–530, 533; "Divine Faith" of, 530

Akhenaten (Amenhotep IV), 53–54

Akkad, 27, 28

Akkadian language, 26, 35, 52

Aksum, 95, 244

Alalakh, 54

Al-Andalus, 259, 292

Alaska, Siberian land bridge and, 8

Ala-ud-Din Khalji, Sultan, 383, 392–393

Albania (Albanians), 618, 733; in Kosovo, 857

Al-Bashir, Omar, 881

Alcoholic beverages: beer, 17, 216, 279, 394, 447, 578, 594 (*illus.*); wine, 149; in trade with Amerindians, 477, 481

Aldrin, Edwin E. "Buzz," 827

Aleppo, Syria, 263, 525, 617

Alexander I (Russia), 627(*illus.*); reforms of, 624, 625

Alexander II (Russia), 623; serfs freed by, 626, 628, 727

Alexander III (Russia), 727

Alexander the Great, 135, 140; Aristotle and, 132; in India, 46, 176(*map*), 184, 186; death of, 135; Mausoleum of, 137

Alexandria, 135, 136, 137; Christianity in, 244, 263; patriarch of, 263, 293, 420

Alexius Comnenus (Byzantium), 274, 275, 293

Algarve, 371

Algeria, 238, 259; as French colony, 675, 753; European settlers in, 753; independence of, 816, 829

Al-Hajj Ahmed, 392

Ali (Muhammad's son-in-law), 252, 254, 256, 526; Fatima and, 254, 268

Al-Jazeera (television network), 891

Al-Kashi, Ghiyas al-Din Jamshid, 331–332

Allende, Salvador, 845

Alliances (allies): Hiram-Solomon, 65–66, 68–69; Mesopotamian, 28; Greek polis, 129–130; of Srivajayan kings, 194–195; in medieval Europe, 280; Mongol marriage and, 323; Mediterranean trade, 409; Portugal-Ethiopia, 417; Spanish-Amerindian, 424–425, 426, 464; French-Amerindian, 482; Congress of Vienna and, 611; balance of power and, 611; British-Amerindian, 654; French-Italian, 718; World War I, 734, 737–738, 749;

Italy-Germany (Axis), 795; World War II, 799(*map*), 800–802, 801(*map*) ; Cold War, 816, 817, 822, 823(*map*); in Japanese industry, 825

All-India Muslim League, 770

Al-Mansur, Ahmad, 537

Al-Nadim, Abu al-Faraj Muhammad, 247, 248

Alpacas, 71, 216, 217, 397, 399. *See also* Llamas

Alphabet: cuneiform and, 52; Phoenician, 68; Greek, 122, 141, 224–225; Armenian, 244; Cyrillic, 275, 288, 625; Roman (Latin), 275–276, 752; Viking runes, 278(*illus.*)

Al-Rashid, Harun, Caliph, 256

Alsace and Lorraine, 720, 742(*map*), 743

Altepetl, 395

Al-Umari, 407

Al-Wahhab, Muhammad ibn Abd, 525

Aluminum, 764(*illus.*), 767

Amarna, 53

Amazon rain forest, 775, 776

Ambergris, from whaling, 537, 694

American Anti-Slavery Society, 657

American Revolution (1775–1783), 595–599, 613; course of, 597–598; France and, 598, 602; frontiers and taxes, 595–597; republican institutions in, 598–599; women in, 596, 599

American system of manufactures, 572

Americas, the (New World; Western Hemisphere). *See also* Amerindians; Caribbean region; Central America; Latin America; North America; *and specific countries*; migrations to, 7(*map*), 8; burial mounds in, 19; domesticated plants and animals in, 16–17; first civilizations of, 198–226; new foods from, 433; Spanish conquistadors in, 423–427, 428; Columbian exchange and, 464–465; chronology (1754–1804), 614; Enlightenment and, 592; constitutional experiments in, 647–648; development and underdevelopment, 662–663, 664–666; foreign interventions and regional wars in, 651–653; social and economic challenges in, 656–667; native peoples and nation-state, 653–655; immigration to, 563–564, 658–660; problem of order in (1825–1890), 646–655; abolition of slavery in, 656–658; personalist leaders in, 648–649; racial discrimination in, 662 (*See also* Mixed-race, in Americas); Spanish conquistadors in, 423–427, 428; threat of regionalism in, 649–651; women's rights in, 661–662

Amerindians (native peoples). *See also* Andean region; Mesoamerica; *specific peoples*; hunting by, 17; Northern peoples, 199, 211–214, 221; Caribbean region, 407–408, 424; disease and, 424, 426; in France, 449; Choctaw, 462, 482; Columbian exchange and, 464–465; epidemics and, 426, 463–464, 465, 468, 470–471, 477, 478; colonial fur trade and, 446, 464, 476, 479, 480–481 *and illus.*; in colonial Latin America, 462, 467–468; horses and, 464–465, 654; labor of, 468–470; lands of, 471, 477, 482, 578, 595, 640, 643; rebellions by, 484–485, 654–655; census of, 670, 671; nation-state and, 653–655, 667

Amnesty International, 886

Amon (god), 43, 53, 54, 55(*illus.*), 94, 955

Amorites, 28, 76, 96

Amritsar massacre (India, 1919), 771

Amsterdam, 447, 460; port of, 460

Amulets, 31, 43, 269(*illus.*)

Amur River Valley, Russia and, 532, 554, 631

Anasazi, 211–212, 213(*illus.*)

Anatolia (modern Turkey), 519, 523. *See also* Ottoman Empire; Turkic (Turkish) peoples; Indo-Europeans in, 19; Çatal Hüyük, 20–21 *and illus.*; in Late Bronze Age, 76; Assyria and, 50, 60; Hittites in, 50–52, 51(*map*), 54, 58, 241; silver in, 50, 55; Troy in, 58; Celts in, 100; Lydia in, 114, 129, 243; Persia and, 114, 129; Greek settlements in, 119; Seleucids in, 136; Christianity in, 156, 244; Seljuk conquest of, 260, 293; Greeks expelled from, 741, 749

ANC. *See* African National Congress

Ancestor cult: Neolithic, 19; Egyptian, 43–44; Chinese, 81, 83, 87, 165, 170, 172; Roman, 172; Southeast Asian, 193; Andean, 202; Maya, 207; Korean, 314; Confucian, 543

Ancien régime (old order), 589; Enlightenment and, 591–593

Andean region, 214–221. *See also* Bolivia; Ecuador; Peru; textiles of, 70, 202, 217; Chavín, 199, 196(*map*), 202–203, 215; Chimú (Chimor), 220–221, 222; cultural response to environment in, 215–216, 222; Mesoamerica compared to, 222; Moche, 216–217, 218–219 *and illus.*, 220; Tiwanaku and Wari, 217–220; Inka Empire, 209(*map*), 397–399, 425(*illus.*), 426–427; Spanish conquest, 426–427; volcanic eruption in, 559; melting glaciers in, 871, 888

Andronicus of Cyrrhus, 139(*illus.*)

Angkor (Cambodia), 378

Anglicanism (Church of England); Henry VIII and, 439, 460; Puritans and, 454, 478; in Africa, 511, 686

Anglo-Saxons, 278

Angola: slave trade in, 490, 504, 508; as Portuguese colony, 509, 510, 511, 590, 682; independence of, 831–832

Angra Mainyu, 117

Animals, 403. *See also* Camels; Cattle; Horses; Hunting; Livestock; Llamas; domestication of, 16–17, 25, 42, 95, 106–108; as source of disease, 18; in Egypt, 42; sacrifice of, 31, 66, 108, 125, 398; jaguar-god, 71, 200, 203; slaughter of, 328; in Columbian Exchange, 424, 464–465

An Lushan rebellion, 302, 303

Anna Comnena, 275

Annam, 318. *See also* Vietnam

Anthony, Susan B., 714

Antigonids, 135, 137

Antigua, plantation scene in, 492(*illus.*)

Antioch, 136, 244; crusaders in, 261, 292, 294; patriarch of, 263

Anyang (Shang capital), 81

Apache peoples, 465, 655

Apartheid, in South Africa, 832

Apedemak (god), 95

Apiru, 64. *See also* Israel

Apollo (god), 123, 125, 126(*illus.*)

Apologus (Basra), 235

Apostles, of Jesus, 156

Appalachian Mountains, 667

Appeasement of Nazi Germany, 795

Appennine Mountains, 144, 148

Aqueducts, 157, 159(*illus.*)

Aquitaine, 286, 294, 369

Arab armies, 255–256, 268, 273; in Spain, 276

Arab caliphate. *See* Caliphates

Arabia (Arabian peninsula). *See also* Saudi Arabia; Yemen (south Arabia); camel domestication in, 237 *and illus.*, 238; before Muhammad, 250–251; chronology (570–1260), 271; origins of Islam in, 250–254; Indian Ocean trade and, 233; pastoralism in, 248, 250; Chinese expeditions to, 339, 340(*map*), 341

Arabian Nights, 247, 256

Arabian Sea, 45, 177, 189, 386, 389, 423

Arabic language, 247, 255, 259, 331, 511; Islam and, 254, 259, 268, 374; works of Aristotle in, 256, 259, 294, 363

Arabic numerals, 188, 190

Arabic script, 387, 526

Arabi Pasha, 683

Arab-Israeli conflict (1947–1973), 838–839

Arab Revolt (1916), 738

Arabs (Arab countries). *See also* Islam; Middle East; Muslims; as merchants, 233, 251, 387, 781; Wahhabism in, 525; Omani, 537, 686; after World War I, 752–753; Palestine question and, 751–752, 754(*map*), 818; Algerian war and, 828

Arab Spring (2010), 881, 882(*illus.*), 886, 891

Arafat, Yasir, 838

Aragon, 371, 409

Aramaic language, 26, 63, 96, 156

Aramaeans, 67, 96

Araucanian people, 655

Arawak, 424; voyages of, 408

Arbenz Guzmán, Jacobo, 833

Arcesilas of Cyrene, 111

Archers. *See* Bows and arrows (archers)

Arches: Roman use of, 157, 159(*illus.*); in Gothic cathedrals, 363

Archilochus, 125–126

Architecture. *See also* Construction materials and techniques; Housing; *and specific types of buildings* (*e.g., churches, pyramids, temples*); in Mesopotamia, 34, 35; Egyptian pyramids, 39, 40 (*illus.*), 44; Mesoamerican, 199, 207 *and illus.*; Toltec, 210; Andean, 219–220; Islamic, 260(*illus.*), 391; Byzantine, 274; Japanese, 346; Chinese, 339; Indian, 391; Russian, 534–535; skyscrapers, 766; International style, 767

Ardashir (Iran), 248

Ares (war god), 98

Argentina: African slaves in, 474; livestock in, 464, 663; independence of, 643, 644 (*map*); black culture in, 662; foreign naval blockade of, 652; immigrants in, 659, 660 *and illus.*, 661, 710; education of women in, 662; tango in, 661; indigenous peoples of, 654; pampas of, 465, 663, 666, 775; railroads in, 663, 705, 775; beef exports of, 709, 710, 775; industrialization in, 775; British investment in, 666, 710, 775; Depression (1930s) in, 776–777; transformation of, 775; Brazil compared to, 775–776; Perón regime in, 777(*illus.*), 778, 845; economic and political crisis in, 846; Mercosur (trade agreement) and, 876

Aristarchus, 139

Aristocracy (nobility). *See also* Elite class; Landowners; Egyptian, 41; Mycenean, 57; Israelite, 66, 67; Assyrian, 60; Carthaginian, 73; early Chinese, 84, 91; Persian, 114, 115; Greek, 124, 131; Roman, 145, 148, 154, 158; Teotihuacan, 204–205; Andean peoples, 216, 221; Chinese imperial, 161, 162, 170, 298, 310; Sasanid, 244, 245(*illus.*); Byzantine, 274, 275; Crusades and, 292, 293, 294; Japanese, 316, 317–318; Mongol, 327, 329, 337; medieval Europe, 279, 280, 281, 351, 368–370; Aztec,

395, 396; Inka, 399; bourgeoisie and, 448, 450; British, 459, 612; Spanish, 453, 470; tax exemption and, 445, 453, 456, 458; Russian (boyars), 533, 535, 727; Enlightenment and, 591; Korean, 546; French, 453, 599, 600, 601; Qing China, 553, 635, 638; European in World War I, 761

Aristotle, 132, 133, 139; Arab translations of, 256, 259, 294, 363; European scholars and, 363; science of, 441

Aritomo, Yamagata, 722, 729

Arizona, native peoples of, 211–212

Arjuna, 174, 186

Arkhangelsk, 532

Ark of the Covenant, 65

Arkwright, Richard, 570, 580, 582

Armed forces (soldiers). *See also* Cavalry; Military; Navy; Red Army (Soviet Union); Warrior elite; *and specific wars*; Mesopotamian, 28, 35; Egyptian, 41; Israelite, 65; Assyrian Empire, 69; early Chinese, 91; Greek (hoplites), 122–123, 124, 127, 129; Macedonian, 135; Persian Empire, 129; Roman, 147, 148 *and illus.*, 149, 155, 156, 157, 172; imperial Chinese, 161, 163–164(*illus.*), 171; Indian, 185, 187–188; Toltec, 210; Arab Muslim, 255, 268, 272, 273, 276; Khitan, 306; Mongol, 324, 334, 345, 346, 353; Conquistadors, 423–427; Holy Roman Empire, 438; Prussian, 456, 724; early modern Europe, 456; French, 456, 603, 607; Ottoman (Janissaries), 516, 519, 524, 525, 618, 620–621; Safavid Iran, 529; Japanese, 546; Manchu, in China, 540; American Revolution, 597, 598; Latin American independence and, 642; Russian, 515, 534; Crimean War, 622–624; Chinese (Bannermen), 630, 633; Brazilian slaves in, 656, 657, 658; South Africa War, 678; American, in Mexico, 697, 698; American, in Philippines, 695; British India (Sepoys), 688; Ethiopian, 684; Islamic *jihad*, 675, 678–679; Prussian, 720; Russian, 727; German, 726, 734, 739–740; Japanese (Meiji),

724, 727; before World War I, 733–734; World War I, 734–737, 738, 740; Guomindang (China), 748, 798, 803–804; Japanese, 795–796; Nazi (Wehrmacht), 778, 799 *and illus.*, 802, 807; Vietnam War, 825–826; Israeli, 883

Armenia (Armenians), 60, 626; Christianity in, 244; Urartu in, 75, 113; in Isfahan, 527, 528; merchants, 515, 527, 535; in Ottoman Empire, 733, 738; Soviet Republic of, 743

Armillary spheres, 330–331 *and illus.*

Armor, body: Greek hoplite, 122–123, 148; of medieval knights, 280, 283, 294(*illus.*); in China, 308; conquistador, 424

Armstrong, Neil A., 827

Arrow War (China, 1856–1860), 633, 635, 722

Art and artists. *See also* Cave paintings; Painting(s); Wall murals (frescoes); Gandhara, 181(*illus.*); Saharan rock art, 2, 235, 236(*illus.*), 240; Byzantine, 275; Renaissance Europe, 367–368, 436–437; Dutch, 446(*illus.*); Persian, 526; post-World War I, 763

Arthashastra, 184

Articles of Confederation (United States), 599, 647

Artillery, 370, 616, 618, 620, 625, 630, 684. *See also* Bombs and bombing; Cannon; World War I, 735

Artisans (craftspeople). *See also specific crafts*; Neolithic, 20; in Mesopotamia, 27, 29; Aegean trade and, 58; Assyrian, 62; Egyptian, 92; Kushite, 92; Scythian, 97 (*illus.*); Greek, 124; Indian guilds, 186, 187; Olmec, 200; Silk Road trade and, 229; Anasazi, 212; Andean, 202, 217, 219; medieval Europe, 289; Kievan Russia, 289; printing, 366; European guilds of, 354; Venetian, 357; Dutch, 446; on sugar plantations, 496; East Asian, 548; Japanese, 547; textile trade, 564; British, 546, 584

Art of War (Sunzi), 85

Aryans (Nazi master race), 793

Aryas, 177, 182, 186

Asante kingdom, 507, 508
Asceticism, 287. *See also*
    Monasteries; in India, 179
Ashikaga shogunate (Japan), 347,
    545
Ashoka (India), 184, 185;
    Buddhism and, 180(*illus.*),
    243
Ashurbanipal (Assyria), 62
Ashur (city), 50, 60, 62
Ashur (god), 60
Asia (Asians). *See also* Central
    Asia; East Asia; Southeast
    Asia; Western Asia; early
    humans in, 3; trade and
    communication routes in, 231
    (*map*); as center of power,
    401; Russia and, 626–627;
    immigrants to Americas from,
    658, 659, 711; chronology
    (1931–1949), 810–811;
    Depression (1930s) in,
    788–789; World War II in,
    800–802 *and map*, 807–808;
    Asian Tigers (industrial
    nations), 844, 852; HIV/AIDS
    in, 861–862; population in
    (1750–2050), 861(*table*);
    financial crisis in, 877–878
Asian Tigers, 852, 853, 864, 871. *See
    also* Hong Kong; Singapore;
    South Korea; Taiwan
Askia Muhammad, 393
Assam, 688, 692
Assassinations: Assassin sect, 330;
    in Mexican civil war, 698;
    anarchists and, 716–717; of
    Russian tsars, 727; beginning
    World War I, 732, 733; in
    Stalin's Russia, 787; in Japan,
    796; in Vietnam, 825; in El
    Salvador, 846
Assemblies: Mesopotamia, 27;
    Carthage, 73; in British
    colonies, 477, 480, 500, 596;
    Athens, 128, 133; Alexandria,
    137; Roman, 145, 153; in
    France, 602; in Prussia, 612;
    in China, 747
Assembly-line manufacturing. *See
    also* Mass production; in
    China, 534; automobile, 746
Assiniboine people, 465
Assyria (Assyrians), 50, 55
Assyrian Empire (Neo-Assyrian
    Empire), 59–63; conquest and
    control in, 60–62 *and map*;
    Egypt and, 60, 75, 94;
    kingship in, 60; mass
    deportations in, 61, 62, 67,
    75, 76; Medes and, 75, 113;
    Persian Empire and, 116;

society and culture, 62–63;
    trade in, 60; tribute and, 60,
    62, 67, 68(*illus.*), 69
Astarte (goddess), 69
Astrakhan, 515, 516; khanate of,
    531
Astrolabe, 330, 411
Astronomy: Mesopotamian, 36;
    Babylonian, 138–140; Olmec,
    200; Greek, 138, 139 *and
    illus.*; Islamic, 264, 337, 348;
    Il-khanate, 331; imperial
    China, 169, 308, 311(*illus.*),
    339; Korean, 345; Jesuit, in
    China, 543; observatories
    and, 331 *and illus.*, 339, 443
    (*illus.*); Copernican, 331, 364,
    442; sunspot activity, 559
Aswan, Egypt, 36, 78, 92; dam at,
    683, 836
Atahuallpa (Inka), 425 *and illus.*,
    426
Atatürk, Mustafa Kemal, 752
Aten (sun-god), 53
Athens, 122, 127–129; acropolis
    in, 128; democracy in, 128,
    129, 130, 131; height of
    power, 130–132; in
    Hellenistic Age, 137; navy of,
    130, 131(*illus.*);
    Peloponnesian War and, 134;
    slavery in, 128, 132; Tower of
    the Winds in, 139(*illus.*);
    Olympics in (1896), 765
Atlantic Ocean: chronology
    (700–1533), 428–429;
    exploration of (before 1450),
    407–408, 431; winds of, 411,
    413; exploration of
    (1450–1550), 411–413, 414
    (*map*), 415; steamships in,
    573 *and illus.*, 663; submarine
    telegraph cables in, 575, 706
Atlantic system (Atlantic economy),
    500–506; African slave trade
    and, 488, 502, 503(*map*), 512;
    Bight of Biafra and Angola,
    508–509; capitalism and
    mercantilism in, 501–502;
    chronology (1611–1713), 514;
    Gold Coast and Slave Coast,
    507–508; New England and,
    479, 504; West Indies and,
    492; Islamic slave trade and,
    509–512, 513; expansion of,
    663
Atman (self), 178, 181
Atomic bombs. *See also* Nuclear
    weapons; bombing of Japan
    (1945), 801 *and map*, 803
    and illus.; development of,
    805

Atomic theory, 126
Auctoritas, of Roman men, 145
Augsburg, Peace of (1555), 452
Augustus (Octavian), 146(*map*),
    157, 172; equites and, 152–153
Aung San Suu Kyi, 881
Aurangzeb, Sultan, 530, 531, 686
Auschwitz death camp, 807
Australia, 702; migration to, 7(*map*),
    8; European immigrants in,
    564, 693, 710; extinctions in,
    10; Aborigines of, 693, 694;
    foraging peoples in, 17; as
    British colony, 693, 694; penal
    colonies in, 693; wool in, 709;
    immigration restrictions in,
    741; Qantas airline in, 764;
    drought in, 888
Australopithecines, 4–5, 9
Australopithecus africanus, 3
Austria-Hungary (1867–1918):
    immigrants from, 711;
    Balkans and, 727; languages
    of, 718, 727; nationalism in,
    724; conservativism in, 724,
    727; German unification and,
    720, 721(*map*); Italian
    unification and, 718–720;
    Serbia and, 733; World War I
    and, 732, 733, 734; division
    of, after World War I,
    742(*map*), 743
Austria (to 1867 and 1918 to
    present): mining in, 354, 356;
    Habsburgs of, 452, 457(*map*);
    Ottomans and, 524; protests
    for reform in, 612; French
    Revolution and, 603, 607;
    conservatism of, 611; after
    World War I, 742(*map*); Nazi
    annexation of (1938), 794; in
    European Community, 819
Austronesian languages, 402, 405
Authoritarianism, 81. *See also*
    Dictatorship; Fascism; Tyrants;
    of Napoleon, 606–607, 613; in
    Ottoman Empire, 620; in
    Brazil and Argentina, 776–777,
    789; in Japan, 796
Automobiles, 845, 868, 880;
    driver's license for, 761;
    mass-production of, 768
Avataras, 182
Averroës (Ibn Rushd), 259
Avianca Airlines, 764
Avicenna (Ibn Sina), 294, 363, 364
Avignon, popes in, 362, 368
Axis powers, World War II, 795,
    808. *See also* Germany; Italy;
    Japan, in World War II
Aya Sofya Mosque (Istanbul),
    517(*illus.*)

Ayllu (Andean clan), 216, 217, 219
Ayrton, William, 709
Azerbaijan, 328, 626, 743
Azores Islands, 407, 410, 411, 413, 469
Aztecs (Aztec Empire), 209(*map*), 394–397. *See also* Mexica; Inka compared to, 399; Toltecs and, 209, 210, 395; Spanish conquest of, 396, 424–426; colonial elite, 466

Baal (Hammon), 66, 74
Baba, Ahmad, 537
Baba of Karo, 680
Babur, Sultan, 529
Babylon (city), 28, 96; New Year's Festival, 31, 32–34; Assyrian conquest of, 75; Cyrus in, 67; Israelites in, 67; renaissance of, 75–76
Babylonia. *See also* Mesopotamia; Creation Myth in, 31, 32–34; Hammurabi's Law Code in, 28, 29; Kassite dynasty in, 50, 52; Neo-Babylonia (Chaldaean), 67, 69, 75, 77; Persian Empire and, 114, 115
Babylonian language, 50
Bactria, 182
Baekeland, Leo Hendrik, 767
Baghdad, 525, 891; books in, 247; caliphate in, 256, 257; decline of, 261; Mongol sack of, 256, 258(*map*), 261, 324, 327, 389, 526; bombing of (2003), 882
Bahamas, Columbus in, 424
Bahmani kingdom, 384
Bahrain, 839
Bakelite (plastic), 766–767 *and illus.*
Bakunin, Mikhail, 716–717
Balance of power, 702–703. *See also* Great powers; in early modern Europe, 436, 456; Congress of Vienna and, 611; Cold War, 825
Balboa, Vasco Núñez de, 426
Balfour, Sir Arthur, 738, 742, 750
Balfour Declaration (1917), 739, 750, 753, 838
Bali, terrorist attack in (2002), 880, 885
Balkans, 335, 725. *See also specific states*; Christians in, 519; Ottoman Empire and, 519, 617, 733; Austria-Hungary and, 726; ethnic cleansing in, 857
Balkh, 327, 329
Ball games, 765; in Mesoamerica, 200, 201, 207(*illus.*).

Baltic region. *See also* Estonia; Latvia; Lithuania; trading fairs in, 287; Germans in, 351–352; trading cities in, 356; Soviet invasion of, 799; independence of, 740, 743, 855
Baluchistan, desert of, 113
Bananas, 192, 234, 240, 241, 377, 394, 407, 464, 493, 832, 833
Bandung Conference (1955), 835 and *illus.*
Bangladesh, 828; flooding and famine in, 813, 889(*illus.*)
Banks and banking: in medieval Europe, 359; Atlantic economy and, 501; Dutch, 447, 459; speculative bubbles and, 458; industrialization and, 566; in Ottoman Empire, 623; Egyptian debts and, 683; World War I loans and, 745; Depression (1930s) and, 787; World Bank, 818, 819, 866; financial crisis (2008), 878–879
Bannermen (China), 630, 633
Bantu language, 242, 537
Bantu migrations, in Africa, 227, 245; iron working and, 241–242
Ban Zhao, 167
Barbados, 827; hurricanes in, 495; sugar economy in, 490, 492, 493
Barbarians: Greeks and, 123, 133; Rome and, 172; China and, 160–161, 170, 172, 300, 303, 405
Barley, 15, 21, 25, 28, 42, 107, 119, 279, 341, 351, 386
Barter: in Mesopotamia, 28; in Rome, 158; in medieval Europe, 279; in Byzantium, 274; Aztec, 396
Basra (Apologus), 235, 255, 263, 266
Bastille, storming of (Paris, 1789), 602
Batavia (modern Jakarta), 538
Bathing (purification) rites: in Israel, 67; in India, 178, 183
Batista, Fulgencio, 816, 833, 834
Batu, Khan, 324, 324(*fig.*), 326(*map*), 328, 332, 334. *See also* Golden Horde
Bayeux Tapestry, 281, 290
Bay of Pigs invasion (Cuba, 1961), 834
Beer making, 17, 216, 394, 447, 578
Beer Street (Hogarth), 594(*illus.*)

Beg, Yaqub, 615
Beijing, 324, 325, 633; Forbidden City in, 336, 339, 341; observatory in, 331; Jesuits in, 450; population of, 758, 865(*table*); British mission in, 556; Manchu armies in, 540, 546, 553; Forbidden City, 748; Western armies occupation of, 729; Nixon in, 837–838; protest in (1989), 853–854
Belgium. *See also* Flanders (Flemish): industrialization in, 565–566, 567, 571, 576, 577(*map*); textile industry in, 571, 573; railroads in, 574; colonies of, 679, 683; World War I in, 734, 735, 741; Nazi invasion of, 799; in European Community, 819; decolonization of, 831–832
Belgrade, 517
Belize (British Honduras), 667
Bell Telephone Laboratories, 890
Benedictine abbey of Cluny, 286, 287
Benedict of Nursia, 285
Benedict XVI, Pope, 884
Bengal (Bengalis), 770; Islam in, 392; East India Company and opium in, 687; independence movement in, 531; famine in (1943), 813
Benin: Portuguese in, 416, 417
Bentham, Jeremy, 583
Berbers, 753; revolts by, 258; in Spain, 255, 259, 276; collapse of Ghana and, 379
Berlin: Olympic Games in, 765; bombing of (1944), 805; blockade and airlift (1948–1949), 822
Berlin Conference (1884–1885), 679, 682
Berlin Wall, 822; fall of (1989), 855–856 *and illus.*
Berytus, 68
Bessemer, Henry, 706
Bhagavad-Gita, 174, 183, 186, 187
Bharatiya Janata Party (India), 881, 884
Bhutto, Benazir, 881
Biafra, Bight of, 508–509
Bible, the: Hebrew (Old Testament), 2, 63–65, 67, 68; Islam and, 251, 252; New Testament, 155, 366; Gutenberg, 367; Luther and, 437; science and, 441; vernacular translations, 440

Bill of Rights (1689, Britain), 455
Bill of Rights (1791, United States), 886
Bindusara (India), 184
Bin Laden, Osama, 885; al-Qaeda and, 849, 874–875, 882; death of, 885
Bipedalism, 4, 5
Bipolar world. *See* Cold War (Bipolar world)
Birth control (contraception), 265, 860; abortion, 762, 791, 862; Sanger and, 762; Soviet policy on, 791; Chinese family planning, 860(*illus.*)
Birthrate. *See also* Fertility rates; late marriage and, 451; plantation slaves, 497, 497(*table*); decline, in industrial nations, 862; in developing world, 862–863; of immigrants, 867
Bisexuality, in ancient Greece, 133
Bishops, 156, 285, 438, 607. *See also* Clergy; appointment (investiture) of, 284; councils of, 250, 282; Ethiopian, 244; African, 686; assassinated, in El Salvador, 846
Bismarck, Otto von, 679, 720, 725–726; German unification and, 720
Bison (buffalo), 17; Amerindians and, 465, 654
Black Death, 351, 353, 355(*map*), 372, 431, 691; Jews and, 358, 362
Blackfoot people, 465
"Black Hole of Calcutta," 687
Black Sea region, 262; colonies in, 97, 123, 356; Italian city-states and, 409; plague in, 353, 355(*map*); Russia and, 532, 534, 619(*map*); Crimean War in, 622–623
"Black ships" of Commodore Perry, 704
Blacksmiths, 52, 67, 283, 378, 496, 706. *See also* Iron industry and tools
Black Thursday (1929), 787
Blitzkrieg warfare, 798
Bloodletting rituals, 200, 207. *See also* Sacrifice
Blyden, Edward Wilmot, 686
Boats. *See also* Canoes; Ships and shipping; Mesopotamian, 28, 35; Kievan Russia, 287; in coastal Pacific, 408
Boccaccio, Giovanni, 365, 366
Bodhisattvas, 182, 195, 244, 299; rulers as, 300, 307
Body armor. *See* Armor, body

Boer War (1899–1902), 678
Bolívar, Simón, 642–643, 648; Gran Colombia and, 643, 648, 649
Bolivia: Tiwanaku in, 217–218; alliance with Peru, 653; mining in, 468, 469, 667; independence of, 643, 644 (*map*), 649; Guevara in, 834; Mercosur (trade agreement) and, 876
Bologna, University of, 364
Bolshevik Revolution (Russia), 740
Bolsheviks, 739, 740, 743. *See also* Communist Party (Soviet Union); women's rights and, 790
Bombay Presidency, 687. *See also* Mumbai
Bombs and bombing (explosives). *See also* Nuclear weapons; Weapons and military technology; anarchist, 716; dynamite, 707; in Sino-Japanese War, 797; in World War II, 798–799, 802; atomic bombing of Hiroshima and Nagasaki, 801 *and map*, 803 *and illus.*; in Arab-Israeli conflict, 883; terrorist, 885
Bonaparte, Joseph, 641
Bonaparte, Napoleon. *See* Napoleon Bonaparte
Boniface VIII, Pope, 368
Book of Changes, 84, 86
Book of Documents, 83, 86
Book of Kells, 286(*illus.*)
Book of Songs, 83, 84, 86
Book of the Dead, Egyptian, 43
Books. *See also* Libraries; Literacy; Printing technology; in Baghdad, 247; in China, 310; Catholic Church and, 442; Dutch, 447
Bordeaux, 279
Borneo, Brunei in, 536
Bornu, 510–511
Borobodur temple (Java), 194(*illus.*), 195
Bose, Hem Chandra, 761
Bose, Pramatha Nath, 770
Bosman, Willem, 507
Bosnia, 617, 733
Bosnia and Herzegovina, 857, 858(*map*)
Boston, colonial era, 479
Boston Massacre (1770), 596
Botany, global economy and, 699–700
Boulton, Matthew, 573
Bourbon dynasty, 454(*table*), 455, 457(*map*), 484

Bourgeoisie, 445–448. *See also* Middle class; French Revolution and, 603; Marx on, 584
Bourke-White, Margaret, 789(*photo*)
Bows and arrows (archers): Iceman, 13 *and illus.*; Mesopotamian, 35; Hyksos, 52; Assyrian, 60; Egyptian, 55 *and illus.*; Nubian, 94; crossbows, 169, 368, 403; Indian, 187–188; Central Asian, 232; flaming arrows, 308, 327, 342 *and illus.*; Mongol, 327; Khitan, 306; in Mali, 381; English longbow, 370
Boxer Uprising (1900, China), 728 *and illus.*, 729
Boycotts. *See also* Protests (demonstrations); in American Revolution, 596, 599; in British India, 770
Boyle, Robert, 443
Bo Zhuyi, 300
Brahe, Tycho, 442, 443(*illus.*)
Brahmanas, 178
Brahmins, 178, 179, 182, 185, 187, 190; oral tradition and, 226; Muslim rule and, 383–384
Brahmo Samaj (Divine Society), 691
Brain size, in early humans, 3, 5, 6(*illus.*), 9, 11
Brandenberger, Jacques E., 767
Brant, Joseph, 598
Brazil, 16; as Portuguese colony, 412, 413, 423, 453, 465, 489; chronology (1530s–1777), 487; native population in, 463; sugar plantations in, 412, 466, 469, 470, 474, 487, 489, 490; cattle in, 464; gold in, 468, 470, 485, 667; coffee production in, 485, 581, 666, 668; slave labor in, 412, 465, 496, 504, 509, 581, 684; runaway slave communities in, 474, 500; Afro-Brazilians, 486 (*illus.*); British naval blockade of, 652; independence in, 644 (*map*), 645; Portuguese royal family in, 641, 645; economic development in, 584; end of slave trade in, 657; free blacks in, 500, 657; women's rights in, 662; immigration to, 659, 712; chronology (1808–1888), 669; war with Paraguay (1865–1870), 657; Depression (1930s) in, 776–777, 789; rain

forest in, 775, 776, 870, 871;
rubber in, 775, 776; Vargas
regime in, 776–777; Argentina
compared, 775–776;
industrialization of, 845, 864;
military rule in, 845;
deforestation in, 776–777,
870; Mercosur trade
agreement and, 876; soap
operas from, 890
Brazza, Savorgnan de, 679
Brazzaville Conference (1944), 831
Brest-Litovsk, Treaty of (1918), 740
Bretton Woods Conference (1946),
818
Brezhnev, Leonid, 822, 854
Bridges: in Rome, 157; in China,
308; iron, in Britain, 572
Britain, 55. See also England;
Great Britain; Celts in, 100,
101, 102; Romans in,
146(map), 158; Viking
raids in, 276
Britain, Battle of (1940), 799
(map), 800
British East India Company (EIC),
555, 556, 586, 596–597;
India and, 555, 586
British Empire (British colonies).
See also Great Britain; India,
under British rule and specific
colonies; in Indian Ocean, 518
(map); in West Indies, 490,
827 (See also Jamaica); in
Southeast Asia, 692; Australia
and New Zealand, 692–694;
financial drain of, 726; free
trade policy in, 701; Hong
Kong, 631; labor migrations
to, 701–702, 712; in Africa,
676, 677–678, 779, 781;
self-rule in, 647, 692;
decolonization and, 830, 831
British Guiana, Asians in, 659, 702
British investment, 709–710; in
Argentina, 666, 709, 775; in
India, 688, 689, 709; in
Mexico, 696
British Navy, 456; Henry VIII and,
439, 456; defeat of Spain by,
456; Dutch and, 456, 459;
Napoleon and, 607–608; end
of slave trade and, 646, 656,
657, 664, 684, 685–686;
steam-powered gunboats,
587; Latin America and, 652;
in Opium War, 630;
supremacy of, 734; in World
War I, 737, 740; in World
War II, 800
British North America, 456,
475–480. See also Canada;

African slaves in, 477, 478;
chronology (1607–1759),
487; Enlightenment in, 592;
French and Indian War in,
482, 483(map); indentured
Europeans in, 476, 489, 491;
Middle Atlantic, 479–480;
New England, 478–479;
reform and reorganization in,
485–486; South, 476–478;
Revolution in, 595–599
British Raj, 687. See also India,
under British rule
British South Africa Company,
678
British West Indies, 497; abolition
of slavery in, 658; Jamaica,
491–493, 494–495, 496
(table), 497(table), 499;
independence of, 827
Bronze. See also Late Bronze Age:
in Mesopotamia, 35; coins,
123–124; in early China, 80,
81, 87(illus.); iron compared
to, 49, 109, 177; in Aegean
Sea region, 58; in Southeast
Asia, 193; for cannon, 335,
342
Brother Industries, Ltd., 759
Bruges, 291, 357
Brunei, 341; Sultanate of, 536
Brutus "the Liberator," 144
Bubonic plague, 274, 327, 633; as
Black Death in Europe, 351,
353, 355(map); at Kaffa, 327,
353
Buddha (Siddhartha Gautama),
180, 181(illus.)
Buddhism; origins of, in India,
179, 180–181, 183–184, 186,
189; cave paintings, 189, 307
(illus.); in Central Asia, 232;
in China, 169, 188, 297, 299,
306, 310; in East Asia,
318–319; in Japan, 316, 347;
in Korea, 314, 315, 345;
Mahayana, 182, 184, 244,
299–300, 306, 316, 318;
missionaries, 193, 297;
pilgrims, 180(illus.), 188; in
Southeast Asia, 392; spread
of, 181–182, 227, 231(map),
243–244; temples, 194(illus.),
195, 299, 316; Theravada,
182, 244; Tibetan, 336, 338,
552; Mongols and, 327, 336,
338; Zen (Chan), 310, 345,
347
Buddhist monasteries (monks and
nuns), 169, 182, 189, 195,
299, 392; in China, 299, 303,
315; gunpowder and, 342

Buenos Aires, 649, 775;
independence movement in,
643; labor activism in, 660
(illus.); growth of, 865(table)
Bukhara, 228; Samanids in, 257,
260(illus.)
Bulgaria, 733, 742(map), 822,
865; fall of communism in,
855, 858(map)
Bureaucracy (bureaucrats). See
also Administration; Civil
service; Sumerian, 27;
Egyptian, 41; Mycenaean
Greek, 56; Israelite, 64;
Hellenistic kingdoms, 136;
Roman, 153; Indian, 187;
Southeast Asian, 193; Chimú
(Peru), 221; Chinese, 168,
297, 310, 314; Inka, 398;
Vietnamese, 348; Delhi
Sultanate, 384; Benin, 416;
European, 456–457, 591;
colonial Latin America, 466;
Japanese, 545, 547; Ottoman
reform, 620–621 and illus.,
624; Russian reform, 627;
Safavid Iran, 529; British
India, 690; World War I, 737;
Soviet Union, 744, 821, 822,
854; United Nations, 818;
African nationalism and, 830
Burgoyne, John, 598
Burials (graves). See also Tombs;
Stone Age, 12; Neolithic, 19;
Egyptian, 54; Mycenaean, 57;
Siberian, 99; Celtic, 103;
Northern Amerindian, 214;
Andean, 217, 218–219 and
illus.; Maya, 218–219 and
illus.; Kievan Russia, 289
Burma (Myanmar), 390;
Buddhism in, 244; British in,
692; Japanese conquest of,
813; independence of, 828;
democratization in, 880–881
Bush, George H. W. (senior), 858
Bush, George W. (junior), 871,
888; war on terrorism and,
885; Iraq invasion and, 883
Business (companies). See also
Capitalism; Corporations;
Entrepreneurs; Industries;
Trade; in China, 313, 337;
English government and, 448,
459; bourgeoisie and, 448;
chartered trading, 447, 489,
501, 502, 504; Japanese, 547;
Ottoman Janissaries and, 524;
insurance, 447, 501; joint-
stock companies, 447, 458,
460, 478, 501, 513, 538, 567,
628; women in, 582,

713–714; laissez faire theory and, 583; cyclical swings of, 709; World War I and, 738; Depression (1930s) and, 788; foreign, in Latin America, 663; nationalized, in Cuba, 834; foreign, in China, 853; eastern European, 880

Buyid family, 257, 260

Byblos, 68

Byron, Lord (George Gordon Noel), 618

Byzantine Empire, 160, 295; (600–1200), 272–276; beleaguered, 273–274; Crusades and, 292; cultural achievements, 275–276; Russia and, 272, 287–288, 289; Sasanid Iran and, 248, 250; scholars in, 363; Seljuk challenge to, 260, 293; society and urban life, 274–275; Ottoman Empire and, 335

Byzantium, 160, 356. See also Constantinople

Cable News Network (CNN), 891

Cabral, Pedro Alvares, 412, 413

Cacao. See Cocoa (cacao)

Cadiz (Gades), 69

Caesar, 149. See also Augustus (Octavian)

Cahokia, mound builders of, 214

Cairo (Fustat), 259, 356, 382, 622 (illus.), 624; Islamic Caliphate and, 259, 263; Mamluks in, 380; modernization of, 683; growth of, 865(table)

Cakchiquel of Guatemala, 463

Calcutta (Kolkata), 691, 758, 770; East India Company in, 687; fingerprint bureau in, 761; projected growth of, 865(table)

Calendars: stone circle, 19; Sumerian, 28; Egyptian, 44, 138; Mesoamerican, 200, 208; Chinese, 308, 311(illus.), 337, 339, 543; Il-khanate, 330; Inka, 398; Korean, 343, 345; French Revolution, 606

Calicut (modern Kozhikode), 389, 403–404; Portuguese and, 420–421, 422

California, 712; gold discovered in, 653

Caliphates (Arab Caliphates, 632–1258 C.E.), 253–262; Abbasid, 257, 258(map), 259, 260, 262; rise and fall of, 254–262; assault on, 260–262; bookstores in, 247; cities of, 263–265; Fatimid,

258(map), 259–260; political fragmentation, 257–260; Umayyad, 254, 255–256, 258 (map), 259, 292; Sokoto, 679

Calixtus II, Pope, 284

Calles, Plutarco Elías, 698, 774

Calpolli, Aztec, 395, 396

Calvin, John, 437

Calvinism, 437, 438, 439. See also Puritans

Cambay (modern Khambhat), 389, 391, 536

Cambodia, 825–826; Angkor, 378

Cambridge University, 364

Cambyses (Persia), 111, 112(map), 114

Camel, Battle of the (656), 254, 268

Camels, 25, 95, 251; domestication of, 55, 107, 238; saddles for, 237 and illus.; Silk Road trade and, 232(illus.); trans-Saharan caravan routes and, 238, 237(illus.), 382; used in warfare, 237

Cameroon, 242, 737, 749

Canaan (Canaanites), 68. See also Phoenicia; Israel and, 65, 66, 76

Canada: as French colony, 480–482 and illus.; Amerindians in, 479, 480–481 and illus., 578; fur trade, 479, 480–481 and illus.; Britain and, 590, 598, 647, 665–666; development in, 663, 666; Dominion of, 647, 694; French-speakers in, 660; immigration to, 564, 659, 663, 666, 710, 711; women's rights in, 662, 762; self-rule in, 647; national parks in, 667; wheat from, 709; immigration restricted in, 741; in World War II, 802; North American Free Trade Agreement and, 876

Canals. See also Irrigation; Suez Canal; in Mesopotamia, 27; in Egypt, 44; in Persia, 114; in China, 169, 298, 337, 556; in Europe, 447, 565; British industry and, 566; in Panama, 699, 846

Canary Islands, 411, 493

Cannon, 343, 359, 370, 516, 529, 625, 707. See also Artillery; bronze for, 335, 342; on ships, 403, 411, 535, 538, 546; conquistador, 426, 426–427

Canoes: in Southeast Asia, 192; of Madagascar colonists, 234; of Polynesian colonists, 405–406; of Canadian fur traders, 481(illus.); of Africans, 242, 408, 684–685

Canon law, 282, 285

Canterbury: archbishop of, 284–285, 353, 439; pilgrimage to, 285

Canterbury Tales (Chaucer), 354, 359, 365

Canton (Guangzhou), 543, 748

Canton system, 555, 556, 629

Cape Coast Castle, 502, 512

Cape Colony, 510, 676–677

Cape Coloureds, 678

Cape Town, 676, 781

Cape Verde, 469

Capitalism. See also Free trade; business cycle in, 709; mercantilism and, 501–502, 583; expansion of, 458; laissez faire, 583; home as refuge from, 713; Marx's view of, 584, 716; Depression (1930s) and, 788; communism and, 818–822

Captain Swing Riots (England), 585

Caracalla (Rome), 155

Caracol, 198

Caramansa, 415–416

Caravan trade and routes. See also Silk Road; Trans-Saharan trade and caravan routes; Egypt and, 41, 54; Nubia and, 92; in Arabia, 251

Caravel (ship), 411, 413

Cárdenas, Lázaro, 774

Caribbean Sea and region (West Indies): Amerindians of, 408; colonization (before 1650), 424; Columbus's exploration of, 413, 424; chronology (ca. 1500–1760), 514; hurricanes in, 494–495 and illus.; sugar and slavery in, 412, 446, 465, 474, 477, 489–500, 505, 506, 581; abolition of slavery in, 657–658; American intervention in (1901–1914), 698–699; Chinese and Indian immigrants in, 659, 668, 701, 712; independence in, 827; population in (1750–2050), 861(table); HIV/AIDS in, 861

Carib people, voyages of, 408

Carolinas, colonial era, 477

Carolingian Empire, 276. See also Charlemagne

Carpet manufacture, in Iran, 528

Carranza, Venustiano, 697, 698
Carrío de la Vandera, Alonso, 472
Carter, James "Jimmy," 846
Carthage (Carthaginians), 69–73;
founding of, 49, 69; child
sacrifice in, 74 and (*illus.*);
commercial empire of, 73;
naval power of, 73, 76; war
and religion,73–75; wars with
Rome, 73, 148–149
Cartier, Jacques, 480
Cartier-Bresson, Henri,
804(*photo*)
Cartography. *See* Mapmaking
Castas, in colonial Americas, 474,
475. *See also* Mixed race, in
Americas
Castes (varna), in India, 178–179,
196, 393, 687, 690, 769
Caste War (Mexico), 655
Castile, 371, 409, 412
Castle of the Mine, 410(*illus.*)
Castro, Fidel, 816, 826, 833–834,
844. *See also* Cuban
Revolution; alliance with
Soviet Union, 816, 826, 834
Çatal Hüyük, 20–21 *and illus.*
Catapults, 134, 327, 342, 346
Cathedrals. *See* Churches
(cathedrals)
Catherine of Aragon, 439, 460
Catherine the Great (Russia), 591,
622
Catholicism (Catholic church),
350; Counter-Reformation
and, 438, 439, 440, 441, 452,
453; English monarchy and,
454–455; in Lithuania, 334;
Inquisition and, 442; wars of
religion and, 444; in colonial
Latin America, 465–466, 467
and *illus.*, 484; in Africa,
416–417; French Revolution
and, 599–600, 603, 607; in
Latin America, 647, 846; in
Mexico, 653, 698; in southern
Germany, 720; in Ireland,
718, 726; in Poland, 807,
855; in Yugoslavia, 857;
conservatism in, 884
Catholic missionaries. *See also*
Dominicans; Franciscans;
Jesuits; in colonial Africa,
416, 686, 780; in China,
542–543; in Latin America,
466
Cattle (cattle herders). *See also*
Oxen; domestication of,
16–17, 22, 96, 107, 235;
Saharan, 2, 235–236 *and
illus.*; Nubian, 92; Celtic, 101;
Israelite, 64; Greek, 119;

Indian, 177; sub-Saharan
Africa, 240, 376; Khitan, 306;
in Egypt, 240; Zimbabwe,
388; in Americas, 464; in
Argentina, 663, 775; Zulu, in
Africa, 676
Caucasus region: Golden Horde
and, 328; Georgia, 529, 622,
623, 743; Russia and, 626,
726–727; Soviet Union and,
743
Caudillos, in Latin America, 648
Cavalry (horsemen). *See also*
Horses; Knights; Assyrian, 60;
Philip II's use of (Macedonia),
135; Chinese, 162, 165, 169;
Indian, 187–188; Scythian,
230; stirrups and, 233, 280,
298, 302(*illus.*); Russian, 289;
Inner Asian, 298, 302(*illus.*);
Khitan, 306; Mongol, 327,
336, 346; conquistador, 424,
425–426; Ottoman, 516, 519;
Safavid Iran, 526; Crimean
War and, 623; United States,
655; Mexican, 697–698;
Polish, 799
Cave paintings: Stone Age, 8–9,
12–13; Saharan rock art, 2,
235, 236(*illus.*); Buddhist, in
India, 189; Buddhist, in
China, 307(*illus.*)
Cavour, Camillo Benso di, 719–720
Ceausescu, Nicolae, 855
Celluloid, 767
Celtic languages, 100, 272(*map*)
Celts (Celtic Europe), 100–103.
See also Ireland (Irish);
Scotland; Wales (Welsh);
belief and knowledge, 103; in
Britain, 100, 101; chronology
(1000–390 B.C.E.), 105;
Druids (priests), 101, 103,
226; legends of, 103, 226;
Romans and, 101, 103, 149;
society of, 101–103; spread
of, 100–101
Censorship, 718; Enlightenment
and, 592
Census: in Israel, 65; in China,
165, 336, 337; identity and,
671; state power and,
670–672
Central America. *See also specific
country*; disease in, 463;
regional disputes in, 649, 651;
United Provinces of, 644(*map*);
American intervention in
(1901–1914), 698–699
Central Asia (Central Asians). *See
also specific country and
people*; pastoralism in, 16–17;

horses from, 55; nomadism in,
186, 189, 193, 304; Rome
and, 146(*map*); Silk Road
and, 189, 228, 230–233;
China and, 300, 302(*illus.*);
chronology (747–1036), 271;
Nestorial Christianity in,
249–250; Turkic peoples of,
257; bubonic plague in, 327;
Chagatai khanate in, 324,
326(*map*), 329; chronology
(1219–1453), 349; Il-khanate
empire in, 326(*map*),
328–332; Yuan China and,
336, 337; Uzbeks of, 529,
626; Qing China and, 615;
Russia and, 727–728
Central Intelligence Agency (CIA):
coup in Guatemala (1954),
833, 834; Cuban invasion
(1961), 834; Iran and, 847
Centralization. *See also* Monarchy;
in Yuan China, 337; in East
Asia (1200–1500), 343–348;
in Delhi Sultanate, 384; in
Europe, 452, 593; in Spain,
453
Central Statistical Bureau (China),
814
Centro Internacional de
Mejoramiento de Maiz y
Trigo, 820
Ceramics. *See also* Porcelain;
Pottery; Olmec, 203;
Hohokam, 211; Andean, 217,
220; Chinese, 343
Cernunnos (god), 102(*illus.*), 103
Cetshwayo (Zulu), 678
Ceuta (Morocco), Portuguese in,
371, 409
Ceylon. *See* Sri Lanka (Ceylon)
Chaco Canyon, 212
Chagatai Khanate, 324–325,
326(*map*), 329
Chaldaean dynasty (Neo-
Babylonian Kingdom), 67, 69,
75, 76, 77, 114
Chamberlain, Neville, 795
Chambers, William, 542(*illus.*)
Chamorro, Violeta, 846
Champa, 318, 340(*map*), Mongols
and, 347
Champagne fairs, 357
Champa rice, 318, 347
Champlain, Samuel de, 480
Chan Chan, 220, 221
Chandra Gupta (India), 187
Chandragupta Maurya (India),
184
Chang'an, 165, 167, 171; Silk
Road trade and, 228; as Sui
and Tang capital, 299, 306

Charcoal: deforestation and, 449, 468; for ironworking, 283, 354, 449

Chariots: in Sahara, 236

Chariot warfare, 35, 57, 60, 66, 174, 185, 232; Egyptian, 50, 52, 55 and illus.; in early China, 81

Charitable trusts, in Ottoman Empire, 621–622

Charles I (Spain) (Charles V, Holy Roman Emperor), 438, 452, 459, 460

Charlemagne, 272, 282; revival under, 276, 285, 363

Charles I (England), 453

Charles II (England), 455, 480, 485

Charles III (Spain), 591

Charles Martel, 276

Charleston, colonial era, 478

Charles V (Holy Roman Emperor) (Charles I of Spain), 438, 452, 459, 460

Charles VII (France), 370

Charles X (France), 611

Chartered trading companies, 447, 489; Atlantic system and, 501, 502, 504

Charter Oath (Japan), 722–723

Chartists (Great Britain), 612

Chaucer, Geoffrey, 354, 359, 365

Chávez, Hugo, 847

Chavín, 199, 215; trade of, 202

Chavín de Huantar, 202, 203, 212, 214

Chechnya (Chechens), 626, 885

Cheka (Russian secret police), 740

Chemical industry (chemistry), 443; Egyptian, 43–44; bleach and dye, 706–707; explosives and, 707; pollution from, 707; plastics, 766–767 and illus.; World War II, 805

Cheras, 187

Chesapeake Bay region, 476, 870

Chess (game), 264(illus.)

Chiang Kaishek (Jiang Jieshi), 748, 797. See also Guomindang (China); civil war (1945–1949) and, 804; Communists and, 748, 796

Chicago, 574, 658, 659, 667, 712, 717; skyscrapers in, 765

Chichen Itza, 209(map), 210

Chickens, 80, 107, 192, 407, 576

Chieftains (chiefdoms): Northern Amerindian, 212, 213–214, 449; Arab, 248, 250; Germanic, 280; Japanese, 316; Liao, 306; Aztec, 395; Inka, 397; Polynesian, 405;

Ottoman Empire, 524–525; Cossack, 532

Child labor: in Britain, 563; on sugar plantations, 496, 498, 500; in textile mills, 580, 581 (illus.); restrictions on, 585

Children, 10, 70, 102, 166. See also Education; Family; Schools; sacrifice of (infanticide), 74 and (illus.), 133; Ottoman education and, 519; in slave trade, 508; working mothers and, 580, 661, 715; abandonment of, in France, 600; Victorian Age, 713; infant mortality, 712, 765; or career, for educated women, 862; Rio de Janiero homeless, 867

Chile: independence of, 643, 644 (map); indigenous peoples of, 655; women's rights in, 662; copper mining in, 663, 667, 668, 789, 832, 845; wars with Bolivia and Peru, 653; socialism and military rule in, 846

Chimú Empire (Chimor), 220, 221

China, early: rice in, 16, 80, 82 (map); agriculture, 80, 83; ancestor worship, 80–81; Yellow River Valley in, 23, 24 (map), 79; bronze in, 80, 81, 87(illus.); Confucianism in, 85–87, 91; Daoism in, 85, 86, 87; divination in, 84; geography and resources, 79–80; Legalism in, 88, 89, 91; monarchy, 81, 83–84; Shang period, 80–83, 82 (map); Warring States period, 88, 91, 98; warrior elite, 81; women and men in, 87, 91; Zhou period, 82(map), 83–85

China, imperial. See also Han Empire; Qing Empire; Song Empire; Tang Empire; and individual emperors; expansion of, 163(map), 165, 171; agriculture in, 163, 171, 310–311, 341; origins of, 160–170; slavery in, 393; Qin, 91, 160–162, 163(map), 314; society in, 167, 308–314; aristocracy in, 161, 162, 170, 299, 310; Rome compared to, 143, 150–152, 169, 171–173; cities, 165, 167, 171, 311, 312, 337–338; nomadic peoples and, 161, 163(map); military of, 161, 165, 168, 170, 298, 312; population of,

165, 312, 351; family in, 86, 165–166, 172, 303, 311; chronology (480 B.C.E.–220 C.E.), 173; Funan and, 193; India and, 193; taxation in, 162, 303, 336, 337, 338; trade in, 299, 312, 313, 338, 386; Buddhist pilgrims from, 180(illus.), 188, 243; women, 300, 302–303, 313–314; chronology (220–1279), 319; rebellions in, 162, 170, 302, 303; Sui Empire, 297, 298; gentry in, 303, 311, 313; Yuan Empire, 325, 335–338, 344, 347; emperors, 164 and illus., 170, 172, 298, 310; chronology (1517–1796), 558; European traders in, 540, 544, 554–555, 586; iron production in, 572; philosopher-kings of, 543, 528; Portuguese trade in, 422–423, 541; rebellions in, 540, 557, 629; agriculture in, 552; famine in, 556; population of, 431 and fig., 556, 629, 745, 859; flooding in, 556, 635; France and, 633, 635; Heavenly Kingdom of Great Peace, 632, 633; Jesuits in, 450, 543–544, 554, 628; Taiping Rebellion in, 631–635; self-strengthening movement in, 728–729; treaty ports in, 631, 728; Boxer Uprising (1900), 728(illus.), 729, 747; Guomindang in (See China, Nationalist)

China, Japan and, 301(map), 306, 337, 721, 744; trade between, 545; war between (1592–1598), 540, 545–546; war between (1894–1895), 694, 729; Boxer Uprising (1900), 729, 747; Twenty-One Demands (1915), 748; Manchuria and, 795–796; war between (1937–1945), 797–798

China, Nationalist (Guomindang). See also Taiwan; Chinese warlords and, 748; collapse, 803–804 and illus.; communists and, 796–797; Japan and, 795; United Nations and, 818, 837

China, People's Republic of (PRC). See also Communist Party (China); famine in (1958–1961), 813–814; Great Leap Forward in, 813, 837;

Mao Zedong and, 804, 837–838; nonaligned countries and, 835, 836; Korean War and, 822; Vietnam and, 824, 825; United Nations and, 837; Cultural Revolution in, 837; Taiwan and, 852; economic boom in, 844, 864; reform in, 852–854; birthrate in, 863; English as second language in, 893; family planning in, 860 (illus.); industrial robots in, 869; in Shanghai Cooperative Organization, 876

Chinampas (floating gardens), 204, 218, 222, 396

Chinese immigrants: in Southeast Asia, 552, 828; to Americas, 659; bubonic plague and, 633; in Caribbean, 659, 660, 668, 701, 710, 712; in Hawaii, 694, 712; World War I and, 737; United States' ban on, 633, 659

Chinese language, 81, 298, 300, 338, 543

Chinggis Khan, 324(fig.), 348; conquests of, 322, 323, 326(map)

Chocolate, 446, 464, 484, 504, 555, 699

Choctaw peoples, 462, 482, 654

Choe dynasty (Korea), 344

Cholas, 187, 196

Cholera, 702, 707; in India, 578, 691

Cholula, 208, 211, 221, 222

Choshu (Japan), 722

Choson kingdom (Korea), 344–346, 550–551

Christianity (Christians). See also Christian Orthodoxy; Missionaries, Christian; Protestantism; and specific sects; Israel and, 63; rise of, 155–157, 173; Jesus Christ and, 155; spread of, 227, 244–245; Zoroastrianism and, 117, 249; Constantine and, 159; conversion to, 159; Egyptian, 256; Ethiopian, 244–245, 380, 388, 417, 683; Islam and, 250, 252, 268, 277(map); Nestorian, 232, 250; pilgrims, 285, 292; protection for Jews, 360–362; scholasticism and, 364; in Africa, 409, 416, 418–420, 511, 780; challenges to, 436; witch-hunts and, 439–441; Amerindians and, 465, 468;

slave owners and, 499; Armenian, 527; Japanese persecution of, 544, 721–722; in Ottoman Empire, 519, 618

Christian militancy, 293, 409. See also Conquistadors; Crusades

Christian missionaries. See Missionaries, Christian

Christian monasteries and convents, 278, 285–287

Christian Orthodoxy. See also Russian Orthodox Church; in Balkans, 617, 857; Byzantine churches, 275, 288, 289; missionaries, 275, 289; schism with Latin Church, 273–274

Christian patriarchs. See Patriarchs

Christian (Western) Church, 282–287. See also Papacy; monasticism, 285–287; politics and, 282–285; schism in, 368

Chunkey (Amerindian game), 214

Churches (cathedrals): Byzantine, 275, 288, 289; Gothic, 359, 363; St. Peter's Basilica, 367, 436

Churchill, Winston; iron curtain speech of, 817, 840; in World War II, 800, 803

Church of England. See Anglicanism

Cimmerians, 97

Cinchona (quinine), 543, 699, 700

Circassians, 262

Cities and towns (urban centers). See also City-states; Urbanization; and specific cities and towns; Neolithic, 20–21; Egyptian, 40, 42–43; Indus Valley, 45–46; Israelite, 66; Nubian, 92, 95; Carthage, 69–71; Chinese, 84, 167, 171; Hellenistic Age, 136; Roman Empire, 153–155, 171; Andean, 202, 222; India, 185, 186; Mesoamerican, 198, 208, 210; Northern Amerindian, 213–214; Olmec, 200–201; Silk Road, 230, 232; Indian Ocean trade and, 233, 421; Islamic caliphate, 259, 260, 263–264; Kievan Russia, 288, 289; revival of, in medieval Europe, 289, 291–292; Mongol siege of, 327; Chinese, 311, 312, 337, 551; late medieval Europe, 356–358, 368; Aztec, 395; Andean, 397, 426; Dutch, 435; social mobility in, 445; poverty in, 449; colonial

American, 476, 479; European bourgeoisie in, 445–447; Ottoman Empire, 527–528 and illus., 623–624; industrialization in, 576, 578; Chinese treaty ports, 631, 728; Taiping rebellion and, 631–632; electricity in, 707–709 and (illus.); street cars and subways in, 708, 712; rickshaws in, 746(illus.), 757, 758; skyscrapers in, 765; automobile suburbs, 765; bombing of, in World War II, 803(illus.), 805; African, 779; migration from rural areas to, 564, 585, 623, 738, 779, 821; global growth of, 865(table)

Citizenship (citizens): Greek, 127, 128; Alexandria, 137; Roman, 144, 148–149, 155, 156; cultural diversity and, 659–660; nationality and, 670; denied to German Jews, 793, 807; denied to South African blacks, 831

City-states: definition of, 26; Mesopotamian, 26; Phoenician, 49, 67, 68, 69, 76; Greek polis, 121–125 (See also Athens; Sparta); Maya, 198, 205; North African, 259; East African ports, 387; Italian, 409; Hausa, 380(map), 382, 510, 511, 679; Singapore as, 828

Civil Code of 1804 (France), 607

Civilization(s): definition of, 20; river valley, 1, 23, 24(map), 25, 47; indicators of, 23; Minoan Crete, 49, 56; Mycenean Greece, 56–58

Civil rights, 826. See also Rights; denied to German Jews, 793

Civil service, 591. See also Bureaucracy; Examinations, for civil servants; Roman, 152, 171; Chinese, 171, 310; Ottoman reforms, 620; Indian (ICS), 690, 691, 769; colonial Africa, 831

Civil wars. See also specific civil wars; in China, 88, 91, 98–99, 170; in Roman Republic and Empire, 149, 153; in Islam, 253; in Inka Empire, 398, 426; in England (1642–1649), 453–454; Choctaw, 462; in China (Taiping), 631–635; in Japan, 317, 347, 545, 722; in United States (1861–1865), 651, 657; in Mexico

(1911–1917), 696–698; in Russia (1921–1922), 743–744; in China (1945–1949), 803–804; in Congo, 831, 881

Cixi, Empress Dowager (China), 634(*illus.*), 635–636, 728–729; Boxer Rebellion and, 728, 729 *and illus.*, 747

Clans. *See also* Kinship systems; Chinese, 87; Japanese, 317; Andean ayllu, 216, 217–218; Aztec calpolli, 394, 395

Classes. *See* Social classes; *and specific classes*

Classic of the Way of Virtue, 86

Claudius (Rome), 146(*map*)

Clawson, Angela, 808

Clean Air Act (United States), 840, 841, 870

Clemenceau, Georges, 741, 743

Cleopatra (Egypt), 136

Clergy. *See* Priests (clergy)

Clermont, Council of (1095), 293

Climate and weather (climate change). *See also* Drought; Monsoons; Rainfall; early humans and, 4; Agricultural Revolution and, 17–18, 22; Saharan, 38; East Asia, 79–80; Southeast Asia, 192; in Iran and Iraq, 260, 261, 291; medieval Europe, 289, 351; tropical environments, 311; Korean meteorology, 343, 345; Vikings and, 407; population and, 430–431 *and fig.*; Little Ice Age, 448, 523, 533, 552, 559–560; global warming, 888–889 *and illus.*

Clive, Robert, 687

Clocks: in China, 311(*illus.*)

Clothing (costume). *See also* Textile industry and trade; Iceman, 12, 13(*illus.*); Celtic warrior, 101; Roman toga, 155; Mesoamerican, 207 *and illus.*; Mongol nobles, 327; urban Islamic, 527, 528 *and illus.*, 848 *and illus.*; Turkish *fez*, 620, 752; Zulu, 677(*illus.*); Japanese westernization, 724; Gandhi and, 771, 772 *and illus.*; cultural diversity in, 895

Clove plantations, 686

Cluny, Benedictine abbey of, 286

CNN (Cable News Network), 891

Cnossus, palace complex at, 56

Coal and coal mining, 335, 795; in Britain, 566; child labor and, 580; in China, 308; coke-iron and, 571–572; in Europe, 577(*map*), 578; in India, 586; pollution from, 576, 707, 713; steam engines and, 572–574 *and illus.*, 707

Coca, 202, 216

Coca-Cola corporation, 853, 869

Cochin, 423

Cocoa (cacao), 201, 218, 222, 396, 493, 513, 565, 567, 682, 775, 779, 831. *See also* Chocolate; in Africa, 700, 779, 831

Coeur, Jacques, 371

Coffee, 493, 504, 521, 555, 831; in Brazil, 485, 581, 666, 668, 699, 775; in Ceylon, 688; in Java, 538; in Kenya, 830; in Yemen, 524; in Colombia, 831

Coins (coinage). *See also* Currency; invention of, 124; devalued Roman, 158; Indian, 185, 186, 187; copper, 243, 337, 552; gold, 124, 255, 256, 259, 291, 411, 458; silver, 124, 255, 291; spread of idea of, 243; Muslim, 247, 248, 249, 263, 291; imperial China, 161, 243, 337, 552; Kievan Russia, 287; Delhi Sultanate, 384; Ottoman, 458

Coke-iron, 572

Colbert, Jean Baptiste, 449, 460, 502

Cold War (Bipolar world; 1946–1991), 815, 816–842. *See also* Superpowers, Cold War; Africa and, 831; capitalism and communism in, 818–822; China in, 823, 837–838; confrontation, 823(*map*); Cuba, 816, 826, 832–834; decolonization (1947–1990), 827–834; in Europe and Korea, 822, 825; Japan and, 836–837; Middle East, 838–839; new nations in South Asia, 827, 828; race for nuclear supremacy, 826–827; Third World and, 835–836 *and illus.*; United Nations and, 817–818; Vietnam and, 825–826; Latin America and, 832–834, 844–847; collapse of Soviet bloc, 844, 855–857, 858(*map*); Soviet Union crisis, 854–855; end of (1989–1991), 846, 854–858

Coleridge, Samuel Taylor, 336

Collectivization: of Soviet agriculture, 768, 785–786, 814; of Chinese agriculture, 837

Colleges and universities: in Athens, 138; in Han China, 164–165; in India, 189; Islamic madrasas, 268, 364; European Renaissance and, 363–365; in colonial Americas, 466, 468; in Istanbul, 620; in Russia, 628; engineering, 707; in India, 691; for women, 714; in Japan, 724; in Middle East, 753; purged, in Iran, 848; English language in, 894; global elite culture and, 894

Cologne, bombing of (1942), 806

Colombia, 832; Gran Colombia and, 644(*map*), 649; independence of, 643, 649; Panama Canal and, 699; German airline in, 764

Colonies (colonialism). *See also* British Empire; Decolonialization; Expansion; French colonies; Imperialism; Portuguese colonies; *and specific colonies and colonial powers*; Phoenician, 69, 70–71, 72(*map*), 75; Greek, 97, 123, 136; Indonesian, in Madagascar, 234; Andean, 216; Black Sea area, 97, 123, 356; Roman, in North Africa, 238; Pacific Islands, 405, 406(*map*); Enlightenment and, 592; extraterritoriality and, 631; European, in Africa, 688–692; Japanese, 723(*map*); mandate system as, 752

Colorado, native peoples of, 212, 213(*illus.*)

Columbian exchange, 463–465; animals in, 424, 464–465

Columbus, Christopher, 321, 372, 403, 412–415, 414(*map*); in Caribbean region, 413, 424

Comanche people, 465, 654

Commerce. *See* Business; Trade (commerce)

Committee of Public Safety (France), 604

Common Market, 819. *See also* European Economic Community

Common Sense (Paine), 597

Commonwealth of Independent States, 856

Communes, in medieval Europe, 291

Communication(s). *See also* Language(s); Telegraph;

Writing; in ancient Egypt, 40; in Assyrian Empire, 61; exchange networks and, 228; and trade, in Asia, 231(*map*); Chinese canal and, 298; Enlightenment and, 598; telephone, 714, 868, 890; in fascist Italy, 792; radio, 760–761, 776, 781, 792, 890; computers and, 868, 869, 891

Communism (communist countries), 716; appeasement of Nazi Germany and, 795; in eastern Europe, 822; in Vietnam, 824, 825; Indonesian, 828; rivalry with capitalism,818–822; Cuban, 834, 844–845; collapse of, 855–857, 858(*map*)

Communist Manifesto (Marx and Engels), 584

Communist Party (China), 748. *See also* China, People's Republic of; Mao Zedong; Guomindang and, 748; Long March (1934–1935) and, 796–797; peasants and, 796, 798; civil war (1945–1949) and victory of, 803–804; Red Guards and, 837; famine and, 813; Tiananmen protests and, 853

Communist Party (Soviet Union), 745, 786–787. *See also* Soviet Union; Russian civil war and (1918), 743; famine and, 743; New Economic Policy in, 744; Stalin's industrialization and, 785; Gorbachev's reforms and, 854; fall of (1990), 855, 858(*map*)

Companies. *See* Business (companies)

Compass, 308, 385, 411

Computers, 868, 869, 891

Comte, Auguste, 583

Concentration camps, World War II, 695, 793, 806(*illus.*), 807

Concordat of 1801 (France), 607

Concordat of Worms (1122), 284, 285

Concrete, invention of, 157

Concubines, 87, 164, 265, 392, 393, 510. *See also* Prostitution

Condorcanqui, José Gabriel, 484–485

Confederacy of Corinth, 135

Confederate States of America (Confederacy), 651

Confederation of 1867 (Canada), 647, 665

Conference on Security and Cooperation in Europe (CSCE), 827

Conflict of the Orders (Rome), 145

Confucianism, 85–87, 91, 297, 543; Buddhism and, 168–169, 300, 302–303, 319; Daoism and, 85, 86, 87; family and, 172; in Japan, 315, 317, 548; in Korea, 550–551; scholar-officials and, 87, 161, 165, 168; Legalism and, 85, 86, 160–161; in East Asia, 314, 318; in Qing China, 543, 555(*illus.*), 557, 631, 635, 747; Song China revival (Neo-Confucianism), 310, 313; in Yuan China, 336, 344–345; examination system and, 341

Confucius (Kongzi), 84; Analects of, 85, 86–87

Congo, 816, 857. *See also* Kongo; civil war in, 831

Congo Free State (Belgian Congo), 679, 680–682

Congo River, 416, 679

Congress of People's Deputies (Soviet Union), 856

Congress of Vienna (1814–1815), 611

Congress Party (India), 881. *See also* Indian National Congress

Congress (United States): Chinese Exclusion Act and, 659; Contra War (Nicaragua) and, 849; League of Nations and, 743; genocide convention and, 886–887

Conquistadors, in Americas, 424–427, 470

Conscription (military draft): in China, 85, 168, 170, 797; in Ottoman Empire, 618; in Japan, 723, 724; of Africans, in World War I, 738; in Nazi Germany, 794

Conservatism: in Europe (1815–1820), 611, 613; nationalism and, 718, 724; Christian, in United States, 884

Constantine (Byzantium), 160

Constantinople, 244, 260, 295. *See also* Istanbul; founding of, 160; Crusade against, 292, 293, 356; Hagia Sophia in, 275; patriarch of, 274, 282, 288; pilgrims in, 275; Russia and, 287–288, 332; Ottoman conquest of, 335, 350, 516; modern Turkey and, 749, 749; population of, 758

Constitutionalists (Mexico), 697, 698

Constitutional monarchy: in Brazil, 645–646; in France, 602, 611; in Italy, 719

Constitutions: British, 453–454; Haitian, 589; France, 603; Ottoman Empire, 624; Mexican, 645, 653, 698, 774, 832; Spanish, 641; Russian, 727; Brazilian, 776; Kenyan, 830–831; Iraqi, 883

Constitution (United States), 599, 649–650, 886; abolition of slavery and, 657; Amendments to, 657, 762; census in, 671

Construction materials and techniques. *See also* Architecture; Engineering; Housing; Neolithic, 15(*illus.*); Mesopotamia, 35; Egyptian pyramids, 39, 40(*illus.*); Indus Valley, 46; Andean, 203; Japanese, 316

Consultative Group on International Agricultural Research, 820

Continental Congress, 593, 597, 598, 599

Contraception. *See* Birth control

Contracts of indenture, 702. *See also* Indentured labor

Contra War (Nicaragua), 846, 849

Cook, James, 692

Cooke, William, 575

Cooking, invention of, 10

Copernicus, Nicholas, 331, 442

Copper, 21, 46; for bronze, 55, 58; Indian, 190–191(*illus.*); Andean, 217; Chinese coins, 243, 337, 552; African, 241, 258, 378, 379 *and illus.*, 388, 393; Hungarian, 354, 359; Chilean, 667, 668, 789, 832, 845

Coptic language, 256

Coral Sea, Battle of (1942), 801(*map*), 802

Le Corbusier (Charles-Edouard Jeanneret), 766

Córdoba, Argentina, 472

Córdova, Spain, 371

Corinth, Confederacy of, 135

Corn. *See* Maize (corn)

Corn Laws (Britain, 1815), 612

Cornwallis, Charles, 598

Corporations. *See also* Business (companies); in Yuan China, 337; Japanese *zaibatsu*, 724, 747, 849; transnational, 663, 869

Corpus Juris Civilis (Body of Civil Law), 275, 285

Corruption: in Catholic Church, 436–437; in Ottoman Empire, 624; in Russia, 739; in China,

557, 635, 798; in South
Vietnam, 825; in Congo, 831;
in Cuba, 833; in Mexico, 832;
in Iran, 847; in Afghanistan,
883–884
Cort, Henry, 572
Cortés, Hernán, 396–397,
424–427, 475, 480
Cosmic order (cosmology). *See
also* Creation myths; Hindu
(Indian), 186, 191; Maya,
206; sub-Saharan Africa, 239;
Chinese, 310; Amerindian,
468
Cosmopolitanism: in Middle East,
50–55, 76; in Hellenistic Age,
136; in Indian Ocean ports,
235; in Tang China, 300; in
Yuan China, 336; in Malacca,
390, 422; in Ottoman Empire,
519; in Istanbul, 528, 620
Cossacks (Russia), 515, 532, 533
Cotton clothing, 582; for
plantation slaves, 565.
Cotton (cotton industry), 699. *See
also* Textile industry and
trade; Anasazi, 211; Andean,
216; Indian, 189, 388, 389,
446; Islamic Iran, 264;
Chinese, 338, 341; Aztec,
396; Hausa, 382; Korean,
345; Italian, 358; Caribbean,
424; Brazilian, 502; British,
580; Egyptian, 586, 624, 683;
Indian, 530, 536, 586, 688,
690; in United States, 571,
578, 580–581, 666;
mechanization of, 565,
570–571, 586
Cotton gin, 345, 571
Coubertin, Pierre de, 765
Council of Clermont (1095), 293
Council of Trent (1545–1563), 438
Councils: in Greek city-states, 124,
128, 137; in Roman towns,
154; of bishops, 282, 283;
Mongol, 323
Counter-Reformation, 438, 440,
441, 452, 453; in Spain, 438,
453
Coureurs de bois, 480–481 *and
illus.*
Craftspeople. *See* Artisans; *specific
crafts*
Creation myths, 2; Babylonian, 31,
32–34; Egyptian, 37; Indian,
178, 191
Credit (loans). *See also* Foreign
debt; in China, 312; in late
medieval Europe, 359; in
Japan, 547–548; in Mexico,
697; triangular flow of, 745

Creoles, in Latin America, 470,
471, 642
Crete, 517, 520–521, 733; Minoan
civilization in, 49, 56–58;
Venetian colony in, 356, 357
Crimea: khanate of, 332; plague
in, 327; Tatars in, 531
Crimean War (1853–1856),
622–624, 626, 734;
modernization of warfare in,
623, 625
Croatia, 857, 858(*map*)
Crompton, Samuel, 570
Cromwell, Oliver, 454
Crossbows, Chinese, 169, 298,
368, 403
Crouching Tiger, Hidden Dragon
(film), 892
Crowther, Samuel Adjai, 686
Crusades (crusaders), 292–295;
Byzantine Empire and, 273;
First, 261; Muslims and, 261,
262, 350; roots of, 292–293;
Second, 294; impact of,
293–295; Third, 294; Fourth,
293, 356; Mongols and,
328–329, 334–335;
Portuguese, 371, 411
Cruzado (coin), 412
Crystal Palace Exhibition
(London), 572
Cuba, 424, 832–834; slave trade
in, 504, 684; abolition of
slavery in, 658, 701; Chinese
immigrants in, 659; revolt
against Spain, 695; sugar
production in, 491, 664–665
and illus., 666, 668, 701, 832;
CIA-sponsored invasion of
(1961), 834; Congo and, 831;
missile crisis in (1962), 816,
826, 834; United States and,
699, 832, 833–834, 844–845
Cuban Revolution (1959), 816,
833–834, 844–845. *See also*
Castro, Fidel
Cubism, in art, 763
Culhuacán, 210
Cults. *See also* Ancestor cults;
Fertility cults; Gods and
goddesses; Shrines; at Çatal
Hüyük, 20; Greek, 124;
Christianity, 157; Egyptian,
42, 241; Roman emperor,
153; of domesticity, 582; of
the modern, 763, 764, 782
Cultural communities, growth of,
227
Cultural diversity. *See* Diversity
Cultural imperialism, 890
Cultural relativism, 763
Cultural Revolution (China), 837

Culture(s). *See also* Art and artists;
Folk culture; Global culture;
Literature; Oral culture;
Westernization; *and specific
cultures*; defined, 9; Ice Age,
8–14; Neolithic, 19; Assyrian,
62–63; Rome and China
compared, 171–172; Hindu-
Buddhist in Southeast Asia,
193; Saharan, 235–236, 238;
African unity, 239–240; great
and small traditions, 239, 245,
262; Byzantine, 275; Kievan
Russia, 289; late medieval
Europe, 353; Russian Empire,
627–628; American, 661;
Mexican, 696; global, 889–896;
media and message, 890–891;
pop, 891–892; English language
and, 893–894; enduring
diversity in, 894–895
Cuneiform writing, 28, 35, 52;
alphabetic systems and, 121
Curie, Marie, 765
Currency. *See also* Coins (coinage);
bars of metal used as, 379;
Chinese paper, 312, 337, 552;
Mongol paper, 329, 332;
exchanges, in Europe, 357;
French paper, 458, 603;
American paper, 596; British
pound sterling, 608, 690;
Ottoman reform, 608;
German inflation and, 724;
euro, 850, 851
Curzon, Lord George, 709, 770
Custer, George Armstrong, 655
Customs and traditions. *See also*
Folk cultures; small *vs.* great
traditions, 239, 245, 262;
Germanic, 276, 279
Cuzco (Inka capital), 397, 398;
Spanish conquest of, 426
Cylinder seals, 29(*illus.*)
Cyprus, 55, 69, 358, 517
Cyrene, 111
Cyrillic alphabet, 275, 288, 625
Cyril (missionary), 275
Cyrus (Persia), 67, 112(*map*), 114,
129
Czechoslovakia (Czechs),
742(*map*), 743; Nazi Germany
and, 794–795; Soviet Union
and, 822; fall of communism
in, 855, 858(*map*)

Dada movement, 763
Daedalus, 56
Da Gama, Christopher, 417
Da Gama, Vasco, 376, 412, 413,
414(*map*), 417; ships of,
404(*illus.*), 420–421 *and illus.*

Dagestan, 626

Dahomey, 507, 508

Daimyo (Japanese warlord), 544, 558, 720–721; Europeans and, 544–545; *seppuku* (suicide) and, 549

Dai Viet, 318, 325. *See also* Vietnam; Mongol attack on, 325

Dakar, Senegal, 781

Dalai Lama, 552

Damascus, 356, 525, 617; Arab Caliphate and, 255, 261, 263

Dams, 338, 377; Aswan (Egypt), 683, 836; hydroelectric, 768, 785, 837

D'Annunzio, Gabriele, 784

Dante Alighieri, 365–366 *and illus.*

Danube River, 15, 114, 157

Daoism, 85, 86, 87, 169, 310

Darby, Abraham, 572

Darby, Abraham, III, 572

Dardanelles Strait, 738, 822

Darius (Persia), 135

Darius I (Persia), 98, 129; expansion under, 112(*map*), 114; Persepolis and, 116, 118(*illus.*)

Dart, Raymond, 3

Darwin, Charles, 3, 725

Darwin, Erasmus, 570

Dasas, 177, 178

Davar, Cowasjee Nanabhoy, 586

David (Israel), 65

Da Vinci, Leonardo, 367

D-day (World War II, 1944), 802

Death penalty. *See also* Assassinations; for witchcraft, 439, 440(*illus.*); forced suicide (*seppuku*), 549; guillotine, 605 *and illus.*; death squads, in Latin America, 845, 846; in United States, 888

De Beers Consolidated, 678

Deborah the Judge, 66

Debt. *See also* Foreign debt (international loans); War debt; Japanese, 852; of Mexican peasants, 697; United States' housing crisis and, 877–878

Debt slavery: in Greece, 124, 128; in Mesopotamia, 29

Decameron (Boccaccio), 366

Deccan Plateau, 187, 191, 384, 389

Deccan region, famine in (1876–1878), 812

Decembrist revolt (Russia), 628

Declaration of Independence (1776, United States), 593, 597, 598, 641; universal rights in, 656

Declaration of the Rights of Man and of the Citizen (1789, France), 603, 641, 886

Decolonization (1947–1990), 827–834. *See also* Independence; of Africa, 828–832; chronology, 841–842; of Latin America, 827, 832–834; nation building and, 827–834; in South and Southeast Asia, 827–828; United Nations and, 818

Deforestation (forest clearing). *See also* Forest products; in China, 343; in Zimbabwe, 388; in Polynesia, 405; in Europe, 354, 449; in American mines, 468, 469; for sugar plantations, 490, 493, 665, 666; soil erosion and, 490, 493, 556, 578, 666; in China, 556; in United States, 666–667; in India, 690, 769; railroads and, 705–706; World War II and, 809; in Brazil, 776–777, 870

De Gaulle, Charles, 831

Deir el-Bahri, 53, 54(*illus.*)

Delhi: as capital of India, 529, 770; durbar pageants in, 689–690; projected growth of, 865(*table*)

Delhi Sultanate (India), 382–384, 389; chronology, 400; expansion of, 382; Gujarat and, 383, 384, 389; Hindu-Muslim relations in, 382–383, 384, 389; slavery in, 392; Timur and, 329, 331, 384; water control systems in, 377–378; women rulers of, 383

Delian League, 130

Delphi (Greece), oracle at, 83, 123, 125

Democracy (democratic reforms): Greek, 125, 128–129, 130, 131, 132; colonial North America, 477; in United States, 599; transition to, in eastern Europe, 844, 880; globalization and, 880–882

Democratic Republic of Congo. *See* Congo

Demographic transition, 463–464, 859–862

Demonstrations. *See* Protests; Strikes

Deng Xiaoping, 853

Denmark, 278. *See also* Scandinavia; science of, 442,

443(*illus.*); in European Community, 819; Nazi invasion of, 799

Deportation: in Assyrian Empire, 61, 62, 67, 75, 76; in Mauryan India, 185

Depression (1930s), 784, 809; economic crisis of, 788; in industrial nations, 788; in nonindustrial regions, 788–789; in Brazil and Argentina, 776–777, 789

Depression (1870s–1880s), 709

Descartes, René, 443, 444

Descent of Man, The (Darwin), 3

De Ulloa, Antonio, 472

Developing nations (Third World). *See also* Nonindustrial world; privileged classes in, 709; raw materials from, 709–710; Cold War and, 835–836 *and illus.*; garbage pickers in, 866(*illus.*), 867; population growth in, 700–701, 843, 859–860, 862–863, 867, 872; environmental degradation in, 870

Devi (goddess), 182, 183

Devshirme system, 372, 519, 525

De Witt Clinton (locomotive), 575(*illus.*)

Dhaka, Bangladesh, 865(*table*)

Dhows (ships), 385 *and illus.*, 386, 403, 420, 422

Diagne, Blaise, 781

Diamond mining, in South Africa, 677, 678

Dias, Bartolomeu, 412

Diaspora, Jewish, 67

Díaz, Porfirio, 640, 697

Dictatorship. *See also* Authoritarianism; Tyrants; Napoleon, 606–607; in Latin America, 648, 653, 789, 844, 845–846; of the proletariat, 716; Guomindang China, 748; Nazi Germany, 793; populist, in Argentina, 777(*illus.*), 778; in Indonesia, 828; in Iraq, 848–849; deposed, in Romania, 855

Diderot, Denis, 591

Dido, 49

Diem, Ngo Dinh, 825

Dienbienphu, Battle of (1954), 824

Diet. *See* Food (diet)

Diocletian (Rome), 158–159

Diplomacy. *See also* Politics; Mongol, 323, 335; European warfare and, 455–456; China trade and, 554–556

Directory (France), 606, 610

Dirty War against Terrorism (Argentina), 845

Discrimination. *See* Racism (racial discrimination)

Disease. *See also* Bubonic plague; Epidemics; in Neolithic Age, 18; plague of Justinian, 274; and diet, in Yuan China, 327; Amerindians and, 424, 426, 433; African slaves and, 497, 498, 506; influenza, 327, 463, 741, 762; typhus (typhoid), 327, 463, 707; in Kongo, 419; malaria, 378, 463, 498, 543, 700, 779; smallpox, 327, 424, 426, 463, 486, 488, 506, 543, 779; yaws, 498; diphtheria, 463; dysentery, 488, 498, 506, 812;
inoculation against, 543; plague, 463, 633; rickets, 578; yellow fever, 463, 610; cholera, 578, 691, 702, 707; in Australia and New Zealand, 693; syphilis and gonorrhea, 779; in colonial Africa, 779; tuberculosis, 779; famine and, 812; HIV/AIDS, 861–862

Di (sky-god), 81, 83

Disraeli, Benjamin, 581

Diu, Portuguese fort at, 423

Diversity (cultural diversity). *See also* Cosmopolitanism; in India, 176(*map*), 196; in Mesoamerica, 211; in Indian Ocean maritime system, 235; in African traditions, 239

Divination, 84; Chinese oracle bones and, 80–81

Divine Comedy (Dante), 365, 366 *and illus.*

Divine kingship: Egyptian pharaohs, 38, 40–41, 43, 47; Chinese Mandate of Heaven, 172; Japanese emperor, 316

Divine Society (Brahmo Samaj), 691

Division of labor, 567, 568–569

Divorce. *See also* Marriage; in Egypt, 42; in Israel, 66; in Islam, 265; in China, 313

DNA evidence, evolution and, 4, 6

Dnieper River, 288

Doctors. *See* Medicine (physicians)

Doctors without Borders, 886

Dogs, domestication of, 16(*illus.*), 22, 106–107

Dome of the Rock (Jerusalem), 838

Domestication. *See also specific animals; food crops*; adrenaline and, 107; of

animals, 16–17, 22, 25, 42, 95, 106–108; of camels, 55, 107, 238; of cattle, 16–17, 96, 107, 235; of horses, 55, 96, 107; of llamas, 17, 216; of pigs, 107, 242, 243; of plants, 15, 16–17, 22, 25, 106, 199

Domesticity, cult of, 582

Domestic servants, women as, 451, 580, 713, 714, 747

Dominican Republic, 699, 765, 891

Dominicans, 364, 466, 467(*illus.*), 542–543

Donkeys, 16, 25, 35, 41, 64, 78, 92, 107, 352, 376

Dos Pilas, 198

Douglass, Frederick, 657

Drama (theater): Greek, 131, 132; Gupta theater-state, 188; Srivijaya theater-state, 195; Japanese, 759–760

Dravidian language, 176 *and map*, 177, 391

Dresden, bombing of (1944), 806

Drew, Richard, 767

Driver, of slaves, 497

Drought: in Andean region, 215, 217, 220; in Chaco Canyon, 212; in Africa, 537; famine and, 812; global warming and, 888–889

Druids (Celtic priests), 101, 103, 226

Druzhina, 288, 289

Dubai, Palm Island in, 877(*illus.*)

Dubois, Eugene, 3

Du Bois, W. E. B., 741, 781, 830

Duke of Zhou, 84

Duma (Russian Parliament), 727

Dunhuang, cave monasteries at, 303, 307(*illus.*)

Dupleix, Joseph François, 531

Durbar pageants, in India, 689

Durkheim, Emile, 763

Dur Sharrukin fortress, 62

Dushan, Stephen, 335

Dutch, in South Africa. *See* Afrikaners

Dutch East India Company, 507, 535; Cape Colony, 510; in Japan, 548–549 *and illus.*; mercantilist capitalism and, 501–502; trade monopoly and, 447, 537

Dutch East Indies. *See also* Indonesia; air travel to, 764; Japanese occupation of, 802, 801(*map*); independence of, 828

Dutch Guiana (Surinam), 658, 827

Dutch Republic. *See* Netherlands (the Dutch, Holland)

Dutch studies, in Japan, 544–545, 722

Dutch West India Company, 447, 479; African slave trade and, 490, 502, 504

Dutch West Indies, 490; abolition of slavery in, 658; independence in, 827

Dyer, Reginald, 771

Dyes: Tyrian purple, 68, 71, 274; indigo for, 477, 707; synthetic, 706–707

Dysentery, 498, 506

Ea (god), 29(*illus.*), 33–34

Earth Day (1970), 840

Earth Mother, 19

Earthquake, 169; in Lisbon (1755), 440; in Caribbean region, 494–495; in Japan (1923), 746–747; and tsunami (2004), 880

East Africa: Great Rift Valley of, 9; Mesopotamian trade with, 234; Muslim travelers in, 374; Chinese voyages to, 340(*map*); Southeast Asians in, 402; Swahili Coast, 380(*map*), 386, 387–388, 404, 422, 536–537; Portuguese in, 417, 420, 422, 537; Muslims in, 536–537, 781; secondary empire in, 686; slave trade in, 537; World War I in, 737; World War II in, 800; decolonization of, 830

East Asia. *See also* Southeast Asia; *and specific countries*; climate zones of, 79–80; Sui and Tang China and, 297; Jin and Liao challenge in, 306–307, 309(*map*); new kingdoms in, 314–318; centralization and militarism in (1200–1500), 343–348; Chinese power in, 403; Europe and, 541–545; Imjin War in, 540, 545–546; porcelain of, 548–549 *and illus.*; events in (1931–1945), 795–798; Chinese Communists and Long March in, 796–797; Manchurian Incident (1931), 795–796; Sino-Japanese War (1937–1945), 797–798

Easter Island, 405, 406(*map*), 407

Eastern Europe. *See also specific countries*; migrations in, 287; Mongol conquest of, 334; new states in, 334–335; serfdom in, 351, 448; Ottoman threat to, 516; Jews from, 659–660; Nazi

Holocaust in, 807; Soviet control of, 818–819, 821–822, 822, 840; Warsaw Pact and, 822, 823(*map*); fall of communist governments in, 855, 858(*map*)

East Germany. *See also* Germany; Berlin Wall and, 822, 856 *and illus.*; reunification and, 855–857

East India Company, British (EIC), 535, 556; American tea boycott and, 596–597; India and, 555, 586

East India Company, Dutch. *See* Dutch East India Company

East India Company, French, 502

East Indies (maritime Southeast Asia). *See also* Indonesia; *specific islands*; Portuguese in, 401, 538; spice trade of, 402–403, 413, 422, 446, 541; Islam in, 536; Dutch, 541; Indian laborers in, 710

East Timor, 880

Ebu's-Su'ud, Mufti of Istanbul, 520–522

Ecological crisis, 10, 17–18. *See also* Environment; in Indus Valley, 47; in Zimbabwe, 388

Ecological zones: in Srivijaya, 195; in Andean region, 202, 398; in Mesoamerica, 199

Economic botany, 699

Economic crisis, 788. *See also* Depression; Inflation; Recession; in Safavid Iran, 528–529; imperial China, 552; French Revolution, 602, 603, 604, 607; in Japan, 849, 852

Economic growth. *See also* Global economy; Industrial Revolution; colonial Americas, 485–486; in China, 551–552, 843; in Japan, 547, 747; railroads and, 640; in United States, 663, 664; Philippines, 695; world market and, 662–663; in Asian tigers, 852, 864; in Africa, 779–780; in Europe, after World War II, 819

Economy (economic factors). *See also* Business; Industrialization; Inflation; Taxation; Trade; Egyptian, 40, 136; Mycenaean Greek, 57; Persian Empire, 115; Athenian, 131; Roman Empire, 158; Chinese, 170; barter, 28, 158, 274, 279;

Islamic caliphate, 259; Byzantine Empire, 272, 274; medieval Europe, 278–280, 289–290; Song China, 308–314, 319; Mongolian Empire, 329, 339; British government and, 459; colonial Americas, 468–470, 480; Atlantic trade, 479–480, 512 (*See also* Atlantic system); French government role in, 460; Ottoman, 524–525; Philippine colonial, 694; imperialism in Latin America and, 695–699; World War I, 737; Nazi Germany, 793; Soviet Union, 744; Algerian, 828–829; British, 726–727; Cold War and, 818; Cuban, 834; Soviet reforms, 855; age distribution and, 863–864

Ecuador, 472–474; trading boats from, 408; Gran Colombia and, 644(*map*), 649; independence of, 643, 649

Edessa, 261

Edict of Milan, 159

Edict of Nantes, 438

Edison, Thomas, 708

Edo. *See* Tokyo (Edo)

Education. *See also* Academies; Colleges and universities; Islamic scholars and schools; Literacy; Schools and scholars; in Han China, 168; European reform, 365; in Islam, 391; in Ottoman Empire, 620; in Egypt, 683; of women, 635, 662, 714; Western ideas and, 691; in Victorian Age, 714; in Japan, 723; nation building and, 724, 725; in Middle East, 753

Edward II (England), 370

Edward III (England), 370

Egypt. *See also* Egypt, ancient; Greek-style cities in, 135; Ptolemaic, 135–137 *and map*; camels in, 238; pork taboo in, 242; Fatimid Caliphate in, 259, 261; Islamic conquest of, 255, 273, 274; Mamluks in, 261, 328, 380, 525; monasticism in, 285; plague in, 327; Ottoman Empire and, 417, 422, 516, 586, 683; French invasion of, 585; Britain and, 586, 683, 753; industrialization in, 585–586; irrigation in, 683; modernization in, 682–684; under Muhammad Ali,

585–586, 616–617, 618, 622, 624, 682–683; under Nasir, 836, 838; foreign debt of, 683; railroads in, 683, 705; Aswan Dam and, 683, 836; Suez Canal in, 624, 683, 706, 753, 794, 836; cotton exports of, 586, 624, 683; World War II and, 799(*map*), 800; Algerian war and, 829; conflicts with Israel, 838–839 *and map*, 839; Arab Spring (2010) in, 881–882, 882(*illus.*)

Egypt, ancient, 36–44; "gift of the Nile," 36–38, 37(*map*); administration and communication, 39–41; agriculture, 41; irrigation, 37, 42; creation myth, 37; ships, 39(*illus.*); Old Kingdom, 37(*map*), 92; Middle Kingdom, 52, 92; pyramids, 39, 40(*illus.*), 44; hieroglyphics, 40; people of, 41–42; women in, 42, 48; megaliths in, 19; belief and knowledge, 42–44; divine kingship (pharaoh), 38–39, 43, 64, 78, 136; Mesopotamia compared, 40, 41, 43, 47–48; New Kingdom, 37(*map*), 52–54, 64, 94; trade, 40, 41, 54–55; Hyksos in, 52, 64, 76; Assyrian invasion of, 60, 75, 94; Israelites in, 64; Nubia and, 36, 41, 52, 55(*illus.*), 58, 92–95, 240; in Persian Empire, 114; treaty with Hittites, 54

Egyptian Book of the Dead, 43

Eiffel Tower, in Paris, 708(*illus.*)

Eightfold Path, in Buddhism, 180

Einstein, Albert, 762, 805

Eisenhower, Dwight D., 824, 826, 834

El Alamein, Battle of, 799(*map*), 800

Elam (Elamites), 26; Assyrians and, 50, 75; Persian and, 116

Elba, Napoleon on, 608

Eleanor of Aquitaine, 294

Electricity, 712–713; Franklin and, 592; home use of, 713, 759; hydroelectric dams, 707, 768, 785, 836, 837; in Paris, 708(*illus.*), 712; in Soviet Union, 785; streetcars and subways, 708, 712, 713; telegraph and, 708; lighting, 707–709, 708(*illus.*), 712, 759

Elephants, 10. *See also* Ivory trade

Elite class (ruling class). *See also* Aristocracy; Planter elite; Warrior elite; Egyptian, 42,

44; Mycenaean, 59; Assyrian, 62; Carthaginian, 69–70; Chinese, 81, 83, 84; Celtic, 100; Roman, 145, 149, 154; Mayan, 199, 207; Mesoamerican, 200, 201, 204, 204; Olmec, 201; Toltec, 210; Andean, 217, 218–219 and illus., 218–219, 230, 399; Cahokian, 214; great traditions and, 239; Byzantine, 274; Confucian, in China, 167–168, 302, 306; Turkic, in China, 298; Annam, 318; Chinese women, 312(illus.), 314; East Asian, 314; Delhi Sultanate, 384, 389; colonial Latin America, 466, 471, 475, 484, 641; colonial North America, 596; Chinese, 543, 551; in Korea (yangban), 551–552; Japanese, 547–550; developing world, 709; British India, 687; industrial, 716; Latin American, 584, 696, 775, 832; colonial Africa, 780; global culture and, 893–894

Elizabeth I (England), 456

Elmina (St. George of the Mine), 416, 490

El Salvador, 846

Emancipation Proclamation (1863), 657

Emmer wheat, 15, 21

Emperors. See Monarchy (kings, emperors)

Empires. See Colonies (colonialism); Expansion; Imperialism; and specific empires and emperors

Empire State Building (New York City), 766

Enclosure movement (England), 564

Encomienda labor, 468–469

Encyclopedias: in China, 341, 343; in France, 565, 591

Engels, Friedrich, 562, 584; Communist Manifesto, 584

Engineering. See also Construction materials and techniques; Mesopotamian, 35; Assyrian Empire, 61; Egyptian, 40(illus.), 44; Macedonian, 134; Roman, 157, 159(illus.); Chinese, 308, 311(illus.), 312; Il-khanate, 331(illus.); European cathedrals, 363; foreign, in Russia, 625; British, 566, 567, 683, 705;

railroads, 705–706; colleges and schools for, 707; foreign, in Japan, 724; in British India, 690, 770; Korean, 852

England. See also British Empire; Great Britain; megaliths in, 19; tin in, 73, 102; Celtic fort in, 101(illus.); Norman invasion of, 278, 281, 292: peasants of, 279; Viking raids on, 276, 278; Henry II and, 284–285; population growth, 290; monarchy in, 369, 370–371; peasants of, 353; war with France, 370, 370–371; wool trade in, 291, 353–354, 358, 370–371; watermills in, 354; revolt in, 353; Dutch rivalry with, 447, 448, 460, 591; monarchy in, 453–455, 454(table); civil war in, 454; Atlantic economy and, 501; iron industry in, 449; science in, 443; South Sea bubble in, 458, 458–459; emigration from, 476, 478, 489, 711; Midlands, 568, 576, 707, 712; population growth in, 563

English Church. See Anglicanism (Church of England)

English colonies. See British Empire (British colonies)

English language, 103; in Ireland, 718; immigrant to United States and, 724; in India, 769; as global second language, 893–894, 894

Enkidu, 23

Enlightenment (Buddhist nirvana), 181–182, 184; bodhisattvas and, 195, 244, 299, 303

Enlightenment (Europe), 444–445, 641, 716; old order and, 591–593; political philosophy in, 455, 591; reforms of, 591, 593–594; science and, 444–445, 591, 670; women and, 592

Entente (France, Great Britain, and Russia), 734

Entrepôts (ports), 332, 405, 422

Entrepreneurs. See also Business; industrialization and, 565–566, 582, 583–584; in British India, 586, 773

Environment (environmental stress). See also Climate and weather; Deforestation; Pollution; in Indus Valley civilization, 44, 177; Andean cultural response to, 215–216,

221; Mongol conquest and, 327–328; Columbian Exchange and, 464; mining and, 468, 667; soil erosion and, 666; industrialization and, 576–578, 668, 707, 776, 870; in Qing China, 556–557, 629; urbanization and, 666, 712; steel industry and, 707; world economy and, 699–702, 707; World War I and, 741; Soviet industrialization and, 785; World War II and, 809; population growth and, 844; Cold War era, 817, 840; industrial nations and, 870, 871; Kyoto treaty and, 871; laws to protect, 840, 870–871

Environmental Protection Agency (United States), 840

Environment and technology: Iceman, 12, 13 and illus.; textiles and dyes, 70 and illus.; astronomy, 138–140 and illus.; Indian mathematics, 190–191 and illus.; camel saddles, 237 and illus.; medieval iron production, 283 and illus.; gunpowder to guns, 342 and illus.; Indian Ocean dhow, 385 and illus.; da Gama's fleet, 404 and illus.; mapping the world, 450 and illus.; sugar plantations, 492–493, 494–495 and illus.; East Asian porcelain, 548–549 and illus.; guillotine, 605 and illus.; industrializing sugar in Cuba, 664–665 and illus.; railroads and immigration, 711 and illus.; industrialized world and, 765–768; new materials, 766–767 and illus.; Green Revolution, 820–821 and illus.; global warming, 888–889 and illus.

Ephesus, 293

Epic of Gilgamesh, 23

Epidemics. See also Bubonic plague; Amerindians and, 426, 428, 439, 462, 463–464, 465, 468; African slaves and, 506; in China, 552, 633; cholera, 578; influenza (1918–1919), 741, 762; plague, 463, 633; smallpox, 463, 779

Epona (goddess), 103

Equality. See Inequality

Equatorial Africa, 678–679; French, 779, 831

Equatorial forests. *See* Tropical rain forest
Equites, in Rome, 153
Erasmus of Rotterdam, 366–367
Eratosthenes, 139
Eretria, 129
Ericsson, Leif, 407
Estado Novo (New State, Brazil), 777
Estates General (France), 371, 455, 602, 608
Estonia, 727; independence of, 855
Ethiopia, 660(*map*); plant domestication in, 15; Aksum in, 95; alliance with Portugal, 417; Christianity in, 244–245, 380, 388, 417; expansion of, 388, 393; modernization in, 682–684; Italian defeat in (1895), 684; Italian invasion of (1935), 778, 781, 794; famine and drought in, 814
Ethnic cleansing, in Balkans, 857
Ethnic minorities. *See also* Racism; *specific minority*; census and, 671; in Ottoman Empire, 733
Ethnography, Greek, 119
Etruscans, 144
Eunuchs (castrates), 302, 393; in harems, 528, 634(*illus.*)
Euphrates River. *See* Tigris and Euphrates Valley
Eurasia: culture and science in, 329–332; Mongol domains in (1300), 326(*map*), 431; land-based empires of, 615, 638 (*See also* Russia; Qing Empire)
Eurasian steppes: China and, 98–100; pastoral nomads of, 95–100, 106(*illus.*); Scythians of, 70(*illus.*), 97–98 *and illus.*, 230
Euro (currency), 876
Europe (1500–1750), 435–461; Atlantic economy and, 500; bourgeoisie, 445–448; Columbian exchange and, 463–465; commercial expansion and risk, 456–460; culture and ideas in, 436–445; early Reformation in, 436–438; Enlightenment, 444–445; Indian Ocean colonies, 538; Mughal Empire and, 529–531; East Asia and, 543–545; Ottoman Empire and, 517, 525; peasants and laborers, 448–449; political innovations, 452–460; population growth in, 563–564; Scientific Revolution in, 441–444;

social and economic life, 445–451; state development in, 452–453; tradition and witch-hunts in, 439–441 *and illus.*; wars of religion in, 436, 438, 444, 452; women and family, 449–451; Russia and, 625–626
Europe, great powers of (1871–1900), 725–728; conservative countries, 725, 727–728; Germany, 726; liberal countries, 726–727; Russia, 726, 727–728
Europe, great powers of (1900–1913), 734
European Economic Community, 819
European expansion (1400–1550), 408–415, 427–428; motives for, 409; Portuguese voyages, 409–412, 414(*map*); Spanish voyages, 412–415 *and map*
European immigrants: in Americas, 659, 859; in North America, 668, 710, 711 *and illus.*; in Argentina, 668, 710, 775; in Australia and New Zealand, 710; in South Africa, 676, 678, 679, 831; World War I refugees, 740
European imperialism, 673. *See also* Imperialism; *specific empires*
European merchants and traders: Atlantic system and, 501, 512; in China, 540, 543, 554–555, 587, 629; in Istanbul, 527; in Japan, 544, 704; joint-stock companies and, 535; proto-industrialization and, 564
European Union (EU), 819, 876; English language in, 893, 894; inequality in, 865–866
Europe (Europeans). *See also* Eastern Europe; Industrial nations; Latin West; Medieval Europe; Roman Empire; western Europe; Neanderthals in, 3; spread of farming in, 15, 18; skin color in, 8; Indo-Europeans in, 19; Celtic peoples of, 100–103; encounters with (1450–1550), 415–427; *ancien régime* in, 589; Napoleonic, 609(*map*); industrialization (ca. 1850), 577(*map*); as advisors in Egypt, 585–586; conservativism in, 611, 613; Greek independence and, 611, 618; Ottoman reforms and,

617–622; nationality and census in, 671–672; voting rights in, 717; World War I in, 734–740; peace and dislocation in (1919–1929), 741–745; architectural innovation, 765–766; cult of the modern in, 763; radio in, 760; Depression (1930s) in, 788; World War II, 799–800 *and map*, 807–808; Bretton Woods Conference (1944), 818–819; demographic transition in, 859; population of (1750–2050), 861(*table*); wealth inequality in, 865–866; guest workers in, 867; industrial robots in, 869
"Everlasting Remorse" (Bo Zhuyi), 300
Evolution: human, 4–6, 6(*illus.*), 21; skin color and, 8
Examinations, for civil servants: in China, 165, 168, 308–310, 632, 745; in India, 690; in Korea, 315, 550–551; in Vietnam, 348
Exchange. *See also* Barter; Trade (commerce); precious metals as medium of, 62; coinage as medium of, 124 (*See also* Coins); in Gupta India, 188; Mesoamerican, 199; in Andean region, 216, 397, 399; networks of communication and, 228; in Kievan Russia, 287; Columbian, 463–465
Exclusif (France), 502
Expansion (expansionism). *See also* Colonies; European expansion; Imperialism; Maritime expansion; *and specific empires and emperors*; Egyptian, 52–53, 54, 94; Assyrian, 50, 59–60; Tyrian, 69; Persian Empire, 112(*map*), 113–114; Roman, 146(*map*), 148–149, 172; Chinese imperial, 163(*map*), 165; Christian, 157; imperial India, 184–192; Andean peoples, 220; Islamic, 255; Mongolian Empire, 321, 322, 323–328, 326(*map*), 356; Mali, 382; Delhi Sultanate, 382–384; Aztec, 395, 396; Ethiopian, 388, 393; Inka, 397; Ottoman Empire, 372, 409; Iberian, 371–372, 408; Spanish Empire, 423–427; Ottoman Empire, 409,

516–517, 518(*map*); Mughal India, 529–530; Qing China, 552–553, 553(*map*), 554, 557; Russian Empire, 457(*map*), 531–535 *and map*, 619(*map*), 624, 626; Napoleonic France, 609(*map*); United States, 649–651 *and map*; world economy, 699–701; railroads, 705–706; Japanese, 723(*map*)

Exploration (expeditions). *See also* Maritime Revolution; Portuguese maritime explorations; *specific explorers*; Phoenician, 72(*map*); Carthaginian, 73; Chinese (Zheng He), 321, 339–340 *and map*, 390, 403–404, 406(*map*); Viking, 407, 431; Malayo-Polynesian, 405, 406(*map*); Spanish maritime, 401, 411–412; in outer space, 827

Explosives, 342, 343, 346, 593. *See also* Bombs and bombing; Gunpowder; dynamite, 707

Extermination camps, 806(*illus.*), 807

Extinction, 10

Extraterritoriality, in China, 624, 631

Ezana (Aksum), 244

Factories. *See also* Manufacturing; child labor in, 580–581, 585; Chinese, 552; in colonial Mexico, 470(*illus.*); in Soviet Union, 785, 786; wages in, 582; women in, 580–581, 585, 714–715; working conditions in, 578–579; World War II, 807–808; robots in, 869

Factory Act of 1833 (Great Britain), 585

Fagan, Brian, 559

Faisal I (Iraq), 738, 742, 753

Faisal II (Iraq), 838

Family. *See also* Ancestor cult; Children; Clans; Marriage; early human, 10–11; Neolithic, 19; Mesopotamian, 26; Israelite, 66; Iranian, 114; Greek, 122; Roman, 145, 172; Chinese, 86, 165, 172, 303, 311; Mongol, 323; colonial American, 478, 480; Istanbul, 527 *and illus.*; Stalin on, 791; Turkish, 752; Victorian Age, 713; working class, 579, 580, 717; automobile suburbs and, 768; colonial African, 779

Family planning. *See also* Birth control; campaign in China, 860(*illus.*)

Famine (food shortage): on Thera, 111; in Europe (1315–1317), 353; in Caribbean, 424; in Europe, 449; in China, 552, 798, 813; in Finland (1695), 559; in French Revolution, 603; in Ireland (1847–1848), 582, 710, 812; in World War I, 737; in World War II death camps, 807; in Russia, 739, 743; in India, 769, 812; in Bengal (1943), 813; in Soviet Union (1933–1934), 786, 814; politics and, 813–814

Farabundo Martí National Liberation Front (El Salvador), 846

Faraday, Michael, 708

Farmers (farming). *See also* Agriculture; Peasants; Rural societies; Neolithic, 15, 18, 19; Mesopotamian, 25, 26, 29; Egyptian, 37; Indus Valley, 44; pastoralists (herders) and, 64, 161, 250; Greek, 119, 120(*map*), 124, 138; Roman, 144–148, 149, 154, 171, 290; Southeast Asian, 192; Mesoamerican, 199, 205; Chinese, 171, 337; Byzantine, 274–275; Kievan Russian, 287, 289; medieval European, 279, 290, 310, 351; three-field system, 351; Korean, 345; tropical, 377; Zimbabwe, 388; Polynesian, 407; colonial America, 479–480; Chinese, 552, 556, 629, 745, 798, 813, 853; colonial Africa, 678; Japanese, 747, 795; Soviet collectivization and, 768, 786; Depression (1930s) and, 788, 795; *kibbutzim*, in Palestine, 753, 755 *and illus.*; tariff protection for, 877

Faruq (Egypt), 838

Fascism (1930s), 792–795; appeasement of, 795; in Hitler's Germany, 793–795 *and illus.*, 810; in Mussolini's Italy, 792, 810; in Brazil, 777

Fathers. *See also* Family; Patriarchy; and Confucianism, in China, 87

Fatima (daughter of Muhammad), 254, 268

Fatimid Caliphate, 258(*map*), 259–260

Faxian, 188, 243

February Revolution (1917, Russia), 739

Feminism (feminists), 582, 877. *See also* Women's rights; Parisian, 604

Feng Guifen, 636

Feng shui, 84

Ferdinand (Aragon), 371–372, 409, 412, 453

Ferdinand VII (Spain), 641, 642, 643

Fertile Crescent region, 25. *See also* Mesopotamia

Fertility cults (deities): at Çatal Hüyük, 20 *and illus.*; Celtic, 101–102; Isis, 43, 95, 157; Cretan, 56; Canaanite, 65, 66; Carthage, 73–75; Cybele, 157; Greek, 124–125, 133; Hindu, 182–183; Mesoamerican, 203–204

Fertility rates. *See also* Birthrates; demographic transition and, 859; for slaves, 498; of immigrant groups, 867

Festivals: Babylonian, 31, 32–34; Egyptian, 43–44; Celtic, 101; Greek, 128, 133; Roman, 154

Feudalism: in China, 83, 84, 163; in India, 190; in medieval Europe, 280

Fez (Turkish hat), 620, 752

Fibonacci, Leonardo, 191

Fief (land grant), 163, 281

Fihrist (al-Nadim), 247

Fiji, 405, 406(*map*), 702

Films (motion pictures), 890; Lumière brothers and, 759–760; Indian, 890–891

Finance. *See also* Banks; Currency; Economy; Fiscal crises; Foreign debt; Inflation; Taxation: in late medieval Europe, 358; Dutch, 447; Ottoman bureau, 621(*illus.*); British, 709, 726; stock exchanges, 447; world trade and, 709–710

Financial crisis (2008–2009), 877–880

Fingerprint bureau, 761

Finland (Finns), 287, 334, 727; famine in, 559; independence of, 740, 743; in European Community, 819

Fire, and cooking, 10

Fire altars, 118

Firearms (guns), 342, 368, 370. *See also* Cannon; Gunpowder; Rifles; Weapons and military technology; Ottoman, 372;

Spanish, 426; African trade in, 416, 507, 511; in slave rebellion, 478; Amerindian trade and, 462, 477, 481 *and illus.*, 654; muskets, 507, 524; Ottoman, 519; Safavid Iran, 529; Japanese, 544; machine guns, 678, 684, 735, 747
First Estate (France), 600
First Sermon (Buddha), 180
First World War. *See* World War I
Firuz Shah, Sultan, 383, 393
Fiscal crises: in Spain, 456; colonial wars and, 590; French Revolution and, 600–602, in Asia (1997), 852
Fishing (fishermen): Stone Age, 12; Amerindian, 17; Mesopotamian, 25; Egyptian, 38, 42; Indus Valley, 46; Andean, 202, 216, 218; African, 242, 831; European, 291; Jurchen, 307; tropical, 376; Polynesian, 407; Dutch, 446(*illus.*); Japanese, 788
Five-year plans (Soviet Union), 785, 786, 809
Flanders (Flemish). *See also* Belgium; trading cities in, 289, 291, 356, 368; painters of, 352(*illus.*), 367; weavers in, 357 *and illus.*, 358
Flooding (floods): in Mesopotamia, 25, 47; Nile River, 15, 37, 47, 138, 809; in China, 556, 809; Indus River, 44; Mekong River, 193; Yellow River, 80, 170, 338, 635, 797; Niger River, 377; in Netherlands, 809; in Bangladesh, 889(*illus.*)
Florence, Italy: banking in, 358, 359; Medici family of, 359, 437
Folk cultures (folk customs): witch-hunts and, 439; popular protest and, 593–595; Mexican, 697
Food crops. *See also specific food crops*; African, in West Indies, 493; African and American, in China, 552; American, 424, 433, 448, 464, 563
Food (diet). *See also* Food production; *and specific foods*; early human, 5; Stone Age, 9, 10, 14; Egyptian, 42; Greek, 122; Andean, 218; pork taboo, 67, 242; medieval European, 279; African slave, 488; animal fat prohibition, 688; improved in industrial

countries, 710; World War I rationing, 737
Food gathering. *See also* Hunter-gatherer peoples; Stone Age, 9, 10, 12; transition to food production, 14–16
Food production. *See also* Agriculture; Farmers; transition from food gathering, 14–16, 18–19; African innovations, 234; Silk Road innovations, 248; Islamic, 264
Food shortage. *See* Famine
Footbinding, of Chinese women, 313–314, 632, 796
Foraging. *See* Food gathering
Forbidden City (Beijing), 336, 339, 341, 748
Ford, Henry, 768, 777
Ford Foundation, 820
Foreign debt (international loans). *See also* War debt; Ottoman, 624; Egyptian, 683; Central America and Caribbean, 699; Greek, 876
Foreign investment: British, 666, 690, 696; in Mexico, 640, 697, 832; Green Revolution and, 820; French, in Africa, 831; in Latin America, 832; American, in Third World, 836; in Chile, 845; in China, 853; in eastern Europe, 844; Asian financial crisis and, 877
Foreign policy: in Egypt, 41; in Carthage, 73; in Sparta, 128; mandala theory, in India, 184
Forest products (management). *See also* Deforestation; Southeast Asia, 192; Maya, 205; Russian, 287, 289; medieval European, 279, 356; colonial Americas, 477, 578; African, 238, 537, 831; Java, 538; tropical hardwoods, 667, 769, 831; economic botany and, 699–700; for railroads, 705
Formosa. *See* Taiwan
Fortifications (walls): Neolithic, 20; Mesopotamian, 27; Indus Valley, 46; early Chinese, 83; Assyrian, 61; Mycenaean, 57; Carthage, 70; Kush, 93; Celtic, 100; Roman, 158, 171; Chinese, 161, 163(*map*), 167, 171; Andean, 221; medieval Europe, 279, 291; Kremlin (Moscow), 333(*illus.*); Japanese, 346; Great Zimbabwe, 387(*illus.*); Portuguese, 423; Spanish,

456; Berlin Wall, 822, 856 *and illus.*
Forty-Seven Ronin incident (Japan), 549, 550 *and illus.*
Forum (Rome), 144, 145
Fossils, of early humans, 3, 5, 6
Four Corners region (North America), 212, 223
"Four Noble Truths" (Buddha), 180
Fourteen Points (Wilson), 740, 750–751
France. *See also under* French; Carthage and, 73; cave paintings in, 8, 12; Celts in, 100, 102; Muslims in, 276; Viking raids in, 276, 278; cathedrals in, 359, 363; monastic reform in, 286–287; peasants in, 279–280, 352(*illus.*); population growth in, 290; plague in, 353; Aquitaine in, 294–295, 369; stone quarries in, 356; trading fairs in, 357–358; Avignon popes and, 362, 368; monarchy in, 369, 370; revolt in, 353; war with England, 370; Enlightenment in, 444–445; wars of religion in, 438; witchcraft in, 441; canals in, 447; deforestation in, 449; peasant rebellions in, 449; monarchy, 455 *and table*, 454; speculative bubble in, 458–459; trading companies of, 502; economic development in, 459; India and, 531; Seven Years' War (1756–1763), 482, 590, 601; American Revolution and, 598, 602; emigrants from, 489, 676; Egypt and, 585, 683; industrialization in, 567, 574; Revolution of 1848 in, 612; railroads in, 574, 705; pin-making shop in, 568–569 *and illus.*; Crimean War and, 622–623, 625; invasion of Mexico by, 652 *and illus.*; Qing China and, 633, 636, 728, 729; worker protests in, 584; as liberal power, 726–727; urbanization in, 712; language and nation in, 718; Suez Canal and, 683; Italian unification and, 718, 719(*map*); voting rights in, 716; war with Prussia (1870–1871), 720, 721(*map*), 724, 734; alliances of, 733–734; World War I and,

734–738 and map, 740, 741; World War I peace and, 741, 742(map), 744, 745; filmmaking in, 759–760; Middle East and, 749, 753, 754 and map; appeasement of Germany by, 795; birthrate in, 762; Depression of 1930s and, 788; World War II and, 799–800, 799(map); United Nations and, 818; in European Community, 819; Serbia and, 857; Suez crisis and, 836; immigrants in, 867

Francis, Pope, 884

Franciscans, 364, 466, 542, 543

Francis I (France), 452

Franco-Prussian War (1870–1871), 721(map), 724, 734, 743

Frankincense and myrrh, 234, 251

Franklin, Benjamin, 592–593

Franks, 350

Franz Ferdinand, assassination of, 732, 733

Franz Joseph (Austria-Hungary), 612

Frederick II (Holy Roman Emperor), 334

Frederick the Great (Prussia), 591

Frederick William IV (Prussia), 612

Free blacks: in West Indies, 494, 499–500; in Haitian rebellion, 589, 608; in Latin America, 474–475, 486(illus.), 642; in United States, 575, 657; in Brazilian army, 657; returning to Africa, 686

Freedom (manumission), for slaves, 475, 500; in United States, 581

Freemasons, in Russia, 628

Free trade (free-market capitalism). See also Capitalism; as British policy, 586, 701; laissez faire and, 583; Lenin and, 744; global economy and, 784; regional trade associations, 876; World Trade Organization and, 877

French and Indian War (1756–1763), 482–483 and map, 596, 597

French colonies (French Empire): fur traders in, 464; Amerindians in, 462, 480–481 and illus.; Indochina, 692; Napoleon and, 607, 609(map); North American, 477, 480–483; in West Indies, 493, 502, 658, 701 (See also St. Dominigue

(modern Haiti)); abolition of slavery in, 589, 610, 612, 658, 701; Vietnam as, 631, 824; in Africa, 679, 682, 682, 779, 831; Algeria, 675, 753, 816; decolonization and, 828, 831

French East India Company, 502

French Equatorial Africa, 779, 831

French Indochina, 692; Japanese occupation of, 800–801, 801(map); communism in, 823–824

French language, 620, 718

French Revolution, 599–608; American Revolution and, 601–602; census in, 670; Haiti and, 608–611; playing cards from, 607(illus.); protest turning to, 602–603; reaction and Napoleon in, 606–608; society and fiscal crisis, 600–602; Terror in, 604–606; women and, 603, 604, 606–607

French West Africa, 679, 682, 831

French West India Company, 502

French West Indies, 493, 502. See also St. Dominigue (Haiti); abolition of slavery in, 657–658, 701; labor migration to, 701–702

Frescoes. See Wall murals (frescoes)

Freud, Sigmund, 763

Front de Libération National (Algeria), 829

Frumentius, 244

Fuad (Egypt), 753

Fuggers of Augsburg, 359

Fujiwara period (Japan), 317–318

Fulani people, 376; Islam and, 392

Fulton, Robert, 574

Funan, 193–194

Fur trade: North American colonies, 446, 464, 476, 479, 480–481 and illus.; Russian, 532

Fustat. See Cairo (Fustat)

Gabriel (Jibra'il), 251, 265

Gades (modern Cadiz), 69, 72(map)

Gage, Thomas, 597

Gaius Marius, 152

Galdan (Mongolia), 552, 554

Galileo Galilei, 442–444

Galley (ship), 357, 411, 519

Gallipoli, Battle of (1915), 738

Gandhara, 342; art of, 181(illus.)

Gandhi, Mohandas K. (Mahatma), 760; militant nonviolence and, 771–772 and illus.

Ganges Plain, 177, 184, 186, 187–188; irrigation in, 377; rice in, 377

Ganges River, 180, 183, 190

Gaozu (China), 162–164

Garibaldi, Giuseppe, 720

Garnet, Henry Highland, 657

Garvey, Marcus, 781, 830

Gas lighting, 578, 712, 713

Gates, Horatio, 598

Gathas (hymns), 117

Gaul (modern France): Celts in, 101–102, 149; Franks of, 276

Gaza Strip, 838, 883

Gebel Barkal, 93(map), 94

Gender roles. See also Men; Women; in Ice Age, 10–11, 21–22; in ancient Egypt, 42; yin/yang, in China, 91; Islam and, 392–394; Aztec, 395; working class, 661–662; Victorian Age, 713; division of labor and, 715

General Assembly, United Nations, 818; Israel and, 818, 838; Palestine and, 883; Universal Declaration of Human Rights and, 886; women's rights and, 887

General Motors corporation, 853

Genetic code, 4

Geneva Convention (1950), 887

Genghis Khan. See Chinggis Khan

Genoa (Genoese), 291, 353, 423; competition with Venice, 356–357

Genocide, 881; Nazi Holocaust, 806(illus.), 807; ethnic cleansing, 857; Convention on (1949), 887

Gens de couleur, in Haiti, 608, 610

Gentry: British, 448, 582, 769; Chinese, 298, 303, 310, 311, 313, 337

George III (Great Britain), 598

Georgia (Caucasus), 529, 616, 622, 624; Soviet Republic of, 743

Georgia (United States), 571

Gerbert of Aurillac, 190

Germany (Germanic peoples). See also Nazi Germany; Prussia; Celts and, 103; Rome and, 146(map), 158; customs of, 276, 279; iron swords of, 283; kingdoms of, 295; migrations of, 287; political order, 278–279; Teutonic Knights, 334–335, 352; mining in, 354; Lutheranism and, 437; witch-hunts in, 440–441; Holy Roman Empire and, 452; mercenaries from, 597; industrialization of, 566, 567, 572, 704–705; customs union in, 583; engineering schools in, 705, 707; Pacific possessions, 694, 749; railroads in, 574, 705; Ruhr district, 576, 577(*map*), 707, 712; immigrants from, 710, 711; voting rights in, 717, 725, 762; chemical industry in, 707; labor unions in, 717; unification of, 612, 720, 721(*map*); as great power, 726, 727; Argentine radio and, 776; autobahn in, 768; African colonies of, 737–738, 749, 778; colonies, 748; navy of, 734; World War I and, 733–734, 737, 739–740; World War I peace and, 741–743 *and map*; hyperinflation in (1923), 745; reparations after World War I, 743, 744–745; treaty with Soviets (1922), 745; Depression (1930s) in, 788, 793; Nazi era, 793; pact with Stalin (1939), 795, 800; Holocaust and, 807; World War II and, 799–800, 806 *and illus.*; fall of Berlin Wall and, 856 *and illus.*; reunification of (1990), 855; immigration to, 867; Greek debt crisis and, 876–877

Ghana, 781, 830. *See also* Gold Coast; Berber conquest of, 379; gold in, 258, 379

Ghazan, Il-khan, 328–329

Ghent, 291, 357

Gibraltar, Strait of, 69, 72(*map*), 73, 258(*map*), 259, 276

Gilgamesh, 23, 48

Giotto, art of, 367

Girondists (Paris), 604

Giza, pyramids at, 39, 40 *and illus.*

Glaciers, melting of, 240–241; in twenty-first century, 871, 888

Glasnost (Soviet openness), 854

Glassmaking, 289; stained glass, 437; Ottoman guild, 523(*illus.*)

Global culture, 815, 889–896; emerging elite, 893–894; enduring diversity in, 894–895; English language and, 893–894, 894; media and message in, 890–891; spread of pop culture, 891–892

Global economy (world economy). *See also* Globalization; botany and, 699; electricity and,

707–708; environment and, 699–702, 707; expansion of, 699–701, 864; chemical industry, 706–707; new technologies and (1850–1900), 705–710; free trade in, 701; steamships and telegraph, 706; steel industry, 706–707; Latin America and, 666; railroads, 705–706; United States and, 664; Japan and, 747; Depression (1930s) and, 788; Chinese integration into, 852–854; new technologies and, 868–869; regional trade associations and, 875–877; financial crisis (2008–2009), 877–880

Globalization, 815, 844; cultural, 890, 893, 894; democracy and, 880–882

Global warming, 888–889 *and illus.*

Global war on terrorism, 885, 887

Glorious Revolution (England), 455, 485

Goa, Portuguese in, 422, 517, 537, 545

Goats, 16, 21, 22, 25, 42, 96, 98, 107–108, 119, 240, 242, 243, 323, 376, 424, 681, 786

Goble, Jonathan, 757

Go-Daigo (Japan), 347

Gods and goddesses. *See also* Divine kingship; Monotheism; Polytheism; Religion(s); Shrines; Temples; *and specific gods and goddesses*; Neolithic, 19; Çatal Hüyük, 20 *and illus.*; Mesopotamian, 28, 29(*illus.*), 30–31, 35–36, 47; Egyptian, 38, 42–43, 47–48, 53; sun-gods, 29(*illus.*), 43, 53, 157, 397, 398; Assyrian Empire, 60; Israelite (Yahweh), 63, 64, 66–67; Chinese, 80–81; Phoenician, 69; Carthaginian, 74; Celtic, 103(*illus.*); Persian Empire, 117–118; Greek, 124, 126 *and illus.*; Roman, 147; Vedic religion, 178; Hindu (India), 174, 181–184; Buddhism and, 299–300; Mesoamerican, 200, 204–205 *and illus.*; Islamic (Allah), 252

Gold Coast (Ghana): Portuguese in, 410(*illus.*), 412, 415; Asante kingdom in, 507, 508; slave trade in, 502, 507–508; British traders in, 682; cocoa farmers in, 779; independence of, 830

Gold coinage, 124, 291; Muslim, 255, 258, 259; Portuguese *cruzado*, 411; French speculators and, 458; Ottoman, 623

Golden Horde khanate, 324, 326(*map*), 332, 531; rivalry with Il-khans, 328–329

Gold (gold trade), 21; Nubian, 41, 55, 92, 94; Aegean region, 57; African, 195, 258, 409, 411, 415; Andean region, 203, 217, 221; Xiongnu, 166(*illus.*); Scythian, 97(*illus.*); Mongolian Empire, 332; Saharan caravan trade and, 259, 371, 379; Portuguese and, 411, 416; salt trade and, 382; Caribbean, 424; Inka, 398, 427; American, 453, 466, 468, 711(*illus.*); mercantilism and, 500; East African, 386, 388, 388, 537; Brazilian, 468, 470, 485, 667; Californian, 653; South African, 677–678; Australian, 693; American reserves, 818

Goldman, Emma, 717

Gomes, Fernão, 412

Good and evil, in Zoroastrianism, 117, 250

Gorbachev, Mikhail, 854; reforms of, 855–856

Goulart, João, 845

Government. *See also* Administration; Bureaucracy; Constitutions; Monarchy; Political systems and institutions; Self-government; ancient Egypt, 39–40; early China, 85, 88; Assyrian Empire, 61–62; Carthage, 70–71, 73–74; Persian Empire, 116, 140; Roman Empire, 149, 150, 155, 158, 159; India, 184–185; Russia, 289; imperial China, 162, 163, 168, 312–313; Islamic caliphate, 254–255; Byzantine Empire, 274; European cities, 291–292; Japan, 316–317; Il-khanate, 329; Vietnam, 348; Yuan China, 336, 339; tropical water systems and, 377, 378; witch-hunts and, 441; Dutch banks and, 447; British business and, 448, 459; tax farmers and, 456, 458; Atlantic system and, 502; colonial Americas, 466; Ottoman, 519, 524, 525, 624; Korean, 550–551; Mughal

Empire, 529–530; imperial China, 552, 557, 636, 729; Enlightenment view of, 591; United States, 598–599; economic growth and, 663; Latin American exports and, 666; power of, and census, 670; British colonial, 688–689; German education and, 725–726; Japanese industry and, 723–724, 837; nationalism and, 724; World War I and, 737, 739; Russian Provisional, 739, 740; Soviet Russia, 785, 787; Guomindang China, 748; colonial Africa, 779; Depression (1930s) and, 788; fascist Italy, 792; European social welfare and, 819; famine and, 812–814; television monopolies, 890–891

Granada, reconquest of, 371–372, 409

Gran Colombia, 644(map); breakup of, 643, 649, 651

Grand Canal (China), 298, 337, 556

Grand National Consolidated Trade Union, 585

Grapes, 119; for wine, 149, 230

Great Britain, 457(map). See also under British; England; India, British rule in; balance of power and, 456; dynasties in, 454(table); Ireland and, 454, 456, 696, 726, 812–813; planter elite in, 499; trade with Spanish colonies, 470; war with France, 482, 590; enclosure movement in, 564; immigrants from, 571, 710; American Revolution and, 595–598; Napoleon and, 608, 609(map); Haitian revolution and, 610; war with United States (1812), 651–652, 654; Qing China and, 556, 587, 629–630, 633, 636; Crimean War and, 622–623, 625; Egypt and, 586, 683; census in, 671; Ethiopia and, 684; Latin American investment and, 666, 697; financial power of, 709; urban growth in, 712; Victorian "separate spheres," 713; voting rights in, 717; foreign investment by, 683, 690, 709–710, 775; vote for women in, 714–715 and illus., 762; labor unions in,

717; as liberal power, 726–727; alliances of, 733–734; World War I and, 734, 735–737; World War I peace and, 741–742, 744; Depression (1930s) and, 788; Jewish homeland and, 739, 750, 754(map), 753; appeasement of Nazis, 795; Middle East and, 753–754 and map, 838; World War II and, 800, 801(map), 805, 817; nationalization in, 819; Cold War and, 818; United Nations and, 817–818; in European Community, 819; nuclear arms race and, 826–827; Suez crisis and, 836; Serbia and, 857

Great Britain, Industrial Revolution in (1760–1851), 565–576; advantages in, 565–567; canal building in, 566; changes in society, 581–582; cities, 562; cotton industry in, 570–571; iron industry in, 571–572; laissez faire, 583; pottery industry, 567–570 and illus.; protests and reforms, 584–585; railroads in, 574, 705–706; steam engines in, 570, 572–574 and illus.; telegraph in, 575–576

Great Britain, Qing China and, 586–587; Macartney mission, 556; opium trade and, 629–630, 728; Opium War (1839–1842) and, 630; Arrow War (1856–1860) and, 633; recovery after Taiping Rebellion, 636, 728–729; Treaty of Nanking (1842), 633

Greater East Asian Co-Prosperity Sphere, 802

Great Famine (Europe, 1315–1317), 353

Great Ice Age. See Ice Age

Great Lakes region (North America), 481, 595, 870

Great Leap Forward (China), 813–814, 837

Great Northern War (1700–1721), 534

Great powers of Europe (1871–1900), 704, 725–728; China, Japan and, 728–729

Great powers of Europe (1900–1913), 733

Great Society reforms (United States), 826

Great traditions, 239, 262, 891

Great Trek, of Afrikaners, 677–678

Great Wall of China, 161, 163(map)

Great War, 673, 734–740, 741, 760, 763, 764–765, 774, 784. See also World War I

Great Western Schism, 368

Great Western (steamship), 570 and illus., 574

Great Zimbabwe, 387(illus.), 388

Greco-Bactrian kingdom, 186. See also Bactria

Greco-Roman traditions, 436, 618; revival, in Renaissance Europe, 365, 367

Greece (Greeks). See also Greek language; Hellenistic Age; agriculture in, 15–16; oracles in, 125; war with Carthage, 73–74; Mycenaean, 49–50, 56–58, 121; Phoenicians and, 121; Archaic period, 121–122; Dark Age in, 59, 121; Celts and, 101; colonies of, 97, 123; Scythians and, 97–98; democracy in, 124, 128–129; rise of, 119–129; geography and resources, 119–121; gods, 124, 126(illus.); inequality in, 132–133; new intellectual currents, 125–127, 131; rivalry with Persia, 111, 116–117, 127, 129–135; transition to literacy in, 122, 131–132, 141, 224–226; Christianity in, 156; Zhou China compared, 141; maritime trade of, 124, 129, 131; medicine of, 111; independence of, 611, 618; Ottoman Empire and, 611, 733; Muslims expelled from, 741, 749; Turkey and, 749, 822; immigrants in, 867; debt burdens of, 876–877

Greek city-states (polis), 114. See also Athens; Sparta; emergence of, 121–125; failure of, 134; Hellenistic Age, 137–140

Greek historians. See Herodotus

Greek language, 59, 121, 137, 155, 225, 332

Greek philosophy, 139, 247, 293, 363

Greenhouse effect, 888

Greenland, Vikings in, 278, 407

Green Revolution, 820–821 and illus.

Gregory VII, Pope, 284, 286
Gregory X, Pope, 360–361
Gregory XIII, Pope, 442
Grenada, American invasion of, 846
Grimké, Sarah, 661
Griot (storyteller), in West Africa, 224, 226
Gropius, Walter, 767
Gross domestic product (GDP): in China, 843, 851; global comparison, 865
Guam, 694, 696
Guangwu (China), 170
Guangxi, 631
Guangzhou. See Canton (Guangzhou)
Guatemala, 667; Maya of, 205–208 and illus., 219 and illus.; Cakchiquel of, 463; CIA-sponsored coup in (1954), 833
Guerrilla warfare: in China, 796, 797; in Vietnam, 825; in Africa, 831; in Argentina, 845; in El Salvador, 846; in Iraq, 882; in Palestine, 753, 838
Guevara, Ernesto "Che," 833, 834
Guianas, 500
Guilds: in Mesopotamia, 28; in India, 186, 188; in Europe, 354, 358, 359; in Ottoman Empire, 523(illus.); in Safavid Iran, 527
Guillotin, Ignace, 605
Guillotine, 605 and illus.
Guinea, independence of, 831
Gujarat, 536; mosque in, 391; Muslim rule of, 389–390; Portuguese and, 422; trade of, 383, 389–390
Gulags (Russian labor camps), 787; Stalin and, 787
Gunboats, 587, 630, 797
Gundestrup cauldron, 102(illus.)
Gunpowder, 335, 343, 345, 348, 507, 516, 630. See also Firearms (guns); flaming arrows and, 308, 335, 342 and illus.
Gunpowder revolution, 409, 558
Guns. See Firearms (guns)
Guomindang (China): Chinese warlords and, 74; communists and, 796; Japan and, 795–796; collapse of, 803–804 and illus.; in Taiwan, 804
Gupta India (320–550 C.E.), 176(map), 187–192; trade of, 189–190; women in, 188–189
Gurkhas (Nepal), 688

Gutenberg, Johann, 367
Gutta-percha, 699
Guyana, 827
Güyük, Great Khan, 324, 324(fig.)

Habsburg dynasty, 452, 454(table), 457(map), 484
Haciendas (Mexican estates), 696, 697, 698
Hadith (sayings of Muhammad), 262–263, 264, 265; women and, 265
Hagia Sofia cathedral, 275
Haile Selassie (Ethiopia), 781
Haiti (St. Domingue): Bolívar and, 642; sugar plantations on, 492; earthquake in, 494; hurricane in, 494–495(illus.); slave rebellion in, 589, 608, 658, 699; revolution in (1789–1804), 608–611, 613, 658; United States and, 699
Hakkas, in China, 632
Hakra (Saraswati) River, 45, 47
Halevi, Judah, 259
Hamas movement, 883
Hamburg, bombing of (1943), 806
Hammurabi, 50; Law Code of, 28, 29, 48
Handwriting. See Script
Han Empire (China), 162–165, 318; decline of, 169–170; expansion of, 163(map); long reign of, 162–165; new forms of thought in, 168–170; nomadic peoples and, 162, 165, 166(illus.); Roman Empire compared to, 143, 150–152, 169, 171–173; Silk Road and, 163(map), 164; society in, 165–168
Han Fei, 85, 88–90
Han'gul (Korean) writing system, 344(illus.), 345
Hangzhou, 308, 312
Hannibal (slave ship), 488
Hanno, 73
Hanoi, Vietnam, 348
Hanoverian dynasty, 454(table)
Hanseatic League, 357, 368
Han Yu, 300
Haque, Azizul, 761
Harappa, 45–46
Harding, Warren, 784
Hargreaves, James, 584
Harkhuf, 78–79, 92
Harness, breast-strap, 290
Harris, Arthur "Bomber," 806
Harsha Vardhana, 190
Hart, Robert, 635
Hatshepsut (Egypt), 53, 54(illus.)
Hattusha, 50, 58

Hausa city-states, 380(map), 382; slave trade and, 510; Sokoto Caliphate and, 679
Havana, Cuba, 456, 491; Castro in, 816
Havel, Vaclav, 855
Hawaiian Islands, 702, 712; Polynesian colonization of, 405, 406(map); Pearl Harbor in, 694–695, 801(map); United States and, 694
Hay, John, 695
Hayford, J. E. Casely, 781
Health care. See also Disease; Medicine (physicians); in colonial Africa, 779, 830; hygiene and, 764; HIV/AIDS and, 861
Heaven (deity), 83, 324. See also Mandate (Son) of Heaven
Heavenly Kingdom of Great Peace (China), 632
Hebrew Bible (Old Testament), 2, 63–64, 66–68, 440. See also Israel; Jews
Hebrew language, 26, 63
Helena (Ethiopia), 417
Heliocentric (Copernican) theory, 331, 364, 442
Hellenistic Age, 135–140, 141; Alexandria in, 135, 136, 137; Antigonids, 137; Ptolemaic Egypt, 135–137; Rome and, 149; Seleucids, 136
Helots, in Sparta, 127
Helsinki Accords, 827
Henry II (England), 284–285, 294
Henry IV (France), 438
Henry IV (Holy Roman Emperor), 284
Henry the Navigator, 410–411
Henry VIII (England), 439, 456, 460
Herat, 330
Herders. See Cattle (cattle herders); Pastoralism
Heresy, 466; Nestorian, 250; in Catholicism, 444, 527
Herodotus, 36, 111, 127, 233; on Scythians, 97–98, 230; on Xerxes, 129–130
Herzl, Theodore, 738, 750
Hesiod, 138
Hezbollah (Lebanon), 883
Hidalgo y Costilla, Miguel, 645, 646(illus.)
Hidden Imam, 526. See also Imam, in Shi'ism
Hideyoshi Toyotomi, 545–546
Hieroglyphics, 52; alphabetic systems and, 121; Egyptian, 40, 95; Maya, 208

Hildebrand. *See* Gregory VII, Pope
Hindi language, 530, 893
Hindu-Buddhist culture, in Southeast Asia, 193
Hindu-Muslim relations: in Delhi Sultanate, 382–383, 383–384, 389; in Mughal Empire, 529–530; in British India, 688, 769–770; Indian independence and, 827; terrorist attacks (2008) and, 881
Hindus (Hinduism): evolution of, 182–184; temples, 175, 183, 189; Delhi sultanate and, 382–383, 383–384; Islam and, 389, 390; *sati* (widow burning) in, 189, 393; social castes and, 403–404, 687; traders, 535; in British India, 687, 688, 691; Bharatiya Janata Party (BJP), 881, 884
Hippalus, 233
Hiram (Tyre), 65, 68
Hirobumi, Ito, 722
Hirohito (Japan), 803
Hiroshima, atomic bombing of, 801 *and map*, 803 *and illus.*
Hisashige, Tanaka, 705
Hispaniola, 424. *See also* Haiti (St. Domingue); Amerindians of, 467
Histories (Herodotus), 127
History (historians): Chinese (Sima Qian), 99, 164, 168, 302; Greek, 126–127; Il-khanate, 329
History Will Absolve Me (Castro), 816
Hitler, Adolf, 768, 792, 793, 794–795; appeasement of, 795; Aryan "master race" and, 793; Holocaust and, 807; pact with Stalin, 795, 800; suicide of, 802
Hittites, 50, 51(*map*), 52; ironworking of, 52, 241; treaty with Egypt, 54
HIV/AIDS, 861–862
Ho Chi Minh, 823–824
Ho Chi Minh City (Saigon), 825
Hogarth, William, 594(*illus.*)
Hohokam, 211
Holland. *See* Netherlands (the Dutch, Holland)
Hollywood films, 781, 890
Holocaust (World War II), 806(*illus.*), 807
Holy Land, 293, 334, 352, 371, 373; Crusades to, 261
Holy Roman Empire, 282, 475(*map*), 452; papacy and,

282, 284; Thirty Years' War and, 455–456
Homer, 58, 124, 125, 224
Hominids, 4–5, 21
Homo erectus, 5, 6, 9–10
Homo floresiensis, 8
Homo habilis, 5–6, 9
Homo sapiens, 5, 6, 8, 10
Homosexuality, in Islam, 268, 528
Honduras, 205, 699
Hong Kong, 631, 633, 852; China and, 864; filmmaking in, 892
Hongwu (China), 339
Hong Xiuquan, 632–633
Hopewell people, 212–213
Hopi people, 2
Hoplites, 124, 129–130, 134, 141; weaponry of, 123, 134, 148
Hormuz, 339, 525; Portuguese in, 422, 517
Horse collar, 169, 290
Horses, 25. *See also* Cavalry; Central Asian steppes, 85, 98–99; domestication of, 55, 96, 107–108; Greek, 119; breast-strap harness for, 290; horseshoes, 290; in medieval Europe, 280, 294(*illus.*), 354; Khitan, 307; Koreans and, 314; plows and, 107, 290, 351; Amerindians and, 464–465, 654; urban pollution and, 713, 768
Horton, James Africanus, 686
Horus, 43
House of Burgesses (Virginia), 477
House of Commons, 371, 454, 479, 612
House of Lords, 371, 454, 771
Housing (dwellings). *See also* Architecture; Construction materials and techniques; Neolithic, 15(*illus.*), 20; Aztec, 396; Carthaginian, 73; Celtic, 101–102; Roman, 154; Andean, 203, 220; Anasazi, 212, 213(*illus.*); Central Asian yurts, 106(*illus.*), 232; Chinese cities, 311; medieval Europe, 352 *and illus.*; for industrial workers, 562; Parisian apartments, 579(*illus.*); of urban poor, 600 *and illus.*, 712; debt crisis in United States, 877–880
Huang Chao, 303, 306
Huang Dao Po, 338
Huanyaputina volcano, 559
Huascar (Inka), 426–427
Huayna Capac (Inka), 399, 426
Hudson River, 479, 481; steamboats on, 574

Huerta, Victoriano, 697
Huitzilopochtli (sun-god), 397
Hülegü, Il-khan, 324(*fig.*), 326(*map*), 328, 330. *See also* Il-khanate Empire (Iran)
Human communities, emergence of, 1; African genesis, 2–8; brain size and, 3, 4, 6(*illus.*), 9; evolution and, 4–6, 6(*illus.*), 21
Humaneness (*ren*), 86, 88–90
Humanists, in Europe, 365–367
Human rights, 815, 844, 846, 887–888. *See also* Rights; Women's rights; universal standards of, 886
Human sacrifice: early China, 81; Kushite, 93; child, in Carthage, 74, 74(*illus.*); Celtic, 101; Mesoamerica, 200, 204; Andean, 218, 220, 398; Cahokia, 214; Aztec, 425
Hume, David, 592
Hundred Years War (1337–1453), 370
Hungary. *See also* Austria-Hungary (1867–1917); copper mining in, 354, 359; Mongols and, 324; Soviet Union and, 822; fall of communism in, 855, 858(*map*)
Huns, 99, 189
Hunter-gatherer peoples. *See also* Food gathering; Hunting; cave paintings, 10, 12; dwellings of, 12; Ice Age, 8–14; women in, 11; Northern Amerindian, 17, 211; in sub-Saharan Africa, 239; in tropics, 376; in Australia, 692
Hunting (hunters): Stone Age, 9–10; dogs and, 16(*illus.*); Amerindian, 17; Çatal Hüyük, 20; Egyptian, 38; Chinese, 81; Saharan, 235; Sasinid kings, 249(*illus.*); Maya, 205; Mongol khans, 327–328; Amerindian, 464, 476, 481, 654; whaling and sealhunting, 537, 693
Husain, Saddam, 848, 883; invasion of Kuwait by, 858, 886
Husayn, Imam, 526–527
Husayn (Jordan), 838
Husayn (Shi'ite martyr), 254
Hussein ibn Ali, 738
Hutu-Tutsi rivalry, in Rwanda, 857
Hyderabad, 531

Hydroelectric dams, 768; in North America, 708; in Soviet Union, 785; in Japan, 837
Hydrogen bomb, 826. *See also* Nuclear weapons
Hyksos, 52, 64

Ibadan, Nigeria, 779
Iberian expansion, 408. *See also* Portuguese maritime explorations; Spanish maritime expeditions; and unification, 371–372
Ibn al-Arabi, 259
Ibn al-Haytham, 265
Ibn Battuta, Muhammad ibn Abdullah, 379; in Delhi, 393; in Mali, 394; in Mogadishu, 374
Ibn Hazm, 259
Ibn Khaldun, 330
Ibn Rushd (Averroës), 259
Ibn Sina (Avicenna), 294, 363
Ibn Tufayl, 259
Ibn Tughluq, Muhammad, Sultan, 383
Ibrahim Pasha (Egypt), 618
Ice Age, 4, 7(*map*), 8, 22; technology and culture in, 8–14; end of, 240
Iceland, Vikings in, 278, 407
Iceman, 12, 13(*illus.*)
Ideas, spread of, 242–245. *See also* Intellectual life (intellectuals); Political thought; Buddhism, 243–244; Christianity, 244–245; material evidence and, 242–243
Identity documents, standardized, 761
Ilanga (Congolese woman), 680–682
Iliad (Homer), 58, 124, 186, 224
Il-khanate Empire (Iran), 326(*map*); culture and science in, 329–332; rivalry with Golden Horde, 328–329; Timurids and, 329
Iltutmish, Sultan, 383
Imam, in Shi'ism, 254, 257, 259, 526–527
IMF. *See* International Monetary Fund
Imjin War, 540, 545–546, 550, 553, 558
Immigrants (immigration). *See also* Chinese immigrants; Migration; acculturation of, 661; in Americas, 470–471, 476, 477, 484, 485, 574, 658–660, 663; in Australia and New Zealand, 564, 692–693,

694; in Hawaii, 694; Indian, 659, 701; Irish, 564, 582, 710; railroads and, 710, 711 *and illus.*; restrictions on, 711, 741; in United States, 564, 658–659, 663, 710, 711 *and illus.*, 724, 809, 862; Jews, in Palestine, 755 *and illus.*; Algerians, in France, 828–829; from Cuba, 834; in industrialized nations, 867–868
Imperialism (1750–1914), 675–703. *See also* Colonies; Expansion; *and specific empires and emperors*; in Africa, 676–686; in Algeria, 675; Australia and New Zealand, 692–694; Berlin Conference, 679, 682; British, in India, 686–692; Chinese responses to, 636–638; free trade and, 701; global economy and, 699–702; in Hawaii and Philippines, 694–695 *and illus.*; industrialization and, 561, 702; Japanese, 727–728, 795; in Latin America, 695–699; new labor migrations, 701–702; in South Africa, 676–678; in Southeast Asia, 692; United Nations and, 818; cultural, 890
Imperial Maritime Customs Service (Britain), 635
Import-substitution industrialization, in Brazil, 845
Indentured labor: in colonial America, 476, 489, 491; in West Indies, 489, 490, 491, 659, 668, 701–702; of Asian immigrants, 659, 668, 701–702, 710–711
Independence (independence movements). *See also* Decolonization (1947–1990); Dutch, 438, 459; Haitian, 608–611; Latin American, 641–646; Serbian, 622; Greek, 611, 618; Mexican, 644(*map*), 645, 646(*illus.*); Panamanian, 699; Philippine, 828; Indian (1905–1945), 674, 769–771; Algerian, 816; Israeli, 838
India, religions of, 191–192. *See also* Hindus; Buddhism, 178, 179–182, 183–184, 185, 186, 392; Jainism, 179–180, 186; Parsees, 118; Vedism, 179–181, 189

India, under British rule, 615, 686–687; Assam and, 688, 692; cholera in, 702, 691; cotton exports, 571, 688, 690; East India Company in, 555, 586, 687–688; fingerprint bureau in, 761; tea production in, 687, 690; labor migration from, 659, 701, 710–712; nationalism in, 691–692, 768, 769–771; opium trade and, 629–630, 687–688; traditions in, 687, 688; political reform and industrial impact, 688–691; railroads in, 586, 690, 696, 705; trade in, 701, 709; Russia and, 626–627, 726; Sepoy rebellion in (1857), 687; World War I and, 737, 770; famine in, 769; independence movement in (1905–1945), 674, 769
India (Indian civilization), 174–197. *See also* India, under British rule; India (1905–present); Mughal Empire (India); Indo-Europeans in, 19; Alexander the Great in, 176(*map*), 184, 186; cattle domestication in, 17; rice cultivation in, 16; Arya-Dasa conflict in, 177; foundations of, 175–184; agriculture in, 177, 187; as subcontinent, 175–177; castes (varna) in, 177–179, 189, 403; chronology (1500 B.C.E.–647 C.E.), 197; commerce and culture, 185–187; Vedic Age, 177–179; epic literature of, 174, 186–187; Mauryan Empire (324–184 B.C.E.), 176(*map*), 184–185, 243; Southeast Asia and, 193–194, 195; women and marriage in, 188–189; Gupta Empire (320–550 C.E.), 176(*map*), 187–192; Chinese silk and, 193; concept of time in, 196; pilgrims in, 180(*illus.*), 188; political fragmentation in, 175, 185–187, 190; widow burning (*sati*) in, 189, 393; Indian Ocean trade and, 233–234; Chinese voyages to, 339–340, 340(*map*); Delhi sultanate in, 377, 382–384; gold trade of, 379; Malabar Coast, 386, 389–390, 389, 420–421, 422, 423; Mughals in, 422; Malabar Coast, 420–421, 422, 423;

Portuguese in, 420, 421 *and illus.*, 422, 517; cotton textiles from, 446, 530, 536, 586

Indian Civil Service (ICS), 690, 769–770

Indian National Congress, 691–692, 770, 771; Nehru and, 773–774

Indian Ocean (Indian Ocean trade), 233–235, 402–405. *See also* East Indies; *and specific states*; Malay explorers, 192; chronology (1st century C.E.), 245–246; origins of contacts and trade, 233; Buddhism and, 231(*map*); Mediterranean trade and, 233–234, 291; Southeast Asia and, 243; impact of, 234–235; monsoons and, 233, 234, 375, 386–387, 388; Aden and Red Sea, 388; Chinese voyagers in, 386, 402–405, 406(*map*); Gujarat and Malabar Coast, 389–390; dhows (ships) in, 385 *and illus.*, 403, 420, 422; Swahili Coast and Zimbabwe, 386, 387–388 *and illus.*; pepper and spices in, 234, 388, 389, 416, 422; chronology (350–1539), 428–429; Portugal and, 412, 418–420, 427–428; Dutch and, 447, 501–502

Indian Removal Act of 1830 (United States), 654

India (1905 to present), 876; chronology (1905–1947), 782–783; Gandhi and, 771–772, 773; Hindu-Muslim relations and, 770–771, 773–774, 827–828; Salt March in, 772 *and illus*; independence movement in, 674, 769–771, 773–774; Indian National Congress and, 770, 771, 773–774; land and people, 769; Nehru and, 773–774, 828; partition and (1947), 773–774; declining birthrate in, 863; Pakistan and, 827–828; economic growth in, 853, 864; English language in, 893; film making in, 890–891

Indigo (indigo plantations), 389, 477–478, 707

Individual rights (individualism): Greek, 124; Buddhism and, 181; Enlightenment view of, 591–592, 593; Declaration of Independence (United States)

and, 597; in Napoleonic France, 607

Indochina. *See also* Burma; Cambodia; Laos; Southeast Asia; Thailand; Vietnam; French in, 692; Japanese occupation of, 800–801, 801(*map*); Communist party in, 824

Indo-European languages, 19, 96, 111; in India 176(*map*), 177, 187

Indo-European speakers, migration of, 56, 96, 177, 176 *and map*

Indonesia, 189, 700. *See also* Dutch East Indies; Java; early humans in, 8; colonists in Madagascar from, 234; Japan and, 828; independence of, 828; relocation program in, 867; financial crisis in, 877; democracy in, 880

Indulgences, sale of, 437

Industrialization. *See also* Industrial nations; Industrial Revolution; in Egypt, 585–587; environmental effects of, 576–578, 668, 707, 776, 870; raw materials for, 578, 656, 699; in United States, 566, 663, 704, 705; imperialism and, 702; British India and, 586, 690, 773; in Germany, 566, 567, 572, 704, 705; in Japan, 704, 724, 746–747, 836–837; urbanization and, 758–759; in Russia, 704, 727; in Brazil and Argentina, 775, 776, 845; in Soviet Union, 744, 785, 787, 819; in Manchuria, 796; in China, 868, 871

Industrial nations (developed world). *See also* Industrialization; Industrial Revolution; new technologies in (1850–1900), 705; overseas trade of, 701, 709; population and migrations, 710–712; urban environments, 712–713; socialism and labor movement, 716–717; women's rights in, 713–715, 762; new technologies and activities, 763–768; personal identity in, 761; transnational corporations and, 869; revolution in sciences, 762; new ways of living, 761–768; cult of the modern in, 763, 764–765, 782; technology

and environment, 765–768; Depression (1930s) in, 788–789 *and illus.*; wealth inequality within, 864; aging population in, 862, 863–864 *and figure*; lower fertility in, 862; wealth gap with poor nations, 865–866; immigration to, 864; environmental concerns in, 869–870, 870, 870–871; global warming and, 888–889

Industrial Revolution (1760–1851), 562–588. *See also* Great Britain, Industrial Revolution in; causes of, 563–567; chronology, 588; cities, 576–578; division of labor in, 569, 568–569; impact of, 576–582; imperialism and, 561; iron industry, 571–572; laissez faire and, 583–584; limits of, outside the West, 585–587; mass production of pottery in, 567–570 *and illus.*; mechanization of cotton industry in, 570–571; new economic and political ideas, 582–585; population growth and, 563–564, 859; protests and reforms in, 584–585; railroads and, 574–575 *and illus.*; rural areas and, 578; steam engines, 572–574 *and illus.*; telegraph and, 575; trade and inventiveness in, 564–565; working women and children in, 578–581

Industry. *See also* Industrialization; Iron industry; Manufacturing; Textile industry; in imperial China, 308, 338; Japanese *keiretsu*, 849; World War II boom, 809; robots for, 869

Indus Valley civilization, 23, 24(*map*) 44–47, 136; natural environment of, 44–45; urban centers in, 46, 47; material culture of, 45–46; trade, 46, 234; transformation of, 47, 48; irrigation in, 46; Persia and, 114; Sind, 255

Inequality. *See also* Wealth inequality; in ancient Greece, 132–133; in Roman society, 145; socialism and, 716; global economy and, 844, 864–866; global poverty and, 843

Infanticide: in Carthage, 74, 74(*illus.*); in Greece, 133

Inflation. *See also* Prices; in ancient Rome, 159; in Spain, 453; in Safavid Iran, 529; in Ottoman Empire, 523; in China, 312, 552, 798; in Paris, 604; in Germany, 744–745, 793; in Argentina and Chile, 845; in Iran, 848

Influenza, 327, 463; epidemic (1918–1919), 741, 762

Inheritance: in Israel, 66; in China, 188; women and, 265; in Islam, 265

Inka (Inka Empire), 209(*map*), 397–399, 465; Spanish conquest of, 426–427; rebellion in, 427, 484–485

Inner Asia. *See also* Central Asia; nomadism in, 230; Buddhism in, 300; China and, 299–300, 301(*map*); Mongols and, 338

Inoculation (variolation), 543

Inquisition: Galileo and, 442–443; in Spain, 372, 441

Institutional Revolutionary Party (Mexico), 832

Insurance companies, 447, 623, 761

Intellectual life (intellectuals). *See also* Philosophy; in Greece, 125–127, 131; in Muslim Spain, 259–260; in imperial China, 168–170, 299; under Charlemagne, 276, 363; in European Renaissance, 363–365; humanism, in Europe, 365; Scientific Revolution, 441–444, 447; Spanish isolation and, 453; Enlightenment, 443–444, 591–593; Qing China, 554; Revolutionary era, 589; Russian, 626, 628; post-World War I, 763; Indian nationalism and, 771

Interchangeable-parts manufacturing, 572

Interest (usury), 359, 450; Japanese rice market and, 547, 548

International Center for the Improvement of Maize and Wheat, 820

International Criminal Court, 881, 887

International Monetary Fund (IMF), 818, 852

International Rice Research Institute, 820

International Statistical Congress (1860), 671

International style, in architecture, 767

International Workingman's Association, 717

Internet (World Wide Web), *815*, 891

Investiture controversy, 284

Investment. *See* Foreign investment

Ionia: Greeks in, 119, 120(*map*), 126; rebellion in, 129

Iran (Iranians), 111–118. *See also* Persia (Persian Empire); Safavid Empire (Iran); Indo-Europeans in, 19; Assyrian Empire and, 59–60; Elamites of, 52; Medes, 75; geography and resources, 113; rise of Persian Empire in, 113–114; Shakas, 186; pork taboo in, 242–243; Silk Road trade and, 230, 231(*illus.*), 248; Sogdiana and, 228; Buyid dynasty in, 257, 260; climate change in, 260, 261; cotton production in, 264; Sasanid Empire, 248–250 *and illus.*, 255, 255, 264, 270; Samanid dynasty in, 257, 259; scholars from, 268, 293; shah of, 248–249 *and illus.*, 250, 255, 256; in Tang China, 298; merchants from, 387–388; Mongol conquest of, 324, 326; Islam in, 256, 263–264, 391, 518(*map*), 521, 526; silk industry in, 524, 528, 529; Mughal India and, 531; Russia and, 626; oil wealth of, 839, 847, 876–877; photography in, 760; universities in, 753; Islamic Republic of, 847–848, 884; nuclear program in, 877, 883; war with Iraq, 848–849

Iraq (Iraqis), 270. *See also* Mesopotamia; Tigris-Euphrates Valley in, 23, 25; Buyid dynasty in, 257; Islam in, 255, 263, 264; climate change in, 260, 261, 291; Mongols and, 327; after World War I, 749, 754(*map*); oil wealth of, 753, 839; war with Iran, 848–849; American war in, 882–884, 891

Ireland (Irish), 714; Celts in, 100, 101, 103; monks from, 286 *and illus.*; English conquest of, 369; Catholicism in, 718, 726; Great Britain and, 454, 456, 696, 726, 812; potatoes in, 448, 582, 812; immigrants from, 564, 582, 711; famine in (1847–1848), 582, 710, 812–813

Irigoyen, Hipólito, 775, 777

Iron Age, 49

Iron curtain, 817, 840. *See also* Cold War; Warsaw Pact

Iron industry. *See also* Steel production; Hittite, 52; Assyrian, 61; Meroë, 95; bronze compared, 49, 109, 177; charcoal for, 283, 354, 449; Indian, 177; steppe nomads and, 230; stirrups, 298, 302(*illus.*); sub-Saharan Africa, 239, 241–242; Chinese, 85, 308–309, 571–572; medieval Europe, 283 *and illus.*, 354; for cannon balls, 342; horseshoes, 290; tropical regions, 378; English, 449, 566, 571–572; European, 577(*map*), 578; Brazilian, 667

Iroquois Confederacy, 479, 480–481; American Revolution and, 598

Irrigation: Mesopotamia, 25, 26, 30; Egypt, 37, 42; Indus Valley, 46; Iran, 113; India, 185; Funan, 193; Anasazi, 211; Mesoamerica, 204, 205, 210; Andean region, 215, 216, 217, 220; China, 298; Muslim lands, 259, 260, 264; Vietnam, 318; Yuan China, 338; Delhi Sultanate, 377–378; dams and, 768; British India, 690, 769; Egypt, 683, 836; Green Revolution and, 820

Isaac (Israel), 64

Isabel (Castile), 371–372, 409, 412–413

Isandhlwana, Battle of (1879), 678

Isfahan, 527–528

Ishmael (Isma'il), 251

Ishtar (goddess), 29(*illus.*)

Isis (goddess), 43, 95, 157

Islamic empires. *See* Caliphates; Mughal Empire; Ottoman Empire; Safavid Empire

Islamic law (Shari'a), 262–263, 265, 528, 530; in Ottoman Empire, 519, 520–522, 618, 620–621; in Southeast Asia, 536; in West Africa, 678–679

Islamic Revolutions, 838, 847–849; in Afghanistan, 848; in Iran, 847–849 *and illus.*

Islamic scholars and schools, 263, 337, 363–364, 391–392, 526; ulama, 260, 268, 617–618; in Africa, 678–679, 780 *and illus.*

Islam (Islamic civilization), 262–270. *See also* Mosques; Muhammad (Prophet); Muslims; Shi'ite Islam; Sufi brotherhoods; African slave trade and, 509–512; meaning of word, 243; origins of, 250–254; Byzantine Empire and, 272–273; Christianity and, 63, 251, 252, 277(*map*); cities in, 259, 260, 263–265; civil war in, 254; conquests of (634–711), 255; conversion to, 255, 257–258, 259, 263–265; Five Pillars of, 253–254; in Spain, 258(*map*), 259–260, 264(*illus.*); polygamy in, 265, 393; revolts within, 257; Kharijites, 254, 256, 258; Quran, 253, 256, 262, 263, 265, 269(*illus.*), 391, 511 620; recentering of, 268–270; slavery and, 265, 268; umma, 253, 257, 260, 262, 268, 270; women in, 30, 265, 264(*illus.*), 268; in Central Asia, 325; in sub-Saharan Africa, 379–382; Mongols and, 325, 328–332, 339; Hellenistic technology and, 354; in Southeast Asia, 390–391, 392; literacy and, 265, 391, 780 *and illus.*; spread of, 389; maritime worlds of (1500–1750), 535–538; in Southeast Asia, 536; in North Africa, 510; in Ottoman Empire, 452, 519; pilgrims in, 423, 511, 536; Wahhabism, 525; West African reforms, 678–679; holy war (*jihad*), 675, 687, 885; slave trade in, 686; in Turkey, 752; terrorist militants in, 849, 874–875

Ismail, Shah, 526–527

Ismail (Egypt), 683

Israel: Egypt and, 836; Suez crisis and (1956), 836; Arab conflict with (1947–1973), 838–839; United States and, 839, 848; ultra-orthodox Jews in, 884; Hamas (Lebanon) and, 883–884

Israel, ancient, 63–67, 96. *See also* Jews; Judaism; Assyrian power and, 66–67; pork taboo and, 67, 242–243; origins, exodus and settlement, 63–65; protests against ruling class in, 66; rise of monarchy, 65–66; trade with Sheba, 66; fragmentation and dispersal, 67–67; Christianity in, 155–157

Istanbul, 516. *See also* Constantinople; elite in, 525; Isfahan compared to, 527–528 *and illus.*; mosques in, 517(*illus.*), 527; Ottoman reforms and, 617; population of, 758

Istanbul University, 620

Italy (Italians): Celts in, 100; Greek colonists in, 123, 126; Roman expansion in, 144, 147–148; Carolingian Empire and, 276; monasticism in, 285; universities in, 364; plague in, 353; trading cities of, 289, 291, 356–357, 409 (*See also* Florence; Genoa; Venice); Renaissance in, 367–368, 409, 436; maize in, 448; immigrants from, 659–660, 661, 710, 711, 775; invasion of Ethiopia by (1895), 684; unification of, 718–720 *and map*; conquest of Libya by, 733; in World War I, 734, 741, 744; *autostrada* in, 768; invasion of Ethiopia by (1935), 778, 781, 794; Mussolini's fascism in, 768, 792; poets of, 784; alliance with Hitler, 795; World War II and, 799(*map*); 800; in European Community, 819; aging population in, 862

Iturbide, Augustín de, 645, 648

Ivan III (Russia), 334

Ivan IV ("the Terrible," Russia), 516, 531

Ivory Coast (Côte d'Ivoire), 831

Ivory trade, 58, 68(*illus.*), 92, 416, 507, 537, 543; in Indian Ocean trade, 234, 386, 388, 389

Jackson, Andrew, 648–649; Indian Removal Act and, 654

Jackson, Michael, 892

Jacobins, in France, 604

Jacob (Israel), 64, 65

Jacquerie revolt (France, 1358), 353

Jaguar-god, 71, 200, 203

Jahiz, 266–267

Jainism, in India, 179–180, 186, 197

Jaja of Opobo, 685(*illus.*), 685

Jakarta, 538

Jamaica, 827; earthquakes and hurricanes in, 494–495; slave life, 493, 494, 496(*table*), 497(*table*); sugar plantations on, 493–499; slave rebellions in, 499

James I (England), 439, 489

James II (England), 455, 479, 485

Jamestown, Virginia, 476

Jammu, 828

Jamshedpur, steel mill in, 770–771

Janissaries (Ottoman military), 372, 519, 524; revolts by, 525, 617, 618; Selim III's reforms and, 617

Japan, China and, 301(*map*), 306, 337, 722, 745–748; war between (1592–1598), 540, 545–546; war between (1894–1895), 694, 729; Boxer Uprising (1900), 729, 747; Twenty-One Demands (1915), 748; Manchuria and, 795–796; war between (1937–1945), 797–798

Japanese Americans, internment of, 809

Japan (Japanese), 315–318. *See also* Japan, China and; migration to, 8; Buddhism in, 316, 347; chronology (645–1185), 319; Confucianism in, 316; Shotoku Constitution in, 305–306, 316; writing in, 316; Fujiwara period, 317; Kamakura shogunate, 317, 346–347; Mongol invasion of, 325, 326, 346–347; Ashikaga Shogunate, 347; piracy and, 341, 347; Europe and, 544–545; civil war in, 545; Dutch studies in, 722; economic growth in, 547–548; elite decline and social crisis, 547–550; Forty-Seven Ronin incident, 550 *and illus.*; reunification of, 546–547; Tokugawa shogunate, 546–547, 557, 720–721; warlords (*daimyo*) of, 544, 545, 546–547, 720–721; immigrants from, 694, 702, 712; pirates from, 545, 552–553, 722; Meiji modernization of, 722–724; Perry's opening of, 704, 722; railroads in, 705–706, 723(*map*); electrical engineers in, 709, 837; women textile workers in, 714; war with Russia (1904–1905), 727, 728, 732; westernization of, 724, 746–747, 894; industrialization of, 704, 724, 746–747; Korea and, 723(*map*), 729, 760; photography in, 760; rickshaw manufacture in, 757, 758; World War I and, 747; sewing machines in, 759; *zaibatsu* (conglomerates), 724, 747, 849; commercial radio in, 760; Depression (1930s) in, 788, 789; filmmaking in, 760; occupation of Burma by, 813; in World War II, 800–802 *and map*; World War II casualties, 803(*illus.*), 805; Southeast Asian nationalists and, 828; economic growth in, 747, 837; U.S. occupation of, 836–837; low fertility in, 862; popular culture of, 892(*illus.*), 894–895; industrial robots in, 869; traditions in, 894

Jati, 178. 769. *See also* Castes, in India

Java, 325; human fossils in, 3, 6; early migration from, 8; Buddhist temples in, 194(*illus.*), 195; Majapahit kingdom in, 390; British in, 692; Dutch in, 538, 542, 692; population growth on, 699–700

Jefferson, Thomas, 603

Jericho, 19, 20

Jerusalem: Temple in, 63, 65–66, 67, 69; Jesus in, 156; Christians in, 156, 244, 263; crusaders in, 261, 292, 293, 334; Holy Sepulchre in, 622; Islamic shrine in, 838

Jesuits (Society of Jesus), 438, 535; in colonial Americas, 481, 484, 485; in China, 450, 543, 554, 628; in Japan, 544

Jesus Christ, 155–157. *See also* Christianity; divinity of, 250, 250

Jewelry: amulets, 28, 43; Indus Valley, 46; Mycenaean gold, 57; Scythian gold, 97(*illus.*); Andean, 217, 218; Anasazi, 212; Indian, 389; Chinese, 543; bakelite, 766(*illus.*)

Jews. *See also* Israel; Judaism; diaspora of, 67; rules and strictures of, 67; in Alexandria, 137, 140; Jesus and, 155–157; Christianity and, 156; in Sasanid Empire, 249; Islam and, 252, 253, 268; in China, 299; in Spain, 259; mapmaking by, 381(*map*); moneylending by, 359; scholars, 363; persecution of, in Europe, 360–362; expelled from Spain, 358, 372, 453;

merchants and traders, 535; in Ottoman Empire, 618–619; eastern European, 660; in Palestine, 738–739, 755 *and illus.*, 818, 838; Russian, 710, 727, 755(*illus.*); Nazi Germany and, 793; Holocaust and, 805–807 *and illus.*; Zionist, 738

Jiang Jieshi. *See* Chiang Kaishek

Jiang Qing, 837

Jihad (holy war), 675, 679, 692; bin Laden and, 885

"Jim Crow" laws (United States), 657

Jin Empire, 308, 315; Mongols and, 336

Jingdezhen, 548, 552; ceramic works at, 343; labor protest at, 552

Jinnah, Muhammad Ali, 773–774

Joan of Arc, 370

João III (Portugal), 418

Joffre, Joseph, 735

John (England), 294, 369 *and illus.*

John Paul II, Pope, 855, 884

Johnson, Lyndon B., 825, 826

Johnson, Samuel, 591

Johnson-Sirleaf, Ellen, 881

John VI (Portugal), 641, 645

Joint-stock companies, 447, 458, 460, 501, 513, 567, 628

Jordan River, 20, 63, 65

Jordan (Transjordan): after World War I, 749, 754(*map*); Palestinian refugees in, 838

Joseph Bonaparte (Spain), 641

Joseph (Israel), 64, 65

Joshua (Israel), 65

Juan, Jorge, 472

Juárez, Benito, 652–653

Judaea, 155, 156

Judah, 66–67, 75

Judaism, 63. *See also* Israel; Jews; Christianity and, 63, 156; Zoroastrianism and, 118, 141; Islam and, 252; Khazar Turks and, 288

Julius Caesar, 152

Jungle, 376. *See also* Tropical rain forest

Junkers, Hugo, 764(*illus.*), 767

Junks (ships), 386, 403, 404(*illus.*), 411, 558

Junta Central (Spain), 641

Juntas, in Latin America, 642, 643

Jurchens, 307–308

Justinian (Byzantine Empire), 274, 275; plague of, 274

Jutland, Battle of (1916), 736

Juvaini, 'Ata-Malik, 329–330

Juvenal, 150–151

Ka'ba (Islamic shrine), 251, 252, 253

Kadesh, Battle at, 54

Kaffa, plague in, 327, 353, 355(*map*)

Kaifeng (Song capital), 307, 309(*illus.*), 311(*illus.*)

K'ak Tiliw Chan Chaak (Maya), 198

Kali (Durga), 183

Kamakura Shogunate (Japan), 317, 346–347

Kamikaze (divine wind), 346

Kamose (Egypt), 52

Kanagawa, Treaty of (1854), 722

Kanem-Bornu, 382, 518(*map*)

Kangxi (China), 543, 554, 555(*illus.*)

Kanishka (Kushan), 243

Kanto earthquake (Japan, 1923), 747

Das Kapital (Marx), 584

Karakorum, 324–325, 326(*map*), 336, 342

Karma, 178

Kashmir, Pakistan-India dispute over, 774, 828

Kassites, 26, 50, 52, 76

Kautilya, 184

Kazakhs, Russia and, 626, 631

Kazan khanate, 531

Keiretsu (Japanese alliances), 849

Kelly, William, 706

Kemal, Mustafa (Atatürk), 749, 752.

Kennedy, John F., 825, 834

Kenya, 240, 537, 679, 779, 781, 830–831, 885; early humans in, 5; independence of, 829 *and illus.*

Kenyatta, Jomo, 829 *and illus.*

Kepler, Johannes, 442

Keraits, 322

Kerensky, Alexander, 739

Kerma, 78, 93, 104

Kew Royal Botanic Gardens, 542(*illus.*)

Khadija (wife of Muhammad), 251, 252, 268

Khadim al-Haramain, 261

Khafre, pyramid of, 39, 40 *and illus.*

Khanates. *See* Golden Horde khanate; Il-khanate Empire (Iran); Jagadai khanate; Yuan Empire (China)

Khans, 324(*fig.*). *See also* Mongolian Empire; *and specific khans*

Kharijite Islam, 254, 256, 258

Khazar Turks, 288

Khipus, 398

Khitan people, 306–308

Khmer Rouge (Cambodia), 825
Khoisan peoples, 240
Khomeini, Ayatollah Ruhollah, 847–848 *and illus.*
Khrushchev, Nikita, 826, 834
Khubilai, Great Khan, 324(*fig.*), 324–325, 326(*map*), 331, 336; invasion of Japan and, 341, 346; Marco Polo and, 336; observatory of, 331
Khufu, pyramid of, 39, 40 *and illus.*
Khurasan, Islam in, 256
Khwarezm, 324
Kibbutzim, in Israel, 753, 755 *and illus.*
Kievan Empire (Russia), 287–288; Byzantium and, 273, 287–288 *and map*, 295; rise of, 287–288; society and culture, 289; Mongol conquest of, 324, 333
Kikuyu people, 830
Kilwa, 388, 389, 537
Kim Jong-il (North Korea), 883
King, Martin Luther, Jr., 826
Kingship. *See* Monarchy (kings, emperors)
King's Peace (England), 284
King's Peace (Greece), 134
Kinship systems. *See also* Clans; Lineages; farming communities, 18–19; Chinese, 87; Celtic, 101; Greek, 123; Northern Amerindian, 213; Indian, 177, 188; Islam and, 252
Kipchak khanate. *See* Golden Horde khanate
Kirov, Sergei, 787
Kitchener, Lord Horatio, 690
Kivas, of Anasazi people, 212
KLM Royal Dutch Airlines, 764
Knights, 280, 368; armor and horses of, 280, 285, 294(*illus.*); Crusades and, 292, 294(*illus.*); Portuguese, 371; Teutonic Knights, 334, 352
Knights of the Hospital of St. John, 517
Koguryo (Korea), 315
Kola nuts, 238, 377
Kollontai, Alexandra, 790–791
Kongo, slave trade in, 416–417, 418–420. *See also* Congo
Kongzi. *See* Confucius (Kongzi)
Korea (Koreans). *See also* North Korea; South Korea; Asian Tigers; Buddhism in, 315; China and, 165, 298, 301(*map*), 306, 314, 315; Choson kings in, 344–346;

printing in, 315, 344(*illus.*), 345–346; *hangul* writing in, 344(*illus.*), 345; technology in, 343, 342; ironclad warships of, 545, 557; Mongol conquest of, 344–345; Imjin War and, 540, 545; Choson, 550–551; Japan and, 729
Korean War (1950–1953), 823, 836, 854
Koryo, 315, 344–345, 551
Kosovo, 857; Battle of (1389), 335, 516, 518(*map*)
Kra, Isthmus of, 193
Kremer, Gerhard (Mercator), 450
Kremlin, in Moscow, 333(*illus.*)
Krishna (god), 174–175, 182, 186
Kshatriyas, 178, 180
Kufa, 255, 263
Kulaks (Soviet peasants), 786
Kush, 36, 93–94. *See also* Nubia
Kushan Empire, 93(*map*), 176(*map*), 186, 187, 231(*map*); Buddhism in, 243
Kuwait, Iraqi invasion of, 858, 873
Kyoto, 316–317, 347, 545, 547, 871; architecture of, 316; Onin War and, 347
Kyoto Protocol (1997), 871, 888
Kyrgyzstan, 631

Labor camps: Russian *gulags*, 532–533, 786, 787; concentration camps, 793, 806(*illus.*), 807
Labor (labor force). *See also* Encomienda labor; Indentured labor; Labor movement; Slaves; Workers; Egyptian, 38; Mesopotamian, 26–27; Assyrian, 62; Persian, 117; Olmec, 201; Chavín civilization and, 202; Chinese, 162; Andean (mit'a), 216, 220–221; Amerindian, 467–470; of children, 496, 497, 500, 580, 581(*illus.*); division of, 567, 568–569; Asian immigrant, 659, 668, 701; African colonial, 779; of women, in World Wars, 736(*illus.*), 737, 808–809
Labor movement (labor protests). *See also* Strikes; in China, 552; immigrants in Americas and, 660(*illus.*), 661
Labor unions (trade unions), 585; socialism and, 716; strikes and, 717; in Poland, 855
Laconia, 127. *See also* Sparta
Laissez faire, 583–584. *See also* Free trade
Lamas (Buddhist priests), 336

Lambeyeque Valley, Peru, 217
Land grants: in Assyrian Empire, 62; in China, 163; in Persian Empire, 115; in Egypt, 136; in India, 190; in Islamic caliphate, 261; in medieval Europe, 281; in Japan, 346; in England, 439; Mughal *mansabs*, 529, 530; in Ottoman Empire, 519, 521, 525; in Russia, 532–533; in Safavid Iran, 529
Landowners (landownership): Mesopotamian, 29; Assyrian Empire, 60; Greek, 124; Persian, 114; Roman era, 144, 153, 154, 158, 172; Chinese (gentry), 84, 161, 171, 172, 310, 311; Byzantine Empire, 274; medieval European, 279, 280–281, 290; East Asian, 314; Korean, 315, 345; Vietnamese, 348; Latin American, 471; Amerindian, 471, 477, 482, 578, 595, 640, 643; British, 353, 448, 564; Russian boyars, 448, 533; French Revolution and, 601; British India, 687; Ottoman, 524; Chinese, 551, 745, 748, 804; colonial Africa, 679; German, 725; Mexican *haciendas*, 696, 697–698; Argentine *oligarquía*, 775
Land reform: Mexican, 697, 698; Chinese, 796, 798, 804; Guatemalan, 833; Cuban, 834
Land speculation, in West Indies, 491
Lane, Edward William, 622(*illus.*)
Language(s). *See also* Arabic language; Writing; Afro-Asiatic, 19; human larynx and, 4; Semitic, 26; Akkadian, 26, 52; Aramaic, 26, 63, 96; Indo-European, 19, 96, 111, 177, 187; Sumerian, 28; Hebrew, 26, 63; Dravidian, 177; Celtic, 100; Meroitic, 95; Chinese, 81, 160, 300, 338; Latin, 144, 155, 350, 364, 366; Persian, 141, 257, 268, 526, 530; Greek, 57, 59, 137, 155, 332; Sanskrit, 178, 187, 190, 297, 299, 391; Bantu, 241; Coptic, 256; Tibetan, 299; Austronesian, 402, 405; Malaccan trader, 390; Malayo-Polynesian, 405, 406(*map*); Slavic, 287, 332; Swahili, 387, 537; vernacular, 365; African slaves and, 477;

Ottoman Empire, 519, 620; Turkish, 99, 519, 620; nationality and, 671, 718, 724; acculturation of immigrants and, 661; French, 620, 718; Indian, 769, 827; colonial African, 781, 830; Russian, 727; Spanish, 672, 724; English, 103, 718, 724, 769, 893–894

Laozi, 86. See also Daoism

Lapita peoples, 405

Las Casas, Bartolomé de, 467

Lascaux (France) cave paintings, 8

Late Bronze Age (1600–1000 B.C. E.), 50–59, 76. See also Assyrian Empire; China, early; in Aegean region, 56–58; fall of, 58–59, 76; in Middle East, 50–55

Lateen sails, 233, 385 and illus., 411

Latifundia (estates), 149

Latin (Roman) alphabet; 275; in Turkey, 752

Latin America. See also Americas, the; Latin America, colonial; *and specific countries*; indigenous peoples, 465; positivism in, 583; constitutional experiments in, 647–648; independence in, 641–646; racial discrimination in, 661–662; underdevelopment in, 662–666; women's rights in, 661–662; census in, 670–672; aviation in, 776; economic imperialism in, 696, 827, 832–833; military dictatorships in, 778, 789, 844; revolutionary movements in (1970s–1980s), 834, 844, 845–846; neoliberalism in, 847, 850; HIV/AIDS in, 861; population growth in, 861(table), 862; immigrants from, 867

Latin America, colonial, 465–475. See also Brazil, colonial; economics of, 468–470; imperial reforms in, 484–485; Northern colonies compared, 476, 477, 485; race and ethnicity in, 472–474; silver mines in, 468–469, 470; slave trade in, 470–471, 472–474, 476; society in, 470–471, 474–475; state and church in, 465–468, 467(illus.)

Latin American independence, 641–646; Bolívar and,

642–643; Brazil, 644(map), 645–646; Mexico (1810–1823), 643, 645, 644(map), 646(illus.); freedom for slaves in, 642, 643; roots of revolution (to 1810), 641–642

Latin Church, 288. See also Catholicism; Christian Church

Latin language, 144, 155; in Europe, 350, 366; in universities, 364

Latin West (Europe 1200–1500), 350–373; civic life, 358–359; Gothic cathedrals, 359, 363; humanists and printers, 365–367; Hundred Years War, 370; Iberian unification, 371–372; famine in (1315–1317), 353; mills and mines, 354–356; monarchs, nobles and church in, 368–370; monarchy in France and England, 370–371; Ottoman frontier, 372; peasants, population and plague in, 351–353; persecution of Jews, 360–362; political and military changes in, 368–372; Renaissance, 363–365, 367–368; rural growth and crisis, 350–356; social rebellion, 353–354; trading cities, 356–358 and map; universities and scholars, 363–365; urban revival, 356–363

Latvia, 727; independence of, 855

La Venta (Olmec center), 200

Law, John, 458

Laws (legal codes). See also Constitutions; Islamic law (Shari'a); of Hammurabi, 28, 29, 48; Israelite, 65; Chinese, 161, 304; Roman, 145, 152–153, 275, 285; church canons, 282, 285; Germanic, 285; Japanese, 315, 547, 548; Vietnamese, 325; English, 354; Spanish colonial, 468; natural, 583; British factory, 586; Napoleonic, 607; Ottoman reforms, 618–620; "Jim Crow" (United States), 657; Natives Land Act (South Africa), 678; working women and, 715; German, 725; Turkish modernization, 752; civil rights, in United States, 826; environmental protection, 840, 870, 871

League of Nations, 745; mandate system and, 749, 754(map);

Germany and, 745, 794; Japan and, 796, 810; passports and, 761; United Nations and, 817–818

Leakey, Louis, 3, 5

Leakey, Mary, 3

Leakey, Richard, 3, 5

Leatherworking (tanning), 382, 389; pollution from, 356

Lebanon, 68. See also Phoenicia; as French mandate in, 749, 753, 754(map); Palestinian refugees in, 838; conflict with Israel, 883

Lebensraum (room to live), 793, 800

Lee, Ang, 892

Legal codes. See Laws (legal codes)

Legalism, in China, 91, 162; Confucianism and, 88, 90, 161

Legislative Assembly (France), 603, 604

Legislature. See also Assemblies; Congress; Parliament; colonial America, 479, 595, 596

Lehman Brothers, 879

Lenin, Vladimir I., 739, 740; economic policy of, 744; Sun Yat-sen and, 747

Leningrad, siege of, 800, 801(map). See also St. Petersburg

Leopold II (Belgium), 679, 682

Leo X, Pope, 437

Lepanto, Battle of (1565), 519

Lesotho, 676

"Lessons for Women" (Ban Zhao), 167

Levant, 41. See also Israel; Lebanon; Syria

Liaodong Peninsula (China), 729

Liao Empire, 306–308, 309(map)

Liberalism: in France and Britain, 726–727; middle class and, 718, 725; nationalism and, 611, 718, 781

Liberia, 686, 881

Libraries. See also Books; in Assyria, 63; in Alexandria, 137; monastic, 286(illus.); in Vatican, 366; in Timbuktu, 391; in Philadelphia, 592; in Sokoto, 679

Libya, 41, 69, 839; Greek colony in, 122, 123; Persians in, 114; Romans in, 240, 290; Italian conquest of, 733; World War II in, 800–802; Arab Spring (2010) in, 881

Life expectancy: for slaves, 497, 497(table), 504; cult of

cleanliness and, 764; aging populations and, 862
Li family, 298
Li Qingzhao, 313
Li Shimin (China), 298, 302(*illus.*)
Li Si, 161
Lighthouse of Alexandria, 137
Lighting: candles and lamps; gas, 578, 712; electric, 707–709, 708(*illus.*), 708, 759
Lima (Peru), colonial, 465
Limbourg brothers, 352(*illus.*)
The Limits of Growth (study), 840
Lincoln, Abraham, 651; Emancipation Proclamation and, 657
Lineages. *See also* Clans; Patriarchy; matrilineage, 19, 95; Maya, 198; Aztec, 395
Linear B (clay) tablets, 57, 59
Linlithgow, Lord, 773
Linnaeus, Carolus, 591
Lisbon, 357; earthquake in (1755), 423
List, Friedrich, 583
Literacy. *See also* Education; Schools; Egyptian, 40; Greek transition to, 122, 131, 141, 224–226; Christian monks and, 285; Chinese, 310, 313; Islam and, 265, 391, 780 *and illus.*; East Asian, 314; Korean, 344(*illus.*), 344; printing press and, 445; Japanese, 722–724
Literature. *See also* Books; Libraries; Poets and poetry; Printing technology; Writing; Chinese, 167, 343; Indian epics, 174, 187; Abbasid Caliphate and, 266–267; Japanese women and, 317; European humanist, 365; Soviet underground, 854; global diversity in, 894
Lithuania, 334, 727; Poland and, 335, 532; independence of, 855; war with Russia, 371
Little Big Horn, Battle of, 655
Little Ice Age, 450–451, 523, 533; Chinese uprisings and, 552, 559–560
Liu Bang, 162
Liverpool and Manchester Railway, 574
Livestock. *See also* Cattle; Columbian exchange, 464; on Caribbean sugar plantations, 493; in Latin America, 468, 666; in Stalin's Russia, 786
Living standards: in United States, 789(*illus.*); Nazi Germany,

793; in western Europe, 819; Soviet decline, 854
Li Zicheng, rebellion of, 540, 553
Llamas, 17, 202, 215, 218; and alpacas, 71, 216, 399
Lloyd George, David, 741
Loans (credit): in China, 312; in late medieval Europe, 359
Locke, John, 455, 591
Loess (soil), 80
Logographers, Greek, 126, 127
London: peasant revolt in, 353; tobacco shops in, 489; growth of, 445, 576, 712, 758; *Beer Street*, 594(*illus.*); Crystal Palace in, 572; Big Stink (1858) in, 707
Longbow, 370
Long March (China), 796–797Looms, 357(*illus.*). *See also* Weaving; power, 571, 582, 724
López, Francisco Solano, 653
Lords and vassals, in medieval Europe, 280, 368
Lorraine. *See* Alsace and Lorraine
Los Angeles, 865(*table*); automobiles in, 765
Louis, Antoine, 605
Louisiana, 571; colonial, 482, 482
Louisiana Purchase, 650(*map*)
Louis Napoleon (Napoleon III), 612
Louis Philippe (France), 611
Louis the Pious, 276
Louis VII (France), 294
Louis XIII (France), 438
Louis XIV (France), 438, 502; Versailles and, 460
Louis XV (France), 601
Louis XVI (France), 601; beheading of, 604
Louis XVIII (France), 611
Lovett, William, 585
Lowell, Francis Cabot, 580
Loyola, Ignatius, 438
Luanda, 490, 509Lü (China), 164
Ludendorff, Erich von, 740
Lugal ("big man"), 27
Lug (god), 103
Lumière, Auguste and Louis, 759
Lumumba, Patrice, 816, 831
Lunar Society, 570
Lunda kingdoms, 509
Luo Guanzhong, 343
Luoyang, 84, 167, 170
Lusitania (ocean liner), 737
Luther, Martin, 437, 442, 452
Lutheranism, German speakers and, 438, 452, 720
Luxembourg, 819, 865
Luxemburg, Rosa, 717
Lyceum, of Aristotle, 132

Lydia, 114, 129; coinage in, 123, 243

Ma'at (divine order), 38
Macao, Portuguese in, 422, 537, 541, 629
Macartney, George (Macartney mission), 556
McDonald's restaurants, 853, 869
Macedonia, 134–135, 733; Antigonids in, 135, 137
Machine guns, 678, 684, 735, 747
Madagascar, Indonesian colonists in, 234; migrations to, 402
Madeira Island, 407, 410, 469
Madero, Francisco I., 697
Madras, 531
Madrasa (Islamic college), 268, 364
Madrid, terrorist bombing in (2004), 885
Magadha, 184, 185
Magellan, Ferdinand, 401, 414(*map*), 413
Maghrib, 753. *See also* Algeria; Morocco; Tunisia
Magic. *See also* Shamans; cave paintings and, 12; in Mesopotamia, 31; in Egypt, 43; in Celtic legends, 103; in China, 169; in Srivijaya, 195; in Africa, 381; witch-hunts and, 439–441
Magi (Persia), 114
Magna Carta (England), 369 *and illus.*
Magnetic compass, 308, 411
Mahabharata, 186
Mahavira, 179
Mahayana Buddhism, 184, 306, 318; bodhisattvas in, 182, 244, 299–300
Mahmud I, Sultan, 382
Mahmud II, Sultan, reforms of, 617, 618, 620, 622
Maimonides, 259
Maine (battleship), 695
Maize (corn), 197, 198, 209, 210, 393, 406, 796; beans, squash, and, 24, 194, 206, 208, 216, 381, 447; in Old World, 430, 447, 540, 550
Majapahit Empire, 390
Malabar Coast (India), 386, 389; Portuguese and, 418–420, 421, 423
Malacca (Melaka), 405, 525; Islamic scholars in, 392; Strait of, 402; port of, 390; Portuguese in, 422, 517; Dutch in, 536, 537, 541; British in, 692; Strait of, 387, 389, 390, 402

Malaria, 342, 378, 464, 498, 779; quinine and, 543, 700

Malaya (Malaysia), 311; tin from, 390; as British colony, 700 and illus.

Malay Federation, 828

Malayo-Polynesian languages, 405, 406(map)

Malay Peninsula (Malays), 189; Indian Ocean trade and, 192, 233, 390; maritime exploration by, 192; Srivijaya and, 194–196

Malcomb, John, 582(illus.)

Mali, 238, 379–382, 781; Ghana and, 258, 379; griot (storyteller), 224; Ibn Battuta in, 394; slave trade in, 393; trans-Saharan trade and, 380(map), 382; women and Islam in, 394; al-Qaeda in, 885

Malindi, 404, 417, 537

Malinke people, 381, 382

Malintzin (Malinche), 425

Malta, 69, 72(map)

Malthus, Thomas, 583, 859, 862

Mamluks (Turks), 260; in Egypt, 261, 326(map), 328, 334, 380, 525; as military slaves, 257, 393; Mongols and, 327, 326(map)

Mammoths and mastodons, 10

Manchester, England, 562, 612; industrial pollution in, 576, 707

Manchukuo, 795. See also Manchuria

Manchuria, 165; China and, 804; Russo-Japanese War (1904–1905), 727, 729; Japanese occupation of, 760, 795–796

Manchurian Incident (1931), 795–796

Manchus, China and, 540, 546, 552, 553. See also Qing Empire (China)

Mandala theory, in India, 184

Mandate (Son) of Heaven: in China, 83, 172; in Japan, 316

Mandate system, 749, 752, 732(map)

Mandela, Nelson, 832, 857, 881

Manet, Edouard, 652(illus.)

Manetho, 38

Mani and Manichaeism, 232, 250

Manila, Philippines, 865(table); economic development in, 695; garbage pickers in, 866(illus.), 867

Manioc (root vegetable), 464

Manco Inka, 427

Manors, in medieval Europe, 279

Mansabs (land grants), 529, 530

Mansa Kankan Musa (Mali), 381(illus.), 382, 407

Mansa Muhammad (Mali), 408

Mansa Suleiman (Mali), 382

Manuel (Portugal), 421

Manufactured goods (manufacturing). See also Industrialization; Industrial Revolution (1760–1851); and specific manufactures; Mesopotamian, 27; Carthaginian, 73; Egyptian, 94; Roman, 154, 238; Indian Ocean trade and, 234; trans-Saharan trade and, 238, 258; caravan trade and, 251; Kievan Russia, 287; medieval Europe, 291, 293, 357; Chinese, 342, 551; Venetian, 358; Gujarati, 389–390; Hausa, 382; Atlantic system, 502, 503(map), 512; Dutch, 445; imported, in Spain, 453; Iranian carpet, 528–529; division of labor in, 567, 568–569; interchangeable parts for, 572; mass production of, 551, 567–570; British Empire and, 485, 690; imported, in Egypt, 586; imported, in Latin America, 666, 696, 775; German tariffs on, 725; new materials for, 766–467 and illus.; overseas market for, 701; Japanese, 547, 850; computers and, 869

Manumission (freedom) for slaves, 475, 499–500; in United States, 580

Manuscripts, 285, 286(illus.)

Manuzio, Aldo, 367

Manzikert, Battle of (1071), 260, 293

Maodun (Xiongnu), 162

Maori people, 692, 694

Mao Zedong, 796, 810. See also China, People's Republic of; Cultural Revolution and, 837; Long March and, 796; Great Leap Forward and, 813, 837; death of, 852

Mapmaking (cartography): Jewish, 381(map); Portuguese, 410(illus.); Chinese, 451; Dutch, 447, 451(illus.)

Mapuche people, 465, 655

Maragheh, observatory at, 330

Marathas, 531, 686

Marduk (god), 31, 32–34

Mari, 54

Maria Theresa (Austria), 670

Marie Antoinette (France), 603

Marinetti, Filippo, 784

Maritime Revolution (to 1550), 401–429; global (before 1450), 402–408; Americas, 423–427; Atlantic Ocean, 407–408; Indian Ocean, 402–405, 406(map); European (1400–1550), 408–415, 414(map); Magellan, 401, 414(map); Pacific Ocean, 405, 406(map); Portuguese in Africa, 410(illus.); Portuguese voyages, 401, 409–412, 414(map); Spanish voyages, 401, 412–415 and map; Africa and, 415–420

Markets. See also Merchants; Trade; Greek agora, 122; Chinese, 7 Kievan Russia, 287–288; Champagne fairs, 357; Aztec, 395; Dutch, 435; Rio de Janiero, 486(illus.); Ottoman, 528; African women and, 394, 486(illus.), 779; telegraph and, 576, 706; Qing China, 586

Marne, Battle of the (1914), 735,

Maroons (runaway slaves), 500.

Marquesas Islands, 405, 406(map)

Marriage. See also Polygamy; Neolithic farmers, 19; Mesopotamian, 26, 28, 30; Egyptian, 42; Israelite, 70; Chinese, 90, 94, 303; Celtic Europe, 104; Alexander and, 135; Greek, 132; Roman, 145, 147; Indian, 182–183, 184–185; intermarriage, 139; divorce, 43, 70, 259, 303; Indian Ocean traders and, 231; Islamic, 259; medieval Europe, 275, 276; Mongol alliances, 314; Delhi Sultanate, 378; Lutheran, 420; Henry VIII and, 422; bourgeoisie and, 431; Ottoman Empire, 528; Hindu-Muslim, 530; Korean, 551; working-class women and, 580, 715; Victorian Age, 714; Turkish, 752; polygamy in Africa, 779; Stalin on, 791

Marshall Plan for Europe, 819

Martí, José, 695

Marv, 255

Marx, Karl, 716, 730; Bakunin and, 716, 717; Communist Manifesto, 584; Mao Zedong and, 796

Mary, mother of Jesus, 250
Maryland, colonial, 476, 485;
Masamune, Date, 544
Masonic lodges, in Russia, 628
Massachusetts: colonial, 478–479,
    485, 504, 596; cotton mills in,
    580
Mass deportation: in Assyrian
    Empire, 61, 67, 75, 76; in
    Mauryan India, 185
Mass production: in China, 308;
    interchangeable parts for,
    572; pottery, 567–570;
    assembly-line, 552, 768;
    consumer goods, 709
Mataram, Sultan of, 538, 542
Mathematics (mathematicians):
    Mesopotamian, 35; Egyptian,
    44; Babylonian, 139; Indian,
    188, 190; concept of zero,
    188, 190, 208; Chinese, 308,
    311(illus.); fractions and, 308;
    Maya, 208; decimals, 332; Il-
    khanate, 330–331, 332;
    Korean, 344; value of pi, 332;
    English, 444; Scientific
    Revolution and, 444
Matrilineal societies, 19; Nubian,
    95; Maya, 198
Matrix (film trilogy), 892
Mau Mau movement (Kenya), 830
Mauritania, 258
Mauritius, Indians on, 701
Mauryan Empire (India),
    176(map), 184–185;
    Buddhism in, 185, 243–244
Maximilian (Mexico), 651–652
    and illus.
Maya, 205–208, 466; ball games
    of, 207(illus.); calendar, 208;
    elite burials, 218, 219(illus.);
    pyramids, 206 and illus.;
    Toltecs and, 209(map), 210;
    urban centers, 198; women in,
    198, 207; writing of, 208;
    rebellion by (1847), 655
May Fourth Movement (China),
    748
Mazzini, Giuseppe, 718
Mbeki, Thabo, 881
Mbuti Pygmies, 239
Meat eating: in Stone Age, 9; in
    Egypt, 42
Mecca: Muhammad in, 251–252,
    253, 264; pilgrimage to, 251,
    253, 382, 423, 511, 536;
    shrines in, 251
Mechanization: in Korea, 345; in
    medieval Europe, 354; in
    colonial Mexico, 470(illus.);
    of cotton industry, 565,
    570–571, 586; protests

against, 584; of sugar refining,
    664–665; industrial robots,
    869
Médecins Sans Frontières (Doctors
    without Borders), 886
Medes, 75, 113–114
Media. See also Motion pictures;
    Newspapers; Radio;
    Television; in Mussolini's
    Italy, 792; global culture and,
    890–891
Medici family, 359, 367 437
Medicine (physicians). See also
    Disease; Health care;
    Egyptian, 44; Greek, 111;
    Indian, 230; Silk Road trade
    and, 229; Islamic, 293;
    Chinese, 337; medieval
    Europe, 353, 363; Kongo,
    420; African slaves and, 488,
    499; Jesuit, in China, 543;
    Ottoman school for, 620;
    radiology, 765; 662; cult of
    cleanliness and, 765;
    antibiotics, 805; Doctors
    without Borders, 886
Medieval Europe (600–1200),
    276–281; Charlemagne, 272;
    Christian church, 277(map),
    282–287; cities in, 289,
    291–292; Crusades, 292–295;
    Germanic kingdoms, 276,
    277(map), 278; Kievan
    Russia, 287–289; monasteries
    in, 285–287 and illus.; revival
    of (1000–1200), 289–292;
    self-sufficient economy,
    278–280; society, 280–281;
    technology in, 283 and illus.,
    290–291; time of insecurity,
    276–278; Viking raids in, 276
Medina, 252, 253, 255, 536
Mediterranean Sea and region. See
    also specific civilizations,
    peoples, and countries;
    Phoenician expansion into,
    68, 69, 71, 72(map), 73, 76;
    Greeks and, 119, 123; climate
    in, 144; Roman expansion in,
    146(map), 148–149; Indian
    Ocean ships compared, 233;
    Fatimid Caliphate power in,
    259; medieval Europe and,
    279; gold coinage in, 292;
    northern Italian cities and,
    291, 356, 358; galleys in, 395;
    trading alliances in, 411;
    Ottoman control of, 452, 525
Medvedev, Dmitri, 880
Megaliths, 19
Mehmed II, "the Conquerer,"
    Sultan, 516

Mehmet II, Sultan, 335
Meiji Restoration (Japan),
    722–724; industrialization in,
    722–724
Mein Kampf (Hitler), 793
Mekong River Delta, 193, 318
Melaka. See Malacca
Melanesia, 692; colonization of,
    405, 406(map)
Melqart (god), 69
"Memorial on the Bone of
    Buddha" (Han), 300
Memphis, Egypt, 38, 39, 43, 94
Men. See also Family; Gender
    roles; Marriage; Patriarchy;
    Women; Ice Age hunters, 11,
    13 and illus.; early agriculture
    and, 14, 30; Israelite, 66; and
    yin/yang concept, 91; fathers,
    in China, 87; Celtic, 101;
    Spartan, 127; bisexual, in
    Greece, 133; Roman, 145;
    Indian ritual and, 183;
    Muslim misogyny and, 265;
    Victorian "separate spheres"
    and, 713
Mencius (Mengzi), 86, 167
Mendoza, Antonio de, 464
Menelik (Ethiopia), 684
Menes (Egypt), 38
Menkaure, pyramid of, 40(illus.)
Mensheviks, 739, 740
Mercantilism, 504; capitalism and,
    501–502, 583
Mercator (Gerhard Kremer), 450 ,
    451(map)
Mercenaries, 831; Mycenaean, 57,
    58; Carthaginian, 73; Greek,
    141; German, 597
Merchant ships. See Ships and
    shipping (merchant marine)
Merchants (traders). See also
    Business; European
    merchants; Markets; Muslim
    merchants; Trade;
    Mesopotamian, 28; Indus
    Valley, 46–47; Assyrian, 50;
    Carthaginian, 73, 76; Cretan,
    58; Phoenician, 69; Greek,
    124; Roman, 155; Silk Road,
    169; imperial China, 167,
    170, 172, 299, 312, 313;
    Indian, 186, 188, 192;
    Persian, 233; Arab, 233, 251,
    386 781; Byzantine, 274;
    Kievan Russia, 287–288;
    European guilds of, 358;
    Indian Ocean trade and, 233,
    387; Chinese, in Southeast
    Asia, 341; Mongolian Empire,
    327, 336–338; taxes on, 370;
    credit and finance for,

358–359; Korean, 345; Gujarati, 389; Italian, 291, 356, 359, 409; Aztec, 395; Calicut, 423; Chinese in Indian Ocean trade, 402, 405; Portuguese, 416; spread of disease and, 431; African slave trade, 491, 508, 509; Armenian, 515, 527, 535; colonial New England, 479; Japanese, 547, 548–549; Timbuktu, 511(*illus.*); Jewish, 535; Chinese opium trade and, 629–631; French, in Africa, 679; West African, 684–686; commercial famines and, 813

Mercosur (Mercado Comun del Cono Sur), 876

Meroë, 94–95, 241

Mesa Verde cliff dwelling, 212, 213(*illus.*)

Mesoamerica: agriculture in, 16; Olmecs, 199–202, 201(*illus.*), 222; classic era (200–900), 203–208; Maya, 198, 205–208; Northern peoples and, 211–214; post-classic era (900–1500), 208–211; pyramids, 200, 201, 206(*illus.*), 206; Teotihuacan, 204–205; Toltecs, 207(*illus.*), 209–211 and map; 221; trade with South America, 408; Aztecs, 394–397, 423–427

Mesopotamia, 25–36. *See also* Assyrian Empire; Babylonia; Iraq; agriculture in, 25; Sumerians in, 26, 27, 30; Tigris and Euphrates Valley, 23, 24(*map*), 25, 50; cities, kings and trade in, 26–28; cylinder seal from, 29(*illus.*); Egypt compared to, 41–44, 47–48; *Epic of Gilgamesh*, 23; Amorites in, 28, 96; city-states, 26; gods, priests, and temples in, 30–31; society, 29–30; technology and science, 31, 34–36; irrigation, 25, 26; Kassites in, 50; Medes and, 113; Persian Empire and, 114, 116, 140; religious diversity in, 249; Seleucids in, 135; Silk Road trade and, 248; Alexander the Great in, 135; trade of, 234; decline of, 75, 261

Messenians, 127

Messiah: in Zoroastrianism, 118; Jesus as, 155; in Islam, 257, 526

Mestizos, 472–474, 475, 696. *See also* Mixed race, in Americas

Metals (metallurgy). *See also* Bronze; Copper; Gold; Iron industry; Mining (minerals); Silver; Steel production; Tin; Çatal Hüyük, 20; Mesopotamian, 35; Indus Valley, 46; Late Bronze Age trade, 55; Kushite, 94; Celtic, 101, 102(*illus.*); Southeast Asian, 193; Andean, 202, 217, 398; coinage and, 243; Song China, 308; Mongol, 335; tropical regions, 378, 379; lost-wax method, 378(*illus.*), 379; Mesoamerican, 408; mercury poisoning, 468; aluminum, 764(*illus.*), 767

Methodius (missionary), 275

Metternich, Klemens von, 611, 612

Mexica, 394–397. *See also* Aztec

Mexican-American War (1846–1848), 651

Mexican Revolution, 696–698; background to, 696–698; civil war (1910–1917), 698; institutionalized (1920s–1940), 774

Mexico City, 652; colonial, 465, 470(*illus.*), 643; boom in (1876–1910), 697; garbage dump dwellers in, 867; growth of, 862, 865(*table*)

Mexico (Mexicans). *See also* Mesoamerica; maize agriculture in, 16; Olmecs in, 199–202; Teotihuacan in, 204–205, 209; Maya in, 205; Mexica people, 394–395, 425; Toltecs in, 207(*illus.*), 204–205 and map; Valley of (1519), 380(*map*); Aztec Empire, 394–397; Spanish conquest of, 423–426; Amerindians in, 463; cattle and horses in, 464; chocolate from, 446; colonial, 465, 468, 470(*illus.*), 475; independence of, 644(*map*), 645, 646(*illus.*); Catholic Church in, 653, 698; French invasion of, 652; mining in, 663, 667, 668; Maya revolt in (1847), 655; civil war in, 696–698; Diaz regime in, 640, 697; oil industry in, 645, 774, 832; railroads in, 640, 705–706; Cárdenas reforms, 774; in United States, 809, 833, 867; economic development in,

584, 864; agricultural research in, 820; birth control policy in, 860; North American Free Trade Agreement and, 876

Michelangelo, 367

Michelino, Domenico di, 366(*illus.*)

Middle Ages, in Europe. *See* Medieval Europe (600–1200)

Middle class: Mesopotamian, 30; Egyptian, 40, 41; Greek, 124, 129; Roman, 145, 171; bourgeoisie, 445–448, 584, 603; Chinese trade goods and, 544; Enlightenment and, 592; cult of domesticity and, 581–582; early industrialization and, 563, 582; French Revolution and, 604, 607; Revolutions of 1848 and, 612; Latin American, 641; liberalism and, 718, 725; Mexican Revolution and, 696–698; urbanization and, 712; industrialized world, 709, 713–714, 761; electricity in homes of, 759; in Brazil and Argentina, 775–776; automobile and, 768; Indian nationalism and, 691, 768; Nazi Germany, 793

Middle East. *See also* Arabs; Islam; *and specific countries, empires, cultures, and regions*; Neanderthals in, 3; burial mounds in, 19; domesticated animals in, 16; early towns in, 19–21; Agricultural Revolution in, 15, 17; beermaking in, 17; trade in, 51(*map*); Late Bronze Age cosmopolitanism in, 50–55; Hellenism in, 141; Chinese trade with, 228, 338; Yuan China and, 336, 337; Muslim traders of, 403; African slaves in, 510, 511; after World War I, 749–754 and map; Arab-Israel conflict and oil in (1947–1973), 838–840 and map; immigrants from, 867; national and religious conflict in, 883–884

Middle Passage, in slave trade, 502, 504–506

Midlands, in England, 568, 576, 707, 712

Midway, Battle of (1942), 801(*map*), 802, 779

Mies van der Rohe, Ludwig, 767

Migration (population movement). *See also* Immigrants; Nomadic peoples; out of Africa, 3, 4, 6–8, 7(*map*); pastoralists and, 16–17; to ancient Egypt, 38; deportations, in Assyrian Empire, 61, 62, 67, 75, 76; Indo-European, 56, 96, 177; Israelite, 64; Kassites, 50; Celtic, 100–101; in China, 170; Greek, 136, 137; in Roman Empire, 159; from China to Southeast Asia, 192; from Southeast Asia to Madagascar, 234; Bantu-speaking peoples, 241–242, 245; Islam and, 263–264; Turkic peoples, 287; East Asian languages and, 315; from Southeast Asia, 405, 406(*map*); and drought, in East Africa, 537; rural-to-urban, 564, 585, 623; labor, in colonial Africa, 780; World War I refugees, 741; partition of India and, 773–774; Vietnam War refugees, 825; World War II, 805, 809; rural-to-urban, 738, 780, 864, 866; global, 867–868

Militarism, in East Asia, 344–348

Military, the. *See also* Armed forces; Navy; War; Weapons and military technology; Mesopotamian, 27, 28, 35; Egyptian, 41; Assyrian Empire, 60–62; Carthaginian, 73; Persian, 115; Spartan, 127; Macedonian, 134–135; Roman, 147, 148, 157; Chinese, 81, 91, 162, 165, 168, 170, 298, 311; Maya, 207; Teotihuacan, 205; Toltec, 209; Andean region, 217, 219; Mamluk, 257; medieval European, 276, 280; Jurchen, 307; Khitan, 306; Crusades and, 292; Delhi Sultanate, 383; Ottoman, 372; Aztec, 395; Prussian, 456; African, 507; Ottoman, 519, 524, 620 (*See also* Janissaries); French, 607; British, 482, 587, 610; Egyptian, 618; Qing China, 632, 633, 747; Zulu, 676, 677 (map); Japanese, 796; Latin American rule, 778, 789, 844, 846

Military draft (conscription): in China, 84, 168, 170, 797; in Ottoman Empire, 618; in

Japan, 724; of Africans, in World War I, 737; in Nazi Germany, 795

Military slaves, 257, 372, 393, 529. *See also* Janissaries

Military technology. *See* Weapons and military technology

Millet (grain), 1580, 239, 240, 307, 341, 377

Mills. *See also* Windmills; on sugar plantations, 492, 493, 665

Milosevic, Slobodan, 857

Minakshi, temple of (Madurai), 175

Mines Act of 1842 (Britain), 585

Ming Empire (China), 545; achievements of, 343; early (1368–1500), 338–343; Mongol foundation of, 338; technology and population, 341, 343; Vietnam and, 339, 340(*map*); Zheng He's voyages in, 321, 339–341 *and map*, 390, 403–404 *and illus.*, 406(*map*); Manchu threat to, 540, 552; rebellion ending, 540, 552, 559

Mining (minerals). *See also* Coal and coal mining; Metals; *and specific metals and minerals*; in east-central Europe, 354; tax on, in China, 341; in tropics, 378–379; in Latin America, 468, 663; environmental impact of, 468, 667; diamond, 677, 678

Minoan Crete, 49, 56–58

Minos (Crete), 56

Minotaur, 56

Minyak people, 306

Missionaries, Buddhist, 193, 297

Missionaries, Catholic, 364. *See also* Dominicans; Franciscans; Jesuits; in colonial Africa, 416, 686, 780; in Latin America, 466; in China, 541–543

Missionaries, Christian, 282, 424; in Africa, 244–245, 416; in Caribbean, 424; in French Canada, 480, 481; Nestorian, 250; Orthodox, 275, 288, 532; in Ottoman Empire, 620–621; schools of, 746, 780; in China, 540, 541–543, 631, 746; Protestant, 631

Mississippian culture, 211, 212–214

Mississippi Company bubble, 458

Mississippi River, steamboats on, 574

Mississippi Valley, 462

Mit'a labor, in Peru, 216, 469

Mitanni, 50

Mithra (sun-god), 157

Mitsubishi corporation, 747, 869

Mitsui companies, 547, 747

Mixcoatl (Toltec), 210

Mixed race, in Americas, 478; creoles and, 484; census and, 671; mestizos, 472–474, 475, 475; metís, in Canada, 481; mulattos, 473, 475; Haitian *gens de couleur*, 608; racial discrimination and, 661–662

Mixed race, in South Africa, 832

Mobutu Sese Seko, 816, 831, 857

Mocha (Yemen), 525

Moche, 216–217, 215(*map*), 220; elite burials, 218, 219 *and illus.*

Moctezuma II (Aztec), 396, 425–426 *and illus.*

Modernization. *See also* Industrialization; Westernization; in Russia, 561; of warfare, 623; in British India, 687; in Egypt and Ethiopia, 682–684; in Japan, 722–724; in Turkey, 749; technologies of, 763–765

Mogadishu, 374

Mohenjo-Daro, 45 *and illus*

Moksha (liberation), 179, 183

Moluccas (Spice Islands), 390, 413

Mombasa, 537

Monarchy (kings; emperors). *See also* Constitutional monarchy; Divine kingship; *and specific monarchs and emperors*; Mesopotamian, 28, 32, 35, 47; Egyptian, 38, 39–41, 43; Minoan, 56; Hittite, 58; Assyrian Empire, 60; Israelite, 65–66, 76; Kushite, 94; Nubian, 95; Scythian, 97; Persian Empire, 114, 115, 116; Roman, 149, 155, 172; Chinese, 81, 83–84, 164–165 *and illus.*; Indian, 186, 188; Srivijaya, 195–196; Sasanid Iran, 248, 249(*illus.*); sub-Saharan Africa, 240; Aksumite, 244; Byzantine, 273; Christian church and, 281, 368; English, 295, 368, 369(*illus.*).; German, 276; Buddhism and, 306; Chinese, 299, 308; French, 368, 453–455 *and table*, 456, 599; Mongol (khans), 324–327, 325(*fig.*), 326(*map*); Delhi Sultanate, 382–383; Korean, 344; Serbian, 335; West

African, 378(*illus.*)379, 381–382 *and illus.*; Zimbabwe, 388; Aztec, 395, 425–426 *and illus.*; early modern Europe, 452; Inka, 426; Kongo, 416, 420–421; Portuguese, 421; Spanish, 412, 454(*table*); English, 439, 453–455 *and table*; Enlightenment and, 444, 591; French restored, 611; Qing China, 544; Brazilian, 641, 645–646; Ethiopian, 684; Iran, 847

Monasteries (monks and nuns): Buddhist, 164, 175, 181, 183, 190, 292, 293, 332, 378; Christian, 284–287; Irish, 286 *and illus.*; nuns, 285, 303; closure of, in England, 436

Monetary system. *See also* Banks; Coins; Currency; Chinese paper, 312, 337; Mongol paper, 329, 332; capitalist *vs.* communist, 818–822

Moneylenders, 359. *See also* Loans (credit); in Indian villages, 769

Möngke, Great Khan, 324(*fig.*)

Mongolia (Mongols), 877; iron working in, 230; Liao capital in, 307; Galdan in, 552; sack of Baghdad by, 526; China and, 553, 629

Mongolian Empire (Mongols), 322–338, 348–349. *See also* *specific khans*; Khanates; sack of Baghdad by, 256, 258(*map*), 261, 324, 328, 389; in China (*See* Yuan Empire); conquests of (1215–1283), 321, 322, 324–327, 326(*map*); culture and science in, 329–332; invasion of Japan by, 325, 346–347; Islam and (1260–1500), 325, 328–332, 338; Korea and, 344; in Middle East (*See* Il-khanate); Ming China and, 338; nomadism and, 323–324; rise of (1200–1260), 323–328; Russia and, 323, 324, 326(*map*), 332–334; Silk Road trade and, 322, 337; trade and disease in, 327–328; Vietnam and, 325, 347–348; women in, 323

Monks. *See* Monasteries (monks and nuns)

Monophysite theology, 250

Monopolies, trading: Carthage, 73; Egyptian, 136; Chinese, 165, 312; Indian, 165;

Byzantine, 274; Portuguese, 412; West African, 424, 416; Dutch, 447, 538; French government and, 458; British government and, 459; colonial Latin America, 479, 484, 485; Chinese government, 746; British, in India, 772; government broadcasting, 890–891

Monotheism: Egyptian, 53; Israelite, 66, 67; Zoroastrianism, 117; Christianity, 156, 173; Islamic, 252

Monsoons: China and, 79, 82(*map*); India and, 44, 177; Indian Ocean trade and, 234, 234, 375, 386, 389, 403; Korea and, 314; Southeast Asia and, 192, 194, 377; failure of, and famine, 769, 813

Moon landing (1969), 827

Morality: abolition of slavery and, 656; Victorian, 713, 763

Morelos, José María, 645

Morelos (Mexico), revolt in, 697

Morocco, 69, 259, 675, 828; Portuguese in, 371, 409, 537; Songhai and, 510; French army in, 753

Moro Wars, in Philippines, 536

Morse, Samuel, 575

Mosaics: Northern Amerindian, 211; Roman, 238

Moscow, 531, 628, 758; Kremlin in, 333(*illus.*); Mongol conquest of, 324, 332–334; Napoleon in, 607, 625; Lenin in, 744(*illus.*); in World War II, 799, 800;

Moses (Israel), 64–65

Mosques, 264; in India, 382–383, 391; in Iran, 526, 527; in Istanbul, 517(*illus.*)

Most-favored nation status, 631

Mosul, 263

Mother goddess. *See* Earth Mother; Fertility cults

Motion pictures (film), 890; Lumière brothers and, 759–760; Indian, 892

Mound builders, Amerindian, 212–214

Mountain, the (France), 604

Movable type, in printing: in Europe, 367; in Korea, 310, 315, 344–346 *and illus.*, 550; in Song China, 310

Mozambique: Portugal and, 537, 682; independence of, 831

Mozambique Channel, 234

Mu'awiya, 254

Mugabe, Robert, 881

Mughal Empire (India), 423, 434; expansion of, 518(*map*); Hindu-Muslim coexistence in, 529, 530; political foundations, 529–530; Portugal and, 422; decay of, and regional challenges to, 531, 686–687

Muhammad, Mansa, 408

Muhammad Ali (Egypt), 618, 624; Britain and, 586; industrialization and, 585–586; modernization of, 682; reforms of, 620; Syria and, 622

Muhammad (Prophet), 227, 270. *See also* Islam; in Mecca and Medina, 251–252, 264; sayings of (hadith), 262, 264, 265; succession to, 253–254

Muir, John, 667

Mule (spinning device), 570

Mumbai (Bombay), 865(*table*); film industry in, 892; terrorist attack in, 881, 885

Mummification, 43, 44, 95

Munich Conference (1938), 795

Mural painting. *See* Wall murals (frescoes)

Muscovy, 531. *See also* Moscow

Museum of Alexandria, 137

Musharraf, Pervez, 881

Music: in early China, 87(*illus.*); African, 240; Byzantine, 274; European troubadour, 294; Chinese women and, 312(*illus.*); of immigrants, 661; Russian, 763; global culture of, 891

Muskets, 507, 524, 630

Muslim Brotherhood, 881

Muslim-Hindu relations, in India, 688; Delhi Sultanate, 382–384, 383–384, 388; Mughal Empire, 529, 530; in British India, 689, 770–771;

Muslim League, All-India, 770, 774

Muslim merchants (traders), 390, 391, 394, 403, 535; in Africa, 382; in Mocha, 525; Portuguese and, 422

Muslims (Muslim countries). *See also* Arabs; Islam; Muslim-Hindu relations; pork taboo and, 242; Crusades against, 261, 292–293, 350; meaning of word, 242; in France, 276; in Spain, 259–260 *and map*,

264(*illus.*), 294; in North Africa, 291; in China, 339; driven from Iberian peninsula, 371; hospitality and, 374; Italian cities allied with, 358, 409; in Red Sea region, 388; driven from Spain, 409, 453; in West Africa, 678–679; in Central Asia, 727–728; expelled from Greece, 741, 749; in Ottoman Empire, 452, 617; in Algeria, 675; in Sudan, 684; shrines in Jerusalem and, 838; al-Jazeera television and, 891; birthrates in, 863; terrorists, 881, 884, 885; women's rights and, 887–888

Mussolini, Benito, 768, 792, 800, 810

Mutsuhito (Japan), 722

Myanmar (Burma): British in, 692; Japanese conquest of, 813; independence of, 828

Mycenaean Greece, 49, 56–58, 121

Myrrh, 41, 53, 54(*illus.*), 234, 251

Nabopolassar (Neo-Babylonia), 75

Nabta Playa, 241

Nadir, Shah (Iran), 531

NAFTA (North American Free Trade Agreement), 876

Nagasaki, 704; Dutch studies in, 544, 722; atomic bombing of, 801(*map*), 803, 803(*illus.*)

Nairobi, Kenya, 887

Nalanda, Buddhist center at, 189, 392

Namibia (Southwest Africa), 737, 749, 832

Nanjing (Nanking), 339, 747; Taiping Rebellion and, 631; Treaty of (1842), 630, 633; Japanese in (1937–1938), 797

Nantes, Edict of, 438

Napata, 94, 95

Napoleon Bonaparte, 606–608; authoritarianism of, 606–607, 613; Europe of, 609(*map*); Haitian revolution and, 611; invasion of Russia by, 607–608, 609(*map*), 624

Napoleonic Civil Code, 607

Napoleonic Wars, 566–567, 607, 609(*map*), 675

Napoleon III (Louis Napoleon), 612, 653

Naqsh-i Rustam, 117

Nara (Japan), 316

Naranjo, 198

Naser al-Din, Shah, 760

Nasir, Gamil Abd al-, 836, 838

Nasir al-Din Tusi, 330

Natal, 677, 702

National Assembly (France), 602–603

National Colored Convention (United States), 657

National Convention (France), 604, 606–607, 610

Nationalism. *See also* Decolonization; Independence; in Revolutionary era (1775–1850), 590, 612; Greek, 618; liberalism and, 611, 718; state power, census and, 670; Austria-Hungary, 724; German, 437, 452, 720, 721(*map*); language and, 718, 724; Italian, 718–720 *and map*, 722–724; Japanese, 346, 795, 796; Social Darwinism and, 724–725; World War I and, 733; Zionist, 738; in colonial Africa, 780–781, 829; Indian, 691, 768, 769–771, 893; Vietnamese, 824; Palestinian, 838; economic, in Latin America, 832; and religion, in eastern Europe, 855; Hindu, in India, 881

Nationalist China. *See* Guomindang (China)

Nationality: census and, 671; language and, 671, 718

Nationalization (expropriation): in Russia, 740; in Mexico, 774 in Britain and France, 819; in Chile, 845; in Cuba, 816, 834; in Egypt, 836; in Iran, 847; in Nicaragua, 845

National liberation movements, 835, 846

National parks, in North America, 667

National People's Party. *See* Guomindang (China)

National Revolutionary Party (Mexico), 774

National Socialist German Workers' Party (Nazis), 793. *See also* Nazi Germany

Natives Land Act (South Africa, 1913), 678

NATO (North Atlantic Treaty Organization), 817, 822, 823(*map*); air war in Serbia, 857, 858(*map*); in Afghanistan, 884

Natural disasters. *See also* Drought; Flooding (floods); Volcanic eruptions; Indus

Valley and, 47; Moche decline and, 217

Natural law, 583

Natural resources. *See* Raw materials (natural resources)

Natural rights, 591. *See also* Rights

Natural selection, 3, 725

Nature. *See also* Environment (environmental stress); Daoism and, 87; Chinese deities and, 168; Scientific Revolution and, 441–444

Navajo people, 464, 654(*illus.*)

Navarino, Battle of (1829), 618

Navigation Acts (Great Britain), 485, 502

Navigation (navigational tools). *See also* Sailing (seafaring); Ships and shipping; in Southeast Asia, 193; rear-positioned rudders, 385; astrolabe, 411; magnetic compass, 308, 385, 411; Polynesian, 405; Portuguese, 411; Viking, 407

Navy (warships). *See also* British Navy; Pirates; Carthaginian, 69, 73–75; Athenian, 129–133, 132(*illus.*); Persian, 129; Chinese, 339; Mongol, 346; Portuguese, 417, 421, 422, 424, 428; Ottoman, 422, 516, 519, 618; Spanish, 456, 484; Korean, 546, 558; Russian, 534, 619(*map*), 727; French, 652; German, 734, 737; Perry's "black ships,", 704, 722; steam-powered gunboats, 587; in Spanish-American War (1898), 695–696; in World War I, 735–737, 740; Japanese, 727, 796, 797; submarine warfare, 737, 740, 798, 802, 785; in World War II, 799, 800–802; aircraft carriers, 799; United States, 800, 848–849, 885

Nawabs (governors), 531, 686

Nazi Germany (1933–1945), 792–795, 810. *See also* Hitler, Adolf; appeasement of, 794; economic and social policies, 793; Holocaust and, 806(*illus.*), 807; Argentina and, 777–778; Wehrmacht (army), 793 *and illus.*, 798, 800, 802, 807

Nazi-Soviet Pact (1939), 795

Ndebele people, 678

Neanderthals, 3, 8

Nebuchadnezzar (Neo-Babylonia), 67, 75

Nefertiti (Egypt), 53
Nehru, Jawaharlal, 835(*illus.*), 836; Indian independence and, 773, 828
Nemesis (gunboat), 587
Neo-Assyrian Empire. *See* Assyrian Empire
Neo-Babylonian kingdom: Chaldaean dynasty, 67, 69, 75; Persian Empire and, 114, 115
Neo-Confucianism, 310, 345
Neoliberalism: in Latin America, 847, 850; women's rights and, 850–851
Neolithic Age (New Stone Age), 9, 14–21; agricultural revolution in, 14–18; life in communities of, 18–21; in China, 80
Nepal, Gurkhas of, 688
Nepotism, 282
Nerchinsk, Treaty of (1689), 554
Nestorian Christianity, 232, 250, 299
Netherlands (the Dutch; Holland). *See also under* Dutch; art of, 446(*illus.*); Tulipmania in, 435; mapmaking in, 447; revolt in, 452, 459, 472; rivalry with England, 447, 459, 460, 590; textile trade of, 446; trade of, 435, 446–447, 459; urban poverty in, 449; Brazil and, 489, 590; independence of, 438, 459; North American colony, 479; slave trade and, 491; Atlantic economy and, 501, 502; Cape Colony, 510, 676; Japan and, 544, 548; slavery abolished in colonies of, 658; in East Indies, 538; Nazi occupation of, 799; flooding of, 809; decolonization of, 827; in European Community, 819; oil embargo and, 839
Nevskii, Alexander, 332, 334, 335
Nevskii, Daniel, 332
Newcomen steam engine, 572
New Deal (United States), 788
New Economic Policy (Soviet Union), 744
New England: Amerindians of, 463; colonial, 478–479, 485, 596; cotton mills in, 571, 580–581, 714
Newfoundland, 278, 480
New France, 480–482 *and illus.*
New Guinea, 8, 405, 406(*map*), 694
New Imperialism, 729
New Jersey, 599, 761
New Laws of 1542 (Spain), 467

Newly industrialized economies (NIEs), 852
New Mexico, native peoples of, 212
New Netherland, 479
New Orleans, 477; Battle of (1815), 649
New Spain, Viceroyalty of, 649, 649. *See also* Mexico, colonial
Newspapers: Crimean War and, 623; Turkish, 620; Indian, 769; nationalism and, 724; photography in, 760
New Stone Age. *See* Neolithic Age
New Testament (Bible), 155, 366
Newton, Isaac, 444, 445, 459
New Year's Festivals, 35, 36–37, 119
New York City, 745; birth control clinic in, 762; colonial, 479, 485; electrification of, 707–708; growth of, 576, 712, 758, 865(*table*); skyscrapers in, 765; stock market crash (1929) in, 787, 809; World Trade Center attack (2001), 874–875, 885
New York state, Women's Rights Convention in, 661
New Zealand, 405, 406(*map*); British colonization of, 693–694; European immigrants to, 710; immigration restrictions in, 741; Maori in, 692, 694; whaling off, 693
Nguni peoples, 676
Niagara Falls, power plant at, 708
Nian rebellion (China, 1850s), 633
Nicaragua, 667; United States and, 699, 846, 849; Sandinista revolution in, 845, 846; Contra war in, 846, 849
Nicholas I (Russia), 625, 627, 628
Nicholas II (Russia), 727, 739
Nicholas IV, Pope, 328
Nicholas V, Pope, 366
Niger, 238, 831
Niger Delta: 377; Benin, 416; palm oil trade in, 684–685, 779
Nigeria: colonial rule in, 680, 779; palm oil in, 779; Ibadan in, 779; radio in, 781; independence of, 830; democracy in, 857
Niger River, 239; flooding of, 377; gold mining in, 382
Niger Valley, copper in, 241
Nile River, 36–38, 241; canal to Red Sea, 114; flooding of, 15, 37, 47, 138, 683; geography of, 37(*map*); in Nubia, 92,

93(*map*); Aswan Dam on, 683, 836
Nile Valley, 23, 24(*map*). *See also* Egypt, ancient; migration to, 15, 240–241
Niña (ship), 413
Nishapur, 263
Nitroglycerin, 707
Nixon, Richard M., 837, 845
Nizam al-Mulk, 531
Nkrumah, Kwame, 830, 836
NKVD (Soviet secret police), 786
Nobel, Alfred, 707
Nobility. *See* Aristocracy (nobility)
Nomadic peoples (nomadism). *See also specific peoples;* Mesopotamia and, 28; Semites, 26; Egypt and, 41; Israelites and, 63; early China and, 82(*map*), 85; Meroë and, 95; in Eurasian steppes, 95–100, 106(*illus.*); China and, 161, 163(*map*); Silk Road trade and, 189, 193; Central Asian, 186, 230; Saharan, 236; Arab, 248, 250; Kievan Russia and, 287; Inner Asian, 323; in Iran, 529
Nonaligned nations, Cold War, 835–836 *and illus.*
Nongovernmental organizations (NGOs), 886
Nonindustrial world. *See also* Developing nations; limits of industrialization in, 585–587; global economy and, 709; raw materials from, 709; new technology in, 758–761, 761; Depression (1930s) in, 788–789
Nonviolence, Gandhi and, 771–772
Normandy invasion (1944), 799(*map*), 802
Normans. *See also* Vikings; conquest of England (1066), 278; in Sicily, 278, 292
North Africa. *See also specific peoples and countries;* cattle in, 16; Carthage and, 49; Phoenician colony in, 69, 241; Greek colony in, 111, 136; Rome and, 158, 238; camels in, 95, 238; Arab city-states in, 259; Berbers of, 256, 379; trading cities of, 291; Portuguese in, 409; Muslim rule in, 379, 409, 452, 510; Ottoman Empire and, 510; pirates in, 537; World War II in, 799(*map*), 800; immigrants from, 867

North America. *See also* Americas;
British North America;
Canada; United States;
Amerindians of, 211–214, 222;
mound builders, 212–214;
Southwestern desert cultures,
211–212, 213(*illus.*); Vikings
in, 276, 407; European claims
in (1755–1763), 483(*map*); fur
trade in, 446, 464, 480–481
and illus.; French and Indian
War (1756–1763), 482 *and
map*; immigrants in, 668, 710,
711 *and illus.*; industrial
economies of, 709; commercial
radio in, 760; electric power in,
707–709; mass consumption
in, 763; population in
(1750–2050), 861(*table*)
North American Free Trade
Agreement (NAFTA), 876
North Atlantic Treaty
Organization (NATO), 817,
822, 823(*map*); air war in
Serbia, 857, 858(*map*); in
Afghanistan, 884
North China Plain, 80, 81,
82(*map*), 103, 335
Northern Rhodesia (Zambia), 678,
679, 789
North German Confederation,
720, 720(*map*)
North Korea, 823, 823; nuclear
weapons in, 883
North River (steamboat), 574
North Sea region, 291
North Vietnam, 823–826. *See also*
Vietnam; treaty with United
States (1973), 823
Norway, 278, 762. *See also*
Scandinavia; Vikings; Nazi
invasion of, 802
Novgorod, 357, 531; Rus of, 288,
289
Nubia, 92–95; Egypt and, 36, 41,
52, 55(*illus.*), 58, 78, 92–95,
240; gold of, 41, 55, 92, 94;
Christianity in, 244, 380;
Meroë and, 94–95; Persian
expedition to, 114
Nuclear weapons: atomic bombs,
in World War II, 803(*illus.*),
805; Cuban missile crisis
(1962), 816, 826, 834;
proliferation of, 826; in Iran,
877; in North Korea, 883
Number system. *See also*
Mathematics; Mesopotamian,
35; Indian, 187, 188, 190;
Roman, 190
Nuns, 285, 303, 482. *See also*
Monasteries

Nur al-Din ibn Zangi, 261
Nuremburg, Nazi rallies at, 794(*illus.*)

Obama, Barack, 879, 880; on
climate change, 888; terrorism
and, 884
Obasanjo, Olusegun, 857
Obregón, Alvaro, 697, 698, 774
Observatories: in China, 330, 339;
in Persian Il-khanate, 332; in
Europe, 443(*illus.*)
Obsidian (stone), 20, 201, 210
Oceania. *See* Pacific Ocean (Oceania)
O'Connor, Fergus, 585
Octavian. *See* Augustus (Octavian)
October Revolution (1917,
Russia), 740
Oda Nobunaga, 545
Odyssey (Homer), 124
Ogé, Vincent, 610
Ögödei, Great Khan, 324,
326(*map*), 335
Ohio River Valley, Amerindians
of, 211, 212–214
Oil (oil-exporting nations): Mexico,
663, 774, 860; Arab-Israel
conflict and (1947–1973),
814(*map*), 838–839; World
War II, 800, 801; British
military and, 753, 755;
embargo (1972), 839 *and illus*;
in Kuwait, 858; organization
of (OPEC), 839, 876; Persian
Gulf states, 876, 877(*illus.*);
world economy and, 875–877
Oil palms, 684–685, 700, 779
Okinawa, 545, 552
Old Stone Age (Paleolithic), 8–14,
240
Old Testament. *See* Hebrew Bible
Olduvai Gorge, 5
Oligarchy: in Greece, 124; in Meiji
Japan, 722, 729; in Argentina
(*oligarquía*), 775, 777
Olives and olive oil, 119, 128, 129,
238
Olmecs, 199–202; stone heads,
200, 201(*illus.*); urban
centers, 199–201
Olympic Games, in Athens, 765
Oman, Indian Ocean trade and,
234; Musqat in, 537; Sultan
of, 686
Omar Khayyam, 330
Onin War (1477, Japan), 347
On the Origin of Species (Darwin),
725
OPEC. *See* Organization of
Petroleum Exporting
Countries
Opium trade, 624, 728, 884; British
India and, 629–630, 687

Opium War (1839–1842),
629–631
Opobo, Jaja of, 685 *and illus.*
Oracles: Assyrian, 60; Chinese,
80–81; Greek, 124
Oral culture (orality): Israelite, 64;
Celtic legends, 100, 226;
Greek, 122, 126, 131; Indian
Brahmins, 226; literacy and,
122, 131, 224–226; West
African griot, 224
Orange Free State, 677, 678
Organization of European
Economic Cooperation
(OEEC), 819
Organization of Petroleum
Exporting Countries (OPEC),
839, 876
Origin of Species (Darwin), 3
Orthodox Christianity, *See also*
Russian Orthodox Church;
Byzantine churches, 274, 287,
288, 289; missionaries, 275,
288; schism with Latin
Church, 273–274; Balkan,
617, 857
Osaka, 547, 707
Osiris (god), 43
Osman, 516
Osmanli language, 519
Ottoman Empire (Ottoman
Turks). *See also* Turkey;
conquest of Constantinople
by, 335, 350; Egypt and, 417,
422, 516, 586, 683;
expansion of, 372, 409, 516,
518(*map*); Portuguese and,
517; central institutions, 519,
522–523; economic changes
in, 524–525; Safavid Iran and,
518(*map*), 519, 521, 524,
526; siege of Vienna by, 452,
517, 524; Islamic law in,
520–522, 618, 620;
Janissaries in, 519, 522–523,
524; as "sick man of Europe,"
626, 733; Greece and, 611,
733; women, 621–622; Russia
and, 524, 533, 619(*map*),
625, 628; Tanzimat reforms,
618, 620, 621(*illus.*), 627,
628, 733; tobacco in, 524;
European reform model for,
616–622; Crimean War and,
622–624; ethnic minorities in,
733; Algeria and, 675; World
War I and, 738–739; division
of, after World War I, 749,
750, 754(*map*), 755
Owen, Robert, 585
Oxen, plows and, 15, 25, 107,
108, 177, 290, 351

Oxford University, 364
Oyo kingdom, 507

Pacific Islanders, 701. *See also specific islands*
Pacific Ocean (Oceania), 413; Amerindian trade in, 408; exploration of (before 1450), 192; Polynesian migration in, 405, 406(*map*); Magellan's crossing of, 401, 413–415, 414(*map*); Balboa and, 426; German possessions in, 694, 749; World War II in, 800–802 *and map*; population (1750–2050), 861(*table*)
Paekche kingdom (Korea), 315
Páez, José Antonio, 648–649
Pahlavi, Muhammad Reza, Shah, 847
Painting(s). *See also* Art and artists; cave, 8–9; Aegean frescoes, 56, 58; Greek vase, 126(*illus.*); Roman frescoes, 154; Buddhist caves, 189 *and illus.*, 307(*illus.*); Chinese, 312(*illus.*); Flemish, 367; Renaissance, 366(*illus.*), 367; Iranian miniature, 330, 526 *and illus.*, 527; Mughal miniature, 530; French, 652(*illus.*); post-World War I trends, 763
Pakistan, 186, 876; Punjab in, 135; Gandhara in, 342; Indus Valley civilization in, 23, 24(*map*) 44–47, 255; Kushans in, 186; Multan merchants in, 530; partition of 1947 and, 773–774; population of, 862; India and, 827, 828, 881; Muslims in, 827, 881; secession of Bangladesh from, 828; Afghan Taliban and, 849, 854; age distribution in, 863 *and figure*; bin Laden in, 885; nuclear program in, 883
Palanquins, 758
Palembang, 187(*map*), 194, 196, 390
Palenques, 474
Paleolithic (Old Stone Age), 9–14, 240
Palestine Liberation Organization (PLO), 838
Palestine (Palestinians), 94, 883. *See also* Israel; Syria-Palestine region; Crusaders in, 293; Britain and, 738–739, 750, 753(*map*), 754; division of (1947), 818, 838; in Gaza and West Bank, 739, 838, 883, 884; Jewish homeland in,

738–739, 750, 838 *and illus.*, 755
Palestinian Governing Authority, 883
Palmares (slave community), 474. *See also* Quilombos
Palm oil trade, 238, 684–686, 699, 779
Pampas, of Argentina, 465, 655, 663, 666, 775
Pan-Africanists, 741, 781
Panama, 16; American intervention in, 698; Isthmus of, 426
Panama Canal, 699, 846
Pan American Airways, 776
Pandyas, 187
Pankhurst, Emmeline, 714 *and illus.*, 715
Pan-Slavism, 626
Papacy (popes), 282–285, 855. *See also specific popes*; schism with Orthodox Church, 273–274; monarchs and, 282–284; excommunication and, 284, 334, 361; Crusades and, 293; Jews protected by, 358, 360–362; Peter's pence and, 359; building program of, 367; schism within, 368; treaty negotiation by, 413; building projects, 436; Protestant Reformation and, 436–438; Henry VIII and, 439; Jesuits and, 543; conservatism of, 884
Papal states, 719 *and map*
Papermaking: papyrus for, 38, 68; in China, 169; in Middle East, 247, 256
Paper money: in China, 311, 337; in Mongolian Empire, 329, 332; French speculators and, 458; Chinese, 551; in colonial America, 596; French Revolution, 603
Papyrus, 40, 41, 68
Paraguay, 643, 644(*map*), 645; dictatorship in, 648; war with Brazil (1865–1870), 657; Mercosur trade agreement and, 876
Paris: watermills in, 354; University of, 364; apartment house in, 579(*illus.*); growth of, 445, 758; Enlightenment salons in, 590; French Revolution and, 600 *and illus.*, 602, 603, 604; Revolution of 1848 and, 612; as "city of lights," 708(*illus.*), 712; Olympics in (1900), 765

Paris, Treaty of (1783), 598
Paris Peace Conference (1919), 741, 748, 749
Parkes, Alexander, 767
Parlement of Paris, 441, 601
Parliament (Britain), 356, 371, 439; House of Commons, 454, 479; House of Lords, 371, 454, 771; American Revolution and, 595; child labor law and, 585
Parsees, 118. *See also* Zoroastrianism
Parthenon, in Athens, 131
Parthians, 248, 249; Rome and, 100, 146(*map*), 158
Passports, 761; in Mongolian Empire, 325(*illus.*), 333
Pastoralism (pastoralists). *See also* Cattle (cattle herders); animal domestication and, 16–17; gods of, 19; Israelite, 63–64; Central Asian, 17; trade with farmers, 64, 161; on Eurasian steppes, 95–100, 106(*illus.*); in Africa, 238; Arab, 248, 250; in tropics, 375–376
Pataliputra (modern Patna), 185, 187
Paterfamilias, in Rome, 145
Patriarchs: of Alexandria, 244, 263, 420; of Antioch, 263; of Constantinople, 274, 282, 288; of Serbia, 335
Patriarchy: in Iran, 114; in Rome, 145; in India, 177; in colonial societies, 464
Patrick (Saint), 296
Patrilineage, 19
Patrona Halil rebellion, 525
Patron/client relationship, 145
Paul (apostle), 156, 437
Pax deorum (peace of the gods), 148
Pax romana (Roman peace), 154
Peacekeeping, United Nations and, 818
Peace of Augsburg (1555), 452
Pearl Harbor (Hawaii), 694; Japanese attack on (1941), 800–801, 801(*map*)
Peasants (peasantry). *See also* Farmers; Rural areas; ancient Egyptian, 41; Late Bronze Age, 50; Mycenaean, 57; Israelite, 66; Tunisian, 73; Chinese, 84–85, 161, 170; Persian, 114; Greek, 124; Roman, 149; Mesoamerican, 204–205; European, 279–280, 351–353 *and illus.*, 448–449; Ottoman, 519;

Russian (serfs), 289, 333, 532, 534; Chinese, 556, 745; rebellions by, 353, 598; French Revolution and, 602; Brazilian, 777; Egyptian, 587, 682–683; freedom for Russian, 626–627, 628, 727; Indian, 189, 687, 769; Mexican, 696–697; in Soviet Union, 739, 742, 785, 786, 814; Middle Eastern, 750; Chinese, 745, 748, 796, 797, 804, 813

Pedro I (Brazil), 645

Pedro II (Brazil), 646

Pei, W. C., 3

Peking man, 3, 6

Peloponnesian League, 128

Peloponnesian War, 134

Penal colonies. See also Prisons and prisoners; in Siberia, 532; in Australia, 692–693

Penn, William, 480

Pennsylvania, 701, 874; colonial, 480

People of the Book, 268. See also Christians; Jews; Zoroastrians

Pepi II (Egypt), 78

Pepin (Franks), 276, 282

Pepper trade, 416, 423, 536, 692. See also Spice trade

Perestroika (Soviet reform), 854

Pericles (Greece), 128, 131, 134

Periplus of the Erythraean Sea, 245

Perkin, William, 706

Perón, Eva Duarte, 778

Perón, Isabel Martínez de, 645

Perón, Juan, 777(illus.), 778, 845

Perry, Matthew C., opening of Japan by, 704, 722

Persepolis (Parsa), 116, 118(illus.)

Pershing, John, 698

Persian Gulf region: Medes and, 113–114; Indian Ocean trade and, 233, 234–235, 385; shipbuilding in, 308; Chinese expeditions to, 339, 340(map); Ottoman control of, 422; Hormuz and, 422, 517; oil wealth in, 876, 877(illus.); Qatar, 839, 891; United States Navy in, 849

Persian Gulf War (1990–1991), 858, 891

Persian language, 141, 257, 270, 391, 526, 530

Persian Wars, 129–130, 135

Persia (Parsa), 26, 233

Persia (Persian Empire), 112–118. See also Iran; chronology (1000–30 B.C.E.), 142; ideology and religion,

118–119, 120, 140; kingship in, 120–121; organization of, 117–118; rise of, 116–118; rivalry with Greece, 111, 116, 127, 128, 129, 133; Alexander's conquest of, 135; Scythians and, 98

Personal identification, 761

Personalist leaders, 648–649

Peru. See also Inka; textiles of, 70; Chavín of, 202–203; Chimú Empire in, 220–221; Moche of, 216–217 and map, 219 and illus.; Wari of, 220; colonial, 465, 468, 470–471, 475; Amerindian revolt in, 484–485; volcanic eruption in, 559; independence of, 642, 643; alliance with Bolivia, 643; Chinese immigrants in, 659; shrinking glaciers in, 871

Peter's pence, 359

Peter the Great, (Russia), 533–535 and illus., 627

Petrarch, Francesco, 365, 366

Petrograd, 739, 740. See also St. Petersburg

Petroleum. See Oil (oil-exporting nations)

Pharaohs, of Egypt, 53–54, 64; crowns of, 38

Philadelphia: colonial, 480, 592; Constitutional Convention in, 598

Philip II (Macedonia), 132, 133–134 and illus.

Philip II (Spain), 438, 452, 459; Counter-Reformation and, 438, 453; Dutch revolt and, 453, 459, 489

Philippine Islands (Filipinos): Magellan in, 401, 414(map); Spanish and, 401, 413, 536, 541; Muslims in, 536; labor migrations from, 694, 712; United States and, 694–695 and illus., 693; in World War II, 801(map); independence of, 828

Philip "the Fair" (France), 368

Philip V (Spain), 484

Philistines, 58; Israel and, 63, 65, 68, 76

Philosophy. See also Confucianism; Daoism; Political thought; and specific philosophers; Greek, 126, 131, 293, 363; in Islamic Spain, 259–260; Enlightenment, 591–593; Chinese philosopher-kings, 543, 628; positivism, 583

Phoenician language, 26

Phoenicia (Phoenicians), 61(map), 76; alliance with Israel, 65, 68; city-states, 52, 67, 68, 69; colonies of, 71, 72 and map, 75, 76, 241; dyes and textiles of, 68, 70–71; explorations of, 72(map), 233; trade of, 68, 72 and map; writing of, 68, 121, 224

Photography, 760

Physics, revolution in, 441, 762

Picasso, Pablo, 763

Piccolomini, Aeneas Silvius, 350

Piedmont-Sardinia, 719, 719(map)

Pigs, 21, 80; domestication of, 107–108, 242–243; taboo on eating (pork), 242

Pilgrims (pilgrimages): Buddhist, 180(illus.), 188, 195, 243–244, 297; Hindu, 183, Mesoamerican, 205, 211; Mississippian, 213; East Asian, 193; Christian, 284; Islamic (Mecca), 251, 252, 253, 382, 511, 536; in New England, 478; in India, 690, 691

Pillow Book (Sei), 317

Pimiko (Himiko), 315

Pin-makers' workshop, 568–569 and illus.

Pinochet, Augusto, 84

Pinta (ship), 413

Piraeus, 131, 134

Pirates. See also Vikings; Greek, 57; Southeast Asian, 195, 390; Japanese, 341, 347, 545, 552, 722; North African, 537; European, 541; Zheng family, 557

Pisa, Italy, 291

Pisistratus, 128

Pius IX, Pope, 718

Pizarro, Francisco, 426, 471

Plague, 463, 633. See also Bubonic plague; of Justinian, 274

Planck, Max, 762

Plantation societies, 513. See also Rubber plantations; Sugar plantations; in American South, 476–467; indigo, 477, 707; clove, on Zanzibar, 686

Planter elite (plantocracy): in American South, 476, 477; in West Indies, 493, 494, 498; Haitian Revolution and, 561, 589, 608–611

Plastic, 766 and illus.

Plato, 131, 132, 363

Platt Amendment (United States), 699

Pleiades (star cluster), 138
Pleistocene epoch, 6
Plows, 17, 275, 289, 310, 347; horses and, 107, 290, 351; oxen and, 25, 107, 108, 177, 290, 354; steel, 665
Plutarch, 74
Plymouth colony (Massachusetts), 478
Poets and poetry. *See also* Literature; Egyptian, 42; Greek, 125–126 (*See also* Homer); Roman, 148, 150; Arab and Islamic, 255; Chinese, 84, 170, 228, 302, 313; European troubadour, 294; Japanese, 317; Italian, 365; Persian (Safavid), 515, 519; Chinese, 543; Italian, 784
Poison gas, in warfare, 737, 807
Poland-Lithuania, 335, 532
Poland (Poles), 292; Mongols and, 324; immigrants from, 710; Russia and, 574, 740; independence of, 741, 743 *and map*; Nazi invasion of, 795, 802; World War II casualties, 805, 807; Soviet invasion of, 799; communist regime in, 822; Roman Catholicism in, 807, 855; fall of communism in, 855, 858(*map*)
Polar regions, warming in, 823
Polis (city-state), in Greece, 121–125. *See also* Athens; Sparta
Political corruption. *See* Corruption
Political reforms. *See* Reforms
Political systems and institutions. *See also* Administration; Government; Monarchy; Political thought; *and specific institutions;* Mesopotamian, 25; Athenian, 128; Indian, 174, 185–187, 190; Olmec, 199; Anasazi, 211; imperial China, 297; Japanese, 346–348; Aztec alteptl, 394, 395; challenges to, in Europe, 436; in British America, 476, 479
Political thought (ideology). *See also* Confucianism; Legalism, in China, 88, 89, 91; democracy, in Greece, 124; Locke and, 455, 591; liberalism, 611; Russian Pan-Slavism, 626; Industrial Revolution and, 584; of Gandhi, 760

Politics. *See also* Political systems and institutions; Sasanid Iran, 248; fragmentation of Arab caliphate and, 255–260; Christian Church and, 282–285; Mongol, 323; religion and, 437; European innovations, 452–460; planter elite in, 499; Russian, 532; chronology (1853–1910), 730–731; French, 726; in British India, 770; famine and, 813; in colonial Africa, 780–781; religion and, 884–886
Pollution: from coal burning, 576, 707; from mining, 667; horses and, 713, 768; of rivers, 576–578, 707; legislation to control, 841, 870
Polo, Marco, 327, 385, 389; route of, 326(*map*)
Pol Pot (Cambodia), 825
Polygamy: in Mesopotamia, 25; in Egypt, 54; in Israel, 64; of Kushite kings, 94; of Persian kings, 115; of Alexander the Great, 135; in Islam, 265, 392; in Kievan Russia, 289; in China, 313
Polynesia. *See also specific islands;* colonization of, 405, 406(*map*); Maori of New Zealand, 692–693, 694
Polytheism: Olmec, 204; Teotihuacan, 204–205; Maya, 205–208; Moche, 216–217; Aztec, 394; Inka, 394; Semitic, 251; Christian church and, 282; Kievan Russian, 289; West African, 378
Pondicherry, 531
Pontiac (Ottawa chief), 595
Pontius Pilate, 156
Poor countries. *See also* Poverty; Third World (developing nations); population growth in, 844, 864, 870; urban growth in, 865(*table*), 866–867
Pope, Alexander, 444
Popes. *See* Papacy (popes); *specific popes*
Popular authoritarianism, of Napoleon, 606–607, 613
Popular culture. *See also* Folk cultures; global spread of, 891–892
Popular sovereignty, 597, 602, 646, 829
Population movement. *See* Immigrants; Migration (population movement)

Population (population growth). *See also* Birthrates; agriculture and, 17, 18, 22, 177, 430; Indus Valley, 47; Carthage, 69–70; Greece, 122, 123; Mesoamerica, 205, 206; Andean, 219; imperial China, 165–166, 312, 337, 343; late medieval Europe, 289; South Asia, 377; Inka, 397; agriculture and increase in, 430, 464; climate and, 430–431 *and fig.*; Amerindian, 463; colonial Americas, 485; food supply and, 583; imperial China, 556, 629, 745, 859; industrialized Europe, 563, 710, 725, 859; Japan, 548, 746; census and, 670–672; immigration in United States and, 663; Australia, 692–693; India, 769–770; Africa, 828–829; developing nations, 700, 845, 859, 862, 867, 872; urbanization and, 712, 758; challenge of, 859–863; demographic transition and, 859–862; industrialized nations, 864; age structure comparison, 863–864 *and figure*; largest urban areas, 865(*table*); world (2000–2050), 872
Populist dictatorship, in Argentina, 777(*illus.*), 777–778
Porcelain, 565. *See also* Pottery; Chinese, 343, 347, 404, 543, 548; Japanese, 546, 549 *and illus.*
Pork. *See also* Pigs; taboo on eating, 67, 242
Porres, Martín de, 467(*illus.*)
Portsmouth, Treaty of (1905), 729
Portugal (Portuguese). *See also* Portuguese maritime explorations; African slave trade and, 411, 416, 417, 418, 419, 508; in North Africa, 371, 409; claim to Brazil, 412, 413; Lisbon earthquake, 440; in East Africa, 417–420, 422, 537; navy of, 417, 421, 422, 423, 428 ; Iberian unification and, 371; Indian Ocean trade and, 412, 415, 417, 420–421, 433 *and illus.*; Napoleon's invasion of, 607, 609(*map*), 641; Ottoman Empire and, 516, 519; in European Community, 819; Brazilian soap operas in, 890

Portuguese colonies. *See also* Brazil, as Portuguese colony; sugar plantations, 489; in Africa, 508, 511, 590, 682, 831; Macao, 422, 537, 541, 629; decolonization, 831

Portuguese maritime explorations, 401, 408, 411, 414(*map*); in Africa, 410(*illus.*), 411, 414(*map*), 415–416, 417; in Atlantic, 407, 414(*map*); da Gama, 412, 417(*map*), 417, 420–421

Poseidon (god), 124

Positivism, 583

Postal system, in Arabic Caliphate, 257–258

Potatoes, 199, 216, 218, 424, 448, 564, 737; sweet, 216, 341, 405, 424, 464, 556; Irish famine and, 580, 812

Potosí, silver mines at, 468

Potter's wheel, 35, 46, 80

Pottery. *See also* Ceramics; Porcelain; Mesopotamian, 35; Cretan, 56, 58; Greek vases, 58, 126(*illus.*); Southwestern desert cultures, 211; Chinese, 234, 299; Korean, 344, 546; mass production of, 567–570 *and illus.*

Pound sterling (British currency), 623, 709

Poverty (the poor). *See also* Poor countries; in Roman Empire, 152, 154; in Europe, 351, 359, 445, 448, 449; of rural-to-urban migrants, 585; French Revolution and, 600; housing for, 713; immigrants and, 711; nationalist appeals to, 724; of industrial workers, 576, 582–583; cotton clothing for, 580–581; in British India, 690, 769–770, 771–772; of Japanese farmers, 795; Depression of 1930s, 788–789 *and illus.*, 795; in Latin America, 776; global trends in, 864–866; in China, 797, 843

Power. *See* Balance of power; Great powers

Power looms, 571, 582

Po Zhuyi, 228

Prakrits (languages), 187

Prices (price inflation). *See also* Inflation; in Roman Empire, 158; in China, 551; Japanese speculators, 547; French Revolution and, 598, 599; opium trade, 624; Depression (1930s) and, 776; oil demand and (1973–2000), 839 *and illus.*, 840, 847, 849, 876

Priests (clergy). *See also* Bishops; Brahmins; Papacy; Religion(s); Mesopotamian, 31, 32; Egyptian, 42–43; Indus Valley, 45(*illus.*); Assyrian, 59; Israelite, 62, 66; Celtic druids, 100, 101, 103, 224; Iranian (Magi), 114; Roman, 147; Mesoamerican, 200, 205, 208; Andean, 202; Christian, 156, 283; Zoroastrian, 250; European monks, 285–286; Kievan Russia, 287, 289; Muslim clerics, 391, 846, 847; Tibetan lamas, 336; tax exemption and, 456; colonial Latin America, 467–468; African, 511; Christian, in Japan, 544; French Revolution and, 600, 601, 602, 603, 607; Mexican independence and, 643, 646(*illus.*); Ukrainian, 627; Salvadorean death squads and, 823; Polish Solidarity and, 829

Primogeniture, 161

Princip, Gavrilo, 732

Printing technology. *See also* Books; in China, 310; Korean, 310, 315, 344–346 *and illus.*, 550; woodblock, 269(*illus.*), 310, 315, 344–346; movable type, 310, 315, 344–346 *and illus.*, 550; humanists in Europe and, 365 ; Luther and, 437; European literacy and, 444; Dutch, 446; in colonial Americas, 465; woodblock, 550(*illus.*), 760; for cotton textiles, 571

Prisoners of war, 81. *See also* Slaves, prisoners of war; World War II, 799; Geneva Conventions and, 887

Prisons and prisoners: penal colonies, in Australia, 693; reconcentration camps, in Philippines, 695; Russian *gulags*, 532, 787; concentration camps, World War II, 793, 806(*illus.*), 807; Japanese American internment, 809

Proclamation of 1763 (Britain), 595

Progress, belief in, 445, 762; imperialism and, 699

Propaganda: in Assyria, 50; Persian kings and, 114, 116, 118; in China, 797; Crimean War, 622; European fascist, 792; in Soviet Russia, 786; World War II, 782, 830; al-Qaeda, 874

Property rights. *See also* Inheritance; Landowners (landownership); in China, 161; of women, 42, 265, 379, 527, 621; of free blacks, in West Indies, 494; in France, 607; middle class and, 612

Prophets: Israelite, 66, 67, 68; Islamic (*See* Muhammad)

Prophet (Tenskwatawa), 654

Prostitution, 23, 690, 795. *See also* Concubines

Protestantism. *See also specific denominations;* Reformation, 436–438; witch-hunts and, 439, 440; science and, 441; wars of religion and, 444; in England (*See* Anglicanism); and conservatism, in United States, 883

Protests (demonstrations). *See also* Strikes; in Argentina, 775; in China, 551, 853; in colonial Americas, 595–596; folk cultures and, 593–595; industrial reforms and, 584–585; Indian independence and, 769, 770, 772 *and illus.*, 773; South African, 831; Iranian, 847; against World Trade Organization, 577; unemployment, 879(*illus.*); Arab Spring (2010), 881, 882(*illus.*), 891

Proxy wars, in Cold War era, 844

Prussia, 352, 357, 457(*map*), 761; army of, 456, 723; French Revolution and, 603, 607; Jews in, 358; railroads in, 574; conservatism in, 611; German unification and, 612, 720, 721(*map*); war with France (1870–1871), 720, 721(*map*), 723, 734

Psychoanalysis, 763

Ptolemaic Egypt, 135–136

Ptolemy, Claudius, 140

Pueblo peoples, 211–212

Puerto Rico (Borinquen), 408, 495; abolition of slavery in, 658; United States and, 695

Puja (service to gods), 183

Punjab, 45, 135, 184

Punt, 41, 53

Purification rites: in Israel, 67; in India, 178, 183

Puritans (Calvinists), 439, 454; in colonial Massachusetts, 478
Putin, Vladimir, 880
Pygmies, of Central Africa, 376
Pyramids: Egyptian, 39, 40(illus.), 44; Nubian, 92; Mesoamerican, 199, 202, 206(illus.), 207

Qadi (Islamic judge), 520
Al-Qaeda militants, 849, 874, 885
Qajar dynasty (Iran), 627
Qantas Airlines, 764
Qatar, 839, 891
Qianlong (China), 554, 556, 558
Qin China, 160–162, 163(map); Korea and, 314
Qing Empire (China), 540, 552–557; Emperor Kangxi, 554, 555(illus.); tea and diplomacy in, 554–556; Russia and, 554; Jesuits in, 554, 628; Korea and, 550, 552; expansion of, 553(map), 554, 557; population and environmental stress in, 556–557; chronology (1794–1877), 639; corruption in, 557, 635; economic and social disorder in, 629; Opium War and aftermath, 629–631; Taiping Rebellion in, 631–635; decentralization at end of, 635–638; Central Asia and, 615; Boxer Uprising (1900), 728, 739 and illus., 747; social and economic change, 745–747
Qing Empire, Great Britain and, 587; Macartney mission, 555–556; Arrow War (1856–1860) and, 633; opium trade and, 629–630, 631; Opium War (1839–1842), 630; recovery after Taiping Rebellion, 636, 728; Treaty of Nanking (1842), 630
Quakers, 480, 499
Quaque, Philip, 512
Quebec, colonial, 480, 488, 595
Quetzalcoatl, 204, 210
Quilombos, 474. See also Palmares
Quinine, malaria and, 543, 700
Quinoa (grain), 202, 216
"Quit India" campaign, 773
Quito, Ecuador, 472–474
Quran, 247, 253, 256, 269(illus.), 511; literacy and, 265, 391
Quranic schools, 620, 679, 780 and illus. See also Islamic schools and scholars
Quraysh, 251, 254

Racism (racial discrimination). See also Mixed race, in Americas;
in Haiti, 608; anti-Asian, in Americas, 659; in Americas, 662; in British India, 688, 769; census taking and, 671; Social Darwinists and, 724; in Nazi Germany, 793; in colonial Africa, 778–779, 780; in South Africa, 831; birth control in poor countries and, 860
Radio, 760–761; in colonial Africa, 781; Italian fascists and, 792; Latin American cartel, 776; transistors, 890
Raffles, Thomas Stamford, 692
Railroads: in Britain, 574, 705; in Canada, 663, 7005; in United States, 575 and illus., 640, 705; in Egypt, 683; in Europe, 574, 577(map); in India, 586, 690, 696, 705; in France, 705; in Latin America, 696; in Mexico, 640, 696, 705; in Russia, 625, 705; telegraph and, 575, 696; in Argentina, 662, 705, 775; in Japan, 705, 723(map); immigration and, 710, 711 and illus.; world economy and, 696; World War I mobilization and, 734; Manchurian, 796; in Africa, 779; famine prevention and, 812, 813
Rainfall. See also Drought; Monsoons; in Africa, 15; in Punjab, 45; in Greece, 119; in Korea, 345; in sub-Saharan Africa, 560
Rain forests. See Tropical rain forest
Rajputs, 530
Ramayana, 186
Ramesses II (Egypt), 55, 55(illus.)
Rashid al-Din, 330
Raw materials (natural resources). See also Metals (metallurgy); Mining; and specific raw materials; Egyptian, 36; Indus Valley, 45; Carthaginian trade in, 69; Phoenician trade in, 68, 72(map); Greece and, 119, 120(map), 122; Japanese, 347, 747; Chinese, 298; Indian export of, 586; American, 668; industrialized countries and, 578, 699, 701; African export of, 682; world economy and, 699, 709, 864; World War II, 781, 779, 800–802, 809; conservation of, 869, 870
Razin, Stenka, 515

Raziya, Sultan, 383
Reagan, Ronald, 846, 849; Nicaraguan Contras and, 846, 849
Rebellions (revolts). See also Civil wars; in Persian Empire, 129–130; in Roman Judaea, 156; within Islam, 256; Berber, 257–258; by Spanish Muslims, 372; in China, 162, 170, 302, 303, 338, 339; in Mali, 379; in France, 353; in Delhi Sultanate, 384; Arawak, 408; Aztec, 426; Inka, 426, 484–845; European peasant, 350, 449, 450, 602; Scottish, 454; Dutch, 453, 459, 489; slave, 474, 478, 497, 499; in Ottoman Empire, 519, 524, 525, 617, 618; in China, 540, 557, 629, 631–635; Decembrist, in Russia, 628; Maya, 655; in British India, 687–688; Cuban, 695; Filipino, 695; in Argentina, 777–778; in Japan, 722; Panamanian, 699; Arab, 738; in eastern Europe, 822; in Afghanistan, 849
Recession (2008–2010), 843, 853, 864, 867, 871; drop in consumption, 870; unemployment protest, 879(illus.)
Reconcentration camps, in Philippines, 695
Red Army (Soviet Union), 733, 743; in World War II, 799, 800, 801, 809; Stalin's purges of, 786; revolts in eastern Europe and, 822; in Korean War, 822; in Afghanistan, 849
"Red Eyebrow" uprising, in China, 170
Red Guard (China), 837
Red Sea region: Egypt and, 53; canal linking Nile to, 114; Aksum, 244; Muslims in, 417; trade in, 388; African slave trade in, 510; Ottoman control of, 422, 516; Ethiopia and, 684
Red Shoes (Shulush Homa), 462
Reformation, Protestant, 436–438. See also Protestantism; specific sects; witch-hunts and, 439–441
Reforms: Akhenaten (Egypt), 53–54; Roman Empire, 159; Chinese, 169; Christian, 286; Truce of God, 292; Taika

(Japan), 316; colonial America, 484–486; British, 612; Enlightenment, 591, 593; industrial protests and, 584–585, 612; Qing China, 561; Russian, 625, 626, 627; Ottoman Empire, 561, 617, 622, 623, 624, 626, 627, 733; British India, 687, 688, 691; Islamic, in West Africa, 678; Mexican Revolution, 697, 698, 774; Turkish, 749; women and, 762; Great Society, in United States, 825; socialist, in Chile, 845; Soviet Union, under Gorbachev, 854; economic, in China, 843, 844, 852, 853

Regional trade associations, 875–877

Reichstag (Germany), 725

Reign of Terror (France, 1793–1794), 604–606

Reincarnation: Celtic belief in, 103; in Vedic religion, 178, 181

Religion(s). *See also* Afterlife, belief in; Buddhism; Christianity; Creation myths; Cult(s); Gods and goddesses; Hinduism; Islam; Judaism; Priests (clergy); Sacrifice; Shrines; Supernatural, the; *and specific religions;* Stone Age, 9, 12; Neolithic, 18; Mesopotamia, 28; Carthaginian, 73; Egyptian, 42–43, 52; Assyrian, 59; Olmec, 199–200; Chinese, 169 (*See also* Buddhism; Confucianism); Persian (*See* Zoroastrianism); Greek, 124, 126(*illus.*); Maya, 206; Teotihuacan, 204, 205; Toltec, 208; pork taboo in, 242; Sasinid Iran, 249–250; Shinto (Japan), 316; Lithuania-Russia war and, 368; Aztec, 397; Protestant Reformation, 436–438; Scientific Revolution and, 441, 442; African slave, 499; European wars of, 435, 437, 439, 444, 452; Mughal India, 530; abolition of slavery and, 656; Heavenly Kingdom of Great Peace, 632, 633; Durkheim on, 763; colonial Africa, 779; eastern European nationalism and, 855; politics and, 884–885

Religions, of India, 182. *See also* Hindus; Buddhism, 178, 179, 181, 185, 186, 392; Jainism, 179, 180, 186, 189; Parsees, 118; Vedism, 181, 189

Religious orders. *See also* Jesuits; Sufi brotherhoods; Dominicans, 364, 466, 467 *and illus.*; Franciscans, 364, 466, 542

Religious tolerance, 322, 383, 389; in Holland, 446; in Mughal Empire, 530; in British India, 688

Renaissance: in Babylon, 75; Italian, 363, 409, 436; artists of, 367–368 *and illus;* universities and, 363–364

Renfrew, Colin, 18

Republican institutions, 598–599. *See also* Democracy; Voting rights

Re (sun-god), 43

Revolution, 716–717. *See also* Maritime Revolution; Rebellions; Revolution, in Atlantic world; Neolithic, 14–17; scientific, 441–444; Mexican, 696–698; socialism and, 716–717; anarchism and, 717; Guomindang, in China, 748; Russian (1905), 727; Russian (1917), 739–740; scientific, 762; Stalin's Soviet Union, 785–787; Cuban (1959), 816, 833, 834, 844–845; Green, 820 *and illus.;* Cultural (China, 1966), 837; Latin American (1970s), 844, 846; Islamic, 844, 847–849

Revolution, in Atlantic world (1750–1850), 589–612; prelude to eighteenth-century crisis, 591–595; in British North America, 595–599; chronology, 617; Congress of Vienna and, 611; Enlightenment and old order, 591–593; in France, 599–608; in Haiti (1789–1804), 589, 610–611, 658; Napoleonic Europe, 609(*map*); nationalism, reform and, 611–612; in Latin America, 641–645 *and map*; popular sovereignty in, 597, 601; Revolutions of 1848, 612, 718

Revolutionary Alliance (China), 747

Rhetoric, Greek, 131

Rhineland, 720, 794

Rhine River, 157, 158

Rhode Island, colonial, 504

Rhodes, Cecil, 678

Ricardo, David, 583

Ricci, Matteo, 450, 543

Rice and rice cultivation: domestication of, 15, 22; in Java, 195; in China, 80, 82(*map*), 307, 310, 341; in Southeast Asia, 15, 186192, 377; in East Asia, 314; Champa, 318, 347; in Ganges Plain, 377; in Vietnam, 193, 318; in Japan, 316, 347; in tropical lands, 377; in Bengal, 392; in colonial Americas, 477, 478; in Japan, 547, 548; in Burma, 813; miracle, 820–821 *and illus.*

Richard I, the Lion-Hearted, 294

Rickshaws, 746(*illus.*); claims of invention, 757; palanquins compared, 758

Rifles, 532, 678, 684, 697, 707, 747; breech-loading, 623; Enfield, 688; muskets, 507, 524, 630; percussion-cap, 628, 630

Righteous Fists (China), 728(*illus.*), 747

Rights. *See also* Individual rights; Voting rights; Women's rights; in British America, 477; natural, 590; Napoleonic France, 607; denied German Jews, 793; human rights, 844, 846, 886

Rig Veda, 178

Rio de Janeiro, 775; market women in, 486(*illus.*); street children in, 867; rural migrants in, 779, 866

Rio de la Plata, 465. *See also* Argentina; Paraguay; Uruguay; United Provinces of, 643, 644(*map*)

The Rite of Spring (Stravinsky), 763

Rituals (rites). *See also* Religion; at Çatal Hüyük, 20; Mesopotamian, 30, 31; Canaanite, 66–67; Chinese, 86, 87; Greek, 126(*illus.*), 133; Indian, 179, 183, 184; Olmec, 200; Andean peoples, 219; Maya, 205, 208; Northern Amerindian, 211, 212; pork taboo in, 242; Aztec, 397; local religion and, 439; Shi'ite Islam, 526–527

Rivers. *See also* Flooding; *specific rivers;* early civilizations and, 24(*map*); of sub-Saharan Africa, 238–239; in Kievan Russia, 287, 288; in Vietnam, 193, 318; watermills on, 354; pollution of, 576–577, 707

River Valley civilizations
(3500–1500 B.C.E.), 1, 23,
24(*map*), 25, 47, 103. *See also*
Egypt, ancient; Indus Valley
civilization; Mesopotamia
Roads: in Mesopotamia, 27; in
Persian Empire, 112(*map*),
115; in Roman Empire, 154,
156; in China, 163(*map*), 169;
in India, 186; in Japan, 547;
industrialization and, 565;
automobiles and, 765
Robespierre, Maximilien, 604
Rock art, in Sahara, 2, 235,
236(*illus.*), 240
Rockefeller, John D., 820
Rockefeller Foundation, 820
Rocket (locomotive), 574
Roman (Latin) alphabet, 275
Roman Catholicism. *See*
Catholicism
Romance of the Three Kingdoms,
343
Roman Empire (31–476 C.E.),
146(*map*), 240. *See also*
Greco-Roman civilization;
and individual emperors;
army of, 148, 152, 155, 156,
157, 171; Celts and, 101, 102,
103; China compared to, 143,
150–152, 169, 170, 171;
Christianity in, 155–156;
chronology, 173; Constantine
and, 159–160; Germanic
peoples and, 146(*map*), 158,
278; Parthians and, 99,
146(*map*), 158; Principate in,
152–153; technology,
157–158; third-century crisis
in, 158, 159; trans-Saharan
trade and, 238, 239; medieval
Europe and, 279
Romania, 733, 822, 866; Crimean
War in, 622; fall of Ceausescu
regime in, 855
Romania (Dacia), 146(*map*)
Romanization, 155
Roman law, 145, 152–153;
Corpus Juris Civilis, 275, 285
Roman numerals, 191
Romanov, Michael, 533
Roman Republic (507–31 B.C.E.),
144–152; Carthage and, 73,
148; chronology, 173;
expansion of, 148–149;
failure of, 149–152; patron-
client relations in, 145; slavery
in, 149; women in, 145, 147
Rome (city), 153–154, 171.
founding of, 144; grain
imports by, 149, 152; housing
in, 154; Constantinople

compared, 274; pilgrims in,
285; Jews in, 346; St. Peter's
Basilica in, 354, 418
Romero, Oscar, assassination of,
846
Romulus (Rome), 144
Roosevelt, Franklin D., 788, 805
Roosevelt, Theodore, 667, 699
Rousseau, Jean-Jacques, 591–592,
604
Roy, Rammohun, 691
Royal African Company, 502,
504, 507
Royal Botanic Gardens (Kew),
542(*illus.*)
Royal charter, in New England, 478
Royal monopoly, 501
Royal Society (London), 443, 444
Rubber, synthetic, 805
Rubber plantations, 769; in Brazil,
775, 776; in Congo, 682; in
Southeast Asia, 700 *and illus.*,
775
Ruhr (Germany), 576, 707, 744
Rule of Benedict, 285
Ruling class. *See* Elite class (ruling
class)
Rural areas. *See also* Farmers;
Peasants; Villages;
Mesopotamian, 37; Greek,
123; Roman Empire, 154,
159; Mesoamerican, 201; late
medieval Europe, 350–356;
Chinese, 552; colonial Latin
America, 468; deforestation
in, 578; Ottoman, 519, 524;
French Revolution and, 602;
Vietnamese, 347;
industrialization in, 564, 576;
protests against
mechanization in, 584
Rural-to-urban migration. *See*
Migration (population
movements)
Russian language, 332, 727
Russian Orthodox Church,
287–288, 289, 295, 332, 334,
625, 626; missionaries and,
275, 288, 532; tsars and, 532
Russian Republic (1991 to
present): end of Soviet Union
and, 855, 858(*map*); under
Putin, 880; oil wealth of, 876;
in Shanghai Cooperation
Organization, 876
Russian Revolution (1905), 727
Russian Revolutions (1914–1918),
739–740; women and family
values in, 790–791
Russia (Russian Empire). *See also*
Russian Republic; Soviet
Union (USSR); Kievan,

287–289; Mongols and, 323,
324, 326(*map*), 332–333, 348
(*See also* Golden Horde
khanate); chronology
(1221–1505), 349; Cossacks
in, 515; forest resources of,
532; witch-hunts in, 439;
Central Asia and, 626;
chronology (1547–1712),
539; Europe and, 534, 615,
625–626; expansion of,
457(*map*), 531–533,
619(*map*), 624, 626; North
American (Alaska), 482;
Ottoman Empire and,
524–525, 533, 619(*map*),
625, 628–629; Peter the Great
and, 532–533, 534 *and illus.*;
westernization of, 534, 538;
Napoleon's invasion of, 607,
609(*map*), 625; Qing China
and, 554; society and politics,
532; Sweden and, 531, 532,
534; chronology (1801–1861),
617; Crimean War and, 622,
623, 625; cultural trends,
626–628; railroads in, 625,
705; serfs, 532, 534, 626, 627;
Jews in, 710, 727, 755(*illus.*);
conservatism in, 611,
726–727; industrialization in,
704, 728; immigrants from,
713; Russification in, 724; war
with Japan (1904–1905), 727,
729, 732; ethnic diversity in,
726–727; in World War I,
733–734, 739–740; double
Revolution in, 739–740; civil
war in, 743
Russo-Japanese War (1904–1905),
728, 729, 732
Rwanda, genocide in, 857

Sa'adi family, 537
Saarinen, Eero, 767
Saba (Sheba), 66, 388
Sabbath, 65
Sacrifice. *See also* Human sacrifice;
Mesopotamian, 30, 31;
animal, 31, 66, 108 ; Persian,
114; Greek, 124, 126(*illus.*);
Indian, 178, 181; Roman, 147
Sadat, Anwar al-, 836
Safavid Empire (Iran), 433;
chronology (1502–1747),
517; Isfahan in, 527–528 *and
illus.*; Ottoman rivalry with,
518(*map*), 519, 520, 525,
526; society and religion,
526–527; economic crisis and
collapse of, 528–529
Sagres, 410

Sahara region, 376. *See also* Trans-Saharan trade and caravan routes; rock art in, 2, 235, 236(*illus.*), 240; climate changes in, 38; drought in, 240; pastoralism in, 17, 235, 236, 376; Tuareg of, 237, 238(*illus.*)

Sahel (Africa), 239; herders of, 236(*illus.*); salt trade in, 238, 258

Sailing (seafaring). *See also* Navigation; Ships and shipping; Indian Ocean trade and, 384–386 *and illus.*; lateen sails, 233, 385 *and illus.*, 411; Polynesian, 405

St. Domingue (modern Haiti): sugar plantations on, 491–492, 493; categories of free people in, 499; earthquakes on, 495; hurricane in, 494(*illus.*); slave rebellion in, 589, 608, 610, 656, 684; revolution in (1789–1804), 608–609, 610–611; United States and, 699

St. George of the Mine (Elmina), 416, 490

St. Helena, Napoleon on, 608

St. Lawrence River, 480

St. Peter's Basilica (Rome), 367–368, 436

St. Petersburg, 534; monument in, 627(*illus.*); as Petrograd, 739, 740; as Leningrad, 799 *and map*

Saint-Simon, duke of, 583

Sakhalin (Karafutu), 723(*map*)

Salah-al-Din (Saladin), 261, 294

Salt (salt trade), 200; trans-Saharan, 238, 258, 382; protest in British India, 771–772

Salvation: in Zoroastrianism, 117; in Buddhism, 179, 339; Lutheran, 437; Calvinist, 437

Samanid dynasty (Iran), 257, 259

Samaria, 66

Samarkand, 228, 329, 330; observatory in, 331

Samarra, 257

Samizdat writings, in Soviet Union, 854

Samoa, 405, 406(*map*); Americans in, 694

Samurai warriors (Japan), 317, 545, 546, 547; Forty-Seven Ronin incident and, 550 *and illus.*

Sanchi, Great Stupa at, 180(*illus.*)

Sandinistas (Nicaragua), 845, 846

Sandino, Augusto César, 845

Sanger, Margaret, 762

Sanitation. *See also* Sewage systems; urbanization and, 707, 712; cult of cleanliness, 764

San Lorenzo, 200, 201

San Martín, José de, 643

Sanskrit language, 178, 190, 299, 391; writings (texts), 179, 297

Santa Maria (ship), 413

Santiago de Compostela, 292

Santo Domingo, 610

São Paulo, Brazil, 758, 776, 865(*table*)

São Tomé, 412, 416, 469

Saqqara, 39

Sarai (Old Sarai), 328, 332, 333, 336

Sarajevo, 732

Saratoga, Battle of, 598

Sardinia, 69, 72(*map*), 73, 149

Sardinia-Piedmont, 719 *and map*

Sargon (Akkad), 27

Sasanid Empire (Iran), 247, 248, 250, 264; politics and society, 248; religions and, 249–250, 269; shahs (kings), 250, 249(*illus.*), 250, 255, 256

Satavahana dynasty (India), 187

Satellites, 827

Sati (widow burning), 189, 393, 691, 769

Satraps, in Persia, 115

Satsuma (Japan), 722

Saudi Arabia, 751; Afghan rebels and, 849; al-Qaeda and, 874; oil wealth of, 839; Persian Gulf War and, 858

Saul (Israel), 65

Savanna, in sub-Saharan Africa, 238

Savannah (steamship), 574

Scandinavia, 292. *See also* Denmark; Finland; Norway; Sweden; Vikings; Christian morality in, 285; Lutheranism in, 437; immigration from, 710

Schism, in Christianity, 274, 368

Schliemann, Heinrich, 57

Scholasticism, in Europe, 364

Schools and scholars. *See also* Education; Islamic scholars and schools; Assyrian, 62–63; Athenian, 132; in Alexandria, 137; Confucian, in China, 87, 160, 165, 167, 543; Korean, 344, 346; legal, in Italy, 364; colonial American, 466, 468; Jewish, 364; Russian, 628;

women teachers in, 661; mission, in colonial Africa, 686, 780; engineering and technical, 705, 724; mission, in China, 746

Science. *See also* Astronomy; Chemical industry; Engineering; Mathematics; Technology; Chinese, 169; Islamic, 264, 330–332; Enlightenment, 442–443, 590, 670; Industrial Revolution and, 565; economic botany, 700; Social Darwinism and, 724; social sciences, 763; World War II, 805; standardization in, 893

Scientific Revolution, 442–444; twentieth century, 762–763

Scotland (Scots), 103, 369, 456, 725; witch-hunts in, 440; rebellion in, 455

Scribes, 121; Mesopotamian, 30, 116; ancient Egyptian, 40; Assyrian, 60; Israelite, 67; Phoenician, 68; Maya, 208, 220; in Islam, 265; Christian monks, 286

Script. *See also* Writing (written language); Egyptian, 40; Mycenaean, 57, 59; Phoenician, 65; Japanese women and, 317; Arabic, 391, 526

Scythians, 114; Herodotus on, 97–98, 230; ironworking by, 230

Seal hunting, off New Zealand, 692

Seal stones: Mesopotamian, 29(*illus.*); Indus Valley, 46, 47

Seasoning, of slaves, 498

Seclusion and veiling, of women, 264 *and illus.*, 268, 274

Second Estate (France), 601, 602

Second Treatise on Civil Government (Locke), 455

Second World War. *See* World War II

Secret police: in fascist Europe, 792; in Russia, 740, 787

Security Council, United Nations: permanent members and veto of, 817–818; Korean War and, 822; China (PRC) on, 838

Seine River, watermills on, 354

Sei Shonagon, 317

Sékou Touré, 831

Seleucid kingdom, 136

Self-government (self-rule). *See also* Independence; Nationalism; Revolutions of 1848 and, 612; in Africa, 829,

831; in British colonies, 647, 694, 770; League of Nations and, 741, 749; in Middle East, 751

Selim I, Sultan, 516, 525

Selim II, Sultan, 520

Selim III, Sultan, 617

Seljuk Turks, 330; Byzantines and, 273, 293; Crusades and, 260, 261

Semites: Sumerians and, 26, 30; Hyksos, 53; polytheism of, 250–251

Senate: Carthage, 70, 73; Rome, 144, 152

Seneca Falls Women's Rights Convention (1848), 662

Senegal, 257, 678, 780

Senior, Nassau, 562, 576

"Separate spheres," in Victorian age, 713–714

Sepoys (India), 687; rebellion of (1857), 687–688

Seppuku (ritual suicide), 549, 550

September 11 terrorism (2001), 874–875, 885

Serbia: Patriarchate of, 335; Austria-Hungary and, 733, 734; Ottoman Empire and, 516, 518(map), 617; independence of, 622; NATO war against (1999), 857, 858(map)

Serfs (serfdom), 279–280. See also Peasants; freedom for, 291, 350–351, 353–354; end of European, 448; Russian, 533, 535; freeing of Russian, 626, 627, 727

Sevastopol, 623

Seven Years' War (1756–1763), 482, 590, 601

Seville (Spain), 258, 259

Sèvres, Treaty of (1920), 749

Sewage systems, 578, 691, 712, 765

Sewing machine, 795

Sexuality. See also Prostitution; Stone Age, 10; prostitution, 23; bisexuality, in Greece, 133; male homosexuality, in Islam, 268, 528; prostitution, 690, 795; sexually-transmitted diseases, 779

Shaft graves, at Mycenae, 57

Shahs, of Iran, 248, 249(illus.), 250, 255, 256

Shaitans and jinns, 252

Shakas, 186

Shaka (Zulu), 676

Shamans (shamanism): Olmec, 200; Maya, 208; Japanese,

315; Korean, 314, 551; Mongol, 323, 328

Shamash (sun-god), 29(illus.)

Shams al-Din, Sayyid Ali, 337

Shangdu (Xanadu), 336

Shanghai, 745, 748; Bund in, 746(illus.); growth of, 634, 758, 865(table); radio in, 760; sale of gold in, 804(illus.)

Shanghai Cooperation Organization (SCO), 876

Shang period (China), 80–83 and map; bronze in, 80, 81; oracle bones in, 80–81

Shang (Qin), 91

Shari'a (Islamic law), 262, 265, 528, 530; in Ottoman Empire, 519, 520–522, 620; in Southeast Asia, 536; in West Africa, 678–679

Sharif, Nawaz, 881

Sharpeville massacre (South Africa, 1960), 832

Shawabti figurines, 44, 95

Sheba, Israelite trade with, 65, 388

Sheep, 64, 101, 250, 353, 464. See also Wool trade; and goats, 16, 21, 22, 25, 96, 107, 108, 119, 241

Shifting cultivation. See Swidden agriculture

Shi Huangdi, 160–161; tomb of, 162, 164(illus.)

Shi'ite Islam, 254; Buyid dynasty and, 257, 260; Il-khans and, 329; in Iran, 256, 263, 264, 391, 518(map), 520, 526, 527, 847, 848; rivalry with Sunnis, 254, 257, 260, 261, 262, 883; Assassin sect of, 330

Shinto, in Japan, 316

Ships and shipping (merchant marine). See also Navigation; Navy; Pirates; Steamships; Carthaginian, 69; Celtic, 101; Greek, 119; Indian Ocean trade, 233–234, 384–386 and illus.; lateen sails for, 233, 385 and illus., 410; Viking, 276, 407; Mediterranean, 58, 279; cannon on, 403, 411, 538; in coastal Pacific, 408; European trading cities and, 356; galleys, 356, 411, 519; Indian (dhows), 385 and illus., 403, 420, 421; Portuguese (caravels), 411, 418–420; Portuguese taxation of, 422; Polynesian canoes, 405; Chinese (junks), 308, 385, 403, 404 and illus.; Dutch,

447, 456; slave trade, 409, 488, 502, 504–506; Canadian canoes, 481(illus.); African canoes, 408, 685; shipping lines, 706; Suez Canal and, 709; refrigerated, 663, 775; Japanese, 837

Shipyard Diary of a Woman Welder (Clawson), 808

Shiva (god), 182–183

Shoa kingdom, 684

Shoguns, 547. See also Japan; specific shogunate

Shona peoples, 678

Shotoku (Japan), 304–305, 316

Shrines: Çatal Hüyük, 20; Mesopotamian, 34; Israelite, 64; Chinese, 169; Hindu, 183; Buddhist, in India, 180(illus.); Islamic, 251, 838; Christian, in Europe, 292, 366

Shudras, 178, 184

Shulush Homa (Choctaw), 462

Siam. See Thailand (Siam)

Siberia, 554; land bridge, 8; penal colony in, 532. See also Gulags; steppe nomads of, 70(illus.); burial mounds in, 99

Sibir khanate, 532

Sicily, 69, 72(map), 123, 144, 358, 363, 719, 720(map), 802; Rome and, 148; Normans in, 278, 292

Siddhartha Gautama (Buddha), 180, 181(illus.)

Sidon, 68

Siege weapons and tactics. See also Fortifications; Weapons and military technology; Mesopotamian, 35; Assyrian, 60; Roman, 157; catapults, 134, 327, 346; Khitan, 306; Mongol, 327

Sierra Leone, 686; Portuguese in, 410(illus.), 411; Christianity in, 686; radio in, 781

Sijilmasa, 258

Sikhism (Sikhs), 688

Silk industry: Chinese, 80, 404, 543; Southeast Asia trade and, 192; Mongol nobles and, 327–328; Iranian, 524, 527, 528

Silk Road, 163(map), 228; origins and operations of, 165; Buddhism and, 169, 231(map), 243; chronology (247 B.C.E.–400 C.E.), 230; cities on, 257; nomadic peoples and, 189, 193; impact of, 230–232; Mesopotamia and, 248; Mongol diversion of, 262, 322, 337

Silla (Korea), 315
Silphium, 111
Silver, 21; Celtic, 102(*illus.*); from
    Anatolia, 50, 54; as medium
    of exchange, 62; Sasanid,
    249(*illus.*); coins, 123, 255,
    291; in Mongolian Empire,
    332, 333; French speculators
    and, 458; Inka, 426;
    mercantilism and, 501;
    inflation and, 453, 523, 529,
    552; from Americas, 453,
    468, 470, 484, 503(*map*),
    540, 541, 620; in China trade,
    339, 540, 551, 587
Sima Qian, 99, 164, 168
Simony, 282
Sinai Peninsula, 838
Sind, 255
Singapore: British in, 555, 630,
    692; economic growth in,
    852, 895; independence of,
    828
Sinhalese, in Sri Lanka, 377
Sino-Japanese Wars: Imjin War
    (1592–1598), 540, 545, 547,
    553; (1894), 694, 729;
    (1937–1945), 797–798
Sino-Tibetan languages, 19
Sioux people, 465, 654
Sipán, Peru, Moche tomb at,
    218–219 *and illus.*
Sirius (steamship), 573–574 *and
    illus.*
Skin color, 8, 41; in India,
    177–178
Sky gods, 19, 81, 124, 147, 178,
    324
Skyscrapers, 765–766
Slash-and-burn agriculture. *See*
    Swidden (shifting) agriculture
Slave Coast, 507–508. *See also*
    Slave trade, African
Slave rebellions, 474, 478, 497,
    499, 658; on St. Domingue,
    589, 608, 610, 657, 684
Slavery, abolition of. *See* Abolition
    (abolitionists)
Slave soldiery, 372, 529. *See also*
    Janissaries; Mamluk, 261,
    393
Slaves (slavery). *See also* Slaves
    (slavery), African; in
    Mesopotamia, 29; Israelite,
    64; prisoners of war, 61, 81,
    116, 152, 268; in Greece, 124,
    129; in Roman Republic and
    Empire, 152; Islamic, 265,
    268; Aztec, 395; Varangian
    trade in, 287; Mongol, 323; in
    India, 393; prisoners of war,
    323, 372, 508, 509, 511, 547;

in Korea, 551; sugar
    plantations, 358, 411, 416;
    serfdom compared to, 532
Slaves (slavery), African, 447; in
    Brazil, 474–475, 485; in
    British North America, 476,
    478, 480; chronology
    (1807–1867), 677; food crops
    of, 494; manumission
    (freedom) for, 474–475,
    499–500, 643; Niger Delta,
    686; runaway slave
    communities, 474–475, 500;
    on sugar plantations, 469,
    474, 475, 490–500; in Cape
    Colony, 510; in United States,
    581, 599, 649, 651; in
    Venezuela, 641; in West
    Indies, 412, 446, 466, 474,
    476, 489–500, 504, 581
Slave trade, African, 382, 393,
    409; Atlantic system and, 488,
    491(*fig.*), 502–508; in
    colonial Latin America, 470,
    472–473, 476; Dutch and,
    489–490; Islamic and
    European contacts, 510–512;
    Portugal and, 412, 416, 417,
    420, 421; Brazil and, 465,
    645; recaptive settlement,
    686; in Eastern Africa, 537;
    sugar plantations and, 490;
    British Navy and, 645, 657,
    658, 664, 684, 686; slave
    ships, 409, 488, 502,
    504–506; malaria and, 463; in
    Zanzibar, 686; end of, 645,
    658, 664; transition from,
    684–686
Slavic languages, 287, 332
Slavophiles, in Russia, 625–626
Slavs (Slavic peoples), 273, 295.
    See also Eastern Europe;
    specific Slavic countries;
    Hitler and, 793, 799; in
    Kievan Russia, 287–288;
    Mongols and, 334; Orthodox
    Christianity and, 275,
    287–288, 289; in Austria-
    Hungary, 727, 733
Slovenia, 857, 858(*map*)
Slumdog Millionaire (film), 892
Smallpox, 328, 424, 426, 779;
    Amerindians and, 463;
    inoculation against, 544
Small traditions, 239, 245. *See also*
    Folk cultures; Traditions;
    Islam and, 262, 269
Smith, Adam, 583; on division of
    labor, 568–569
Social classes (social hierarchy).
    See also specific classes;

Mesopotamian, 29, 47;
    Egyptian, 41; Persian, 114;
    Athenian, 128; Andean
    peoples, 217; Indian (castes),
    178, 189, 403, 687, 769;
    colonial Latin America,
    470–474; African, 240; in
    colonial North America, 478;
    Industrial Revolution and,
    565–566; Parisian housing
    and, 579(*illus.*); Marxism
    and, 584; in China, 746
The Social Contract (Rousseau),
    591
Social Darwinism, 724
Socialism. *See also* Marx, Karl;
    labor movements and,
    716–717; in Chile, 852
Social media, 891
Social sciences, 763
Social welfare: in Germany, 725; in
    western Europe, 819; for
    aging population, 862, 863
Society (social conditions). *See also*
    Social classes; *and specific
    societies and social issues;*
    Stone Age, 10–11;
    Mesopotamian, 29–30;
    Assyrian, 62–63; Roman,
    145, 153–154; imperial
    China, 85, 165–166,
    308–314; Anasazi, 211;
    Sasanid Iran, 248; medieval
    Europe, 280–281; Byzantine
    Empire, 274–275; Kievan
    Russia, 289; colonial Latin
    America, 470–475; Safavid
    Iran, 526–527; Japanese, 746;
    Russian, 532; French
    Revolution, 600–601;
    Industrial Revolution and,
    581–582; socialism and labor
    movements, 716–717; spread
    of Islam and, 392–394;
    changes in (1850–1900),
    710–715; population and
    migrations (1850–1914),
    710–712; urbanization and,
    712–713; women's work and,
    714–715; Middle East,
    750–752
Socrates, 131
Soga clan (Japan), 315–316, 317
Sogdiana, 228
Soil erosion: cotton production
    and, 666; deforestation and,
    490, 493, 556, 578, 666
Soil (loess), 80
Sokoto Caliphate, 679
Solidarity (Poland), 855
Solomon (Israel), 65, 68; Sheba
    and, 66, 388

Solon (Athens), 128
Solzhenitsyn, Alexander, 854
Somalia (Horn of Africa), 66, 341;
    Islam in, 392
Somme, Battle of (1916), 736
Somoza, Anastasio, overthrow of,
    845
Song Empire (China), 297,
    306–314, 342; economy and
    society in, 308–314, 319;
    industries of, 308; Korea and,
    315; Liao and Jin challenge
    to, 306–308, 309(*map*);
    neo-Confucianism in, 310;
    Southern Song, 308,
    309(*map*); Vietnam (Annam)
    and, 318, 347–348; women
    in, 312–314 *and illus.*
Songhai, 393, 510
Soninke people, 258
Son of Heaven. *See* Mandate of
    Heaven
Sons of Liberty, 596
Sophists, 131
Sorghum (grain), 15, 240, 377
South Africa: Cape Colony, 676;
    Afrikaners (Dutch), 676–678;
    Zulu of, 676–677 *and illus.*,
    677; diamond mining in, 677;
    native landownership in, 678;
    English language in, 678;
    European immigrants in, 679,
    831; gold in, 377, 378, 789;
    nationalism in, 781; railroads
    in, 705; Mandela and, 832,
    857, 881; racial apartheid in,
    832, 833–834; trade
    agreement (SADC), 876
South African Broadcasting
    Corporation, 781
South African War (1899–1902),
    678–679
South America. *See also* Andean
    region; Latin America; *and
    specific countries;* Amerindian
    voyages from, 407; migration
    to, 7(*map*), 8; Columbus in,
    413; Polynesian voyagers in,
    405; trade with Mesoamerica,
    408; Old World diseases in,
    464; horses and cattle in, 464;
    chronology (1808–1888),
    642; Polynesian voyagers in,
    405; trade with Mesoamerica,
    408
South Arabia. *See* Yemen (south
    Arabia)
South Asia. *See also* India; Sri
    Lanka; chronology
    (1206–1500), 377; miracle
    rice in, 821(*illus.*);
    decolonization in, 827–828

South Asia, empires in. *See* Delhi
    Sultanate (India); Gupta
    India; Mauryan Empire
    (India)
South Carolina, colonial,
    477–478, 479–480
South China Sea, 232, 386, 390,
    402, 557
Southeast Asia, 192–196. *See also*
    East Indies (maritime
    Southeast Asia); *and specific
    countries;* migration to, 8; rice
    cultivation in, 14, 190, 377;
    early civilizations, 192–194;
    geography and climate of,
    192; Indian Ocean trade and,
    223, 235, 389; spice trade in,
    192; chronology (2000 B.C.
    E.–1025 C.E.), 177; Srivijaya,
    194–196; Funan and, 188;
    Hindu-Buddhist culture in,
    192, 194; pig domestication
    in, 242, 243; chronology
    (1283–1500), 324; fishing in,
    376; Angkor (Cambodia),
    378; migration from, 407,
    406(*map*); Islam in, 391, 392;
    trade networks from, 402;
    migration from, 407,
    406(*map*); Muslims in, 536;
    Chinese immigrants in, 552,
    712; Dutch colonies in, 692;
    imperialism in, 692–693,
    672(*map*); Japanese invasion
    of, 800, 801(*map*); rubber in,
    700 *and illus.*, 775;
    communism in, 825; miracle
    rice in, 821(*illus.*);
    decolonization in, 828; trade
    associations in, 876
Southern Rhodesia (Zimbabwe),
    678, 831, 881
Southern Song (China), 308;
    Mongols and, 323, 326(*map*),
    336
South Korea, 877. *See also* Korea;
    Korean War and, 822, 824;
    economic growth in, 849,
    852, 894; age distribution in,
    863 *and figure*
South Sea Company, 456, 458–459
South Sudan, Republic of, 881
South Vietnam, 824 *and illus. See
    also* Vietnam
Southwest Africa (Namibia), 738,
    749
Southwestern desert cultures,
    North America, 211–212,
    213(*illus.*)
Soviet Union (USSR), 743–744.
    See also Red Army (Soviet
    Union); Russia; New

Economic Policy in, 744;
    collectivization of agriculture
    in, 785–786, 813; Communist
    Party in, 743, 744, 745;
    famine in, 787, 813; Five-Year
    Plans in, 785, 786;
    industrialization in, 785, 787;
    pact with Germany, 745, 795;
    peasants in, 785–786, 813;
    Stalin Revolution in,
    785–787; terror and
    opportunities in, 787;
    women's rights in, 789–791;
    in World War II, 799 *and
    map*, 800, 817; World War II
    casualties, 805
Soviet Union (USSR), Cold War
    era (1946–1991). *See also*
    Cold War (Bipolar world);
    China and, 822, 837, 838;
    command economy of,
    818–819, 821–822; Cuba
    and, 816, 826, 831, 834; race
    for nuclear supremacy,
    826–827; rivalry with United
    States, 822, 834, 839, 844;
    Third World and, 834, 835;
    United Nations and, 817;
    Vietnam and, 824; Warsaw
    Pact and, 817, 823(*map*);
    crisis in, 854–855;
    environmental damage in,
    869; war in Afghanistan, 847,
    849, 854, 855; Gorbachev's
    reforms in, 855; collapse of,
    847, 855–857, 858(*map*)
Space exploration, 827
Spain (Spanish Empire). *See also*
    Latin America, colonial;
    Celtiberian culture of, 100,
    103; Phoenician colonies in,
    69, 72(*map*); Carthage and,
    73; Berbers in, 254, 259;
    Rome and, 149, 159(*illus.*);
    agriculture in, 259; Jews in,
    259; women in, 258(*illus.*);
    Ummayyad Caliphate in, 259
    and map, 276; Viking raids
    on, 276; Visigoths in, 276;
    pilgrimage in, 292; Muslims
    in, 259–260, 258(*map*),
    264(*illus.*), 294, 330, 409;
    windmills in, 354; Jews
    expelled from, 358, 372;
    Muslims driven from, 371;
    unification of, 372, 409;
    Muslims driven from, 409,
    453; Philippines in, 401, 415;
    unification of, 409; Aztecs
    and, 396, 424–426;
    conquistadors and, 423–427;
    Inkas and, 426–427; Armada

defeated, 438, 456; Catholicism in, 452, 454; Dutch independence and, 459, 489; dynasties in, 454(*table*); in Caribbean, 491, 494; War of Spanish Succession and, 456; Philippines, 401, 415, 536, 541; immigrants from, 477, 484, 489, 643, 660 *and illus.*, 710, 775; Napoleon's invasion of, 607, 609(*map*), 641; Junta Central in, 641; Mexico and, 643; abolition of slavery in, 658; in European Community, 819; immigrants in, 867; housing speculation in, 879; terrorism in, 886

Spanish-American War (1898–1899), 695–696

Spanish language, 672, 724

Spanish maritime expeditions, 401, 412–415 *and map*; Columbus, 412, 413–415 *and map*; Magellan, 401, 414(*map*), 413

Sparta (Spartans), 127, 128, 129; in Hellenistic Age, 136; Peloponnesian War and, 134; women in, 132

Spear, Percival, 772

Speculative market. *See also* Stock exchanges; Tulipmania, in Holland, 435; in France and England, 436–460, 501; in West Indies, 491; in Japan, 548; in United States, 878–879

Speech, development of, 4, 5. *See also* Language(s)

Spencer, Herbert, 725

Spice Islands (Moluccas), 390

Spice trade, 192, 291, 356, 402, 413, 446, 541; cloves, 686; Indian Ocean trade and, 233, 388, 389; pepper, 416, 423, 536, 692; Portuguese and, 422, 537

Spinning jenny, 570, 584

Spinning wheels: in England, 358; in Korea, 345; in India, 394

Spring and Autumn Annals, 84, 86

Sputnik satellite (1957), 827

Sri Lanka (Ceylon), 402; Buddhism in, 243, 244; as Indian tributary state, 384; irrigation in, 377; Sinhalese in, 377; Tamils in, 885; coffee in, 688; English language in, 893

Srivijaya, 194–196

Staffordshire pottery, 570

Stalin, Joseph, 809; famine and, 786, 813; Hitler's pact with

(1939), 794, 799; revolution of, 744, 785–787; on women and abortion, 791

Stalingrad (Volgograd), siege of, 799(*map*), *800*

Stalinism, Soviet rejection of, 837

Stamp Act (1765), 596

Standardization, 28, 46; in Qin China, 160; in identification documents, 761

Stanley, Henry Morton, 679

Stanton, Elizabeth Cady, 714

Statistics, nation-states and, 670–672

Steam engines, 565, 570, 571, 572–574; railroads and, 574–575 *and illus.*, 707; coal for, 572, 573, 707; in sugar refining, 664–665 *and illus.*

Steamships, 578, 663; in British India, 690; warships (gunboats), 587; transatlantic, 573 *and illus.*, 663; in Russia, 625; shipping lines, 706; Perry's "black ships," 704; Suez Canal and, 706; global economy and, 706, 709; immigration and, 710, 711

Steel production (steel mills). *See also* Iron industry; Chinese, 84, 308; Japanese, 343, 346; for swords, 346, 424, 425; for plows, 666; in United States, 665; stainless, 767; in India, 770–771; in Japan, 837; world economy and, 706

Stele (stone monuments), 198

Stephenson, George, 574

Steppes (prairies), 338; Eurasian, 95–100; sub-Saharan, 239

Stirrups, 230, 280, 298, 302(*illus.*)

Stock exchanges: in Amsterdam, 447; crash (1929), 788, 874

Stone Age, 9–13. *See also* Ice Age; Neolithic Age; cave paintings, 8, 12; clothing, 12, 13(*illus.*); food gathering and tools, 9–10. 12, 13(*illus.*); gender roles and social life in, 10–12; hearths and culture in, 12–14

Stone construction: megaliths, 19, 241; Egyptian pyramids, 39, 40 *and illus.*; Buddhist temples, 194(*illus.*), 195; by Andean peoples, 219; Maya, 206(*illus.*), 207(*illus.*); stele, 198; in France, 356; Gothic cathedrals, 359, 363; in Great Zimbabwe, 387(*illus.*); Inka, 398

Stone heads, Olmec, 200, 201(*illus.*)

Stonehenge, in England, 19

Stone tools, 9–10, 11 *and illus.*, 14, 15; at Çatal Hüyük, 20; in Mesopotamia, 35; in ancient Egypt, 39; obsidian, in Mesoamerica, 201, 210

Straits Settlements, 692. *See also* Singapore

Strasbourg, burning of Jews in, 362; cathedral of, 362

Stravinsky, Igor, 763

Streetcars and subways, 708, 712, 713

Strikes: in Argentina, 660(*illus.*); in China, 552; worker, 554, 676; fascist repression of, 782

Strogonov family (Russia), 532

Stuart dynasty, 439, 454(*table*)

Stupas (Buddhist shrines), 180(*illus.*)

Submarine telegraph cables, 575, 706

Submarine warfare: in World War I, 737, 740; in World War II, 798, 802, 809

Sub-Saharan Africa, 238–242. *See also specific countries*; farming in, 15, 377; Egypt and, 41, 53; Carthage and, 73; Nubia and, 92, 95; cattle in, 240; trans-Saharan trade and, 238; Bantu migrations, 241–242, 245; cultural unity in, 239–240, 245; geography of, 239; ironworking in, 241–242; Islam and literacy in, 391; Islamic Empires in, 379–384; gold trade and, 409; Islam and slave trade in, 511, 513; rainfall in, 560; new media in, 781; colonialism in (1900–1945), 778–781; economic and social changes, 779–780; religious and political changes in, 780–781; declining birthrate in, 862; independence in, 828–832; urban water resources in, 866

Subway trains. *See* Streetcars and subways

Sudan, 376. *See also* Mali; Bornu in, 510; coppersmiths of, 378(*illus.*), 379; Islamic empires in, 379–382; Egypt and, 753; Muslims in, 684, 781; famine and drought in, 813; genocide in Darfur, 881; mosques in, 391

Suez Canal, 624, 706, 753, 794; opening of (1869), 683; Egypt-Israeli tensions and, 836

Suffrage. *See* Voting rights (suffrage)

Suffragists, women as, 714, 715(*illus.*). *See also* Voting rights, for women

Sufi brotherhoods, 268–269, 391, 536, 675, 781

Sugar, 565; in Atlantic system, 503(*map*), 504

Sugar cane, 264, 377

Sugar plantations, 501; on Atlantic islands, 411, 416, 469; in colonial Brazil, 447, 466, 469, 470, 474, 487; deforestation for, 490, 493, 664, 666; slave labor on, 358, 411, 416, 469, 474, 491–500, 581; technology and environment, 492–493; abolition of slavery in, 658; in West Indies, 412, 446, 466, 474, 477, 489–500, 581, 712; in Cuba, 491, 664 *and illus.*, 666, 668, 832

Sui Empire (China), 297–298

Suiko (Japan), 316

Sukarno, Achmad, 828, 835

Suleiman the Magnificent, Sultan, 516, 533

Sultans, 260. *See also* Delhi Sultanate; Mughal Empire; Ottoman Empire

Sulu Empire (Philippines), 536

Sumatra, 341; Srivijaya and, 194–196; Buddhism in, 244; pirates in, 390; Portuguese and, 517; Dutch in, 538, 692; Acheh in, 536, 538, 692, 880

Sumerian language, 27

Sumerians. *See also* Mesopotamia; gods of, 30; kings of, 37; Semites and, 26, 30

Summa Theologica (Aquinas), 360, 364

Sunda Strait, 402

Sundiata (Mali), 381–382

Sun-gods: Shamash, 29(*illus.*); Re, 43; Aten, 53; Mithra, 157; Aztec, 397; Inka, 398

Sunni Islam: Il-khans and, 329; Shi'ite rivalry with, 254, 257, 260, 261, 263, 518(*map*), 883; Wahhabism and, 525

Sun Yat-sen, 747

Sunzi, 85

Supernatural, the. *See also* Magic; Religion(s); Egyptian belief in, 47; Celtic belief in, 103; in Mesoamerica, 200, 207 Mongol, 324; spread of disease and, 426; witch-hunts and, 440

Superpowers, Cold War, 854. *See also* Cold War; Soviet Union,

Cold War era; United States, Cold War era; Arab-Israeli conflict and, 839; environment and, 839–840; Islamic Revolutions and, 849; nonaligned nations and, 836; nuclear weaponry of, 826; proxy wars of, 844, 871

Surinam (Dutch Guiana), 658, 827

Surrealist art, 763

Survival of the fittest, 725

Susa, 116

Su Song, clock of, 311(*illus.*)

Swahili Coast, 380(*map*), 391, 404, 536–537; Indian Ocean trade and, 385, 387, 388; slave trade in, 393; China trade and, 404; Portuguese and, 422

Swahili language, 387, 537

Swaziland, 676

Sweden (Swedes). *See also* Scandinavia; ironworking in, 283, 449; Varangians, 278, 287; witch-hunts in, 439; army of, 456; Russia and, 532, 533, 534; in European Community, 819; aging population in, 862, 863–864 *and figure*

Sweet potatoes, 199, 341, 405, 424, 464, 556. *See also* Yams

Swidden (shifting) agriculture, 15; in Southeast Asia, 192; Maya, 205; in Kievan Russia, 289; in Japan, 317; in tropical lands, 377

Swift, Jonathan, 444

Switzerland, witch-burning in, 440(*illus.*)

Swords: Greek, 123; Germanic, 282; Japanese, 341, 346, 347; Mongol, 346; Indian, 378; conquistador, 424, 427

Sybil, or, The Two Nations (Disraeli), 581

Sylvester II, Pope, 190

Synagogue, 67

Syria (Syrians), 839. *See also* Syria-Palestine region; Assyria and, 58; cities in, 26, 52; Seleucids in, 135; Seljuks in, 260; Islamic conquest of, 254, 255, 261, 273, 274; Mongol defeat in, 261; Crusaders in, 293; caravan trade and, 251; Umayyad caliph in, 276; Ottoman Empire and, 516, 518(*map*), 618; Egypt and, 622; French mandate in, 749, 753 *and map*; General Syrian Congress (1919), 751–752;

Palestinian refugees in, 838; civil war in, 881

Syria-Palestine region, 58 *See also* Canaan; Israel; Phoenicia (Phoenicians); Aramaeans in, 67, 96; Assyrian invasions of, 60, 69; Egypt and, 52, 54, 136; Christianity in, 156

Tabriz, 330, 336

Tacky (slave rebel), 499

Taft, William, 699

Tahert, 258

Taika reform, in Japan, 316

Taiping Rebellion (China, 1850–1864), 631–635; Nanjing in, 632; recovery after, 635

Taiwan (Formosa), 541, 642, 837; pirates in, 552–553, 557; Japan and, 723(*map*), 760; Guomindang (nationalists) in, 804; economic growth in, 852, 895

Takrur (Sudan), 381

Talas River, Battle of (751), 298, 301(*map*), 303

The Tale of Genji, 317

The Tale of the Heike, 317

Taliban (Afghanistan), 849, 881, 884

Tamerlane. *See* Timur

Tamil kingdoms, 187

Tang Empire (China), 299–306, 315; Buddhism and, 297, 299–300, 303, 314; cities in, 298; as cosmopolitan era, 300; East Asia and, 314; end of, 303, 306; law code, 304; powerful women in, 300, 302; upheavals and repression in, 300, 302–303; Vietnam and, 318, 347

Tanggut, 306; Mongols and, 324, 336

Tanit (goddess), 74

Tanning. *See* Leatherworking

Tanzania: early humans in, 5; embassy bombing in (1998), 885

Tanzimat reforms (Ottoman Empire), 618, 620, 621(*illus.*), 624, 627, 628

Tariffs: Egyptian, 586; German, 583, 725; Chinese, 631; global economy and, 709; Indian industry and, 773; Depression of 1930s and, 788; lowering of, in Europe, 819; Brazilian, 845; Japanese and, 850; local farmers and, 877

Taro (root vegetable), 377, 407

Tarquinus Superbus (Rome), 144
Tarragona, Roman aqueduct near, 159(*illus.*)
Tata, Dorabji and Jamsetji, 770
Taxation (taxes): Egypt, 39, 53; Assyrian Empire, 59–60, 62; Israel, 65; early China, 85; Persian Empire, 115; Roman Empire, 149, 155, 158; India, 184; Arab caliphate, 257; imperial China, 162, 303, 336, 337; Russia, 289, 333; English wool, 370; French monarchy, 370; Delhi Sultanate, 383, 384; Portuguese, 422; Spanish, 453; French, 455, 460; nobles exempt from, 445, 453, 456–457; English, 454, 459, 460; colonial Americas, 466, 484, 485; Ottoman Empire, 519, 617; American Revolution and, 596; French Revolution and, 601; British India, 687; Egyptian, 683; Chinese, 745, 748, 804
Tax farming: in Iran and Iraq, 261; in China, 313, 335, 337; in Europe, 456; Il-khanate, 329; in Ottoman Empire, 524, 618
Teachers, women as, 662, 714. *See also* Schools and scholars
Tea trade, 699; American boycott of, 596; China and, 543, 555; in British India, 688, 769; sugar and, 504
Technology. *See also* Engineering; Environment and technology; Manufacturing; Science; Technology, Industrial Revolution and; Weapons and military technology; of early humans, 4; Ice Age culture and, 8–14; defined, 31; in Mesopotamia, 34; in Roman Empire, 157–158; in China, 169, 341, 343; in medieval Europe, 283 *and illus.*, 290–291; world economy and, 705–710; in middle-class homes, 713, 759; of modernity, 713; in British India, 770; in nonindustrial countries, 758–761; computers, 868–869; environmental change and, 868–871; industrial robots, 869; world economy and, 868–869; cultural globalization and, 890
Technology, Industrial Revolution and,567–576. *See also*

Railroads; chronology (1702–1851), 588; division of labor, 567, 568–569; iron industry, 571–572; in Japan, 704; mass-produced pottery, 567–570; mechanization in cotton industry, 570–571; steam engine, 572–574 *and illus.*; telegraph, 575–576
Tecumseh (Shawnee), 654
Teheran (Iran), 758; hostage crisis (1979), 848
Telegraph, 575–576, 663, 707–708; in India, 586, 690; railroads and, 575, 697; submarine cables for, 575, 706
Telephone, 714; cell phones, 868, 891
Telescope, of Galileo, 442
Television, 890–891
Temples: Mesopotamian, 27, 31; Egyptian, 43, 53, 54(*illus.*); Phoenician, 69; in Jerusalem, 63, 66, 67, 69; Nubian, 94, 95; Greek, 128, 131; Hindu, 175, 183, 189; Buddhist, 194(*illus.*), 195, 299, 316; Mesoamerican, 204, 204, 206; Zoroastrian, 260(*illus.*); Kievan Russia, 288; Aztec, 397; Inka, 398
Temüjin, 322. *See also* Chinggis Khan
Ten Commandments, 64
Tenochtitlan, 209 *and map*, 395, 397, 398; Spanish conquest of, 425–426
Teotihuacan, 204–205, 209–210; pyramids in, 204.
Terracing: in Andes, 204, 216; in Mesoamerica, 205, 210
Terror (terrorism): in Assyrian Empire, 61; Mongols and, 335; in France (1793–1794), 604, 606; Stalin's purges, 786–787; Dirty War, in Argentina, 845; September 11 (2001), 874–875, 885; Muslim, 881, 884, 885; global war on, 885
Terry, Eli, 572
Tet Offensive (1968), 825
Teutonic Knights, 334, 335, 352
Téwodros II (Ethiopia), 684
Texas, 571; cattle in, 464; independence of, 652
Textile industry and trade. *See also* Clothing; Cotton (cotton industry); Weaving; Wool trade; Scythian, 70(*illus.*); Tyrian purple, 69, 70, 274;

Islamic, 264; Andean, 202, 217, 399; Flemish, 357 *and illus.*; women's role in, 217, 359, 399; Gujarati, 389; Dutch, 446–447; African, 507; industrialization in, 564, 565; child labor in, 580, 581(*illus.*); silk, 404, 524, 528, 529, 543; Indian cotton, 446, 530, 536, 586, 688; steam engines in, 573; women in, 580, 581(*illus.*), 661, 714, 747; wool, 570, 571; British, 690; Japanese, 714, 724, 747; relocation of, 869
Thailand (Siam), 311, 390, 692, 877; Buddhism in, 244
Theater (drama): Greek, 131, 132; Gupta theater-state, 188; Srivijaya theater-state, 195; Japanese, 759–760
Thebes, Egypt, 39, 43, 52, 53; Assyrian invasion and, 94
Theology, 364, 366. *See also* Religion(s); Monophysite, 250; Reformation and, 437
Thera, 111
Theravada Buddhism, 182, 244
Thesmophoria festival, 133
Third Dynasty of Ur, 28
Third Estate (France), 601, 602
Third Geneva Convention (1950), 887
Third Reich, 793. *See also* Nazi Germany
Third Satire (Juvenal), 150–151
Third World (developing nations). *See also* Nonindustrial world; *and specific countries*; Cold War and, 835–836; privileged classes in, 709; raw materials from, 709; Cold War and, 835–836 *and illus.*; garbage pickers in, 866(*illus.*), 867; population growth in, 700–701, 843, 859, 862–863, 867, 872 environmental degradation in, 870
Thirty Years' War (1618–1648), 455
Thomas à Becket, 284–285, 365
Thomas Aquinas, 351; *Summa Theologica*, 360, 364
Thrace, 114
Three-field system, 351
Thucydides, 128
Tiamat, 32–33
Tiananmen Square massacre (1989), 853
Tian (Heaven), 83–84
Tiberius (Rome), 156
Tiber River, 144

Tibet, 631; Buddhism in, 244, 552; China and, 300, 301(*map*)
Tibetan language, 300
Tiglathpileser III (Assyria), 60
Tigris and Euphrates Valley, 46, 261. *See also* Iraq; floods in, 47; Mesopotamia and, 23, 24(*map*), 25, 50
Tikal, Great Plaza at, 206(*illus.*)
Timbuktu, 382, 511(*illus.*); library in, 391
Timekeeping. *See also* Calendars; Indian concept of, 196; clocks, 311(*illus.*)
Timor and Ambon, 538, 541
Timur (Tamerlane), 330, 335; Delhi and, 329, 331, 384
Tin, 28, 73, 102, 390; for bronze, 50, 55, 58
Tiwanaku, 217–220 *and illus.*
Tlatelolco, 395, 396
Tlaxcalans of Mexico, 425, 426
Tobacco, 424, 441, 446; in Brazil, 470, 504; in Caribbean, 489, 490, 491; in colonial Mexico, 470(*illus.*); in colonial Virginia, 446, 476, 489
Tocqueville, Alexis de, 729
Togo, 737, 749
Tokugawa Ieyasu, 546
Tokugawa shogunate (Japan), 546–548, 557, 720; opening of Japan in, 720; rebellion ending, 722–723
Tokyo (Edo), 547, 707; bombing of, World War II, 802, 806; population growth in, 712, 758, 865(*table*)
Toledo (Spain), 259, 363, 371
Toltecs, 207(*illus.*), 209–211, 395; Maya and, 211
Tombs. *See also* Burials (burial practices); Egyptian, 38, 41, 43–44, 47; Celtic, 102; Chinese, 81, 162, 164(*illus.*); Persian kings, 117; Moche, 219 *and illus.*; Samanid, in Bukhara, 260(*illus.*)
Tonga, 405, 406(*map*)
Tools. *See* Iron industry; Stone tools; Technology
Tophets (Carthage), 74, 74(*illus.*)
Topiltzin (Toltec), 210
Tordesillas, Treaty of (1494), 414(*map*), 413–415
Torture and cruelty: witch burning, 440(*illus.*); in Latin America, 845; human rights activism and, 886
Tours, Battle of (732), 276
Toussaint L'Ouverture, François Dominique, 589, 610

Towns. *See* Cities and towns (urban centers)
Toyoda Sakichi, 724
Toyota Motor Company, 849, 853; origins of, 724
Tractors, 768
Trade associations, regional, 876
Trade (commerce). *See also* Barter; Business; Free trade; Merchants; Ships and shipping; Spice trade; Trade routes; *and specific commodities*; Çatal Hüyük, 20–21; Mesopotamian, 28; Egyptian, 40, 41, 54–55; Indus Valley, 46; Nubian, 92; Middle East, 51(*map*); Minoan and Mycenaean, 49, 57, 59; Assyrian Empire, 62; Israelite, 63, 65; Phoenician, 68, 72 *and map*; Carthaginian, 69–73; Celtic Europe, 102; coinage and, 124; Greek, 124, 129, 131; Hellenistic Age, 136; Roman Empire, 154, 158; Indian, 186, 189; Islamic world, 264; Srivijaya and, 195; Andean region, 202, 218; Mesoamerican, 199, 201, 396; Northern Amerindian, 213–214; Kievan Russia, 287, 288, 289; spread of ideas and, 245; medieval Europe, 289, 291–292, 356–358; imperial China, 300, 312, 313, 341; Mongolian Empire, 327–328, 337–338; Delhi Sultanate, 384; Italian city-states, 356, 409; Japanese, 347; Zimbabwe, 388; Dutch, 435, 447, 459; Anglo-Dutch rivalry, 447; North American colonies, 479; Ottoman, 524, 623; Mughal Empire, 530; East African ports, 537; European expansion, 564–565; Japanese, 548–549, 850–851; British Empire, 470, 586, 699, 701; Chinese, 586; "legitimate," with Africa, 684; British India, 701, 709; Depression (1930s) and, 788; e-commerce (Internet), 891; regional associations, 876–877
Trade entrepôts (hubs), 332, 405, 422
Trade monopoly. *See* Monopolies, trading
Trade routes, 227. *See also* Caravan trade and routes;

Indian Ocean trade; Silk Road; Trade; Trans-Saharan trade and caravan routes; Aegean Sea, 58; Late Bronze Age, 54, 55; Assyrian control of, 50; China and, 163(*map*), 165; Meroë and, 95; India and, 187; Southeast Asia and, 193, 402; Asian, 231(*map*); Southeast Asia and, 402
Trade unions, 585. *See also* Labor unions
Trading companies, 673, 682, 687. *See also specific companies*
Traditions: great and small, 239, 245, 262; Germanic custom, 276, 279; African slave, 499; in British India, 687, 689; in Mexico, 697
Trafalgar, Battle of (1805), 609(*map*)
Trajan (Rome), 146(*map*)
Tran Hung Dao, 325
Transnational corporations, 663, 815, 869
Transportation. *See also* Automobiles; Canals; Railroads; Roads; Ships and shipping; in Mesopotamia, 35; in Late Bronze Age, 55; llamas used for, in Andean region, 202; streetcars and subways, 708, 712; rickshaws, 746(*illus.*), 757, 758
Trans-Saharan trade and caravan routes, 235–238; African gold in, 259, 371, 379, 411; camels in, 238, 237(*illus.*), 382; early Saharan cultures and, 235–238 *and illus.*; salt trade, 237, 258; Tuareg and, 238, 237(*illus.*), 376; Mali and, 380(*map*), 381, 382; Portuguese and, 371, 411; slave trade in, 371, 510, 511; Songhai and, 510
Trans-Siberian Railway, 727
Transvaal, 677, 678
Travel (travelers). *See also* Exploration (expeditions); Pilgrimages; Roads; Ships and shipping; Trade routes; Transportation; in ancient Egypt, 53; Romans in China, 143; Silk Road, 228; Muslim (*See* Ibn Battuta; Zheng He); Marco Polo, 326(*map*), 327, 389; Amerindians, in Europe, 449; passports for, 325(*illus.*), 335, 761; Peter the Great in Europe, 533–534; Turks in Europe, 620

Treaty ports, in China, 631, 728, 746. *See also* Hong Kong; Shanghai

Trench warfare, World War I, 735

Trent, Council of (1545–1563), 438

Tres Zapotes (Olmec center), 200

Trevithick, Richard, 574

Tribute systems: Egyptian, 53; Assyrian Empire, 60, 62, 67, 68(*illus.*), 69; Persian, 115; Cahokian elite and, 214; Andean peoples, 221; Chinese, 299, 301(*map*), 307, 338, 546, 554; colonial Americas, 471; Vietnam, 318; Japanese, 346, 545; Mongol, 323, 324, 338, 348; South Asian, 384; Aztec, 396; Oyo kingdom and, 508; Ottoman, 517

Trinidad Tobago, 827; Indian laborers in, 702

Triple Alliance (World War I), 734

Tripoli, 261

Trireme (ships), 130, 132(*illus.*)

Tropical rain forest, 375–376, 667, 700; in Brazil, 775, 776, 871; in sub-Saharan Africa, 239; in Southeast Asia, 376

Tropics (tropical ecology). *See also specific tropical countries and regions*; Africa and Asia, 375–379; environment, 375–376; human ecosystems, 376–377; mineral resources, 378–379; social and cultural change, 390–394; water systems and irrigation, 377–378; world economy and exports from, 699, 710

Trotsky, Leon, 744

Troubadours (poets), 294

Troy, siege of, 58

Truce of God, 292

Trung sisters, of Vietnam, 318

Tsars, of Russia, 334, 335, 531, 624. *See also specific tsars*

Tuareg people, 237(*illus.*), 238, 376, 382

Tuberculosis, 779

Tudor dynasty (England), 454(*table*)

Tughluq, Sultan, 383, 393

Tughril Beg (Seljuk), 260

Tula (Toltec capital), 208, 209(*illus.*), 210–211, 222, 223

Tulipmania, in Holland, 435, 460

Tulip Period (Ottoman Empire), 525, 533

Tunisia, 49, 70, 73, 753, 828. *See also* Carthage

(Carthaginians); Arab conquest of, 255, 273; camel saddles in, 237; farmers in, 290; Fatimid Caliphate in, 259, 268; Arab Spring (2010) in, 881

Tupac Amaru II (Quechua), 484–485

Turkey (Turks). *See also* Anatolia; Ottoman Empire; rise of, 749, 752, 754(*map*); women's rights in, 752, 762; Greece and, 749, 822

Turkic (Turkish) peoples, 273–274. *See also* Mamluks; Xiongnu; ironworking by, 230; Khazar, 288; Uighurs, 300, 330; Central Asian, 257; migration of, 287; Keraits, 322; Seljuks, 260, 261, 273, 293, 330; Mongols and, 325, 338; Delhi Sultanate, 382; Russia and, 532

Turkish language, 99, 519, 620

Turkmenistan, 250

Turquoise, 211

Tutankhamun (Egypt), 53

Tutsi-Hutu rivalry, in Rwanda, 857

Twenty-One Demands (Japan), 748

Tyler, Wat, 353

Tyrants. *See also* Dictatorship; in Greece, 124, 128; in Korea, 344; immigration and, 711

Tyre, 65, 76; Assyria and, 69, 75; Carthage and, 49; colonies of, 72 *and map*; purple cloth of, 68, 71

Ugarit, 52, 54, 58

Uighur language, 300

Uighurs, 330

Ukraine, 287, 800; Scythians in, 97 *and illus.*, 230; Mongol conquest of, 332, 333; Russia and, 627, 628, 727; Soviet Republic of, 743

Ulama (Islamic scholars), 260, 268; Ottoman reforms and, 617, 618

Ulugh Beg, 331

Umar, Caliph, 255

Umayyad Caliphate, 254, 255, 258(*map*), 276; Al-Andalus and, 259, 292

Umma (Islam), 257, 260, 262, 268, 270; formation of, 253

Union of South Africa, 678. *See also* South Africa

Union of Soviet Socialist Republics. *See* Soviet Union (USSR)

United Arab Emirates, 839, 877(*illus.*)

United Fruit Company, 833

United Nations (UN), 863; Charter, 817; China and, 852; Cold War and, 817–818; partitioning of Palestine and, 818, 838; Food and Agriculture Organization (FAO), 818, 820; General Assembly, 816, 818, 838, 883, 886; Iraq and, 858, 882; Security Council, 817–818, 823, 837; peacekeeping by, 818; English language and, 893; human rights and, 886; women's rights and, 887

United Provinces of the Free Netherlands. *See* Netherlands, the (the Dutch, Holland)

United Provinces of the Río de la Plata, 643, 644(*map*). *See also* Argentina; Paraguay; Uruguay

USS Cole (destroyer), 885

United States. *See also* United States, Cold War era; colonial era, 475–480; revolution in, 595–599; steamboats in, 574; cotton industry in, 571, 578, 580; chronology (1789–1890s), 669; expansion of, 650(*map*), 651; industrialization of, 565, 662, 704; railroads in, 574, 575(*illus.*), 640, 663, 705; slavery in, 580, 651; telegraph in, 575; war with England (1812), 651, 654; war with Mexico (1846–1848), 651, 653; abolition of slavery in, 656, 684; civil war (1861–1865) in, 651, 657; racial discrimination in, 662; women's rights in, 661–662, 762; Chinese immigration banned, 634, 659; immigration to, 564, 658, 663, 710, 711 *and illus.*, 724, 833, 862; Qing China and, 629, 630, 635, 729; deforestation in, 666–667; Depression (1930s) in, 788, 789(*illus.*); economic development of, 663; steel production in, 665; census in, 670; Latin America and, 666, 696; Hawaii and, 694; Philippines and, 694–695; war with Spain (1898–1899), 694–695; British investment in, 710; wheat from, 709;

intervention in Caribbean and Central America, 699; intervention in Mexico by, 697, 699; Japan and, 720, 796, 849; as great power, 729; World War I and, 737, 738, 740; voting rights in, 714, 717, 739, 826; immigration restrictions in, 741; post-World War I boom in, 745; automobiles in, 768; in World War II, 802–803, 803, 805, 808–809, 817, 819; labor unions in, 717; national parks in, 667; passports in, 761; environmental concerns in, 840, 870; per capita wealth in, 865; industrial robots in, 869; rising oil demand in, 876; North American Free Trade Agreement and, 876; Kyoto Protocol and, 871; cultural imperialism of, 888; terrorist attacks in (9/11), 874–875, 885; housing debt crisis in, 877–878; genocide convention and, 887; death penalty in, 888; drought in, 888

United States, Cold War era (1946–1991): Cuba and, 816, 832, 833–834, 844; United Nations and, 818; interventions in Latin America, 833, 834, 845, 846; Japan and, 837–838; China and, 837; Korean War and, 823; monetary policy, 818; nonaligned countries and, 836; Philippines and, 828; race for nuclear supremacy and, 826–827; rivalry with Soviet Union, 826, 834, 839, 844; support of Israel by, 839; Vietnam War and, 825–826 and illus.; oil embargo and, 839 and illus.; Iranian hostage crisis and, 848

Universal Declaration of Human Rights (United Nations), 886

Universal male suffrage, 585, 717, 730, 775. See also Voting rights

Universities. See Colleges and universities

Untouchables, in India, 178

Upanishads, 179, 691

Upper class. See Elite class (ruling class)

Ur, Third Dynasty of, 28

Urartu, 75, 113

Urban II, Pope, 293

Urbanization. See also Cities and towns; in Americas, 204; in Islamic civilization, 263–264; in Ottoman Empire, 624; industrialization and, 707; population growth and, 712, 758–759; new technology and, 758; environmental costs of, 666, 712

Urdu language, 391, 530

Ure, Andrew, 580

Uriburu, José, 777

Uruguay, 464; independence of, 643, 644(map), 646, 649, 653; education of women in, 662; Mercosur (trade agreement) and, 876

Uruk, 34

Usury, 359. See also Interest

Uthman, Caliph, 254

Uzbekistan (Uzbeks), 186, 529, 626

Vaishyas, 178

Valiente, Juan, 471

Valois dynasty (France), 438, 454(table)

Van Eyck, Jan, 367

Van Ostade, Adriaen, 446(illus.)

Varangians (Swedes), 278, 287

Vargas, Getulio, 776–777

Variolation, disease and, 543

Varnas (castes), in India, 178, 189, 403, 687, 769

Vassals. See Lords and vassals

Vatican. See also Papacy (popes); library in, 366; Sistine chapel in, 367; Japan and, 544

Vedic Age, in India, 177–179

Vedism (Vedic religion), 181, 189

Venezuela: in Gran Colombia, 644(map), 649; independence of, 642, 643, 648; under Chávez, 847; Mercosur (trade agreement) and, 876

Venice (Venetians), 291, 423; colonies of, 356; Ottoman rivalry with, 517, 520; printing in, 366; sack of Constantinople and, 293, 356; sea power of, 358

Verdun, Battle of (1916), 735

Verdun, Treaty of (843), 276

Vernacular languages, 439

Versailles, 455, 460; French Revolution and, 602, 603

Versailles, Treaty of (1919), 743; Hitler's violation of, 793, 794

Vertical exchange, in Andes, 216, 397

Vespucci, Amerigo, 413

Viceroyalties, in South America, 465. See also Latin America, colonial; New Spain; Rio de la Plata

Victor Emmanuel (Italy), 719

Victoria (Great Britain), 688, 713

Victorian Age, 713

Victorian morality, 713, 763

Victoria (ship), 401

Vienna, 612; Ottoman siege of, 452, 517, 524; Congress of (1814–1815), 611

Viet Cong, 825

Viet Minh, 824

Vietnam (Vietnamese): Funan, 193; Annam, 318; emergence of (1200–1500), 347–348; China and, 165, 298, 311, 318, 339, 340(map), 347; women of, 318; Mongol invasion of, 325, 348; French colonization of, 631; nationalism in, 824

Vietnam War, 826–826 and illus.

Vijayanagar Empire, 384

Vikings, 278; Atlantic exploration by, 276, 407, 431; runestone, 278(illus.)

Villa, Francisco "Pancho," 698

Villages. See also Rural areas; Neolithic, 19; Mesopotamian, 26; Egyptian, 38, 41; Chinese, 83, 338; Nubian, 92; Greek, 122; Indian, 188, 189, 377; Southeast Asian, 192; Bantu, 242; Arab, 250; medieval Europe, 279; tropical lands, 399; folk custom in, 439; Balkan, 519; Chinese, 629, 837; Indian, 691; Mexican, 696; Sino-Japanese War and, 797; Vietnam War and, 824(illus.); Kikuyu in Kenya, 830

Vindication of the Rights of Woman (Wollstonecraft), 582

Vinland, Vikings in, 278, 407

Virginia, colonial, 476; tobacco from, 446, 476, 489

Vishnu (god), 182–183, 191

Visigoths, in Spain, 276

Vladimir I (Russia), 288

Vladivostok, 626

Volcanic eruptions, 192, 559; in Mesoamerica, 199, 204

Volga River, 287, 288, 515, 625; Golden Horde and, 324, 328, 332

Volta, Alessandro, 575

Voltaire (FranÇois-Marie d'Arouet), 444–445, 544, 591

Voting rights (suffrage): denied to African Americans, 661; in France, 612; in United States, 714, 717, 730, 826; universal male, 585, 717, 730, 775; denied to native peoples, 672,

694; in Europe, 730; in Germany, 717, 725; for women, 657, 661, 714 *and illus.*, 762; in Argentina, 775

Wac-Chanil-Ahau (Maya), 198, 207
Wafd (Nationalist) Party, in Egypt, 753
Wages: in colonial Africa, 779, 789; in Cuba, 834; factory worker, 582; immigrant labor and, 582, 660; women's, 580, 582, 713–714
Walesa, Lech, 855
Wales (Welsh), 369, 563, 726; Celts in, 101, 102
Wall fortifications. *See* Fortifications (walls)
Wall murals (frescoes): Çatal Hüyük, 20; Egyptian, 55(*illus.*); Minoan, 56; Mycenaean, 57; Roman, 154; Indian cave shrines, 189 Teotihucan, 205; Moche, 217; Central Asian, 232; Italian Renaissance, 367
Wallpaper, Chinese, 543
Wang Mang (China), 170
War debt: British, 458, 459, 590, 596; French, 601–602, 675; World War I, 745; American, 878
Wari, 217, 220
Warlords, in Japan. *See Daimyo*
War of the Austrian Succession (1740–1748), 590, 601
War of the Pacific (1879–1883), 653
War of the Spanish Succession (1701–1714), 456, 590
Warring States period (China), 88, 91, 98
Warrior elite: Chinese, 81; steppe nomads, 96; Celtic, 101, 102(*illus.*); Iranian, 114, 116; Indian, 174, 177, 191; Mesoamerican, 210; Moche, 217, 218; Arab, 256; Turkic mamluks, 256, 260; Viking, 276; European knights, 279, 280, 292, 294(*illus.*); Mongol, 323, 346; Aztec, 395; Indian (Rajputs), 530; Japanese (samurai), 317, 347, 545, 547, 549, 550(*illus.*); Russian (cossacks), 515, 532
Warsaw Pact, 817, 822, 823(*map*), 827; Egypt and, 836; collapse of, 855
Warships. *See* Navy (warships)

War (warfare). *See also* Armed forces; Chariot warfare; Civil wars; Cold War; Guerrilla warfare; Military, Navy; Weapons and military technology; World Wars; *and specific wars;* early China, 85, 91; Celtic, 101; among Greek city-states, 134; Greek-Persian, 129–130, 135; Roman expansion and, 148–149; Rome-Carthage, 73, 148–149; Chavín, 203; Maya, 207; Andean, 220; medieval Europe, 280; Crusades, 261, 292–295; Mongol, 323; Hundred Years', 370; Aztec, 395; Polynesian, 407; religious, in Europe, 435, 438, 444; Anglo-Dutch, 448, 459, 460; colonial North America, 481, 482, 483(*map*); Imjin War (East Asia), 540, 545, 553; Napoleonic, 566–567, 607, 609(*map*), 675; Russia-Sweden, 534; Crimean, 622–624; Islamic *jihad*, 675, 679, 885; South African, 676, 678, 703; oil and, 838; Italian poets on, 784; Nazi *Blitzkrieg*, 798; Pakistan-India, 827; Arab-Israeli, 836–837, 838; global war on terrorism, 885
Washington, George, 597, 647; as general, 596–597, 598
Water buffalo, domestication of, 17
Water control systems. *See also* Canals; Dams; Irrigation; Roman aqueducts, 157, 159(*illus.*); in China, 311(*illus.*), 312; in tropics, 377–378; watermills, 169, 354, 356
Water frame, 570
Waterloo, Battle of, 608
Water Margin, 343
Water power (hydroelectricity), 768; for sugar mills, 492–493; for cotton mills, 570; in North America, 708; in Soviet Union, 785; in Japan, 837
Water supplies. *See also* Irrigation; disease and, 691; sewage treatment and, 578, 691, 765
Waterways. *See* Canals; Irrigation; Rivers
Water wheels, 570; in China, 308, 311(*illus.*), 338; in Japan, 347; in Korea, 345
Watt, James, 573, 574
Wavell, Lord, 813

Wealth inequality. *See also* Inequality; in Europe, 448; in Mexico, 832; worldwide, 864–866, 878(*map*)
The Wealth of Nations (Smith), 568–569, 583
Weapons and military technology. *See also* Armor; Artillery; Bombs and bombing; Bows and arrows; Cannon; Chariot warfare; Firearms; Gunpowder; Nuclear weapons; Swords; Assyrian, 61; Greek hoplite, 122, 134, 148; siege, 35, 61, 134, 157, 307; Islamic chemistry and, 268; Silk Road trade and, 232; stirrups, 232, 280, 298, 302(*illus.*); catapults, 134, 327, 346; European crusader, 294, 295; explosives, 308, 343, 346, 707; Chinese, 298, 302(*illus.*), 308, 343, 342 *and illus.*; Japanese, 341, 346; Korean, 343, 346; Mongol, 327, 346; Hundred Years' War, 368; Portuguese, 421; conquistador, 424, 426, 427; transition to modern warfare, 623, 625; Qing China, 747; Ethiopian modernization, 682–684; in Mexican civil war, 697, 698; Zulu, 677(*illus.*); poison gas, 737, 807; World War I, 737; World War II, 798–799, 804, 807, 809; Cold War rivalry and, 849
Weapons of mass destruction (WMDs), 882, 883. *See also* Nuclear weapons
Weather. *See* Climate and weather
Weaving. *See also* Spinning; Textile industry and trade; women and, 208, 217, 359; Anasazi, 212; Andean, 217, 398; Chinese, 343; medieval European, 357(*illus.*), looms, 357(*illus.*); Navajo, 464; mechanization of, 582; Indian, 690
Webb, James L. A., Jr., 560
Weber, Max, 735
Wedgwood, Josiah, 568–570
Wehrmacht (Nazi German army), 793 , 794(*illus*), 798, 800, 802, 807
Wei River Valley, 83, 91, 160; Chang'an in, 167
Weizmann, Chaim, 738, 742
Weld, Theodore, 656
Welfare. *See* Social welfare

Wen (China), 83
West Africa. *See also specific countries;* Yoruba people of, 2, 378(*illus.*); farming in, 15; griot in, 224; Saharan culture patterns in, 236; Islamic Empires in, 379–382; encounters with Europe, 415–417; gold in, 379; ironworking in, 378; coppersmiths of, 378(*illus.*); market women in, 394; Portuguese in, 410(*illus.*), 412, 413; slave trade in, 411, 488, 507–508, Songhai Empire of, 510; Sokoto Caliphate in, 679; palm oil trade in, 684–686, 779; French colonies, 679, 831; World War I in, 737; independence of, 830; trade agreement in (ECOWAS), 876
West Bank, 749, 838, 883
Western Asia, 53. *See also* Middle East; chronology (2000 B.C.E.–612 B.C.E.), 77; Late Bronze Age in, 50–55; Persian Empire and, 114, 140; Greek culture in, 136
Western Eurasia, Mongol Empire and, 332–335
Western Europe. *See also* Latin West (Europe 1200–1500); Medieval Europe (300–1200); Roman Empire; Celts in, 100–103; Byzantium and, 273; cities and trade in, 291–292; chronology (711–1095), 296; revival of (1000–1200), 289–292; Crusades and, 292–295; technology in, 290–291; Russia and, 626, 628; economies of, 709, 818; Marshall Plan for, 819; NATO and, 817; low fertility rates in, 862; improved air quality in, 870
Western Front (World War I), 735, 741
Western Hemisphere. *See* Americas, the (New World; Western Hemisphere)
Western imperialism, 893; *See also* Imperialism; *specific Western empires;* Chinese response to, 636–638; Meiji Japan and, 722
Westernization (Western culture). *See also* Industrialization; Modernization; in Egypt, 683; in Russia, 534, 538, 625; in West Africa, 686; in British

India, 687; of Japan, 724, 747, 894; in Middle East, 750–752; cultural imperialism and, 890; Muslim response to, 848, 890
Western Sudan (Mali), 379–382. *See also* Mali; Sudan
West Germany, 822. *See also* Germany; in European Community, 819; reunification and, 855
West India Company, Dutch, 447, 456, 479
West India Company, French, 502
West Indies. *See* Caribbean Sea and region
Whaling, 537, 693
Wheat, 22, 238, 377, 448, 464, 586, 820; in Argentina, 775; in China, 80, 82(*map*), 307, 341; emmer, 15, 21; in North America, 709, 710
Wheatstone, Charles, 575
Whistler, James McNeill, 625
White, Emma, 686
White Horde (khanate), 332
White Lotus Rebellion (China, 1794–1804), 629
Whitney, Eli, 571, 572
Whydah, 488, 507
Widow burning (*sati*), 189, 393, 691, 769
Wilhelm I (Germany), 720
Wilhelm II (Germany), 726
William and Mary (Britain), 485
William the Conquerer (England), 278, 280
William the Pious, 286
Wilson, Henry Lane, 697
Wilson, Woodrow, 699; Fourteen Points, 740; League of Nations and, 743, 749; Mexico and, 697
Windmills: in Caribbean, 492; in Europe, 354–356
Winds. *See also* Monsoons; hurricanes, in Caribbean, 494 *and illus.*; *kamikaze*, in Japan, 346; westerlies, in Atlantic, 411, 413
Wine, 149
Witch-hunts, 439–441 *and illus.*, 444
Wojtyla, Karol (John Paul II), 855
Wollstonecraft, Mary, 582, 592
Women. *See also* Family; Fertility rates; Gender differences; Marriage; Women's rights; Ice Age, 11; Neolithic Age, 15; Çatal Hüyük, 20; Mesopotamian, 30; Egyptian, 42, 48; Cretan, 56; Nubian

queens, 95; Celtic, 102; Israelite, 66; Persian, 115, 116; Chinese, 163, 167; Greek, 133, 135; Roman, 145, 147; Indian, 179, 183; widow burning (*sati*), 189, 393, 691, 769; Maya elite, 199, 208; Anasazi, 212; Central Asian nomads, 230; Indian Ocean trade and, 235; Iranian dancing girls, 228; as nuns, 285, 303, 482; seclusion and veiling of, 264(*illus.*), 265, 266; weaving by, 70, 212, 217, 359; Islamic, 30, 265–268, 392; Byzantine Empire, 274; medieval European, 281, 351, 352(*illus.*), 359; Kievan Russia, 289; as concubines and prostitutes, 87, 265, 300, 392, 510, 690, 796; Vietnamese, 318, 348; Japanese, 316, 317; Chinese, 300–303, 313–314; Mongol, 323; Delhi Sultans, 383; Dutch, 446(*illus.*); European, 451; witch-hunts and, 439–441 *and illus.*; African slave, 493, 496, 499–500, 509, 510; in colonial America, 473, 475; Acheh Sultans, 536; African, in markets, 486(*illus.*); seclusion and veiling of, 527, 887; carpet making by, 528; Korean, 550–551; American Revolution and, 596, 599; Enlightenment salons, 592; French Revolution and, 603, 604, 607; industrial work and, 579–580, 661; in textile industry, 580, 661, 747; cult of domesticity and, 582; abolitionist, 656; education of, 635, 662, 714; as teachers, 662, 714; footbinding in China and, 313, 631; as doctors and nurses, 662; colonial African, 680–682, 779, 789; as domestic servants, 451, 580, 713, 714, 747; German socialists, 717; Victorian separate sphere of, 713; working-class, 714–715; in Olympic Games, 765; labor of, in World Wars, 736(*illus.*), 737, 808–809; social reform and, 762; Nazi German, 793, 808; cult of cleanliness and, 765; Soviet Union, 787, 788–789; Iranian revolution and, 848 *and illus.*; in Arab Spring protests, 882(*illus.*)

Women's rights: abortion and, 762, 790–791; in Americas, 656, 661, 762; in Ottoman Empire, 621; to property, 42, 265, 348, 527, 621–622; in Turkey, 752, 762; in Soviet Union, 790–791; voting rights (suffrage), 657, 661, 714–715 *and illus.*, 762; Chinese Communists and, 797; neo-liberalism and, 850–851; Western feminists and, 887–888

Women's rights conferences: New York state (1848), 661; Nairobi (1985), 887

Wonhyo (Buddhist monk), 315

Woodblock printing, 550(*illus.*); in Islamic lands, 269(*illus.*); in China, 310; in Korea, 315, 344–346; movable type, 310, 315, 367; in Japan, 760

Wool trade. *See also* Sheep; Australian, 709; Mycenaean Greek, 57; Andean peoples, 70, 202, 216, 399; English, 291, 353, 358, 370; Flemish, 357; mechanization of, 571; British, 570

Woren, 636–637

Workers (working class). *See also* Labor; Peasants; Slaves; Persian Empire, 116; French Revolution and, 604, 606; Revolutions of 1848 and, 612; housing for, 562; Industrial Revolution and, 578–581; poverty of, 583; Marxist proletariat, 584, 716; Mexican Revolution and, 697; street cars and subways for, 712; women, 579–580, 661, 713–714, 717, 808–809; industrialized world, 709, 765, 768; Russian Revolution and, 739; Soviet Russia, 785; in Argentina and Brazil, 775, 776, 777; guest workers in Europe, 867

Works and Days (Hesiod), 138

World Bank, 818, 820, 866

World economy. *See* Global economy

World maps. *See* Mapmaking (cartography)

World Trade Center, attack on (2001), 874, 885

World Trade Organization (WTO), 877

World War I (1914–1918), 732–743; aircraft in, 737, 764;

alliances and military strategy in, 733–734; origins of the crisis, 732–734; stalemate (1914–1917), 734–737; nationalism in, 733–734; casualties, 735–736, 740; homefront and economy, 737; impact of, 741; Indians in, 737, 770; Africans in, 737, 781; Japan in, 747; Ottoman Empire and, 738–739; Russian Revolutions and, 739–740; Western Front, 735, 741; end of, in western Europe, 740; peace treaties, 741–743; reparations for, 744–745; territorial changes after, 742(*map*), 755

World War II (1939–1945), 674, 798–809; Africa and, 781; alliances in, 799(*map*), 801, 801(*map*), 817; appeasement leading to, 795; in Asia and the Pacific, 801(*map*), 802–803 *and map*; bombing raids in, 806; Brazil in, 777; character of warfare in, 805–809; Chinese civil war and, 803–804; chronology, 810–811; environment in, 809; in Europe and North Africa, 799–800; Germany in, 799–800 *and map*, 805; Holocaust in, 807; homefront in, 808–809; India and, 773; Japan in, 802 *and map*, 803 *and illus.*; science and technology of, 805; United States in, 801(*map*), 802–803, 803, 805, 819, 867; as war of movement, 798–799; end of, 800–802 *and illus.*

World Wide Web (the Web), 891

Worms, Concordat of (1122), 284

Wright, Frank Lloyd, 767

Wright, Orville and Wilbur, 764

Writing (written language). *See also* Literacy; Scribes; Mesopotamian (cuneiform), 27, 34–35, 52; Egyptian (hieroglyphics), 40, 52, 95; Linear B tablets (Mycenaean), 57, 59; in Indus Valley, 46; Phoenician, 68, 121, 224; Sanskrit, 178, 297; Greek, 122; Chinese, 81, 161, 299; Maya, 198, 208; Olmec, 200; oral societies and, 224–226; Cyrillic, 275, 288; Japanese, 316, 317; Korean, 550; Korean (han'gul), 316, 345; Persian, 526

WTO (World Trade Organization), 877

Wu (China), 83, 164; Sima Qian and, 99, 164, 168

Wu Sangui, 540

Wu Zhao (China), 300

"Xanadu" (Coleridge), 336

Xavier, Francis, 544

Xenophanes, 125

Xerxes (Persia), 112(*map*), 129; Persepolis and, 116, 118(*illus.*)

Xhosa people, 677

Xia dynasty (China), 80

Xinjiang, 615

Xiongnu, 99, 163; Confederacy of, 162, 165; gold belt buckle, 166(*illus.*)

X-rays, 765

Xunzi, 86

Yahweh (god), 64–65, 66

Yam, 78. *See also* Nubia

Yamamoto, Isoroku, 801

Yamatai (Japan), 1–2

Yams (vegetable), 15, 234, 240, 377, 407

Yangban class (Korea), 551

Yang Guifei, 300, 302

Yangzi River, 79, 298, 338

Yangzi River Valley, 79, 298

Yaws (disease), 498

Yazdigird III, Shah, 255

Yazid, 254

Yellow fever, 464, 610

Yellow River, 23, 24(*map*), 79, 161; flooding of, 80, 170, 338, 635, 797

Yeltsin, Boris, 855

Yemen (south Arabia), 66; Aden in, 388; camel saddles in, 237 *and illus.*; Ethiopia and, 234, 244; myrrh from, 234; coffee from, 524; al-Qaeda in, 885

Yin/yang concept, 91

Yi Songgye, 345

Yi SunShin, 546

Yohannes IV (Ethiopia), 684

Yongle (China), 339, 341

Yorktown, Battle of (1781), 598 *and map*

Yoruba people, 2, 378(*illus.*)

Yosef (Jew), 388

Young Ottomans (Turks), 624, 628, 733

Ypres, 291; weavers of, 357(*illus.*)

Yuan Empire (China), 325, 335–338. *See also* Khubilai, Great Khan; early Ming and, 338; fall of, 338; Korea and, 344; Vietnam and, 347

Yuan Shikai, 747
Yucatán, Maya of, 210
Yuezhi, 99
Yugoslavia, 836; formation of, after World War I, 743; Soviet Union and, 822; ethnic cleansing in, 857; NATO war in, 857, 858(*map*)
Yurts (felt huts), 106(*illus.*), 232

Zagros Mountains, 50, 55, 113
Zaibatsu (conglomerates), 724, 747, 849
Zaire River, 239
Zambezi River, 239; gold mines on, 379, 388
Zambia (Northern Rhodesia), 678, 679, 789
Zamorin of Calicut, 389

Zamzam, 251
Zanzibar, 686
Zapata, Emiliano, 697
Zarathushtra, 117. *See also* Zoroastrianism
Zardari, Asif Ari, 881
Zebu cattle, 17
Zeila, 388, 393
Zen (Chan) Buddhism, 310, 347
Zheng Chenggong, 555
Zeng Guofan, 635
Zero, concept of, 188, 190, 208
Zetkin, Clara, 717
Zeus (god), 124
Zhang Jian, 233
Zheng (China), 161
Zheng family, 557
Zheng He, voyages of, 321, 341 and *map*, 386, 403–404 *and illus.*, 406(*map*)

Zhou period (China), 82(*map*), 83–91; Confucianism and Daoism in, 85–91; Greece compared, 140–141; Warring States Period, 88, 91, 98
Zhu Xi, 310
Zhu Yuanzhang, 338, 339
Ziggurat, 31, 35
Zimbabwe, 387–388 *and illus.*; gold in, 388; Southern Rhodesia, 678, 831, 881
Zionism, 738, 750, 751, 753, 838. *See also* Israel
Zollverein (German union), 583
Zoroastrianism, 117–118, 141, 232, 244; Christianity and, 118, 249, 270; fire temple, 118, 260(*illus.*); good and evil in, 117, 250
Zulu kingdom, 676 *and illus.*, 677